CRITICAL SURVEY OF

Long Fiction

Fourth Edition

CRITICAL SURVEY OF

Long Fiction

Fourth Edition

Volume 1
Kōbō Abe—Hermann Broch

Editor
Carl Rollyson
Baruch College, City University of New York

SALEM PRESS
Pasadena, California   Hackensack, New Jersey

Editor in Chief: Dawn P. Dawson

Editorial Director: Christina J. Moose   *Research Supervisor:* Jeffry Jensen
Development Editor: Tracy Irons-Georges   *Research Assistant:* Keli Trousdale
Project Editor: Judy Selhorst   *Production Editor:* Joyce I. Buchea
Manuscript Editor: Desiree Dreeuws   *Design and Graphics:* James Hutson
Acquisitions Editor: Mark Rehn   *Layout:* William Zimmerman
Editorial Assistant: Brett S. Weisberg   *Photo Editor:* Cynthia Breslin Beres

Cover photo: Samuel Beckett (The Granger Collection, New York)

Some of the essays in this work, which have been updated, originally appeared in the following Salem Press publications: *Critical Survey of Long Fiction, English Language Series* (1983), *Critical Survey of Long Fiction, Foreign Language Series* (1984), *Critical Survey of Long Fiction, Supplement* (1987), *Critical Survey of Long Fiction, English Language Series, Revised Edition* (1991; preceding volumes edited by Frank N. Magill), *Critical Survey of Long Fiction, Second Revised Edition* (2000; edited by Carl Rollyson).

∞ The paper used in these volumes conforms to the American National Standard for Permanence of Paper for Printed Library Materials, Z39.48-1992 (R1997).

Library of Congress Cataloging-in-Publication Data

Critical survey of long fiction / editor, Carl Rollyson. — 4th ed.
    p. cm.
  Includes bibliographical references and index.
  ISBN 978-1-58765-535-7 (set : alk. paper) — ISBN 978-1-58765-536-4 (vol. 1 : alk. paper) —
ISBN 978-1-58765-537-1 (vol. 2 : alk. paper) — ISBN 978-1-58765-538-8 (vol. 3 : alk. paper) —
ISBN 978-1-58765-539-5 (vol. 4 : alk. paper) — ISBN 978-1-58765-540-1 (vol. 5 : alk. paper) —
ISBN 978-1-58765-541-8 (vol. 6 : alk. paper) — ISBN 978-1-58765-542-5 (vol. 7 : alk. paper) —
ISBN 978-1-58765-543-2 (vol. 8 : alk. paper) — ISBN 978-1-58765-544-9 (vol. 9 : alk. paper) —
ISBN 978-1-58765-545-6 (vol. 10 : alk. paper)
 1. Fiction—History and criticism. 2. Fiction—Bio-bibliography—Dictionaries. 3. Authors—Biography—Dictionaries. I. Rollyson, Carl E. (Carl Edmund)
  PN3451.C75 2010
  809.3—dc22

2009044410

First Printing

PRINTED IN CANADA

CONTENTS

PUBLISHER'S NOTE

The Critical Survey series provides students and general readers with in-depth profiles of major authors in one of the major literary genres—in this case, long fiction (the novel, novella, and related long forms). While the profiled authors may have written in other genres as well, sometimes to great acclaim, the focus of this set is on their most important works of long fiction.

Critical Survey of Long Fiction was originally published in 1983 and 1984 in separate English- and foreign-language series; combined revised editions in 1991 and 2000 provided a selection of authors. The *Fourth Edition*, however, includes all 581 original author essays (reinstating 117 authors) and then adds 97 new authors, covering 678 novelists and expanding from eight to ten volumes. The writers covered in this set represent more than sixty countries and the literary history of long fiction from the tenth century to the early twenty-first century.

In addition to these author essays, the final volume provides informative and insightful overviews organized by time period, country, ethnicity, and subgenre as well as valuable resource material. Author portraits are included as available, and bylines appear for all essays.

NEW MATERIAL

More than 20 percent of the text of the *Fourth Edition* is new to the Critical Survey series, and this edition features 35 percent more material than the previous one. In selecting the 97 new authors, a significant effort was made to add more women writers; they constitute fully half of the new authors and include such important novelists as Julia Alvarez, A. S. Byatt, Annie Dillard, Cynthia Kadohata, Terry McMillan, Sue Miller, Bharati Mukherjee, E. Annie Proulx, Marilynne Robinson, and Susan Sontag. Many authors with works in English translation are covered for the first time in this edition. These authors include Roberto Bolaño, Maryse Condé, Umberto Eco, Ismail Kadare, Haruki Murakami, Amos Oz, José Saramago, and W. G. Sebald. Also added are several prominent authors of young adult literature, including Robert Cormier, S. E. Hinton, Walter Dean Myers, Gary Paulsen, and J. K. Rowling.

New subgenre overview essays were commissioned on the following topics: "The Academic Novel," "The Espionage Novel," "The Legal Novel," "The Modern Novel," "The Political Novel," "The Postmodern Novel," "Sports Long Fiction," and "Young Adult Long Fiction." Four completely new Resources can be found at the end of the final volume: the "Bibliography," a general listing of print sources, with annotations; the "Guide to Online Resources," a directory of Web sites and electronic databases, with annotations; "Major Awards," lists of award-winning novelists and works; and the "Time Line," a chronological survey highlighting milestones in literary history.

In addition, phonetic pronunciation is now provided for foreign-language or unusual last names of profiled authors upon first mention in the main text. A Pronunciation Key appears at the beginning of each volume.

UPDATING THE ESSAYS

Librarians and their patrons often wonder what a publisher means by "updating"—especially for sets such as this one that include writers who are still contributing to their respective bodies of work. All parts of the essays were scrutinized: The authors' latest works of long fiction were added to front-matter listings, other significant publications were added to back-matter listings, new translations were added to listings for foreign-language authors, and deceased authors' listings were rechecked for accuracy as well as currency. Those original articles identified by the editor, Carl Rollyson, as not needing substantial updating were nevertheless reedited by Salem Press editors, and all essays' bibliographies—lists of sources for further consultation—were revised to provide readers with the latest information.

In addition, the 130 original author essays that required updating by academic experts received similar and even fuller attention: Each section of text was reviewed to ensure that major awards appear in the "Achievements," that new biographical details are incorporated into the "Biography" for still-living authors, and that the "Analysis" examines one or more recently published works of long fiction. The updating experts' names were added to essays, and each essay's bibliography was revised. Every original overview essay was read and updated in a similar manner.

FORMAT AND CONTENT

The first nine volumes of the *Fourth Edition* contain 678 essays on novelists likely to be studied in most high school and undergraduate courses in the English-speaking world. Essays are arranged alphabetically by author's last name. Following full data on alternate or birth names and dates and places of birth and death, the ready-reference top matter provides a list of the author's "Principal Long Fiction" that includes the original title and date of publication and the English title in translation and translation date as applicable. The brief overview of "Other Literary Forms" places the author in a larger literary context. Two longer sections, "Achievements" and "Biography," follow. The former summarizes the author's innovations and contributions to literature as well as noting any major honors and awards. The latter chronicles the author's basic life events, from birth and upbringing to death (or the present day, for living authors).

The core of each author essay is found in the section headed "Analysis," in which the author's work in the long fiction form is described and examined in terms of its themes, typical concerns, characters, and motifs. Subsections within this part of the text are headed with the titles of works that receive special attention. In these subsections, students and general readers will find descriptions and analyses of selected significant novels.

The final section of each of the author essays is the "Bibliography," which lists both classic and updated resources deemed most useful to those approaching the writer's work for the first time. These entries include biographies, literary surveys, monographs, and other book-length secondary works geared to a student or general audience; occasionally, journal and magazine articles, interviews, or chapters in books are also listed—particularly where book-length works are less likely to be widely available (as for contemporary novelists).

The last third of volume 9 and all of volume 10 are devoted to 61 surveys of long fiction, arranged in four sections: Long Fiction in History (chronological overviews), World Long Fiction (covering major regions of the world), North American Long Fiction (covering various groups and subgenres in the United States and Canada), and Genre Overviews (addressing prominent ongoing subgenres, from the detective novel to feminist fiction).

FEATURES AND RESOURCES

At the beginning of each volume are a list of Contents for that volume as well as a Complete List of Contents for the entire set. Volume 10 ends with several tools for further research and points of access to the wealth of information contained in the *Fourth Edition*. In addition to the "Bibliography," "Guide to Online Resources," "Major Awards," and "Time Line," an updated "Glossary of Literary Terms" defines basic literary concepts; the "Chronological List of Authors" organizes the novelists covered in these volumes by year of birth, allowing readers to identify contemporaries quickly; the "Geographical Index of Authors and Essays" and "Categorized Index of Authors" (both formerly lists, now with page numbers) group authors and overviews by country or region and profiled authors by culture, subgenre, and subject matter, respectively. Finally, the Subject Index lists all titles, authors, subgenres, and literary movements or terms that receive substantial discussion in these volumes.

ACKNOWLEDGMENTS

Wherever possible, the original contributors of these essays were invited to update their own work; we also owe our gratitude to the outstanding academicians who took on the task of updating or writing new material for the set. Their names and affiliations are listed in the "Contributors" section that follows. Finally, we are indebted to our editor, Professor Carl Rollyson of Baruch College, City University of New York, for his development of the table of contents for the *Fourth Edition* and his advice on updating the original articles to make this comprehensive and thorough revised edition an indispensable tool for students, teachers, and general readers alike.

CONTRIBUTORS

Contributors to the *Second Revised Edition* and the *Fourth Edition*

Carl Rollyson, Editor
Baruch College,
City University of New York

Randy L. Abbott
University of Evansville

McCrea Adams
Los Angeles, California

Michael Adams
CUNY Graduate Center

Patrick Adcock
Henderson State University

M. D. Allen
University of Wisconsin-Fox Valley

Daniel Altamiranda
University of Buenos Aires

Heather Russell Andrade
Florida International University

Andrew J. Angyal
Elon University

Gerald S. Argetsinger
Rochester Institute of Technology

Karen L. Arnold
Columbia, Maryland

Tel Asiado
Chatswood, New South Wales

Jane L. Ball
Yellow Springs, Ohio

Patricia Kennedy Bankhead
University of South Carolina

Thomas Banks
Ohio Northern University

Carl L. Bankston III
Tulane University

James Barbour
Oregon State University

Paula C. Barnes
Hampton University

David Barratt
Farnsfield, England

Laura Barrett
Wilkes Honors College at Florida
Atlantic University

Alvin K. Benson
Utah Valley University

Jacquelyn Benton
Metropolitan State College of Denver

Cynthia A. Bily
Adrian, Michigan

Margaret Boe Birns
New York University

Nicholas Birns
The New School

Mary A. Blackmon
Hardin-Simmons University

B. Diane Blackwood
International Press Club of Chicago

Franz G. Blaha
University of Nebraska-Lincoln

Steve D. Boilard
Legislative Analyst's Office

Bernadette Lynn Bosky
Yonkers, New York

Jay Boyer
Arizona State University

William Boyle
University of Mississippi

Virginia Brackett
Triton Community College

Harold Branam
Savannah, Georgia

James S. Brown
Bloomsburg University of
Pennsylvania

Mary Hanford Bruce
Monmouth College

Faith Hickman Brynie
Bigfork, Montana

Susan Butterworth
Salem State College

Ann M. Cameron
Indiana University Kokomo

Edmund J. Campion
University of Tennessee

Amee Carmines
Hampton University

Henry L. Carrigan, Jr.
Northwestern University

Thomas Cassidy
South Carolina State University

Nancy E. Castro
Baruch College, CUNY

Laurie Champion
San Diego State University

Allan Chavkin
Texas State University-San Marcos

C. L. Chua
California State University, Fresno

Robin Payne Cohen
Texas State University-San Marcos

David W. Cole
University of Wisconsin Center-Baraboo

David Conde
Metropolitan State College of Denver

Julian W. Connolly
University of Virginia

Richard Hauer Costa
Texas A&M University

David Cowart
University of South Carolina

Marsha Daigle-Williamson
Spring Arbor University

Anita Price Davis
Converse College

Clark Davis
University of Denver

Joseph Dewey
University of Pittsburgh at Johnstown

M. Casey Diana
Arizona State University

Margaret A. Dodson
Boise, Idaho

Thomas Du Bose
Louisiana State University in Shreveport

Stefan Dziemianowicz
Bloomfield, New Jersey

Anita M. Eckhardt
Satellite Beach, Florida

Julie M. Elliott
Indiana University South Bend

Jack Ewing
Boise, Idaho

Grace Farrell
Butler University

Nettie Farris
University of Louisville

Cristina Farronato
San Diego, California

Thomas R. Feller
Nashville, Tennessee

T. A. Fishman
Purdue University

Rebecca Hendrick Flannagan
Francis Marion University

Robert J. Forman
St. John's University

Tom Frazier
Cumberland College

Miriam Fuchs
University of Hawaii at Manoa

Kelly Fuller
Claremont Graduate University

Joe B. Fulton
Dalton State College

Ann D. Garbett
Averett University

Keith Garebian
Mississauga, Ontario

Marshall Bruce Gentry
Georgia College and State University

Craig Gilbert
Portland State University

Sheldon Goldfarb
University of British Columbia

Lucy Golsan
Stockton, California

Charles A. Gramlich
Xavier University of Louisiana

Jeffrey Greer
Detroit, Michigan

John L. Grigsby
Appalachian Research and Defense Fund of Kentucky

L. M. Grow
Broward College

Elsie Galbreath Haley
Metropolitan State College of Denver

Richard A. Spurgeon Hall
Methodist College

Renata Harden
Fort Valley State University

Betsy P. Harfst
Kishwaukee College

June Harris
Texas A&M University-Commerce

Stephen M. Hart
University College London

Peter B. Heller
Manhattan College

Diane Andrews Henningfeld
Adrian College

Cynthia Packard Hill
University of Massachusetts Amherst

Arthur D. Hlavaty
Yonkers, New York

Nika Hoffman
Crossroads School for Arts and Sciences

William Hoffman
Fort Myers, Florida

John R. Holmes
Franciscan University of Steubenville

Gregory D. Horn
*Southwest Virginia Community
    College*

Pierre L. Horn
Wright State University

E. D. Huntley
Appalachian State University

Mary Hurd
East Tennessee State University

Julie Husband
SUNY-Buffalo

Earl G. Ingersoll
SUNY-College at Brockport

Charles Israel
Columbia College

Sheila Golburgh Johnson
Santa Barbara, California

Harland W. Jones III
University of South Carolina

Theresa M. Kanoza
Lincoln Land Community College

Leela Kapai
Prince George's Community College

Steven G. Kellman
University of Texas at San Antonio

Howard A. Kerner
Polk Community College

Mabel Khawaja
Hampton University

Leigh Husband Kimmel
Indianapolis, Indiana

Anne Mills King
Prince George's Community College

Grove Koger
Boise State University

Margaret Krausse
Linfield College

Rebecca Kuzins
Pasadena, California

Brooks Landon
University of Iowa

Ralph L. Langenheim, Jr.
*University of Illinois at Urbana-
    Champaign*

Michael J. Larsen
Saint Mary's University

Eugene Larson
Pierce College

William Laskowski
Jamestown College

Linda Ledford-Miller
University of Scranton

Christine Levecq
Michigan State University

Leon Lewis
Appalachian State University

Stanley Vincent Longman
University of Georgia

Bernadette Flynn Low
*Community College of Baltimore
    County-Dundalk*

Carol J. Luther
*Pellissippi State Technical
    Community College*

R. C. Lutz
Madison Advisors

Janet McCann
Texas A&M University

Joanne McCarthy
Tacoma, Washington

Andrew F. Macdonald
Loyola University New Orleans

Gina Macdonald
Nicholls State University

Ron McFarland
University of Idaho

Richard D. McGhee
Arkansas State University

Edythe M. McGovern
West Los Angeles College

S. Thomas Mack
University of South Carolina Aiken

Joseph McLaren
Hofstra University

David W. Madden
*California State University,
    Sacramento*

Mary E. Mahony
Wayne County Community College

Daryl F. Mallett
Sahuarita, Arizona

Lois A. Marchino
University of Texas at El Paso

John L. Marsden
Indiana University of Pennsylvania

Charles E. May
*California State University,
    Long Beach*

Laurence W. Mazzeno
Alvernia College

Cecile Mazzucco-Than
Port Jefferson, New York

Patrick Meanor
SUNY-College at Oneonta

Jaime Armin Mejía
Texas State University-San Marcos

Siegfried Mews
*University of North Carolina at
    Chapel Hill*

Julia M. Meyers
Duquesne University

Vasa D. Mihailovich
University of North Carolina at Chapel Hill

P. Andrew Miller
Northern Kentucky University

Modrea Mitchell-Reichert
Texas State University-San Marcos

Christian H. Moe
Southern Illinois University at Carbondale

Kathleen N. Monahan
Saint Peter's College

Robert A. Morace
Daemen College

Toni J. Morris
University of Indianapolis

Sherry Morton-Mollo
California State University, Fullerton

Charmaine Allmon Mosby
Western Kentucky University

Roark Mulligan
Christopher Newport University

Donna Munro
Bee & Flower Press

Daniel P. Murphy
Hanover College

William Nelles
University of Massachusetts Dartmouth

Allan Nelson
Caldwell College

Elizabeth R. Nelson
Saint Peter's College

John Nizalowski
Mesa State College

Holly L. Norton
University of Northwestern Ohio

Jim O'Loughlin
Penn State Erie, The Behrend College

Bruce Olsen
Clarksville, Tennessee

James Norman O'Neill
Bryant College

Lisa Paddock
Cape May Court House, New Jersey

Robert J. Paradowski
Rochester Institute of Technology

David B. Parsell
Furman University

Susie Paul
Auburn University, Montgomery

David Peck
Laguna Beach, California

William E. Pemberton
University of Wisconsin-La Crosse

Susana Perea-Fox
Oklahoma State University-Stillwater

Marion Petrillo
Bloomsburg University of Pennsylvania

Allene Phy-Olsen
Austin Peay State University

Adrienne I. Pilon
North Carolina School of the Arts

Mary Ellen Pitts
Rhodes College

Troy Place
Western Michigan University

Marjorie Podolsky
Penn State Erie, The Behrend College

Andrew B. Preslar
Lamar State College-Orange

Victoria Price
Lamar University

Maureen J. Puffer-Rothenberg
Valdosta State University

John D. Raymer
Holy Cross College

Rosemary M. Canfield Reisman
Charleston Southern University

Martha E. Rhynes
Stonewall, Oklahoma

Mark Rich
Cashton, Wisconsin

J. Thomas Rimer
University of Pittsburgh

Dorothy Dodge Robbins
Louisiana Tech University

DaRelle M. Rollins
Hampton University

Carl Rollyson
Baruch College, CUNY

Paul Rosefeldt
Delgado Community College

Robert L. Ross
University of Texas at Austin

Sabah A. Salih
Bloomsburg University

Elizabeth Sanders
Nicholls State University

Vicki A. Sanders
Gainesville, Georgia

Elizabeth D. Schafer
Loachapoka, Alabama

Beverly Schneller
Millersville University

Chenliang Sheng
Northern Kentucky University

Nancy E. Sherrod
Georgia Southern University

R. Baird Shuman
University of Illinois at Urbana-Champaign

Paul Siegrist
Fort Hays State University

Anne W. Sienkewicz
Monmouth, Illinois

Thomas J. Sienkewicz
Monmouth College

Charles L. P. Silet
Iowa State University

Nirmala Singh
University of Michigan

Amy Sisson
Houston Community College

Genevieve Slomski
New Britain, Connecticut

Marjorie Smelstor
Kauffman Foundation

Gilbert Smith
North Carolina State University

Rebecca G. Smith
Barton College

Roger Smith
Portland, Oregon

Traci S. Smrcka
Hardin-Simmons University

Jean M. Snook
Memorial University of Newfoundland

George Soule
Carleton College

Brian Stableford
Reading, England

Isabel Bonnyman Stanley
East Tennessee State University

Joshua Stein
Los Medanos College

Karen F. Stein
University of Rhode Island

Judith L. Steininger
Milwaukee School of Engineering

J. David Stevens
Seton Hall University

Theresa L. Stowell
Adrian College

Gerald H. Strauss
Bloomsburg University

Geralyn Strecker
Ball State University

Trey Strecker
Ball State University

Philip A. Tapley
Louisiana College

Judith K. Taylor
Erlanger, Kentucky

Christine D. Tomei
Columbia University

Richard Tuerk
Texas A&M University-Commerce

Scott D. Vander Ploeg
Madisonville Community College

Dennis Vannatta
University of Arkansas at Little Rock

Steven C. Walker
Brigham Young University

Jaquelyn W. Walsh
McNeese State University

Gary P. Walton
Northern Kentucky University

Qun Wang
California State University, Monterey Bay

Gladys J. Washington
Texas Southern University

Shawncey Webb
Taylor University

Dennis L. Weeks
Schenectady County Community College

Lynn Wells
University of Regina

John T. West III
Northwest Arkansas Community College

Gary Westfahl
University of California, Riverside

James Whitlark
Texas Tech University

Albert Wilhelm
Tennessee Technological University

Thomas Willard
University of Arizona

Donna Glee Williams
North Carolina Center for the Advancement of Teaching

Tyrone Williams
Xavier University

Judith Barton Williamson
Sauk Valley Community College

James A. Winders
Appalachian State University

Michael Witkoski
Columbia, South Carolina

Scott D. Yarbrough
Charleston Southern University

Gay Pitman Zieger
Santa Fe College

Contributors to the *Critical Survey of Long Fiction, English Language Series*; the *Critical Survey of Long Fiction, Foreign Language Series*; the *Critical Survey of Long Fiction, Supplement*; and the *Critical Survey of Long Fiction, English Language Series, Revised Edition*

Timothy Dow Adams
S. Krishnamoorthy Aithal
Terry L. Andrews
Stanley Archer
Edwin T. Arnold III
Marilyn Arnold
Bryan Aubrey
Linda C. Badley
Peter Baker
Dean R. Baldwin
Thomas P. Baldwin
Jane L. Ball
Lowell A. Bangerter
Thomas Banks
Stanisław Barańczak
Dan Barnett
Carol M. Barnum
Jean-Pierre Barricelli
Fiora A. Bassanese
Joseph F. Battaglia
Robert Becker
Kirk H. Beetz
Kate Begnal
Todd K. Bender
Richard P. Benton
Frank Bergmann
Randi Birn
András Boros-Kazai
Frederick Bowers
Harold Branam
Anne Kelsch Breznau
J. R. Broadus
Joseph Bruchac
Carl Brucker
Domenic Bruni
Mitzi M. Brunsdale
Hallman B. Bryant
Paul Budra
C. F. Burgess
Suzan K. Burks
Jean-Pierre Cap

Karen Carmean
John Carpenter
Leonard Casper
Edgar L. Chapman
Luisetta Elia Chomel
John R. Clark
Samuel Coale
John L. Cobbs
Richard N. Coe
Steven E. Colburn
John J. Conlon
Mark Conroy
Deborah Core
Natalia Costa
David Cowart
Carol I. Croxton
Diane D'Amico
Reed Way Dasenbrock
J. Madison Davis
Mary E. Davis
Frank Day
Paul J. deGategno
Bill Delaney
Joan DelFattore
Lloyd N. Dendinger
A. A. DeVitis
Richard H. Dillman
Thomas Di Napoli
Lillian Doherty
Robert Dombroski
Henry J. Donaghy
David C. Dougherty
Virginia A. Duck
Paul F. Dvorak
David B. Eakin
Roberto González Echevarría
Grace Eckley
Wilton Eckley
Bruce L. Edwards, Jr.
Robert P. Ellis
Ann Willardson Engar

Thomas L. Erskine
Howard Faulkner
William L. Felker
John H. Ferres
Richard A. Fine
Bruce E. Fleming
Margot K. Frank
Howard Fraser
June M. Frazer
Kenneth Friedenreich
Miriam Fuchs
Robert L. Gale
Honora Rankine Galloway
Kristine Ottesen Garrigan
James R. Giles
L. H. Goldman
Dennis Goldsberry
Peter W. Graham
John R. Griffin
James Grove
Stephen I. Gurney
Franz P. Haberl
Angela Hague
Jay L. Halio
David Mike Hamilton
Robert D. Hamner
Todd C. Hanlin
Terry L. Hansen
Klaus Hanson
John P. Harrington
Robert Hauptman
Melanie Hawthorne
William J. Heim
Terry Heller
Greig E. Henderson
Robert Henkels
David K. Herzberger
Erwin Hester
Marie-France Hilgar
Jane Hill
James L. Hodge

Watson Holloway

Linda Howe

Helen Mundy Hudson

Edward W. Huffstetler

Barbara L. Hussey

Mary Anne Hutchinson

Archibald E. Irwin

Joe W. Jackson, Jr.

Abdul R. JanMohamed

Angela M. Jeannet

Alfred W. Jensen

Clarence O. Johnson

D. Barton Johnson

Judith L. Johnston

Betty H. Jones

Jane Anderson Jones

Feroza Jussawalla

Djelal Kadir

Lothar Kahn

Deborah Kaplan

Irma M. Kashuba

Anna B. Katona

Richard Keenan

Catherine Kenney

Sue L. Kimball

Anne Mills King

Charles L. King

James Reynolds Kinzey

John V. Knapp

Paula Kopacz

Sarah B. Kovel

Lawrence F. Laban

Jeanne Larsen

Donald F. Larsson

Paul LaValley

Norman Lavers

Penelope A. LeFew

Robert W. Leutner

Avril S. Lewis

Ward B. Lewis

Henry J. Lindborg

Naomi Lindstrom

Robert Emmet Long

Michael Lowenstein

Philip A. Luther

James J. Lynch

John D. Lyons

Tim Lyons

Barbara A. McCaskill

James C. MacDonald

Fred B. McEwen

Dennis Q. McInerny

Iole F. Magri

Carol S. Maier

Bryant Mangum

Patricia Marks

Bruce K. Martin

Paul Marx

Anne Laura Mattrella

Charles E. May

Richard A. Mazzara

Jeremy T. Medina

Jean-Pierre Metereau

Siegfried Mews

N. J. Meyerhofer

Jennifer Michaels

George Mihaychuk

Joseph R. Millichap

Kathleen Mills

Mark Minor

Sally Mitchell

Harold K. Moon

Gene M. Moore

Robert A. Morace

Carole Moses

Christer L. Mossberg

C. Lynn Munro

Carol J. Murphy

Earl Paulus Murphy

Brian Murray

John M. Muste

William Nelles

F. William Nelson

Stella A. Nesanovich

Martha Nochimson

George O'Brien

James O'Brien

John C. O'Neal

Robert M. Otten

Cóilín Owens

Donald Palumbo

Robert J. Paradowski

Makarand Paranjape

Ana María F. Parent

John G. Parks

David B. Parsell

Carole Deering Paul

William Peden

William E. Pemberton

Genaro J. Pérez

Janet Pérez

Robert C. Petersen

Peter Petro

Alice Hall Petry

Linda Schelbitzki Pickle

Janet Polansky

Karen Priest

Charles H. Pullen

Philippe Radley

Victor J. Ramraj

K. Bhaskara Rao

Paul Reichardt

Edward C. Reilly

Rosemary M. Canfield Reisman

Helene M. Kastinger Riley

Michael Ritterson

Samuel J. Rogal

Deborah D. Rogers

Carl Rollyson

Joseph Rosenblum

Sven H. Rossel

Victor Anthony Rudowski

Murray Sachs

David Sadkin

F. C. St. Aubyn

Jan St. Martin

Arthur M. Saltzman

Dale Salwak

John K. Saunders

June H. Schlessinger

Joachim Scholz

Thomas C. Schunk

Lucy M. Schwartz

Kenneth Seib

Joan Corey Semonella

Lynne P. Shackelford
Vasant A. Shahane
Millicent Sharma
Walter Shear
Frank W. Shelton
John C. Shields
T. A. Shippey
Jack Shreve
R. Baird Shuman
William L. Siemens
Anne W. Sienkewicz
Thomas J. Sienkewicz
Charles L. P. Silet
Linda Simon
Armand E. Singer
Jan Sjåvik
Carol J. Sklenicka
Gilbert Smith
Katherine Snipes
Philip H. Solomon
Sherry G. Southard
Sharon Spencer

Brian Stableford
Sonja G. Stary
Wojtek Stelmaszynski
Irwin Stern
William B. Stone
W. J. Stuckey
Mary Ellen Stumpf
Stan Sulkes
James Sullivan
Eileen Tarcay
Thomas J. Taylor
Victor Terras
Christopher J. Thaiss
Lou Thompson
Gary Topping
Charles Trainor
Janet G. Tucker
Linda F. Tunick
Kim Vivian
Hans Wagener
Nancy Walker
Ronald G. Walker

John Michael Walsh
Bernice Larson Webb
Judith Weise
Steven Weisenburger
John P. Welle
Craig Werner
Joan M. West
Dexter Westrum
David Allen White
Bruce Wiebe
Roger E. Wiehe
Raymond L. Williams
James A. Winders
Chester L. Wolford
Timothy C. Wong
Philip Woodard
Jennifer L. Wyatt
Sanroku Yoshida
Michele Wender Zak
Harry Zohn
Leon Zolbrod

COMPLETE LIST OF CONTENTS

VOLUME 1

VOLUME 2

Contents. xxxv

Complete List of Contents xxxvii

Pronunciation Key. xlvii

VOLUME 3

VOLUME 4

VOLUME 5

VOLUME 6

VOLUME 7

VOLUME 8

VOLUME 9

Contents clxxi
Complete List of Contents clxxiii
Pronunciation Key clxxxiii

LONG FICTION IN HISTORY

WORLD LONG FICTION

VOLUME 10

PRONUNCIATION KEY

Foreign and unusual or ambiguous English-language names of profiled authors may be unfamiliar to some users of the *Critical Survey of Long Fiction*. To help readers pronounce such names correctly, phonetic spellings using the character symbols listed below appear in parentheses immediately after the first mention of the author's name in the narrative text. Stressed syllables are indicated in capital letters, and syllables are separated by hyphens.

VOWEL SOUNDS

Symbol	*Spelled (Pronounced)*
a	answer (AN-suhr), laugh (laf), sample (SAM-puhl), that (that)
ah	father (FAH-thur), hospital (HAHS-pih-tuhl)
aw	awful (AW-fuhl), caught (kawt)
ay	blaze (blayz), fade (fayd), waiter (WAYT-ur), weigh (way)
eh	bed (behd), head (hehd), said (sehd)
ee	believe (bee-LEEV), cedar (SEE-dur), leader (LEED-ur), liter (LEE-tur)
ew	boot (bewt), lose (lewz)
i	buy (bi), height (hit), lie (li), surprise (sur-PRIZ)
ih	bitter (BIH-tur), pill (pihl)
o	cotton (KO-tuhn), hot (hot)
oh	below (bee-LOH), coat (koht), note (noht), wholesome (HOHL-suhm)
oo	good (good), look (look)
ow	couch (kowch), how (how)
oy	boy (boy), coin (koyn)
uh	about (uh-BOWT), butter (BUH-tuhr), enough (ee-NUHF), other (UH-thur)

CONSONANT SOUNDS

Symbol	*Spelled (Pronounced)*
ch	beach (beech), chimp (chihmp)
g	beg (behg), disguise (dihs-GIZ), get (geht)
j	digit (DIH-juht), edge (ehj), jet (jeht)
k	cat (kat), kitten (KIH-tuhn), hex (hehks)
s	cellar (SEHL-ur), save (sayv), scent (sehnt)
sh	champagne (sham-PAYN), issue (IH-shew), shop (shop)
ur	birth (burth), disturb (dihs-TURB), earth (urth), letter (LEH-tur)
y	useful (YEWS-fuhl), young (yuhng)
z	business (BIHZ-nehs), zest (zehst)
zh	vision (VIH-zhuhn)

CRITICAL SURVEY OF

Long Fiction

Fourth Edition

A

KŌBŌ ABE
Kimifusa Abe

Born: Tokyo, Japan; March 7, 1924
Died: Tokyo, Japan; January 22, 1993
Also known as: Kimifusa Abe

OTHER LITERARY FORMS

Kōbō Abe (ahb-eh) gained international renown not only for his novels but also for his short stories, plays, essays, radio dramas, and film scenarios. As the title of his collection of essays *Mōken-no kokoro-ni keisanki-no te-o* (1957; with the hand of an adding machine in the heart of a vicious dog) suggests, virtually all of his writings reflect—in however oblique a way—moral indignation at the state of humankind. Abe tried to expose the alienation and despair that so easily possess lonely and isolated people, particularly in modern urban society. He demonstrated a willingness to experiment, and his stage pyrotechnics, as well as his halting and fragmented mode of narration, were deliberately calculated to expose the irony and paradox of human existence.

ACHIEVEMENTS

By means of his short stories, which were first published in journals and then collected in books during the early 1950's, Kōbō Abe carved a special niche in the postwar Japanese literary scene. His story "Akai mayu" ("Red Cocoon"), first published in December, 1950, was awarded the Postwar Literature Prize. His first collection of short stories, *Chin'nyūsha* (1952; intruders), took its title from one of his best-received tales, a satiric allegory on counterfeit democracy in postwar Japan. Later, he transformed the title story, "Intruders," into the play *Tomodachi* (pr., pb. 1967; *Friends*, 1969). Two of Abe's early stories, "Kabe" ("The Wall") and "S. Karuma-shi-no hanzai" ("S. Karuma's Crime"), were awarded the coveted Akutagawa Prize for portraying a Kafkaesque world that stresses the qualities of irrationality, surrealism, and frustration in contemporary life. His radio drama *Bō ni natta otoko* (pr., pb. 1969; *The Man Who Turned into a Stick*, 1975—a later version for theater) received a Cultural Festival Prize. Another of his radio dramas earned a second-place prize in the Public Broadcasting Cultural Festival in 1958. His masterpiece novel, *The Woman in the Dunes*, won the Yomiuri Literature Prize in 1960 on the basis of an earlier, serialized version. As the doyen of living Japanese writers who enjoyed an international reputation, Abe transcended the cultural code of his native country. His works deal with issues that relate to individuals and societies everywhere. The basic themes that underlie his best-known novels are those of alienation and identity, two poles that regulate human existence in social groups.

BIOGRAPHY

The son of a physician on the staff of the Manchurian School of Medicine in Mukden (now Shenyang, China), Kimifusa Abe was born in Tokyo, Japan, while his father was there on a research assignment. The circumstances of Abe's early life and education suggest why he was especially predisposed to treat the issues of alienation and identity with clinical detachment as well as with verve and imagination. When Abe was barely a year old, the family returned to Mukden, where Abe lived until the age of sixteen. His early life and schooling, partly in Mukden and partly in Tokyo, took place during a turbulent period of social and political unrest in northern China. Japanese military occupation included the area where he lived. In due course, World War II broke out, and eventually Tokyo and the other main cities of Japan were devastated by bombs and fire. All of this was part of Abe's direct experience. It is no wonder that his novels are dotted with references to warfare and human conflict.

Exempted from military service because of a respiratory illness, Abe stood apart from other young men of his age. Being forcibly separated from the place where he grew up by virtue of the Japanese defeat in the war, he became almost a displaced person in his own country. His birthplace was Tokyo, yet his youth had been spent mostly in Mukden. His official family residence was on the northern island of Hokkaidō. Abe himself later said that he was a man without a homeland. After going back to Tokyo in 1941 for schooling and military training and traveling under wartime conditions several times between Japan and Manchuria, Abe eventually finished medical school in 1948. Deciding against medical practice, however, in favor of a writing career, Abe allied himself with a literary group led by Kiyoteru Hamada; the group was committed to the goal of fusing surrealistic techniques with Marxist ideology. Taking the pseudonym Kōbō Abe, he published works in an avant-garde, experimental style that quickly won praise from the younger generation of readers, who admired his short stories, novels, and plays that exposed the emptiness of life in modern society.

ANALYSIS

Human loss, disappearance, allocation of responsibility, anguish, and futility stand out as the main issues that figure in Kōbō Abe's writings. At first, Abe treated such matters mostly in a serious way. Gradually, from the underlying absurdity and irrationality of the imaginary situations about which he wrote, a kind of gallows humor emerged, giving a sense of situation comedy, albeit black comedy. Abe recognized, on one hand, that without cohesive units of interdependent people, human life could scarcely exist; on the other hand, he also observed that people everywhere suffer under the pressure to model their behavior on conventionally accepted manners and mores. Abe's characters' resistance to such pressures (or perhaps their unconscious wish to suffer) results in their desire to assert their individuality. Ironically, such assertion leads to alienation, creating a Catch-22 situation and a sense of absurdity.

In Abe's novels, human relationships are shown to be in disorder, partly reflecting the particular quality of his artistic imagination and partly reflecting his own youthful experiences. Except for the case of *The Woman in the Dunes*, which is set in a remote seaside hamlet, the main action in his narratives typically takes place against the urban landscape and amid the impersonalized locations and institutions with which modern city dwellers are most familiar—hospitals, offices, laboratories, department stores, movie theaters, waiting rooms, and apartments. Conversation and human intercourse are fragmented and interrupted, contributing to a sense of incompleteness. Success, fruition, and fulfillment constantly evade his protagonists, who are usually depicted as well-educated people, deserving to reap the rewards of their prudence and perseverance. The underlying irony of Abe's narratives suggests that human beings have learned to govern many of the forces of their external environment, but they know so little about themselves that they struggle helplessly at the mercy of satanic workings that lurk in the irrational depths of the mind. Sexuality in many of Abe's novels perversely turns out to exert a divisive impact on men and women, reducing them to a bestial level.

Sometimes, it would seem, gratuitous detail clogs Abe's narratives, slowing down the forward thrust of the action and creating what amounts to a form of static. The sequence of time is often juggled, creating a confusion of past and present. Lists of objects, minute descriptions of surface appearances, and clinical analyses of emotional responses try the reader's patience, giving an impression of awkwardness. Actually, however, what appear as technical deficiencies contribute to the overall effectiveness of the author's style. Aside from imparting a sense of verisimilitude to the situations described—however absurd and irrational they would seem to be—the interruptions, false starts, and narrative shifts convey the state of suffering from which the characters in the end find it impossible to be freed; periodic breaks in the flow of a story are essential to the ultimate completion of the event.

Another intrusive characteristic in Abe's novels that deserves mention relates to the didactic impulse. As critics have recognized, the novels are imbued with an implicit desire for men and women, parents and children, and family or community to work for social good. A strong social conscience drives all the novels like a compelling organic force. It is easy to understand why at the beginning of his career Abe immersed himself in philosophical writings. He not only felt empathy for Marxism but also studied Friedrich Nietzsche, Martin Heidegger, and Karl Jaspers. As a founding member of two postwar Japanese groups of left-wing authors as well as someone involved in a cross section of European literary movements, Abe, like Jean-Paul Sartre and Albert Camus, stands out as an intellectual writer of cosmopolitan bent who deals not in themes of localized scope but with universal problems. As such, he deserves to be counted as the leading Japanese exponent of the novel of ideas.

In pinpointing the sources of Abe's moral sensibility, however, one must go beyond twentieth century ideologies and consider the same Chinese and South Asian Buddhist and Confucian sources that led earlier Japanese authors, such as Kyokutei Bakin (1767-1848), to treat themes touching on good and evil behavior and on the individual's place in the larger framework of human society. For example, in terms of theme, Abe's idea that the search for the other—typically a missing or estranged person—becomes a search for the self relates to fundamental insights of Zen. Similarly, the concept of a realm of nothingness owes as much to Buddhist philosophy as to modern nihilism. Social criticism based on the tech-

Kōbō Abe. (Library of Congress)

niques of irony and satire recalls popular Japanese literature of the late eighteenth and early nineteenth century, with its pronounced Confucian orientation and its express purpose of encouraging good and castigating evil.

Even in terms of technique, the idea of a postscript in the author's voice, which suggests removal of the narrator's mask, resembles Bakin's practice. The ending of *Inter Ice Age 4*, for example, insists on the open-ended nature of literature and fiction, in which each person must form his or her own conclusion about the meaning of the tale, yet Abe in his own voice observes in the last words of the postscript, "The most frightening thing in the world is discovering the abnormal in that which is closest to us." Few modern authors would dare to make such an observation about their own fiction, at least in the text itself, but Bakin frequently did so in his day. Nevertheless, unlike Bakin, Abe refrains from simplistic characterization of certain kinds of behavior as praiseworthy or reprehensible.

Paradox and irony in Abe's writings give rise to positive and negative polarities. On the negative side are situations such as running away, disappearing, loss of identity, and desiring to escape, all of which lead to destruction, loss, and denial of self. On the positive side, a sense of rebirth, regeneration, and reshaped identity emerges from the narratives. *The Woman in the Dunes*, in particular, suggests a case in point. Toward the end of the story, the omniscient narrator states pointedly about the protagonist, "Perhaps, along with the water in the sand, he had found a new self." Returning to a communal structure, as Niki Jumpei does, binds and imprisons but also shelters and supports.

The constituent elements of Abe's long fiction may be summed up as follows. His main theme involves exposition of the condition of the outsider in modern society. His technique is based on allegory, irony, and satire. His narratives are often constructed by means of a series of reverses. Whenever some hopeful sign appears that communication between people is about to take place, some obtrusion appears that renders further development impossible, as if the lights were suddenly turned on in a lovers' bedroom or someone knocked on the door. His style is often stiff and formal, like a student in a celluloid collar always preparing for examinations. Order is what one arbitrarily imposes on experience. Logic represents an abstraction incapable of fathoming reality, which constantly changes in shape and inexorably exerts the power to move people, however reluctant they may be.

In cumulative effect, Abe creates parable and myth. By inverting, destroying, or denying meaning to the rational foundations of society and its values, Abe invents a new reality that takes the shape of an ironic affirmation of a future without form. Brief discussion of a few of Abe's works of long fiction that have appeared in English translation will serve to demonstrate the salient characteristics of Abe's art and philosophy.

INTER ICE AGE 4

Essentially about artificial intelligence, computers, and the moral issues that surround abortion, *Inter Ice Age 4* involves a scientist and laboratory administrator, Dr. Katsumi (whose name literally means "win-see"), who supervises the reduction of a slain man's intelligence to a computer program. Toward the end of the novel, Dr. Katsumi is ordered killed by the computer that

he himself programmed. Mostly in the form of a first-person narrative, the novel combines elements of murder mystery and science-fiction fantasy. In a subplot, aborted fetuses are kept alive, and, by means of sordid biological experimentation that involves "planned evolution," a new form of human life is created—namely, "aquans." Aquans become heirs to the earth, owing to climatic change that brings a dramatic warming of temperatures and a precipitous rise in the level of the sea.

Ironically, the investigators turn out to be the perpetrators of the crime. In addition to murder, racketeering in human fetuses, computer programming, and aquan research, the bizarre plot includes strange telephone calls and the intense rivalry that can lead scientists into reckless or irresponsible behavior. As a computer designed to predict the future comes to speak with its own intelligence, gothic horror merges with science fiction. Dr. Katsumi's own wife unknowingly contributes her aborted fetus to aquan research. "Was I . . . trying to protect her or was I . . . trying to use her . . . ?" muses the husband. "Compared with this fate, infanticide was a refined and humane act."

In the climactic episode, Dr. Katsumi's subordinate colleagues place him on trial in a kangaroo court. Such a development suggests victimization, lynching, and scapegoating, which abound in Abe's work and which Rene Girard has treated in his book *"To Double Business Bound": Essays on Literature, Mimesis, and Anthropology* (1978). Characteristically, the narrative mode of *Inter Ice Age 4* changes toward the end to a representational mode. Televised pictures of an aquan breeding farm are described with commentary by the scientist in charge, Professor Yamamoto, who serves partly as a foil and partly as a double for Dr. Katsumi. *Inter Ice Age 4* originally appeared in serial form from July, 1958, through March, 1959, in the wake of the Soviet Union's 1957 launch of the first human-made satellite, *Sputnik 1*, and in an atmosphere of heightened awareness of futuristic science and technology.

THE WOMAN IN THE DUNES

The Woman in the Dunes is Abe's most widely read novel. It has been translated not only into English but also into more than twenty other languages. A film adaptation directed by Hiroshi Teshigahara was released in 1964 to huge commercial success. As William Currie has noted, *The Woman in the Dunes* is a narrative of "almost mythic simplicity" in which Abe probes the "roots of existence" and the "difficulty people have in communicating with one another," touching on the "discrepancy between the mind and the external world, or between inner and outer reality."

Central to the novel is the metaphor of sand. It suggests the shifting reality with which the protagonist, Niki Jumpei, must come to terms. Often used in Buddhist scriptures, the image of sand represents both that which is universal and that which can grind or pulverize other material. Niki Jumpei's name has a significance that goes beyond his identity as a schoolteacher who likes to travel to remote places to collect insects. Written with Chinese characters that may be translated as "humanity-tree conform-to-average," the name suggests allegorically a kind of victimized Everyman.

From the narrative, the idea emerges that people living under conditions of permanent crisis are, on one hand, forced by public circumstances to pull together, but on the other hand, private desires and primitive instincts compel them to withdraw into isolation. The specific conditions that led Abe to grapple with people's contradictory impulses in literary and imaginative terms may well derive from his own experience of coming of age during wartime and witnessing the social disorder and transformation that came in the wake of defeat. This is not to imply, however, that Abe's work is limited to any special time or place. The beauty of *The Woman in the Dunes* lies in the work's transcendence of any locality or period. It reminds one that life everywhere, now as always, lurches from crisis to crisis. The future remains as uncertain as the shifting sands on the shore. A person's well-being depends on a precarious balance between identity with others and alienation from a social group.

Alienation and identity, the paired concepts crucial to an appreciative reading of Abe's novels, also figure prominently in *The Face of Another*. The idea of deceitfully masking one's true identity and thereby alienating oneself from the possibility of love is developed in a first-person narrative that involves a brilliant scientist who has lost his face in a laboratory explosion. By creating a new face mask, he acquires a new self, which, as Philip Williams has observed, "ironically leads to his own psychological death as a person."

THE RUINED MAP *and* THE BOX MAN

The Ruined Map is a first-person narrative about a detective who has been hired by a woman to search for her missing husband. In a metamorphosis resembling that of *Inter Ice Age 4*, the detective is transformed into the ghostly man whom he is relentlessly pursuing. As his own personality progressively disintegrates, he is carried to the edge of madness. By the end of the novel, he has given up "looking for a way to the past." As the woman—his wife or the person who hired him to find her husband—apparently gives up searching for him, he leaves his "crevice in the darkness." He begins "walking in the opposite direction," relying on a map he does not comprehend, "perhaps in order to reach her." Such is the nature of the paradox and irony that distinguish Abe's mode of narration.

Similarly, *The Box Man* describes a person's futile effort to escape from himself. Here the protagonist tries to achieve this end by cutting a peephole in a large cardboard box and placing the box over his head. Thus he expects to walk away from his anxieties. The main danger for the character lies in the possibility of his meeting another "box man." Part of the narrative involves intercourse between a true box man and a fake box man, suggesting the literary device of doubling and splitting. As Abe himself said in discussing the novel, "Being no one means at the same time that one can be anyone." Aversion to ordinary existence and the question of what is genuine and what is counterfeit are expressed by means of the box as a shield from the world, a symbol that represents disposability and concealment.

One unusual feature of *The Box Man* is the inclusion of nine leaves of photographs, all but one of which have enigmatic or aphoristic captions. For example, the text for the fifth of these, the photo in the middle position, reads as follows:

> In seeing there is love, in being seen there is abhorrence. One grins, trying to bear the pain of being seen. But not just anyone can be someone who only looks. If the one who is looked at looks back, then the person who was looking becomes the one who is looked at.

The appropriateness of such a graphic and textual appendage to *The Box Man* stems from the former identity of the fictional narrator, who has become a box man. He was a photographer, albeit not of portraits or landscapes but rather of such prosaic subjects as women's underwear and incidents in public parks. He took surreptitious snapshots—seeing without being seen.

SECRET RENDEZVOUS

Secret Rendezvous is a surrealistic detective story about an unidentified thirty-two-year-old man, a director of sales promotion for "jump shoes," special athletic footwear with "air-bubble springs" built into the soles. Early one morning, his wife, who was perfectly healthy, suddenly disappears, a typical occurrence in Abe's fictional world. An ambulance comes to pick her up and take her to a hospital, and when the husband attempts to check into the situation, he encounters a tangle of red tape and is unable to obtain any solid information.

Among the underlying social issues in this novel are the quality and the dependability of health care. Titillating and yet frightening incidents take place, such as "a deliberate prearranged rendezvous" with a physician. In a narrative that mixes both first- and third-person modes, one of the suspected doctors turns out to be involved in collecting his own sperm for sale to an agency that offers artificial insemination.

In addition to the matter of inexplicable loss and the struggle to come to terms with a reality that lies beyond the power of human comprehension (elements common to all of Abe's principal works of long fiction), *Secret Rendezvous* involves the puzzling business of human sexuality and issues of institutional continuity. It also deals with the provision of effective health care in a world marred by petty jealousies, internecine rivalries, and haphazard medical diagnoses. "Secret rendezvous among patients" are handled as common occurrences, and hospital surveillance techniques necessitate "automatic recording of love scenes." Abe's topsy-turvy world, which inexorably requires scapegoats and hapless victims, unfolds in such a way that it becomes impossible for the protagonist to distinguish the aggressor from the victim.

Outwardly stiff and awkward, Abe's novels reveal the author's preoccupation with ideas rather than style. Using concepts and language drawn from science and philosophy, Abe trains a critical focus on human society and institutions. Allegory, irony, and satire lend artistic force and credibility to his concern for the dangers of alienation from society and the difficulty of achieving a constructive identity of the self within the confines of the social groups among which an individual must live.

Leon Zolbrod

OTHER MAJOR WORKS

SHORT FICTION: *Kabe*, 1951; *Suichū toshi*, 1964; *Yume no tōbō*, 1968; *Four Stories by Kōbō Abe*, 1973; *Beyond the Curve*, 1991.

PLAYS: *Seifuku*, pr., pb. 1955; *Yūrei wa koko ni iru*, pr. 1958 (*The Ghost Is Here*, 1993); *Omae ni mo tsumi ga aru*, pr., pb. 1965 (*You, Too, Are Guilty*, 1978); *Tomodachi*, pr., pb. 1967 (*Friends*, 1969); *Bō ni natta otoko*, pr., pb. 1969 (*The Man Who Turned into a Stick*, 1975); *Gikyoku zenshū*, pb. 1970; *Gaido bukku*, pr. 1971; *Imeji no tenrankai*, pr. 1971 (*The Little Elephant Is Dead*, pr. 1979); *Mihitsu no koi*, pr., pb. 1971 (*Involuntary Homicide*, 1993); *Midoriiro no sutokkingu*, pr., pb. 1974 (*The Green Stockings*, 1993); *Ue: Shin doreigari*, pr., pb. 1975; *Three Plays*, 1993.

POETRY: *Mumei shishū*, 1947.

NONFICTION: *Uchinaro henkyō*, 1971.

MISCELLANEOUS: *Abe Kōbō zenshū*, 1972-1997 (30 volumes).

BIBLIOGRAPHY

Cassegård, Carl. *Shock and Naturalization in Contemporary Japanese Literature*. Folkestone, England: Global Oriental, 2007. Uses the concepts of "naturalization" and "naturalized modernity" to analyze how modernity has been experienced and depicted in post-World War II Japanese literature. Emphasizes the works of Abe as well as writers Yasunari Kawabata, Haruki Murakami, and Ryū Murakami.

Cornyetz, Nina. *The Ethics of Aesthetics in Japanese Cinema and Literature: Polygraphic Desire*. New York: Routledge, 2007. Explores Japanese literature and film from the 1930's through the post-World War II period by studying the ethical dimensions of Japanese aesthetics. Describes how works by Abe and others were influenced by changing artistic, political, and intellectual issues.

Currie, William. "Abe Kōbō's Nightmare World of Sand." In *Approaches to the Modern Japanese Novel*, edited by Kinya Tsuruta and Thomas E. Swann. Tokyo: Sophia University, 1976. Contribution to an informative and comprehensive collection of essays on twentieth century Japanese fiction presents a detailed analysis of *The Woman in the Dunes*.

Iles, Timothy. *Abe Kōbō: An Exploration of His Prose, Drama, and Theatre*. Fucecchio, Italy: European Press Academic Publishing, 2000. Study devotes individual chapters to Abe's prose, drama, and techniques for training actors. Examines numerous themes in Abe's work, including the function of existentialism and the absurd, the relationship between society and the individual, and Abe's attempts to reshape humankind into a form capable of dealing with modern society's urbanization, alienation, and fragmentation.

Keene, Donald. *Five Modern Japanese Novelists*. New York: Columbia University Press, 2003. The chapter devoted to Abe in this volume features biographical material as well as commentary on *The Woman in the Dunes* and his other novels.

Olsen, Lance. *Ellipse of Uncertainty: An Introduction to Post-modern Fantasy*. Westport, Conn.: Greenwood Press, 1987. In one of the first studies to examine the intersection of fantasy and postmodernism in literature, Olsen develops working definitions of these terms and then analyzes various postmodernist fantasy works.

Pollack, David. *Reading Against Culture: Ideology and Narrative in the Japanese Novel*. Ithaca, N.Y.: Cornell University Press, 1992. Investigates works by Japanese novelists in terms of their ideology, use of narrative, and treatment of the self and of Japanese culture. Chapter 6 is devoted to discussion of Abe's *The Woman in the Dunes*.

Rimer, J. Thomas. *A Reader's Guide to Japanese Literature*. 2d ed. New York: Kodansha International, 1999. Comprehensive volume provides an introductory overview of Japanese literature. Includes a short exploration of *The Woman in the Dunes*.

Schnellbächer, Thomas. *Abe Kōbō, Literary Strategist: The Evolution of His Agenda and Rhetoric in the Context of Postwar Japanese Avant-Garde and Communist Artist's Movements*. Munich, Germany: Iudicium, 2004. Examines the essays Abe wrote between 1947, when he was repatriated from Manchuria, and 1962, when he was expelled from the Communist Party, by placing these writings within the context of the political and artist groups in which he was active and the broader issues in post-World War II Japanese literature.

PETER ABRAHAMS

Born: Brookline, Massachusetts; June 28, 1947

PRINCIPAL LONG FICTION

The Fury of Rachel Monette, 1980
Tongues of Fire, 1982
Red Message, 1986
Hard Rain, 1988
Pressure Drop, 1989
Revolution Number Nine, 1992
Lights Out, 1994
The Fan, 1995
A Perfect Crime, 1998
Crying Wolf, 2000
Last of the Dixie Heroes, 2001
The Tutor, 2002
Their Wildest Dreams, 2003
Down the Rabbit Hole: An Echo Falls Mystery, 2005
Oblivion, 2005
Behind the Curtain: An Echo Falls Mystery, 2006
End of Story, 2006
Nerve Damage, 2007
Delusion, 2008
Into the Dark: An Echo Falls Mystery, 2008

OTHER LITERARY FORMS

Peter Abrahams is known primarily for his novels, which have been translated into several languages, including Chinese, Dutch, Greek, Hungarian, Japanese, Polish, Russian, and Swedish, indicating the breadth of his appeal.

ACHIEVEMENTS

With the publication of his first novel, *The Fury of Rachel Monette*, Peter Abrahams was widely recognized as an important new voice in the genre of crime fiction. His subsequent novels have strengthened his hold on the imagination of critics and general readers alike. In an interview, Abrahams expressed great admiration for the works of American-Canadian crime novelist Ross Macdonald and others like him. Abrahams particularly noted that Macdonald's main character, detective Lew Archer, was developed by Macdonald to grow over the years as a human being and to become more interesting and complex. Furthermore, Archer was given a broader understanding of life and began to respond more deeply

to the inevitable messiness of human experience. One recognizes the same qualities in characters created by Abrahams.

Abrahams effectively uses the conventions of the melodramatic crime thriller to create intense reader involvement. His novels also rise above others with their sophisticated rendering of flesh-and-blood individuals caught up in the dilemmas of contemporary life.

Lights Out was nominated for an Edgar Award, and *Down the Rabbit Hole* won an Agatha Award. The Edgar and Agatha awards (named for Edgar Allan Poe and Agatha Christie) are among the most prestigious awards for mystery fiction. *The Fan* was made into a 1996 feature film starring Robert De Niro and Wesley Snipes.

BIOGRAPHY

Peter Abrahams was born and reared in Massachusetts. His father was a dentist, and his mother a writer. He acquired a love of reading from his mother, from whom he also learned the basic rules of writing fiction, the most important of which is to be original. As a boy, he particularly loved adventure stories, such as Robert Louis Stevenson's *Treasure Island* (1883). Like those stories, Abrahams's works are notably effective in creating suspense.

Abrahams was graduated from Williams College in Massachusetts with a bachelor of arts degree in 1968. He then spent two years in the Bahamas, working as a spear fisherman. From there he went to Toronto, Canada, where he worked for a time in radio as a producer for the Canadian Broadcasting Corporation. His novels reflect these international experiences in a number of ways, particularly in his exploration of the United States' relationship with and impact upon other regions of the world.

In 1978, Abrahams married Diana Gray, a teacher. They had four children, two daughters and two sons. Soon after his marriage, Abrahams began to publish his critically and commercially successful fiction at the rate of one novel every other year.

The reading interests of Abrahams's children seem to have influenced him to try his hand at

Peter Abrahams. (Dan Cutrona/Courtesy, HarperCollins Publishers)

writing fiction for younger readers. In 2005, he published *Down the Rabbit Hole*, a mystery story with parallels to Lewis Carroll's *Alice's Adventures in Wonderland* (1865). Other mystery novels for young readers include *Behind the Curtain* and *Into the Dark*, and they, too, have enjoyed great popularity and recognition.

ANALYSIS

In his fiction, Peter Abrahams often employs variations on the double motif, that is, paired characters that suggest the duality of human beings or the self as other, such as one finds in Stevenson's *Strange Case of Dr. Jekyll and Mr. Hyde* (1886). This technique is especially useful for a writer who sees the criminal world as an inverse image of the conventional world, with disturbing correlations. In *Revolution Number Nine*, for example, a gentle, reclusive, middle-age man must confront the extremist youth he once was, after his former identity and violent past are uncovered. In *Crying Wolf*, a brilliant professor and a dim-witted thug are linked by blood and a shared conviction of their superiority to human laws and moral restraints. In *The Tutor*, a disturbed young man tries to model himself on a charismatic teacher who intends to destroy him. In *Their Wildest Dreams*, a Russian American gangster is an outsized version of the protagonist's husband in mad pursuit of the American Dream. In *The Fan*, a disturbing symbiosis develops between a professional athlete and an obsessive fan.

Where many of his American contemporaries in the crime and mystery genre have a distinct regional focus in terms of setting (Robert B. Parker's Boston, Sara Paretsky's Chicago), Abrahams is much more likely to set his stories in various locales around the United States, as well as abroad. He intends to capture as many dimensions of America as possible, with novels set in widely different states and areas of the country: New Hampshire, Vermont, Louisiana, and Arizona, among others.

A PERFECT CRIME

A Perfect Crime is a fine example of Abrahams's strengths as a novelist. Set in contemporary New England, with allusions to Nathaniel Hawthorne's *The Scarlet Letter* (1850), the story is about the adulterous affair of Francie, an art dealer, and Ned, a radio personality who dispenses advice to people with relationship prob-

lems. Francie has been married to the brilliant but brittle Roger Cullingwood for over fifteen years, but the marriage has unraveled because of his inability to father a child, his recent loss of employment, and his increasingly militant attempts to control all aspects of his domestic life, including his wife.

As with many of Abrahams's stories, *A Perfect Crime* moves back and forth between two dominant points of view, in this case from that of wife Francie, who is seeking love and fulfillment, to that of husband Roger, who moves from suspicion to blazing anger to coldly plotting "the perfect crime" when he discovers his wife's infidelity.

Ned and Francie have an apparently ideal place to conduct their affair, a cottage on a small island surrounded by a lake in bucolic New Hampshire. The cottage is owned by one of Francie's wealthy clients, who is currently living in Europe. Nothing can link the cottage in any obvious way to either of the lovers. The setting, which turns from idyllic to deadly with the first snowstorm, is an effective counterpoint to the emotions generated by this affair.

Francie began her affair with Ned out of desperation, as a response to an attractive man at a time when she felt increasingly thwarted and diminished by her husband's inadequacies and abuse. She was vulnerable, Ned was sympathetic. The reader notices questionable things about Ned that Francie is inclined to overlook for some time, such as his insistence that he could never leave his wife because of its potential impact on their daughter, and his almost obsessive insistence on absolute secrecy. Nevertheless, the affair unlocks deep and powerful reserves of sexuality, creativity, and profound love in Francie, dimensions of self that she was unaware of, or despaired of being able to express. Roger, noting the changes, quickly intuits the reason, and finds a way to confirm his suspicions about his cheating wife. He immediately decides on revenge as his only possible response, assessing how to get the most satisfaction for the least amount of investment and risk.

In his portrayal of Roger, Abrahams limns the sort of character that reappears in various guises in his fiction, the calculating narcissist who thinks he is smarter than everyone else, for whom all others are chess pieces in a game to be moved about at his will. Roger is nearly as clever as he thinks he is. His plan, from which much of the story's narrative energy derives, is brilliant.

The plan is also diabolical; it brings into play a grotesque criminal who is Roger's dark double and his instrument of retribution. This criminal, an unstable mix of psychosis and sexual deviance, is on parole after long years in prison for killing a police officer's wife in the same area of the country as the hideaway cottage. It is this same police officer who has the task of piecing together the clues from a bewildering and brutal murder.

OBLIVION

In *Oblivion*, Nick Petrov is a Los Angeles private investigator specializing in missing-persons cases. In his early forties, Petrov is intelligent, imaginative, and relentless; he is also famous as the detective who solved the baffling case of a particularly gruesome serial killer named Gerald Reasoner, who preyed on young women. The case provided the basis for a television movie, and one of the interesting variations on the double motif in this novel is the counterpoint between the actual case and its widely viewed film version.

As the story opens, Liza, an attractive woman in her early thirties, hires Petrov to find her missing fifteen-year-old daughter, Amanda. Petrov is reluctant to take the case at first, because Liza's account of herself, her daughter, and the disappearance seems constructed and implausible. He is persuaded, finally, to take the case because a child is involved and the mother seems genuinely desperate. As he begins investigating, Petrov experiences a sudden, severe headache accompanied by a flood of very early childhood memories. The headaches recur periodically, and with increasing intensity.

Petrov learns that Amanda once confided to a school friend that her birth mother was murdered. This apparent bit of adolescent melodrama adds to Petrov's unease about his client's story, so he surreptitiously searches Liza's house for something that might confirm Amanda's parentage. While there, he is surprised to get a telephone call from a former professional associate, and lover, Elaine Kostelnik, whom he has not seen in years. Kostelnik, recently appointed as the first female chief of police of the Los Angeles Police Department, also played a role in solving the Reasoner case. That role propelled her professionally, owing partly to the image of her created by the film.

Petrov's sleuthing uncovers some intriguing facts. Thus, he learns that Amanda's grandfather played football in high school, coached by Kostelnik's father. Moreover, the grandfather had two daughters. Lara, the older of the two, was murdered some years earlier, reportedly the seventh and last victim of Reasoner. Liza, the younger sister, is Petrov's unreliable client. This cluster of apparent coincidences sends Petrov back to the decade-old murder case to see what connections might exist between the present and the past.

Petrov follows an acquaintance of Amanda to Reasoner's former home, where he committed the atrocities, and he discovers Amanda inside. However, instead of being grateful for a rescue, she is convinced he is there to kill her, suggesting that she has found proof that Lara was not killed by Reasoner but by others, who now want her dead as well. At this point, Petrov experiences a blinding headache; he collapses and is taken to the hospital, where he is diagnosed with a brain tumor. After days of tests, he is sent home with a grim prognosis.

One of the finest aspects of this novel, which excels in so many ways, is the portrayal of Petrov's physical deterioration and the mental and emotional adjustments he makes to what is happening to him. Also brilliant is Abrahams's innovative use of the double motif here, as he portrays Petrov in search of his own self that existed prior to his collapse.

Liza and Amanda have disappeared. So, too, has Petrov's memory of them and of much else as well. However, provocative bits and pieces of the recent case are noticeable around his home and office. Unable to resist the dictates of his nature and the habits of many years, he sets out to put those pieces together. In doing so, he discovers the shocking truth about Amanda's disappearance and Lara's murder; he also uncovers disturbing truths about himself, a self that the current Petrov is prepared to leave behind as he tries to construct a more fulfilling life in the short time he has to live.

NERVE DAMAGE

Nerve Damage is the story of Roy Valois, a Vermont artist who is working on a very large modernist steel sculpture of his late wife, Delia. Delia, it seems, had worked for the Hobbes Institute, a nongovernmental organization that addresses the needs of the developing world. She died fifteen years earlier, and according to official reports, she was killed in a helicopter accident in Central America while on a work assignment; yet she lives on in Roy's memory, imagination, and art. Early in the story, Roy learns that he has a terminal disease. The narrative is propelled by the main character's increasing sense of urgency, and is pervaded by his deepening awareness of human limitations and mortality.

While talking with his lawyer and close friend about his last will and testament, Roy begins to wonder how he will be described in his obituary. This seemingly innocuous though morbid line of thought leads to a morbid fact: Obituaries of public figures and celebrities are often prepared in advance, leaving the final details to be filled in at the appropriate time. Roy persuades a local young man to hack into the *New York Times* computer system to find the artist's draft obituary. Most of the draft is as expected, except for one detail: It reports that Delia worked for the United Nations. It is a small discrepancy, but for Roy, who idealizes his late wife, an intolerable one, and so he sets out to correct it by contacting a *New York Times* staff writer.

In very short order, the young hacker disappears, the staff writer is murdered, and ominous signs indicate that Roy himself is under surveillance, by persons unknown. Roy's sense of identity, of selfhood, is challenged by the physical threat of extinction, owing to his disease and the danger unleashed by his inquiries, but even more so by the recognition that much of his past might not be as he imagined. He sets out to find the truth about his late wife, and thus about himself and their life together.

One of the most intriguing aspects of the story is Abrahams's grimly realistic portrayal of Roy's interaction with the cancer specialist in charge of his treatment. The doctor's cool, analytical handling of Roy the patient, as he swings between hope and despair, is as chilling as the dangers Roy encounters in pursuit of the truth about Delia's real work, and the circumstances of her death. This pursuit eventually takes Roy to Washington, D.C., and to the highest offices of the U.S. government. There, he finally uncovers the secrets of his wife and her past; in doing so, he also rescues an authentic part of their shared life and love that will live on after his death.

Another important dimension of this novel is its portrait of Roy the artist. Throughout the story, Roy continues to work on Delia's sculpture, which is described in great detail as it takes shape. His quest for the facts about his wife, therefore, is partly driven by his understandable curiosity regarding the most important person in his life. It is also driven by the artist's uncompromising dedication to finding and expressing the most profound human truth through making art. In this way, and others, the novel signals Abrahams's conviction regarding the critical importance of art, its role as discovery and revelation. This conviction is amply supported by Abrahams's substantial body of work.

Michael J. Larsen

OTHER MAJOR WORKS

SHORT FICTION: *Up All Night: A Short Story Collection*, 2008 (with others).

NONFICTION: *Turning the Tide: One Man Against the Medellin Cartel*, 1991 (with Sidney D. Kirkpatrick).

YOUNG ADULT LITERATURE: *Reality Check*, 2009.

BIBLIOGRAPHY

Abrahams, Peter. http://www.peterabrahams.com. Author's Web site features biographical information, author commentary, and reviews of major works. Provides a useful introduction and overview to Abrahams's work.

Oates, Joyce Carol. "Unforgettable." Review of *Oblivion*, by Peter Abrahams. *The New Yorker*, April 4, 2005. Highly respected novelist Oates provides an overview of *Oblivion* as well as insightful commentary on Abrahams's major themes and methods.

Scaggs, John. *Crime Fiction*. New York: Routledge, 2005. Part of the New Critical Idiom series, this brief but comprehensive book surveys the field of crime fiction. An excellent general overview of the genre.

Winks, Robin, and Maureen Corrigan, eds. *Mystery and Suspense Writers: The Literature of Crime, Detection, and Espionage*. New York: Scribner & Sons, 1998. An invaluable guide to major mystery writers and genres.

CHINUA ACHEBE

Born: Ogidi, Nigeria; November 16, 1930
Also known as: Albert Chinualumogu Achebe

PRINCIPAL LONG FICTION

Things Fall Apart, 1958
No Longer at Ease, 1960
Arrow of God, 1964
A Man of the People, 1966
Anthills of the Savannah, 1987

OTHER LITERARY FORMS

The short stories of Chinua Achebe (ah-CHAY-bay), written over a period of twenty years, were first published in England by Heinemann under the title *Girls at War, and Other Stories* (1972), although most of them had already appeared in various periodicals and in a Nigerian publication, *The Sacrificial Egg, and Other Short Stories* (1962). Achebe's poems, most of them written during the Biafran crisis (1967-1970), came out soon after the war as *Beware: Soul Brother, and Other Poems* (1971) and a year later in an enlarged edition. Doubleday then published this Heinemann collection in the United States as *Christmas in Biafra, and Other Poems* (1973). Additional poems and an essay by Achebe were combined with photographs by Robert Lyons in a full-color coffee-table book, *Another Africa* (1998), which provided an overview of the beauty and complexity of modern Africa. Achebe has gathered together various autobiographical, political, literary, and cultural essays under the intriguingly optimistic title *Morning Yet on Creation Day* (1975), published by both Doubleday and Heinemann. In 1983, Heinemann published his short book *The Trouble with Nigeria*, which challenged his contemporaries to overcome their growing resignation. *Hopes and Impediments* (1988) brings together some fifteen essays, mainly on literature and the writer's role and covering a twenty-three-year period, some of them previously published, including five from *Morning Yet on Creation Day*. Achebe has also written the children's stories *Chike and the River* (1966) and, jointly with John Iroaganachi, *How the Leopard Got His Claws* (1972). Achebe has also collaborated in editing several volumes of poetry and short stories.

ACHIEVEMENTS

From the beginning of his literary career, with the publication of *Things Fall Apart*, Chinua Achebe recognized and accepted his role as that of a spokesman for black Africa. The primary function of that role was to reinterpret the African past from an African's point of view. This he successfully does in *Things Fall Apart* and *Arrow of God*, which correct the imperialist myth of African primitivism and savagery by re-creating the Igbo culture of the Eastern Region of Nigeria, its daily routines, its rituals, its customs, and especially its people, dealing with one another in a highly civilized fashion within a complex society. The reinterpretation necessitated, as well, a look at the invading culture; Achebe tilted the balance in the Africans' favor by depicting individuals in the British administration as prejudiced, imperceptive, unnecessarily bureaucratic, and emotionally impotent. As his main subject was the African crisis, he did not go to great pains to explore the private lives of the British or to mollify the British public. He needed to show that white civilization and white people were not intrinsically superior, and to restore to Africans a respect for their own culture and their own lives.

Achebe did not conceive his role as that of a mere propagandist, however, as any reader of the novels would acknowledge. His interpretation paid due respect to Western civilization and seriously criticized aspects of his own. In spite of certain fictional shortcuts—which some critics regard as crucial flaws—Achebe's attempt was to arrive at an objective appraisal of the conflict between Africa and the West. In fact, the central focus of his three other novels—*No Longer at Ease*, *A Man of the People*, and *Anthills of the Savannah*—set in contemporary times, is on the failure of Africans to meet challenges in the modern world. Of these, the first two are satirical attacks; the third is a subtle blend of irony, compassion, traditional wisdom, and a sane perspective on the chaotic Nigerian scene.

Achebe's importance as a spokesman for and to his own people has drawn criticism from some Western readers who are more interested in the quality of a novel than in its social function. Achebe has had several angry words to say to such aesthetically minded critics. His defense is that literature is a human and humane endeavor, not primarily a formal one. Still, one can easily defend his novels on aesthetic grounds, even arguing, as Charles Larson has done, that Achebe is actually an innovative writer who has transformed the novel to suit the African setting. Certainly, the most remarkable thing that Achebe has done, especially in *Things Fall Apart* and *Arrow of God*, is to transform the English language itself into an African idiom. Bernth Lindfors and others have noted the skill with which Achebe uses imagery, allusions, figures of speech, proverbs, sentence patterns, Standard English, and various forms of non-Standard English to capture a particular historical moment as well as the African mentality and—just as important—to unify the novels around major motifs and themes. Achebe has not written mere social documents or social manifestos, but creditable works of literature that can stand the test of critical analysis; his contribution to the African world goes far beyond his five novels, but they are his major literary achievement.

As a consequence of his achievement as a novelist, Achebe was named chairman of the Society of Nigerian Authors and became a Member of Council at the University of Lagos. He also received the New Statesman Award for his third novel, *Arrow of God*. Among other honors were a Rockefeller Travel Fellowship to East and Central Africa (1960) and a United Nations Educational, Scientific, and Cultural Organization (UNESCO) Travel Fellowship to the United States and Brazil (1963). In 1989, Achebe was elected the first president of the Nigerian chapter of the International Association of Poets, Playwrights, Editors, Essayists, and Novelists (PEN), although he was living in the United States at the time.

Some twenty American, European, and African institutions, including Dartmouth College, Stanford University, the Open University of Great Britain, and the University of Port Harcourt in Nigeria, have granted Achebe honorary degrees. He holds the influential position of founding editor of the African Writers Series, which, more than any other publisher, is responsible for the worldwide recognition of literary talent from Africa. *The Times* of London included Achebe among its 1993 list of one thousand "Makers of the Twentieth Century," and in 1996 he received the Campion Award, which is

presented by the Catholic Book Club to honor a "Christian person of letters" who combines faith and literary talent. In 2007, he was awarded the Man Booker International Prize for his body of work. *Things Fall Apart* has been translated into more than forty-five languages and has sold millions of copies, making it one of the most widely read and influential African novels ever written.

BIOGRAPHY

Albert Chinualumogu Achebe was born on November 16, 1930, in Ogidi, in the Eastern Region of Nigeria. He gives some details about his family and his early life in an essay titled "Named for Victoria, Queen of England" (1973, in *Morning Yet on Creation Day*). His parents, Isaiah and Janet Achebe, were both Christian, his father an evangelist and church teacher. His maternal grandfather, like the character Okonkwo in *Things Fall Apart*, was a wealthy and distinguished community leader. He was not Christian, but he exercised tolerance when Achebe was converted. Achebe was baptized Albert Chinualumogu, named for Queen Victoria's consort, but he dropped the Albert while at university, evidently as a reaction against the British and his Christian heritage. He has explained, however, that he was never really torn between the two cultures. He experienced none of the agony that is often evidenced in the works of other African writers, such as Cheikh Hamidou Kane. Achebe enjoyed the rituals of both religions. He did come to wonder if the apostates were not the Christians rather than the pagans, but he noted some advantages brought in by Christianity: education, certain humane reforms, paid jobs. Achebe seems to have exhibited a pragmatic and tolerant strain from the beginning.

For his secondary education, Achebe attended Government College, Umuahia (1944-1947), and he received a bachelor of arts degree from University College, Ibadan, in 1953. During the next twelve years he worked for the Nigerian Broadcasting Corporation, first as producer in Lagos (1954-1958), then as controller in Enugu (1959-1961), and finally as director of external broadcasting in Lagos (1961-1966). In 1961, he married Christiana Chinwe Okoli, and they had two sons and two daughters. Also during these years Achebe wrote his first four novels, beginning with his most famous, *Things Fall Apart*, in 1958, and ending with *A Man of the*

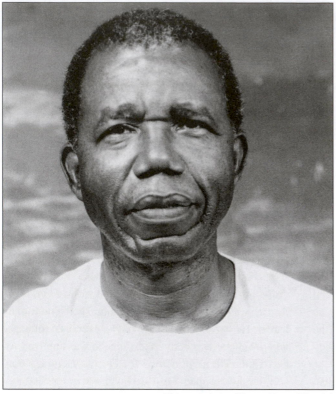

Chinua Achebe. (Rocon/Engu, Nigeria)

People in 1966. Achebe explains his novelistic career as the result of a revolution in his thinking during the nationalist movement after World War II. He decided that foreigners really could not tell the Nigerian story adequately. Joyce Cary's *Mister Johnson* (1939) was a prime example of this failure. Achebe regarded *Things Fall Apart* as an atonement for his apostasy, a ritual return to his homeland.

By 1966, Achebe was a distinguished member of the international literary community. In 1967, however, his career was interrupted by the outbreak of the war in Biafra, Achebe's Igbo homeland in the Eastern Region of Nigeria. The conflict came to be essentially a civil war. Achebe joined the Biafran Ministry of Information and played a diplomatic role in raising money for the Biafran cause. Bound as he was by emotional ties and personal commitment to his country's fate, Achebe had no time to write novels. All he could manage were short poems, which were published a year after the war was over (1971).

Achebe's career after the war was taken up primarily by the academic world. In 1972, he was a senior research fellow at the Institute of African Studies at the University of Nigeria in Nsukka. From 1972 to 1975, he was a professor at the University of Massachusetts at Amherst, and in the 1975-1976 academic year he was employed at the University of Connecticut. He then became a professor at the University of Nigeria, Nsukka, and ten years later was again at the University of Massachusetts. Three of his publications during that time were a collection of short stories, *Girls at War, and Other Stories*, written over a period of years going back to his university days; a collection of essays, *Morning Yet on Creation Day*, that gave his views on a number of issues, from the Biafran war to the problems of African literature in the Western world; and a book-length essay on the Nigerian situation, *The Trouble with Nigeria*. When it seemed that Achebe had left his career as a novelist behind him, twenty-one years after *A Man of the People*, he produced the carefully crafted *Anthills of the Savannah*, bringing up to date the apparently futile attempts to end the vicious cycles of corruption and coups in Nigeria.

In March, 1990, while en route to the airport in Lagos, Nigeria, Achebe was involved in a serious car accident and suffered a spinal injury that left him confined to a wheelchair. After nearly six months of recovery in various hospitals, he accepted an endowed professorship at Bard College in New York. For the next several years he turned his energies increasingly to the academic world, teaching, editing, and writing political and critical nonfiction.

ANALYSIS

Chinua Achebe is probably both the most widely known and the most representative African novelist. He may very well have written the first African novel of real literary merit—such at least is the opinion of Charles Larson—and he deals with what one can call the classic issue that preoccupies his fellow novelists, the clash between the indigenous cultures of black Africa and a white, European civilization. He avoids the emotionally charged subject of slavery and concentrates his attention on political and cultural confrontation. His five novels offer, in a sense, a paradigm of this clash. He begins in *Things Fall Apart* with the first incursion of the British into the Igbo region of what became the Eastern Region of Nigeria, and his subsequent novels trace (with some gaps) the spread of British influence into the 1950's and beyond that into the postindependence period of the 1960's. The one period he slights, as he himself admits, is the generation in transition from traditional village life to the new Westernized Africa. He had difficulty imagining the psychological conflict of the African caught between two cultures. There is no example in Achebe of Cheikh Hamidou Kane's "ambiguous adventure." Achebe does, however, share with Kane and with most other African novelists the idea that his function as a writer is a social one.

Achebe insists repeatedly on this social function in response to Western critics who tend to give priority to aesthetic values. He seems to suggest, in fact, that the communal responsibility and the communal tie are more fundamental than artistic merit for any writer, but certainly for the African writer and for himself personally at the present stage in African affairs. He describes himself specifically as a teacher. His purpose is to dispel the colonial myth of the primitive African and to establish a true image of the people and their culture. This message is intended, to some extent, for a Western audience, but especially for the Africans themselves, since they have come to believe the myth and have internalized the feeling of inferiority. Achebe's aim is to help them regain their self-respect, recognize the beauty of their own cultural past, and deal capably with the dilemmas of contemporary society.

It is important, however, that Achebe is not fulfilling this role as an outsider. He returns to the traditional Igbo concept of the master craftsman and to the *Mbare* ceremony to explain the functional role of art in traditional society. He insists that creativity itself derives from a spiritual bond, the inspiration of a shared past and a shared destiny with a particular people: Alienated writers, such as Ayi Kwei Armah, cannot be in tune with themselves and are therefore likely to be imitative rather than truly creative. It would appear, then, that Achebe values originality and freshness in the management of

literary form but considers these attributes dependent on the sensitivity of writers to their native settings.

Whereas Achebe's motivation in writing may be the restoration of pride in the African world, his theme—or, rather, the specific advice that he offers, albeit indirectly—is much more pragmatic. He does not advocate a return to the past or a rejection of Western culture. Like other African writers, he decries the destructive consequences of colonial rule: alienation, frustration, and a loss of cohesiveness and a clear code of behavior. He recognizes as well, however, that certain undesirable customs and superstitions have been exposed by the foreign challenge. His practical advice is that Africans should learn to cope with a changing world. He teaches the necessity of compromise: a loyalty to traditional wisdom and values, if not to tribal politics and outmoded customs, along with a suspicion of Western materialism but an openness to Western thought. He notes that in some cases the two cultures are not so far apart: Igbo republicanism goes even beyond the British-American concept of democracy, a view that the Ghanaian novelist Armah has developed as well. Unlike the negritude writers of francophone Africa, Achebe, in his attempt to reinterpret the African past, does not paint an idyllic picture. He regrets the loss of mystery surrounding that past, but he chooses knowledge because he considers judgment, clarity of vision, and tolerance—virtues that he locates in his traditional society—to be the way out of the present confusion and corruption.

This key idea of tolerance pervades Achebe's work. One of his favorite stories (Yoruba, not Igbo) illustrates the danger in dogmatism. The god Echu, who represents fate or confusion, mischievously decides to provoke a quarrel between two farmers who live on either side of a road. Echu paints himself black on one side and white on the other, then walks up the road between the two farmers. The argument that ensues concerns whether the stranger is black or white. When Echu turns around and walks back down the road, each farmer tries to outdo the other in apologizing for his mistake. Achebe's most pervasive vehicle for this idea of tolerance, however, is in the concept of the *chi*, which is central to Igbo cosmology. Achebe interprets it as the ultimate expression of individualism, the basic worth and independence of every person. Politically it means the rejection of any authoritarian rule. Morally it means the responsibility of every person for his or her own fate. The *chi* is one's other self, one's spiritual identity responsible for one's birth and one's future. Thus, while one's *chi* defines one's unique-ness, it also defines one's limitations. As Achebe fre-quently notes in his novels, no one can defeat his or her own *chi*, and the acceptance of one's limitations is the beginning of tolerance.

It is the social purpose, this "message" of tolerance, in Achebe's novels that dictates the form. His plots tend to be analytic, static, or "situational," as Larson argues, rather than dynamic. Instead of narrative movement, there is juxtaposition of past and present, of the tradi-tional and the modern. Achebe achieves balance through comparison and contrast. He uses exposition more than drama. His main characters tend to be representational. Their conflicts are the crucial ones of the society. The protagonists of the two novels set in the past, *Things Fall Apart* and *Arrow of God*, are strong men who lack wis-dom, practical sense, an ability to accept change, and a tolerance for opposing views. The protagonists of *No Longer at Ease* and *A Man of the People* are weak and vacillating. They accept change but are blinded by van-ity and have no satisfactory code of conduct to resist the unreasonable pressures of traditional ties or the cor-ruption and attractions of the new age. The two male pro-tagonists of *Anthills of the Savannah*, also hindered by vanity, prove inadequate idealists in a power-hungry en-vironment and wake up too late to their lack of control over events.

An even more predominant feature of the five novels is their style. Achebe makes the necessary compromise and writes in English, a foreign tongue, but manipulates it to capture the flavor of the native Igbo expression. He does this through dialect, idiom, and figurative language as well as through proverbs that reflect traditional Igbo wisdom, comment ironically on the inadequacies of the characters, and state the central themes.

Achebe thus manages, through the authorial voice, to establish a steady control over every novel. To some ex-tent, one senses the voice in the proverbs. They represent the assessments of the elders in the clan, yet the wisdom of the proverbs is itself sometimes called into question, and the reader is invited to make the judgment. In gen-eral, it is Achebe's juxtaposing of character, incident,

proverb, and tone that creates the total assessment. Against this background voice one measures the pride, vanity, or prejudice of the individuals who, caught in the stressful times of colonial or postcolonial Nigeria, fail to respond adequately. The voice does not judge or con-demn; it describes. It reminds the Nigerian of the danger of self-deception. It also recognizes the danger of failing to communicate with others. Achebe keeps ever in mind the tale (found in numerous versions all over Africa) of humankind whose message to Chukwa (the supreme de-ity) requesting immortality is distorted by the messenger and thus fails in its purpose. The voice he adopts to avoid the distortion is one of self-knowledge, practical sense, pragmatism, and detachment but also of faith, convic-tion, and humor. The voice is, in a sense, the message it-self, moderating the confrontation between Africa and the West.

THINGS FALL APART

Significantly, Achebe takes the title of his first novel, *Things Fall Apart*, from William Butler Yeats's 1920 apocalyptic poem "The Second Coming," which proph-esies the end of the present era and the entrance on the world's stage of another that is radically different. *Things Fall Apart* treats the early moments of that transi-tion in an Igbo village. For the people of the village, the intrusion of the British is as revolutionary as the coming of a second Messiah, Yeats's terrible "rough beast."

To some extent, Achebe creates a mythic village whose history stretches back to a legendary past. Chap-ters are devoted to the daily routines of the people, their family lives, their customs, their games and rituals, their ancient wisdom, their social order, and their legal prac-tices. Achebe remains a realist, however, as he identifies also certain flaws in the customs and in the people. Su-perstition leads them to unnecessary cruelties. The pro-tagonist, Okonkwo, reflects a basic conflict within the society. He is, on one hand, a respected member of the society who has risen through hard work to a position of wealth and authority. He conscientiously accepts the re-sponsibilities that the elders lay on him. At the same time, he is such an individualist that his behavior runs counter to the spirit of traditional wisdom. His shame over his father's weak character provokes him to be ex-cessive in proving his own manhood. A defensiveness and uncertainty lie behind his outward assertiveness. It is true that the clan has its mechanisms to reprimand and punish Okonkwo for errant behavior. Nevertheless, even before the British influence begins to disturb the region, the cohesiveness of the clan is already in question.

One particular chink in Okonkwo's armor, which identifies a weakness also in the clan as it faces the foreign threat, is his inflexibility, his inability to adapt or to accept human limitations. Since he, in his youth, overcame adversity (familial disadvantages, natural forces such as drought and excessive rains, challenges of strength as a wrestler), he has come to believe that he has the individual strength to resist all challenges to his personal ambition. He cannot accept the presence of forces beyond his control, including the forces of his own personal destiny. It is this and the other aspects of Okonkwo's character that Achebe develops in the first section of the novel against the background of the tribe to which he belongs.

Part 1 ends with the symbolic act of Okonkwo's accidentally killing a young man during a funeral ceremony. Like death, the act is beyond his control and unexplainable, yet it is punishable. The elders exile him for seven years to the village of his mother's family. This separation from his village is itself symbolic, since in a way Okonkwo has never belonged to the village. While he is away, the village changes. With the coming of the missionaries, traditional religious practices begin to lose their sanction, their absoluteness. In part 3, Okonkwo returns from exile but finds that his exile continues. Nothing is as it was. Open hostility exists between the new religion and the traditional one. The British government has begun to take over authority from the elders. The novel ends with Okonkwo's irrational killing of a messenger from the British district officer and with his subsequent suicide. Okonkwo rightly assumes, it would seem, that no authority now exists to judge him: The old sanctions are dead, and he refuses to accept the new ones. He must be his own judge.

There is, however, if not a judge, a voice of reason and compassion, detached from the action but controlling its effects, that assures Okonkwo of a fair hearing. The voice is heard in the proverbs, warning Okonkwo not to challenge his own *chi* (his own spiritual identity and destiny), even though another proverb insists that if he says yes his *chi* will say yes too. It is heard in the deci-

sions of the elders, the complaints of the wives, and the rebellion of Okonkwo's own son, Noye, who turns to Christianity in defiance against his father's unreasonableness. It is found in the tragic sense of life of Okonkwo's uncle, Uchendu, who advises this man in exile to bear his punishment stoically, for his sufferings are mild in comparison with those of many others.

Achebe locates his voice in one particular character, Obierika, Okonkwo's closest friend and a man of thought rather than, like his friend, a man of action. In the important eighth chapter, Achebe measures his protagonist against this man of moderation, reflection, and humor, who can observe the white invader with tolerance, his own society's laws with skepticism, and, at the end of the novel, his dead friend with respect and compassion. Achebe's voice can even be seen in the ironically insensitive judgment of the district commissioner as the novel closes. As superficial and uninformed as that voice might be in itself, Achebe recognizes that the voice nevertheless exists, is therefore real, and must be acknowledged. The final view of Okonkwo and of the village that he both reflects and rejects is a composite of all these voices. It is the composite also of Okonkwo's own complex and unpredictable behavior, and of his fate, which is the result of his own reckless acts and of forces that he does not comprehend. Amid the growing chaos one senses still the stable influence of the calm authorial voice, controlling and balancing everything.

NO LONGER AT EASE

From the early twentieth century setting of *Things Fall Apart*, Achebe turns in his second novel, *No Longer at Ease*, to the mid-1950's, just before independence. The protagonist, Obi Okonkwo, grandson of the tragic victim who lashed out against British insolence in his first novel, resembles to some extent his grandfather in his inadequacy to deal with the pressures of his society, but he has far different loyalties. The novel begins after things have already fallen apart; Nigeria is between societies.

Obi no longer belongs to the old society. His father is the rebellious son of Okonkwo who left home for the Christian church and was educated in mission schools. Obi received a similar education and was selected by his community to study in England. The financial and personal obligation this creates plagues Obi throughout the novel, for after he receives his Western education he no longer shares the old customs and the old sense of loyalty. He considers himself an independent young man of the city, with a Western concept of government and administration. After his return from England he receives a civil service job and has visions of reforming the bureaucracy. The story is thus about the practical difficulties (it is not really a psychological study) of an ordinary individual separating himself cleanly from the past while adapting to the glitter and temptations of the new.

Obi faces two particular problems. He has chosen to marry a woman, Clara, who belongs to a family considered taboo by the traditional community. He attempts to resist family and community pressure, but he eventually succumbs. Meanwhile, Clara has become pregnant and must go through a costly and embarrassing abortion. Obi essentially abandons his responsibility toward her in his weak, halfhearted respect for his family's wishes. He likewise fails at his job, as he resists self-righteously various bribes until his financial situation and morals finally collapse. Unfortunately, he is as clumsy here as in his personal relations. He is arrested and sentenced to prison.

As in Achebe's first novel, the subject of *No Longer at Ease* is the individual (and the society) inadequate to the changing times. The author's main concern is again a balanced appraisal of Nigerian society at a crucial stage in its recent history, because the greatest danger, as Achebe himself observes, is self-deception. He presents a careful selection of characters whose vanity, prejudice, or misplaced values allow them only a partial view of reality. Obi is, of course, the main example. He leaves his home village as a hero, is one of the few Nigerians to receive a foreign education, and, as a civil servant and proud possessor of a car, becomes a member of the elite. His vanity blinds him to such an extent that he cannot assess his proper relationship to his family, to Clara, or to his social role. His father, caught between his Christian faith and tribal customs, cannot allow Obi his independence. Mr. Green, Obi's British superior at the office, is trapped by stereotypical prejudices against Africans. There is no one individual—such as Obierika in *Things Fall Apart*—within the novel to provide a reasonable interpretation of events.

One nevertheless feels the constant presence of

Achebe as he balances these various voices against one another. Achebe also assures perspective by maintaining a detached tone through irony, wit, and humor. The narrator possesses the maturity and the wisdom that the characters lack. This novel also shows Achebe experimenting with structure as a means of expressing the authorial voice. *No Longer at Ease* opens—like Leo Tolstoy's *Smert' Ivana Il'icha* (1886; *The Death of Ivan Ilyich*, 1887)—with the final act, the trial and judgment of Obi for accepting a bribe. Achebe thus invites the reader to take a critical view of Obi from the very beginning. There is no question of the reader's becoming romantically involved in his young life and career.

This distancing continues in the first three chapters as Achebe juxtaposes present and past, scenes of reality and scenes of expectation. The real Lagos is juxtaposed directly against the idyllic one in Obi's mind. A picture of the later, strained relationship between Obi and Clara precedes the romantic scenes after they meet on board ship returning from England. Through this kind of plotting by juxtaposition, Achebe turns what might have been a melodramatic story of young love, abortion, betrayal, and corruption into a realistic commentary on Nigerian society in transition. In *Things Fall Apart* he rejects a paradisiacal view of the African past; in *No Longer at Ease* he warns against selfish, irresponsible, and naïve expectations in the present.

ARROW OF GOD

In his third novel, *Arrow of God*, Achebe returns to the past, taking up the era of British colonization a few years after the events of *Things Fall Apart*. The old society is still intact, but the Christian religion and the British administration are more firmly entrenched than before. Achebe again tries to re-create the former Igbo environment, with an even more elaborate account of daily life, customs, and rituals, and with the scattering throughout of traditional idioms and proverbs. The foreigners, too, receive more detailed attention, though even the two main personalities, Winterbottom and Clarke, achieve hardly more than stereotyped status. Rather than work them late into the story, this time Achebe runs the two opposing forces alongside each other almost from the beginning in order to emphasize the British presence. Now it is the political, not the religious, power that is in the foreground, suggesting historically the second stage of foreign conquest, but the Christian church also takes full advantage of local political and religious controversy to increase its control over the people.

Achebe continues to be realistic in his treatment of traditional society. It is not an idyllic Eden corrupted by satanic foreign power. In spite of the attractive pictures of local customs, the six villages of Umuaro are divided and belligerent, and, in two instances at least, it is ironically the British government or the church that ensures peace and continuity in the communal life. By this stage in the colonization, of course, it is difficult (and Achebe does not try) to untangle the causes of internal disorder among the Igbo.

Like Okonkwo, the protagonist in *Arrow of God*, Ezeulu, is representative of the social disorder. In him Achebe represents the confidence in traditional roles and beliefs challenged not only by the new British worldview but also by forces within. Personal pride, egotism, and intolerance sometimes obscure his obligation to the welfare of the community. Whereas Okonkwo is one among several wealthy members of the clan, Ezeulu occupies a key position as the priest of Ulu, chief god of the six villages. The central cohesive force in the society is thus localized in this one man. Ezeulu differs from Okonkwo in another way as well: Whereas Okonkwo stubbornly resists the new Western culture, Ezeulu makes such gestures of accommodation that his clan actually accuses him of being the white man's friend. Instead of disowning his son for adopting Christianity, he sends Oduche to the mission school to be his spy in the Western camp.

Ezeulu's personality, however, is complex, as are his motives. Accommodation is his pragmatic way of preserving the clan and his own power. When the opportunity arises for him to become the political representative of his people to the British government, he refuses out of a sense of loyalty to his local god. This complexity is, however, contradictory and confusing, thus reflecting again the transitional state of affairs during the early colonial period. Ezeulu does not always seem to know what his motives are as he jockeys for power with Winterbottom and with the priest Idemili. In trying to save the community, he sets up himself and his god as the sole sources of wisdom. As priest—and thus considered half man and half spirit—he may, as Achebe

seems to suggest, confuse his sacred role with his human vanity.

It is in the midst of this confusion that Achebe again questions the existence of absolutes and advises tolerance. The central concept of the *chi* reappears. Does it say yes if humanity says yes? If so, humankind controls its own destiny. If not, it is severely limited. In any case, the concept itself suggests duality rather than absoluteness. Even Ezeulu, while challenging the new power, advises his son that one "must dance the dance prevalent in his time." Chapter 16, in which this statement appears, contains the key thematic passages of the novel. In it, one of Ezeulu's wives tells her children a traditional tale about a people's relation with the spirit world. The story turns on the importance of character—the proper attitude one must have toward oneself and toward the gods. A boy accidentally leaves his flute in the field where he and his family had been farming. He persuades his parents to let him return to fetch it, and he has an encounter with the spirits during which he demonstrates his good manners, temperance, and reverence; this encounter leads to material reward. The envious senior wife in the family sends her son on a similar mission, but he exhibits rudeness and greed, leading only to the visitation of evils on human society. The intended message is obvious, but the implied one, in the context of this novel, is that traditional values appear to be childhood fancies in the face of contemporary realities.

At the end of the chapter, Ezeulu puts those realities into focus. He describes himself as an arrow of god whose very defense of religious forms threatens the survival of his religion, but he goes on to suggest the (for him) terrifying speculation that Oduche, his Christian son, and also Christianity and the whites themselves, are arrows of god. At the end of his career, Ezeulu is opening his mind to a wide range of possibilities. This tolerance, however, is double-edged, for, as Achebe seems to suggest, humanity must be not only receptive to unfamiliar conceptions but also tough enough to "tolerate" the pain of ambiguity and alienation. Ezeulu is too old and too exhausted to endure that pain. The final blow is his son's death, which occurs while he is performing a ritual dance. Ezeulu interprets this as a sign that Ulu has deserted him.

Indeed, the voice in *Arrow of God* is even more ambiguous than that in the first two novels. There is no Obierika to correct Ezeulu's aberrations. Akueke, Ezeulu's friend and adviser, is not a sure guide to the truth. Achebe works through dialogue in this novel even more than in *Things Fall Apart*, and the debates between these two men do not lead to a clear answer. Akueke cannot decipher the priest's motives or anticipate his actions. Ezeulu, as a strange compound of spirit and man, is to him "unknowable." Nor does Achebe make the task any easier for the reader. Ezeulu does not seem to understand his own motives. He considers himself under the spiritual influence of his god. His sudden, final decision not to seek a reconciliation with his people he imagines as the voice of Ulu. He thus sacrifices himself and his people (as well as the god himself) to the will of the god. Achebe remains silent on the issue of whether the voice is the god's or Ezeulu's. One can only speculate that since the society created the god in the first place (or so the legend went), it could also destroy him.

A MAN OF THE PEOPLE

Like *No Longer at Ease*, Achebe's fourth novel, *A Man of the People*, seems rather lightweight in comparison with the two historical novels. It takes place not in Nigeria but in an imaginary African country, a few years after independence. Achebe seems to be playing with some of the popular situations in contemporary African literature, as though he were parodying them. The main character, Odili, has relationships with three different women: Elsie, a friend from the university who functions as a sort of mistress but remains a shadowy figure in the background; Jean, a white American with whom he has a brief sexual relationship; and Edna, a beautiful and innocent young woman with whom he "falls in love" in a rather conventional Western sense. There is also the typical estrangement of the university-educated son from his traditionally oriented father. Achebe contrives a somewhat romantic reconciliation during the last third of the novel. Finally, while all of Achebe's novels are essentially political, this one pits two candidates for public office against each other, with all the paraphernalia of personal grudges, dirty tricks, campaign rhetoric, and even a military coup at the end that ironically makes the election meaningless. (In fact, it was already meaningless because the incumbent, Nanga, had arranged that Odili's name not be officially registered.) Furthermore,

the contest is a stock romantic confrontation between the idealism of youth and the corrupt opportunism of an older generation. While the story might at first glance appear to be a melodramatic rendering of the romantic world of love and politics, it so exaggerates situations that one must assume Achebe is writing rather in the comic mode.

Along with this choice of mode, Achebe also creates a more conventional plot line. The rising action deals with the first meeting after sixteen years between Odili, a grammar school teacher, and Nanga, the "man of the people," Odili's former teacher, local representative to parliament, and minister of culture. In spite of his skepticism toward national politics, Odili succumbs to Nanga's charm and accepts an invitation to stay at his home in the city. The turning point comes when Odili's girlfriend, Elsie, shamelessly spends the night with Nanga. Odili sees this as a betrayal by Elsie, even though he himself feels no special commitment to her. More important, Odili feels betrayed and humiliated by Nanga, who does not take such incidents with women at all seriously. His vanity touched by this rather trivial incident, Odili suddenly reactivates his conscience over political corruption and vows to seek revenge. The attack is twofold: to steal Edna, Nanga's young fiancé, who is to be his second wife, and to defeat Nanga in the next elections. Odili's motives are obviously suspect. The rest of the novel recounts his gradual initiation into love and politics. The revenge motive drops as the relationship with Edna becomes serious. The political campaign fails, and Odili ends up in the hospital after a pointless attempt to spy on one of Nanga's campaign rallies. Again, it is tempting to treat this as a conventional initiation story, except that Odili's experiences do not really cure him of his romantic notions of love and politics.

For the first time, Achebe elects to use the first-person point of view: Odili tells his own story. This may be the reason that the balancing of effects through juxtaposition of scenes and characters does not operate as in the earlier works. The tone is obviously affected as well: Odili is vain and pompous, blind to his own flaws while critical of others. Hence, Achebe has to manipulate a subjective narrative to express the objective authorial voice, as Mark Twain does in *Adventures of Huckleberry Finn* (1884) or (to use an African example) as Mongo Beti does in *Le Pauvre Christ de Bomba* (1956; *The Poor Christ of Bomba*, 1971). The primary means is through Odili's own partial vision. Odili frequently makes criticisms of contemporary politics that appear to be just and therefore do represent the judgment of Achebe as well. At the same time, Odili's affected tone invites criticism and provides Achebe with an occasion to satirize the self-deception of the young intellectuals whom Odili represents. Achebe also expresses himself through the plot, in which he parodies romantic perceptions of the contemporary world. In addition, he continues to include proverbs in the mouths of provincial characters as guides to moral evaluation.

Achebe emphasizes one proverb in particular to describe the political corruption in which Nanga participates. After a local merchant, Josiah, steals a blind beggar's stick to make his customers (according to a figurative twist of reasoning) blindly purchase whatever he sells, the public reacts indignantly with the proverb: "He has taken away enough for the owner to notice." Unlike Achebe's narrator in the first three novels, Odili cannot allow the proverb to do its own work. He must, as an academic, analyze it and proudly expand on its meaning. He had done this before when he became the "hero" of Jean's party as the resident expert on African behavior and African art. He may very well be correct about the political implications of the proverb, that the people (the owners of the country) are now being blatantly robbed by the politicians, but he fails to identify emotionally with the local situation. Nor is he objective enough to admit fully to himself his own immoral, hypocritical behavior, which he has maintained throughout the novel. He is an egotist, more enchanted with his own cleverness than concerned about the society he has pretended to serve.

In like manner, at the close of the story Odili turns the real death of his political colleague, Max, into a romantic fantasy of the ideal sacrifice. Totally pessimistic about the reliability of the people, he returns once again to the proverb to illustrate their fickle behavior as the melodramatic villains: They always return the Josiahs to power. Achebe may to some extent share Odili's view of the public and the national leadership it chooses, but he is skeptical of the Odilis as well, and hence he positions the reader outside both the political structure and Odili as an observer of the society. Achebe, then, even in this first-person narrative, does not abandon his authorial voice, nor does he abandon the role of social spokesman that he had maintained in all his other novels.

ANTHILLS OF THE SAVANNAH

Achebe's fifth novel, *Anthills of the Savannah*, written twenty-one years after his fourth, shares some of the preceding novel's interests. Achebe once again makes the situation political and the setting contemporary. As in *A Man of the People*, the country, Kangan, is fictitious (though the resemblance to Nigeria is again hardly disguised), but the time is somewhat later in the independence period, perhaps in the 1970's or the early 1980's. Also, once again, the main actors in the drama knew one another under different circumstances in the past. Whereas the former relationship between Nanga and Odili was teacher and student, the three male protagonists of *Anthills of the Savannah* are of the same generation and first knew one another as fellow students at Lord Lugard College when they were thirteen years old. The novel deals with their lives during a period of twenty-seven years, including their experiences in England at the University of London, their adventures in love, and their choices of careers. These years are shown only through flashbacks, however, for the focus is on a two-week period in the present, on the edge of a political crisis, when the characters are forty years old.

Achebe does not present his narrative in a straight chronological line; in addition to flashbacks, even during the two-week present he recounts, or has his characters recount, events out of chronological order—a technique he used in his other novels as well to control reader response. The events of this two-week period begin, as the novel does, on a Thursday morning as Sam, now president of Kangan, presides over his weekly cabinet meeting. Sam had decided long before, following the advice of his headmaster at Lord Lugard College, to choose the army over a medical career because it would turn him into a "gentleman." His choice proved to be a good one when, after a military coup two years earlier, he was named president of the new government. A fellow student at Lord Lugard, Christopher Oriko, became his minister of information. Chris used his influence over Sam to name five of the twelve cabinet members and to appoint another old school friend, Ikem Osodi, editor of the *National Gazette*. The political conflict in the novel focuses on these three men, although Sam as a character remains largely in the background.

The relationship between Chris and Sam has become increasingly strained over the two-year period, as Sam has expanded his drive for status into an ambition to be president for life with total authority. He is now highly suspicious of Chris and has appointed the tough, ruthless Major Johnson Ossai as his chief of staff and head of intelligence. Chris, meanwhile, as he himself admits in the opening chapter, has become an amused spectator and recorder of events, almost indifferent to the official drama before him. Such an attitude has also driven a wedge between him and Ikem, who, as a crusading journalist, has continued to attack government incompetence and to represent and fight for the hapless public, while Chris has counseled patience and diplomacy in dealing with Sam.

The inciting force on this Thursday is a delegation from Abazon—the northern province of Kangan devastated, like Nigeria's own northern regions, by drought—that has come to the capital city of Bassa to seek relief. Ikem has only recently written an editorial, his allegorical "Hymn to the Sun" that dries up the savannah, accusing the president (the sun) of responsibility and promoting the delegation's cause. Sam at first feels threatened by the loud demonstrations outside his office, but when he learns that the delegation consists of only six elders and that the rest of the demonstrators are Bassa locals, he decides to use the situation to rid himself of his old school buddies and to entrench himself in power surrounded by loyal henchmen such as Ossai.

Chris and Ikem do not realize what is going on behind the scenes—nor does the reader—until events get beyond their control. Within hours, Sam has Ikem arrested and murdered (though the official version is that he was shot while resisting arrest for plotting "regicide"), the Abazon delegation put in prison, and Chris declared an accomplice of both. Chris himself has managed to escape; he hides out with friends and sympathizers and eventually, in disguise, travels by bus past roadblocks to the Abazon province. There he learns that a military coup has toppled Sam from his throne and that Sam has mysteriously disappeared. Ironically, at this very moment, in the midst of riotous celebration at a roadblock,

Chris is shot by a police sergeant while trying to prevent the man from abducting and raping a girl. The novel leaves no hope that the next regime will offer Kangan any better leadership.

The men in this modern African state consistently fail to bring the persistent political incompetence under control. Sam is a variation on the Nanga type, the amoral, self-interested servant of power who does not foresee the consequences of his ruthless treatment of others. This naïveté of the tyrant is matched by the naïve idealism of the moral crusader, Ikem, and the naïve detachment of the philosophical observer, Chris. While most of the novel is an omniscient third-person narrative, with Achebe providing a clear, balanced perspective, five of the first seven chapters are told in first person, with Chris and Ikem being two of the three narrators. Inside their minds, the reader sees a false self-confidence that Achebe eventually parlays into a chauvinism, apparently characteristic of the African male. For the first time in his novels, Achebe takes up the feminist theme, stating flatly that women need to be a major part of the solution to Africa's woes. Sam, as perceived by the third character-narrator, Beatrice, Chris's fiancé, treats women as sex objects, as he invites Beatrice to a dinner party at his lake retreat, assuming that she will be honored to serve her president. The two male protagonists, Ikem and Chris, innocent carriers of long-held assumptions, treat the women they love too lightly, and neither understands until only days before his death the wisdom and spiritual power of Beatrice, the central female character in the novel.

In fact, Beatrice herself seems only half aware of her strength until the crisis in Kangan puts it to the test. In chapters 6 and 7, which she narrates, she reveals the change that takes place in her. Chapter 6 is her account of the visit to Sam's retreat, where her defensiveness and vanity obscure her actual superiority over the other guests, including a young American female reporter who uses her sexuality to gain access to Sam. Beatrice sees herself, rather vaingloriously at this point, as a sacrificial shield to protect Sam—a symbol for her of the African leader—from the white temptress. Still, she rebuffs Sam's sexual advances, and he, insulted and humiliated, sends her home in ignominy. Beatrice sees dimly, however, the role that she must play. In chapter 7, she receives help from Ikem, who visits her for the last time before his death. With her help he has made a great discovery, for she had long accused him of male chauvinism, and he reads to her the "love letter" that she has inspired. It is a feminist recantation of his chauvinism, a rejection of the two traditional images of women found in both biblical and African sources: the woman as scapegoat, the cause of evil and men's suffering, and the woman idealized as the mother of the male god, called upon to save the world when men fail. His final word on the insight she had given him, however, is that the women themselves must decide their role; men cannot know. Beatrice tells this story of Ikem's last visit in her journal, written months after Ikem has died. Only then is she able to put the pieces of the tragedy together in her mind.

Chris, too, begins to see a special power in Beatrice during the weeks of crisis. She becomes for him a priestess of sexual and spiritual resources who could, as a prophetess, tell the future. Indeed, it is Beatrice (a literary allusion to Dante's Beatrice, only one of several whimsical allusions in the novel) who warns Chris and Ikem that they must mend their relationship, that tragedy is in store not only for them but also for Sam. They do not take her seriously enough, however, as they soon discover. Achebe, however, does not allow the elevation of Beatrice into the traditional Igbo role of half woman, half spirit (the Chielo of *Things Fall Apart*, as Beatrice herself notes), to be the work of the characters alone. In chapter 8, Achebe himself, as omniscient narrator, recounts the Igbo legend of the sun-god who sent his daughter to earth as a harbinger of peace. This legend suggests that henceforth women must stand as mediators between men and their desires, but this too is not Achebe's final word on the subject. As Ikem says in his confession to Beatrice in chapter 7, "All certitude must now be suspect."

In the last chapter, Achebe tries to bring together his thoughts on women and numerous other themes throughout the novel. The scene is Beatrice's apartment, and the time is nine months after the tragedy. Those present are a family of friends, including Elewa, Ikem's fiancé; Agatha, Beatrice's housekeeper; and Abdul Medani, the army captain who secretly helped Chris escape from Bassa. The occasion is the naming ceremony for Elewa and Ikem's twenty-eight-day-old daughter. The women, along with the men present, are trying to put their lives and, symbolically, the lives of their countrymen in order. Beatrice fears, however, that they are all fated pawns of "an alienated history." They acknowledge the value of people and the living ideas that they leave behind, the importance of humor and the need to laugh at oneself, the "unbearable beauty" even of death, and the community of all religions that can dance the same dance. They learn that women can perform tasks usually reserved for men; since Ikem is not present, Beatrice, the priestess, names the child: Amaechina, the path of Ikem, a boy's name for a baby girl. Elewa's uncle, a male representative of traditional thinking, arrives to preside over the naming but instead pays homage to the young people in the room. "That is how to handle this world," he says, "give the girl a boy's name," make her "the daughter of all of us."

It is important not to take oneself too seriously. Sam, Ikem, and Chris forgot, as Beatrice had to remind them, that their story is not "the story of this country," that "our story is only one of twenty million stories." That reminder may be the main message of *Anthills of the Savannah*, that the other millions of people are not ants caught in a drought, retreating from the sun into their holes, but people with their own stories. As the elder in the Abazon delegation reminds Ikem, the story is the nation's most valued treasure, the storyteller possessed by Agwu, the god of healers and the source of truth. Beatrice, like Ikem and Chris, is a writer, a teller of stories. Uchendu, in *Things Fall Apart*, warns that all stories are true; this fifth novel, itself full of proverbs, stories, legends, and political allegory of the sun shining on the anthills of the savannah, is an ambitious exposé and a compassionate vision of the future.

Thomas Banks
Updated by Cynthia A. Bily

OTHER MAJOR WORKS

SHORT FICTION: "Dead Men's Path," 1953; *The Sacrificial Egg, and Other Stories*, 1962; *Girls at War, and Other Stories*, 1972.

POETRY: *Beware: Soul Brother, and Other Poems*, 1971, 1972; *Christmas in Biafra, and Other Poems*, 1973; *Collected Poems*, 2004.

NONFICTION: *Morning Yet on Creation Day*, 1975; *The Trouble with Nigeria*, 1983; *Hopes and Impediments*, 1988; *Conversations with Chinua Achebe*, 1997 (Bernth Lindfors, editor); *Home and Exile*, 2000.

CHILDREN'S LITERATURE: *Chike and the River*, 1966; *How the Leopard Got His Claws*, 1972 (with John Iroaganachi); *The Drum*, 1977; *The Flute*, 1977.

EDITED TEXTS: *Don't Let Him Die: An Anthology of Memorial Poems for Christopher Okigbo, 1932-1967*, 1978 (with Dubem Okafor); *Aka weta: Egwu aguluagu egwu edeluede*, 1982 (with Obiora Udechukwu); *African Short Stories*, 1985 (with C. L. Innes); *Beyond Hunger in Africa*, 1990 (with others); *The Heinemann Book of Contemporary African Short Stories*, 1992 (with Innes).

MISCELLANEOUS: *Another Africa*, 1998 (poems and essay; photographs by Robert Lyons).

BIBLIOGRAPHY

Achebe, Chinua. "The Art of Fiction: Chinua Achebe." Interview by Jerome Brooks. *The Paris Review* 36 (Winter, 1994): 142-166. In this interview, Achebe discusses his schooling, work as a broadcaster, and views on other writers as well as the nature of his writing process and the political situation in Nigeria.

_____. *Home and Exile*. New York: Oxford University Press, 2000. An exploration, based on Achebe's own experiences as a reader and a writer, of contemporary African literature and the Western literature that both influenced and misrepresented it.

Bolland, John. *Language and the Quest for Political and Social Identity in the African Novel*. Accra, Ghana: Woeli, 1996. This volume examines Achebe's novel *Anthills of the Savannah*, among others, but it is valuable for its examination of African fiction and history, touching on themes found in Achebe's short stories.

Booker, M. Keith, ed. *The Chinua Achebe Encyclopedia*. Westport, Conn.: Greenwood Press, 2003. A helpful reference in an encyclopedia format featuring several hundred alphabetically arranged entries. Some of the entries are summary discussions of Achebe's major works of fiction, nonfiction, and poetry.

Carroll, David. *Chinua Achebe: Novelist, Poet, Critic*. Rev. 2d ed. Basingstoke, England: Macmillan, 1990.

Includes historical details concerning Africa, colonialism, and twentieth century Nigerian political history. Contains a sizable bibliography and an index.

Ezenwa-Ohaeto. *Chinua Achebe: A Biography*. Bloomington: Indiana University Press, 1997. Full-length biography benefits from its author's insights as a former student of Achebe, a native of Nigeria, and a speaker of Igbo. Examines Achebe's life and literary contributions and places them within their social, historical, and cultural contexts. Written with the cooperation of Achebe and his family, the book includes several rare and revealing photographs. Includes bibliographical references and an index.

Innes, C. L. *Chinua Achebe*. New York: Cambridge University Press, 1990. Gives a detailed analysis of each of Achebe's novels, showing how Achebe adapted what he found in Western fiction to create a new literary form—the Africanized novel. Includes a chapter on Achebe's critical and political writings, demonstrating how the Nigerian civil war changed his politics and his fiction.

Iyasere, Solomon O., ed. *Understanding "Things Fall Apart": Selected Essays and Criticism*. Troy, N.Y.: Whitston, 1998. Nine essays demonstrate the breadth of approaches taken by critics. They include a reading of Okonkwo as a tragic hero, a discussion of the rhythm of the novel's prose as it echoes African oral tradition, and a discussion of how Achebe successfully transformed the colonizers' language to tell the story of the colonized.

Lindfors, Bernth, ed. *Conversations with Chinua Achebe*. Jackson: University Press of Mississippi, 1997. In twenty interviews, Achebe discusses African oral tradition, the need for political commitment, the relationship between his novels and his short stories, his use of myth and fable, and other issues concerning being a writer.

Mezu, Rose Ure. *Chinua Achebe: The Man and His Works*. London: Adonis & Abbey, 2006. Mezu, a Nigerian-born scholar and literary critic, analyzes Achebe's novels and other writings, comparing them with other works of literature by African and African American authors, including Olaudah Equiano and Zora Neale Hurston.

Morrison, Jago. *The Fiction of Chinua Achebe*. New

York: Palgrave Macmillan, 2007. Analyzes Achebe's major novels, focusing on *Things Fall Apart*, as well as his short fiction, outlining areas of critical debate, influential approaches to his work, and the controversies his work has engendered.

Muoneke, Romanus Okey. *Art, Rebellion, and Redemption: A Reading of the Novels of Chinua Achebe*. New York: Peter Lang, 1994. Examines Achebe's role as a public chronicler of Nigeria's social, economic, and political problems in order to explore the larger issues of the writer's redemptive role in society. Argues that Achebe's novels challenge colonialism and negritude, two forces that have distorted the African image.

ALICE ADAMS

Born: Fredericksburg, Virginia; August 14, 1926
Died: San Francisco, California; May 27, 1999
Also known as: Alice Boyd Adams

PRINCIPAL LONG FICTION

Careless Love, 1966
Families and Survivors, 1974
Listening to Billie, 1978
Rich Rewards, 1980
Superior Women, 1984
Second Chances, 1988
Caroline's Daughters, 1991
Almost Perfect, 1993
A Southern Exposure, 1995
Medicine Men, 1997
After the War, 2000

OTHER LITERARY FORMS

Alice Adams was a prolific writer. In addition to her novels, she published several short-story collections, including *Beautiful Girl* (1979), *To See You Again* (1982), *Molly's Dog* (1983), *Return Trips* (1985), *After You've Gone* (1989), *The Last Lovely City: Stories* (1999), and *The Stories of Alice Adams* (2002). Although noted primarily for these short-story collections, Adams also published widely in top literary magazines during the 1970's and 1980's. Her work appeared regularly in *The New Yorker*, *The Atlantic Monthly*, *Mademoiselle*, *Virginia Quarterly Review*, *The New York Times Book Review*, and *The Paris Review*.

ACHIEVEMENTS

Alice Adams won several prestigious awards during her career, including a Guggenheim Fellowship in 1978 and a National Endowment for the Arts fiction grant in 1976. She also was recognized for her short stories with awards in 1976, 1992, and 1996, and she won two American Academy of Arts and Letters awards (1984 and 1992).

BIOGRAPHY

Alice Boyd Adams was born August 14, 1926, in Fredericksburg, Virginia, the only child of Nicholson B. Adams, a professor, and Agatha Erskine Boyd Adams, a writer. She entered Radcliffe College at the age of sixteen and graduated with a B.A. in 1946. She married Mark Linenthal, Jr., a university professor, in 1947.

Adams relocated to California with her husband, who had found a teaching job at San Francisco State University beginning in the early 1950's. Adams would base many of her novels and short stories in and around San Francisco. The couple's son, Peter, was born in 1951. Holding down various jobs such as a clerk, a secretary or a bookkeeper, following her divorce from Linenthal in 1958, Adams was the character later portrayed in her own books and stories: She was an intelligent, vibrant woman with much to offer the world, struggling to find her talent and voice.

Adams's first short story, "Winter Rain" appeared in *Charm* in July, 1959. She has been described by writer Mary Gaitskill as having "intense elegance" and "grace," and possessing "an organic mental integrity." Later in

Adams's career, she taught creative-writing courses at Stanford University and the University of California, Davis, and Berkeley. She was always supportive of younger writers.

ANALYSIS

The novels and short stories of Alice Adams are excellent studies in time and place. Adams captures the setting and surroundings and, more important, the dialogue, which is never forced. A native of Virginia, Adams is especially adept at drawing southern characters and giving them authentic voices and believable motivations. As one critic wrote, "she depicts with sensitivity and intelligence the contemporary woman's search for self-identity, independence, and stable relationships with both men and women."

Alice Adams. (AP/Wide World Photos)

This search is especially evident in Adams's best-selling book *Superior Women*, one of her more critically acclaimed novels. The four women in this story learn and grow in their relationships and in their roles as modern women, establishing themselves in careers, meeting the social struggles of their day, and following their hearts to realize their dreams and ambitions. *Superior Women*, along with *Rich Rewards*, *Second Chances*, and *A Southern Exposure*, are the best-received of Adams's longer works of fiction.

A SOUTHERN EXPOSURE

A Southern Exposure is set in Pinehill, a beautiful southern college town, in the 1930's. The novel begins with the locally celebrated Byrd family—Russ and Sallyjane (whom Russ calls Brett) and their five children—driving back from a trip to California, where Russ has earned a good deal of money from his most recent play. Unknown to Russ, Brett had her own reasons for visiting California. She got an abortion, a fact she is keeping from everyone.

Driving through Kansas, Russ nearly runs off the road and kills what he at first believes is a small child walking with her mother. The child turns out to be a pig, and the odor of pig feces fills the air. Russ scrambles to repay Ursula, the pig's owner, for her loss.

Back home in Pinehill, Russ buys a second house as a hideaway for himself and his beautiful young girlfriend, Deirdre Yates; the two have a child together, Graham. Pinehill is full of secrets, and gossip is shared over cold drinks on the veranda. These secrets, of course, are hinted at in the most cloying of terms and through innuendo, the knowing smile, and the clever nuances that plainly reveal what is intended to be hidden.

The story also features the Baird family: Harry and Cynthia, with their daughter, Abigail. The Bairds had moved to Pinehill in the hope of escaping their expensive and complicated lives in Connecticut. Cynthia has chosen this community for one reason: to meet and fall in love with poet James Russell Lowell Byrd, that is, Russ Byrd.

Another character, Jimmy Hightower, has built his dream home just up the road from the

Byrds, hoping some of Russ's celebrity might rub off on him; but it does not. Russ is not interested in people who might be interested in him. In the meantime, the Bairds insert themselves into Pinehill society, adopt the local accent, and keep from "rocking the boat" on the issue of "coloreds."

Adams has drawn convincing portraits in this novel and as well as those of Southern women who are stylish, genteel, and predictably small minded. Cynthia Baird's closest friend, Dolly Bigelow, has trouble with her "help," a tall, somber black woman named Odessa, who has an unerring eye for interior design. Cynthia recognizes Odessa's talent and works behind the scenes to empower her to leave Dolly and change her fortunes.

Sallyjane, who now insists that she no longer be called Brett, drifts slowly into depression and steadily gains weight. Clyde Drake, a local psychiatrist, "adopts" Sallyjane and Russ and moves in with them. Dr. Drake's nymphomaniac wife, Norris, is another woman—like Deirdre, Cynthia, and Sallyjane—who has fallen in love with the idea of Russ the southern poet. Sallyjane dies during electroshock therapy, clearing the way for Russ to have a passionate affair with Cynthia; he eventually marries Deirdre, however, after she becomes pregnant with their second child.

A Southern Exposure is an excellent novel, another work that displays Adams's talent for characterization and capturing a sense of place and time. The wisteria, the hydrangeas, the magnolia blossoms of Pinehill fill every page. The reader encounters a theme like that of Margaret Mitchell's novel *Gone With the Wind* (1936), a time in the American South facing radical change and grasping at the prejudices handed down through the generations.

ALMOST PERFECT

Stella Blake is half Mexican, the only child of a not-quite-famous writer, the prodigal son of East Coast old money. Stella, whose mother is deceased, is estranged from her father and his latest wife. Stella lives in San Francisco and is a writer herself, penning feature articles for newspapers and the occasional magazine. She is poor, and once was the very young lover and companion to an aging film director. She has been cut off from the money of her father's family and lives hand-to-mouth in a small, dreary apartment.

Richard Fallon is a narcissist, a womanizer, a closeted bisexual, a genius with design, a drunk, a great cook, and a high school dropout. He grew up poor in Patterson, New Jersey, and makes his living—on those rare occasions when he works—in advertising. Though Richard has many talents and skills, he mostly relies on his good looks to get through life's rough spots. His former wife, Marina, whom he met and married in New Jersey, calls him to encourage him to face his many creditors and pay his ongoing debts. His former girlfriend, Claudia, calls him for the occasional sexual liaison, and his gay friend, Andrew, calls him to tempt him with new possibilities.

Stella and Richard first meet when Stella interviews Richard for an article she is writing. As it turns out, she never writes the article. Their encounter leads to a two-year romance, one in which Richard grows steadily weaker and Stella grows progressively stronger. Stella is not Richard's type. He prefers women who look like him: blond, tall, blue-eyed, Nordic types. Stella, who is short, dark complected, and intelligent is everything Richard is not. She is far more in love with Richard than he is with her.

Throughout the novel, Stella and Richard drink too much. They have a small circle of friends from both sides of their relationship. Richard has an enormous studio, attractively decorated by him with mostly junk. He also has a spectacular house in the country, which he designed. Stella and Richard, however, spend most of their time in Stella's newly renovated apartment, which Richard has transformed from drab to dreamy. They make love often, cook dinners for each other, and drink.

Stella's writing finds an audience in New York, and a major literary magazine begins buying her stories; the magazine soon signs her to a lucrative contract. Richard, it seems, has a number of promising projects, but those opportunities slowly evaporate into the black fog of San Francisco. Richard, in yet another affair with tall blonds (this newest one lives in Germany), cheats on Stella.

With Stella's success, the relationship is thrown out of balance, and Richard retreats to booze, more sex, and thoughts of suicide. His decline finds him fleeing the Bay Area to Mexico City, where he and his dying friend, Andrew, are spending Andrew's money. Stella slowly begins to recover from the loss of Richard and meets a young doctor who is the son of one of Richard's friends. Stella moves from San Francisco, too, and she moves from memories of her two years with Richard and learns what it is like to be loved rather than used by the one loved.

SUPERIOR WOMEN

In *Superior Women*, four Radcliffe College graduates in the early 1940's share their dreams, their fears, their lovers, and, eventually, more than forty years of their lives. The cast of "superior women" includes Lavinia, a Southern belle in the proudest tradition, who is blond, incredibly well-bred, and a horrible bigot to her bones. Despite her lack of character, she is the novel's scene stealer. She is larger than life, and she embodies every negative stereotype of the sophisticated, image-conscious, backbiting society princess. She respects money and everything it will buy her. She is highly practical and calculating, and is intolerant of everyone she perceives as not being her equal, which includes almost everyone. She serves masterfully as the character readers love to hate.

Lavinia, of course, cannot be the central character in the book because she is not sympathetic. The lead role in the novel goes to Megan, an outsider. Born and raised in California, Megan is jealous of what she perceives as East Coast sophistication. A little pudgy, Megan is a people person and is popular with the boys. She winds her way through the novel encountering a series of lovers. Her most important lover is the tall, dark-eyed intellectual Henry, who has been having an ongoing affair with Lavinia for years. Megan never marries or has children, but at the novel's end she forms her own modern family, a mixture of her actual relatives, her lovers, and some of her friends and their lovers.

Adams does not develop her next two characters, Peg and Cathy, as strongly as she does Lavinia and Megan. Peg is rich enough to impress even Lavinia; however, she is more overweight than Megan and marries the first man who has sex with her and knows her family has money. Peg moves to Texas, raises four children, and becomes active in the Civil Rights movement. She ultimately embraces her homosexuality and leaves her husband to move with her companion to open a shelter for homeless women in Georgia.

Finally, Cathy is more of a stereotype than even Lavinia. Trapped by her Catholic upbringing, Cathy finds herself loving a priest, getting pregnant by him, and then hiding the truth from her family and friends. Cathy moves to San Francisco and raises her son with the help of her mother but without the son's father.

This novel is reminiscent of "girls' stories" from the early twentieth century, in which friends take divergent paths through life. At the heart of *Superior Women* are issues of strength, style, and class. These superior women reveal their talents, weaknesses, desires, doubts, and passions through long years of association.

Randy L. Abbott

OTHER MAJOR WORKS

SHORT FICTION: *Beautiful Girl*, 1979; *To See You Again*, 1982; *Molly's Dog*, 1983; *Return Trips*, 1985; *After You've Gone*, 1989; *The Last Lovely City: Stories*, 1999; *The Stories of Alice Adams*, 2002.

NONFICTION: *Mexico: Some Travels and Some Travelers There*, 1990.

BIBLIOGRAPHY

Blades, Larry T. "Order and Chaos in Alice Adams' *Rich Rewards*." *Critique* 27, no. 4 (Summer, 1986): 187-195. Blades examines the interplay of order and chaos in Adams's novel *Rich Rewards*.

Herman, Barbara A. "Alice Adams." In *Contemporary Fiction Writers of the South: A Bio-bibliographical Sourcebook*, edited by Joseph M. Flora and Robert A. Bain. Westport, Conn.: Greenwood Press, 1993. Herman situates Adams within the great pantheon of American southern writers of the twentieth century.

Kerrison, Catherine. *Claiming the Pen: Women and Intellectual Life in the Early American South*. Ithaca, N.Y.: Cornell University Press, 2006. A scholarly study that speaks to the lives of the strong, smart women in Adams's novels of the American South. Kerrison examines topics such as female authorship and the female intellectual.

RICHARD ADAMS

Born: Newbury, Berkshire, England; May 9, 1920

Also known as: Richard George Adams

PRINCIPAL LONG FICTION

Watership Down, 1972

Shardik, 1974

The Plague Dogs, 1977

The Girl in a Swing, 1980

Maia, 1984

Traveller, 1988

The Outlandish Knight, 2000

Daniel, 2006

OTHER LITERARY FORMS

Richard Adams has written two collections of short fiction, one of which, *Tales from Watership Down* (1996), is in part a sequel to his most famous novel. His other works include several illustrated children's books in verse; an illustrated series of nature guides; an account of a journey to Antarctica, *Voyage Through the Antarctic* (1982), cowritten with Ronald M. Lockley, the author of the factual work that became the basis for *Watership Down*; and an autobiography covering the first part of his life through his demobilization after World War II, *The Day Gone By* (1990).

ACHIEVEMENTS

Called by English writer A. N. Wilson "the best adventure-story-writer alive," Richard Adams is most famous for taking the talking-animal story out of the genre of children's literature and informing it with mature concerns and interests, as in his first great success, *Watership Down*, which won the Carnegie Award and the Guardian Children's Fiction Prize. He continued this transformation in *The Plague Dogs* and *Traveller*. Adams also made his mark in fantasy literature; his imaginary kingdom of Bekla is the backdrop for *Shardik* and *Maia*, novels whose main concerns, slavery and warfare, definitely remove them from the realm of children's literature. He also wrote a less successful full-length ghost story, *The Girl in the Swing*, and later two

historical novels, *The Outlandish Knight* and *Daniel*, the latter of which returns to his concern with the subject of slavery.

BIOGRAPHY

The youngest of three children, Richard George Adams spent an idyllic childhood ("the happiest [days] of my life") growing up on the outskirts of Newbury, England. His father, a local doctor, transmitted his knowledge of and love for the flora and fauna of the region to his son, whose later devotion to animal welfare was additionally inspired by Hugh Lofting's Dr. Dolittle books. Adams's father also instilled in his son a lifelong interest in storytelling, which Adams later honed in bedtime tales told to roommates at prep school. Other important influences included the Uncle Remus stories of Joel Chandler Harris, *Uncle Tom's Cabin* (1852) by Harriet Beecher Stowe, *The Three Mulla-Mulgars* (1910) by Walter de la Mare, and the silent Rin-Tin-Tin films. All would later echo in his fiction.

Although his time at prep school was often unpleasant, Adams thoroughly enjoyed his public school experience at Bradfield. The school put on a yearly play in its open-air theater, often a classical Greek drama, and Adams called the theater the place where he was "more consistently happy than anywhere else." Bradfield also encouraged his love of literature, the Greek and Roman classics, and history, the subject in which Adams won a scholarship to Worcester College, Oxford, in 1938. Adams was grateful to Oxford for its acceptance of what he calls one's "fantasy potential."

Adams's Oxford years were interrupted, as were those of so many others, by World War II. Adams chose to serve in the Royal Army Service Corps (RASC), which is mainly concerned with transport and communication duties, but later he volunteered for the airborne arm of the RASC and served in the Middle East and in Singapore. On his return to England, Adams was shocked to learn how many of his Oxford companions had died during the war.

After demobilization, Adams soon met Elizabeth Acland, whom he would later marry and with whom he would have two daughters. In 1948 he joined the British civil service, but he never abandoned his love for storytelling. *Watership Down* began, like many other "children's" classics, as a story initially told by the author to his children (in this case to entertain them on a long car trip); two years after its publication, Adams was able to retire from the civil service and write full time at his various homes in the south of England.

ANALYSIS

In each of his novels, Richard Adams adopts a different individual narrative voice: easygoing and colloquial in *Watership Down* and *Maia*, stately and epic in *Shardik*, ironic and densely allusive in *The Plague Dogs*, and the very different first-person voices in *The Girl in a Swing* and *Traveller*. On the surface, Adams's natural gift as a storyteller is his strongest talent, but his novels deserve to be read more for his habitual concerns: a love for "the surface of the earth," as George Orwell called it, as manifested in the English countryside and the creatures who inhabit it; a hatred for the cruelties that human beings inflict on the other inhabitants of this world as well as on themselves; and an acute awareness of the transitory nature of existence and the evanescence of friendship and love.

WATERSHIP DOWN

Watership Down burst on the literary scene in 1972, as unlikely a success as J. R. R. Tolkien's *The Lord of the Rings* (1955) had been almost two decades earlier. Its plot and characters seemed those of a children's book: A group of rabbits leave their threatened burrow and make a dangerous journey to find a new home as well as enough new rabbits to ensure its continuation. In its length and often violent action, however, it certainly went beyond the boundaries of a children's work, and it succeeded with many adults. It even led to some shameless imitations, such as William Horwood's mole epic, *Duncton Wood* (1980), but none had the imagination and freshness of the original.

As Tolkien did with the Hobbits, Adams made his exotic characters familiar by giving them an easily identifiable demotic speech. Hazel, Bigwig, and the others speak much as did the originals on which they are modeled: Adams's companions in the 205th Company of the RASC during World War II. (Hazel, according

to Adams, is his commanding officer, John Gifford, and Bigwig is Paddy Kavanagh, who was killed in battle.) The rabbits, like their soldier counterparts, are believable everyday heroes. Their persistence in the face of daunting odds, their relatively unflappable demeanor as they are introduced into new and dangerous surroundings, their ingenuity in overcoming their difficulties—all recall the best qualities of those soldiers in the war.

The familiar speech is also reproduced in the novel's narrative voice, which is often that of a good oral storyteller; as Adams has noted, "A true folk-tale teller is usually rather colloquial." This informality helps to disguise the classical underpinnings of the work, the main one of which is Vergil's *Aeneid* (c. 29-19 B.C.E.; English translation, 1553). There are also echoes of Xenophon's *Kyrou anabasis* (c. fourth century B.C.E.; *Anabasis*, 1623) and Homer's *Iliad* (c. 750 B.C.E.; English translation, 1611) and *Odyssey* (c. 725 B.C.E.; English translation, 1614), with Hazel as a more trustworthy Odysseus and Bigwig a less belligerent Achilles. These archetypal characters and plot devices are also supported by the scientific accuracy of the details of the rabbits' lives, which Adams culled from *The Private Life of the Rabbit* by R. M. Lockley (1964). Familiar yet exotic characters, an epic story, and verisimilitude of milieu contribute to the lasting and deserved appeal of *Watership Down*. (*Tales from Watership Down*, in its latter half a sequel to the novel, also serves as an answer to those who accused the original of, among other charges, sexism.)

SHARDIK

Adams's next novel, *Shardik*, disappointed many of his readers, for although on the surface, like *Watership Down*, a fantasy, it was far removed from the first novel in setting, characters, and plot. Adams constructs the mythical land of Bekla, whose precarious peace is shattered by the emergence of a great bear, which is taken by many to be the avatar of the god Shardik. After a short rule by the bear's chief follower, Kelderek, the bear escapes, and Kelderek must learn the real meaning of the irruption of Shardik into the lives of so many people. For much of the book, the characters are unlikable, the setting is foreign without being exotic, and the plot seems to be nothing but one violent incident after another. The narration is also different from that in *Watership*

Down, much more stately and epic in tone, with self-consciously Homeric similes interrupting the narrative flow.

In the end, however, *Shardik* is satisfying, once the reader grasps the greater themes of the novel. Shardik's reign has allowed slavery to flourish once again in Bekla, and only by suffering and death can Shardik and Kelderek redeem themselves and society. Adams's own horror at slavery, both literary and real, echoes in the plot: The evil slaver Genshed is consciously modeled on Stowe's great villain in *Uncle Tom's Cabin*, Simon Legree, and the mutilated beggar boys whom Adams had seen from a troop train in India are reproduced in some Beklan slaves. Adams's own hatred of war causes the first half of the book to be almost antiepic in its drive: The religious war it depicts is nasty, brutish, and long. Once the arc of the plot is evident, *Shardik* can be seen as an epic indictment of the horrors of epic war.

THE PLAGUE DOGS

The Plague Dogs is the most tendentious of Adams's novels. The title characters are trying to escape from a laboratory in England's Lake Country, where they have been subjected to cruel and unnecessary experiments. Although seemingly a return to the mode of his greatest success, the grown-up animal novel, it is much more a satire, filled with savage indignation at the lengths to which humans will use and abuse other species, a satire that gains effect from Adams's experience working in government bureaucracies. Like *Shardik*, it is an investigation of cruelty, this time toward what the novel calls "animal slaves": "It's a bad world for the helpless," as one of its characters says. Once again Adams adopts a new narrative voice, particularly in the sections concerning humans, this one arch and packed with literary allusions. The novel is not totally one-sided, the case being made near the end for useful animal medical experimentation. Yet again it is in his animal portrayals that Adams best succeeds, particularly those of the dog Snitter, whose nonsense language, caused by a brain operation, echoes that of dramatist William Shakespeare's fools, and of the wild fox, whose feral otherness seems to be an answer to criticisms of Adams's cozy rabbits.

THE GIRL IN A SWING

Adams's next two novels are major departures, explorations of the themes of sexuality and love, subjects he touched on only tangentially in previous work. *The Girl in a Swing* is nominally a ghost story, but in reality it is more a depiction of the obsessive love that the hero, Alan Desland, feels for Käthe, a German girl whom he meets in Copenhagen and swiftly marries, not knowing that she is trying to escape a ghost from her past. The work contains echoes of Emily Brontë's *Wuthering Heights* (1847), with Käthe as Cathy Earnshaw, but Alan is no Heathcliff, and while Adams's depictions of local scenery remain one of his strengths—much of the locale is again borrowed from Adams's childhood—the end of the novel is more deflationary than chilling. Adams has said that ghosts in English horror writer M. R. James's short stories are knowingly artificial, but the one in *The Girl in a Swing* is unfortunately no less an *umbra ex machina*, a ghost from the machine.

MAIA

Maia returns to the fantasy world of Bekla, which Adams created in *Shardik*, to tell the story of the eponymous heroine, who undergoes a transformation from literal sex slave to country matron, all described at sometimes tedious length, in more than twelve hundred pages. Adams's narrative style here is more familiar than that in *Shardik*, his similes shorter, homelier, and less epic. However, the reproduction of the girl's countrified speech becomes irritating, and anachronisms such as discussions of infection and primitive vaccination are annoying. The plot is basic: Girl meets boy, girl loses boy, girl gets boy. The girl does not even meet the boy until almost halfway through the novel, however, making for difficult reading.

The underlying theme of *Maia* is much the same as that of *Shardik*, as the good side attempts to eradicate slavery in the Beklan empire, but this time the scenes of sadism that Adams describes become extremely uncomfortable. In *Shardik* such scenes had a moral point, but here their purpose seems cloudier: We know these characters are villains, so several scenes explicitly depicting their villainy are uncalled for. On the positive side, Adams once again depicts actions that undercut fantasy epic conventions: Maia's most heroic actions are undertaken to prevent, and not to further, violence and warfare. At the end, however, when Maia has become a contented country wife and mother, the reader wonders how this matron grew out of the girl who, some nine hundred pages earlier, had realized she possessed "an exceptional erotic attitude" and proceeded to use and enjoy it.

TRAVELLER

Traveller is basically the story of the Civil War seen through the eyes and told by the voice of Confederate general Robert E. Lee's famous horse. In this novel, Adams plays to all his strengths, including a new narrative voice, this one a modification of Joel Chandler Harris's in the Uncle Remus stories; a singular, believable animal persona through which the action is described; and a depiction of his favorite themes—hatred of war, admiration for those who must suffer through it, and sorrow over the ephemerality of comrades and friendship. The bravery of Lee's Army of Northern Virginia is, as Adams elsewhere has noted, a reflection of Adams's own pride in the gallantry of the British First Airborne Division in the battle of Arnhem. Lee is Adams's quintessential hero because he treats both animals and people with dignity and respect. Traveller, like satirist Jonathan Swift's Houyhnhnms, a race of intelligent horses in *Gulliver's Travels* (1726), is aghast at humankind's capacity for cruelty, but he is not keen enough (or anachronistic enough) to see the cruelty that slavery commits. Traveller is, as another horse calls him, "thick": At Gettysburg, he thinks Pickett's charge succeeds, and at Appomattox, he thinks the Federals have surrendered to "Marse Robert." However, he gets the basic truth right: "Horses [are] for ever saying goodbye." It was the lesson Adams learned when he returned to Oxford after the war to learn of his friends' deaths, and it is the grave lesson that has informed his best fiction.

William Laskowski

OTHER MAJOR WORKS

SHORT FICTION: *The Unbroken Web: Stories and Fables*, 1980 (also known as *The Iron Wolf, and Other Stories*); *Tales from Watership Down*, 1996.

NONFICTION: *Nature Through the Seasons*, 1975 (with Max Hooper); *Nature Day and Night*, 1978 (with Hooper); *Voyage Through the Antarctic*, 1982 (with Ronald M. Lockley); *A Nature Diary*, 1985; *The Day Gone By*, 1990 (autobiography).

CHILDREN'S LITERATURE: *The Tyger Voyage*, 1976; *The Adventures of and Brave Deeds of the Ship's Cat on the Spanish Maine: Together with the Most Lamentable*

Losse of the Alcestis and Triumphant Firing of the Port of Chagres, 1977; *The Legend of Te Tuna*, 1982; *The Bureaucats*, 1985.

EDITED TEXTS: *Sinister and Supernatural Stories*, 1978; *Occasional Poets: An Anthology*, 1980.

BIBLIOGRAPHY

Adams, Richard. *The Day Gone By*. London: Hutchinson, 1990. Provides information on Adams's childhood, his service in World War II, and how he developed both a love of nature and a skill for storytelling that would lead to his becoming a writer.

_____. "Richard Adams: Some Ingredients of *Watership Down*." In *The Thorny Paradise: Writers on Writing for Children*, edited by Edward Blishen. Harmondsworth, England: Penguin Books, 1975. Adams is one of more than twenty authors who contributed essays to this collection about why and how they write. His chapter focuses on *Watership Down*.

Bridgman, Joan. "Richard Adams at Eighty." *Contemporary Review* 277, no. 1615 (August, 2000): 108. Overview of Adams's personal and professional life, placed within the broader context of children's literature published in the United Kingdom and featuring an evaluation of *Watership Down*.

Harris-Fain, Darren. *British Fantasy and Science-Fiction Writers Since 1960*. Vol. 261 in *Dictionary of Literary Biography*. Detroit, Mich.: Gale Group, 2002. A brief biography of Adams and analysis of his books, along with a list of his works and a bibliography, are included in this standard reference book.

Kitchell, Kenneth F., Jr. "The Shrinking of the Epic Hero: From Homer to Richard Adams's *Watership Down*." *Classical and Modern Literature* 7 (Fall, 1986): 13-30. Detailed analysis of *Watership Down* makes a convincing argument that the novel is a twentieth century epic that treats its rabbit protagonist as a classical hero.

Meyer, Charles. "The Power of Myth and Rabbit Survival in Richard Adams' *Watership Down*." *Journal of the Fantastic in the Arts* 3, no. 4 (1994): 139-150. Examines the novel's treatment of reason and intuition and shows the connections between *Watership Down* and R. M. Lockley's *The Private Life of the Rabbit*.

Perrin, Noel. "An Animal Epic: Richard Adams, *Watership Down*." In *A Child's Delight*. Hanover, N.H.: University Press of New England, 1997. Collection of essays about thirty children's books that Perrin describes as "neglected," "ignored," or "under-appreciated" includes a brief discussion of *Watership Down*.

Watkins, Tony. "Reconstructing the Homeland: Loss and Hope in the English Landscape." In *Aspects and Issues in the History of Children's Literature*, edited by Maria Nikolajeva. Westport, Conn.: Greenwood Press, 1995. Assesses the treatment of the landscape in several works of English children's literature. Focuses on Kenneth Grahame's *The Wind in the Willows*, comparing it with *Watership Down* and J. R. R. Tolkien's *The Lord of the Rings* trilogy.

JAMES AGEE

Born: Knoxville, Tennessee; November 27, 1909
Died: New York, New York; May 16, 1955
Also known as: James Rufus Agee

PRINCIPAL LONG FICTION

The Morning Watch, 1951 (novella)
A Death in the Family, 1957

OTHER LITERARY FORMS

The first book that James Agee (AY-jee) published, *Permit Me Voyage* (1934), was a collection of poems; his second was a nonfiction account of Alabama sharecroppers during the Great Depression. He and photographer Walker Evans lived with their subjects for eight weeks in 1936 on a *Fortune* magazine assignment, and a number of critics hailed the resulting book, *Let Us Now Praise Famous Men* (1941), as Agee's masterpiece. From 1941 through 1948, Agee wrote film reviews and feature articles for *Time* magazine and *The Nation*; thereafter, he worked on film scripts in Hollywood, his most notable screenplay being his 1952 adaptation of C. S. Forester's novel *The African Queen* (1935). He also wrote an esteemed television script on Abraham Lincoln for the *Omnibus* series in 1952. *Letters of James Agee to Father Flye* (1962) contains his thirty-year correspondence with an Episcopalian priest who had been his teacher.

ACHIEVEMENTS

The prestigious Yale Series of Younger Poets sponsored James Agee's first book, and Archibald MacLeish contributed its introduction. Agee went on to gain an unusual degree of literary fame for a man who published only three books, two of them slim ones, in his lifetime. Sometimes accused of wasting his talent on magazine and film "hack" work, Agee lavished the same painstaking attention on film reviews as he did on his carefully crafted books. His film work was highly prized by director John Huston, and Huston and Agee's collaboration on *The African Queen* resulted in a film classic. Agee's greatest fame developed posthumously, however, when his novel *A Death in the Family* won the Pulitzer Prize in 1958. Three years later, Tad Mosel's adaptation of the novel for the stage, titled *All the Way Home* (pr. 1960), earned another Pulitzer. The continued popularity of Agee's work is testament to the author's vast human sympathy, his unusual lyrical gift, and his ability to evoke the tension and tenderness of family life in both fiction and nonfiction.

BIOGRAPHY

Born in Knoxville, Tennessee, on November 27, 1909, James Rufus Agee was the son of Hugh James Agee, from a Tennessee mountain family, and Laura Whitman Tyler, the well-educated and highly religious daughter of a businessman. His father sang mountain ballads to him, and his mother passed on to him her love of drama and music. Hugh Agee's death in an automobile accident in the spring of 1916 profoundly influenced young Rufus, as he was called in the family.

Agee received a first-rate education at St. Andrew's

School, near Sewanee, Tennessee, where he developed a lifelong friendship with Father James Harold Flye; at Phillips Exeter Academy, Exeter, New Hampshire; and at Harvard College, where in his senior year he edited the *Harvard Advocate*. Upon his graduation from Harvard in 1932, he went immediately to work for *Fortune* and later worked for its sister publication, *Time*. Over a sixteen-year period, he did a variety of staff work, reviewing, and feature stories while living in the New York metropolitan area.

From 1950 on, Agee spent considerable time in California working mostly with John Huston, but his health deteriorated. Highly disciplined as a writer, Agee exerted less successful control over his living habits, and chronic insomnia and alcohol use contributed to his having a succession of heart attacks beginning early in 1951. Agee was married three times and had a son by his second wife and three more children by his third, Mia Fritsch, who survived him. He succumbed to a fatal heart attack in a New York City taxicab on May 16, 1955, at the age of forty-five.

ANALYSIS

Neither James Agee's novella *The Morning Watch* nor his novel *A Death in the Family* offers much in the way of plot. The former covers a few hours of a boy's Good Friday morning at an Episcopalian boys' school, the latter a few days encompassing the death and funeral of a young husband and father. Agee's fiction develops a remarkable lyric intensity, however, and dramatizes with sensitivity the consciousness of children. Agee presents the minutiae of life as experienced by his characters at times of maximum awareness and thereby lifts them out of the category of mere realistic detail into the realm of spiritual discovery.

Even a cursory glance at the facts of Agee's life reveals how autobiographically based his fiction is. There is no reason to doubt that St. Andrew's, where he spent the years from ages ten to sixteen, supplies the framework for *The Morning Watch*, or that Agee's own family, seen at the time of Hugh Agee's fatal accident, furnishes the building blocks of the more ambitious *A Death in the Family*. At the same time, Agee permitted himself artistic freedom in selecting, altering, and arranging the facts of raw experience. It is clear that his lit-

erary appropriation of his childhood owes much to reflection and interpretation in the light of maturity.

Agee was a writer who stayed close to home in his work. His fiction displays no trace of the two-thirds of his life spent mainly in New England, New York, and California. As is so often the case with writers from the American South, Agee's work is imbued with a sense of his origins, of folk traditions viewed in their own right and in competition with the emerging urban culture. The South, with its insistence on the primacy of personal and familial relationships, was in the author's bones. In keeping to his earliest and most vividly felt years, Agee created a convincing context in which experiences of universal significance could unfold.

THE MORNING WATCH

At the beginning of *The Morning Watch*, a preadolescent boy and several of his classmates are awakened in the wee hours of Good Friday morning to spend their assigned time in an overnight vigil in the school chapel as part of the Maundy Thursday-Good Friday devotions. Anyone who has experienced a period of religious scrupulosity in childhood will respond to Agee's presentation of Richard. While his friends fumble and curse in the darkness, Richard prepares for adoration. Once in the chapel before the veiled monstrance, he strives to pray worthily despite the inevitable distractions of potentially sinful thoughts, the dangers of spiritual pride, and the torture of the hard kneeling board. Richard wonders whether he can make a virtue of his discomfort: To what extent is it proper for him to suffer along with the crucified Savior? Agee brings Richard intensely alive and conveys the power and the puzzlement of mighty spiritual claims at this stage of life.

The narrative also develops from the start Richard's sense of his relationships with the other boys, most of whom, he realizes, lack his delicate spiritual antennae. After the stint in the chapel is over, he and two classmates do not return to the dormitory as expected but decide to take an early-morning swim. Their adventure is presented in a heavily symbolic way. Richard dives into deep water at their swimming hole, stays down so long that his friends begin to worry, and emerges before his lungs give out. The boys torture and kill a snake, with Richard (who, like Agee himself, cannot bear to kill) finishing off the job. He debates in his mind whether the snake is poisonous and whether to wash the slime from his hand, deciding finally in the negative. He carries back to the school a locust shell he has found on the way. The snake, which seemingly cannot be killed, suggests both ineradicable evil and, in its victimization, Christ; the locust shell, which he holds next to his heart, seems to represent suffering in a purer form. Richard's dive into the water and subsequent resurfacing obviously symbolize his own "death" and "resurrection" in this Christian Holy Week.

Some critics have noted the influence of James Joyce on this novella. Certainly Richard resembles in certain ways the young protagonists of some of Joyce's *Dubliners* (1914) stories as well as Stephen Dedalus in *A Portrait of the Artist as a Young Man* (1916). Attracted by religious mysteries and artifacts, Richard wishes to appropriate them for his own purposes. He senses the conflict of religion with the world, evinces distaste for the practices of the latter, and hopes to fashion a life that blends the best of both. While Richard's appropriation of religious rite and doctrine is less consciously the artist's than is that of Stephen Dedalus, the reader senses that Richard's individualistic spirituality will inevitably bring him into a Joycean conflict with conservative religious practice.

A DEATH IN THE FAMILY

Since *The Morning Watch*, despite its provocatively ambiguous conflict between the world and the spirit, is somewhat labored and precious, and since Agee's short stories were few and insignificant, his reputation as an important American novelist rests primarily on one book that he did not quite complete before his early death, *A Death in the Family*. As he left it, the story begins at the supper table of the Follet household in Knoxville, Tennessee, in about 1915 and ends just after Jay Follet's funeral on the third day following. Agee had written a short descriptive essay, "Knoxville: Summer 1915" (which makes an appropriate preface to the novel), and six additional sections, which together make up about one-fifth the length of the narrative.

Although all the six scenes (as they will be termed here) pertain to times prior to that of the main story, it remains unclear where Agee intended to place them or whether he would have used stream-of-consciousness flashbacks, a story-within-a-story technique, or perhaps

James Agee. (Library of Congress)

another method suggested by his cinematic experience to incorporate them. Surely he intended to use them, for they illuminate and enrich the death story despite the absence of any formal linkage among them or collectively to the narrative. The editorial decision to print three of them after each of the first two parts of the three-part narrative seems as logical as any other way under the circumstances.

The novel has no single protagonist. Jay Follet, strong, tall, and taciturn, is described most specifically, at one point being compared to President Abraham Lincoln, although Follet is apparently more handsome. Last seen alive one-third of the way through the narrative, he appears in five of the six scenes and remains the main object of the other characters' thoughts in the last two parts of the narrative. At various stages, each important family member reflects on him: his wife, Mary; his son, Rufus, his brother, Ralph; Mary's parents, Joel and Catherine; Mary's aunt, Hannah, and her brother, Andrew; and even Jay and Mary's three-year-old daughter, also named

Catherine. Agee focuses most frequently on Rufus and Mary.

No point of view outside the family circle intrudes, and, except on two occasions when the six-year-old Rufus interacts with neighborhood children outside, attention is focused on family members exclusively. Throughout the novel, Agee juxtaposes the tensions and tendernesses of domestic life. The reader is constantly made to feel not only how much the family members love one another but also how abrasive they can be. Recognizing that a family does not succeed automatically, Agee portrays a continual struggle against external divisive pressures and selfishness within.

Jay and Mary's marriage has withstood a number of strains. First of all, their origins differ greatly. Mary's people are the citified, well-educated Lynches; the Follets are Tennessee mountain folk. The couple's ability to harmonize their differences is exemplified in the second of the six scenes. Rufus notes that when his parents sing together, his father interprets music flexibly, "like a darky," while his mother sings true and clear but according to the book. Rufus particularly admires his father's sense of rhythm. Sometimes, the boy observes, his mother tries to sing Jay's way and he hers, but they soon give up and return to what is natural for themselves.

Jay's father, who indirectly causes Jay's death, is one point of difference. Mary's antipathy to him is known to all the Follets, but even Jay realizes that his likable father is weak of character. When Jay's brother calls and informs him that their father is very ill, Jay wastes no time in preparing to go to him, despite his suspicion that the unreliable Ralph has greatly exaggerated the danger. It is on his return trip, after learning that his father is all right, that a mechanical defect in Jay's car causes the crash that kills him instantly.

Jay's drinking problem, a Follet weakness, has also distressed his wife, and Jay has vowed to kill himself if he ever gets drunk again. In one of the scenes, Rufus, aware that whiskey is a sore point between his parents, accompanies his father when he stops at a tavern, and it appears that he has overcome his habit of excess, but his reputation has spread. Both the man who finds Jay's body and the children who later taunt Rufus on the street corner attribute his accident to drunken driving, and

Mary has to fight off the temptation to consider the possibility.

Religion is another divisive issue. Jay does not appear to be a denominational Christian, while Mary is, like Agee's own mother, a fervent Episcopalian. The men on both sides of the family are either skeptics or thoroughgoing unbelievers. A devotee of Thomas Hardy's fiction, Mary's father, Joel, has little use for piety or what he calls "churchiness." Although he originally disapproved of Mary's marriage to Jay, he has come to terms with Jay, whom he views as a counterweight to Mary's religiosity. Mary's brother carries on open warfare with the Christian God; when Andrew first hears of Jay's accident, Mary senses that he is mentally rehearsing a speech about the folly of belief in a benevolent deity. Even young Rufus is a budding skeptic. Told that God has let his father "go to sleep," he ferrets out the details and concludes that the concussion he has heard about, "not God," has put his father to sleep. When he hears that his father will wake up at the Final Judgment, he wonders what good that is. The women accept the inscrutable as God's will, but the men take an agnostic stance and fear the influence of the church. Father Jackson, the most unpleasant person in the novel, ministers to Mary in her bereavement. Rufus quickly decides that the priest's power is malevolent and that, were his real father present, the false father would not be allowed into his home.

Some hours after the confirmation of Jay's death, Mary feels his presence in the room, and although Andrew and Joel will not concede any kind of spiritual visitation, they acknowledge that they too felt "something." Later, Andrew tells Rufus of an event he considers "miraculous": the settling of a butterfly on Jay's coffin in the grave and the creature's subsequent flight, high into the sunlight. The men's unbelief, then, is not positivistic; they recognize the possibility of a realm beyond the natural order, but they bitterly oppose the certified spiritual agent, Father Jackson, as too self-assured and quick to condemn.

To counter the estrangements brought on by cultural and religious conflicts in the family, reconciliations dot the narrative. Rufus senses periodic estrangements from his father and then joyful feelings of unity. Jay frequently feels lonely, even homesick. Crossing the river between Knoxville and his old home, he feels restored. To go home is impracticable, bound up with a vanished childhood. In one of the scenes, the family visits Rufus's great-great-grandmother, taking a long, winding journey into the hills and into the past. It is apparent that none of the younger generations of Follets has gone to see the old woman in a long time. Rufus, who has never been there, comes home in a way impossible to his father. The old woman, more than one hundred years old, barely acknowledges any of her numerous offspring, but she clasps Rufus, the fifth-generation descendant, who is joyful to her. On other occasions, Jay, by imaginative identification with Rufus, can feel as if he is his "own self" again.

Mary also feels alternate waves of friendship with and estrangement from her father. He, in turn, has a wife with whom communication is difficult because of her deafness. When Catherine cannot hear her husband, she seldom asks him to repeat himself, as if fearful of exasperating him. In this way, she is insulated from his unbelief. Although they talk little, they communicate by gestures and physical closeness. Agee shows him taking her elbow to help her over a curb and carefully steering her up the street toward their home. Rufus and his father are usually silent on their walks; they communicate by sitting together on a favorite rock and watching passersby.

Much of the talk following Jay's death is irritable and nerve-shattering. Andrew dwells thoughtlessly on the one-chance-in-a-million nature of Jay's accident, for which his father rebukes him. Mary implores Andrew to have mercy and then hysterically begs his forgiveness, upon which her aunt censures her for unwarranted humility. Both Mary and Andrew are enduring crises, however, and are hardly responsible for what they say. She is resisting the temptation to despair of God's mercy; he is trying to come to terms with a possibly meaningless universe. Andrew communicates best through service; during the hours of distress, he is unfailingly helpful.

The truest communication exists between Jay and Mary. When he is not silent, he can be sullen or wrathful. As he prepares to set forth on his journey to his father's, Mary dreads the "fury and profanity" she can expect if, for example, the car will not start, but this sometimes harsh husband stops in the bedroom to recompose their bed so it will look comfortable and inviting when she returns to it. She disapproves of his drinking strong coffee, but she makes him some very strong coffee on this occasion because she knows he will appreciate it. By dozens of such unobtrusive deeds, Jay and Mary express their love, which prevails over the numerous adverse circumstances and personal weaknesses that threaten it.

Long before he began work on *A Death in the Family*, Agee expressed his intention to base a literary work on his father's death. The eventual novel is thus deeply meditated and very personal. At the same time, it attains universality by means of its painstaking precision. In the Follets can be seen any family that has striven to harmonize potentially divisive differences or has answered a sudden tragedy courageously. As in loving families generally, the tensions do not disappear. At the end, Andrew, for the first time in his life, invites Rufus to walk with him. Sensing the negative feelings in his uncle, Rufus nevertheless is afraid to ask him about them. Walking home with this man who can never replicate his father but who will fill as much of the void as possible, Rufus comes to terms with his father's death in the silence that in Agee's fiction communicates beyond the power of words. In this reconstruction of his own most momentous childhood experience, Agee portrays the most difficult reconciliation of all.

Robert P. Ellis

OTHER MAJOR WORKS

SHORT FICTION: "A Mother's Tale," 1952; *Four Early Stories by James Agee*, 1964; *The Collected Short Prose of James Agee*, 1968.

POETRY: *Permit Me Voyage*, 1934; *The Collected Poems of James Agee*, 1968.

SCREENPLAYS: *The Red Badge of Courage*, 1951 (based on Stephen Crane's novel); *The African Queen*, 1952 (based on C. S. Forester's novel); *The Bride Comes to Yellow Sky*, 1952 (based on Crane's short story); *Noa Noa*, 1953; *White Mane*, 1953; *Green Magic*, 1955; *The Night of the Hunter*, 1955; *Agee on Film: Five Film Scripts*, 1960.

NONFICTION: *Let Us Now Praise Famous Men*, 1941; *Agee on Film: Reviews and Comments*, 1958; *Letters of James Agee to Father Flye*, 1962; *James Agee: Selected Journalism*, 1985; *Brooklyn Is: Southeast of the Island, Travel Notes*, 2005 (wr. 1939).

BIBLIOGRAPHY

Barson, Alfred. *A Way of Seeing: A Critical Study of James Agee*. Amherst: University of Massachusetts Press, 1972. A revisionist view of Agee, whose earliest critics thought that his talents were dissipated by his diverse interests but who judged him to have been improving at the time of his death. Barson inverts this thesis, stating that Agee's finished work should not be so slighted and that his powers were declining when he died. Includes notes and an index.

Bergreen, Laurence. *James Agee: A Life*. New York: E. P. Dutton, 1984. One of the best biographies of Agee available, thorough and well researched. Presents critical analyses that are cogent and thoughtful, written in an appealing style. Includes illustrations, notes, a bibliography of Agee's writings, a bibliography of works about him, and an index.

Folks, Jeffrey J. "Art and Anarchy in James Agee's *A Death in the Family*." In *In Time of Disorder: Form and Meaning in Southern Fiction from Poe to O'Connor*. New York: Peter Lang, 2003. Essay focusing on *A Death in the Family* is included in a volume that examines how Agee and other southern writers sought to create a sense of social order in their work in response to perceptions that society was unjust, chaotic, and governed by random chance.

Hughes, William. *James Agee, "Omnibus," and "Mr. Lincoln": The Culture of Liberalism and the Challenge of Television, 1952-1953*. Lanham, Md.: Scarecrow Press, 2004. Resurrects *Mr. Lincoln*, the five television programs Agee wrote about Abraham Lincoln's early life, which for many years were not available to the public. Places the scripts within the culture of American Cold War liberalism and describes how Agee's experiences, political leanings, and film writings influenced his re-creation of the Lincoln legend.

Kramer, Victor A. *Agee and Actuality: Artistic Vision in His Work*. Troy, N.Y.: Whitston, 1991. Delves into the aesthetics of Agee's writing and provides a valuable resource for identifying the controlling themes that pervade the author's work.

_____. *James Agee*. Boston: Twayne, 1975. Well-written work remains one of the more valuable sources on Agee available to the nonspecialist, useful for its analyses, its bibliography, and its chronology of the author's life.

Lofaro, Michael A., ed. *Agee Agonistes: Essays on the Life, Legend, and Works of James Agee*. Knoxville: University of Tennessee Press, 2007. Compilation of seventeen essays from the James Agee Celebration, which was held at the University of Tennessee in April, 2005. The essays are divided into four parts, addressing Agee's influences and syntheses, Agee's films, Agee's literature, and Agee's correspondence. Also features new photographs, previously unknown correspondence, and a remembrance by Agee's daughter.

_____. *James Agee: Reconsiderations*. Knoxville: University of Tennessee Press, 1992. The nine essays in this slim volume are carefully considered. Mary Moss's bibliography of secondary sources is especially well crafted and eminently useful, as are penetrating essays by Linda Wagner-Martin and Victor A. Kramer.

Madden, David, and Jeffrey J. Folks, eds. *Remembering James Agee*. 2d ed. Athens: University of Georgia Press, 1997. The twenty-two essays in this volume touch on every important aspect of Agee's life and work, ranging from the reminiscences of Father Flye to those of his third wife, Mia Agee. The interpretive essays on his fiction and films are particularly illuminating, as are the essays on his life as a reporter and writer for *Fortune* and *Time*.

Spiegel, Alan. *James Agee and the Legend of Himself*. Columbia: University of Missouri Press, 1998. This critical study of Agee's writing offers especially sound insights into the role that childhood reminiscence plays in the author's fiction and into the uses that Agee makes of nostalgia. The extensive discussion of *Let Us Now Praise Famous Men* represents one of the best interpretations of this important early work. Teachers will appreciate the section titled "Agee in the Classroom."

SHMUEL YOSEF AGNON
Shmuel Yosef Czaczkes

Born: Buczacz, Galicia, Austro-Hungarian Empire (now Buchach, Ukraine); July 17, 1888
Died: Rehovoth, Israel; February 17, 1970
Also known as: Shmuel Yosef Czaczkes

PRINCIPAL LONG FICTION
Hakhnasat kala, 1931 (*The Bridal Canopy*, 1937)
Bi-levav yamim: Sipur agadah, 1935 (*In the Heart of the Seas: A Story of a Journey to the Land of Israel*, 1947)
Sipur pashut, 1935 (*A Simple Story*, 1985)
Oreach nata lalun, 1939 (*A Guest for the Night*, 1968)
Temol shilsom, 1945 (*Only Yesterday*, 2000)
Shirah, 1971 (*Shira*, 1989)
Bachanuto shel Mar Lublin, 1974

OTHER LITERARY FORMS
Many of the works written by Shmuel Yosef Agnon (AHG-nahn) are available in two comprehensive collections, both titled *Kol sippurav shel Shmuel Yosef Agnon*. The first volume of the first collection appeared in 1931 in Berlin. The collection included two novels, *The Bridal Canopy*, parts 1 and 2, and *A Simple Story*, and three collections of short stories, *Me-az ume-'ata* (1931; from then and from now), *Sipure ahavim* (1931; stories of lovers), and *Beshuva vanachat* (1935; with repentance and joy). This edition was expanded to eleven volumes: Volumes 7 and 8, including the novel *A Guest for the Night* and a collection of stories, *Elu ve'elu* (1941; of this and that), were printed in Jerusalem. Volumes 9 through 11, published both in Jerusalem and Tel Aviv, included the novel *Only Yesterday* and two more volumes of short stories, *Samukh venir'e* (1951; near and apparent) and *Ad hena* (1952; *To This Day*, 2008). The second comprehensive collection of Agnon's work was published in Tel Aviv in eight volumes, seven of them in 1953 and another in 1962.

In addition to his fiction, Agnon published a number of nonfiction works. They include *Yamim nora'im* (1938; *Days of Awe*, 1948), an anthology of High Holi-day traditions; *Sefer, sofer, vesipur* (1938; book, writer, and story), excerpts on booklore from various sources; *Atem re'item* (1959; *Present at Sinai: The Giving of the Law*, 1994), a compilation of rabbinic responsa; and *Sifrehem shel tsadikim* (1961; tales of the Zaddikim), stories of the Baal Shem Tov and his disciples. Posthumous publications of Agnon's works include the two novels *Shira* and *Bachanuto shel Mar Lublin* (in Mr. Lublin's store); three collections of stories, one concerning Agnon's hometown in Galicia, titled *'Ir u-melo'ah* (1973; a city and the fullness thereof), and two others, *Lifnim min hachomah* (1975; inside the wall) and *Pitche dvarim* (1977; introductions); a book of Agnon's letters and speeches, *Meatsmi el atsmi* (1976; from myself to myself); and a work tracing Agnon's family tree, *Korot batenu* (1979; pillars of our house). Some of his works have been translated into French, Spanish, and German.

ACHIEVEMENTS
Affectionately known in Israel by the acronym "Shai," Shmuel Yosef Agnon was during his lifetime, as one critic notes, "uncontestably the dean" of Hebrew letters. He is widely read and almost a household word in Israel but is not as well known to English-speaking audiences. His works, although deceptively simple, are so complex that they do not lend themselves well to translation. He was a prolific writer, the author of more than one hundred tales, yet for many years relatively few of his major works were available in English translation.

Agnon is unique in many respects: He was a religious Jew who wrote fiction rather than biblical commentaries, an intellectual writer who appeals to the simple as well as to the highly sophisticated. Most of his writings appeared in local periodicals, either in Europe or in Israel, prior to their incorporation in the volumes of collected works. In his extraordinary Hebrew prose style, which assimilates biblical phrases and talmudic parables, Agnon insists on a return to Jewish sources. He is an allusive writer who writes with the erudition of his rabbinic background, using the language of the Jewish scholar. His Hebrew is classical rather than modern.

Agnon's works have a timeless, dreamlike, magical quality that takes them beyond the reality he presents. The issues with which Agnon deals are not explicit; they are veiled in layers of symbolism, making his works so elusive that scholars are reluctant to attempt translations. The surface of his fiction, however, is realistic, offering a detailed picture of Eastern European Jewry of the nineteenth and twentieth centuries.

Agnon was the recipient of numerous honors and prizes. In 1966, with poet Nelly Sachs, he received the Nobel Prize in Literature—the first time this award was granted to a Hebrew-language writer.

BIOGRAPHY

The oldest of five children, Shmuel Yosef Agnon was born Shmuel Yosef Czaczkes in the small village of Buczacz in Eastern Galicia (a small East European province that has belonged alternately to Poland and to Austria). His father, Shalom Mordecai, an ordained rabbi, earned his livelihood as a fur merchant. Religiously, the family was traditionally observant; economically, it was strongly bourgeois; culturally, it was erudite in Jewish literature. Agnon received a traditional and liberal education, studying the Talmud, Midrash, Jewish medieval philosophers, and Hasidic and rabbinic lore as well as the early Galician enlightened writers, modern Hebrew and Yiddish literature, and German literature. His broad education developed in him two loves, which became his modus vivendi: his love for literature and for Zion.

In his Nobel Prize speech, Agnon claimed that he wrote his first poem at the age of five as a tribute to his father, who was away on a business trip, because he missed him. His early interest in writing was no doubt generated by a desire to emulate both his father, who wrote poetry and scholarly articles, and his cousin, Hayim Czaczkes, a writer whose works were often published in the Galician press. He was fortunate that his family was well-off and did not need his help in its support, and he was encouraged to pursue his own interests. At fifteen, he published his first poem in the Kraków Hebrew weekly. By the time he was eighteen, he was considered a promising young writer.

Agnon, a strong Zionist, left for Palestine in 1907, and although he returned to Buczacz twice, in 1913 and in 1930, he could stay only for short periods. His journey

to Eretz Yisrael, the Land of Israel, was a difficult one, requiring a train trip to Trieste and then a sea voyage to Jaffa. Agnon's short novel *In the Heart of the Seas* records this hazardous trip. Upon entering Palestine, he settled in Jaffa, the scene of a number of his stories, including his first published tale in 1908, titled "Agunot" ("Deserted Wives"). Following a trend adopted by earlier Hebrew writers, such as Mendele Mokher Sefarim (pseudonym for Shalom Jacob Abramovich) and Sholom Aleichem (pseudonym for Sholom Rabinowitz), young Shmuel Yoseph Czaczkes signed this tale with the name of "Agnon," adopting it officially as his family name in 1924.

It is significant that he chose this particular name, for it would seem to indicate his own relationship to the world. In Jewish law, the *agunah*, or deserted woman, is not free to remarry, because she has not been divorced. She is anchored in a relationship that can last forever. This image of being in limbo was pursued a decade after Agnon's story by S. Ansky in his classical drama *The Dybbuk* (1916; English translation, 1917) and some thirty-five years later by Saul Bellow in his depiction of the *Dangling Man* (1944). In all three cases, the characters are not free. They are constricted by invisible threads that they do not control and cannot sever. This condition is not a form of alienation, an estrangement from a person or society; rather, it suggests an eternal rootedness that cannot be easily extirpated. At the age of twenty, Agnon felt like the *agunot* of his tales: uprooted, yet eternally bound to his native village of Buczacz and the world of his youth. In 1911, he moved to Jerusalem and settled permanently in that city, even though he left it for one extended period and other brief periods. He was proclaimed an honorary citizen of Jerusalem in 1962.

Agnon went to Berlin in 1913. The time he spent in Germany proved to be very significant to him. (He made a brief trip to his hometown to visit his ailing father, who died November 20, 1913. His mother had died earlier, in 1908.) There he met Zalman Schocken, a merchant and Zionist and patron of the Jewish arts who became Agnon's admirer, his patron, and his sole publisher. Agnon was one of those fortunate artists who never had to struggle for a livelihood and was thus free to concentrate on his writing.

Germany was then a hub of cultural activity, and

Shmuel Yosef Agnon. (© The Nobel Foundation)

In 1929, Agnon lost his home again, this time to marauding Arabs, who attacked numerous Jewish settlements in that year. The family escaped unhurt, but his house and library were in shambles. In a letter to his friend Schocken, he described the scene and wrote that he was able to save his manuscripts, but most of his archives and the history of Eretz Yisrael were destroyed. His new library of three thousand books, many of which he had inherited from his father-in-law, also suffered: Books had been "overturned and scattered and torn" in the attack.

The loss of his home a second time was a crushing blow to Agnon. The family spent four months at his wife's sister's home in Bat Galim, near Haifa. In January, 1930, Agnon traveled to Germany to see Schocken, who had decided to publish Agnon's collected works. During this time, Agnon also made a trip to Buczacz. He stayed only a week, but this trip provided the material for his novel *A Guest for the Night*.

The Berlin edition of his collected works was enthusiastically received, and from that time on, Agnon's life was a series of artistic and critical triumphs. Since his death in Israel on February 17, 1970, his daughter has edited a number of his works, many of which have been published by Schocken Books.

ANALYSIS

Two dominant forces ruled Shmuel Yosef Agnon's life: the Torah as the essence of a meaningful life and Eretz Yisrael, the Land of Israel, as the ancestral homeland for the Jew. On a personal basis, Agnon integrated these passions into his existence at an early age. He was brought up in a religious home. For a brief time, he abandoned his piety, but he shortly realized that his life was empty without it. He returned to his Orthodox ways and lived as a Jew committed to the Torah, albeit in secular surroundings. He made Eretz Yisrael his home when most religious Jews still looked upon the Holy Land as a suitable burial place but not a place to live. They felt that settlement in Israel could take place only with the advent of the Messiah.

Agnon moved in a dynamic circle of philosophers, writers, Zionist leaders, and industrialists. In 1920, he married Esther Marx, a member of one of Germany's most respected Jewish families. The couple moved to Homburg, where their two children were born, a daughter, Emunai, in 1921, and a son, Hemdat, in 1922. Agnon's years in Germany were productive ones, but in 1924 his home there was destroyed by a fire that consumed much of his unpublished material. He never entirely recovered from the trauma of this loss. In his Nobel speech, he claimed to have lost, at that time, not only everything he had written after he left Israel but also a rare library of four thousand Hebrew books. After the fire, he returned to Jerusalem alone, sending his wife and children to her parents' home. In 1925, his family joined him, and they made their home in Talpiot, a suburb of Jerusalem. Agnon was busy at this time working on his epic novel *The Bridal Canopy*.

On an artistic level, Agnon's early works, those that are best known and have been widely translated, present a nostalgic evocation of the milieu of the Eastern European shtetl—specifically, his native village of Buczacz. The works that are set in the nineteenth century depict a hermetically sealed community governed by piety and love and watched over by the omnipresent and benevolent Almighty. Agnon, however, was a man of his times, fully aware of contemporary events and their effects on the Jewish community. Eretz Yisrael is a motif in all of his works, which reflect the ongoing dissolution of the shtetl as it became increasingly vulnerable to the intrusions of the age. Although Agnon made brief visits to Buczacz as an adult, all of his works are drawn from his childhood memories of his hometown. The images are at times ebullient and joyful, as in *The Bridal Canopy*; at times fanciful, as in *In the Heart of the Seas*; and at other times somber and depressing, as in *A Guest for the Night*.

THE BRIDAL CANOPY

The Bridal Canopy is the first novel of a trilogy in which Agnon deals with the experience of Eastern European Jewry. Written in 1931 (although based on a short story completed in 1920), a time of upheaval between two major wars, the novel focuses on the Jewish community in Galicia of the 1820's. In a mood of fantasy and nostalgia, Agnon presents a work that is both realistic and unrealistic: realistic in its depiction of the Jewish milieu, the piety of the Jew, and his devotion to the Torah; unrealistic in its childlike attitude toward life, where the concerns of men are limited to the amassing of a bridal dowry and to the telling of tales of past saints and wonder-workers.

The theme of this major work, as suggested in the title, is the brotherhood of the Jewish people, which is achieved through the upholding of God's commandments, especially those of charity and hospitality. The original title, *Hakhnasat kala*, a Hebrew idiom meaning bridal dowry, was loosely translated as *The Bridal Canopy* for the English translation of the novel by I. M. Lask, but this is misleading. The focus of the work is on the collection of the dowry; the wedding itself, which takes place under the "bridal canopy," is of relatively minor significance. Agnon deals with the marriage process, which involves not only the protagonist, Reb Yudel, but also the entire Jewish community. All participate in the preservation of the social institution of marriage and in the fulfillment of God's commandment of procreation. The bridal dowry, an ancient concept—well known in the time of Abraham, who sent his servant, Eliezer, loaded with gifts, to seek a wife for his son, Isaac—is an integral element of the traditional Jewish marriage.

With this initial novel, Agnon falls into the category of Jewish writers who depict Jewish social institutions humorously. Many of them, such as Yosef Perl and Mendele Mokher Sefarim, writing during the period of the Haskalah—the Enlightenment—parodied and satirized traditional Jewish customs. Agnon's novel more closely resembles the work of Israel Zangwill, who in the late nineteenth century wrote the marvelously funny work *The King of Schnorrers* (1894), depicting, with a combination of humor and love, the Jewish mendicant, who is considered a vital aspect of the community. It is through him that the community is able to fulfill God's commandment of charity. The protagonist, the schnorrer, never allows the community to forget that he is the instrument of their salvation. Similarly, in Agnon's work, Reb Yudel, by raising a bridal dowry for his daughter, allows the community to participate both in hospitality to a stranger and in charity to the poor. Through the peregrinations of Reb Yudel, one sees a cohesive Jewish community, its members flawed but united, a community wherein each is his brother's keeper.

The plot is simple, if somewhat improbable. Provoked by his wife's complaints, the protagonist leaves the relative comforts of his home and the house of study in his native village of Brod and travels to various neighboring communities to raise enough money for the bridal dowry of his eldest daughter. He is accompanied by his faithful friend, the wagon-driver Nota, and Nota's trusty and intelligent horses, Mashkeni and Narutza. (These names whimsically play on a passage in the Hebrew Bible's Song of Songs, where the beloved says to her betrothed, "Draw me after thee"—*mashkeni*—"and we will run together"—*narutza*.) After spending months on the road, he yearns for a return to the simple life and decides to make up for lost time by settling in at an inn, studying the Torah, and using the collected dowry money to pay for his stay. While at the inn, he is mistaken for a wealthy man who coincidentally happens to bear his same name and lives in the same town as he does. This mistaken identity is the vehicle for the ensuing events: an alliance in the form of an engagement with a wealthy family, the return to his home, the inadvertent intercession of the aristocratic Yudel Nathanson, who unwittingly becomes the patron of Yudel the Hasid, the discovery of the treasure in a cave, the wedding itself, Yudel's blessed and prosperous life, and his eventual settling in the Land of Israel.

Agnon's language in *The Bridal Canopy* is a combination of the Yiddish vernacular and biblical and postbiblical Hebrew. It was the medium of popular Hebrew texts of the seventeenth, eighteenth, and nineteenth centuries and also the language of the pious Jew of the period depicted. Eclectic in style, the novel is essentially a series of tales or anecdotes held together by the tale of Reb Yudel. Most of the tales in *The Bridal Canopy* were published as individual stories; some are well integrated into the novel, whereas others seem superimposed. These tales are, at times, didactic, at other times fanciful. Some are folktales; others are Agnon's own creations. The narrative of Reb Yudel's odyssey and the tales within the narrative illuminate the character of the protagonist and the inhabitants of the community of Brod, his hometown, and those whom he meets in the neighboring villages. The tale within the tale is also symbolic of the Jew within the Jewish community: Each has his or her own personality, and together they make up a larger entity.

The novel itself is a depiction not so much of Reb Yudel as it is of the entire environment he traverses. It establishes Agnon's posture in his fictive world as well, an attitude of respect for religious tradition in spite of instances of hypocrisy and ignorance. The work is divided into two parts. Book 1 deals with the departure of Reb Yudel, the raising of the bridal dowry, and the quest for a successful match for his daughter; book 2 deals with his return home and the wedding.

The opening chapter describes Reb Yudel's high spiritual aspirations and his lowly material circumstances. He lives in an unfurnished cellar. His only possession is a rooster, known as Reb Zerach, that functions at the beginning of the work simply as an alarm clock, awakening Reb Yudel at dawn for the morning worship. At the end of the work, it becomes clear that the rooster's function is a more subtle one.

Reb Yudel's character, as the work progresses and he becomes a wanderer, combines three Jewish stock figures: the *batlon* (the idler), the *meshulach* (the messenger or schnorrer), and the *maggid* (the itinerant preacher and storyteller). Reb Yudel, a *batlon*, known affectionately, if somewhat ironically, as "the Chasid," the student, is one of that society's pious men who is incapable of earning a living and spends all day in the house of study. Agnon indicates his attitude toward the protagonist (and the work itself) by referring to him by the descriptive diminutive "Reb Yudel" or "little Jew." It is the name given to a child or to one of lowly stature, *dos kleine Mensch*, and lacks the reverence that would be found in the scholar's appellation. At no time is the character referred to as "Rav Yehuda ha Chasid"—Rabbi Judah, the pious. Agnon wants his audience to recognize the humble nature and childlike quality of his protagonist as well as the inherent comedy of the work. This is reflected not only in Yudel's naïveté but also in his attitude toward life and the world at large, an attitude indicated in the subtitle of the book, *The Wonders of Reb Yudel, the Chasid from Brod . . .* , which supports the mood of fantasy and nostalgia in which this novel was written. Reb Yudel is not a saint and does not perform miracles, but he depends on and believes in miracles. Like a child, Reb Yudel interprets experiences and expressions in their most literal contexts. Like the unscholarly, nonsaintly individual, he misquotes the sages, misapplies biblical and talmudic sayings, and misassesses situations.

Agnon's depiction of Reb Yudel is not harshly critical. Reb Yudel represents a world that no longer exists, a world that was reassuring in its simplicity, in its belief in the goodness of God and humankind, a world where one could spend one's life recounting the marvels of the sages while enjoying the hospitality of one's host and brethren. Some critics find a troubling ambiguity in the novel, an uncertain combination of acceptance and rejection of the world so painstakingly delineated. Readers are likely to feel this ambiguity only if they mistake Agnon's comedy for criticism. In fact, Agnon wrote as a devoted traditionalist; he makes this obvious in his depiction of Heshel, the *maskil*, the man of the Enlightenment whom Reb Yudel meets during his odyssey. Heshel, ready to discard tradition without replacing it with anything substantial ("Grammar is the foundation of the world," he claims), receives the harshest treatment of any character in the work. He begins as a wealthy man, and Yudel goes to him for a contribution to his bridal fund, but he ends in a state of abject penury, ill clothed, pockets empty, starving. He comes as a beggar to the wedding of Yudel's daughter. The point Agnon makes is obvious: Life is impoverished when it is devoid of tradition. In contrast to Heshel, Reb Yudel, the believer, is amply rewarded for his faith with material fortune, a prosperous life with its spiritual culmination in the Land of Israel, where he settles in his old age.

It has been suggested that *The Bridal Canopy* is modeled on Miguel de Cervantes' *Don Quixote de la Mancha* (1605, 1615) and that Agnon treats his protagonist ambivalently, as both saint and fool. Actually, Agnon's style, like Sholom Aleichem's, more closely resembles that of the American humorist Mark Twain in its use of the vernacular, folk humor, tall tale, literal interpretation of metaphor, and comic treatment of cloistered religion. The protagonist, Reb Yudel, is not a romantic; he does not fight windmills, nor does he reach for the impossible dream, as does Don Quixote. He is a firm believer in the beneficence and magnanimity of God and has utmost faith that all of his needs will be met, and, ultimately, they are. This is not a romantic concept but a religious one.

The Bridal Canopy is an eclectic work. In his Nobel speech, Agnon voiced his indebtedness to the Jewish sources: to the Bible and to its major commentator, Rashi; to the Talmud and *Shulhan ʿarukh*; to Jewish sages and authorities on Jewish law; to medieval poets and thinkers, especially Moses Maimonides; and to contemporary Hasidim and pious men with whom he had spent time.

In the Heart of the Seas

In the Heart of the Seas, the second of the trilogy begun with *The Bridal Canopy*, is a shorter novel that has much in common with its predecessor. The time period of the second novel is the same as that of the earlier work, about 1820; the milieu, the city of Buczacz (instead of the village of Brod) in Galicia. While *The Bridal Canopy* ends with Reb Yudel's ascent to the Holy Land, *In the Heart of the Seas* begins with the last-minute preparations for the departure of a group of pious Hasidim who

have decided to emigrate to Eretz Yisrael. The work deals with the journey itself, the perils, trials, and anguish involved in this trip, and the determination of the pilgrims in spite of all hardships.

It is a tale that commingles reality and fantasy. In 1934, the year the novel was published, Agnon was witness to the Fifth Aliya (ascent to the Land of Israel), which brought some 250,000 Jews to the country. Most of them were refugees from Nazi Germany who managed to leave before all exits were closed. They were not necessarily religious people; they were those who had the means and the foresight to leave. In *In the Heart of the Seas*, Agnon reflects on what it would be like to emigrate to the Holy Land out of love and religious commitment rather than the political necessity of the times. It is a fantastic concept. The single individual may move whenever he or she desires, but communities of people are not so mobile and will reestablish themselves, or move from the security of their environment, only when forced to do so. This was the case with the Jewish community of Eastern Europe. *In the Heart of the Seas* is a wistful tale with a realistic veneer.

The work assumes even greater significance if considered in the context of the secular writings of the Hebraists and the cultural climate of the time. Zionism was viewed mainly as a secular and political movement within the Jewish world and was frowned upon by religious Jews who, like the rabbi of Buczacz in *In the Heart of the Seas*, believed that it was sacrilege to go to Israel prior to the coming of the Messiah. Agnon takes the traditional image of Zion, which the ancient poets and pietists glorified in psalms and poetry, and transforms it into a realistic destination of the pious Hasidim of this Eastern Galician village.

Although the action takes place in the early part of the nineteenth century, the author includes himself as one of the travelers. He is the last to join the group. He is mentioned by name, Rabbi Shmuel Yosef, the son of Rabbi Shalom Mordechai ha-Levi, who is married to a woman named Esther and who has a penchant for storytelling. The tale is related by an omniscient narrator who is replaced at times by the author's own persona. He purports to be chronicling the adventures of a man named Chananiah exactly as he heard them.

On a literal level, Chananiah is the character who

frames the story. The story starts with him and ends with him. Chananiah—meaning "God has graced"—is a saintly mysterious stranger, an evanescent figure. He joins the group of Hasidic pilgrims to the Holy Land. Before they start out on their journey, he tells them his own story, a tale of robbers, immoral men, and their hideouts in a country that knows no Sabbath; the chief of the villains wears phylacteries (leather boxes containing biblical passages that are traditionally worn by Orthodox Jews during prayer), even though he is not Jewish. Chananiah is a jack-of-all-trades; he emerges in time of need to help the travelers with their preparations, making boxes for their belongings while keeping his own in a kerchief. He disappears for the voyage itself but is seen riding the waves on this same kerchief, and he reaches the destination much before his fellow travelers. He also appears on the last page of the work, where the narrator states that the book is a tribute to the memory of Chananiah. This would seem to suggest a realism that is contradicted by the subtitle of the story, *Sipur agadah* (*An Allegorical Tale*). In its allegorical context, the work suggests that all of life is a pilgrimage fraught with dangers and hardships, cloaked in mystery. The good, those "graced by God," will ride the rough seas under his aegis, protected by his garment. The work, then, becomes a tribute not to the evanescent Chananiah of this particular tale but to all of those Chananiahs who embark on the journey into time or who journey from night to day, from ignorance to illumination, donning the protective mantle of God's covering, the Torah.

Chananiah is also the author himself, who narrates allegorical tales for the reader to interpret. The kerchief is the imagination of the author, which can take him over the seas, or back in time, or anywhere he desires to go.

The style of this work is, like that of *The Bridal Canopy*, eclectic. Agnon draws from biblical sources, the book of Jonah, Psalms, Song of Songs, the Midrash, among others, and also from travel literature describing voyages to the Holy Land, especially a work published in 1790 titled *Ahavat Zion*, an autobiographical account of Rabbi Simcha of Zalozitz's voyage to Eretz Yisrael. Less fanciful than *The Bridal Canopy* despite its allegorical quality, *In the Heart of the Seas* acts as a bridge to the realism and sobriety of the last novel of the trilogy, *A Guest for the Night*, Agnon's greatest work.

A GUEST FOR THE NIGHT

In *A Guest for the Night*, Agnon changes his mode of storytelling from the comic and fanciful to the tragic. Originally published in daily installments in *Ha'aretz*, a Tel Aviv newspaper, from October 18, 1938, to April 7, 1939, the novel reflects the unrelenting gloom that pervaded both Europe and Palestine during this period.

Agnon, distraught upon losing his home for the second time, made a sentimental journey to his native village of Buczacz in 1930, attempting to recapture some of the serenity and security of his childhood. He was unsuccessful; within five days, Agnon realized that he could not reenter the protective womb of his childhood. The key to his security was not to return to or re-create a chimerical past but to build a strong foundation in the present, to ensure a firm and stable future. The novel is an extended re-creation of this visit. It deals with the return of the narrator to his native town of Shibush (the Hebrew word for "error") after his home in Jerusalem has been destroyed by Arab marauders. It is a bleak work, evincing none of the gaiety and merriment of Agnon's previous novels. Realistically drawn, it reveals Agnon at the height of his powers.

In a complex interweaving of historical and psychological themes, Agnon develops the idea that an adult's recollection of childhood is best left to the imagination. Reality belongs to the present, and the real present can never be as beautiful as the imagined past. The theme of the ēgun, the "dangling man," is used to convey the character of the protagonist. He is a man in limbo, ejected from his home, estranged from his family. Just as the *agunah*, the deserted woman, is still tied down to her evanescent husband, and just as the dangling man dangles from the end of an imperceptible cord, so the protagonist of *A Guest for the Night* is securely linked to the home and land from which he flees, to the family from which he separates and the traditions that bind him for all time.

Early in the novel, the narrator is given the key to the *bet midrash* (house of study) by the townspeople of his native village. On a literal level, the key opens the door to the house of study. The narrator, however, misplaces the key immediately and must have a new one made. The old key turns up once again at the end of the story, when the narrator has returned to Jerusalem; his wife finds it in a corner of his suitcase. The villagers have no need for the key. Most of the old-timers have left town, and those who remain await an opportune moment to leave. The new key suggests that the house of study needs new life to restore its grandeur. The narrator's presence is temporary, and his effect on the town is limited. Symbolically, the old key represents the old tradition, which has served the townspeople in the past but seems to be in disharmony with the present time and inadequate to meet contemporary needs. One character's story of a wartime comrade who was shot while still wearing his phylacteries illustrates this point. That the old key reappears at the end of the story, when the protagonist has returned to his home in Jerusalem, suggests Agnon's concept of tradition: It recedes into the background when it is unceremoniously dropped; it will, however, resurface eventually to take its necessary place within one's life. On a psychological level, the key opens the door for the narrator to a secure world where he can close himself off from harm, and although he allows everyone to enter, he knows that whoever comes is a countryman and friend. The four walls of the house of study represent a return to the secure embrace of his childhood.

Eretz Yisrael is another primary theme in this work. Agnon settled in Israel during the time of the Second Aliya, the second wave of Zionist emigration to Israel, which spanned the decade from 1904 to 1914. Those who participated in this *aliya* (literally, "ascent") were mainly from Eastern Europe. Many of them became workers and settled in the port city of Jaffa, where Agnon himself settled before moving to Jerusalem. Others settled in existing *moshavim* (agricultural settlements) or established kibbutzim. Agnon depicts this period of Zionism in *A Guest for the Night* in his portrayal of the members of the Jewish pioneer group preparing themselves for life in Israel by working as a group on a farm in Poland and also in vignettes of the various members of the Bach family, including the patriarch, Reb Shlomo Bach, who settles in Israel in his old age. The narrator has left Israel after the attack on his home, but he considers his leaving a form of therapy and not a permanent emigration. He expresses his love for Eretz Yisrael by the tales he tells and by his positive attitude toward the Holy Land in conversations with various members of the community. In fact, at one point he says that one of the reasons he does not like to visit with the local rabbi

is that he is disturbed by the rabbi's antagonism toward Israel.

In *The Bridal Canopy*, Reb Yudel's journey to Israel is the culmination of his life, and he settles there in his old age. In *In the Heart of the Seas*, an entire Hasidic group, a quorum of ten, moves to the Holy Land. In *A Guest for the Night*, young and old strive to achieve the same goal. Not all are fortunate in their endeavors. Some cannot make it for familial, economic, or political reasons. Zvi, the young man who prepares himself for life in the Land of Israel by working on a farm in Poland, cannot afford the cost of proper papers and attempts to enter the country illegally; he is turned back by the British. Some who do make it are disillusioned and do not stay, as is the case with Yerucham Freeman. In fact, Yerucham Freeman's harsh criticism of the protagonist's relationship to Israel and his influence on others illuminates another theme of this work: illusions and realities.

For most of the Jews of Eastern Galicia (and, for that matter, worldwide), the Land of Israel at this period was indeed a dream, the subject of poetry, literature, prayers, and communal deliberations. It gave direction to one's life, but it remained generally an unattainable quest, an illusion, as it were. The narrator of this work, having settled in the Land of Israel while still a youth, transforms this illusion into a reality for his community. He becomes an exemplar for others and, in time, personifies Israel itself. Yerucham Freeman also falls in love with the Land of Israel, but he does not realize that he is exchanging one illusion for another. For this reason, he cannot find fulfillment when he does emigrate to the Holy Land. Entering the new country, he finds that the narrator has left for a sojourn abroad. This information shatters Yerucham's dream, which was thoroughly interwoven with its personification, and (expelled from the Land of Israel for communist activities) he returns to his native village to gain a foothold in reality.

The narrator makes a similar movement, but for opposite reasons. Reality for him is the home he has established for himself in the Land of Israel, encompassing both its beauty and its harshness. The narrator would like to erase its harshness by returning to a state of illusion—a return to his childhood and his juvenile vision of the Holy Land. His prolonged stay in Shibush demonstrates that one cannot go "home" again, one cannot recapture the past. The narrator arrives in Shibush on the eve of Yom Kippur, the most solemn day in the Jewish calendar, a day of judgment for all. By bringing the narrator in at the onset of this holy day, Agnon suggests that the protagonist needs to take stock of himself and repent for his sins, the most obvious of which is his decision to leave his family and home in the Land of Israel. Just as Shibush is no longer the place that he knew, so must Israel take a more realistic place in his life. Reality may at times be beautiful, but it is also brutal.

All the themes of the novel coalesce within a historical perspective spanning two time periods. The work was written during a six-month span from October, 1938, to April, 1939, a period that witnessed the upheaval of the Jewish communities in Europe prior to the outbreak of World War II and the ultimate destruction of the shtetl way of life. Indeed, *A Guest for the Night* has been referred to as "an elaborate elegy on the lost shtetl culture." The story itself takes place in 1930, a time between wars, a time when the entire European world had not had a chance to recover from the devastating effects of the maelstrom of World War I before it was thrown into another cycle of death and destruction. The Jewish community was caught in this vertigo. Agnon's work captures all the bleakness of this "no exit" situation: Europe, the shtetl, could no longer be the home of the Jew, and Eretz Yisrael, the Land of Israel, was not considered a viable alternative. As a British mandate, Palestine was inhospitable and unsympathetic to Jewish immigration, while the Yishuv, the Jewish settlement in Israel, was not developed sufficiently to be a replacement for the Jewish community of the shtetl. Agnon re-creates this dilemma in the narrative of *A Guest for the Night*. Allegorically, the title (taken from Jeremiah 14:8) suggests the historical situation of the Jew, who comes as a guest to a foreign country, intending to stay for a short while, and remains for as long as he can maintain his status as a guest; then, when the realities of life force him to do so, he leaves.

Agnon is above all a storyteller, and although the mood of *A Guest for the Night* differs from that of *The Bridal Canopy*, the style is characteristically Agnon's. In both works, the inn or the house of study represents the centrifugal force of the novel: The protagonist employs his vantage point as a hotel guest to narrate his own tales and the tales of the people with whom he comes in contact or allows them to tell their own tales. The protagonists of both novels are passive characters and sedentary people; they are not adventure seekers. Agnon's heroes are humble, gentle, and compassionate people who are imbued with a love and fear of God and a love for their fellow human beings. Their tales comprise the chronicles of the Jewish people.

Agnon's later works continue to reflect on the situation of the Jew in modern society. Although the Holocaust is not a major theme of his works, it is an underlying current in many of his novels. In *A Guest for the Night*, the gloom and sterility of the village seem to foreshadow the destruction of the culture about to take place. Agnon's next novel, *Only Yesterday*, set in Palestine in the early part of the twentieth century, symbolically suggests, with its protagonist's being eaten by a mad dog, the fate of the Jewish people.

Perhaps what has endeared Agnon so much to his people is the love that he expresses for them throughout his writings and his understanding and compassion for their situation, one of uprootedness, which he echoed in the name he adopted for himself. In a fluctuating, chaotic world, his steadfast traditionalism, coupled with his artistic complexity, is appreciated by a general audience as well.

L. H. Goldman

OTHER MAJOR WORKS

SHORT FICTION: "Agunot," 1909 (English translation, 1970); "Vehaya he-'akov lemishor," 1912; *Me-az ume-'ata*, 1931; *Sipure ahavim*, 1931; "Ha-mitpahat," 1932 ("The Kerchief," 1935); *Sefer hama'asim*, 1932 (reprints 1941, 1951); "Pat Shelema," 1933 ("A Whole Loaf," 1957); *Beshuva vanachat*, 1935; *Elu ve'elu*, 1941; *Shevu'at emunim*, 1943 (*Betrothed*, 1966); *Ido ve'Enam*, 1950 (*Edo and Enam*, 1966); *Samukh venir'e*, 1951; *Ad hena*, 1952 (*To This Day*, 2008); *Al kapot hamanul*, 1953; *Ha-Esh veha'etsim*, 1962; *Two Tales*, 1966 (includes *Betrothed* and *Edo and Enam*); *Selected Stories of S. Y. Agnon*, 1970; *Twenty-one Stories*, 1970; *'Ir u-melo'ah*, 1973; *Lifnim min hachomah*, 1975; *Pitche dvarim*, 1977; *A Dwelling Place of My People: Sixteen Stories of the Chassidim*, 1983; *A Book That Was Lost, and Other Stories*, 1995.

POETRY: *Agnon's Alef Bet: Poems*, 1998.

NONFICTION: *Sefer, sofer, vesipur*, 1938; *Yamim nora'im*, 1938 (*Days of Awe*, 1948); *Atem re'item*, 1959 (*Present at Sinai: The Giving of the Law*, 1994); *Sifrehem shel tsadikim*, 1961; *Meatsmi el atsmi*, 1976; *Korot batenu*, 1979.

MISCELLANEOUS: *Kol sippurav shel Shmuel Yosef Agnon*, 1931-1952 (11 volumes); *Kol sippurav shel Shmuel Yosef Agnon*, 1953-1962 (8 volumes).

BIBLIOGRAPHY

Aberbach, David. *At the Handles of the Lock: Themes in the Fiction of S. J. Agnon*. New York: Oxford University Press, 1984. Sets out the major patterns in Agnon's writing on a work-by-work basis and features discussion of his novels as well as his short fiction. Includes detailed notes and a list of references.

Band, Arnold J. *Nostalgia and Nightmare: A Study in the Fiction of S. Y. Agnon*. Berkeley: University of California Press, 1968. Covers Agnon's literary development text by text and is very useful for the historical background to, and context of, Agnon's work. Discusses Agnon's life and his career as a writer and includes both primary and secondary bibliographies, informative appendixes, and a general index.

_____. *Studies in Modern Jewish Literature*. Philadelphia: Jewish Publication Society, 2003. Anthology of Band's essays written from the 1960's to the early twenty-first century includes a section titled "Modern Hebrew Literature" that includes four essays devoted to discussion of Agnon's work.

Ben-Dov, Nitza. *Agnon's Art of Indirection: Uncovering Latent Content in the Fiction of S. Y. Agnon*. New York: E. J. Brill, 1993. Discusses a number of themes in Agnon's work; of particular interest is a chapter titled "The Web of Biblical Allusion." Includes bibliography and index.

Fisch, Harold. *S. Y. Agnon*. New York: Frederick Ungar, 1975. Part of a series on literary greats, this work includes a useful chronology and a brief biography of Agnon's life. An in-depth discussion of individual writings follows the biographical section. Supplemented by notes, primary and secondary bibliographies, and an index.

Fleck, Jeffrey. *Character and Context: Studies in the Fiction of Abramovitsh, Brenner, and Agnon*. Chico, Calif.: Scholars Press, 1984. Places Agnon's work alongside that of his contemporaries, especially in the first chapter, "Modern Hebrew Literature in Context." Focuses on one of Agnon's novels in another chapter, "Man and Dog in *Only Yesterday*."

Green, Sharon M. *Not a Simple Story: Love and Politics in a Modern Hebrew Novel*. Lanham, Md.: Lexington Books, 2001. Examines Agnon's novel *A Simple Story* and argues that Agnon was a Jewish nationalist and secular modernist whose critical depictions of modern Jewish life were not meant to demean Jews; rather, the author's intention was to demonstrate how the Jewish community could thrive by recapturing its sense of self-respect, heroism, and romantic love.

Hochman, Baruch. *The Fiction of S. Y. Agnon*. Ithaca, N.Y.: Cornell University Press, 1970. Presents a detailed interpretation of Agnon's major works, placing them in the context of the time and place in which they were written. A primary bibliographical note aids readers in locating translations of the original works, and notes on all the chapters are supplied at the end of the book, as is an index.

Negev, Eilat. *Close Encounters with Twenty Israeli Writers*. London: Vallentine Mitchell, 2003. Negev, a literary correspondent for the Israeli journal *Yedioth Achronot*, presents twenty profiles of prominent contemporary Israeli writers, including Agnon, based on her interviews with the writers and other research.

Shaked, Gershon. *Shmuel Yosef Agnon: A Revolutionary Traditionalist*. New York: New York University Press, 1989. Details Agnon's progression as a writer, including biographical events that influenced his development and analysis of his novels. Includes index, notes, and select bibliography.

DEMETRIO AGUILERA MALTA

Born: Guayaquil, Ecuador; May 24, 1909
Died: Mexico City, Mexico; December 29, 1981

PRINCIPAL LONG FICTION

Don Goyo, 1933 (English translation, 1942, 1980)

C.Z. (Canal Zone): Los Yanquis en Panamá, 1935

¡Madrid! Reportaje novelado de una retaguardia heróica, 1937

La isla virgen, 1942

Una cruz en la Sierra Maestra, 1960

El Quijote de El Dorado: Orellana y el río de las Amazonas, 1964

La caballeresa del sol: El gran amor de Bolívar, 1964 (*Manuela, la Caballeresa del Sol*, 1967)

Un nuevo mar para el rey: Balboa, Anayansi, y el Océano Pacífico, 1965

Siete lunas y siete serpientes, 1970 (*Seven Serpents and Seven Moons*, 1979)

El secuestro del general, 1973 (*Babelandia*, 1985)

Jaguar, 1977

Réquiem para el diablo, 1978

Una pelota, un sueño, y diez centavos, 1988

OTHER LITERARY FORMS

In addition to his novels, Demetrio Aguilera Malta (ah-gee-LAYR-ah MAWL-tah) wrote, in collaboration with Joaquín Gallegos Lara and Enrique Gil Gilbert, *Los que se van* (1930; those who leave). He also published several dramas of importance: *España leal* (pb. 1938; loyalist Spain), *Lázaro* (pb. 1941), *Sangre azul* (with Willis Knapp Jones, pb. 1948; *Blue Blood*, 1948), *No bastan los átomos* (pb. 1955; atoms are not enough), *Dientes blancos* (pb. 1955; *White Teeth*, 1963), *El tigre* (pb. 1956; the tiger), *Honorarios* (pb. 1957; honorariums), *Fantoche* (pb. 1970), *Infierno negro* (1967; *Black Hell*, 1977), and *Muerte, S.A.* (pb. 1970; Murder, Inc.). His poetry is collected in *Primavera interior* (1927; spring interior) and *El libro de los mangleros* (1929; the book of the mangleros), and his nonfiction works in-

clude *La revolución española a través de los estampas de Antonio Edén* (1938; the Spanish revolution through the engravings of Anthony Eden) and *Los generales de Bolívar* (1965: Bolívar's generals).

ACHIEVEMENTS

Demetrio Aguilera Malta has been hailed as the initiator of Magical Realism in Latin America. This innovative literary tendency constitutes a new way of perceiving the reality of the New World by searching for the collective consciousness of the Latin American countries, probing their history, legends, and psychology. Stylistically, Magical Realism departs from fiction's traditional linear structure, chronological ordering of events, and logic in order to juxtapose past and present; intermix history, legend, and psychology; and integrate multiple elements of time, space, and reality on the same narrative level.

The introduction and development of this new literary tendency reflects Aguilera Malta's dedication to fostering new ideological and aesthetic trends in Latin America. Although he perfected the sophisticated narrative techniques of the vanguard, he looked to the familiar landscapes of his childhood in Ecuador and to the traditions of its people for the expression of his strong sense of social obligation.

BIOGRAPHY

Demetrio Aguilera Malta was born on May 24, 1909, in Guayaquil, Ecuador. One of the most important aspects of his youth that later influenced his literary production was his contact with the countryside and the peasants on the island of San Ignacio, which was owned by his father. He spent much time there and witnessed the massacre of the workers on the island in November, 1922. In this insular environment, he developed an understanding and sympathy for his surroundings and for the island's inhabitants, the *cholos*.

After completing his bachelor's degree at a school in Guayaquil, he enrolled simultaneously in the law school and in the school of fine arts of Guayaquil University in 1928. He abandoned his studies after two years and in

1930 went to Panama, where he worked for four years as a journalist. In 1936, Aguilera Malta went to Spain to study the humanities at the University of Salamanca, but the Spanish Civil War thwarted his plans and he was forced to return to Ecuador. In 1937, he became a professor at the institution where he received his secondary education and was also appointed subsecretary of public education. He remained in these positions until 1943 and then served several cultural and consular missions in Chile. In 1958, he moved to Mexico. During the course of his lifetime, Aguilera Malta visited almost all the countries of Europe and the Americas. He offered courses and gave conferences in universities in Chile, Brazil, and Colombia as well as in universities in Mexico, Central America, and the United States.

Although he was noted for his friendliness, the most outstanding features of Aguilera Malta's personality were his versatility and dynamism. From his first days as a writer, he was known for his generous and enthusiastic spirit. He was a member of the Generacíon del Treinta (generation of the thirties), so called because the year 1930 saw the publication of *Los que se van*, the emblematic work of the movement during its first years. Within the Generación del Treinta, he belonged to the division known as the Grupo de Guayaquil, a literary group composed of José de la Cuadra, Alfredo Pareja Diezcanseco, Joaquín Gallegos Lara, and Enrique Gil Gilbert. The works of these authors are marked by denunciation of elite white-power groups and protest against the living and working conditions of the Latin American Indians, with the goal of emancipating them from a feudal system that was suffocating them.

Analysis

Demetrio Aguilera Malta's long fiction can be divided into three categories: Magical Realist, historical, and journalistic fiction. The novels that introduce Magical Realism and develop it as a major literary movement in Latin America are considered to be his best and most important. These are *Don Goyo*, *La isla virgen*, *Seven Serpents and Seven Moons*, and *Babelandia*.

Don Goyo

Don Goyo, like most of the works of Aguilera Malta's generation, is a novel of social protest. Unlike the traditional novels of its kind, however, its message is expressed on a narrative level that fuses objective reality with magical reality. Magical reality is expressed through the fusion of mythical, legendary, and supernatural elements in the form of animism, totemism, eroticism, and the superhuman powers of some of the characters. The narrative techniques of flashback, stream of consciousness, and metaphor contribute stylistically to convert objective reality into magical reality.

Animism is a primitive vision of nature and the universe that holds that good and evil spirits are responsible for natural phenomena. It also allows human beings to perceive the cosmic unity of the universe from a simplistic viewpoint. In this environment, humankind is never alone, because nature fully participates in the actions of humans and reflects their emotional states. In *Don Goyo*, the mangle, the native tree of the Guayas Islands, walks, talks, and shares the same emotions and fate as the *cholos* (a group of aborigines believed to be Asiatic immigrants from the Yellow Sea during prehistoric times). For example, until the arrival of the white man on the islands, there existed a special reciprocal relationship of dependency between the mangle and the *cholo*. When the white man arrived, he immediately began to use the mangle for commercial purposes. Not only the *cholos* but also the mangles rebelled.

Totemism is a primitive vision of nature that espouses the belief that each human being shares a kinship with a totem, be it animal or plant, which is thought to have a human soul and superhuman qualities. In this novel, Don Goyo and the oldest mangle on the island share the same destiny. During the course of their discussions, the relationship between the two becomes evident. The mangle is the only one on the island who addresses him familiarly as Goyo. Their kinship is most evident when the protagonist dies. Don Goyo's wife becomes concerned when her husband leaves home and is gone for a long time. She summons everyone on the island to look for him. During their long and frustrating search, the *cholos* hear a loud, trembling noise reverberating throughout the entire island, caused by the oldest mangle on the island falling to die near the oldest man on the island, Don Goyo. The searchers later find Don Goyo dead next to the mangle, his totem.

Eroticism in *Don Goyo* is of the kind that occurs in the natural habitat and has a positive connotation. In the environment of the Guayas Islands, eroticism forms part of the procreative force of nature. It is not, however, limited to the human species. The relationship between human beings and nature is also erotic. The human is reduced to a primitive state, governed by instinct, and all the elements of nature participate in the sexual act. There is a fusion and total harmony among all the species and all the objects of nature. For example, after Don Goyo arrived on the islands, they willingly gave themselves to be possessed and conquered by him in a human sexual way.

The two characters who most identify with the magical reality of the novel are Don Encarnación and Don Goyo. Don Encarnación is considered to be part warlock, more mythical than real. He is popular with the *cholos* because of his strong belief in supernatural events and his ability to recount them. For example, he recounts the story of Ño Francia, a black warlock who predicted a great flood. The white man did not believe in witchcraft, made a mockery of him, and in the end was punished for his disbelief by drowning in the flood. Don Encarnación also tells other stories about great natural disasters by magical forces.

Don Goyo is the incarnation of supernatural powers. It is rumored that he is more than 150 years old. He is regarded as the mythical patriarch of the islands and the only one who can control nature. He is also thought to possess magical cures for illnesses that white city doctors have not yet been able to conquer. Don Goyo is phantasmal and human at the same time. In the first two parts of the novel, he rarely appears in human form but seems to be omnipresent. He assumes human form only when he defends the mangle against the exploitation of the white man. The third part of the novel reinforces the human dimension of Don Goyo by recounting stories of his marriages and children. After his death, Don Goyo becomes a legend. Shortly after Don Goyo and the mangle are found together, uprooted and dead, he appears to his daughter Gertrú and the caretaker of the mangles, Cusumbo. Don Goyo and the mangle are firmly implanted in the consciousness of the *cholo*.

LA ISLA VIRGEN

La isla virgen is a continuation of the world of *Don Goyo*: the Guayas Islands, the primitive environment of the *cholos*, and a magical vision of reality. It forms part of Aguilera Malta's tendency to look to the land to find the identity and roots of the Latin American people. This is done on both a real and a mythical level; many times in the novel, nature is perceived through magical rites, legends, and indigenous religious beliefs.

As in his other works, Aguilera Malta's message of social protest is clear in *La isla virgen*. It is more forceful in this novel because nature itself is the chief protagonist; nature must always be on the defensive against white civilized man, who wishes to exploit it. Unlike the situation in *Don Goyo*, in which nature cooperates willingly with the *cholos*, who learn to understand it and live within its confines in perfect union, nature in *La isla virgen* is hostile and defensive.

La isla virgen recounts the story of Don Nestor, a rich white man who suffers financial failure when his crops are destroyed by a disease called witches'-broom. He loses all of his possessions except the island of San Pancracio. He decides to go there to cultivate it and recover his fortune. His plan fails, however, and he dies.

Magical Realism is present in the novel in the savage forces of nature, the story of the tiger, the characters of Don Guayamabe and Don Nestor, the triumph of the *cholo* Don Pablo, and the skillful use of narrative techniques. The savagery of nature manifests itself in a phantasmagoric scene in which all the magical forces on the island unite and awaken all the souls of the dead to protest the presence of the white man. It is further reinforced in the episode of the tiger, which depicts the raw power of nature, controllable only by a brave man such as Don Guayamabe, the only one capable of killing the tiger.

Like Don Goyo, Don Guayamabe is a mythical character who understands the mysteries of the islands. He has supreme wisdom and a superior knowledge of life on the islands. He has conquered nature in a positive way and is therefore tranquil in the face of adversity, while others manifest panic and desperation. He always knows in advance the fate of Don Nestor's projects but obeys the white owner unfailingly and without question. Don Nestor is the primary victim of the magical forces of the island. Throughout the novel, there is a constant antagonism between his original intention of coming to the island to get rich and his sense of masculinity, which comes alive in the primitive environment. There are moments when his economic goal is totally forgotten, superseded by his emotional state. For example, upon his arrival on the island, nature forces him to lose all capacity to reason. During a later monologue, the erotic aspect is introduced when he expresses his sexual desire to possess the land physically.

The magical forces of the island also surface in the character of Don Pablo Melgor, the son of the *cholo* worker killed by Don Nestor. Don Pablo is Don Guayamabe's godson and has inherited his supernatural wisdom and ability to dominate the brutal forces of nature. Don Pablo declares himself to be the enemy of the white man and avenges his father's death by orchestrating the final downfall of Don Nestor.

The narrative techniques of interior monologue and stream of consciousness allow the reader to become submerged in the mental processes of the characters, in a dream state between reality and fantasy. For example, Don Nestor's monologue occurs while he finds himself in a prerational mental state. Aguilera Malta applies this vanguard technique to a primitive environment, integrating everything in a magical vision.

SEVEN SERPENTS AND SEVEN MOONS

Like the works described above, *Seven Serpents and Seven Moons* takes place on the Guayas Islands. Again, Aguilera Malta's strong sense of social obligation is clearly evident. The central theme of this novel is the clash between good and evil, which results in the exposure of a corrupt political system, social exploitation, the prejudice between races, and the corruption of religion. It is in *Seven Serpents and Seven Moons* that Magical Realism realizes its fullest expression. It is the unifying element of this novel and is expressed through the use of classical themes, miracles, psychic phenomena, superstitions, myth, witchcraft, and zoomorphism. The narrative structure further reinforces the magical reality of the novel.

Crisístomo Chalena, with the help of the Devil, to whom he has sold his soul, succeeds in exploiting the poor *santoronteños*, inhabitants of the mythical island of Santorontón. This classic theme of selling souls to the Devil adds a mythical dimension to the portrayal of social injustice. Since the main theme deals with the clash of forces between good and evil, the conflict is elevated to a more transcendental level, represented by the clash between Christ and the Devil. Miracles are supernatural forces capable of altering the natural laws of the uni-

verse. In this novel, both Christ and the Devil possess the ability to perform miracles and do so quite frequently.

Psychic phenomena are manifested in two notable examples: First, the presence of Christ very often seems to be a psychic phenomenon in the minds of the two priests. Second, Clotilde's trauma when the man she saw assassinate her parents also rapes her is manifested in her hatred for men; in a psychic state, she often imagines herself having sexual relations with men and later castrating them. Although this vision exists initially only in Clotilde's mind, it is later converted into an island legend.

The narration is also governed by magical forces resulting from superstitions. For example, the origin of the Tin-tines and the episodes with Dominga are effectively explained through resort to popular beliefs and superstitions. The mythical aspect is developed in the episode of the pirate Ogazno. He is created as an archetype of all the pirates who have sacked Guayaquil throughout the ages. He represents all pirates, a fact that places him in a mythical time frame, blurs the borders between history and legend, and transcends reality and temporality. Bulu-Bulu is the incarnation of witchcraft in the novel. His onomatopoeic name, which means "capable of curing people," contributes to the primitive dimension of magical reality in the novel. Like Don Goyo and Don Guayamabe, Bulu-Bulu is privy to all of nature's secrets. The zoomorphic aspect of Magical Realism is evidenced by the characters' ability to metamorphose into animals: Calendario can become an alligator, Chalena a toad, and Bulu-Bulu a tiger.

The structural elements that contribute to create magical reality in the novel are interior monologue, the chaotic temporal structure (which erases the dividing line between the real and the unreal), and the use of collective mentality (which allows an action or event to be transformed into legend). The language, which is metaphoric and onomatopoeic, infuses the narrative with magical lyricism.

BABELANDIA

In *Don Goyo*, *La isla virgen*, and *Seven Serpents and Seven Moons*, Aguilera Malta uses literature as a vehicle for achieving social reform. In these novels, the language and literary techniques characteristic of Magical Realism create the illusion of a primitive world in which all components coexist in perfect harmony. *Babelandia* treats the same themes and utilizes the same literary techniques as these three earlier novels, but the result is totally different. It shows a new direction in and a new attitude toward literature.

Like *Seven Serpents and Seven Moons*, *Babelandia* deals with the theme of good and evil. The forces of good are represented by the Amautas and the forces of evil by the dictatorship of Holoformes Verbofilia in the mythical land of Babelandia. Babelandia and the characters that represent these two opposing forces are archetypes. As such, they transcend the physical laws of time and space. Babelandia is illustrative of any underdeveloped nation. The forces of good are represented by a trinity of characters: Fulgido Estrella, who is a symbol of the eternal revolutionary, similar to Jesús in *Seven Serpents and Seven Moons*; María, who has been converted into an archetype of the Virgin Mary by the people because she is a young virgin whose husband died on their wedding day before consummating the marriage; and Eneas Roturante, who personifies forgiveness. Their victory represents the beginning of a more humanitarian epoch in Babelandia, where all inhabitants are vehemently opposed to any political system that wishes to dehumanize them.

The forces of evil are represented by the dictatorial government of Babelandia. The dictator himself, Holoformes Verbofilia, is a parody of death. He is portrayed as a skeleton who speaks through cassettes that are inserted into his throat. He exemplifies the destructive and annihilating force of human ideals, creativity, and vitality. He is also impotent with his wife. General Jonas Pitecantropo is a caricature of the military man. He symbolizes the military's obsession with power and the destructive force of the army. He suppresses journalistic freedom and destroys any vestige of humanitarianism in the fight against the Amautas. Like the dictator, he is also impotent with women. The remaining government officials, who also represent the forces of evil, are zoomorphic characters who typify egotism, political and human corruption, and lust.

In this archetypal world, the characters who represent the forces of evil are associated with the stylistic devices of expressionism and distortion. Each character is the physical symbol of a political or social problem. Exterior physical reality is deformed to express an interior reality in order to portray the mechanical, unemotional way of life in Babelandia: The dictator is a skeleton who speaks through cassettes; the military's obsession with power and authority is illustrated through the portrayal of the colonel as a military uniform. Such grotesque and absurd effects efficiently typify the corrupt mechanism of the dictatorship, a totally dehumanized world in which the dictator and his subordinates are reduced to robots and puppets.

Zoomorphism also contributes to the grotesque aspect of the novel. Unlike Aguilera Malta's preceding works, it has a negative connotation in this novel. It has a metaphoric function: The characters undergo zoomorphism only when they try to express their suppressed emotions. For example, when Banquero is speaking to the foreigner about business matters, his laughter is compared to that of a defenseless rabbit in an alfalfa field. Esquino Cascabel, one of the dictator's most servile employees, is converted into a horse.

Aguilera Malta's long fiction is a testimony to the depth of his social commitment to the portrayal of the social reality of his day. The themes of war, colonialism, exploitation, and oppression are presented from many perspectives. Their unifying component is Aguilera Malta's desire to promote an awareness of these themes and thereby activate a spirit of reform, not only in Ecuador but also in the entire Spanish-speaking world. Although Aguilera Malta's novels of Magical Realism are perhaps his most powerful in the expression of his message, all of his works exude his strong compassion for the underprivileged, his strong sense of nationalism, and his strong commitment to social reform.

Anne Laura Mattrella

OTHER MAJOR WORKS

SHORT FICTION: *Los que se van*, 1930 (with Joaquín Gallegos Lara and Enrique Gil Gilbert); *El cuento actual latino-americano*, 1973 (with Manuel Mejia Valera); *Hechos y leyendas de nuestra América: Relatos hispanoamericanos*, 1975.

PLAYS: *España leal*, pb. 1938; *Lázaro*, pb. 1941; *Sangre azul*, pb. 1948 (with Willis Knapp Jones; *Blue Blood*, 1948); *Dos comedias fáciles*, 1950 (includes *El pirata fantasma* and *Sangre azul*); *"No bastan los átomos" y "Dientes blancos,"* 1955; *Dientes blancos*, pb. 1955 (*White Teeth: A Play in One Act*, 1963); *El tigre*, pb. 1956 (one act); *Honorarios*, pb. 1957; *Trilogía ecuatoriana: Teatro breve*, 1959 (includes *Honorarios*, *Dientes blancos*, and *El tigre*); *Infierno negro: Pieza en dos actos*, pb. 1967 (*Black Hell*, 1977); *Teatro completo*, 1970 (includes *España leal*, *Lázaro*, *No bastan los átomos*, *Honorarios*, *Dientes blancos*, *El tigre*, *Fantoche*, *Muerte, S.A.*, and *Infierno negro*).

POETRY: *Primavera interior*, 1927; *El libro de los mangleros*, 1929.

SCREENPLAYS: *La cadena infinita*, 1948; *Entre dos carnavales*, 1951; *Dos ángeles y medio*, 1958.

NONFICTION: *Leticia: Notas y comentarios de un periodista ecuatoriano*, 1932; *La revolución española a través de los estampas de Antonio Edén*, 1938; *Los generales de Bolívar*, 1965; *Guayaquil 70: Metropoli dinámica*, 1970 (with Juan Aguilera Malta, Fausto Aguilera Malta, and Fernando Aguilera Malta).

BIBLIOGRAPHY

Angulo, María-Elena. "Two Ecuadorian Novels of Realismo Maravilloso of the 1970's: Demetrio Aguilera Malta's *Siete lunas y siete serpientes*, Alicia Yanez Cossio's *Bruna, soroche y los tios*." In *Magic Realism: Social Context and Discourse*. New York: Garland, 1995. Chapter discussing Aguilera Malta's novel is part of an analysis of five modern Latin American novels that focuses on how the authors use Magical Realism to illuminate problems of class, gender, and race within Latin American society.

Brushwood, John S. "The Year of *Don Goyo*." In *The Spanish American Novel: A Twentieth Century Survey*. Austin: University of Texas Press, 1975. Brushwood, who translated Aguilera Malta's novel *Don Goyo*, analyzes that book and places it within the larger context of other works by Latin American novelists.

Diez, Luis A. "The Apocalyptic Tropics of Aguilera Malta." *Latin American Literary Review* 10, no. 20 (Spring/Summer, 1982). Provides a brief introduction to Aguilera Malta's work before focusing on *Seven Serpents and Seven Moons*, discussing what Diez calls "the magic apocalypse" of that novel.

Rabassa, Clementine Christos. *Demetrio Aguilera-Malta and Social Justice: The Tertiary Phase of Epic Tradition in Latin American Literature*. Rutherford, N.J.: Fairleigh Dickinson University Press, 1980. Places Aguilera Malta within the epic tradition, examining the roles of such natural elements as topography, vegetation, and animal life in his fiction. Discusses justice in the epic tradition and Aguilera Malta's works, focusing particularly on divine retribution and poetic justice.

Siemens, William L. "The Antichrist-Figure in Three Latin American Novels." In *The Power of Myth in Literature and Film*, edited by Victor Carrabino. Tallahassee: University Presses of Florida, 1980. Compares Aguilera Malta's treatment of the Antichrist in *Seven Serpents and Seven Moons* with the treatments of Antichrist figures in Gabriel García Márquez's *Cien años de soledad* (1967; *One Hundred Years of Solitude*, 1970) and Guillermo Cabrera Infante's *Tres tristes tigres* (1967, 1990; *Three Trapped Tigers*, 1971).

Wishnia, Kenneth J. A. *Twentieth-Century Ecuadorian Narrative: New Readings in the Context of the Americas*. Lewisburg, Pa.: Bucknell University Press, 1999. Examines works by several Ecuadoran writers, including Aguilera Malta. Chapter 2 discusses what Wishnia describes as the "demythication of history" in *Don Goyo*; chapter 4 compares Aguilera Malta's play *El tigre* with Eugene O'Neill's play *The Emperor Jones* (pr. 1920) to delineate the playwrights' different assumptions about surviving in a mythological jungle.

CONRAD AIKEN

Born: Savannah, Georgia; August 5, 1889
Died: Savannah, Georgia; August 17, 1973
Also known as: Conrad Potter Aiken; Samuel
Jeake, Jr.

PRINCIPAL LONG FICTION

Blue Voyage, 1927
Great Circle, 1933
King Coffin, 1935
A Heart for the Gods of Mexico, 1939
Conversation: Or, Pilgrim's Progress, 1940
The Collected Novels of Conrad Aiken, 1964

OTHER LITERARY FORMS

Conrad Aiken (AY-kuhn) was one of the most prolific of modern American writers, publishing more than forty separate volumes of poetry, novels, plays, short stories, and criticism. Aiken published five collections of stories, culminating in the *Collected Short Stories of Conrad Aiken* (1966). He is the author of *Mr. Arcularis* (pb. 1957; pr. as *Fear No More* in 1946), a play based on an adaptation by Diana Hamilton of his short story of the same title. His nonfictional writing includes introductions to *Two Wessex Tales by Thomas Hardy* (1919) and *Selected Poems of Emily Dickinson* (1924) as well as a lifetime of reviews, originally published in such leading journals as *The New Republic, Poetry, The Dial, The Nation*, and *The New Yorker* and collected in *A Reviewer's ABC: Collected Criticism of Conrad Aiken from 1916 to the Present* (1958). An earlier critical work was *Skepticisms: Notes on Contemporary Poetry* (1919). His most famous nonfiction work, and one of his most lasting contributions to American literature, is his third-person autobiography *Ushant: An Essay* (1952). He published twenty-nine collections of poetry; the best of his early poems were collected in *Selected Poems* (1929), and the best of his total poetic output can be found in *Collected Poems* (1953, 1970). In addition, Aiken served as editor for numerous anthologies of poetry, including *A Comprehensive Anthology of American Poetry* (1929, 1944), and was a contributing editor of *The Dial* during the period 1917-1918. Finally, under the pseudonym Samuel Jeake, Jr., Aiken was a London correspondent for *The New Yorker* from 1934 to 1936.

ACHIEVEMENTS

Conrad Aiken's literary reputation is based on his poetry, for which he received the Pulitzer Prize in 1930, the National Book Award in 1954, and the Bollingen Prize in 1956. Despite these major awards, his reputation seems fixed among the most major of minor poets, a position that virtually all of his critics agree is too low. Of his fiction, the short stories "Silent Snow, Secret Snow" and "Mr. Arcularis" are often anthologized and discussed, although few of his others are ever mentioned. His reputation as a novelist is even more tenuous; none of his novels is in print in the early twenty-first century, and few critical articles have been published about any of them. When his first novel, *Blue Voyage*, appeared, its initial reputation as an experimental novel and its personal revelations about Aiken's interior life brought the book some notoriety. Subsequent critical opinion, however, has treated *Blue Voyage* as an inferior version of James Joyce's *A Portrait of the Artist as a Young Man* (1916) or *Ulysses* (1922). *Great Circle*, Aiken's second novel, was praised by literary critics as a psychological case study and was admired by neurologist Sigmund Freud himself for its Freudian overtones. Aiken's last three novels received little praise or attention. *A Heart for the Gods of Mexico* was not even published in the United States until the collected edition of his novels appeared. Aiken himself considered *King Coffin* a failure; he admits in *Ushant* that his last novels were unsuccessful and says that he does not mind his relative obscurity, but in a letter to his friend Malcolm Cowley he wrote, "Might I also suggest for your list of Neglected Books a novel by c. aiken called *Great Circle*, of which the royalty report, to hand this morning, chronicles a sale of 26 copies in its second half year?" Later critics, like Aiken's contemporaries, saw the major value of his novels in their experimental nature, their Freudian images, and their amplification of the themes of Aiken's poetry.

BIOGRAPHY

Conrad Potter Aiken was born in Savannah, Georgia, on August 5, 1889. Both of his parents were New Englanders. His mother, Anna Potter Aiken, was the daughter of William James Potter, minister of the Unitarian First Congregational Society of New Bedford, Massachusetts, and a friend of the essayist and poet Ralph Waldo Emerson. His father, William Ford Aiken, was a physician educated at Harvard. The central event of his childhood—and in fact of his whole life—took place in 1900, when, at the age of eleven, he discovered the dead bodies of his parents. Aiken's father had killed his mother with a revolver and then shot himself. This event remained forever embedded in his psyche. As Aiken writes in *Ushant*, "He had tiptoed into the dark room, where the two bodies lay motionless, and apart, and, finding them dead, found himself possessed of them forever."

Conrad Aiken. (Library of Congress)

Following this crucial event, Aiken's two brothers were separated from him, and he spent the remainder of his childhood living with a great-great-aunt in New Bedford. He attended the Middlesex School in Concord and, in 1907, entered Harvard University during the same period as T. S. Eliot, John Reed, Walter Lippmann, E. E. Cummings, and Robert Benchley. At college, Aiken was president of the *Harvard Advocate* literary magazine, a frequent contributor to the *Harvard Monthly*, and a leader among his classmates in literary discussions, but he also established a pattern that was to hold true throughout his life—he was always a loner, following neither particular schools of criticism nor prevailing literary styles. Placed on probation for poor class attendance as a senior, Aiken left Harvard in protest and spent half a year in Europe, thus establishing another constant pattern: For the remainder of his life he made frequent trips to Europe, living as often abroad as at home until World War II, after which he lived in New England, primarily in Brewster, Massachusetts.

Following his return to Harvard, Aiken graduated in 1912 and immediately began writing poems for his first collection, *Earth Triumphant, and Other Tales in Verse* (1914). For the rest of his life, Aiken supported himself solely with his writing, except for a brief stint as an English tutor at Harvard in 1927. He married three times. He divorced his first wife, Jessie McDonald, after eighteen years of marriage and the rearing of three children; his second wife, Clarissa Lorenz, he divorced after seven years. He remained married to his third wife, Mary Hoover, from 1937 until his death from a heart attack on August 17, 1973, in Savannah, Georgia, the city of his birth, to which he had returned to complete the great circle of his life.

For most of his career, Aiken worked simultaneously on his poetry, fiction, and criticism. From 1925 to 1935, he alternated short-story collections with novels. In 1939 and 1940, he published his last two novels, *A Heart for the Gods of Mexico* and *Conversation*; thereafter he concentrated on poetry and criticism. During the 1920's and 1930's, Aiken was involved with such American expatriates as T. S. Eliot, Ezra

Pound, and Malcolm Lowry, yet he was always deliberately apart from the center of artistic circles, choosing, for example, to live in London and Brewster rather than Paris and New York. The best source of information about Aiken's relation with other writers is *Ushant*, in which Eliot, Pound, and Lowry appear as the Tsetse, Rabbi Ben Ezra, and Hambo.

ANALYSIS

The central event in Conrad Aiken's personal life—the murder-suicide of his parents—was also the central event of his artistic life, for all of his literary work is in some way aimed at coming to terms with the childhood tragedy. In *Ushant*, Aiken says of his parents that "he was irrevocably dedicated to a lifelong—if need be—search for an equivalent to it all, in terms of his own life, or work; and an equivalent that those two angelic people would have thought acceptable." The search for understanding of his personal tragedy motivated Aiken to try to understand the universal tragedy of modern humankind, what Joseph Warren Beach called "moral terror," the basic question of good and evil in the human heart that American writers have been struggling with since the advent of American letters.

Aiken's search for a way to maintain equilibrium in the face of his contradictory love for his parents and his revulsion for their deaths lies outside theological or conventional ethical questions; his search centered on his own consciousness, on himself. The major subject of each of his five novels is a search for self, an interior exploration—often expressed metaphorically as a circular journey. *Blue Voyage* and *Great Circle* focus on psychological understanding in which the protagonist attempts to get back to himself through a circular analysis of his past. *King Coffin* is a psychological horror story of a madman's decision to murder a complete stranger, a decision that eventually leads the protagonist around full circle until he kills himself. *A Heart for the Gods of Mexico* presents a literal journey—a train trip from Boston to Mexico—in which the narrator attempts to reconcile the beauty and strangeness of the changing landscape with the impending death of his woman companion. Finally, *Conversation* describes the circular arguments in a lovers' quarrel that eventually runs its course, returning to its starting place.

In each novel, Aiken's chief character is trying to complete what in plane geometry is called a great circle of a sphere, a circle whose plane passes through the center of the sphere. For Aiken's protagonists, the circle is a descent into their pasts, and the sphere is the shape of their lives. Because of this self-analysis, each novel is introspective and confessional. Taken together, the novels chart a series of points on Aiken's great circle, a graphic display of his search for an understanding of his own life. Each novel is based, in varying degrees, on autobiographical details from his life, and each is discussed in *Ushant*, where Aiken says, "The artificer, in the very act of displaying himself in the new shape of the artifact, must remain wholly neutral to that part of himself which is his subject—which is to say, his all."

Aiken's attempts to get to the bottom of, or to the other side of, his parents' deaths led him on a series of physical voyages between the United States and Europe and on a series of literary voyages between poetry and fiction that in his 1958 poem "The Crystal" he called "the westward pour of the worlds and the westward pour of the mind." In both his life and his art, he speaks of a constant tension between two opposing forces: a desire for artistic expression, for bringing art to bear on the chaos of human existence, which is in constant confrontation with what Frederick Hoffman calls "the shock of reality, which continually challenges the creative spirit and, in moments of terror or violence, may even severely dislocate it." Although the shortest distance between two points may be a straight line, when those points are located within these opposing spheres, then the shortest arc between the comfort of art and the moral terror of reality becomes the great circle that Aiken so thoroughly and so gracefully traced in his novels.

BLUE VOYAGE

Writing in 1952 about his first novel, *Blue Voyage* (which in *Ushant* he calls, half-ironically, *Purple Passage*), Aiken said it was "a compromise in which the voice of Joyce had been too audible." This Joycean comparison refers to the hero of the novel, William Demarest, who has booked a second-class passage aboard a steamship en route to England, ostensibly to search for his lost love, Cynthia, but actually to search within himself for an explanation of his feelings about Cynthia and about himself as a writer. Demarest clearly resembles Aiken, both in autobiographical detail (when Demarest's parents die he is sent as a boy to live in New Bedford) and in critical reputation (Demarest names as his literary weakness the inability to present a "theme energetically and simply" instead of dressing it "in tissue upon tissue of proviso and aspect . . . from a hundred angles"). The novel is also Joycean in style, for when Demarest discovers that Cynthia is actually on board the ship, he returns to his stateroom and launches himself into a lengthy regression that Jay Martin, in his *Conrad Aiken: A Life of His Art* (1962), calls a "preconscious monologue." This regression is filled with allusions to self-crucifixion, bizarre sexual dreams, fragments of popular songs, bits of English poetry, extended lists of numbers, noises, and a constant repetition of the capitalized word MISERY, all accompanied by the incessant throbbing of the ship's engines.

Martin sees *Blue Voyage* as an attempt to combine the confessional and the aesthetic novel, and, like Joyce's *A Portrait of the Artist as a Young Man*, Aiken's first novel includes discussions of its hero's theories about art and literature with Aiken's Cranley/Lynch figure, a man named Silverstein, who acts as Demarest's psychoanalyst. *Blue Voyage* tries to go beyond Joyce's early work in terms of experimentation, for in the sixth chapter, Aiken presents a lyrical out-of-body experience in which the main characters of the novel perform a hallucinatory ritualistic parody of the Crucifixion that results in Cynthia's being metamorphosed into a Gothic stained-glass window. The book ends with a series of undelivered letters written by Demarest to Cynthia that alternate between intense self-loathing and a passionate attempt to explain the letter writer to his lost love and to himself—and, by extension, to explain Aiken to his readers. As Demarest says in his second letter, "It is precisely the sort of thing I am always trying to do in my writing—to present my unhappy reader with a wide-ranged chaos—of actions and reactions, thoughts, memories and feelings—in the vain hope that at the end he will see that the whole thing represents only *one moment, one feeling, one person*."

GREAT CIRCLE

In his autobiography, Aiken's second novel, *Great Circle*, appears as *Dead Reckoning*, a punning title that encompasses the major themes of the novel: navigation

along the great circle as a metaphor for exploration of the psyche of a man whose world, like the author's, turns over with the horrifying discovery of his parents' betrayal by sudden death. *Great Circle* opens with its protagonist, Andrew Cather, on board a train to Cambridge, where he will surprise his wife in the act of adultery, an act that was forewarned both by a friend and by signs the protagonist has refused to see. Andrew Cather, who is often called One-eye Cather because of an ambiguously explained injury to one eye, is not able to stop the marital infidelity he knows is coming, any more than the Cyclops in Homer's epic can avoid Odysseus's prophesied appearance.

Cather's discovery leads him to Aiken's familiar dilemma: how to maintain balance in the face of moral terror. Cather's initial response is to avoid the terror by avoiding consciousness of it, at first by maintaining a false air of melodrama about the situation and then by repeatedly drinking himself into a stupor. The combination of drunkenness and estrangement from his wife, whose adultery was consummated with Cather's best friend, causes him to fall into the lengthy reverie about his childhood that constitutes all of chapter 2, the most successfully sustained section in all of Aiken's prose fiction. This section is a sensually lyrical evocation of the summer in Cather's childhood in Duxbury, Massachusetts, during which he first felt the strangeness of his father's absence and his mother's attachment to his Uncle David. The chapter is Joycean in style and Faulknerian in content, full of lyrical passages that call up ocean and shore. Like Maisie from Henry James's *What Maisie Knew* (1897) or William Faulkner's Quentin Compson from *The Sound and the Fury* (1929), the young Andy Cather slowly comes to awareness about the sexuality of the adults who move around him. Reading a letter from his father to his mother, Andy Cather realizes imperfectly that his mother is having an affair with his uncle. The chapter ends with Andy's terrible discovery of the bodies of his mother and her lover, who drowned during a storm. Speaking of this chapter, Jay Martin says, "Aiken intends it to be real, an exact and complete account of his experience insofar as it entered the consciousness of the boy."

The third chapter of *Great Circle* consists of a night-long amateur psychoanalysis session in which Cather speaks an exhaustive monologue in an attempt at talking through his marital problems in the present, the horror of his childhood discovery, and the interconnection between the two events. Realizing that he unconsciously associates the physical intimacies of marriage with the discovery of his mother, dead in his uncle's embrace, Cather makes an actual trip to Duxbury, thus confronting and completing the great circle voyage through his past and his psyche. Aiken's novel reflects Henry David Thoreau's argument at the conclusion of *Walden: Or, Life in the Woods* (1854) that "our voyaging is only great-circle sailing," for the horrible scene from his protagonist's childhood is, of course, suggestive of Aiken's own childhood tragedy.

The image of circularity echoes throughout the novel, from the title to the description of Cather "hurrying from point to point on the earth's surface, describing his swift little arc" to the later statement that he is running "round in mad circles, like a beheaded hen." Later, Cather says to himself about the origin of his problems, "It is your own little worm-curve; the twist that is your own life; the small spiral of light that answers to the name of Andrew Cather." The entire second chapter is enclosed within outsized parentheses, suggestive of the great circle, and in one of his childhood revelations, Cather remembers an old riddle—"Rats live on no evil star," a palindrome, a sentence that "spells the same thing backward"—which reminds the reader that Andrew Cather's initials backward are Conrad Aiken's, and that Cather's attempt to rescue his marriage through a series of therapeutic returns to his childhood is also Aiken's attempt to resolve his own problems by writing about them in novels.

KING COFFIN

Aiken's third novel, *King Coffin*, is the only one he leaves out of *Ushant*, probably because he considered it to be a major failure, unredeemable through subsequent analysis. Although most critics refer to *King Coffin* as a failure, if they mention it at all, Aiken's best critic, Jay Martin, argues that the author meant *King Coffin* as a parody of a psychological novel, playing "lightly with a serious psychological subject while still retaining a real sense of its dignity and importance." The subject of the novel is an insane plan conceived half in jest by Jasper Ammen (a name suggestive of Edwin Arlington Robinson's *King Jasper*, 1935) to demonstrate his innate supe-

riority by murdering an ordinary person chosen at random—a person Ammen comes to call "a specimen man" or "the anonymous one." The motive for the murder is the achievement of a perfectly pure relationship, in Ammen's simplification of Nietzschean/Emersonian ideas, between the superior man and the ordinary one. Initially, Ammen claims he has chosen his victim and is studying the dailiness of the man's life as background for a novel about "pure" murder, a novel he plans to call *King Coffin*.

As the actual novel progresses, Ammen begins to think of Jones, his intended victim, as "one-who-wants-to-be-killed." This short novel ends with Ammen's too-close identification with his victim; seeing that Jones's wife's newborn baby has died, Ammen decides that the perfect ending to his plan would be his own murder, thereby bringing the novel full circle: The random victim has unconsciously caused Ammen to kill himself. Although Martin sees *King Coffin* as its protagonist's "attempt to recognize and resolve his own strangeness, to realize his ego completely by fully understanding its complexity," most critics have seen the book as a competent murder mystery at best, clearly the least successful of Aiken's novels. Because Jasper Ammen is labeled a psychotic at the start of the novel, the rationalizations he uses for his bizarre plan never become compelling; they are neither the ravings of a madman nor the thoughts of a superior human. Instead they fall somewhere in between. *King Coffin* is considerably shorter than Aiken's previous novels and interesting mainly for its conception: Aiken creates a psychopathic killer who pretends to write the book that Aiken actually writes, just as the narrator of *Ushant*, a character Aiken calls only D., discusses his attempt at writing the very autobiography in which one reads his discussion.

A HEART FOR THE GODS OF MEXICO

Aiken's penultimate novel, *A Heart for the Gods of Mexico*, returns to the author's now-familiar themes. The story tells of a lengthy train trip from Boston to Mexico by day coach, taken by a woman who knows she is soon to die of heart failure; her fiancé, who is unaware of her condition; and her friend, who is half in love with her. Noni, the young woman who is soon to die, puzzles over her upcoming death in a manner that recalls *King Coffin*: "It seems so ridiculously random . . . it's *that*

that's so puzzling." Unlike the psychopathic protagonist of the earlier novel, however, the young woman is a sympathetic character. She and her friend are constantly struggling with such questions as whether the subterfuge is ethical, whether the trip is hastening her inevitable death, and whether the startling tropical beauty of Mexico should make them forget the impending death or revel in it.

Both critics and its author have described *A Heart for the Gods of Mexico* as a curious failure; the novel contains brilliant landscape scenes, strong and affecting portrayals of character, particularly Noni's, and a passionate depiction of the travelers' meeting in Cuernavaca with Hambo, Aiken's name for Malcolm Lowry, the author of *Under the Volcano* (1947). Unlike *Blue Voyage* and *Great Circle*, however, this book lacks form. The trip is too long in getting started, and too much local color is presented along the way. *A Heart for the Gods of Mexico* is the shortest of Aiken's novels. The book offers no flashbacks, no self-analysis, no sense of any concentric structure except for the shape imposed on the novel by the narrative of the trip itself, Noni's "great-circle to Mexico" upon which she takes her "heart as an offering to the bloodstained altar of the plumed serpent."

CONVERSATION

Aiken's last novel, *Conversation*, records the bitterly circular quarrel of Timothy and Enid Kane, whose marital argument, like the one in *Great Circle*, is (on the surface, at least) about infidelity, this time on the part of the husband. In some ways, the novel deals with feminism; Enid wants to live in an urban environment, whereas her husband, a painter, wants to live in the country on Cape Cod rather than remain in the city painting commissioned portraits. Timothy sees the journey to the country as a chance to get back in touch with his natural artistic creativity; his wife sees the move as "all that nonsense of yours about plain living and high thinking, about living the natural and honest life of our Pilgrim ancestors, and being independent—but it's no good for a woman."

While Enid is wrong in thus belittling her husband's desire to paint freely, Timothy is also wrong in hiding the fact that the move is partly to get away from his in-town affair. The bucolic escape turns into a series of get-togethers with bohemian Greenwich Village artists and

poets, such as Karl Roth, who represents the poet Maxwell Bodenheim. Enid's reference to the pilgrims suggests one of the connections between this portrait of the artist as a young married man, the novel's subtitle, and the excerpts from *A Journal of the Pilgrims at Plymouth* (1962) that head each chapter of the novel. Like the early visitors to Massachusetts, Timothy wants to recapture a spirit of freedom so that he can overcome the sterility he has felt, both in his art and in his life, since the birth of his daughter. Although his daughter's birth represents in his wife's mind the highest womanly creative act, and although his daughter's freshly imaginative outlook on nature is exactly the kind of artistic rebirth Timothy is looking for, he comes to see during the course of the long, circuitous argument that his repressed anxieties about the physical details of his daughter's birth are the cause of his inability to hold a conversation with his wife. Like Andrew Cather, who is disgusted by the "filthy intimacies" of marriage, Timothy Kane finds the effect of childbirth, what his friend calls "that butcher-shop and meaty reality," to be "something for which love's young dream hadn't at all been prepared. A loss of belief."

The argument in *Conversation* continues along Aiken's familiar circular path until, like a snake with its tail in its mouth, it comes back to where it began and resolves itself with the reunion of the Kanes and a decision to have a son; however, since no one can predict the sex of an unborn child before conception, it is clear that this resolution will likely lead the couple back onto another loop of their argument. In the middle of his last novel, Aiken presents a scene in which Timothy Kane is comparing his idea of marriage while still engaged with his vision after his child's birth. Using the metaphors of poetry and prose, Timothy gives Aiken's final critical assessment of the relationship between his own work in the two genres: "The poetry had been too pure a poetry, its further implications (of all that the body, and passion, could exact, or time and diurnal intimacy dishevel and destroy) had been too little understood; and when the prose followed, it had inevitably seemed only too ingrainedly prosaic."

This assessment is accurate. Despite their relative merits, Aiken's five novels would probably not continue to find readers were it not for the reputation of their author as a poet. In his autobiography, Aiken says of his parents' deaths that "he was to discover, while at Harvard, that the staining sense of guilt and shame had been mysteriously exorcised, as no longer there," but clearly some degree of both guilt and shame must have remained throughout the author's life, despite the therapy he gained from writing these five novels.

Timothy Dow Adams

OTHER MAJOR WORKS

SHORT FICTION: *The Dark City*, 1922; *Bring! Bring!, and Other Stories*, 1925; *Costumes by Eros*, 1928; "Silent Snow, Secret Snow," 1932; *Impulse*, 1933; *Among the Lost People*, 1934; "Round by Round," 1935; *Short Stories*, 1950; *Collected Short Stories*, 1960; *Collected Short Stories of Conrad Aiken*, 1966.

PLAYS: *Fear No More*, pr. 1946 (pb. 1957 as *Mr. Arcularis: A Play*).

POETRY: *Earth Triumphant, and Other Tales in Verse*, 1914; *The Jig of Forslin*, 1916; *Turns and Movies, and Other Tales in Verse*, 1916; *Nocturne of Remembered Spring, and Other Poems*, 1917; *The Charnel Rose*, 1918; *Senlin: A Biography, and Other Poems*, 1918; *The House of Dust*, 1920; *Punch: The Immortal Liar*, 1921; *Priapus and the Pool*, 1922; *The Pilgrimage of Festus*, 1923; *Changing Mind*, 1925; *Priapus and the Pool, and Other Poems*, 1925; *Prelude*, 1929; *Selected Poems*, 1929; *Gehenna*, 1930; *John Deth: A Metaphysical Legend, and Other Poems*, 1930; *The Coming Forth by Day of Osiris Jones*, 1931; *Preludes for Memnon*, 1931; *And in the Hanging Gardens*, 1933; *Landscape West of Eden*, 1934; *Time in the Rock: Preludes to Definition*, 1936; *And in the Human Heart*, 1940; *Brownstone Eclogues, and Other Poems*, 1942; *The Soldier: A Poem by Conrad Aiken*, 1944; *The Kid*, 1947; *The Divine Pilgrim*, 1949; *Skylight One: Fifteen Poems*, 1949; *Wake II*, 1952; *Collected Poems*, 1953, 1970; *A Letter from Li Po, and Other Poems*, 1955; *The Fluteplayer*, 1956; *Sheepfold Hill: Fifteen Poems*, 1958; *Selected Poems*, 1961; *The Morning Song of Lord Zero*, 1963; *A Seizure of Limericks*, 1964; *Cats and Bats and Things with Wings: Poems*, 1965; *The Clerk's Journal*, 1971; *A Little Who's Zoo of Mild Animals*, 1977.

NONFICTION: *Skepticisms: Notes on Contemporary Poetry*, 1919; *Ushant: An Essay*, 1952; *A Reviewer's ABC: Collected Criticism of Conrad Aiken from 1916 to the Present*, 1958; *Selected Letters of Conrad Aiken*, 1978.

EDITED TEXTS: *A Comprehensive Anthology of American Poetry*, 1929, 1944; *Twentieth Century American Poetry*, 1944.

BIBLIOGRAPHY

Aiken, Conrad. *Selected Letters of Conrad Aiken*. Edited by Joseph Killorin. New Haven, Conn.: Yale University Press, 1978. Includes a representative sample of 245 letters (from some 3,000) written by Aiken. A cast of correspondents, among them T. S. Eliot and Malcolm Lowry, indexes to Aiken's works and important personages, and a wealth of illustrations, mostly photographs, add considerably to the value of this volume.

Butscher, Edward. *Conrad Aiken: Poet of White Horse Vale*. Athens: University of Georgia Press, 1988. The first installment of a projected two-volume psychobiography focuses on the years 1899-1925. Includes information about Aiken's childhood in Savannah, Georgia, and Massachusetts, his years at Harvard University, and his friendships and involvements with other poets, including T. S. Eliot, Ezra Pound, and Amy Lowell. Also analyses and traces the development of Aiken's literary works.

Cowley, Malcolm. "Conrad Aiken: From Savannah to Emerson." In *New England Writers and Writing*, edited by Donald W. Faulkner. Hanover, N.H.: University Press of New England, 1996. This essay discussing Aiken's work and its relation to New England is part of a collection of essays that analyze nineteenth and twentieth century authors from that region.

Hoffman, Frederick J. *Conrad Aiken*. New York: Twayne, 1962. Presents a useful overview of Aiken's work and examines his attitude toward New England, his obsession with "aloneness," and his concern about human relationships. Contains a chronology, a biographical chapter, and an annotated bibliography.

Lorenz, Clarissa M. *Lorelei Two: My Life with Conrad Aiken*. Athens: University of Georgia Press, 1983. Aiken's second wife discusses the 1926-1938 years, the period when he wrote his best work. Covers his literary acquaintances, his work habits, and the literary context in which he worked. Well-indexed volume also includes several relevant photographs.

Seigel, Catharine F. *The Fictive World of Conrad Aiken: A Celebration of Consciousness*. De Kalb: Northern Illinois University Press, 1993. Features chapters on the Freudian foundation of Aiken's fiction, on his New England roots, and on many of his novels. Concluding chapters discuss Aiken's autobiography *Ushant* and provide an overview of his fiction. Includes notes, selected bibliography, and index.

Spivey, Ted R. *Time's Stop in Savannah: Conrad Aiken's Inner Journey*. Macon, Ga.: Mercer University Press, 1997. Examines Aiken's life and works to uncover his literary, spiritual, and psychological development. Describes how he used his writing as a way to heal the pain of his parents' deaths.

Spivey, Ted R., and Arthur Waterman, eds. *Conrad Aiken: A Priest of Consciousness*. New York: AMS Press, 1989. Focuses on Aiken's poetry but includes information on his novels. Provides an extensive chronology of Aiken's life and a lengthy description of the Aiken materials housed at the Huntington Library.

Womack, Kenneth. "Unmasking Another Villain in Conrad Aiken's Autobiographical Dream." *Biography* 19 (Spring, 1996): 137. Examines the role of British poet and novelist Martin Armstrong as a fictionalized character in Aiken's *Ushant* and argues that Aiken's attack on Armstrong is motivated by revenge for Armstrong's marriage to Aiken's first wife.

WILLIAM HARRISON AINSWORTH

Born: Manchester, Lancashire, England; February 4, 1805
Died: Reigate, Surrey, England; January 3, 1882
Also known as: T. Hall

PRINCIPAL LONG FICTION

Sir John Chiverton, 1826 (with John Partington Aston)
Rookwood, 1834
Crichton, 1837
Jack Sheppard, 1839
The Tower of London, 1840
Guy Fawkes, 1841
Old Saint Paul's, 1841
The Miser's Daughter, 1842
Windsor Castle, 1843
Saint James's: Or, The Court of Queen Anne, 1844
James the Second, 1848
The Lancashire Witches, 1849
The Flitch of Bacon, 1854
The Star-Chamber, 1854

The Spendthrift, 1856
Mervyn Clitheroe, 1858
Ovingdean Grange, 1860
The Constable of the Tower, 1861
The Lord Mayor of London, 1862
Cardinal Pole, 1863
John Law, 1864
Auriol, 1865
The Spanish Match, 1865
The Constable de Bourbon, 1866
Old Court, 1867
Myddleton Pomfret, 1868
The South-Sea Bubble, 1868
Hilary St. Ives, 1869
Talbot Harland, 1871
Tower Hill, 1871
Boscobel, 1872
The Manchester Rebels of the Fatal '45, 1872 (originally published as *The Good Old Times*)
Merry England, 1874
The Goldsmith's Wife, 1875

Preston Fight, 1875
Chetwynd Calverley, 1876
The Leaguer of Latham, 1876
The Fall of Somerset, 1877
Beatrice Tyldesley, 1878
Beau Nash, 1879
Stanley Brereton, 1881

OTHER LITERARY FORMS

Most of the work that William Harrison Ainsworth (AYNZ-wurth) produced in forms other than the novel was limited to juvenilia. Before he had reached the age of nineteen, he had published dramas, poems, essays, tales, and translations in local Manchester periodicals. He also wrote several short books of verse and a brief political pamphlet before he became known as a novelist. Later, he contributed some reviews and verse to annuals and magazines. The songs and ballads scattered throughout his novels were collected for separate publication in 1855 and reprinted in 1872. Ainsworth's association with periodicals was long and significant, and most of his novels were first published as magazine serials. He served as editor with the periodicals *Bentley's Miscellany* (1839-1841 and 1854-1868), *Ainsworth's Magazine* (1842-1854), and the *New Monthly Magazine* (1846-1870).

ACHIEVEMENTS

William Harrison Ainsworth has often been considered the heir of Sir Walter Scott. After writing two books that were criticized for glamorizing criminals, he produced dozens of solid historical novels that were entertaining, moral, and educational. Some of these works feature real historical figures; others use invented characters who take part in significant historical events. Ainsworth's books have vivid scenes and exciting conflicts. They are filled with accurate details about costume, food, ceremony, and architecture. Although *Windsor Castle* and *The Tower of London* are novels, generations of tourists used them for guidebooks. Ainsworth covered the significant monarchs that were too recent to be in William Shakespeare's plays. Most ordinary people in the nineteenth century gleaned their sense of English history largely from the works of Scott, Shakespeare, and Ainsworth.

Ainsworth, however, contributed virtually nothing to the development of the novel as a literary form; he merely did what Scott had done before him—and not nearly so well. The literary novel was turning to realistic social and psychological examinations of contemporary life. Ainsworth is significant for the roles he played as an author and as an editor of popular literature. His books refined and preserved elements of popular theater and gothic fiction, adapting them to mid-nineteenth century modes of publication. His novels are characterized by heightened confrontations and recurring climaxes; the techniques of suspended narration and the resources of serial construction; supernatural excitements, vivid tableaux, and memorable spectacles; a preference for romantic underdogs; and moral simplicity. Ainsworth made these touchstones of popular writing briefly respectable and then handed them down to the authors who catered to the much broader mass reading public of the late nineteenth century.

BIOGRAPHY

William Harrison Ainsworth was born February 4, 1805, to a prosperous family in Manchester, England. His father was a solicitor who had a substantial house on a good street, a suburban summer residence, and a fondness for collecting information about crime and criminals. Even before he could read, Ainsworth adored his father's stories of highwaymen and ghosts. Although he was brought up in a strict atmosphere of Whiggism and Nonconformity, Ainsworth also grew to love lost causes. From early youth he adopted Jacobite and Tory ideals.

When he was twelve years old, Ainsworth was sent to the Manchester Free Grammar School. He became passionately fond of the stage, and from the age of fifteen wrote and acted in plays with schoolboy friends. One of them, *Giotto: Or, The Fatal Revenge*, included a dreadful storm, terrible and mysterious events, signs of the supernatural, and minute descriptions of scenery, buildings, and costumes.

In the next few years, Ainsworth published anonymous or pseudonymous pieces in a number of magazines, briefly edited a periodical of his own, and wrote to Charles Lamb for advice about two metrical tales and three short songs that he published in 1822 as *Poems* by Cheviot Ticheburn. Leaving school at seventeen, Ainsworth became an articled clerk; in 1824, when his father died, he went to London for further legal education. At the age of twenty-one he qualified as a solicitor. In 1826, however—almost as soon as he had finished preparing to practice law—he published the historical romance he had written with a fellow clerk in Manchester, married Anne Frances "Fanny" Ebers, and took over the publishing and bookselling branches of his father-in-law's business.

Ainsworth hoped to conduct a gentlemanly trade that would publish good books that were not popular enough for other publishing houses, but he soon found the prospects were not what he had imagined; although he met many authors and produced some good works, his firm's biggest success was a cookbook. In 1829, after returning briefly to law, he became part of the circle formed by William Maginn to contribute to *Fraser's Magazine for Town and Country*—a circle that included Theodore Hook, Samuel Taylor Coleridge, Thomas Carlyle, and William Makepeace Thackeray and was therefore intimately linked to literary fashion. Ainsworth started begging friends for plots. Finally, inspired by Ann Radcliffe's gothic fiction, he published *Rookwood* in April, 1834, a work that was an immediate success with both critics and public.

The next ten or twelve years were Ainsworth's best. His novels sold phenomenally. For much of the time he was producing two at once: *Guy Fawkes* ran in *Bentley's Miscellany* between January, 1840, and November, 1841, while at the same time *The Tower of London* came out in monthly parts in 1840, and *Old Saint Paul's* was serialized in the *Sunday Times* during 1841. Even while writing two novels at once, Ainsworth was a successful and conscientious editor. He succeeded Charles Dickens at the helm of *Bentley's Miscellany* in 1839 and then, in 1842, began *Ainsworth's Magazine*. He was also a social celebrity who gave elaborate dinners for friends, including virtually everyone active in literature in England during the 1840's.

By the decade's end, Ainsworth was rerunning his early novels in *Ainsworth's Magazine* and repeating scenes and characters in the new books he wrote. In 1853

William Harrison Ainsworth. (Getty Images)

he moved to Brighton. Although he continued to write constantly for almost thirty more years and although, as an editor, he still influenced the course of popular fiction, he was no longer—physically, creatively, or socially—at the heart of nineteenth century literature.

Almost nothing is known of Ainsworth as a private person. Neither of his wives shared his public life. Fanny, who bore him three daughters, separated from him three years before she died in 1838. Sarah Wells, who gave him another daughter in 1867, was married to Ainsworth secretly sometime before they moved to Reigate in 1878. There he continued to write for whatever he could earn. His last novel was being serialized in a provincial newspaper when he died on January 3, 1882.

ANALYSIS

Popular fiction requires, above all else, a work that holds the reader's interest. The best popular authors, furthermore, are generally those who believe and delight in the books they write. William Harrison Ainsworth began to publish just after Sir Walter Scott's death. At that time there was as yet no clearly discernible indication of the direction fiction would take, but there was a vogue for stories about history and crime. These topics suited Ainsworth's personal taste—his early interest in his father's tales, his love of acting exciting roles, his fondness for Scott, Lord Byron, Christopher Marlowe, and for gothic novelists such as Matthew Gregory Lewis and Ann Radcliffe. Before long, the vogue for such stories had passed. Its other practitioners, including Charles Dickens, moved on to different styles and themes, but Ainsworth remained in the groove he had carved. His method of composition bred a narrative technique that secured the reader's involvement but did not encourage analytical thought.

Ainsworth's mind was attracted by snatches of legend, by the mood surrounding a place, by the intensely realized scenes without antecedents or consequences that often feature in daydreams. His books have very complicated stories but often lack plot in the sense of shape, point, or consequence. His most successful works gain apparent unity because they are linked to a single place or use a well-known historical event as a frame. Ainsworth was not creative in the broad sense; he depended on research because it supplied a mass of details that helped disguise the fact that he lacked Scott's ability to create the texture and spirit of the past. The accurate details also gave Ainsworth's books respectability for a mass public that was becoming increasingly self-conscious; historical distance permitted both Ainsworth and his readers to be emotionally involved in scenes of horror, conflict, and danger.

Ainsworth's stories are far too complicated to summarize. In each novel, at least three or four series of events move simultaneously; typically, one is historical, one uses fictional characters acting in historical events, and a third involves comic figures. Each individual story line is itself intricate. In any plot, at any moment, present action may be suspended by the entrance of a stranger who proceeds to recount the course of his life to date, and the stranger's narrative may itself be suspended for its own internal interruptions. The method is not, strictly speaking, dramatic, because the reader is likely to forget just what question is driving the story onward. The individual scenes, however, are vividly realized. Inevitably, at the end of an installment, one set of characters is left dangling, and a new set is taken up in the next. Ainsworth's creative use of the breaks imposed by the medium (in this case serialization) and his control of lighting effects and angles of vision anticipate the techniques of popular film and television.

Especially useful for creating effects, the topics of history and the supernatural were used by Ainsworth because they supplied cruelty, torture, flight, combat, and chills down the spine, tools for the manipulation of emotions. The supernatural elements that appear in almost all of Ainsworth's novels are used primarily for effect; Ainsworth neither explains the uncanny events nor (as serious gothic novelists would) explores the mystery of evil. Elements of reality, such as murders, storms, and riots, arouse emotional responses, and the unreality of the supernatural may, like the distance of history, help rationalist readers from an industrialized world to release emotions that are no longer acceptable in daily life.

Ainsworth virtually always includes at least one character who is disguised, who is using a false name, or who has mysterious, confused, obscure parentage. Readers of Ainsworth's books soon learn that they can never be certain who the characters really are. The stories of concealed parentage and shifting identity allow readers in the most humdrum circumstances to step imaginatively into the shoes of a countess, a knight, or even royal offspring, secure in the expectation that anyone might turn out to be royalty in disguise. The device is a psychological strategy for Ainsworth, the bourgeois son of a Nonconformist family from a bleak industrial town who chose to become a Royalist, a Tory, and a Jacobite. It is also a paradigm for the escapism beloved by readers who found themselves increasingly interchangeable cogs in the nineteenth century's bureaucratic and commercial machines.

ROOKWOOD

An immediate best seller, *Rookwood* not only is typical Ainsworth but also might serve as a model to teach generations of adventure writers about constructing narrative books. The opening sentence reveals two people seated in a burial vault at midnight. The rest of the long first paragraph holds the reader's curiosity about these people in abeyance while it describes the architecture and effigies of the mausoleum in order to create an air of foreboding. The first chapter alternates passages of partial exposition with scenes of strong emotion, and the second chapter is a chase built from a series of captures, struggles, and escapes. At the second chapter's climax, Luke Rookwood—the protagonist—dives into a pool and does not emerge; the chapter ends, leaving him underwater. The next several chapters introduce other characters, new lines of action, and a great deal more historical exposition before telling the reader what happened to Luke.

Rookwood virtually catalogs the devices made popular by gothic novelists thirty years earlier. In the opening chapter, Ainsworth introduces the inheritance theme and Luke's confused parentage, a death omen, croaking ravens, a Gypsy queen, a preserved corpse with a significant ring on its finger, an evil Jesuit, a moving statue, a dead hand, and writing on a wall. The rest of the book supplies duels between relatives, a deathbed curse, a runaway bride, a portrait that changes expression, underground caverns, a supernatural summons, a miniature with an inscription that gives a clue to the past, a rediscovered marriage certificate, secret passageways, stormy nights, an interrupted burial, a purely incidental death by thunderbolt, corpses swaying from a gibbet, talismans, a deserted priory where Gypsies dwell, a character who masquerades as a ghost, infallible prophecies in verse, love potions, a marriage in a subterranean shrine (formerly an anchorite's cell) with a corpse on the altar, disguises, a bride substituted for another in the dark, a heroine drugged into passivity, a battle between Gypsies and highwaymen, and a faithless lover who dies from kissing a poisoned lock of hair. In the final scene, the villainess is shoved by a statue into a sarcophagus, where she perishes.

Like the typical gothic romance, *Rookwood* has a Byronic hero of mixed good and evil (Luke), a persecuted maiden (Eleanor), and a romantic hero who gets the girl (Ranulph). Ranulph and Eleanor are uninteresting, and even Luke is not very successful; he arouses some sympathy at the outset because he is an underdog, but his transformation to villain is not explored fully enough to be convincing. To berate Ainsworth for lack of originality, however, is to miss the point. He used the traditional gothic devices for the very reason that they were conven-

tional; they had become a code, an emotional shorthand that triggered known responses. Ainsworth was thus able to control the reader's mood, orchestrate the emotional response, and build to repeated transports of excitement.

The most interesting character in *Rookwood* is Dick Turpin, the highwayman. He appears in an outstanding sequence that has little to do with the book's plot: After accidentally killing one of his friends, Turpin rides on horseback with a pistol in each hand and the reins between his teeth, barely ahead of pursuers, the entire distance from London to York. The action peaks every twenty miles or so when Turpin encounters characters from the main plot or exerts a superhuman effort to outfight or outrun the law.

Rookwood was almost totally unplanned; Ainsworth's visit to a gloomy mansion inspired him to attempt a deliberate imitation of the work of Ann Radcliffe. He researched thieves' cant so he could include English highwaymen in place of Italian bandits; he interspersed dramatic songs, comic ballads, and Gypsy dances as if he were writing a melodrama for the stage; and he decided how to solve the mysteries as he went along. The most telling indication of Ainsworth's relationship to his work is that he wrote the twenty-five thousand words of Turpin's ride to York in a day and a night of work. He was so fully absorbed by the scene and its emotion that he wrote continuously until it was finished.

THE TOWER OF LONDON

Setting remained an essential stimulus to Ainsworth's imagination. The architectural-historical books, of which *The Tower of London* is a good example, were largely responsible for his reputation as a novelist who supplied education along with excitement. The single setting and the historical events should have helped Ainsworth focus the novel. The story that he chose, however, illuminates the artistic difficulties that grew from his ability to become wholly absorbed in his characters' emotions.

The Tower of London covers the struggle for the throne between the Protestant Lady Jane Grey and the Catholic Queen Mary. The book opens with a magnificent processional, described in exhaustive detail from contemporary sources. Within the frame of this processional, Ainsworth dangles passages of historical exposition, scenes from an assassination conspiracy, confrontations between as-yet-unidentified characters, a thunderstorm, a warning from an old crone, a moment of love at first sight, and other elements that establish emotional tone and provide the narrative hook. The handling of the historical plot line, however, shows how little the story element mattered to Ainsworth; he frequently reminds readers of the outcome already determined by history, so that curiosity about the ending is not a prime motive for reading on.

The book is a good example of Ainsworth's visual imagination and the reciprocal influence of novel and stage. Ainsworth worked closely with his illustrator, George Cruikshank. After their previous collaboration on *Jack Sheppard*, they had seen that Cruikshank's illustrations were almost immediately turned into living tableaux for stage versions of the book. Before beginning each monthly part of *The Tower of London*, Ainsworth and Cruikshank visited the Tower together and decided on the exact setting. They examined the architectural detail, explored the possibilities for light and shadow and composing human forms, and decided what events would take place. Ainsworth apparently learned from the stage how to control the source of light. He conceals the identities of characters by showing them in profile against backlight, he blinds onlookers with sudden brightness, and, inevitably, he extinguishes candles or torches at crucial moments.

Ainsworth continued to manipulate feelings by using dungeons, secret passageways, and torture chambers; he describes—with full detail—a martyr burned at the stake and a prisoner gnawed by rats. The humor supplied in *The Tower of London* in a running subplot about three giants and a dwarf is also largely visual.

Ainsworth has trouble linking the characters from history with the fictional people acting out his typical story of concealed birth, attempted seduction, and true love. The historical scenes are sometimes well realized, in particular the scenes between Lady Jane and Lord Dudley that dramatize the conflict of patriotism and faith. Nevertheless, Ainsworth's emotional connection to the characters—which makes the scenes so powerful—virtually prevents him from shaping any opinion on the moral conflict. Although the book depicts a struggle in which Queen Mary is generally seen as the villain, he cannot despise her. At any given moment, his sympathy is entirely engaged by the character at the center of the scene he is writing. Thus, even with the Tower imposing unity, the book remains a collection of vivid fragments.

OLD SAINT PAUL'S

By the time of *Old Saint Paul's*, serious literary critics were beginning to dismiss Ainsworth and his novels. The best they could say was that his books were educational, but critic Richard Henry Hengist Horne, in *A New Spirit of the Age* (1844), objected that even the history was nothing but "old dates, old names, old houses, and old clothes" and called *Old Saint Paul's* "generally dull, except when it is revolting." Part of the problem, for critics, was the simple fact that Ainsworth had become so popular. *Old Saint Paul's* was apparently the first novel serialized in an English newspaper. The *Sunday Times* paid Ainsworth one thousand pounds for first rights alone; after the book had run in weekly installments through 1841, he was able to sell it again in monthly parts, in three volumes, and in a steady stream of cheap, illustrated, and popular editions.

Artistically, the book is one of Ainsworth's most competent; a coherent invention integrates the history, the melodrama, and even the comedy. The story follows London grocer Stephen Bloundel and his family through the plague of 1665 and the fire of 1666. Most of the characters are fictional, although one historical person, the libertine earl of Rochester, provides a unifying strand by pursuing the grocer's blue-eyed daughter Amabel from one end of the tale to the other. The story lines are adroitly interwoven (perhaps because Ainsworth was not tied to actual historical confrontations), and the comic subplot involving a hypochondriac servant advances and comments on the main action while it supplies laughs. Memorable minor characters include the plundering nurse Judith Malmayns and the religious fanatic Solomon Eagle.

As always, Ainsworth is best at painting scenes. The novel features unforgettable pictures of London with green grass in the streets, of live burials and mass graves, of Saint Paul's filled with victims of plague, of King Charles II in a mad masque of death. In *Rookwood* (as in gothic novels in general) the past simply provides distance and strangeness; it gives readers an excuse to enjoy vicariously passion, cruelty, and sheer excitement. *Old*

Saint Paul's allows the same indulgence of feelings, but the novel's scenes of death and sexual passion have a legitimate relationship to the heightened sense of life and death implicit in the historical events.

The moral outlook of *Old Saint Paul's* suggests one reason Ainsworth remained popular with middle-class and lower-middle-class readers long after the literary mainstream had left him behind. The grocer Stephen Bloundel is a rock of individualism and self-sufficiency; as a husband and a father he knows what is best for his family, rules with an iron hand, and preserves not only their lives but also (even in the face of fire) most of their goods. The protagonist—Bloundel's apprentice Leonard Holt—is intelligent, industrious, ambitious, loyal, and as successful as any Horatio Alger hero. His master makes him a partner; his suggestions about fighting the fire are so practical that King Charles gives him a title. Furthermore, his girlfriend turns out to be an heiress in disguise and somehow, during a week of unrelieved firefighting, he manages to acquire new clothes suited to his improved station in life. Although Rochester and his crowd are seen as evil libertines through most of the book, Leonard has no ill feeling toward them at the end. This paradoxical moral attitude—which despises the upper classes for idleness and sexuality yet rewards the industrious hero by giving him wealth and a title—is virtually universal in the cheap literature of the mid-nineteenth century.

LATER CAREER

The historical vein supplied boundaries and permissible exaggerations that gave free play to what Ainsworth could do well. He was much less successful when he attempted a partly autobiographical book in the manner of Dickens's *David Copperfield* (1849-1850, serial; 1850, book)—Ainsworth's was titled *Mervyn Clitheroe*—or when he wrote sensation novels (including *Old Court, Myddleton Pomfret*, and *Hilary St. Ives*). The most popular form of the 1860's (and the direct ancestor of thrillers and detective stories), the sensation novel required tight plotting and a convincing contemporary milieu; Ainsworth's modern tales used his typical devices of misplaced inheritance, concealed identity, and inexplicable supernatural events, but the gaps tended to show when the actors wore modern dress.

If he was not particularly adept at writing sensation novels, however, Ainsworth was good at finding people who could. His middlebrow popular magazines effectively encouraged tight serial construction, the accumulation of incidents, and the interweaving of plots so that each installment could end in suspense. He discovered and encouraged two of the best-selling authors of the 1860's and 1870's, Ouida (Marie Louise de la Ramée) and Mrs. Henry Wood, whose famous *East Lynne* was written for *New Monthly Magazine* between 1859 and 1861, when Ainsworth was its editor. He reputedly read all submissions and wrote letters of advice to young authors. He also knew how to promote himself and was not above giving dinners to cultivate the influential librarian Charles Edward Mudie.

After the success of *Rookwood* in 1834, Ainsworth was a novelist everyone read. His first books were reviewed by leading journals; Ainsworth's *Jack Sheppard* sold more copies on first appearance than did Dickens's *Oliver Twist*, which came out at the same time. By the late 1860's, however, some of Ainsworth's novels were published only in penny magazines and sixpenny paperback editions. By the end of the century, his works were generally considered boys' reading; he became known as a novelist to be classed with such writers as Frederick Marryat and G. A. Henty.

Ainsworth had not changed; the novel and the reading public had. The division between mass literature and serious literature grew wider as the number of literate consumers for popular fiction burgeoned. Eight of Ainsworth's novels ran as serials in *Bow Bells*, a penny-weekly magazine that featured household advice and needlework patterns; the romantic-historical-gothic mode continued popular in *Bow Bells* and persisted as a women's escapist form into the twentieth century. At a Manchester testimonial in 1881, it was said that the Free Library had 250 volumes of Ainsworth's works in order to meet the demand by readers from the artisan class. The influence of his technique can be traced, finally, through the Jack Harkaway serials at the end of the century and on into the Hardy Boys books, which share with Ainsworth's best novels the spooky buildings, caves and underground passages, effective use of lighting, suspended narration, and exclamation marks at the ends of chapters.

Sally Mitchell

OTHER MAJOR WORK

POETRY: *Ballads*, 1855.

BIBLIOGRAPHY

Abbey, Cherie D., ed. *Nineteenth-Century Literature Criticism*. Detroit, Mich.: Gale Research, 1986. Presents information on Ainsworth's writing in its two forms, the Newgate novels and the historical romances, and includes some biographical details. Also includes extracts from reviews and essays from the 1830's through 1979, which are helpful in assessing critical responses to Ainsworth.

Carver, Stephen James. *The Life and Works of the Lancashire Novelist William Harrison Ainsworth, 1805-1882*. Lewiston, N.Y.: Edward Mellen Press, 2003. Provides extensive analysis of Ainsworth's writings and outlines the contributions Ainsworth made to periodical literature. Includes bibliographies of both Ainsworth's work and secondary literature.

Collins, Stephen. "Guy Fawkes in Manchester: The World of William Harrison Ainsworth." *Historian* 188 (Winter, 2005): 34-37. Explores Harrison's life and works. Maintains that Harrison was one of the nineteenth century authors "responsible for placing some of the most memorable historical legends in the public psyche," as illustrated by his novels about Dick Turpin and Jack Sheppard. Focuses on Ainsworth's novel *Guy Fawkes*, in which the author sets the Gunpowder Plot in his native Manchester.

Hollingsworth, Keith. *The Newgate Novel, 1830-1847: Bulwer, Ainsworth, Dickens, and Thackeray*. Detroit, Mich.: Wayne State University Press, 1963. Discusses the Newgate theme in nineteenth century literature, including critical commentary on Ainsworth's Newgate fiction and his association with Charles Dickens. Valuable for placing Ainsworth within this genre. Also covers his later writings and his work as editor of *New Monthly Magazine*.

Kelly, Patrick. "William Ainsworth." In *Victorian Novelists After 1885*. Vol. 1 in *Dictionary of Literary Biography*, edited by Ira B. Nadel and William E. Fredeman. Detroit, Mich.: Gale Research, 1983. Provides some helpful background information on Ainsworth's early years, the influences on his writing, and his later years as an editor. Cites *Rookwood* and *Jack Sheppard* as novels worthy of attention, and also discusses the novel *Crichton*. Notes the influence of Sir Walter Scott on Ainsworth's historical novels.

Mitchell, Rosemary. "Experiments with History: The Later Novels of W. H. Ainsworth and Their Illustrations and the Decline of the Picturesque Historical Novel." In *Picturing the Past: English History in Text and Image, 1830-1870*. New York: Oxford University Press, 2000. Chapter on Ainsworth's later historical novels is part of a study of nineteenth century history books, history textbooks, and historical novels that focuses on Victorians' attitudes toward British history. Demonstrates how the text and images in popular and scholarly publications contributed to Victorian cultural identities.

Sharpe, James. *Dick Turpin: The Myth of the English Highwayman*. London: Profile, 2004. Biography explores how the criminal's legend was recounted in eighteenth and nineteenth century literature, including a discussion of Ainsworth's treatment of Turpin in his historical novel *Rookwood*.

Worth, George J. *William Harrison Ainsworth*. New York: Twayne, 1972. Discusses the major aspects of Ainsworth's writing and provides background information on his long life. Describes the author as an "intriguing novelist" who "deserves to be read."

VASSILY AKSYONOV

Born: Kazan, Russia, Soviet Union (now in Russia);
  August 20, 1932
Died: Moscow, Russia; July 6, 2009
Also known as: Vassily Pavlovich Aksyonov

PRINCIPAL LONG FICTION

Kollegi, 1960 (*Colleagues*, 1962)
Zvezdnyi bilet, 1961 (*A Starry Ticket*, 1962; also
  known as *A Ticket to the Stars*)
Apelsiny iz Marokko, 1963 (*Oranges from
  Morocco*, 1979)
Pora, moi drug, pora, 1965 (*It's Time, My
  Friend, It's Time*, 1969)
Zatovarennaya bochkotara, 1968 (*Surplussed
  Barrelware*, 1985)
Stalnaya ptitsa, 1977 (novella; *The Steel Bird*,
  1979)
Poiski zhanra, 1978
Zolotaya nasha Zhelezka, 1979 (*Our Golden
  Ironburg*, 1986)
Ozhog, 1980 (*The Burn*, 1984)
Ostrov Krym, 1981 (*The Island of Crimea*, 1983)
Bumazhnyi peizazh, 1983
Skazhi izyum, 1985 (*Say Cheese!*, 1989)
Moskovskaia saga: Trilogiia, 1993-1994
  (includes *Pokolenie zimy*, *Voina i tiurma*
  [*Generations of Winter*, 1994], and *Tiurma i
  mir* [*The Winter's Hero*, 1996])
Novyi sladostnyi stil, 1997 (*The New Sweet Style*,
  1999)
Kesarevo svechenie, 2001
Volteryantsy i Volteryanki, 2004
Redkiezemli, 2007

OTHER LITERARY FORMS

Vassily Aksyonov (uhk-SYUH-nuhv) was primarily
a novelist, but he also worked in many other genres. As a
young Soviet writer, he produced short stories in the
1960's that were enormously popular among Russian
readers. He was also the author of numerous Russian
film scripts and several plays, of which the best is
Tsaplya (pb. 1979; *The Heron*, 1987). Children's books

and a fictionalized biography, *Lyubov k elektrichestvu*
(1971; love for electricity), are also found in his oeuvre.
His travel writings, especially *Kruglye sutki: Non-stop*
(1976; around the clock nonstop), a collage account of a
visit to the United States, are a remarkable blend of fantasy and reportage. A steady stream of diverse journalism also came from his pen, particularly after his emigration to the United States.

ACHIEVEMENTS

Vassily Aksyonov holds a unique position in modern
Russian literature. From the early 1930's until the death
of dictator Joseph Stalin in 1953, Soviet literature stag-
nated under the official aesthetic doctrine of Socialist
Realism. Aksyonov, as a controversial leader of the
"young prose" movement in the post-Stalin period, revitalized Russian prose by introducing fresh themes, characters, and living speech into his work. He was an idol of
and spokesman for the new generation of young Soviet
technocrats, who dreamed of a Western-oriented humanist socialism. As the dream dimmed, Aksyonov was
forced to turn to "writing for the drawer," knowing his
work could not be published in the Soviet Union. These
new works, increasingly surrealistic, detailed the disillu-
sion of the young intelligentsia. Published in the West
only after Aksyonov's emigration, they confirm his reputation as the preeminent chronicler of his generation as
well as its most innovative literary stylist.

BIOGRAPHY

Vassily Pavlovich Aksyonov was born in Kazan,
Russia, on August 20, 1932. His parents, both committed Communists, were falsely arrested as "enemies of
the people" in 1937. The future writer rejoined his freed
mother and stepfather, a Catholic doctor-prisoner, in Siberia at age seventeen. Because "it's easier for doctors in
the camps," it was decided that Aksyonov would attend
medical school in Leningrad, from which he graduated
in 1956, the year in which Premier Nikita S. Khrushchev
denounced the crimes of Stalin. Taking advantage of the
cultural "thaw," the young practitioner began writing.
After his successful first novel, *Colleagues*, was pub-

lished in 1960, Aksyonov turned to full-time writing. The early "optimistic" period of his career came to an end on March 8, 1963, when Khrushchev himself publicly demanded recantation of his work. Publication became increasingly difficult, especially after the Soviet invasion of Czechoslovakia in 1968, but Aksyonov was permitted to accept a one-term Regents' Lectureship at the University of California at Los Angeles in 1975.

In the late 1970's, Aksyonov and a number of colleagues boldly undertook to publish an uncensored literary anthology to be called *Metropol*. Those involved were subjected to reprisals, and Aksyonov was, in effect, forced to emigrate in 1980. In the United States, Aksyonov published several works written earlier and taught at various universities. He was also a fellow at the prestigious Woodrow Wilson International Center. As a resident of Washington, D.C., Aksyonov continued to write novels, including *Say Cheese!*, a fictionalized version of the *Metropol* affair. An energetic publicist, Aksyonov occupied a leading position in émigré cultural affairs.

In 2004, Aksyonov and his wife, Maya, moved back to Russia, taking an apartment in Moscow. They retained a second home in Biarritz, France, however, and Aksyonov made it clear that if the Russian federal government should begin heroizing Stalin once again, he would disown his own country. Aksyonov died in Moscow on July 6, 2009.

ANALYSIS

The major theme in Vassily Aksyonov's fiction is the nature and fate of the Soviet Union and the role of Aksyonov's generation in trying to reshape the nation after the death of Stalin. His works chronicle these years first from the optimistic perspective of a generation on the rise, confident that a new day has dawned, then from the perspective of growing doubt, and finally in a mood of despair.

A TICKET TO THE STARS

A Ticket to the Stars is a landmark book that became the rallying point for the new generation. The young people it portrays and those whom it inspired when it appeared took the name "star boys" as their banner. Conservatives of the older generation used the name as a term of condemnation. The story begins in the early summer in Moscow, circa 1960. Three friends who have just finished high school are hanging out in the courtyard of their apartment building. The neighbors look askance at their clothes and the music blaring from their tape recorder. All three are from professional families, and all are headed for college and careers in accord with the expectations of society and the wishes of their families. Dimka Denisov, the ringleader, confides to his older brother Victor that he and his friends have decided to kick over the traces, defy their parents, and head for the Baltic seacoast for the summer, and perhaps longer.

Vassily Aksyonov. (AP/Wide World Photos)

Victor, who narrates parts of the story, is twenty-eight, a doctoral candidate in space medicine. A model son, a scholarship student, he looks with affection but mild alarm at his aimless younger brother and his friends. Victor's goal in life is represented by the night view from his bedroom window, from which he can see a small rectangle of sky dotted by stars. The sight reminds him of a tram ticket punched with star-shaped holes.

The teenagers pass their summer on the beach. Among their haunts is a restaurant bar with a star-painted ceiling. As their money disappears, they join an Estonian collective fishing enterprise. The young Muscovites at first find their companions crude and the work difficult, but at length they begin to take pride in the endeavor. Victor, now on the verge of a brilliant career, comes to visit Dimka, who is still wary of a "programmed" future. Suddenly called back to Moscow, Victor is killed in a plane crash. After the funeral, Dimka lies on Victor's bed and sees for the first time "the starry ticket." It is now his ticket to the stars, but where will it take him?

At the time *A Ticket to the Stars* was published, Soviet readers, unlike their Western counterparts, were not accustomed to sympathetic accounts of youthful alienation. Even though the story has a reassuring ending, readers were shocked by the novel's racy language and its young heroes' flippant attitude toward authority.

THE STEEL BIRD

The Steel Bird, written in 1965 but not published until 1977, marks a crucial turning point in Aksyonov's writing both stylistically and thematically. His earlier novels are stylistically within the limits of realism, and their themes are more social than political. The young heroes, whose rebellion is against cant and excessive conformity, ultimately affirm the values of a socialist society. *The Steel Bird* is a political allegory in a modernist stylistic framework. In the spring of 1948, an odious creature named Popenkov (who subsequently proves to be part human and part mechanical bird) presents himself at a large, decaying Moscow apartment building and begs a corner in the entry-hall elevator. As the years pass, the creature expands his domain and enlists the residents in an illegal fake antique tapestry business. Eventually the tenants, a diverse cross section of Soviet society, are reduced to entering the building through a cramped back door.

The 1960's arrive. Soviet life has changed for the better. The residents of the older generation are retired, and their children are making their mark as leaders of a cultural revolution. The apartment building, weakened by age and Popenkov's constant remodeling, is on the verge of collapse. The Steel Bird nevertheless decides that for the convenience of his nocturnal flights the elevator should be extended through the roof. Seeing their home in danger, the residents finally rise. A coalition of worker-tenants and the young cultural leaders confront the Steel Bird on the roof, but as the residents drive off his minions, the building starts to crack. The building collapses, but all the residents are saved and moved to a splendid new building, while the Steel Bird remains perched atop the old elevator shaft. Months later, as bulldozers start to clear the rubble, Popenkov slowly flies off. The spirit of Stalinism departs, but it may return at any time.

The story, told by means of third-person narrative, eyewitness accounts, official reports, interludes of poetry, and authorial asides, is punctuated by the Stalinist house manager's cornet improvisations, thus echoing the story's themes. The Steel Bird increasingly lapses into using an autistic bird language.

THE BURN

The Burn, written in the post-Czech invasion years (1969-1975), presents a far bleaker stage in the evolution of Aksyonov's views. The events of *The Burn*—a long, complex, often hallucinatory novel—are perceived through the alcoholic haze that is the response of the intelligentsia to the demise of their hopes for a new Russia. The novel features five more or less interchangeable heroes—or rather antiheroes—all members of Aksyonov's generation, all liberals, all superstars in their professions. Kunitser is a physicist; Sabler, a jazz saxophonist; Khvastishchev, a sculptor; Malkolmov, a physician; and Pantelei, a writer whose past resembles that of author Aksyonov. Although the men have certain almost identical and seemingly concurrent experiences, they lead independent existences. The narrative focus alternates among them, and on occasion they change identities. Most remarkably, they share flashbacks to a single, common childhood, when they were Tolya von Steinbock.

The heroes have retreated before a renascent (but

much milder) Stalinism, withdrawing into their creative work, sex, and alcohol. On the evening of the first day portrayed in the novel, they individually encounter an old friend, Patrick Thunderjet, a visiting Anglo-American who is obviously their Western counterpart. The day's drinking expands into a binge that takes the collective hero, a friend, and Thunderjet through a set of bizarre experiences ending in the Crimea, where they are ultimately arrested and confined to the drunk tank. The collective hero, too valuable an asset to Soviet society to be abandoned, is sent to a detoxification hospital. Released, the protagonists undertake a sober life, each engaged in a major creative endeavor. Soviet society, however, is too corrupt for their survival. Each has a professional colleague, a close friend from the heady days of the early 1960's. The old friends, who have compromised with the authorities, betray the trust of the heroes, who again succumb to drink. Now merged into a single nameless "I," the protagonist descends into alcoholic hallucinations, ultimately leaping to his death while fantasizing a lunar space flight.

The main story line of *The Burn* describes the smashed hopes of a generation. There is also a story behind the story. The five heroes share a childhood very much like Aksyonov's. Tolya von Steinbock joins his mother in Siberia when she is released from a ten-year sentence toward the end of Stalin's reign. He wants nothing more than to be a model Soviet youth and is vaguely embarrassed by his ex-prisoner mother and stepfather, a doctor and Catholic lay priest of German origin. Among a group of new women prisoners, he sees a girl of Polish-English origin named Alisa and dreams of a daring rescue. As he daydreams, another young man, a former prisoner, offers modest aid to the girl. Tolya becomes friends with the young man, Sanya Gurchenko, who is a friend of his stepfather. Their courage and idealism greatly impress him. Tolya's mother is soon rearrested, as is Sanya. They are interrogated, Sanya brutally, by two political police officers. Sanya eventually escapes to the West, where he becomes a Catholic priest and, years later, briefly encounters the hero.

These events of twenty years before lie deeply buried in the minds of the successful heroes, who do not wish to confront either their impotent past or their compromised present. The past, however, is very much with them.

Wherever they go, they encounter two figures, cloak-room attendants, drunk-tank aides, and the like, vaguely reminiscent of the former police officials. They also yearn for a beautiful, promiscuous woman who moves in corrupt, elite Moscow circles and seems to resemble the Polish-English Alisa. The heroes, however, remain incapable either of vengeance or of rescuing their ideal. Unlike Sanya, who actively resisted evil, they have tacitly compromised with the system.

It is Sanya, the priest, who offers Aksyonov's solution with his philosophy of "the third mode." Its basic postulate is that all human beings, atheists and believers alike, seek God. There are always two models: an idea and its antithesis. One must seek a third, qualitatively different model through which one may strive to see the face of God. Humankind comes close to it only in moments of free, irrational creativity, the "burn" of the book's title. The higher emotions, such as compassion for one's neighbor, charity, and the urge for justice, are rationally and biologically inexplicable, fantastic. Christianity, precisely because it is concerned with these emotions, is sublime. Christianity is likened to a breakthrough into space, an image that corresponds to the hero's final, hallucinatory suicide flight. *The Burn*, Aksyonov's most important novel, is a diagnosis and indictment of his generation.

THE ISLAND OF CRIMEA

The Island of Crimea, written between 1977 and 1979, continues some of the themes of *The Burn*, but with a different emphasis. Although more traditional in style, *The Island of Crimea* is based on two fantastic premises. The Crimea, in reality a peninsula in the Black Sea, is, in the novel, an independent island-country. Historically, the Red Army defeated the White Armies during the Russian Civil War, and the Whites were driven into overseas exile. Fictionally, the Whites have successfully defended the island of Crimea and established a capitalistic Western political democracy that, in the late 1970's, is a fabulously wealthy, technological supercivilization.

Andrei Luchnikov, a jet-set member of one of the country's most prominent White émigré families, is the editor of an influential liberal newspaper. Luchnikov's political program, which reflects his generation's nostalgia for Mother Russia, calls for the voluntary reunification of the Crimea with Russia. Although realizing that the Soviet Union is, by the standards of the Crimea, politically and economically primitive, he believes that the historical motherland is moving forward and that both countries would profit from a symbiotic union. Eventually, the island's voters approve the reunification. The Soviet government, unable to comprehend the idea, responds with a massive military invasion in which most of Luchnikov's family dies, Luchnikov goes mad, and his son flees into exile. The novel, which reads like a James Bond thriller, is, in some sense, a very black comedy.

The Island of Crimea sums up Aksyonov's twenty-year meditation on the nature, history, and fate of his native country. From *A Ticket to the Stars* to *The Island of Crimea*, Aksyonov charted the evolution of the Russian intelligentsia: from the optimism of the early 1960's through the cynicism and despair of the late 1960's and early 1970's, to dissidence and emigration. It is the saga of a generation.

GENERATIONS OF WINTER

In his 1985 novel *Say Cheese!*, a largely autobiographical novel in which Aksyonov reflects on his emigration to the United States, he permits free rein to his satirical side, poking playful fun at the foibles of Soviet society. However, Aksyonov would soon prove himself capable of very serious historical writing as well as satiric comedy. In 1993, only two years after the Soviet Union's collapse and replacement by a new, democratic Russian Federation, he published *Generations of Winter*, a generational saga of a family living in the Soviet Union under Stalin, intended to be a masterpiece on the level of Leo Tolstoy's *Voyna i mir* (1865-1869; *War and Peace*, 1886).

In the beginning of *Generations of Winter*, the big family headed by renowned surgeon Boris Nikitich Gradov is enjoying the prosperous last few years of the New Economic Policy, the program of limited small-business capitalism that was permitted by Soviet leader Vladimir Ilich Lenin as a means of rebuilding prosperity after the catastrophe of the Russian Civil War. Boris is roped into the medical conspiracy that results in the death of military leader Mikhail Vasilievich Frunze, and as a result the family becomes entangled in a sequence of major events during the Great Purges and World War II.

In several cases, sons or grandsons redeem the memories of their forebears through acts of courage in situations that parallel earlier acts of cowardice. For instance, whereas the patriarch Boris Gradov acted in cowardice and became complicit in the death of Frunze, his grandson, also named Boris, protects a Jewish colleague who was falsely implicated in the Doctors' Plot, the infamous attacks on high-ranking Jewish physicians that many historians believe to have been intended as the beginning of a new round of purges on the level of the 1930's Great Terror, which was stopped only by Stalin's sudden death. Similarly, as Boris's son Kiril is haunted by pangs of conscience for having helped to suppress the Krondstadt rebellion, his son, also named Kiril, refuses to betray a group of Polish soldiers in World War II to whom he had promised safe passage. Although it may not be strictly realistic that so many members of a single family keep encountering high-ranking individuals at key turning points in history, this conceit permits Aksyonov to comment on these events more pungently than would be possible if he always kept the great actors of Soviet history strictly at arms' length, in the tradition of Sir Walter Scott's historical novels.

THE NEW SWEET STYLE

In 1997, Aksyonov published *The New Sweet Style*, the story of Aleksandr Iakovlevich Korbakh, a Russian émigré who rises from pushing drugs on the streets of Los Angeles to being a respected professor in Washington, D.C. Although there are certain autobiographical elements in this novel, Aksyonov plays fast and free with his character to create the literary effects he wants. In no way should any particular scene in the novel be seen as a confession of the author's personal history, although it is clear that Aksyonov's own experiences informed many of the scenes.

KESAREVO SVECHENIE

With the new millennium, Aksyonov returned to work that borders on science fiction. In *Kesarevo svechenie* he portrays a future in which his heroes wrest numerous wonderful inventions from the vaults of a greedy oil company that had hidden them away to protect its own profits. These inventions had been bought from their inventors and sequestered because they promise the generation of limitless clean, green power. Releasing them to the world brings the protagonists only a moral victory, however—not material rewards. In the final scenes, set sometime in the middle of the new century, they have become very old but are still too poor to afford a fully robotic home or lifesaving medical treatments; they have withered into miserable and ridiculous elders, tormented by their own frailties. They finally have clones made of themselves, and only when they themselves die do the clones finally attain the radiance of the original characters.

In a sense, Aksyonov himself came full circle as a writer in this work, returning to his original satirical roots, but for new reasons. In the old, repressive Soviet Union, satirical works set in fantastical worlds could often slip subtly political messages past the censors. In the post-Soviet world, where there are no longer official government censors, humor becomes a way to handle ideas that would be dismissed as mere conspiracy theory if they were presented as straight narrative. By taking the reader on a wild and delightful romp through an imaginary future, Aksyonov can slip a few heavy ideas past the reader's own internal censor.

D. Barton Johnson
Updated by Leigh Husband Kimmel

OTHER MAJOR WORKS

SHORT FICTION: *Katapulta*, 1964; *Na polputi k lune*, 1965; *Zhal, chto vas ne bylo s nami*, 1969; *The Steel Bird, and Other Stories*, 1979; *Pravo na ostrov*, 1983; *The Destruction of Pompeii, and Other Stories*, 1991; *Negativ polozhitel'nogo geroia*, 1996.

PLAYS: *Potselui, Orkestr, Ryba, Kolbasa . . .* , pb. 1964; *Vsegda v prodazhe*, pr. 1965; *Chetyre temperamenta*, pb. 1967 (*The Four Temperaments*, 1987); *Aristofaniana s lyagushkami*, pb. 1967-1968; *Vash ubiytsa*, pb. 1977 (*Your Murderer*, 1999); *Tsaplya*, pb. 1979 (*The Heron*, 1987); *Aristofaniana s lygushkami: Sobranie pes*, 1981 (includes *Potselui, Orkestr, Ryba, Kolbasa . . .* , *Vsegda v prodazhe*, *Chetyre temperamenta*, *Aristofaniana s lygushkami*, and *Tsaplya*).

NONFICTION: *Lyubov k elektrichestvu*, 1971 (biography); *Kruglye sutki: Non-stop*, 1976; *V poiskakh grustnogo bebi*, 1987 (*In Search of Melancholy Baby*, 1987).

EDITED TEXT: *Metropol: Literaturnyi almanakh*, 1979 (*Metropol: Literary Almanac*, 1982).

MISCELLANEOUS: *Quest for an Island*, 1987 (plays and short stories); *Sobranie sochinenii*, 1994- (works; 5 volumes).

BIBLIOGRAPHY

Dalgard, Per. *Function of the Grotesque in Vasilij Aksenov*. Translated by Robert Porter. Århus, Denmark: Arkona, 1982. Discusses how Aksyonov portrays commonplace things and events as grotesque or ridiculous, often as a method of social criticism.

Kustanovich, Konstantin. *The Artist and the Tyrant: Vassily Aksenov's Works in the Brezhnev Era*. Columbus, Ohio: Slavica, 1992. In-depth study examines how Aksyonov uses satirical and fantastical motifs to criticize the failings and evils of the Soviet regime. Includes analysis that compares motifs found in Aksyonov's plays with those in his prose works.

Lowe, David. "E. Ginzburg's *Krutoj marsrut* and V. Aksenov's *Ozog:* The Magadan Connection." *Slavic and East European Journal* 27 (Summer, 1983). Examines the biographical connections between Aksyonov's *The Burn* and his mother's account of her exile.

Matich, Olga. "Vasilii Aksyonov and the Literature of Convergence: *Ostrov Krym* as Self-Criticism." *Slavic Review* 47, no. 4 (1988). Provides in-depth discussion of *The Island of Crimea*.

Mozejko, Edward, Boris Briker, and Peter Dalgård, eds. *Vasily Pavlovich Aksenov: A Writer in Quest of Himself*. Columbus, Ohio: Slavica, 1986. Collection of essays addresses various aspects of Aksyonov's writing, including his novels.

Proffer, Ellendea. "The Prague Winter: Two Novels by Aksyonov." In *The Third Wave: Russian Literature in Emigration*, edited by Olga Matich and Michael Heim. Ann Arbor, Mich.: Ardis, 1984. Essay focusing on *The Burn* and *The Island of Crimea* is part of a collection devoted to the works of Russian authors.

Simmons, Cynthia. *Their Fathers' Voice: Vassily Aksyonov, Venedikt Erofeev, Eduard Lemonov, and Sasha Sokolov*. New York: Peter Lang, 1994. Compares and contrasts the works of three leading writers of the post-Stalin generation.

ALAIN-FOURNIER
Henri-Alban Fournier

Born: La Chapelle-d'Angillon, France; October 3, 1886

Died: Near Les Éparges, France; September 22, 1914

Also known as: Henri-Alban Fournier

Principal long fiction

Le Grand Meaulnes, 1913 (*The Wanderer*, 1928; also known as *The Lost Domain*, 1959)

Colombe Blanchet, 1922, 1924 (fragment)

Other literary forms

In addition to *The Wanderer*, on which his fame principally rests, Alain-Fournier (ah-LAN FEWRN-yay) published stories, poems, and essays. His correspondence with Jacques Rivière (collected by Alain-Fournier's sister, Isabelle, in a posthumous edition) is especially noteworthy; indeed, it is generally regarded as among the most valuable cultural documents to come out of France at the beginning of the twentieth century. As a painstaking record of the growth of a novel and the evolution of an aesthetic, these letters are comparable to the journals of André Gide; as a scrupulous exercise in psychological introspection and as meditations on and records of the contemporary arts in the Paris of the belle époque, they are of inestimable value. Similarly, Alain-Fournier's letters to his family and to his friend René Bichet are distinguished by the same arresting qualities that inform *The Wanderer*: an ability to describe impressions suggestively and economically, a keen and nostalgic sense of what is irretrievable in human experience, and a lucid and discriminating appreciation of human character.

In addition to the letters are the stories, poems, and reviews edited by Jacques Rivière under the title *Miracles* (1924). Most of these works bear the earmarks of Alain-Fournier's early infatuation with the French Symbolists, and they betray the hand of an apprentice. There are, however, an equal number of pieces in this collection—especially "Le Miracle des trois dames"—that prefigure the tempered artistry of *The Wanderer*. Finally, Alain-Fournier produced unfinished sketches for a play, "La Maison dans la forêt," and a novel left incomplete at the time of his death.

Achievements

Alain-Fournier's novel *The Wanderer* is universally regarded as one of the signal achievements of French fiction in the first half of the twentieth century. In a review that appeared on April 19, 1953, in *The Observer*, the eminent English critic Sir Harold Nicolson claimed, "Were I asked what was the most impressive novel published in France during my own lifetime, I should answer 'Alain-Fournier's *Le Grand Meaulnes*.'" He concluded his evaluation of Alain-Fournier's novel with the following critical judgment: "Certainly I should place this novel among those which every literate person should have read."

Scholars of French literature have demonstrated an indefatigable interest in this writer. In volume 6 of *A Critical Bibliography of French Literature* (1980), Alain-Fournier—along with Marcel Proust, Gide, and a handful of other writers—is accorded a separate chapter of eighteen double-columned pages. The quarterly journal of the Association des Amis de Jacques Rivière et Alain-Fournier is devoted to essays, notes, and reviews on the lives and works of these two authors. In Paris, there is a famous bookstore called Au Grand Meaulnes, and the local high school, or *lycée*, in Bourges is named for Alain-Fournier. In 1967, a film version of *Le Grand Meaulnes*, directed by Jean-Gabriel Albicocco from a screenplay by Albicocco and Alain-Fournier's sister, Isabelle Rivière, was released in France (it was released in the United States as *The Wanderer* in 1969); the film has gone on to become a veritable *object de culte* among discriminating French moviegoers. Another film version, directed by Jean-Daniel Verhaeghe, was released in France in 2006. In short, on the level of both critical appreciation and popular response, *The Wanderer* has achieved the status of a classic in modern French fiction.

BIOGRAPHY

Henri-Alban Fournier (Alain-Fournier is a partial pseudonym) was born October 3, 1886, at La Chapelle-d'Angillon. After a childhood passed in Sologne and the Bas-Berry, where his parents were schoolteachers, he began his secondary education in Paris and then prepared in Brest for entry into the École Novale. Unable to suppress a passionate attachment to the countryside of his childhood, he returned closer to home and enrolled in a course of philosophical studies at Bourges. He subsequently attended the Lycée Lakanal at Sceaux, where he met and developed a profound friendship with the future editor of the *Nouvelle Revue française*, Jacques Rivière; in 1909, Rivière married Alain-Fournier's younger sister, Isabelle.

Together, Alain-Fournier and Rivière dedicated themselves to the study, evaluation, and analysis of the contemporary arts: painting, music (especially the music of Claude Debussy), and, above all, literature. They were among the first to discover and celebrate those writers destined to become the acknowledged masters of twentieth century French literature, including Paul Claudel, Charles-Pierre Péguy, and Gide.

On Ascension Day of June, 1905, while leaving an exhibition of contemporary art in Paris, Alain-Fournier encountered the woman whom he subsequently transformed into the heroine of *The Wanderer*, Yvonne de Galais. Yvonne de Quièvrecourt (her real name) was the daughter of a French naval officer and, in consequence, moved in a higher social milieu than the young Alain-Fournier. A brief conversation they once had as they strolled by the Seine was abruptly terminated when the young lady responded to Alain-Fournier's importunities with the following remark: "À quoi bon?" ("What's the use?"). These are the precise words that Yvonne de Galais addresses to Augustin Meaulnes in Alain-Fournier's novel. Despite the brevity of this colloquy, Alain-Fournier regarded his encounter with Yvonne as the most decisive event in his life. Eight years later, after ineffectual attempts to renew relations, he met her for a second time: She was then married and the mother of two children.

Alain-Fournier's studies were interrupted in 1907 by two years of military service. In the meantime, he had begun to publish diverse poems, essays, and studies (later collected by Rivière in the volume *Miracles*). His work

on *The Wanderer*, however, was painstaking and slow. It was several months after the second encounter with Yvonne that *The Wanderer*, the novel in which Alain-Fournier's years of ineffectual devotion are enshrined, finally appeared. A year later, the author was dead.

Alain-Fournier was one of the first casualties of World War I. The young French lieutenant was struck down during an ambush of his troop on September 22, 1914, at Les Éparges. According to the accounts of survivors, Alain-Fournier raised his hand in a gesture of command when a bullet passed through it. He fell to one knee but was lost sight of in the ensuing confusion and presumed dead. His body was never recovered.

After the death of Rivière in 1925, Isabelle published the correspondence between her husband and her brother as *Correspondance avec Jacques Rivière, 1905-1914* (1926-1928); this volume was followed by *Lettres au petit B.* (1930; letters to René Bichet, a young comrade of Alain-Fournier at Lakanal) and *Lettres d'Alain-Fournier à sa famille, 1905-1914* (1930).

ANALYSIS: THE WANDERER

In *The Wanderer*, Alain-Fournier has written one of those few novels whose riches are not exhausted by analysis, however prolonged. Its multivalent textures, organic use of imagery, psychological depth, and contrapuntal themes reveal a structural integrity that is peculiarly modern. At the same time, the novel summarizes and brings to consummate expression a variety of concerns, preoccupations, and attitudes germane to the French Symbolists. It may be construed simply and straightforwardly as a novel of adventure or, on a complementary level, as a quest for the Absolute that makes abundant, though discreet, reference to medieval legend, ancient myth, folktale and fairy tale, and the symbols and procedures of religious initiation. It may be relished for the haunting, restrained lyricism of its prose, its delicate evocations of a landscape flickering with impressionist light and Symbolist overtones, its unprecedented fusion of fantasy and factuality, its insights into adolescent psychology, and, finally, its depiction of a mythopoeic search for salvation.

PLOT

François Seurel, the narrator of the story, recounts the events associated with his family's move, fifteen years earlier, to the village of Sainte-Agathe. A shy and reclusive adolescent suffering from a slight limp, Seurel is gradually cured after the arrival of a dynamic and imperious youth named Augustin Meaulnes. Dominant and intense, the seventeen-year-old Meaulnes becomes the accepted leader of the other schoolboys. When Monsieur Seurel (François's father) chooses another student to join François in meeting his grandparents at the local train station, Meaulnes rebels by stealing a horse and cart and taking off on his own.

Meaulnes soon becomes lost and, after a night in the woods, arrives at an isolated château where, as he later discovers, festivities are in preparation for a marriage between the spoiled son of the house, the sixteen-year-old Frantz de Galais, and his fiancé, an impoverished seamstress named Valentine Blondeau. After entering the château through a window, Meaulnes is mistaken for a guest and subsequently joins in a masked ball arranged by the children of the domain. Diverted, along with the other revelers, by the antics of a costumed Pierrot, Meaulnes soon retires to a secluded portion of the house, where his attention is arrested by the sound of a distant piano. Entering a small chamber occupied by children turning the pages of storybooks, Meaulnes beholds, seated at a piano, a young girl who later proves to be Frantz's sister, Yvonne de Galais.

The next day, during a boating party, Meaulnes meets and talks briefly with Yvonne. He returns to the château to find the revelers in a state of consternation and disarray. Frantz has failed to return with his bride, and the guests, tired of waiting, grow restless, moody, and cynical, entertaining one another with bawdy songs and off-color jokes.

As he is about to leave, Meaulnes is accosted by a youth in naval costume; this youth turns out to be Frantz de Galais. His fiancé, mistrusting the effects of his lofty ideals, has abandoned him. Frantz orders Meaulnes to suspend the proceedings. As Meaulnes is hurried from the château in a rolling carriage, a flash of light accompanied by the report of a gun explodes from the depths of the forest. This is followed by the apparition of the costumed Pierrot carrying the inert body of Frantz de Galais.

The rest of the novel is devoted to Meaulnes's unsuccessful attempt to return to the lost domain. After a brief interval following Meaulnes's return to Sainte-Agathe, a

mysterious stranger, his head wrapped in bandages, arrives at the village in the company of a dissolute strolling player named Ganache. (They turn out to be Frantz and the erstwhile Pierrot.) Before disclosing any information concerning the whereabouts of his sister, Frantz departs, having chosen to lead the itinerant life of a gypsy.

Meaulnes travels to Paris in the hope of seeing Yvonne at the Galaises' city residence, but the house is abandoned. Waiting outside the house, like Meaulnes, is another figure: a girl, dressed in black with a white collar like a "pretty Pierrot." Like Meaulnes, she is companionless. Despairing of ever seeing Yvonne again, Meaulnes accepts Valentine (for this chance-met girl is indeed Frantz's former fiancé) as his mistress.

In the meantime, Seurel has discovered the whereabouts of Yvonne. She is a regular customer at his uncle's country store. Having lived vicariously for so long in Meaulnes's adventure (and knowing nothing of Meaulnes's relations with Valentine), Seurel now hopes to bring Meaulnes and Yvonne together. He arranges to meet Meaulnes at his parental home but is astonished at Meaulnes's apparent reluctance to give up an intended journey. (As is later disclosed, Meaulnes had abandoned Valentine after discovering that she was Frantz's fiancé. Hence, Seurel's arrival with news of Yvonne synchronizes unmercifully with Meaulnes's intention to find and retrieve the self-destructive Valentine.)

In any event, Seurel convinces Meaulnes to meet Yvonne at a country outing organized by Seurel and Monsieur de Galais. The meeting proves to be a disaster. To Yvonne's mortification (for her father has lost his fortune in paying off the accumulated debts of his son), Meaulnes dwells obsessively on the vanished splendor of the lost domain. Finally, Meaulnes starts an argument with Yvonne's father over his imprudence in saddling the broken-down cart horse, Belisaire. That evening, in a fit of remorse, Meaulnes asks Yvonne to be his wife.

On the evening of the wedding, Frantz returns. He persuades Meaulnes to accompany him on a search for his lost fiancé. To Seurel's incredulity and dismay, Meaulnes departs with Frantz. Seurel becomes, in consequence, both surrogate husband to Yvonne and substitute father to the child conceived on the night before Meaulnes's departure. Following the birth of her child, Yvonne dies and Seurel is appointed guardian. After an indeterminate interval, Meaulnes returns, having successfully reunited Frantz with Valentine. Presently Meaulnes departs with his daughter to a nameless destination. Seurel is left with nothing save a host of indelible memories and the book in which they are enshrined.

THEMES

The opening pages of *The Wanderer* immediately enunciate the themes and dramatic situations subsequently borne out by the novel's hapless protagonists: François Seurel, the diffident yet deeply compassionate narrator; Augustin Meaulnes, the figure of youthful valor who betrays his best impulses and precipitates those around him into tragedy and regret; and Frantz de Galais, the wayward, erratic embodiment of those demoniac forces that explode toward the novel's conclusion. These characters, although sharply differentiated and thoroughly believable as dramatic figures, are, to a certain extent, psychological counterparts of one another. (Triadic figures are, of course, common ingredients of fairy tales, as in "Goldilocks and the Three Bears" or "The Three Little Pigs.") Here, however, the three protagonists represent, on a psychological level, individual aspects of a single, fragmented ego. The resemblance between the names "Frantz" and "François" is not merely fortuitous, nor is it merely accidental that Meaulnes, at one point in the novel, sustains wounds to the head and knee—the respective locations of Frantz's scar and François's affliction.

The very first words of the novel evoke that sense of an irretrievable happiness that, through François's delicate and subtly cadenced prose, envelops the characters, scenes, and situations of *The Wanderer* with a profound and poignant sense of nostalgia. After mentioning a nameless "He" who will turn out to be the principal subject of the book, François remarks of the house, the neighborhood, and the countryside of his early adventures that "we shall not be going back to it." Here, then, is one of the themes, casually broached and tentatively suggested, that colors the lives and attitudes of the chief characters—namely, the search for a lost paradise variously identified with an idealized childhood, an uncorrupted heart, or a state of pure and disinterested love. "My credo in art and literature," wrote Alain-Fournier, "is childhood: to render this state without puerility, but with a profound sense of its mystery."

Childhood is, of course, the period of human life most frequently extolled by the Romantic school of the nineteenth century. The child enjoys a continued imaginative transformation of reality; the boundaries between ego and world are nebulous. Hence the child becomes the type and emblem of the poet. Moreover, the sense of oneness with the whole of Being is more readily available in childhood (before the process of ego building has begun) than at any other period. In consequence, the child's unconscious participation in the whole of reality is analogous to the conscious awareness of that wholeness that is deliberately cultivated by the mystic. It is one thing to be an adult, however, and to cherish childhood as emblematic of the spiritually awakened conscience; it is another thing altogether to be an adult and wish to return to a condition from which, by virtue of one's temporality, one is debarred.

The Wanderer is informed by a growing awareness that the celebration of childhood, when protracted beyond its limits, becomes demoniac and obsessive; concomitant with this awareness emerges a collateral theme: "the dialectic of desire." This dialectic, as outlined by C. S. Lewis in his preface to *The Pilgrim's Regress* (1933), may be described as follows. Human beings are so constituted that they perpetually feel the paucity of present satisfactions. In order to hide this emptiness and discontent, one is perennially engaged in the search for some object that can fill the vacuum of existence. Each object pursued or desired is inevitably disappointing insofar as it fails to secure everlasting happiness. In consequence, one scuttles from object to object, goal to goal, in the hope of securing that without which one is miserable. The fallacy inherent in the pursuit becomes evident, however, when the attainment of some cherished and sought-for treasure does not produce the lasting effect desired. Sometimes, when present objects do not satisfy expectations, one wrongly believes that if it were in one's power to return to some luminous moment in the past, one could again be happy. Such a return, however, would reveal only that the "luminous" moment similarly involved the pursuit of a distant goal or the longing for a vanished past. Hence one is obliged to resign oneself to a moody cynicism or, through an act of secondary reflection, to arrive at a greater understanding of the dilemma—namely, a recognition that one is created to enjoy a felicity not available in the world of spatiotemporal objects. The things sought—the wonder of childhood, the purity of first love, the ecstasy of sexual union—have an analogous relationship to the true object of the quest but should not be confused with it.

SEA IMAGERY

The divine discontent of Romanticism points, then, to a reality of ultimate and transcendent worth, and it is the recognition of this reality (or the failure to recognize it) that is thematically central to *The Wanderer*. Indeed, one of Alain-Fournier's signal achievements in this novel lies in his ability to make the reader conscious of that reality as it impinges on human existence, and it is through an especially cunning stylistic device—the consistent use of marine imagery—that this effect is achieved. Through repeated and strategic references to the sea, Alain-Fournier is able to achieve that sense of what the French call *dépaysment*, the feeling of being transported from one's present surroundings into a more mysterious dimension of existence. In a letter to Rivière, Alain-Fournier claimed that his intention in the novel was not simply to reproduce the sights, sounds, and impressions associated with his childhood home in the landlocked region of the Sologne but to capture "that other mysterious landscape" at which the real landscape hints or that it suggests, to "insert the marvellous into reality" without straining credulity or surpassing the world of concrete objects and living forms. To achieve his effects, Alain-Fournier fused the idealized conventions of romance narrative with the low mimetic style of realistic fiction.

Thus, after a matter-of-fact inventory of the household and schoolroom associated with Meaulnes's adventure, Seurel suddenly introduces an image that has the effect of transposing the reader above the immediate scene into an atmosphere of haunting suggestivity and alien coldness: "This was the setting in which the most troubled and most precious days of my life were lived; an abode from which our adventurings flowed out, to flow back again like waves breaking on a lonely headland." The haunting image of the "lonely headland" coupled with the fairy-tale superlatives "most troubled" and "most precious" has the effect of jolting the reader out of the present and into that vast Symbolist "beyond" that Alain-Fournier inherited from the poets and artists of his generation. Throughout the novel, sea imagery is used to expand the sense of horizon, to make the reader conscious of a quest that is essentially religious. Significantly, as the novel progresses and the characters fail to live up to their early impulses, the imagery darkens, as connotations of shipwreck and loss supplant the first hopeful sense of adventure.

SYMBOLISM

Notwithstanding the intricacies of the narrative, the reader is aware from the very beginning that the plot—like a bass line in music—sustains an imposing edifice of suggestive details, symbolic episodes, and allegorical events. Virtually every paragraph hints of or highlights the book's implicit themes or comments, through oblique but dexterously chosen effects, on the significance of the characters and dramatic situations. When, for example, Seurel as a small boy first arrives at Sainte-Agathe under the protection of his parents, the first problem that concerns his mother is the distressing abundance of doors and windows that need to be "blocked before the place is habitable." From this point on, images of doors and windows ramify in an exceedingly suggestive manner. They belong to that network of images in the novel that opposes interiors to exteriors, warmth to cold, and darkness to light. For Seurel, the warmth and security of the maternal home is both a starting point and orientation. Throughout the novel, he persists in identifying happiness or fulfillment with the domestic hearth. Meaulnes, on the other hand, is associated with roads and cold. In fact, his arrival occurs on "a cold Sunday in November," and it is he who, as Seurel later reflects, "extinguishes the lamp around which we had been a happy family group at night-time when my father had closed all the wooden shutters." Unlike Seurel, however, Meaulnes is continually tempted by the allure of a ceaseless journey toward an indeterminate goal.

Meaulnes is the demoniac force that makes Seurel and the other schoolboys conscious of their limitations. He initiates the transition to adulthood by compelling his schoolfellows to recognize impulses that no longer pertain to the period of childhood. In the final analysis, however, Meaulnes is less a hero than an antihero. He is able to carry the urge to self-actualization only so far; he arrives at the threshold of adult reality but remains, to the last, unable to pass through the door. It is not surprising that Seurel first glimpses Meaulnes as he stands in the shadowed contours of a door frame—a literal threshold that is the first of several that make the reader conscious of the opposition between interiors and exteriors and that highlight Meaulnes's tendency to vacillate between antagonistic impulses.

Meaulnes's first action at Sainte-Agathe epitomizes his power to evoke mystery and magic in the realm of the humdrum and mundane. When he sets off a skyrocket in the school courtyard, the crepuscular glow that illuminates the humble village of Sainte-Agathe is a tangible emblem of his ability to transfigure reality. The burst of black-and-red light at this moment is replicated in subsequent situations: the sparks in the shadowed smithy where Meaulnes conceives of stealing the horse and cart, the blast of Frantz's pistol, the wavering candlelight by which Meaulnes discovers Frantz, the red light of Ganache's Gypsy caravan, the red-and-black drapes in the room that Meaulnes shares with Valentine, and, finally, the black-frocked priest and the boy "wearing the red cap of an acolyte," both of whom Seurel confronts as a portent of Yvonne's death. The imagery, with its increasingly sinister connotations, mirrors Meaulnes's failure to develop; it further parallels the manner in which creative potential, distorted or frustrated by the hero's immaturity, turns into its destructive opposite. Significantly, Meaulnes's appearance at Sainte-Agathe occurs on a day when Seurel comments, apropos of the village bells: "Then, abruptly, the pealing of the baptismal bells left off—as though someone issuing a joyous summons to a *fête* had become aware of a mistake in the date, or the parish." The canceled baptism prefigures Meaulnes's aborted rite of passage, and the reference to a *fête* anticipates the broken-off wedding party at Les Sablonnières, where Meaulnes will remain, in an emotional sense, permanently arrested.

The *fête étrange* itself is at once the starting point and the goal of the novel's various adventures. In consequence, it carries enormous symbolic weight, notwithstanding the matter-of-fact account to which it is reduced in the increasingly disenchanted context of the novel's third and last part. It is especially here, however, that the reader recognizes Alain-Fournier's dexterity in weaving commonplace incidents into a highly wrought fabric that blends the marvelous with reality. Meaulnes's adventure, it should be noted, begins as an inglorious schoolboy prank; it is only gradually, as he becomes lost, that the suggestive details that heighten the sense of mystery begin to build imperceptibly. (Hence Meaulnes falls asleep immediately before his arrival and after his departure from the domain. This adds to its dreamlike quality but also underlines its significance as a symbolic projection of unconscious processes unfolding in the adolescent Meaulnes.)

Moreover, the whole journey to the *fête étrange* not only bears the earmarks of the Grail legend but also duplicates the customary rites and events associated with primitive initiation rituals. Like an archetypal hero of medieval or ancient mythology, Meaulnes strays from the limited and myopic confines of Sainte-Agathe, engages in the quest for a nameless goal that transfigures his existence, and then returns to his former state with the presumed intent of lifting his associates to an awareness of their potentialities. It is at this point, however, that the analogy between Meaulnes and the legendary hero of romance breaks down. Although Meaulnes's journey reflects the tripartite movement of separation, initiation, and return (which Joseph Campbell notes, in his 1949 book *The Hero with a Thousand Faces*, is paradigmatic in Western myth), Meaulnes fails to complete the return journey successfully. Instead of pointing the way to his fellow students, Meaulnes remains stuck in one phase of his development. Instead of accepting a workaday existence and transforming it from the perspective of his adventure, he clings to the thrills and trappings of the mysterious *fête*, refusing to accept anything of lesser intensity or to prize any goal of slighter significance. In a word, Meaulnes's journey to the domain bears the earmarks of a rite that misses completion.

After coming to a crossroads (which is perhaps more significant when understood psychologically than when viewed topographically), Meaulnes, in descending from the cart, stumbles, hurting both his head and his knee. Not only do these wounds connect him symbolically with Frantz and Seurel but they are also equivalent to the symbolic wounds sustained in primitive cultures by young novices in preparation for adulthood. These wounds represent the death of the old unawakened self and signal the candidate's rebirth into a higher, more complex plane of existence. Moreover, Meaulnes's first glimpse of the domain is provided by children (who, the reader simultaneously learns, are totally in charge of the proceedings), and, on the evening prior to his "initiation," Meaulnes sleeps in an abandoned sheepfold, where, in an effort to keep warm, he wraps himself in his smock, drawing up his knees in an embryonic pose. As Mircea Eliade has demonstrated in his book *Le Sacré et la profane* (1956; *The Sacred and the Profane: The Nature of Religion*, 1959), the primitive initiation rite customarily begins with a ceremony in which the novice is cared for and led by the hand like a child; rebirth requires a preliminary reversion to the state of primal virtuality associated with infancy. Meaulnes's symbolic pose and his return to childhood are thus preparatory to his rebirth as an adult.

On the two evenings prior to his first glimpse of Yvonne, moreover, Meaulnes has a series of dreams—one of his mother seated at the piano, the other of a girl sewing in a long green room—that forecast his encounter with Yvonne. (As Eliade has noted, the rite of passage involves the recognition of three dimensions of existence: sexuality, death, and the sacred. Meaulnes's meeting with Yvonne reflects the first of these dimensions.) Interestingly, pianos and sewing machines function as symbolic counterparts throughout the novel and connect each of the female figures with Meaulnes's subconscious image of the "eternal feminine." Seurel's mother is a seamstress who makes her own hats; Yvonne is first seen, like Meaulnes's mother in his dream, seated at the piano; and Valentine earns her living as a seamstress. Each of these women is a variant of that buried feminine component that each man carries in his unconscious—what the Swiss psychologist Carl Jung calls the "anima," or feminine portion, of the male ego. At the moment of "falling in love," according to Jung, this unconscious image—partly derived from ancestral memories, partly colored by the child's first contact with women—attaches itself to a particular woman; hence the coalescent images of femininity that cluster about Yvonne. (Significantly, both Meaulnes's mother and Yvonne are associated with mother hens whose fledglings are missing from their brood.)

Meaulnes's courtship of Yvonne at the lost domain involves both of them in a primitive reversion to childhood—a reversion that is not that unusual when placed in the context of modern psychology. Scientists have ob-

served that the mating calls of birds resemble the sounds of fledglings in their nests, and everyone is familiar with the endearing diminutives and the so-called billing and cooing that characterize the private talk of lovers. Unfortunately for Meaulnes, however, this stage of psychological projection and childhood reverie, which diversifies the initial stages of courtship before the lovers are "reborn" into the world of adult responsibility, is never transcended; in consequence, he fails to discriminate between the projected image of Yvonne and the real flesh-and-blood woman with distinct needs and perceptions of her own. Moreover, it is his failure to integrate his concept of woman into a composite whole that divides him between Yvonne and Valentine. Each of the women is associated with a fragmentary portion of Meaulnes's anima. In consequence, Meaulnes remains divided between the chaste and disincarnate image of Yvonne and the seductive, potentially explosive image of Valentine. It would be a mistake, however, to assume that the episode of the *fête étrange* is entirely reducible to clinical psychology. Meaulnes's predicament has both ethical and religious dimensions, which Alain-Fournier is at pains to suggest.

The sleep with which Meaulnes's adventure is rounded out not only connects the events at the lost domain with Meaulnes's subconscious but also hints of the atemporal nature of Meaulnes's experience. Commenting on that moment in the rite of passage when the novice reverts to a childlike state, Eliade observes that "this state is not meant only in terms of human physiology but also in terms of a regression to virtual, precosmic life: the womb of uncreated Being." In short, the *fête étrange* involves a recognition of that second component in the rite of passage: the reality of the sacred. Like the Gardens of Adonis in Edmund Spenser's *The Faerie Queene* (1590, 1596), the lost domain represents the original ground of being or "pre-cosmic womb" out of which all life proceeds. Thus, the revelers dress in period costumes, embracing and, hence, transcending the manifold changes of history. The party itself is a Saturnalia and takes place during Christmas. Although it is midwinter, a springlike warmth in the air adds to the sense of atemporality. "Midwinter spring is its own season/ Sempiternal though sodden towards sundown" writes T. S. Eliot on the moment of Pentecost in *Four*

Quartets (1943). Here, too, a "midwinter spring" suggests the moment of the intersection of eternity with time, the sense of an infinite present, an eternal now, which both Alain-Fournier and Eliot associated with the immediacy of childhood. (Significantly, Alain-Fournier was Eliot's French tutor, so the connection is less fortuitous than it might seem.)

Why, then, given all of these positive ingredients and connotations, is Meaulnes irretrievably ruined by the experience of the *fête*? To answer this question, one must turn to Yvonne's brother, Frantz de Galais. If Seurel comes close to embodying Meaulnes's ethical sense, then Frantz is representative of Meaulnes's id—that is, the urge to self-gratification regardless of consequences. Frantz's love for Valentine caricatures Meaulnes's love for Yvonne in the same way that Frantz's gypsylike wanderings are a distorted and counterfeit version of Meaulnes's quest for the ideal. Meaulnes progressively succumbs to the lure of Frantz's emotional restlessness. While childhood and adolescence are celebrated in this novel as stages that, in the development of the ego, must be assimilated rather than left behind, Alain-Fournier demonstrates, in the character of Frantz, the fatal consequences that befall those who fail to integrate the freshness of childhood and the self-dedication of adolescence into the mature perspectives of adulthood. Frantz is the "spoiled child" unable to apply an inner check to his expansive impulses.

Despite his efforts to return to the lost domain, Meaulnes finally prefers to live on the memory of Yvonne and in the spell of his former adventure. When he meets Yvonne a second time at the outing arranged by Seurel, he evokes two items (significantly compared to bits of "wreckage") from his first night's stay at Les Sablonnières: the lute with the broken strings and the large oval mirror. The broken lute recalls the figure of Orpheus; the mirror, Narcissus. Like the mythic poet Orpheus, Meaulnes fails to retrieve his lost Eurydice from the underworld (which, in Meaulnes's instance, must be construed as a failure to dissociate and, hence, liberate Yvonne from her status as an idealized projection of Meaulnes's ego); like Narcissus, Meaulnes never outgrows the self-infatuation of adolescence. (The episode at the *fête* in which Meaulnes admires his reflection in a standing pool is especially pertinent.)

The items that clutter Meaulnes's bed at Les Sablonnières (the candelabra and broken lute) point to the sexual element in Meaulnes's rite of passage. They are symbolic descendants of the lance and cup sought by the Knights of the Holy Grail; like the lance and cup, they may be construed, on one level, as emblems of sexual fertility. Meaulnes's polarized conception of femininity—Yvonne and Valentine, virgin and whore—is never fully resolved; in consequence, he vacillates between opposing images of womanhood and fails to establish an authentic relationship with either his mistress or his wife. In addition, Meaulnes remains hopelessly divided between opposing impulses: celibacy contra marriage, the contemplative life contra the domestic life. At one point, he writes to Seurel apropos of his experience at the domain: "Our adventure is ended. The winter of this year is as dead as the grave. Perhaps when we come to die, death will be the meaning and the sequel and the ending of this unsuccessful adventure." Meaulnes, here, demonstrates a clear-sighted Christian stoicism. Rejecting the "dialectic of desire," he recognizes that, for him, the lost domain must not be construed narrowly as a final resting place or identified simplistically with the figure of Yvonne. A return to the scene of his former inspiration would not produce the desired effect; as his words denote, it is only in another dimension that he will find the elusive essence that he seeks. Unfortunately, this insight is not sustained for long. Immediately following his letter to Seurel, Meaulnes engages in an affair with Valentine Blondeau—entirely unconscious of her former relations with Frantz.

At this point, the novel deepens in moral complexity. Is the reader to believe, as Meaulnes would have it, that if Valentine had remained faithful to Frantz (instead of retreating in the face of her fiancé's lofty ideals), an unbroken felicity would have been guaranteed for all? When Meaulnes discovers Valentine's identity, he throws this accusation in her face and abandons her to what, in the context of the novel's Victorian mores, is her only alternative: a life of prostitution. Meaulnes's accusation, however, is more accurately applicable to himself: If *he* had remained faithful to his former impulses, if he had clearly discriminated between the love of woman and the search for the absolutes of perfection, if he had been able to recognize the difference between emotional restlessness and divine discontent, then Valentine, Yvonne, Seurel, and he would not be subject to the disequilibrium of Meaulnes's undisciplined will. In a preliminary version of the novel, Alain-Fournier intended to have Meaulnes pursue a religious vocation (an ending that the author wisely revised on recognizing its incompatibility with the novel's elusive textures); traces of Meaulnes's religious orientation are preserved in the following words, which he addresses to Seurel:

> But how can a man who has once strayed into heaven ever hope to make terms with the earth! What passes for happiness with most people seemed contemptible to me. And when I tried deliberately and sincerely to live like the rest of them I stored up enough remorse to last me a very long time.

(Significantly, even Seurel is not devoid of culpability; he entirely misses the point of Meaulnes's words and pushes his friend in the direction of Yvonne without reflecting on Meaulnes's unfitness for domestic life.)

Meaulnes's remorse is associated with his treatment of Valentine, but it is not Valentine alone who is victimized by his vacillation. On the evening of his marriage to Yvonne, Meaulnes abandons his bride, presumably to assist Frantz in recovering his fiancé. Although Meaulnes is able to reunite Frantz and Valentine, his exertions on Frantz's behalf are self-deceiving. The short-lived nature of Frantz's liaison with Valentine becomes apparent when, on their return to Les Sablonnières, they enter the playhouse formerly constructed by Monsieur de Galais for his errant son. They are no more than two children "playing house" before the onset of a mutual, estranging tantrum. On the pretext of aiding his friend, Meaulnes has been able to circumvent his greatest fear: a candid and responsible relationship with a mature woman.

THE HEROINE

A final word remains to be said about the novel's enigmatic heroine, Yvonne de Galais. It is difficult to assess the precise nature of her role in the novel. On one hand, she is tender, domestic, maternal, and down-to-earth. Seurel finds her, after all, in the least exotic of settings: the country store of his Uncle Florentin. Moreover, she enunciates a position that is in every way antagonistic to the romantic excesses of her brother and

would-be lover. As she says to François on learning that he intends to teach school like his father,

> But most of all, I would teach those boys to be sensible. I'd impress upon them a kind of wisdom I do know something about. I wouldn't fill their heads with a desire to go roaming about the world, as you will probably do, Monsieur Seurel, once you're an instructor. I'd teach them how to find the happiness which, if they only knew it, is within easy reach.

At the same time, Yvonne is regarded, at least by Meaulnes and Seurel, as a sort of Dantesque mediator between the divine and the human: a breathing incarnation of the absolutes of purity and grace.

To the end, however, these estimates of Yvonne are ambiguous. Like Simone Weil's God, a "beggar waiting for our love," she waits patiently and without censure for the love that neither Frantz nor Meaulnes is mature enough to give, yet this uncritical acceptance of her brother's petulance and her husband's shortcomings contributes to her demise. Whether she is considered a pathetically exploited victim or a Christ figure, she is, at any rate, destroyed by a male mentality that distorts the interpersonal situation of love by regarding the woman almost exclusively from an aesthetic point of view. Only Seurel can see her from a point of view other than his own.

It is especially in her death that Yvonne repudiates the emotional restlessness of the male protagonists and reaffirms her conviction that authentic existence is to be grasped not in some remote and alluring never-never land but in the quotidian world of relationships and commitments. When her coffin proves too bulky to fit up the stairs, one of the bearers suggests that it may be hoisted up through the window and lowered in the same way. At this point, Seurel intervenes and carries the inert body of Yvonne down the steps in a sequence that lends a cruel irony to the traditional image of a groom carrying his bride over the threshold. (This episode, with its macabre sexual overtones, reveals that Seurel, as Meaulnes's follower, is equally afflicted with a fear of women: It is only in death that Yvonne may be safely embraced.) Yvonne cannot be lowered through the window, for, from the inception of the novel, window imagery repeatedly signals a flight from reality or a transposition to another dimension of experience. Meaulnes's arrival at Sainte-Agathe is heralded by his mother tapping on Seurel's window; both Meaulnes and Frantz enter the lost domain through a window, and Meaulnes is awakened in the carriage bearing him away from his adventure by a tap on the window. Frantz's disruption of Meaulnes's happiness is foreshadowed by the sound of a dead rose branch tapping the window of the newlyweds' cottage; it is at the shuttered windows of the Galaises' Parisian residence that Meaulnes stands vigil prior to his meeting with Valentine. Before her death, Yvonne watches steadfastly at the window for Meaulnes's return; yet inasmuch as, at the end of the novel, the window imagery loses its initial connotations of mystery, transcendence, and wonder and declines into a motif associated with irresponsible escapism, it is impossible, given her scale of values, for Yvonne to pass through a window, even in death.

By the same token, one of Yvonne's last gestures summarizes and brings to final significance the pattern of images associated with birds and nests. In an evening walk prior to her confinement, Yvonne and Seurel are caught in a sudden rain shower that obliges them to seek shelter in the abandoned playhouse of Frantz. On the threshold, they discover a brood of newly hatched chickens, most of which have died. Yvonne separates the living ones in a gesture of maternal solicitude. This moment consummates the series of images that, from the novel's inception, foreshadow disaster and defeat. Meaulnes's mother, upon her first appearance at Sainte-Agathe, is described as having "the look of a hen whose wild changeling is missing from the brood." When Meaulnes meets Seurel's mother, she clutches her hat (which is compared to a nest) close to her breast in a gesture with strong psychological overtones: The domestic nest needs to be protected against an intruder like Meaulnes. The dead squirrel, in a basket brought by a student on the day of Meaulnes's departure, is a permutation of the same image. Ganache supports himself and Frantz by stealing chicken eggs, and on the day when Seurel receives a hint of Meaulnes's lost trail, the other schoolboys are "playing hooky" to hunt for nest eggs. The violated or overturned nest becomes, in consequence, another image that obliquely comments on the novel's themes: the molestation of childhood, the loss of

innocence, the failure to develop emotionally and spiritually.

By the end of the novel, this failure, beginning with Meaulnes, radiates outward and affects everyone with whom he comes in contact. Hence, Meaulnes's head wound on the way to the lost domain is reiterated in the bruised head of his baby, the wound that Yvonne sustains as she rushes outside to intercept her brother and bring back her husband, and the scar that disfigures the forehead of Frantz de Galais.

A CAUTIONARY TALE

The Wanderer, ultimately, is a cautionary tale; it embodies a sense of reality that is distinctly antiromantic and implicitly warns against the extravagances to which an untempered romanticism is prone. Its hero, Meaulnes, is a conspicuous example of bad faith. He leaves Yvonne for the putative purpose of reuniting Valentine with Frantz—but the reader realizes, and so must he, that such a union is ill-advised and without substance. He seeks for a purity that is not of this world, but he marries a woman who exists for him exclusively as a symbol of that purity. He both solicits and recoils from the demands of marriage and the responsibilities of parenthood, confusing Heaven with earth, the supernatural with the natural, the divine with the human. Desiring all or nothing, he wrecks the happiness that comes with an acceptance of human limit yet lacks the dedication, the disdain for comfort, and the single-minded tenacity of the hero or the saint. A final estimate of Meaulnes is leavened with compassion, however. Seurel's grave and musical prose, his sense of the sadness and inscrutability of human existence, and his fidelity to the memories of Meaulnes and Yvonne are a palliative to the novel's grim conclusion and temper the tragedy with grace notes.

Stephen I. Gurney

OTHER MAJOR WORKS

NONFICTION: *Correspondance avec Jacques Rivière, 1905-1914*, 1926-1928; *Lettres au petit B.*, 1930; *Lettres d'Alain-Fournier à sa famille, 1905-1914*, 1930; *Towards the Lost Domain: Letters from London, 1905*, 1986 (W. J. Strachan, editor).

MISCELLANEOUS: *Miracles*, 1924 (poetry and short stories).

BIBLIOGRAPHY

Cancalon, Elaine D. *Fairy-Tale Structures and Motifs in "Le Grand Meaulnes."* New York: Peter Lang, 1975. Provides a stimulating discussion of an important element in Alain-Fournier's novel.

Ford, Edward. *Alain-Fournier and "Le Grand Meaulnes" ("The Wanderer").* Lewiston, N.Y.: Edwin Mellen Press, 1999. Discusses Alain-Fournier's life and his interest in primitivism, arguing that *Le Grand Meaulnes* is a primitivist novel. Explains the novel's structure, the literary influences that shaped Alain-Fournier's work, and the novel's influence on other writers.

Gibson, Robert. *Alain-Fournier: "Le Grand Meaulnes."* London: Grant & Cutler, 1986. Brief yet excellent in-depth study of the novel is the work of a scholar many consider to be the leading authority on Alain-Fournier in the English-speaking world.

_____. *The End of Youth: The Life and Work of Alain-Fournier.* Exeter, England: Impress, 2005. Gibson, who published his first biography of Alain-Fournier in 1953, reassesses the author's life and work based on newly discovered information. Includes new material about the two great loves of Alain-Fournier's life, Yvonne de Quièvrecourt and "Simone," the leading boulevard actress of her day, as well as many letters from Alain-Fournier's friends and fellow writers, a compilation of his work as a literary gossip columnist, the complete drafts of his second novel, and the plays left unfinished when he went off to war in 1914.

Gurney, Stephen. *Alain-Fournier.* Boston: Twayne, 1987. Presents an informative general introduction to the life and work of Alain-Fournier.

Turnell, Martin. *The Rise of the French Novel: Marivaux, Crèbillon fils, Rousseau, Stendhal, Flaubert, Alain-Fournier, Raymond Radiguet.* New York: New Directions, 1978. Discussion of important French authors devotes a chapter to Alain-Fournier, providing biographical information as well as analysis of *The Wanderer* and *Miracles*.

Ullmann, Stephen. "The Symbol of the Sea in *Le Grand Meaulnes*." In *The Image in the Modern French Novel: Gide, Alain-Fournier, Proust, Camus.* 1960. Reprint. Westport, Conn.: Greenwood Press, 1977. Chapter examining sea imagery in Alain-Fournier's novel is part of a larger work on the use of symbolism by four important modern French novelists.

LEOPOLDO ALAS

Born: Zamora, Spain; April 25, 1852
Died: Oviedo, Spain; June 13, 1901
Also known as: Leopoldo Enrique García Alas y Ureña; Clarín

PRINCIPAL LONG FICTION

La regenta, 1884 (2 volumes; English translation, 1984)
Su único hijo, 1890 (*His Only Son*, 1970)

OTHER LITERARY FORMS

In addition to two major novels, Leopoldo Alas (AHL-ahs) published more than eighty short stories or novelettes, including "Pipá," "Doña Berta" (English translation), "El sombreto del señor cura," "¡Adiós, Cordera!" (English translation), "Dos sabios," and "Zurrita." Many of these pieces have been collected and republished under such titles as *Cuentos morales* (1896, 1973), *¡Adiós, Cordera! y otros cuentos* (1944), *Cuentos de Clarín* (1954), and *Cuentos escogidos* (1964). Alas's collections of literary and political essays include *El derecho y la moralidad* (doctoral thesis, 1878), *Solos de Clarín* (1881, 1971), *La literatura en 1881* (1882; with Armando Palacio Valdés), *Nueva campaña, 1885-1886* (1887), *Mezclilla* (1889), *Ensayos y revistas* (1892), *Palique* (1893, 1973), and *Galdós* (1912). His only attempt at theater is the play *Teresa* (pr., pb. 1895). An important general compilation of Alas's work is that of

Juan Antonio Cabezas, *Obras selectas* (1947, 1966), which includes both of the major novels, twenty-five short stories, and thirty-seven articles.

ACHIEVEMENTS

Leopoldo Alas, frequently known by his pseudonym Clarín, is considered one of the four or five most important figures of nineteenth century Spanish realism, along with Benito Pérez Galdós, Emilia Pardo Bazán, Juan Valera, and José María de Pereda. While Alas was recognized early in his literary career for the excellence of his short stories and for the biting criticism of his essays, he was, like Stendhal, generally misunderstood by his own generation. His fame now rests primarily on his two major and lengthy works, particularly *La regenta*, considered by many critics as the second greatest novel in the Spanish language, after Miguel de Cervantes' *Don Quixote de la Mancha* (1605, 1615). Since the centennial celebration of Alas's birth in 1952, studies of his best short stories and of *His Only Son* have finally brought about a relatively balanced view of his artistic achievements.

Alas was one of the most prolific and certainly one of the most feared of all literary critics in Spain during the second half of the nineteenth century. By the end of his life, he could lash out mercilessly at a mistake in grammar by some aspiring writer or politician and, by a single stroke of the pen, destroy that person's career. With respect to literary ideology, his essays call, above all, for a realism based on exactness of observation and psychological depth, within a moral framework. Alas also was one of the few to insist that his contemporaries inform themselves of literary developments taking place north of the Pyrenees.

BIOGRAPHY

Leopoldo Enrique García Alas y Ureña, the third son of a local civil governor, was born on April 25, 1852, in Zamora, a town some 250 kilometers (155 miles) northwest of Madrid, Spain. At the age of seven, he was sent to the Jesuit *colegio* of San Marcos in León, where he spent several happy months despite the fact that his blond hair, short and slight stature, and myopic vision set him apart somewhat from his schoolmates. It was there that he began to develop both the sentimentality and the sense of

moral discipline that were to become so evident in his later thought and writing.

The following summer, Alas and his family moved to the northern city of Oviedo, where he was to spend the rest of his life and which was to be the setting for his masterpiece *La regenta*. While working for his *bachillerato*, he continued to develop an extremely competitive spirit, as he strove to compensate for physical weaknesses by a precocious and inquiring mind. During his fourth year of study, Alas and his classmates were profoundly moved by the revolution of General Juan Prim and its aftermath, and it was during this period that Alas began to contemplate the complexities of social justice and the disillusionments that arise when idealized hopes are dashed by the harsh realities of political life.

At age twenty, Alas was in Madrid, preparing for his doctorate and feeling nervous, melancholy, and increasingly homesick for his native Asturias. A naturally critical temperament and a stubborn reluctance to embrace philosophical or literary fads delayed his acceptance of Sanz del Río's Krausism and the naturalistic approach being preached by Émile Zola, but, as with his subsequent ideological views, once these ideas were accepted, Alas was to defend them with sincerity and passion.

At age twenty-three, Alas began publishing articles in Madrid-based journals, and in October, 1875, he adopted the pseudonym Clarín. The name was chosen perhaps in lighthearted recognition of Pedro Calderón de la Barca's famous gracioso in *La vida es sueño* (1635; *Life Is a Dream*, 1830) or perhaps because of the musical tradition of the time, by which an orchestra might pause to allow for a clear, often moving solo by the clarion, or *clarín*. Alas's barbs soon produced many enemies, and it was not long before he found himself forced to change sidewalks to avoid confrontations; he took to target shooting and fencing lessons in preparation for some inevitable duels.

One immediate result of Alas's critical pen came when the minister of public instruction, one of the figures whom the young writer had derided in print, rejected him for the *cátedra*, or professorship, of political economy at the University of Madrid, despite the youth's having clearly surpassed his competitors in the *oposiciones*. This experience was a bitter lesson in social and political realities, one that would be reflected in the biting satire of *La regenta* and in some of the short stories.

Two years of happiness followed, however, as Alas fell in love with and married Onofre García Argüelles and was awarded two *cátedras*, first in Zaragoza and then, in 1883, at the University of Oviedo. There followed a period of intense writing, with little sleep and but a few mouthfuls of food a day. A feverish creative effort produced the second volume within six months, despite the severe emotional impact of his father's death. Not surprisingly, Alas's health began to fail. Increasingly disillusioned with society, he continued to produce articles exposing truths few wanted to hear. In some areas, his power became immense, as illustrated by the firing of a public official because of Alas's anger at the official's mispronunciation of a single word.

During the summer of 1892, while secluded in his beloved country retreat at Guimarán, Alas suffered a severe mental crisis, but he soon recovered with the rediscovery of the sentimentality and religious contentment of his youth. This change became evident immediately afterward in some of his short stories, particularly "Cambio de luz" and, later, those in *Cuentos morales*. Alas's long resistance to proper medical care finally caught up with him, however, and, overcome by intestinal tuberculosis, he died on June 13, 1901.

ANALYSIS

The realistic novel in Spain arose out of a particular set of historical circumstances and from diverse streams of intellectual growth. These included social and economic factors (the rise of a middle-class, materialistic society, the Revolution of 1868, and the underlying political, religious, and economic corruption of the Restoration period) and scientific influences (positivism, Darwinism, and the Industrial Revolution). They also included philosophical currents (the eighteenth century position that truth can be discovered through the senses and, later, the influence of Krausism), and, most particularly, such literary developments as the influence of and reaction against Romanticism, currents from France (the realism of Honoré de Balzac, Gustave Flaubert, and Stendhal, and Zola's naturalism), and the rediscovery of Cervantine and traditional Spanish realism.

The Spanish realistic novel, particularly as exemplified by Alas, revealed some points of emphasis that differed from the French: a stronger continuity of thought and feeling with previous Romantic tendencies, a more pronounced stress on spiritual and religious matters, a regionalist framework (such as Alas's focus on Asturias and Oviedo), and the constant presence of the Cervantine influence. The last characteristic included the special use of character and authorial perspectives that expose the ambiguity and complexity of reality, a distinctive brand of literary irony, and devices that produce the effect of character autonomy.

Within this general framework, Alas's linguistic refinements and extremely subjective point of view deviated from the slightly more objective approach of many of his own Spanish contemporaries. Furthermore, while all realistic writers were critical of their environment, Alas, more than most, failed to camouflage his didactic stance. His realism, rather, is to be found in the solidity and extraordinary depth of his major psychological studies, his powers of observation and the resulting exactness of detail, and his intricate play of character-author perspectives. Like most of the major novelists of the second half of the nineteenth century in Spain, Alas evolved somewhat in his later years away from the realistic-naturalistic focus toward a more "idealistic" inspiration. Leo Tolstoy, rather than Balzac or Zola, became the most significant foreign influence during this period. The Asturian writer came to abandon, to an extent, his preoccupation with aesthetic theory and literary novelty in the search for a more transcendent, spiritual, often symbolic approach.

LA REGENTA

La regenta, Alas's first and greatest novel, stands as one of the supreme achievements of nineteenth century realism in Spain and the rest of Europe. In it, one can see a reawakening in the Iberian Peninsula of what György Lukács called the "novel of romantic disillusionment." Certainly, it is one of the most powerful creations of modern psychological realism. In *La regenta*, all of Alas's literary theories were put into effect: A strong, ideological tone and theme provided a framework for exploring psychological motivations; the actualities of contemporary Spanish society are portrayed; and the smallest of details contributes to artistic ends.

The work reflects the author's conception of art as an *ancha ventana abierta* (wide-open window), in which Alas the critic could search for justice, Alas the educator could search for truth, and Alas the artist could search for beauty.

The book is many things in one: an autobiography (in its reflection of the author's own personality, culture, ideology, and actual experiences); a regional novel (to the extent that its setting, called Vetusta, is the city of Oviedo); a treatise on national traits, both historical and contemporary; and the greatest of all Spanish "naturalistic" creations. (One must add, immediately, that none of the major realistic novelists in Spain subscribed totally to Zola's concept of philosophical determinism or to full descriptive treatment of grotesque or crude realities.)

Despite the novel's length and complexity, the basic threads of the action can be summarized in a few sentences. In broadest terms, the plot traces the process by which the heroine, Ana Ozores, is drawn into an adulterous relationship with an aristocratic Don Juan, Alvaro Mesía. Conflict arises from Ana's physical attraction to Alvaro, which battles against idealistic, spiritual impulses nurtured by her confessor, Don Fermín de Pas, and natural inclination versus conjugal duty. The rest of the plot is a study of these figures and the behavior of literally hundreds of other characters who inhabit a city plagued by political corruption and social and moral degeneration. Ana's vacillations—the very basis for the action as well as the novel's style and structure—dramatize the need for love, both in the form of human companionship and in what Sherman Eoff has called "a personal and sympathetic relationship with Deity."

Alas's tone, his approach to his characters, and his setting are not "realistically" neutral. The author's own feelings range through sarcasm, criticism, displeasure, hatred, sympathy, derision, and open, light humor. Just as evident, if not as pertinent to the work's artistry, however, are Alas's ideological, utilitarian themes; his condemnation of indifference, narrowness, provincialism, ignorance, pedantry, moral degradation, religious hypocrisy, and political corruption; and his dissection of a city in which, as Michael Nimetz puts it, "sex and religion occupy the same shrine and neutralize each other in the process," thus producing a state of general frustration.

Alas's irony is present everywhere. The many types and variations of ironic comment range from those that are primarily linguistic ("Vetusta, la muy noble y leal ciudad . . . hacía la digestión del cocido y de la olla podrida") to those directed toward characterization, as in descriptions of such minor characters as Don Saturnino; those related to manners or customs of the general population, as in the description of the casino library, where the books are "de más sólida enseñanza" but where "la llave de aquel departamento se había perdido"; and those that present purer, more open humor (as in Don Víctor's reenactments of Calderonian honor plays).

The implied author's actual position—that is, his presence as it relates to the action—can best be described in the words of Frank Durand.

> Alas believed the author (as opposed to a character within the novel) to be best qualified to interpret a character's thoughts, actions, and motivations. . . . Because Alas knows all, the reader not only sees characters through the author's eyes but, entering their consciousness, sees reality through the eyes of the characters themselves. Thus the author's omniscient point of view carries within itself, so to speak, narrower individual points of view. The resultant multiple perspectives serve to delineate the different characters as well as to develop the major themes and the main action of the novel.

At times the author himself is clearly speaking. At other moments, the reader is projected into the thoughts and feelings of the major characters. The judicious combination of these two points of view allows for an extensive as well as an intensive view of the characters and the city, and serves also to maintain a high level of interest throughout an extremely lengthy narrative.

With respect to language, realism is enhanced by the following elements: the inclusion of extremely exact detail, a frequent appeal to the senses, vivid imagery designed to highlight the animal nature of the city and its inhabitants, and a nearly constant sense of theatrical immediacy. Some stylistic traits, however, reveal the author's conscious attempt to draw attention to language itself and thus to rise above realism: the use of reiteration, frequent "extremist" tendencies (antithetical expressions, hyperboles, paradoxes), and authorial allusions (usually ironic) to art or literature.

Much of Alas's realism depends on the creation of what might be called a total atmospheric reality. With the exception of Pèrez Galdós's *Fortunata y Jacinta* (1886-1887; *Fortunata and Jacinta: Two Stories of Married Women*, 1973), *La regenta* captures the urban social and physical milieu more completely than any single Spanish work of the nineteenth century. Few modern readers would deny that the novel is too long. The outcome of Ana's story is powerful, however, precisely because the process preceding it goes on for so long. The background descriptions are, at the least, needed for an understanding of the external pressures and the heaviness of the material world that contribute to the denouement. The atmosphere of Vetusta (Oviedo) is in itself a major antagonist in the novel. Above all, the novel's descriptions contribute to the author's central goal: character study, the attempt to reveal the psychological complexity that positivistic naturalism had reduced to a series of systematized formulas. While the secondary figures are meant to represent types, Ana Ozores and Don Fermín de Pas are remarkably real and autonomous.

Several significant methods are used to achieve this depth. Alas reveals his characters from multiple perspectives: To the reader, the characters appear as what they are, what they think they are, and what others think they are. Frequently, actual mirrors are used to dramatize this complex play of perspectives. All the major characters are actors. The reader, also engulfed in so many points of view, tends also to confuse illusion and reality. The result is a sense of the characters' distance and autonomy from authorial control, a Cervantine appearance of verisimilitude. The use of purposeful contrasts and parallels among the major and minor figures—such as de Pas's spiritual motivations versus Alvaro's licentious intentions, Don Víctor's preoccupations versus Ana's troubles, Obdulia versus Visitación, Camoirán or Cayetano versus Mourelo—constitutes another means of making the characters more vivid and more plausible.

Alas traces, carefully and logically, the historical and environmental origins and the subsequent development of Ana's predicament: her need for love and her yearning for a child. The factors presented include the lack of a mother's presence, the frequent absence of her father, the cruelty of her nurse Doña Camila, a frightening night when she is stranded alone on a boat with her childhood playmate, the later treatment she receives from an indifferent father, the hypocrisy and cruelty of her aunts, her escape through a marriage without love, the depressive atmosphere of Vetusta, the plots of Visitación and Alvaro to effect her downfall, and the advice of Don Fermín. Her turn to religion (in the person of her confessor, Don Fermín), of course, thwarts even further her psychological, sexual, and maternal cravings. Ana is an individualistic creation, neither all good nor all evil. An inherent vanity, for example, offsets the purity of her intentions. Nevertheless, she also offers a mixture of traits and perspectives that is definitely representative of the Spanish people: a quixotic "madness," masochistic tendencies, mystical inclinations, the need for love and approval, a strong sense of pride and individuality, and, above all, a romantic, idealistic nature.

The author seems to have had even closer affinity to the personality and aspirations of the other main character. Although Don Fermín's flaws occasionally suggest a symbolic role of evil incarnate (vanity, hypocrisy, cruelty, desire for power), he is, nevertheless, a completely convincing, individualized figure. Conflicting desires for power and for escape from the vulgar existence of Vetusta create many of his frustrations. Dominated from childhood by an overpowering, ambitious mother and lacking, like Ana, the love and affection that go with a normal upbringing, he sees the regenta as a threefold means of achieving his own mental stability and satisfaction: He can help another human being by offering spiritual assistance; he can satisfy his need to dominate; and, unconsciously, he can find sexual release. Ironically, the last two impulses, his desire for conquest and his passion, lead him to forget the wisest means of approach. The first motivation, of course, reveals that he is not entirely evil. In essence, he is an ambiguous creation.

La regenta is thus fundamentally the story of two individuals who are frustrated by their environment and by the absence of love; each is trapped within a social role (wife, priest), and each sees in the other a chance for salvation. Both exemplify vividly the metaphysical conflict between a single perceiving consciousness and the social environment, between aspiration and realization, between illusion and reality—warring factors that constitute the basis of Alas's realism as well as the approach of the Spanish realistic movement in general.

The other characters function mainly in relation to these two figures and exemplify type portraiture: Alvaro as a cowardly and calculating Don Juan, the symbol of *poder laico*; Doña Paula (see María Remedios in Pèrez Galdós's *Doña Perfecta*, 1876; English translation, 1880) typifying the forces of avarice and tyranny; the maid Petra as the marvelous embodiment of what one critic calls "suspicacia y socarronería de personaje de clase popular . . . muy español"; and so on.

Alas's artistry is revealed in many ways that surpass the usual limits of nineteenth century realistic delineation. His use of symbolism (for example, the banquet scene in the casino, which ironically parallels Leonardo da Vinci's depiction of the Last Supper) and meticulous structural planning demonstrate clearly the depth of his originality. With respect to the latter element, such critics as J. I. Ferreras and Durand have analyzed in detail the complicated network of parallels and calculated contrasts, the elements of a "circular" nature and the complex system of flashbacks that constitute the novel's narrative construction.

Contrary to the opinion of many critics, *La regenta* is not a simple example of Zolaesque naturalism. Ana's personality and her downfall are not the direct result of the moral laxity around her; they stem, rather, from her reactions against the city. Her adultery is a kind of triumph of love, possible only after twenty-eight chapters of careful, convincing preparation. The final *desenlace* (conclusion) is brought about by fortuitous circumstances (Petra's actions). Alas is saying that the pressures of the environment are strong and, in fact, may cause changes in a person's life. Yet the instances of free will in *La regenta*, along with the moments of humorous satire mentioned above, illustrate the author's rejection of Zola's sweeping pessimism and the maintenance of a more traditionally Spanish point of view.

In *La regenta*, Alas demonstrates most clearly his own particular version of the Spanish realistic formula. His utilitarian approach, his highly subjective irony and satire, his deliberate artistry in manipulating language—these and other elements reflect the author's conscious rejection of strictly realistic writing. In his usually explicit statement of themes, he departed from the norm of his Spanish contemporaries, yet his attention to exactness and detail, the numerous variations on authorial and character perspective, and the profundity of the novel's psychological studies reveal a true attempt to achieve a complete or total transcription of genuine human conflicts and aspirations.

HIS ONLY SON

If *La regenta* is characterized by the ridicule of provincial customs through carefully detailed description, *His Only Son* reduces society to its most dominating, abstract features: The precise delineation of physical settings and realistic conflicts is replaced by an operatic universe of melodramatic contrivances and the invisible, inner elements of psychological reverie. *His Only Son* is a novel of transition, reflecting the decline of naturalism and the competing influence of various fin de siècle trends: Idealistic, symbolic, and decadent elements combine with a distinctly modern flavor, a purposeful ambiguity that forces the reader to participate more actively in the interpretation of events. Masculine and feminine roles are confused or reversed, the plot exhibits surprising turns of direction, and a more "authentic," alienated protagonist anticipates the problematic hero of the *generación del 98*, or Generation of '98. Its first readers saw the novel as a Zolaesque study of eroticism and physiological needs, and its emphasis on psychology over externality and its very subjective comic vein reveal a distinct divergence from naturalistic practices.

Critics have been particularly perplexed by the work's ambiguity (the time and setting are indefinite, the question of the hero's paternity is left unresolved, and so on), not realizing until years later that Alas was attempting a very Cervantine statement concerning the relativism and lack of clarity of everyday reality. The plot line itself is simple and, in fact, almost insignificant. In a poor, provincial town, Bonifacio Reyes (Bonis), of a family in decline, marries the despotic Emma Valcárcel but soon becomes the lover of Serafina Gorgheggi, a member of an opera company. Emma, amid an atmosphere of corruption and abulia and provoked by the entrance into her house of the Italian singers, becomes involved in an affair with the baritone Minghetti. Eventually, Bonis's main preoccupation turns from the romantic fantasies of his *tertulia* to a fanatic belief in the importance of the family, seeing in the birth of a son ("su único hijo," a phrase from the Apostles' Creed laden with symbolic ramifications) a means of self-redemption.

In the church where the child's baptism is to take place, Serafina avenges her lover's change of heart by claiming that the father is actually Minghetti. As the novel closes, Bonis denies this and quixotically insists that the child is his. The reader is struck by the similarity to the closing of *La regenta* (the protagonist is in a church and, in each case, tormented by rejection), but Bonis's case is more pathetic than tragic. He has been misled by the private cult of the family and fatherhood, not by any kind of Christian mysticism or belief in dogma. If Ana's end demonstrates the double failure of love and an exalted religiosity, the protagonist's downfall here is one of both the romantic ideal and of "la religión del hogar."

Like the characters of *La regenta*, the figures here attempt to project fiction on reality (the *Don Juan Tenorio* play in the first novel, the world of opera here), and in both works a chorus of gossip and *murmuración* provides the ironic backdrop. In *His Only Son*, however, the characters are archetypal, skeletal abstractions, often presented through hyperbolic caricature, in consonance with exaggerated, theatrical melodrama. This is evident in such scenes as Bonis and Serafina's lovemaking, Emma and Bonis's marital crises, and Emma's hysteria and fears of miscarriage. Gone are the positive-negative tensions of *La regenta*, replaced by a general world of resentment in which, by a few relatively simple strokes, Alas constructs a society of degenerate romantics, a few ridiculous human beings, sometimes grossly deformed and almost always repugnant. The author's irony remains, but a more ambiguous perspective forces the reader to look for essences, not explanations.

The six secondary figures are nonindividualistic representatives of but a few social traits, usually within a dualistic framework: Don Juan Nepomuceno hides carnal desire by a romantic facade; Korner is a "spiritual" dreamer but also a materialistic glutton; Mochi and Minghetti use personal attraction for economic gain; and Marta hides her sensuality, ego, and greed by an appearance of idealism. Serafina is even more systematically presented as a dual figure: beautiful and ugly, the angel and the devil, the voluptuous temptress and the serene madonna, romantic and sensuous, loving and materialistic. She is the embodiment of the conflict between good and evil, and evil triumphs in the end. Her English-

Italian background and even her name reinforce this aspect of duality: "Serafina," meaning celestial seraph; her family name "Gorgheggi," broken down to "gorgo," meaning vortex or abyss, and "gorgone," the mythological Gorgon, suggesting the Medusan female. The secondary characters all use an "attractive" front to win over others, while a real, negative side leads them to exploit those around them.

Bonis is the clearest example of psychological duality in the novel, alternatively ridiculous and moving, comic and sad, indecisive and creative, in need of erotic excitement yet searching for peace. He vacillates between romantic fantasy and bourgeois needs (symbolized by his flute and slippers, respectively), both of which represent ways to escape reality. The disintegration of his personality is the result of his inability to reconcile these two forces. Bonis feels hatred for the materialistic world, yet in fact he is a typical *burgués* (bourgeois). The key to his personality (and, indeed, to the whole novel) is the ambivalence inherent in his description as a *soñador sonoliento*. Alas himself is not sure whether to like or hate his protagonist's delicate, dreaming, gentle nature, whether to identify and commiserate with him or to poke fun at him.

From a broader viewpoint, Bonis is a caricature of nineteenth century Romanticism in crisis. He is the archetypal figure of the nonhero who wants to be a hero. Alienated both from society and from himself, he sees the exploration of his own identity—in the form of an inner journey to the past and to his father's nature—as a heroic venture. In comparison with Ana, however, there is no heroism in his victimization; his conflict is more with self than with others, and there is no wall of misunderstanding between him and society, as in *La regenta*. In contrast to Ana, he shows no initiative, no capacity to try to rise above his vulgar surroundings. In *His Only Son*, the importance of the will is seen either in its misdirection (Emma) or in its nonexistence (Bonis). The only vestige of the hero's grandeur is the protagonist's readiness to sacrifice himself for his son's future.

Bonis's attraction to Serafina stems in part from a romantic attachment to the memories of his mother. Eroticism and filial love are combined and linked with nostalgia for the past. At times, one feels that he uses his love for the mother figure as a way to repress his sensuality.

Then, as the novel progresses and Bonis sees a heavenly "Annunciation" of his future son's birth in Serafina's song (chapter 12), he concludes that divine coincidence has brought about the revelation of Emma's pregnancy on the same day that he breaks with Serafina. His longing for a child subsequently develops to the point of a religious cult, where fatherhood and motherhood join in him as a kind of *sacerdote*, or priest: Like God, he will offer "his only son" as a benefit for all humankind. In this thought, and in the notion that the earth is ruled by paternal Providence, he seems to find the security he needs and the moral support or atonement for his past conduct. Romantic raptures thus give way to fatherly love as the focus of ideality; at the same time, his longing for a son represents his need for another *yo* (or "I"), for a new beginning.

Emma ("Emma," perhaps a reminder of the twisted views of Gustave Flaubert's Emma Bovary; "Valcárcel," "val" or valley, as in an open sewer; and "carcel," imprisonment for Bonis) is basically a type character, a study in diabolical deformation that anticipates some of Ramón María del Valle-Inclán's depictions a few decades later. She is the epitome of the decadent *fuerza maléfica*, a malevolent force: perverse, spoiled, capricious, morbidly sensual, neurotic, and unnatural in her rejection of motherhood. Bonis and Alas think of her in terms of archetypal epithets: a Fury, witch, dragon, vampire; the proverbial femme fatale, as opposed to Serafina, who comes to represent angelic maternalism.

The reader is thus thrown into a world of characters exhibiting surprising traits: The man is more feminine than the aggressive, nonmaternal woman; his lover comes to personify domesticity and his wife to represent perverse eroticism; Emma finds her own lover when she learns of Bonis's relationship with Serafina, rather than resigning herself to her fate, as would other nineteenth century female characters. The unpredictable nature of human reality set forth in the novel is one of the work's many modern attributes.

Thematically, *His Only Son* is not particularly original, presenting a somewhat traditional, ironic exposure of the failings of idealized concepts and dogmas, when a simplified or falsified viewpoint clashes with the true complexity of reality. Rather than making a direct attack on pseudo-Romanticism per se, Alas is deriding the

maintenance of any form of belief determined by other than spontaneous, internal motives. There are, he says, no exterior, abstract, or secondhand formulas for life. Reality cannot be reduced to either matter or mind but, rather, is characterized by the vacillation between the physiological and the spiritual. Other ideas in the novel—the need to face oneself rather than attempt to escape, the possible exaltation of family roots, an attack against a life oriented toward physical pleasure—are corollaries of the central theme. All of these concepts, finally, are seen in the context of personal and universal values rather than a framework of national or societal decay, as is the case in *La regenta*.

Alas's novelistic production can be viewed as a reflection of the disillusionments and frustrations of his own life and of his critical stance toward society. His two major novels have much in common—psychological depth, authorial irony, and explicit thematic statement—but the passage from *La regenta* to *His Only Son* reveals a number of significant developments in technique and characterization. These differences, in turn, relate to the change from a period in which realistic and naturalistic elements were dominant to one in which the influences of symbolism, decadence, and idealistic spirituality are more evident.

Alas's initial preoccupation with the problems of Spanish society places him clearly in a literary line that runs from Francisco de Quevedo y Villegas (1580-1645) to Mariano José de Larra (1809-1837) and, later, to the Generation of '98. He was among the very few writers of his time who were able to utilize much of Spain's literary heritage, particularly Cervantine elements, while still anticipating a number of twentieth century techniques.

Jeremy T. Medina

OTHER MAJOR WORKS

SHORT FICTION: *Pipá*, 1886; *Doña Berta, Cuervo, Superchería*, 1892; *Cuentos morales*, 1896, 1973; *El señor y lo demás, son cuentos*, 1900; *¡Adiós, Cordera! y otros cuentos*, 1944; *Cuentos de Clarín*, 1954; *Cuentos escogidos*, 1964; *Superchería, Cuervo, Doña Berta*, 1970; *El gallo de Sócrates, y otros cuentos*, 1973; *Ten Tales*, 2000.

PLAY: *Teresa*, pr., pb. 1895.

NONFICTION: *El derecho y la moralidad*, 1878 (doctoral thesis); *Solos de Clarín*, 1881, 1971; *La literatura en 1881*, 1882 (with Armando Palacio Valdés); *Sermón perdido*, 1885; *Cánovas y su tiempo*, 1887; *Nueva campaña, 1885-1886*, 1887; *Mezclilla*, 1889; *Rafael Calvo y el teatro español*, 1890; *Ensayos y revistas*, 1892; *Palique*, 1893, 1973; *Crítica popular*, 1896; *Siglo pasado*, 1901; *Galdós*, 1912; *Doctor Sutilis*, 1916; *Páginas escogidas*, 1917; *Epistolario de Menéndez y Pelayo y Leopoldo Alas*, 1941; *Leopoldo Alas: Teoría y crítica de la novela española*, 1972; *Preludios de 'Clarín,'* 1972; *Obra olvidada*, 1973.

MISCELLANEOUS: *Obras selectas*, 1947, 1966.

BIBLIOGRAPHY

DuPont, Denise. *Realism as Resistance: Romanticism and Authorship in Galdós, Clarín, and Baroja*. Lewisburg, Pa.: Bucknell University Press, 2006. Explores the boundaries between realism and Romanticism in novels by three Spanish authors: Alas's *La regenta*, Benito Pérez Galdós's first series of *Episodios nacionales*, and Pío Baroja's *The Struggle for Life*. All three novels feature quixotic characters who act as authors, a theme DuPont traces to the influence of Spanish writer Miguel de Cervantes.

Franz, Thomas R. *Valera in Dialogue = In Dialogue with Valera: A Novelist's Work in Conversation with That of His Contemporaries and Successors*. New York: Peter Lang, 2000. Chronicles the debate among Alas and his contemporaries Juan Valera and Benito Pérez Galdós over the aesthetics of Spanish realist fiction, and how this debate influenced Alas's successors, namely Miguel de Unamuno y Jugo and Ramón María del Valle-Inclán.

Gilfoil, Anne W. "Disease as a Dis/Organizing Principle in Nineteenth-Century Spain: Benito Pérez Galdós, Leopoldo Alas, and Emilia Pardo Bazán." In *Science, Literature, and Film in the Hispanic World*, edited by Jerry Hoeg and Kevin S. Larsen. New York: Palgrave Macmillan, 2006. Gilfoil's essay and the others in this book chart the relationship between literature and science in Hispanic literature and culture by analyzing Spanish-language literature and films.

Goode, Stephen. "Return of a Nineteenth-Century Classic." *Washington Times*, February 18, 2007. Goode expresses his praise for *La regenta*, arguing that the novel is "surprisingly modern" and that its "well-rendered interior monologues, carried on in the minds" of its characters "lift this book out of the late Victorian era when it made its appearance, and make it feel truly at home today."

Medina, Jeremy T. *Spanish Realism: The Theory and Practice of a Concept in the Nineteenth Century*. Potomac, Md.: José Porrúa Turanzas, 1979. Medina analyzes works by Alas and other nineteenth century Spanish authors, discussing how and why these works exemplified the realistic literature of that time and place.

Sinclair, Alison. *Dislocations of Desire: Gender, Identity, and Strategy in "La regenta."* Chapel Hill: University of North Carolina, Department of Romance Languages, 1998. Sinclair takes a psychoanalytical approach to Alas's novel, examining how the narration and text of *La regenta* are similar to the workings of the human psyche.

Valis, Noel. "Death and the Child in *Su único hijo*." *Hispanic Review* 70, no. 2 (Spring, 2002). An analysis of Alas's novel *His Only Child*, focusing on the chimerical son, who is the object of protagonist Bonifacio Reyes's desire and obsession.

LOUISA MAY ALCOTT

Born: Germantown, Pennsylvania; November 29, 1832

Died: Boston, Massachusetts; March 6, 1888

Also known as: A. M. Barnard

PRINCIPAL LONG FICTION

Moods, 1864 (revised 1881)

Little Women, 1868

Little Women, Part 2, 1869 (also known as *Good Wives*, 1953)

An Old-Fashioned Girl, 1870

Little Men, 1871

Work: A Study of Experience, 1873

Eight Cousins, 1875

Rose in Bloom, 1876

A Modern Mephistopheles, 1877

Under the Lilacs, 1878

Jack and Jill, 1880

Jo's Boys, and How They Turned Out, 1886

A Long Fatal Love Chase, 1995 (wr. 1866)

The Inheritance, 1997 (wr. 1850)

OTHER LITERARY FORMS

In addition to her novels, Louisa May Alcott authored a collection of fairy tales, *Flower Fables* (1854); several short-story collections, notably *Aunt Jo's Scrap-Bag* (1872-1882, 6 volumes), *A Garland for Girls* (1887), and *Lulu's Library* (1895); a nonfiction work, *Hospital Sketches* (1863); a collection of plays, *Comic Tragedies Written by "Jo" and "Meg" and Acted by the "Little Women"* (1893); a few poems; and some articles and reviews for major periodicals. Alcott's surviving letters and journal entries were edited and published in 1889 by Ednah D. Cheney.

ACHIEVEMENTS

Louisa May Alcott first gained the recognition of a popular audience and then acceptance by the critics as a serious writer, becoming a giant in the subgenre of adolescent girls' novels and the family story. She was unique in having moral lessons exemplified by her characters' actions, thus avoiding the sermonizing of her contemporaries. Her heroes and heroines are flawed humans often trying to overcome their weaknesses. Much of the time, Alcott managed to avoid making her novels a vehicle to promote social or political issues, which was a fairly common practice of the day. She was a master of character development, and, despite adverse scholarly criticism and changing literary tastes among readers, her novels endure for what they offer in support of timeless values: the importance of a strong family life and honest, hard work.

BIOGRAPHY

Louisa May Alcott was the second daughter of Abby May and Amos Bronson Alcott, a leader in the Transcendentalist movement headed by essayist and poet Ralph Waldo Emerson. When it became evident that Bronson Alcott would not be a reliable provider, Louisa perceived it as her mission in life to support the family. The death of her younger sister and the marriage of her older sister were traumatic experiences for her; partly to fill the void left by their absence and partly to seek some purpose in life and to participate in the Civil War in the only way open to women, Alcott became an army nurse in Washington, D.C. After six weeks, she contracted typhoid fever, an illness from which she never fully recovered, owing to the effects of mercury poisoning from her medication. Alcott recorded her experiences during this time in *Hospital Sketches*, the work that would establish her as a serious writer.

Alcott had also begun writing gothic thrillers, which brought in money for the family but did not enhance her literary reputation. Her first novel appeared in 1864. In 1865, Alcott toured Europe, and soon after her return she became editor of the children's magazine *Merry's Museum*. About that time, the editor Thomas Niles urged Alcott to write a novel for girls; the result was *Little Women*, an overnight success. After her father suffered a stroke in 1882, Alcott moved him to Boston, where she continued to try to write. Sensing by this time that she would not regain her health, she adopted her nephew, John Sewell Pratt, who would become heir to her royalties and manage her affairs after her death. Louisa May

Alcott died on March 6, 1888, two days after the death of her father. The two are buried in the Sleepy Hollow Cemetery in Concord, Massachusetts.

ANALYSIS

Versatility characterizes the canon of Louisa May Alcott, which includes children's literature, adult novels, gothic thrillers, autobiography, short stories, poetry, and drama. While Alcott's works for children may be distinguished from those of other writers of children's stories in some important ways, they nonetheless fit into the broader context of American literature of the time. What set Alcott's children's novels apart from the rest was her careful avoidance of the overt didacticism and sermonizing that characterized many others. A code of proper behavior is implicit in the novels, but it is detected in situations rather than showcased by authorial intrusion. In the juvenile novels, with the exception of the March family works, Alcott wrote less from her own experiences, and she was more prone to rewrite earlier works. The most enduring of Alcott's collection are the girls' novels and the family stories, which continue to be read because of the vitality of the characters—how they deal with life situations and challenges with humor, even fun—and the way Alcott uses detail to present simple, honest lives. Although critics of the late twentieth century and early twenty-first century found the children's novels to be overly sentimental, readers of the day enjoyed them.

Alcott's works for adults portray a less simplistic view of life than do the children's stories. Readers meet people with boring, unhappy, or even sordid lives, lives that would not be deemed suitable for those works that earned Alcott the epithet "children's friend." Alcott's skill in building character, in using dialogue, and in exploring social issues of the day is evident.

MOODS

Moods, Alcott's first and favorite novel, was published in 1864. Having been advised to cut its length by about half, Alcott submitted a text that was predictably unsatisfactory both to her and to her critics. Some twenty years later, a new edition was published with some deletions and the restoration of former chapters. The basic story remained the same: The heroine, Sylvia Yule, is dominated by mood swings. Governed more by feelings than by reason, she is prone to making misguided judg-

Louisa May Alcott.

ments in love. She loves Adam Warwick, a model of strength, intellect, and manliness, but she learns, too late, that he uses others to serve his own purposes and then shuns them. After Adam leaves Sylvia, his best friend, Geoffrey Moor, becomes a true friend to Sylvia, but he mistakes the friendship for love. He is totally unlike Adam Warwick: slight of build, sweet, and tranquil. Sylvia decides to marry Geoffrey because he is a "safe" choice, not because she loves him. When Sylvia finally confesses to Geoffrey her love for Adam, Geoffrey leaves for one year to see if his absence will help her learn to love him. The plan works, but on his way back to claim her love, Adam, Geoffrey's traveling companion, is drowned. Though saddened, Sylvia and Geoffrey are reunited, wiser and more cognizant of the value of their mutual love. In the 1864 edition of the book, Sylvia develops tuberculosis, and when Geoffrey returns, he nurses her through her terminal illness before she dies in his arms. In the 1881 edition, in which Sylvia falls ill but recovers and accepts Geoffrey's love, Alcott focuses more clearly on the theme of moods rather than of marriage, and plot and characterization are more even.

LITTLE WOMEN

Although Louisa May Alcott was already an established author when *Little Women* was published, it was that novel that brought her an enduring reputation. *Little Women* was written quickly; the original manuscript was completed in six weeks. Because the public clamored for a sequel revealing how the sisters married, Alcott obliged with *Little Women, Part 2* (later published as *Good Wives*) one year later. The two were subsequently published as a single novel.

Little Women is based on the fictionalized life of the Alcott sisters at their house in Concord. The plot is episodic, devoting at least one chapter to each sister. The overall theme is the sisters' quest to face the challenges of life and to overcome their personal "burdens" so that they may develop into "little women." The chief burden of Meg, the eldest, is vanity. Jo, like her mother, has a temper that she must learn to control if she is to become a "little woman." Beth, thirteen, is already so nearly perfect that her burden is simply to overcome her shyness. Amy is the proverbial spoiled baby in the family, and she must try to overcome her impracticality and thoughtlessness. When the sisters are not sharing intimacies and producing dramatic productions for entertainment, they interact with the next-door neighbors, Mr. Laurence and his orphaned grandson, Laurie. Laurie is wealthy in material things but longs to have family; he often enjoys the March girls' activities vicariously, from a window.

Mrs. March, affectionately called Marmee, is a central character in the novel. The girls know that they can confide in their mother about anything, and at any time. She is strong, wise, and loving, clearly the anchor of the family. Mr. March is a clergyman who has gone to serve in the Civil War and so is absent during the course of the novel. Among the events of the novel is the tragic death of Beth from a terminal illness. The story ends with the engagement of Meg, the eldest sister, with Jo's decision to become a writer and to leave her tomboyish childhood for a mature relationship, and with Amy's betrothal to Laurie. *Little Women* was an overnight success, and the public eagerly awaited the sequel, provided in *Little Women, Part 2.*

LITTLE WOMEN, PART 2

The sequel to *Little Women* was released in January of 1869. *Little Women, Part 2* begins with Meg's wedding day; she settles into a conventional marriage in which her husband is the breadwinner and she is the docile, dependent wife. They have two children, Daisy and Demi-John. For a time, Alcott allows Jo to be happy being single, enjoying her liberty. After she has married Amy off to Laurie in another conventional romantic marriage, however, she bows to the wishes of her readers and has Jo marry Professor Bhaer, the kindly older man about whom Jo became serious in *Little Women*. With this union, Jo is able to maintain a degree of freedom and to pursue intellectual interests in a way that conventional marriages of the day would not have allowed. Together, Jo and the Professor operate the Plumfield School, whose pedagogy parallels the philosophy of Alcott's father in his Temple School; the success of Plumfield is thus a tribute to Bronson Alcott.

AN OLD-FASHIONED GIRL

Alcott's novel *An Old-Fashioned Girl*, published in 1870, was not as commercially successful as were the books about the March family. The theme of *An Old-Fashioned Girl* is that wealth in itself does not bring happiness. Polly Milton pays an extended visit to her wealthy friend Fanny Shaw, only to realize that Fanny's very "new-fashioned" family is not much of a family at all: Brother Tom is left uncared-for by everyone except his grandmother, who is also ignored by the rest of the family; Maud, the six-year-old sister, is a petty, ill-tempered child; the father gives himself wholly to his work; the mother neglects the household largely because of a self-proclaimed invalidism; and Fanny herself is lazy and shallow. Polly Milton's family, on the other hand, though poor, is noble. The Reverend Milton is a country parson who provides for his loving and happy family's needs. Mrs. Milton, like Marmee of *Little Women*, is a wise and caring confidant who sees to it that Polly is dressed appropriately for her age and who teaches respect and charity by word and deed. She is an able seamstress and cook, and she operates the household economically and within the family's means. Polly helps improve the Shaw family, and she returns unspoiled to her loving family. She becomes a music teacher so that she can send her brother to college. Polly is not perfect, however; her flaw is vanity. As a working woman without a fashionable wardrobe, she does not enjoy full social acceptance.

Polly seeks proper marriages for the Shaw children. A reversal of financial circumstances in the Shaw family forces Fanny to learn from the Miltons how to make do with little, but it is a blessing because both Tom and Fanny become better people. By the end of the novel, marriages have been planned for all except Maud, who remains a happy spinster.

LITTLE MEN

Little Men, published in 1871, employs the episodic technique of Alcott's earlier novels to continue the story that *Little Women* began. The focus is on Professor and Jo March Bhaer and their students at Plumfield. Jo and her husband have two sons, Rob and a lovable baby boy named Teddy; Daisy and Demi, Meg's twins, are now old enough to be students at the school, as is Bess, Laurie and Amy's daughter. Professor Bhaer's nephews, Emil and Franz, are senior students. Other students include the stock characters Stuffy Cole, Dolly Pettingill, Jack Ford, Billy Ward, and Dick Brown. Four other students are more fully developed: Tommy Bangs, an arsonist; Nat Blake, who loves music and tells lies; Nan, a girl who wanted to be a boy and becomes a physician; and Dan Kean, a troublemaker who threatens to upset the reputation the Bhaers have gained for success in reforming wayward students. The children are rarely seen in the classroom, carrying out Bronson Alcott's Temple School principle of cultivating healthy bodies and spirits as well as developing the intellect. Corporal punishment of students is not practiced, and the school is coeducational. Under the guidance of the long-suffering Professor Bhaer and the now-motherly Jo, the school is like a magnet that draws its former charges back to its stable shelter.

WORK

Some critics consider *Work* to be Alcott's most successful novel for adults. Christie Devon, an orphan, leaves home to seek independence. She goes through a number of jobs quickly—a chapter is given to each one, in episodic fashion—before she meets Rachel, a "fallen" woman whom she befriends. When Rachel's past is discovered, she is fired from her job, as is Christie for remaining her friend. Christie becomes increasingly poor,

hungry, lonely, and depressed, to the point of contemplating suicide. Rachel comes along in time and takes Christie to a washerwoman who introduces her to the Reverend Thomas Power. He arranges for Christie to live with the widow Sterling and her son David, a florist. Christie tries to make David heroic, which he is not, but in time they are married, just before David goes off to war. He is killed, and Christie, who is pregnant, goes to live with David's family. Rachel turns out to be David's sister-in-law. The novel focuses on the loneliness and frustration of women in situations such as these. Like Alcott, they find salvation in hard work, and although the financial recompense they receive is paltry, the work is not deemed beneath their dignity. More than in her other novels, in *Work* Alcott realistically portrays relationships between men and women.

EIGHT COUSINS

In *Eight Cousins*, which appeared in 1875, Alcott does not resort to the episodic technique she used in earlier novels as she focuses clearly on the character Rose Campbell, also the heroine of the sequel to *Eight Cousins*, *Rose in Bloom*. A ward of her Uncle Alex, the orphaned heiress Rose comes to live with her relatives. Her six aunts all have strong opinions about Rose's education, but her schooling merely crams Rose full of useless facts; she is not really educated. Eventually, Uncle Alex takes over her education and provides her with "freedom, rest, and care," echoing Bronson Alcott's educational philosophy. Rose is in frequent contact with her seven male cousins, to whom she becomes a confidant. She submits to Uncle Alex's wholesome regimen, but she has her ears pierced despite his disapproval, and she admires what is fashionable even though she dresses as her uncle suggests.

The central theme of the novel is a woman's education. It prescribes physical exercise, housework, and mastery of some kind of trade. The novel promotes courses that were nontraditional for women at the time the work appeared as well as education that rests on practical experience rather than reading of books, although reading is respected. Although the novel clearly has in mind a treatment of various social issues, it succeeds nevertheless because of Alcott's development of the child characters and the humor with which she views the foibles of the adult characters.

A MODERN MEPHISTOPHELES

In 1877, Alcott's publisher requested from her a novel that could be published anonymously in the No Name series of works by popular writers. Alcott chose a manuscript she had written ten years earlier that had been deemed sensational. Revising this work enabled her to write in the gothic mode without compromising her reputation as a children's writer. Furthermore, she had been impressed with Johann Wolfgang von Goethe's drama *Faust: Eine Tragödie* (pb. 1808; *The Tragedy of Faust*, 1823), and the parallels to Goethe's masterpiece are obvious. Just when Felix Canaris, an aspiring but rejected poet, is contemplating suicide, Jasper Helwyze comes along, rescues Felix, and befriends him, promising to make him successful. Within a year, Felix has indeed found success as a poet. He falls in love with Olivia, a former love who had rejected Jasper, but Gladys, an orphan protégé of Olivia, also falls in love with Felix. Completely under Jasper's influence, Felix is forced to marry Gladys instead of Olivia. Jasper harasses the young couple in various ways. As they look forward to life with a child, Jasper forces Felix to reveal his secret to Gladys: He has no real talent—Jasper has been writing his poetry. Gladys does not reject Felix, but after she goes into premature labor, she and the baby both die. Before her death, she implores Felix and Jasper to forgive each other. Felix is thus freed from his bondage to Jasper and goes on to live a worthwhile life; Jasper has a stroke.

A Modern Mephistopheles is not simply a rewritten *Faust*; the novel adds to the story the dominant theme of the power of women, both wives and mothers, to save men from themselves, an idea of high interest to the readers of the day. The work employs a great deal of foreshadowing, partly because of its parallels to *Faust*. In this work Alcott explores the darker side of human nature in a way that she could not, or would not, do in her works for children.

JACK AND JILL

The episodic plot of *Jack and Jill* may be explained by the fact that it was first serialized in the *St. Nicholas* magazine in 1879 and 1880, although several of Alcott's other novels also employed this technique. Alcott called it a "village story," with Harmony Village as a fictionalized Concord. Jack and Frank are modeled on Anna Alcott's sons, and Ed is based on Ellsworth Devens, a Concord friend. Jack and Jill are recovering from a serious sliding accident, and the novel concerns the way the other children in Harmony Village are inspired by the near tragedy to improve their ways, both physically and morally. Like Beth of *Little Women*, Ed is almost too good to be true, foreshadowing his early death. This novel, like *Little Men*, is an educational novel.

JO'S BOYS

In 1886, Alcott brought closure to the March family novels with a final story portraying the changes that occurred within the previous ten years. Mr. Laurence, the kind next-door neighbor of *Little Women*, endows a college next door to the Plumfield School of *Little Women, Part 2* and *Little Men*. Meg notes the absence of the beloved Marmee, Beth, and her late husband John. Readers learn that Demi has gone into the publishing business; Daisy is a "little woman" who marries Nat Blake, and Nan becomes a doctor. Nat completes his musical education in Germany; Emil becomes a ship's officer who takes charge of a lifeboat when the captain becomes ill; Dan, who decided to seek his fortune in the West, kills a man in self-defense when a crooked card game goes sour. It is remembering and upholding the honor of Plumfield that guides these young men. The one character who cannot return to the inner circle of the March family is the "bad boy," Dan Kean. He does come back to Plumfield after he is wounded while working with Native Americans in the West, but he is not allowed to marry Beth, the daughter of Amy March and Laurie Laurence. Feminism is the main focus of the novel; all of the young women succeed in careers that were denied the title characters in *Little Women*.

Victoria Price

OTHER MAJOR WORKS

SHORT FICTION: *Flower Fables*, 1854; *On Picket Duty, and Other Tales*, 1864; *Morning-Glories, and Other Stories*, 1867; *Aunt Jo's Scrap-Bag*, 1872-1882 (6 volumes); *Silver Pitchers, and Independence: A Centennial Love Story*, 1876; *Spinning-Wheel Stories*, 1884; *A Garland for Girls*, 1887; *Lulu's Library*, 1895; *Alternative Alcott*, 1988; *A Double Life: Newly Discovered Thrillers of Louisa May Alcott*, 1988; *Louisa May Alcott: Selected Fiction*, 1990; *Freaks of Genius: Unknown Thrillers of Louisa May Alcott*, 1991; *From Jo March's*

Attic: Stories of Intrigue and Suspense, 1993; *Louisa May Alcott Unmasked: Collected Thrillers*, 1995; *The Early Stories of Louisa May Alcott, 1852-1860*, 2000.

PLAYS: *Comic Tragedies Written by "Jo" and "Meg" and Acted by the "Little Women,"* 1893.

POETRY: *The Poems of Louisa May Alcott*, 2000.

NONFICTION: *Hospital Sketches*, 1863 (essays); *Life, Letters, and Journals*, 1889 (Ednah D. Cheney, editor); *The Journals of Louisa May Alcott*, 1989 (Joel Myerson and Daniel Shealy, editors); *The Sketches of Louisa May Alcott*, 2001.

BIBLIOGRAPHY

Boyd, Anne E. *Writing for Immortality: Women and the Emergence of High Literary Culture in America*. Baltimore: Johns Hopkins University Press, 2004. Explores efforts by Alcott and other female writers living in mid-nineteenth century New England to achieve recognition as authors equal to that given to their male counterparts in both Europe and the United States.

Clark, Beverly Lyon, ed. *Louisa May Alcott: The Contemporary Reviews*. New York: Cambridge University Press, 2004. Collection of reviews of Alcott's work that appeared when it was published in the nineteenth century. Provides insights into the author's reception by her contemporaries in addition to information about the attitudes toward popular fiction and women writers in that period.

Delamar, Gloria T. *Louisa May Alcott and "Little Women."* London: McFarland, 1990. Unlike many other Alcott biographies, this work includes reviews and critical analyses of Alcott's work.

Eiselein, Gregory, and Anne K. Phillips, eds. *The Louisa May Alcott Encyclopedia*. Westport, Conn.: Greenwood Press, 2001. Six hundred alphabetically arranged entries provide information about Alcott's family and personal life and place her work within historical and cultural contexts, including various reform movements, the American Civil War, and other major events. Also addresses Alcott's position in the nineteenth century publishing world.

Elbert, Sarah. *A Hunger for Home: Louisa May Alcott and "Little Women."* Philadelphia: Temple University Press, 1984. A feminist study of Alcott, this critical biography analyzes the connections between Alcott's family life and her work, placing Alcott squarely within the reform tradition of the nineteenth century and the debate over the proper role of women.

Meigs, Cornelia. *Invincible Louisa: The Story of the Author of "Little Women."* 1933. Reprint. Boston: Little, Brown, 1968. Biography emphasizes Alcott's work with young people and her belief that children must have the opportunity to earn independence. Also discusses Alcott's assistance to soldiers during the Civil War and her trip to Europe. Includes a fine chronology of Alcott's life.

Saxton, Martha. *Louisa May Alcott: A Modern Biography*. 1977. Reprint. New York: Farrar, Straus and Giroux, 1995. Depicts Alcott as an ambivalent rebel and irreverent feminist who, despite her bitter childhood with an oppressive father, became famous for writing a sweet story about a happy family.

Showalter, Elaine. *Sister's Choice: Traditions and Change in American Women's Writing*. Oxford, England: Clarendon Press, 1991. Chapter 3 discusses the wide variance in feminist critical reception of Alcott's *Little Women:* Some feel that bowing to pressures of the time kept Alcott from fulfilling her literary promise; others see the novel as an excellent study of the dilemma of a literary woman writing in that age.

Stern, Madeleine B. *Louisa May Alcott: A Biography*. 1950. Reprint. Boston: Northeastern University Press, 1999. Considered to be the standard biography of Alcott since its initial publication in 1950, this reprint features a new introduction by Stern, a rare-book dealer who has written several books about Alcott and has edited anthologies of her work.

_____. *Louisa May Alcott: From Blood and Thunder to Hearth and Home*. Boston: Northeastern University Press, 1998. Collection of essays analyzes Alcott's key themes, including her love for the theater and feminism, and examines her "double literary life" as an author who wrote both domestic dramas and "blood-and-thunder" thrillers.

Strickland, Charles. *Victorian Domesticity: Families in the Life and Art of Louisa May Alcott*. Tuscaloosa: University of Alabama Press, 1985. Surveys the range of Alcott's ideas about domestic life and considers Alcott's literary treatment of women, families, and children within the various fictional forms in which she chose to work.

Trites, Roberta Seelinger. *Twain, Alcott, and the Birth of the Adolescent Reform Novel*. Iowa City: University

of Iowa Press, 2007. Analyzes the work of Alcott and Mark Twain to delineate how they helped change the nature of American adolescence, viewing it as a time in which children expressed a great potential for change and reform.

RICHARD ALDINGTON

Born: Portsmouth, Hampshire, England; July 8, 1892
Died: Sury-en-Vaux, France; July 27, 1962
Also known as: Edward Godfree Aldington

PRINCIPAL LONG FICTION

Death of a Hero, 1929
The Colonel's Daughter, 1931
All Men Are Enemies, 1933
Women Must Work, 1934
Very Heaven, 1937
Seven Against Reeves, 1938
Rejected Guest, 1939
The Romance of Casanova, 1946

OTHER LITERARY FORMS

Richard Aldington was one of the principal Imagist poets. Each of his Imagist poems renders one impression of a scene, and most of these poems are short. "Whitechapel," which is frequently anthologized, evokes the sounds and sights of the section of London for which the poem is titled. Aldington's poems were collected in small volumes, including *Images, 1910-1915* (1915) and *Images of War* (1919), among many others. The full range of his poetic skills can be seen in *The Complete Poems of Richard Aldington* (1948).

Aldington also conceived masterfully ironic short stories. Set in England in the modern period, these stories frequently pit an individual idealist against a hypocritical society. The collections *Roads to Glory* (1930) and *Soft Answers* (1932) contain the best of these contemporary sketches. In addition, Aldington's translations of French, Italian, Greek, and Latin poems, fiction,

and prose number more than twenty-eight volumes, including poems by Folgóre da San Gimignano that Aldington titled *The Garland of Months* (1917), Voltaire's *Candide, and Other Romances* (1927), Julien Benda's *The Great Betrayal* (1928), and *The Decameron of Giovanni Boccaccio* (1930).

Aldington's literary reviews and critical studies demonstrate his scholarship, his genial wit, and his delight in the critical evaluation of contemporary and classical literature. His astounding capacity for work enabled him to produce hundreds of entertaining and informative essays of literary history and criticism. His introductions to the 1953 Penguin editions of D. H. Lawrence are valuable for their personal and critical insight. Aldington's volumes of short essays, most of them originally published as review essays in periodicals, include *Literary Studies and Reviews* (1924), *French Studies and Reviews* (1926), and *Artifex: Sketches and Ideas* (1935).

His biographical and critical studies delighted and infuriated readers. Aldington wrote his first biography, *Voltaire* (1925), about the satirist who shared Aldington's skepticism. The next two biographies championed the work of a contemporary novelist who was then under attack: *D. H. Lawrence: An Indiscretion* (1927) and *D. H. Lawrence: A Complete List of His Works, Together with a Critical Appreciation* (1935). *The Duke, Being an Account of the Life and Achievements of Arthur Wellesley, First Duke of Wellington* (1943) was Aldington's most popular historical biography; for this rollicking life story, Aldington won the James Tait Black Memorial Prize in 1947. The great majority of his critical biographies were published after Aldington ceased writing satiric fiction. Of interest to literary historians are his later studies of contemporary writers: *D. H. Lawrence: Portrait of a Genius But . . .* (1950), *Ezra Pound and T. S. Eliot, a Lecture* (1954), *A. E. Housman and W. B. Yeats, Two Lectures* (1955), and *Lawrence L'Imposteur: T. E. Lawrence, the Legend and the Man* (1954). The Prix de Gratitude Mistralienne was awarded to Aldington's *Introduction to Mistral* (1956).

ACHIEVEMENTS

Judged on the basis of his contemporary influence as a poet, reviewer, and novelist, Richard Aldington should be regarded as one of the major modernists; that his current reputation fails to match his achievements evidences the uncertainties of literary fame. His best-selling novel *Death of a Hero*, despite its enormous popularity in the decade after its publication in English and its many translations, has been out of print since the 1980's and is likely to remain unavailable. Sparked by the publication of various collections of his letters, there has been a revival of interest in Aldington as a literary figure who knew other writers, but no comparable resurgence of scholarly interest in Aldington's work has taken place. His biographical studies of D. H. Lawrence and T. E. Lawrence were widely read and almost as widely denounced when first published, because they presented brutally honest portraits of their subjects; in the context of current literary biographies, their critical attitude toward lionized literary greats seems measured, and perhaps even mild. Aldington's literary essays are models of clear, evaluative prose. His Imagist poems, which were lauded by other poets and critics of poetry when first published, still seem fresh, though the Imagist movement ended more than seventy years ago. Aldington's long fiction appealed to a large reading public, who delighted in his satire, his wit, and his richly detailed portraits of contemporary culture.

BIOGRAPHY

Richard Aldington was born Edward Godfree Aldington in Portsmouth, England, on July 8, 1892. *Life for Life's Sake: A Book of Reminiscences* (1941), his genial autobiography, presents an amusing, cordial, and meticulously honest persona to his readers. That version of Aldington's personality is also celebrated in *Richard Aldington: An Intimate Portrait* (1965), sketches written by twenty-two people who knew him (including Roy Campbell, Lawrence Durrell, T. S. Eliot, Herbert Read, Alec Waugh, and Henry Williamson), and lovingly collected by Alister Kershaw and Frédéric-Jacques Temple. Those letters that have been published—*A Passionate Prodigality*, Aldington's letters to Alan Bird, 1949-1962 (1975) and *Literary Lifelines*, correspondence between Richard Aldington and Lawrence Durrell (1981)—reveal a witty, considerate, and self-deprecating egotist, who could, when angered by incompetence, hypocrisy, or prejudice, portray his target in pitiless satire; he could also ridicule weaknesses in friends and in writers he greatly admired. The subjects were not always able to see the humor in his satiric sketches.

Contradicting the more generous interpretations of Aldington's character and behavior is the unflattering fictionalized portrait of Rafe in *Bid Me to Live* (1960), a novel by H. D. (Hilda Doolittle, who was married to Aldington from 1913 to 1938, though their marriage dissolved during World War I). Charles Doyle's 1989 biography of Aldington provides one of the most detailed accounts of his life currently available. In general, it is possible to divide Aldington's long literary career into four broad phases: Imagist poet from 1912 to 1919, literary essayist and translator from 1919 to 1928, novelist from 1928 to 1938, and critical biographer from 1939 to 1957.

From his childhood, Aldington recalled with pleasure long walks through the English countryside unspoiled by automobile traffic, his observations as an amateur naturalist and astronomer, and freely reading romances and British poetry in his father's large, general library. He also remembered, and satirized in his novels, the sentimentality, patriotic chauvinism, and narrow philistine manners of middle-class, Victorian citizens in the city of Dover. Like the hero of his novel *Rejected Guest*, Aldington attended University College, London, and, like the hero of *Very Heaven*, he was forced to leave college by his father's financial failure. In 1911, Aldington began his professional career by reporting sporting events for a London newspaper and, in his spare time, writing poetry for publication. He was introduced to Ezra Pound and H. D. by Brigit Patmore, and he soon met Harold Monro, William Butler Yeats, May Sinclair, and Ford Madox Ford.

Aldington's first literary life, which ended in World War I, was given focus by his relationship with H. D. (they were married in October, 1913) and his involvement in the Imagist movement in poetry. Aldington credited H. D. with writing the first Imagist poems, influenced by Greek forms, written in the free verse of the French Symbolists. The Imagists avoided the florid language of Georgian poetry by paring images to concrete, exact details and revising for concise, clear diction. In Aldington's view, H. D.'s aesthetic sense influenced his poetry, and also that of D. H. Lawrence and Amy Lowell. The point of Aldington's exaggeration, surely, was to remove Pound from the leadership of the Imagists. Aldington insisted that Pound merely named the group, arranged for the first publications in the Chicago magazine *Poetry* in 1912, and organized the first anthology, titled *Des Imagistes*, in 1914. Critical of Pound's despotic editorship, Aldington clearly preferred the democratic efficiency of Lowell, who organized and published three volumes titled *Some Imagist Poets* in 1915, 1916, and 1917. These three volumes included the work of Aldington, H. D., John Gould Fletcher, F. S. Flint, Lawrence, and Lowell. Aldington himself organized one more collection, *Imagist Anthology* (1930), but his Imagist poetry, which was written simultaneously with that of H. D., belongs to his prewar world. The English periodical that became home for Imagist poetry was *The Egoist*, formerly *The New Freewoman*, managed by Dora Marsden and Harriet Shaw Weaver, with Aldington as its literary editor from 1914 to 1916, sharing the post with H. D. once he entered the army.

Aldington's attitude toward fiction writing and some of his style as a novelist were certainly influenced by Ford, whom Aldington served as a private secretary while Ford was composing *The Good Soldier* (1915), his novel about the collapse of an era, and *When Blood Is Their Argument* (1915), a propagandist attack on German culture. The psychologically unbalanced narrator, the convoluted time of the narrative, and the ranting tone of Aldington's *Death of a Hero* owe much to Ford's writing during the first year of the war. Aldington singled out Ford's war tetralogy *Parade's End* (1924-1928, 1950) for praise, and it is useful to remember that Aldington wrote his own war book after Ford's had been published. Ford assumes an almost mythic place in Aldington's literary history, as one of the last Englishmen to believe in and support a republic of letters. For Aldington, the war destroyed that idealistic world, and the war itself forced a painful break in his life.

Feeling his duty but denying all moral aims of war, Aldington volunteered in 1916 and served until February of 1919, concluding his service as a captain in the army and returning to England with lingering shell shock. His wartime experiences appear in deliberately phantasmagoric descriptions in *Death of a Hero*, and his postwar nightmares are described in *All Men Are Enemies*. During the war, he had begun an affair with Dorothy Yorke (their relationship continued until 1928) and separated from his wife. A fictionalized account of Aldington's choice between wife and lover may be found in George Winterbourne's complicated relations with Elizabeth and Fanny in *Death of a Hero*, but the physical appearances of the two women have been inter-

Richard Aldington. (Library of Congress)

changed. Aldington's version of H. D.'s wartime life, her refusal of sexual relations with him, the birth of her daughter, Perdita (whose father's identity she concealed), her subsequent pneumonia, and her recovery under the care of Bryher (Winifred Ellerman) may be found fictionalized in *Women Must Work*.

The second phase in Aldington's literary career began when Ellerman persuaded her father, Sir John Ellerman, to use his influence to arrange a job for Aldington as a critic of French literature with *The Times Literary Supplement*. With that steady income and the royalties from his poems and translations, Aldington and Yorke settled in a cottage in Berkshire formerly occupied by D. H. Lawrence. Aldington satirizes the stultifying social hierarchy and the narrow cultural life of provincial England after the war in *The Colonel's Daughter*. During this period, Aldington developed his new friendships with Herbert Read, who shared his experience in the war, and T. S. Eliot, whom he later portrayed satirically in *Stepping Heavenward* (1931). In 1926, during Great Britain's general strike, Aldington, like the hero of *All Men Are Enemies*, worked to bring out *The Times*, and he witnessed the violence between workers and police. He also strengthened his old friendship with D. H. Lawrence as the two men discussed their growing alienation from their native land.

The beginning of the third phase in Aldington's literary life was in 1928: He began writing his first novel, he decided to leave England, and he broke off his affair with Yorke to begin one with Brigit (Ethel Elizabeth) Patmore (their relationship lasted until 1938). By 1928, Aldington was receiving an adequate income in royalties from his accumulated publications, and he was able to move to Paris. There he met Hart Crane, Ernest Hemingway, James Joyce, and Thomas Wolfe, and became close friends with French literary critic and publisher Jean Paulhan. He began writing *Death of a Hero* in Paulhan's resort house on Isle de Port-Cros. *Death of a Hero* was an enormously popular success, was published in numerous translations, and increased Aldington's financial security. During the decade of 1928 to 1938, he wrote seven novels satirizing British culture. His travels through Italy, Spain, and Portugal made him acutely aware of the changing political scene, and in 1935 he relocated to the New World, as Lawrence had done earlier.

After a short period in New York City, he moved to a farm in Connecticut, where he remained during World War II.

In 1938, Aldington broke off his relationship with Patmore, divorced H. D., and married Netta McCulloch, the former wife of Patmore's son. His new marriage produced a much-beloved daughter, Catherine, who remained with her father after the marriage dissolved in 1950. From July, 1944, through April, 1946, Aldington worked in Los Angeles, writing movie scripts and completing *The Romance of Casanova*. At the end of that period, disenchanted with American culture, Aldington returned to France.

Aldington wrote no more novels, concentrating on critical biographies, including *Lawrence L'Imposteur*, which demythologized Lawrence of Arabia, with disastrous consequences to his own reputation and sales. Aldington's carefully researched book demolished the heroic myth that T. E. Lawrence had created in *Seven Pillars of Wisdom* (1922; revised 1926, 1935), but the reading public chose to remain loyal to the romantic Lawrence of Arabia. That critical biography so damaged Aldington's credibility that his novels declined in popularity and in critical acclaim. Aldington's satiric fiction became associated with his attack on Lawrence, and a myth of Aldington as a bitter, unbalanced, even envious writer overshadowed most subsequent evaluations of his work.

Financial difficulties resulting from the hostile response to *Lawrence L'Imposteur* led Aldington to live a quiet life in a cottage near Suryen-Vaux. In his seventieth year, he accepted an invitation to visit the Soviet Union, where he was lionized for his sharp critiques of British culture (his equally biting satires of Communist fanatics were quietly ignored). Shortly after his return to France in 1962, Aldington died.

ANALYSIS

Richard Aldington, one of the generation who were young adults in 1914, felt compelled to chronicle the impact of World War I on English culture and society, and all seven of his novels published between the world wars explore some aspect of that obsession. Only the first of these novels describes the war itself, but all of them portray the social degeneration that Aldington connected with World War I. This fiction satirizes English class snobbery, moral hypocrisy, selfish commercialism, insensitivity to art, faddish adherence to publicized avant-garde figures, and a culpable ignorance of sexual feelings, which the Victorian generation repressed and the generation of 1914 indulged without restraint, with disastrous consequences.

DEATH OF A HERO

Aldington's great war novel, *Death of a Hero*, though a popular success, was sharply criticized as a ranting, inartistic piece of writing. D. H. Lawrence, having read the manuscript, warned his friend, "If you publish this, you'll lose what reputation you have—you're plainly on your way to an insane asylum." Early reviewers found the novel's style "uncontrolled," "exasperatingly diffuse," and "puerile." Aldington let himself in for a flood of misguided critical response because he disregarded the modernist preference for authorial impassivity. Eschewing the example of Gustave Flaubert and Joyce, Aldington found his models in Laurence Sterne and Ford Madox Ford. In *Death of a Hero*, as in Sterne's *The Life and Opinions of Tristram Shandy, Gent.* (1759-1767) and Ford's *The Good Soldier*, readers find discursive narration, defense of feeling, confusion of author and narrator, temporal dislocation, polemical intrusion, and a tone shifting unexpectedly from angry indignation to ironic self-mockery.

Working through a monomaniacal narrator, Aldington nevertheless orders his madman's chaotic discourse by suggesting three formal analogies for the novel: a threnody, a tragedy, and a symphony. A threnody is a funeral lamentation that may be written as a choral ode or as a monody; Aldington chose the single-voiced monody, and the narrator's personality, disturbed by his war experience, distorts the story significantly, as a detailed analysis of the novel reveals. For example, the narrator begins speculating, "I sometimes think that George committed suicide in that last battle of the war," but by the time he narrates the death, the suicide is not a speculation but a fact. By revealing the death of his hero at the beginning, the narrator rejects suspense; as in the performance of a Greek tragedy, the emotive and intellectual response of the audience is manipulated not by the facts of the case but by the rendition. Although the narrator specifically mentions Aeschylus's *Oresteia* (458 B.C.E.; English

translation, 1777), the analogy to his tragic tale is by contrast. Both heroes are tormented by Furies, but Athena, goddess of war and wisdom, intervenes at Orestes' trial to give Apollo's logic triumph over the Furies' passion; in George's war, there is no logical resolution, and the desire for revenge creates a war of attrition—significantly, George dies in the final year of World War I.

The symphonic form of *Death of a Hero* is emphasized in the tempo markings given to the four sections. The prologue, dealing with the postwar world, is marked "allegretto," suggesting the spasmodic grasping for pleasures as a response to the suppressed guilt of the survivors in the 1920's. In part 2, "vivace" sets the pace of England's economic growth in the 1890's, which is connected with the fanatical patriotism of the Boer War, with an affected enthusiasm for culture, and with hypocritical attitudes toward sexuality. In part 3, "andante cantabile" marks the self-satisfied ease of the Georgian era, just before the war. The war itself is treated in part 4, "adagio," a funeral march commemorating the death of George's generation. As in a symphony, there are several repeated and counterpointed motifs. "Bread and babies" is one of these motifs, linking economic growth and demands with increased population and ignorance about contraception. The "bread and babies" motif is heard in the narration of George's marriage and early career, in the sordid story of his parents' courtship and marriage, and, during the war, as one analysis of the forces making war inevitable. This motif is interwoven with others throughout the narrative, creating a complex pattern unlike the linear structure of a polemical speech. Neither an unedited memoir of a shell-shocked veteran nor a propagandistic tract, this novel is distinguished by its formal composition.

Aldington's deliberate use of sentiment, of repetition, of discontinuities in narrative time, of digressions, and of sudden shifts in mood reflects not only his narrator's postwar hysteria but also his decision to address his readers' affective responses. Working in the tradition of Sterne and Ford, Aldington wrote a satiric novel that attempted to chronicle the transitional years from 1890 to 1918 in English cultural history.

THE COLONEL'S DAUGHTER

Aldington's second novel, *The Colonel's Daughter*, demonstrates his control of a satiric narrative and his mastery of psychological and realistic detail, but the subject, Georgie Smithers, while sympathetically analyzed, is a caricature. A plain girl, Georgie fully shares the narrow cultural and moral perspective of her parents, unquestioning servants to the British Empire. Despite her service as a volunteer nurse, she has been untouched by the revolution in manners and morals introduced by war. She still wears her hair long, unbobbed, and her dress resembles a Girl Guide uniform. A knowledgeable narrator presents Georgie's actions and some of her thoughts, offering occasional judgments; supplementing the narrator is a skeptical character, Purfleet, whose attitude toward Georgie shifts from amusement to pity to infatuation to calculating irony.

Naïvely, Georgie reveals her desire to be married in her declaration, "I adore babies," and she would make any sincere man of her class a docile, faithful wife; unfortunately, there are few such relics left in her world. The one candidate who fortuitously appears, having been isolated from change by his position as a civil servant in the colonies, treats her as a sister and is easily seduced by a more fashionably amoral girl. Georgie shows her compassionate nature and essential human goodness as she defends a working-class girl who has become pregnant out of wedlock. Once Georgie overcomes her shock, she acts generously and intelligently to arrange a marriage, a job, and a home for the girl. As the reader contrasts Georgie's character with the mean-spirited people around her, Aldington's critique of English morality emerges. Under Purfleet's guidance, Georgie awakens to her own sexual desires, but she attracts no acceptable mate. After her father's death, Georgie finds herself fully conscious of being trapped in her poverty, in her duty to her mother, and in her solitude.

Appended to *The Colonel's Daughter* is a short satiric and farcical epilogue in which Bim and Bom, two Russians, attack the economic and social bases of English culture. In style and mood, this epilogue differs radically from the body of the sentimental, psychologically realistic novel, but Aldington's attack on hypocrisy, materialistic values, social injustice, and prudery remains the same.

ALL MEN ARE ENEMIES

All Men Are Enemies, Aldington's third novel, presents the odyssey of Anthony Clarendon from 1900 to 1927. Like Homer, Aldington begins his modern odyssey with a council of gods determining the fate of his hero. Athena, goddess of wisdom, gives the hero the gift of loving truth—clearly not the gift of devious Odysseus. Aphrodite places him under her erotic influence. Artemis, goddess of pain in childbirth, promises to stir up hatred for Clarendon. Ares promises him strength. The exiled goddess Isis, whom Aldington introduces to Zeus's council, dooms the hero to seek a lost beauty and an impossible perfection. Until the last pages of this novel, the curse of Isis prevails.

The first part of Clarendon's life includes his intellectual and emotional education, his first loves, and ends in 1914 as he parts from his perfect mate, Katha, an Austrian with whom he has enjoyed an ideal affair. The literary source of Katha's primal eroticism may be glimpsed in the D. H. Lawrentian name of her English aunt, Gudrun. The war separates these lovers, and the remaining three-fourths of the novel chronicles Clarendon's long, painful journey back to Katha.

Aldington skillfully describes the vivid nightmares and suicidal apathy of the war veteran Clarendon, who condemns the meaningless frivolity and opportunism of postwar society. Clarendon's roots in prewar English culture have been destroyed, not only by his wartime experience of the blind hatred, or by the deaths, but also by the pressures to conform. He observes, with profound regret, a friend encased by "a facetious social personality so long and carefully played up to that it had ended by destroying the real personality." He avoids that fate by leaving England, separating from his wife, and aimlessly traveling in Europe. By chance, a mutual acquaintance helps him relocate Katha, and they are reunited after a speedy automobile pursuit, a rough boat ride, and a tenderly hesitant courtship. As Odysseus is reconciled with Penelope, so Clarendon and Katha resume their idyllic love. The novel's conclusion celebrates the future happiness of these two battered survivors, their passion freely expressed. However improbable, the romantic denouement seems to fulfill Clarendon's wish that the postwar world not be as superficial as he had believed. Aldington's subsequent novels are less optimistic.

WOMEN MUST WORK

Women Must Work addresses the tragedy, as Aldington sees it, of the liberated career woman, who, despite her idealistic dreams, becomes selfish, unconsciously repeats the mistakes of her parents' generation, and, consequently, fails to enjoy her financial and social success. Etta Morison's culturally narrow childhood in a bourgeois family instills in her a desire to escape from restraint. Introduced to the woman suffrage movement by a friend named Vera, Etta plans her escape, learning the clerical skills by which she hopes to earn an independent living. Her strategy, advancement through education, has been a successful formula for heroes of the bildungsroman, but for a young woman education opens fewer doors. Without her family's approval, Etta flees to London, finds a cheap room in a nearly respectable boardinghouse, and takes an underpaid job she hopes will lead to advancement; instead, it leads to near starvation and an improper proposal from her boss.

Unlike the unfortunate, fallen heroines of the naturalistic novel, Etta escapes the corrupting forces of her environment and moves into a better situation. She throws herself on the mercy of a kind, wealthy woman devoted to woman suffrage and is hired as the woman's personal secretary. As in a traditional romance, Etta falls in love with her boss's attractive young nephew, but she scruples to take advantage of her position within her benefactor's house. The war separates the confessed lovers and then almost unites them, but Etta, after preparing for and promising her lover all the sexual joy she had previously denied him, again refuses, because her brother has been declared missing at the front. The young man, frustrated and uncomprehending, does not communicate with her again until the war's end, when he returns to attempt a reconciliation, only to find Etta pregnant by a wartime lover who has abandoned her.

Unable to trust a man's fidelity, Etta rejects her soldier and turns to Vera, and the two women retreat to a pastoral cottage, where Etta's daughter is born. Their futile attempts to manage a farm reflect Aldington's own postwar experience and also demonstrates the impracticality of a pastoral retreat from the problems of the modern world. Casting off the faithful Vera, Etta rises again with the assistance of yet another woman, who launches her on a successful career in advertising—an occupation selected to symbolize the postwar commercial society. There is no moral triumph in her success once she returns to the city; Etta succeeds in advertising because she has

learned to use people and to manipulate their desires to meet her own.

Etta's story resolves into a series of renunciations and frustrations that transform her personality, so that the idealistic young woman who longed to be independent becomes a hard, competitive, selfish, and tyrannical success in the business world. She has survived, but at a cost that seems too great. Aldington's judgment is clear in his portrayal of Etta's unintentional alienation of her own rebellious, independent daughter. Despite herself, Etta repeats her parents' mistake by determining the life she wishes for her daughter rather than allowing her daughter the liberty to choose for herself.

In its narrative, *Women Must Work* records the successive failure of several traditional fictional forms. The bildungsroman, the naturalistic novel, the romance, the novel of the soil, and the urban success story all collapse as models for Etta's life. In Aldington's nightmare, the postwar degeneration of cultural and moral norms abandons both the novelist and the hero in a wilderness.

VERY HEAVEN

Aldington's fifth novel, *Very Heaven*, a nostalgic return to the outmoded *Künstlerroman*, portrays a sensitive, intelligent individualist, Chris Heylin, as he encounters his society's hypocritical ethical codes, dullness, and huddling homogeneity. Forced to leave college by his incompetent father's financial failure, Chris confronts his mother's calculating plans for advancement through marriage. Although unable to prevent his sister's unwise union with a rich older man (who later infects her with venereal disease), he denounces her exchange of sex for money. Refusing a similarly advantageous marriage with an older, richer woman with whom he has enjoyed an affair, Chris makes his way alone in London, living in a small, dirty apartment, toiling as an underpaid librarian and flunky to a condescending and conceited man with great wealth and a desire to flaunt it. His life brightens with the addition of a lover who has no sexual inhibitions and who perfectly understands his problems. (Given the implicit determinism of Aldington's fictional world, the reader wonders what parents and what sort of upbringing produced this idyllic modern woman.)

After the hero has apparently attained happiness in the prospect of a teaching job at a private school, a continuing love affair, and an extended European tour, he suffers a double disappointment, losing his promised job through rumors of his immoral affair and losing the sponsor of his European tour through arguments over religious and intellectual independence. The novel expires in Chris's lengthy meditation on his future, as he faces the sea and contemplates suicide. His meditation concludes with his refusal of despair, his renunciation of all formal codes, and his determination to try once more. The hero's final act, turning to walk toward the light of the town, deliberately recalls the end of D. H. Lawrence's *Sons and Lovers* (1913). This ending, inappropriate to the social reality depicted in Aldington's novel, seems unsuited to the practical character of Chris, whose idealism has been tempered by his contact with postwar materialism. Chris has been portrayed as a survivor, not a dreamer. This odd conclusion belongs to a novel written before World War I.

SEVEN AGAINST REEVES

Seven Against Reeves offers a sympathetic though comical portrait of a retired businessman besieged by his ungrateful, socially ambitious family and by a series of leeches—gentry and artists—who want some of his earned money. Despite the punning allusion of its title, this novel does not resemble Aeschylus's tragedy *Hepta epi Thēbas* (467 B.C.E.), the English title of which is *Seven Against Thebes* (translation 1777). The picaresque adventures of Reeves, at home, in Venice, and on the Riviera, pit English generosity, shrewdness, and misplaced self-confidence against various exploiters, domestic and foreign.

Reeves's gullibility and good intentions dimly reflect England's political history in the period between the wars, though Aldington's aim is less political than moral. The denouement, which is probably farcical, celebrates the authoritarian in Reeves as he asserts his own will over his wayward family; the parallel with the dictatorships briefly mentioned throughout this 1938 novel is unfortunate, for Aldington seems to be echoing or mocking a popularly sentimental conclusion. The father's strict authority over his family cannot be expected to solve their various complicated problems, nor will his return to business restore moral order to English society.

REJECTED GUEST

Rejected Guest, which vividly portrays the life of the idle rich in the late 1930's, originates in the social disruption of World War I. Aldington consciously takes up one of the stereotyped stories of that social disruption, that of the illegitimate war baby, and uses it as a vehicle for exploring the postwar dislocation of values. Exposing the hypocrisy of assertions that, in this modern age, illegitimacy arouses no shameful prejudice, Aldington presents society's repeated rejection of David Norris. David's father was killed in the war; his mother abandoned him to his maternal grandparents to make a respectable marriage. Hurt by the ostracism of his hometown and seeking to escape the poverty of his maternal family, David enrolled in University College, London, but lacked sufficient funds to complete his degree. Desperate, he applied to his wealthy paternal grandfather, who, moved by sentiment and remorse, and checked by shame, supplied a stipend large enough for David to live luxuriously, on the conditions that David live abroad and never claim kinship. Suddenly, with the values imposed by years of poverty, David finds himself living with a playboy guardian among the wealthy elite on the Riviera. He adapts, but, through his outsider's observations on the customs and morals of the international set, Aldington continues his satiric attack on postwar society.

Aldington's indictment of hypocrisy and selfishness seems, once again, to be mitigated by eros, as David falls helplessly in love with Diana, an independent and passionate young woman. Swimming, sailing, and making love in the blue Mediterranean, they plan a yearlong sail through the tropics. When the Munich crisis threatens war, however, Diana's selfish instincts reassert their control, and she abandons David. The wealthy grandfather dies without having provided for David in his will, and the young man is forced to accept a job as an office boy in London. The war baby finds no home among the people who produced him, for, as a living reminder of their failure in World War I, David disrupts their comfortable illusions. The political parallel in Aldington's ironic moral fable may be heard when David's playboy guardian advises him, "Kindly remember that I am only acting in your own interests," and David interrupts, "as the Nazi said when he robbed the Jew." The social elite of England and Europe, playing on the Riviera, choose to ignore their world's political affairs until war threatens to spoil their idleness. Aldington's critique of their selfish indifference is unambiguous.

THE ROMANCE OF CASANOVA

Aldington's eighth and final novel, the historical fantasy *The Romance of Casanova*, abandons the social and psychological problems of the twentieth century. This purely entertaining novel presents Giacomo Casanova as an elderly man wondering if he was ever loved for himself rather than for his reputation or his skill as a lover. Answering that doubt, Casanova narrates his affair with Henriette, the romance of his youth. He was captivated with her beauty even before learning her name, and he describes their lovemaking in passionate detail. Their affair was destroyed by his own infidelity and by his ambitious involvement in political intrigues. The novel was perhaps influenced by Aldington's measure of Hollywood's standards, clearly lower than his own as a novelist of the 1930's.

In her *Composition as Explanation* (1926), Gertrude Stein wrote that the most significant effect that World War I had on literature was to force a contemporary self-consciousness. Her suggestion helps explain not only the themes but also the experimental forms of Aldington's long fiction. His contemporary self-consciousness demanded affective response to the war and its aftermath. He rejected Joyce's method in *Ulysses* (1922), which he found vulgar and incoherent, and embraced D. H. Lawrence's eroticism and the cult of personality. Though he denied that he was an interpreter of his age, he believed that an author's composition is shaped by the spirit of the time. Like Stein, he believed that the attitude of the writer had changed as a result of World War I; writers of his own age, he felt, were reacting against stagnation. His own fiction, reacting against the stagnation of old forms and the formlessness of modernist prose, provoked much hostile literary criticism yet won a following of appreciative readers. The uneven reputation of Aldington as a novelist validates Stein's paradoxical 1926 dictum: "The creator of a new composition in the arts is an outlaw until he is a classic."

Judith L. Johnston

OTHER MAJOR WORKS

SHORT FICTION: *At All Costs*, 1930; *Last Straws*, 1930; *Roads to Glory*, 1930; *Two Stories: "Deserter" and "The Lads of the Village,"* 1930; *A War Story*, 1930; *Stepping Heavenward*, 1931; *Soft Answers*, 1932.

PLAY: *A Life of a Lady*, pb. 1936 (with Derek Patmore).

POETRY: *Images, 1910-1915*, 1915 (enlarged 1919); *The Love of Myrrhine and Konallis, and Other Prose Poems*, 1917; *Reverie: A Little Book of Poems for H. D.*, 1917; *Images of Desire*, 1919; *Images of War: A Book of Poems*, 1919; *War and Love, 1915-1918*, 1919; *The Berkshire Kennet*, 1923; *Collected Poems, 1915-1923*, 1923; *Exile, and Other Poems*, 1923; *A Fool i' the Forest: A Phantasmagoria*, 1924; *Hark the Herald*, 1928; *Collected Poems*, 1929; *The Eaten Heart*, 1929; *A Dream in the Luxembourg*, 1930; *Movietones*, 1932; *The Poems of Richard Aldington*, 1934; *Life Quest*, 1935; *The Crystal World*, 1937; *The Complete Poems of Richard Aldington*, 1948.

NONFICTION: *Literary Studies and Reviews*, 1924; *Voltaire*, 1925; *French Studies and Reviews*, 1926; *D. H. Lawrence: An Indiscretion*, 1927; *Remy de Gourmont: A Modern Man of Letters*, 1928; *Artifex: Sketches and Ideas*, 1935; *D. H. Lawrence: A Complete List of His Works, Together with a Critical Appreciation*, 1935; *W. Somerset Maugham: An Appreciation*, 1939; *Life for Life's Sake: A Book of Reminiscences*, 1941; *The Duke, Being an Account of the Life and Achievements of Arthur Wellesley, First Duke of Wellington*, 1943; *Four English Portraits, 1801-1851*, 1948; *Jane Austen*, 1948; *The Strange Life of Charles Waterton, 1782-1865*, 1949; *D. H. Lawrence: Portrait of a Genius But . . .*, 1950; *Ezra Pound and T. S. Eliot, a Lecture*, 1954; *Lawrence L'Imposteur: T. E. Lawrence, the Legend and the Man*, 1954; *Pinorman: Personal Recollections of Norman Douglas, Pino Orioli, and Charles Prentice*, 1954; *A. E. Housman and W. B. Yeats, Two Lectures*, 1955; *Lawrence of Arabia: A Biographical Inquiry*, 1955; *Introduction to Mistral*, 1956; *Frauds*, 1957; *Portrait of a Rebel: The Life and Work of Robert Louis Stevenson*, 1957; *Richard Aldington: Selected Critical Writings, 1928-1960*, 1970 (Alister Kershaw, editor); *A Passionate Prodigality*, 1975 (Alan Bird, editor); *Literary Lifelines*, 1981 (Lawrence Durrell, editor).

TRANSLATIONS: *Latin Poems of the Renaissance*, 1915; *The Poems of Anyte of Tegea*, 1915; *The Garland of Months*, 1917 (of Folgóre da San Gimignano's poetry); *Greek Songs in the Manner of Anacreon*, 1919; *The Poems of Mealeager of Gadara*, 1920; *The Good-*

Humoured Ladies, 1922; *French Comedies of the XVIIIth Century*, 1923; *Voyages to the Moon and the Sun*, 1923 (of Cyrano de Bergerac's novel); *A Book of "Characters" from Theophrastus*, 1924; *Dangerous Acquaintances*, 1924 (of Pierre Choderlos de Lacos's novel); *Candide, and Other Romances*, 1927 (of Voltaire's novels); *Fifty Romance Lyric Poems*, 1928; *The Great Betrayal*, 1928 (of Julien Benda's essay); *Remy de Gourmont, Selections from All His Works*, 1929; *Alcestis*, 1930 (of Euripides' play); *The Decameron of Giovanni Boccaccio*, 1930; *Great French Romances*, 1946.

EDITED TEXT: *The Viking Book of Poetry of the English-Speaking World*, 1941.

BIBLIOGRAPHY

Ayers, David. "Proto-Fascism of Richard Aldington's *Death of a Hero*." In *English Literature of the 1920's*. Edinburgh: Edinburgh University Press, 1999. Examination of *Death of a Hero* focuses on the novel's relationship to fascism and its treatment of war, women, and male-male relations. Part of a larger work that places novels and other English literature within the context of social issues and the literary history of the 1920's.

Doyle, Charles. *Richard Aldington: A Biography*. Carbondale: Southern Illinois University Press, 1989. Comprehensive biography does ample justice to Aldington's multifaceted gifts as a writer. The chapter "The T. E. Lawrence Affair, 1950-55," concerning Aldington's biography of Lawrence, makes fascinating reading not only for Aldington's debunking of the Lawrence myth but also for its depiction of the legal intricacies involved in publishing controversial material. Includes a valuable contribution to secondary material on Aldington.

_____, ed. *Richard Aldington: Reappraisals*. Victoria, B.C.: English Literary Studies, University of Victoria, 1990. Collection of essays reconsiders Aldington's reputation as poet, novelist, and writer of nonfiction. The assumption behind this collection is that Aldington was unjustly blacklisted as a result of his frank treatment of T. E. Lawrence.

Gates, Norman T., ed. *Richard Aldington: An Autobiography in Letters*. University Park: Pennsylvania State University Press, 1992. Comprehensive selection of letters presents a recounting of Aldington's life story through the author's own words. The letters provide the author's opinions of other modernist writers; describe his love for his wife, the American poet H. D., and for his mistresses; discuss his work on the editorial staffs of *The Egoist* and the *Criterion*; and offer information about other aspects of his life.

Goldman, Jane. "*The Egoist*, War, Hell, and Image: T. S. Eliot, Dora Marsden, John Rodker, Ezra Pound, and Richard Aldington." In *Modernism, 1910-1945: Image to Apocalypse*. New York: Palgrave Macmillan, 2004. Aldington is one of the authors whose work is examined in this study of the rise and development of modernist and avant-garde literature and literary theory from the heyday of Imagism to the apocalypse movement.

Kershaw, Alister, and Frédéric-Jacques Temple, eds. *Richard Aldington: An Intimate Portrait*. Carbondale: Southern Illinois University Press, 1965. Anthology presents favorable commentary on Aldington from various distinguished persons, including T. S. Eliot, Lawrence Durrell, Sir Herbert Read, and C. P. Snow. Includes an excellent bibliography of Aldington's writings.

McGreevy, Thomas. *Richard Aldington: An Englishman*. 1931. Reprint. New York: Haskell House, 1974. Early, appreciative study of Aldington provides critical commentary on his works up to 1931. Covers Aldington's poetry and his novels, with emphasis on *Death of a Hero*.

Smith, Richard Eugene. *Richard Aldington*. Boston: Twayne, 1977. Comprehensive survey of Aldington's work includes criticism of Aldington's major novels as well as his work as a biographer, translator, and critic. Notes that his leadership in the Imagist movement during the 1920's was but a small part of his varied and productive literary career.

Willis, J. H., Jr. "The Censored Language of War: Richard Aldington's *Death of a Hero* and Three Other War Novels of 1929." *Twentieth Century Literature* 45, no. 4 (Winter, 1999): 467-487. Critiques four novels written after World War I—Aldington's *Death of a Hero*, Ernest Hemingway's *A Farewell to Arms*, Erich Maria Remarque's *All Quiet on the*

Western Front, and Frederick Manning's *The Middle Parts of Fortune*—to demonstrate how these authors responded to the obscenity laws of the 1920's, which made it difficult for writers to portray realistically the bitter experiences of modern warfare.

Zilboorg, Caroline. "'What Part Have I Now That You Have Come Together?': Richard Aldington on War, Gender, and Textual Representation." In *Gender and Warfare in the Twentieth Century: Textual Representations*, edited by Angela K. Smith. New York: Manchester University Press, 2004. Analysis of *Death of a Hero* focuses on the novel's treatment of World War I and its depiction of the relationships between men and women during the war.

THOMAS BAILEY ALDRICH

Born: Portsmouth, New Hampshire; November 11, 1836

Died: Boston, Massachusetts; March 19, 1907

PRINCIPAL LONG FICTION

Daisy's Necklace and What Came of It, 1857
The Story of a Bad Boy, 1869
Prudence Palfrey, 1874
The Queen of Sheba, 1877
The Stillwater Tragedy, 1880
The Second Son, 1888 (with Margaret Oliphant)

OTHER LITERARY FORMS

During his prolific literary career, Thomas Bailey Aldrich (AWL-drihch) published short stories, poems, essays, and verse plays. Many of his letters are included in Ferris Greenslet's *The Life of Thomas Bailey Aldrich* (1908).

ACHIEVEMENTS

Thomas Bailey Aldrich was one of the best-known literary figures in the United States during the latter half of the nineteenth century. As a poet, he was already a popular success in 1855—at age nineteen. Ten years later, after having his more mature and less sentimental poetry praised by Henry Wadsworth Longfellow, Ralph Waldo Emerson, James Russell Lowell, and Oliver Wendell Holmes, he was considered worthy enough to be included in the prestigious Blue and Gold Series of verse published by Ticknor & Fields. He further enhanced his reputation when he turned to fiction in the late 1860's.

The Story of a Bad Boy was enormously popular, and Aldrich's short stories soon were a consistent feature of *The Atlantic*. For the rest of his career, this magazine was his favorite place of publication, for its predominantly genteel audience enjoyed his serialized novels and his clever, well-crafted short stories with surprise endings.

Aldrich's stature as a major writer, strengthened during his successful tenure as editor of *The Atlantic*, was certainly apparent in 1884 when *The Critic*, a New York literary magazine, asked readers to name the forty most important American writers. Aldrich finished seventh, outpolling Henry James, Mark Twain, Walt Whitman, and Bret Harte. Twenty years later his importance was again strikingly affirmed when he was one of the first fifteen artists named to the National Academy of Arts and Sciences.

Aldrich's reputation plummeted after his death, however. Critics such as H. L. Mencken, C. Hartley Grattan, and Vernon Louis Parrington denigrated his accomplishments, dismissing him as shallowly optimistic, blindly conservative, and uninteresting. They believed that he had nothing to say to the modern, post-World War I reader. Aldrich's stock has never recovered, and now he is interesting primarily to those who study the relationship between the genteel tradition and the growth of realism, particularly how his poetry possibly foreshadows the Imagists; how his *The Story of a Bad Boy* broke ground for Twain's "boys' books"; how his female characters reflect his age's literary treatment of women; and how *The Stillwater Tragedy* fits into the history of the American economic novel.

BIOGRAPHY

Thomas Bailey Aldrich was born on November 11, 1836, in Portsmouth, New Hampshire, the sleepy seaport town he nostalgically re-created in much of his fiction—most notably in *The Story of a Bad Boy*, his autobiographical homage to adolescence. He was an only child, and his early years were a bit unsettled because his father, in a restless search for business success, first moved the family to New York City in 1841 and then to New Orleans in 1846. In 1849, Aldrich's parents sent him back to Portsmouth for a better education, but his plans eventually to enter Harvard suddenly ended when his father died of cholera. In 1852, because of his family's uncertain financial state, Aldrich had to accept a job as a clerk in his uncle's New York City counting house.

In 1855, after publishing his first book of poems (filled with echoes of John Keats, Alfred, Lord Tennyson, and Longfellow) and after having become well known with his sentimental and extremely popular poem "The Ballad of Babie Bell," Aldrich left his uncle's business. Having decided to be a man of letters, he spent the rest of the 1850's publishing more poetry, beginning his career as an editor by working for the *Home Journal* (1855-1859) and the *Saturday Press* (1859-1860), and writing his first novel, *Daisy's Necklace and What Came of It*—a confused, uninteresting attempt to burlesque the saccharine fiction of "the Feminine Fifties." At the same time, he was moving back and forth between two New York social-literary crowds: the genteel circle that included Bayard Taylor, E. C. Stedman, and Richard Stoddard, and the radical, bohemian circle that included Walt Whitman.

Temperamentally uncomfortable with the rebellious, flamboyant bohemians, Aldrich in the 1860's inevitably found his intellectual home in the more conservative group. He felt, in fact, that the luckiest day of his life was when he moved to Boston in 1866 to be the editor of the periodical *Every Saturday*. Married by then, he settled into the fashionable life of Beacon Hill and became, as he once proudly noted, "Boston-plated." Deeply committed to this genteel society, Aldrich, unlike his friend William Dean Howells, never seriously questioned its values, and his art reflects this acceptance.

From 1868 to 1873, Aldrich turned from poetry and devoted himself to fiction, publishing *The Story of a Bad Boy* and his most famous short story, "Marjorie Daw." In 1874, after *Every Saturday* failed, he moved to the village of Ponkapog, twelve miles from Boston, and spent six quiet, happy, and productive years writing poems, novels, and sketches. This idyll ended in 1881 when he replaced Howells as the editor of *The Atlantic*, a position Aldrich held until 1890. From 1890 to his death in 1907, Aldrich spent his time writing, traveling overseas, and supervising the collecting of his works.

ANALYSIS

In *The Rise of the American Novel* (1948), Alexander Cowie calls Thomas Bailey Aldrich an "Indian Summer writer." By this he means that Aldrich's art represents a late and pleasantly light blooming of the genteel New

Thomas Bailey Aldrich. (Library of Congress)

England literary tradition. It is an easygoing, entertaining, and edifying art that attempts to break no new ground and usually does not disturb its readers. Cowie's description is apt because it points to the conservatism and optimism resting at the heart of Aldrich's novels. Always ready to defend the traditional way, Aldrich reacts against the forces that threaten the established, secure order. Thus he nostalgically celebrates the idyllic, old-fashioned New England village while looking with disgust on modern, industrialized towns and cities; he promotes the beauties of American capitalism while warning against the dangers of labor unions; he trusts the security of orthodox religious beliefs while shying away from the uncertainties of modern thought; and he affirms the ideal of the prudent, measured life while suspecting all types of erratic, impulsive behavior. In his fiction, tradition continually collides with the disruptive energy of change, and Aldrich usually depicts the triumph of orthodox values in such a struggle.

To make sure that his readers understand this conservative position, Aldrich clarifies and stresses it through his use of the narrative voice. Continually entering the novels, this voice always belongs to a cultured man who is a mirror image of Aldrich himself. In *Daisy's Necklace and What Came of It*, he is a well-read young writer grappling with a first novel filled with pastoral reveries, literary criticism (including an offhand attack of Walt Whitman), and editorials espousing various traditional beliefs. In *The Story of a Bad Boy*, he is this same young man grown a bit older. He now meditates on his lost youth and lingers over his birthplace, the ancient town of Rivermouth. Like Twain's St. Petersburg in *The Adventures of Tom Sawyer* (1876), this setting is enveloped in a romantic mist; its gigantic elms, its old houses, its crumbling wharves, and its memories of past glories evoke a time of past innocence for the narrator. This persona in Aldrich's next two novels, *Prudence Palfrey* and *The Queen of Sheba*, becomes an anonymous Victorian gentleman who is distanced from the Rivermouth setting, imperiously commenting on the struggles of young love, on the town's foibles, and on the dangers of rash behavior. Finally, in *The Stillwater Tragedy*, Aldrich uses this same gentleman to defend ardently the American businessman against the demands of the radical workingman.

Aldrich's faith in the superiority of the genteel value system, a faith embodied in these narrators, helped him to maintain his conviction that art should be optimistic and instructive. He believed that art should never be morbid because it then has a subversive, unhealthy, and depressing effect on the audience. Also, it should avoid the low and vulgar areas of life, for such material inevitably undercuts the beauties of literature. Instead, the artist should work to maintain a hopeful, buoyant, noble tone in the creation of wholesome, affirmative, radiant works. Then the artist will succeed in uplifting the audience.

This view of art, which centers on not upsetting or challenging an audience's existing value system, helps explain Aldrich's reservations about the poetry of Whitman and Emily Dickinson as well as his antipathy toward the naturalism of Émile Zola. It also accounts for his urge to create happy endings within his novels and his usual unwillingness to stare too long at the darker sides of life. For example, *Prudence Palfrey*, *The Queen of Sheba*, and *The Stillwater Tragedy* all end with young lovers realizing their marriage plans after melodramatically overcoming various tensions and hardships. In each case, the narrative voice makes certain to assure the reader that the couple will go on to live happily together.

This is not to say that Aldrich never treats the more somber aspects of human existence. Most notably, in every novel Aldrich creates orphaned, vulnerable protagonists who experience loneliness and alienation while missing the guidance of strong parental figures. Through them, Aldrich, who shared his culture's devotion to the family, tries to objectify the emotional trauma he felt when his father died. This darker side of his vision also appears when he examines—sometimes in a truncated way—the more irrational sides of human behavior: jealousy in *Prudence Palfrey*, madness in *The Queen of Sheba*, and uncontrollable rage in *The Stillwater Tragedy*. In the end, however, Aldrich usually avoids fully confronting this intriguing part of his fictional world. As a result, he is able to maintain the sunny climate of his novels—although the reader finds it difficult to forget or ignore the moments of danger and sadness haunting Aldrich's Indian Summer writing.

THE STORY OF A BAD BOY

Early in 1869, *The Story of a Bad Boy* first appeared as a serial in the juvenile magazine *Our Young Folks*.

Apparently Aldrich felt that it would appeal primarily to an adolescent audience; however, the novel's widespread popularity during the remainder of the nineteenth century indicates that it attracted older readers as well. To a great extent, its general success stemmed from Aldrich's realistic treatment of his hero, Tom Bailey. He wanted the boy to be different from the saintly and unbelievable "little grown-ups" moralizing their way through the popular fiction of his time. This is why Aldrich calls Tom a "bad boy": It is his striking way of stressing that he will not create a pious stick figure; rather, his boy will be an amiable, impulsive, flesh-and-blood human being who, like most healthy children, gets into a bit of trouble. Tom's badness, then, is not that of a subversive, delinquent child. Usually he respects adult authority, whether it emanates from his father, grandfather, or schoolteacher. He also frequently agrees with their criticisms of his occasionally wayward behavior. Tom is thus Aldrich's realistic version of the genteel adolescent, and the boy's respectability explains why the novel has only the illusion of conflict between Tom and his community.

This conception of Tom seems quite conventional now, but the boy's "badness" was a refreshing change for Aldrich's audience, who had grown tired of reading about perfect children. William Dean Howells, for example, in his review of the novel, praised its resolution to show a boy's life as it is, not as it ought to be. In addition, as Walter Blair has noted, *The Story of a Bad Boy* might have spurred Twain's conception of *The Adventures of Tom Sawyer*. Although Twain was not much impressed when he first read Aldrich's novel in 1869, it probably helped him see the potential in writing a more realistic "boys' book." It also provided Twain with an example of the narrative strategy he would eventually employ, with variations, in his own novel: Aldrich generates a type of double perspective by having an adult narrator re-create an adolescent's vision of the world. This structure enables Aldrich to create a sense of tension as he moves the reader back and forth between the viewpoints of Tom Bailey the boy, who is spontaneous and sometimes adventurously foolish, and Tom Bailey the man, who is prudent and nostalgic.

When Aldrich locates the reader within the boy's perspective, he concentrates on dramatizing, rather than explaining, Tom's experiences. There are many of these moments, and they accumulate to give a strong sense of the everyday reality of childhood. They include Tom's boring Sundays in his grandfather's religious household, his trips to the woods and cliffs, his scuffles with other boys, his playacting, his winter exploits, and his elaborate pranks designed to upset temporarily the staid life of Rivermouth. These moments also include the novel's darker times. For example, in one of the most haunting scenes in Aldrich's fiction, Tom witnesses the death of his playmate Binny Wallace. The horrified Tom watches as the helpless boy, trapped on a runaway boat, drifts out to sea toward certain destruction. The boat gets ever smaller, the sea grows choppier, and then Binny disappears into the night, which suddenly seems to sob with the cries of ghosts. Here Aldrich lets Tom's consciousness tell the story, and consequently the incident is alive in all its terror. Moreover, at other times, Aldrich objectifies his own sense of familial loss through Tom's perception (when the lonely boy yearns to be reunited with his parents and when he grieves over the death of his father); these episodes represent Aldrich's most personal examination of his bittersweet childhood.

In all these episodes, however, no matter how deeply Aldrich immerses the reader within the boy's consciousness, the reader rarely forgets the adult point of view always hovering over Tom's story. Employed for many purposes, this voice speaks directly to both the adolescents and the adults in Aldrich's audience. When the narrator speaks to the young, he becomes the friendly Victorian moralist drawing lessons from his own childhood and instructing them about the evils of smoking, the advantages of a boy learning how to box, the value of working hard, and the dangers in being impulsive. He is the voice of mature wisdom, and his prudence is often set in polite opposition to the values of Tom Bailey the boy. This strategy, which allows Aldrich to critique as well as to appreciate Tom's adventures, thus protects the novel from becoming a hymn to the anarchy of adolescence.

The narrator, however, becomes much more appealing (because he is not so smug or patronizing) when he speaks to adults. Intensely nostalgic, he luxuriates in remembering, with great detail, the Rivermouth of his youth. At the same time, his awareness of being caught in time occasionally makes him brood about death. He thinks about the fates of his boyhood chums who have already died. He also thinks about his dead father—confessing that he has never completely recovered from losing this sacred companion (here Aldrich directly states his feelings through the narrator). With these recollections and musings, Aldrich succeeds in creating a sharp, often poignant juxtaposition of childhood and adulthood. He touches on the adult reader's desire to freeze time so that cherished moments and people can be rescued from the always withering past. Most important, in catching this desire, he makes *The Story of a Bad Boy* more than a book only for boys.

PRUDENCE PALFREY

Like *The Story of a Bad Boy*, Aldrich's *Prudence Palfrey* is a readable, episodic work set in Rivermouth and narrated by a persona closely aligned to Aldrich's conservative values. It is not nearly as autobiographical as its predecessor, however, and Aldrich's decreasing reliance on his personal experiences results in a weak plot. Having to create most of the story out of his imagination or from materials outside the realm of his immediate experience, Aldrich too often falls back on melodramatic strategies to further the plot. The hero, John Dent, loves Prudence Palfrey, a young woman having the qualities found in the stereotypical heroine of the popular genteel novel: She is earnest, pale, attractive, and, as her name indicates, prudent. The lovers are separated when Dent travels to the West to make his fortune, for without money, he cannot marry her. In a long section not well integrated into the novel, Aldrich describes John's western experiences as the young man makes a fortune, loses it to a villain, and then wanders in despair. In the meantime, the villain—who has an unnatural hatred for John—goes to the East, enters Rivermouth under the guise of being the town's new minister, and begins courting Prudence. Finally, in a thoroughly contrived denouement, complete with a secret will, striking coincidences, treacherous schemes, and sudden revelations, John returns home, unmasks the villain, suddenly becomes rich, and marries Prudence.

Such a plot hardly makes for great fiction. Still, in two ways, the work is important to an understanding of how Aldrich's aesthetic vision developed. First, it points to his changing conception of his genteel narrative voice, setting the direction for the magisterial persona of his next two novels, *The Queen of Sheba* and *The Stillwater*

Tragedy. Less personal, less nostalgic, and less vulnerable than Tom Bailey in *The Story of a Bad Boy*, the anonymous narrator of *Prudence Palfrey* does not describe and relive his own childhood experiences. He is much more removed from the action that he oversees, and this distance allows him to assume a more objective stance toward Rivermouth. Thus, while he obviously respects the town's backwoods tranquillity and its preservation of traditional moral values, the narrator also can be quite critical. This tougher side of his perspective leads him to comment sarcastically on the pretensions of the town's wealthy inhabitants, to chide the gossips, to laugh at the town's taste in architecture, and to note that it desperately needs new blood because it is in danger of becoming a sterile place.

In addition to its employment of the narrative voice, *Prudence Palfrey* is interesting because, more than any of Aldrich's other novels, it reflects the author's devotion to the ideals of work, duty, discipline, and prudence. At times, it almost seems to be a casebook espousing the Victorian values affirmed by Thomas Carlyle in *Sartor Resartus* (1836); the major tensions in *Prudence Palfrey* invariably arise because the novel's two most interesting characters, John Dent and his uncle Ralph Dent, fail to follow the model of the one-dimensional Prudence, who always behaves with restraint.

John Dent, for example, must curb his immoderate, often self-indulgent behavior before he can be worthy enough to marry Prudence. At the beginning of the novel, the narrator (who repeatedly celebrates the disciplined life) warns that John, whose father has just died, is in a perilous position. Because he is orphaned, he lacks necessary guidance, and the narrator suggests that this loss of a loving but restraining hand makes John more susceptible to the specious attraction of the romantic quest. For John, this quest is linked to his desire to become suddenly rich in the gold fields: He dreams of a big nugget waiting for him and therefore rejects the Victorian ethic of working hard for long-term, more enduring rewards. Further, he rashly declares that he will come back rich or not come back at all.

Like all of Aldrich's undisciplined characters, John suffers. He becomes immersed in the outlaw society of the western mining towns and yearns for the ordered Rivermouth. He becomes the victim of his dishonest partner. Finally, because of his lack of inner strength, he loses faith in himself after his reversals and sinks into self-pity. All this suffering, however, eventually purges him of his arrogance, light-mindedness, and impetuosity. A chastened John returns to Rivermouth—which he now values for its old-fashioned peace and integrity—and behaves like a conscientious young gentleman worthy of inheriting the money left to him by Parson Hawkins. (Even the parson's will upholds the Victorian belief in work—it stipulates that John must try to become self-reliant before he can receive the money.)

For the first half of *Prudence Palfrey*, Ralph Dent struggles, like his nephew, to control his emotions. Caught between his strong sense of duty as Prudence's surrogate father (the orphaned young woman is his ward) and his increasing sexual attraction toward her, the elder Dent frequently lets jealousy rule him. It leads him to instigate the dismissal of Parson Hawkins, whose friendship with Prudence seems to be standing between Dent and his ward. This action, along with his equally rash championing of the new liberal minister without examining his background, causes Rivermouth to lose its conservative, safe old minister and to become victimized by the impostor. In addition, Dent's jealousy makes him react too violently to his nephew's desire to marry Prudence. As a result, instead of helping the confused young man, he spurs John's wild decision to go to the West.

At times, Ralph Dent is almost reminiscent of the evil stepfathers of melodrama, yet the reader finally sees him as a much more intriguing and sympathetic figure than these cardboard characters. As he confronts, with horror, the true nature of his attraction to Prudence and as he tries to overcome his passion, Dent becomes a complex portrait of a man frightening in his inability to control his feelings, pathetic in his love for the unsuspecting Prudence, and honorable in his efforts not to violate her trust in him. He is thus potentially Aldrich's most tragic character. Aldrich abruptly defuses Dent's inner conflict before the halfway point of the novel, however, by having him suddenly conquer his passion. In the name of duty, Dent buries it for the rest of the novel—and the reader feels shortchanged. It is not unbelievable that the uncle would eventually stifle his passion, but it is inconceivable, after the way he has struggled, that he should suddenly succeed so easily. Aldrich appears to have shied away from the full implications of this character, perhaps because be was afraid that Dent's dilemma was about to upset the comic intent of the novel.

THE STILLWATER TRAGEDY

The Stillwater Tragedy, Aldrich's contribution to the plethora of economic novels written in the United States during the last quarter of the nineteenth century, is his most ambitious attempt at long fiction. In his previous novels, he had not openly confronted social issues, although the pressures of the Gilded Age, the Industrial Revolution, and urban life are in the backgrounds of *The Story of a Bad Boy*, *Prudence Palfrey*, and *The Queen of Sheba*. Such issues, however, come to the forefront in *The Stillwater Tragedy*, as Aldrich leaves his usual Rivermouth setting to concentrate on the conflict between business and the rising labor unions in a small New England factory town. Most important, in depicting this struggle, Aldrich uses his fiction to express, as Walter Fuller Taylor explains in *The Economic Novel in America* (1942), a right-center, moderately conservative, middle-class economic vision. He attacks labor unions as disruptive forces endangering the American Dream while sympathizing with and often idealizing businessmen.

Aldrich tries to appear open-minded about the labor question, so he creates some "good" workers who are honest, simple, hardworking men. He also has his hero, Richard Shackford, acknowledge that workers, if unjustly treated, have a right to strike. Aldrich finally fails in his attempt to be objective, however, because he spends most of the novel depicting what he sees as the usual strike: an absurd, destructive act in which radical labor organizers, whom he calls ghouls, mislead the confused workers into betraying their fair-minded employers.

In building his conservative case. Aldrich overtly ties the passions motivating the labor union to one of the primary themes in his fiction: the dangers of any type of excessive human behavior. Therefore he argues, often through his narrator, who is an apologist for American business, that the labor unions' stubborn, irrational demands (especially their not permitting owners to hire apprentices to fill out the workforce) ultimately hurt the workers by keeping the economic market unnaturally depressed. Aldrich also argues that most of the labor troubles are caused by foreign anarchists who enter the United States still nurturing their wild Old World anger. Finally, he explicitly portrays the "good" worker as the man who respects law and order, reasons out his position, and consequently obeys the commonsense policies of his farseeing employer. In contrast, the "bad" worker permits his emotions to rule him; this behavior is evidenced in the actions of the novel's two most important agitators—Torrini, a self-destructive, ungrateful drunkard who uses his eloquence to inflame the workers, and Durgin, a spiteful parasite who eventually commits murder.

To reinforce this theme, Aldrich goes so far as to show that Shackford's weakest moment in the novel is when the young man lowers himself to Torrini's level of behavior. Having always been cursed with a terrible temper, Aldrich's hero becomes outraged by the Italian's insubordination and gets involved in a physical confrontation with the worker. The workers, in response to this incident, admire Shackford for his use of force. Aldrich makes sure that the reader takes a wider perspective, however, for he has Shackford's fiancé, Margaret Slocum— another of Aldrich's perfectly prudent genteel heroines—rebuke her young man for not showing "the beauty of self control." Here Margaret is certainly speaking for Aldrich, who has pitted two different value systems against each other in this episode to stress the moral superiority of the more sophisticated one. It is this superiority that makes Margaret's father so magnanimous toward his prodigal workers, causes Margaret to become an administering angel during the strike as she brings food to the workers' suffering families, and leads Shackford to forget Torrini's past abuses as he nurses the mortally injured worker. Obviously, Aldrich does everything he can to make the upper-class characters above criticism.

This obvious bias is one of the three major reasons the novel fails. In devoting so much of his energy to elevating the Slocums and Shackford, Aldrich never treats with any complexity the other side of the conflict. He rarely examines with sympathy or understanding the reasons that many workers in the late 1870's felt the need to strike, and he never makes any of the workers more than one-dimensional—probably because he was too divorced from the lives of workingmen to create complex characterizations.

The novel also fails because Aldrich cannot seem to decide whether he is writing a murder mystery, an antiunion polemic, or a conventional love story. As a result, the three story lines do not cohere into a whole, although they sometimes merge temporarily. Finally, *The Stillwater Tragedy* suffers because Aldrich's intrusive narrator tends to explain away the work's conflicts. After listening to his dogmatic and sometimes strident comments, the reader better understands why Howells frequently lamented Aldrich's reliance on this type of authorial voice. Howells felt that it undercut the fictional illusion and made his friend too often appear more like an essayist than a novelist. Even Aldrich at times felt that such intrusions could be a liability; for example, he criticized Henry James's *The American* (1877) for not being dramatic enough because of its omnipresent narrative voice. This criticism is strikingly ironic in the light of the fact that James eventually made the dramatic method the cornerstone of his fiction, while Aldrich never escaped his tendency to disrupt the dramatic flow of his narratives through editorializing.

James Grove

OTHER MAJOR WORKS

SHORT FICTION: *Out of His Head: A Romance*, 1862; *Marjorie Daw, and Other People*, 1873; *Two Bites at a Cherry, with Other Tales*, 1893; *A Sea Turn, and Other Matters*, 1902.

POETRY: *The Bells: A Collection of Chimes*, 1855; *The Ballad of Babie Bell, and Other Poems*, 1859; *Cloth of Gold, and Other Poems*, 1874; *Flower and Thorn: Later Poems*, 1877; *Mercedes and Later Lyrics*, 1884; *Wyndham Towers*, 1890; *Judith and Holofernes*, 1896; *Unguarded Gates, and Other Poems*, 1896; *The Poems of Thomas Bailey Aldrich: The Revised and Complete Household Edition*, 1897.

NONFICTION: *From Ponkapog to Pesth*, 1883; *An Old Town by the Sea*, 1893; *Ponkapog Papers*, 1903.

miscellaneous: *The Works of Thomas Bailey Aldrich*, 1970.

BIBLIOGRAPHY

Aldrich, Mrs. Thomas Bailey. *Crowding Memories*. Boston: Houghton Mifflin, 1920. Written after Aldrich's death, this biography by his wife presents a noncritical view of the author. Interesting for its anecdotal stories about Aldrich and illustrations of the author, his residences, and his friends.

Cohoon, Lorinda B. "Necessary Badness: Reconstructing Post-bellum Boyhood Citizenships in *Our Young Folks* and *The Story Of a Bad Boy*." *Children's Literature Association Quarterly* 29 (Spring, 2004): 5-31. Analyzes Aldrich's novel *The Story of a Bad Boy* and *Our Young Folks*, a nineteenth century children's magazine, to demonstrate how post-Civil War children's literature began promoting the idea that American boyhood was a time when boys rebelled and rejected contemporary concepts of citizenship by engaging in pranks or taking trips into the wilderness.

Cowie, Alexander. *The Rise of the American Novel*. New York: American Book Company, 1948. Classic work provides analysis of Aldrich's narrative style and other aspects of his novels. Cowie calls Aldrich a vital writer whose contribution to American literature can be measured in terms of authenticity.

Greenslet, Ferris. *The Life of Thomas Bailey Aldrich*. 1908. Reprint. Port Washington, N.Y.: Kennikat, 1965. Comprehensive biography details Aldrich's youth and apprenticeship, with significant attention given to Aldrich's editorship of *The Atlantic* during the 1880's and to his novels and poetry. Includes illustrations and an excellent bibliography.

_____. *Thomas Bailey Aldrich*. Boston: Houghton Mifflin, 1908. Official Aldrich biography contains numerous letters not available anywhere else. Describes Aldrich's friendship with William Dean Howells, his influence on American literary life in the last half of the nineteenth century, and his editorship of *The Atlantic*.

Jacobson, Marcia Ann. *Being a Boy Again: Autobiography and the American Boy Book*. Tuscaloosa: University of Alabama Press, 1994. Focuses on a literary genre that flourished between the Civil War and World War I, the American boy book. Examines how the boy books differed from earlier and more didactic stories for boys, discusses how and why the genre developed, and explains why it disappeared. Includes discussion of works by Aldrich, William Dean Howells, Mark Twain, Stephen Crane, and Booth Tarkington.

Prchal, Tim. "The Bad Boys and the New Man: The Role of Tom Sawyer and Similar Characters in the Reconstruction of Masculinity." *American Literary Realism* 36 (Spring, 2004): 187-205. Analyzes the depiction of adolescent boys in Aldrich's *The Story of a Bad Boy*, Mark Twain's *The Adventures of Tom Sawyer*, and other books from the mid-nineteenth century. Describes how their treatment of boyhood and masculinity reflected the cultural changes of their era.

Samuels, Charles E. *Thomas Bailey Aldrich*. New York: Twayne, 1965. Literary biography provides a useful general introduction to Aldrich's life and work, including information about his novels. Features chapter notes, index, and bibliography.

Sattelmeyer, Robert, and J. Donald Crowley, eds. *One Hundred Years of Huckleberry Finn: The Boy, His Book, and American Culture*. Columbia: University of Missouri Press, 1985. Extensive collection of essays includes comparative analyses of Aldrich's and Mark Twain's works, especially in terms of Aldrich's *The Story of a Bad Boy*. In his essay "'I Did Wish Tom Sawyer Was There': Boy-Book Elements in *Tom Sawyer* and *Huckleberry Finn*," Alan Gribben briefly but astutely argues that Aldrich's novel has not received due analysis in terms of its influence on *The Adventures of Tom Sawyer*.

Yardley, Jonathan. "Thomas Bailey Aldrich." *The Washington Post*, May 13, 2001. Discusses *The Story of a Bad Boy*, including its reception when it initially appeared, the novel's view of adolescence as a time when boys behave badly, and how the concept of the American "bad boy" has changed since the book's publication.

CIRO ALEGRÍA

Born: Hacienda Quilca, Sartimbamba district, Peru;
  November 4, 1909
Died: Chaclacayo, Peru; February 17, 1967
Also known as: Ciro Alegría Bazán

PRINCIPAL LONG FICTION

La serpiente de oro, 1935 (*The Golden Serpent*,
  1943)
Los perros hambrientos, 1938
El mundo es ancho y ajeno, 1941 (*Broad and
  Alien Is the World*, 1941)
Siempre hay caminos, 1969
Lázaro, 1973
El dilema de Krause: Penitenciaria de Lima,
  1979

OTHER LITERARY FORMS

In addition to his works of long fiction, Ciro Alegría (ahl-ay-GREE-ah) wrote short stories that have been published in several collections, including *Duelo de caballeros* (1963) and *Siete cuentos quirománticos* (1978). His nonfictional works include *La revolución cubana: Un testimonio personal* (1973) and *Mucha suerte con harto palo: Memorias* (1976), and early in his career he published the poetry volume *Cantos de la revolución* (1934).

ACHIEVEMENTS

Imprisoned in his native Peru for his liberal, antidictatorial convictions and political activism, then exiled to neighboring Chile, Ciro Alegría wrote the three prizewinning novels that echoed around the world as a powerful voice for the rights of the oppressed and exploited Indians of his native country. These *novelas indigenistas* (indigenist novels, so called because they deal with the problems of the indigenous peoples of Latin America) are lyric, direct, and honest, portraying the hard lives of the Indians and *cholos* (those of mixed Indian and white blood) of the Andes with deep sympathy and condemning the actions of their persecutors. His third novel, *Broad and Alien Is the World*, was awarded the Latin American Novel Prize in 1941. Despite this tremendous

beginning, however, Alegría did not continue to write novels, and, apart from his posthumously published works—including *Lázaro*, which he wrote in Cuba in 1953 and never quite finished—these three first novels remain his entire opus in the genre.

Though written with freshness and vigor, Alegría's novels were in a style reminiscent of the best nineteenth century fiction, and so to a later, post-World War II generation, which witnessed the rise of a new, technically more sophisticated school of Latin American fiction, Alegría's indigenist realism seemed too one-dimensional and too undisciplined structurally. Unfortunately, this postwar reappraisal kept the author from writing any further novels, and so from 1941 until 1963, Alegría went into a period of total literary silence. Indeed, his novels do have a loose, rather jumbled structure, yet they also have great emotional and aesthetic impact because they portray a sector of human life with great credibility and humanitarianism and because they are vibrant with the author's commitment to human rights.

BIOGRAPHY

Ciro Alegría Bazán was born on November 4, 1909, in Sartimbamba district, Huamachuco province, in Peru. During his childhood on his family's ranch, he learned a great deal about the life and problems of the Peruvian Indians, and his grandfather taught him to sympathize with their hard life. When Alegría was in high school, one of his teachers, the famous poet César Vallejo, influenced his political thinking and encouraged him to write. Alegría's career as a journalist began in 1925; two years later, at the age of eighteen, he was already editor in chief of *El norte*, an opposition newspaper, and a member of Alianza Popular Revolucionaria Americana, a group advocating democratic socialism.

Alegría registered at the University of Trujillo in 1930 but dropped out after half a year and returned to journalism. Soon he was arrested and given a ten-year jail sentence for his editorials against the government. After serving two years of his sentence, he emigrated to Chile, where he wrote his three famous novels in order to win prize money to supplement his scanty earnings as a reporter. During his Chilean exile, two attempts on his life as well as a kidnapping attempt were made by the Peruvian secret service. His first novel, *The Golden Serpent*, won a coveted literary prize. As a result of hunger and hardships suffered in prison, Alegría contracted tuberculosis and spent some time in a sanatorium in Chile, where he wrote his second novel, *Los perros hambrientos* (the hungry dogs). The English translation of his third novel, *Broad and Alien Is the World*, was published in the United States even before the Spanish-language edition appeared. The book was quickly translated into sixteen other languages, making Alegría world-famous.

During his twenty-six-year exile from his native Peru, Alegría taught literature at Columbia University, at the University of Puerto Rico, and later at Oriente University in Cuba. He finally returned to Peru in 1960 and was elected senator as a member of the social democratic Acción Popular Party. He died in Lima, Peru, in 1967, at the age of fifty-seven.

ANALYSIS

Ciro Alegría's novels are distinguished from prior works in the Latin American tradition of indigenist literature because they depict the Andes Indians realistically, and they avoid the extremes of either an exotic picturesque idealization of the "noble savage" or a warped negative portrayal of criminalistic and pathological primitivism amid the crudest living conditions. Like other novelists of the school of indigenist realism, which thrived in the 1920's and 1930's throughout Latin America, Alegría wrote novels of protest against the hard lot and oppressed condition of the Indians and was not concerned primarily with literary quality for its own sake. His works, perhaps for that very reason, give an impression of great spontaneity and directly perceived reality.

THE GOLDEN SERPENT

Alegría's first novel, *The Golden Serpent*, focuses not on the tribal Indians, who appear occasionally in the background, but on the *cholo* river men in a jungle valley along the treacherous Marañon River, where they earn their living as ferrymen transporting people, goods, and cattle on their balsa rafts at the risk of their lives. The great struggle of the book is between the rushing river—

with its dangerous currents and rapids, its cliffs, jungles, and sandy, gold-dust-rich beaches—and the men who match their wits and brawn with the river's primeval power.

The title *The Golden Serpent* refers to the river; this metaphor is applied to it by a young engineer from Lima, Don Osvaldo, because from a cliff top this "world of yellow mud" looks like a "great yellow serpent"; its secondary reference is to a company by the same name that the engineer plans to establish to obtain financing and machinery to mine the river's rich gold deposits. The title also references the little yellow viper that bites the engineer fatally in the neck, preventing him from ever returning to civilization. All three meanings intermingle in the chthonic symbolism of the river and its jungles, teeming with both life and death. In Alegría's rich, poetic prose, the river becomes a symbol of life itself, powerful and multivalent: "Life always triumphs. Man is like the river, deep, having his ups and downs, but always stouthearted." "Not everything went smoothly, for life is like the river, full of turns and rough crossings." Such comparisons, both explicit and implicit, are woven into the texture of many vivid descriptions of the tropical environment.

In *The Golden Serpent*, the central focus is on humankind's struggle with nature—the exploitation or oppression of human beings by other humans plays only a small role here. The river, whose ominous roar can always be heard in the background, is the main challenge as well as the life-giving force. Among its more tangible dangers are landslides, treacherous rapids, seasonal floods that sweep away whole settlements, and tremendous logjams that fling the flimsy balsa rafts of the *cholos* against jutting cliffs or cause them to be swallowed up by whirlpools. The deadly disease *uta*, which rots the flesh off a person's living bones, affects mainly outsiders who venture into the tropical valleys. Snakes, mosquitoes, and other vermin are ubiquitous, and larger denizens of the jungle also make their presence felt; in one chapter, a *cholo* woman outwits and kills a puma that has been slaying the farm animals and spreading panic in the village. Early in the novel, Alegría graphically describes the plight of two brothers stranded in the middle of the shallows in the low-water season, separated from shore on both sides by deep water and steep cliffs and slowly starving. Only one of the brothers survives; the other is caught in the swift current and drowns when he makes a desperate but unwise attempt to swim to shore.

The *cholo* men are uneducated, heavy drinkers, hard workers, impetuous, proud of their hazardous life, and grateful to the river for their livelihood, aware of its beauty and its unexpected dangers, which could kill them suddenly when they least expect it. They face its challenges boldly, matching their courage to its strength.

The narrative perspective of the novel is quite complex. The overall narrative vantage point is the first-person plural, denoting "we *cholos*"—as opposed, on one hand, to the pure-blooded tribal Indians who are further from civilization and, on the other, to the occasional representatives of white, civilized authority, both of whom appear only rarely and peripherally to the lives of the *cholo* river-valley dwellers in their remote habitat. Gradually, a first-person-singular narrator emerges out of the plural "we" and becomes a particular *cholo* close to the main protagonists, though his name, Lucas Vilca, is not mentioned until near the end of the book in a chapter in which, by falling hopelessly in love with the widow of one of his dead friends, he momentarily becomes no longer merely a sympathetic observer but the main protagonist. Framed within the comprehensive unity of the *cholo* river man Vilca's "we" and "I" narrative are numerous stories-within-a-story told by other narrators, so that the result is a colorful patchwork quilt of narrative perspective.

Los perros hambrientos

Los perros hambrientos begins with an idyllic scene that sets the tone for the entire first part of the book: A shepherd girl, La Antuca, is herding a large flock of sheep high in the mountains with the help of four faithful dogs. Between sorties to bring back various stray sheep, her companion dog, Zambo, snuggles close to her so that they "mutually share the warmth of their bodies" against the cold wind and mist. The dogs have been raised to be sheepdogs from birth, and they enjoy their work and perform it intelligently. The girl, too, is happy at this lonely work, sometimes singing or calling to the elements, sometimes remaining still "as if united with the vast and profound silence of the *cordillera*, which consists of rock and immeasurable, lonely distances."

The shepherd girl's father, Simón Robles, is famous throughout the region for this breed of dogs as well as for his other talents, such as playing the flute and the drum, telling stories, and exercising sound, humane judgment. The dogs are not purebred, but of a stock "as mixed as that of Peruvian man." They are "*mestizos* like their master." The dogs share the simple but good life of their masters "fraternally," and they feel attached to their owners. Even in the idyllic first part of the novel, however, some mishaps occur. One dog is accidentally blown to bits by exploding dynamite; another is killed with a single jugular-severing bite by a vicious dog that belongs to the local feudal landlord.

The exploits of Robles's dogs are described with pride. They never mistreat the sheep but get them to obey by yapping at their ears. One dog is skilled at partridge hunting; another keeps a frightened herd of cattle from turning back disastrously at midstream in a swift river. They all are courageous and feel a comradeship with humans. The birth and naming of new pups is an occasion of joy. Sometimes they receive traditional names: For example, two dogs are called *Pellejo* (skin) and *Güeso* (bones), and Simón Robles, the great storyteller, jovially explains how once an old widow, guessing that a thief was hiding in her house, kept saying more and more loudly, as if to herself, "All I am is *skin and bones*, that's all, just *skin and bones*," until her two dogs by those names finally heard and came to her rescue. Sometimes, a dog gets its name from a special occasion. One pup is the perpetual companion of Robles's little grandson Damián. "He seems just like his brother," the boy's mother remarks. The little boy overhears and keeps repeating his baby version of the word "brother" (*hermano*), *mañu*, and so the dog is named Mañu. It is a good life, in which each being, human or animal, feels sheltered within the communal pattern of existence.

Two major parallel events signaling the approaching end of the idyllic phase of the novel are the coerced conscription of Damián's father into military service (he is never to return) and the stealing of La Antuca's lead sheepdog by two cattle rustlers. By chapter 7, the dismal anti-idyllic phase begins with the words "It was a bad year," which in agrarian language means "a year without good crops." Both people and animals are put on half rations. Eventually all the chickens have been eaten, and even wheat is in short supply. After a hard year, Simón

Robles is still able to make his family laugh by telling a funny story, which—practical man that he is—he follows up by giving the order for a sheep to be killed the next day. The plight of the dogs "at half ration" is somewhat worse. They "cannot tell or listen to stories," and they have "sheep to guard but not to slaughter." So they howl continuously at night and roam the fields in search of food. Some raid a fenced field of standing green corn and blunt their hunger with the unripe grain, until the owner ambushes them and shoots three of them. The next calamity involves the political machinations that lead to the siege of the two cattle rustlers, Julián and Blás Celedón, and their death by poisoning, while Güeso, who has meanwhile become their faithful companion, dies attacking their killers.

The next year's crop also fails, and now truly dire times are upon the land. Simón Robles forgets his stories. The dogs are no longer fed at all. People are haggard and sad-faced. The social contract between human beings and between humans and animals begin to fall apart, for "the animal loves the one who feeds him. No doubt, the same is true of that higher animal which is man, though he receives his ration in less ostensible equivalencies." Even toward the higher forces, Christian or pagan, this contract seems broken. Ironically, during a procession along a mountain road, as the crowd is singing a hymn, "This and much more/ Our Lady deserves," the statue of the Virgin Mary falls off its stand and is smashed to pieces at the bottom of a cliff. By the end of chapter 14, La Antuca, in a sad scene that counters the opening idyll, is seen again herding her considerably diminished flock on the mountain slopes. She still calls to the elements, "Cloud, cloud, cloooud . . . ," and "Wind, wind, wiiind . . . ," but it is not as before, for "with the pantheistic sentiment of her Indian ancestor she understood that the dark and powerful forces of nature had turned against animal and man." As humankind feels abandoned by nature, so the hungry dogs feel abandoned by humans; the dog Wanka kills a sheep and the other dogs join her in devouring it, atavistically, like prehistoric dogs in the Stone Age.

When the dogs finally return to Robles's farm, they are chased away with sticks and stones, because once a dog has begun to kill the herd, that dog will not stop unless killed or driven away. The dogs thus begin the sad life of homeless marauders. Meanwhile, Damián, abandoned by his mother, who has gone to seek her husband, dies of starvation on the road to his grandfather's village, and his faithful dog, Mañu, tries to protect the little corpse against scavenging condors. For a time, Mañu then helps to guard La Antuca's sheep, but eventually, unfed and uncaressed, he, too, joins the "nomadic" dogs, for "the suffering of the outcasts was his own, and moreover he no longer had any ties to man."

Eventually, two parallel attacks on the big landowner's house result in tragedy for the respective invaders. First, the desperate dogs invade the big house itself, slaying domestic animals, and the landowner kills most of them by laying out poisoned meat. In the second incursion, some fifty *cholos* and Indians appear at the big house, and Simón Robles, their spokesman, questions the landowner's claim that there is no food to be distributed to the starving:

> Master, how can there be nothing? Your mules and horses are eating barley. Isn't a person worth more than an animal? . . . But now the time has come to kill your animals so that your people can eat. We are worse than dogs. . . . Yes, we are just like hungry dogs.

Simón then asserts that all the landowner's harvests, and whatever he and his animals eat, have been accumulated through the peasants' work. Instead of showing commiseration, the landlord harps snidely on his feudal right: "Isn't the land mine? Do you think I give you the land for your pretty faces?" The outraged peasants then attempt to capture the big house but are routed by a barrage of rifle fire and suffer three deaths.

Finally the drought ends, and the only surviving dog, Wanka, mother of the rest, returns to Robles's farm. Simón Robles bursts into tears and, feeling the dog's sufferings to be his own, he caresses her and says, "You know what it is when the poor man and the animal have no land and water. . . . You know, and so you have come back. Wanka, Wankita, . . . you have returned like the good rain."

The great all-encompassing theme of *Los perros hambrientos* is life itself. Although the negative drought-ridden second part of the book is longer than the idyllic first five chapters, the picture of a happier life in more normal times is portrayed convincingly as the more usual lot of human beings and animals, so that even under crushing adversity, the memory of a happy life lingers hauntingly. The times of extreme hardship serve as a touchstone for social inequity, tearing asunder the social arrangements that had been considered quite adequate by the frugal peasants during times of less stress. These lower classes, the *cholo* tenant farmers and the landless Indian farmhands, ranked little above the dogs in the economy of things when the landlord had to choose between them and his livestock. They are not revolutionary firebrands, however; all they seek is "a tiny place" within the broad horizon of the world.

Alegría got the idea for *Broad and Alien Is the World* while writing *Los perros hambrientos*. Like the dog Wanka that returns from her outcast state to the warmth and social functionality of human companionship as soon as living conditions permit, so Simón Robles and his peers, after the famine is over, gladly return to the feudal order, which allows them to till the land and draw a modest livelihood from it. *Los perros hambrientos* is a masterpiece in its depiction of the brave, robust, and generous character of the simple, uneducated men and women of the Andes highlands; in its use of the dog perspective to represent the nobility and basic claims of life itself on an elemental level and as an allegory of the socially low status of the unpropertied classes; and, finally, in its breathtaking beauty and grandeur in some scenes set in the great Andean *cordillera*.

BROAD AND ALIEN IS THE WORLD

Alegría's third novel, *Broad and Alien Is the World*, deals with an organized tribal community of full-blooded Indians. A proud and simple people, the Indians of the Andean village of Yumi live free and independent lives as the novel opens, working hard on their communal property and sharing the produce equitably. Theirs is an almost idyllic existence. Under the wise leadership of their elected mayor, old Rosendo Maqui, the village thrives and the people live happily within their communal system—a relic of the pre-Columbian Inca order that they retain because "work ought not to be to prevent someone from dying or falling sick but to provide well-being and happiness."

Then, in the person of a powerful and ruthless neighbor and rancher, Don Alvaro Amenábar, disaster strikes: Rosendo is imprisoned, and troops attack the village,

leaving it a ghost town, an empty, uninhabited shell of the once-happy place it had been. Some of the Yumi dwellers are scattered in all directions and are reduced to a subhuman state of semiserfdom in the mines or on coconut and rubber plantations in the coastal jungles, where they eke out an exploited and unfree existence and eventually die of hunger and exhaustion. Another part of the Yumians stay together and retreat even higher into the mountains to steeper, less fertile land, where they establish a harsher, scantier semblance of their former, comparatively opulent community. Even this does not satisfy the rancher: What he wanted, in destroying the village, was not primarily the land; rather, he wanted the people themselves to use as cheap labor on his land and in his house. Troops are sent, the Indians are defeated in battle, many of them are killed, and even the second Yumi is left desolate and vacant.

The title *Broad and Alien Is the World* expresses the Indians' hopeless final state when they realize how defenseless and exposed they are—unable to defend their most basic rights or even their very lives. Neither legal means nor armed self-defense proves adequate. Their power within the "broad" society is nil, and so they feel "alienated" from it. The broad society does not provide the foundation for them to maintain their integrity and dignity or even their physical existence within its framework; the broad society does not provide the proper sociopolitical context for their village, which, with its rich interpersonal links and close relation to the soil and to their mountainous habitat, represents home to them, as opposed to the "alien" outside world; the broad society fails to recognize even their most vital interests and leaves them prey to human predators who covet not only their property but also their very persons, subjecting them to inhuman drudgery, exploitation, and death. The destruction of the village of Yumi marks the destruction of the humanity of the individuals who composed it. It is a crime bordering on genocide, because it destroys their dignified life of self-sustaining cooperative labor in their own community and replaces it with loneliness, pain, servitude, and death in a cruel and impersonal society.

By traditional standards, *Broad and Alien Is the World* suffers from a serious structural disunity. The first half of the book has a close perspectival unity centering mostly on the observations of the wise old mayor Rosendo Maqui, but when the villagers are scattered, and especially after Rosendo has been killed, the perspective necessarily shifts away from this internal, character-linked viewpoint to that of a more anonymous omniscient narrator orchestrating the whole, which leaves the reader with an impression of a breach of style. This shift, however, permits Alegría to follow the various fates of individual villagers scattered to all parts of the country after their community has been destroyed.

Alegría's overriding concern was not stylistic unity but thematic comprehensiveness: He was writing the story not of just one person but of an entire village, and it was essential to this purpose to follow the outcome of its destruction for at least a cross section of the villagers. Also, consonant with the epic treatment typical of the indigenist genre, Yumi represents all similarly oppressed Indian villages of Peru; it gives a collective picture of the status of the Indians in Peruvian society at the time (1910 to 1928). This panoramic perspective, which gradually replaces the more intimate personal vantage point of the first part of the book, corresponds to the work's intention to be a realistic exposé and sociological documentary; the persecutions (jail, exile, murder, and kidnapping attempts) the author suffered from the Peruvian authorities, as well as the great acclaim given him and the political office to which he was elected at the end of his twenty-five-year exile, prove amply that the political and humanitarian message of his works was understood by his countrymen—however unreceptive to this message they were for many years.

Ana María F. Parent

OTHER MAJOR WORKS

SHORT FICTION: *Duelo de caballeros*, 1963; *La ofrenda de piedra*, 1969; *Sueño y verdad de América*, 1969; *Siete cuentos quirománticos*, 1978.

POETRY: *Cantos de la revolución*, 1934.

NONFICTION: *Gabriela Mistral íntima*, 1969; *La revolución cubana: Un testimonio personal*, 1973; *Mucha suerte con harto palo: Memorias*, 1976.

BIBLIOGRAPHY

Early, Eileen. *Joy in Exile: Ciro Alegría's Narrative Art*. Washington, D.C.: University Press of America, 1980. Presents an excellent overview and study of Alegría's major books. Particularly useful for English-speaking readers, as Early explains Alegría's background and references clearly.

Foster, David William. *Peruvian Literature: A Bibliography of Secondary Sources*. Westport, Conn.: Greenwood Press, 1981. Compilation of critical works includes a chapter on Alegría that offers an extensive bibliography.

Higgins, James. *A History of Peruvian Literature*. Wolfeboro, N.H.: F. Cairns, 1987. Historical overview provides a lucid summary of Alegría's novels. Higgins, a professor of Latin American literature, has written numerous books and articles about the literature of Peru. Includes indexes and bibliography.

_____. *The Literary Representation of Peru*. Lewiston, N.Y.: Edwin Mellen Press, 2002. Comprehensive work examines more than four hundred years of writings by Peruvian authors to analyze the how these works reflect Peruvian society's response to modernity.

Kokotovic, Misha. *The Colonial Divide in Peruvian Narrative: Conflict and Transformation*. Eastbourne, East Sussex, England.: Sussex Academic Press, 2005. Describes how the colonial divide between Peru's indigenous people and the descendants of Spanish conquerors is expressed in Peruvian literature. Includes an analysis of the narrative form used by Alegría in *Broad and Alien Is the World*.

Onis, Harriet de. Afterword to *The Golden Serpent*, by Ciro Alegría. New York: American Library, 1963. The translator of this edition provides informative commentary on the novel and on its author.

Vázquez Amaral, José. *The Contemporary Latin American Narrative*. New York: Las Americas, 1970. Alegría is one of the novelists whose works are discussed in this overview of Latin American fiction. Includes bibliographical references and index.

SHOLOM ALEICHEM

Born: Pereyaslav, Russia (now Pereyaslav-
    Khmelnitsky, Ukraine); March 2, 1859
Died: New York, New York; May 13, 1916
Also known as: Sholom Naumovich Rabinowitz

PRINCIPAL LONG FICTION

Natasha, 1884
Sender Blank und zayn Gezindl, 1888
Yosele Solovey, 1890 (*The Nightingale*, 1985)
Stempenyu, 1899 (English translation, 1913)
Blondzne Shtern, 1912 (*Wandering Star*, 1952)
Marienbad, 1917 (English translation, 1982)
In Shturm, 1918 (*In the Storm*, 1984)
Blutiger Shpas, 1923 (*The Bloody Hoax*, 1991)

OTHER LITERARY FORMS

Sholom Aleichem (ah-LAY-kehm) is best known for his short narratives, impressionistic sketches, and literary slices of life. The stories surrounding two of his characters—Tevye, the milkman, and Menahem-Mendl, the unsuccessful jack-of-all-trades—are frequently brought together in collections that form episodic but coherent wholes. The adventures of a third character, Mottel, the cantor's son, are sometimes published as young adult fiction, though divisions of Aleichem's audience according to age distinctions are artificial. Aleichem's stories have been published throughout Europe, in Israel, and in the United States. At least eight separate compilations are now available in English.

Some of Aleichem's writings, descriptions, or reactions to events and people are difficult to classify and are sometimes labeled simply "miscellany." Even his autobiography—*Fun'm yarid*, 1916 (*The Great Fair: Scenes from My Childhood*, 1955)—contains as much fantasy as fact. Although he had planned the book for many years, it was left incomplete at his death and covers only his youth.

ACHIEVEMENTS

Sholom Aleichem is regarded as one of the founders of Yiddish literature and is perhaps the most beloved writer in that language. While his longer fiction adds little to the development of the novel, even these works demonstrate the strengths for which he is loved throughout the Jewish world. Although, like most educated East European Jews of his time, he began by writing in Hebrew, the language of sacred learning and of scholarship, he soon discovered that Yiddish was the proper vehicle for relating the exploits of people like those he had known in his youth. The wisdom, the humor, and even the foolishness of these folk could be fully captured only as they actually spoke. In his hands, this despised "jargon" became a vivid, lively, literary instrument. Fluent in the Russian language, and a correspondent with Leo Tolstoy and Anton Chekhov, Aleichem brought to Yiddish fiction the compassion for the insulted and injured that was such a dominant note in classic Russian fiction.

By the end of the twentieth century, Yiddish was spoken only in small pockets of the United States, East Europe, and Israel, and was spoken chiefly by older people. The Yiddish newspapers had almost disappeared, and the theater was preserved only as a relic. Though much of the humor was lost in translation, Aleichem's writing survived and reached large Gentile as well as Jewish audiences in English, Russian, Hebrew. and other languages. Aleichem's fictional characters were introduced to even wider audiences with the popularity of his Broadway musical *Fiddler on the Roof* (pr. 1964), adapted from his Tevye tales, and an operatic adaptation of the novel *The Nightingale* (music by Noam Elkies and libretto by Jeremy Dauber), which was performed at Harvard University in 1999.

Aleichem's central value, though, is his preservation in fiction of a milieu that has vanished, of a people dispersed through pogroms, immigration, revolution, assimilation, and the Holocaust. His books are populated by rabbis, cantors, religious teachers, and kheder students, and yet his books have social and political dimensions. The society of the shtetl (a small Jewish townlet) is already changing in these writings. Revolutionaries who identify themselves as Russians more than as Jews and seek to rid their lives of czars, bishops, and rabbinical tyrants alike begin to appear in his novels. Other characters dream of wealth in America, while Zionists preach a return to the land of their spiritual ancestors.

Along with a large continuing readership, Aleichem has received many posthumous honors, including, in his name, statues in Russia's Kiev and Moscow and a street in New York City. His likeness is also on postage stamps in East Europe and Israel. His home in Kiev is now a place of literary pilgrimage.

BIOGRAPHY

Sholom Aleichem was born Sholom Naumovich Rabinowitz in 1859 in Pereyaslav, Russia (now in Ukraine), to a family of means, although family fortunes fluctuated during his childhood as they did throughout his entire life. His family moved to Voronkov, a small town nearby, which would be the model for his fictional town of Kasrilevke. Even though he received a traditional Jewish religious education, his father was aware of his talents and made sure they were supplemented by training at a Russian secondary school.

Sholom was thirteen years old when his beloved mother died. According to Jewish custom, it was not long before he had a stepmother; in this case, she could have stepped from the tales of the Brothers Grimm. However, she inspired his first published Yiddish work, a dictionary of humorous curses commonly uttered by stepmothers.

Because of the precarious financial situation of his family, young Sholom accepted a position as a government rabbi, an elected but despised functionary who mediated between the czarist government and the Jewish community. Later he was able to find more congenial employment as tutor to Olga Loyeff, daughter of a wealthy Jewish family. Falling in love and fearing her father's disapproval, Aleichem and Loyeff eloped. Their marriage lasted until his death.

Around 1883, Sholom wrote a humorous sketch that appeared in a Yiddish paper under the pseudonym Sholom Aleichem, a Hebrew greeting meaning "Peace unto you." He used the pseudonym initially as an apology for not writing in Hebrew, but he would come to use this pen name exclusively, just as he would continue to write in Yiddish. As business concerns and stock-market speculation took him to cities such as Kiev, Odessa, Paris, and Vienna, his writing continued, with brief nar-

ratives, character sketches, extended anecdotes, and even poems. Also a skilled reader, he was soon in demand as a performer, reading his own stories.

As times became ever more difficult in the Pale of Settlement (the area of the czarist empire in which Jews were permitted to live), immigration to the United States became an attractive possibility. In 1905, a devastating pogrom in which many Jews perished convinced Aleichem to relocate his family to the United States, where he was widely read and the Yiddish theater promised a decent livelihood.

It was in his later years that Aleichem aspired to be a playwright. His ear for the rhythms of speech of many different personalities, along with his imaginative portrayal of different character types, would seem to have fitted his work for the stage. However, he had limited success in the American Yiddish theater.

Even as his sales mounted on two continents, Aleichem, who was not an especially skilled businessman, received limited royalties and often was compelled to earn his living with lectures and readings. Never fully

Sholom Aleichem. (Library of Congress)

at home in the United States, he died in New York City in 1916. Enormous crowds attended his funeral, acknowledging him as a folk hero. His plays met with some acclaim after his death.

ANALYSIS

Sholom Aleichem excelled in character development. The personalities of his protagonists unfold through their thoughts, desires, dreams, worries, and hopes; their interactions with others; and, most of all, through their speech. Their language—a lively, colloquial Yiddish—is rhythmic and rustically poetic. They curse one another, express affection, identify with animals, misquote Scripture, and misuse Talmudic lore, though, even in their innocent, or calculated, mangling of Scripture and tradition, they often reveal a higher folk wisdom.

Because Aleichem was basically a writer of short impressionistic sketches, it is difficult to diagram a clear plot in his narratives. He was largely indifferent to the literary architecture required of longer works. His novels, often picaresque, are therefore disjointed and episodic. He may introduce a character, leave him or her for several chapters, take up another character, and only later return to the first. The natural environment is rarely or only briefly described, yet the little towns and bustling cities through which his characters move come alive as they struggle to survive in whatever setting God has placed them.

The most famous Aleichem characters struggle with poverty, dream of what it would be like to be rich, and ultimately accept their plight. They are not, however, above arguing with the Deity. There is frequently a nearly magical, even mystical element in some of Aleichem's writing, which may reflect the influence of his grandfather, a Hasidic Jew and Kabbalistic mystic.

Preferring the epistolary narrative form or the monologue, Aleichem allows his protagonists to speak for themselves. Sometimes they address their unseen listener respectfully, but the author appears rarely to interfere with them. This encourages the reader to laugh with rather than at the characters so compassionately presented. In his novels, Aleichem appears to be telling rather than writing a story.

It has been customary to refer to Aleichem as the Jewish Mark Twain. There is a story, almost certainly apocryphal, of his meeting with the American humorist: When introduced, Twain is modestly rumored to have said "I understand that I am the American Sholom Aleichem." Certainly, in their use of first-person narrative, often in dialect, to individualize their fictional creations and bring out the humor of situations, the two are similar. They are alike in their kindly satire, as they comment on the foibles of society. However, Aleichem, as several critics have suggested, might more appropriately be compared to Charles Dickens, who displays, as does Aleichem, a stoic quality of writing and a "laughter through tears" humor.

IN THE STORM

An early short novel presented as if it were a two-act play, *In the Storm* is a story of three different families who live together at one address in Russia in 1905. In the background are revolution, pogroms, and riots. The characters try to cope through assimilation, religion, and rebellion against tradition. Jews of three different social classes further represent different economic orders. One family is headed by a prosperous businessman who bullies his way through the Jewish community; another father is a struggling druggist, trying to assimilate. The third head of household is a shoemaker, very conscious of his poverty. Although there is little sustained action, the novel is a fine mirror of its time and place.

STEMPENYU

Stempenyu, the novel's title character, is a fiddler, with the soul of an artist. He has made an unfortunate marriage to Friedl, a shrew. He meets the gentle Rachel, and the two fall in love. She, too, is unhappily married, to a rich young man who ignores her in his enthusiasm for Talmudic study. Stempenyu and Rachel meet only a few times, once significantly against a monastery wall, and their love is never consummated. Rachel's virtue is, in fact, rewarded, when her husband is exhorted by his mother that his family is as important as his religion. While the chief interest of the novel is its examination of Jewish life in the Pale of Settlement, with its arranged marriages, the narrative also enables Aleichem to express his rejection of sentimental romances and the adulterous tradition of "love in the Western world." In Jewish life, readers are reminded, love comes in marriage, not before or apart from it.

WANDERING STAR

Aleichem's final attempt at sustained fiction allowed him to express his opinion of actors, the Yiddish stage, and theatrical promoters. This novel is strung together by a thin love story about two youths who escape their oppressive homes to become wandering performers. The main interest of *Wandering Star*, however, resides in descriptions of the magic of theater, reflections on the differences between sacred and secular music, and a lively review of the history of Yiddish theater. Aleichem focuses on the theater's origins in Romania to its degeneration in New York City at the hands of impresarios more interested in money than in Jewish folk art.

THE BLOODY HOAX

The Bloody Hoax is a novel based on a real event, known as the Beiliss affair, in which a Ukrainian Jew was accused of a ritual murder in 1911. In Aleichem's recasting of events, two friends, one Jewish and the other Gentile, decide to exchange places in order to expand their experience of life. The Gentile boy initially encounters problems through his inability to speak Yiddish, but his trouble really begins with the surfacing of "the blood libel," an unfounded but pervasive accusation made against Jews in times of persecution. He is accused of using Gentile blood to make Passover bread. Despite its serious subject, the novel is marketed as a comedy, and it is especially notable in its treatment of Russian Jewish intellectuals and the Zionist movement at the beginning of the twentieth century.

Allene Phy-Olsen

OTHER MAJOR WORKS

SHORT FICTION: *Tevye der Milkhiger*, 1894-1914 (*Tevye's Daughters*, 1949; also known as *Tevye the Dairyman*); *Menakhem-Mendl*, 1895 (*The Adventures of Menachem-Mendl*, 1969); *Der farkishnefter Shnayder*, 1900 (*The Bewitched Tailor*, 1960); *Mottel, Peyse dem Khazns*, 1907-1916 (*The Adventures of Mottel, the Cantor's Son*, 1953); *Jewish Children*, 1920; *The Old Country*, 1946; *Inside Kasrilevke*, 1948; *Selected Stories of Sholom Aleichem*, 1956; *Stories and Satires*, 1959; *Old Country Tales*, 1966; *Some Laughter, Some Tears*, 1968; *Holiday Tales of Sholem Aleichem*, 1979; *The Best of Sholom Aleichem*, 1979 (Irving Howe and Ruth R.

Wisse, editors); *Tevye the Dairyman and the Railroad Stories*, 1987; *The Further Adventures of Menachem-Mendl*, 2001.

PLAYS: *A Doktor*, pr. 1887 (*She Must Marry a Doctor*, 1916); *Yakenhoz*, pr. 1894; *Mazel Tov*, pr. 1904; *Tsuzeyt un Tsushpreyt*, pr. 1905; *Die Goldgreber*, pr. 1907; *Samuel Pasternak*, pr. 1907; *Stempenyu*, pr. 1907; *Agenten*, pb. 1908; *Az Got Vil, Shist a Bezem*, pb. 1908; *Konig Pic*, pb. 1910; *Shver Tsu Zein a Yid*, pb. 1914; *Dos Groyse Gevins*, pb. 1915 (*The Jackpot*, 1989); *Menshen*, pb. 1919; *Der Get*, pr. 1924; *The World of Sholom Aleichem*, 1953; *Fiddler on the Roof*, pr. 1964.

NONFICTION: *Fun'm yarid*, 1916 (*The Great Fair: Scenes from My Childhood*, 1955); *Briefe von Scholem Aleichem und Menachem Mendl*, 1921.

BIBLIOGRAPHY

Butwin, Joseph, and Frances Butwin. *Sholom Aleichem*. Boston: Twayne, 1977. A general review of the life and work of Aleichem, with insightful descriptions of all major writings and critical reactions to them. Part of Twayne's World Authors series.

Halberstam-Rubin, Anna. *Sholom Aleichem: The Writer as Social Historian*. New York: Peter Lang, 1989. A scholarly consideration of Aleichem's reconstruction of his native East European Jewish community written as a background study for the Broadway production of *Fiddler on the Roof*.

Howe, Irving. *World of Our Fathers: The Journey of the East European Jews to America and the Life They Found and Made*. New York: Simon & Schuster, 1976. A thorough examination of East European Jewish immigrants in the United States, the role of Yiddish in their lives, and their love of the Yiddish theater and Yiddish writers. This is the world Aleichem entered in his later years.

Liptzin, Solomon. *A History of Yiddish Literature*. New ed. Middle Village, N.Y.: Jonathan David, 1985. A thorough survey of the entire sweep of Yiddish literature and Aleichem's dominant place within it. Especially helpful are the discussions of characteristic Yiddish humor and the problems of translation. Equally pertinent is the examination of the rise and ultimate decline of Yiddish as a language of literature, theater, and cultural exchange.

Samuel, Maurice. *The World of Sholom Aleichem.* New York: Random House, 1973. A readable reconstruction of the world about which Aleichem wrote, the towns and villages of the Jewish Pale of Settlement. Illustrations are taken from the writings of Aleichem, in a demonstration of the ways in which fiction can imaginatively recapture an actual time and place now vanished.

Silverman, Erica, and Mordicai Gerstein. *Sholom's Treasure: How Sholom Aleichem Became a Writer.* New York: Farrar, Straus and Giroux, 2005. An illustrated biography aimed at younger readers. Covers events of the author's early life, including his problems with a difficult stepmother and his fascination with Jewish folklore.

Waife-Goldberg, Marie. *My Father, Sholom Aleichem.* New York: Schocken Books, 1971. A loving, carefully prepared biography of the author by his youngest daughter. Waife-Goldberg discusses the reception of Aleichem's works, the fluctuations in his career, and his sometimes-precarious financial situation even after he became famous as a writer.

SHERMAN ALEXIE

Born: Spokane Indian Reservation, Wellpinit, Washington; October 7, 1966

Also known as: Sherman Joseph Alexie, Jr.

PRINCIPAL LONG FICTION

Reservation Blues, 1995
Indian Killer, 1996
The Absolutely True Diary of a Part-Time Indian, 2007
Flight, 2007

OTHER LITERARY FORMS

Sherman Alexie initiated his literary career with an unusual collection of poems and very short stories titled *The Business of Fancydancing: Stories and Poems*, published in 1992 by a small press, Hanging Loose, in Brooklyn, New York. Of the forty-two titles in that small book, only six could be confidently described as "short stories," and the longest of these runs only nine pages. Before his thirtieth birthday, Alexie had published six more full-length books, three of which were collections of poetry, and two chapbooks of poetry. His first book of short fiction, *The Lone Ranger and Tonto Fistfight in Heaven*, was published in 1993 to considerable acclaim, and he has followed that with two other books of short fiction. Alexie's short fiction has evolved in various ways. While the average length of the twenty-four stories in *The Lone Ranger and Tonto Fistfight in Heaven* is just nine pages, the nine stories that make up *The Toughest Indian in the World* (2000) average twenty-five pages in length, and one story, the ominously allegorical "The Sin Eaters," runs almost to novella length at forty-four pages. Similarly, the first of the nine stories in his third collection, *Ten Little Indians* (2003), runs fifty-two pages and the last runs forty-eight.

Some readers admire Alexie's poetry over his prose. He has had several books of poetry published, including the limited edition chapbook *Dangerous Astronomy* (2005). Alexie has also written screenplays for two films drawn from his literary work, *Smoke Signals* (1998) and *The Business of Fancydancing* (2002).

ACHIEVEMENTS

Among other recognitions that Sherman Alexie has received for his writing, his novel *The Absolutely True Diary of a Part-Time Indian* received the 2007 National Book Award for Young People's Literature. In the fall of 2007, Alexie was honored by the Western Literature Association with its Distinguished Achievement Award. Two of his stories have appeared in *The Best American Short Stories* anthologies (1994, 2004), and one of his poems was selected for the *Best American Poetry* anthology in 1996. His first novel, *Reservation Blues*, won the American Book Award for 1996, and his second novel,

Sherman Alexie. (© Marion Ettlinger)

Indian Killer, was listed as a *New York Times* Notable Book the same year. His short-story collection *The Toughest Indian in the World* was recognized with a PEN/Malamud Award for Short Fiction from the PEN/Faulkner Foundation in 2001.

BIOGRAPHY

Born with hydrocephalus (water on the brain), Sherman Joseph Alexie, Jr., grew up on the Spokane Indian Reservation in Wellpinit, Washington. His father was a member of the Coeur d'Alene tribe, his mother a Spokane. An operation when he was six months old placed him at risk of mental retardation, but Alexie survived to become a voracious reader early on. Feeling ostracized on the reservation, partly because of his intellectual pursuits, he transferred to the all-white high school in Reardan, twenty-two miles away, where he was a popular student and starred on the basketball team. After two years at Gonzaga University, Alexie transferred to

Washington State University, where his initial interest in pursuing a medical career ended when he fainted in a human anatomy class. His poetry workshop teacher, Alex Kuo, encouraged his writing, and with the assistance of a Washington State Arts Commission fellowship in 1991, he finished his first books of poetry. In his review of *The Business of Fancydancing* for *The New York Times Book Review*, James Kincaid hailed Alexie as "one of the major lyric voices of our time." Following this initial acclaim, Alexie gave up drinking, and he has spoken out against alcohol abuse, particularly on the reservation, both in his public appearances and in his subsequent writings.

Alexie married Diane Tomhave, of Hidatsa, Ho-Chunk, and Potawatomi heritage, in 1995. They would have two sons, Joseph (born 1997) and David (born 2001). Alexie's move to Seattle is reflected in the shift of settings in his first two novels, from the Spokane reservation in *Reservation Blues* to Seattle in *Indian Killer*, which was published one year later. His involvement in film, which started with *Smoke Signals* in 1998, is consistent with his flair for public performance and stage presence. Alexie takes pride in having won the World Heavyweight Poetry Bout (slam poetry) in 1998 and each of the next three years as well, and his credits include stand-up comedy and various television appearances, including the Public Broadcasting Service's program *A Dialogue on Race with President Clinton* in 1998. With Colville Indian musician Jim Boyd, Alexie has also collaborated on several musical recordings.

Owing to an administrative oversight, Alexie's bachelor's degree was not awarded by Washington State University until 1994; his alma mater recognized him in 2003 with a Regents' Distinguished Alumnus Award. He also holds honorary degrees from Seattle University and Columbia College (Chicago).

ANALYSIS

In his poetry volume *Old Shirts and New Skins* (1993) Sherman Alexie offers a formula that he attributes to one of his recurring characters, Lester FallsApart: "Poetry = Anger × Imagination." The formula appears slightly altered in a story in *The Lone Ranger and Tonto Fistfight in Heaven*, where "Poetry" is replaced with "Survival." A more accurate formula might require that

Anger and its multiple, Imagination, be divided by Humor or Wit, for what makes Alexie's anger tolerable for many readers is not so much his imagination, which is sometimes visionary and suggests certain features of Magical Realism, but his comic, generally satiric sensibility. Alexie's comedy is often dark, and he frequently employs insult humor, as in *Reservation Blues*, when Chess, a Flathead Indian woman, tells Veronica, an Indian wannabe, that "a concussion is just as traditional as a sweatlodge." This passage exemplifies another facet of Alexie's perspective on Indianness. He has described himself as having been influenced as much by 1970's family television program *The Brady Bunch* as by tribal traditions.

Part of what makes Alexie so popular with academic audiences is his blending of pop-culture elements with historical and literary allusion. In *The Absolutely True Diary of a Part-Time Indian*, for instance, young Arnold Spirit, Jr., reflects on the opening sentence of Leo Tolstoy's *Anna Karenina* (1875-1877). *Reservation Blues* is constructed on the Faust legend as embodied in the historical blues guitarist Robert Johnson, but the novel is also haunted by such historical figures as Colonel George Wright, who had nine hundred Spokane horses shot in 1858. Two New Age white groupies who hang out with the reservation blues band are named Betty and Veronica, straight out of the Archie comic books. Female characters figure prominently and powerfully in Alexie's fiction. He consistently assails racist and sexist attitudes, and he has taken a strong stand against homophobia and gay bashing.

Dreams and memories, sometimes historically based like the murder of Crazy Horse, tend to haunt Alexie's fiction. These combine with characters such as Big Mom, who appears to have mystical powers, to lend otherworldly or surreal overtones. A basketball game might dissolve into fantasy. A magical guitar might burst into flame. In *Flight*, the teenage protagonist experiences a series of metamorphoses, inhabiting multiple bodies, both white and Indian, before he returns to himself in the body of his runaway father, which prompts him to reflect on William Shakespeare's *Hamlet* (pr. c. 1600-1601).

With certain exceptions, as in *Indian Killer* and some of the later stories, Alexie prefers uncomplicated syntax and colloquial dialogue; short paragraphs predominate.

These stylistic features combine with others, including Alexie's disinclination toward complex imagery and metaphor, to make his fiction readily accessible.

RESERVATION BLUES

The three predominant characters in his first novel, *Reservation Blues*, Alexie has described as "the holy trinity of me": Victor Joseph (angry, physical, inclined to drink), Junior Polatkin (the "intellectual" because he went to college for a couple of years), and Thomas Builds-the-Fire (the storyteller, spiritual, given to memories and dreams). When they acquire legendary blues singer Robert Johnson's magic guitar, this trio forms the nucleus of the reservation blues band, Coyote Springs, which is joined by two Flathead Indian sisters, Chess and Checkers Warm Water. Their success arouses the enmity of their fellow Spokanes, notably in the person of the tribal chair, David WalksAlong.

Thomas and Chess (predictably, the more intellectual of the sisters) form a couple, and record producers from the East, Phil Sheridan and George Wright (both named after historically renowned Indian fighters), offer them an audition with Cavalry Records. Despite Big Mom's assistance, however, the recording session ends disastrously, and when the band members return to the reservation, Junior commits suicide. Ironically, the record company finds Betty and Veronica to be "Indian enough" and signs them to a contract, the refrain to one song being "Indian in my bones." Thomas stomps on the tape.

When Thomas, Chess, and Checkers leave the reservation to move to the city of Spokane, Big Mom organizes reconciliation with the tribe at the longhouse. One important theme of the novel concerns the importance of maintaining blood quantum through the marriage of Thomas and Chess. Alexie also deals with the dangers of alcohol and violence (the beverage of choice at the longhouse is Pepsi). While he does not reject traditional tribal values (Big Mom teaches a song of survival at the end of the novel), Alexie implicitly underscores the benefits of leaving the reservation, as he himself elected to do.

INDIAN KILLER

In *Indian Killer*, a wealthy white couple from Seattle adopts an infant from an unspecified Indian reservation. John Smith (the name ironically echoes the historical

Captain John Smith of Jamestown fame) consequently grows up tribeless and confused as to his identity. A loner and apparently a paranoid schizophrenic, John suffers from various delusions and violent fantasies. When a serial killer scalps victims and leaves owl feathers with their bodies, the reader tends to side with characters in the novel who suspect an Indian (likely John) is the killer.

Opposite John Smith stands Marie Polatkin, a self-assured Spokane Indian activist and University of Washington student (majoring in English), who ably puts down the arrogant professor of Native American literature, Dr. Clarence Mather. It could be argued that racial profiling or stereotyping runs throughout this often-foreboding novel. It seems unlikely, for example, that any teacher in Mather's position would offer Forrest Carter's controversial 1976 novel *The Education of Little Tree* as required reading in a college course on Indian writers, and the virulently racist shock-jock radio talk-show host Truck Schultz is as exaggerated a caricature as a Charles Dickens villain. Suzanne Evertsen Lundquist has connected the faux-Indian novelist Jack Wilson with the Paiute Ghost Dance prophet Wovoka. Daniel Grassian has observed that the novel arose from Alexie's "anger and dissatisfaction" regarding non-Indians who write "Indian books."

The killer is not identified, and although some readers may assume it is John Smith, who commits suicide by leaping from the skyscraper on which he has been working, Alexie never states for certain that the killer is in fact an Indian. Moreover, it may be debatable whether John himself is truly "Indian"; he never appears to acquire a confident sense of who he is. Reviewers have characterized *Indian Killer* as "angry" and even "ugly," but its sinister theme calls for such pejorative qualifiers: the white control, denial, even eradication of the Indian's identity or possession of self and the violence resulting from that act.

FLIGHT

Flight, a short novel (at fewer than forty thousand words, more aptly "novella"), opens with the fifteen-year-old protagonist declaring, in the mode of Herman Melville's Ishmael, from *Moby Dick* (1851), "Call me Zits." The streetwise, angry-and-sad, mixed-blood product of multiple foster homes and various types of abuse

describes himself as "a blank sky, a human solar eclipse," but he adopts a darkly comic perspective and refuses to feel sorry for himself. A white boy allegorically named Justice gets Zits involved in a bank robbery armed with both a real pistol and a paint gun. When he is fatally shot during the robbery, however, Zits begins a series of five transformations (metempsychoses) in which he inhabits various male bodies, starting with that of a white agent of the Federal Bureau of Investigation (FBI) in 1975 Idaho (the action recalls events that took place at Wounded Knee, South Dakota).

As he occupies other bodies, ranging from that of a mute Indian boy at the Battle of the Little Bighorn to that of a guilt-ridden pilot who has taught a Muslim terrorist how to fly a plane, Zits participates in acts of violence, but he also witnesses compassionate and heroic behavior, notably on the part of white characters. After occupying his Indian father's body, Zits is brought to an understanding of why his father deserted his mother, who died soon afterward. When he returns to himself, Zits leaves the bank and hands his guns to a friendly white police officer named Dave, who arranges to have Zits adopted by his brother and his wife, who introduces the boy to acne medicine. In the last sentences of the novella, Zits reveals his actual name, "Michael."

In *Flight* Alexie offers readers who might have been alarmed at certain ominous aspects of *Indian Killer* a more hopeful solution to the problem of Indian identity and to an apparently inescapable cycle of violence in contemporary American (especially urban) society. Although this book has not been identified as young adult fiction, the protagonist's age and the elements of fantasy and time travel are likely to appeal to that readership.

THE ABSOLUTELY TRUE DIARY OF A PART-TIME INDIAN

Although the page count of *The Absolutely True Diary of a Part-Time Indian* is higher than that of *Flight*, this autobiographical novel runs about the same length (that is, around forty thousand words) and so might also be designated a "novella." Marketed as young adult fiction, the book features a fourteen-year-old protagonist, Arnold Spirit, Jr., who resembles Alexie in every way, including his hydrocephalic birth; his move from the reservation town of Wellpinit to Reardan, which he sees as necessary to his hopes but also as possible betrayal of his tribe; and his popularity in the white world and his success as a basketball player and as a student.

Divided into twenty-nine very short chapters and illustrated by Seattle artist Ellen Forney (Arnold says that he draws cartoons because he finds words "too predictable" and "too limited"), the novella moves rapidly, as does most of Alexie's fiction. That is, the fast pace encountered here is not necessarily a function of the novel's intended audience. Alexie's tendency to promote dialogue as opposed to narrative paragraphs is common to most of the short stories of *The Lone Ranger and Tonto Fistfight in Heaven* and to both *Reservation Blues* and *Flight*. Only in some of the stories of *The Toughest Indian in the World* and *Ten Little Indians* and in the novel *Indian Killer* does Alexie more frequently employ paragraphs that run longer than half a page.

If *The Absolutely True Diary of a Part-Time Indian* were to be read as memoir, it would likely be described as a "success story," particularly success achieved by overcoming adversity that involves poverty and racial prejudice. Like Alexie, the adolescent Arnold chooses, at some personal risk, to redefine himself in the broader world outside the reservation. Although this decision temporarily costs him his best friend, appropriately named Rowdy, Arnold finds himself welcome (surprisingly, both for him and for the reader) in the white world of small farm-town Reardan. The hopeful story is darkened, however, by the deaths of Arnold's grandmother, his sister, and his father's best friend, all of which involve alcohol in some way. Alexie's cautionary tale for young Indian readers is clear: Avoid alcohol and accept the challenge of leaving the apparently secure but perilously limiting world of the reservation.

Ron McFarland

OTHER MAJOR WORKS

SHORT FICTION: *The Lone Ranger and Tonto Fistfight in Heaven*, 1993; *The Toughest Indian in the World*, 2000; *Ten Little Indians*, 2003; *War Dances*, 2009.

POETRY: *I Would Steal Horses*, 1992; *Old Shirts and New Skins*, 1993; *The Man Who Loves Salmon*, 1998; *One Stick Song*, 2000; *Dangerous Astronomy*, 2005.

SCREENPLAYS: *Smoke Signals*, 1998; *The Business of Fancydancing*, 2002.

MISCELLANEOUS: *The Business of Fancydancing:* *Stories and Poems*, 1992; *First Indian on the Moon*, 1993; *The Summer of Black Widows*, 1996 (poems and short prose).

BIBLIOGRAPHY

Alexie, Sherman. "Sherman Alexie, Literary Rebel: An Interview." Interview by John Bellante and Carl Bellante. *Bloomsbury Review* 14 (May/June, 1994): 14. Published before any of his long fiction appeared, this interview touches on important aspects of Alexie's "minimalism" (a term he does not care for), the "holy trinity of me," and various thematic issues.

Andrews, Scott. "A New Road and a Dead End in Sherman Alexie's *Reservation Blues*." *Arizona Quarterly* 63, no. 2 (Summer, 2007): 137-152. Reflects on the ambiguities of the novel's ending, in which the blues band fails and the principal characters leave the reservation.

Chen, Tina. "Toward an Ethics of Knowledge." *MELUS* 30, no. 2 (Summer, 2005): 157-173. Discusses Alexie's *Indian Killer* as well as Cynthia Ozick's *The Shawl* (1989) and Julie Otsuka's *When the Emperor Was Divine* (2002). Advises proceeding from an ethical understanding of racial and cultural differences when dealing with these novels.

Christie, Stuart. "Renaissance Man: The Tribal 'Schizophrenic' in Sherman Alexie's *Indian Killer*." *American Indian Culture and Research Journal* 25, no. 4 (2001): 1-19. Addresses Alexie's treatment of Native American characters and how, in Anglo-European cultural contexts, tribal identity may lead to a pathological state for Native Americans.

Grassian, Daniel. *Understanding Sherman Alexie.* Columbia: University of South Carolina Press, 2005. First book-length work offering commentary on Alexie's poetry and fiction pays ample attention to reviews and other published discussions of his writings. Provides biographical details as well as analysis and interpretation of the fiction through *Indian Killer*.

Lundquist, Suzanne Evertsen. *Native American Literatures: An Introduction.* New York: Continuum, 2004. Section on Alexie (in the chapter titled "The Best and the Best Known") includes summaries of important critiques of *Reservation Blues* and *Indian*

Killer that question his representation of Native American cultural values and reservation life as well as issues of "hybridity" and "essentialism."

SAIL: Studies in American Indian Literature 9, no. 4 (Winter, 1997). Special issue devoted to Alexie's fiction includes an interview with Alexie as well as essays by such scholars as Karen Jorgensen ("White Shadows: The Use of Doppelgangers in Sherman Alexie's *Reservation Blues*"), Janine Richardson ("Magic and Memory in Sherman Alexie's *Reservation Blues*"), and P. Jane Hafen ("Rock and Roll, Redskins, and Blues in Sherman Alexie's Work").

NELSON ALGREN
Nelson Ahlgren Abraham

Born: Detroit, Michigan; March 28, 1909
Died: Sag Harbor, New York; May 9, 1981
Also known as: Nelson Ahlgren Abraham

PRINCIPAL LONG FICTION

Somebody in Boots, 1935
Never Come Morning, 1942
The Man with the Golden Arm, 1949
A Walk on the Wild Side, 1956
The Devil's Stocking, 1983

OTHER LITERARY FORMS

Although Nelson Algren (AWL-gruhn) is known primarily as a novelist, some critics believe that the short story, because it does not make the structural demands the novel does, was a more appropriate genre for him, and his *The Neon Wilderness* (1947) has been acclaimed one of the best collections of short stories published in the 1940's. *Chicago: City on the Make* (1951) is a prose poem that has been variously described as a social document and a love poem to the city that serves as the center of Algren's fictional world. Similar nonfiction writings include *Who Lost an American?* (1963), a self-described "guide to the seamier sides" of several cities, including Chicago, and *Notes from a Sea Diary: Hemingway All the Way* (1965); both books combine travel writing and personal essays. What little poetry Algren wrote that is not included in his novels (*The Man with the Golden Arm*, for example, concludes with a poem of the same title that Algren terms an "epitaph") is included in *The Last Carousel* (1973), along with some unpublished stories and sketches. He also collaborated with H. E. F. Donohue on the book *Conversations with Nelson Algren* (1964), a series of interviews. *Nelson Algren's Own Book of Lonesome Monsters* (1962), an anthology to which he contributed a preface and the concluding story, sounds Algren's recurring theme: Human beings are always alone.

ACHIEVEMENTS

Although Nelson Algren's first novel, *Somebody in Boots*, failed commercially, it drew the attention of serious literary critics, who were even more impressed by his second novel, *Never Come Morning*, which won for Algren in 1947 one thousand dollars from the American Academy of Arts and Letters. Also in 1947, he received a grant from the Newberry Library to assist him in the writing of *The Man with the Golden Arm*, which subsequently received the National Book Award in 1950. Since many of the stories in *The Neon Wilderness* had previously appeared in the O. Henry Memorial collections or in *The Best American Short Stories*, Algren's stature as a first-class writer of fiction was assured by 1950. Because his fictional world, for the most part, was Chicago, Algren is frequently linked with James T. Farrell and Richard Wright, who belong to what some critics have termed the "Chicago school." While he denied any literary indebtedness to Farrell and Wright, Algren admitted that his work was influenced by Carl Sandburg, partly because Algren's prose tends to the poetic, so much so that he was termed by the famous literary historian Malcolm Cowley "the poet of the Chicago slums."

Maxwell Geismar termed Algren a "neo-naturalist" with roots in the American realistic tradition of Stephen Crane, Theodore Dreiser, and Ernest Hemingway (Algren acknowledged his debt to Hemingway, who in return hailed Algren as, after William Faulkner, among America's first writers). Unfortunately, critics, including Geismar, have also found many of the excesses of naturalism—melodrama, romanticism, oversimplification of characters and motives, and "overwriting"—in Algren's work, which has also been assailed for its formlessness. What Algren lacks in style and form, however, he more than compensates for in rich detail and insightful observations about what George Bluestone has called the "world's derelicts," those unfortunates who had largely been ignored, even by those writers who were ostensibly concerned with the "lumpen proletariat." In fact, so preoccupied is he with the victims of the American Dream, those losers customarily associated with the Great Depression, that one seldom encounters the other America in his fiction. Consequently, some readers have found his work dated, and although *The Man with the Golden Arm* and *A Walk on the Wild Side* were both adapted to film (the motion pictures were released in 1955 and 1962, respectively), thereby testifying to Algren's popularity, his critical standing declined. From 1945 to 1960, however, he was among the most acclaimed writers in the United States because of his focus and his vision, both of which were compatible with post-World War II America.

BIOGRAPHY

Nelson Algren was born Nelson Ahlgren Abraham in Detroit, Michigan, on March 28, 1909, to second-generation Chicagoans; the family moved back to Chicago when Algren was three years old. From 1912 until 1928, Algren absorbed the Chicago environment that was to become the center of his fictional world. After receiving his journalism degree from the University of Illinois in 1931, he began traveling across the Southwest, working at odd jobs (door-to-door coffee salesman in New Orleans, migrant worker, co-operator of a gasoline station in Texas, and carnival worker) and gathering the raw material that he later transformed into his fiction, particularly *A Walk on the Wild Side*. After serving time for stealing a typewriter (an oddly appropriate theft for a

writer), he returned to Chicago, where he continued his "research" on the Division Street milieu and began to write short stories, poems, and his first novel, *Somebody in Boots*, a Depression tale about the Southwest that became, after extensive revision, *A Walk on the Wild Side*.

After World War II—he served three years in the U.S. Army—Algren legally shortened his name, returned again to Chicago, and within five years enjoyed a reputation as one of America's finest fiction writers. *The Man with the Golden Arm* received the National Book Award, and several of his short stories were also recognized for their excellence. It was during this period that Algren had his now-famous affair with French novelist and philosopher Simone de Beauvoir. *A Walk on the Wild Side* and its subsequent filming, as well as the cinematic adaptation of *The Man with the Golden Arm*, brought Algren to the height of his popularity during the 1950's and 1960's, but aside from some travel books and his last novel, his writing career essentially ended in 1956. In his later years, he taught creative writing before spending his last years on *The Devil's Stocking*, a thinly veiled fictional treatment of the murder trial and imprisonment of Rubin "Hurricane" Carter, a middleweight boxer. This "novel" did little to restore Algren's literary reputation.

ANALYSIS

Whether the setting is Chicago or New Orleans, Nelson Algren's characters live, dream, and die in an environment alien to most Americans, many of whom have achieved the financial success and spiritual failure endemic to the American Dream. His characters are, at their best, losers in the quest for success; at their worst, they are spectators, not even participants, in that competitive battle. Although his protagonists do aspire to escape from their environments, to assume new identities, and to attain that American Dream, they are so stunted by their backgrounds and so crippled by their own guilt that their efforts are doomed from the start, and their inevitable fates often involve the punishment that their guilt-ridden souls have unconsciously sought. In *Never Come Morning*, Bruno cannot escape his guilt for allowing Steffi to be raped by his gang and almost welcomes his punishment for the murder of another man; in *The Man with the Golden Arm*, Frankie Machine cannot es-

Nelson Algren. (Library of Congress)

cape his guilt for the accident that incapacitates his wife and so can end his drug addiction only by hanging himself; in *A Walk on the Wild Side*, Dove cannot escape his guilt for having raped Terasina, to whom he returns after having been blinded in a fight. In all three novels, the guilt that the man experiences from having abused a woman leads to a self-destructive impulse that negates his attempt to escape from his environment and produces the punishment he seeks.

NEVER COME MORNING

Although it is not his first published novel, *Never Come Morning* is Algren's first major novel. As the chronicle of a young man's passage from boyhood to manhood, *Never Come Morning* is another, albeit more cynical, American initiation novel, in which Bruno Bicek's initiation leads to his death. Like many young men, Bruno dreams of escaping from the ghetto through

professional sports, either boxing or baseball ("Lefty" Bicek is a pitcher), but Algren quickly indicates, through similar chapter headings, that Bruno shares a "problem" with Casey Benkowski, his idol, whose defeat in the boxing ring foreshadows Bruno's eventual defeat in life. Bruno's dreams are illusory, the product of the media: He reads *Kayo* magazine, sees pictures of boxers on matchbook covers, and watches James Cagney films. His dream of becoming a "modern Kitchel" (Kitchel was a former Polish American boxing champion) reflects his desire to become someone else, to define his success in terms of other people, not himself. To become a successful man, he seeks status as the president and treasurer of the Warriors, his street gang, but his allegiance to the gang reflects his childish dependence on the group, not his adult leadership of it. His "other-directedness" also affects his relationship with Steffi, whom he seduces partly in order to gain status from the Warriors, who subsequently assert their own sexual rights to her. Rather than defend her and reveal the very "softness" that wins the reader's respect, he yields to the Warriors, thereby forsaking independence and manhood and incurring the guilt that eventually destroys him.

Like most of Algren's women, Steffi has a supporting role and exists primarily in terms of the male protagonist. She is the agent by which Bruno comes of age sexually, acquires his spiritual guilt, eventually becomes an independent man, and, finally, since she has alienated the informant Bonifacy, is doomed. Despite being the victim of a gang rape, Steffi retains her capacity for love and forgiveness, limited as that is, and becomes the stereotyped "whore with a heart of gold" whose love enables the "hero," antiheroic as he is, to overcome the odds. Her passivity is reflected symbolically through Algren's description of a fly without wings in Steffi's room: After he "seduces" her, Bruno destroys the fly. Later, when Bruno wins a Kewpie doll and subsequently and unthinkingly destroys it, Algren ties the fate of the doll, an appropriate symbol, to Steffi, who is won and destroyed by Bruno. Steffi's fate seems even crueler than Bruno's, as he will "escape" in death but Steffi will remain trapped with the other prostitutes who endure at "Mama" Tomek's brothel.

Before he is incarcerated, Bruno does mature through a series of tests that prove his manhood. Although he cannot articulate his love and desire for forgiveness, he does come to understand that love is compatible with manhood. When he arranges a fight for himself with Honeyboy Tucker, he acts independently; when he overcomes Fireball Kodadek and Tiger Pultoric, Bonifacy's thugs, he overcomes his fear of physical mutilation (Fireball's knife) and of his idol and father figure (Pultoric is the former champion). Before he can "be his own man," Bruno must overcome his childish dependence and hero worship. Bruno's subsequent victory over Tucker makes his earlier symbolic victory official and gives him the identity he seeks as a promising "contender," but that identity is destroyed when he is arrested only minutes later and sent to jail.

Images of imprisonment pervade the novel, which is concerned with the institutions that house inmates. When Bruno first serves time, Algren digresses to describe prison life, just as he digresses when he recounts Steffi's life at the brothel, where she is no less a prisoner. While she is there, she dreams of a "great stone penitentiary" and of the "vault" that is the barber's room. The prison and the brothel are appropriate institutions for a city that Algren compares to a madhouse. (Algren also sees the prostitutes as inmates of an insane asylum.) There is no escape for Steffi or Bruno, just as there is no real morning in this somber tale of darkness and night. Algren's Chicago is America in microcosm: As madhouse, prison, and brothel, it is an insane, entrapped world where people "sell out," thereby prostituting themselves.

THE MAN WITH THE GOLDEN ARM

In *The Man with the Golden Arm*, also set in Polish American Chicago, Algren reiterates many of the themes, images, and character types that exist in *Never Come Morning*. Although the novel's controversial theme of drug addiction has received much attention, Algren is not concerned with drug addiction per se but rather with the forces, external and internal, that lead to the addictive, dependent personalities that render people unable to cope with their environments or escape from them. Once again, Algren's characters are life's losers, "the luckless living soon to become the luckless dead," the "wary and the seeking, the strayed, the frayed, the happy and the hapless, the lost, the luckless, the lucky and the doomed" who become the "disinherited," those who emerge "from the wrong side of its [America's] billboards." The "hunted who also hope" in *Never Come Morning* become the "pursued" in *The Man with the Golden Arm*, which also relies on naturalistic metaphors comparing people and animals.

Given that the characters are themselves victims of a system that excludes them, it seems ironic that they should experience guilt, but Algren's protagonist, Frankie Machine, is trapped by the guilt he feels at having been responsible for the car accident that has paralyzed Sophie, his wife. (Since Sophie has induced the paralysis—there is nothing physically wrong with her—his guilt is even more ironic.) Sophie uses Frankie's guilt to "hook" (a word suggesting addiction) him, punish him, and contribute to their self-destructive mutual dependence. Algren describes Frankie's guilt as "slow and cancerous" and even has Louie, the pusher, attribute drug addiction to the desire for self-punishment. Frankie, the "pursued," is not alone in his guilt, for Algren portrays Record Head Bednar, the "pursuer," as also afflicted by a consuming guilt. As the agent of "justice," he feels "of all men most alone, of all men most guilty of all the lusts he had ever condemned in others." Bednar, who is hardly without sin, must nevertheless "cast the first stone."

Sin and guilt permeate this novel, which belabors religious imagery, particularly that concerning the Crucifixion of Christ. The controlling metaphor in the novel is Sophie's "luminous crucifix," which she uses to enslave Frankie. Sophie states, "My cross is this chair. I'm settin' on *my* cross. . . . I'm *nailed* to mine." When her friend Violet suggests that she is driving in her own "nails," Sophie evades the issue because her "crucifixion," while voluntary, is not selfless but selfish. Algren observes the parallels between Sophie and Christ—both have been betrayed and bleed for the sins of others. Sophie lacks love, however. In another parody of the Crucifixion, Sparrow protests to Bednar, "You're nailin' me to the cross, Captain"; Bednar responds, "What the hell you think they're [the politicians] doin' to me?" Although they have enough religious teaching to mouth biblical allusions, Algren's characters use Christianity only as popular culture, as a source, like advertising and films, of reference to their own ego-centered worlds. Although Algren suggests that "God had forgotten His own," at least in Frankie's case, it is at least equally true that, as Sophie confesses, she and Frankie have forgotten God. Sophie's pathetic, self-centered musing about God having gone somewhere and keeping his distance indicate that God has no place in the world of Division Street. Surely Algren's allusion to the gamblers' God, who watches Sparrow's "fall," reflects the post-Christian modern world.

In Algren's naturalistic world, the characters are seen as caged animals waiting to be slaughtered. At the beginning of the novel, Frankie, who waits for justice from Bednar, watches a roach drowning in a bucket and is tempted to help it, but the roach dies before he intercedes, just as Frankie dies without anyone interceding for him. Algren's metaphor for the trapped Sophie is equally flattering. When she hears the mousetrap in the closet snap shut, she feels "it close as if it had shut within

herself, hard and fast forever." Even Molly Novotny, who resembles Steffi in *Never Come Morning* in that she is a "fallen woman" and agent of redemption, is depicted as living in a "nest." In fact, Algren uses animal imagery to suggest Frankie's impending fate. When Frankie is apprehended for stealing irons, Algren describes the saleswomen as "over-fed hens" and "bosomy biddies" and then has Frankie glimpse "a butcher holding a broken-necked rooster." Since Frankie finally hangs himself, the glimpse is ironically prophetic. Frankie's addiction is also expressed in animal terms: Frankie has a "monkey on his back," and although he temporarily rids himself of the monkey, permanent escape is impossible. The two caged monkeys at the Kitten Klub shriek insults at the patrons and serve as the metaphor incarnate for Frankie's addiction.

Frankie's addiction is also expressed in terms of an army buddy also addicted to morphine, Private McGantic, whose "presence" is akin to the monkey's. By the end of the novel, Frankie has "become" Private McGantic: Frankie calls himself "Private Nowhere," suggesting both the identification and the lack of direction. "Private McGantic" is, however, only one of Frankie's identities; the novel recounts his futile attempt to become someone other than Frankie Machine (the assumed name reflects his lost humanity), the Dealer. He wants Molly to call him "the Drummer," not "the Dealer," but he never becomes a professional musician, and part of his tragedy is that he does not know who he is: "Who am I anyway, Solly?" The answer Solly (Sparrow) gives, "Be yourself," is a meaningless cliché, an example of circular reasoning because Frankie does not know what his "self" is. The official inquest into the death of Francis Majcinek (Frankie's "real" name) establishes nothing of consequence (his addiction is not even alluded to) except that he is "the deceased," one of the "luckless dead" Algren mentions earlier in the novel. Even his fictional life is not "real": It is a "comic strip" from birth to death.

A Walk on the Wild Side

A Walk on the Wild Side, Algren's fourth novel, is a reworking of *Somebody in Boots*, published some twenty years earlier. As a result, although it resembles Algren's other works in its characters, loose structure, and imagery, it also looks back to an earlier time, the Great Depression, and its setting is New Orleans rather than Chicago. Once again, Algren focuses on prison inmates, whose "kangaroo court" justice is superior to the justice they receive "outside," and on prostitutes, who also "serve their time" and are compared to caged birds (the brothel is an "aviary"). Despite their situation and their pasts, they are "innocent children" in their naïveté and illusions, and one of them is the means by which the hero is redeemed. Other notable characters include the freaks and the cripples who frequent Dockerty's "Dollhouse" and who are the physical counterparts of the emotional cripples in the novel. Achilles Schmidt, legless former circus strongman, is the exception, for he has found psychological strength through the accident that should have "crippled" him. It is only when Dove Linkhorn, the protagonist, is blinded and therefore "crippled" by Schmidt that he rids himself of the illusions that have weakened him.

A parody of the Horatio Alger myth of the American Dream, *A Walk on the Wild Side* concerns an ambitious young man who "wants to make something of himself" and leaves the farm to find fame and fortune in the city. Dove's journey is "educational" in terms of the reading instruction he receives and the culture he acquires as well as the "lessons" he learns about capitalism and life in general. At the beginning of the novel, Dove is an "innocent," as his name suggests, but that "innocence" is not sexual—he rapes Terasina, the earth mother who is also his first "mentor"—but experiential, in that he believes in the "Ladder of Success" with "unlimited opportunities" for "ambitious young men." Algren offers Dove a naturalistic parable of capitalism, particularly on the tenuous nature of life at the top. The headless terrapin in the fish market struggles to the top by using its superior strength in "wading contentedly over mothers and orphans," but its reign as king of the turtles is short-lived, and it has literally and symbolically "lost its head." Algren adds that Dove does not know that "there was also room for one more on the bottom." Before he reaches the bottom, Dove becomes a salesman, the epitome of the enterprising capitalist; the coffee scam and the phony beauty-parlor certificate racket, while illegal, are also seen as integral parts of capitalism.

Before he achieves his greatest success as a "salesman" of sex, Dove works, appropriately, in a condom manufacturing plant, which also sells sex. In his role as "Big Stingaree" in Finnerty's brothel, he is paid to perform an art that involves the "deflowering" of "virgins," who are played by prostitutes. In effect, the brothel, the primary setting of the novel, also serves as the symbolic center, as Algren presents a society that has sold itself—prostituted itself—to survive. Ironically, the real prostitutes in the brothel are morally superior to the "prostitutes" in mainstream American society, the "Do-Right Daddies," the powerful people who crusade against sin but also sin within the laws they create.

Hallie Breedlove, a prostitute, "sins," but she is capable of love and compassion, first with Schmidt and then with Dove, with whom she leaves the brothel. The "escape" is futile, however, for Hallie's subsequent pregnancy, in the light of her black "blood," threatens their future, and she believes that she can have her child only if she returns to her past, the mulatto village where she was born. Dove lacks her insight and, in his attempt to find her, he is jailed, is released, and then loses his sight in a battle with Schmidt. Metaphorically, however, in searching for her, he finds himself, and in losing his vision, he gains insight. Having learned that the "loser's side of the street" is superior to the "winners' side," Dove abandons his quest for success and returns to his Texas hometown to be reconciled with Terasina. Unlike Bruno and Frankie, Dove not only survives but also resolves to deal constructively with the guilt caused by his sin against his woman.

THE DEVIL'S STOCKING

Algren's last novel, *The Devil's Stocking*, is not so much a novel as a fictional treatment of the trial and imprisonment of Hurricane Carter. What began as an assignment for *Esquire* magazine, covering a boxer's murder trial, grew to "novel" proportions, probably because of the boxing and the trial, both of which appear in his other novels. The Algren characters—prostitutes, gamblers, police officers, and petty crooks—reappear in the novel about Carter, renamed Ruby Calhoun for fictive purposes. Because of its geographic and chronological distance from his earlier novels, as well as its blending of fact and fiction, *The Devil's Stocking* is not among the works for which Algren will be remembered.

Despite the qualified optimism of *A Walk on the Wild Side*, Algren's novels tend to paint a negative image of capitalistic American society, with its nightmarish

American Dream. Chicago and New Orleans become microcosms of America, a country marked by images of madness, imprisonment, and prostitution. In that world, virtue, such as it is, resides on the "loser's side of the street," in the prisons and the brothels. Constricted by their backgrounds, Algren's male protagonists typically strive to escape and assume new identities, sin against women (thereby incurring guilt that compounds their problems), serve time in prison (presented as a place of refuge), and pursue a self-destructive course that leads inevitably to death or mutilation.

Thomas L. Erskine

OTHER MAJOR WORKS

SHORT FICTION: *The Neon Wilderness*, 1947; *The Last Carousel*, 1973 (also includes sketches and poems); *The Texas Stories of Nelson Algren*, 1995.

NONFICTION: *Chicago: City on the Make*, 1951; *Who Lost an American?*, 1963; *Conversations with Nelson Algren*, 1964 (with H. E. F. Donohue); *Notes from a Sea Diary: Hemingway All the Way*, 1965; *Nonconformity: Writing on Writing*, 1996.

EDITED TEXTS: *Nelson Algren's Own Book of Lonesome Monsters*, 1962.

BIBLIOGRAPHY

Algren, Nelson. *Conversations with Nelson Algren*. Interviews by H. E. F. Donohue. New York: Hill & Wang, 1964. Collection of conversations between Donohue and Algren about Algren's life and work, arranged chronologically, provides interesting biographical information. Valuable also for Algren's comments on writing, writers, and politics.

Cappetti, Carla. *Writing Chicago: Modernism, Ethnography, and the Novel*. New York: Columbia University Press, 1993. Includes a chapter on Algren that focuses primarily on *Never Come Morning*. Discusses how his fiction interrupts historicity and factuality with poetic devices that prevent the reader from lapsing into simple referentiality.

Cox, Martha Heasley, and Wayne Chatterton. *Nelson Algren*. Boston: Twayne, 1975. Excellent assessment of Algren's life and work. Provides a chronology, a biographical chapter, an annotated bibliography, and a helpful index.

Drew, Bettina. *Nelson Algren: A Life on the Wild Side*. New York: G. P. Putnam's Sons, 1989. Well-researched and readable biography mixes material about Algren's life with publication details about his work. Supplemented by a bibliography of Algren's work.

Giles, James R. *Confronting the Horror: The Novels of Nelson Algren*. Kent, Ohio: Kent State University Press, 1989. Presents an analysis of Algren's novels that is most helpful in relating the author's naturalism to a literary tradition that extends to later writers, such as Hubert Selby, Jr., and John Rechy. Argues that Algren's fiction reflects the author's despair over the absurd state of humankind and the obscenity of death.

_____. "Encountering the Urban Grotesque: Nelson Algren's *Man with the Golden Arm*." In *The Naturalistic Inner-City Novel in America: Encounters with the Fat Man*. Columbia: University of South Carolina Press, 1995. Examines Algren's novel within the context of a group of twentieth century novels that depict urban slum dwellers in an increasingly familiar and humane manner.

Horvath, Brooke. *Understanding Nelson Algren*. Columbia: University of South Carolina Press, 2005. Features a brief introduction to Algren's life and work and provides detailed analysis of *Never Come Morning, The Man with the Golden Arm, A Walk on the Wild Side*, and other writings. Examines Algren's literary style, including his lyricism and humor, as well as the social and political concerns expressed in his work.

Pitts, Mary Ellen. "Algren's El: Internalized Machine and Displaced Nature." *South Atlantic Review* 52 (November, 1987): 61-74. Focuses on Chicago's elevated railway (or "el") as a symbol of entrapment in the inner city in Algren's major works. Argues that the prisonlike bars of the el's framework symbolize the circumscription of the characters' lives and echo the "danger" of technology—the enclosing of the human mind that occurs when technology is unquestioned.

Ray, David. "Housesitting the Wild Side." *Chicago Review* 41 (1995): 107-116. Anecdotal discussion of Ray's acquaintance with Algren in the 1950's and 1960's. Discusses Algren's connection with Chicago, his relationship with Simone de Beauvoir, and efforts to structure and organize Algren's manuscripts.

Ward, Robert, ed. *Nelson Algren: A Collection of Critical Essays*. Madison, N.J.: Fairleigh Dickinson University Press, 2007. Essays include discussions of *The Man with the Golden Arm* and *Never Come Morning*, Algren's life and work within the context of Chicago history, and the paperback revolution and how it affected Algren's reputation.

ISABEL ALLENDE

Born: Lima, Peru; August 2, 1942

PRINCIPAL LONG FICTION

La casa de los espíritus, 1982 (*The House of the Spirits*, 1985)

De amor y de sombra, 1984 (*Of Love and Shadows*, 1987)

Eva Luna, 1987 (English translation, 1988)

El plan infinito, 1991 (*The Infinite Plan*, 1993)

Hija de la fortuna, 1999 (*Daughter of Fortune*, 1999)

Portrait sépia, 2000 (*Portrait in Sepia*, 2001)

Zorro, 2005 (English translation, 2005)

Inés del alma mía, 2006 (*Inés of My Soul*, 2006)

OTHER LITERARY FORMS

Isabel Allende (ah-YEHN-day) was a journalist before she turned to fiction, and she has published widely in many forms. In addition to news and feature articles, Allende has written fiction for children, including *La gorda de porcelana* (1984) and her internationally popular trilogy *Ciudad de las bestias* (2002; *City of the Beasts*, 2002), *El reino del dragón de oro* (2003; *Kingdom of the Golden Dragon*, 2004), and *El bosque de los Pigmeos* (2004; *Forest of the Pygmies*, 2005). Her humor pieces include the essay collection *Civilice a su troglodita: Los impertinentes de Isabel Allende* (1974), and *Cuentos de Eva Luna* (1990; *The Stories of Eva Luna*, 1991) is a collection of her short stories. Allende has also written many essays, television scripts, and film documentaries. Her book-length memoir of her daughter's illness and death, *Paula* (1994; English translation, 1995), includes excursions into her own life, and in 2007 she published a second memoir, *La suma de los días* (*The Sum of our Days*, 2008). Her book *Afrodita: Cuentos, recetas, y otros afrodisiacos* (1997; *Aphrodite: A Memoir of the Senses*, 1998) is unclassifiable by genre, being a mingling of erotic recipes, stories, old wives' tales, and advice about food and sex. Some of Allende's work blurs the boundaries between novel and creative nonfiction. The real people and events of her own and her country's past figure largely in her fiction writing, and "magical" elements, such as telepathy and clairvoyance, sometimes appear in her nonfiction.

ACHIEVEMENTS

Isabel Allende's books have been translated into more than twenty-seven languages and have been best sellers in Europe, Latin America, and Australia as well as the United States. A few of the dozens of awards and honors Allende has won include Chile's Best Novel of the Year award in 1983 for *The House of the Spirits*, France's Grand Prix d'Evasion in 1984, Mexico's Best Novel Award in 1985 for *Of Love and Shadows*, a German Author of the Year prize in 1986, and an American Critics' Choice Award in 1996. Her work has been celebrated by major honors in more than a dozen countries, the range of awards reflecting her mixed popular and scholarly audience. She has also been awarded numerous honorary degrees from institutions including Bates College, Dominican College, New York State University, Florida Atlantic University, Columbia College Chicago, Lawrence University, Mills College, and Illinois Wesleyan University. Her version of Magical Realism has greatly influenced a new generation of experimental writers.

BIOGRAPHY

Isabel Allende was born in Lima, Peru, and moved to Chile when she was three years old; she comes from a major Chilean political family and identifies herself as a Chilean. Her childhood was spent with her maternal grandparents in Santiago, Chile, following the divorce of her parents. She represents her grandparents as Esteban and Clara Trueba in her best-known novel, *The House of the Spirits*. Educated partly in England and Europe, Allende returned to Chile in her early twenties to become a journalist and to involve herself in feminism and political causes. She spent the years 1964 through 1974 writing articles and editing journals; she also worked on television shows and film documentaries. Her early experiences before the 1973 military coup in Chile, which changed her life, included editing *Paula* magazine and conducting interviews for television stations.

Isabel Allende. (Reuters/Gustau Nacarino/Archive Photos)

Allende was married to engineer Miguel Frias in 1962 and was divorced from him in 1987; her two children, Paula and Nicholas, were born of this union. Her daughter Paula's illness and death, the major tragedy of Allende's adult life, are recounted in the memoir *Paula*. In 1988 Allende married William Gordon.

The daughter of a cousin of Chilean president Salvador Allende, Isabel Allende has always been preoccupied with Chilean history and politics, particularly the events leading to Salvador's death during a military coup in 1973 that overthrew his socialist government and led to military commander Augusto Pinochet Ugarte's dictatorship. Chile's internal problems have always been a major factor in her works. Allende at first attempted to help the forces attempting to overthrow the new regime, but she was forced to escape with her family to Venezuela in 1974. Following her exile, she lived in various parts of the world and taught in a number of institutions, including in the United States at the University of Virginia, Barnard College, and the University of California at Berkeley. In 2003 she was granted U.S. citizenship and moved to California. She has written about California, too, especially about the points at which its history and myth intersect with those of Spain—her popular 2005 novel *Zorro* is set in both countries.

ANALYSIS

Isabel Allende's work is at the forefront of the Magical Realism movement. Magical Realism is, in essence, the putting together of realistic events with fantastic details in a narrative that is written as if it were factual. Although it is practiced by authors worldwide, Magical Realism is associated mostly with Latin American writers such as Gabriel García Márquez, whose novel *Cien años de soledad* (1967; *One Hundred Years of Solitude*, 1970) is perhaps the prototypical Magical Realist novel. Magical Realism equates intuitive knowledge with factual knowledge, so that readers' definitions of reality are challenged and they are able to understand the importance of all types of knowledge. Allende adds another dimension to Magical Realism, because she often uses it to examine women's issues and problems in Latin American society. Critic Patricia Hart has asked, "Has [Allende] by her politics, her commitment to women's issues, her liberal, liberated female characters, and even her gender forged a new category that we might call magical feminism?" It seems clear from her works that she is not merely another Magical Realist writer. Her magical elements tend to define a concept of the feminine that equates it with fruition, generation, and the spiritual and allows hope for the future through womankind. Thus the green hair of Clara in *The House of the Spirits* may be seen as a complicated symbol suggesting intuition, passion, feminine nature, and growth.

Allende's novels are many-layered, which may account for their tremendous popularity worldwide and their translation into so many languages. Each contains a striking narrative, often with elements of the surreal woven into the story so flawlessly that readers are forced to accept the fantastic premises (such as women being born with green hair, levitating, or reading minds) as though these were ordinary physical facts. (Allende's later works, however, excluding the children's trilogy, have less recognizable Magical Realism in them.) The narratives build up lively suspense, and the intriguing plots and unusual, yet somehow believable, characters contribute to the appeal. Allende uses startling symbolism to define the male and female realms of power and influence and to show how women manage to achieve power for good even in societies that greatly repress them. Allende also makes use of the political narrative, which may not be fully understandable to readers unfamiliar with Latin American history. However, the representation of history is also woven into the narrative fabric, so readers do not feel their lack of knowledge; rather, they learn without effort. Allende is that rarity, a popular novelist whose work has literary complexity and merits rereading.

THE HOUSE OF THE SPIRITS

The House of the Spirits, Allende's first novel, remains her most widely read book. It is based on the events of her childhood and on the Chilean political situation that resulted in the death of her cousin Salvador Allende. It tells the story of three generations of women, from the traditionally feminine Clara, based in part on Allende's own grandmother, to Blanca, her daughter, who appears to conform to the family's expectations, to Alba, Clara's grandchild and the revolutionary who barely holds on to her life. Despite their differences, the three women—whose names mean "clear" (Clara) or

"white" (Blanca and Alba)—have deep unconscious bonds that help them survive overwhelming odds. These bonds include the inheritance of extrasensory perception, which, most vivid in the child Clara and in her beautiful doomed sister Rosa, begins the story. The women could be seen as simply swept along in the masculine-dominated course of events, but they are not: Although their actions and motivations are markedly different from the men's, and although their actions are circumscribed by custom, the women play an important role. The climax of the story, a bloody confrontation between the aristocrats and the socialist government of Chile, is an account of the actual military coup that resulted in Salvador Allende's death and Isabel Allende's exile from Chile.

The novel traces the lives of the women and their men, three generations of masculine pride and feminine intuition, of bloodshed and love. The frame story involves the healing of wounds between the granddaughter Alba and her dying grandfather, Esteban Trueba, whose unyielding pride has caused much grief for many. This healing is facilitated by the reading of grandmother Clara's diaries, which help Alba to understand her grandfather and her family's and country's history.

Sex roles are clearly defined in the story: the men from the old tradition associated with conquering and controlling, the women left to a kitchen role and keeping their values and hopes alive through their intuitions and their spiritual communication. As the society becomes more modern, these gender definitions change somewhat, but they are never eliminated. The change gives rise to hope that new politics may bring about a new understanding between the sexes, which will allow more freedom to both.

OF LOVE AND SHADOWS

Of Love and Shadows is less a Magical Realist novel than is *The House of the Spirits*. It is based on a real event, the finding of fifteen bodies in a secret grave in the Chilean countryside. This novel also uses the paranormal in a factual way, but the "miracles" are marginal to the story of love and death in a world that mirrors dictator Pinochet's.

The story has a fairy-tale beginning, describing the switching of two identically named babies. One baby grows into an epileptic seer whose disappearance will be investigated by Irene Beltran and Francisco Leal, the daughter of a wealthy family and the son of a Spanish Civil War exile. These two work together as reporter and photographer to unravel a mystery. Several members of the *sindicato agrícola*, a farmers' organization set up during the brief agrarian reform, have mysteriously vanished. When Evangelina Ranquileo, an adolescent mystic, publicly accuses Juan de Dios Ramírez of the crime, she disappears too. Irene and Francisco work toward the foregone conclusion: discovery of massive political corruption and murder.

The "shadows" of the title refer to this sinister event; the "love" of the title refers to the affair that takes place between Irene and Francisco after Irene leaves her less-intellectual soldier lover. Widely read in the wake of *The House of the Spirits*, this novel is less popular with scholars, partly because its political message and its love story are less neatly woven together than in the earlier novel, and partly because the magical and realistic elements of the story do not form the seamless unity seen in *The House of the Spirits*. Nevertheless, the persuasive political message and the ebullient, passionate love story make *Of Love and Shadows* memorable reading, and while Allende's characteristic magical elements are less highlighted than previously, they are present with their symbolic force.

EVA LUNA

In *Eva Luna*, Magical Realism reasserts itself, in a book that is as complex and as playful about serious concerns as *The House of the Spirits*. Eva Luna, the narrator, tells the story of her life, which includes the stories of countless other lives. The line is thin between Eva's made-up world ("I describe life as I would like it to be") and the real world from which she draws her stories. Eva is a hapless child born of a servant girl's desire to comfort a South American Indian dying of a snakebite. However, the painful and odd things that happen to her do not leave her embittered; rather, she becomes open to others' experiences and empathizes with them. As critic Alan Ryan commented, "For Eva Luna, everything that happens in life is a conjunction of countless stories already in progress and, at the same time, the starting point for others not yet told. . . . Stories, for her, transform life. When a character tells Eva of the sad death of his sister, Eva invents another story: 'All right, she died, but not

the way you say. Let's find a happy ending for her.' And so it is. . . ."

Latin American political events are present in this novel too, but they are not so well known as those in *The House of the Spirits*, nor are the political messages so clearly underscored as those in *Of Love and Shadows*. The casual or uninformed reader may miss them. Some critics have found the story sentimental because of the improbable happy ending and the irrepressible good nature of the main character, despite some Candide-like misfortunes. Other critics have balked at the number of stories left open-ended, situations never resolved. Still, the structure of the novel represents the incoherent tangle of lives. This novel blurs the real and the surreal and provides a constant challenge to linear thinking.

PORTRAIT IN SEPIA

Portrait in Sepia, a companion to the novel that preceded it, *Daughter of Fortune*, tells the story of Aurora del Valle, a young woman who does not remember her early childhood. The mystical, matriarchal family of both *Daughter of Fortune* and Allende's most famous work, *House of the Spirits*, endures more of the turbulent Chilean history of the nineteenth and twentieth century. Eliza Sommers, the protagonist of *Daughter of Fortune*, is here the grandmother of this story's main character, Aurora del Valle. Aurora is the relative and contemporary of Clara del Valle of *House of the Spirits*. The three novels share the theme of women's special gifts and abilities within a violent society run by men.

Aurora tells of her birth in San Francisco in 1880 and her inability to remember what her life was like before she was taken to live in Chile with her grandmother, Paulina del Valle. She decides at a plateau in her life that she needs to find out who she is before she can commit herself to another and live her life. She is a photographer, and she uses photographs to find as well as to define herself as she travels from relative to relative, finding pieces of a puzzle that will at last yield her completed past. She learns ultimately of the events surrounding her mother's and grandfather's deaths and the history that led to her being reared in Chile. Her discoveries, though horrifying, free her at last to move toward a positive future.

Much of the story in *Portrait in Sepia* consists of Aurora's memories of growing up in Chile and of her relationships with the strong women who played major parts in her life. These mysterious, sometimes clairvoyant women stand out in strong opposition to the shadowy men who exert political power for political ends.

INÉS OF MY SOUL

Inés of My Soul is a fairly straightforward historical novel; Allende has described it as "a work of intuition" but added that "any similarity to events and persons relating to the conquest of Chile is not coincidental." It reaches further back into the Chilean past than her other novels to tell the story of Inés Suárez, a sixteenth century woman who was married to a conquistador and played an important part in the foundation of Chile.

The novel is a romanticized version of Inés's life. The bloody Spanish conquest and the upheavals surrounding it serve as background for her tale of passion involving several men who played major parts in the conquest. While the novel does not exactly glorify the conquistadors, it does throw a veil of the romantic over this shameful period in Spain's history. In this book, however, the romance is paramount; history serves romance.

This extraordinary woman rose from seamstress to a position of power, even wielding swords with the band of Pedro de Valdivia, who became her most passionate lover. After their affair and the conquest are over, she marries Rodrigo de Quiroga and settles down with this man, governor and conquistador, for whom she feels "a mature, joyful sentiment" rather than the excess and abandon of her passion for Valdivia. Inés is a widow close to the end of her life when she narrates the story to Isabel, daughter of her late husband. The subtleties of Allende's trademark Magical Realism and its multilayered symbolism are mostly lacking in this fast-paced narrative, which has a strong appeal to romance readers as well as history buffs.

Janet McCann

OTHER MAJOR WORKS

SHORT FICTION: *Cuentos de Eva Luna*, 1990 (*The Stories of Eva Luna*, 1991).

NONFICTION: *Civilice a su troglodita: Los impertinentes de Isabel Allende*, 1974; *Paula*, 1994 (English translation, 1995); *Conversations with Isabel Allende*, 1999; *Mi país inventado*, 2003 (*My Invented Country: A Nostalgic Journey Through Chile*, 2003); *La suma de los días*, 2007 (*The Sum of Our Days*, 2008).

CHILDREN'S LITERATURE: *La gorda de porcelana*, 1984; *Ciudad de las bestias*, 2002 (*City of the Beasts*, 2002); *El reino del dragón de oro*, 2003 (*Kingdom of the Golden Dragon*, 2004); *El bosque de los Pigmeos*, 2004 (*Forest of the Pygmies*, 2005).

MISCELLANEOUS: *Afrodita: Cuentos, recetas, y otros afrodisiacos*, 1997 (*Aphrodite: A Memoir of the Senses*, 1998).

BIBLIOGRAPHY

Allende, Isabel. *Conversations with Isabel Allende*. Edited by John Rodden. Austin: University of Texas Press, 1999. Collection of interviews with the author sheds some light on her life and work.

_____. *My Invented Country: A Nostalgic Journey Through Chile*. New York: HarperCollins, 2003. Memoir presents Allende's reflections on the land of her youth, the people she knew, and history. This work illuminates the author's semiautobiographical novels.

Bloom, Harold, ed. *Isabel Allende*. New York: Chelsea House, 2002. Collection of essays on Allende's work includes an informative editor's introduction as well as analyses by other major scholars.

Correas Zapata, Celia. *Isabel Allende: Life and Spirits*. Translated by Margaret Sayers Peden. Houston: Arte Público Press, 2002. First biographical discussion of Allende in book form, written by an admiring but scholarly friend of the novelist, provides an intimate glimpse into Allende's life.

Cox, Karen Castellucci. *Isabel Allende: A Critical Companion*. Westport, Conn.: Greenwood Press, 2003. Presents down-to-earth analysis of Allende's novels through *Portrait in Sepia*. Includes a biographical sketch.

García Pinto, Magdalena, ed. *Women Writers of Latin America: Intimate Histories*. Austin: University of Texas Press, 1991. Contains an excellent interview with Allende that provides a great deal of insight into the way she views her writing. Allende mentions that she sees herself as a troubadour going from village to village, person to person, talking about her country.

Gough, Elizabeth. "Vision and Revision: Voyeurism in the Works of Isabel Allende." *Journal of Modern Literature* 27, no. 4 (2004): 93-120. Offers an insightful and readable analysis of photography, spying, and hidden observation as themes in Allende's work.

Hart, Stephen M. *White Ink: Essays on Twentieth-Century Feminine Fiction in Spain and Latin America*. London: Tamesis, 1993. Sets Allende's work within the context of women's writing in the twentieth century in Latin America. Examines the ways in which Allende fuses the space of the personal with that of the political in her fiction and shows that, in her work, falling in love with another human being is often aligned with falling in love with a political cause.

Levine, Linda Gould. *Isabel Allende*. New York: Twayne, 2002. Good introductory work presents analysis of Allende's works. Includes bibliographical references and index.

Rojas, Sonia Riquelme, and Edna Aguirre Rehbein, eds. *Critical Approaches to Isabel Allende's Novels*. New York: Peter Lang, 1991. Collection of essays provides in-depth discussion of Allende's first three novels.

Swanson, Philip. *The New Novel in Latin America: Politics and Popular Culture After the Boom*. New York: Manchester University Press, 1995. Chapter 9 contains a discussion of the use of popular culture in Allende's fiction, showing that the people and popular culture are seen to challenge official culture and patriarchy in her work. Also has a good introduction that sets Allende's work in the context of the works of other post-Latin American boom novelists.

JULIA ALVAREZ

Born: New York, New York; March 27, 1950

Also known as: Julia Altagracia Maria Teresa Alvarez

PRINCIPAL LONG FICTION

How the García Girls Lost Their Accents, 1991
In the Time of the Butterflies, 1994
¡Yo!, 1997
In the Name of Salomé, 2000
The Cafecito Story, 2001
Saving the World, 2006

OTHER LITERARY FORMS

Julia Alvarez has written in several genres, something for which, she says, "I blame my life." Her publications include the nonfiction *Once upon a Quinceañera: Coming of Age in the USA* (2007), which she was invited to write. She also has written numerous essays, including the autobiographical *Something to Declare* (1998). Her favorite genre is poetry, and she has published many poems in literary journals, plus several books of poems, including *The Other Side/El otro lado* (1995) and *Seven Trees* (1998), which features prints by her daughter-in-law, artist Sara Eichner. She also has drawn on her Latino heritage for a substantial number of books for children and young adults, notably *Before We Were Free* (2002) and *How Tía Lola Came to Stay* (2001).

ACHIEVEMENTS

Julia Alvarez's books have been published in at least eleven languages and are widely available around the world. Some are bilingual (English and Spanish) editions. She has won a number of prizes for her poetry, including from the Academy of American Poetry in 1974, and was awarded a Robert Frost Fellowship in Poetry in 1986. Three of her works, *How the García Girls Lost Their Accents*, *In the Time of the Butterflies*, and *Before We Were Free*, were chosen as Notable Books by the American Library Association (ALA); the latter also received the ALA's Pura Belpré Award, presented for an outstanding literary work for youth and children that "best portrays, affirms, and celebrates the Latino cultural experience." Alvarez has received honorary degrees from John Jay College of the City University of New

York and from Union College of Schenectady, New York. Her works have contributed substantially to the Latina voice in contemporary American literature.

BIOGRAPHY

Julia Alvarez was born Julia Altagracia Maria Teresa Alvarez in New York City in 1950, the second of four daughters, but her family returned to the Dominican Republic when she was still an infant. Her mother and her father, a doctor, both came from large, affluent Dominican families that had respect for and connections to the United States. Alvarez and her sisters grew up in a large and traditional extended family; she remembers the men going to work and the children being raised with their cousins by a large group of aunts and maids. She came to recognize the restrictions these women faced: One aunt was trained as a physician but did not practice; another aunt, known as the one who read books, was unconventional and unmarried. This "reading aunt" gave Alvarez a copy of the classic collection of folktales *One Thousand and One Nights*, introducing her to her "first muse," Scheherazade, a princess who was dark-skinned and resourceful. Alvarez, fascinated by the possibilities of storytelling, would draw on her experiences with her aunts, maids, cousins, and siblings for several of her novels, notably *How the García Girls Lost Their Accents*.

Alvarez was ten years old when her father's involvement in a plot to overthrow Dominican dictator Rafael Trujillo was discovered. With the help of a U.S. agent, the family escaped and returned to New York City. Although Alvarez yearned for this "homecoming," the adjustment was difficult for all. Her father had to retrain as a physician. The family lived in a small apartment in Queens, isolated from other Dominicans and without the support of their extended family. Alvarez herself was homesick and faced the prejudice of her classmates. This experience as an immigrant would be a major focus of her writing.

Alvarez went to college in the late 1960's and early 1970's, struggling to reconcile her traditional Dominican background with her new and chaotic culture. She earned her bachelor's degree at Middlebury College in

Julia Alvarez.

Vermont in 1971 and her master's degree in creative writing from Syracuse University in 1975. She married and divorced twice before she was thirty years old, unable to combine marriage with the life of writing that had become her passion. For a number of years, she worked at part-time and temporary academic jobs to support herself. Both Alvarez's professional and personal lives stabilized at the end of the 1980's. In 1988, she began a long-term association as a professor at Middlebury; in 1998, she entered a new arrangement with the college, becoming a writer-in-residence so that she would have more time for writing.

In 1989, Alvarez was married a third time, this time to Bill Eichner, a doctor and son of a Nebraska farm couple. This relationship gave Alvarez a new culture to negotiate, a new appreciation for farming and gardening, and a new project. She and Eichner started a sustainable organic-coffee farm and a school to teach reading and writing to illiterate coffee farmers and their families in the Dominican Republic. This project is the subject of the novel *The Cafecito Story*, which Alvarez calls an "eco-parable" and a love story, written primarily for young readers.

ANALYSIS

If Julia Alvarez's life were a novel, postmodern, postcolonial, and feminist critics, especially, would be interested in analyzing it. She has referred to herself as a "Dominican hyphen American," adding, "As a fiction writer, I find that the most exciting things happen in the realm of that hyphen—the place where two worlds collide or blend together." This is the place postcolonial writers call the liminal space, the "place between." It is the place where Alvarez has lived her life, and it is the setting of her fiction.

Alvarez considers herself an American, but her writing is concerned with both Dominican and American culture and with the dilemma of immigrants trying to bridge the gaps. Because she is aware that most of her American readers, like her young American classmates from the past, will not be familiar with anything Dominican, she also patiently works to bridge this gap as well. It is understandable, given this focus, that some scholars consider her a Caribbean writer, connecting her to Edwidge Danticat and Jamaica Kincaid, among others.

Alvarez's sense of living in liminal space and having to deal with the collision of cultures is mirrored in the fragmented form of her novels, which some scholars consider short stories; in her fluid use of time; and in her use of multiple points of view. This style results in a confusion between reality and fiction. While Alvarez addresses general concerns of the postcolonial and postmodern, her novels focus primarily on how these issues affect women. Through her numerous female characters, she examines sexism in Latino culture, pressures faced by women living in dictatorships, and misogyny in both external and internal forms. It is not coincidental that her most intriguing characters are women who rebel against the existence of repressive boundaries (for example, Yo in *How the García Girls Lost Their Accents* and Miranda in *The Time of the Butterflies*).

Alvarez is not only interested in examining cultural, ethnic, and gender boundaries; another main concern in her work is language—its use to define and limit, especially immigrants and the lower classes, and its possibilities for a writer, especially a bilingual one. Her childhood experience in an oral culture, her own love of poetry, and her struggles to learn English and to maintain her fluency in Spanish all contribute to her thoughtful use of language in her writings.

HOW THE GARCÍA GIRLS LOST THEIR ACCENTS

Alvarez's first novel is based on the experiences of her own family. The book is divided into three sections by time, which moves backward in this account. Each section is subdivided into five vignettes, stories focused on a single character or group of characters. To aid her readers, Alvarez provides a genealogical chart at the beginning of the book, tracing both the de la Torreses (Mami's family) and the Garcías to the conquistadores. Readers also become aware of where the four García girls—Carla, Sandra (Sandi), Yolanda (Yo), and Sofia (Fifi)—fit in these two large and important families. Alvarez has noted that Yo's name is a play on the Spanish word for self or "I"; indeed, Yo is the storyteller in this work.

The first section (1989-1972) details Yo's return to the Dominican Republic after a five-year absence, looking for a home but not finding it. This section presents the aging of the parents and the marriages and struggles, including Sandi's breakdown, of the adult "girls." The second section (1970-1960, the ten years after the family's exile) focuses on the parents' struggle to adjust to American life, the father's acceptance that conditions in his homeland mean staying in the United States, and the tensions between the parents and their daughters, who are having their own problems in the United States in the 1960's. During this period, the parents decide that summers with the family on the island will help solve the problems, but the sisters have to "rescue" Fifi from the prospect of a traditional island marriage with her sexist cousin, Manuel. The final section, 1960-1956, depicts life on the island before the family's exile, when America was represented by toys from FAO Schwarz. Because of the reverse chronology, readers get a clear picture of what the García family gained—and lost—when they were exiled.

IN THE TIME OF THE BUTTERFLIES

Alvarez's second novel is a fictionalized account of the story of the three Mirabel sisters, Patria, Minerva, and Maria Teresa (Maté), who were brutally murdered by Trujillo in November, 1960, shortly after the Alvarez family fled to the United States. *Las Mariposas* (the butterflies, which was the code name of the sisters) were among the founders of the underground resistance to which Alvarez's father belonged. Alvarez refers to this book as one she felt compelled to write.

In this account, Alvarez focuses on the characters, beginning with the surviving sister, Dede, in 1994, as she is waiting to talk to a "gringo writer," clearly Alvarez, coming to interview her about her sisters. Dede, now in her sixties, still maintains a museum in honor of *Las Mariposas*; she has become their storyteller. Although the rest of the book is written in the first person, from the rotating viewpoints of the three butterflies, Dede's sections are third-person, limited point of view, which emphasizes her distance from the others and their story.

In the Time of the Butterflies is divided into three parts, starting in the late 1930's and moving to November 25, 1960, the day the sisters were murdered. Each sister has one chapter in each of the sections; Dede speaks the epilogue, using first person for the first time. Each sister is presented clearly. Patria, the oldest, is the most traditional. A devout Catholic, she marries young and focuses on her husband, his family farm, and her children. She is brought to the revolution through the church: along with her priest and others, she is radicalized during a retreat in the mountains after they witness a government massacre of peasants, one of whom looks like Patria's young son.

Minerva is always rebellious, understanding even as a youth the nature of Trujillo and his dictatorship. She is attracted to a mournful classmate, whose sorrow she finds has been caused by Trujillo's murder of all male members of her family, including a young brother. Minerva witnesses Trujillo's seduction of the most beautiful and accomplished young woman in her school, whose life is destroyed by this attention. Minerva's own beauty attracts Trujillo's notice, and she puts herself and her family in jeopardy when she publicly slaps him. She becomes a revolutionary early, is attracted to two young radicals, and marries one of them.

Alvarez presents Maté, the youngest sister, through the pages of Maté's diary. At first, the entries seem typical of any young girl and are even a bit silly. As the story progresses, Maté matures, and the diary and its ominously torn-out pages symbolize how even innocent thoughts can be dangerous in a dictatorship.

Dede stays outside the intrigue because of the attitude of her husband, but ironically, she divorces him after the death of her sisters. Dede, though devastated by her loss, rallies to take care of her extended family, including her sisters' children. Hers is a feminist voice, criticizing the sisters' husbands, who are eventually released from prison and go on with their lives and to new families. The epilogue suggests, however, that she is finally ready to embrace her own life, including herself, "the one who survived," as part of the story.

In a postscript, Alvarez discusses her connection to the history of the Mirabel sisters and her approach to telling their story. She has also included an essay titled "Chasing the Butterflies" in *Something to Declare*, which discusses her 1986 trip to the Dominican Republic and her first interviews with people who knew the Mirabel sisters or had witnessed parts of their last day. *In the Time of the Butterflies* was made into a feature film (2001) starring Salma Hayek.

¡YO!

Alvarez has said that *¡Yo!* is not a sequel to her successful first novel, but there is a clear connection. Yo, the writer of her own successful novel, has angered her family and friends for turning them into "fictional fodder." This novel is their answer; in fifteen separate pieces, the novel presents varied perspectives on Yo, including an ironic one from her mother, a poignant one from a landlady, a frightening one from a stalker, and a tender one from her father. Alvarez creates believable characters with distinctive voices; at the same time, she presents a complex portrait of Yo.

Elsie Galbreath Haley

OTHER MAJOR WORKS

POETRY: *Homecoming: Poems*, 1984 (revised and expanded 1996 as *Homecoming: New and Collected Poems*, 1996); *The Other Side/El otro lado*, 1995; *Seven Trees*, 1998; *Cry Out: Poets Protest the War*, 2003 (multiple authors); *The Woman I Kept to Myself*, 2004.

NONFICTION: *Something to Declare*, 1998; *Once upon a Quinceañera: Coming of Age in the USA*, 2007.

CHILDREN'S/YOUNG ADULT LITERATURE: *The Secret Footprints*, 2000; *How Tía Lola Came to Stay*, 2001; *Before We Were Free*, 2002; *Finding Miracles*, 2004; *A Gift of Gracias*, 2005.

EDITED TEXT: *Old Age Ain't for Sissies*, 1979.

BIBLIOGRAPHY

Johnson, Kelly Lyon. *Julia Alvarez: Writing a New Place on the Map*. Albuquerque: University of New Mexico Press, 2005. The first book-length examination of Alvarez's writings. Johnson explores shared themes, ideals, and issues of understanding cultural identity in a global society. Notes that Alvarez embraces the notion of *mestizaje*, the mixing of races.

Luis, William. "A Search for Identity in Julia Alvarez's *How the García Girls Lost Their Accents*." *Callaloo* 23, no. 3 (Summer, 2000): 839-849. A study of Alvarez's tale of the search for identity in the "space" between two homelands.

Oliver, Kelly. "Everyday Revolutions, Shifting Power, and Feminine Genius in Julia Alvarez's Fiction." In *Unmaking Race, Remaking Soul: Transformative Aesthetics and the Practice of Freedom*, edited by Christa Davis Acampora and Angela L. Cotten. Albany: State University of New York Press, 2007. In this collection of essays on the power of creativity to transform the lives of women of color, Oliver explores how Alvarez's female characters use their everyday genius to counter, for example, sexism and misogyny. Oliver places this "feminine genius" on similar footing with the genius of larger-scale revolutionary acts.

Sirias, Silvis. *Julia Alvarez: A Critical Companion*. Westport, Conn.: Greenwood Press, 2001. A basic guide to Alvarez's works, with chapters on four of her novels. Includes chapters examining Alvarez's life as well as the Latino/Latina novel.

Socolovsky, Maya. "Patriotism, Nationalism, and the Fiction of History in Julia Alvarez's *In the Time of the Butterflies* and *In the Name of Salomé*." *Latin American Literary Review* 34, no. 68 (July-December, 2006): 5-24. Socolovsky is concerned with Alvarez's ability in these novels to walk the line between remembering historical events and the risk of hagiography, or forgetting the events by overmemorializing them.

JORGE AMADO

Born: Ferradas, near Ilhéus, Bahia, Brazil; August 10, 1912

Died: Salvador, Bahia, Brazil; August 6, 2001

PRINCIPAL LONG FICTION

O país do carnaval, 1931
Cacáu, 1933
Suor, 1934
Jubiabá, 1935 (English translation, 1984)
Mar morto, 1936 (*Sea of Death*, 1984)
Capitães da areia, 1937 (*Captains of the Sand*, 1988)
Terras do sem fim, 1942 (*The Violent Land*, 1945)
São Jorge dos Ilhéus, 1944 (*The Golden Harvest*, 1992)

Seara vermelha, 1946
Os subterrâneos da liberdade, 1954 (includes *Agonia da noite*, *A luz no túnel*, and *Os ásperos tempos*)
Gabriela, cravo e canela, 1958 (*Gabriela, Clove and Cinnamon*, 1962)
Os velhos marinheiros, 1961 (includes *A morte e a morte de Quincas Berro Dágua* [*The Two Deaths of Quincas Wateryell*, 1965] and *A completa verdade sôbre as discutidas aventuras do Comandante Vasco Moscoso de Aragão, capitão de longo curso* [*Home Is the Sailor*, 1964])
Os pastores da noite, 1964 (*Shepherds of the Night*, 1967)

Dona Flor e seus dois maridos, 1966 (*Dona Flor and Her Two Husbands*, 1969)

Tenda dos milagres, 1969 (*Tent of Miracles*, 1971)

Tereza Batista cansada de guerra, 1972 (*Tereza Batista: Home from the Wars*, 1975)

Tiêta do Agreste, 1977 (*Tieta, the Goat Girl*, 1979)

Farda fardão, camisola de dormir, 1979 (*Pen, Sword, Camisole*, 1985)

Tocaia Grande: A face obscura, 1984 (*Showdown*, 1988)

O sumiço da santa: Una história de feitiçaria, 1988 (*The War of the Saints*, 1993)

A descoberta da América pelos Turcos, 1994

Capitán de altura, 2000

OTHER LITERARY FORMS

Although known primarily for his long fiction, the prolific Jorge Amado (uh-MAH-doo) also wrote much nonfiction, including works of journalism and several books. His nonfiction indicates his interests even more obviously than does his fiction, as the translations of the following titles show: *Guia das ruas e dos misterios da cidade do Salvador* (1945; guide to the streets and mysteries of Salvador), *Homens e coisas do Partido Comunista* (1946; men and facts of the Communist Party), *União Soviética e democracias populares* (1951; the Soviet Union and popular democracies), and *Bahia boa terra Bahia* (1967; Bahia, sweet land Bahia). Also pertinent here are two biographies of Brazilians, *ABC de Castro Alves* (1941), about a Romantic nineteenth century abolitionist poet known as the poet of the slaves, and *Vida de Luíz Carlos Prestes* (1942), featuring a twentieth century revolutionary and Marxist hero. Amado's efforts in other genres include a collection of prose poems, *A estrada do mar* (1938); a play, *O amor de Castro Alves* (pb. 1947; also known as *O amor do soldado*); and various film scenarios.

ACHIEVEMENTS

During the first stage of his career, in the 1930's, Jorge Amado was frequently criticized for writing propagandistic novels, for allowing his left-wing politics to take precedence over his novelistic art. Although Amado proudly admitted such a priority, part of the explanation for his early awkwardness is that he was only beginning to learn his art. Of his novels of the 1930's, the most notable is *Jubiabá*. Although Amado's early novels are his least read, with many still untranslated into English, they do establish his credentials as a writer of the people and help account for his 1951 Stalin International Peace Prize.

With *The Violent Land*, Amado's first acknowledged masterpiece, his politics became less overt. Samuel Putnam, Amado's early translator into English, maintained that Amado succumbed to the repressive censorship of the Getúlio Vargas dictatorship in Brazil, but if this is so, Fred P. Ellison has argued, the ironic result was more effective art. Part of the explanation again seems to be that Amado's art simply matured in *The Violent Land*, that he developed from thesis novels to a fuller version of reality.

Gabriela, Clove and Cinnamon, Amado's next masterpiece, marked another shift in his career—adoption of a humorous stance. The entertaining novels of this period represent the height of Amado's art. Other comic masterpieces include *Dona Flor and Her Two Husbands* and the volume *Os velhos marinheiros*, which contains two novels translated as *The Two Deaths of Quincas Wateryell* and *Home Is the Sailor*.

With *Tereza Batista*, *Tieta, the Goat Girl*, and his later novels, Amado's art became hackneyed, as he indulged in shallow (and wordy) repetition of previously successful formulas, such as centering a novel on a sexy woman. The effect of his formulaic prose is magnified in translation, wherein Amado's famed lyricism is mostly lost, but even in the original Portuguese, Amado was prone to repeat himself from novel to novel and even within the same novel.

Despite his limitations, Amado is an immensely popular writer, the best-known Brazilian novelist in his country and in the world. His work has been translated into more than fifty languages and has gained mass circulation through radio and film. Amado always had a good eye for popularity, even in his early days, when proletarian novels were in vogue. Perhaps his popularity explains why he was a perennial candidate for the Nobel Prize in Literature.

BIOGRAPHY

A *Nordestino* (a person from the Brazilian northeast), Jorge Amado wrote about the people and places he experienced at first hand: the cacao plantations and seacoast towns of his native state of Bahia. Son of João Amado de Faria and Eulália Leal Amado, he was born August 10, 1912, on his father's cacao plantation near Ilhéus. When he was old enough, Amado spent his summers working in the cacao groves with other Bahian laborers. These early experiences among Brazil's impoverished provided an invaluable learning experience for Amado and a foundation for much of his writing.

It was a turbulent and violent period, as documented in *The Violent Land*, where Amado depicts himself as a fascinated child observing a highly publicized murder trial. He attended primary school in Ilhéus; his headmistress, Dona Guilhermina, appears briefly in *Gabriela,*

Jorge Amado. (Bernard Gotfryd/Archive Photos)

Clove and Cinnamon, where her reputation for severity is "legendary." Amado went on to secondary school in Salvador, first at the strict Jesuit Colégio Antánio Vieira (from which he ran away) and then at the progressive Ginásio Ipiranga. He attended law school at the Federal University of Rio de Janeiro, receiving his degree in 1935.

Appreciating Amado's penchant for social realism requires an understanding of the sociopolitical climate in which he first began to write. Following a global economic crisis that shattered the coffee industry and forced masses of Brazilians into poverty, Brazil's 1930 presidential election was also turbulent. When the liberal challenger Getúlio Vargas met with apparent defeat, he led an armed rebellion against the state and gained control of civilian and military institutions, disbanded the congress, and issued a decree of absolute power for his government. Initially, the overthrow of the old order produced a renaissance of sorts among Brazil's writers. Vargas publicly advocated achievement and reform, and many writers were quick to adopt this spirit of social renewal. The new literature of Brazil revealed the squalor of the country's lower classes and offered solutions for a nation needing change.

While a student at the Ginásio Ipiranga, Amado began writing for newspapers and magazines and joined the Academia dos Rebeldes (academy of rebels), a bohemian group of writers and artists. He continued similar activities in Rio de Janeiro, where he published his first novel when he was nineteen. By that time, he was already attracted to leftist politics, and his second novel, *Cacáu,* branded subversive, landed him briefly in jail. Thus began a whole series of clashes with censors, detentions and imprisonments (1935-1936, 1938), and exiles (1936-1937, 1941-1943, 1948-1952).

In 1945, Amado married Zélia Gettai of São Paulo; they would have two children, João Jorge and Paloma. Also in 1945, after the military overthrew the Vargas dictatorship, Amado, running on the Communist Party ticket, was elected federal deputy of the Brazilian parliament and helped draft a new constitution. His political career ended in 1948 after the Communist Party was outlawed and Amado was forced into exile. During his exiles, Amado traveled through the rest of South America as well as through Mexico, the United States, Western and Eastern Europe, and Asia, living perhaps for the longest periods in Mexico, Argentina, Uruguay, France, Czechoslovakia, and Poland.

After 1952, as Amado's worldwide popularity increased, conditions improved for him in Brazil. From 1956 to 1959, he edited *Para todos*, a prominent cultural periodical in Rio de Janeiro. In 1961, he was appointed to the Literary Committee of the Conselho Nacional de Cultura (national council of culture) and was elected to the Academia Brazileira de Letras. In 1962 Amado traveled to Cuba and Mexico shortly after the death of his father, and in 1963 he and his family returned to Salvador to live.

After traveling through Europe and North America, Amado became a writer-in-residence at Pennsylvania State University in 1971. During the 1990's he spent much of his time in Paris and London after his Salvador home began attracting hordes of tourists. He returned to Brazil in 1996 to undergo heart surgery, and he died in Salvador on August 6, 2001.

ANALYSIS

Some critics are made uneasy by the coexistence in Jorge Amado of Marxist commitment and the Bahian version of *far niente*, or "Let the good times roll." Amado's duality was evidenced by his popularity on both sides of the Iron Curtain and by the unlikely conjunction of his early propagandistic novels and his later spate of sexy best sellers. There is more consistency in Amado's career than first appears, however. As Amado himself maintained, his sympathies throughout his writing were with the working class and the poor. In part, Amado's metamorphoses indicate his strategy: He had to present his case in the face of disinterest, opposition, and censorship. After all, if sex and humor could be used to sell toothpaste and automobiles, then they could be used to sell Marxist views. Amado also answered the question of what to do while one waits for the revolution: One has a good time and invites the rich to a party. Indeed, in Amado's easygoing Marxism, revolution might not even be necessary, as modern society seems to be evolving on its own toward a humane civilization free of want, repression, and prejudices.

The duality in Amado's outlook is reflected in his depiction of the working-class poor. They are ground down by hunger and serfdom, yet, paradoxically, they are also heroic. As a class they are heroic because it is mainly with their blood, sweat, and tears that civilization has been built. The working class also furnishes most of Amado's individual heroes and heroines. In the early novels, heroic proletarians abound, the most notable being the black António Balduíno, who becomes a labor leader in *Jubiabá*. Later examples are the mulatto beauties Gabriela and Tieta, who subvert the bourgeois social order with their sexual freedom. The Syrian immigrant Nacib Saad, who has to choose between Gabriela and bourgeois macho respectability, might also be included here. In general, the Bahian poor, with their urge to enjoy life, best exemplify Amado's ideal of humane civilization, whereas the repressed bourgeoisie are driven by greed, puritanism, snobbery, and other demons. The bourgeoisie rule, but when they want a good time they have to go to the poor. Through the interaction of these two classes, Amado shows the evolution of society taking place.

THE VIOLENT LAND

The most primitive stage of social organization is represented in *The Violent Land*, set in early twentieth century Bahia. Although Bahia has been at least sparsely settled for centuries, frontier conditions reminiscent of the Wild West of North America still prevail in the novel. The main enemy is the dark rain forest, the Sequeiro Grande, full of fearsome animals and imagined goblins presided over by an old witch doctor who delivers his curse. The jungle constantly threatens to reclaim the cacao plantations carved from it, a threat symbolized by the cries of frogs being swallowed by snakes in a pond next to a plantation house. The darkness lurking in the hearts of men and women—ignorance, lawlessness, amorality, and greed—also threatens. To bring order out of this impending chaos and drive the wedge of conquest deeper into the jungle requires a few strongman types; therefore, the resulting social order is a feudal plantation system presided over by the strongmen-owners, such as Sinhô and Juca Badaró and Colonel Horacio da Silveira.

The defects of this feudal strongman system, however, are immediately apparent. Only the strongmen (the "colonels") and their close henchmen benefit substantially; the workers live at a subsistence level, laboring long hours daily and completely subject to the will of the strongmen. The social order achieved at such high cost is minimal: The only law is the whim of the strongmen. Corrupted by their power, the strongmen corrupt their followers; this moral morass is symbolized by the sticky cacao ooze that clings to the hands and feet of the workers, who can rise in the order only by becoming assassins for their bosses (a description that also gives some notion of how the social order is enforced). The only ideal is a macho code of personal courage (which, however, is flexible enough to allow bullying and bushwhacking; beating women is also considered acceptable). Most of the women serve as cooks or prostitutes, though Ana Badaró impresses everyone with her ability to shoot as straight as any man.

Paradoxically, the strongman social order is very weak. Dependent on the headman, it waits for his orders before anything gets done, and then it is limited by his vision. The system's fragility is demonstrated most clearly when the strongmen clash, as happens in *The Violent Land*. The principle of survival of the fittest returns: In the cacao war between Colonel Horacio and the Badarós, the Badarós are decimated and their plantation burned to the ground.

Amado thus shows the feudal strongman system to be only one step beyond the jungle, a primitive stage that belongs to a civilized country's past. As long as it stays in the past, it can be celebrated, and *The Violent Land* thus possesses epic qualities: a grand design, sweeping action, a lyric prose style that breaks out into ballads. The colorful characters tend toward the mock-heroic—gamblers, whores, assassins, adulterers, colonels. Above all, Amado has an epic theme: the struggle and sacrifice required to achieve progress. He never tires of saying that the land was fertilized by human blood, mainly the blood of workers. To lose what has been achieved at such great cost would be a betrayal.

GABRIELA, CLOVE AND CINNAMON

Gabriela, Clove and Cinnamon shows the next step up for society, the transition from a feudal order to a crude form of democracy. The novel is set in Ilhéus in 1925-1926, during a boom period for the cacao industry.

Significantly, material change, especially the growth of cities, has preceded political change. Representing the old feudal order is the octogenarian Colonel Ramiro Bastos, in addition to a clutch of other colonels, some sporting scars of the cacao wars. Representing the new order is the cacao exporter Mundinho Falcão, who gathers a following of town dignitaries and a few enlightened colonels. Ruling by decree, Colonel Ramiro Bastos stands in the way of further progress—schools, roads, sewers, and especially a port that will accommodate large ships. Throughout the novel, the political campaign between Colonel Ramiro and Mundinho Falcão heats up. Colonel Ramiro's followers propose to bring back the old-style violence, but their plans fizzle when the old man dies. Ultimately the issues are settled peacefully, by an honest election, itself an innovation for the region.

Significantly, the agent of change, Mundinho Falcão, is not a native of the region but the youngest son of a rich and politically prominent Rio de Janeiro family. Another, humbler agent of change is also an outsider: the Syrian Nacib Saad, owner of the Vesuvius Bar. The novel's other main line of action concerns Nacib's love for the beautiful backlander Gabriela, a mulatto whom he hires as cook at a migrant labor pool called the Slave Market. When Gabriela proves to be as good in bed as she is in the kitchen ("color of cinnamon, smell of clove"), Nacib marries her. A flower of the people, generous and loving, Gabriela seems an ideal woman, but the marriage is a mistake, like the caged bird Nacib gives her as a present. Free and easy as a bird, Gabriela cannot stomach the middle-class restrictions of marriage in Ilhéus.

When Nacib finds Gabriela in bed with the town Romeo, he is faced with a dilemma: The old macho code decrees that he must kill her and her lover, but the easygoing Nacib, however heartbroken, is no killer. The solution is another triumph for civilization in the region: Nacib and Gabriela's marriage is declared legally void, and, after a period of separation, they go back to living and loving together. The triumph is underlined when a cacao colonel who had killed his wife and her lover is sent to prison—the first such conviction in Ilhéan history.

These cases and others are discussed nonstop in the

homes, businesses, and taverns of Ilhéus, especially in the Vesuvius Bar. Amado's characters like to talk, and they tell all. As Amado notes here and elsewhere, the main entertainment in small-town Bahia is gossip. Obviously the Ilhéans are well entertained, as are Amado's readers. In *Gabriela, Clove and Cinnamon*, a masterpiece of plotting, character, and theme, gossip is raised to a fine art.

THE TWO DEATHS OF QUINCAS WATERYELL

A smaller masterpiece is Amado's *The Two Deaths of Quincas Wateryell*. Here, in a funny, fantastic little story that verges on allegory, Amado attacks middle-class pretensions and restrictions head-on. His hero is Joaquim Soares da Cunha, an exemplary family man and bureaucrat who, at the age of fifty, retires from the State Rent Board and inexplicably leaves his home and family to become a bum, roaming the slummy Salvador waterfront in the company of drunks and whores. In his new identity, Joaquim Soares da Cunha becomes Quincas Wateryell, named after the outraged scream he lets out when he drinks a glass of water thinking it is white rum. After ten years, Quincas's convivial life of drinking, whoring, and gambling catches up with him: When the novella opens, he lies dead on a rancid flophouse bed, his big toe sticking out of a hole in his dirty sock. Still, there is a smile on the corpse's face.

As his relatives gather to give Quincas a "decent" burial, his reason for running away from home becomes clear. His straitlaced family, scandalized and mortified all of those years, is finally relieved by his death. In particular, his smug daughter, Vanda, determines to put the domestic screws to Quincas in death, just as her "saintly" mother did in life. That is, she symbolically dresses him up and has the undertaker make him up as Joaquim Soares da Cunha. Nothing, however, can be done about his immoral smile, which Vanda thinks is mocking her. Indeed, she thinks she hears the corpse whistle and call her "Viper!" Her efforts to reclaim Quincas for respectability are defeated when four of his buddies appear at the wake. Left alone with the corpse, they revive it with rum and take it for a last night on the town, including a fight in a bar and a visit to Quincas's mistress. The drunken party ends up at sea in a fishing boat, from which the corpse "leaps" to its death in the cleansing waters—a proper end for an old salt like Quincas.

DONA FLOR AND HER TWO HUSBANDS

After *Gabriela, Clove and Cinnamon*, *Dona Flor and Her Two Husbands* is perhaps the best known of Amado's novels. *Dona Flor and Her Two Husbands* is the story of a young lower-middle-class cooking teacher named Florípedes Paiva. The story is set in the Salvador, Bahia, of the 1920's and 1930's. Florípedes's marriage to the promiscuous and gambling Vadinho Guimarães is suddenly terminated by his premature death. Flor is devastated, despite his exploitation and abuse of her, because he was the source of her greatest pleasure, with a zest for life and passionate lovemaking.

Despite serious misgivings, the widowed Flor accepts the marriage proposal of a respectable but dull local pharmacist, Dr. Teodoro Madureira. Her newfound security and respectability are not able to satisfy her needs, however. In response to Flor's emotional and sexual vulnerability, Vadinho reappears as a ghost, overcomes her defenses, and regains his place in her marriage bed. Soon, however, he begins to disappear as the result of a Bahian Candomblé ritual that Flor had earlier ordered in an effort to halt his illicit advances. It is only through Flor's personal intercession that the decision of the gods is later reversed, thus allowing her to enjoy the best of both Vadinho and Teodoro.

To critics, it appeared strange that such a politically engaged author should publish an apparently frivolous work just two years after the imposition of a brutal military dictatorship. Consequently, some critics viewed the two husbands, diametrically opposed to each other, as metaphors for two contradictory political forces in Brazil: the leftist populism of the 1950's and early 1960's versus the opposing military and technocratic forces. The heroine's magical solution, which grants her the best of both her husbands, could be read as a statement about the problems of and answers for the Brazilian people. On one level, no one narrow sociopolitical philosophy is, in Amado's opinion, capable of meeting the country's needs, whether it be populist and democratic in nature or technocratic and military, whether it is oriented to the values and demands of the working classes or to those of the bourgeoisie. Only through the combination of both these forces can an effective society be achieved. Brazil, like Flor, is otherwise left vulnerable, unsatisfied, and incomplete.

TIETA, THE GOAT GIRL

A similar attack on bourgeois values informs *Tieta, the Goat Girl*, an example of Amado's later work. *Tieta, the Goat Girl*, however, is neither little nor a masterpiece. The wordy, rambling story runs on interminably (672 pages in the English translation), and it is as silly as it is raunchy. The first half or so details the 1966 return of a "prodigal daughter," Tieta "the goat girl," to her poor hometown of Agreste on the Bahian seacoast. Twenty-six years before, her father beat her and drove her from home for giving away sexual favors. Now, supposedly the widow of a rich São Paulo industrialist, the beautiful and generous Tieta is enfolded in the bosom of her family, and the dazzled town declares her a saint. The joke is that Saint Tieta became rich by learning to sell her sexual favors, eventually becoming madam of the fanciest whorehouse in Brazil. When this joke wears thin, Amado tries, in the book's last half, to whip up reader enthusiasm for an ecological battle: A polluting titanium dioxide factory wants to move into town and spoil the beaches and fishing.

Despite the novel's sophomoric plot and characters, *Tieta, the Goat Girl* is entertaining. Amado's unrestrained style is not merely wordy; it has a veritably Rabelaisian range and exuberance. Consistent with his uninhibited style is Amado's satiric attack on bourgeois hypocrisy and greed, including recent extremes manifested in consumer society and destructive industries. Amado's attack reaches its literal and symbolic climax in Tieta's seduction of her nephew Ricardo, a seventeen-year-old seminarian. Saint Tieta, the expert, teaches Ricardo a new life-affirming religion, as Ricardo is assured by the liberation theologian Frei Thimóteo, a Franciscan friar. Other characters representing this religion in the novel are a group of hippies who visit the fabulous beach of Mangue Seco and a group of fishing families who have always lived there.

Coming from another direction, but deriving its inspiration from Marx as well as Jesus, liberation theology is not too far away from Amado's own easygoing Marxism. The appearance of liberation theology in recent decades supports Amado's view that modern society—at least in Brazil—is evolving toward a humane civilization free of want, repression, and prejudice. Both liberation theology and Amado represent the frustration and optimism of Brazil—and the new combinations of thought emanating from that vital land.

THE WAR OF THE SAINTS

In *The War of the Saints*, Amado creates a tale of Magical Realism that reverberates with the sights, sounds, smells, and tastes of a carnival. The novel opens with the description of a statue of Saint Barbara of the Thunder, famed for her eternal beauty and miraculous powers. The statue has just been transported from the altar of a provincial church across the Bay of All Saints to Bahia for an exhibition of religious art. Soon after the ship docks, the statue takes life and disappears into the crowd. The icon is transformed into the living African deity Saint Barbara Yansan. The novel recounts the magical events of the next forty-eight hours. If the mulatto culture of this part of Brazil, which is based on the mixture of Roman Catholicism and West African animism, is the underlying subject of the novel, it is clear that the author's sympathy lies nearly entirely with the latter religion. Candomblé, an Afro-Brazilian religion partly of Yoruba origin, is the book's true protagonist and winner in the cultural struggle depicted in the novel.

Saint Barbara Yansan has come to rescue Manela, a young girl who is in love with a taxi driver named Miro, from the puritanical clutches of her devoutly Catholic aunt, Adalgisa. Being a goddess, Saint Barbara naturally succeeds. Along the way, she permits her humble servant, the author, to create a riotously satiric epic that pokes fun at critics and professors, Marxists and fascists, generals and judges, priests, politicians, and policemen—in short, anyone with any power in Brazil. Concurrently, however, Amado paints a loving portrait of Bahia's powerless, particularly artists, poets, musicians, lovers, and the priests and priestesses of Candomblé. The book is a consummate celebration of life amid misery, and it is unabashedly triumphant.

Harold Branam
Updated by Genevieve Slomski

OTHER MAJOR WORKS

PLAY: *O amor de Castro Alves*, pb. 1947 (also known as *O amor do soldado*).

POETRY: *A estrada do mar*, 1938.

NONFICTION: *ABC de Castro Alves*, 1941 (biography); *Vida de Luíz Carlos Prestes*, 1942; *Bahia de todos os santos*, 1945 (travel sketch); *O cavaleiro da esperança*, 1945 (biography); *Guia das ruas e dos misterios da cidade do Salvador*, 1945; *Homens e coisas do Partido Comunista*, 1946; *O mundo da paz*, 1951 (travel sketch); *União Soviética e democracias populares*, 1951; *Bahia boa terra Bahia*, 1967; *Bahia*, 1971 (English translation, 1971); *O menino grapiúna*, 1981; *Navega ção de Cabotagem*, 1992.

CHILDREN'S LITERATURE: *O gato malhado e a andorinha sinhá: Uma historia de amor*, 1976 (*The Swallow and the Tom Cat: A Love Story*, 1982).

BIBLIOGRAPHY

Brookshaw, David. *Race and Color in Brazilian Literature*. Metuchen, N.J.: Scarecrow Press, 1986. Brookshaw detects racial stereotyping and prejudice in Amado's characterization of blacks in *Jubiabá*; *Gabriela, Clove and Cinnamon*; and *Tent of Miracles*. Includes a bibliography.

Brower, Keith H., Earl E. Fitz, and Enrique Martínez-Vidal, eds. *Jorge Amado: New Critical Essays*. New York: Routledge, 2001. In addition to analyses of specific novels, including *Dona Flor and Her Two Husbands* and *Gabriela, Clove and Cinnamon*, this collection features a comparison of the work of Amado and John Steinbeck and a description of a visit to Pennsylvania State University that Amado and his wife made in 1971.

Chamberlain, Bobby J. *Jorge Amado*. Boston: Twayne, 1990. Provides excellent and detailed analysis of Amado's later works of fiction. Discusses Amado as a writer, social critic, and politician and places his works within their social, political, and historical context. Concluding chapter discusses the author's contradictory status as a man of letters and a literary hack. Includes biographical information, chronology, and bibliography.

Dineen, Mark. "Change Versus Continuity: Popular Culture in the Novels of Jorge Amado." In *Fiction in the Portuguese-Speaking World: Essays in Memory of Alexandre Pinheiro Torres*, edited by Charles M. Kelley. Cardiff: University of Wales Press, 2000. Examination of Amado's novels is presented within a collection of sixteen essays that analyze major fiction writers from Portugal, Brazil, and Portuguese-speaking Africa.

Lowe, Elizabeth. *The City in Brazilian Literature*. Madison, N.J.: Fairleigh Dickinson University Press, 1982. Characterizes Amado's depiction of Salvador, Bahia, as "picturesque exoticism" and his portrayal of the urban poor as "carnivalization." Includes bibliography and index.

Patai, Daphne. *Myth and Ideology in Contemporary Brazilian Fiction*. Madison, N.J.: Fairleigh Dickinson University Press, 1983. Chapter 5 presents a critique of Amado's *Tereza Batista*, which Patai believes undercuts itself ideologically. Criticizes Amado for his use of the supernatural, for his use of humor (which she feels trivializes social injustice), and for what Patai regards as his patronizing view of the poor. Argues that Amado's work blurs the distinction between history and fiction. Includes bibliography.

Pescatello, Ann. "The Brazileira: Images and Realities in the Writings of Machado de Assis and Jorge Amado." In *Female and Male in Latin America: Essays*, edited by Ann Pescatello. Pittsburgh, Pa.: University of Pittsburgh Press, 1973. Compares and contrasts female characters in several of Amado's major novels with those of Joaquim Maria Machado de Assis. Detects a preoccupation with race and class in both writers' female characterizations. Includes a bibliography.

Richardson, Daniel C. "Towards Faulkner's Presence in Brazil: Race, History, and Place in Faulkner and Amado." *South Atlantic Review* 65, no. 4 (2000): 13-27. Argues that previous studies have traced William Faulkner's literary presence in the Spanish-speaking countries of Latin America while ignoring his reception in Brazil and addresses this absence by comparing Faulkner's work to that of Amado.

Wyles, Joyce Gregory. "Boundless Love and Death in Bahia." *Americas* 54, no. 1 (January/February, 2002): 22. Biographical article discusses Amado's life and death in Bahia, some of his novels, the impact of Salvador, Bahia, on the characters in his fiction, his style of writing, and the plots and themes of his books.

KINGSLEY AMIS

Born: London, England; April 16, 1922
Died: London, England; October 22, 1995
Also known as: Kingsley William Amis; Robert Markham

PRINCIPAL LONG FICTION

Lucky Jim, 1954
That Uncertain Feeling, 1955
I Like It Here, 1958
Take a Girl Like You, 1960
One Fat Englishman, 1963
The Egyptologists, 1965 (with Robert Conquest)
The Anti-Death League, 1966
Colonel Sun: A James Bond Adventure, 1968 (as Robert Markham)
I Want It Now, 1968
The Green Man, 1969
Girl, 20, 1971
The Riverside Villas Murder, 1973
Ending Up, 1974
The Crime of the Century, 1975 (serial), 1987 (book)
The Alteration, 1976
Jake's Thing, 1978
Russian Hide-and-Seek, 1980
Stanley and the Women, 1984
The Old Devils, 1986
Difficulties with Girls, 1988
The Folks That Live on the Hill, 1990
The Russian Girl, 1992
You Can't Do Both, 1994
The Biographer's Moustache, 1995

OTHER LITERARY FORMS

Kingsley Amis (AY-mihs) is best known as a novelist, but readers have turned often to his other writings for the insights they provide into the man and his fiction. Many of the themes that are explored in depth in his novels are expressed indirectly in the peripheral works. He published several collections of short stories: *My Enemy's Enemy* (1962), *Collected Short Stories* (1980), and *Mr. Barrett's Secret, and Other Stories* (1993). *Dear Illusion*, a novella, was published in 1972 in a limited edition of five hundred copies. His collections of poetry include *Bright November* (1947), *A Frame of Mind* (1953), *A Case of Samples: Poems, 1946-1956* (1956), *The Evans Country* (1962), *A Look Round the Estate: Poems, 1957-1967* (1967), and *Collected Poems: 1944-1979* (1979). Amis published his opinionated *Memoirs* in 1991. His criticism covers an extremely wide range; in addition to studies of figures as diverse as Jane Austen and Rudyard Kipling, he published one of the first significant critical books on science fiction, *New Maps of Hell: A Survey of Science Fiction* (1960), a work that did much to encourage academic study of the genre and to win recognition for many gifted writers. *The James Bond Dossier* (with Ian Fleming; 1965), several volumes of collected science fiction edited with Robert Conquest and titled *Spectrum: A Science Fiction Anthology* (1961-1965), and *The King's English: A Guide to Modern Usage* (1997) offer further evidence of the extraordinary range of his work.

ACHIEVEMENTS

Almost from the beginning of his career, Kingsley Amis enjoyed the attention of numerous commentators. Because his works are filled with innovations, surprises, and variations in techniques and themes, it is not surprising that critics and reviewers alike found it difficult to make a definitive statement about his achievements. The range of his work is extraordinary: fiction, poetry, reviews, criticism, humor, science fiction, and biography. Of all his writings, however, his achievement depends most on his novels.

Amis's early novels are considered by many critics to be "angry" novels of protest against the contemporary social, political, and economic scene in Britain. The themes include resentment of a rigid class stratification, rejection of formal institutional ties, discouragement with the economic insecurity and low status of those without money, loathing of pretentiousness in any form, and disenchantment with the past. Because many of Amis's contemporaries, including John Wain, John Osborne, John Braine, and Alan Sillitoe, seemed to express similar concerns, and because many came from working-class or lower-middle-class backgrounds, went to Oxford or Cambridge University, and taught for a time at a provincial university, journalists soon spoke of them as belonging to a literary movement.

The "Angry Young Men," as their fictional heroes came to be called, were educated men who did not want to be gentlemen. Kenneth Allsop called them "a new, rootless, faithless, classless class" lacking in manners and morals; W. Somerset Maugham called them "mean, malicious and envious . . . scum" and warned that these men would some day rule England. Some critics even confused the characters with the writers themselves. Amis's Jim Dixon (in *Lucky Jim*) was appalled by the tediousness and falseness of academic life; therefore, Dixon was interpreted as a symbol of anti-intellectualism.

Dixon taught at a provincial university; therefore, he became a symbol of contempt for Cambridge and Oxford. Amis himself taught at a provincial university (Swansea); therefore, he and Dixon became one and the same in the minds of many critics. Like all literary generalizations, however, this one was soon inadequate. The most that can be said is that through Amis's early heroes there seemed to sound clearly those notes of disillusionment that were to become dominant in much of the literature of the 1950's.

Because it seems so artless, critics have also found Amis's fiction difficult to discuss. His straightforward plotting, gift for characterization, and ability to tell a good story are resistant to the modern techniques of literary criticism. Because Amis's work lacks the obscurity, complexity, and technical virtuosity of the fiction of James Joyce or William Faulkner, some critics have suggested that it is not to be valued as highly. In many of the reviews of his early work, Amis was described as essentially a comic novelist, an entertainer, or an amiable satirist not unlike P. G. Wodehouse, the Marx Brothers, or Henry Fielding. Furthermore, his interest in mysteries, ghost stories, James Bond thrillers, and science fiction confirmed for some critics the view that Amis was a writer lacking serious intent.

Looking beyond the social commentary and entertainment found in Amis's work, other critics have found a distinct relationship between Amis's novels and the "new sincerity" of the so-called Movement poets of the 1950's and later. These poets (including Amis himself, Philip Larkin, John Wain, and D. J. Enright, all of whom also wrote fiction) saw their work as an alternative to the symbolic and allusive poetry of T. S. Eliot and his followers. In a movement away from allusion, obscurity, and excesses of style, the Movement poets encouraged precision, lucidity, and craftsmanship. They concentrated on honesty of thought and feeling to emphasize what A. L. Rowse calls a "business-like intention to communicate with the reader." Amis's deceptively simple novels were written with the same criteria he imposed on his poetry; one cannot read Amis with a measure suitable

Kingsley Amis. (© Washington Post; reprinted by permission of the D.C. Public Library)

only to Joyce or Faulkner. Rather, his intellectual and literary ancestors antedate the great modernist writers, and the resultant shape is that of a nineteenth century man of letters. Amis's novels may be appreciated for their commonsense approach. He writes clearly. He avoids extremes or excessive stylistic experimentation. He is witty, satiric, and often didactic.

Amis's novels after 1980 added a new phase to his career. One of the universal themes that most engaged Amis was that of relationships between men and women, both within and outside marriage. After 1980, he moved away from the broad scope of a society plagued by trouble to examine instead the troubles plaguing one of that society's most fundamental institutions—relationships—and the conflicts, misunderstandings, and drastically different responses of men and women to the world. Most of his characters suffer blighted marriages. Often they seem intelligent but dazed, as if there were something they had lost but cannot quite remember. Something has indeed been lost, and loss is at the heart of all of Amis's novels, so that he is, as novelist Malcolm Bradbury calls him, "one of our most disturbing contemporary novelists, an explorer of historical pain." From the beginning of his canon, Amis focused on the absence of something significant in modern life: a basis, a framework, a structure for living, such as the old institutions like religion or marriage once provided. Having pushed that loss in societal terms to its absolute extreme in the previous novels, Amis subsequently studied it in personal terms, within the fundamental social unit. In *The Old Devils*, for example (for which he won the 1986 Booker Fiction Prize), his characters will not regain the old, secure sense of meaning that their lives once held, and Amis does not pretend that they will. What success they manage to attain is always partial. What, in the absence of an informing faith or an all-consuming family life, could provide purpose for living? More simply, How is one to be useful? This is the problem that haunts Amis's characters, and it is a question, underlying all of his novels, that came to the forefront near the end of his life.

In looking back over Amis's career, critics have found a consistent moral judgment quite visible beneath the social commentary, entertainment, and traditional techniques that Amis employs. Beginning in a world

filled with verbal jokes, masquerades, and incidents, Amis's view of life grew increasingly pessimistic until he arrived at a fearfully grim vision of a nightmare world filled with hostility, violence, sexual abuse, and self-destruction. Critics, therefore, view Amis most significantly as a moralist, concerned with the ethical life in difficult times. Amis's response to such conditions was to use his great powers of observation and mimicry both to illuminate the changes in postwar British society and to suggest various ways of understanding and possibly coping with those changes. For all these reasons, one can assert that Amis achieved a major reputation in contemporary English fiction, and, as is so often the case, his is an achievement that does not depend on any single work. It is rather the totality of his work with which readers should reckon.

BIOGRAPHY

Kingsley William Amis was born in London on April 16, 1922. His father, William Robert Amis, was an office clerk with Coleman's Mustard and fully expected his only child to enter commerce. His son's intention, however, was to be a writer—a poet, really—though it was not until the publication of his rollicking and irreverent first novel, *Lucky Jim*, in 1954 that Amis achieved his goal.

By Amis's own account, he had been writing since he was a child. Writing became for him a means of coming to terms with certain fears. As a boy he suffered from the routine terrors of childhood—fear of the dark, fear of the future, fear of other children, fear of his parents' disapproval—but as he grew older the subjects of his fears changed. He was a complicated individual; depression alternated with laughter, and an inner loneliness counterbalanced his social charm. Typically, one fear involved his health. Like many of his characters, one of his strongest fears was and continued to be the fear of loneliness. "Being the only person in the house is something I wouldn't like at all," he said, years later. "I would develop anxiety. By this I mean more than just a rational dislike of being alone and wanting company but something which means, for me, becoming very depressed and tense. I've always been terribly subject to tension. I worry a lot."

Kingsley Amis as an author and his characters themselves often seem to be running scared, playing out their lives while always looking over their shoulders, afraid that the truth of life's meaninglessness will catch up to them. Amis admitted that writing fiction encourages the illusion that there is some sense in life. "There isn't," he said, "but if that's all you thought, you'd go mad." In his fiction, if not in life, he was able to pretend that there is a pattern in events and that the suffering of his characters can be justified, or explained, or atoned for, or made all right. Such power to conjure up meaning where it otherwise may not exist brought with it the "wonderful feeling of being Lord of Creation."

Long before Amis was to experience this power, he was merely a schoolboy at St. Hilda's local fee-paying school. At St. Hilda's he learned French from Miss Crampton and also developed a crush on his English teacher, Miss Barr, "a tall, Eton-crowned figure of improbable eloquence." It is in these inauspicious surroundings, he said, humorously, that perhaps "we can date my first education into the glories of our literature." Perhaps because of Miss Barr, but more probably because of his temperament and interests, he developed a fascination for anything to do with writing—pens, paper, erasers.

His interest may have been piqued at St. Hilda's, but his first literary efforts occurred at Norbury College. There he was exposed to the vast entertainment that the days held for a British public school boy in the 1930's: Under the tutelage of his teachers, he began to write stories and poems. His first published work of fiction, a three-hundred-word adventure story called "The Sacred Rhino of Uganda," appeared in the school magazine. In the fall of 1934, he entered the "really splendid" City of London School—a day school of seven hundred boys that overlooked the Thames by Blackfriars Bridge. Amis read much during this period. He specialized in the classics until he was sixteen, then switched to English, but later he would wish that he had been more interested in scripture and divinity at the time and had been touched by the wings of faith, a wish that his fiction would ultimately demonstrate. He also read French. Early artistic delights included watercolors, Dadaism, and architecture. He especially loved to read poetry, and with his keen mind and quick sensibilities he could take in a considerable amount of material quickly.

In the prewar year of 1939, while he was in the sixth form, Amis and many of his school chums were suddenly surprised to find themselves being evacuated from London for their safety, sent to Marlborough College in Wiltshire; there he spent the next five terms. He found himself in the small country town of Marlborough, one of the most undisturbed countrysides remaining in the southwest of England. There, in vivid contrast to the suburbia he knew in Clapham, Amis was initiated into the beauties and mysteries of nature, and for the rest of his life he would carry images of Marlborough with him and re-create them in his fictional country scenes.

Amis's first novel, written while he attended St. John's College at the University of Oxford (1941-1942, 1945-1947), was rejected by fourteen publishers. Eventually Amis abandoned it altogether, having come to regard it as boring, unfunny, and derivative. Although his studies at Oxford were interrupted by the war, Amis persisted, earning his B.A. (with honors) and M.A. degrees in English.

Several factors influenced Amis's development into a writer whose stories and style are unique. His comic proclivities were encouraged by his father—a man with "a talent for physical clowning and mimicry." Amis described himself as "undersized, law-abiding, timid," a child able to make himself popular by charm or clowning, who found that at school he could achieve much by exploiting his inherited powers of mimicry. His school friends testified to Amis's capacity for making people laugh. Philip Larkin's description of their first meeting (1941) in the introduction to the 1964 edition of his own novel, *Jill* (first published in 1946), suggests that it was Amis's "genius for imaginative mimicry" that attracted him: "For the first time I felt myself in the presence of a talent greater than my own." John Wain also recalled how, in the "literary group" to which both of them belonged, Amis was a "superb mimic" who relished differences of character and idiom.

This period of "intensive joke swapping," as Larkin called it, continued when Amis entered the army in 1942. He became an officer, served in the Royal Signals, and landed in Normandy in June, 1944. After service in France, Belgium, and West Germany, he was demobilized in October, 1945. This period was to provide material for such stories as "My Enemy's Enemy," "Court of

Inquiry," and "I Spy Strangers," but its immediate effect was to open his eyes to the world, to all sorts of strange people and strange ways of behaving.

Amis's status as an only child also contributed to his development as a writer, for he found himself looking at an early age for "self-entertainment." He satisfied this need by reading adventure stories, science fiction, and boys' comics. During these years, too, Amis became interested in horror tales. He recalled seeing the Boris Karloff films *Frankenstein* (1931) and *The Mummy* (1932) and Fredric March in *Dr. Jekyll and Mr. Hyde* (1932). After that time, Amis was interested in what might be called the minor genres on grounds of wonder, excitement, and "a liking for the strange, the possibly horrific." Amis became aware that the detective story, various tales of horror or terror, and the science-fiction story provided vehicles for both social satire and investigation of human nature in a way not accessible to the mainstream novelist.

Along with his natural comic gifts, his interest in genre fiction, and his war experiences, Amis was influenced in his development by his early exposure to an English tradition that resisted the modernist innovations so influential in the United States and Europe at the time. His dislike for experimental prose may be traced in part to the influence of one of his tutors at Oxford, the Anglo-Saxon scholar Gavin Bone, and to his readings of certain eighteenth century novelists whose ability to bring immense variety and plentitude to their work without reverting to obscurity or stylistic excess appealed to the young Amis.

Amis attributed his personal standards of morality both to his readings in Charles Dickens, Fielding, and Samuel Richardson and to the training in standard Protestant virtues he received while growing up at home. Both of his parents were Baptists, but in protest against their own forceful religious indoctrination, they attended church less and less frequently as they grew older. Any reader of Amis's works soon becomes aware that there is in his writings a clear repudiation of traditional Christian belief. Nevertheless, from his parents he received certain central moral convictions that crystallized a personal philosophy of life and art. Hard work, conscientiousness, obedience, loyalty, frugality, patience—these lessons and others were put forward and later found their way into his novels, all of which emphasize the necessity of good works and of trying to live a moral life in the natural—as opposed to the supernatural—world.

Despite these convictions, however, Amis was not able to live his private life impeccably—as he himself would ultimately testify. His long-standing marriage to Hilary Bardwell, which produced a daughter and two sons, including novelist Martin Amis, was marred by his frequent infidelities and was ultimately destroyed by his romantic involvement with fellow novelist Elizabeth Jane Howard. Amis and Hilary were divorced in 1965. Amis's subsequent marriage to Howard was not happy, however, and the two separated in 1980. Misogynistic novels such as *Jake's Thing* and *Stanley and the Women* mirror Amis's dissatisfaction with his relationship with Howard in particular and with relations between the sexes in general.

The sunnier aspect of Amis's final novels—especially *The Old Devils* and *The Folks That Live on the Hill*—owes its character to Amis's reconcilement (of sorts) with his first wife. In 1981 Amis, Hilary, and her third husband, Alistair Boyd (Lord Kilmarnock), set up housekeeping together. The arrangement was to last until Amis's death in late 1995. During this final period Amis received Britain's highest literary award, the Booker Prize, for *The Old Devils*. His unusual domestic arrangements are described in detail in Eric Jacobs's *Kingsley Amis: A Biography* (1998). Amis's final novel, *The Biographer's Moustache*, reflected his somewhat uneasy feelings over having his biography written. According to Jacobs, Amis remained a writer until his death in 1995. During his last illness he was busy compiling notes about hospital routines to be incorporated into yet another novel.

ANALYSIS

Kingsley Amis's fiction is characterized by a recurring preoccupation with certain themes and concepts, with certain basic human experiences, attitudes, and perceptions. These persistent themes are treated with enormous variety, however, particularly in Amis's novels that draw on the conventions of genre fiction—the mystery, the spy thriller, the ghost story, and so on. Of the more than twenty novels Amis published, his development as a seriocomic novelist is especially apparent in *Lucky Jim*, *Take a Girl Like You*, *The Anti-Death League*, *The Green Man*, *The Old Devils*, *The Folks That Live on the Hill*, and *The Russian Girl*, his most substantial and complex works, each of which is representative of a specific stage in his career. All these novels are set in contemporary England. Drawing on a variety of traditional techniques of good storytelling—good and bad characters, simple irony, straightforward plot structure, clear point of view—they restate, in a variety of ways, the traditional pattern of tragedy: A man, divided and complex, vulnerable both to the world and to himself, is forced to make choices that will determine his destiny. Built into this situation is the probability that he will bring down suffering on his head and injure others in the process.

In *Lucky Jim*, for example, Amis establishes a comic acceptance of many of life's injustices in the academic world. The novel is distinguished by clear-cut cases of right and wrong, a simple irony, and knockabout farce. Because he has neither the courage nor the economic security to protest openly, the hero lives a highly comic secret life of protest consisting of practical jokes and rude faces, all directed against the hypocrisy and pseudo-intellectualism of certain members of the British establishment. While only hinted at in *Lucky Jim*, Amis's moral seriousness becomes increasingly evident beginning with *Take a Girl Like You*. Whereas in *Lucky Jim* the values are "hidden" beneath a comic narrative, gradually the comedy is submerged beneath a more serious treatment. *Take a Girl Like You* is thus a turning point for Amis in a number of ways: The characterization is more complex, the moral problems are more intense, and the point of view is not limited to one central character. Distinguished also by a better balance between the comic and the serious, the novel is more pessimistic than its predecessors, less given to horseplay and high spirits.

In later novels such as *The Anti-Death League* and *The Green Man*, Amis continues to see life more darkly, shifting to an increasingly metaphysical, even theological concern. Contemporary England is viewed as a wasteland of the spirit, and his characters try vainly to cope with a precarious world filled with madness and hysteria, a world in which love and religion have become distorted and vulgarized. Threatened with death and ugly accidents by a malicious God, Amis's characters

feel powerless to change and, in an attempt to regain control of their lives, act immorally. Amis's ultimate vision is one in which all of the traditional certainties—faith, love, loyalty, responsibility, decency—have lost their power to comfort and sustain. Humanity is left groping in the dark of a nightmare world. In the later *The Old Devils*, Amis's study of a Wales and a Welshness that have slipped out of reach forever clearly shows a culmination of his increasing damnation of Western society, portrayed through the microcosm of human relationships. The final picture is one of the aimlessness of old age, the meaninglessness of much of life itself.

LUCKY JIM

In *Lucky Jim*, a bumbling, somewhat conscientious hero stumbles across the social and cultural landscape of contemporary British academic life, faces a number of crises of conscience, makes fun of the world and of himself, and eventually returns to the love of a sensible, realistic girl. This is the traditional comic course followed by Amis's first three novels, of which *Lucky Jim* is the outstanding example. Beneath the horseplay and high spirits, however, Amis rhetorically manipulates readers' moral judgment so that they leave the novel sympathetic to the hero's point of view. By triumphing over an unrewarding job, a pretentious family, and a predatory female colleague, Dixon becomes the first in a long line of Amis's heroes who stand for common sense and decency, for the belief that life is to be made happy now, and for the notion that "nice things are nicer than nasty things."

To develop his moral concern, Amis divides his characters into two archetypal groups reminiscent of the fantasy tale: the generally praiseworthy figures, the ones who gain the greatest share of the reader's sympathy; and the "evil" characters, those who obstruct the good characters. Jim Dixon (the put-upon young man), Gore-Urquhart (his benefactor or savior), and Christine Callaghan (the decent girl to whom Dixon turns) are among the former, distinguished by genuineness, sincerity, and a lack of pretense. Among the latter are Professor Welch (Dixon's principal tormentor), Welch's son, Bertrand (the defeated boaster), and the neurotic Margaret Peele (the thwarted "witch"), all of whom disguise their motives and present a false appearance.

One example should be enough to demonstrate

Amis's technique—the introduction to the seedy, absentminded historian, Professor Welch. In the opening chapter, Amis establishes an ironic discrepancy between what Welch seems to be (a scholar discussing history) and what he is in reality (a "vaudeville character" lecturing on the differences between flute and recorder). Although he tries to appear a cultured, sensitive intellectual, all of the images point to a charlatan leading a boring, selfish life. His desk is "misleadingly littered." Once he is found standing, "surprisingly enough," in front of the college library's new-books shelf. Succeeding physical description undercuts his role-playing: He resembles "an old boxer," "an African savage," "a broken robot." What is more, his speech and gestures are mechanized by cliché and affectation. Professing to worship "integrated village-type community life" and to oppose anything mechanical, he is himself a virtual automaton, and he becomes more so as the novel progresses. Although Amis does not term Welch a ridiculous phony, the inference is inescapable.

Central to the novel's theme is Dixon's secret life of protest. Although he hates the Welch family, for economic reasons he dares not rebel openly. Therefore, he resorts to a comic fantasy world to express rage or loathing toward certain imbecilities of the Welch set. His rude faces and clever pranks serve a therapeutic function—a means by which Dixon can safely release his exasperation. At other times, however, Dixon becomes more aggressive: He fantasizes stuffing Welch down the lavatory or beating him about the head and shoulders with a bottle until he reveals why he gave a French name to his son.

In Amis's later novels, when the heroes' moral problems become more intense, even life-threatening, such aggressive acts become more frequent and less controlled. In this early novel, however, what the reader remembers best are the comic moments. Dixon is less an angry young man than a funny, bumbling, confused individual for whom a joke makes life bearable. There are, of course, other ways in which one might react to an unjust world. One can flail at it, as does Jimmy Porter in John Osborne's drama *Look Back in Anger* (pr. 1956). One can try to escape from it, as will Patrick Standish in *Take a Girl Like You*, or one can try to adapt to it. Like Charles Lumley's rebellion against middle-class values in John

Wain's *Hurry on Down* (1953; also known as *Born in Captivity*), Dixon's rebellion against the affectations of academia ends with an adjustment to the society and with a partial acceptance of its values. By remaining in the system, he can at least try to effect change.

TAKE A GIRL LIKE YOU

Ostensibly another example of the familiar story of initiation, Amis's fourth novel, *Take a Girl Like You*, contains subtleties and ironies that set it apart from *Lucky Jim*. The characterization, the balance between the comic and the serious, and the emphasis on sexual behavior and the pursuit of pleasure blend to make this novel a significant step forward in Amis's development as a novelist.

The plot of this disturbing moral comedy is built around a variety of motifs: the travelogue and the innocent-abroad story, the theme of love in conflict with love, and the country-mouse story of an innocent girl visiting the big city for the first time. Jenny Bunn, from whose point of view more than half of the novel is narrated, is the conventional, innocent young woman who has not been touched by deep experience in worldly matters. Like Jim Dixon, she finds herself in an unfamiliar setting, confronting people who treat her as a stranger with strange ideas. Out of a simpleminded zeal for the virtues of love and marriage, she becomes the victim of a plausible, nasty man.

Jenny carries out several artistic functions in the story. She is chiefly prominent as the perceptive observer of events close to her. Again like Dixon, she is able to detect fraud and incongruities from a considerable distance. When Patrick Standish first appears, for example, she understands that his look at her means he is "getting ideas about her." Amis draws a considerable fund of humor from Jenny's assumed naïveté. His chief device is the old but appropriate one of naïve comment, innocently uttered but tipped with truth. Jenny, a young girl living in a restrictive environment and ostensibly deferential toward the attitudes and opinions of the adults who compose that environment, yet also guided by her own instinctive reactions, may be expected to misinterpret a great deal of what she observes and feels. The reader follows her as she is excited, puzzled, and disturbed by Patrick's money-mad and pleasure-mad world—a world without fixed rules of conduct. Many of the "sex scenes" between them are built on verbal jokes, comic maneuvers, digressions, and irrelevancies, all of which give life to the conventional narrative with which Amis is working.

Patrick Standish is the antithesis of the good, moral, somewhat passive Jenny. Like the masterful, selfish Bertrand Welch, he is a womanizer and a conscious hypocrite who condemns himself with every word he utters. In spite of Patrick's intolerable behavior and almost crippling faults, Amis maintains some degree of sympathy for him by granting him more than a surface treatment. In the earlier novels, the villains are seen from a distance through the heroes' eyes. In *Take a Girl Like You*, however, an interior view of the villain's thoughts, frustrations, and fears allows the reader some measure of understanding. Many scenes are rhetorically designed to emphasize Patrick's isolation and helplessness. Fears of impotence, cancer, and death haunt him. He seeks escape from these fears by turning to sex, drink, and practical jokes, but this behavior leads only to further boredom, unsatisfied longing, and ill health.

Also contributing to the somber tone of the novel are secondary characters such as Dick Thompson, Seaman Jackson, and Graham MacClintoch. Jackson equates marriage with "legalised bloody prostitution." MacClintoch complains that, for the unattractive, there is no charity in sex. Jenny's ideals are further diminished when she attends a party with these men. The conversation anticipates the emotional barrenness of later novels, in which love is dead and in its place are found endless games. Characters speak of love, marriage, and virtue in the same tone as they would speak of a cricket game or a new set of teeth.

With *Take a Girl Like You*, Amis leaves behind the hilarity and high spirits on which his reputation was founded in order to give expression to the note of hostility and cruelty hinted at in *Lucky Jim*. Drifting steadily from bewilderment to disillusionment, Jenny and Patrick signal the beginning of a new phase in Amis's moral vision. Life is more complex, more precarious, less jovial. The simple romantic fantasy solution at the end of *Lucky Jim* is not possible here.

THE ANTI-DEATH LEAGUE

The Anti-Death League represents for Amis yet another extension in philosophy and technique. The con-

ventions of the spy thriller provide the necessary framework for a story within which Amis presents, from multiple viewpoints, a worldview that is more pessimistic than that of any of his previous novels. A preoccupation with fear and evil, an explicit religious frame of reference, and a juxtaposition of pain and laughter, cruelty and tenderness all work to create a sense of imminent calamity reminiscent of George Orwell's *Nineteen Eighty-Four* (1949). No longer does Amis's world allow carefree, uncomplicated figures of fun to move about, relying on good luck and practical jokes to see them through their difficulties. Life has become an absurd game, and the players are suffering, often lonely and tragic individuals, caught in hopeless situations with little chance for winning the good life, free from anxieties, guilt, and doubts.

As the controlling image, the threat of death is introduced early in the novel in the form of an airplane shadow covering the principal characters. Related to this scene is an elaborate metaphor drawn from the language of pathology, astronomy, botany, and thermonuclear war. Part 1 of the three-part structure is titled "The Edge of a Node"—referring to Operation Apollo, an elaborate project designed to destroy the Red Chinese with a horrible plague. As the narrative progresses, the characters are brought to the edge or dead center of the node.

Related to this preoccupation with death is the sexual unhappiness of the characters. Jim Dixon's romps with Margaret are farcical and at times rather sad. Patrick Standish's pursuit and conquest of Jenny Bunn are disgusting and somewhat tragic. In *The Anti-Death League*, the characters' pursuit of love and sex leads only to unhappiness and even danger. Two disastrous marriages and several unhappy affairs have brought Catherine Casement to the brink of madness. An unfaithful husband and a possessive lover have caused Lady Hazell to avoid any emotional involvement whatsoever. A desire to get away from love impels Max Hunter, an alcoholic and gay, to join the army.

Along with the inversion of love, Amis dramatizes an inversion of religion. In place of a benevolent supreme being, Amis has substituted a malevolent God whose malicious jokes lead to death and tragic accidents. In protest, Will Ayscue, the army chaplain, declares war on Christianity as the embodiment of the most vicious lies ever told. Max Hunter writes a poem against God ("To a Baby Born Without Limbs"), organizes the Anti-Death League, and demolishes the local priory. James Churchill cites Hunter's alcoholism, the death of a courier, and Catherine's cancer as reasons for retreating from a world gone bad. Whereas in the preceding novels laughter helps the heroes cope with specific injustices, in *The Anti-Death League*, laughter only intensifies the horror, the pain. Sometimes Amis shifts abruptly from laughter to pain to intensify the pain. A lighthearted moment with Hunter in the hospital is followed by a depressing scene between Catherine and Dr. Best. News of Catherine's cancer is juxtaposed with Dr. Best's highly comic hide-and-seek game.

Hysteria, depression, boredom—these are some of the moods in the army camp, bespeaking a malaise and a loss of hope from which neither sex nor religion nor drink offers any escape. Although both condemning and laughing at the characters' foibles, the reader feels a personal involvement with them because the suffering is seen through the sufferers' eyes. Alone, trying to regain control of their lives, they act irresponsibly and immorally. Only Moti Naidu—like Gore-Urquhart in *Lucky Jim*, a moral voice in the novel—speaks truth in spite of the other characters' tragic mistakes. His recommendations that they aspire to common sense, fidelity, prudence, and rationality, however, go unheeded.

THE GREEN MAN

Although *The Green Man* offers the same preoccupation with God, death, and evil as *The Anti-Death League*, the novel is different from its predecessor in both feeling and technique. The work is, to begin with, a mixture of social satire, moral fable, comic tale, and ghost story. Evil appears in the figure of Dr. Thomas Underhill—a seventeenth century "wizard" who has raped young girls, created obscene visions, and murdered his enemies and now invades the twentieth century in pursuit of the narrator's thirteen-year-old daughter. God also enters in the person of "a young, well-dressed, sort of after-shave lotion kind of man," neither omnipotent nor benevolent. For him, life is like a chess game, the rules of which he is tempted to break. A seduction, an orgy, an exorcism, and a monster are other features of this profoundly serious examination of dreaded death and all its meaningless horror.

The novel is narrated retrospectively from the point of view of Maurice Allington. Like Patrick Standish and James Churchill, he spends most of his time escaping, or trying to escape, from himself—and for good reason. Death for him is a fearful mystery. Questions of ultimate justice and human destiny have been jarred loose of any religious or philosophical certainties. He suffers from "jactitations" (twitching of the limbs) as well as unpleasant and lengthy "hypnagogic hallucinations." What is more, problems with self extend to problems with his family and friends: He is unable to get along well with his wife or daughter, and his friends express doubts about his sanity. In fact, the only certainty Maurice has is that as he gets older, consciousness becomes more painful.

To dramatize Maurice's troubled mind, Amis employs supernatural machinery as an integral part of the narrative. The windowpane through which Maurice sees Underhill becomes a metaphor for the great divide between the known, seen world of reality and the unknown, hence fearful, world of the supernatural. Dr. Underhill, a doppelgänger, reflects Maurice's own true nature in his selfish, insensitive manipulation of women for sexual ends. Also, Underhill's appearances provide Maurice with an opportunity to ennoble himself. In his pursuit and eventual destruction of both Underhill and the green monster, Maurice gains self-knowledge—something few of Amis's characters ever experience. He realizes his own potential for wickedness, accepts the limitations of life, and comes to an appreciation of what death has to offer as an escape from earthbound existence. For the first time in his life, Maurice recognizes and responds to the loving competence of his daughter, who looks after him when his wife leaves.

On one level, this elaborately created story is a superbly entertaining, fantastic tale. On another level, it is a powerful and moving parable of the limitations and disappointments of the human condition. Unlike *Lucky Jim* and *Take a Girl Like You*, both of which are rooted in the real world and are guided by the laws of nature, *The Green Man*—and to some extent *The Anti-Death League*—employs fantastic and surreal elements. Ravens, specters, and vague midnight terrors, all associated with guilt and despair, provide fitting emblems for Maurice's self-absorbed condition.

THE OLD DEVILS

The Old Devils is not an easy book to read, but it is an almost irresistibly easy book to reread. It is one of Amis's densest novels, its many different characters and their stories diverging, interweaving, and dovetailing with a striking precision that requires the utmost concentration of the reader. The novel has no central hero-narrator; each of the major characters claims his or her own share of reader attention. Though the characters' talks and thoughts wander from topic to topic casually, appearing aimless and undirected, actually the inner workings of the characters are carefully regulated, as are the descriptive comments by the omniscient narrator, to support, define, develop, and ultimately embody the novel's themes.

In terms of narrative, the story itself is painted in muted tones. Alun Weaver has chosen to retire from his successful television career in London as a kind of "professional Welshman" and third-rate poet and return after thirty years with his beautiful wife, Rhiannon, to South Wales. The novel explores, over a span of a few months, the effect of this return on their circle of old friends from university days. The old devils—a group of Welsh married couples all in their sixties and seventies—include Malcolm Cellan-Davies, an unsung local writer, and his wife, Gwen; Peter Thomas, a chemical engineer, and his wife, Muriel; Charlie Norris, the proprietor of a restaurant, and his wife, Sophie; Percy and Dorothy Morgan; and Garth Pumphrey, a former veterinarian who with his wife, Angharad, now attends to business at a local pub. Of the five couples, the first three have never left their hometown or accomplished anything very remarkable; their lives have passed them by. They are old now, retired from their professions, and do little else but drink heavily, a device Amis often uses to lower his characters' defenses and reveal their true emotional states. As Sophie says of her husband, "I never realised how much he drank till the night he came home sober. A revelation, it was."

The physical ill health the cronies worry about extends to the spiritual health of their marriages. With the exception of Rhiannon, her daughter Rosemary, and a few minor characters, the women in this novel not only are plain, hard, sharp, critical, or cross but also lack any reasonable relationships with their husbands that would make significant communication possible. Only Alun

and Rhiannon, married for thirty-four years, seem still to have an appetite for life and love as well as drink, and most of their misunderstandings lead only to teasing, not to disaster. Their arrival, however, arouses conflict among their old friends. "You know," says Muriel early in the novel, "I don't think that news about the Weavers is good news for anyone." The conflict comes in part because their return revives memories of various youthful liaisons and indiscretions, and also because the egotistical Alun immediately sets out to woo again the three women with whom he had affairs in the old days.

The Old Devils is about more than an aging present, however; it is also very much about the past and its impingements on everyone. Many of the characters in *The Old Devils* are carrying scars from bitterness and regret because of things that happened in their lives long ago, things they hide carefully from the world but on which their conscious attention is fixed. Past choices weigh heavily on all of them. These memories, like the memories of the aging characters in earlier novels, touch various notes—some sweet, some sour, some true, and others a bit off pitch. Indeed, these old devils are bedeviled by worries and fears of all kinds that deepen their uncertainty about life and increase their preoccupation with the past. Amis points out that one of the reasons old people make so many journeys into the past is to satisfy themselves that it is still there. When that, too, is gone, what is left? In this novel, what remains is only the sense of lost happiness not to be regained, only the awareness of the failure of love, only the present and its temporary consolations of drink, companionship, music, and any other diversions they might create, only a blind groping toward some insubstantial future. Neither human nor spiritual comfort bolsters their sagging lives and flagging souls; Malcolm speaks for all the characters, and probably for Amis himself, when he responds to a question about believing in God: "It's very hard to answer that. In a way I suppose I do. I certainly hate to see it all disappearing."

As in earlier novels, Amis finds in the everyday concerns of his ordinary folk a larger symbolic meaning that carries beyond the characters to indict a whole country. By the end of the novel, one character after another has uncompromisingly attacked television, the media, abstract art, trendy pub decor, rude teenagers, children, shoppers, rock music, Arab ownership of shops and pubs, and anything that smacks of arty or folksy Welshness. The point, says Malcolm, sadly, is that Wales is following the trends from England and has found a way of destroying the country, "not by poverty but by prosperity." The decline and the decay, he says, are not the real problem. "We've faced that before and we've always come through." What he abominates is the specious affluence. "It's not the rubble I deplore," he says, "it's the vile crop that has sprung from it." Both extremes—decay and affluence—are suggested by the homes the characters occupy, and unhappiness characterizes either extreme. Amis's awareness of rooms, of houses, and of what they reveal about their inhabitants is a critical commonplace. Here, in each instance, the description of a character's personal environment is a means of rendering his or her appalled and irritated perception of the world.

Amis's characterization in *The Old Devils*, however, goes beyond a study of that final form of human deterioration. Rather, the novel examines an often debilitating process of moral and spiritual decay, a lessening of these people as human beings as life goes on and their hopes have dimmed along with their physical and mental powers. Perhaps Rhiannon, the most well-rounded of Amis's female characters in a novel, has kept her spiritual core more intact than any of the old devils. Without a doubt she holds a certain moral superiority over her husband in a way that is reminiscent of Jenny Bunn in *Take a Girl Like You*, and the differences in husband and wife are played against each other. Rhiannon emerges as the voice of common sense in the novel, serene and utterly down-to-earth; Alun is condemned, by his actions and words, as a shallow, worldly, selfish man. In the end, he meets death while Rhiannon survives and, in fact, looks ahead to future happiness. The two are unreconciled at Alun's death; no mention is made of her mourning, no homage is paid to his memory, and at the end of the novel she turns to Peter, her lover of forty years before. She finally forgives him for his long-ago abandonment, and the two begin to look forward to spending their last years together.

That event is one of two at the end of the novel that vitiate its undertone of pain, despair, and anxiety. The other positive event is the wedding of Rosemary, the Weavers' daughter, to William, the son of Peter and Muriel, suggesting the replacing of the older generation by the new, which in one sense is heralded by the author as a sign of progress and fulfillment. The reader feels that the young couple will go on to live somewhat happy, placid lives. Despite the overriding negativism in the novel, there is some possibility of redemption. In *The Old Devils*, Amis pictures two relatively attractive people who show promise of living and working together peacefully, using their energy to make a new world instead of destroying an existing one.

The Folks That Live on the Hill

The Folks That Live on the Hill appeared only four years after *The Old Devils*, and while the two share certain similarities—especially the deployment of a wide, even panoramic, cast of characters—the latter work exhibits a greater degree of acceptance of humankind's foibles. This attitude is displayed in particular by the novel's protagonist, Harry Caldecote, a retired librarian who cannot help caring about—and caring for—other people. These include a widowed sister who keeps house for him in the London suburb of Shepherd's Hill, a niece by marriage whose alcoholism is reaching catastrophic proportions, and a brother whose mediocre poetry Harry nevertheless shepherds toward publication. Providing a kind of running commentary on the novel's hapless characters are two immigrant brothers, a pair of bemused outsiders who see the follies of the "folks" all too clearly. When offered an attractive job in the United States, Harry chooses to remain where he is, partly through inertia but largely because he knows he is needed where he is. Harry is recognizably an Amis character, however, and a distinctly male one at that. Twice married and twice divorced, he is largely intolerant of women, other classes, and their annoying patterns of speech.

The Russian Girl

The Russian Girl encapsulates many of Amis's perennial motifs and patterns, yet the gentler note sounded in *The Folks That Live on the Hill* remains. The novel's protagonist is Richard Vaisey, an opinionated professor of Russian literature and language who is fighting to maintain the integrity of his subject in the face of academic progress. (It seems that Richard's considerable knowledge of his subject "dates" him.) Richard's wife Cordelia is perhaps the most harpylike of all Amis's female characters, a rich, sexually attractive but wholly villainous creation noted for her absurd but attention-getting accent. The "girl" of the title is Anna Danilova, a visiting Russian poet who becomes involved with Richard. Their affair propels Richard from his comfortable, sheltered existence into a life of possibility.

Saving the novel's plot from a certain predictability is the fact that Anna, like Harry's brother Freddie in *The Folks That Live on the Hill*, is not a good poet. (To drive the point home, Amis reproduces an embarrassingly poor poem Anna has written in loving tribute to Richard.) This is a situation that Richard understands yet ultimately chooses to accept. In turn, Anna senses Richard's true opinion of her work and accepts it as well. Although not Amis's final novel, *The Russian Girl* represents in many ways the culmination of the author's career in fiction. More sharply focused than many of its predecessors, it forces its protagonist through very difficult moral and intellectual choices. Anna, too, achieves a kind of dignity because of, not despite, her very lack of talent and emerges as one of Amis's most gratifyingly complex female characters.

In retrospect, it is clear that Kingsley Amis is a moralist as well as a humorist. The early novels exhibit a richly comic sense and a considerable penetration into character, particularly in its eccentric forms. With *Take a Girl Like You*, Amis begins to produce work of more serious design. He gives much deeper and more complex pictures of disturbing and distorted people, and a more sympathetic insight into the lot of his wasted or burnt-out characters. In all of his novels, he fulfills most effectively the novelist's basic task of telling a good story. In his best novels—*Lucky Jim, Take a Girl Like You, The Anti-Death League, The Green Man, The Old Devils, The Folks That Live on the Hill*, and *The Russian Girl*—Amis tries to understand the truth about different kinds of human suffering, then passes it on to the reader without distortion, without sentimentality, without evasion, and without oversimplification. His work is based on a steadying common sense.

Dale Salwak
Updated by Grove Koger

OTHER MAJOR WORKS

SHORT FICTION: *My Enemy's Enemy*, 1962; *Collected Short Stories*, 1980; *We Are All Guilty*, 1991; *Mr. Barrett's Secret, and Other Stories*, 1993.

POETRY: *Bright November*, 1947; *A Frame of Mind*, 1953; *A Case of Samples: Poems, 1946-1956*, 1956; *The Evans Country*, 1962; *A Look Round the Estate: Poems, 1957-1967*, 1967; *Collected Poems: 1944-1979*, 1979.

NONFICTION: *New Maps of Hell: A Survey of Science Fiction*, 1960; *The James Bond Dossier*, 1965 (with Ian Fleming); *What Became of Jane Austen? and Other Questions*, 1970; *On Drink*, 1972; *Tennyson*, 1973; *Rudyard Kipling and His World*, 1975; *An Arts Policy?*, 1979; *Everyday Drinking*, 1983; *How's Your Glass?*, 1984; *Memoirs*, 1991; *The King's English: A Guide to Modern Usage*, 1997; *The Letters of Kingsley Amis*, 2000 (Zachary Leader, editor).

EDITED TEXTS: *Spectrum: A Science Fiction Anthology*, 1961, 1962, 1963, 1965 (with Robert Conquest); *Harold's Years: Impressions from the "New Statesman" and "The Spectator,"* 1977; *The Faber Popular Reciter*, 1978; *The New Oxford Book of Light Verse*, 1978; *The Golden Age of Science Fiction*, 1981; *The Great British Songbook*, 1986 (with James Cochrane); *The Amis Anthology*, 1988; *The Pleasure of Poetry: From His "Daily Mirror" Column*, 1990; *The Amis Story Anthology: A Personal Choice of Short Stories*, 1992.

BIBLIOGRAPHY

Amis, Martin. *Experience*. New York: Talk/Miramax Books, 2000. Kingsley's son, Martin Amis, a highly regarded novelist in his own right, discusses his relationship with his father and the crises in his father's life.

Bell, Robert H., ed. *Critical Essays on Kingsley Amis*. New York: G. K. Hall, 1998. Thirty-two new and reprinted essays analyze Amis's work. Contributors include writers such as John Updike and V. S. Pritchett. Bell provides an introduction in which he discusses Amis's major novels. Includes bibliography and index.

Bradbury, Malcolm. *No, Not Bloomsbury*. London: Deutsch, 1987. Devotes a chapter to Amis's comic fiction through *The Old Devils*, charting Amis's course from anger to bitterness. Discusses Amis's moral seriousness, honesty, and humor. Includes chronology and index.

Bradford, Richard. *Kingsley Amis*. London: Arnold,

1989. Key study shows how Amis confounds customary distinctions between "popular" and "literary" fiction. Argues that it is time to readjust the criteria for judging literary worth. Includes secondary bibliography and index.

_____. *Lucky Him: The Biography of Kingsley Amis*. London: Peter Owen, 2001. Although Amis often denied that his fiction was based on his life, this important reassessment of the author demonstrates that his work contains many autobiographical elements.

Gardner, Philip. *Kingsley Amis*. Boston: Twayne, 1981. This first full-length study of Amis's life and career treats his novels (through *Jake's Thing*) and nonfiction, paying particular attention to the recurrence of certain themes and character types, to his modes of comedy, and to the relationship between his life and fiction. Supplemented by a chronology, notes, bibliographies, and index.

Jacobs, Eric. *Kingsley Amis: A Biography*. New York: St. Martin's Press, 1998. A readable, sometimes painfully candid biography written with Amis's full cooperation. Includes photographs, notes, bibliography, and index. This American edition includes material that did not appear in the first (British) edition of 1995.

Laskowski, William. *Kingsley Amis*. New York: Twayne, 1998. Stresses Amis's overall accomplishment as a man of letters. Divides his output into letters, genre fiction, and mainstream novels and devotes equal consideration to each category. Published soon after Amis's death, this volume surpasses the coverage of Philip Gardner's study cited above but does not replace it.

Leader, Zachary. *The Life of Kingsley Amis*. New York: Pantheon Books, 2007. Voluminous, engrossing biography pays equal attention to discussion and analysis of Amis's literary output. Draws on unpublished works, correspondence, and interviews with many of Amis's friends, relatives, fellow writers, students, and colleagues.

McDermott, John. *Kingsley Amis: An English Moralist*. Basingstoke, England: Macmillan, 1989. This first British book-length study of Amis's work seeks to show that the novels are serious as well as funny, that they are distinctively English, and that they offer a wide range of approaches to significant aspects of human behavior. Includes substantial primary and secondary bibliographies and an index.

Moseley, Merritt. *Understanding Kingsley Amis*. Columbia: University of South Carolina Press, 1993. Short survey stresses Amis's accomplishments as a professional man of letters, with special emphasis on his novels. Includes an annotated secondary bibliography and an index.

MARTIN AMIS

Born: Oxford, England; August 25, 1949
Also known as: Martin Louis Amis

PRINCIPAL LONG FICTION

The Rachel Papers, 1973
Dead Babies, 1975 (also known as *Dark Secrets*, 1977)
Success, 1978
Other People: A Mystery Story, 1981
Money: A Suicide Note, 1984
London Fields, 1989
Time's Arrow: Or, The Nature of the Offence, 1991
The Information, 1995
Night Train, 1997
Yellow Dog, 2003
House of Meetings, 2006

OTHER LITERARY FORMS

In addition to novels, essays, criticism, and cultural history have provided important literary outlets for Martin Amis (AY-mihs). *Invasion of the Space Invaders*

(1982) is a history of video games, while *The Moronic Inferno and Other Visits to America* (1986) is a collection of journalistic essays. *Visiting Mrs. Nabokov, and Other Excursions* (1993) and *The Second Plane: September 11, Terror, and Boredom* (2008) are collections of some of Amis's essays on literature, politics, sports, and popular culture. His short stories, which include some of his most imaginative writing, are collected in *Einstein's Monsters* (1987) and *Heavy Water, and Other Stories* (1998).

ACHIEVEMENTS

Martin Amis has been a force on the modern literary scene since his first novel, *The Rachel Papers*, won the Somerset Maugham Award for 1974. Critical and popular acclaim accompanied his sixth novel, *London Fields*, which was a best seller on both sides of the Atlantic. *Time's Arrow* was short-listed for the Man Booker Prize for Fiction, and *Yellow Dog*, for the British Book Awards, for literary fiction. In 2000, for *Experience*, he won the James Tait Black Memorial Prize for biography.

Amis has a powerfully comic and satiric vision of the ills of contemporary society, which he caricatures in a way that has reminded many reviewers of Charles Dickens. Amis spares his reader little in his depiction of low-life characters in all their physical grossness and emotional aridity. The emptiness and corruption inherent in a materialistic culture are recurring themes in his work. In spite of the often-sordid subject matter, however, Amis's novels are illuminated by their stylistic exuberance and ingenuity. More than one critic has remarked on the American flavor of Amis's work, and he is regularly compared to Tom Wolfe and Saul Bellow.

BIOGRAPHY

The son of the novelist Kingsley Amis, Martin Louis Amis spent his early years in Swansea, in south Wales, where his father held a teaching position at Swansea University. The family spent a year in Princeton, New Jersey, in 1959, and then moved to Cambridge, England. Amis's parents were divorced when Amis was twelve, and this had a disruptive effect on his schooling: He attended a total of fourteen schools in six years. As a teenager he had a brief acting career, appearing in the film *A High Wind in Jamaica* (1965). In 1968 he entered Exeter

College, Oxford, and graduated in 1971 with first-class honors in English. He immediately became editorial assistant for *The Times Literary Supplement* and began writing his first novel, *The Rachel Papers*. In 1975 Amis became assistant literary editor of the *New Statesman*, and his second novel, *Dead Babies*, was published in the same year.

In 1980, when Amis was a writer and reviewer for the London newspaper *The Observer*, he reported his discovery that the American writer Jacob Epstein had plagiarized as many as fifty passages from *The Rachel Papers* for his own novel *Wild Oats* (1979). The accusation created a storm in the literary world. Epstein quickly conceded that he had indeed copied passages from Amis's novel and others into a notebook that he had then inadvertently used for his own novel. Thirteen deletions were made for the second American edition of Epstein's book, but Amis was infuriated because he thought that the revisions were not sufficiently extensive.

Martin Amis married Antonia Phillips, an American professor of aesthetics, in 1984, and they had two sons, Louis and Jacob. The controversy that has often accompanied Amis's writings spilled over into his private life from 1994 to 1996. First, he left his wife for American writer Isabel Fonseca. Then he fired his agent, Pat Kavanagh, when Kavanagh was unable to obtain a large advance from his publisher, Jonathan Cape, for his next novel, *The Information*. Amis's new agent, the American Andrew Wylie, eventually made a deal with Harper-Collins, and the whole proceedings were reported in the British press with an intensity rarely given literary figures such as Amis. The controversy was compounded by reports that Amis spent part of his new earnings for extensive dental work in the United States. In 1996, it was revealed that Amis was the father of a twenty-year-old daughter from a 1975 affair. In 2007, Amis accepted the position of professor of creative writing at the University of Manchester's Centre for New Writing.

ANALYSIS

Martin Amis remarked in an interview that he writes about "low events in a high style," and this comment gives a clue to the paradox his work embodies. Although the content of his novels is frequently sordid and nihilistic—dictated by the depressing absence in his characters of traditional cultural values—Amis's rich, ornate, and continually inventive style lifts the novels to a level from which they give delight. "I would certainly sacrifice any psychological or realistic truth for a phrase, for a paragraph that has a spin on it," Amis has commented. The result is that Amis's novels, in spite of the fact that they are often uproariously hilarious, do not make easy or quick reading. Indeed, Kingsley Amis has remarked that he is unable to get through his son's novels because of their ornate style, which he attributes to the influence of Vladimir Nabokov.

THE RACHEL PAPERS

Amis's first novel, *The Rachel Papers*, set the tone for most of his subsequent work, although his later novels, beginning with *Money*, have exhibited greater depth and range, as the force of his satire—his immense comic hyperbole—has steadily increased. Furthermore, one senses a sharp moral awareness in *Money* and *London Fields*, although Amis chooses not to offer any solutions to the individual and social ills he identifies so acutely.

The Rachel Papers is a lively but fairly innocuous satire about the turbulent adolescence of Charles Highway, the first-person narrator. Highway is a rather obnoxious young man, a self-absorbed intellectual studying for his Oxford examinations and aspiring to become a literary critic. The action takes place the evening before Highway's twentieth birthday and is filled out by extensive flashbacks. A substantial portion of Highway's intellectual and physical energy is devoted to getting his girlfriend, Rachel, into bed and to writing in his diary detailed descriptions of everything that happens when he succeeds. Amis's hilarious and seemingly infinitely inventive wordplay is never more effectively displayed than when Highway is describing his sexual adventures.

DEAD BABIES

Dead Babies, which chronicles the weekend debaucheries of a group of nine privileged young people, is considerably less successful than Amis's first novel, and Amis has since declared his own dislike for it. The theme seems to be a warning about what happens when traditional values (the dead babies of the title) are discarded. For the most part, however, the characters are too repul-

Martin Amis. (Cheryl A. Koralik)

sive, and their indulgence in drugs, sex, alcohol, and violence too excessive, for the reader to care much about their fate.

SUCCESS

In *Success*, Amis chronicles a year in the lives of two contrasting characters. The handsome and conceited Gregory comes from an aristocratic family and appears to have all the worldly success anyone could want. He shares a flat in London with his foster brother Terry, who from every perspective is Gregory's opposite. Terry comes from the slums, he is physically unattractive and has low self-esteem, and he is stuck in a boring job that he is afraid of losing. The two characters take turns narrating the same events, which they naturally interpret very differently. As the year progresses, there is a change. Gregory is gradually forced to admit that his success is little more than an illusion. He has been fooling himself most of the time, and realization of his true ineptitude and childlike vulnerability causes him to go to pieces.

Meanwhile, Terry's grim persistence finally pays off: He makes money, loses his self-hatred, and finally acquires a respectable girlfriend. For all of his crudity and loutishness, he is more in tune with the tough spirit of the times, in which traditional values are no longer seen to be of any value and those who in theory represent them (like Gregory) have become effete.

Success is a clear indication of Amis's pessimism about life in London in the 1970's. Frequently employing extremely coarse language, the novel depicts some of the least attractive sides of human nature, and although this grimness is relieved (as in almost all of Amis's books) by some ribald humor, on the whole *Success* is a depressing and superficial book. Indeed, it had to wait nine years after publication in Great Britain before an American publisher would take it on.

OTHER PEOPLE

In Amis's fourth novel, *Other People: A Mystery Story*, he appears to have been trying to write something with more philosophical and existential depth than the satires that came before. This time the protagonist is a young woman who suffers from total amnesia. Released from the hospital, she wanders alone through alien city streets, viewing other people as a separate species and virtually unable to distinguish between animate and inanimate things. Taking the name Mary Lamb, she experiences life in complete innocence, having to relearn everything that being alive involves—not only who she is but also the purpose of everyday things such as shoes and money. She mixes with a range of people, from drunks and down-and-outs to upper-class degenerates, at the same time edging closer to a discovery of her real identity. It transpires that her real name is Amy Hide and that everyone thinks she had died after being brutally attacked by a man. Adding to the surreal atmosphere of the novel is a mysterious character called Prince, whom Mary/Amy keeps encountering. Prince seems to fulfill many roles: He is a policeman, perhaps also the man who attacked her, and a kind of tutelary spirit, an awakener, under whose guidance she discovers her own identity.

Other People was written according to what is known in Great Britain as the Martian school of poetry, a point of view in which no knowledge about human life and society is assumed. This technique is intended to allow the most mundane things to be examined in a fresh light. Although Amis achieves some success in this area, the novel is spoiled by excessive obscurity. The novelist has simply not left enough clues to his intention, and the reader is left to grasp at bits of a puzzle without being able to construct an intelligible whole. Realizing that few people had grasped his meaning, Amis explained in an interview what his intention had been the following:

> Why should we expect death to be any less complicated than life? Nothing about life suggests that death will just be a silence. Life is very witty and cruel and pointed, and let us suppose that death is like that too. The novel is the girl's death, and her death is a sort of witty parody of her life.

This may not be of much help to readers who are especially puzzled by the novel's concluding pages. Perhaps the most rewarding parts of the novel are Amis's depictions of the characters Mary encounters; their physical and mental deformities are captured with merciless wit.

MONEY

In *Money: A Suicide Note*, Amis continues to devote attention to what he undoubtedly depicts best: people who have been deformed, who have failed to reach their full human growth, by the shallow materialism of the age. The scope of *Money* is far wider and more impressive than anything Amis had produced before, however: Not only is it much longer, but it also fairly rocks with vulgar energy. Clearly, at this point in his career Amis has finished his writing apprenticeship and is moving into top gear.

The protagonist of *Money* is John Self, a wealthy, early-middle-aged maker of television commercials who is visiting New York to direct what he hopes will be his first big motion picture. The project runs into every difficulty imaginable, and after a series of humiliating experiences Self ends up back in London with nothing. The problem with Self is that although he is wealthy, he is uneducated and lacks all culture. He lives at a fast pace but spends his money and his time entirely on worthless things—junk food, alcohol, pornography, television. Satisfying pleasures continually elude him. Amis has commented on Self: "The world of culture is there as a sort of taunting presence in his life, and he wants it but he doesn't know how to get it, and all his responses are being blunted by living in the money world."

LONDON FIELDS

Amis's attack on the "money world" continues in *London Fields*, although Amis's finest novel is far more than that. It is at once a comic murder mystery and a wonderfully rich and varied evocation of the decline of civilization at the end of the millennium. Many of the comic scenes are worthy of Charles Dickens, and the plot is acted out against a cosmic, apocalyptic background, as the planet itself seems to be on the brink of disintegration.

Set in post-Thatcherite London in 1999, the plot centers on three main characters. The first is the antiheroine Nicola Six. Nicola has a gift for seeing the future, and she has a premonition that on her next birthday, which happens to be her thirty-fifth, she will be murdered by one of two men she meets at a London pub called the Black Cross. She sets out to avenge herself in advance by using her sexual power to entice both men and draw them to ruin. Nicola is a temptress of the first magnitude, and Amis employs comic hyperbole (as he does throughout the novel) to describe her: "Family men abandoned sick children to wait in the rain outside her flat. Semiliterate builders and bankers sent her sonnet sequences."

The second character, one of the possible murderers, is Keith Talent. Talent is probably Amis's finest creation, a larger-than-life character who might have stepped out of the pages of Dickens. He is a petty criminal, compulsive adulterer, wife beater, and darts fanatic. He makes a living by cheating people, whether it be by selling fake perfume, running an outrageously expensive taxi service, or doing botched household repair jobs. He earns more money than the prime minister but never has any, because he loses it each day at the betting shop. Keith is not totally bad but wishes that he were: He regards his redeeming qualities as his tragic flaw. Obsessed with darts and television (which for him is the real world), he is driven by his ambition to reach the televised finals of an interpub darts competition. The miracle of the novel is that Amis succeeds, as with John Self in *Money*, in making such a pathetic character almost likable.

The second possible murderer is Guy Clinch. Clinch is quite different from Keith Talent. He is a rich, upper-class innocent "who wanted for nothing and lacked everything." One of the things he lacks is a peaceful home life, after his wife, Hope, gives birth to Marmaduke, a ferocious infant who almost from the day he is born is capable of acts of quite stunning malice and violence. (The only nurses who can cope with him are those who have been fired from lunatic asylums.) Once more the comedy is irresistible.

The convoluted plot, with its surprise ending, is narrated by a terminally ill American writer named Samson Young, who is in London on a house swap with the famous writer Mark Asprey. That the absent Asprey's initials are the same as those of Martin Amis is perhaps no coincidence. Young is in a sense the author's proxy, since he is himself gathering the material and writing the story of *London Fields* for an American publisher. To make matters even more subtle, a character named Martin Amis also makes an appearance in the novel, just as there is a Martin Amis character in *Money*. Deconstructing his own fictions in this manner, Amis reminds the reader that in the manipulative world he depicts, he himself is the chief manipulator, but his own novel is only one fiction in a world of fictions.

The setting of *London Fields* is integral to the plot. The London of the near "future" (which 1999 was at the time of the novel's publication in 1989) possesses an oppressive, almost Blakean apocalyptic atmosphere. Not only has urban prosperity evaporated—parts of the city have sunk back into squalor—but the natural environment is in rapid decay also. Everyone is talking about the weather, but it is no longer simply small talk. Weather patterns are violently unstable; the sun seems to hang perpetually low in the sky, and rumors of impending cosmic catastrophe abound. The threat of a nuclear holocaust remains. When Nicola Six was a child, she invented two imaginary companions and called them Enola Gay and Little Boy. *Enola Gay* is the name of the airplane that dropped the first atom bomb, nicknamed Little Boy, on Hiroshima in 1945. Yet Samson Young, the narrator, calls nuclear weapons "dinosaurs" when compared to the environmental disasters that now threaten the earth. Eventually Young refers to the situation simply as "The Crisis," a term that also well describes the human world that Amis ruthlessly exposes, in which love, decency, and genuine feeling have been superseded by violence, greed, and lust. Microcosm and macrocosm are joined in a kind of horrible, frenzied dance of death. The world of *London Fields*, in which people and planet hurtle helplessly toward disaster, is where all Amis's fiction has been leading.

TIME'S ARROW

Time's Arrow is an unusual departure for Amis. Not only does this most contemporary of writers deal with the past, but he also does so with a less realistic and more overtly moralistic approach than in his other novels. A Nazi doctor's life is told in reverse order from his death in the United States to his birth in Germany, though his true identity is not apparent until more than halfway through the narrative. While many of Amis's narrators may not be completely reliable, the narrator of *Time's Arrow* is relatively innocent. The physician's reverse life is told by his alter ego, who stands outside the action until finally merging with the protagonist near the end.

Time's Arrow also deals with the question of identity in the twentieth century, as Tod Friendly progresses from an elderly, rather anonymous man into a Massachusetts physician; into another physician, this time in New York City, named John Young; into an exile in Portugal named Hamilton de Souza; into his true identity as Odilo Unverdorben, a concentration camp doctor and protégé of the ominous Auschwitz monster he calls Uncle Pepi. In telling Friendly's increasingly complicated tale, Amis tries to encompass much of the history of the twentieth century, with particular attention to the Vietnam War era and the Cold War.

By telling the story backward, Amis also explores such themes as the banality of human communication, exemplified by conversations appearing with the sentences in reverse order—answers coming before questions. Amis gets considerable comic mileage out of the horrifying images of such acts as eating and excreting depicted backward. In this ironic, perverse universe, suffering brings about joy. The narrator, one of several Amis doppelgängers, is alternately irritated and disgusted by Friendly's behavior, particularly his crude treatment of his longtime American lover, Irene. The narrator also professes his affection for and admiration of Jews before finally admitting that he and Unverdorben are one, a highly ironic means of accepting responsibility for one's actions.

Many critics have dismissed *Time's Arrow* as a narrative stunt. In an afterword, Amis acknowledges that other writers have also employed reverse narratives,

mentioning the famous account of a bomb traveling backward to its origins underground in Kurt Vonnegut's *Slaughterhouse-Five: Or, The Children's Crusade, a Duty-Dance with Death* (1969) as a particular influence. *Time's Arrow* is most notable for Amis's less subtle presentation of his moral concerns, which have often been compared to those of Saul Bellow.

THE INFORMATION

With *The Information*, Amis returns to more typical themes. Two writers, best friends, are contrasted by their success, fame, and sex lives. Richard Tull, author of two little-read novels, edits *The Little Magazine*, a minor literary journal, serves as director of a vanity press, and writes reviews of biographies of minor writers. Gwyn Barry, on the other hand, has published a best seller and is a major media figure. Married, with twin sons, Richard lusts after Lady Demeter, Gwyn's glamorous wife. Richard is not jealous of Gwyn's success so much as resentful that Gwyn's book is so universally beloved when it is completely without literary merit, an assessment with which both their wives agree. All of Richard's plans for revenge backfire, including hiring Steve Cousins, a mysterious criminal known as Scozzy, to assault Gwyn.

In addition to addressing his usual topics—sex, violence, greed, and chaos—Amis presents a satirical view of literary infighting and pretensions. Richard creates primarily because of his need for love and attention. He perceives the world as an artist would, but he is unable to transform his vision into accessible literature: When editors read his latest effort, they become ill. Only the psychotic Scozzy seems to understand what he is trying to say. Richard cannot give up writing, however, because then he would be left with nothing but the tedium of everyday life. Gwyn is equally ridiculous. Obsessed by his fame, he reads newspaper and magazine articles about all subjects in hopes of seeing his name. The two writers are like a comic pair of mismatched twins.

The Information is also a typical Amis work in that it is highly self-conscious. The narrator who explains the warped workings of Scozzy's mind makes occasional appearances, first as "I," then as "M. A.," and finally as "Mart," yet another of Amis's cameo roles in his fiction. The narrator seems, as when he tries to explain that he cannot control Scozzy, to call attention to the artifice of the novel and to force the reader, as a willing participant in this satire, to share responsibility for the world's chaos.

NIGHT TRAIN

For his next novel, *Night Train*, Amis appropriates the form of the hard-boiled detective novel, although his aim seems more that of undermining the genre than of paying tribute to it. Detective Mike Hoolihan, the policewoman narrator, speaks with an almost unremittingly harsh voice that is as masculine as her first name. Hoolihan once suffered from alcoholism to the point of nearly dying, and much of her hardness, and of her unwillingness to show emotional reaction, arises from her fight against her old self. Perhaps because of this hardness, within the department she is called out for no-win cases, such as the one she now accepts: to investigate the suicide of the chief's daughter. The chief is a father figure to Hoolihan, since he saw her through her alcoholic crisis, and the now-dead daughter had sat at Hoolihan's side. The case is, as she knows from the beginning, the worst of her career.

Amis unfolds his subversion of the detective novel gradually. Hoolihan studies the facts of the suicide, investigating it as possible murder, then closes the case in the negative. New leads force her to reconsider, however, with each new lead pointing a new direction. The dead woman, a brilliant astronomer, made a massive mistake at her job just before her death—perhaps intentionally. A traveling businessman calls, saying he has a date with the deceased, on the sole date after her suicide marked in the dead woman's date book. She had given the man not her own phone number, however, but the detective's.

By the end of her investigations, Hoolihan sees all the clues as red herrings—intentional ones, and directed at herself. Rather than being the one who finds meaning within disparate, seemingly unrelated facts, the detective is instead confronted with a void bereft of meaning. Hoolihan takes this to heart in a way that makes her conclusion, as detective, seem an act of self-discovery.

YELLOW DOG

A complex exploration of the sleazy world of tabloid journalism and pornographic filmmaking, *Yellow Dog* takes place in a world that is not quite like the reader's own. In perhaps the most pronounced difference, British royal power is invested in a King Henry IX, to be passed along to his daughter, Victoria. One of the novel's several narrative strands follows Henry, who faces a dilemma. He has been sent a film that shows Victoria in her bath. The footage seems real. The king, who lives a life constrained by minor social occasions and royal duties, is not a person of action. How to tell Victoria? How to deal with the press and the greater world?

In the main narrative strand, writer and actor Xan Meo is assaulted and does not know why. He is beaten to the point of brain damage, and his recovery seems doubtful at times. When he at last emerges from the hospital, he descends into callous sexual behavior with his wife and develops a fixation on his own daughter. A third strand follows Clint Smoker, journalist with *Morning Lark*, a pornographic tabloid sparingly sprinkled with actual news. His troubles, as he sees them, are sexual in nature, and to his relief he receives a series of e-mails that seem finally to match him with a perfect mate. Hanging over all is the apocalyptic threat of a near-Earth comet, the erratic course of which might deliver it into Earth's atmosphere.

As the various narrative strands converge, reality deals the characters different hands. The central character Meo emerges, as do other Amis characters, with a triumph that partakes of emptiness: As he recovers from his head injury, Meo learns that he was attacked because of a literary allusion he made—one that a criminal took, wrongly, as factual revelation about him.

HOUSE OF MEETINGS

The Amis character driven by a need for survival, and perhaps equally by an obsession with recovering the past, takes new form in *House of Meetings*, a novel whose main setting is in the Russian gulag of the years after World War II. The narrator describes himself as a foul-mouthed old man, now in his eighties. He is aboard a Russian tourist ship heading for Norlag in Siberia, where he was once imprisoned. As narrator, writing an account of his past, he remains a nameless cipher, embodying the depersonalized anonymity of the prisoner.

He was a soldier, one whose violent acts included the rape of East German women during the war. In Norlag, he accepts the power hierarchies within the prison camp and acts out the intrinsic violence of those hierarchies, to the point of committing murder. The story of his imprisonment, however, begins when his half brother, Lev, arrives in the same camp. Lev has a misshapen, troglodyte-like appearance, but he is not violent, and he avoids the gamesmanship required to obtain creature comforts. He becomes the butt of others' aggression, against which his more violent-minded brother gives protection.

In their younger years, the narrator fell deeply in love with a woman named Zoya. The surprise he experiences in seeing Lev arrive in Norlag turns to dismay when he learns the ugly Lev has married the beautiful Zoya. Zoya has remained in the narrator's mind, as a symbol of the life behind him and, he hopes, the life ahead. Even with Lev as Zoya's husband, that goal remains before him, up to the moment he finds an opportunity to have sex with her, essentially to rape her. He then experiences a revelation of the utter emptiness of the desire that has ruled his life.

Amis captures much of the narrator's fate in the House of Meetings of the title. It is a small building in the camp that is reserved for those prisoners who are allowed visits from their spouses. It is the place for the longed-for moment of sexual love, for the affirmation of carnal being. Because of the ill-fed and weakened state of the prisoners, however, most believe not a single act of sex takes place within it. Lev, however, says otherwise, and the narrator's fixations lead him to return now, as an aged tourist. He finds the building a ruin.

Although some feminist critics have expressed reservations about Amis's work (and it is true that most of his male characters treat their women with contempt), Amis is a formidable and critically acclaimed writer, certainly one of the most accomplished of the generation of English writers who came of age in the 1970's. Few others could have attempted a work on the scale of *London Fields*, for example. Together with Salman Rushdie, Julian Barnes, and Peter Ackroyd—in their different ways—Amis has broken through the neat, middle-class boundaries of much contemporary English fiction and reached out toward a fiction that is more challenging and comprehensive in its scope.

Bryan Aubrey; Michael Adams
Updated by Mark Rich

OTHER MAJOR WORKS

SHORT FICTION: *Einstein's Monsters*, 1987; *Heavy Water, and Other Stories*, 1998.

NONFICTION: *Invasion of the Space Invaders*, 1982; *The Moronic Inferno and Other Visits to America*, 1986; *Visiting Mrs. Nabokov, and Other Excursions*, 1993; *Experience*, 2000; *The War Against Cliché: Essays and Reviews, 1971-2000*, 2001; *Koba the Dread: Laughter and the Twenty Million*, 2002; *The Second Plane: September 11, Terror, and Boredom*, 2008.

MISCELLANEOUS: *Vintage Amis*, 2004.

BIBLIOGRAPHY

Alexander, Victoria N. "Martin Amis: Between the Influences of Bellow and Nabokov." *Antioch Review* 52, no. 4 (1994): 580-590. Investigates the links between Amis and two of the authors whom he most reveres, Saul Bellow and Vladimir Nabokov.

Diedrick, James. *Understanding Martin Amis*. 2d ed. Columbia: University of South Carolina Press, 2004. Expansion of the first book-length study of Amis's fiction and career looks at all aspects of this multifaceted writer, including his criticism. Discusses the novels through *Yellow Dog*.

Edmondson, Elie H. "Martin Amis Writes Postmodern Man." *Critique* 42 (Winter, 2001): 145-154. Explicates the techniques that Amis uses to revise reader expectations of the traditional novel. Focuses particularly on the novel *Money*.

Finney, Brian. *Martin Amis*. New York: Routledge, 2008. Provides an introduction to Amis's novels, with discussion of critical approaches to the work. Includes biographical information.

_____. "Narrative and Narrated Homicides in Martin Amis's *Other People* and *London Fields*." *Critique* 37 (Fall, 1995): 3-15. Argues that in these two novels, by using manipulative, self-conscious narrators who victimize the other characters, Amis forces his readers to recognize how the characters are both immersed in and outside the action.

Keulks, Gavin. *Father and Son: Kingsley Amis, Martin Amis, and the British Novel Since 1950*. Madison: University of Wisconsin Press, 2003. Ambitious chronicle of a literary dynasty places both father and son within the contexts of their times.

Moyle, David. "Beyond the Black Hole: The Emergence of Science Fiction Themes in the Recent Work of Martin Amis." *Extrapolation* 36 (Winter, 1995): 305-

315. Shows how Amis adapts traditional science-fiction themes, such as time travel, concern about the end of the world, and a Dr. Frankenstein-like lack of regard for conventional morality, in *Time's Arrow* and *London Fields*.

Stout, Mira. "Martin Amis: Down London's Mean Streets." *The New York Times Magazine*, February 4, 1990. Lively feature article in which Amis, prodded by Stout, discusses a range of topics, including *London Fields*, his interest in the environment, his early

life and career, his relationship with his father, the state of the novel as a form, the Thatcher government, middle age, and his daily work routine.

Tredell, Nicolas, ed. *The Fiction of Martin Amis: A Reader's Guide to Essential Criticism*. New York: Palgrave Macmillan, 2002. Collection of reviews, critical essays, and other materials presents discussion of a wide range of topics concerning Amis's fiction, including the author's use of language and his representation of sexuality.

RUDOLFO ANAYA

Born: Pastura, New Mexico; October 30, 1937
Also known as: Rudolfo Alfonso Anaya

PRINCIPAL LONG FICTION

Bless Me, Ultima, 1972
Heart of Aztlán, 1976
Tortuga, 1979
The Legend of La Llorona, 1984
Lord of the Dawn: The Legend of Quetzalcóatl, 1987
Alburquerque, 1992
Zia Summer, 1995
Jalamanta: A Message from the Desert, 1996
Rio Grande Fall, 1996
Shaman Winter, 1999
Jemez Spring, 2005

OTHER LITERARY FORMS

Rudolfo Anaya has written short stories, children's literature, essays, plays, allegories, screenplays, and poetry, including a mock-heroic epic poem in barrio street slang. His early short stories are collected in *The Silence of the Llano* (1982). His children's stories include *The Farolitos of Christmas: A New Mexico Christmas Story* (1987) and *The Santero's Miracle: A Bilingual Story* (2004). Anaya's essay output largely results from his many lectures. *A Chicano in China* (1986) recounts a visit to China in 1984. *The Anaya Reader* (1995) con-

tains representative works, including his play *Who Killed Don José?* (pr. 1987).

ACHIEVEMENTS

The "godfather" of Chicano literature and the "foremost" Chicano novelist of the twentieth century, Rudolfo Anaya gained recognition in his mythopoetic field as the late 1960's Chicano movement gained strength. He battled publisher prejudices against bilingual works, turning to small Chicano presses such as Quinto Sol before going mainstream with Warner Press in 1993. His first novel, *Bless Me, Ultima*, won the Premio Quinto Sol literary award in 1972, putting Anaya at the center of Chicano issues. Publication of *Heart of Aztlán* made him a force in Chicano letters and the term "Aztlán" (the legendary Aztec homeland and symbol of Chicano unity) important in literature. Anaya's Sonny Baca detective stories placed him in the Magical Realism movement, and the successes of mentored students (including Denise Chavez) mark his far-reaching community influence.

Anaya has received numerous awards for achievements in Chicano literature, including El Fuego Nuevo Award (1995), De Colores Hispanic Literature Award (2000), the National Medal of Arts in Literature (2001), the Wallace Stegner Award (2001), and the Champions of Change Award (2002). *Alburquerque* won the International Association of Poets, Playwrights, Editors, Essayists, and Novelists (PEN Club) Center West Award for fiction (1992). The 1995 illustrated edition of *The Farolitos of Christmas*, a warm tale of family love, received the Southwest Texas State University Tomás Rivera Mexican-American Children's Book Award, and Anaya received the award again in 2000 for *Elegy on the Death of César Chávez* (2000), a work in verse celebrating that Chicano national hero. At least six universities have awarded Anaya honorary doctorates. While Anaya speaks to the long history of the Mexican American community in the southwestern United States, he also provides others a Chicano worldview in a wide variety of literary forms, converging the mestizo identity in the varied cultures that infuse the New Mexican community. He revives an American vision of assimilation that encompasses the best of mixed heritages.

BIOGRAPHY

Rudolfo Alfonso Anaya was born in Pastura, New Mexico, on October 30, 1937, one of seven children, the only male among his siblings to attend school (his three brothers fought in World War II). His mother (Rafaelita Mares), a devout Catholic, came from a farming community; his father (Martín Anaya) grew up among nomadic herders on the eastern plains and worked as a cowboy. The family moved to Santa Rosa, New Mexico, while Rudolfo was still a child, then, in 1952, to the tough Albuquerque barrios, where he attended high school. The young Anaya, who spoke only Spanish before he entered school, struggled with English immersion. Spanish oral storytelling enlivened his childhood as the barrio life of music, street gangs, racism, and closed community did his adolescence. As a high school sophomore, Anaya broke two vertebrae diving in an irrigation ditch, necessitating a long, painful convalescence. These experiences were crucial to his first three novels: his early countryside years inspiring *Bless Me, Ultima*, his Albuquerque experiences influencing *Heart of Aztlán*, and his painful injury leading to *Tortuga*.

After studying accounting at Browning Business School (1956-1958), Anaya transferred to the University of New Mexico at Albuquerque, where he earned a bachelor's degree in English in 1963. There he reflected on his cultural identity: a Latino for whom English remained a second language thrust into a culturally diverse

Rudolfo Anaya. (Michael Mouchette)

community that lacked literature about Mexican American life and that assumed Mexican Americans make better laborers than scholars.

Following college, Anaya taught for three years at a small-town school while he wrote poetry and novels exploring his questions about existence, belief, and identity; he burned all these early manuscripts, however. His desire to mentor young people led him to teach for seven years in the Albuquerque public schools and to serve as a school guidance counselor for three more years. During this time, he married Patricia Lawless (1966), who proved an excellent, supportive editor. Anaya returned to the University of New Mexico to earn master's degrees in literature (1968) and counseling (1972).

While teaching, Anaya had struggled to write *Bless Me, Ultima*, until a creative vision of an elderly woman in black (a traditional Mexican figure) inspired Ultima, his strongest character, the spiritual mentor for both protagonist and novelist. However, finding a publisher for a bilingual book took seven years. Anaya finally found acceptance at Quinto Sol Publications, a small Chicano press in Berkeley, California. An award for the best Chicano novel published in 1972 brought him an English professorship at the University of New Mexico, where he taught for fourteen years, received emeritus status in 1993, and led workshops in creative writing for years thereafter.

In the early 1990's, Anaya began a quartet of linked books set in New Mexico combining world mythologies, the motifs of dream visions and collective memory, the realism of murder mysteries, the allegory of folklore tales, and the fantasy of Magical Realism. The results— *Alburquerque*, *Zia Summer*, *Rio Grande Fall*, *Shaman Winter*, and *Jemez Spring*—reestablished Anaya's reputation as the foremost Chicano writer of his generation. Anaya is known internationally as a storyteller and writer, a mentor to all aspiring to his craft. Since his retirement, he continues to reside in Albuquerque, but he also travels widely throughout Central and South America. Throughout his life, Anaya has tirelessly promoted Chicano literature—editing anthologies, translating works into English, lecturing, and writing reviews and essays, both academic and nonacademic. He writes about the personal (family, community, ties to the land, and personal struggle) but employs world myth to attain the universal.

ANALYSIS

A significant figure in Chicano literature, Rudolfo Anaya speaks for the ethnically and culturally mixed voices of New Mexico, the American Southwest, and the United States in general, to unite and inspire. Anaya's works use Magical Realism and archetypal symbols to connect fragmented contemporary life with a unified heroic past. His principal characters struggle with the duality of Chicano identity—an Aztec-Spanish past, an English-speaking present. Anaya celebrates Mexican American and Native American heritage throughout his canon, connecting the Aztec sun god with Trojan gold and Greek myth. Anaya seeks answers to life's mysteries in his personal cultural background and in the mythos of ethnically mixed peoples. In interviews he has called ancestral values the "substratum" of his oeuvre. His fiction promotes education, including mentoring by wise elders, to bridge differences and promote understanding.

His work testifies to the values of family, harmony, and balance in reconciling disparate life choices.

BLESS ME, ULTIMA

Bless Me, Ultima, the first novel in a loose trilogy and arguably Anaya's most famous, defines the modern Mexican American experience in a psychological and magical maturation story. It includes biographical parallels that provided Anaya detailed realities to strengthen his fiction. Set in the 1940's and 1950's, the novel features first-person narrator Antonio Marez, who must master competing realities interwoven with symbolic characters and places to mature. Ultima, a *curandera* (herbal healer), evokes a timeless pre-Columbian world, while a golden carp swims supernatural river waters to offer a redemptive future.

Like Anaya, Antonio is born in Pastura, on the eastern New Mexican plain. Later his family moves to a village across the river from Guadalupe, where Antonio spends his childhood. His father, a roving cattleman, and his mother, from a settled farming family, epitomize the contradictions Antonio must resolve within himself. His father wants him to become a horseman like his ancestors. His mother wants him to become a priest to a farming community, an honored tradition. The parents' wishes are symptomatic of a deeper spiritual challenge facing Antonio, involving his Catholic beliefs and the magical world of the pre-Columbian past. Ultima, a creature of both worlds, guides Antonio's understanding of these challenges. She supervises his birth; she moves in with the family when Antonio is seven years old and becomes his spiritual mentor. On several occasions, Antonio witnesses her power in life-and-death battles, including when Ultima saves Antonio's uncle from witches' curses. However, she brings on herself the wrath of the witches' father, Tenorio Tremelina.

Antonio's adventure takes him beyond the divided world of farmer and horseman, beyond Catholic ritual, with its depictions of good and evil. With Ultima's help, he channels these opposites into a new cosmic vision of nature represented by the river, which flows through two worlds, and the golden carp, which points to a new spiritual covenant. The novel ends with Tenorio killing Ultima's owl, and thus Ultima herself, as the owl carries her spiritual presence. Her work is complete, however: Antonio can now choose his own destiny.

HEART OF AZTLÁN

Also highly biographical, *Heart of Aztlán*, second in the trilogy and another psychological and magical quest for Chicano empowerment, expresses solidarity with Chicano laborers. In the novel, the Chávez family leaves the Guadalupe countryside for a better life in Albuquerque, but the family members discover that their destinies lie in a lost past. They move to Barelas, a real barrio on the west side of the city where other immigrants reside, as did Anaya. The Chávezes soon learn their lives are not their own. Clemente Chávez and his son Jason illustrate the pitfalls of barrio life: for Jason, gangs, drugs, and devastating gossip; for Clemente, the forces of industry and politics. Jason encounters wide class divisions, gang rivalry, and dangerous marijuana dealers; he saves his younger brother from the dealers but brings upon himself the vengeance of a violent former reformatory inmate, Sapo, for slights and grievances. Clemente learns that industrial interests (particularly Santa Fe Railroad interests), a compromised union, and corrupt politicians control the barrio. Mannie García, the owner of *el super* (a supermarket), controls the populace and delivers the community vote. Individual needs (providing for families) crush all attempts of the barrio inhabitants to organize. Clemente's disobedient daughters reject his insistence on traditional respect and his control. Clemente loses his railroad yard job during a futile strike, becomes an alcoholic, and attempts suicide.

With the mystical help of Crespín, a blind musician representing eternal wisdom, Clemente solves the riddle of a magical stone, journeys to a mountain lake, and enters the heart of Aztlán (the source of Chicano empowerment, held by *la India*, a dark sorceress), where he undergoes a magical rebirth. Community members initially debate whether he has obtained magical knowledge or has gone insane. Clemente turns first to the Catholic Church and then to *el super*, the religious and political powers of barrio life, but neither has the compassion or the motivation to unify the Chicano population. When he tries to inspire striking workers to seek inner strength, they purposefully misinterpret his words and violently attack the railroad. Clemente's power to incite violence leads the dual forces of business and Church to try to pay him to leave town; he refuses.

Jason is falsely accused of fathering a bastard child and lying during confession—lies to turn the community against the Chávezes. Sapo forces Jason's defenseless girlfriend, Cristina, to attend a dance with him, then forces Jason's brother, Benjie, up the railroad water tower. Shot in the hand, Benjie falls; he is completely paralyzed as a result of his injuries. A grief-stricken Clemente attacks the water tower with a hammer but cannot bring down the structure (a symbol of industrial might) alone. When a crowd gathers outside the hospital where his son is being treated, Clemente is finally ready to lead his community, not in violent protest but in accessing their inner pride and unifying their struggle for social and economic justice.

TORTUGA

The trilogy that concludes with *Tortuga*, winner of the Before Columbus American Book Award (1980), takes the protagonists into the past and into the physical and mythical landscapes of the southwestern present, revealing their relationship to the social and political power structure of mainstream America. *Tortuga* records a year-long journey to self-realization and supernatural awareness. Benjie Chávez, paralyzed after his fall in *Heart of Aztlán* and transported south to the Crippled Children and Orphans Hospital for rehabilitation, undergoes a symbolic rebirth to replace Crespín, a blind guitarist and the keeper of Chicano wisdom, upon Crespín's death. Benjie's entry into the labyrinthine hospital symbolizes his entry into a world of supernatural transformation.

The hospital sits at the foot of Tortuga Mountain, from which flow mineral springs with healing waters. Fitted with an immobilizing body cast, Benjie is nicknamed Tortuga (turtle). A physically and psychologically painful ordeal follows, exposing Tortuga to suffering, deformed children. Nothing prepares him for the "vegetable" ward of immobile children, unable to breathe without iron lungs. There, Salomón, a vegetable with supernatural insight into the human condition, enters Tortuga's psyche and guides him toward spiritual renewal. Like baby sea turtles that must dash to the ocean after hatching on the beach, most of which are devoured by other creatures, Tortuga must endure danger to arrive at his true destiny, "the path of the sun." When the bully Danny pushes him into the swimming pool, Tortuga almost drowns, surviving only because others rush to his aid. Symbolically, this is Tortuga's safe arrival to and from the sea. The vegetables are not so lucky, for Danny turns off the power to their ward. Without the iron lungs, they all die. The novel's end and Tortuga's rehabilitation confirm that Crespín, the magical helper of Tortuga's neighborhood, has died. Benjie inherits Crespín's blue guitar, a symbol of universal knowledge.

THE LEGEND OF LA LLORONA

The Legend of La Llorona merges the traditional stories of Doña Marina, "La Malinche," the Aztec interpreter and lover of Spanish conquistador Hernán Cortéz, with the Mexican folkloric figure of *la llorona* (the weeping woman), one seduced, abandoned, and driven by grief and revenge to kill her babies before forever mourning their loss. The first evokes scorn for a traitor; the second, sympathy for a woman scorned by a rake. Thereby, Anaya redeems a historical figure, redefining her as a double victim of Aztec cruelty and male indifference.

The birth of Marina's brother ends her value for the family. Sold into slavery, then passed on to curry European favor at Tabasco, she quickly masters Spanish and translates for the Spaniards taking Tenochtitlán in 1521. Cortez's mistress, she bears his mestizo son in 1522, but he abandons her in favor of his wife, and their son dies during a failed insurgency—a matter of indifference to the Spaniard. Doña Marina, like her people, is dismissed, and any opportunity for assimilating two peoples is lost. Anaya asserts that, like La Llorona of legend, this proud woman was seduced and abandoned by a wealthy, dashing outsider. La Malinche as La Llorona confirms the brutalizing effects of the Spanish conquistadores, the complexity produced by accommodation and assimilation, and the ambiguity of human behavior.

ALBURQUERQUE

Originally, *Alburquerque* was intended to initiate an Alburquerque quartet, but Anaya focused on private detective Sonny Baca in later books and dropped *Alburquerque* from the set. The novel explores the ethnically mixed roots of Albuquerque, New Mexico, the lost "r" in the name of which resulted from Anglo mispronunciation. As developers and politicians unscrupulously promote city expansion, the community seeks to retain its culturally diverse heart. Abrán Gonzalez, a young man proud of his barrio upbringing by adoptive

Mexican American parents but disturbed by his lighter skin, is a former Golden Gloves boxing champion turned college student. At age twenty-one, he learns that his birth mother was a respected Anglo artist, knowledge that calls into question his Chicano identity. Lucinda Córdova, the nurse who was present at his mother's death, helps Abrán search for his real father, becomes his fiancé, and shares his dreams of starting a health clinic.

Abrán's quest provides the book's underlying structure, as he is drawn into city politics, first by wealthy mayoral candidate Frank Dominic, who uses Abrán's boxing talent to attract voters; then by the seductive present mayor, Marisa Martínez, a friend of his dead mother and briefly his lover; and later by Abrán's friend Jose Calabasa, a Santo Domingo Indian and veteran of the Vietnam War. Jose, who opposes the city developers' plans, learns that Ben Chávez, a University of New Mexico creative-writing instructor, is Abrán's father. Jose, Ben, and Lucinda try to use this information to persuade Abrán to renege on a boxing match he is losing badly, since he no longer needs Dominic's help finding his father, but the knowledge that he is a Chicano with respected parents inspires Abrán to make a comeback in the ring, knock out his opponent, and become the city hero. City and city defender merge, and the knockout blow ends the developers' attempted takeover and Dominic's political aspirations. Abrán and Lucinda return to the simplicity of mountain village life, while Ben uses his art to provide the community with cultural symbols.

Alburquerque satirizes self-aggrandizing politicians who value power over community welfare, use others ruthlessly, and deny their cultural heritage. It mocks Anglo bigots like Walter Johnson, who forces his supposed daughter Cynthia to put her half-Mexican child up for adoption. Its mix of magic and realism (Pueblo trickster Coyote and the Mexican folkloric figure La Llorona alongside real characters) reflects the Indian, Mexican, Spanish, and Anglo blend that makes the city of Albuquerque a microcosmic image of the American Southwest.

ZIA SUMMER

Zia Summer, the first novel in the Sonny Baca seasonal series and the second in the originally planned Alburquerque quartet, sets the pattern for Anaya's later books. In the series, a modern investigator examines his personal and cultural history in dream and family myth to unravel the secrets of his present and to combat an evil that has haunted his mixed genetic line for five centuries. The series blends crime fiction with terrorist threats and the Magical Realism inherent in Latin American and Native American literatures, merging the ordinary and supernatural, the logical and the extrasensory. The ramifications of the ritual murder of Baca's cousin, Gloria Dominic (body drained of blood, stomach carved with a Zia sun sign) and of an ecoterrorist scheme to blow up a truck transporting highly radioactive nuclear waste extend into the community's ancestral memories and mixed mythological inheritance. Baca feels Gloria's spirit seeking revenge, and Gloria's husband, who is running for mayor of Albuquerque, encourages him to search throughout the moneyed communities of the New Mexico South Valley (artists, environmentalists, land developers, even self-styled witches).

Baca, a wily survivor associated with the southwestern trickster/creator Coyote, counters Raven, a shapeshifting shaman who promoting mayhem, who extends his reach through cult followers and black magic. Readers have the unsettling experience of learning about the management of nuclear wastes in the context of two different cultures and different creation stories, as Raven and Baca battle each other in the Sandia Mountains north of Albuquerque. This personal conflict becomes a universal one of dark versus light, evil versus good. An ancient Aztec mystical medallion brings chaos but also deflects a bullet that would have ended Baca's life.

RIO GRANDE FALL

Rio Grande Fall, second in the Sonny Baca seasonal series, once again works Mexican and Indian folklore and myth into a detective story that bursts the seams of the genre, as logic and detection slide into dream country. Baca again tackles Raven, who supposedly died in a flash flood but has returned, more powerful than ever. A healing ritual to cleanse the dark images that cloud Baca's mind produces a vision of a falling woman. Indeed, Veronica Worthy, Raven's wife, a key witness against a murderer, falls from a hot-air balloon during the Albuquerque International Balloon Fiesta. Hired witnesses claim Veronica was alone in the balloon, but others report seeing someone push her over.

Baca believes Raven pushed his wife to her death, and the directors of the fiesta hire Baca to investigate. Red herrings lead Baca to local police, federal agents, and even fiesta manager Madge Swensen. When two more balloonists die, Baca ties the balloons to drug smuggling, the Medellín drug cartel, and the U.S. Central Intelligence Agency. When Raven kidnaps Baca's girlfriend, Rita, the ensuing battle pits coyote wiliness against Raven duplicity. Protected by a spiritually powerful Zia medallion, Baca challenges Raven to a psychological and spiritual duel across the landscape; ritual tools and ancient mythologies turn a detective story into a hybrid tall tale in which identifying particular hit men responsible for drug killings takes second place.

SHAMAN WINTER

Shaman Winter, third in the Sonny Baca series, draws its title from the mythology of seasons, with winter associated with death—in this case, a shaman-induced nuclear winter involving the destruction of Baca's past to end his present and future. Raven's operatives have infiltrated a Los Alamos nuclear project to steal plutonium to turn the fire and light that the Raven of Native American mythology gave humankind into a destructive force (a massive bomb). Meanwhile, white supremacists under orders from Raven kidnap the mayor's teenage daughter. A wheelchair-bound Sonny Baca, badly injured at the end of *Rio Grande Fall*, no longer scoffs at dreams as another reality, and he conducts his investigation mainly in dreams inhabited by mythic figures reenacting the histories of ancient native peoples (Aztec, Anasazi, Toltec, Pueblo), including the arrival of the Spanish conquistadores in the sixteenth century, the coming of European settlers, and the relocation of indigenous peoples to reservations. The dreams are all located in sacred places, and Anaya's discussion of them reflects a New Age vision of a collective memory affecting the present.

In the real world, Baca depends on traditional clues to find four kidnapped girls (including the mayor's daughter), all of whom represent Baca's own female ancestors. However, Don Eliseo, a Pueblo Indian elder and Baca's kindly neighbor, guides Baca through the spirit world, teaching him that attaining his goals requires reconnecting with his unique ancestry (Indian, Spaniard, Anglo) and with the Sangre de Cristo Mountains (historically his spiritual center), and then fighting his battles in the dreamworld. As Baca experiences each period in the racial and cultural heritage of modern-day New Mexico, he meets his own genetic predecessors—all beleaguered by a dark *brujo*. This witch figure, Raven, haunts Baca's dreams, destroying his female ancestors to eliminate his history (the Pueblo Indian genetic line is matrilineal). Baca evolves into a shaman himself, representative of the sun, bringing light to dispel the darkness and winter of Raven's world of death and destruction.

In this novel, Anaya transcends the detective genre that dominated the earlier series books to create southwestern landscapes (mental and historical) and mystical battles between allegorical forces. The concept of destroying an individual's history by changing that person's dreams approaches the level of science fiction.

JEMEZ SPRING

Jemez Spring, another Baca story, begins with the governor of New Mexico drowned in a hot tub at Jemez Springs, where Baca has a private residence that he visits to escape urban life. Driving there, Baca meets Naomi, an Aztec snake-woman prototype, who insinuates herself into his investigation. The murder involves a statewide conspiracy including police officers. When Raven volunteers to disarm a dirty bomb set to detonate within a few hours near the Los Alamos National Laboratories, Baca knows that Raven, not terrorists, has an ulterior motive connected to who controls water. Anaya pits aggressive Anglo perspectives against bucolic Indo-Hispanic perspectives and time-driven projects against timeless pastoral visions.

Don Eliseo, now a guiding spirit, steers Baca aright, warning that bullets cannot stop Raven, whose power is darkly spiritual, and advising Baca to use rather than be overpowered by the dreamworld. He gives Baca a dream catcher, a spiderweb-like tool used by Native American shamans for catching good dreams and letting bad dreams pass through. Baca's friends, his beloved Rita, and even his feisty, one-eyed dachshund, Chica, are at risk. Images of one-eyed people and animals fill Baca's dreamscape as he enters Raven's inner circle and faces his demons, only to be tricked as aroma therapist Sybil Sosostris helps Raven snatch the protective Zia stone. Raven's misdirection includes psychic projections of twin daughters Rita had miscarried. Baca's obsession with these lost dead nearly costs him his life. When Ra-

ven snatches Chica, Baca meets him at the river in equal contest. Rescue from an unexpected quarter leaves the plot open for a return of Raven, for this is an ongoing match between spiritual forces. For the moment, however, Baca—Chica and Zia stone in hand—goes home to Rita.

Ultimately, by associating Chicano life with heroic motifs from Homer's *Odyssey* (c. 725 B.C.E.; English translation, 1614), mystic symbols from the Pueblo Indians, and the pastoral dream of Aztlán, Anaya ties Mexican Americans to a mythic past to ennoble their present.

David Conde
Updated by Gina Macdonald with Elizabeth Sanders

OTHER MAJOR WORKS

SHORT FICTION: *The Silence of the Llano*, 1982; *Serafina's Stories*, 2004; *The Man Who Could Fly, and Other Stories*, 2006.

PLAYS: *The Season of La Llorona*, pr. 1979; *Who Killed Don José?*, pr. 1987; *Billy the Kid*, pb. 1995.

POETRY: *The Adventures of Juan Chicaspatas*, 1985 (epic poem); *Elegy on the Death of César Chávez*, 2000 (juvenile).

SCREENPLAY: *Bilingualism: Promise for Tomorrow*, 1976.

NONFICTION: *A Chicano in China*, 1986; *Conversations with Rudolfo Anaya*, 1998.

CHILDREN'S LITERATURE: *The Farolitos of Christmas: A New Mexico Christmas Story*, 1987 (illustrated edition 1995); *Maya's Children: The Story of La Llorona*, 1997; *Farolitos for Abuelo*, 1998; *My Land Sings: Stories from the Rio Grande*, 1999; *Roadrunner's Dance*, 2000; *The Santero's Miracle: A Bilingual Story*, 2004 (illustrated by Amy Cordova, Spanish translation by Enrique Lamadrid); *The First Tortilla: A Bilingual Story*, 2007 (illustrated by Cordova, Spanish translation by Lamadrid).

EDITED TEXTS: *Voices from the Rio Grande*, 1976; *Cuentos Chicanos: A Short Story Anthology*, 1980 (with Antonio Márquez); *A Ceremony of Brotherhood, 1680-1980*, 1981 (with Simon Ortiz); *Voces: An Anthology of Nuevo Mexicano Writers*, 1987; *Aztlán: Essays on the Chicano Homeland*, 1989; *Tierra: Contemporary Short Fiction of New Mexico*, 1989.

MISCELLANEOUS: *The Anaya Reader*, 1995.

BIBLIOGRAPHY

Baeza, Abelardo. *Man of Aztlan: A Biography of Rudolfo Anaya*. Austin, Tex.: Eakin Press, 2001. Concise biography offers a fresh look at the man behind the classic novels. Includes bibliographical references.

Dick, Bruce, and Silvio Sirias, eds. *Conversations with Rudolfo Anaya*. Jackson: University Press of Mississippi, 1998. Collection of interviews with the author is designed to present Anaya's point of view and philosophy. Appropriate for students and general readers. Includes index.

Fernández Olmos, Margarite. *Rudolfo A. Anaya: A Critical Companion*. Westport, Conn.: Greenwood Press, 1999. Provides biographical material and discusses Anaya's literary influences as well as the themes, characters, and structures of individual works.

González-Trujillo, César A., ed. *Rudolfo A. Anaya: Focus on Criticism*. La Jolla, Calif.: Lalo Press, 1990. Collection of critical articles by American and European scholars is presented by an eminent scholar and critic of Anaya.

González-Trujillo, César A., and Phyllis S. Morgan. *A Sense of Place: Rudolfo A. Anaya—An Annotated Bio-bibliography*. Berkeley: University of California Press, 2000. Locates Anaya's real and mythic geography. Includes maps by Ronald L. Stauber.

Klein, Dianne. "Coming of Age in Novels by Rudolfo Anaya and Sandra Cisneros." *English Journal* 81, no. 5 (September, 1992): 21-26. Presents an insightful comparative study of the bildungsroman as written by the two authors.

Vassallo, Paul, ed. *The Magic of Words: Rudolfo A. Anaya and His Writings*. Albuquerque: University of New Mexico Press, 1982. Collection of essays provides interesting readings and discussion of Anaya's early fiction.

SHERWOOD ANDERSON

Born: Camden, Ohio; September 13, 1876
Died: Colón, Panama Canal Zone; March 8, 1941

PRINCIPAL LONG FICTION

Windy McPherson's Son, 1916
Marching Men, 1917
Winesburg, Ohio: A Group of Tales of Ohio Small Town Life, 1919
Poor White, 1920
Many Marriages, 1923
Dark Laughter, 1925
Beyond Desire, 1932
Kit Brandon, 1936

OTHER LITERARY FORMS

In addition to *Winesburg, Ohio*, which some critics regard as a collection of loosely related short stories, Sherwood Anderson produced three volumes of short stories: *The Triumph of the Egg* (1921); *Horses and Men* (1923); and *Death in the Woods, and Other Stories* (1933). He published two books of prose poems, *Mid-American Chants* (1918) and *A New Testament* (1927). *Plays: Winesburg and Others* was published in 1937. Anderson's autobiographical writings, among his most interesting prose works, include *A Story Teller's Story* (1924), *Tar: A Midwest Childhood* (1926), and the posthumously published *Sherwood Anderson's Memoirs* (1942). All three are such a mixture of fact and fiction that they are sometimes listed as fiction rather than autobiography. Anderson also brought out in book form several volumes of journalistic pieces, many of which had appeared originally in his newspapers: *Sherwood Anderson's Notebook* (1926), *Perhaps Women* (1931), *No Swank* (1934), *Puzzled America* (1935), and *Home Town* (1940). *The Modern Writer* (1925) is a collection of lectures.

ACHIEVEMENTS

Sherwood Anderson was not a greatly gifted novelist; in fact, it might be argued that he was not by nature a novelist at all. He was a brilliant and original writer of tales. His early reputation, which brought him the homage of writers such as James Joyce, Ford Madox Ford, Gertrude Stein, Ernest Hemingway, and F. Scott Fitzgerald, was established by the stories published in *Winesburg, Ohio*, *The Triumph of the Egg*, and *Horses and Men*. Anderson had published two novels before *Winesburg, Ohio* and was to publish five more, but none of these achieved the critical success of his short pieces.

Anderson's difficulties with the novel are understandable when one sees that his great gift was for rendering moments of intense consciousness—"epiphanies," as James Joyce called them—for which the short story or the tale is the perfect vehicle. The novel form requires a more objective sense of a world outside the individual consciousness as well as the ability to move characters through change and development and to deal to some extent with the effect of character on character. The best parts of Anderson's novels are those scenes in which he deals, as in the short stories, with a minor character trapped by his own eccentric nature in a hostile world.

Another serious limitation to Anderson's talent as a novelist was his inclination to preach, to see himself as a prophet and reformer and to make sweeping generalizations that are as embarrassing as they are inartistic. Even in *Poor White*, probably his best novel, his characters run to types and become, finally, representative figures in a social allegory. In his worst novels, the characters are caricatures whose absurdity is not perceived by their author. Anderson's style, which could at times work brilliantly, became excessively mannered, a kind of self-parody, which was a sure sign that he had lost his grip on the talent that had produced his best and earlier work.

Winesburg, Ohio is without doubt Anderson's great achievement. It is a collection of tales striving to become a novel; indeed, most critics regard it as a novel, a new form of the novel, which, though perhaps first suggested by Edgar Lee Masters's *Spoon River Anthology* (1915), took on its own expressive form and became the model for later works such as Hemingway's *In Our Time* (1924) and William Faulkner's *The Unvanquished* (1938). A few of the Winesburg stories, such as "Godliness," are marred by a tendency to generalization, but on the whole they assume the coherence and solidity of such

masterpieces as Mark Twain's *Adventures of Huckleberry Finn* (1884) and Stephen Crane's *The Red Badge of Courage* (1895), which bristle with implications not only about the life of their times but also about the present. If Anderson had published only *Winesburg, Ohio*, he would be remembered and ranked as an important minor American novelist.

BIOGRAPHY

Sherwood Anderson was born September 13, 1876, in Camden, Ohio, to Irwin and Emma Anderson. When he was eight years old, his family moved to Clyde, Ohio, where Anderson spent his most impressionable years. In later life, Anderson remembered Clyde as an ideal place for a boy to grow up; it became a symbol of the lost innocence of an earlier America. Many of his best stories have a fictionalized Clyde as their setting, and his memory of it shaped his vision of the American past and became a measure of the inadequacies of the industrialized, increasingly mechanized America of city apartments and bloodless sophistication.

Anderson's family was poor. Irwin Anderson, a harness maker, was thrown out of work by industrialization and periods of economic instability. Thus he was forced to work at various odd jobs, such as house painter and paper hanger. Anderson's mother took in washing, while Sherwood and his brother did odd jobs to help support the family. In his autobiographical accounts of growing up, *A Story Teller's Story*, *Tar*, and *Memoirs*, Anderson expresses his humiliation at his impoverished childhood and his resentment toward his father for the inability to support his family. Anderson was particularly bitter about the hardship inflicted on his mother, to whom he was deeply attached. He held his father accountable for his mother's early death, and in *Windy McPherson's Son* one may see in the portrait of the father Anderson's view of his own father as a braggart and a fool whose drunkenness and irresponsibility caused the death of his wife. In time, Anderson's attitude toward his father softened; he came to see that his own gifts as a storyteller were derived from his father, who was a gifted yarn spinner.

Even more important in Anderson's development as a writer was the sympathy awakened in him by his father's failures. A braggart and a liar, Irwin Anderson nevertheless had romantic aspirations to shine in the eyes of the world; his pathetic attempts to amount to something made him grotesque by the standards of the world. An underlying tenderness for his father grew stronger as Sherwood Anderson grew older, enabling him to sympathize with those people in life who become the victims of the wrong kinds of dreams and aspirations. The portrayal of the narrator's father in "The Egg" is one example of Anderson's eventual compassion for such individuals.

Anderson's youth, however, was marked by a rejection of his father and a worship of progress and business success. He eagerly embraced the current version of the American Dream as exemplified in the Horatio Alger stories: the poor boy who becomes rich. Anderson's own career followed that pattern with remarkable fidelity. He took any odd job that would pay, whether it was selling papers or running errands, and earned himself the nickname Jobby. After a brief stint in the U.S. Army during the Spanish-American War and a year at the Wittenburg Academy completing his high school education, Anderson started in advertising in Chicago and moved up the financial ladder from one position to the next until he became the owner of a paint factory in Elyria, Ohio, the success of which depended on his skill in writing advertising letters about his barn paint.

Anderson's personal life also developed in a traditional way. In 1904, he married a young woman from a middle-class family, had three children, and associated with the "best" people in Elyria. Around 1911, however, contradictory impulses at work in Anderson precipitated a breakdown. He worked hard at the paint factory and at night spent increasing amounts of time in an attic room writing fiction. The strain eventually took its toll, aided by the pressures of conflicting values: Anderson wanted business and financial success, yet, deep down, he believed in something very different. One day, without warning, he walked out of his paint factory and was later found wandering about the streets in Cleveland, dazed and unable to give his name and address. After a short stay in the hospital, Anderson returned to Elyria, closed out his affairs, and moved to Chicago.

Anderson later told the story of his departure from the paint factory and each time he told it, the details were different. Whatever the exact truth, the important fact appears to be that his breakdown was the result of serious strain between the kind of life he was leading and the kind of life something in him was urging him to live. Rex Burbank in *Sherwood Anderson* (1964) remarks that the breakdown was moral as well as psychological; it might be called spiritual as well, for it had to do with feelings too vague to be attached to questions of right and wrong. Anderson, in his best work, was something of a mystic, a "Corn Belt mystic" one detractor called him, and his mystical sense was to be the principal source of his gift as a fiction writer, as well as his chief liability as a novelist.

Anderson's life after he left the paint factory in Elyria was a mixture of successes and failures. He wandered from Chicago to New York to New Orleans and finally to Marion, Virginia, in 1927, where he built a house and became the publisher of two local newspapers. His first

Sherwood Anderson. (Library of Congress)

marriage had ended in divorce shortly after he moved to Chicago; he married three more times, his last to Eleanor Copenhaver, a Virginian. Anderson's financial status was always somewhat precarious. His reputation had been established early among Eastern intellectuals who were attracted to what they saw as Anderson's primitivism, a quality he learned to cultivate. Except for *Dark Laughter*, however, which was something of a best seller, none of his books was very successful financially, and he was forced to lecture and to do journalistic writing. His most serious problem, however, was the waning of his creative powers and his inability after 1923 to equal any of his earlier successes. During his later years, before his final and happiest marriage, Anderson often was close to a breakdown.

During his years in Virginia and under the influence of his fourth wife, Anderson increasingly became interested in social problems. He visited factories, wrote about labor strife, and lent his name to liberal causes. His deepest commitment, however, was not to politics but to his own somewhat vague ideal of brotherhood, which he continued to espouse. In 1941, while on a goodwill tour to South America for the U.S. State Department, he died of peritonitis.

ANALYSIS

All novelists are to some extent autobiographical, but Sherwood Anderson is more so than most; indeed, all of Anderson's novels seem to arise out of the one great moment of his life, when he walked out of the paint factory and left behind the prosperous middle-class life of Elyria. In his imagination, his defection from material success took on great significance and became not only the common paradigm for his protagonists but also the basis for his message to the modern world. Industrialization and mechanization, money making, advertising, rising in the world, respectability—all of which Anderson himself had hankered after or had sought to encourage in others—became in his fiction the target of criticism. This is not to accuse him of insincerity, but only to point out the extent of his revulsion and the way in which he made his own personal experience into a mythological history of his region and even of the modern world. Anderson's heroes invariably renounce materialism and economic individualism and their attendant social and

moral conventions and seek a more spiritual, more vital existence.

WINDY McPHERSON'S SON

Anderson's first published novel, *Windy McPherson's Son*, though set in Caxton, Iowa, is clearly based on Anderson's boyhood in Clyde, Ohio, and his later years in Elyria and Chicago. Sam McPherson is a fictionalized version of Jobby Anderson, with his talent for money-making schemes; his father, like Anderson's own, is a braggart and liar who frequently disgraces his hardworking wife and ambitious son in front of the townspeople of Caxton. After his mother's death, Sam leaves Caxton and takes his talent for money making to Chicago, where in effect he takes over management of an arms manufacturing plant. Sam becomes rich and marries the boss's daughter, but, instead of finding satisfaction in his wealth and position, he discovers that he is dissatisfied with business success and his childless marriage. He walks out of the business, abandons his wife, and wanders through the country attempting to find meaning in existence. After discovering that "American men and women have not learned to be clean and noble and natural, like their forests and their wide, clean plains," Sam returns to his wife Sue, bringing with him three children he has adopted. Out of some sense of responsibility, he allows himself to be led back into the darkened house from which he had fled, a curious and unsatisfactory "happy" ending.

MARCHING MEN

Marching Men, Anderson's second novel, repeats the same basic pattern: success, revolt, search, revelation, elevation—but in a less convincing way. The setting is Coal Creek, a Pennsylvania mining town. The hero is Beaut McGregor, who rebels against the miners' passive acceptance of their squalid existence and escapes to Chicago, where he becomes rich. McGregor continues to despise the miners of Coal Creek until he returns for his mother's funeral; then, he has an awakening, a sudden illumination that gives him a spiritual insight that alters his existence. He sees the miners as men marching "up out of the smoke," and that insight and the marching metaphor become the inspiration for McGregor's transformation.

Back in Chicago, McGregor becomes the leader of a new movement called the "marching men," an organization as vague and diffuse as its aim: to find "the secret of order in the midst of disorder," in order that "the thresh of feet should come finally to sing a great song, carrying the message of a powerful brotherhood into the ears and brains of the marchers." A great march takes place in Chicago on Labor Day, and though the marching of the men makes its power felt when the day is over, it is clear that the movement, whatever its temporary success, has no future. The marchers disperse in roving gangs, and an "aristocratic" opponent of the movement muses on its success and failure, wondering whether in deliberately turning away from the success of business and embracing the ultimate failure of the marching men, Beaut McGregor did not achieve a higher form of success.

Though a failure as a novel, *Marching Men* is interesting as Anderson's attempt to give expression to his own kind of achievement and as a place to experiment with concepts successfully handled later in *Winesburg, Ohio*. Anderson had given up success in the business world for a precarious career as a writer; he saw himself as a prophet preaching ideals of brotherhood that had nothing to do with political movements or social programs, but that expressed a mystical yearning for order and unity. The metaphor of the marching men was intended to express this vague ideal. The quest for order and brotherhood was a theme to which Anderson was to return in his next novel, *Winesburg, Ohio*, where he found the form best suited to its expression. The format of *Marching Men*, with its lack of convincing motivation and realistic development, exposed the inadequacy of Anderson's marching metaphor for sustaining a full-length realistic novel.

WINESBURG, OHIO

Winesburg, Ohio is Anderson's masterpiece, a collection of interrelated stories that are less like chapters than like the sections of a long poem; within these pieces, however, there is what might be called a submerged novel, the story of George Willard's growth and maturation. Willard appears in many of the stories, sometimes as a main character, but often as an observer or listener to the tales of other characters. There is the story of Alice Hindeman, who refuses to elope with Ned Curry because she does not want to burden him and eventually runs naked out into the rain. There is also Wing Biddlebaum in "Hands" and Elmer Cowley of "Queer," who desperately try to be normal but only succeed in being stranger than ever. There is the Reverend Curtis Hartman, who spies through a chink in his study window the naked figure of Kate Swift and ends by having a spiritual insight: Christ manifest in the body of a naked woman. These minor characters raise an important critical question: What bearing have they on the submerged bildungsroman?

In five stories, beginning with "Nobody Knows" and ending with "Sophistication" and including "The Thinker," "An Awakening," and "The Teacher," George Willard moves from a lustful relationship with Louise Trunion to a feeling of respectful communion with Helen White, discovering the ultimate reverence for life that Anderson describes as the only thing that makes life possible in the modern world. The discovery was one Anderson himself had made in the early years of his newfound freedom in Chicago, following his escape from the paint factory. In "An Awakening," the pivotal story in the submerged novel, George is made to undergo a mystical experience in which he feels himself in tune with a powerful force swinging through the universe; at the same time, he feels that all of the men and women of his town are his brothers and sisters and wishes to call them out and take them by the hand, including, presumably, the so-called grotesques of the other stories.

The precise relationship of these other stories to those that constitute the growth and maturation of George Willard is a matter of continual critical conjecture, for *Winesburg, Ohio* is the kind of book that does not give up its meanings easily, partly because the kind of meaning the book has can only be suggested and partly because Anderson's way of suggesting is so indirect, at times even vatic. Anderson was possibly influenced by the French post-Impressionist painters such as Paul Cézanne and Paul Gauguin, whose works he had seen in Chicago, and his interest in rendering subjective states indirectly might well parallel theirs. Whether such influences were in fact exerted is arguable. What is clear, however, is that Anderson was by temperament an oral storyteller and that he depended on tone, colloquial language, and folk psychology rather than the more formal structures of the novelist. In *Winesburg, Ohio* he was also a poet, working by suggestion and indirection, a method that produces intellectual and narrative gaps that the reader is obliged to cross under his or her own power.

One of the chief critical issues of *Winesburg, Ohio* is the nature of Anderson's characters. In an introductory story, "The Book of the Grotesque" (an early title for the novel), Anderson supplied a definition of a grotesque as one who took a single idea and attempted to live by it, but such a definition, while it can be applied to some characters such as Doctor Parcival of "The Philosopher," hardly fits others at all. In an introduction to the Viking edition of *Winesburg, Ohio* (1960), Malcolm Cowley suggested that the problem of the Winesburg characters was an inability to communicate with one another. Jarvis Thurston's article in *Accent* (1956) offers a more compelling view; the Winesburg characters, Thurston says, are all on a spiritual quest, and their often violent behavior is symptomatic, not of their inability to communicate, but of a blockage of the spiritual quest. Only George Willard succeeds in that quest, when he undergoes, in "An Awakening," a transcendent experience. Burbank, however, in *Sherwood Anderson*, emphasizes the difference between Willard and the other characters of *Winesburg, Ohio* in this way: They are all "arrested" in a state of loneliness and social isolation. George, on the other hand, because he has heard the stories of the grotesques and has absorbed their lives, has managed to break out of a meaningless existence into a meaningful one. Burbank calls George "an artist of life."

Whatever view one takes of Anderson's characters, it is clear that no simple explanation will suffice, especially not the old writer's, though some critics think of him as Anderson's spokesman. Indeed, the prospect of a single idea summarizing and explaining all of the characters seems ironic in the light of the old writer's assertion that such simplemindedness produces grotesques. *Winesburg, Ohio* has its own kind of unity, but it has its own kind of complexity as well. It is a book of contradictory impulses that stands conventional judgment on its head; at times it is funny and often at the same time profoundly sad. It is a book in praise of the emotions, but, at the same time, it is aware of the dangers of emotional excess.

Winesburg, Ohio was well received by reviewers and even had a moderate financial success. It also confirmed, in the minds of Eastern critics such as Van Wyck Brooks

and Waldo Frank, Anderson's authentic American genius. He was seen as part of that native American tradition that came down through Abraham Lincoln, Walt Whitman, and Mark Twain, expressing the essential nature of American life, its strengths, its weaknesses, and its conflicts.

Winesburg, Ohio has not been without its detractors. From a certain point of view, the antics of a character such as Alice Hindeman dashing naked into the rain are ridiculous, and Anderson's style at times slips into the mode of the fancy writer of slick fiction; even his mysticism can be ridiculed if one sees it as Lionel Trilling does in *The Liberal Imagination* (1950) as a form picking a quarrel with respectable society. Despite its faults, however, *Winesburg, Ohio* still lives—vital, intriguing, moving. It remains a modern American classic, expressing in its eccentric way a certain quality of American life that is all but inexpressible.

POOR WHITE

Anderson's next novel was to be a more traditional sort of work with a hero and a heroine and a "happy" ending that included the requisite embrace, though the hero and the embrace were anything but popularly traditional. Hugh McVey, the protagonist of *Poor White*, is the son of a tramp, born on the muddy banks of the Mississippi and content to live there in a dreamy, sensual existence until taken up by a New England woman who does her best to civilize him. Hugh is tall and lanky, rather like Lincoln in appearance if more like Huck Finn in temperament. When Sarah Shepard, the New England woman, leaves Missouri, Hugh goes east to the town of Bidwell, Ohio, where he becomes the town's telegrapher, and then, out of boredom, begins inventing labor-saving machinery. Being naïve and something of a social outcast, Hugh is unaware of the changes his inventions make in Bidwell. He thinks he is making life easier for the laborers, but opportunists in the town get hold of Hugh's inventions; the factories they bring into being exploit both Hugh and the farm laborers, who, without work in the fields, have swarmed into the new factories, slaving long hours for low pay. Inadvertently, Hugh has succeeded in corrupting the lives of the very people he had set out to help.

Clearly, the story of Hugh's "rise" from a dreamy loafer into a rich inventor and the changes that take place in Bidwell from a sleepy farm community into a bustling factory town are meant to tell the story of mid-America's transformation from a primitive, frontier society of hard-working, God-fearing people to an urban society that differentiates between the rich and the poor, the exploiters and the exploited, the slick new city types and the country-bred factory hands. It is meant to be a pathetic story. In welcoming industry and mechanization—and for the best of reasons—America has managed to stamp out and stifle the older, more primitive but vital life of the frontier. Hugh's "love" affair is less clearly and convincingly done. He marries, is separated from, and then reunited with the daughter of the rich farmer who exploits him. This part of the novel attempts to make a statement, presumably, about emotional life in the new industrial period, but it seems contrived and mechanical compared with the chapters dealing with Hugh's rise.

Poor White, then, is not an entirely successful novel. There are too many flat statements and not enough scenes; the character of Hugh McVey—part Lincoln, part Finn, part Henry Ford—seems at times too mechanical. Still, *Poor White* has its moments; it is an ambitious attempt to deal fictionally with the changes in American life that Anderson himself had experienced in his journey from poor boy to businessman to writer. It is by common assent his best novel after *Winesburg, Ohio.*

MANY MARRIAGES *and* DARK LAUGHTER

After *Poor White*, Anderson's career as a novelist seriously declined. He continued to write and to publish novels: *Many Marriages* in 1923, and in 1925, *Dark Laughter*, which became a best seller. Both novels, however, betray what Anderson himself condemned in other writers: the tendency to oversimplify the psychological complexities of human nature. Both novels are anti-Puritan tracts, attacking sexual repression, which writers and popular critics of the day singled out as the source of so much modern unhappiness. In *Many Marriages*, John Webster, a washing-machine manufacturer who has found true sexual fulfillment with his secretary, decides to liberate his militantly virginal daughter by appearing naked before her and lecturing her and her mother on the need to free their sexual impulses. *Dark Laughter* retells the story of Anderson's escape from the paint factory by inventing an improbable hero who gives up his career as a journalist and goes back to the town in which he grew

up. There he becomes the gardener and then the lover of the factory owner's wife, an experience meant to suggest the interrelation of physical and spiritual love.

Both *Many Marriages* and *Dark Laughter* suffer from Anderson's inability to think through the implications of his theme and to dramatize it effectively with developed characters and situations. The same limitations are reflected in his last two published novels, *Beyond Desire*, a novel about labor unions and strikes, which is badly confused and poorly written, and *Kit Brandon*, the story of a young woman who is the daughter-in-law of a bootlegger. The weaknesses of these last four novels show that Anderson's talent was not essentially novelistic. His real strengths lay in rendering an insight or an illumination and in bodying forth, often in a sudden and shocking way, an unexplained and unexplainable revelation: Wash Williams smashing his respectable mother-in-law with a chair, or the Reverend Curtis Hartman rushing out into the night to tell George Willard that he had seen Christ manifest in the body of a naked woman. Both of these scenes are from *Winesburg, Ohio*, a book that by its structure did not oblige Anderson to develop or explain his grotesque characters and their sudden and violent gestures. In *Many Marriages* and *Dark Laughter*, scenes of nakedness and sexual awakening are made ridiculous by Anderson's attempt to explain and develop what is better left evocative.

After his death in 1941, Anderson was praised by writers such as Thomas Wolfe and Faulkner for the contribution he had made to their development and to the development of modern American fiction. Though he was limited and deeply flawed as a novelist, he ranks with Twain, Crane, and Hemingway as an important influence in the development of American prose style, and he deserves to be remembered as the author of *Winesburg, Ohio* and a number of hauntingly evocative short stories.

W. J. Stuckey

OTHER MAJOR WORKS

SHORT FICTION: *The Triumph of the Egg*, 1921; *Horses and Men*, 1923; *Death in the Woods, and Other Stories*, 1933; *The Sherwood Anderson Reader*, 1947; *Certain Things Last: The Selected Short Stories of Sherwood Anderson*, 1992.

PLAY: *Plays: Winesburg and Others*, 1937.

POETRY: *Mid-American Chants*, 1918; *A New Testament*, 1927.

NONFICTION: *A Story Teller's Story*, 1924; *The Modern Writer*, 1925; *Sherwood Anderson's Notebook*, 1926; *Tar: A Midwest Childhood*, 1926; *Hello Towns!*, 1929; *Perhaps Women*, 1931; *No Swank*, 1934; *Puzzled America*, 1935; *Home Town*, 1940; *Sherwood Anderson's Memoirs*, 1942; *The Letters of Sherwood Anderson*, 1953; *Selected Letters*, 1984; *Letters to Bab: Sherwood Anderson to Marietta D. Finley, 1916-1933*, 1985; *Southern Odyssey: Selected Writings by Sherwood Anderson*, 1997.

MISCELLANEOUS: *Sherwood Anderson: Early Writings*, 1989 (Ray Lewis White, editor).

BIBLIOGRAPHY

Anderson, David D. *Sherwood Anderson: An Introduction and Interpretation*. New York: Holt, Rinehart and Winston, 1967. This critical biography argues that all of Anderson's work, not just *Winesburg, Ohio*, must be considered when attempting to understand Anderson's career and his place in the literary canon.

Appel, Paul P. *Homage to Sherwood Anderson: 1876-1941*. Mamaroneck, N.Y.: Author, 1970. A collection of essays originally published in homage to Anderson after his death in 1941. Among the contributors are Theodore Dreiser, Gertrude Stein, Thomas Wolfe, Henry Miller, and William Saroyan. Also includes Anderson's previously unpublished letters and his essay "The Modern Writer," which had been issued as a limited edition in 1925.

Bassett, John E. *Sherwood Anderson: An American Career*. Selinsgrove, Pa.: Susquehanna University Press, 2006. Bassett reevaluates the accomplishments in *Winesburg, Ohio* and Anderson's other novels and short stories, but focuses more than previous studies on his nonfiction, autobiographical, and journalistic writing. Also discusses how Anderson coped with the cultural changes of his time.

Campbell, Hilbert H., and Charles E. Modlin, eds. *Sherwood Anderson: Centennial Studies*. Troy, N.Y.: Whitston, 1976. Written for Anderson's centenary, these eleven previously unpublished essays were solicited by the editors. Some of the essays explore Anderson's relationship with other artists, including Edgar Lee Masters, Henry Adams, Alfred Stieglitz, and J. J. Lankes.

Dunne, Robert. *A New Book of the Grotesques: Contemporary Approaches to Sherwood Anderson's Early Fiction*. Kent, Ohio: Kent State University Press, 2005. Offers a new interpretation of Anderson's early fiction by looking at it from a postmodern theoretical perspective, especially from poststructuralist approaches. Describes how the early novels laid the groundwork for *Winesburg, Ohio* before it examines that novel.

Howe, Irving. *Sherwood Anderson*. Toronto, Ont.: William Sloane, 1951. This highly biographical work explores why Anderson, a writer with only one crucial book, remains an outstanding artist in American literature. The chapters on *Winesburg, Ohio* and the short stories are noteworthy; both were later published in collections of essays on Anderson.

Papinchak, Robert Allen. *Sherwood Anderson: A Study of the Short Fiction*. New York: Twayne, 1992. Introduction to Anderson's short stories examines his search for an appropriate form and his experimentations with form in the stories in *Winesburg, Ohio*, as well as the short stories that appeared before and after that book. Deals with Anderson's belief that the most authentic history of life is a history of moments when a person truly lives, as well as his creation of the grotesque as an American type that also reflects a new social reality. Includes comments from Anderson's essays, letters, and notebooks, as well as brief commentaries by five other critics.

Rideout, Walter B., ed. *Sherwood Anderson: A Collection of Critical Essays*. Englewood Cliffs, N.J.: Prentice-Hall, 1974. Treats Anderson from a variety of perspectives: as prophet, storyteller, and maker of American myths. Three of the essays deal with *Winesburg, Ohio*, including a discussion of how Anderson wrote the book. Includes an appreciation of Anderson's work by William Faulkner and a chronology of significant dates.

Small, Judy Jo. *A Reader's Guide to the Short Stories of Sherwood Anderson*. New York: G. K. Hall, 1994. Provides commentary on every story in *Winesburg, Ohio*, *The Triumph of the Egg*, *Horses and Men*, and

Death in the Woods. Small summarizes the interpretations of other critics and supplies historical and biographical background, accounts of how the stories were written, the period in which they were published, and their reception.

Townsend, Kim. *Sherwood Anderson*. Boston: Houghton Mifflin, 1987. Biography in which Townsend focuses, in part, on how Anderson's life is reflected in his writings. Supplemented by twenty-six photographs and a useful bibliography of Anderson's work.

White, Ray Lewis, ed. *The Achievement of Sherwood Anderson: Essays in Criticism*. Chapel Hill: University of North Carolina Press, 1966. This collection of essays treats an important variety of subjects, including isolation, Freudianism, and socialism in Anderson's texts, as well as his development as an artist.

IVO ANDRIĆ

Born: Dolac, Bosnia, Austro-Hungarian Empire (now in Bosnia and Herzegovina); October 10, 1892

Died: Belgrade, Yugoslavia (now in Serbia); March 13, 1975

PRINCIPAL LONG FICTION

Gospodjica, 1945 (*The Woman from Sarajevo*, 1965)

Na Drini ćuprija, 1945 (*The Bridge on the Drina*, 1959)

Travnička hronika, 1945 (*Bosnian Story*, 1958; better known as *Bosnian Chronicle*)

Priča o vezirovom slonu, 1948 (*The Vizier's Elephant: Three Novellas*, 1962; includes *Pričo o vezirovom slonu* [*The Vizier's Elephant*], *Anikina vremena* [*Anika's Times*], and *Zeko* [English translation])

Prokleta avlija, 1954 (novella; *Devil's Yard*, 1962)

OTHER LITERARY FORMS

Ivo Andrić (AHN-dreech) began his writing career with two volumes of poems in 1918 and 1920 and continued to publish poetry in magazines throughout his life. During the 1920's and 1930's, he published several volumes of short stories and brought out a fourth volume in 1948. His essay "Conversations with Goya" (1934) sets out his creed as a writer and a humanist. Between 1945 and his death in 1975, he also published essays on various philosophical, aesthetic, and literary subjects. A selection of his short stories from all periods of his career, *The Pasha's Concubine, and Other Tales*, was published in English in 1968.

ACHIEVEMENTS

Ivo Andrić is undoubtedly best known in the English-speaking world as the author of what has been called one of the great novels of the twentieth century, *The Bridge on the Drina*. Primarily for this novel, and for two others about life in his native Bosnia published at the same time, he was awarded the Nobel Prize in Literature in 1961. Until this "Bosnian trilogy" brought him considerable fame, he had not been widely known outside his own country. His reputation has gone through three distinct phases. From 1918 to 1941, Andrić came to be recognized, primarily in Yugoslavia, as that nation's leading writer of short stories and as one of its better poets and essayists. The second phase, from 1941 to 1961, established his fame as a writer of novels and novellas, culminating in his winning the Nobel Prize. In this period, especially in the 1950's, he gained his first wide readership throughout the Western Hemisphere. Finally, in the period from the Nobel Prize onward, he gained worldwide recognition, with his novels and short stories translated into more than thirty languages and appearing in many paperback reprints.

Andrić is one of a very few Nobel Prize winners whose work continues to be admired equally by both professional critics and the general public. As a novelist, he has been praised especially for his vivid and lifelike characterizations, for his ability to relate individual dilemmas to larger social forces, and for "the epic force with which he has depicted themes and human destinies drawn from the history of his country," in the words of the Nobel Prize Committee. It was Andrić's fame that first drew the attention of the rest of the world to the high quality of Yugoslav literature in general.

BIOGRAPHY

Ivo Andrić's family origins embody that ethnic, religious, and cultural diversity of modern Yugoslavia that has always been one of the underlying subjects of his fiction. He was born in the tiny hamlet of Dolac in what is now Bosnia and Herzegovina (then a province of the Austro-Hungarian Empire) on October 10, 1892. His father, a Serb of the Orthodox faith, was a poor coppersmith; his mother was a Croat and a Roman Catholic. When Ivo was an infant, his father died, and his mother took him to live with her parents in the eastern town of Višegrad, where he played on the bridge erected by the Turks that was later to be the location and subject of his greatest novel. A brilliant student, he had translated some of Walt Whitman's poetry into Serbo-Croatian by the time he was nineteen. His education was interrupted by his political activities, however. As a youth he had joined Young Bosnia, an organization dedicated to creating an independent nation for the South Slavs. After another member of the organization assassinated the heir to the Austro-Hungarian throne, Archduke Francis Ferdinand, in 1914 (the event that precipitated World War I), Andrić was arrested and imprisoned for three years.

Andrić always said that his imprisonment forced him to mature rapidly, both as a writer and as a human being. He read extensively, especially the Danish philosopher Søren Kierkegaard, whose work gave substance to Andrić's already developing pessimism. Released from prison in 1917, he began to publish poetry he had written while incarcerated, joined the editorial staff of a literary journal, and resumed his academic career. During the next six years, Andrić studied languages, philosophy, and history at universities in Poland, Austria, and Yugoslavia, earning a Ph.D. in history in 1923 from the University of Graz in Austria. His work on his doctoral the-

Ivo Andrić. (© The Nobel Foundation)

sis, a study of Bosnian spiritual and intellectual life during four centuries of Turkish rule, provided a solid underpinning of historical knowledge for his later novels and stories of Bosnian life. That same year, Andrić, then thirty-one, joined the diplomatic corps of the new Kingdom of the Serbs, Croats, and Slovenes, a country roughly equivalent to what later became Yugoslavia, created out of the ruins of the Austro-Hungarian and Ottoman empires after World War I. He served in a variety of posts in Rome, Madrid, Budapest, Geneva, Trieste, Graz, and Bucharest over the next eighteen years, rising to be the Yugoslav ambassador to Germany from 1939 to 1941.

Andrić had published his first piece of fiction, the long story "Voyage of Ali Djerzelez," in 1920 while still in the university, but his diplomatic career allowed little time for sustained writing. He did manage to write and publish three volumes of short stories—in 1924, 1931, and 1936—but had to postpone writing several novels for which he had developed sketches and done considerable research. His diplomatic career ended, and his years as a novelist began, with the Nazi invasion of Yugoslavia in April of 1941. Arriving in Belgrade just ahead of the first German bombers, Andrić placed himself under voluntary house arrest in his apartment. There he spent the remainder of the war, enduring the destruction around him and writing novels and short stories. He refused to flee the city in the periodic bombardment and panic because, he said later, "I had nothing to save but my life and it was beneath human dignity to run for that." The three novels he wrote at that time all deal with the suffering and endurance of his native Bosnia at various times in its history.

With the end of the war in 1945, Andrić quickly published *Bosnian Chronicle*, *The Bridge on the Drina*, and *The Woman from Sarajevo* as well as a volume of translations from Italian. Yugoslavia had become a Communist Federated Republic under Marshal Tito. Andrić joined the Communist Party, served as president of the Yugoslav Writers' Union, and in subsequent years sat as a representative for Bosnia in the Yugoslav parliament. Throughout the 1940's and 1950's, he continued to write prolifically, publishing four novellas, a number of short stories, philosophical and travel essays, and critical studies of key figures in Western art, including Petrarch and Francisco de Goya. He won many awards in Yugoslavia for his writing, and, in 1961, he was awarded the Nobel Prize in Literature. Advancing age and the burdens of fame slowed Andrić's output after that time. A bachelor for most of his life, he married Milica Babić, a well-known painter and theatrical designer, in 1959. He died in Belgrade at the age of eighty-two on March 13, 1975.

ANALYSIS

Ivo Andrić's native Bosnia, the setting for almost all of his fiction, functions as a microcosm of human life. It is for his characters a land of fear, hatred, and unrelenting harshness. To all who enter it, mere survival becomes a victory. Its effect on outsiders especially is one of confusion, panic, and sometimes even insanity. Bosnia's strategic location in southern Europe has given it a peculiar character that Andrić exploits fully in his novels. In an-

cient times, it formed a border between Eastern and Western empires, and later between Roman Catholic and Eastern Orthodox forms of Christianity and culture. In the sixteenth century, it became an outpost of the Ottoman Empire, which was Turkish and Muslim. All of these religions, in addition to Judaism, existed in uneasy juxtaposition in Bosnia, with periodic outbursts of religious, ethnic, and political violence between various religious and ethnic groups.

Subject to constant nationalistic upheaval, foreign conquest, and the crude violence of Turkish rule, Bosnian history is for Andrić the epitome of the dangers, sufferings, and uncertainties of human life. All people live in a kind of prison as they struggle against one another and against their own fears and insecurities. Undoubtedly, certain facts of Andrić's life help to explain his views. He spent both world wars in confinement, able to write yet unable to act in other ways. His efforts to keep Yugoslavia out of World War II failed, showing him his powerlessness as a diplomat to change the course of history. Finally, the literary heritage of Bosnia that Andrić knew so thoroughly offers several important writers and cultural figures with similar views of human life.

Andrić's fiction is concerned not only with the unpredictability of human life but also with his characters' attempts to understand their place in history, to escape their fears, and to find some measure of constancy and hope. He presents his characters against a background of the inexorable flow of time and its cumulative effect on future generations. His concept of history is not one of discrete periods of time but rather of the constant change that is to him the basic fact of human existence. His characters fail whenever they attempt to relive time rather than to understand its flow, when they concentrate on mere memory of the past rather than on its meaning for the future. In an essay, Andrić stated: "Only ignorant and unreasonable men can maintain that the past is dead and by an impenetrable wall forever separated from the present. The truth is rather that all that man once thought and did is invisibly woven into that which we today think, feel, and do."

Andrić has been praised most often for the masterful character portrayals in his novels. His main characters are usually figures of relatively low social importance—

priests, consuls, wealthy local farmers, petty bureaucrats, and small merchants—chosen by Andrić for detailed treatment because on such persons the whole weight of the injustices, cruelties, and irrationalities of life tend to fall most heavily. As he says of his protagonist in *Bosnian Chronicle:* "He is one of those men who are predestined victims of great historic changes, because they neither know how to stand with these changes, as forceful and exceptional individuals do, nor how to come to terms with them, as the great mass of people manage to do."

His other characters are drawn with equal skill. It has been said that there is no such thing as a flat character in an Andrić novel. This pattern results from the fact that he explores carefully the background of every person whom he introduces, however briefly each appears. As a result, the reader knows all the characters intimately, yet the narrative flow is never unnecessarily interrupted in order to impart this information. It is a technique that serves Andrić's thematic purposes as well, for it embeds his characters more deeply in the stream of time. The plots of his novels develop out of this careful delineation of his characters' pasts. The meaning of their lives is the product of that confluence of personal and national history of which all humans are made and yet relatively few novelists have portrayed as successfully as has Andrić.

BOSNIAN CHRONICLE

Although Andrić's first three novels were published simultaneously in 1945, *Bosnian Chronicle* was the first to be written after he returned to Belgrade in 1941. He began writing, he says, because

> it was a way of surviving. I remembered the moments in history when certain peoples seemed to lose out. I thought of Serbia and Bosnia blacked out in the Turkish tide of the sixteenth century. The odds against one were so monstrous . . . even hope was an aspect of despair. . . . I pulled the past around me like an oxygen tent.

The act of writing under these conditions, he goes on, was "like drawing up a testament."

Bosnian Chronicle is set in the town of Travnik during the period when French emperor Napoleon I was at the height of his power, from 1806 to 1814. Its main characters are the consuls and viziers who represent the various governments having an interest in Bosnia. The Turkish vizier is there because his empire "owns" Bosnia; the French consul, because the French are trying to extend their power inland from the coast; the Austrian consul, because the Austrians fear French power as a threat to their own. The protagonist of the novel is the French consul, Jean Daville, and the plot grows out of his efforts as a European to comprehend the strange mixture of Eastern and Western cultures that is Bosnia. He is alternately bewildered, frustrated, and horrified at the barbarity of Turkish rule, the ignorance of the peasantry, and the endless intrigues of the contending powers represented in Travnik. Daville's ideals, formed during the French Revolution, are slowly being eroded and betrayed in this outpost of the empire; he comes to see that he is merely a pawn in a game of international politics played without principle or mercy.

Daville has trouble working with his friends as well as with his enemies. He and his assistant, Desfosses, a generation apart in age, epitomize the opposite approaches that Westerners take toward the Orient. Daville follows the "classical" strategy: He emphasizes order and form, tradition, pessimism about sudden change, and a refusal to take local culture seriously. Desfosses, on the other hand, follows the "Romantic" attitude: He approaches problems with optimism, energy, impatience with tradition, and a great respect for local culture.

The several Turkish viziers with whom the French consul must deal present him with complex moral and political dilemmas. The first one, Husref Mehmed Pasha, poisons an emissary from the sultan who has come to order Husref Pasha's removal. Daville is shocked but can see no ready way to deal with the situation or even to reveal it to anyone. The second vizier, Ibrahim Halimi Pasha, is, like Daville, incurably pessimistic, but he is even more violent than Husref Pasha. Just when Daville believes he has found someone with whom he can solve diplomatic problems rationally, Ibrahim Pasha gives Daville a present of a sack full of ears and noses purportedly severed from the heads of rebellious Serbs; in actuality, the body parts were taken from Bosnian peasants who were massacred at a religious festival. Ibrahim Pasha also shoots one of his own army captains merely because the Austrians ask him to do so. Daville must acknowledge that "morbid circumstances, blind chance, caprice and base instincts" are simply taken for granted in Bosnia. A mindless anarchy seems to pervade everything when the bazaar riots against some captured Serbs, brutally torturing and executing some of them in the town square. The third vizier to appear in Travnik, Silikhtar Ali Pasha, makes no pretense of using anything but unbridled terror as his main instrument of policy.

One of Andrić's most common themes involves the various ways human beings attempt either to live with or to escape from the dismal conditions of human life. Desfosses and the Austrian consul's wife try to escape through sexual desire, but their efforts are frustrated by chance and, in the wife's case, by extreme instability. Cologna, physician at the Austrian consulate, converts to Islam to save his wife during the bazaar riots but is found dead the next morning at the base of a cliff. Daville himself attempts to bring order to his life through an epic he is writing about Alexander the Great; he never finishes it because, the narrator implies, he has no roots in this culture and therefore no way to nourish his creativity. Only Daville's happy family life keeps him from losing his reason as the years pass. As he nears the end of his tenure in Travnik (Napoleon has been defeated in Russia and will soon abdicate), he concludes that there is really no such thing as progress in human affairs:

> In reality all roads led one around in a circle. . . . The only things that changed were the men and the generation who travelled the path, forever deluded. . . . One simply went on. The long trek had no point or value, save those we might learn to discover within ourselves along the way. There were no roads, no destinations. One just travelled on . . . spent oneself, and grew weary.

Even though the reader undoubtedly must take Daville as a "chorus" character reflecting Andrić's own views, Daville does not have the last word in the novel. The work begins and ends not with Europeans but with native Bosnians in the small coffeehouses as they assess the import of the events in their region. The narrator shows that, ultimately, the Bosnian people will survive these various foreign occupations, their character having been tested in these trials of the body and spirit. As one of them says to Daville while the latter prepares to leave Bosnia forever: "But we remain, we remember, we keep a tally of all we've been through, of how we have defended and preserved ourselves, and we pass on these dearly bought experiences from father to son." The stream of history carries away much good along with the bad, but their cumulative knowledge has formed the bedrock of the Bosnian character, and they will survive.

The fact that Andrić did not write his first novel until he had more than twenty years' experience with successful short stories meant that *Bosnian Chronicle* emerged as an unusually mature work. One of its weaknesses, however, is the characterization of its protagonist, Jean Daville. Even though the story is narrated from his point of view, he is never as fully developed or as believable as most of the other characters in the novel. The plot also suffers from being too episodic, lacking the sense of direction that a journey, for example, can give an episodic plot. Nevertheless, *Bosnian Chronicle* remains an impressive work, showing Andrić's extraordinary descriptive powers and his great gift for developing a memorable group of characters.

THE BRIDGE ON THE DRINA

Nowhere in Andrić's fiction is the handling of the great flow of history more impressive than in his novel *The Bridge on the Drina*. This work is a marvelous condensation of four centuries of Bosnian culture as acted out in the town of Višegrad and on its bridge across the Drina, linking Bosnia and Serbia, East and West. In its structure, this novel, too, is episodic, a fact that Andrić emphasizes by labeling it a "chronicle." Yet its plot is more successful than that of *Bosnian Chronicle* because the episodes, though they cover many years, are unified by the novel's two great symbols, the bridge and the river. In addition, the author wisely devotes about half of the novel to the fifty-odd years before the destruction of the bridge at the beginning of World War I, the years in which all those things the bridge represents are most severely tested.

The bridge originated in the sixteenth century in the dreams of the grand vizier of the Ottoman Empire, Mehmed Paşha Sokollu. As a young peasant growing up in the nearby Bosnian village of Sokolovići, he had witnessed the horror of children being ferried across the Drina as blood sacrifices for the empire. Later, though he was to serve three sultans for more than sixty years and win battles on three continents, he would still remember his boyhood home by ordering that a bridge be built across the Drina at Višegrad as a way of exorcising his memory of the ferry of death. Ironically, in the first of many arbitrary deaths in the novel, Mehmed Paşha himself is assassinated shortly after the bridge is completed.

The Bridge on the Drina, like all of Andrić's fiction, is filled with memorable characters. Early in the novel there is Abidaga, the ruthless supervisor of construction of the bridge. In what is undoubtedly one of the most horrifying scenes in Western literature, Abidaga catches a young Bosnian attempting to sabotage the project and has him impaled alive on a huge stake. There is Fata Avdagina, the ravishingly beautiful merchant's daughter on her way to a wedding that will join her with a man she does not want to marry. There is Alihodja Mutevelic, the Muslim merchant and cleric whose fate in the last half of the novel personifies that of the bridge and of the Ottoman Empire: He dies gasping on the hill above the town, old and worn out, as the bridge just below him is destroyed by the opening salvos of what will become a world war. He cannot believe that a work made centuries ago for the love of God can be destroyed by human beings. There is Salko Corkan, the one-eyed vagabond who, drunk one night, dares to attempt what no one has before: to walk the ice-covered parapet of the bridge. He succeeds and becomes in later generations part of the folklore of the town. There is Milan Glasicanin, a wealthy young man who cannot stop gambling. One night on the bridge, he meets a mysterious stranger who, in a game of chance, takes him for everything he has. Andrić had a great interest in and respect for the folklore of Bosnia. His merging of history and folklore in *The Bridge on the Drina* is one of the novel's most impressive characteristics.

The symbolic function of the bridge and the river is obvious enough, verging on cliché, yet in Andrić's hands these obvious symbols become profoundly suggestive of what is ephemeral and what is permanent in human life. The river represents, above all, the ceaseless flow of time and history that continually threatens to obliterate all evidence of human effort. The bridge is many things. It is permanence and therefore the opposite of the river: "Its life, though mortal in itself, resembled eternity, for its end could not be perceived." It is the perfect blend of beauty and utility, encouraging and sym-

bolizing the possibilities of endurance: Life is wasted, and life endures. It is a symbol of humankind's great and lasting works, of the finest impulses as expressed in the words of its builder: "the love of God." Like all great works of art, though it is not completely safe from the ravages of time, it remains for generations and centuries to inspire humankind, to provide comfort and constancy in an uncertain universe. The bridge says to human beings that they need not become paralyzed by fear and by change. In this novel, as in Andrić's other fiction, no one can escape the fear and uncertainty that is the human lot, but the bridge enables the reader to perceive those aspects of life in their true proportions. In the end, the people will endure, because the bridge sustains their vision as well as their commerce.

THE WOMAN FROM SARAJEVO

Ivo Andrić's achievement in the novels written during World War II is all the more remarkable in that the three works he produced are so different in purposes, plots, and settings. In *The Woman from Sarajevo*, instead of the vast canvas of four centuries of history or the political intrigues of diplomats, he concentrates on one ordinary person: a moneylender, Raika Radakovich. "Miss," as she is universally known, lives an outwardly uneventful life, dying old and alone in a Belgrade apartment in 1935. Yet Miss Raika becomes for Andrić an example of how human beings often attempt, unsuccessfully, to fend off the dangers and uncertainties of life. His exploration of the development of her personality from childhood to old age is one of the masterpieces of characterization in world literature.

Miss Raika can deal with life only through an extreme miserliness. For her, thrift is something almost spiritual in character. Her miserliness originates in her youth, when the father whom she idolizes loses everything and dies a pauper. On his deathbed, he tells her she must suppress all love of luxury, "for the habit of thrift should be ruthless, like life itself." Thereafter, as a young woman in Sarajevo, she becomes an extremely shrewd manager of her money, relishing the power that having money to lend gives her over the lives of other people. Money enables her, she believes, to avoid the desperation and unhappiness that she perceives in the eyes of those who come to her to borrow. If through thrift and careful lending she can become a millionaire, only then will she be able to atone for her father's death. She vows never to make his mistakes, such as feeling compassion for or generosity toward another human being. If one has no emotional ties to anyone, then one is not obligated to be compassionate.

The outbreak of World War I seriously threatens Miss Raika's financial situation. Surrounded by people who feel intensely the great social and political changes then taking place in Bosnia and in Eastern Europe, she searches desperately for someone with whom she can have a strictly "business" relationship, but there is no one except the memory of her dead father. Shunned by the town as a "parasite," abandoned by her advisers (who are ruined by the war), unable to lend money at interest, she leaves Sarajevo in 1919 and moves to Belgrade. There, among relatives whom she detests, she resumes her career.

In one of the most revealing episodes in the novel, she repeatedly loans money to a charming young man despite clear evidence of his irresponsibility. The narrator makes the point that because her miserliness never allowed her to develop either knowledge of others or self-knowledge, she cannot prevent herself from making the same mistake again and again. Her last years are increasingly lonely, as money turns out not to be the protection against unhappiness that she had imagined. More and more fearful of robbery, she bars doors and windows to guard her gold. In the powerful last scene of the novel, Miss Raika dies of a heart attack brought on by her irrational fear that every sound she hears is that of a thief breaking in to steal her money.

In this novel, as in his others with much vaster canvases, Andrić's strength is to be able to relate the life of Miss Raika to the historical currents of her time and place. The acid test for Andrić's characters is always how well they can adapt to the constant change and uncertainty that is human life and human history. Miss Raika fails not simply because hoarding money is somehow "wrong" but because, in being a miser, she fails to understand either her own life or the lives of others. There is perhaps also a hint that Miss Raika fails because she represents the decay of the capitalist ethic, which can think of no other response when its values are challenged but to hoard what it has left. More tightly plotted than *Bosnian Chronicle* or *The Bridge on the Drina*, *The*

Woman from Sarajevo is, in its structure and in the characterization of its protagonist, Andrić's most successful novel.

THE VIZIER'S ELEPHANT

In answer to an interviewer's question, Andrić stated that he thought the novella form more congenial to the Yugoslav temperament than the full-length novel. *The Vizier's Elephant*, one of three novellas that Andrić wrote in the first few years after World War II, is based on a kind of folktale that circulated unrecorded in Bosnia during the nineteenth century. The story takes place in Travnik in 1820 (in the same location as, and only a few years later than, *Bosnian Chronicle*). A new vizier, Sayid Ali Jelaludin Pasha, proves to be unusually cruel even for a Turkish imperial official. The Ottoman Empire is decaying in its outlying regions, so the sultan has sent a man known for his viciousness to conquer the anarchic Bosnian nobility. The new vizier has a two-year-old pet elephant that, in its rambunctiousness, destroys the town market, frightens people away, and in general causes havoc in the town. The vizier's retinue makes things worse by punishing anyone who dares to object to the elephant's behavior. Finally, the merchants decide they must act. One of their number, Alyo, volunteers to go see the dreaded vizier about the problem. He is too frightened to go into the palace, however, so instead he fabricates a story about his "visit," claiming that he has told the vizier that the people of the town love the elephant so much, they wish to have more elephants. Finally, the merchants make repeated attempts to poison the beast—attempts that never succeed—until the vizier himself commits suicide when he learns he is to be replaced because his cruelties have created more, not less, anarchy.

As always, Andrić tells an interesting story, but *The Vizier's Elephant* is perhaps his least successful novella, especially in its halting attempts to attach a larger significance to the eccentricities of its characters. The narrator encourages the reader to view the elephant as a symbol of the empire: Causing constant fear and apprehension, behaving in a mindless, destructive way, the elephant is ungainly and out of place in a changing world. Andrić, however, never commits himself completely to this or any other narrative approach. The vizier and Alyo never emerge as more than stereotypes, and Alyo's motives especially are too often left unexplained. The work is less successful in depicting the anguish of human existence than are most of Andrić's stories; the comic effects of the elephant's behavior are not developed enough to make the humor dominant, yet these same comic effects dilute the force of the tragedy that lies behind the vizier's cruelties.

ANIKA'S TIMES

Anika's Times, a novella also published in 1948, is more complex and satisfying than *The Vizier's Elephant*. It is set in the village of Dobrun in two different time periods. The first part concerns Father Vuyadin Porubovich, the Orthodox parish priest, and takes place in the 1870's. After the death of his wife in childbirth, Father Vuyadin gradually loses his grip on reality. He comes to feel enormous disgust for the people whose spiritual needs it is his job to satisfy. His behavior becomes erratic, and he refuses to speak to anyone. Finally, no longer able to stand the strain of his own hypocrisy, he seizes his rifle and fires at some peasants visible from his window. He then flees into the night but is later captured and confined to an insane asylum. How, the narrator asks, is one to explain the priest's behavior?

The narrator's "answer" to this question takes the reader back to the time of Vuyadin's grandparents. The story at this point concerns a beautiful young woman named Anika, her feebleminded brother, Lale, and the various men who cannot resist Anika's charms. She first has an affair with a young man named Mihailo. They break up, and Mihailo takes up with a married woman whose husband he unintentionally helps the wife to murder. Although he returns to Anika in the hope of forgetting his guilt, Mihailo cannot hold her, and she develops into the classic "evil woman," inflaming men and causing them to act like fools. She takes up with Yaksha Porubovich, the future grandfather of Father Vuyadin. This is too much for Yaksha's father, who calls the police to have Anika arrested. Hedo Salko, the chief of police, is reluctant to carry out the order. He believes that no problem is ever solved: "Evil, misfortune and unrest are constant and eternal and . . . nothing concerning them can be changed." On the other hand, he says, "every single problem will somehow be resolved and settled, for nothing in this world is lasting or eternal: The neighbours will make peace, the murderer will either surrender himself or else flee into another district." Because

Salko will not act, the mayor intervenes, but Anika seduces the mayor.

Anika's tangled love affairs now begin to trap her. When she visits a religious festival in Dobrun, huge mobs surround her, and Yaksha's father attempts to shoot her from the same window from which his great-grandson Vuyadin will try to kill the peasants seventy years later. The family steps in, however, and Yaksha's father can only curse Anika from his darkened room. Yaksha himself attempts to kill the mayor in a fit of jealousy, but he fails and flees into the hills. It is here that Andrić shows his supreme skill at managing the climax of a narrative involving many characters. Mihailo reappears, still haunted by the murder of the husband eight years before and convinced that the husband's death foretold his own. No longer able to distinguish Anika from the married woman he had also loved, he goes to her house intending to kill her, but he finds that someone else has already done it and fled. No one is arrested, though it appears that Lale may have been the killer. Yaksha is reconciled with his father, but his father predicts that Anika will poison the town for a century.

Andrić's handling of theme and atmosphere in *Anika's Times* is similar to that in many stories of the American writer Nathaniel Hawthorne. Like Hawthorne, Andrić in this novella is concerned with the ways in which "the sins of the fathers are visited on the sons." He is able to suggest in subtle and complex ways how behavior patterns in the village are constantly changing yet remain fundamentally the same. A number of his characters, even those, such as Salko, who appear only briefly, come vividly alive. Andrić knows how mysterious human behavior can be, and how ambiguous and tentative explanations of it must often remain.

ZEKO

The longest of the three novellas published in 1948, *Zeko* is Andrić's only piece of long fiction concerned with the World War II period in Yugoslav history. It is the story of a meek little man, Isidore Katanich, nicknamed Zeko (meaning "Bunny"), who in the course of his various tribulations comes to understand the meaning of his own and his country's life during the years of depression and war. The other main character aside from Zeko is his domineering wife, Margarita—nicknamed Cobra. She is full of aggressive energy, constantly twitching, with "greedy, mistrustful, deadly eyes." Her occupation is managing the apartment building that she and Zeko own. They have a son, Mihailo, a handsome, egocentric, and entirely shiftless young man without moral values; his nickname is "Tiger." The son and his mother take sides constantly against Zeko, and it is an uneven match: Cobra and Tiger versus Bunny.

There are signs in the book that Andrić intends Zeko's life to parallel and therefore to comment on the development of the Yugoslav people during the twentieth century. Although not strictly speaking an allegory, *Zeko* shows through its protagonist the developing national consciousness and desire for freedom of the South Slavs. Zeko had been a gifted artist, but he lost confidence in himself and went to law school at the time of the Austrian annexation of Bosnia in 1908. When the 1912 Balkan War begins, Zeko joins the army but suffers continually from typhus and is finally forced to return home. He marries Margarita, but World War I intervenes. He returns home in 1919 to find his wife a horrible shrew. He hears rumors that Mihailo was fathered by someone else while he was away at war, but he cannot establish the truth or falsehood of the rumor. "Everything around him was changed, turbulent, shattered . . . this was a time of fatigue and of the acceptance of half-truths." As the years go on, Zeko is increasingly desperate to find a way out of his marriage (his years with Margarita corresponding to the years of the "marriage" of the Serbs, Croats, and Slovenes in the Kingdom of Yugoslavia—that is, 1919 to 1941).

Zeko finds several forms of escape. He associates more and more with his sister-in-law and her family, and he discovers the subculture of those who live on and by the Sava River. Their lives are uncertain and dangerous—what the narrator calls "the true life of most people." Zeko does manage to find true peace and acceptance among these "strenuous, unsettled lives, full of uncertainty, where efforts invested in work were out of proportion to the rewards." The members of his sister-in-law's family become Communists, and, symbolically, as it were, Zeko gravitates increasingly toward their values, away from the greed and selfishness of his capitalistic wife and son. Zeko becomes, then, a true man of the people and, in embracing their fate and their future, finds meaning for his own life.

With the coming of Adolf Hitler's invasion, Cobra and Tiger, because of their fear and lack of self-knowledge, do not have the inner resources necessary to withstand the despair of war. Zeko, however, does: Becoming more aware of the need for meaningful action, he is less tempted to hide from conflict, as he had done on the river: "The most important thing was to do away, once and for all, with a barren and undignified life, and to walk and live like a man." Like Yugoslavia itself, Zeko learns the value of independence. He finally joins the Partisans (Tito's anti-Nazi guerrilla organization) while his wife and son, finding it difficult to orient themselves amid the suffering of war, flee Belgrade and disappear. On Zeko's first mission against the Germans, he is caught in an ambush and, attempting to flee, drowns in the Sava River. Zeko's death is not a defeat, however, for, like his country, he was finally learning how to live with dignity; like his country, he had finally decided what creed he would follow.

One of the chief virtues of *Zeko* is that Andrić allows the parallels between Zeko and Yugoslavia to resonate within the story without ever forcing them on the reader. The other main characters have a vividness that prevents them from fading into stereotypes. The gradual awakening of Zeko's consciousness is portrayed with much of the same skill that Andrić displayed in the characterization of Miss Raika in *The Woman from Sarajevo*.

DEVIL'S YARD

If each of Andrić's novels and novellas employs important images representing the dangers and uncertainties characteristic of human life, in his last novella, *Devil's Yard*, such an image for the human condition comes to dominate everything in the story: Devil's Yard, the notorious prison in Istanbul under the Ottoman Empire. One can be thrown into this prison on suspicion of almost anything, on the principle that it is easier to release a man who has been proved innocent than to track down one who has been proved guilty. The inmates are mostly the weak, the poor, the desperate of society. In Devil's Yard (and in roughly the first half of the novella), the dominant character is the warden, Karadjos. His name means "shadow show," and he will appear anywhere in the prison without warning, trying to trick or frighten a confession out of a prisoner. He is overweight, horribly ugly, with a powerful, piercing eye. His governing principle is that, because everyone is guilty of something, everyone who ends up in Devil's Yard belongs there, whether guilty or not of the particular crime with which he is charged.

In *Devil's Yard*, the prison is a metaphor for human life, with Karadjos as its "god," or fate. He is inscrutable, unpredictable, and tyrannical. In addition to the constant fear felt by the inmates, there is the constant mingling of truth, half-truth, and falsehood that, according to Andrić, is a basic characteristic of human existence. Karadjos fosters this climate of rumor and suspicion with an endless series of threats, cajolery, incredible jokes, and surprise remarks. The prisoners "complained about him the way one complains about one's life and curses one's destiny. Their own damnation had involved them with him. Therefore, despite their fear and hate, they had grown to be one with him and it would have been hard for them to imagine life without him."

Devil's Yard is Andrić's only piece of long fiction told as a story within a story (in fact, it includes several stories within stories). This technique, which Andrić handles with great ease, seems meant to reinforce the notion that in life itself there are layers of truths, half-truths, and falsehoods among which one must try to distinguish. The outermost frame of the story concerns a young monk: He is helping sort through the effects of another monk named Brother Petar, who has recently died. As the young monk does so, he recalls Brother Petar's story of having once been held for several months in Devil's Yard while on a visit to Istanbul. The next frame is that of Brother Petar narrating his stay in the prison. While there, he meets a young, educated Turk, Djamil Effendi. The story of Djamil's life is actually narrated by Haim, a depressed, apprehensive, and talkative Jew from Smyrna. Haim has "a passion for narrating and explaining everything, for exposing all the errors and follies of mankind." The story he tells of Djamil's life, although at times incredible, has a ring of truth about it simply because its teller has such a passion for the truth, or at least for detail.

It seems that Djamil has studied the history of the Turkish Empire to the point where he has begun to imagine himself one of its ill-fated sultans—Djem Sultan, who in the late fifteenth century was bested in a struggle for the throne by his brother. When Djamil himself returns to the prison yard after several days' interrogation, he tells Petar the story of Djem Sultan. Djamil's story of Djem Sultan is the innermost tale in this intricately narrated novella. He has been confined in Devil's Yard because his complete identification with Djem Sultan bears an uncomfortably close resemblance to the life of the current sultan, whose own throne is threatened by his own brother. Djamil thus seems to illustrate the danger of people accepting too completely the accounts of their own history and therefore the meaning of their lives as embodied in that history. Djamil finally disappears, and the very mystery of his fate—Is he free? Was he murdered? Is he confined in a hospital for the insane?—only underlines the confusion that passes for human knowledge.

As his imprisonment drags on, apparently for no reason except the arbitrary will of some higher authority, Brother Petar realizes that he is becoming irrational. He cannot find anyone whose talk seems sane. The brutal Karadjos has dominated the first half of the novella, and Djamil Effendi, equally irrational, has dominated the second half. Under their influence, Brother Petar could not have retained his own sanity had he remained in prison much longer. Like most of Andrić's protagonists, Brother Petar has had to spend all of his energy simply to escape madness and despair. When the first narrator, the young monk, resumes his own tale at the end of *Devil's Yard*, he is forced out of his reverie by the "dull clang of metal objects thrown on the pile" of Petar's earthly possessions. This is a "reality" that the reader views in a light far different from that of any earlier impression.

There is no use pretending that Andrić was an optimist about the human condition. His impressive accomplishments in the novel and the novella hinge on other things: an impeccable style; a depth of insight into human motivation almost unmatched in Western literature; a profound sympathy for the sufferings of his characters; vivid dramatization of the ethnic character of his province, built up over the centuries against oppression and civil war; and, perhaps most important, an ability to turn local history into universal symbols, so that readers knowing nothing of Bosnia can see in his fiction the common lot of humankind.

Mark Minor

OTHER MAJOR WORKS

SHORT FICTION: *Pripovetke*, 1924, 1931, 1936; *Nove pripovetke*, 1948; *Odabrane pripovetke*, 1954, 1956; *Panorama*, 1958; *The Pasha's Concubine, and Other Tales*, 1968.

POETRY: *Ex Ponto*, 1918; *Nemiri*, 1920; *Šta sanjam i šta mi se dogadja*, 1976.

NONFICTION: *Die Entwicklung des geistigen Lebens in Bosnien unter der Einwirkung der türkischen Herrschaft*, 1924 (*The Development of Spiritual Life in Bosnia Under the Influence of Turkish Rule*, 1990); *Zapisi o Goji*, 1961; *Letters*, 1984.

MISCELLANEOUS: *Sabrana dela*, 1963.

BIBLIOGRAPHY

Hawkesworth, Celia. "Ivo Andrić as Red Rag and Political Football." *Slavonic and East European Review* 80, no. 2 (April, 2002): 201. Hawkesworth, who has written extensively on Serbo-Croatian literature and translated Andrić's books, profiles the author, discussing the content and interpretation of his works and his educational and career background. Also addresses Bosnian nationals' criticisms of his fiction for its portrayal of Muslim characters.

_____. *Ivo Andrić: Bridge Between East and West*. London: Atholone Press, 1984. Provides a comprehensive introduction to Andrić's work, including verse, short stories, novels, essays, and other prose. Includes notes on the pronunciation of Serbo-Croatian names and a bibliography.

Juričič, Želimir B. *The Man and the Artist: Essays on Ivo Andrić*. Lanham, Md.: University Press of America, 1986. The first book on Andrić written in English offers an insightful analysis into his personal life, describing how his fiction reflects his experiences as a young man.

Mukerji, Vanita Singh. *Ivo Andrić: A Critical Biography*. Jefferson, N.C.: McFarland, 1990. Often cited along with Hawkesworth's book *Ivo Andrić: Bridge Between East and West* as providing the best biographical and critical introduction to the author. Includes biography and index.

Sendich, Munir. "English Translations of Ivo Andrić's *Travnicka hronika*." *Canadian Slavonic Papers* 40 (September-December, 1998): 379-400. Analyzes *Bosnian Chronicle* by closely examining various English-language translations of the work. Describes some of the difficulties involved in translating Serbo-Croatian and the "Turkisms" in the original text.

Talmor, Sascha. "Europe Ends at Travnik: Ivo Andrić's *Bosnian Chronicle*." *European Legacy* 3, no. 1 (February, 1998): 84. Discusses *Bosnian Chronicle*, focusing on how the novel's account of political conflict and warfare in that region in the nineteenth century could help readers understand the causes of the ethnic and political war that was waged in Yugoslavia in the 1990's.

Vucinich, Wayne S., ed. *Ivo Andrić Revisited: The Bridge Still Stands*. Berkeley: University of California Press, 1995. Collection of essays includes discussion of Andrić and his times, his short stories, his views of Yugoslavia and of history, Bosnian identity in his work, and his handling of grief and shame, women, the folk tradition, and narrative voice. Vucinich's introduction is a good place to begin a study of Andrić's role in the history of Yugoslavia and its literary traditions.

Wachtel, Andrew B. "Ivan Meštovič, Ivo Andrić, and the Synthetic Yugoslav Culture of the Interwar Period." In *Yugoslavism: Histories of a Failed Idea, 1918-1992*, edited by Dejan Djokič. London: Hurst, 2003. Essay about Andrić is part of an examination of Yugoslavian history, from the country's creation in 1918 to its dissolution in the early 1990's. The collection as a whole demonstrates how the concept of "Yugoslavia" differed at various times and was interpreted differently among the various Yugoslavian nations, leaders, and social groups.

AHARON APPELFELD

Born: Czernowitz, Romania (now Chernovtsy, Ukraine); February 16, 1932

PRINCIPAL LONG FICTION

Ke-ishon ha-'ayin, 1972

Badenheim, 'ir nofesh, 1975 (*Badenheim 1939*, 1980)

Tor ha-pela'ot, 1978 (*The Age of Wonders*, 1981)

Kutonet veha-pasim, 1983 (*Tzili: The Story of a Life*, 1983)

Nesiga mislat, 1984 (*The Retreat*, 1984)

Be-'et uve-'onah ahat, 1985 (*The Healer*, 1990)

To the Land of the Cattails, 1986 (also known as *To the Land of the Reeds*)

Al kol hapesha'im, 1987 (*For Every Sin*, 1989)

Bartfus ben ha-almavet, 1988 (*The Immortal Bartfuss*, 1988)

Katerinah, 1989 (*Katerina*, 1992)

Mesilat barzel, 1991 (*The Iron Tracks*, 1998)

Timyon, 1993 (*The Conversion*, 1998)

Layish, 1994

Unto the Soul, 1994

'Ad she-ya'aleh 'amud ha-shahar, 1995

Mikhreh ha-kerah, 1997

Kol asher ahavti, 1999 (*All Whom I Have Loved*, 2006)

Masa' el ha-horef, 2000

Polin erets yerukah, 2005 (*Poland, a Green Country*, 2005)

Pirhe ha-afelah, 2006 (*Blooms of Darkness*, 2006)

OTHER LITERARY FORMS

Aharon Appelfeld's writing career began with poetry published in the 1950's and progressed through short stories to novellas and longer fiction. He has been a prolific writer in Hebrew of countless poems, hundreds of stories, and more than twenty volumes of fiction and essays. Many of his short stories have been published in English-language periodicals, and one collection is available in English, *In the Wilderness* (1965). Like his longer fiction, Appelfeld's short stories revolve princi-

pally around the events preceding and following the Holocaust and deal in large part with Jews separated from the mainstream who manage to maintain themselves in a non-Jewish world. Prominently mentioned in significant discussions of his work are the stories "Berta," "The Journey," "The Betrayal," "The Pilgrimage to Kazansk," "Regina," "Kitty," and "1946."

ACHIEVEMENTS

Although Aharon Appelfeld has been published since the 1950's and emerged in the 1960's as a leading Israeli writer, it was only in the 1980's that his genius was recognized outside Israel, with the publication of several of his novels in English. Prior to that time, however, he had been recognized with several major Israeli awards, including one for his poetry in 1960 and the Bialik Prize in 1978. He was also the recipient of the Israel Prize for Literature in 1983 and the National Jewish Book Award for fiction in 1989. His autobiography *The Story of a Life* (2004) was awarded the Prix Médicis in France, and in 2005 Appelfeld received the Nelly Sachs Prize, a literary award presented every two years by the German city of Dortmund.

Most critics writing in English have concentrated on Appelfeld's reputation as one of the great voices of the Holocaust (Alan Mintz asserts that "Greenberg and Appelfeld are the two great writers of the Holocaust in Hebrew literature") and on his writing techniques of simplicity and understatement and their relationship to the techniques of Franz Kafka. Appelfeld himself has commented on these evaluations of his work, disagreeing in part with both: "I am not writing what is called 'Holocaust literature.' . . . I'm just telling stories about Jews—to Jews—at a certain period in their history. . . . If my work has echoes of both *Kohelet* [Ecclesiastes] and Kafka, that's because I see them both in the tradition of Jewish minimalist literature." Appelfeld's writing achievements are perhaps characterized better by Irving Howe: "No one surpasses Aharon Appelfeld in portraying the crisis of European civilization both before and after the Second World War. . . . He is one of the best novelists alive."

BIOGRAPHY

Aharon Appelfeld was born in Czernowitz, Bukovina, Romania, in 1932, into an assimilated Jewish family whose language of choice was German. When Appelfeld was eight, he and his family were removed from their environment. His mother was taken by the Nazis, and he was separated from the rest of his family and shipped to a concentration camp in Transnistria, from which he escaped. After three perilous years of wandering through the forests of Eastern Europe with temporary stays with various refugees along the way, he joined the Russian army in 1944, at age eleven, in the Ukraine as a field cook. At twelve, Appelfeld joined a gang of war orphans who made their way south, living off the land. He was the youngest member and was to remain in touch with others of the gang. Upon their arrival in Italy, the gang members were befriended by a priest and lived for a time at his church, singing in the choir. After this interlude, the gang went on to Naples, where they met a Youth Aliya group and were persuaded to go to Israel. Appelfeld has related that the gang's last night in Naples was spent at a brothel, where he sat up all night in a chair.

After his arrival in Israel in 1947, Appelfeld began writing poetry in his newly acquired language, Hebrew. The Jerusalem editor to whom he sent his poetry corrected it and rejected it for three years, after which time the editor instructed the poet not to send him any more poetry until he learned to write Hebrew. Ten years later, in 1960, Appelfeld has noted, he received an award for his poetry, the award named after the same editor, who had recently died.

In 1962, Appelfeld's first short-story collection was published by an eccentric publisher who had not read the material but liked the author's looks. The book, although not distributed to bookstores initially, enjoyed critical acclaim and started Appelfeld's literary career as a short-story writer and novelist. A graduate of Hebrew University in Jerusalem, Appelfeld teaches Hebrew literature at Ben Gurion University of the Negev in Beersheba, Israel, and makes his home in a suburb of Jerusalem.

ANALYSIS

Careful analysis of Aharon Appelfeld's writing suggests that his works consist of detailing different elements of one story, his own story. The seemingly auto-biographical aspects of these novels, however, reveal Appelfeld's unusual ability to retell visions and motifs in ever-changing and fascinating literary hues and designs. Appelfeld himself has said,

> It's usually pointed out that I draw on my own experience for my stories and novels. I acknowledge that. Yet I have no interest in writing autobiography. . . . Memory can't create a story; the author must. So I objectify my own experience by recreating it in the stories of others.

As noted above, critics have also referred to Appelfeld as one of the great producers of Holocaust literature. Although accurate, that judgment is ironic, for Appelfeld never specifically names or addresses events of the Holocaust in his writing. Nevertheless, in his sparsely written recounting of the pre-Holocaust period, the author evokes the horrors to come by stirring the memories and imagination of those who read with a historical perspective. In like manner, in his stories about those who sur-

Aharon Appelfeld. (© Jerry Bauer)

vived the years of hiding or after being "sucked into" railroad cars, both recurring motifs in Appelfeld's works, he forces the reader's imagination to develop the pictures he never paints but that are responsible for the broken, imperfect souls of the post-Holocaust experience. Appelfeld himself has spoken of this technique: "You can never understand the meaning of the Holocaust. You can just come to the edges of it. If you wrote about it directly, you'd end up trivializing it."

The novels discussed below, in fact, can be placed into two simple categories: those that describe pre-Holocaust European Jewish society and begin and end with no hope for the future (*Badenheim 1939* and *The Retreat*) and those that seem to indicate that the return to roots, the finding of the true secrets of Jewishness, permits the survival of youth into the post-Holocaust period (*The Age of Wonders, Tzili, To the Land of the Cattails*). All these novels share a common base of retold experience, literary techniques, motifs, themes, and symbols, woven into magic by a masterful storyteller. The retold experience is Appelfeld's own life and its connection with the Holocaust. Although, as stated earlier, the Holocaust is never named and its too-familiar scenes of horror are never drawn, the dreamlike superimposition of allegory and realism immerses the reader in visions of impending horror. The reader's historical memory and imagination fill in what Appelfeld's novels do not provide, especially since the understated, simple, spare, and matter-of-fact text demands these additions.

Appelfeld's images and themes are recurrent. The most devastating images recall, with chilling understatement and deceptively simple, direct language, the naïve willingness of European Jews to accept resignedly the events, indignities, and humiliations that preceded the Holocaust, and their destructive self-abnegation and anti-Jewish behavior. Appelfeld accents these characteristics by emphasizing stereotypical differences between pre-Holocaust Jews and non-Jews. Jews were timid figures whose long faces were pale from lack of outdoor activity and whose bodies were undeveloped by physical exercise. On the one hand were the intellectual Jews who had assimilated into Western European culture, abandoning their traditions and the Yiddish language; on the other hand were the *Ostjuden* (Jews from the east, Poland in particular), who lacked refinement and who were

known for their single-minded pursuit of mercantile occupations and their observance of traditional ways. The two groups disliked each other intensely. Travel, trains, disdaining intellectuals, culpable *Ostjuden*, forests, abandoned children, lost mothers, ugly fathers, unpleasant Jewish characteristics, and the coarse, peasantlike behavior of non-Jews—these are the recurring motifs that Appelfeld weaves into an allegorical but realistic fictional world that intensifies the reader's vision of the Holocaust. These recurrent themes testify to the ugliness of prewar Jewish society, its emphasis on assimilation and self-hate, its rejection of the essence of Judaism, its inability to "raise a hand" against its oppressors. Opposed to this are the themes of inner peace, salvation, and even survival achieved through the finding and acceptance of the secrets of basic Judaism.

Recurrent symbols and motifs include forests and nature—havens in Appelfeld's own life, symbolizing peace and safety. Trains and other forms of transportation, by contrast, lead to uncertain destinations usually invoking premonitions of the impending Holocaust. Love of books and humanizing education, as opposed to rigidly enforced study in the Austrian *gymnasium*, indicate characters' acceptance of Judaism and humanism, whereas descriptions of people eating usually indicate coarse, peasantlike cruelty to man and beast and are associated with non-Jews.

Although the novels discussed here are based on retold experience and recurrent themes, symbols, and motifs, each also presents a different view of the same problems, thus affording a multifaceted, in-depth analysis of factors preceding the Holocaust. Although readers can share Appelfeld's stories, they are also left to complete them and draw their own conclusions.

BADENHEIM 1939

Badenheim 1939, the first of Appelfeld's novels to be translated into English, recounts with chillingly understated simplicity the naïve response by a broad spectrum of Jews to unmistakable warning signals just prior to the Holocaust. By not using historical terminology for the victims, the victimizers, or the impending events, Appelfeld increases the horror of his story: The reader is wrenched by historical knowledge of the impending disaster posed against the unawareness of the victims and their almost giddy efforts to ignore what is clear.

The book opens in 1939 as the Austrian resort town of Badenheim slips from sluggish winter into tentative spring, bringing with it a mélange of sybaritic visitors who wait for the entertainment to begin. Dr. Pappenheim, the "impresario," is responsible for providing summer-long entertainment for the guests, many of whom are regulars at Badenheim. To introduce his major theme of willful Holocaust unawareness, Appelfeld introduces the character of Trude, wife of the pharmacist. Like an unwelcome Elijah, Trude is consumed by what the others view as a manic-depressive illness that allows her no peace, as she is obsessed by her vision of a "transparent . . . poisoned and diseased world" in which her absent daughter is "captive and abused" by her non-Jewish husband. She also describes the resort-goers as "patients in a sanitorium."

Additional disharmonies surface when Dr. Pappenheim is disappointed by the musicians' greed and he himself displays melancholic longing for his *Ostjuden* Polish roots. Even more ominous is the increasingly authoritative role taken by the Sanitation Department, which "took measurements, put up fences and planted flags" as "porters unloaded rolls of barbed wire, cement pillars, and all kinds of appliances." Characteristically, the naïve vacationers interpret these preparations as signs of a particularly successful summer festival; otherwise, "why would the Sanitation Department be going to all this trouble?" The palpably clear answer is accentuated by the appearance of the twin performers, "tall, thin and monkish," whose forte is the death poetry of Rainer Maria Rilke and who "rehearsed all the time with morbid melody throbbing in their voices."

The themes of assimilation and levels of Jewishness surface when a "modest announcement" appears on the notice board, saying that all citizens who are Jews must register with the Sanitation Department by the end of the month. Heated discussions among the guests about who must comply, based upon class distinctions that elevate the importance of Austrian Jews and denigrate the *Ostjuden*, increase strife.

All the while, the Sanitation Department has continued its work. It now holds detailed records of each person's heritage and begins to display inviting posters of Poland. Concurrently, the department prohibits access to or exit from the town, stops all incoming and outgoing

mail, and closes the resort pool. As fear and despair begin to envelop the people, "an alien orange shadow gnawed stealthily at the geranium leaves," and the Jews are put into quarantine.

What has been considered up to this time as disease or infection, an unnamed fear in some hearts such as Trude's, becomes real. Delusions disappear and weaker people ignore basic social rules as they loot the pharmacy and consume all the food. The musicians steal the hotel dishes, and even the dogs become uncontrollable. At the same time, another force begins to operate in the face of chaos. With the common experience of deprivation and fear of the unknown future, the edges of dissension among the people start to smooth and closer common bonds draw the captives together.

Badenheim 1939 ends with the recurring Appelfeld image of trains and journeys signaling a hopeless future. Still uncomprehending, the victims refuse to recognize the facts, clinging to the illusion that deportation to Poland is only a "transition." Old and young Austrian Jews, *Ostjuden*, and those who are part Jewish are "all sucked in as easily as grains of wheat poured into a funnel [into] four filthy freight cars." The last irony is voiced by Dr. Pappenheim, who observes, "If the coaches are so dirty it must mean that we have not far to go."

THE AGE OF WONDERS

Badenheim 1939 re-creates Appelfeld's memory of the European pre-Holocaust world, but the narrator's voice is objective; the characters in this novel cannot be linked directly with Appelfeld or with those around him. *The Age of Wonders*, Appelfeld's second book in English translation, on the other hand appears to be closer to fictionalized biography; in it Appelfeld's own feelings are more visible. *The Age of Wonders* also affords the reader a view of both the pre-Holocaust and the post-Holocaust periods, and as a result it is a more complete and stronger novel than its predecessor.

In the first part of *The Age of Wonders*, the "ugly orange fog" felt in *Badenheim 1939* is an omnipresent, identifiable antagonist. The viscous, threatening suffocator of the pleasure-seeking vacationers in Badenheim is a major character in *The Age of Wonders* as it envelops and destroys Austrian-Jewish lives in pre-Holocaust Vienna. Repeated evocations of Jewish decadence prior to the war enforce the realization that the horror could perhaps have been averted had the Jews reversed the course of assimilation and self-hatred.

The three-year prewar history of a doomed intellectual family in Vienna is reviewed and dispassionately related by the only child, whose name, Bruno, is not revealed until the second part of the book. The action begins with the mother and Bruno traveling by train from their last carefree summer vacation in a forested, "little known retreat." The first clear indication of the impending Holocaust comes when all the passengers who are non-Christian by birth are commanded to leave the train and register during an unscheduled stop at an old sawmill.

Appelfeld's recurring theme of Jewish alienation from Jews is introduced when Bruno's relatives come to celebrate his eleventh birthday. Cousin Charlotte, who has been fired from her position as an actor with the National Company, represents the reality of Jews being ostracized from the Austrian culture and also Jewish self-delusion (she acts foreign roles). Uncle Carl Landman, an attorney, expresses his outrage at Jewish "vulgarity"; some Jews refuse the customs of the prevailing culture. Bruno's Uncle Salo represents the Jewish merchant who flirts with Gentile women and is despised by the intellectuals, such as Landman and Bruno's father. The party ends with bitter debate about what Jewish life should be and displays of hate among the guests; the gathering represents a microcosm of Jewish life before the Holocaust and seems to indicate that Appelfeld sees these divisions as a precursor to the Holocaust.

Bruno's father, a nationally known and acclaimed author/intellectual, despises observant Jews and the *Ostjuden* entrepreneurs, whom he charges with "dark avarice" and whom he believes "should be wiped off the face of the earth, because they ruin everything they touch." Speaking of his own heritage, he says, "My Jewishness means nothing to me." Ironically, the father's anti-Semitism, which is a theme in his own works, is used against him by another, similarly minded Jew. Michael Taucher destroys the author's reputation and career via repeated attacks in the press. Supported by non-Jewish editors who allow Taucher all the space he can fill, the critic finally writes, about Bruno's father, "the Jewish parasite must be weeded out," and then, having served his purpose, he himself disappears.

Another important thread that unwinds as months go by is the high attrition rate among traditionally observant Jews, as the older generation dies off and the younger traditionalists feel the scorn of their contemporaries. When Bruno's Aunt Gusta dies and is buried according to traditional Jewish rites, Bruno describes the scene as "ugly and shameful."

Kurt Stark, a sculptor and longtime friend of Bruno's father, illustrates the almost militant Jewish opposition to the contemporary traditionalists who wanted to preserve religious observance and practices. In a theme shown in several of Appelfeld's works, notably *To the Land of the Cattails*, Stark, the son of a Jewish mother and an Aryan father, seeks refuge from his "tortured [and] cruel perplexities" by conversion to Judaism. In spite of all the difficult hurdles, Stark reaches his goal, but he and his life are horribly altered. After his circumcision, he barely exists in the Paul Gottesman Almshouse for Jews, a dreadful place devoid of spiritual or physical beauty and inhabited by old, dying men. Stark has become a stereotypical Appelfeld Jew—retiring, weak, pale, and unhealthy—whereas before his conversion he had been the stereotypical Aryan—strong, robust, and physically aggressive.

With the family's growing sense of isolation and their increasingly frequent contacts with homeless, dispossessed Jews, Bruno's father seeks escape by appealing to non-Jewish friends. He is representative of the male characters in Appelfeld's works, most of whom are neither strong nor admirable. Bruno's mother, on the other hand, like Tzili in *Tzili* and Toni and Arna in *To the Land of the Cattails*, gathers strength and courage to do what she can to maintain order, even after her husband abandons the family and escapes to Vienna and a non-Jewish woman. In one of the most violent scenes in Appelfeld's fiction available in English, all of the town's Jews are herded into and locked in the synagogue, where the frenzied prisoners decide that the rabbi, who represents Judaism, is the source of their misery and beat him almost to death.

Book 1 of *The Age of Wonders* shares the hopelessness of *Badenheim 1939* but appears to place the blame for the coming disaster on the Jewish people themselves, their assimilation, and their self-chosen alienation from Judaism. In Bruno and his family can be seen the autobiographical elements of Appelfeld's own separation from mother and father prior to the Holocaust, and the images of Bruno's summer vacations in the forest as restorative and saving are unmistakably autobiographical.

The darkness of book 1 is mitigated by book 2, which introduces hope through survival. Book 2 takes up the same motif with which book 1 begins and ends: Bruno is again on a train, but now he is alone, returning thirty years later to the town of his birth, Knospen, Austria. Bruno comes back with memories of the war years mentioned only in reference to towns—Auschwitz and Thereisenstadt—with the burden of a wife and a failing marriage in Jerusalem, and with an inherited and continuing dislike of Jews as part of his emotional foundation. Although his reason for returning is unclear to both Bruno and the reader, what Bruno experiences is depressingly morbid. Bruno finds only the memories of his town of birth and revisited aspects of the countryside pleasant. In contrast, memories of people and places such as school, perhaps some of them once pleasant, become unwholesome and diseased in revisitation.

The Henrietta Bar, which Bruno frequents and leaves "dull with drink," reveals unpleasant postwar realities. As bizarre as the four swarthy Singapore midgets who entertain bar patrons, not with their talent but with their freakish appearance and wild dancing, are the strange, half-breed waitress and her friends, half-Jewish misfits who have no real identity or past other than their existence. Among these Bruno discovers a half cousin, a bastard daughter of his Uncle Salo. Finally, he confronts old Brum, a prototype of prewar denial and cowardice who echoes Bruno's father. Demanding that Bruno leave because he is stirring up "evil spirits . . . Jews again . . . the old nightmare," Brum arouses unexpected violence in Bruno by stating, "My hatred for Jews knows no bounds." Bruno hits the Jewish anti-Semite in the face and displays no emotion except vengeance as the old man, a both real and symbolic specter of the past, lies bleeding on the ground.

Never going back to see what happens to Brum, Bruno quietly leaves town early the next morning. The phrase "It's all over" echoes in his mind as epiphany relieves Bruno of a heavy emotional burden. Ironically, even though the Jews Bruno meets on his return initially

repel him, he becomes increasingly tolerant of their weaknesses. In a total reversal, Bruno becomes violent against the disease of prewar Jews—the same one he himself had displayed—Jewish anti-Semitism.

Unlike *Badenheim 1939*, *The Age of Wonders* reflects hope and rebirth after death. Bruno, by surviving and returning to his roots, finds truth and reaffirms the faith of his long-dead Aunt Gusta. He becomes a vibrant, unafraid, and robust Jew. The antithesis of prewar stereotypical Jews who hated themselves, their heritage, and would not raise their hands against attack, Bruno undergoes conversion and remains strong and vital.

TZILI

Appelfeld's third novel to appear in English translation, *Tzili*, continues in the pattern of *The Age of Wonders* with a strong autobiographical element, pre- and post-Holocaust segments, and the tempering of pessimism by the survival of youth. Appelfeld's use of allegory in *Tzili* sets it apart from his other novels. The minimalist approach places an even greater responsibility on the reader to interpret meaning while multiple levels of interpretation are added to each word and scene. This approach makes *Tzili* possibly the most rewarding reading of the novels discussed here.

As a young child, Tzili is ignored by her invalid father and shopkeeper mother and is left during summer days to sit alone behind the shop in the dirt and ashes. Feebleminded and unable to learn when she is finally sent to school at age seven, Tzili is scolded by her parents, who are extremely anxious that their children attain high academic goals, and she is ridiculed by her Gentile classmates, who are particularly gleeful at the spectacle of a Jewish child who cannot learn. The parents engage an old Jewish tutor to instruct their youngest child in Jewish customs and laws, but Tzili can manage only to repeat the Judaic formulas drilled into her by rote. Her tutor appreciates the irony, wondering "why it had fallen to the lot of this dull child to keep the spark [of Judaism] alive." Indeed, only the tutor's visits keep the child from total wretchedness. Unintentionally, as a last resort, her parents have unwittingly provided Tzili with the source of her future salvation as well as her present strength—a strong faith.

When troops appear just outside town, the family deserts Tzili; after charging her to "take care of the property," the rest of them flee to what they mistakenly believe will be safety. Tzili survives an undescribed night of massacre, but her family is never mentioned again. Indeed, Tzili repeatedly escapes death as if she were divinely protected. In a long, circular journey that never takes her far from her birthplace, Tzili moves from childhood to young adulthood. Her survival is both a celebration of indomitable human courage and an allegorical reference to the undying spirit of Judaism, as she survives as if by miracles a series of deadly episodes during the Holocaust years.

When the war ends, Tzili is fifteen, pregnant, and abandoned by her lover-companion, Mark. She falls into the company of liberated but disturbingly petty, quarreling Jews. They ignore Tzili's pain and their own as they travel, but, surprisingly, when Tzili's fragile condition prevents her from keeping up with the group, a fat, former cabaret dancer demands that the group stop for the girl, and they do. A stretcher is constructed, upon which Tzili is carried aloft for the rest of the long journey amid "a rousing sound, like pent-up water bursting from a dam." The stretcher bearers are joined by the entire group, who roar, "We are the torch bearers." Tzili, symbol of the Jewish spark noted by her former tutor, unites the group, gives them strong purpose, and helps them survive. Tzili's destiny ultimately leads her aboard a ship bound for Palestine, perhaps with others of the group. While the fate of her assimilated parents and intellectually superior siblings is unknown, the "chosen" child is saved for entrance to the Chosen Land, Palestine.

THE RETREAT

In *The Retreat*, except for the restorative nature of the forest and other recurring motifs, Appelfeld seems to eliminate the strong autobiographical elements seen in *The Age of Wonders*, *Tzili*, and *To the Land of the Cattails* as well as their theme of youth and survival. Instead, this book is an echo of *Badenheim 1939*, concentrating, in a very different environment, on the ugliness of the pre-Holocaust Jewish milieu and the assimilation and breakdown of Jews and their community because of self-hatred. There is no hint of a future, no youth present who, like Tzili, can be viewed as a living symbol of the enduring spirit of Judaism. The chilling shadow of the Holocaust comes closer as the narrative continues, and the only hope offered is that the Jews in the Retreat, an iso-

lated mountaintop house that has been established as an "Institute for Advanced Study," will help one another and will not abandon anyone; in a time of extremes, they discover that they need one another for support and comfort.

Lotte Schloss, the novel's protagonist, is the listener among the other castoffs at the Retreat; she is a prototype of the metamorphosis and becomes an important part of the group's final support system. The "great Balaban," founder of the institute, envisions his Retreat as a place where Jews can learn to divest themselves of their ugly Jewish characteristics and become more like the Gentiles around them. Thwarted in this goal, Balaban dies unmourned, but ironically he has prepared the members of the group to shift for themselves, help one another, and therefore survive.

At the end of *The Retreat* a faint glimmer of hope for survival through unity appears, but Appelfeld destroys any possibility of salvation: "At night, of course, people were afraid. But they helped one another. If a man fell or was beaten, he was not abandoned." Unity is all the group has.

TO THE LAND OF THE CATTAILS

Appelfeld returns to autobiographical material in his fifth novel published in English, *To the Land of the Cattails*. Its blend of allegory and realism explores what Appelfeld has called a "a love story between a mother and a son," and it ends, as did Appelfeld's own childhood, with the mother lost and leaving her son to find his own way to Jewishness. Although this narrative ends before the Holocaust is at its height, it shares with *The Age of Wonders* and *Tzili* a sense of fulfillment in the characters' acceptance of their Jewishness, and it marks a further development of Appelfeld's almost mystical ability to evoke the Holocaust while never naming it or describing it concretely.

To the Land of the Cattails, interspersing flashbacks and current happenings, recounts a two-year journey during which the two major characters undergo dramatic metamorphoses. In the autumn of 1938, thirty-four-year-old Toni Strauss (née Rosenfeld) and her fifteen-year-old son, Rudi, begin a long journey by horse and carriage from the bustling city of Vienna back to the mother's birthplace of Dratscincz, Bukovina, on the river Prut. Rudi resembles his father, a Gentile "through and through," in appearance and interests. Toni is fearful lest her son also become callous and brutal and abandon her, as his father had fourteen years earlier. She therefore resolves to return to her parents, whom she has not seen since she eloped at seventeen with August Strauss, a Gentile. In addition to fulfilling her own yearning to return from exile, Toni also has a "strong wish for [Rudi] to be Jewish."

Although Rudi considers himself a Jew, Toni tells him at the beginning of their journey, "Certainly you are a Jew, but you need a few more things, not many, not difficult . . . you are a Jew in every fibre of your being. And here, in these regions, you will learn the secret easily." Thus the story of Rudi's metamorphosis begins. In the course of their long journey, however, Rudi returns to his Gentile roots rather than becoming more Jewish. Toni watches the transformation with dread. Her own total commitment to Judaism accomplished, she decides to go on alone to her parents' home. Rudi soon follows after her, but his mother is gone, having been "easily sucked in" with other compliant Jews to waiting railway cars and an unknown future.

Rudi wanders off, blaming his mother for leaving him and angry that she did not wait for him, but he suddenly understands what he has guessed, that his mother is in danger. That understanding begins the final stage of Rudi's metamorphosis, achieved through his friendship with Arna, a thin, thirteen-year-old Jewish girl who also has been separated from her family. Arna believes in God and teaches Rudi the ways of observant Jews; she has brought him a "kind of hidden promise." Rudi falls critically ill, and as Arna takes care of him, he wishes for death. During his illness, he hears Arna intone "Hear, O Israel."

Rudi learns the Jewish secrets well, so well that his physical presence changes to match his spiritual change. His gait, which was once swaggering and self-assured, is different after his illness. In fact, Rudi is so different that "he himself did not know how much he had changed." As the narrative ends and the transformation is complete, Rudi and Arna stand at a railroad station watching a train approach: "It was an old locomotive, drawing two old cars . . . the local apparently. It went from station to station, scrupulously gathering up the remainder." Hope remains that Rudi and Arna, young, vigorous, and secure

in their Jewishness, will somehow survive the ensuing Holocaust years and share what they have learned with a future generation.

June H. Schlessinger

OTHER MAJOR WORKS

SHORT FICTION: *'Ashan*, 1962; *Ba-gai ha-poreh*, 1963; *In the Wilderness: Stories*, 1965; *Kefor 'al ha-arets*, 1965; *Be-komat ha-karka'*, 1968; *Adne ha-nahar*, 1971; *Ke-me a edim*, 1975; *Shanim ve-sha ot*, 1975.

NONFICTION: *Masot be-guf rishon*, 1979; *What Is Jewish in Jewish Literature? A Symposium with Israeli Writers Aharon Appelfeld and Yoav Elstein*, 1993; *Beyond Despair: Three Lectures and a Conversation with Philip Roth*, 1994; *Sipur hayim*, 1999 (*The Story of a Life*, 2004); *'Od ha-yom gadol: Yerushalayim, ha-zikaron veha-or*, 2001 (*A Table for One: Under the Light of Jerusalem*, 2005); *Encounter with Aharon Appelfeld*, 2003 (Michael Brown and Sara R. Horowitz, editors).

BIBLIOGRAPHY

Appelfeld, Aharon. *Beyond Despair: Three Lectures and a Conversation with Philip Roth*. Translated by Jeffrey M. Green. New York: Fromm International, 1994. Series of lectures contains useful biographical information on Appelfeld. In an interview that first appeared in *The New York Review of Books* in 1988, Roth and Appelfeld explore the biographical and literary sources of Appelfeld's works.

Bauer, Yehuda, et al., eds. *Remembering for the Future*. 3 vols. Elmsford, N.Y.: Pergamon Press, 1989. Includes many informative essays on Appelfeld, especially "Aharon Appelfeld and the Uses of Language and Silence," in which Lawrence I. Langer explores irony in Appelfeld's work, and "To Express the Inexpressible: The Holocaust Literature of Aharon Appelfeld," in which Nurit Govrin treats Appelfeld's fiction in the context of his essays.

Budick, Emily Miller. *Aharon Appelfeld's Fiction: Acknowledging the Holocaust*. Bloomington: Indiana University Press, 2005. Presents philosphical analyses of Appelfeld's major novels, including *Badenheim 1939*, *Tzili*, and *The Iron Tracks*, addressing how these fictional works support understanding of true historical events.

Fridman, Lea Wernick. "The Silence of Historical Traumatic Experience: Aharon Appelfeld's Badenheim 1939." In *Words and Witness: Narrative and Aesthetic Strategies in the Representation of the Holocaust*. Albany: State University of New York Press, 2000. Analyzes Appelfeld's novel *Badenheim 1939* along with other Holocaust literature to demonstrate how Appelfeld and other writers invent techniques to represent this "unrepresentable" tragedy.

Ramras-Rauch, Gila. *Aharon Appelfeld: The Holocaust and Beyond*. Bloomington: Indiana University Press, 1994. Provides biographical information on Appelfeld as well as critical discussion of his works.

Schwartz, Yigal. *Aharon Appelfeld: From Individual Lament to Tribal Eternity*. Translated by Jeffrey M. Green. Hanover, N.H.: University Press of New England/Brandeis University Press, 2001. Discusses three major themes in Appelfeld's work: the recovery of childhood and memory, the creation of place, and the religious stance of the Holocaust writer. Maintains that Appelfeld's underlying concerns transcend his experiences as a Holocaust survivor to include larger issues of Jewish identity.

Wisse, Ruth R. "Aharon Appelfeld, Survivor." *Commentary* 76, no. 2 (August, 1983): 73-76. Contains an early appraisal of Appelfeld's fiction.

REINALDO ARENAS

Born: Holguín, Oriente, Cuba; July 16, 1943
Died: New York, New York; December 7, 1990

PRINCIPAL LONG FICTION

Celestino antes del alba, 1967 (revised as *Cantando en el pozo*, 1982; *Singing from the Well*, 1987; part 1 of *The Pentagonía*)

El mundo alucinante, 1969 (*Hallucinations: Being an Account of the Life and Adventures of Friar Servando Teresa de Mier*, 1971; also translated as *The Ill-Fated Peregrinations of Fray Servando*, 1987)

El palacio de las blanquísimas mofetas, 1975 (as *Le Palais des très blanches mouffettes*, 1980; *The Palace of the White Skunks*, 1990; part 2 of *The Pentagonía*)

La vieja Rosa, 1980 (novella; *Old Rosa*, 1989)

Otra vez el mar, 1982 (*Farewell to the Sea*, 1986; part 3 of *The Pentagonía*)

Arturo, la estrella más brillante, 1984 (novella; *The Brightest Star*, 1989)

La loma del ángel, 1987 (*Graveyard of the Angels*, 1987)

Old Rosa: A Novel in Two Stories, 1989 (includes the novella *Old Rosa* and the novella *The Brightest Star*)

El portero, 1989 (*The Doorman*, 1991)

Viaje a La Habana, 1990

El asalto, 1991 (*The Assault*, 1994; part 5 of *The Pentagonía*)

El color del verano, 1991 (*The Color of Summer: Or, The New Garden of Earthly Delights*, 2000; part 4 of *The Pentagonía*)

OTHER LITERARY FORMS

In addition to novels, Reinaldo Arenas (ah-RAY-nahs) wrote several collections of short stories, political essays, plays, poems, and an extensive autobiography, *Antes que anochezca* (1992; *Before Night Falls*, 1993). His short-story collections include *Con los ojos cerrados* (1972), *Adiós a mamá: De La Habana a Nueva York* (1995), and *Mona, and Other Tales* (2001). His poetry collections include *El central* (1981; *El Central: A Cuban Sugar Mill*, 1984) and *Voluntad de vivir manifestándose* (1989).

ACHIEVEMENTS

Reinaldo Arenas's first novel, *Singing from the Well*, was awarded first place by the Cuban Writers Union in 1965. *Singing from the Well* also was awarded a prestigious French literary award, the Prix Medici, in 1969. In the same year, *Hallucinations* received the award for

Best Foreign Novel from *Le Monde* (France). In 1980, he was awarded the Cintas Foundation's Fellow honor. This was followed by other fellow honors, including from the Guggenheim Foundation in 1982 and the Wilson Center Foundation in 1987. His autobiography, *Before Night Falls*, was listed among the top ten books of the year by *The New York Times* in 1993. These literary awards were enhanced when the film based on his autobiography received both the Grand Jury Prize at the Venice International Film Festival (1999) and Movie of the Year award from the American Film Institute (2000).

Reinaldo Arenas. (Getty Images)

BIOGRAPHY

Reinaldo Arenas was born on July 16, 1943, in Holguín, Oriente, Cuba. He was born into a rural setting, and his family suffered extreme poverty. According to his autobiography and interviews, his childhood was one of hunger and neglect. While a youth in rural Cuba under the harsh dictatorship of Fulgencio Batista, Arenas was marginally involved in the building insurrection that would eventually topple the oppressive regime in 1959. Several years after the Cuban Revolution, he moved to Havana (1961). He studied at the Universidad de Havana but did not graduate. Arenas also worked for a while in the José Martí National Library (1964).

In 1967, at the age of twenty-four, Arenas published his first novel, *Singing from the Well*. This work somewhat mirrored his childhood, presenting a young protagonist who suffers poverty—both physical and mental. It features a boy who must use independent thought to survive an oppressive reality. Arenas's literary works are not exemplary of the realism that the revolutionary authorities wanted to see published. His open advancement of independent thinking, coupled with his open homosexuality, soon led to his works being labeled antirevolutionary; they were then censored and banned in Cuba.

Nonetheless, Arenas secretly smuggled his writings out of Cuba. His works were published in Europe and the

United States, where they received critical acclaim but led to further reprisals from the Cuban revolutionary regime. His works were removed from the lists of official Cuban literature and were confiscated throughout Cuba. Arenas was imprisoned several times for his defiant attitude. He was tortured in prison and forced to renounce his own works and his homosexuality. Although he was a nonperson in Cuba, he was not allowed to emigrate. His life was reduced to one of minimal existence in Havana, seeking marginal employment to survive. Because of a bureaucratic mistake, he emigrated to the United States in the 1980 exodus known as the Mariel Boat Lift.

In the United States, Arenas was free to publish and criticize the regime of revolutionary leader Fidel Castro. He insisted that his criticism was not only of the Cuban situation but of all types of dogmatic ideologies as well. His literary forms expanded to include poetry, essays, short stories, and journalism. On December 7, 1990, shortly after writing his definitive autobiography, Arenas committed suicide in New York City. In his parting words in a suicide letter, he made it clear that he was not leaving this world as a victim of the Cuban Revolution. To the contrary, he described his life as one of struggle and hope. He expressed his desire that one day all Cubans would be free, stating eloquently that in his death, he already was.

ANALYSIS

Reinaldo Arenas uses the written word to criticize all forms of authoritarianism, especially that which impedes independent thought and action. His most fervent and defiant works condemn the dictatorial regime of the post-Batista revolutionary junta in Cuba, headed by Castro (during Arenas's lifetime). However, he does not limit his criticism to Cuba. He once stated that both capitalism and communism severely limit freedom and expression, but in a capitalist society, one is free to complain openly; in a communist society, one must quietly accept repression. Many of Arenas's works also condemn adult authority over children. As in all authoritarian situations (political, societal, and familial), adult authority stifles the independence of children and adolescents. Arenas's works also contain much psychological and physical abuse.

Arenas presents the reader with a world where the protagonists must use their intellectual skills to survive in a world that is not logical, or just. The reader is confronted with unreliable narrations, descriptions, and dialogue. Indeed, Arenas writes as if truth is only to be found between fantasies, lies, distortions, exaggerations, and hyperbole. His works are often confusing counterpoints within perceived truths. For Arenas, truth is not universal, so the reader of his work is forced to decide for himself or herself what truth is being presented. Arenas reveals a society of humans who struggle for self-expression and self-esteem.

Arenas's textual style varies. In some novels, he uses neither paragraphs nor chapters. In others, he employs an inordinate amount of chapters and textual divisions. His language is generally quite graphic, to the point of being repugnant to some readers. Arenas is not concerned with convincing his readership of the innocence of his characters. To the contrary, he presents their actions as forms of fantasy, and it is up to readers to accept or deny the "reality" of the characters' actions. Extraordinary events are mingled with deceptions, half-truths, distortions, and confusion. The fictional is not obvious and neither is the truth. Furthermore, although Arenas's works are often fantastical and even magical, they are not examples of the Magical Realism employed by many Latin American writers.

SINGING FROM THE WELL

Singing from the Well is the first novel in a five-book series that Arenas called *pentagonía*, or five agonies. *Singing from the Well* is the first and only novel by Arenas to be published in Cuba. (His later works were banned there as well.) Like many of his works, there is no definite chronological order to the story, nor does it clearly delineate its characters. The only consistent linking of time and space is the dysfunctional relationship between the principal protagonist, a young boy growing up in rural poverty and confusion, and his mother. He is never named, unlike his imagined cousin, Celestino.

The world of the boy is a bizarre mixture of nightmare, punishment, and repression. His mother disciplines him with an ox prod, his cousins conspire to kill their grandfather, and his grandmother burns his beloved crosses. To survive this world of cruel fantasies, the boy splits himself into another imaginary being: Celestino, his deceased cousin. Celestino is a poet who carves his poems into trees and leaves.

The reader is never exposed to Celestino's poetry directly. Nonetheless, it is obvious that his poems are attempts to face the bleakness of his life. The wondrous world of nature that the boy and his imaginary cousin inhabit and narrate (through their poetry) is their imagined "real" world. The boy's grandfather, who cannot decipher the strangely coded texts that Celestino carves into trees and other plants, displays an ignorance and distrust that leads him to try to eliminate the texts by chopping them up with a hatchet. The word *hacha*, or hatchet, is used by Arenas more than hundred times over the course of one page of the novel.

Singing from the Well presents a poignant tale of imaginative self-expression. As with other novels by Arenas, the reader encounters a text full of dissonance and fantasy, and without normally accepted logic. The reader must determine the story's merits and truths.

THE PALACE OF THE WHITE SKUNKS

In *The Palace of the White Skunks*, the childlike Celestino is replaced by an older adolescent narrator, Fortunato. Although not overtly stated, Fortunato is a chronological extension of the young boy from *Singing from the Well*. It is also an analogical extension of the anti-Batista revolutionary epic of rural Cuba.

In this work, there is a definite historical setting and time period: the revolutionary rebels fighting against the Batista regime in the Sierra Maestra of Cuba. The novel again describes a dysfunctional family and society. Fortunato faces many real challenges that often overlap with fantasy. The events could be described as forms of magical absurdism: Fortunato conversing with deceased characters, stabbing himself while continuing to amble along, and ghosts and demonic ghouls dancing in the home. Here, also, Fortunato's life is a series of frustrations, deceptions, and rejections. Extreme poverty, problems with the revolutionary insurrection, distrust and insults from family members, and even the sexual frustrations of others enter into impossible and improbable realities. The history presented is reliable, but the events and voices contained in the novel are inconsistent, conflicted, and confusing.

Arenas once again confronts the reader with surreal situations and characters that are not logically reliable. The reader must attempt to sort out the myriad textual transgressions and diversions. Fortunato realizes that he must find a form of self-expression to survive the oppressive situation in which he finds himself. He does so by starting to write his responses to the forces that are limiting his independent choices in life. Fortunato steals paper from his grandfather and begins to secretly express his inner revulsion with the outer life that he is experiencing. The reader is not privy to the actual words of the adolescent. However, it becomes clear that the writings represent a desperate defense mechanism. The text reveals a youth who is literally sweating-out a confrontation with an absurd reality that lurks in the background. He writes instead of sleeping or eating. As with other Arenas novels, the reader finds a protagonist who seeks to find an aesthetic and pure inner textual world that will address his need for self-expression.

FAREWELL TO THE SEA

In this novel, the reader finds an adult reincarnation of the central characters found in *Singing from the Well* and *The Palace of the White Skunks*. The main protagonist, Hector, lives in the institutionalized revolution of modern Cuba. He suffers for attempting to express independent thoughts and writings. In this work, Arenas confronts the Castro regime openly, presenting a post-revolution Cuba as intolerable of dissent. Hector confronts this world with a desperate desire to express his independence. He is an unpublished author, but in this novel, the reader is allowed to view his writings and hear his *cantos* (songs).

This novel is divided into two parts that feature events that follow Hector and his wife's return from the beach after six days of vacation from the totalitarian government in Havana. Part one consists of six chapters (one for each day at the beach) that straightforwardly reveal the unnamed wife's descriptions of a life devoid of tolerance, of unfulfilled intellectual and sexual expression. Part two is narrated by Hector and has six components labeled *cantos*. They are a blend of prose and poetry, fantasy and fact (as perceived by Hector).

As the couple approaches the outskirts of Havana, the reader discovers that the wife is actually a nonexistent creation of Hector. The car begins to accelerate, and the implied ending is that death by suicide is better than returning to a life of intolerance, oppression, and repression.

The reader is confronted by various analogies. The most obvious is the parallel of Hector's life with that of the author. Furthermore, this work was clearly important for Arenas, as he rewrote it twice, each time after it had been confiscated by the Castro government.

Paul Siegrist

OTHER MAJOR WORKS

SHORT FICTION: *Con los ojos cerrados*, 1972 (revised as *Termina el desfile*, 1981); *Adiós a mamá: De La Habana a Nueva York*, 1995; *Mona, and Other Tales*, 2001.

PLAY: *Persecución: Cuatro piezas de teatro experimental*, pb. 1986.

POETRY: *El central*, 1981 (*El Central: A Cuban Sugar Mill*, 1984); *Voluntad de vivir manifestándose*, 1989.

NONFICTION: *Necesidad de libertad*, 1986; *Antes que anochezca*, 1992 (*Before Night Falls*, 1993).

BIBLIOGRAPHY

Browning, Richard L. *Childhood and the Nation in Latin American Literature*. New York: P. Lang, 2001. A discussion of various Latin American authors and the specific correlations between their childhoods and the literature they produced as adults. Includes bibliographical references.

Ocasio, Rafael. *Cuba's Political and Sexual Outlaw: Reinaldo Arenas*. Gainesville: University Press of Florida, 2003. Good source for information on the life and self-exile of Arenas. Describes the relationship between his quest for self-determinism and living as an out gay man in Cuba and the United States. Includes bibliographical references.

Soto, Francisco. *Reinaldo Arenas*. Boston: Twayne, 1998. A comprehensive literary critique of most of the literature by Arenas. Includes bibliographical references and an index.

Vargo, Marc. *Scandal: Infamous Gay Controversies of the Twentieth Century*. New York: Harrington Park Press, 2003. A collection documenting the "gay" scandals of the twentieth century, including the political scandals involving an out Arenas in an intolerant Cuba. Includes bibliographical references.

Yozell, Erica Miller. "Writing Resistance Through Melancholy: Reinaldo Arenas's *El palacio de las blanquísimas mofetas* and *Otra vez el mar*." *MLN* 123, no. 2, (March, 2008): 308-330. Argues that Arenas employs a "discursive melancholy" in these two novels "as a means of both resistance and escape."

AYI KWEI ARMAH

Born: Takoradi, Gold Coast (now Ghana); 1939

PRINCIPAL LONG FICTION

The Beautyful Ones Are Not Yet Born, 1968
Fragments, 1969
Why Are We So Blest?, 1972
Two Thousand Seasons, 1973
The Healers, 1978
Osiris Rising, 1995
KMT in the House of Life: An Epistemic Novel, 2002

OTHER LITERARY FORMS

Although Ayi Kwei Armah (awr-MAW) is primarily a novelist, he has written and published in other forms as well. Among his short stories, "Yaw Manu's Charm" appeared in *The Atlantic Monthly* (1968) and "The Offal Kind" in *Harper's* (1969). His poem "Aftermath" is included in *Messages: Poems from Ghana* (1970). Armah also has worked as a translator for *Jeune Afrique* and the Algerian-based *Révolution Africaine*. His polemical essay "African Socialism: Utopian or Scientific?" appeared in *Présence Africaine* (1967).

ACHIEVEMENTS

Ayi Kwei Armah has become Ghana's best-known writer on the international scene, but he would probably prefer to measure his achievement by the reception of his African audience. He has been vulnerable to suspicion and resentment both in Africa and abroad. Not only has he been in exile from his own nation, choosing to live in other African countries, in Paris, and in the United States, but he has also attacked virulently the corruption and materialism of his country's elite and has absolutely condemned the white race (whether European or Arab) for its perverted mentality and for its past and present role in the destruction of African culture.

There is an abrasive quality about Armah's early novels—their oppressive naturalism, their sadomasochistic sexuality, their melodramatic casting of blame—that demands more than mere tolerance on the part of his audience. These novels require the reader to go beyond the vehicle to the attitude and the argument that it reveals. A reasonably careful reading will get beyond this abrasiveness and may even dispel the suspicion and resentment, because Armah's real achievement lies in his making the novel not a simple outlet for his venom but a functional instrument in the African cause. Armah is one of the few truly experimental African novelists. He takes a Western literary form and shapes it into a voice for the African in the modern world.

In his first novel, Armah turns naturalism and romantic irony into a symbolic, existential statement. In the next two novels, he experiments with narration through multiple points of view. In all three cases, his purpose is to explore the isolation of the individual African in his transformed society. It is evident that Armah is searching for a voice. In his later novels the voice is that of the traditional historian and storyteller of the tribe. The Western concept of point of view merges with the oral tradition, and fictional realism merges with history, legend, and myth. In *Osiris Rising*, his sixth novel, Armah returns to the realism of his earliest work but imbues this with a new symbolic undercurrent based on the Osiris and Isis myth cycle, one of Africa's earliest foundational stories. Armah does not engage in experimentation for its own sake: Technique and form are in the service of the larger human concern, the preservation of a culture and the fulfillment of his role within it.

BIOGRAPHY

Ayi Kwei Armah was born in 1939 in the seaport town of Sekondi-Takoradi in western Ghana. Unlike the unnamed protagonist of his first novel, Armah was able to attend mission schools and Achimota College, near the capital city of Accra. He then received scholarships to continue his education in the United States. Like the "man" in his first novel, *The Beautyful Ones Are Not Yet Born*, however, his early life was dramatically influenced by the effects of colonial rule. During World War II, the British sent Ghanaians to fight in Burma (Myanmar) and on other battlefields; the postwar period in Ghana was marked by economic crises, social unrest and strikes, the rise of political parties, and the achieving of independence.

Armah did not experience directly the events after independence. In 1959, he received a scholarship to attend Groton School in Massachusetts. He went on to Harvard, where he graduated summa cum laude in sociology. In 1963, he visited Algeria and worked as translator for *Révolution Africaine*. He saw firsthand what was happening in African countries after independence: a con-

tinuation of the old policies, of African subservience, and of poverty. The novel *Why Are We So Blest?* appears to be a distillation of Armah's experiences during these years.

During his brief return to Ghana in 1966, Armah attempted to apply his American education and his talents as a writer in various ways. He was a research fellow at the university, a journalist, a teacher of English, and a television scriptwriter. His second novel, *Fragments*, appears to be a spiritual biography of this frustrated attempt to adapt himself again to his society. In 1967, Armah was again in the United States, attending Columbia University on a writing fellowship, and then in Paris as editor-translator for the newsmagazine *Jeune Afrique*. In 1968, he taught at the University of Massachusetts and published *The Beautyful Ones Are Not Yet Born*, which traces the Ghanaian experience from World War II to the overthrow of Kwame Nkrumah in 1966 but concentrates on the corruption in Ghanaian society around the time of the coup.

Armah continued to teach at universities in diverse locales, both in Africa and abroad. He held academic appointments at the Teachers' College in Dar es Salaam, Tanzania; the University of Lesotho; the University of Wisconsin at Madison; and in Nigeria. Armah settled in Popenguine, Senegal. In the mid-1990's, he and some friends formed a cooperative printing and publishing company dedicated to the promotion of the local African book industry.

ANALYSIS

Ayi Kwei Armah's novels have provoked conflicting reactions. On one hand, one can argue that Armah is essentially Western, not African. He is certainly not African in the manner of the Nigerian novelist Chinua Achebe. While Achebe's works are to some degree "social documents," Armah moves rapidly from social realism to a symbolic level, even within his first novel. His succeeding novels move away from external detail toward the inner life and the idealism of legend and myth. Achebe is a realist, Armah a romantic. Achebe maintains an objective stance in his analysis of the colonial and postcolonial eras in Nigeria, while Armah's voice is strident and polemical. Whereas Achebe is likely to make the society itself as important a "character" as the individual protagonist, Armah, in his early works at least, focuses on the individual consciousness.

Armah's novels thus bear the obvious marks of contemporary European and American fiction. His protagonists are alienated antiheroes who deserve sympathy and who are essentially correct in their moral attitudes, but who are ineffectual misfits. The society itself is clearly wrong but defeats the individual moral person through sheer force of numbers, viewing such protagonists as mad or criminal. In fact, this society is the typical twentieth century wasteland, whether it is in Ghana, northern Africa, or the United States. Armah's Ghanaians resemble black Americans trying to be white in order to participate fully in the technological age. Finally, the protagonist within this society resembles, and often in fact is, the isolated artist—a typical Western figure, not at all African.

One can easily argue that if these are not incidental features, they are at least sketched into a larger picture that identifies Armah with an essentially African sensibility. Judging from his first five novels and not emphasizing simply the early works, one could conclude that Armah is an African writing for Africans. For him, the identity of the African artist is inseparable from the society that he serves. He would not want to be judged according to the Western criterion of art for its own sake, or by Western standards of what makes a satisfactory novel. He tries to make his novels functional within an African context. His primary stress is on the individual African sensibility isolated from his society. His novels are a search not so much for private redemption as for communal salvation, and in this respect he reflects an essentially African rather than Western mentality.

Armah is a philosophical novelist: Realism is in the service of, or sacrificed to, an idea. He is a social critic searching for a philosophical and historical framework. His protagonists are social failures but heroes in the cause of the greater Africa. His ultimate purpose is pan-African in scope, and his experimentation with technique and form, even though the source may be Western, is a search for the appropriate voice to further the end of common understanding.

Although each novel individually could not be called a bildungsroman, together they appear, in retrospect, to trace the individual protagonist from confusion and frus-

tration to a sense of wholeness and communal belonging. The "man" in *The Beautyful Ones Are Not Yet Born* cannot be sure of his own identity or his moral values because he receives no reinforcement from his society, while Densu in the fifth novel, *The Healers*, rejects his immediate society and joins a small outcast community that understands the larger African tradition.

Armah has some interesting things to say sociologically as well. Like most contemporary African novelists, he deals with the traumatic experience of colonialism, the rapid change from traditional to modern society, the effects of the slave trade and of Western influence in general, the difficulties of adapting to the technological age, the political corruption immediately after independence, and the cultural vacuum. His novels move from the narrow confines of one Ghanaian city in *The Beautyful Ones Are Not Yet Born* to the larger international scene of America, Europe, and North Africa, to show at first hand those forces that helped create the filth and artificiality surrounding his protagonist. In *Two Thousand Seasons* and *The Healers*, Armah leaves the 1960's to give a picture of African society in the distant and recent past. In general, he argues that foreign exploitation has perverted the traditional communal values, which are, if anything, superior to the ones that have replaced them. What seems to concern Armah particularly, however, are the psychological implications of this displacement.

The protagonists of the second two novels are mentally disturbed and require professional therapy or convalescence. Juana of *Fragments* is a psychologist, and the outcast priests of *Two Thousand Seasons* and *The Healers* are practitioners of traditional therapies. The essential problem that Armah identifies is the impotence and extreme depression of the sensitive individual rejected by the westernized African society. In addition, Armah explores the nightmares and dreams of his frustrated protagonists, and in his novels he seeks an answer to frustration through the revival of racial consciousness in myth and legend. The ultimate purpose of his novels is therapeutic.

THE BEAUTYFUL ONES ARE NOT YET BORN

If the central issue in Armah's novels is the relationship between the individual and his (or her) community, then *The Beautyful Ones Are Not Yet Born* is a depress-

ing omen. The main character, the center of consciousness, has no name—not so much because he represents
all men or even because he represents the man of integrity, though these are possible readings, but because he is
anonymous. Society does not recognize his existence.
He is an outcast because he attempts to hold on to moral
values while the rest of society has succumbed to bribery, corruption, and materialism. This isolation is total.
Even his own family urges him to advance himself for
their benefit within the corrupt system. The isolation,
however, extends beyond family and community. Even
in this first novel, Armah introduces the historical context. The "man" is trapped within the present. He has no
sense of belonging to a Ghanaian or to an African tradition. He cannot identify the source of his integrity or of
his moral judgment. Hence, he resides in a historical
void, which makes him question the very values that
give him sustenance. Honesty seems unnatural, cruel,
obstinate, even criminal and insane.

The story evolves at a specific time in the contemporary history of Ghana. Though Armah does not give
dates, it is clear that the early episodes (chapters 1-12)
take place late in Kwame Nkrumah's reign, in the mid-
1960's. The final three chapters deal with the hours just
after Nkrumah's fall in February, 1966. The "man" is a
controller for the railroad, a husband, and the father of
two children. Armah describes in naturalistic detail a day
in the man's life, his journey to and from work, the op-
pressiveness of the physical surroundings, the boring
and insignificant responsibilities of his job, and the return home to an unsympathetic and accusing wife. The
only dramatic event in these first chapters is the man's
rejection of a bribe.

To seek relief and reassurance, he pays a visit to his
former teacher, who shares his moral awareness and can
explain to some extent the origin of the present malaise,
but who has withdrawn from society. The teacher has no
family and hence no compelling responsibility. He refuses to participate in the corruption but also declines to
fight it. All he can do for the man is understand his situation. He is, nevertheless, the first of a series of figures in
the five novels who represent the wisdom of a way of life
that Ghana no longer knows. Within this realistic and
cynical first novel it is not surprising that the teacher
lacks the confidence and the vision necessary to save the

man or his society. In spite of this, Armah leaves no
doubt as to the importance of the teacher and his philosophical appraisal of contemporary Ghana. He places
the visit at the very center of the novel. From this point,
the man must accept total isolation. He cannot lean on
his elder and former guide: He must find his own solution.

The problem that faces the man in the final third of
the novel involves him in the corruption of an old classmate who is a minister under Nkrumah. His wife and
mother-in-law agree to participate in the illegal purchase
of a fishing boat, which is primarily for the benefit of
Minister Koomsan. When the man refuses complicity,
he becomes even more of an outcast within the family.
His wife constantly measures him against the successful
Koomsan, who has surrounded himself with the things
of modern civilization. The last three chapters, however,
reverse the situation. Nkrumah falls. Koomsan, a piti-
fully frightened victim of the coup, comes to the man for
aid. The two escape from the house just as the authorities
arrive, and the man leads him to the fishing boat and to
exile. The man himself swims back to shore and to his
family. Though he has involved himself in the corruption he despises, the act of saving Koomsan must be seen
as a heroic and humane gesture. The man's wife, at least,
now recognizes his courage and his worth. The novel
thus moves from almost total submergence in the repulsive details of daily life to a romantic but ironic act of
heroism, whose ultimate significance is nevertheless left
ambiguous.

Armah is already suggesting the larger movement
from realism to myth in the figurative and even symbolic
dimension of the narrative. What first strikes the reader's
attention, in fact overwhelms him or her, is the vivid and
disgusting insistence on the filth, the excrement, and the
vomit that one touches and breathes in the city. Yet this
physical reality is at the same time the political and
moral corruption that the society discharges as it continues to pursue and consume the "things" of Western technology. Koomsan's escape through the latrine is symbolically a wallowing in his own excrement. A second
symbol special to this novel is the chichi dodo bird,
which despises excrement but subsists on the worms that
the excrement nourishes: the man, as much as he may try
to remain free of taint, is implicated in the social guilt.

Finally, Armah uses a third image, the stream, that recurs in all the other novels. He seems to identify water in a traditional way as a purifying agent. During one of his walks, the man notices, in an otherwise muddy stream, a perfectly clear current that seems to have no source. He associates it with a gleam of light—his own moral awareness—a clarity of vision that he cannot trace to any source. He sets this clarity against the brightness of new things imported from the West, but it is not strong enough or permanent enough to give him hope. In spite of his heroism, his baptismal dip in the ocean, and his "rebirth," he still must recognize at the end that "the beautyful ones are not yet born."

FRAGMENTS

In *Fragments*, Armah continues the exploration of the individual and his obligation to both family and community. The scene again takes place in the later 1960's, but the situations are considerably changed. Baako Onipa (the hero now has a name, which means "Only Person") is a "been-to," a member of the educated elite who has spent five years studying in the United States. In this respect, he resembles Armah himself, an American-educated intellectual who must have had similar difficulties readjusting to Ghanaian society.

Like Armah, Baako is a writer searching for a role within his newly independent nation. No longer is the protagonist buried in lower-class poverty. His education gives him access to prominent men in the community and to the things of modern technology. He thus has the means to satisfy the expectations of his family, especially his mother. He resembles the man, however, in his inability to sacrifice his personal integrity to take advantage of his opportunities. In a sense, his situation is even more critical than that of the man. He is a highly sensitive artist. Whereas the man has perceived the "madness" of his obstinacy, Baako has already experienced insanity in America and is on the edge of it again throughout this novel, the title of which, *Fragments*, is thus particularly appropriate.

The story does not follow a clear chronological path, because Armah has chosen to present it through three centers of consciousness. The emphasis is thus not on the exterior world but, much more obviously than in *The Beautyful Ones Are Not Yet Born*, on the psychological responses to the world of the two main characters, Baako

and Juana, a Puerto Rican psychologist who becomes Baako's confidant, and of Baako's grandmother, Naana, who represents the traditional wisdom of the people. The novel opens with Naana recalling Baako's ritual departure five years before and her anticipation of his cyclical return. Baako does return, unannounced, however, to avoid the inevitable ritual ceremony. He dreads to face his family because he brings no gifts and because he knows that he will be unable to fulfill his mother's expectations. His mother expects what the man's wife expected in *The Beautyful Ones Are Not Yet Born*, money and the comforts of the modern age. Baako, in his rebellion against this imitation of Western values, goes to his former teacher, Ocran, for advice. Ocran has himself chosen to pursue his profession as an artist in solitude, because he sees no possibility for useful work within contemporary Ghanaian society.

Against Ocran's advice, the less experienced Baako has decided to make the attempt by turning his talents as novelist to a more public role as a television scriptwriter. He hopes to transform popular Ghanaian myths into scripts for television, and in general to raise the consciousness of the people by introducing them to the true traditions of Ghana. The authorities, preferring to use the television screen as an instrument of propaganda, reject this proposal as dangerous. Baako goes back to the privacy of the writing table and, thus isolated, gradually loses his mind. His family places him in an asylum, from which he is about to be rescued by Juana as the novel closes.

The threat of insanity, in fact, has plagued Baako from the very beginning. He goes to Juana for help early in the novel. She becomes his lover and, along with Ocran, his spiritual guide. The novel thus ends as does *The Beautyful Ones Are Not Yet Born*, ambiguously—but with a note of hope, and with the nucleus of a new community, two Ghanaians and the outsider, Juana, who represents not the evils of white society but the sensitivities of a minority. Furthermore, Ocran seems to offer a temporary compromise between the two extremes that have driven Baako to insanity, a compromise that Armah develops in the later novels. Whereas society and family demand that Baako yield to their values, and Baako, while recognizing his inherent need for identity within the community, must maintain his integrity, Ocran proposes a kind of synthesis: Baako cannot expect to achieve his goal immediately. He must submit to a temporary isolation from the present society and work for the larger community of the future. Naana reinforces this view as her commentary closes the novel with a picture of contemporary Ghana in fragments. This novel thus has raised the argument to a more philosophical level than that of *The Beautyful Ones Are Not Yet Born* by using four different characters who reflect on the problem of the perceptive individual within a materialistic society.

In other ways, too, Armah moves away from the naturalism of his first novel. Even the naturalistic scenes, such as the killing of the "mad" dog, are obviously symbolic of something beyond themselves. Just as Juana observes a crowd of soldiers who close in on a dog that they only suspect to be mad, so she watches the community and the family judge and incarcerate Baako for his "insane" ideas. The novel also incorporates ritualistic and religious elements. Naana contrasts the unifying role of traditional ritual with the fragmentation of the present. The mother appeals to an itinerant, spiritualist preacher to aid her in praying for Baako's return. Baako and Juana discuss the similarities between Catholicism and animism, as opposed to the isolating force of Protestantism. Baako is concerned in particular with myth: He contrasts his overseas experience with the traditional hero's departure and triumphal return to save the community. He and Juana repeat the myth of Mame Water, who rises from the sea periodically to meet her lover and give him special powers, but at the same time leaves him with an excruciating sense of isolation. The water itself, like the stream from *The Beautyful Ones Are Not Yet Born*, flows into *Fragments*. Baako pictures himself swimming upstream against a cataract; water still seems to be a purifying force and the stream itself the natural flow of history.

WHY ARE WE SO BLEST?

In retrospect, *Why Are We So Blest?* appears to be a transition between Armah's first two novels and the mythical ones to follow. It continues the trend away from realistic description toward a study of multiple consciousness, a philosophical reflection, a larger international context, and an emphasis on personal relationships. The time of the novel, however, remains the same, the mid- to late 1960's, as does the central premise: the individual isolated from his community and hence from his own identity.

Again, Armah seems to be drawing from his own experience, this time as a student in an American university, and from the guilt feelings that inevitably arise in one who is given special treatment while his country suffers from the very hands that feed him. In a sense, the Ghanaian character, Modin, is Baako receiving the education that is so useless to him upon his return, though Armah has a far different fate for this avatar. The other major African character, Solo, shares with Modin a situation that Armah has not created in the first two novels. They both remain abroad, completely detached from their societies, Modin as a student and would-be revolutionary, Solo as a disillusioned revolutionary in exile. Solo, the dispassionate observer, finds in Modin a reincarnation (with variations) of his own past fascination with revolution and with a Western woman. This third major character is Aimée Reitsch, a white American of German ancestry, whose perverted fascination with Africa and with Modin precipitates his destruction.

The narrative in *Why Are We So Blest?* resembles that of *Fragments* in that it, too, has three centers of consciousness. The two principal actors in the drama, Modin and Aimée, have kept journals about their experiences, which Aimée leaves with Solo after Modin's death. Solo thus functions as editor, providing personal information and commentary and arranging the journal entries to reconstruct the story of their lives and his encounter with them in northern Africa. He opens the novel with an account of his own life before he met them and fills out this autobiography at intervals throughout the book. He is a reviewer of books eking out an existence in the fictional town of Laccryville (Algiers) and making occasional visits to the headquarters of a revolutionary organization that he once wished to join.

The story of Modin and Aimée, as Solo reconstructs it, goes back to Modin's days as a scholarship student in African studies at Harvard. Immediately after arriving, he receives a warning from Naita, the black secretary of his sponsor, that he must not trust those who have brought him to the United States. They actually consider him their property. Modin eventually realizes that she is right about the white race in general being the black person's destroyer, but makes the mistake of considering Aimée an exception. He leaves for Africa with her to join the revolutionary organization in Laccryville. Its leaders are suspicious of Aimée and hence reject them both. Solo meets them and would like to do something to save Modin, but realizes that he is doomed. Modin and Aimée take off on a futile hitchhiking journey across the Sahara, only to be picked up by white male racists who sexually abuse them and leave Modin to die. Aimée returns to her middle-class life in America and Solo is left frustrated in his isolation. It would seem, however, that Solo as author has finally found his voice, and is fulfilling a useful function after all in this "book" that he is offering to the public. That is, Solo has discovered the role that Armah himself has chosen.

In this respect, *Why Are We So Blest?* looks forward to the positive and hopeful tone of the next three novels. What the "man" and Baako lacked, Solo has discovered. In other ways, too, this novel looks forward. The stream as a motif reappears, but it is no longer muddy as in *The Beautyful Ones Are Not Yet Born*, and the swimmer is no longer fighting against the current. Instead, Solo is observing its continuous flow and waiting for a place to enter and become a part of it. Madness, obsession, and psychological tension continue to be significant motifs, but while *Fragments* ends with Baako in an asylum, this novel opens with Solo's overcoming a bout of mental depression by committing himself to a month's convalescence in a hospital. His return to health accompanies a transformation in his view of society, the nature of revolution, and the role of militants.

By this third novel, also, Armah has transformed the African female figure into a kind of soul mate. Naita possesses sexual purity, a natural grace, and a wisdom that could have been Modin's salvation. She attains an almost mythical dimension. The most significant symbol in the novel, in fact, is sexuality. Through it, Armah exposes the selfish aggressiveness of the white female and the cruel fascism of the white male. The novel announces with violent acerbity a thesis that appears for the first time in Armah's fiction, the essential animosity between black and white. It bears the sure stamp of the Black Muslim movement that must have deeply affected him in America. The white race becomes identified as the destroyer, the enemy. The African has lost his or her identity because the white race has taken away the tradition and the community that gave him or her meaning.

TWO THOUSAND SEASONS

In *Two Thousand Seasons*, Armah prophesies a more fruitful course. He makes a leap of faith in his narrative style and, more important, in his promise of an answer to the frustrated heroes of the first three novels. This novel has no hero, unless it be the community itself. No isolated personality is trapped within his own consciousness. The narrator, as character, is the ubiquitous member of every generation who knows the true history of the tribe. He is the griot, the tribal historian, the wise man, the poet. He is a member of the select few whose task it is to maintain the spiritual coherence of the group. The story he tells is the group's chronicle. Thus Armah, as author, effaces himself by adopting the traditional and anonymous role of historian—a significantly symbolic act since Armah must recognize that he too finds his identity only if he merges with the community.

The chronicle begins one thousand years (two thousand seasons) ago, when the Akan tribe, probably intended to represent the black race, living in peace, harmony, and "reciprocity" on the edge of the desert, succumbs to the "predators" of the north, the Arab-Muslim civilization of North Africa. The narrator describes the destruction of the social order and the enslavement of the people. It is here that the community first loses its cohesiveness. A small nucleus of people, particularly women of the tribe, initiate and lead a revolt, and then a migration away from the desert toward the south. The eventual destination is present-day Ghana, but the people arrive only to find another threat from the sea. The Europeans have begun their exploitation of the continent.

The last half of the novel concentrates on the disintegration of the tribe as the forces from without create division within. The narrator focuses on one particular period, when one generation of youths undergoing initiation escapes into the forest and organizes a resistance movement. A seer named Isanusi leads them and trains them in the "Way," the traditional values of the tribe. Their king, Koranche, subsequently persuades them to return, deceives them, and sells them into slavery. They are able to escape from the slave ship and make their way back to the forest retreat, bringing with them new recruits. These guerrilla warriors, the "beautyful ones," operate against the oppressive authorities who have betrayed the tribal traditions.

Armah has thus solved the essential problem facing the protagonists of the early novels. He has achieved the synthesis adumbrated by Ocran in *Fragments*. Though it may be impossible to join and serve the particular society in Ghana today, it is possible to participate spiritually in the larger society and in the genuine traditions of the people. This solution certainly explains the mythical and romantic mode of this novel in contrast to the naturalism or realism at the base of the first three. No longer caught within the contemporary world of the 1960's, the initiates of *Two Thousand Seasons* belong to an ancient tradition. A mythical pattern controls the novel. The tribe begins in Eden, falls from grace, and moves toward the cyclical return. It is this confidence in the future and in the total pattern of life that separates this novel from its predecessors.

The racism of *Why Are We So Blest?* becomes a struggle for cultural identity on a panoramic scale. The whites, whether Muslim or Christian, are the enemy. Their culture is oppressive and destructive to blacks. They represent class divisions and hierarchical structures. The African "way" is reciprocity, equality, and a sharing of responsibility and power. Armah is obviously dealing in romantic terms. He is also trying to find his own modus vivendi: a justification of his "exile" and a role within the larger pattern of his nation's fate.

THE HEALERS

Armah called *The Healers* a historical novel. It is, to be sure, based on particular events in the 1870's during the Second Asante War, and Armah's purpose—as in the previous novels, especially *Two Thousand Seasons*—is to offer an interpretation of Ghanaian (African) society and to reevaluate African history. His method, however, is not so much historical as romantic and mythical. The story is a mixture of fact and fiction, and the characters and events conform to an idea of the essential African mentality and the future of the African continent. It thus continues the optimistic chronicle of the previous novel.

The storyteller is again the "anonymous" griot. The tale begins as an epic, in medias res. It proceeds immediately to narrate the initiation of nine Asante boys into manhood. Densu is obviously a young man of heroic proportions. He refuses to engage in the wrestling contest because the competition required violates the spirit of cooperation that he values. He nevertheless demonstrates his superior strength and grace in this and other games, while finally refusing to win to avoid being named the next chief in the tribe. He resists this temptation held out by Ababio, the evil adviser who remains Densu's nemesis throughout the novel. Densu's ambition is to join the spiritual ones, the "priests" or "healers" who live as outcasts in the forest and who preserve the values of the community that are being perverted by ambitious men such as Ababio. Before he can realize this goal, however, he must not only convince Damfo, the chief healer and his spiritual guide, that he can truly sacrifice the things of common life but also overcome Ababio's scheme to condemn him falsely for murder and to engage in the war against the British as General Nkwanta's aid. The novel ends melodramatically, with the betrayal and defeat of the Asante army, the last-minute acquittal of Densu at the murder trial, and the various African tribes dancing on the beach, ironically brought together by the invading British.

Armah thus suggests a future pan-African unity. For the present, however—if the events of the 1870's offer a paradigm for the contemporary situation—the solution to the sociological and psychological problems facing Ghanaians is much the same as that proposed in *Two Thousand Seasons*. The perceptive individual who works for a solution must not expect an immediate communal identity. Again, Armah clarifies the choices available through romantic simplification. In *Two Thousand Seasons*, the proponents of the Way face a challenge from the white predators and destroyers and from the zombies among their own people. In *The Healers*, the choice is between competition and manipulation on one hand and cooperation and inspiration on the other. Densu chooses to leave his tribe because he knows that the leaders and the people are not ready for the essential virtues of the true community. Instead, he is initiated by Damfo into the community of healers. Damfo, in his dealings with other people, never resorts to manipulation or even persuasion, but rather relies on spiritual understanding and respect. This is presented as the only way to establish a genuine community.

In this fifth novel, Armah seems to be consciously drawing in all the threads from his early works. The beautyful ones, it would seem, are born, but they reside outside the society itself, preparing for the future. Unlike the "man," they fully accept the pain of nonconformity. The healer, Damfo, fulfills the tasks that frustrate the teacher, Ocran, Juana, Naana, and Solo. In his conversations with Densu, he employs a method of instruction that is both Socratic and therapeutic. The philosophical and psychological conflicts that plague the early heroes thus find their resolutions in the spiritual communication and intimate friendship between priest and initiate. Nightmares become dreams of self-discovery. Body, mind, and spirit achieve harmony in Densu. He sees the chaos of the present within the perspectives of history. He is also at home in the natural world.

The stream that flows as a minor motif through the other novels is a significant part of the setting in *The Healers*. Densu wins the swimming contest not by competing but by becoming at one with the natural element. He later escapes arrest by holding on to roots at the bottom of the stream and breathing through a hollowed-out cane. Even later, he and Damfo master the stream in a long journey against the current. Finally, in this river of life Densu contemplates his own image and purpose. Clearly, Armah creates a hero in *The Healers* who has found his place in the stream of history, a hero who gives meaning to Armah's own chosen role in his community.

OSIRIS RISING

Osiris Rising, Armah's sixth novel—and his first in seventeen years—represents a further evolution of his perspective along this axis. The old themes are once again in evidence: pan-African unity, historical consciousness, intellectual nonconformity, and disgust with the corrupt African leadership. The Osiris and Isis myth alluded to in the title provides an important symbolic background for this otherwise realistic text. As a genuinely African myth of origin, the Osiris legend mirrors a major theme of the novel, which explicitly deals with the need for Africa to put its own culture at the center of its historical consciousness. The magnificence of ancient Egypt then serves as the perfect and natural locus for this shift.

The novel tells the story of Ast, a young African American Egyptologist who feels displaced in America and thus "goes home" to Africa in search of her roots and a sense of belonging. She is also following Asar, her college lover who has returned to his homeland in Africa to fight against the injustices of the postindependence puppet regimes. Significantly, the country to which she travels (and where the rest of the novel takes place) is never named directly. Armah's pan-Africanism makes him more interested in the symbolic aspects of the story than in its relevance to any single national entity. In Africa, Ast comes across another acquaintance from her university days, Asar's longtime rival and countryman Seth, who has risen in the corrupt administration to become chief of security for the entire nation. The action of the novel revolves largely around Ast's and Asar's grassroots political organizing on the campus where they both teach, set against the insipid political machinations of Seth, who sees Asar in particular as a threat to his way of life. Ultimately, Seth appears to "win" at the close of the novel as Asar's body is literally blown into fragments by the guns of Seth's death squad.

When considered alongside the informing Osiris myth, however, Seth's victory is exposed as transitory and futile against the greater advances for which Asar's teaching has set the stage. The myth tells of Osiris and his sister and wife Isis, who ruled Egypt as king and queen. Their brother Seth murdered Osiris and scattered fragments of the body across Egypt, which historically accounted for the spread of the Osiris cult. Isis then raised their son, Horus, to manhood, at which time he avenged his father's murder by deposing Seth and assuming power as king of the living. Osiris, reassembled by Isis, became lord of the underworld. With this in mind, an allegorical reading of the novel becomes clear: Asar, who has clearly stated throughout the novel that his death would be an insignificant obstacle for the widespread communal movement for African unity, is the martyr Osiris, and the rising alluded to in the title suggests that indeed the movement will yet prevail. Likewise, that Ast is pregnant with Asar's child would seem to prophesy the child's ultimate defeat of Seth and victory for the representatives of African justice.

OTHER MAJOR WORKS

SHORT FICTION: "Yaw Manu's Charm," in *The Atlantic*, 1968; "The Offal Kind," in *Harper's*, 1969.

POETRY: "Aftermath," in *Messages: Poems from Ghana*, 1970.

NONFICTION: "African Socialism: Utopian or Scientific?," in *Présence Africaine*, 1967; *The Eloquence of the Scribes: A Memoir on the Sources and Resources of African Literature*, 2006.

Thomas Banks
Updated by Harland W. Jones III

BIBLIOGRAPHY

Fraser, Robert. *The Novels of Ayi Kwei Armah: A Study in Polemical Fiction*. London: Heinemann, 1980. An excellent starting place for general readers. The first chapter provides the context of liberation and resistance informing Armah's work and is followed by five chapters on individual novels. Includes a bibliography and an index.

Lazarus, Neil. *Resistance in Postcolonial African Fiction*. New Haven, Conn.: Yale University Press, 1990. Full-length study that focuses on the politics and ideology of Armah's first three novels. A cogently argued critique of early postcolonial nationalism.

Ogede, Ode. *Ayi Kwei Armah: Radical Iconoclast*. London: Heinemann, 1999. Full-length study of Armah's entire oeuvre, from one of the most prolific Armah scholars. Focuses on the juxtapositions of "imaginary" worlds with the "actual." A volume in the Studies in African Literature series.

Okolo, M. S. C. *African Literature as Political Philosophy*. New York: Palgrave Macmillan, 2007. While focusing on works by Chinua Achebe and Ngugi wa Thiong'o, Okolo places these writings within the broader context of postcolonial African literature, including a discussion of Armah's work. Okolo argues that Armah, Achebe, and Thiong'o have been profoundly affected by the continent's political situation and have helped create a new African political philosophy.

Palmer, Eustace. "Negritude Rediscovered: A Reading of the Recent Novels of Armah, Ngugi, and Soyinka." *International Fiction Review* 8 (1981): 1-11. This discussion of the concept of negritude pays particular attention to three works: Soyinka's *Season of Anomy*, Ngugi's *Petals of Blood*, and Armah's *Two Thousand Seasons*. Includes notes.

Research in African Literatures 18 (Summer, 1987). A special issue on Ayi Kwei Armah that includes three articles, a bibliography of studies in African literature, and seventeen book reviews.

Wodajo, Tsegaye. *Hope in the Midst of Despair: A Novelist's Cures for Africa*. Trenton, N.J.: Africa World Press, 2004. Examines five novels—*The Beautyful Ones Are Not Yet Born*, *Fragments*, *Two Thousand Seasons*, *The Healers*, and *Osiris Rising*—to focus on the characters' protests against Africa's sociopolitical and economic institutions. Wodajo argues that the first two novels meticulously describe the deterioration of these institutions, providing a rationale for the protagonists of the last three novels, who openly resist the continent's corrupt ruling elite and the complicity of their foreign collaborators.

Wright, Derek. *Ayi Kwei Armah's Africa: The Sources of His Fiction*. London: Hans Zell, 1989. Traces the African background of Armah's fiction, particularly the early novels, and provides a broad cultural and anthropological context. Useful for the student and reader already familiar with Armah's work and seeking more specialized analysis. Includes chapter notes, a bibliography, and an index.

_____, ed. *Critical Perspectives on Ayi Kwei Armah*. Boulder, Colo.: Three Continents Press, 1992. Collection of twenty-two essays on Armah's early career. Includes four general essays and seven on *The Beautyful Ones Are Not Yet Born*, with the rest evenly distributed among four other early novels. Extensive and valuable bibliography and notes on contributors.

Yankson, Kofi E. *The Rot of the Land and the Birth of the Beautyful Ones: The World of Ayi Kwei Armah's Novels*. Accra: Ghana Universities Press, 2000. A text of a lecture delivered in 1994, in which Yankson critiques *The Beautyful Ones Are Not Yet Born*, *Fragments*, *Why Are We So Blest?*, *Two Thousand Seasons*, and *The Healers*. Maintains that these novels depict two types of souls—diseased and healthy. Focuses on the nature and causes of the diseased souls who, according to Armah, constitute the rot of the African continent.

HARRIETTE ARNOW

Born: Wayne County, Kentucky; July 7, 1908
Died: Ann Arbor, Michigan; March 22, 1986
Also known as: Harriette Louisa Simpson;
   H. L. Simpson

PRINCIPAL LONG FICTION

Mountain Path, 1936
Hunter's Horn, 1949
The Dollmaker, 1954
The Weedkiller's Daughter, 1970
*The Kentucky Trace: A Novel of the American
   Revolution*, 1974
Between the Flowers, 1999 (wr. late 1930's)

OTHER LITERARY FORMS

Harriette Arnow wrote two well-received social histories of the Cumberland River basin, an area that encompasses parts of Kentucky and Tennessee. *Seedtime on the Cumberland* (1960) focuses more on the lives and work of individual pioneers of the period from 1780 to 1803, while *Flowering of the Cumberland* (1963) concentrates on the social activities of the same time, relating to education, industry, professions, and entertainments. Arnow wrote *Old Burnside: A Memoir of a Southern Girlhood* (1977) as a reminiscence of her growing up in Burnside, Kentucky. Though not a prolific short-story writer, Arnow wrote several stories, which are gathered in *The Collected Short Stories of Harriette Simpson Arnow* (2005). Her most widely published short story is "The Washerwoman's Day," about the hypocrisy behind a charitable deed.

ACHIEVEMENTS

Harriette Arnow's critics consider her an underrated writer who deserves wider recognition. She is especially credited for her role in the development of Appalachian literature. Critics have observed that her specific portrayals of a particular region, like any good fiction, also connect to more universal themes.

Arnow, and her novel, received many awards and other honors. *Hunter's Horn* was a *Saturday Review* national critics' poll winner for best novel and was nomi-

nated for the National Book Award. For *The Dollmaker*, Arnow won the Friends of American Writers award, and the novel was a runner-up for the National Book Award, was a *Saturday Review* national critics' poll cowinner for best novel, won the Berea College Centennial award, and won the *Woman's Home Companion* Silver Distaff award. For *Seedtime on the Cumberland*, Arnow won a commendation from the Tennessee Historical Commission. She also received an Award of Merit from the American Association for State and Local History, an Outstanding Alumni award from the University of Louisville, the Kentucky Governor's Award in the Arts for outstanding artistic contribution, an Outstanding Alumni Award from Berea College, and the Mark Twain Award from the Society for the Study of Midwestern Literature. She was inducted into the Michigan Women's Hall of Fame in 1984 and has honorary degrees from Albion College (1955), Transylvania University (1979), and University of Kentucky (1981).

BIOGRAPHY

Harriette Louisa Simpson Arnow was born in 1908 in Wayne County, Kentucky. When she was five years old, her family moved to Burnside. Five of her six novels are set in this southern Kentucky area. Arnow was the second oldest of six children. Her father was a teacher, farmer, and oil-well driller; her mother was a teacher. When she was sixteen years old, she attended Berea College for two years and then taught in rural schools similar to the one she writes of in *Mountain Path*. She taught until she was able to return to college, this time at the University of Louisville. In 1931, she completed a bachelor of science degree in education. After a few years of teaching, she decided to devote herself to writing.

In 1934, Arnow moved to Cincinnati, Ohio. She wrote, read widely, and supported herself with a variety of jobs, including waitress and typist. The publication of her first short stories brought her to the attention of a publisher, who brought out her first novel. Her second novel, *Between the Flowers*, did not satisfy publishers; it was published posthumously in 1999. Arnow also was employed by the Federal Writers Project of the Works

Progress Administration (WPA) in Cincinnati, where she met Harold Arnow of Chicago, a newspaper reporter. They married in 1939.

Arnow and her husband tried farming in the Big South Fork area of Kentucky, but farm work left them little time for writing. After the birth of their daughter Marcella, they moved to Detroit, Michigan, where Harold worked for the *Detroit Times*. For a time, Arnow lived in a Detroit housing project much like the one described in *The Dollmaker*. Their son, Thomas, was born in Detroit. Arnow's second published novel, *Hunter's Horn*, received positive reviews and popular acclaim. Later, the Arnows moved to the country near Ann Arbor, Michigan, where they lived for the rest of their lives.

In 1954, *The Dollmaker* was published to critical and popular success. In her later years, Arnow taught writing workshops and continued with her own writing. At the time of Arnow's death in 1986, she was working on a novel about the Cumberland River area at the time of the American Civil War.

ANALYSIS

With the exception of *The Weedkiller's Daughter*, Harriette Arnow writes of Appalachian characters and settings. Even though she disliked labels, she nevertheless helped to create the genre of modern Appalachian literature and to separate it from local color or regional realism, in which an outside narrator describes the quaint or picturesque way of life of an isolated group of people as a means of entertainment. Arnow, in contrast, writes with sympathy and understanding of rural people and presents them as individuals, not stereotypes. She focuses on the everyday lives of working people, often centering on women, and she excels in depicting the details of their lives and work. Arnow also is careful to present the dialect of these characters as part of her realism, but the unusual spellings can occasionally become distracting.

Often, Arnow's characters find themselves in conflict with a powerful outside force, such as history, culture, economics, or social rules and pressures to conform. This conflict has led many to see a deterministic strain in her works. For example, World War II, the economic situation of her family, and the pressure to conform to materialistic values confront Gertie Nevels, the

protagonist of *The Dollmaker*. This determinism is also seen in Arnow's frequent portrayal of the limitations of women's lives in traditional patriarchal society (Suse and Lureenie in *Hunter's Horn*). Often her characters refuse to conform to the strict religious beliefs of their communities. In spite of the dark fates of some of her characters, Arnow usually holds out hope with characters who make connections through the bonds of common humanity. For example, while encountering prejudice against hillbillies in a wartime Detroit housing project, Gertie is also the recipient of kindness and compassion from the other women in the alley, in spite of their different backgrounds.

Another feature of Arnow's fiction is an ecological awareness. Arnow chronicles the loss of natural habitats due to expanding civilization and urbanization. She notes the damage to land due to poor farming practices. Most of her works also celebrate the beauty and power of nature and her characters' emotional responses to it.

Arnow's first three published novels are often referred to as her Kentucky trilogy. She considered them stories of the erosion of a traditional way of life, as the geographically isolated characters increasingly come into contact with the outside world. *Mountain Path* presents the traditional rural community of the late 1920's. By the late 1930's of *Hunter's Horn*, a gravel road has reached close enough to the community to bring in both positive and negative influences of society beyond. At the time of the World War II setting of *The Dollmaker*, the rural community has become depopulated as the men have gone off to war or to work in factories, often never to return. Taken together, the three novels trace social change in the region.

THE DOLLMAKER

The Dollmaker is Arnow's most widely read and best-known work. Novelist and critic Joyce Carol Oates calls it the "most unpretentious American masterpiece." It is historically important in documenting the great Appalachian out-migration and in presenting a vivid picture of life and work in a wartime housing project in Detroit.

In the novel, Gertie Nevels and her family move to Detroit from Kentucky during World War II so that Clovis, Gertie's husband, can work in one of the war-effort factories. Life in the crowded Detroit housing project where they live contrasts with the peaceful farm life they left behind. For Gertie, whose dream is to buy a small farm, Detroit is a nightmare.

Gertie is a memorable literary creation. A large, powerful woman who finds it difficult to verbalize her thoughts, she often expresses herself by quoting the U.S. Constitution or the Bible, even though she is not conventionally religious. She is an artist, though she calls her wood carvings "whittling" or "foolishness." She grapples with big ideas. For example, in trying to find a face for a figure she is carving in a large block of wood, she considers several possibilities and often wonders if perhaps it is Judas, leading her to speculate on questions of free will, guilt, betrayal, and responsibility.

A major conflict in *The Dollmaker* is that of individualism versus conformity. Even in Kentucky, Gertie is something of an outsider, but with the move to Detroit, she finds herself at odds with almost everything. Gertie is told that she will have to "adjust," meaning, to conform. Two of Gertie's children easily adopt the materialistic values and consumerism of Detroit, but two others struggle. Even though Gertie has doubts about the value of adjusting, she encourages both of them to try to be more like the others in hopes that this will help their unhappiness. Both reject her advice, and she loses them both, albeit in different ways.

The block of wood that Gertie has been carving throughout the story develops as a powerful symbol with several possible meanings. The carving could represent Gertie's role as an artist, her religious ideas, her sense of self, or her ability to help her family. Her destruction of the block of wood at the end of the novel has different meanings, then, depending on what it symbolizes. To help her family financially, Gertie destroys the block to have wood to make small carvings. The splitting of the carving may be viewed as a symbol of hope and of Gertie's reassertion of her ability to provide for her family. Some have called Gertie's obliteration of her art a Christlike sacrifice, but the splitting of the carving may also symbolize the various ways that Gertie and her family have been destroyed by city life. One can also suggest that the demolishing of the figure is Gertie's final adjustment to Detroit. Those interested in learning what happens to Gertie will find her as a minor character in *The Weedkiller's Daughter*, which is set in the late 1960's.

MOUNTAIN PATH

In *Mountain Path*, a coming-of-age novel, the plot is structured around two patterns: the outsider coming to a community and a love story. In the late 1920's, Louisa Sheridan begins teaching in a one-room school in a remote Kentucky valley reachable only by horseback on a rough path. She boards with the school trustee, Lee Buck Cal, who, unknown to her, is a moonshiner. She has accepted the job with reluctance, only so that she can earn enough money to continue her own education. The novel follows her development as she tests her book learning and narrow experience with the reality of life in the valley. Although the plot involves such common topics for fiction as moonshining, a feud, and murder, Arnow avoids cliché by focusing on the women's perspective of these events. The women anxiously wait for the results of their men's actions and then must cope with the outcomes. Louisa comes to admire the locals despite the educational and cultural gulf between herself and them.

Louisa's romantic attraction to Chris Bledsoe, a relative of Lee Buck Cal, brings her into greater sympathy with the ways of her hosts. Chris is hiding out with the family because he has killed a deputy in Tennessee in revenge for his brother's death. The plot is not a conventional romance, although Louisa entertains the fantasy that she could marry Chris and make a life in the valley as a teacher. Chris cannot escape vengeance, and Louisa then desires revenge for what happens to him. She has gone beyond mere understanding.

HUNTER'S HORN

Nunnely Ballew's obsession to track down the destructive fox called King Devil shapes the plot of *Hunter's Horn*. Nunn's decisions early in the novel start a chain of events that lead to neglect of and harm to his family. King Devil is a plague to the region because he snatches hens and kills lambs, so in addition to the pleasure of the hunt, there are practical reasons for killing him. When Nunn has the chance to kill him by spotlighting him when he is nearly cornered, he does not because doing so is not the honorable way to kill a fox. Instead, Nunn vows to chase him down. To that end, he purchases two expensive purebred foxhound puppies to train. The care of these two puppies causes him to shortchange his family in supplies, leads him to neglect his farm, and ultimately lands him in debt. Nunn is aware that his obsession with the fox is harming his family, but he will not abandon his quest. His misplaced sense of honor causes him to shirk his moral responsibility to his family. His hounds eventually do run down King Devil, but not as Nunn expects.

While Nunn is the main character, Arnow also creates a gallery of other characters, which shows the interconnected life of the entire community. The women play important roles but have little choice outside tradition; biology, in the form of pregnancy, determines the destiny of several characters. A subplot centers on Nunn's daughter, Suse, who wants to continue on to high school in town so that she can eventually get away from the farm. However, her father's neglect and bad luck conspire to thwart her dreams and condemn her to a sad fate.

Carol J. Luther

OTHER MAJOR WORKS

SHORT FICTION: *The Collected Short Stories of Harriette Simpson Arnow*, 2005.

NONFICTION: *Seedtime on the Cumberland*, 1960; *Flowering of the Cumberland*, 1963; *Old Burnside: A Memoir of a Southern Girlhood*, 1977.

BIBLIOGRAPHY

Chung, Haeja K., ed. *Harriette Simpson Arnow: Critical Essays on Her Work*. East Lansing: Michigan State University Press, 1995. This volume contains twenty essays divided into three sections: Arnow's life and general essays on her work, critical essays on individual works, and interviews with or essays by Arnow. Some of the essays are reprinted from other sources.

Hobbs, Glenda. "Starting Out in the Thirties: Harriette Arnow's Literary Genesis." In *Literature at the Barricades: The American Writer in the 1930's*, edited by Ralph F. Bogardus and Fred C. Hobson. Tuscaloosa: University of Alabama Press, 1982. Hobbs examines *Mountain Path* and *Between the Flowers* in the light of the interest in the southern rural poor in the 1930's and the stereotypes about them that influenced the content and reception of her work.

Miller, Danny L. *Wingless Flights: Appalachian Women in Fiction*. Bowling Green, Ohio: Bowling Green State University Popular Press, 1996. In chapter 6 of this work, Miller discusses the women of Arnow's Kentucky trilogy, emphasizing their strength. Though often victimized, characters such as Corie Cal, Milly Ballew, and Gertie Nevels are not defeated. Gertie embodies the best in Appalachian women.

Oates, Joyce Carol. "On Harriette Arnow's *The Dollmaker*." In *An American Vein: Critical Readings in Appalachian Literature*, edited by Danny L. Miller, Sharon Hatfield, and Gurney Norman. Athens: Ohio University Press, 2005. In one of the most influential essays on *The Dollmaker*, Oates comments on the novel's reflection of American themes and conflicts. She remarks on the conflict between the competing views of God as love and God as vengeance. The novel explores also the themes of individualism versus conformity and the crushing nature of industrial society.

SHOLEM ASCH

Born: Kutno, Poland, Russian Empire (now in Poland); November 1, 1880
Died: London, England; July 10, 1957
Also known as: Szulim Asz; Shalom Ash

PRINCIPAL LONG FICTION

Dos Shtetl, 1905 (*The Little Town*, 1907)
Amerike, 1911 (*America*, 1918)
Motke Ganev, 1916 (*Mottke the Thief*, 1917)
Onkl Mozes, 1918 (*Uncle Moses*, 1920)
Kiddush Hashem, 1920 (English translation, 1926)
Toyt Urteyl, 1926 (*Judge Not*, 1938)
Khayim Lederers Tsurikkumen, 1927 (*Chaim Lederer's Return*, 1938)
Farn Mabul, 1927-1932 (*Three Cities*, 1933)

Der Tilim Yid, 1934 (*Salvation*, 1934)
Three Novels, 1938 (includes *Uncle Moses*,
    Judge Not, and *Chaim Lederer's Return*)
The Nazarene, 1939
The Apostle, 1943
Ist River, 1946 (*East River*, 1946)
Mary, 1949
Moses, 1951
Der Novi, 1955 (*The Prophet*, 1955)

OTHER LITERARY FORMS

Although Sholem Asch (ahsh) is remembered chiefly as a novelist, much of his early work consists of dramas. When *Der Got fun Nekome* (pr. 1907; *The God of Vengeance*, 1918) was performed on Yiddish stages in Russia and Poland, Max Reinhardt, who understood Yiddish, decided to produce it at the Deutsche Theater. This was the first time that a Yiddish work had appeared in the international literature. This play, in which a brothel owner purchases a Torah to place in his daughter's room, hoping it will protect her from the impurities in the apartment below, was widely condemned as sacrilegious. Many other dramas followed, including adaptations of such novels as *Mottke the Thief*, which enjoyed considerable success on Yiddish stages.

Asch also published *From Many Countries: The Collected Stories of Sholem Asch* (1958) and other collections of short fiction, as well as an autobiographical essay, *What I Believe* (1941), in which he reacted to criticism levied against him by the Jewish community.

ACHIEVEMENTS

Until 1950, Sholem Asch was indisputably the best-known, most translated, most successful Yiddish writer. More than anyone before him, he managed to inject the Yiddish word into world culture, making the world aware of a major literature that had been unjustly ignored. This broader world sometimes seemed more kindly disposed to him than the segment of his Jewish readers who objected to his delineation of the seamier aspects of Jewish life in some works and to his sympathetic treatment of Christianity in others. The bulk of his Jewish readers remained faithful and recognized in him a lover of the poor and weak, a God-seeker, a gentle soul keenly aware that humans did not live by bread alone.

In spite of his high regard for Christianity, Asch remained faithful to Jewish life and tradition, acutely aware of the anti-Semitism all around him. While his characters accept this intolerance as a fact of life, Asch himself could not always assume the same stance. He returned a medal awarded to him by the Polish government when he realized that the policies of that government permitted a heightened anti-Jewish feeling.

A student of the revered I. L. Peretz, whose influence he acknowledged as late as 1951, Asch went beyond the teachings of this master and dealt with topics that Yiddish literature had theretofore avoided. His work marks an abandonment of the rational ways that the Jewish enlightenment had made obligatory for Jewish writers. Like Isaac Bashevis Singer, who replaced him as *the* Yiddish writer on the world stage, Asch was attracted to folkloristic and irrational elements. Because of the diversity of his oeuvre, critics have found it difficult to classify Asch. There is the Romantic who idealized the life of simple Jews and insisted on the primacy of tradition and faith in faith; there is the naturalist who brilliantly depicted the milieus of thieves, jugglers, and prostitutes; there is the didactic moralist who strove to teach the meaning of the good life. There is even a hint of the publicist who fought Hitlerite anti-Semitism by underscoring the basic nobility of Jewish existence and demonstrating the common bonds uniting Judaism and Christianity. This very multiplicity suggests Asch's enduring appeal.

BIOGRAPHY

The tenth child of a pious and prosperous Hasid, Sholem Asch underwent an early formal education in Hebrew language and literature, especially the Bible. His progress indicated sufficient promise for his father to entertain hopes for him in a rabbinic career. As a teenager, Asch came upon his first secular book and became "enlightened." He found employment as a scribe, writing letters for the illiterate, which likely gave him unique insights into the human psyche. At the same time, he was teaching himself German, Russian, and Polish and reading whatever books by major writers became available to him.

At the age of sixteen, Asch visited Peretz, whose stories he had admired, and requested that the master comment on his own efforts, which he was then writing in Hebrew. Peretz liked what he read but urged the youngster to change to Yiddish. Asch's first story, "Moshele," appeared in *Der Jud* in late 1900. A collection of Hebrew stories published in 1902 was followed in 1903 by another in Yiddish. (His writing then, as later, was colored by the dark and dingy places in which he had lived and the hunger he had suffered and which he was never to forget.) Asch married Mathilda Shapiro, the daughter of a teacher and minor poet. In 1904, he serialized his "poem in prose" *The Little Town* in *Der Freint*; in 1905, it was published as a book that quickly established him at the forefront of Yiddish writers.

Asch visited Palestine in 1907 and the United States in 1909. He was awed by biblical sites in Palestine and the evidence of Jewish and Christian events. In America, the landscapes impressed him, but he was repelled by the sweatshops, the tenements, and the quality of the life he observed.

In the ten years preceding World War I, Asch completed ten plays. He lived mostly in France but was forced to leave upon the outbreak of the conflict. In addition to *Mottke the Thief*, his wartime writing, emanating mostly from New York City, included *Uncle Moses*, a novel of immigrants in their initial years in New York.

After the war, Asch revisited Eastern Europe as the representative of a Jewish relief agency. He was horrified by the slaughter of Jews at the hands of Cossacks and White Russians. What he saw reminded him of a seventeenth century Ukrainian slaughterer of Jews whose soldier-peasants terrorized the countryside. The result was the first of his historical novels, *Kiddush Hashem* (sanctification of the name).

In the words of Sol Liptzin, Asch in the postwar years continued "glorifying Jewish deeds of brotherly love and quiet heroism." Before Adolf Hitler rose to power, Asch believed that contrasting such quiet deeds of Jews with the crude Hitlerite reliance on force would be his way of fighting the Nazi menace. *Salvation*, written in 1932, was the most spiritual novel he wrote, and he was embittered by its poor reception.

Asch's spiritual orientation, accompanied by the desire to strengthen the Jewish position, led to novels on Jesus (*The Nazarene*), Paul (*The Apostle*), and Mary (*Mary*). These works alienated his Jewish readers, who feared a case of apostasy at a time when Hitler was decimating European Jewry. *The Nazarene* was published in English before a Yiddish publisher would touch it. The controversy continued for nearly a decade. The resilience of European Jews and the establishment of a Jewish state tore Asch out of his isolation and prompted him to turn to *Moses*, which he had begun long before and had laid aside in favor of his Christian novels.

In 1954, having lived in the United States and France, Asch settled permanently in Israel, where he wrote *The Prophet* (1955). As the chronicler of a world that had disappeared, Asch became again an object of admiration—a condition that his insatiable ego demanded. In 1957, he suffered a mild stroke. While in London for an operation, he died before surgery could be performed.

Sholem Asch. (Library of Congress)

Analysis

Nearly all of Sholem Asch's works are related, in a broad sense, to some religious concern. His many themes are clearly intertwined: the simple, traditional life of the Jew; saintliness in the quest for God and service to humans; the ugliness of poverty but the distinct possibility of meaningful beauty even in poverty; the emptiness of a purely material existence; the Jewish roots of Christianity and the need to close the gap between the two faiths. In fact, faith in both its meanings—trust in God and different institutionalized ways of reaching Him—is a thread running through all of Asch's works, but especially his later works.

The Little Town

Even in his first major work, *The Little Town*, Asch had romanticized the inwardness of Jewish life in the shtetl, a different approach from the ridicule usually heaped upon the backward enclaves in literature. Asch perceived nobility and charm in the poverty-ridden, filth-infested shtetl.

Similarly, Asch dealt with spiritual and sacrificial heroism before dealing with it directly in *Kiddush Hashem*. Living far out in the Padolian steppe, a Jewish innkeeper, Mendel, dreams of the day when other Jews will join him in the town and enable him to build a synagogue and lead a Jewish existence. Mendel eventually overcomes the threats of the local priest, and a small but flourishing Jewish community comes into being. Mendel and the congregation are dangerously sandwiched between the machinations of the Catholic priest and the Greek Orthodox priest. The former is intent on humbling the latter. What better means of debasing his rival than to force him to go to the Jew Mendel to obtain the key to his own church? In his frustration, the Orthodox priest threatens Mendel: Sooner or later "the little brothers" will come to liberate the peasants from the Polish lords and the filthy Jews.

The little brothers eventually come, under the leadership of Bogdan Chmelnitzky, and lay waste not only to Mendel's but also to every Jewish community far and wide. Mendel's attachment to his synagogue is such that he refuses to leave, but the rabbi reminds him that the synagogue is only stone, while a human life is a human life. Mendel's Jews flee, joining the stream of refugees; they put up a heroic fight with virtually no weapons.

They are finally conquered through the betrayal of the Polish lords, who are only too willing to sacrifice their Jewish allies in the mistaken belief that they can thereby save themselves.

Through Mendel and his family, which includes a learned son and his beautiful wife, Asch depicts the simplicity and piety of Jewish life and the Jews' willingness to live and die for "the sanctification of the name." Jews are offered a chance to save their lives by bowing before the Cross, but they will bow only before their one and only God. All resist the easy way out, sacrificially preferring to suffer cruelty, death, and martyrdom. Although the body may be destroyed, the will and spirit are indestructible. Asch only implies that the Jews' imperishable faith in God has ensured their survival in the past and will ensure it in the future.

Charles Madison has stated that "Asch's compassionate brooding gives the tragic tale the poignant quality of imaginative truth." This critic has also distinguished between two forms of martyrdom—Mendel's, which is not a pure martyrdom in that it is wholly passive, and his daughter-in-law's, which is active: She persuades the Cossack captor who loves her that he should shoot her, on the pretense that no bullet can hurt her.

Kiddush Hashem

Kiddush Hashem is perhaps Asch's only novel in which religious motifs and Jewish historical destiny, especially the Jews' suffering for their survival as a group, fuse successfully. The structure of the novel, on the other hand, is awkward, which prevents it from becoming the masterpiece it might have been.

Mottke the Thief

If *The Little Town* and *Kiddush Hashem* are, to use Liptzin's words, in a Sabbath mood, *Mottke the Thief* is decidedly workaday. Asch abandons the idealized Jews of earlier works to offer such sad human specimens as Blind Layb and Red Slatke, Mottke's parents. Layb is a vicious, irresponsible father whose only guidance to his child is the lash, which he uses freely and cruelly. Not only is Jewish life imperfect in *Mottke the Thief*, in spite of some obedience to forms and tradition, but it also exists on the lowest levels of humanity. Asch shows an exceptional virtuosity in this novel. The first half combines picaresque with gargantuan, larger-than-life features; the second half is Zolaesque in its depressing naturalism.

The abused Mottke, first open enough to seek affection even from a curious dog, is transformed into a callous pimp and murderer, a development that calls for considerable skill, which Asch demonstrates in good measure.

Asch's earlier work might have given rise to the impression that there was something do-goodish in the writer, that his feet were not firmly planted on the ground. With the creation of Mottke, this impression was swept aside. From the moment Mottke joins a group of vaudevillians, uses and abuses them, seduces or is seduced by Mary, the rope dancer, and competes with the treacherous Kanarik, he becomes a character apart from any that Asch had previously created. The erstwhile thief's descent into total depravity continues. With Mary's help, he kills Kanarik, assumes Kanarik's identity, and acquires his own small staff of prostitutes. Yet the Mottke who had once enjoyed something of a Jewish upbringing, however atypical, is not wholly dead. He is fatally attracted to a decent girl, and his love generates decent impulses that have long been submerged. The desire for chastity, piety, and living in the love of and reverence for God, however, has been resurrected too late. Perhaps Mottke's conversion, which comes to naught, is not the most persuasive part of the book; in any case, Mottke is betrayed by the sweet girl he loves. Yet even in the novel's variety of depressing settings, Asch still emerges as a man with a profound faith in faith.

SALVATION

Salvation, a story of the saintly Jekhiel and his quest for God and ways of serving humanity, is more in the mainstream of Asch's fiction than is *Mottke the Thief*. It is probably the most purely "spiritual" of Asch's novels—a term he himself used to describe it—and he attributed its relative failure with the reading public to the refusal of the modern world to address spiritual questions.

Jekhiel's father was a Hasid who left his wife and younger son to join his rabbi in study. Jekhiel was a deep disappointment to him, for, unlike Jekhiel's older brother, Jekhiel has failed to grasp the subtleties of the Talmud. Jekhiel, oppressed by a sense of failure, helps his mother eke out a bare living in the marketplace. She dies, and the youngster serves as tutor to an innkeeper's children, to whom he teaches the elements of the Hebrew language. Jekhiel is heartened one day by a wise stranger, who tells him that knowing the Psalms, with their simple yet warm teachings, is every bit as important in the sight of God as the subtle shadings of talmudic disputation. Soon Jekhiel is known as the Psalm-Jew (which was, indeed, the original Yiddish title of the novel).

In this first half of *Salvation*, Asch poses several questions, to which his answers are clear. He is not enamored of the father, who puts study—however strong an ethic in Jewish tradition—ahead of his familial obligations; Asch does not place learning the Talmud above simpler aspects of the Jewish obligation to ponder the ways of God. A cold, rational approach to religion attracts him less than a warmer, human, perhaps less rational mode.

Jekhiel, without wishing it, develops a following of his own, becoming the rabbi of the Psalms, simple and humble. He is also known for miracles, for which, however, he claims no credit. On one occasion, Jekhiel, under great pressure, commits God to giving a child to a hitherto barren woman. A girl is born. When Jekhiel's wife dies shortly thereafter, the pious rabbi sees it as a sign from Heaven. He leaves home and, in the manner of ascetic saints of all faiths, roams the countryside in rags. He is finally recognized and forced to return.

The years pass, and the girl whose birth he had promised has grown to maturity and fallen in love with a strapping young Polish soldier. They plan to marry. In preparation for her conversion to Catholicism, she enters a convent. There is consternation in the girl's family. Torn by conflicting pressures, the girl jumps to her death. Jekhiel, who had fought the conversion, is troubled for the second time: Has he overstepped proper bounds again? Was not human life and the search for God more precious than the particular way of reaching Him: the Jewish or the Christian?

Asch's implied tolerance of intermarriage again brought him into conflict with his Jewish readers. *Salvation* paved the way for a work that would nearly lead to a rupture with these readers: the story of Jesus of Nazareth, whose emphases within Judaism were not that different from those of Jekhiel the Psalm-Jew.

THE NAZARENE

The problem of Christian anti-Semitism is omnipresent in the oeuvre of Sholem Asch. Considering the author's vision of Jesus, an extension of his characterization of Jekhiel, it is not surprising that Asch often felt bitter about the crimes against Jews committed in the name of the saintly Nazarene. Throughout *The Nazarene*, Asch has his Rabbi Jeshua repeat that he has not come to destroy the Law but to fulfill it. Jeshua observes all but one or two of the ritual commandments, but it is his failure to observe those that his wealthy detractors use against him. Asch's Jesus is learned in the Torah; the character appears to be depicted in the tradition of the great teacher Hillel; he has infinite wisdom and compassion. If, in spite of its strengths, *The Nazarene* fails to satisfy completely, that failure must be attributed to the nature of the subject.

Jeshua as a man, as a self-revealed Messiah, and as a Son of Man (interpreted to mean the Son of God) is a difficult fusion to achieve. Asch is as successful as any novelist who has ever attempted it or, for that matter, biographers and interpreters. There are times, however, when Jeshua, ever mysterious—now very human, now very enigmatic, even furtive—suggests ever so slightly the religious charlatan. Yet this was far from Asch's intent and has not been the impression of all readers.

Jeshua's teachings are within the frame of Jewish tradition, but as he himself says, the fulfillment of that tradition requires new interpretations and emphases. The occasional impressions of hucksterism are held only by the more cynical modern reader, reacting to Jesus' refusal to answer questions directly, to speak in parables only, to select carefully his moments of healing and revealing, to satisfy the doubts of the most searching and spiritually avid of his disciples and admirers. Rabbi Jeshua has a talent for the grand gesture and for the attention-getting phrase or figure of speech, but this image is not one created by Asch; it is, rather, inherent in the subject matter, which he derives entirely from New Testament sources. There are few famous sayings of Jesus that are not quoted, and the endless quotations, although necessary, at times slow the pace of the narrative.

Asch underscores the innovations of the teachings of Jesus: compassion for the poor, the sick, the neglected; the emphasis on the spirit, not the forms, of observance; the primacy of faith; a piety that adds to fervor of the divine humility and an all-encompassing pity; and an involvement in the affairs of humans. Jesus attacks privi-

lege, be it hereditary or earned. The task of involving oneself in the suffering of others must be never-ending; it must lead to the more fortunate assisting those who are suffering. Rabbi Jeshua's leniency toward the sinner, reassurance of the untutored and ignorant, and forbearance vis-à-vis those who have disappointed him all contribute to making him an innovative teacher and preacher. In the end, Jeshua dies, like so many of Asch's noble characters, for the sanctification of the name.

Asch was attracted to the story of Jesus on an early trip to Palestine, but he did not turn to writing it until decades later, when the need for closer Jewish-Christian ties seemed to him highly desirable. The device he finally employed for telling it was ingenious: A half-demented anti-Semitic Polish scholar, imagining that he was Pontius Pilate's right-hand man, relates the first third of the novel. Judas Ischariot, Jesus' most learned disciple, whom Asch rehabilitates in the novel, tells the next third in the form of a diary. The final third, recounted by a Jewish disciple of Nicodemus, a rabbi sympathetic to Jeshua, reports on the political and religious evasions within the Sanhedrin and Pilate's desire to rid himself of the troublemaking revolutionary.

Again, Asch displays his mastery of painting different milieus. The messianic craving among lowly and wealthy Jews, the Roman cynicism toward this strangest of peoples, the Jews, the doings in the Temple, the political rivalries between priests and scholars, the evocation of historical figures, the atmosphere of Jesus' preaching and reception in Galilee—all come alive in Asch's prose. If Rabbi Jeshua is only partly convincing, it is because his dual status as man and Messiah may well elude even the most skillful of writers.

EAST RIVER

Set on New York's East Side, another radically different milieu, *East River* is hardly one of Asch's better novels. The writing, even the syntax, appears a bit sloppy, and the work bears the marks of haste. The novel does, however, pull together many of Asch's most typical themes and interests: the poor sorely tried, and not by poverty alone; one son given to learning, the other to practical pursuits; traditional Jewish religious learning transformed into secular equivalents; anti-Semitism and the need for Jewish-Christian dialogue; the spirit of a religion versus its mere forms. Intermarriage, which unleashed a minor religious war between contending religious leaders in *Salvation*, is treated here with sympathy and understanding.

To be sure, Moshe Wolf, symbol of the old life, cannot reconcile himself to his wealthy son's intermarriage, but neither can he accept—in spite of, or because of, his own poverty—this son's exploitation of Jewish and Christian workers. Wolf, a near saint, accepts with love and understanding the burdens imposed on him by God: his beloved older son's crippling polio, this son's failure to use his dazzling intelligence to study Scripture, applying it instead to secular ideas, which often frighten the traditional Jew in him. Wolf's wife, Deborah, thoroughly Americanized, has more understanding for the tycoon son than for the "cripple." For her, the former has succeeded; the latter, with his superfluous learning, is useless.

The Catholic girl who originally loved the cripple but then married the tycoon is treated sympathetically and is ultimately accepted by Wolf as a God-loving, God-seeking human being. Mary breaks with her pathologically anti-Semitic failure of a father and leads her husband back to the ways of decency and righteousness. Mary's relationships with her father and husband are not credible and detract seriously from any power the novel might have. Yet for whatever it is worth, Mary convinces her husband not to live only for himself or even his immediate family, but to enlist himself in the war against poverty, injustice, and cruelty. The old lesson is repeated here in less subtle form: Humans do not live by bread, or money, alone.

Asch's daring in tackling milieus that cannot have been close to him is admirable: a grocery store, Tammany Hall, sweatshops, synagogue politics, Jewish-Irish relations, the garment industry. It is interesting to speculate what this book would have been like at the height of Asch's literary power. A courageous failure, it testifies to the profoundly ecumenical spirit of his fiction.

Lothar Kahn

OTHER MAJOR WORKS

SHORT FICTION: *From Many Countries: The Collected Stories of Sholem Asch*, 1958.

PLAYS: *Tsurikgekumen*, pr. 1904; *Der Got fun Nekome*, pr. 1907 (*The God of Vengeance*, 1918).

NONFICTION: *What I Believe*, 1941; *One Destiny: An Epistle to the Christians*, 1945.

BIBLIOGRAPHY

Brodwin, Stanley. "History and Martyrological Tragedy: The Jewish Experience in Sholem Asch and Andre Schwarz." *Twentieth Century Literature* 40 (1994): 72-91. An excellent comparative analysis of Asch's novel *Kiddush Hashem* and Andre Schwarz-Bart's *Le Dernier des justes*. The novels focus on the biblical injunction of *Kiddish hashem*, in which both the Jewish individual and the Jewish community are called upon to sanctify the name of God by suffering martyrdom.

Fischthal, Hannah Berliner. "Christianity as a Consistent Area of Investigation of Sholem Asch's Works Prior to *The Nazarene*." *Yiddish* 9 (1994): 58-76. Focuses on how Asch treated Christianity in the works he wrote prior to *The Nazarene*, his controversial 1939 novel based on the life of Jesus Christ.

Lieberman, Herman. *The Christianity of Sholem Asch*. New York: Philosophical Library, 1953. Lieberman, a columnist for the Yiddish-language newspaper *Forward*, provides a scathing denunciation of *The Nazarene*, claiming that Asch's novel about the life of Jesus "may lure away ignorant Jewish children into worshipping foreign gods."

Norich, Anita. *Discovering Exile: Yiddish and Jewish American Culture During the Holocaust*. Stanford, Calif.: Stanford University Press, 2007. Studies the writings of Asch and other Jewish authors who published works in both Yiddish and English during the Holocaust to demonstrate how the Yiddish- and English-speaking worlds of the 1930's and 1940's drew upon each other for inspiration.

Siegel, Ben. *The Controversial Sholem Asch: An Introduction to His Fiction*. Bowling Green, Ohio: Bowling Green State University Press, 1976. Often cited as the best introduction to Asch's life and work, this book is especially good for its examination of the controversy that followed the publication of *The Nazarene*. Includes a chronology, bibliography, and detailed index.

Slochower, Harry. "Franz Werfel and Sholem Asch: The Yearning for Status." In *No Voice Is Wholly Lost:*

Writers and Thinkers in War and Peace. New York: Creative Age Press, 1945. This essay is another good comparative analysis to be read in conjunction with that of Stanley Brodwin.

Stahl, Nanette, ed. *Sholem Asch Reconsidered*. New Haven, Conn.: Beinecke Rare Book and Manuscript Library, Yale University, 2004. Reprints lectures delivered at a conference held at Yale in 2000, in which Yiddish literary critics reevaluated Asch's work. Includes a discussion of his christological novels, plays, and American fiction, as well as his novels dealing with the radical change and dislocation experienced by European Jews at the beginning of the twentieth century. Also includes an overview of Asch's life by his great-grandson, David Mazower.

Steinberg, Theodore. L. "Sholem Asch's *Three Cities*." In *Twentieth-Century Epic Novels*. Newark: University of Delaware Press, 2005. Steinberg analyzes *Three Cities* and four novels by other authors to demonstrate how the novels' themes and contents, especially their heroic elements, qualify them as modern epics.

ISAAC ASIMOV

Born: Petrovichi, Russia, Soviet Union (now in Russia); January 2, 1920
Died: New York, New York; April 6, 1992
Also known as: Paul French; Isaak Ozimov

PRINCIPAL LONG FICTION

Pebble in the Sky, 1950
Foundation, 1951
The Stars Like Dust, 1951
The Currents of Space, 1952
Foundation and Empire, 1952
Second Foundation, 1953
The Caves of Steel, 1954
The End of Eternity, 1955
The Naked Sun, 1957
The Death-Dealers, 1958 (also known as *A Whiff of Death*)
Fantastic Voyage, 1966
The Gods Themselves, 1972
Murder at the ABA: A Puzzle in Four Days and Sixty Scenes, 1976
Foundation's Edge, 1982
The Robots of Dawn, 1983
Foundation and Earth, 1985
Robots and Empire, 1985
Fantastic Voyage II: Destination Brain, 1987
Azazel, 1988

Prelude to Foundation, 1988
Nemesis, 1989
Robot Dreams, 1989
Robot Visions, 1990
Nightfall, 1991 (with Robert Silverberg)
The Ugly Little Boy, 1992 (with Silverberg)
Forward the Foundation, 1993
The Positronic Man, 1993 (with Silverberg)

OTHER LITERARY FORMS

Isaac Asimov (AZ-eh-mof) was an unusually prolific author with more than five hundred published books in his bibliography, including fiction, autobiographies, edited anthologies of fiction, and nonfiction works ranging in subject from the Bible to science, history, and humor; only his most famous major novels are listed above. His series of juvenile science-fiction novels about the character Lucky Starr first appeared under the pseudonym Paul French. Asimov also regularly wrote articles on science and literature, and he lent his name to a science-fiction magazine for which he wrote a monthly article. The magazine has continued in publication since Asimov's death.

Asimov wrote three autobiographies: *Before the Golden Age* (1974); *In Memory Yet Green* (1979), which covers his life from 1920 to 1954; and *In Joy Still Felt* (1980), which continues from 1954 to 1978. In *I. Asi-*

mov: A Memoir (1994), he addresses the events of his life in more anecdotal form. *Yours, Isaac Asimov: A Lifetime of Letters* (1995) is a posthumous collection of excerpts from letters written by Asimov, edited by his brother Stanley Asimov. In 2002, Asimov's wife, Janet Jeppson Asimov, published an edited condensation of Asimov's three autobiographies titled *It's Been a Good Life*. This consolidation includes the short story "The Last Question," personal letters to the editor, and an epilogue by Jeppson giving details on Asimov's illness and death.

ACHIEVEMENTS

Isaac Asimov was widely known as one of the "big three" science-fiction writers, the other two being Robert A. Heinlein and Arthur C. Clarke. In addition to obtaining a doctorate in biochemistry from Columbia University, Asimov was awarded fourteen honorary doctoral degrees from various universities. He won seven Hugo Awards (for achievements in science fiction) in various categories. He was awarded the Nebula Award (awarded by the Science Fiction Writers of America) in 1972 for *The Gods Themselves* and again in 1977 for the novelette *The Bicentennial Man* (later expanded by Robert Silverberg to *The Positronic Man*). In 1987, Asimov received the Nebula Grand Master Award, the eighth to be given; all seven of the previous awards had been given to science-fiction authors who were still living and had begun publication before Asimov. Earlier, the American Chemical Society had given Asimov the James T. Grady Award in 1965, and he received the Westinghouse Science Writing Award in 1967. Asimov wrote on a huge number of subjects, and he has at least one book numbered in each of the ten Dewey Decimal Library System's major classifications.

BIOGRAPHY

Isaac Asimov emigrated to the United States with his Russian Jewish parents when he was three years old; they settled in Brooklyn, New York. Unsure of his actual birthday, due to poor record keeping in Russia at the time, he claimed January 2, 1920. Encountering early science-fiction magazines at his father's candy store,

Isaac Asimov. (Library of Congress)

where he began working when his mother was pregnant with his brother, led him to follow dual careers as scientist and author. Asimov was the eldest of three children; he had a sister, Marcia, and a brother, Stanley. He considered himself an American and never learned to speak Russian; in later life he studied Hebrew and Yiddish. In high school, Asimov wrote a regular column for his school's newspaper. He entered Columbia University at age fifteen, and by age eighteen, he sold his first story to the magazine *Amazing Stories*.

Graduating from Columbia with a B.S. in chemistry in 1939, Asimov applied to all five New York City medical schools and was turned down. He was also rejected for the master's program at Columbia but convinced the department to accept him on probation. He earned his master's degree in chemistry in 1941. His doctoral program was interrupted by his service in World War II as a junior chemist at the Philadelphia Naval Yard from 1942 through 1945. He worked there with fellow science-fiction writer Robert A. Heinlein.

Asimov earned his doctorate in biochemistry in 1948, and after graduation he worked for a year as a researcher at Columbia before becoming an instructor at Boston University School of Medicine. He was granted tenure there in 1955, but he gave up his duties to write full time, while retaining his title. The university promoted him to the rank of full professor in 1979.

Asimov married Gertrude Blugerman in July of 1942. They had two children, a son named David and a daughter named Robyn Joan. They were divorced on November 16, 1973, and Asimov married Janet Opal Jeppson fifteen days later. They had no children, but they wrote the Norby robot children's books together. Asimov was afraid of heights and flew in airplanes only twice in his life. On the other hand, he enjoyed closed-in places, and he thought that the city he describes in his book *The Caves of Steel* would be a very appealing place to live. Asimov was not religious but was proud of his Jewish ethnic heritage. He enjoyed public speaking almost as much as he enjoyed writing and had an exuberant personality. He died in New York City on April 6, 1992, at the age of seventy-two.

ANALYSIS

Isaac Asimov was especially known for his ability to explain complicated scientific concepts clearly. Although his reputation as a writer is based primarily on his science fiction, his nonfiction writings are useful reference works on the many subjects he covered. His goal was not only to entertain but also to inform.

Most of Asimov's novels are science fiction, and, of these, fourteen novels are tied together at some point with part of the Foundation series. Early in his writing career Asimov established four series of stories: the Empire series, consisting of three novels and collections of short stories; the Foundation series, consisting of seven novels, with more that Asimov outlined to be finished by other authors; the Robot series, consisting of four novels and collections of short stories; and the Lucky Starr series, a collection of six works for children not related to the Foundation series. Asimov borrowed heavily from history, specifically the history of the Roman Empire,

to create his plot lines for the Foundation books. Of all his novels, *The Gods Themselves*, a Hugo and Nebula Award winner, was Asimov's favorite.

EMPIRE SERIES

The Empire series consists of three novels, *Pebble in the Sky*, *The Stars Like Dust*, and *The Currents of Space*. Later Foundation series books attempt to tie these three into that series. Asimov's first published novel, *Pebble in the Sky*, is the best of these. The writing is not Asimov's most polished, but the hero, Joseph Schwartz, provides an interesting middle-aged counterpoint to Bel Arvardan, a younger man of action coping with a postapocalyptic, radioactive Earth.

FOUNDATION SERIES

The Foundation series began as a trilogy. The first three Foundation books, known for some time as the Foundation trilogy, were written in the 1950's and took much of their plot lines from the history of the Roman Empire. Because of the length of the trilogy, it is rarely taught in schools, but the first two of the three books, *Foundation* and *Foundation and Empire*, are examples of Asimov's fiction at its best.

The hero of these novels is Hari Seldon, a mathematician who invents the discipline of psychohistory. Using psychohistory, Seldon is able to predict the coming fall of the empire and to help set up the Foundation in order to help humankind move more quickly through the coming "dark ages" that will be caused by the collapse of the empire. Psychohistory is unable to predict individual mutations and events in human history, however, so Seldon's Foundation is unable to predict the rise of the Mule, a mutant of superior intelligence, to the position of galactic overlord. Asimov's introduction of the concept of psychohistory, a science that could predict the future course of humankind, has inspired many scholars of history, psychology, sociology, and economics and was significant in the creation of an actual psychohistory major at some colleges and universities.

By the third book, *Second Foundation*, Asimov was tired of the Foundation story and came up with two alternate endings that he hoped would let him be free of it. In the first, the Mule discovers the secret second Foundation and destroys it, thereby ending Seldon's plan. Asimov's editor talked him out of this ending, so he wrote another, in which the Second Foundation triumphs. Seldon's plan is restored to course and nothing of interest happens again to the human species—thus freeing Asimov from the need to write further Foundation novels. Time and financial incentives eventually overcame Asimov's boredom with the Foundation trilogy, however, and thirty years later, in the 1980's and 1990's, he began filling in the gaps around the original stories with other novels. He went on to produce *Foundation's Edge*, *Foundation and Earth*, *Prelude to Foundation*, and *Forward the Foundation*. None of these has quite the same magic as the first two Foundation novels.

ROBOT SERIES

The ideas introduced by Asimov in the Robot series are perhaps his most famous. Asimov's robots are human in form and have "positronic" brains. In the late 1980's and 1990's, the television program *Star Trek: The Next Generation* and the feature films based on it contributed to public awareness of this concept through the character of the android Data, who, like Asimov's robots, has a positronic brain. Asimov also invented the three Laws of Robotics, which he tended not to let other people use. His invention of mechanical creatures with built-in ethical systems is used freely, however, and from that standpoint Data is an Asimovian robot. The concept of a tool designed for safety in the form of a robot was new to science-fiction writing when Asimov introduced it, and it stood in sharp contrast to the usual mechanical men of science-fiction pulp magazines, which tended to run amok in dangerous fashion.

Exciting ideas and parts are to be found in each of the four Robot novels, *The Caves of Steel*, *The Naked Sun*, *The Robots of Dawn*, and *Robots and Empire*. *The Caves of Steel* is a good place to start. The character R. Daneel Olivaw is introduced in this novel and appears in six additional novels. The "R." in his name stands for "robot." This particular novel is also notable for its blending of two genres, science fiction and mystery. Additionally, the title describes Asimov's solution to an overcrowded Earth, an incredible complex of multilayered megacities covering the entire planet.

Another part of the Robot series is Asimov's short-story collection *I, Robot*. This work lent its title and character names to a motion picture released in 2004. The 1999 film *Bicentennial Man* is also based on Asimov's Robot series.

LUCKY STARR SERIES

Because he was intentionally writing the Lucky Starr juvenile novels for a hoped-for television series and was afraid that they would affect his reputation as a serious science-fiction writer, Asimov originally published them under the pseudonym Paul French. In these novels, David Starr and his friend Bigman Jones travel around the solar system in a spaceship. Asimov adapted the stereotypes of the Western genre to create the books' plots, but he used his amazing ability to explain science to create plot devices and solutions based on science.

THE GODS THEMSELVES

The Gods Themselves is one of Asimov's best novels and one of the few unrelated to any others. To single it out as a stand-alone work, however, would be to imply that the books of his series are dependent upon one another, which is not true. *The Gods Themselves* is one of the few Asimov novels dealing with aliens.

The Gods Themselves (the title is taken from a quote by German dramatist Friedrich Schiller, "Against stupidity the gods themselves contend in vain") is actually a series of three interrelated stories treating stupidity and responses to it. Humans exchange energy with aliens in a parallel universe with the Inter-Universe Electron Pump. When one human realizes the pump will eventually cause the sun to explode, he works to warn others, but nobody listens. Meanwhile, in the parallel universe, one of the "para-men" also attempts to shut down the pump. Although neither succeeds, owing to stupidity on the part of his peers, the problem eventually is solved by others in one of the parallel universes, and the human universe is saved.

MYSTERIES

Another fiction genre in which Asimov enjoyed writing was the mystery. He published ten mystery short-story collections and the novel *Murder at the ABA: A Puzzle in Four Days and Sixty Scenes*. This novel is a roman à clef, as the main character is Asimov's friend and fellow science-fiction writer Harlan Ellison, as portrayed by the character Darius Just (pronounced dar-I-us, to rhyme with bias). Asimov appears in the novel, and it includes footnoted comments by both Asimov and Darius Just. The action takes place at the hotel where the American Booksellers Association's annual convention is being held. During the convention, Darius Just's protégé, Giles Devore, is found dead in the bathtub of his hotel room. The police treat the death as an accident, but certain factors about the state of the hotel room make Darius suspect that it is murder.

Darius sets out to prove that it is indeed murder, and along the way he has a couple of sexual interludes, one with a friend from the book-publishing world and another with an attractive hotel liaison. Several of the key conversations leading up to the death of Giles Devore occur during meals eaten at social events during the convention. In order to prove that Giles has been murdered, Darius interviews everyone who has worked with Giles during the twenty-four hours preceding his death. He discovers during this process that Giles indulged in an unusual sexual practice in addition to his compulsive behavior regarding pens and clothing.

Asimov's mysteries, like his other fiction work, tend to focus on the cleverness of situations or on science rather than on any deep individual characterization. The Black Widowers collections of short stories, such as *Tales of the Black Widowers* (1974) and *Banquets of the Black Widowers* (1984), like *Murder at the ABA*, follow the roman à clef style; they are based on the monthly meetings during which Asimov and his friends would have dinner and discuss science, writing, history, and world events.

NOVELETTES

As a publishing ploy, it was arranged that science-fiction novelist Robert Silverberg would expand three of Asimov's best and most famous novelettes—*Nightfall*, *The Bicentennial Man* (which became *The Positronic Man*), and *The Ugly Little Boy*—into full novels. Although Silverberg is an excellent and literary writer, his style and Asimov's do not blend particularly well. Given the opportunity, readers would be well served by reading the original award-winning works. The original version of *Nightfall*, in particular, has won worldwide acclaim and is the most mentioned and remembered of Asimov's novelettes. Its premise concerns what happens to the psyches of a people who live in a world that experiences total darkness only once every two thousand years.

The original novelette *Nightfall* has twice been the basis for motion pictures; the first film adaptation, titled *Nightfall*, was released in 1988 (retitled *Isaac Asimov's Nightfall* for a video release in 2000), and the second,

which retained the underlying science concept of Asimov's work, was released in 2000 as *Pitch Black*. *Nightfall* tells the story of a world in a solar system with six suns. Because the suns never set, it has been daylight on the planet for more than two thousand years. The work presents a sociological exploration of the reactions of the inhabitants of this world when a total eclipse of the suns occurs and they are thrown into darkness for the first time in one hundred generations.

B. Diane Blackwood

OTHER MAJOR WORKS

SHORT FICTION: *I, Robot*, 1950; *The Martian Way*, 1955; *Earth Is Room Enough*, 1957; *Nine Tomorrows*, 1959; *The Rest of the Robots*, 1964; *Asimov's Mysteries*, 1968; *Nightfall, and Other Stories*, 1969; *The Early Asimov*, 1972; *Tales of the Black Widowers*, 1974; *Buy Jupiter, and Other Stories*, 1975; *The Bicentennial Man, and Other Stories*, 1976; *More Tales of the Black Widowers*, 1976; *Good Taste*, 1977; *The Key Word, and Other Mysteries*, 1977; *Casebook of the Black Widowers*, 1980; *Computer Crimes and Capers*, 1983; *The Union Club Mysteries*, 1983; *The Winds of Change, and Other Stories*, 1983; *Banquets of the Black Widowers*, 1984; *The Disappearing Man, and Other Mysteries*, 1985; *Alternative Asimovs*, 1986; *Isaac Asimov: The Complete Stories*, 1990-1992 (2 volumes); *The Return of the Black Widowers*, 2003.

NONFICTION: *The Chemicals of Life: Enzymes, Vitamins, Hormones*, 1954; *Inside the Atom*, 1956; *The World of Carbon*, 1958; *The World of Nitrogen*, 1958; *Realm of Numbers*, 1959; *Words of Science and the History Behind Them*, 1959; *The Intelligent Man's Guide to Science*, 1960; *The Wellsprings of Life*, 1960; *Life and Energy*, 1962; *The Search for the Elements*, 1962; *The Genetic Code*, 1963; *Asimov's Biographical Encyclopedia of Science and Technology*, 1964; *The Human Body: Its Structures and Operation*, 1964; *The Human Brain: Its Capacities and Functions*, 1964; *Planets for Man*, 1964 (with Stephen H. Dole); *A Short History of Biology*, 1964; *The Greeks: A Great Adventure*, 1965; *The New Intelligent Man's Guide to Science*, 1965; *A Short History of Chemistry*, 1965; *The Genetic Effects of Radiation*, 1966; *The Neutrino: Ghost Particle of the Atom*, 1966; *The Roman Republic*, 1966; *Understanding Phys-*

ics, 1966; *The Universe: From Flat Earth to Quasar*, 1966; *The Egyptians*, 1967; *The Roman Empire*, 1967; *The Dark Ages*, 1968; *Science, Numbers, and I*, 1968; *Asimov's Guide to the Bible*, 1968-1969 (2 volumes); *The Shaping of England*, 1969; *Asimov's Guide to Shakespeare*, 1970 (2 volumes); *Constantinople: The Forgotten Empire*, 1970; *Electricity and Man*, 1972; *The Shaping of France*, 1972; *Worlds Within Worlds: The Story of Nuclear Energy*, 1972; *The Shaping of North America from Earliest Times to 1763*, 1973; *Today, Tomorrow, and . . .* , 1973; *Before the Golden Age*, 1974 (autobiography); *The Birth of the United States, 1763-1816*, 1974; *Earth: Our Crowded Spaceship*, 1974; *Our World in Space*, 1974; *Our Federal Union: The United States from 1816 to 1865*, 1975; *Science Past—Science Future*, 1975; *The Collapsing Universe*, 1977; *The Golden Door: The United States from 1865 to 1918*, 1977; *A Choice of Catastrophes: The Disasters That Threaten Our World*, 1979; *Extraterrestrial Civilizations*, 1979; *In Memory Yet Green: The Autobiography of Isaac Asimov, 1920-1954*, 1979; *The Annotated "Gulliver's Travels,"* 1980; *Asimov on Science Fiction*, 1980; *In Joy Still Felt: The Autobiography of Isaac Asimov, 1954-1978*, 1980; *In the Beginning*, 1981; *Visions of the Universe*, 1981; *Exploring the Earth and the Cosmos: The Growth and Future of Human Knowledge*, 1982; *The Roving Mind*, 1983; *The History of Physics*, 1984; *Asimov's Guide to Halley's Comet*, 1985; *The Edge of Tomorrow*, 1985; *Exploding Suns*, 1985; *Robots: Machines in Man's Image*, 1985 (with Karen A. Frenkel); *The Dangers of Intelligence, and Other Science Essays*, 1986; *Beginnings: The Story of Origins—of Mankind, Life, the Earth, the Universe*, 1987; *Past, Present, and Future*, 1987; *Asimov's Annotated Gilbert and Sullivan*, 1988; *The Relativity of Wrong*, 1988; *Asimov on Science*, 1989; *Asimov's Chronology of Science and Discovery*, 1989; *Asimov's Galaxy*, 1989; *Frontiers*, 1990; *Asimov's Chronology of the World: The History of the World from the Big Bang to Modern Times*, 1991; *Atom: Journey Across the Subatomic Cosmos*, 1991; *I. Asimov: A Memoir*, 1994; *Yours, Isaac Asimov: A Lifetime of Letters*, 1995 (Stanley Asimov, editor); *It's Been a Good Life*, 2002 (condensed version of his 3 volumes of autobiography; Janet Jeppson Asimov, editor); *Conversations with Isaac Asimov*, 2005 (Carl Freedman, editor).

CHILDREN'S LITERATURE: *David Starr: Space Ranger*, 1952; *Lucky Starr and the Pirates of the Asteroids*, 1953; *Lucky Starr and the Oceans of Venus*, 1954; *Lucky Starr and the Big Sun of Mercury*, 1956; *Lucky Starr and the Moons of Jupiter*, 1957; *Lucky Starr and the Rings of Saturn*, 1958.

BIBLIOGRAPHY

Asimov, Isaac. *Asimov's Galaxy*. Garden City, N.Y.: Doubleday, 1989. Compilation of sixty-six essays presents readers with Asimov's unique perspective on a genre to which he made many important contributions. Topics addressed include religion and science fiction, women and science fiction, time travel, science-fiction editors, and magazine covers. Particularly interesting are the items in the final section, "Science Fiction and I," in which Asimov writes frankly about his life and work.

"A Celebration of Isaac Asimov: A Man for the Universe." *Skeptical Inquirer* 17 (Fall, 1992): 30-47. Praises Asimov as a master science educator, perhaps the best of all time, given that he was responsible for teaching science to millions of people. Includes tributes from Arthur C. Clarke, Frederik Pohl, Harlan Ellison, L. Sprague de Camp, Carl Sagan, Stephen Jay Gould, Martin Gardner, Paul Kurtz, Donald Goldsmith, James Randi, and E. C. Krupp.

Chambers, Bette. "Isaac Asimov: A One-Man Renaissance." *Humanist* 53 (March/April, 1993): 6-8. Discusses Asimov's stature as a humanist and his presidency of the American Humanist Association. Also addresses Asimov's support for the Committee for the Scientific Investigation of Claims of the Paranormal and his thoughts on censorship and creationism, pseudoscience, and scientific orthodoxy.

Fiedler, Jean, and Jim Mele. *Isaac Asimov*. New York: Frederick Ungar, 1982. Brief volume serves as a primer on Asimov's work as a science-fiction writer. Provides descriptions of most of his writings in the genre, including the Foundation trilogy, the Robot series, and the juvenile books. Provides a clear and nonacademic treatment of Asimov's major works in addition to giving some of his less well-known works long-overdue recognition. Includes notes, bibliography, and index.

Freedman, Carl, ed. *Conversations with Isaac Asimov.* Jackson: University Press of Mississippi, 2005. Collection of interviews with the author spans the period from 1968 to 1990. Asimov discusses such topics as the state of science-fiction writing and his own opinions about his classic novels. Includes chronology, list of Asimov's books, and index.

Gunn, James. *Isaac Asimov: The Foundations of Science Fiction.* Rev. ed. Lanham, Md.: Scarecrow Press, 1996. Gunn, a professor of English, science-fiction writer, historian and critic of the genre, and longtime friend of Asimov, shows how science fiction shaped Asimov's life and how he in turn shaped the field. Presents painstaking analyses of Asimov's entire science-fiction corpus. Includes a chronology, a checklist of works by Asimov, a select list of works about him, and an index.

Hutcheon, Pat Duffy. "The Legacy of Isaac Asimov." *Humanist* 53 (March/April, 1993): 3-5. Biographical account discusses Asimov's efforts to encourage an understanding of science and his desire to make people realize that to study humanity is to study the universe, and vice versa. Asserts that Asimov saw the possibility of an eventual organization of a world government and predicted the end of sexism, racism, and war.

Palumbo, Donald. *Chaos Theory, Asimov's Foundations and Robots, and Herbert's "Dune": The Fractal Aesthetic of Epic Science Fiction.* Westport, Conn.: Greenwood Press, 2002. Looks at the history of epic science fiction through its two most outstanding examples. Includes bibliographical references and index.

Touponce, William F. *Isaac Asimov.* Boston: Twayne, 1991. Offers a good introduction to the life and works of the author. Includes bibliographical references and index.

White, Michael. *Asimov: A Life of the Grand Master of Science Fiction.* New York: Carroll & Graf, 1994. First full-length biography of the author provides a detailed look at his life and work. Includes a general bibliography, a bibliography of Asimov's fiction, a chronological list of his books, and an index.

MIGUEL ÁNGEL ASTURIAS

Born: Guatemala City, Guatemala; October 19, 1899
Died: Madrid, Spain; June 9, 1974
Also known as: Miguel Ángel Asturias Rosales

PRINCIPAL LONG FICTION

El Señor Presidente, 1946 (*The President*, 1963)
Hombres de maíz, 1949 (*Men of Maize*, 1975)
Viento fuerte, 1950 (*The Cyclone*, 1967; better known as *Strong Wind*, 1968)
El papa verde, 1954 (*The Green Pope*, 1971)
Los ojos de los enterrados, 1960 (*The Eyes of the Interred*, 1973)
El alhajadito, 1961 (*The Bejeweled Boy*, 1971)
Mulata de tal, 1963 (*Mulata*, 1967)
Maladrón, 1969

OTHER LITERARY FORMS

Although known primarily as a novelist, Miguel Ángel Asturias (ah-STEWR-yahs) produced work in a variety of literary forms, including several volumes of short stories, a few plays, and two substantial collections of verse. In addition, Asturias published a number of sociological and journalistic works.

Most of Asturias's works, regardless of genre, are interrelated in one way or another. The short stories collected in *Week-end en Guatemala* (1956), for example, are integral parts of the political and artistic statements of the novels of the Banana trilogy (*Strong Wind, The Green Pope,* and *The Eyes of the Interred*). Similarly, the play *Soluna* (pb. 1955; sun-moon) provides a helpful introduction to the novels *Men of Maize* and *Mulata* and presents an overview of primitive magic lacking in the novels. The complementarity between individual works has led many critics to regard Asturias's oeuvre as a unified whole and to analyze it on that basis.

ACHIEVEMENTS

The works of Miguel Ángel Asturias are the expression of a mind intensely engaged with the essence of America. A virtuoso in the use of language and a master of many genres, Asturias focused his craft on a great variety of issues and themes. Two of these concerns had special importance for him, and a majority of his published works can be identified as explorations of those topics. His achievements were identical with his interests: the combination of Mayan cosmology with an aesthetic technique often called Magical Realism for the purpose of making a unique interpretation of modern Indian and mestizo reality, and a blend of social protest and art that attacked dictatorship and imperialism through the forum of world literature.

Asturias's concerns ran parallel with those of his generation. With the passing of Romanticism and *Modernismo* in the first decades of the twentieth century, Latin American writers began to seek inspiration in native rather than European themes. Realistic and naturalistic traditions in the novel developed into an original "literature of the land" that sought to portray a distinctively American experience. Peasants, supposedly in harmony with their surroundings but exploited by other elements of society, increasingly became the subjects of important works of fiction. The American landscape in art and literature changed from the idealized, idyllic paradise it had often been in nineteenth century fiction and poetry to an unforgiving wilderness.

Asturias's literary use of Indian myth was the most elaborate application of Native American lore in the history of Central American letters and represented a total break with European themes. The main works of his Mayan cycle, *Leyendas de Guatemala* (1930), *Men of Maize*, and *Mulata*, present a kaleidoscopic view of Indo-America, redefining it with an often startling freedom of interpretation and with a philosophy of the novel that respects few traditional preconceptions about plot.

The political fiction of Asturias is equally innovative and American. *The President*, possibly the most significant and accomplished novel ever published by a Guate-

malan author, along with *Week-end en Guatemala* (1956) and the books of his Banana trilogy, form a literary parallel with Guatemala's liberal revolution of 1946 to 1953, confronting the misuse of economic, military, and political power. Asturias strengthened the role of literature in national life by including in his fiction, as part of its legitimate function, inquiry into the forces that control Guatemala. He was rewarded in 1967 with the Nobel Prize in Literature.

BIOGRAPHY

The son of a magistrate and a schoolteacher, Miguel Ángel Asturias belonged to Ladino (non-Indian) upper-middle-class society. When he was about six years old, the family moved to a farm of his paternal grandparents in Baja Verapaz. The move to the country was caused by his father's political difficulties with the dictator of Guatemala, Manuel Estrada Cabrera, and the family's three-year retreat away from the city was significant in Asturias's development, introducing him to the effects of dictatorship as well as to the countryside and its people.

When the political crisis was over, Asturias's family returned to Guatemala City, and Asturias began his studies at the Instituto Nacional de Varones (National Men's Institute) in 1912. Although student unrest crystallized into isolated protests against Estrada Cabrera between 1910 and 1920, Asturias was generally apolitical during his early school years. He participated in one disorder, a window-breaking spree with political overtones, but otherwise he refrained from attacks on the dictatorship until the formation of the Unionist Party in 1919. He signed a student manifesto against the government in August of that year, his first public stand against Estrada Cabrera.

After the Unionist victory, Asturias became a leader in the reform movement. He and his friends founded a popular university dedicated to educating the poorer classes, with the ultimate goal of bringing the country into the twentieth century. Asturias's concerns were expressed in the dissertation he wrote for his law degree, but he was not able to find a local outlet for his social conscience after graduation because political pressures made necessary his departure from the country. He traveled to England and then to France. In Paris, he studied anthropology at the Sorbonne, under George Raynaud and, with the help of another student, translated the Mayan documents *Popol Vuh* (c. 1550) and *Annals of the Cakchiquels* (sixteenth century) from Raynaud's French versions into Spanish. This apprenticeship to Indian literature and tradition had a profound effect on Asturias and deeply influenced his literary production. His first book, *Leyendas de Guatemala*, was the direct result of his work in Paris.

In 1933, Asturias returned to Guatemala, where he managed his radio news program *El diario del aire*. He began his political career as a deputy to the national congress in 1942, and, after the fall of Guatemalan president Jorge Ubico Casteñeda in 1944, he was made cultural attaché to Mexico. It was there that he arranged to have his first novel, *The President*, published privately. In 1947, he was named cultural attaché to Buenos Aires,

Argentina, a position he held for six years. That period was one of intense literary activity during which he wrote two volumes of his Banana trilogy as well as *Men of Maize*.

In June of 1954, Colonel Carlos Castillo Armas, with a small army and American support, invaded Guatemala and toppled President Jacobo Árbenz Guzmán, of whom Asturias was a firm supporter. Castillo Armas deprived Asturias of his citizenship, and the author took refuge in South America. He stayed for a time with poet Pablo Neruda in Chile, where he completed *Week-end en Guatemala*, a series of stories condemning the military intervention of 1954 and describing the causes and effects of the coup.

Throughout his exile, Asturias wrote steadily and continued to publish. The avant-garde play *Soluna* ap-

Miguel Ángel Asturias. (Archive Photos)

peared in 1955, and another play, *La audiencia de los confines* (border court), in 1957. The final volume of the Banana trilogy appeared in 1960; subsequently, *The Bejeweled Boy* and *Mulata*, his most elaborate and complex fictions, complemented the nonpolitical cycle of his works. In 1966, he was awarded the Lenin Peace Prize in recognition of the anti-imperialist thrust of his oeuvre, and, on his birthday in 1967, he received the Nobel Prize in Literature. Asturias's diplomatic career resumed with a change of government in Guatemala, and he was ambassador to France from 1966 to 1970. He continued to live and write in Europe until his death in Madrid on June 9, 1974.

ANALYSIS

The writers who formed Guatemala's Generation of '20—which included Miguel Ángel Asturias—were typical of numerous Latin American intellectuals of the early twentieth century who questioned the values of the past and the relevance of European traditions. The authors of that group were disheartened over the failures of Western civilization in World War I and had lost confidence in what had always been considered foreign superiority. Feeling that they had nowhere to turn except to themselves, Asturias and his contemporaries began to study factors that distinguished their peoples from the French and the Spanish.

The cultural pendulum swung away from the escapism of preceding decades toward a confrontation with the essence of America. Central American history was reappraised, and that revision of ideas was disseminated through the free popular university that Asturias helped to found. In attempting to come to terms with Guatemalan reality, Asturias and others also became aware of the importance of the Central American Indians, who formed the excluded, oppressed majority in that nation's society. Not only was it believed that no truly nationalistic philosophy or literature could evolve until all aspects of the racial issue were considered, but it also was believed that any progress was impossible until Indian oppression had been resolved. Literary clubs and magazines were formed to express progressive Guatemalan aesthetics and to encourage the creation of a national folklore. Journals such as *Ensayos*, *Cultura*, *Tiempos nuevos*, and *Claridad*, which flourished briefly in the

1920's and on many of which Asturias collaborated, created a distinctive literary environment. Although Asturias left Guatemala shortly after his graduation from San Carlos and spent much of his life in Europe or South America, the formative issues of the Generation of '20, the concerns with authenticity and social reform, were his persistent literary obsessions.

Asturias's interests went far beyond political protest and literary re-creation of the Mayan spirit, but his most significant vision of Central America can be found in the books of those two cycles. Most of his later works do not fit easily into the two principal types of fiction—political and Mayan. *The Bejeweled Boy*, for example, which explores the inner world of a child, is interesting from a psychological and technical point of view, but it does not create the kind of thematic drama that characterizes his earlier writings. His other plays, fiction, and poetry, as well as the previously unpublished material being published posthumously from the Fons Asturias in Paris, add depth and complexity to a body of writing that has yet to be fully viewed and understood. It is possible that, as additional works are published, critics will find more meaningful interpretations of his earlier books and redefine the borders of the cycles.

By the time Asturias died in 1974, the political dreams of Guatemala's Generation of '20 had not come true. The new Guatemala that might have replaced that of Estrada Cabrera and Ubico Casteñeda fell to Castillo Armas and another series of strongmen. In literature, however, Asturias and his contemporaries such as Flavio Herrera, David Vela, and Rafael Arévalo Martínez brought their country into the mainstream of Latin American letters. Writer Epaminondas Quintana has remarked that the award of the Nobel Prize to his friend Asturias amounted to worldwide recognition not only of the writer himself but also of his generation and its ideals. To many Guatemalans, this is a significant part of Asturias's achievement.

The heart of Asturias's Guatemalan perspective was the acceptance of Mayan theology as an intellectual superstructure for his art, and the effects of his study and translation of the *Popul Vuh* and the *Annals of the Cakchiquels* are clearly visible in his first collection of tales, *Leyendas de Guatemala*. Written between 1923 and 1928, the tales reflect a non-Western worldview of the Mayan documents on which Asturias was working at the time. These "legends" foreshadow the techniques that he employed in his Mayan cycle—notably a surrealistic presentation of scenes that blends everyday reality with bizarre fantasy to create a Magical Realism. The lyricism of the author's language, his fondness for elaborate wordplay and Guatemalan puns, combined with his exposition of an Indian worldview and his use of an exotic tropical setting, produced the radical transformation of national aesthetics sought by the Generation of '20. In French translation, with a preface by Paul Valéry, *Leyendas de Guatemala* won the Prix Sylla Monsegur.

MEN OF MAIZE

Men of Maize, which appeared nineteen years after *Leyendas de Guatemala*, is a much longer and more complex vision of the Guatemalan people and landscape. Asturias's inspiration for the novel was, again, traditional Indian texts. There is no clearly defined plot in this second work of the Mayan cycle; rather, Asturias presents a series of events and a gallery of characters united by themes that reflect a Mayan frame of reference.

In the first part of the novel, Indians violently object to the commercial growing of corn, a crop that they consider sacred. Troops are sent to rescue the growers, and the military commander, Colonel Godoy, succeeds in quieting the revolt by having its leader poisoned. Subsequently, a curse is put on Godoy and his accomplices, all of whom die within seven years. The second section of the novel is concerned with María Tecún, a child of one of the unfortunate conspirators, who leaves her beggar husband, Goyo Yic. The latter spends most of his life looking for María; he does not find her until the final pages of the book. The third part of *Men of Maize* is the story of Nicho Aquino, an Indian mail carrier who also loses his wife; his search for her is fruitful in that, although he finds that she has been killed accidentally, he meets a mysterious seer, Seven Year Stag, who teaches him the lost wisdom of the race.

Asturias was criticized by a number of prominent Latin American scholars for the seemingly unrelated events of the novel's separate sections; however, themes such as metamorphosis and *nahualismo* (a belief that people have alter egos in certain plants or animals) give *Men of Maize* unity on a level other than plot.

SOLUNA

Open to widely divergent interpretations, *Men of Maize* can be less than satisfying to the uninitiated. It is of some use, however, to compare this novel with other major pieces of the Mayan cycle, the play *Soluna* and and the novel *Mulata*. The former concerns the personal crisis of Mauro, the owner of a country estate, whose wife, Ninica, has just left him. Mauro consults Soluna, a shaman, who gives him a mask to help him solve the problem. When Mauro falls asleep with the mask on his lap, he dreams an elaborate dream in which Ninica finally returns. When he wakes up, he finds that his wife's train has derailed, and she, having reassessed her relationship with her husband, has come back to stay. From the dreamlike action of the play and the unlikely details of its plot emerges the story of a modern, Westernized Guatemalan who, in the middle of a deep trauma, finds consolation in superstition. There is a similarity between Mauro's search for a resolution of his crisis in the irrational and Nicho Aquino's experience in which Seven Year Stag plays such an important role in *Men of Maize*.

MULATA

Mulata is a surrealistic tale about Yumi, an Indian peasant who sells his wife to Tazol, the corn-husk spirit, to achieve wealth and fulfillment. Yumi's near-fatal mistake is lusting after an apparently sensuous *mulata* (a mulatto woman) who, in fact, is hardly sexual and proves to have supernatural powers. After a series of strange adventures, Yumi succeeds in regaining his wife, who assists him in trying to avoid the vengeance of the *mulata*. Here, as in *Leyendas de Guatemala*, *Soluna*, and *Men of Maize*, it is perhaps easier to take all the grotesque, extraordinary episodes at face value, accepting them for what they are in themselves, like a series of painted scenes, rather than trying to find logical connections between events. Indeed, it is possible to argue that Asturias had no intention of making each individual portion of these works relate to other sections and that, collectively, the scenes convey the nonrational cosmos and the dense theological texture of the Indian mentality better than could any logical, consecutive narrative.

THE PRESIDENT

In the political cycle of his fiction, Asturias turns away from the totally Indian universe that dominates the

Mayan cycle and concentrates instead on ruthless dictatorship and unscrupulous imperialism in Central America. The shift of theme is accompanied by a change in structure and style. The political novels and stories have more recognizable and traditional plotting than *Men of Maize* and *Mulata*, although Asturias never abandons his lyrical, surrealistic style.

The President is one of Asturias's most polished works. This first novel is a carefully constructed critique of the dictatorship of Estrada Cabrera, and it vividly evokes the climate of fear and repression that permeated Guatemalan life in the early decades of the twentieth century. The novel's main character is Miguel Cara de Ángel, the president's right-hand man. He is told to kill General Canales, who has lost favor with the dictator; Cara de Ángel, however, takes pity on Canales and his daughter, Camila, and helps them to escape. The general dies before he has the chance to start his own revolution, and Camila, rejected by the rest of her family for fear of reprisal by the president, is saved by Cara de Ángel, who falls in love with her. As she hides from government spies in the back room of a tavern, she becomes ill with pneumonia. On the advice of an occultist, Cara de Ángel marries her "because only love can stand up to death." After her recovery, they consummate the marriage, and Camila becomes pregnant. Cara de Ángel is soon arrested, jailed, and never heard from again, and Camila gives birth to their son, Miguelito, whose name means "little Miguel."

Throughout the development of the plot, there is less political propaganda than vivid description of the brutal abuse of power. Asturias allows the actions of the president to speak for themselves. The book's message is enhanced by the fact that Camila and Cara de Ángel are not political characters. The former is an innocent victim of her father's unpopularity with the dictator, but she is not necessarily of the innocent masses; nor is Cara de Ángel a revolutionary hero who fights injustice. He is human and flawed, and his break with the president is caused by indiscretion, not by ideology. His actions toward Camila are motivated by love, not by his desire to save his people from the tyrant.

The President is one of the most successful and moving protests against dictatorship in the history of modern fiction. In addition, its craftsmanship contrib-

uted to making it one of the few Latin American novels published before 1950 to reach more than a local audience. *The President* also played no small role in elevating Asturias from the status of a talented Guatemalan author in exile to recipient of the Nobel Prize in Literature.

BANANA TRILOGY

Between the publication of *Men of Maize* and *Mulata*, Asturias was preoccupied with four works of fiction that complement the position taken in *The President*. The three novels of his Banana trilogy, *Strong Wind*, *The Green Pope*, and *The Eyes of the Interred*, as well as the collection of stories *Week-end en Guatemala*, are among the strongest statements in Central American literary history against the presence of the United States in that region. Far more polemical and political in tone than *The President*, these works provide a sensitive analysis of the problems associated with colonialism: economic exploitation of people and natural resources, the corruption of government officials who betray their nation to foreign interests, and military intervention.

STRONG WIND

The trilogy documents the history of the United Fruit Company and portrays both North Americans and Guatemalans whose lives are dominated by the company. *Strong Wind* provides a broad panorama of the extent of the United Fruit Company's influence as well as an introduction to the people who have been victimized by the fruit monopoly.

An intensely drawn tropical environment, prominent in all of Asturias's fiction, is the setting for the story of Lester Mead, a planter and member of the corporation. Mead lives and works incognito with the exploited Guatemalans to bring about change from within the system. His struggles form the principal line of action around which Asturias depicts the extensive corruption brought about by the United Fruit Company.

THE GREEN POPE

The Green Pope, which appeared four years later, follows a similar pattern of presenting history and characterization with a clearly political purpose. The first part of the novel concentrates on a detailed accounting of the United Fruit Company's development in the country, while the second continues the train of events from *Strong Wind*. *The Green Pope* is essentially the saga of George Maker Thompson, another North American who, in alliance with the Lucero family, eventually becomes the major stockholder in the company and then its president. As in *Strong Wind*, the machinations of the United Fruit Company are exposed and severely criticized.

THE EYES OF THE INTERRED

The final work of the trilogy, *The Eyes of the Interred*, finished while Asturias was in exile, completes the dream of reform begun in the other works and traces the efforts of Octavio Sansor to form a union and establish worker control over the company. Although he first plans a revolution and a violent end to dictatorship and foreign economic control, Sansor ultimately chooses nonviolence, and his victory is the organization of the workers' syndicate, a general strike, the resignation of the president, and company concessions to the union.

William L. Felker

OTHER MAJOR WORKS

SHORT FICTION: *Leyendas de Guatemala*, 1930; *Week-end en Guatemala*, 1956; *El espejo de Lida Sal*, 1967 (*The Mirror of Lida Sal*, 1997); *Novelas y cuentos de juventud*, 1971; *Viernes de dolores*, 1972.

PLAYS: *Cuculcán*, pb. 1930; *Soluna*, pb. 1955; *La audiencia de los confines*, pr., pb. 1957; *Chantaje*, pr., pb. 1964; *Dique seco*, pr., pb. 1964; *Teatro*, 1964.

POETRY: *Sien de alondra*, 1949; *Bolívar*, 1955; *Clarivigilia primaveral*, 1965.

NONFICTION: *Sociología guatemalteca: El problema social del indio*, 1923 (*Guatemalan Sociology: The Social Problem of the Indian*, 1977); *La arquitectura de la vida nueva*, 1928; *Rumania: Su nueva imagen*, 1964 (essays); *Latinoamérica y otros ensayos*, 1968 (essays); *Tres de cuatro soles*, 1977.

MISCELLANEOUS: *Obras completas*, 1967 (3 volumes).

BIBLIOGRAPHY

Barrueto, Jorge J. "A Latin American Indian Re-Reads the Canon: Postcolonial Mimicry in *El Señor Presidente*." *Hispanic Review* 74, no. 3 (Summer, 2004). Barrueto reevaluates *The President*, considered a novel of political criticism that ascribes the problems of Guatemala to the nation's indigenous peoples. Barrueto seeks to broaden analysis of the novel by examining the book from the perspective of the Guatemalan Indians.

Brotherston, Gordon. *The Emergence of the Latin American Novel*. New York: Cambridge University Press, 1977. This scholarly work is intended as an introduction to the Latin American novel, particularly from the 1950's to the 1970's. The chapter on Asturias discusses the author's work in the light of his politics, culture, and literary influences. Contains a general bibliography of secondary works on Latin American literature as well as a list of works by and on the major authors mentioned in the text. Accessible to general readers.

Callan, Richard J. *India's Mythology in the Novel "El Alhajadito" ("The Bejeweled Boy") by Miguel Ángel Asturias*. Lewiston, N.Y.: Edwin Mellen Press, 2003. Callan analyzes *The Bejeweled Boy* within the context of Hindu mythology. He describes how Hinduism informed Asturias's plot and characterization and how Asian deities and beliefs are expressed in Asturias's metaphors, reflecting Asturias's conviction that mythology is the ancient literary means for expressing the doubts, desires, and conflicts of human experience.

_____. *Miguel Ángel Asturias*. New York: Twayne, 1970. Callan's book both acquaints English-speaking readers with the author's works and ideas and outlines the substructure of Asturias's work: the depth psychology of Carl Jung. Beyond sketching the historical and cultural context of Asturias's work, Callan plunges into its essential depths. Supplemented by an annotated bibliography, a chronology, and notes.

Gonzalez Echevarria, Roberto. *Myth and Archive: A Theory of Latin American Narrative*. New York: Cambridge University Press, 1990. Although the book focuses on other writers, Asturias's work is briefly discussed and placed within the context of other Latin American novels. A very helpful volume in coming to terms with Asturias's unusual narratives.

Harss, Luis, and Barbara Dohmann. "Miguel Ángel Asturias: Or, The Land Where the Flowers Bloom." In *Into the Mainstream: Conversations with Latin-American Writers*. New York: Harper & Row, 1967.

Based on interviews, the section devoted to Asturias offers useful information on the author's thought.

Henighan, Stephen. *Assuming the Light: The Parisian Literary Apprenticeship of Miguel Angel Asturias*. Oxford, England: Legenda, 1999. Henighan focuses on Asturias's time in Paris during the 1920's and 1930's, which, he argues, was the most crucial and least understood period of the author's career. Henighan studies *The President* and other works to demonstrate how Asturias shaped his definitions of Guatemalan cultural identity and Spanish-American modernity from a French perspective.

Prieto, Rene. *Miguel Ángel Asturias's Archaeology of Return*. New York: Cambridge University Press,
1993. An excellent study of the novelist's body of work. Prieto discusses both the novels and the stories, taking up issues of their unifying principles, idiom, and eroticism. Prieto's measured introduction, in which he carefully analyzes Asturias's reputation and identifies his most important work, is especially useful. Includes detailed notes and a bibliography.

Williams, Raymond Leslie. *The Modern Latin American Novel*. New York: Twayne, 1998. This examination of Latin American novelists includes a chapter on Asturias and places his work within the general tradition of modernist Latin American fiction. Includes a bibliography and an index.

MARGARET ATWOOD

Born: Ottawa, Ontario, Canada; November 18, 1939
Also known as: Margaret Eleanor Atwood

PRINCIPAL LONG FICTION

The Edible Woman, 1969
Surfacing, 1972
Lady Oracle, 1976
Life Before Man, 1979
Bodily Harm, 1981
The Handmaid's Tale, 1985
Cat's Eye, 1988
The Robber Bride, 1993
Alias Grace, 1996
The Blind Assassin, 2000
Oryx and Crake, 2003
*The Penelopiad: The Myth of Penelope and
     Odysseus*, 2005

OTHER LITERARY FORMS

A skillful and prolific writer, Margaret Atwood has published many volumes of poetry. Collections such as *Double Persephone* (1961), *The Animals in That Country* (1968), *The Journals of Susanna Moodie* (1970), *Procedures for Underground* (1970), *Power Politics*
(1971), *You Are Happy* (1974), *Two-Headed Poems* (1978), *True Stories* (1981), *Interlunar* (1984), and *Morning in the Burned House* (1995) have enjoyed a wide and enthusiastic readership, especially in Canada. During the 1960's, Atwood published in limited editions poems and broadsides illustrated by Charles Pachter: *The Circle Game* (1964), *Kaleidoscopes Baroque: A Poem* (1965), *Speeches for Dr. Frankenstein* (1966), *Expeditions* (1966), and *What Was in the Garden* (1969).

Atwood has also written books for children, including *Up in the Tree* (1978), which she also illustrated, and *Rude Ramsay and the Roaring Radishes* (2004). Her volumes of short stories, a collection of short fiction and prose poems (*Murder in the Dark*, 1983), a volume of criticism (*Survival: A Thematic Guide to Canadian Literature*, 1972), and a collection of literary essays (*Second Words*, 1982) further demonstrate Atwood's wide-ranging talent. In 1982, Atwood coedited *The New Oxford Book of Canadian Verse in English*. She has also written articles and critical reviews too numerous to list. She has contributed prose and poetry to literary journals such as *Acta Victoriana* and *Canadian Forum*, and her teleplays have been aired by the Canadian Broadcasting Corporation.

Margaret Atwood. (Courtesy, Vancouver International Writers Festival)

ACHIEVEMENTS

Early in her career, Margaret Atwood received critical recognition for her work. This is particularly true of her poetry, which has earned her numerous awards, including the E. J. Pratt Medal in 1961, the President's Medal from the University of Western Ontario in 1965, and the Governor-General's Award, Canada's highest literary honor, for *The Circle Game* in 1966. Twenty years later, Atwood again won this prize for *The Handmaid's Tale*. Atwood won first prize in the Canadian Centennial Commission Poetry Competition in 1967 and won a prize for poetry from the Union League Civic and Arts Foundation in 1969. She has received honorary doctorates from Trent University and Queen's University. Additional honors and awards she has received include the Bess Hoskins Prize for poetry (1974), the City of Toronto Award (1977), the Canadian Booksellers Association Award (1977), the St. Lawrence Award for Fiction (1978), the Canada Council Molson Prize (1980), and the Radcliffe Medal (1980). *The Blind As-*

sassin won the 2000 Booker Prize, and Atwood received Spain's Prince of Asturias literary prize for 2008.

BIOGRAPHY

Margaret Eleanor Atwood was born in Ottawa, Ontario, Canada, on November 18, 1939, the second of Carl Edmund Atwood and Margaret Killam Atwood's three children. At the age of six months, she was backpacked into the Quebec wilderness, where her father, an entomologist, pursued his special interests in bees, spruce budworms, and forest tent caterpillars. Throughout her childhood, Atwood's family spent several months of the year in the bush of Quebec and northern Ontario. She did not attend school full time until she was twelve.

Though often interrupted, Atwood's education seems to have been more than adequate. She was encouraged by her parents to read and write at an early age, and her creative efforts started at five, when she wrote stories, poems, and plays. Her serious composition, however, did not begin until she was sixteen.

In 1961, Atwood earned her B.A. in the English honors program from the University of Toronto, where she studied with poets Jay Macpherson and Margaret Avison. Her M.A. from Radcliffe followed in 1962. Continuing graduate work at Harvard in 1963, Atwood interrupted her studies before reentering the program for two more years in 1965. While she found graduate studies interesting, Atwood directed her energies largely toward her creative efforts. For her, the Ph.D. program was chiefly a means of support while she wrote. Atwood left Harvard without writing her doctoral thesis.

Returning to Canada in 1967, Atwood accepted a position at Sir George Williams University in Montreal. By this time, her poetry was gaining recognition. With the publication of *The Edible Woman* and the sale of its film rights, Atwood was able to concentrate more fully on writing, though she taught at York University and was writer-in-residence at the University of Toronto. In 1973, Atwood divorced her American husband of five years, James Polk. After the publication of *Surfacing*, she was able to support herself through her creative efforts. She moved to a farm near Alliston, Ontario, with Canadian novelist Graeme Gibson; the couple's daughter, Eleanor Jess Atwood Gibson, was born in 1979. In 1980, Atwood and her family returned to Toronto, where Atwood and Gibson became active in the Writers' Union of Canada, Amnesty International, and the International Association of Poets, Playwrights, Editors, Essayists, and Novelists (PEN).

ANALYSIS

For Margaret Atwood, an unabashed Canadian, literature became a means to cultural and personal self-awareness. "To know ourselves," she writes in *Survival*, "we must know our own literature; to know ourselves accurately, we need to know it as part of literature as a whole." Thus, when she defines Canadian literary concerns she relates her own as well, for Atwood's fiction grows out of this tradition. In her opinion, Canada's central reality is the act of survival: Canadian life and culture are decisively shaped by the demands of a harsh environment. Closely related to this defining act of survival, in Atwood's view, is the Canadian search for territorial identity—or, as literary theorist Northrop Frye put it, "Where is here?"

Atwood's heroines invariably discover themselves to be emotional refugees, strangers in a territory they can accurately label but one in which they are unable to feel at home. They are alienated not only from their environment but also from language itself; for them, communication becomes a decoding process. To a great degree, their feelings of estrangement extend from a culture that, having reduced everything to products, threatens to consume them. Women are particularly singled out as products, items to be decorated and sold as commodities, though men are threatened as well. Indeed, Canadian identity as a whole is in danger of being engulfed by an acquisitive American culture, though Atwood's "Americans" symbolize exploitation and often turn out to be Canadian nationals.

Reflective of their time and place, Atwood's characters are appropriately ambivalent. Dead or dying traditions prevent their return to the past, a past most have rejected. Their present is ephemeral at best, and their future inconceivable. Emotionally maimed, her heroines plumb their conscious and unconscious impressions, searching for a return to feeling, a means of identification with the present.

Atwood often couches their struggle in terms of a journey, which serves as a controlling metaphor for inner explorations: The unnamed heroine of *Surfacing* returns to the wilderness of Quebec, Lesje Green of *Life Before Man* wanders through imagined Mesozoic jungles, Rennie Wilford of *Bodily Harm* flies to the insurgent islands of Ste. Agathe and St. Antoine. By setting contemporary culture in relief, these primitive sites define the difference between nature and culture and allow Atwood's heroines to gain new perspectives on their own realities. They can see people and places in relation to each other, not as isolated entities. Ultimately, however, this resolves little, for Atwood's novels end on a tenuous note. Although her heroines come to terms with themselves, they remain estranged.

Supporting her characters' ambivalence is Atwood's versatile narrative technique. Her astringent prose reflects their emotional numbness; its ironic restraint reveals their wariness. Frequent contradictions suggest not only the complexity of her characters but also the antagonistic times they must survive. By skillful juxtaposition of past and present through the use of flashbacks, Atwood evokes compelling fictional landscapes that ironically comment on the untenable state of modern men and women. Still, there remains some hope, for her characters survive with increased understanding of their world. Despite everything, life does go on.

SURFACING

The first of Atwood's novels to arouse critical praise and commentary, *Surfacing* explores new facets of the bildungsroman. What might have been a conventional novel of self-discovery develops into a resonant search for self-recovery imbued with mythic overtones and made accessible through Atwood's skillful use of symbol and ritual. At the same time, Atwood undercuts the romantic literary conventions of ultimate self-realization as a plausible conclusion. To accept the heroine's final emergence as an end in itself is to misread this suggestively ironic novel.

The unnamed heroine of *Surfacing*, accompanied by her lover, Joe, and a married couple named David and Anna, returns to the Canadian wilderness where she was reared in hopes of locating her missing father. His sudden disappearance has recalled her from a city life marked by personal and professional failures that have left her emotionally anesthetized. While her external search goes forward, the heroine conducts a more important internal investigation to locate missing "gifts" from both parents. Through these, she hopes to rediscover her lost ability to feel. In order to succeed, however, she will need to expose the fiction of her life.

At the outset of her narrative, the heroine warns her readers that she has led a double life when she recalls Anna's question, "Do you have a twin?" She denies having one, for she apparently believes the elaborate fiction she has created, a story involving a spurious marriage, divorce, and abandonment of her child. As additional protection, the heroine has distanced herself from everyone. She refers to her family as "they," "as if they were somebody else's family." Her relationship with Joe is notable for its coolness, and she has known Anna, described as her best friend, for only two months.

By surrounding herself with friends whose occupation of making a film significantly titled *Random Samples* reveals their rootlessness, the heroine seeks to escape the consequences of her actions. Indeed, she describes herself both as a commercial artist, indicating her sense of having sold out, and as an escape artist. Reluctantly approaching the past she sought to escape, the heroine feels as if she is in foreign territory.

That she feels alienated by the location of her past is not surprising, for she is an outsider in a number of telling ways: of English descent in French territory; a non-Catholic, indeed nonreligious, person among the devout; a woman in a man's world. Her French is so halting that she could be mistaken for an American, representing yet another form of alienation, displacement by foreigners. Most of all, she is a stranger to herself. Rather than focusing on her self-alienation, she is consumed by the American usurpation of Canada, its wanton rape of virgin wilderness; this allows her to avoid a more personal loss of innocence.

Canada's victimization by Americans reflects the heroine's victimization by men. Having been subjected to the concept that "with a paper bag over their head they're all the same," the protagonist is perceived as either contemptible or threatening. Her artistic skills are denigrated by a culture in which no "important" artists

have been women. Even her modest commercial success is treated as a personal assault by Joe, who has an "unvoiced claim to superior artistic skills." By telling herself that the wilderness can never recover from abuse, the protagonist denies her own recovery. Although she feels helpless at the beginning of the novel, she soon rediscovers her own capabilities, and as these are increasingly tested, she proves to be a powerful survivor. Thus, the wilderness, a self-reflection, provides the key to self-discovery.

Perhaps the most important lesson the heroine learns is that the wilderness is not innocent. Her encounter with and response to a senselessly slaughtered heron evoke a sense of complicity, leading her to reflect on similar collusion in her brother's animal experiments when they were children. Finding her refuge in childhood innocence blocked, the heroine goes forward with her search. Once again, nature provides information, for in discovering her father's body trapped under water, she finally recognizes her aborted child, her complicity in its death by yielding to her lover's demands. On a broader scale, she acknowledges death as a part of life and reclaims her participation in the life process by conceiving a child by Joe.

In a ceremony evocative of primitive fertility rites, she seduces her lover. Then, assured of her pregnancy, she undergoes a systematic purgation in order to penetrate to the very core of reality. During this process, the protagonist discovers her parents' gifts—her father's sense of sight and her mother's gift of life. With body and mind reunited, she takes an oath in which she refuses to be a victim. Whole, she feels free to reenter her own time, no longer either victim or stranger.

Atwood's procedure for bringing her heroine to this state of consciousness is remarkable for its intricacy. Though she distrusts language, the protagonist proceeds to tell her story by describing what she sees. Since she has lost her ability to feel, much of this description seems to be objective—until the reader realizes just how unreliable her impressions can be. Contradictions abound, creating enormous uncertainty as intentional and unintentional irony collide, lies converge, and opinion stated as fact proves to be false. Given this burden of complexity, any simple conclusion to *Surfacing* is out of the question. Clearly, Atwood hints at a temporary union with

Joe, but this is far from resolving the heroine's dilemma. Outer reality, after all, has not altered. Atwood's open-ended conclusion is thus both appropriate and plausible, for to resolve all difficulties would be to give in to the very romantic conventions that her fiction subverts.

LIFE BEFORE MAN

Coming after the gothic comedy of *Lady Oracle*, *Life Before Man* seems especially stark. Nevertheless, its similarity with all of Atwood's novels is apparent. A penetrating examination of contemporary relationships, it peels away protective layers of deceptions, stripping the main characters until their fallible selves are presented with relentless accuracy. Lesje Green and Elizabeth and Nate Schoenhof are adrift in a collapsing culture in which they struggle to survive. As she focuses on each character, Atwood reveals unrecognized facets of the others.

In this novel, wilderness and culture converge in the Royal Ontario Museum, where Lesje works as a paleontologist and Elizabeth works in public relations. There is little need for the bush country of Quebec, since culture is something of a jungle itself. Unlike the Mesozoic, however, the present anticipates its own extinction because of abundant evidence: pollution, separatist movements, political upheaval, lost traditions, disintegrating families. Humanity is in danger of drowning in its own waste. Whatever predictability life held in the past seems completely absent; even holidays are meaningless. Still, the novel is fascinated with the past, with the behavior of animals, both human and prehistoric, and with the perpetuation of memory, particularly as it records the history of families.

As in *Surfacing*, a violent death precipitates emotional withdrawal. Most affected is Elizabeth Schoenhof, whose lover Chris has blown off his head as a final gesture of defiance, the ultimate form of escape. His act destroys Elizabeth's sense of security, which resides both in her home and in her ability to manipulate or predict the actions of others. A supreme manipulator, Elizabeth attempts to make everyone act as reasonably as she. Not surprisingly, Elizabeth has at least two selves speaking different languages, genteel chic and street argot, and what passes for "civilized" behavior is merely an escape from honest confrontation with such basic human emotions as love, grief, rejection, and anger. In fact, all of the

novel's characters prefer escape to self-realization, and while they pay lip service to social decorum, they quietly rebel.

Their rebellious emotions are reflected in the larger world, a political world aflame with separatist zeal. René Lévesque, with whom Nate identifies, is gaining momentum for the separation of Quebec and the reestablishment of French as the major language, threatening to displace the English. Indeed, the world seems to be coming apart as international, national, and personal moves toward separation define this novel's movement. As a solution, however, separation fails to satisfy the characters' need to escape, for no matter how far they run, all carry the baggage of their past.

Elizabeth in particular has survived a loveless past, including abandonment by both parents, the painful death of her alcoholic mother, her sister's mental breakdown and drowning, and her Auntie Muriel's puritanical upbringing. All of this has turned Elizabeth into a determined survivor. Beneath her polished exterior is a street fighter from the slums, a primitive. Indeed, Elizabeth recognizes an important part of herself in Chris. Nate and Lesje share a different kind of past, where love created as much tension as affection. Lesje's Jewish and Ukrainian grandmothers treated her as disputed territory, speaking to her in languages she could not understand and driving her to seek refuge in her fantasy world of Lesjeland.

Feeling like a refugee in treacherous territory, each character attempts to build a new, stable world, notwithstanding the continual impingement of the old, messy one. Nate, having forsaken his mother's futile idealistic causes to save the world, falls in love with Lesje, whom he envisions as an exotic subtropical island free from rules. For a time, Elizabeth inhabits a clean expanse of space somewhere between her bed and the ceiling, and Lesje explores prehistoric terrain, wishing for a return to innocence. When these fantasies diminish in power, the characters find substitutes, challenging the reader to reexamine the novel's possibilities.

Despite its bleak tone, its grimy picture of a deteriorating culture, its feeling of estrangement and futility, and its rejection of simplistic resolutions, *Life Before Man* is not without hope. Each character emerges at the end of this novel with something he or she has desired.

Nate has Lesje, now pregnant with his child—a child who, in turn, confirms Lesje's commitment to life by displacing her preoccupation with death. Having exorcised the evil spirits of her past, Elizabeth experiences a return of direct emotion.

There is, however, a distinct possibility that the apparent resolution is as ambivalent as that of *Surfacing*. What appears to be a completely objective third-person point of view, presiding over chapters neatly cataloged by name and date, sometimes shifts to the first person, an unreliable first person at that. Through her revolving characters, their identification with one another, and their multiple role reversals, Atwood creates contradictory, problematic, and deceptive human characters who defy neat categorization. Taken separately, Nate, Elizabeth, and Lesje can easily be misinterpreted; taken as a whole, they assume an even more complex meaning, reflecting not only their own biased viewpoints but also the reader's. Atwood's ability to capture such shifting realities of character and place is one of her chief artistic distinctions.

Bodily Harm

Rather like the narrator of *Surfacing*, Rennie Wilford in *Bodily Harm* has abandoned her past, the stifling world of Griswold, Ontario, to achieve modest success as a freelance journalist. To Rennie, Griswold represents values of duty, self-sacrifice, and decency found comic by modern-day standards. It is a place where women are narrowly confined to assigned roles that make them little better than servants. Rennie much prefers city life, with its emphasis on mobility and trends such as slave-girl bracelets and pornographic art. In fact, Rennie has become an expert on just such trends, so adept that she can either describe or fabricate one with equal facility. Having learned to look only at surfaces, Rennie has difficulty accepting the reality of her cancerous breast, which *looks* so healthy.

Her cancer serves as the controlling metaphor in the novel, spreading from diseased personal relationships to a political eruption on St. Antoine. Indeed, the world seems shot through with moral cancer. The symptoms are manifest: Honesty is a liability, friends are "contacts," lovers are rapists, pharmacists are drug pushers, and no one wants to hear about issues. What should be healthy forms of human commerce have gone out of control, mirroring the rioting cells in Rennie's breast. When confronted by yet another manifestation of this malaise, a would-be murderer who leaves a coil of rope on her bed, Rennie finds a fast escape route by landing a magazine assignment on St. Antoine.

Her hopes of being a tourist, exempt from participation and responsibility, are short-lived as she is drawn into a political intrigue more life-threatening than her cancer. Before reaching St. Antoine, she learns of its coming election, ignoring Dr. Minnow's allusions to political corruption and makeshift operations. What puzzles her most about their conversation is his reference to the "sweet Canadians." Is he being ironic or not, she wonders. Her superficial observations of island life reveal little, though plenty of evidence points to a violent eruption. Rennie seems more concerned about avoiding sunburn and arrest for drug possession than she is about the abundant poverty and casual violence. Her blindness allows her to become a gunrunner, duped by Lora Lucas, a resilient survivor of many injurious experiences, and Paul, the local connection for drugs and guns, who initiates Rennie into genuine, albeit unwilling, massive involvement.

As a physical link to life, Paul's sexual attention is important to Rennie, who appreciates the value of his touch. His hands call forth the "missing" hands of her grandmother, her doctor's hands, and Lora's bitten hands, hands that deny or offer help. Paul's "aid" to the warring political factions, like Canada's donation of canned hams and Rennie's assistance, is highly questionable, and the results are the reverse of what was planned. Trying to escape from his botched plan, Rennie is brought to confront her own guilt.

Again, Atwood uses flight as a route to self-discovery and deprivation as a source of spiritual nourishment. In Rennie's case, however, these are externally imposed. In her underground cell, with only Lora as company, Rennie ultimately sees and understands the violent disease consuming the world, a disease growing out of a human need to express superiority in a variety of ways and at great spiritual expense. Rennie becomes "afraid of men because men are frightening." Equally important, she understands that there is no difference between *here* and *there*. Finally, she knows that she is not exempt: "Nobody is exempt from anything."

If she survives this ordeal, Rennie plans to change her life, becoming a reporter who will tell what truly happened. Once again, however, Atwood leaves this resolution open to questions. Rennie is often mistaken about what she sees and frequently misinterprets events. Her entire story may well be a prison journal, an account of how she arrived there. When projecting her emergence from prison, she uses the future tense. For Atwood's purposes, this is of relative unimportance, since Rennie has been restored in a way she never anticipated. In the end, stroking Lora's battered hand, Rennie finally embodies the best of Griswold with a clear vision of what lies beneath the surface of human reality.

THE HANDMAID'S TALE

In *The Handmaid's Tale*, Atwood's fiction turns from the realistic to the speculative, though she merely takes the political bent of the 1980's to its logical—and chilling—conclusion. Awash in a swill of pollution, promiscuity, pornography, and venereal disease, late twentieth century America erupts into political and religious battles. Rising from the ashes is the Republic of Gilead, a theocracy so conservative in its reactionary bent that women are channeled into roles as Daughters, Wives, Marthas (maids), Econowives, or Handmaids (mistresses).

The narrator, Offred (referring to her status as a possession *of* her master), is among the first group of Handmaids, fertile women assigned to high-ranking government officials. Weaving between her past and present in flat, almost emotionless prose, Offred draws a terrifying picture of a culture retreating to religious fundamentalist values in the name of stability. At first her prose seems to be accurate, a report from an observer. Deeper in the story, readers come to understand that Offred is numb from all that has changed in her life. Besides, she does not trust anyone, least of all herself. Still, as a survivor, she determines to stay alive, even if that means taking risks.

Her loss of freedom and identity create new hungers in Offred: curiosity about the world, a subversive desire for power, a longing for feeling, a need to take risks. In many ways, *The Handmaid's Tale* is a novel about what loss creates. Gilead, in fact, is created partially in response to men's loss of feeling, according to Fred, Offred's Commander. Offred, however, takes little comfort in his assurance that feeling has returned.

As she knows, feeling is ephemeral, often unstable, impossible to gauge. Perhaps this is why her characterization of others in the novel seems remote. While Offred observes gestures, facial movements, and voice tone, she can only guess at intent. Implicit in the simplest statement may be an important message. Offred thus decodes all kinds of communication, beginning with the Latin inscription she finds scratched in her wardrobe: "Nolite te bastardes carborundorum." Even this injunction, however, which becomes her motto, is a corruption. Though desperate for communication, Offred cautiously obscures her own message. Her struggle to understand reflects Atwood's familiar theme of the inability for an individual truly to understand another person, another situation.

By having Offred acknowledge the impossibility of accurately decoding messages, Atwood calls attention to the narrative itself. Another interesting fictional element is the narrative's remove in time. Offred tells her story in the present, except when she refers to her life before becoming a Handmaid. Ironically, readers learn that not only is she telling her story after events, but her narrative has been reconstructed and presented to an audience at a still greater temporal remove. All of this increases the equivocal quality of the novel and its rich ambiguity.

While Atwood demands attention, she provides direction in prefatory quotations. Most revealing is her quotation from Jonathan Swift's "A Modest Proposal." Like Swift's satire, Atwood's skates on the surface of reality, often snagging on familiar actions and only slightly exaggerating some attitudes, especially those commonly held about women. Perennial issues of a woman's place, the value of her work, and her true role in society are at the center of this novel.

CAT'S EYE

These concerns appear again in *Cat's Eye*, but in a more subdued form. In subject and theme, *Cat's Eye* is an artistic retrospective. Elaine Risley, a middle-aged painter, is called to Toronto to prepare for her first artistic retrospective. Risley takes the occasion to come to terms with the dimensions of self in time, which she perceives as a "series of transparencies, one laid on top of another." Her return to Toronto, where she grew up, gives her an opportunity to look through the layers of people and events from her present position on the curve of time. This perspective, often ironic and tenuous, allows Risley to accept herself, including her foibles.

Cat's Eye takes full advantage of Atwood's visual style as it reiterates the importance of perspective in relation to change. The novel's art theme emphasizes interpretation while simultaneously satirizing the kind of inflated yet highly subjective criticism published for public consumption. Atwood's most personal novel to date, *Cat's Eye* tackles the physics of life and art and arrives at Atwood's least ambiguous conclusion. Returning to her family in Vancouver, Risley notes that the starlight she sees is only a reflection. Still, she concludes, "it's enough to see by."

THE ROBBER BRIDE

In *The Robber Bride* communication as a decoding process occurs both figuratively and literally, as one of the four protagonists, the historian Antonia "Tony" Fremont, seeks to discover the underlying meaning of the past. In her own storytelling she sometimes uses a reverse code, transforming herself into her imagined heroine Ynot Tnomerf. In fact, each of the women in the novel has renamed herself to gain distance from past traumas: Karen becomes Charis to cast out the memory of sexual abuse; Tony hopes to escape the "raw sexes war" that characterized her family; Roz Grunwald becomes Rosalind Greenwood as her family climbs the social ladder.

Although cast in comic form, the novel explores issues of identity, reality versus fiction, and women's friendship. The three friends meet for lunch and reminisce about their betrayal at the hands of Zenia, a mysterious femme fatale who seduced Tony's and Roz's husbands and Charis's lover. Zenia has multiple stories about her origins, all dramatic but plausible. She ensnares her victims by preying on their fears and hopes. Speaking about the novel, Atwood has remarked that Zenia is the equivalent of the fiction writer, a liar, a trickster who creates stories to captivate her audience.

ALIAS GRACE

Alias Grace is a historical novel based on the real case of Grace Marks, a nineteenth century Irish immigrant to Canada who was accused of being an accomplice in the murder of her employer and his housekeepermistress. The novel combines gothic elements, social commentary, and conventions of nineteenth century fiction to tell its story. Spinning out several parallel courtship plots, the novel elucidates the implications of class and gender: Servant women were often the victims of wealthy employers or their employers' bachelor sons. Grace's friend Mary Whitney dies of a botched abortion when she becomes pregnant.

The story is told through letters and narration by Grace and Dr. Simon Jordan, a young physician who has been employed by Grace's supporters to discover the truth of the murder. Dr. Jordan is a foil to Grace: As her fortunes rise, his fall. Hoping to win a pardon from her prison sentence, the shrewd Grace narrates her life story in great detail but claims she cannot clearly remember the events surrounding the murder. Dr. Jordan hopes to restore her faulty memory and to learn the facts of the case. However, in an ironic twist of plot, he becomes embroiled in a shabby romantic liaison and, to avoid the consequences, flees Canada in haste. He is injured while serving as a physician in the American Civil War and loses his recent memory. Grace is released from prison, given a job as a housekeeper, and marries her employer. Dr. Jordan remains in the care of his mother and the woman she has chosen to be her son's wife. At the end of the novel all the plot threads are conveniently tied together as in the conventional nineteenth century novel, but at the heart of the story Grace herself remains a mystery.

THE BLIND ASSASSIN

Some of Atwood's loyal readers may have looked to *The Blind Assassin* as an opportunity for the Nobel Committee to grace the author with its literature prize. It is a "big novel," not merely because it runs well over five hundred pages but also because it offers a large slice of Canadian history in the twentieth century—or, perhaps more accurately, modern history, in its sweep through the two world wars and the Great Depression. It is a family chronicle of at least three generations of the Chase family, a wealthy, socially prominent family whose progenitor enriched his heirs from the manufacture of buttons and underwear. Stylistically, *The Blind Assassin* is an especially complex text, a series of nested narratives, for the most part under the control of the novel's octogenarian narrator, Iris Chase Griffen, telling the story as a memoir of essentially how she has survived the rest of her family. Because she has a heart condition, Iris is racing against time to finish her story, the most important prospective reader of which is her lost granddaughter Sabrina.

Iris begins with the blunt statement, "Ten days after the war [World War II] ended, my sister Laura drove a car off a bridge," which this memoir promises to explain. Many readers of *Alias Grace* were disappointed because they expected to know eventually whether or not Grace was guilty of murder, but the opening pages of *The Blind Assassin* give a strong sense that Iris not only knows "whodunit" but will eventually divulge that information.

Before Iris can do so, she must explain everything that led up to that fatal day in 1945. She tells how her father survived World War I—unlike his brothers—and struggled with his business through the Depression to save his workers' jobs, only to accept a merger that cost them those jobs and doomed Iris to a loveless marriage with his business rival, who delighted in leaving bruises on her body where only he could enjoy them as the stigmata of his domination. In rapid fashion Iris loses the only man she ever loved, then her sister and her husband to suicide, and finally her daughter is taken from her as well—a tragic sequence of events reminiscent of Greek tragedy.

ORYX AND CRAKE

Atwood has encouraged readers to approach *Oryx and Crake* as a "bookend" to *The Handmaid's Tale*. *Oryx and Crake* is also set in a future United States. It involves speculation concerning humankind's uses of science, but Atwood rejects the term "science fiction" for this novel as well as for *The Handmaid's Tale*, preferring instead to call them "speculative fiction." She has been adamant in arguing that all the scientific elements she needed for *Oryx and Crake*'s future world, in which global warming and genetic engineering are the dominant forces, are either already in play or merely extensions of the present.

Oryx and Crake represents a new departure for the author as her first novel with a male viewpoint character. Snowman, short for "The Abominable Snowman," struggles to survive in a postapocalyptic world. Snowman was once "Jimmy," the childhood chum of Crake, a boy wonder of bioengineering. In its earlier stages, bioengineering was a boy's game of dreaming up hybrids

such as the "rakunk," a mixture of raccoon and skunk. Now the field has developed into procedures such as NooSkins, which gradually replace human skin for a youthful appearance.

As a young man, Crake moves into a powerful position in which he seduces Oryx, whom Jimmy and Crake "met" as boys surfing child pornography online, as well as Jimmy, as his instruments in a master plan to eradicate humanity and replace it with the Children of Crake, creatures he has genetically engineered to survive, as *Homo sapiens* no longer can, in the global swamp generated by contamination of the atmosphere and the melting of the polar icecaps. These Frankenstein's "monsters" will inherit a brave new world from which Snowman and a few remaining humans will soon depart.

THE PENELOPIAD

Commissioned by Canongate Books for its series The Myths, *The Penelopiad* offers the long-suffering wife of Odysseus an opportunity to tell her side of the story from the Underworld more than three millennia after her death. Half of the novel is her memoir, a genre to which Atwood has become attracted in her later years.

Penelope begins with her unhappy childhood as the daughter of an indifferent water spirit and a royal father who foolishly sought immortality by attempting to drown her when the Oracle prophesied that Penelope would weave his shroud—actually it was her father-in-law whose shroud she would famously weave—but she was saved by a flotilla of ducks, thus earning the nickname "Duckie." From childhood she was tormented with the name by her beautiful cousin Helen, whose abduction by or elopement with Prince Paris would start the Trojan War.

Accordingly, if Penelope would cast herself as a figure in Greek tragedy—Atwood's theater adaptation has been successfully staged—Helen is the nemesis who brought about a fall from the good fortune of her early married life with Odysseus, whom she grew to love, even if she could never trust him because he was a "storyteller" and because he had his eye on Helen. Like Iris with her writer-lover, Penelope learned to tell stories after making love. Almost obsessed with her cousin as rival for Odysseus's love, Penelope devotes her energies to managing Ithaca so well that Odysseus upon his return will tell his wife she is worth a thousand Helens.

Atwood has stated that she took the Canongate assignment because she had been haunted as an early teenager by the summary execution of Penelope's twelve maids by Odysseus and Telemachus. The maids function as a Greek chorus of cynical commentary on the royals. They are Penelope's confidants, spies, and helpers with the unweaving of the shroud their mistress must finish before choosing a new husband. At least one disclosed the shroud ruse, and Penelope may have feared they would accuse her of adultery. The big question is whether Penelope colluded in their murder. Like Grace, Penelope never reveals any guilt.

Atwood's vision is as informed and humane as that of any contemporary novelist. Challenging her readers to form their own judgments, she combines the complexity of the best modern fiction with the moral rigor found in the works of the great nineteenth century novelists. Atwood's resonant symbols, her ironic reversals, and her example challenge readers and writers alike to confront the most difficult and important issues of today's world.

Karen Carmean; Karen F. Stein
Updated by Earl G. Ingersoll

OTHER MAJOR WORKS

SHORT FICTION: *Dancing Girls, and Other Stories*, 1977; *Bluebeard's Egg*, 1983; *Murder in the Dark: Short Fictions and Prose Poems*, 1983; *Wilderness Tips*, 1991; *Good Bones*, 1992 (also known as *Good Bones and Simple Murders*, 1994); *Moral Disorder*, 2006.

POETRY: *Double Persephone*, 1961; *The Circle Game*, 1964 (single poem), 1966 (collection); *Kaleidoscopes Baroque: A Poem*, 1965; *Talismans for Children*, 1965; *Expeditions*, 1966; *Speeches for Dr. Frankenstein*, 1966; *The Animals in That Country*, 1968; *What Was in the Garden*, 1969; *The Journals of Susanna Moodie*, 1970; *Procedures for Underground*, 1970; *Power Politics*, 1971; *You Are Happy*, 1974; *Selected Poems*, 1976; *Two-Headed Poems*, 1978; *True Stories*, 1981; *Snake Poems*, 1983; *Interlunar*, 1984; *Selected Poems II: Poems Selected and New, 1976-1986*, 1987; *Selected Poems, 1966-1984*, 1990; *Poems, 1965-1975*, 1991; *Poems, 1976-1989*, 1992; *Morning in the Burned House*, 1995; *Eating Fire: Selected Poems, 1965-1995*, 1998; *The Door*, 2007.

NONFICTION: *Survival: A Thematic Guide to Canadian Literature*, 1972; *Days of the Rebels, 1815-1840*, 1977; *Second Words: Selected Critical Prose*, 1982; *Margaret Atwood: Conversations*, 1990; *Deux sollicitudes: Entretiens*, 1996 (with Victor-Lévy Beaulieu; *Two Solicitudes: Conversations*, 1998); *Negotiating with the Dead: A Writer on Writing*, 2002; *Moving Targets: Writing with Intent, 1982-2004*, 2004 (also known as *Writing with Intent: Essays, Reviews, Personal Prose, 1983-2005*, 2005); *Waltzing Again: New and Selected Conversations with Margaret Atwood*, 2006 (with others; Earl G. Ingersoll, editor); *Payback: Debt and the Shadow Side of Wealth*, 2008.

CHILDREN'S LITERATURE: *Up in the Tree*, 1978; *Anna's Pet*, 1980 (with Joyce Barkhouse); *For the Birds*, 1990; *Princess Prunella and the Purple Peanut*, 1995 (illustrated by Maryann Kowalski); *Bashful Bob and Doleful Dorinda*, 2004 (illustrated by Dušan Petričić); *Rude Ramsay and the Roaring Radishes*, 2004 (illustrated by Dušan Petričić).

EDITED TEXTS: *The New Oxford Book of Canadian Verse in English*, 1982; *The Oxford Book of Canadian Short Stories in English*, 1986 (with Robert Weaver); *The CanLit Foodbook: From Pen to Palate, a Collection of Tasty Literary Fare*, 1987; *The Best American Short Stories 1989*, 1989 (with Shannon Ravenel); *The New Oxford Book of Canadian Short Stories in English*, 1995 (with Robert Weaver).

MISCELLANEOUS: *The Tent*, 2006.

BIBLIOGRAPHY

Bloom, Harold, ed. *Margaret Atwood*. Philadelphia: Chelsea House, 2000. Collection of essays by literary critics provides analyses of Atwood's major novels. Includes brief biography, chronology of Atwood's life, and an informative editor's introduction.

Brown, Jane W. "Constructing the Narrative of Women's Friendship: Margaret Atwood's Reflexive Fiction." *Literature, Interpretation, Theory* 6 (1995): 197-212. Argues that Atwood's narrative reflects the struggle of women to attain friendship and asserts that Atwood achieves this with such reflexive devices as embedded discourse, narrative fragmentation, and doubling.

Cooke, Nathalie. *Margaret Atwood: A Biography*. Toronto, Ont.: ECW Press, 1998. Although this is not an authorized biography, Atwood answered Cooke's questions and allowed her access, albeit limited, to materials for her research. A more substantive work than Sullivan's biography *The Red Shoes* (cited below).

Howells, Coral Ann. *Margaret Atwood*. New York: St. Martin's Press, 1996. Lively critical and biographical study elucidates issues that have energized all of Atwood's fiction: feminist issues, literary genres, and her own identity as a Canadian, a woman, and a writer.

_____, ed. *The Cambridge Companion to Margaret Atwood*. New York: Cambridge University Press, 2006. Collection of twelve excellent essays provides critical examination of Atwood's novels as well as a concise biography of the author.

McCombs, Judith, ed. *Critical Essays on Margaret Atwood*. Boston: G. K. Hall, 1988. Indispensable volume comprises thirty-two essays, including assessments of patterns and themes in Atwood's poetry and prose. Discusses her primary works in chronological order, beginning with *The Circle Game* and ending with *The Handmaid's Tale*. An editor's introduction provides an illuminating overview of

Atwood's writing career. Includes a primary bibliography to 1986 and a thorough index.

Stein, Karen F. *Margaret Atwood Revisited*. New York: Twayne, 1999. Presents a thorough overview of Atwood's writings in all genres. Includes references and a selected bibliography.

Sullivan, Rosemary. *The Red Shoes: Margaret Atwood, Starting Out*. Toronto, Ont.: HarperFlamingo Canada, 1998. Biography focuses on Atwood's early life, until the end of the 1970's. Attempts to answer the question of how Atwood became a writer and to describe the unfolding of her career.

Wilson, Sharon Rose. *Margaret Atwood's Fairy-Tale Sexual Politics*. Jackson: University Press of Mississippi, 1993. One of the most extensive and thorough investigations available of Atwood's use of fairy-tale elements in her graphic art as well as her writing. Covers her novels up to *Cat's Eye*.

_____, ed. *Margaret Atwood's Textual Assassinations: Recent Poetry and Fiction*. Columbus: Ohio State University Press, 2003. Collection of scholarly essays examines Atwood's work, with a focus on her writings published since the late 1980's. Includes discussion of the novels *Cat's Eye*, *The Robber Bride*, *Alias Grace*, and *The Blind Assassin*.

LOUIS AUCHINCLOSS

Born: Lawrence, New York; September 27, 1917
Also known as: Louis Stanton Auchincloss;
   Andrew Lee

PRINCIPAL LONG FICTION

The Indifferent Children, 1947 (as Andrew Lee)
Sybil, 1951
A Law for the Lion, 1953
The Great World and Timothy Colt, 1956
Venus in Sparta, 1958
Pursuit of the Prodigal, 1959
The House of Five Talents, 1960
Portrait in Brownstone, 1962

The Rector of Justin, 1964
The Embezzler, 1966
A World of Profit, 1968
I Come as a Thief, 1972
The Partners, 1974
The Dark Lady, 1977
The Country Cousin, 1978
The House of the Prophet, 1980
The Cat and the King, 1981
Watchfires, 1982
Exit Lady Masham, 1983
The Book Class, 1984
Honorable Men, 1985

Diary of a Yuppie, 1986
The Golden Calves, 1988
Fellow Passengers, 1989
The Lady of Situations, 1990
Three Lives, 1993 (novellas)
The Education of Oscar Fairfax, 1995
Her Infinite Variety, 2001
The Scarlet Letters, 2003
East Side Story, 2004
The Headmaster's Dilemma, 2007
Last of the Old Guard, 2008

OTHER LITERARY FORMS

Although best known as a novelist, Louis Auchincloss (AW-kihn-klahs) has been a prolific and successful
writer in a variety of other literary forms. Among his
strongest collections of short fiction are the early volumes *The Romantic Egoists* (1954), *Powers of Attorney*
(1963), and *Tales of Manhattan* (1967), each of which
presents stories linked by narration, characters, or theme
in such a way as to resemble a novel. An accomplished
critic, Auchincloss has published studies of a wide range
of writers, from William Shakespeare to Edith Wharton;
among his best-known critical works are *Reflections of a
Jacobite* (1961) and *Reading Henry James* (1975). *Life,
Law, and Letters: Essays and Sketches* (1979) consists
chiefly of essays on literary subjects, while the autobiographical memoir *A Writer's Capital* (1974) provides
valuable insight into the formation of Auchincloss's outlook. Auchincloss has also published several heavily illustrated biographies and works of nonfiction intended
for a general readership; among these works are
Richelieu (1972), *Persons of Consequence: Queen Victoria and Her Circle* (1979), *False Dawn: Women in the
Age of the Sun King* (1984), *The Vanderbilt Era: Profiles
of a Gilded Age* (1989), and *La Gloire: The Roman Empire of Corneille and Racine* (1996).

ACHIEVEMENTS

During the 1950's, Louis Auchincloss emerged as a
strong social satirist and novelist of manners, rivaling in
his best work the accomplishments of John P. Marquand
and John O'Hara. Unlike those writers, however, Auchincloss was clearly an "insider" by birth and breeding, belonging without reservation to the social class and power

structure that he so convincingly portrayed. With the
waning of the tradition represented by figures such as
Marquand and O'Hara, Auchincloss stands nearly alone
as an American novelist of manners, unrivaled in his
analysis of social and political power.

Freely acknowledging his debt to Henry James and
Edith Wharton as well as to Marcel Proust and the Duc
de Saint-Simon, Auchincloss transforms the stuff of success into high art, providing his readers with convincing
glimpses behind the scenes of society and politics, where
top-level decisions are often made for the most personal
and trivial of reasons. As a rule, his featured characters
are credible and well developed, if often unsympathetic;
Auchincloss's apparent aim is to describe what he has
seen, even at the risk of alienating readers who care so
little about his characters as not to wonder what will become of them. At the same time, Auchincloss's characteristic mode of expression leaves him open to accusations that he is an "elitist" writer, featuring characters
who are almost without exception white, Anglo-Saxon,
and Protestant. Such accusations, however, do little to
undermine the basic premise that emerges from the body
of Auchincloss's work: For good or for ill, the people of
whom he writes are those whose decisions and behavior
have determined the shape of the American body politic.
In 2005, in recognition of his body of work as a writer,
Auchincloss was awarded the National Medal of Arts.

BIOGRAPHY

Louis Stanton Auchincloss was born September 27,
1917, in Lawrence, New York, a village on Long Island
where his parents owned a vacation house. Their permanent residence was New York City's upper East Side,
where Auchincloss has spent his entire life except for his
years of education and military service. His parents, Joseph and Priscilla Auchincloss, were related to many
prominent families in New York City society. Auchincloss attended the Bovee School for Boys and graduated
from the prestigious Groton School, where his English
teacher, Malcolm Strachan, fostered his literary interests. He entered Yale University in 1935 with plans to
become a writer, only to withdraw several months short
of graduation in 1939 after his initial efforts at publication had been rejected. Deciding instead to pursue a
career in law, he received his degree from the University

of Virginia in 1941 and worked briefly for the firm of Sullivan and Cromwell in New York before joining the U.S. Navy.

During World War II, Auchincloss served in Naval Intelligence in the Panama Canal Zone and as a gunnery officer on landing ship tanks off the coast of France. Later he was commanding officer on similar craft in the Pacific Ocean. Returning to Sullivan and Cromwell after World War II, Auchincloss again tried his hand at creative writing, this time with demonstrable success. His first novel, *The Indifferent Children*, incorporated some of his experiences in the Navy and used an upper-class military officer as its protagonist, but it was published under the pseudonym Andrew Lee. Auchincloss's parents disapproved of the novel because they thought it might diminish his social standing and harm his legal career.

In 1951, Auchincloss withdrew from the practice of law and devoted himself to writing full time, only to decide after some three years that law and literature were indeed compatible, even symbiotic, and that the writer's life excluding all other pursuits was a bore. During this period he also had intensive psychotherapy. In 1954, he returned to the practice of law with the Manhattan firm of Hawkins, Delafield, and Wood, of which he became a partner in 1958. The previous year, he had married the former Adele Lawrence, to whom he dedicated several of his publications. Three children were born to them: John Winthrop Auchincloss in 1958, Blake Leay Auchincloss in 1960, and Andrew Sloane Auchincloss in 1963. Auchincloss retired from Hawkins, Delafield, and Wood in 1986.

In the 1960's Auchincloss achieved critical acclaim, but during the next decade he experienced persistent doubts about his creative ability and his reputation as a writer. After several years in which he wrote mainly nonfiction, he became more productive and began to explore new forms. After 1980 he wrote historical fantasies such as *Exit Lady Masham* and stories that are more decidedly comic, such as those in *Narcissa, and Other Fables* (1983).

In addition to his work as writer and lawyer, Auchincloss has been active in civic and cultural affairs. He served as president of the Museum of the City of New York and was a member of the advisory board of *Dictio-*

nary of Literary Biography. He also became a life fellow of the Pierpont Morgan Library.

ANALYSIS

For a writer with a full-time professional career, Louis Auchincloss proved astoundingly prolific, producing nearly one book of fiction or nonfiction each year from the 1950's through the 1990's. Like that of many highly prolific writers, the quality of his work is decidedly uneven. At his best, however, Auchincloss meets and surpasses the standard set by John P. Marquand and John O'Hara for twentieth century American social satire, displaying a resonant erudition that somehow eluded the two older writers even in their brightest moments. Even in the best of his novels, the results of Auchincloss's erudition are sometimes too conspicuous for the reader's comfort, but they can easily be overlooked in favor of the authenticity displayed by characters portrayed in convincing situations.

Auchincloss's reputation as a major writer rests primarily on novels written during the 1960's, a time some-

Louis Auchincloss. (© Jerry Bauer)

what past the vogue of social satire in the United States but coinciding neatly with the author's full maturity: The worst of his mistakes were behind him, and he had not yet experienced the temptation to repeat himself. *Pursuit of the Prodigal*, published in 1959, shows Auchincloss approaching the height of his powers, yet not quite free of his earlier mode as he portrays the tribulations of a "maverick" lawyer who is uncomfortable with the conventions into which he was born. Set in the immediate postwar years, *Pursuit of a Prodigal*, despite the distinct insider's voice, shows a clear indebtedness to Marquand's *Point of No Return* (1949), published a decade earlier. The following year, however, Auchincloss broke new and enviable ground with *The House of Five Talents*, ostensibly the memoirs, composed in 1948, of the septuagenarian Miss Gussie Millinder, heiress to and survivor of an impressive nineteenth century New York fortune. The author's demonstrated skill at characterization and narration served clear notice of his new, mature promise, soon to be fulfilled with *Portrait in Brownstone*, *The Rector of Justin*, and *The Embezzler*, any one of which would suffice to confirm Auchincloss's reputation as the successor to O'Hara and Marquand as a master observer of American society and a superior stylist.

It is hardly surprising that Auchincloss achieved his greatest success with books narrated by the characters themselves, frequently by two or more characters in successive sections of one novel. Although his early novels and certain of his short stories bear witness to his control of third-person narration, Auchincloss is doubtless at his best when assuming the voice and persona of a featured character, striking a thoroughly convincing tone of vocabulary, style, and reflection. At times, his narrators are authentically unreliable without, however, approaching the virtuoso performances sought and achieved by Marquand in such works as *The Late George Apley* (1937) or *H. M. Pulham, Esquire* (1941). Unlike Marquand, Auchincloss seeks less to ridicule his characters than to represent them true to life, allowing readers to draw their own conclusions. It is to Auchincloss's credit that he can credibly assume such diverse personae as those of Miss Gussie Millinder and the three main characters of *The Embezzler*, as well as the slightly fussy schoolmaster who narrates *The Rector of Justin*.

Given the fact that Auchincloss has chosen to serve

as a chronicler of his generation and those immediately preceding, it stands to reason that a number of his featured characters are drawn rather closely upon recognizable models—perhaps too closely in *The House of the Prophet*, rather less so in *The Embezzler* and *The Rector of Justin*. Such a practice has both its benefits and its pitfalls. At his best, Auchincloss meets and surpasses the aims of the finest historical fiction, showing rounded characters where the record presents only flatness. On other occasions, however, his presentation is so sparse as to require the readers' knowledge of the facts behind the fiction. This is not to say, however, that any of Auchincloss's novels are simple *romans à clef*; in each case, Auchincloss is careful to discover and point a message that goes far deeper than a simple recitation of documented facts.

Together with the highest minded of his characters, Auchincloss exhibits and values a strong sense of moral and ethical responsibility; unlike certain of his predecessors and erstwhile competitors in the genre, he never indulges in sensationalism or exposé for its own sake. Even when scandal invades the lives of his characters, as often it must, there is no perceptible intent to scandalize or titillate readers. Indeed, given the Proustian atmosphere that reigns in many of Auchincloss's novels, readers often wait in vain for the comic catharsis, however slow to build, with which Marcel Proust frequently rewards his readers' patience. Still, it must be noted that Auchincloss presents all but the meanest of his characters with considerable indulgence, providing a human warmth that is totally lacking in the work of such satirists as Sinclair Lewis and often absent in the more bitter works of O'Hara and Marquand.

A New Yorker by proclivity as well as by birth, Auchincloss remains, above all, a New York novelist; his characters spend most of their time in the metropolis, leaving it only for such traditional watering-places as Newport and Bar Harbor or for higher civic duty in Washington, D.C. The author's sense of place serves to illustrate and to explain the dominant role traditionally played by New Yorkers in the shaping of American society.

THE HOUSE OF FIVE TALENTS

In the first work of his "mature" period, *The House of Five Talents*, Auchincloss undertakes a personal record of upper-level Manhattan society through the still-perceptive eyes of one Augusta Millinder, age seventy-five, whose immigrant grandfather, Julius Millinder, founded one of the less conspicuous but more durable of the major New York fortunes. The Millinders had, by the time of Augusta's birth in 1873, established a position of quiet dominance, based upon diversified investments. The world in which Augusta and her more attractive elder sister Cora grew to maturity was thus one of easy movement and understated privilege, pursued frequently aboard yachts and in private railroad cars. As a memoirist, Augusta remains securely inside the closed world that she describes, yet she is privileged to have a gift for shrewd observation.

As the second and less attractive of two daughters, "Gussie" Millinder learned at an early age to view male admiration with a jaundiced eye. Indeed, the only man to whom she ever became engaged had proposed several years earlier to her vacuous sister Cora, who subsequently married a French prince. Although it seems likely that Lancey Bell, a rising young architect, has proposed to Gussie in good faith, she remains so skeptical that she breaks the engagement, having developed such inner resources that she no longer believes marriage to be necessary or desirable. In fact, the marriages in and around Gussie's family do little to encourage her faith in that institution. Soon after ending her engagement, Gussie becomes a reluctant participant in the dismantling of her own parents' marriage and household. Her father, aged sixty, has become enamored of a former actor half his age and wishes to marry her, supported in his folly by Gussie's older brother Willie and sister-in-law Julia.

Although the divorce and remarriage eventually take place as planned, Gussie has discovered in the meantime her own increasingly formidable talent for high-minded meddling. She has also begun to explore the extent of a freedom uniquely available to rich and well-read spinsters. Although dissuaded from attending college in her youth, she has taken enough courses at Columbia during her early adulthood to qualify her for part-time teaching in a private school. Later, around the age of forty, she becomes deeply involved in volunteer work. By 1948, when she at last addresses herself to her memoirs, she has led a life both independent and fulfilling, but not without its disappointments.

Appropriately, Gussie's greatest disappointments have less to do with spinsterhood than with her various relatives, many of whom seem to have a singular talent for ruining their lives, at least when measured by Gussie's demanding but forgiving standards. Gussie's personal favorite appears to have been her nephew Lydig, a versatile and talented former army flight instructor who tries his hand at various pursuits successfully but without commitment, only to seek fulfillment in a life of adventure. Having taken up mountain climbing, he dies in an avalanche around the age of thirty, a year before the stock market crash of 1929.

The changes wrought by the Depression and its consequences upon the Millinders are recorded with a sympathetic but dispassionate eye by Gussie, whose own personal fortune is sufficiently great to sustain major loss without requiring more than minimal changes in her privileged lifestyle. Among the few things she is obliged to forfeit is her private railroad car, while the chauffeured limousine remains. To the others, Gussie remains a rock of stability in a river of change, able to avert disaster with a well-placed loan (or gift) and a bit of timely meddling. At seventy-five, however, she admits that her interventions have not always been the right ones, much as they may have seemed so at the time. Several marriages remain broken beyond all possible repair and certain of her cousins face congressional investigation for their leftist sympathies.

Self-aware, yet not too much so for credibility, Gussie Millinder remains one of Auchincloss's most engaging narrators and one of his most satisfying creations, combining in her large and slightly outrageous person the best qualities of observer and participant in the action that she records.

PORTRAIT IN BROWNSTONE

Auchincloss's next novel, *Portrait in Brownstone*, attempts a broader picture of New York society. While fulfilling much of the promise held forth by *The House of Five Talents*, it falls short of its predecessor in tightness of construction, in part because of a multiplicity of narrative voices and viewpoints. Each chapter is presented from the viewpoint of a particular character, and while certain characters speak for themselves, others do not, presumably because their self-awareness is so limited as to require the author's third-person intervention.

The principal character of *Portrait in Brownstone*, although never a viewpoint character, is one Derrick Hartley, a minister's son from New England whose Harvard education and contacts facilitate his rapid rise within the presumably closed world of New York high finance. In the hands of O'Hara or Marquand, such a character as Derrick would emerge as a perceptive outsider with just a hint of the romantic hero; Auchincloss, however, presents Derrick as a thoroughgoing professional and opportunist, quick to impose his own stamp upon the closed world that almost did not allow him within its confines. He is also quick to enjoy and exploit the attentions of two female cousins, nieces of the employer whom he will eventually replace.

Set principally in the period during and surrounding World War I, *Portrait in Brownstone* underlines the contrast between "old money" and well-bred industry. Derrick, although polished and considerably less of an arriviste than certain of Auchincloss's later protagonists, has a talent for making money that renders him conspicuous among the Denison descendants, for whom the presence of money has obviated the need for making it.

After a brief and disastrous infatuation with the treacherous and ultimately unhappy Geraldine, Derrick returns his attentions to the younger, somewhat plainer cousin, Ida Trask, who had been his first love. Although disabused of her earlier illusions, Ida agrees to marry Derrick and soon bears him two children, a daughter and then a son. Ida, as a main viewpoint character, narrates much of the novel's action, developing considerably as a character in proportion to a growing awareness of her own innate strengths; Ida is a survivor, a resourceful, intelligent woman who, born in a later time, might well have rivaled her own husband's success. In any case, she is the only woman in the novel who could possibly handle the strains of marriage to a hard-driving businessman such as Derrick, whose strongest attentions and affections are reserved for his work. Like Gussie Millinder, Ida has developed character and intelligence in the absence of great beauty. Unlike Gussie, however, she is willing and able to function competently within the demands of marriage and parenthood. Because of her intelligence and understanding, her marriage to Derrick survives a number of shocks, including their daughter's marital problems and a late-blooming affair between Derrick and Geraldine.

Minor character that she may be, it is Ida's cousin Geraldine whose life and eventual suicide polarize the action of the novel. Although it is Ida who should resent Geraldine and not the other way around, Geraldine continues to envy Ida's relatively stable marriage and often genuine happiness. As Ida observes, "She remained to the end the little girl who had come down with a bright face and bright flowing hair to find in her Christmas stocking a switch and a book of sermons while mine was crammed with packages that I dared not open." Childless despite several marriages, resentful of Derrick's mechanical approach to lovemaking during their brief affair, Geraldine begins drinking heavily to dull the pain of bright promise unfulfilled.

Among the other characters portrayed in some detail are the Hartleys' two children, born shortly before World War I. Dorcas, who has inherited her father's temperament but little of his discipline, seeks a career of her own in publishing that is cut short by her marriage to a rebellious young editor who accepts the Hartley's largesse while professing to scorn its source. Eventually, Dorcas enters into a second marriage with one Mark Jesmond, an associate of Derrick who, during an earlier career as a lawyer, had handled the details of her divorce from the editor. Dorcas at last finds fulfillment of sorts in assisting Mark in efforts to "depose" her father from headship of his firm, much as Derrick himself had done years earlier to Ida's uncle Linnaeus Tremain. Dorcas's brother Hugo, meanwhile, is beginning to enter adulthood at the age of thirty-five, thanks mainly to his mother's direct intervention in the choice of his wife and career: Ida, it seems, has begun to assert herself as a matriarch.

Although marred by loose construction and a multiplicity of viewpoints, *Portrait in Brownstone* is notable for the keenness of its observation and the presentation of several memorable scenes. In any case, Auchincloss's readers did not have long to wait before the publication of *The Rector of Justin*, considered by several critics to be the finest of his novels.

THE RECTOR OF JUSTIN

Despite the fact that it shares with *Portrait in Brownstone* the potential pitfalls of loose construction and multiple viewpoints, *The Rector of Justin* is considerably more successful both as novel and as document. Auchincloss manages to broaden the appeal of the novel through his choice of subject matter, focusing upon the concept and execution of the American preparatory school. In analyzing the life and career of one Francis Prescott, founder of "Justin Martyr, an Episcopal boys' boarding school thirty miles west of Boston," Auchincloss provides through various viewpoint characters a thoughtful examination of a powerful American institution.

The main narrator of *The Rector of Justin* is Brian Aspinwall, whose arrival at Justin coincides with the outbreak of World War II in Europe. Brian has recently returned to the United States after several years of study at Oxford, where doctors have diagnosed a heart murmur that renders him unfit for service in the British Army. Unsure as yet of his vocation to become an Episcopal priest, Brian welcomes the prospect of teaching at Justin as an opportunity to test his suitability for the priesthood as well as for teaching, another possibility. Drawn gradually deeper into the affairs of the school and its founder-headmaster, Brian records his observations and experiences in a journal that forms the backbone of the book. Later, as the idea of recording the school's history begins to take form in his mind, he includes the testimony—both oral and written—of Dr. Prescott's family, friends, and former students. The result is thus more unified and better organized than *Portrait in Brownstone*, despite the old-maidish Brian's obvious limitations both as narrator and as observer.

By the time of Brian's arrival, Francis Prescott is nearly eighty years of age and long overdue for retirement; as both founder and headmaster, however, he is such an institution that no one has given serious thought to replacing him. Brian vacillates between admiration and harsh criticism for the old man and his "muscular Christianity." To Brian's incredulity, the aging Prescott remains unfailingly democratic in pronouncements both public and private, seemingly unaware of the fact that he and his school have helped to perpetuate an American class system that Prescott personally deplores. This basic irony continues to animate the novel, providing as it does the subject matter for Brian's continuing research.

Early in the novel, Brian learns that Prescott, as a young man, took pains to examine at close range the British public-school system preparatory to founding a boarding school of his own; at no point does Prescott or anyone near him appear to have considered the differ-

ence between British aristocracy and American democracy. In fact, many of the questions raised in Brian's mind are left hanging, at least for readers, calling attention to the anomalous role of private education in America. Prescott, for his part, continues to deny the existence of an American ruling class even when faced with evidence to the contrary from his own alumni rolls.

Brian's continuing research gradually uncovers a wealth of conflicting evidence concerning Prescott's accomplishment. It is clear in any case that the realization of Prescott's lifelong dream has been achieved only at great personal cost. Brian finds the darker side of Justin's history in both a document penned by the long-dead son of the school's charter trustee, on whose behalf Prescott's efforts failed miserably, and in the spoken recollections of Prescott's youngest daughter, ironically named Cordelia. When Brian meets her, Cordelia is in her middle forties, an unreconstructed Greenwich Village bohemian with nymphomaniacal tendencies that, on one occasion, send Brian fleeing for his life. Prescott, it seems, did much to ruin not only her early first marriage but also a later liaison with a mortally wounded veteran of World War I. Cordelia ascribes much of her unhappiness to the fact that both men, as "old boys" of Justin Martyr, perceived a higher obligation to her father than to herself.

Ending with Prescott's death in retirement at age eighty-six, *The Rector of Justin* concludes much as it began, undecided as to the ultimate value of Prescott's achievement. Brian, however, has made a decision; now a fully ordained priest, he continues as a member of the faculty at Justin Martyr.

Together with *The House of Five Talents*, *The Rector of Justin* stands as one of Auchincloss's more impressive accomplishments; in few of his other novels are the interdependent questions of privilege and responsibility discussed with such thoughtfulness or candor. If the book has a major weakness it is that the characters, especially Prescott himself, are often stretched so flat as to strain the readers' belief; even then, it is possible to accept flatness in the case of a character who adamantly refuses to admit life's ambiguities.

THE EMBEZZLER

Published two years after *The Rector of Justin*, *The Embezzler* builds on the author's known strengths to provide a strong social satire in the tradition of O'Hara and Marquand, yet it transcends the accomplishments of both authors with its spareness and authority. Recalling in its essentials one of the subplots in *The House of Five Talents*, wherein Gussie Millinder reluctantly covers the defalcations of a distant relative threatened with exposure, *The Embezzler* credibly re-creates the heyday of high finance in America before, during, and after the crash of 1929.

The title character and initial narrator of *The Embezzler* is Guy Prime, writing in 1960 to set straight the record of his notoriety some twenty-five years earlier. His antagonist and eventual successor as narrator is Reginald (Rex) Geer, an erstwhile friend and associate since college days. The gathering tension between the two men, reflected in the conflict between their recollections of the same events, provides the novel with its major human interest. Throughout the novel, it is up to readers to weigh conflicting testimony and to form their own considered judgments.

Grandson of a former Episcopal bishop of New York, Guy Prime has grown up less rich than other of Auchincloss's main characters. His breeding and Harvard education, however, qualify him to function competently at the upper reaches of Manhattan's financial establishment. His classmate Rex Geer, like Derrick Hartley the son of a rural New England parson, is perhaps even better suited than Guy to the "art" of making money. Rex is not, however, a social climber; to interpret him as such, as a number of the characters do, is to oversimplify a personality of multiple and often conflicting motivations. Guy, for his part, is hardly less complex, an essentially humane man whose interactions with his fellow mortals are inevitably compounded by a flair for the dramatic and a tendency toward hero worship.

From the start, the friendship of Guy Prime and Rex Geer is complicated by their interlocking relationships with women whom neither man quite understands. The first of these is Guy's wealthy cousin Alix Prime, a doll-like heiress with whom Rex falls suddenly and disastrously in love, quite to his own consternation. Although ambitious and industrious, Rex is immune to the blandishments of inherited wealth and quite undone by the common opinion that he covets Alix

for her money. The second woman is Guy's wife Angelica, reared mainly in Europe by her expatriate mother. An affair in middle life between Rex and Angelica permanently alters the lives of all three characters, serving at least in part as Guy's justification for his ventures into thievery. To Guy's way of thinking, the affair between his wife and his best friend suffices to suspend his belief in permanent values; the fact remains, however, that Guy has already begun to borrow large sums of money from Rex to cover high-risk stock market activities. With the increase of risk, Guy "simply" begins to pledge the value of securities that have been left in trust with his firm.

Later testimony supplied by Rex (and by Angelica herself in a short concluding chapter) casts serious doubt upon some of the assertions made by Guy in the brief memoir that has been discovered following his death in 1962. Even so, there are few hard-and-fast answers to the questions that remain in the readers' mind. Auchincloss does not make any serious attempt to justify the plainly unethical conduct of his principal character; what he seeks, rather, is a credible re-creation of a significant moment in recent American history, leading immediately to the extensive financial reforms implemented by the administration of Franklin D. Roosevelt. To a far greater degree than in his earlier novels, Auchincloss presents characters caught and portrayed in all their understandably human ambiguity. Despite its limited scope and relative brevity, *The Embezzler* may well be the tightest and finest of Auchincloss's novels to date.

THE HOUSE OF THE PROPHET

A prophet, according to Scripture, is not without honor save in his own house. In *The House of the Prophet*, Auchincloss, drawing from that proverb, has fashioned a novel based loosely on the life of the prominent political journalist Walter Lippmann. The novel's protagonist, Felix Leitner, a respected attorney, widely read pundit, and adviser to presidents, emerges diminished from the examination of his life undertaken by Roger Cutter, an erstwhile assistant and aspiring biographer. A variety of lesser narrative voices, including those of Leitner's two former wives, do their best to show the private truth behind the public image.

As in many of his later efforts, Auchincloss in *The*

House of the Prophet returns with diminished success to a number of conventions and devices that have served him well in the past: The basic format of the novel, including the fussy, would-be "historian," owes much to *The Rector of Justin*, while Leitner, speaking occasionally in his own voice, recalls both Rex Geer and Guy Prime of *The Embezzler*. Although the action and characters are both credible and engrossing, *The House of the Prophet* gives the disturbing impression of a novel that one has already read, in which only the names and certain of the circumstances have been changed.

In its weakest moments, *The House of the Prophet* borders upon self-parody. Roger Cutter, the "main" narrator whose memories and intentions form the backbone of the novel, often comes across as Brian Aspinwall in caricature: Rendered impotent for life by a diabetic crisis sustained in early adulthood, Roger is (even more obviously than the old-maidish Brian) cast in the role of house eunuch, free to observe and record the master's movements while remaining immune to any possible entanglement with the numerous female characters. Only in its documentary interest and its plausible interpretations of recent American history does *The House of the Prophet* bear serious comparison with the strongest of the author's earlier novels.

Viewed purely as a "political" novel, *The House of the Prophet* is a creditable example of the genre, showing that Auchincloss, when he chooses, can examine politics with the same shrewd powers of observation that he customarily applies to business and the law. As Leitner the pundit grows increasingly conservative with the onset of old age, his changing opinions are attributed less to the ossification of his mind than to the necessary tension between the "prophet" and his changing times. Toward the end of his life, for example, Leitner prepares a brilliant but outrageous column suggesting that America, through the forced resignation of Richard Nixon, "is engaging in one of the most ancient of tribal rituals: the burial of the fisher king." Roger Cutter, appalled by the likely consequences should such opinions be allowed to appear in print under Leitner's respected byline, acts quickly and effectively to have the column suppressed. Leitner's intelligence, however touched by senility, remains as keen and sensitive as ever; he has simply outlived his own time.

HONORABLE MEN

Political controversy provoked by the Vietnam War is an important issue in *Honorable Men*, but this novel remains primarily a treatment of personal and family crises. Spanning four decades (the 1930's through the 1960's), the book displays the troubled lives of Chip Benedict and his wife Alida. Sections of the novel focusing on Chip use third-person narration, but Alida's sections use the first person and thereby elicit more sympathy.

As a young woman, Alida Struthers dabbles in adolescent rebellion but eventually re-creates herself as the most famous debutante in America. By this means she escapes the genteel poverty into which her family has fallen and marries the rich and handsome Chip.

Chip is the only male descendant in a New England family who has become wealthy from manufacturing glass, a commodity as fragile as many relationships in the novel. Born with great privileges but also burdened by family expectations, Chip displays both self-righteous hypocrisy and guilt at his own inadequacies. He continually searches for Puritanical moral certainty as a buttress against his own less honorable impulses. As his name implies, he can scarcely define himself except as a chip off the family block. In a key episode that echoes the novel's title, Chip forces his best friend to resign from law school for presumably violating the honor code. Chip's action shows that he can adhere rigidly to the rules but has no larger faith that might give real meaning to the code of honor.

Chip's actions always appear good, but eventually his active support of the Vietnam War shatters his family. Alida leaves him, his daughter becomes an antiwar activist, and his son goes to Sweden to escape the draft. In an ending that some readers may find too facile, Chip finally receives assurance of his mother's unqualified love and apparently finds happiness by marrying his adoring secretary.

THE EDUCATION OF OSCAR FAIRFAX

In *The Education of Oscar Fairfax* Auchincloss revisits much of the territory explored in *Honorable Men* and other novels. Spanning seventy years, the narrative takes Oscar through a New England boys' school, on to Yale University, and eventually to a partnership in the Wall Street law firm founded by his grandfather. The chapters are loosely linked, but each episode provides an opportunity for Oscar's further enlightenment.

At St. Augustine's School, for example, he learns the possible dangers of close male relationships and saves a senior master from damaging accusations. At Yale he regretfully acknowledges the limits of his own literary talents but heartily condemns the ruthless tactics of a more brilliant classmate. As a wealthy and successful lawyer, Oscar repeatedly ponders the appropriate use of his power—in influencing the opinion of a Supreme Court justice regarding New Deal legislation, in introducing an idealistic young man from Maine into his own jaded social and professional realm, in meddling with his son's rigorous ethics. Early in the novel Oscar's future wife accuses him of caring more for art than for people. Throughout the book, however, Oscar is a keen observer of all those around him. In keeping his eyes open and exercising subtle power, he also manages to change the lives of many for the better.

David B. Parsell
Updated by Albert Wilhelm

OTHER MAJOR WORKS

SHORT FICTION: *The Injustice Collectors*, 1950; *The Romantic Egoists*, 1954; *Powers of Attorney*, 1963; *Tales of Manhattan*, 1967; *Second Chance: Tales of Two Generations*, 1970; *The Winthrop Covenant*, 1976; *Narcissa, and Other Fables*, 1983; *Skinny Island: More Tales of Manhattan*, 1987; *Fellow Passengers: A Novel in Portraits*, 1989; *False Gods*, 1992 (fables); *The Collected Stories of Louis Auchincloss*, 1994; *Tales of Yesteryear*, 1994; *The Atonement, and Other Stories*, 1997; *The Anniversary, and Other Stories*, 1999; *Manhattan Monologues*, 2002; *The Young Apollo, and Other Stories*, 2006; *The Friend of Women, and Other Stories*, 2007.

NONFICTION: *Reflections of a Jacobite*, 1961; *Pioneers and Caretakers: A Study of Nine American Women Novelists*, 1965; *Motiveless Malignity*, 1969; *Edith Wharton: A Woman in Her Time*, 1971; *Richelieu*, 1972; *A Writer's Capital*, 1974; *Reading Henry James*, 1975; *Life, Law, and Letters: Essays and Sketches*, 1979; *Persons of Consequence: Queen Victoria and Her Circle*, 1979; *False Dawn: Women in the Age of the Sun King*, 1984; *The Vanderbilt Era: Profiles of a Gilded Age*, 1989; *J. P. Morgan: The Financier as Collector*, 1990; *Love Without Wings: Some Friendships in Literature and Politics*, 1991; *The Style's the Man: Reflections on Proust, Fitzgerald, Wharton, Vidal, and Others*, 1994; *La Gloire: The Roman Empire of Corneille and Racine*, 1996; *The Man Behind the Book: Literary Profiles*, 1996; *Woodrow Wilson*, 2000; *Theodore Roosevelt*, 2001; *Writers and Personality*, 2005.

BIBLIOGRAPHY

Auchincloss, Louis. "The Art of Fiction: Louis Auchincloss." Interview by George Plimpton. *The Paris Review* 36 (Fall, 1994): 72-94. Auchincloss discusses his fiction and nonfiction, commenting on his relationships with editors, how important plot and character are in his fiction, and his notion of literary style as a reflection of the personality of the writer.

Bryer, Jackson R. *Louis Auchincloss and His Critics*. Boston: G. K. Hall, 1977. Comprehensive annotated bibliography is the first secondary sourcebook dealing exclusively with Auchincloss and his work. Remains authoritative in its record of his developing reputation as a writer; lists works by and about Auchincloss from 1931 to 1976.

Dahl, Christopher C. *Louis Auchincloss*. New York: Frederick Ungar, 1986. First book-length study of Auchincloss's work examines his novels and stories in chronological order and offers a balanced view of his accomplishments. Of special interest is the investigation of the boundaries between Auchincloss's fiction and fact, in which possible historical antecedents are noted for characters and plot in *The Embezzler*, *The House of the Prophet*, and *The Rector of Justin*.

Gelderman, Carol. *Louis Auchincloss: A Writer's Life*. Rev. ed. Columbia: University of South Carolina Press, 2007. Good biography addresses the events and contradictions of the writer's life. Includes photographs and index.

Milne, Gordon. *The Sense of Society*. Rutherford, N.J.: Fairleigh Dickinson University Press, 1977. Provides an overview of the American novel of manners, with a chapter devoted to Auchincloss in which his characterizations and prose style are examined.

Parsell, David B. *Louis Auchincloss*. Boston: Twayne, 1988. Presents a good overview of Auchincloss's work. Chapter titled "The Novel as Omnibus: Auchincloss's Collected Short Fiction" is recommended for those seeking to explore Auchincloss's singular approach to both short and long fiction.

Piket, Vincent. *Louis Auchincloss: The Growth of a Novelist*. New York: Macmillan, 1991. Offers a critical look at the evolution of Auchincloss's writing career. Includes bibliographical references and index.

JANE AUSTEN

Born: Steventon, Hampshire, England;
    December 16, 1775
Died: Winchester, Hampshire, England; July 18,
    1817

PRINCIPAL LONG FICTION

Sense and Sensibility, 1811
Pride and Prejudice, 1813
Mansfield Park, 1814
Emma, 1816
Northanger Abbey, 1818
Persuasion, 1818
Lady Susan, 1871 (novella)
The Watsons, 1871 (fragment)
Sanditon, 1925 (fragment), 1975 (completed
    by Anne Telscombe)

OTHER LITERARY FORMS

In addition to writing novels, Jane Austen (AWS-tuhn) was the author of various short juvenile pieces, most of them literary burlesques mocking the conventions of the eighteenth century novel. Her other works are *Lady Susan*, a story told in letters (written c. 1805); *The Watsons*, a fragment of a novel written about the same time; and *Sanditon*, another fragmentary novel begun in 1817. All these pieces appear in *Minor Works* (volume 6 of the *Oxford Illustrated Jane Austen*, 1954), edited by R. W. Chapman. Jane Austen's surviving letters have also been edited and published by Chapman.

ACHIEVEMENTS

Jane Austen, who published her novels anonymously, was not a writer famous in her time, nor did she wish to be. From the first, however, her novels, written in and largely for her own family circle, gained the notice and esteem of a wider audience. Among her early admirers were the Prince Regent and the foremost novelist of the day, Sir Walter Scott, who deprecated his own aptitude for the "big Bow-Wow" and praised Austen as possessing a "talent for describing the involvements and feelings and characters of ordinary life which is to me the most wonderful I ever met with." Since the days of Scott's somewhat prescient praise, her reputation has steadily grown. The critical consensus now places Jane Austen in what F. R. Leavis has termed the "Great Tradition" of the English novel. Her talent was the first to forge, from the eighteenth century novel of external incident and internal sensibility, an art form that fully and faithfully presented a vision of real life in a specific segment of the real world. Austen's particular excellences—the elegant economy of her prose, the strength and delicacy of her judgment and moral discrimination, the subtlety of her wit, the imaginative vividness of her character drawing—have been emulated but not surpassed by subsequent writers.

BIOGRAPHY

Jane Austen's life contained little in the way of outward event. Born in 1775, she was the seventh of eight children. Her father, the Reverend George Austen, was a scholarly clergyman, the rector of Steventon in rural Hampshire, England. Mrs. Austen shared her husband's intelligence and intellectual interests, and the home they provided for their children was a happy and comfortable one, replete with the pleasures of country life, genteel society, perpetual reading, and lively discussion of ideas serious and frivolous. Jane Austen, who never married, was devoted throughout her life to her brothers and their families, but her closest relationship was with her older sister Cassandra, who likewise remained unmarried. Austen relied on Cassandra as her chief critic, cherished her as a confidant, and admired her as the ideal of feminine virtue.

On the rector's retirement in 1801, Austen moved with her parents and Cassandra to Bath. After the Reverend George Austen's death in 1804, the women continued to live for some time in that city. In 1806, the Austens moved to Southampton, where they shared a house with Captain Francis Austen, Jane's older brother, and his wife. In 1808, Edward Austen (who subsequently adopted the surname Knight from the relations whose two estates he inherited) provided his mother and sisters with a permanent residence, Chawton Cottage, in the Hampshire village of the same name. At this house, Austen was to revise her manuscripts that became *Sense and Sensibility*, *Pride and Prejudice*, and *Northanger Abbey* and to write *Mansfield Park*, *Emma*, and *Persuasion*. In 1817, it became evident that she was ill with a serious complaint whose symptoms seem to have been those of Addison's disease. To be near medical help, she and Cassandra moved to lodgings in Winchester in May, 1817. Austen died there less than two months later.

Jane Austen. (Library of Congress)

ANALYSIS

Jane Austen's novels—her "bits of ivory," as she modestly and perhaps half-playfully termed them—are unrivaled for their success in combining two sorts of excellence that all too seldom coexist. Meticulously conscious of her artistry (as, for example, is Henry James), Austen is also unremittingly attentive to the realities of ordinary human existence (as is, among others, Anthony Trollope). From the first, her works unite subtlety and common sense, good humor and acute moral judgment, charm and conciseness, deftly marshaled incident and carefully rounded character.

Austen's detractors have spoken of her as a "limited" novelist, one who, writing in an age of great men and important events, portrays small towns and petty concerns, who knows (or reveals) nothing of masculine occupations and ideas, and who reduces the range of feminine thought and deed to matrimonial scheming and social pleasantry. Though one merit of the first-rate novelist is the way his or her talent transmutes all it touches and

thereby creates a distinctive and consistent world, it is true that the settings, characters, events, and ideas of Austen's novels are more than usually homogeneous. Her tales, like her own life, are set in country villages and at rural seats from which the denizens venture forth to watering places or to London. True, her characters tend to be members of her own order, that prosperous and courteous segment of the middle class called the gentry. Unlike her novel-writing peers, Austen introduces few aristocrats into the pages of her novels, and the lower ranks, though glimpsed from time to time, are never brought forward. The happenings of her novels would not have been newsworthy in her day. She depicts society at leisure rather than on the march, and in portraying pleasures her literary preference is modest: Architectural improvement involves the remodeling of a parsonage rather than the construction of Carlton House Terrace and Regent's Park; a ball is a gathering of country neighbors dancing to a harpsichord, not a crush at Almack's or the duchess of Richmond's glittering fete on the eve of Waterloo.

These limitations are the self-drawn boundaries of a strong mind rather than the innate restrictions of a weak or parochial one. Austen was in a position to know a broad band of social classes, from the local lord of the manor to the retired laborer subsisting on the charity of the parish. Some aspects of life that she did not herself experience she could learn about firsthand without leaving the family circle. Her brothers could tell her of the university, the navy in the age of Horatio Nelson, or the world of finance and fashion in Regency London. Her cousin (and later sister-in-law) Eliza, who had lost her first husband, the comte de Feuillide, to the guillotine, could tell her of Paris during the last days of the Old Regime.

In focusing on the manners and morals of rural middle-class English life, particularly on the ordering dance of matrimony that gives shape to society and situation to young ladies, Austen emphasizes rather than evades reality. The microcosm she depicts is convincing because she understands, though seldom explicitly assesses, its connections to the larger order. Her characters have clear social positions but are not just social types; the genius of such comic creations as Mrs. Bennet, Mr. Woodhouse, and Miss Bates is that each is a sparkling refinement on a quality or set of qualities existing at all times and on all levels. A proof of Austen's power (no one questions her polish) is that she succeeds in making whole communities live in the reader's imagination with little recourse to the stock device of the mere novelist of manners: descriptive detail. If a sparely drawn likeness is to convince, every line must count. The artist must understand what is omitted as well as what is supplied.

The six novels that constitute the Austen canon did not evolve in a straightforward way. Austen was, memoirs relate, as mistrustful of her judgment as she was rapid in her composition. In the case of *Pride and Prejudice*, for example, readers can be grateful that when the Reverend George Austen's letter offering the book's first incarnation, titled "First Impressions" (1797), to a publisher met with a negative reply, she was content to put the book aside for more than a decade. *Sense and Sensibility* was likewise a revision of a much earlier work. If Austen was notably nonchalant about the process of getting her literary progeny into print, one publisher with whom she had dealings was yet more dila-

tory. In 1803, Austen had completed *Northanger Abbey* (then titled "Susan") and, through her brother Henry's agency, had sold it to Crosby and Sons for ten pounds. Having acquired the manuscript, the publisher did not think fit to make use of it, and in December, 1816, Henry Austen repurchased the novel. He made known the author's identity, so family tradition has it, only after closing the deal. For these various reasons, the chronology of Austen's novels can be set in different ways; here they are discussed in order of their dates of publication.

SENSE AND SENSIBILITY

Sense and Sensibility, Austen's first published novel, evolved from "Elinor and Marianne," an epistolary work completed between 1795 and 1797. The novel is generally considered her weakest, largely because, as Walton Litz convincingly argues, it strives but fails to resolve "that struggle between inherited form and fresh experience which so often marks the transitional works of a great artist." The "inherited form" of which Litz speaks is the eighteenth century antithetical pattern suggested in the novel's title. According to this formula, opposing qualities of temperament or mind are presented in characters (generally female, often sisters) who, despite their great differences, are sincerely attached to one another.

In *Sense and Sensibility*, the antithetical characters are Elinor and Marianne Dashwood, the respective embodiments of cool, collected sense and prodigal, exquisite sensibility. In the company of their mother and younger sister, these lovely young ladies have, on the death of their father and the succession to his estate of their half brother, retired in very modest circumstances to a small house in Devonshire. There the imprudent Marianne meets and melts for Willoughby, a fashionable gentleman as charming as he is unscrupulous. Having engaged the rash girl's affections, Willoughby proceeds to trifle with them by bolting for London. When chance once again brings the Dashwood sisters into Willoughby's circle, his manner toward Marianne is greatly altered. On hearing of his engagement to an heiress, the representative of sensibility swoons, weeps, and exhibits her grief to the utmost.

Meanwhile, the reasonable Elinor has been equally unlucky in love, though she bears her disappointment quite differently. Before the family's move to Devonshire, Elinor had met and come to cherish fond feelings for her sister-in-law's brother, Edward Ferrars, a rather tame fellow (at least in comparison with Willoughby) who returns her regard—but with a measure of unease. It soon becomes known that Ferrars's reluctance to press his suit with Elinor stems from an early and injudicious secret engagement he had contracted with shrewd, base Lucy Steele. Elinor high-mindedly conceals her knowledge of the engagement and her feelings on the matter. Mrs. Ferrars, however, is a lady of less impressive self-control; she furiously disinherits her elder son in favor of his younger brother, whom Lucy then proceeds to ensnare. Thus Edward, free and provided with a small church living that will suffice to support a sensible sort of wife, can marry Elinor. Marianne—perhaps because she has finally exhausted her fancies and discovered her latent reason, perhaps because her creator is determined to punish the sensibility that throughout the novel has been so much more attractive than Elinor's prudence—is also provided with a husband: the rich Colonel Brandon, who has long loved her but whom, on account of his flannel waistcoats and his advanced age of five-and-thirty, she has heretofore reckoned beyond the pale.

The great flaw of *Sense and Sensibility* is that the polarities presented in the persons of Elinor and Marianne are too genuinely antithetical to be plausible or dynamic portraits of human beings. Elinor has strong feelings, securely managed though they may be, and Marianne has some rational powers to supplement her overactive imagination and emotions, but the young ladies do not often show themselves to be more than mere embodiments of sense and sensibility. In her second published novel, *Pride and Prejudice*, Austen makes defter use of two sisters whose values are the same but whose minds and hearts function differently. This book, a complete revision of "First Impressions," the youthful effort that had, in 1797, been offered to and summarily rejected by the publisher Cadell, is, as numerous critics have observed, a paragon of "classic" literature in which the conventions and traditions of the eighteenth century novel come to full flowering yet are freshened and transformed by Austen's distinctive genius.

PRIDE AND PREJUDICE

The title *Pride and Prejudice*, with its balanced alliterative abstractions, might suggest a second experiment in schematic psychology, and indeed the book does show some resemblances to *Sense and Sensibility*. Here again the reader encounters a pair of sisters, the elder (Jane Bennet) serene, the younger (Elizabeth) volatile. Unlike the Dashwoods, however, these ladies both demonstrate deep feelings and perceptive minds. The qualities alluded to in the title refer not to a contrast between sisters but to double defects shared by Elizabeth and Fitzwilliam Darcy, a wealthy and well-born young man she meets when his easygoing friend Charles Bingley leases Netherfield, the estate next to the Bennets' Longbourn. If so rich and vital a comic masterpiece could be reduced to a formula, it might be appropriate to say that the main thread of *Pride and Prejudice* involves the twin correction of these faults. As Darcy learns to moderate his tradition-based view of society and to recognize individual excellence (such as Elizabeth's, Jane's, and their Aunt and Uncle Gardiner's) in ranks below his own, Elizabeth becomes less dogmatic in her judgments and, in particular, more aware of the real merits of Darcy, whom she initially dismisses as a haughty, unfeeling aristocrat.

The growing accord of Elizabeth and Darcy is one of the most perfectly satisfying courtships in English literature. Their persons, minds, tastes, and even phrases convince the reader that they are two people truly made for each other; their union confers fitness on the world around them. Lionel Trilling has observed that, because of this principal match, *Pride and Prejudice* "permits us to conceive of morality as style." Elizabeth and Darcy's slow-growing love may be *Pride and Prejudice*'s ideal alliance, but it is far from being the only one, and a host of finely drawn characters surround the heroine and hero. In Jane Bennet and Charles Bingley, whose early mutual attraction is temporarily suspended by Darcy and the Bingley sisters (who deplore, not without some cause, the vulgarity of the amiable Jane's family), Austen presents a less sparkling but eminently pleasing and well-matched pair.

William Collins, the half-pompous, half-obsequious, totally asinine cousin who, because of an entail, will inherit Longbourn and displace the Bennet females after Mr. Bennet's demise, aspires to marry Elizabeth but, when rejected, instead gains the hand of her plain and practical friend Charlotte Lucas. Aware of her suitor's absurdities, Charlotte is nevertheless alive to the advantages of the situation he can offer. Her calculated decision to marry gives a graver ring to the irony of the novel's famous opening sentence: "It is a truth universally acknowledged, that a single man in possession of a good fortune, must be in want of a wife."

The last of the matches made in *Pride and Prejudice* is yet more precariously based. A lively, charming, and amoral young officer, George Wickham, son of the former steward of Pemberley, Darcy's estate, and source of many of Elizabeth's prejudices against that scrupulous gentleman, first fascinates Elizabeth and then elopes with her youngest sister, the mindless, frivolous Lydia. Only through Darcy's personal and financial intervention is Wickham persuaded to marry the ill-bred girl, who never properly understands her disgrace—a folly she shares with her mother. Mrs. Bennet, a woman deficient in good humor and good sense, is—along with her cynical, capricious husband, the ponderous Collins, and the tyrannical Lady Catherine De Bourgh—one of the great comic creations of literature. Most of these characters could have seemed odious if sketched by another pen, but so brilliant is the sunny intelligence playing over the world of *Pride and Prejudice* that even fools are golden.

MANSFIELD PARK

Mansfield Park, begun in 1811 and finished in 1813, is the first of Austen's novels to be a complete product of her maturity. The longest, most didactic, and least ironic of her books, it is the one critics generally have the most trouble reconciling with their prevailing ideas of the author. Although *Mansfield Park* was composed more or less at one stretch, its conception coincided with the final revisions of *Pride and Prejudice*. Indeed, the critics who offer the most satisfying studies of *Mansfield Park* tend to see it not as a piece of authorial bad faith or self-suppression, a temporary anomaly, but as what Walton Litz calls a "counter-truth" to its immediate predecessor.

Pleased with and proud of *Pride and Prejudice*, Austen nevertheless recorded her impression of its being "rather too light, and bright, and sparkling"—in need of shade. That darkness she found wanting is supplied in *Mansfield Park*, which offers, as Trilling observes in his well-known essay on the novel, the antithesis to *Pride and Prejudice*'s generous, humorous, spirited social vi-

sion. *Mansfield Park*, Trilling argues, condemns rather than forgives: "Its praise is not for social freedom but for social stasis. It takes full notice of spiritedness, vivacity, celerity, and lightness, only to reject them as having nothing to do with virtue and happiness, as being, indeed, deterrents to the good life."

Most of the action of *Mansfield Park* is set within the little world comprising the estate of that name, a country place resembling in large measure Godmersham, Edward Austen Knight's estate in Kent; but for her heroine and some interludes in which she figures, Austen dips into a milieu she has not previously frequented in her novels—the socially and financially precarious lower fringe of the middle class. Fanny Price, a frail, serious, modest girl, is one of nine children belonging to and inadequately supported by a feckless officer of marines and his lazy, self-centered wife. Mrs. Price's meddling sister, the widowed Mrs. Norris, arranges for Fanny to be reared in "poor relation" status at Mansfield Park, the seat of kindly but crusty Sir Thomas Bertram and his languid lady, the third of the sisters. At first awed by the splendor of her surroundings, the gruffness of the baronet, and the elegance, vigor, and high spirits of the young Bertrams—Tom, Edmund, Maria, and Julia—Fanny eventually wins a valued place in the household.

During Sir Thomas's absence to visit his property in Antigua, evidence of Fanny's moral fineness, and the various degrees in which her cousins fall short of her excellence, is presented through a device that proves to be one of Austen's most brilliant triumphs of plotting. Visiting the rectory at Mansfield are the younger brother and sister of the rector's wife, Henry and Mary Crawford, witty, worldly, and wealthy. At Mary's proposal, amateur theatricals are introduced to Mansfield Park, and in the process of this diversion the moral pollution of London's Great World begins to corrupt the bracing country air.

Just how the staging of a play—even though it be *Lovers' Vows*, a sloppy piece of romantic bathos, adultery rendered sympathetic—can be morally reprehensible is a bit unclear for most modern-day readers, especially those who realize that the Austens themselves reveled in theatricals at home. The problem as Austen presents it lies in the possible consequences of role-playing: coming to feel the emotions and attitudes one presents on the stage or, worse yet, expressing rather than suppressing genuine but socially unacceptable feelings in the guise of mere acting. In the course of the theatricals, where Fanny, who will not act, is relegated to the role of spectator and moral chorus, Maria Bertram, engaged to a bovine local heir, vies with her sister in striving to fascinate Henry Crawford, who in turn is all too ready to charm them. Mary Crawford, though it is "her way" to find eldest sons most agreeable, has the good taste to be attracted to Edmund, the second son, who plans to enter the clergy. Mary's vivacity, as evidenced by the theatricals, easily wins his heart.

Time passes and poor Fanny, who since childhood has adored her cousin Edmund, unintentionally interests Henry Crawford. Determined to gain the affections of this rare young woman who is indifferent to his charms, Crawford ends by succumbing to hers. He proposes. Fanny's unworldly refusal provokes the anger of her uncle. Then, while Fanny, still in disgrace with the baronet, is away from Mansfield Park and visiting her family at Portsmouth, the debacle of which *Lovers' Vows* was a harbinger comes about. The *homme fatal* Henry, at a loss for a woman to make love to, trains his charms on his old flirt Maria, now Mrs. Rushworth. She runs away with him; her sister, not to be outdone in bad behavior, elopes with an unsatisfactory suitor. Mary Crawford's moral coarseness becomes evident in her casual dismissal of these catastrophes. Edmund, now a clergyman, finds solace, then love, with the cousin whose sterling character shines brightly for him now that Mary's glitter has tarnished. Fanny gains all she could hope for in at last attaining the heart and hand of her clerical kinsman.

EMMA

Austen's next novel, *Emma*, might be thought of as harmonizing the two voices heard in *Pride and Prejudice* and *Mansfield Park*. For this book, Austen claimed to be creating "a heroine whom no one but myself will much like," an "imaginist" whose circumstances and qualities of mind make her the self-crowned queen of her country neighborhood. Austen was not entirely serious or accurate: Emma certainly has her partisans. Even those readers who do not like her tend to find her fascinating, for she is a spirited, imaginative, healthy young woman who, like Mary Crawford, has potential to do considerable harm to the fabric of society but on whom,

like Elizabeth Bennet, her creator generously bestows life's greatest blessing: union with a man whose virtues, talents, and assets are the best complement for her own.

Emma's eventual marriage to Mr. Knightley of Donwell Abbey is the ultimate expression of one of Austen's key assumptions, that marriage is a young woman's supreme act of self-definition. Unlike any other Austen heroine, Emma has no pressing need to marry. As the opening sentence of the book implies, Emma's situation makes her acceptance or rejection of a suitor an act of unencumbered will: "Emma Woodhouse, handsome, clever, and rich, with a comfortable home and happy disposition, seemed to unite some of the best blessings of existence; and had lived nearly twenty-one years in the world with very little to distress or vex her."

Free though circumstance allows her to be, Emma has not been encouraged by her lot in life to acquire the discipline and self-knowledge that, augmenting her innate intelligence and taste, would help her to choose wisely. Brought up by a doting valetudinarian of a father and a perceptive but permissive governess, Emma has been encouraged to think too highly of herself. Far from vain about her beauty, Emma has—as Mr. Knightley, the only person who ventures to criticize her, observes—complete yet unfounded faith in her ability to judge people's characters and arrange their lives. The course of *Emma* is Miss Woodhouse's education in judgment, a process achieved through repeated mistakes and humiliations.

As the novel opens, the young mistress of Hartfield is at loose ends. Her beloved governess has just married Mr. Weston, of the neighboring property, Randalls. To fill the newly made gap in her life, Emma takes notice of Harriet Smith, a pretty, dim "natural daughter of somebody," and a parlor-boarder at the local school. Determined to settle her protégé into the sort of life she deems suitable, Emma detaches Harriet from Robert Martin, a young farmer who has proposed to her, and embarks on a campaign to conquer for Harriet the heart of Mr. Elton, Highbury's unmarried clergyman. Elton's attentiveness and excessive flattery convince Emma of her plan's success but at the same time show the reader what Emma is aghast to learn at the end of book 1: that Elton scorns the nobody and has designs on the heiress herself.

With the arrival of three new personages in Highbury, book 2 widens Emma's opportunities for misconception. The first newcomer is Jane Fairfax, an elegant and accomplished connection of the Bates family and a girl whose prospective fate, the "governess trade," shows how unreliable the situations of well-bred young ladies without fortunes or husbands tend to be. Next to arrive is the suave Mr. Frank Churchill, Mr. Weston's grown son, who has been adopted by wealthy relations of his mother and who has been long remiss in paying a visit to Highbury. Finally, Mr. Elton brings home a bride, the former Augusta Hawkins of Bristol, a pretentious and impertinent creature possessed of an independent fortune, a well-married sister, and a boundless fund of self-congratulation. Emma mistakenly flatters herself that the dashing Frank Churchill is in love with her and then settles on him as a husband for Harriet; she suspects the reserved Miss Fairfax, whose cultivation she rightly perceives as a reproach to her own untrained talents, of a clandestine relationship with a married man. She despises Mrs. Elton, as would any person of sense, but fails to see that the vulgar woman's offensiveness is an exaggerated version of her own officiousness and snobbery.

Thus the potential consequences of Emma's misplaced faith in her judgment intensify, and the evidence of her fallibility mounts. Thoroughly embarrassed to learn that Frank Churchill, with whom she has shared all her hypotheses regarding Jane Fairfax, has long been secretly engaged to that woman, Emma suffers the deathblow to her smug self-esteem when Harriet announces that the gentleman whose feelings she hopes to have aroused is not, as Emma supposes, Churchill but the squire of Donwell. Emma's moment of truth is devastating and complete, its importance marked by one of Jane Austen's rare uses of figurative language: "It darted through her, with the speed of an arrow, that Mr. Knightley must marry no one but herself!" Perhaps the greatest evidence of Emma's being a favorite of fortune is that Mr. Knightley feels the same as she does on this matter. Chastened by her series of bad judgments, paired with a gentleman who for years has loved and respected her enough to correct her and whom she can love and respect in return, Emma participates in the minuet of marriage with which Austen concludes the book, the other couples so united being Miss Fairfax and Mr. Churchill

and Harriet Smith (ductile enough to form four attachments in a year) and Robert Martin (stalwart enough to persist in his original feeling).

Emma Woodhouse's gradual education, which parallels the reader's growing awareness of what a menace to the social order her circumstances, abilities, and weaknesses combine to make her, is one of Austen's finest pieces of plotting. The depiction of character is likewise superb. Among a gallery of memorable and distinctive characters are Mr. Woodhouse; Miss Bates, the stream-of-consciousness talker who inadvertently provokes Emma's famous rudeness on Box Hill; and the wonderfully detestable Mrs. Elton, with her self-contradictions and her fractured Italian, her endless allusions to Selina, Mr. Suckling, Maple Grove, and the *barouche landau*. Life at Hartfield, Donwell, and Highbury is portrayed with complexity and economy. Every word, expression, opinion, and activity—whether sketching a portrait, selecting a dancing partner, or planning a strawberry-picking party—becomes a gesture of self-revelation. *Emma* demonstrates how, in Austen's hands, the novel of manners can become a statement of moral philosophy.

NORTHANGER ABBEY

Northanger Abbey was published in a four-volume unit with *Persuasion* in 1818, after Austen's death, but the manuscript had been completed much earlier, in 1803. Austen wrote a preface for *Northanger Abbey* but did not do the sort of revising that had transformed "Elinor and Marianne" and "First Impressions" into *Sense and Sensibility* and *Pride and Prejudice*. The published form of *Northanger Abbey* can therefore be seen as the earliest of the six novels. It is also, with the possible exception of *Sense and Sensibility*, the most "literary." *Northanger Abbey*, like some of Austen's juvenile burlesques, confronts the conventions of the gothic novel or tale of terror. The incidents of her novel have been shown to parallel, with ironic difference, the principal lines of gothic romance, particularly as practiced by Ann Radcliffe, whose most famous works, *The Romance of the Forest* (1791) and *The Mysteries of Udolpho* (1794), had appeared several years before Austen began work on her burlesque.

Like *Emma*, *Northanger Abbey* is centrally concerned with tracing the growth of a young woman's mind and the cultivation of her judgment. In this less sophisticated work, however, the author accomplishes her goal through a rather schematic contrast. As an enthusiastic reader of tales of terror, Catherine Morland has gothic expectations of life despite a background most unsuitable for a heroine. Like the gothic heroines she admires, Catherine commences adventuring early in the novel. She is not, however, shipped to Venice or Dalmatia; rather, she is taken to Bath for a six-week stay. Her hosts are serenely amiable English folk, her pastimes the ordinary round of spa pleasures; the young man whose acquaintance she makes, Henry Tilney, is a witty clergyman rather than a misanthropic monk or dissolute rake. Toward this delightful, if far from gothic, young man, Catherine's feelings are early inclined. In turn, he, his sister, and even his father, the haughty, imperious General Tilney, are favorably disposed toward her. With the highest expectations, Catherine sets out to accompany them to their seat, the Abbey of the novel's title (which, like that of *Persuasion*, was selected not by the author but by Henry Austen, who handled the posthumous publication).

At Northanger, Catherine's education in the difference between literature and life continues. Despite its monastic origins, the Abbey proves a comfortable and well-maintained dwelling. When Catherine, like one of Radcliffe's protagonists, finds a mysterious document in a chest and spends a restless night wondering what lurid tale it might chronicle, she is again disappointed: "If the evidence of her sight might be trusted she held a washing-bill in her hand." Although Catherine's experience does not confirm the truth of Radcliffe's sensational horrors, it does not prove the world a straightforward, safe, cozy place. Catherine has already seen something of falseness and selfish vulgarity in the persons of Isabella Thorpe and her brother John, acquaintances formed at Bath. At Northanger, she learns that, though the general may not be the wife murderer she has fancied him, he is quite as cruel as she could imagine. On learning that Catherine is not the great heiress he has mistakenly supposed her to be, the furious general packs her off in disgrace and discomfort in a public coach.

With this proof that the world of fact can be as treacherous as that of fiction, Catherine returns, sadder and wiser, to the bosom of her family. She has not long to droop, however, for Henry Tilney, on hearing of his fa-

ther's bad behavior, hurries after her and makes Catherine the proposal that he has long felt inclined to offer and that his father has until recently promoted. The approval of Catherine's parents is immediate, and the general is not overlong in coming to countenance the match. "To begin perfect happiness at the respective ages of twenty-six and eighteen is to do pretty well," observes the facetious narrator, striking a literary pose even in the novel's last sentence, "and . . . I leave it to be settled by whomsoever it may concern, whether the tendency of this work be altogether to recommend parental tyranny, or reward filial disobedience."

PERSUASION

Persuasion, many readers believe, signals Austen's literary move out of the eighteenth century and into the nineteenth. This novel, quite different from those that preceded it, draws not on the tradition of the novelists of the 1790's but on that of the lionized poets of the new century's second decade, Sir Walter Scott and Lord Byron. For the first time, Austen clearly seems the child of her time, susceptible to the charms of natural rather than improved landscapes, fields, and sea cliffs rather than gardens and shrubberies. The wistful, melancholy beauty of autumn that pervades the book is likewise romantic. The gaiety, vitality, and sparkling wit of *Pride and Prejudice* and *Emma* are muted. The stable social order represented by the great estate in *Mansfield Park* has become fluid in *Persuasion*: Here the principal country house, Kellynch Hall, must be let because the indigenous family cannot afford to inhabit it.

Most important, *Persuasion*'s heroine is unique in Jane Austen's gallery. Anne Elliott, uprooted from her ancestral home, spiritually isolated from her selfish and small-minded father and sisters, separated from the man she loves by a long-standing estrangement, is every bit as "alienated" as such later nineteenth century heroines as Esther Summerson, Jane Eyre, and Becky Sharp. Anne's story is very much the product of Austen's middle age. At twenty-seven, Anne is the only Austen heroine to be past her first youth. Furthermore, she is in no need of education. Her one great mistake—overriding the impulse of her heart and yielding to the persuasion of her friend Lady Russell in rejecting the proposal of Frederick Wentworth, a sanguine young naval officer with his fortune still to make and his character to prove—is some eight years in the past, and she clearly recognizes it for the error it was.

Persuasion is the story of how Anne and Frederick (now the eminent Captain) Wentworth rekindle the embers of their love. Chance throws them together when the vain, foolish Sir Walter Elliott, obliged to economize or rent his estate, resolves to move his household to Bath, where he can cut a fine figure at less cost, and leases Kellynch to Admiral and Mrs. Croft, who turn out to be the brother-in-law and sister of Captain Wentworth. Initially cool to his former love—or, rather, able to see the diminution of her beauty because he is unable to forgive her rejection—the captain flirts with the Musgrove girls; they are sisters to the husband of Anne's younger sister Mary and blooming belles with the youth and vigor Anne lacks. The captain's old appreciation of Anne's merits—her clear insight, kindness, high-mindedness, and modesty—soon reasserts itself, but not before fate and the captain's impetuosity have all but forced another engagement on him. Being "jumped down" from the Cobb at Lyme Regis, Louisa Musgrove misses his arms and falls unconscious on the pavement. Obliged by honor to declare himself hers if she should wish it, Wentworth is finally spared this self-sacrifice when the susceptible young lady and the sensitive Captain Benwick fall in love. Having discovered the intensity of his devotion to Anne by being on the point of having to abjure it, Wentworth hurries to Bath, there to declare his attachment in what is surely the most powerful engagement scene in the Austen canon.

Though the story of *Persuasion* belongs to Anne Elliott and Frederick Wentworth, Austen's skill at evoking characters is everywhere noticeable. As Elizabeth Jenkins observes, all of the supporting characters present different facets of the love theme. The heartless marital calculations of Mr. Elliott, Elizabeth Elliott, and Mrs. Clay, the domestic comforts of the senior Musgroves and the Crofts, and the half-fractious, half-amiable ménage of Charles and Mary Musgrove all permit the reader to discern more clearly how rare and true is the love Anne Elliott and her captain have come so close to losing. The mature, deeply grateful commitment they are able to make to each other is, if not the most charming, surely the most profound in the Austen world.

Peter W. Graham

Other major works

SHORT FICTION: *Minor Works*, 1954 (volume 6 of the *Oxford Illustrated Jane Austen*; R. W. Chapman, editor).

NONFICTION: *Jane Austen's Letters to Her Sister Cassandra and Others*, 1932 (R. W. Chapman, editor).

CHILDREN'S LITERATURE: *The History of England*, wr. 1791 (published with Charles Dickens's *A Child's History of England* as *Two Histories of England*, 2006); *Catherine*, 1818; *Lesley Castle*, 1922; *Three Sisters*, 1933.

MISCELLANEOUS: *Love and Freindship, and Other Early Works*, 1922.

Bibliography

Austen, Jane. *Jane Austen's Letters to Her Sister Cassandra and Others*. Edited by R. W. Chapman. 2 vols. Oxford, England: Clarendon Press, 1932. The first collection of surviving Austen letters is arranged chronologically in two volumes with appendixes that give summary identifications of anyone who is ambiguously mentioned in the text of the letters. With corrected spelling and punctuation. Includes a map of eighteenth century Berkshire and Surrey, England.

Brown, Julie Prewit. *Jane Austen's Novels*. Cambridge, Mass.: Harvard University Press, 1979. Provides a somewhat feminist perspective on Austen as a conscious artist who masterfully employed ironic comedy and satiric realism. Five chapters explore the purpose and subtleties of each novel. Includes an eye-opening chapter on the artist as a woman writer.

Copeland, Edward, and Juliet McMaster, eds. *The Cambridge Companion to Jane Austen*. New York: Cambridge University Press, 1997. Collection of thirteen essays is divided between those concerning Austen's own world and those that address modern critical discourse, such as Claudia L. Johnson's "Austen Cults and Cultures." Some essays focus on Austen's novels, whereas others deal with broad issues, such as class consciousness, religion, and domestic economy. This excellent overview includes a chronology and concludes with an assessment of late twentieth century developments in Austen scholarship.

Galperin, William H. *The Historical Austen*. Philadelphia: University of Pennsylvania Press, 2003. Careful study provides a fresh explication of Austen's work. Examines how Austen used her fiction to serve as a "social and political" tool.

Halperin, John. *The Life of Jane Austen*. Baltimore: Johns Hopkins University Press, 1984. Biographical study focuses on the association between the life of the artist and the works she produced. Valuable for a realistic look at the life of a legendary figure. Includes illustrations.

Lambdin, Laura Cooner, and Robert Thomas Lambdin, eds. *A Companion to Jane Austen Studies*. New York: Greenwood Press, 2000. Collection of twenty-two essays devoted to Austen's works includes fourteen that examine her novels, including *Sanditon* and *The Watsons*—the two novels she left unfinished.

Lane, Maggie. *Jane Austen's England*. New York: St. Martin's Press, 1986. Fascinating volume is full of illustrations that give Austen's readers a look at the world of her novels. Arranged chronologically, taking the reader to the places Austen would have gone, usually through contemporary paintings. The first chapter, "The England of Jane Austen's Time," gives a good basic summary of social conditions around the beginning of the nineteenth century. Includes specific references to the novels; for example, a quote from the Box Hill episode in *Emma* is accompanied by a painting of Box Hill. Includes map, brief bibliography, and index.

Le Faye, Deirdre. *Jane Austen: A Family Record*. London: British Library, 1989. Revision of the 1913 edition of *Life and Letters of Jane Austen*, written by a descendant of Austen's nephew, James Edward. Thanks to additional extensive contemporary research, provides a thorough look at Austen's life and the close-knit family on which she was financially dependent. Includes illustrations and a thorough chronology of Austen's life.

Lynch, Deidre, ed. *Janeites: Austen's Disciples and Devotees*. Princeton, N.J.: Princeton University Press, 2000. Collection of nine essays explores the novelist as an enduring cultural phenomenon. Topics addressed include Austen's novels as works of Regency pop fiction, Austen's earliest readers and the reception of her work in the United States, and Austen and the discipline of novel studies.

Mooneyham, Laura G. *Romance, Language, and Education in Jane Austen's Novels*. New York: St. Martin's Press, 1986. Theorizes that a relationship exists among language, education, and romance in Austen's work. Asserts that the romance between heroine and hero is in itself educational for the heroine because romance offers the opportunity for open communication. This approach is provocative and useful, especially because it emphasizes Austen's own preoccupations. Covers all six of Austen's complete novels in individual chapters.

Nokes, David. *Jane Austen: A Life*. New York: Farrar, Straus and Giroux, 1997. Biography employs a broad perspective to explore the family in which Austen lived as well as the wider world in which the family belonged.

Selwyn, David. *Jane Austen and Leisure*. London: Hambledon Press, 1999. Examines the manners and customs of Austen's class in her era and how Austen portrays them in her works.

Todd, Janet M. *The Cambridge Introduction to Jane Austen*. New York: Cambridge University Press, 2006. Todd, an Austen scholar and editor of the author's work, provides an overview of Austen's life, her novels, the context in which they were written, and her works' reception. Includes a detailed discussion of each novel, providing a good starting point for the study of her major works.

Tomalin, Claire. *Jane Austen: A Life*. New York: Knopf, 1998. Compelling account of Austen's life is exceedingly well written and attempts to tell the story from the subject's own perspective. Proceeding in chronological order, the book concludes with a postscript on the fates of Austen's family members and two interesting appendixes: a note on Austen's final illness and an excerpt from the diary of Austen's niece Fanny.

PAUL AUSTER

Born: Newark, New Jersey; February 3, 1947
Also known as: Paul Benjamin Auster

PRINCIPAL LONG FICTION

City of Glass, 1985
Ghosts, 1986
The Locked Room, 1986
In the Country of Last Things, 1987
The New York Trilogy, 1987 (includes *City of Glass*, *Ghosts*, and *The Locked Room*)
Moon Palace, 1989
The Music of Chance, 1990
Leviathan, 1992
Mr. Vertigo, 1994
Timbuktu, 1999
The Book of Illusions, 2002
Oracle Night, 2003
The Brooklyn Follies, 2006
Travels in the Scriptorium, 2007
Man in the Dark, 2008
Invisible, 2009

OTHER LITERARY FORMS

As a young man, Paul Auster (AW-stur) distinguished himself in the literary forms of translation and poetry. His well-received translations of the works of French poets Stéphane Mallarmé, Jacques Dupin, Joseph Joubert, and André du Bouchet led to his editing a bilingual anthology titled *The Random House Book of Twentieth-Century French Poetry*, published in 1982. Beginning in 1974, his own poetry was published in reviews and by small presses. The poetry collections *Disappearances: Selected Poems* (1988) and *Ground Work: Selected Poems and Essays, 1970-1979* (1990) were published after Auster made a name for himself in fiction. His nonfiction prose collection *The Art of Hunger, and Other Essays* and his memoir *The Invention of Solitude* were originally published in 1982, and a later memoir, *Hand to Mouth: A Chronicle of Early Failure*, appeared in 1997, after Auster had published eight novels. Scriptwriting is another genre for which Auster is noted. He wrote the screenplays for the films *Smoke* (1995), *Blue in the Face*

(1995), which he also codirected, as well as for *Lulu on the Bridge* (1998). *I Thought My Father Was God, and Other True Tales from NPR's National Story Project* (2001) is another edited volume for which Auster received critical notice. Auster has also been involved in musical recordings and writing song lyrics, notably for his daughter's 2005 album with the New York band One Ring Zero titled *Sophie Auster*. In 2007, Auster's film *The Inner Life of Martin Frost*, which he both wrote and directed, was released; it stars his daughter Sophie Auster as the character Anna James. He adapted his novel *In the Country of Last Things* for a 2008 feature film in English and Spanish, directed by Alejandro Chomski and filmed in Argentina.

ACHIEVEMENTS

Paul Auster's works of fiction have earned him significant recognition. *City of Glass* was nominated for an Edgar Award for best mystery novel in 1986, and *The Locked Room* was nominated for a *Boston Globe* Literary Press Award for fiction in 1990. In 1993, Auster received the Chevalier de l'Ordre des Arts et des Lettres and also won the French Prix Medicis Étranger for foreign literature, for *Leviathan*. In 2006, he was awarded the Spanish Prince of Asturias Award for Letters.

BIOGRAPHY

Paul Benjamin Auster was born in Newark, New Jersey, on February 3, 1947, and grew up in the suburbs of Newark. He benefited early from the influence of an uncle who was a skilled translator and who encouraged his nephew's developing interest in writing and literature. In the summer between high school and college, Auster traveled to Europe, returning to the United States to attend Columbia University. He supported himself during his college years with a variety of freelance jobs, including translation and interpretation. Auster graduated from Columbia in 1969 with a B.A. in English and comparative literature, and he received his M.A. in the literature of the Renaissance the following year. Auster returned to Paris in 1971 and lived in France until 1974.

Back in New York in late 1974, Auster married the

writer Lydia Davis. Together they worked on translations, and Auster began to publish poetry, reviews, and essays. In 1977, their son Daniel was born. Auster was at a low point in his life at this time—his marriage was failing, and he was unhappy with his writing career and having financial difficulties. By 1979 his marriage had ended. When his father died suddenly of a heart attack and left him a small inheritance, Auster was able to write without financial worry. He continued to work on poetry and translation, but by 1980 he had begun work on *The Invention of Solitude*, which includes a tribute to his father.

In 1981, Auster met and married Siri Hustvedt. A fertile time in his writing career began, and during the 1980's he published *The Random House Book of Twentieth-Century French Poetry*, *The Art of Hunger*, and more translations. The three novels of *The New York Trilogy*, as well as *In the Country of Last Things* and *Moon Palace*, received good reviews. He worked as a

teacher of creative writing at Princeton University from 1986 to 1990, and his daughter Sophie was born in 1987.

Auster's next novel, *The Music of Chance*, published in 1990, attracted the attention of the motion-picture industry, and a film version was released in 1993. At the same time, Auster's story "Auggie Wren's Christmas Story" appeared in *The New York Times*, and director Wayne Wang became interested in turning the story into a film. Auster's script became the film *Smoke*, which was followed shortly by the companion piece *Blue in the Face*. By the time the two films were released in 1995, Auster had published two more novels, *Leviathan* and *Mr. Vertigo*. In 1997, the memoir *Hand to Mouth* was released. Auster was a member of the jury for the 1997 Cannes Film Festival; in 1998, the film *Lulu on the Bridge* appeared.

Timbuktu marked Auster's return to novel writing in 1999. The novels *The Book of Illusions*, *Oracle Night*, *The Brooklyn Follies*, *Travels in the Scriptorium*, and *Man in the Dark* appeared in rapid succession through the first decade of the twenty-first century, along with volumes of his collected poetry and nonfiction, collaborations with recording and visual artists, and another film, *The Inner Life of Martin Frost*.

Auster continues to produce novels, screenplays, nonfiction, and collaborative multimedia works. He lives and works in Brooklyn, New York, a location that has influenced much of his work. At the same time, he is deeply connected to Europe, where his work is popularly and critically acclaimed.

ANALYSIS

Paul Auster is best known as a postmodernist writer. "Postmodernism" is an elusive academic term applied to unconventional fiction from the late twentieth century onward that in style and theme investigates the methods of fiction. Beneath a deceptively simple fictional form—the detective novel, science fiction, the picaresque story—lies an intellectually stimulating, thematically complex interplay between reader and author as well as between protagonist and writer. Auster's fiction is accessible on the surface level, yet the subtext is worthy of the term "experimental." The appeal of postmodern fic-

Paul Auster. (© Jerry Bauer)

tion is intellectual; readers are forced to think about the writer's allusions, use of unexpected devices, and breaking of the rules of conventional fiction. Auster's fiction is intelligent and puzzling, influenced by the works of Nathaniel Hawthorne, Edgar Allan Poe, Samuel Beckett, and the French Symbolists.

The three short novels collected as *The New York Trilogy* (*City of Glass*, *Ghosts*, and *The Locked Room*) constitute Auster's most often discussed work. The use of the detective-story form to introduce themes of isolation and the crisis of the individual is taken as a prime example of postmodern literature, writing that may use traditional forms in ironic or displaced ways. Characteristic of postmodernist stories, the protagonists of Auster novels do not reach solutions. Many of his heroes disappear, die mysterious deaths, or lose all of their personal possessions.

Throughout his long fiction, Auster is critically admired for his diversity of form, his intelligence, the agility of his prose, and the complexity of his structure and themes. His writing appeals to a mass audience as well as to literary scholars; his fiction has a cult following among students. He is known for the variety of genres in which he works: poetry, memoirs, essays, and screenplays.

Auster's novels are connected, in many cases by the names of characters who appear in more than one novel, but above all by their abstraction and ambiguity and by their intertwining themes: the role of chance and coincidence and the unstable nature of identity. They feature mazes of story lines and narrative twists and turns in which fiction bleeds into reality. Much of Auster's work is characterized by its examination of language. The protagonist is often a writer, sometimes Auster himself.

THE NEW YORK TRILOGY

The New York Trilogy, composed of the three short novels *City of Glass*, *Ghosts*, and *The Locked Room*, has received more attention from critics than any of Auster's subsequent work. The three novels share a common style, theme, and New York setting. Auster intentionally blurs the distinction between reality and text, placing himself as a character in the first novel. This postmodern device raises questions of identity that resonate throughout the series. Auster takes the convention of mistaken identity and develops it into a metaphor for contemporary urban life.

The first novel, *City of Glass*, opens as a standard detective novel. Quinn, a detective novelist, receives a telephone call intended for a detective named Paul Auster. Quinn decides to take on Auster's identity and accept the case. The job is to tail a madman named Stillman who has recently been released from a mental institution. Once a promising linguist, Stillman had been committed for isolating his son in a locked room for nine years to try to re-create the primitive language of Adam and Eve. Now that Stillman has been released, the son's life is in danger.

The novel subtly shifts from a standard detective story to an existential quest for identity. It moves into the realm of serious literature as it explores themes of the degeneration of language, the shifting of identity, and the struggle to remain sane in the anonymity of the metropolis. Each detail is significant. Coincidences abound, particularly coincidences involving names. Quinn the watcher becomes as seedy and degenerate as Stillman the quarry. True to its postmodern identity, and typical of Auster's work, the novel does not actually offer a resolution. Questions remain unanswered; characters simply disappear.

Ghosts, the second novel of the trilogy, explores many of the same questions of identity and blurred distinctions between watcher and prey, detective and client, but on a more abstract plane. A client named White hires a detective named Blue to follow a man named Black. The three characters merge into one as Blue passes years watching Black writing a book in a room across the street, while Blue records his observations and mails them weekly to White.

Clearly the novel is meant to be a metaphor, and after carefully paying attention to details and clues, as is necessary in a mystery story, the reader is left with the question, What does it all mean? As in the first novel, the detective hired to watch merges into the watched. In this novel, however, neither the reader nor the protagonist knows why the detective is watching his subject.

The final volume in the trilogy, *The Locked Room*, is the richest and most accessible of the three. The narrator is summoned by the wife of his old friend Fanshawe (the name is an allusion to Hawthorne's work), who has disappeared and is presumed dead. Fanshawe, a brilliant writer, has left behind a closetful of manuscripts and instructions for his friend to have them published. The narrator moves into Fanshawe's life, marrying his wife and publishing his work. He has nearly succumbed to believing the rumors that he is actually Fanshawe, or at least the creator of the works, when he receives a communication from the real Fanshawe. The plot becomes suspenseful and dangerous as the narrator follows Fanshawe to the brink of annihilation. He so identifies with Fanshawe that he nearly joins him in his dark night of the soul. Lines between truth and fiction are dramatically blurred in a deeply satisfying conclusion to the trilogy.

IN THE COUNTRY OF LAST THINGS

For *In the Country of Last Things*, Auster also uses an established genre, this time science fiction, to achieve his postmodernist ends. This novel shares stylistic and thematic concerns with *The New York Trilogy*. The protagonist, Anna Blume, travels to a large metropolis on another continent in search of her missing brother. She discovers a city in chaos, a hellish postapocalyptic scene, a futuristic nightmare of doom. At first the reader believes this is a dystopian novel of the future in the tradition of Aldous Huxley's *Brave New World* (1932) or George Orwell's *Nineteen Eighty-Four* (1949). The reader soon realizes, however, that this world represents the ethical, spiritual, and cultural chaos of the urban jungle of the present. Auster concludes that, without art and creativity, life is bleak.

MOON PALACE

Auster's novels following *In the Country of Last Things* cannot be as easily categorized by genre. Looser in structure, *Moon Palace* is sometimes referred to as a picaresque novel, as it follows its young hero's adventures on a journey in search of his lost father. This novel employs some of the familiar motifs of the bildungsroman: the struggling orphan, the lost father, the search for self, the journey as initiation into manhood. The writer-narrator, however, seems unconcerned with creating a realistic or believable plot; in fact, he himself does not seem to believe what he has written. The writer violates realistic conventions intentionally to investigate other functions of the novel. Plot and character are secondary to structure, the relationship between reader and writer, and the act of reading.

THE MUSIC OF CHANCE

The Music of Chance is another accessible story that can be enjoyed on many levels. It opens in the manner of a road-trip novel, as protagonist Jim Nashe takes to the road in search of himself. When his money runs out, he joins a young gambler, Pozzi, in a poker game against two eccentric lottery winners. When Jim and Pozzi fall into debt, they are forced to build a stone wall for the eccentrics as payment.

Critics have faulted this novel for weakness of plot and character, yet once again these "faults" seem to be intentional. In this work, Auster takes the opportunity to explore some of his favorite themes: the roles of coincidence and random chance, the consequences of solitude, the limitations of language and free will. Character and plot are deliberately unconvincing, calling attention to the author's other literary aims. Beneath a conventional exterior, Auster's fiction is disturbing, intellectually challenging, and structurally experimental. The use of gambling as a metaphor for the role of chance in life and the allusions to Samuel Beckett's absurdist and existentialist play *Waiting for Godot* (pb. 1952) in the character names add literary depth to the novel.

LEVIATHAN

Leviathan, published in 1992, is a complex novel in the looser style Auster adopted with *Moon Palace* three years earlier. The climax of the story, the death by explosion of the New York writer Benjamin Sachs, is unveiled on the first page. Another writer, Peter Aaron, becomes obsessed with writing the story of his friend's life, not unlike the narrator's obsession with Fanshawe in *The Locked Room*. Aaron uncovers a world of secrets, multiple and exchanged identities, and previously unknown connections between characters. Readers familiar with Auster's work will recognize such elements as the references to the detective-story framework of *The New York Trilogy*, the self-referential character of the writer-narrator, shifting identities, and the importance of the written word to creating and maintaining identity.

THE BOOK OF ILLUSIONS

The Book of Illusions is a novel that is as much driven by the double themes of chance and blurred identity as any of Auster's previous books. Zimmer, a university professor who has descended into alcoholism and loneliness following the loss of his wife and sons in an accident, happens upon the films of Hector Mann, a star of silent movies who had disappeared at the height of his career some sixty years earlier. Zimmer saves his sanity by writing a book about the film star. Then a letter arrives in Zimmer's mailbox, purported to be from Hector Mann's wife, saying that Mann is alive and would like to meet him. Is this a hoax?

Critics have deemed *The Book of Illusions* Auster's richest work to date, his best book in years. Auster's trademarks—coincidence, disappearance, twists and turns of plot, a writer protagonist, characters whose lives eerily reflect one another, merging identities, random events, the thin line between sanity and madness— merge with a plot-driven, fast-moving story. Allusions to a Hawthorne plot and to a translation from the French autobiography of François-René de Chateaubriand add literary interest. There is a new maturity and tenderness in the ending as the fictional character of Zimmer, now merged with the real writer, Auster himself, reaches a reconciliation of sorts, coming to terms with the deaths of his wife and children.

ORACLE NIGHT

Oracle Night is a book within a book within a book. Its main character, Sidney Orr, is a writer with similarities to Auster, a middle-aged married man who lives in Brooklyn. After recovering from a life-threatening illness, he buys a new blue notebook and begins writing a novel, also titled *Oracle Night*. The stage is set for another novel in which fiction bleeds into reality and identities merge.

While some critics have found the plot of *Oracle Night* even more unbelievable than the plots of most of Auster's other works, others have appreciated the novel's absurdity and have praised it for its chilling ghostliness. Chance and coincidence play major roles in the novel, which has echoes of the eerie mysteries of Edgar Allan Poe. The title suggests that fiction may shape reality, yet the ambiguous ending leaves the possibility of randomness open as well.

THE BROOKLYN FOLLIES

The Brooklyn Follies is a more straightforward, down-to-earth book than Auster's previous two novels. Like *Mr. Vertigo* and *Timbuktu*, *The Brooklyn Follies* is notable for its storytelling, though chance makes an inevitable appearance. All three novels have linear plot

structures, and while they are enjoyable and sold well upon publication, Auster's devoted followers have not all appreciated the author's departure in these novels from his dark existentialism.

The protagonist of *The Brooklyn Follies* is Nathan Glass, a survivor of lung cancer who has come to Brooklyn to die, seeking only solitude and anonymity. He unexpectedly connects with an estranged nephew working in the bookstore of a former forger. In one of Auster's familiar references to Nathaniel Hawthorne, one of the plot twists involves a forgery of the first page of *The Scarlet Letter* (1850). Glass begins work on his own book, which he calls *The Book of Human Folly*, but his own despair is superseded by unexpected connections with other people. A collection of vignettes of typical Brooklyn characters is one of the pleasures of the book. In a novel that is warmer and more cheerful than most of Auster's work, Nathan finds redemption, but the ending darkens as a happy Nathan steps out into the bright sunshine of the morning of September 11, 2001.

TRAVELS IN THE SCRIPTORIUM

Travels in the Scriptorium, a spare, fable-like novella, is pure distilled Auster, reminiscent of *Ghosts* in its abstractness. Mr. Blank has lost all memory of his identity. He finds himself in a locked room, with a few labeled objects—DESK, CHAIR, LAMP—the labels of which mysteriously change places. Language itself is not to be trusted. Blank appears to be undergoing some kind of treatment; he feels a vague sense of guilt. In the room is a manuscript, the story within the story, and Blank begins to read. The narrative seems to be a report, but his doctor tells him it is fiction and suggests that he create an ending to the story as an exercise in "imaginative reasoning." As characters enter the room, Blank writes down their names so that he can remember them. The names he lists have appeared in previous Auster novels. The locked room appears to be Auster's own.

Stories with changing endings, objects with changing labels, characters that move from book to book, fact that is indistinguishable from fiction, loss of identity, a violent and chaotic dystopian society—reading Auster is like wandering in a maze or working a puzzle for which there is no solution. The more Auster one has read, the more intricate the layers become, but the message seems to recede further into abstraction. The elements of the novel are familiar, but the whole is outside conventional meaning.

Susan Butterworth

OTHER MAJOR WORKS

POETRY: *Disappearances: Selected Poems*, 1988; *Ground Work: Selected Poems and Essays, 1970-1979*, 1990; *Collected Poems*, 2004.

SCREENPLAYS: *"Smoke" and "Blue in the Face": Two Screenplays*, 1995; *Lulu on the Bridge*, 1998; *The Inner Life of Martin Frost*, 2007.

NONFICTION: *The Art of Hunger, and Other Essays*, 1982 (also known as *The Art of Hunger: Essays, Prefaces, Interviews*, 1991); *The Invention of Solitude*, 1982, 1988; *Hand to Mouth: A Chronicle of Early Failure*, 1997; *The Red Notebook: True Stories*, 2002; *The Story of My Typewriter*, 2002.

TRANSLATIONS: *A Tomb for Anatole*, 1983 (of Stéphane Mallarmé's poetry); *The Notebooks of Joseph Joubert: A Selection*, 1983.

EDITED TEXTS: *The Random House Book of Twentieth-Century French Poetry*, 1982; *I Thought My Father Was God, and Other True Tales from NPR's National Story Project*, 2001.

MISCELLANEOUS: *Collected Prose: Autobiographical Writings, True Stories, Critical Essays, Prefaces, and Collaborations with Artists*, 2003.

BIBLIOGRAPHY

Auster, Paul. "Interview, 1989-90." Interview by Larry McCaffery and Sinda Gregory. In *The Art of Hunger, and Other Essays*. Berkeley, Calif.: SBD, 1982. Long interview is a rich resource for readers interested in Auster's approach to writing.

Barone, Dennis, ed. *Beyond the Red Notebook: Essays on Paul Auster*. Philadelphia: University of Pennsylvania Press, 1995. Collection of critical essays on Auster's poetry and prose, some previously published in periodicals, addresses many different aspects of his work. Includes a detailed bibliography of works by and about Paul Auster.

_____. "Paul Auster/Danilo Kis Issue." *Review of Contemporary Fiction* 14, no. 1 (Spring, 1994): 7-96. Special issue devoted to the works of these two authors includes essays by scholars such as Charles Baxter, Sven Birkerts, Paul Bray, Mary Ann Caws, Robert Creeley, Alan Gurganus, Mark Irwin, Mark Osteen, Mark Rudman, Katherine Washburn, and Curtis White.

Bloom, Harold, ed. *Paul Auster*. Philadelphia: Chelsea House, 2004. Collection of sixteen critical essays includes discussion of *The New York Trilogy* and the themes of fear of identity loss, chance, and confinement in Auster's novels. Literary critic Bloom provides an informative introduction.

Brown, Mark. *Paul Auster*. New York: Palgrave, 2007. Offers extended analysis of Auster's essays, poetry, fiction, films, and collaborative projects. Traces how Auster's representations of New York and city life have matured from a position of urban nihilism to qualified optimism.

Donovan, Christopher. *Postmodern Counternarratives: Irony and Audience in the Novels of Paul Auster, Don DeLillo, Charles Johnson, and Tim O'Brien*. New York: Routledge, 2005. Explores the role of Auster and three other major contemporary ironic novelists amid questions of social realism and morality in the twenty-first century.

Martin, Brendan. *Paul Auster's Postmodernity*. New York: Routledge, 2008. Theorizes that in creating fictional protagonists who appear to be versions of himself, Auster constructs postmodern autobiography.

Shiloh, Ilana. *Paul Auster and Postmodern Quest: On the Road to Nowhere*. New York: Peter Lang, 2002. Discusses Auster's work from the perspective of the narrative of the quest, focusing on eight novels written between 1982 and 1992.

Springer, Carsten. *A Paul Auster Sourcebook*. New York: Peter Lang, 2001. Outlines many of the real-life sources for Auster's fictions. Also contains an extensive bibliography of his writings and further secondary sources in print, including an extensive list of interviews, newspaper articles, and Web sites.

MARIANO AZUELA

Born: Lagos de Moreno, Jalisco, Mexico; January 1, 1873

Died: Mexico City, Mexico; March 1, 1952

Also known as: Mariano Azuela González

PRINCIPAL LONG FICTION

María Luisa, 1907

Los fracasados, 1908

Mala yerba, 1909 (*Marcela: A Mexican Love Story*, 1932)

Andrés Pérez, maderista, 1911

Sin amor, 1912

Los de abajo, 1915 (serial), 1916 (book; revised 1920; *The Underdogs: A Novel of the Mexican Revolution*, 1929)

Los caciques, 1917 (*The Bosses*, 1956)

Las moscas, 1918 (*The Flies*, 1956)

Las tribulaciones de una familia decente, 1918 (*The Trials of a Respectable Family*, 1963)

La malhora, 1923

El desquite, 1925

La luciérnaga, 1932 (*The Firefly*, 1979)

Precursores, 1935

El camarada Pantoja, 1937

San Gabriel de Valdivias, comunidad indígena, 1938

Regina Landa, 1939

Avanzada, 1940

Nueva burguesía, 1941

La marchanta, 1944

La mujer domada, 1946

Sendas perdidas, 1949

La maldición, 1955

Esa sangre, 1956

Two Novels of Mexico, 1956

Two Novels of the Mexican Revolution, 1963

Three Novels, 1979

OTHER LITERARY FORMS

Apart from his long fiction, Mariano Azuela (ahs-WAY-lah) also tried his hand at theater and biography. He wrote three plays, *Los de abajo*, a dramatization of the novel of the same title that had its premiere in 1929; *Del Llano Hermanos, S. en C.*, based on *Los caciques* and staged in 1936; and *El búho en la noche* (pb. 1938), based on *El desquite*, which never reached the stage. He also wrote biographies: *Pedro Moreno, el insurgente* (1932) and *El padre Don Agustín Rivera* (1942). All these works were made available in volume 3 of Azuela's complete works, put out by the Fondo de Cultura Económica in Mexico City in 1960. Some of Azuela's novels have made their way to the big screen, but it was only the film version of *Los de abajo* (1940), directed by Chano Ureta, with musical accompaniment by Silvestre Revuelta and camera work by Gabriel Figueroa, which met with any real acclaim.

ACHIEVEMENTS

Mariano Azuela's masterpiece, *Los de abajo* (*The Underdogs*), is an important work on the Mexican Revolution. Though largely unrecognized by the literary establishment in his early years, Azuela was showered with literary honors in later life. He was awarded the Premio de Letras by the Ateneo Nacional de Ciencias y Artes in 1940, and he became a member of the Seminario de Cultura Mexicana and of the Academia de la Lengua in 1942. He was one of the founding members of the Colegio Nuevo in 1943.

BIOGRAPHY

Mariano Azuela was born into a provincial, middle-class family in Mexico; his father owned a local grocery store in Lagos de Moreno, a town in eastern Jalisco. In 1887, the young Azuela went to Guadalajara to study for the priesthood but left the seminary two years later, deciding instead to pursue a medical career. He qualified as a doctor at the University of Guadalajara in 1889; during his student days he also read much nineteenth century literature, which influenced the fiction he later wrote. In 1900, he married Carmen Rivera, with whom he had ten children.

Azuela was a supporter of Francisco Madero, who eventually dislodged President Porfirio Díaz in the national elections held in 1912. For his support, Azuela was rewarded with the post of *jefe político* (political chief) in Lagos. Madero, however, was not to remain in power for long (he was murdered and succeeded by his own minister of war, Victoriano Huerta, in 1914) and, given that Azuela supported Madero, it is no wonder that he saw the ensuing events of the Mexican Revolution (with the rapid successions and deaths of leaders Venustiano Carranza, Álvaro Obregón, and Emiliano Zapata) as a process of mindless carnage. He witnessed military action in 1914-1915 while working as a surgeon in the army of Julián Medina, then of revolutionary Pancho Villa.

After the latter's northern division was routed, Azuela crossed the U.S. border in 1915 and took refuge in El Paso, Texas, where he completed the text that would make him famous. *The Underdogs* was published in a local Spanish-language newspaper in El Paso, *El Paso del Norte*, in twenty-three weekly installments from October to November (for which Azuela was paid ten dollars per week). Azuela brought out a revised, expanded version of the novel at his own expense in Mexico City in 1920 and, quite by chance, it caught the attention of the reading public in 1924, bringing him instant fame. As a result, Azuela was able to exchange his stethoscope for the pen, and he remained a writer until the end of his life. Some of his later works, such as *The Trials of a Respectable Family* and *The Firefly*, gave him some notoriety, but it was *The Underdogs* that earned him fame in Mexico and abroad. Azuela died on March 1, 1952, and, in keeping with a writer of his stature, was buried in the Rotunda of Illustrious Men in Mexico City.

ANALYSIS

In the first few decades of the twentieth century, the novel in Latin America focused on two interrelated themes: struggles over political space (that is, the identity of the nation) and struggles over geographic space (namely, national territory). Although Azuela's fiction, like that of his contemporaries, concentrated on the struggle for political and geographic space (specifically in the context of the Mexican Revolution), it had the advantage of offering something entirely new to contemporary readers. Azuela was one of the first writers in Latin America to introduce two of the techniques of cinematography into the novel: the description of the appearance of things as if the camera were simply rolling and the use of the cinematic cross-cut from one scene to the next as a means of echoing the chaos of war. It is noteworthy that, of the twenty-four novels Azuela wrote, nearly two-thirds of them either name a particular individual in the title (such as *María Luisa*) or refer to groups of individuals (such as *los de abajo*, the underdogs), which suggests that the Mexican writer was interested in how individuals function within society—that is, the interplay between individual and collective psychology.

THE UNDERDOGS

Azuela's detractors have argued that *The Underdogs* presents the events of the Mexican Revolution from too provincial a perspective. They also charge its author with failing to understand (or reveal) the ideological causes of the revolution. It is true that the revolution as depicted in this novel is largely confined to Jalisco, Aguascalientes, and Zacatecas (these were the areas in which Azuela had witnessed the events), and that the characters in Azuela's version of the drama seem strikingly ignorant of the larger picture. The decisive battles of the revolution occur "offstage" in Azuela's novel; Demetrio and his followers, for example, only find out about the Battle of Celaya, which occurred in the spring of 1915 and in which Villa was decisively defeated by Obregón, when they question some soldiers they suspect of being deserters. None of the various political manifestos that shaped the course of the revolution is even mentioned by the characters in the book. Pancracio manages to mispronounce Carranza's name, calling him Carranzo, and Valderrama expresses lack of interest in Villa, Obregón, or Carranza; they are simply meaningless names to him.

The geographic limitations of the novel are the judicious restraints of a seasoned artist rather than those of a timid one. Azuela pointed out, for example, in a speech given on January 26, 1950, when he was awarded the Premio Nacional de Ciencias y Artes, that he saw his role as one of describing rather than explaining events. He said, "As a novelist I have tended to describe our evils and point them out; it is the task of others to find a solution for them." Indeed, in this novel Azuela homes in on the dangers involved in an idealized version of reality. The intellectual who accompanies Macías's army, Luis

Cervantes, for instance, describes the revolution as a time when the underdogs will finally be rewarded, but his views are greeted scornfully by his companions, and, indeed, he finally reveals himself to be a smooth-talking opportunist when he escapes to the United States to avoid danger.

Cervantes' name, given the obvious allusion to the Spanish author of the literary masterpiece *Don Quixote de la Mancha* (1605, 1615), Miguel de Cervantes, is also meant to signal his lack of pragmatism. Even Solís, whom a number of critics have seen as a projection of Azuela himself, offers a pessimistic view of the revolution: He refers to the "psychology" of the Mexican people as "summed up" by two words: "robbery and murder." These insights seem borne out by the various events described in the novel, involving violence, vengeance, rape, and pillage. Life is cheap; one soldier boasts how he killed a man because he gave him some currency printed by the enemy Huerta, and another plays sadistically with one of his prisoners, threatening to kill him and then postponing the event until the following day. Culture is systematically destroyed: A typewriter is smashed on the rocks, and Dante's literary masterpiece, *The Divine Comedy* (c. 1320), is torn to shreds. The ending of the novel seems to lend credence to the notion that the revolution is presented as a vicious circle, as readers are left with an image of Macías fighting against impossible odds in exactly the same place that he started. Despite its pessimism, however, *The Underdogs* is unequaled in its vivid re-creation of the daily events of the revolution, its fast-moving narrative pace, which crosscuts from scene to scene, and its racy, colloquial style.

THE TRIALS OF A RESPECTABLE FAMILY

This novel portrays the events that took place in Mexico City in 1916 and 1917 during the administration of President Venustiano Carranza, known in the novel ironically as "el primer Jefe" (the number one boss). The Vázquez Prados, an upper-middle-class family from Zapatecas, take refuge in Mexico City to escape the ravages of the revolution. In the capital, however, the family is overwhelmed by the massive social upheaval created by the war, for it is a world in which cynical opportunists, such as General Covarrubias, use crime as a means of achieving high office. The novel has some compelling scenes, such as the brutality of soldiers' treatment of the civilian population in downtown Mexico City described by Lulú and César, which ensure the novel's place in the Azuela canon as a valuable social document. Procopio, the patriarch of the family, is presented sympathetically; he loses his fortune but comes to terms with his fate when he finds a job as an office employee, a situation he would never have accepted in Zacatecas. The two main themes of this work are the betrayal of the revolution and the virtue of honest work.

THE FIREFLY

The Firefly, which some scholars assert is Azuela's best novel, is a psychological work as well as a work of social protest. It portrays three major characters: Dionisio, his wife Conchita ("the firefly"), and his brother, José María. Like *The Trials of a Respectable Family*, the plot centers on the disastrous decision made by a family to move from the provinces to Mexico City. Dionisio moves his family from Cienguilla in search of a better life, to which end he intends to use Conchita's inheritance of fifteen thousand pesos, a considerable sum in those days. However, once in the capital, Dionisio is robbed by an assortment of unscrupulous businessmen and crooks, and he turns to drink to drown his sorrows. While driving a bus under the influence of alcohol, he loses control of the vehicle and is involved in a collision in which many of the passengers are killed. To make matters worse, his daughter is murdered in a brothel frequented by high-ranking politicians, his son dies of tuberculosis, and his miserly brother refuses to lift a finger to save him from financial ruin.

All is not lost, however, since his wife, Conchita, like a firefly beating back the darkness of sin, returns to Mexico City to save him. The novel uses a number of innovative techniques; most notably, it has a fragmented, nonchronological structure, cutting unexpectedly from one scene to the next, which is an appropriate vehicle with which to express Dionisio's gradual descent into alcoholism. Just as striking, the novel uses the device of indirect interior monologue, whereby the unarticulated and highly subjective thoughts of the three main characters are expressed in third-person prose. A highly experimental novel, *The Firefly* manages to draw vivid, well-rounded characters who capture the reader's imagination.

Stephen M. Hart

OTHER MAJOR WORKS

SHORT FICTION: *María Luisa y otros cuentos*, 1937.

PLAYS: *Los de abajo*, pr. 1929; *Del Llano Hermanos, S. en C.*, pr. 1936; *El búho en la noche*, pb. 1938.

NONFICTION: *Pedro Moreno, el insurgente*, 1933 (serial), 1935 (book); *Cien años de novela mexicana*, 1947; *Páginas autobiográficas*, 1974.

MISCELLANEOUS: *Mariano Azuela: Obras completas*, 1958-1960 (Alí Chumacero, editor); *Epistolario y archivo*, 1969.

BIBLIOGRAPHY

Griffin, Clive. *Azuela: "Los de abajo."* London: Grant and Cutler, 1993. An excellent study of Azuela's masterpiece *The Underdogs*, with separate chapters on the historical backdrop to the Mexican Revolution as well as on realism, characterization, and structure.

Herbst, Gerhard R. *Mexican Society as Seen by Mariano Azuela*. New York: Ediciones ABRA, 1977. Studies eight of Azuela's novels and deduces his vision of Mexican society. Shows that although Azuela became embittered once Pancho Villa, whom he supported, was defeated, he nevertheless maintained a faith in the common person.

Leal, Luis. *Mariano Azuela*. New York: Twayne, 1971. Leal, a prominent scholar of Latin American literature, provides an overview of Azuela's life and work with insightful comments on Azuela the person and Azuela the writer.

Martínez, Eliud. *The Art of Mariano Azuela: Modernism in "La malhora," "El desquite," "La Luciérnaga."* Pittsburgh, Pa.: Latin American Literary Review, 1980. A study of Azuela's lesser-known novels. Particularly good is the chapter on *The Firefly*, which discusses the novel chapter by chapter and shows how Azuela uses avant-garde techniques to enhance his message. Martínez argues that *The Firefly* is Azuela's best novel.

Parra, Max. *Writing Pancho Villa's Revolution: Rebels in the Literary Imagination of Mexico*. Austin: University of Texas Press, 2005. Focuses on *The Underdogs* and novels by other authors as well as on chronicles and testimonials written from 1925 to 1940 to examine how these works depicted Pancho Villa's rebellion and either praised or condemned his style of leadership.

Robe, Stanley L. *Azuela and the Mexican Underdogs*. Berkeley: University of California Press, 1979. Compares the first version of *The Underdogs*, serialized in 1916, with its definitive version, published in 1920. Also provides a detailed picture of the two years of political unrest, 1914 and 1915, in which this novel is set.

Schedler, Christopher. "Mariano Azuela: Migratory Modernism." In *Border Modernism: Intercultural Readings in American Literary Modernism*. New York: Routledge, 2002. Schedler compares the works of Mexican, Native American, and Chicano modernists with their European and Anglo-American counterparts. Concludes that Azuela and other writers who worked in the borderlands of Mexico and the United States produced a new type of literature that sought to modernize the "native" literary traditions of the Americas.

Sommers, Joseph. *After the Storm: Landmarks of the Modern Mexican Novel*. Albuquerque: University of New Mexico Press, 1968. The section on *The Underdogs* was the first to argue convincingly that Azuela's novel focuses so much on the carnage and immediacy of the Mexican Revolution that he does not understand, or indeed reveal, its causes.

B

BERYL BAINBRIDGE

Born: Liverpool, England; November 21, 1933
Also known as: Beryl Margaret Bainbridge

PRINCIPAL LONG FICTION

A Weekend with Claud, 1967 (revised 1981 as *A Weekend with Claude*)
Another Part of the Wood, 1968 (revised 1979)
Harriet Said, 1972
The Dressmaker, 1973 (also known as *The Secret Glass*)
The Bottle Factory Outing, 1974
Sweet William, 1975
A Quiet Life, 1976
Injury Time, 1977
Young Adolf, 1978
Winter Garden, 1980
Watson's Apology, 1984
Filthy Lucre: Or, The Tragedy of Andrew Ledwhistle and Richard Soleway, 1986
An Awfully Big Adventure, 1989
The Birthday Boys, 1991
Every Man for Himself, 1996
Master Georgie, 1998
According to Queeney, 2001

OTHER LITERARY FORMS

Beryl Bainbridge has published a remarkable number of novels, but she is also a well-known short-story writer, journalist, theater critic, and screenwriter. Her short-story collections include *Mum and Mr. Armitage: Selected Stories of Beryl Bainbridge* (1985) and *Collected Stories* (1994). Bainbridge also worked on several television documentaries, including *Emily Brontë and Haworth* (1982) and *English Journey: Or, The Road to Milton Keynes* (1984). She also hosted the series *Forever England: North and South* (1987) and wrote and pub-

lished the companion volume to that series. As a long-time journalist, her columns from the *Evening Standard* newspaper were collected in 1993 and published as *Something Happened Yesterday*. Bainbridge drew on her experiences as an actor and theater critic for the book *Front Row: Evenings at the Theatre, Pieces from "The Oldie"* (2005), a collection of reviews, essays, and a memoir.

ACHIEVEMENTS

Beryl Bainbridge has received both popular and critical praise for her work, which has a wide English-language readership and has been translated into many languages. She was elected a fellow of the Royal Society of Literature in 1978 and was appointed Dame Commander of the British Empire in 2000. In addition, Bainbridge received many literary honors, including being short-listed five times for the Booker Prize: in 1973 for *The Dressmaker*, in 1974 for *The Bottle Factory Outing*, in 1990 for *An Awfully Big Adventure*, in 1996 for *Every Man for Himself*, and in 1998 for *Master Georgie*. She won the Guardian Fiction Award, the Whitbread Novel Award, and the James Tait Black Memorial Prize for fiction. In 2003, she shared the David Cohen British Literature Prize for lifetime achievement with Thom Gunn.

BIOGRAPHY

Beryl Margaret Bainbridge was born on November 21, 1933, in Liverpool, England, during the Great Depression. Her parents were Richard and Winifred Bainbridge, and she had an older brother. Her family moved to the town of Formby when she was still a baby. She was raised and educated in Formby. Although she was encouraged to read and write by her parents, she did not enjoy a happy home life. The stresses and strains of her early years inspired several of her books. The young

Bainbridge, who wrote her first book when she was only ten years old, often used writing as a way to escape from the troubles in her home. At the age of thirteen, she produced a manuscript that would be published as the novel *Filthy Lucre* in 1986.

At the age of sixteen, after her expulsion from school two years earlier, Bainbridge joined the Liverpool Playhouse Company as an assistant stage manager. Many of her experiences at the theater (where she stayed until 1952) are evident in her 1989 novel, *An Awfully Big Adventure*.

Bainbridge married Austin Davies, an artist, in 1954. After five years and two children, however, the marriage ended in divorce. Soon after, she married the author Alan Sharp, with whom she had a daughter; that marriage, too, did not last. Bainbridge once again turned to writing as a means of escape and to provide support for herself and her children. For inspiration, she used stories from newspapers and drew from her own past.

Harriet Said, completed in 1958 but not published until 1972, was the first novel Bainbridge published as an adult. She quickly followed this novel with *A Weekend with Claud*, first published in 1967 and revised and republished as *A Weekend with Claude* in 1981. (She often revised and republished her earlier works.)

Throughout the late 1960's and 1970's, Bainbridge continued to use personal experience as inspiration for her writing. In 1978, she tried alternative history in her novel *Young Adolf*, the story of a fictional journey to Liverpool by Adolf Hitler as a teenager. Bainbridge also wrote about the life of wife murderer John Selby Watson in her 1984 novel *Watson's Apology*. She did not abandon her autobiographical material during this period, however. *An Awfully Big Adventure* returned Bainbridge to her Liverpool roots and to her days as a young actor and stage manager.

The death of Bainbridge's longtime editor, Colin Haycraft, in 1994 coincided with Bainbridge's increas-

Beryl Bainbridge. (Getty Images)

ing turn toward historical fiction. She re-created events such as Robert Falcon Scott's race to the South Pole in *The Birthday Boys*, the sinking of the *Titanic* in *Every Man for Himself*, and the Crimean War in *Master Georgie*.

Bainbridge also was a familiar figure on British television during the 1980's and 1990's. She wrote the scripts for several documentaries, including *English Journey*. In this program, Bainbridge led viewers in the steps of English writer J. B. Priestley as he traveled throughout his native country in 1934.

In the early twenty-first century, Bainbridge continued her ongoing fascination with the re-creation of the past in fiction. Her novel *According to Queeney* examined the relationship of eighteenth century writer and curmudgeon Samuel Johnson with Hester Lynch Thrale, a diarist and the wife of a prosperous beer merchant.

ANALYSIS

Beryl Bainbridge's novels run the gamut from thinly veiled autobiographical fiction to the strange and macabre world of murder and madness. For this reason, it is sometimes difficult for critics to provide a clear overview of her work. Nevertheless, for all their variety, Bainbridge's works do share certain characteristic stylistic and thematic concerns.

All of the novels carry a strong sense of place, created through the use of specific and minute details. Several of Bainbridge's books, for example, are set in postwar Liverpool. Bainbridge knows this setting well because she was a teenager in Liverpool during these same years. The depiction of working-class Liverpool is heartbreaking in its accuracy; bombed-out, gritty, and cold, Liverpool and its residents struggled through the late 1940's and 1950's to regain their footing. Her work is not restricted to Liverpool, however. Bainbridge is equally on target with her descriptions of the Antarctic in *The Birthday Boys*, the bridge of the *Titanic* in *Every Man for Himself*, and eighteenth century England in *According to Queeney*.

What is particularly striking is that Bainbridge's strong and accurate evocation of place is accompanied by her ability to push the edges of narrative reliability. That is, she makes certain in her work that her reader can never be sure that the narrative voice of the novel speaks the truth. For Bainbridge, it seems, there really is no one truth, but rather competing voices, pushing individual perceptions of truth toward the reader.

Many of Bainbridge's books provide dark humor, something that produces unease in readers. She juxtaposes death and tragedy with scenes that provoke laughter. In *An Awfully Big Adventure*, the main character drops the flashlight that represents Tinker Bell in a production of *Peter Pan*; the consternation of the children in the audience is terrible, yet funny. At the same time, one of the main characters is committing suicide offstage.

Bainbridge's characters also tend toward the quirky, eccentric, and pathological. Rarely in her novels do readers encounter truly sympathetic characters, but her characters are rich in their complexity. Like real people, they exhibit both good and bad judgment as well as compassion and coldheartedness. Complicated and complex, Bainbridge's characters are often not likable, but they are always interesting.

THE BOTTLE FACTORY OUTING

The Bottle Factory Outing, which earned for Bainbridge her first Booker Prize nomination as well as the Guardian Fiction Award in 1974, is a story of two women, Brenda and Freda, who work in a bottle factory. Bainbridge used her own experiences for this novel, having worked briefly in a bottle factory when she was younger. Although the events of the novel are purely fiction, the details are based on an actual factory environment.

Brenda is quiet, nervous, and altogether unremarkable, while Freda is bossy and manipulative. When Freda develops an attraction for one of her fellow workers, she organizes a picnic as an opportunity to spend time with the object of her affection. However, at the picnic, Freda is murdered. While Bainbridge does not typically write murder mysteries, the bizarre death of her main character is the kind of unexpected plot twist that Bainbridge's readers have come to expect. The novel also illustrates Bainbridge's ironic bent: Freda expects the picnic to be a sunny, warm, happy event, full of life and love; what she gets is drunkenness and death. In addition, the comic description of Freda's coworkers disposing of her body is at odds with the horror of murder. The tendency toward black humor permeates many of Bainbridge's later novels.

AN AWFULLY BIG ADVENTURE

In *An Awfully Big Adventure*, Bainbridge once again draws on the details of her own life for her setting and plot. This novel is the story of a young Liverpool woman in post-World War II England, a time and place of unyielding deprivation and hopelessness. Stella, abandoned by her mother at birth, is being raised by her aunt and uncle, who encourage her to take a job as an assistant stage manager in a local theater company. The company provides a rich opportunity for Bainbridge to develop the quirky characters so typical of her novels.

The company is preparing to present *Peter Pan*, and the juxtaposition of a children's play with the sometimes sordid and often darkly humorous plot turns underscores Bainbridge's talent for the ironic. Further, the novel demonstrates the way that historic decisions have present consequences, an ongoing concern in Bainbridge's work. At one point in the novel, Stella's mother has a brief affair with an older actor, resulting in Stella's birth. The plot of *An Awfully Big Adventure* winds its way through sixteen years until Stella finds herself confronting the consequences of her mother's decisions.

In addition, Stella's choices throughout the novel, including her penchant for speaking uncomfortable truths, lead to tragic consequences for the other members of the theater company. While many readers will find events in *An Awfully Big Adventure* comic, others may be uncomfortable with the close association of the humorous with emotional trauma and death.

THE BIRTHDAY BOYS

The 1910-1912 expedition of British explorer Robert Falcon Scott and his team provides the fodder for *The Birthday Boys*. Divided into five parts with five different narrators, the novel tells the story of Scott's ill-fated race to reach the South Pole. The irony of the Scott expedition makes it the perfect setting for the novel. Scott's men did indeed reach the South Pole, but they found that Norwegian explorer Roald Amundsen had beat them to it. Scott and his team—Petty Officer Edgar Evans, Dr. Edward Wilson, Lieutenant Henry Robertson Bowers, and Captain Lawrence Edward Oates—died on the return trip, making the expedition virtually meaningless. Bainbridge's ability to re-create historical settings and her thematic concern for the irony of life make the expedition remarkable in its irony.

Using Scott's journals as well as the memoirs of one survivor of the expedition as her source material, Bainbridge is able to creatively imagine lives for the other men who died. By telling the story from so many perspectives and by her frequent use of flashbacks and reminiscences, the story of the Scott expedition grows increasingly contested and unreliable. The competing voices of the five narrators attest to the complexity of historical re-creation in fiction. With beautiful imagery and complete control of her subject, however, Bainbridge provides a strange yet compelling story that offers another way to examine the troubling journey.

EVERY MAN FOR HIMSELF

The sinking of the passenger steamship *Titanic* remains one of the most iconic events of the twentieth century. Just before midnight on April 14, 1912, the supposedly unsinkable *Titanic* hit an iceberg in the North Atlantic and sank within three hours, leading to a great loss of life. Bainbridge opens the story with the ship sinking and then flashes back to the previous four days of the journey. The flashback technique is one that Bainbridge uses in virtually all of her novels.

Bainbridge's inspiration for writing the novel came from the clear irony of the ship's construction. She uses the overconfidence of the ship's manufacturers and owners, and contrasts that overconfidence with the suffering and pain experienced by those on the sinking ship. In addition, Bainbridge had an ongoing thematic interest in the ways that the British class system continued to sustain itself even in extreme circumstances, including during the sinking of the *Titanic*; that interest shows itself in the novel as well.

Diane Andrews Henningfeld

OTHER MAJOR WORKS

SHORT FICTION: *Mum and Mr. Armitage: Selected Stories of Beryl Bainbridge*, 1985; *Collected Stories*, 1994.

NONFICTION: *Something Happened Yesterday*, 1993; *Front Row: Evenings at the Theatre, Pieces from "The Oldie,"* 2005.

BIBLIOGRAPHY

Becket, Fiona. "Singular Events: The 'As If' of Beryl Bainbridge's *Every Man for Himself*." In *British Fic-

tion of the 1990's, edited by Nick Bentley. New York: Routledge, 2005. A chapter-long discussion of Bainbridge's novel about the sinking of the *Titanic*. Becket is particularly interested in the interconnectedness of fact and fiction in this novel, and in Bainbridge's exploration of loss.

Grubisic, Brett Josef. *Understanding Beryl Bainbridge*. Columbia: University of South Carolina Press, 2008. An overview of Bainbridge's life and an analysis of her major novels. An excellent starting place for any study of Bainbridge's work. Includes an extensive bibliography and references.

Rennison, Nick. "Beryl Bainbridge." In *Contemporary British Novelists*. New York: Routledge, 2005. An installment in the Routledge Key Guides series. Offers a biographical overview as well as discussion of key works, including plot devices and themes. Includes a bibliography and a guide to further reading.

Wennö, Elisabeth. *Ironic Formula in the Novels of Beryl Bainbridge*. Göteburg, Sweden: Acta Universitatis Gothoburgensis, 1993. One of the very few book-length studies of Bainbridge, this text provides a key reading of Bainbridge's use of irony throughout her career. While the book is academic and challenging, it is nonetheless an important resource for those studying Bainbridge's work.

JAMES BALDWIN

Born: New York, New York; August 2, 1924
Died: St. Paul de Vence, France; December 1, 1987
Also known as: James Arthur Baldwin

PRINCIPAL LONG FICTION

Go Tell It on the Mountain, 1953
Giovanni's Room, 1956
Another Country, 1962
Tell Me How Long the Train's Been Gone, 1968
If Beale Street Could Talk, 1974
Just Above My Head, 1979

OTHER LITERARY FORMS

Before he published his first novel, James Baldwin had established a reputation as a talented essayist and reviewer. Many of his early pieces, later collected in *Notes of a Native Son* (1955) and *Nobody Knows My Name: More Notes of a Native Son* (1961), have become classics; his essays on Richard Wright, especially "Everybody's Protest Novel" (1949) and "Many Thousands Gone" (1951), occupy a central position in the development of "universalist" African American thought during the 1950's. Culminating in *The Fire Next Time* (1963), an extended meditation on the relationship of race, reli-gion, and the individual experience in America, Baldwin's early prose demands a reexamination and redefinition of received social and cultural premises. His collections of essays *No Name in the Street* (1971) and *The Devil Finds Work* (1976) reflected a more militant stance and were received less favorably than Baldwin's universalist statements. *The Evidence of Things Not Seen* (1985) is a book-length essay on the case known as the Atlanta child murders, and *The Price of the Ticket* (1985) includes all of Baldwin's essay collections as well as a number of previously uncollected pieces. Less formal and intricate, though in some cases more explicit, reflections of Baldwin's beliefs can be found in *A Rap on Race* (1971), an extended discussion between Baldwin and anthropologist Margaret Mead, and *A Dialogue* (1975), a conversation with poet Nikki Giovanni.

Baldwin also wrote children's fiction (*Little Man, Little Man*, 1975), the text for a photographic essay (*Nothing Personal*, 1964, with Richard Avedon), an unfilmed scenario (*One Day, When I Was Lost: A Scenario Based on "The Autobiography of Malcolm X,"* 1972), dramas, and short stories. Most critics prefer Baldwin's first play, *The Amen Corner* (pr. 1954), to his *Blues for Mister Charlie* (pr. 1964) despite the latter's four-month Broadway run. Although he published little short fiction after the collection *Going to Meet the Man* (1965), Baldwin was an acknowledged master of the novella form. "Sonny's Blues" (1957), the story of the relationship of a jazz musician to his "respectable" narrator-brother, anticipates many of the themes of Baldwin's later novels and is widely recognized as one of the great American novellas.

ACHIEVEMENTS

James Baldwin's role as a major spokesman on race guarantees his place in American cultural history. Although not undeserved, this reputation more frequently obscures than clarifies the nature of his literary achievement, which involves his relationship to African American culture, existential philosophy, and the moral tradition of the world novel. To be sure, Baldwin's progression from an individualistic, universalist stance through active involvement with the integrationist Civil Rights movement to an increasing sympathy with militant pan-Africanist thought parallels the general development of African American thought between the early 1950's and the mid-1970's. Indeed, Baldwin's novels frequently mirror both the author's personal philosophy and its social context. Some, most notably *Another Country*, attained a high degree of public visibility when published, leading to a widely accepted vision of Baldwin as a topical writer. Consideration of Baldwin primarily as a racial spokesman, however, imposes a stereotype that distorts many of his most penetrating insights and underestimates his status as a literary craftsman.

More accurate, although ultimately as limited, is the view of Baldwin primarily as an exemplar of the African American presence in the "mainstream" of the American tradition. Grouped with Ralph Ellison as a major "post-Wright" black novelist, Baldwin represents, in this view, the generation that rejected "protest literature" in favor of "universal" themes. Strangely at odds with the view of Baldwin as racial spokesman, this view emphasizes the craftsmanship of Baldwin's early novels and his treatment of "mainstream" themes such as religious hypocrisy, father-son tensions, and sexual identity. Ironically, many younger African American novelists accept this general view of Baldwin's accomplishment, viewing his mastery of Jamesian techniques and his involvement with continental literary culture as an indication of alienation from his racial identity. Recasting political activist Eldridge Cleaver's political attack on Baldwin in aesthetic terms, the African American writer Ishmael Reed dismisses Baldwin as a great "white" novelist. A grain of truth lies in Reed's assertion; Baldwin rarely created new forms. Rather, he infused a variety of Euro-American forms, derived from Wright and William Faulkner as well as from Henry James, with the rhythms and imagery of the African American oral tradition.

Like the folk preacher whose voice he frequently assumed in secular contexts, Baldwin combined moral insight with an uncompromising sense of the concrete realities of his community, whether defined in terms of family, lovers, race, or nation. This indicates the deepest level of Baldwin's literary achievement; whatever his immediate political focus or fictional form, he possessed an insight into moral psychology shared by only a handful of novelists. Inasmuch as the specific circumstances of this psychology involve American racial relations, this insight aligns Baldwin with Wright, Faulkner, Mark Twain, and Harriet Beecher Stowe. Inasmuch as Baldwin's insight involves the symbolic alienation of the individual, it places him with American romantics such as Nathaniel Hawthorne and European existentialists such as Albert Camus. Since his insight recognizes the complex pressure exerted by social mechanisms on individual consciousness, it reveals affinities with James Joyce, George Eliot, and Ellison. As a writer who combined elements of all of these traditions with the voice of the anonymous African American preacher, Baldwin cannot be reduced to accommodate the terms of any one of them. Refusing to lie about the reality of pain, he provided realistic images of the moral life possible in the inhospitable world that encompasses the streets of Harlem and the submerged recesses of the mind.

BIOGRAPHY

James Arthur Baldwin once dismissed his childhood as "the usual bleak fantasy." Nevertheless, the major concerns of his fiction consistently reflect the social context of his family life in Harlem during the Depression. The dominant figure of Baldwin's childhood was clearly that of his stepfather, David Baldwin, who worked as a manual laborer and preached in a storefront church. Clearly the model for Gabriel Grimes in *Go Tell It on the*

Mountain, David Baldwin had moved from New Orleans to New York City, where he married Baldwin's mother, Emma Berdis. The oldest of what was to be a group of nine children in the household, James assumed a great deal of the responsibility for the care of his half brothers and half sisters. Insulated somewhat from the brutality of Harlem street life by his domestic duties, Baldwin, as he describes in *The Fire Next Time*, sought refuge in the church. Undergoing a conversion experience, similar to that of John in *Go Tell It on the Mountain*, at age fourteen in 1938, Baldwin preached as a youth minister for the next several years. At the same time, he began to read, immersing himself in works such as Harriet Beecher Stowe's *Uncle Tom's Cabin* (1852) and the novels of Charles Dickens. Both at his Harlem junior high school, where the African American poet Countée Cullen was one of his teachers, and at his predominantly white Bronx high school, Baldwin contributed to student literary publications. The combination of family tension, economic hardship, and religious vocation provides the focus of much of Baldwin's greatest writing, most notably *Go Tell It on the Mountain*, *The Fire Next Time*, and *Just Above My Head*.

If Baldwin's experience during the 1930's provided his material, his life from 1942 to 1948 shaped his characteristic approach to that material. After he graduated from high school in 1942, Baldwin worked for a year as a manual laborer in New Jersey, an experience that increased both his understanding of his stepfather and his insight into American economic and racial systems. Moving to Greenwich Village in 1943, Baldwin worked during the day and wrote at night for the next five years; his first national reviews and essays appeared in 1946. The major event of the Village years, however, was Baldwin's meeting with Richard Wright in the winter of 1944-1945. Wright's interest helped Baldwin secure first a Eugene F. Saxton Memorial Award and then a Rosenwald Fellowship, enabling him to move to Paris in 1948.

After his arrival in France, Baldwin experienced more of the poverty that had shaped his childhood. Simultaneously, he developed a larger perspective on the psychocultural context conditioning his experience, feeling at once a greater sense of freedom and a larger sense of the global structure of racism, particularly as

James Baldwin. (© John Hoppy Hopkins)

reflected in the French treatment of North Africans. In addition, he formed many of the personal and literary friendships that contributed to his later public prominence. Baldwin's well-publicized literary feud with Wright, who viewed the younger writer's criticism of Wright's novel *Native Son* (1940) as a form of personal betrayal, helped establish Baldwin as a major presence in African American letters. Although Baldwin's first novel, *Go Tell It on the Mountain*, was well received critically, it was not so financially successful that he could devote all of his time to creative writing. As a result, Baldwin continued to travel widely, frequently on journalistic assignments, while writing *Giovanni's Room*, which is set in France and involves no black characters.

Returning to the United States as a journalist covering the Civil Rights movement, Baldwin made his first trip to the American South in 1957. The essays and reports describing that physical and psychological journey propelled Baldwin to the position of public prominence that he maintained for more than a decade. During the height of the movement, Baldwin lectured widely and was present at major events such as the March on Washington and the voter registration drive in Selma, Alabama. In addition, he met with most of the major African American activists of the period, including Martin Luther King, Jr., Elijah Muhammad, James Meredith, and Medgar Evers. Attorney General Robert F. Kennedy asked Baldwin to bring together the most influential voices in the black community; even though the resulting meeting accomplished little, the request testifies to Baldwin's image as a focal point of African American opinion.

In addition to this political activity, Baldwin formed personal and literary relationships—frequently tempestuous ones—with numerous white writers, including William Styron and Norman Mailer. A surge in literary popularity, reflected in the presence of *Another Country* and *The Fire Next Time* on best-seller lists throughout most of 1962 and 1963, accompanied Baldwin's political success and freed him from financial insecurity for the first time. He traveled extensively throughout the decade, and his visits to Puerto Rico and Africa were to have a major influence on his subsequent political thought.

Partly because of Baldwin's involvement with prominent whites and partly because of the sympathy for gays evinced in his writing, several black militants, most notably Eldridge Cleaver, attacked Baldwin's position as "black spokesman" beginning in the late 1960's. As a result, nationalist spokesmen such as Amiri Baraka and Bobby Seale gradually eclipsed Baldwin in the public literary and political spotlights. Nevertheless, Baldwin, himself sympathetic to many of the militant positions, continued his involvement with public issues, such as the fate of the group of North Carolina prisoners known as the Wilmington 10, which he addressed in an open letter to Jimmy Carter shortly after Carter's election to the U.S. presidency. In his later years, though he returned periodically to the South, Baldwin lived for much of the time in France and Turkey. He died in St. Paul de Vence, France, on November 30, 1987.

ANALYSIS

Uncompromising in his demand for personal and social integrity, James Baldwin from the beginning of his career charged the individual with full responsibility for his or her moral identity. Both in his early individualistic novels and in his later political fiction, he insisted on the inadequacy of received definitions as the basis for self-knowledge or social action. Echoing the existentialist principle "existence precedes essence," he intimated the underlying consistency of his vision in the introductory essay in *Notes of a Native Son*: "I think all theories are suspect, that the finest principles may have to be modified, or may even be pulverized by the demands of life, and that one must find, therefore, one's own moral center and move through the world hoping that this center will guide one aright." This insistence on the moral center and movement in the world cautions against associating Baldwin with the atheistic or solipsistic currents of existential thought. Never denying the possibility of transcendent moral power—which he frequently imaged as the power of love—he simply insisted that human conceptions must remain flexible enough to allow for the honest perception of experience. Fully recognizing the reality of existential pain and despair, Baldwin invoked honesty and self-acceptance as the necessary supports for the love capable of generating individual communication and at least the groundwork for political action.

Baldwin's social vision, reflecting his experience in a racist culture, acknowledges the forces militating against self-knowledge and moral responsibility. Each of his novels portrays a series of evasive and simplifying definitions built into religious, economic, and educational institutions. These definitions, which emphasize the separation of self and other, control the immediate contexts of individual experience. As a result, they frequently seem to constitute "human nature," to embody the inevitable limits of experience. While sympathizing with the difficulty of separating the self from context without simultaneously denying experience, Baldwin insists that acquiescing to the definitions inevitably results in self-hatred and social immorality. The individual incapable of accepting his or her existential complexity flees to the illusion of certainty provided by the institutions that assume responsibility for directing moral decisions. This cycle of institutional pressure encouraging existential evasion ensuring further institutional corruption recurs in each of Baldwin's novels. On both personal and social levels, the drive to deny the reality of the other—racial, sexual, or economic—generates nothing save destruction. Derived from the streets of Harlem rather than from Scripture, Baldwin's response echoes Christ's admonition to "love thy neighbor as thyself." The derivation is vital; in Baldwin's novels, those who extract the message from the Bible rather than from their lives frequently aggravate the pain that makes evading reality seem attractive.

The immediate focus of Baldwin's attention gradually shifted from consciousness to context, creating the illusion of a change in his basic concerns. While he always worked in the realistic tradition of the novel, his choice of specific forms paralleled this shift in thematic focus, though again his later work indicates an underlying unity in his fiction. His first novel, *Go Tell It on the Mountain*, employs a tightly focused Jamesian form to explore the developing awareness of the adolescent protagonist John Grimes, who is not yet aware of the evasive definitions conditioning his experience. After a second Jamesian novel, *Giovanni's Room,* Baldwin adapted the relatively unstructured Dreiserian mode in *Another Country* and *Tell Me How Long the Train's Been Gone.* Characters such as Rufus Scott and Vivaldo Moore in *Another Country* continue to struggle for individual awareness, but Baldwin's new narrative stance emphasizes the impact of the limiting definitions on a wide range of particular social circumstances. Attempting to balance the presentation of consciousness and context, Baldwin's last two novels, *If Beale Street Could Talk* and *Just Above My Head,* synthesize the earlier technical approaches. Returning to the immediate focus on the individual consciousness in these first-person narratives, Baldwin creates protagonists capable of articulating their own social perceptions. Consciousness and context merge as Baldwin's narrators share their insights and, more important, their processes with their fellow sufferers.

These insights implicitly endorse William Blake's vision of morality as a movement from innocence through experience to a higher innocence. Beginning with an unaware innocence, individuals inevitably enter the deadening and murderous world of experience, the world of the limiting definitions. Those who attempt to deny the world and remain children perish alongside those who cynically submit to the cruelty of the context for imagined personal benefit. Only those who plunge into experience, recognize its cruelty, and resolve to forge an aware innocence can hope to survive morally. Specifically, Baldwin urges families to pass on a sense of the higher innocence to their children by refusing to simplify the truth of experience. This painful honesty makes possible the commitment to love despite the inevitability of pain and isolation. It provides the only hope, however desperate, for individual or social rejuvenation.

To a large extent, Baldwin's career developed in accord with the Blakean pattern. John Grimes begins his passage from innocence to experience in *Go Tell It on the Mountain*; Rufus Scott and Vivaldo Moore, among others, struggle to survive experience in *Another Country,* which intimates the need for the higher innocence. Baldwin's last two novels portray the entire process, focusing on the attempt first to find and then to pass on the higher innocence. *Just Above My Head,* with its middle-aged narrator and his teenage children, clearly represents a more highly developed and realistic stage of the vision than *If Beale Street Could Talk,* with its teenage-mother narrator and her newborn infant.

GO TELL IT ON THE MOUNTAIN

Go Tell It on the Mountain centers on the religious conversion and family relationships of John Grimes, whose experience parallels that of Baldwin during his youth. Although he believes himself to be the natural son of Gabriel Grimes, a preacher who, like Baldwin's stepfather, moved to New York after growing up in the South, John is actually the son of Gabriel's wife, Elizabeth, and her lover, Richard, who committed suicide prior to John's birth. Growing up under the influence of his hypocritical and tyrannical stepfather, John alternately attempts to please and transcend him. Gabriel expends most of his emotional energy on his openly rebellious son Roy, whose immersion in the violent life of the Harlem streets contrasts sharply with John's involvement with the "Temple of the Fire Baptized," the storefront church where his conversion takes place.

To the extent that Baldwin organizes *Go Tell It on the Mountain* around John's attempt to come to terms with these pressures, the novel appears to have a highly individualistic focus. The overall structure of the novel, however, dictates that John's experience be viewed in a larger context. Of the three major sections of *Go Tell It on the Mountain*, the first, "The Seventh Day," and the third, "The Threshing Floor," focus directly on John. The long middle section, "The Prayers of the Saints," a Faulknerian exploration of history, traces the origins of John's struggle to the experience of his elders, devoting individual chapters to Elizabeth, Gabriel, and Gabriel's sister Florence. Together the prayers portray the Great Migration of African Americans from South to North, from rural to urban settings. Far from bringing true freedom, the movement results in a new indirect type of oppression. As Elizabeth recognizes,

> There was not, after all, a great difference between the world of the North and that of the South which she had fled; there was only this difference: the North promised more. And this similarity: what it promised it did not give, and what it gave, at length and grudgingly with one hand, it took back with the other.

Even in his most individualistic phase, Baldwin is aware of the power of institutional pressures. The origins of John's particular struggle against the limiting definitions go back to their impact on both Elizabeth and Gabriel.

Elizabeth's relationship with John's true father, at least in its early stages, appears to offer hope for at least a limited freedom from external definition. Highly intelligent and self-aware, Richard struggles to transcend the limitations imposed on black aspiration through a rigorous program of self-education, which he shares with Elizabeth. Despite his intelligence and determination, however, Richard maintains a naïve innocence concerning the possibility of self-definition in a society based on racist assumptions. Only when arrested on suspicion of a robbery he had nothing to do with does he recognize that his context defines him as simply another "nigger." Unable to reconcile this imposed definition with his drive for social transcendence, he despairs and commits suicide. This act, in turn, destroys Elizabeth's chance for obtaining a greater degree of freedom. She is not, however, simply a victim. Fearing that Richard will be unable to cope with the responsibility of a family, she fails to tell him of her pregnancy. Far from protecting him, this evasion contributes to his destruction by allowing

Richard to view his situation as purely personal. Elizabeth's own choice, conditioned by the social refusal to confront reality, combines with the racist legal system to circumscribe her possibilities. Forced to care for her infant son, she marries Gabriel, thus establishing the basic terms for John's subsequent struggle.

Seen in relation to John in "The Seventh Day," Gabriel appears to be one of the most despicable hypocrites in American literature. Seen in relation to his own history in "The Prayers of the Saints," however, he appears victimized by the institutional context of his youth. In turn, he victimizes his family by attempting to force them into narrowly defined roles. The roots of Gabriel's character lie in the "temple-street" dichotomy of his southern childhood. Encouraged by his religious mother to deny his sensuality, Gabriel undergoes a conversion experience and immerses himself in the role of preacher. As a result, he enters into a loveless, asexual marriage with his mother's friend Deborah, herself a victim of the racist psychology—enforced by blacks and whites—that condemns *her* after she has been brutally raped by a group of whites.

Eventually, Gabriel's repressed street self breaks out and he fathers a son by the sensual Esther. Again attempting to deny his sensuality, Gabriel refuses to acknowledge this son, Royal. Like John's half brother Roy, the first Royal immerses himself in the street life that Gabriel denies; he dies in a Chicago barroom brawl. Gabriel fears that Roy will share Royal's fate, but his attempt to crush his second son's street self merely strengthens the resulting rebellion. Faced with the guilt of Royal's death and the sense of impending doom concerning Roy, Gabriel retreats into a solipsism that makes a mockery of his Christian vocation. Far from providing a context for moral responsibility, the church—both in the South and in the North—simply replaces the original innocence of religious fervor with a cynical vision of religion as a source of the power needed to destroy the innocence of others.

Against this backdrop, John's conversion raises a basic question that will recur in slightly different circumstances in each of Baldwin's novels: Can an individual hope to break the cycle of evasion that has shaped his or her personal and social context? In John's case, the problem takes on added dimensions, since he remains ignorant of many of the events shaping his life, including those involving his own birth. By framing the prayers with John's conversion, Baldwin stresses the connection between past and present, but the connection can be perceived as either oppressive or liberating. The complex irony of "The Threshing Floor" section allows informed readings of John's conversion as either a surrender to evasion or a movement toward existential responsibility. Focusing primarily on John's internal experience as he lies transfixed on the church floor, "The Threshing Floor" revolves around a dialogue between an "ironic voice" that challenges John to return to the street and the part of John that seeks traditional salvation. Throughout John's vision, the narrative voice shifts point of view in accord with John's developing perception. As John accepts the perceptions implied by his vision, the ironic voice shifts its attention to yet deeper levels of ambiguity. To the extent that John resolves these ambiguities by embracing the Temple, his experience seems to increase the risk that he will follow Gabriel's destructive example.

Several image patterns, however, indicate that John may be moving nearer to a recognition of his actual complexity. Chief among these are those involving the curse of Ham, the rejection of the father, and the acceptance of apparent opposites. From the beginning of the vision, the ironic voice ridicules John for accepting the curse of Ham, which condemns him both as son and as "nigger." Manipulating John's sense of guilt for having indulged his street self by masturbating, the ironic voice insists that John's very existence "proves" Gabriel's own sexual weakness. If Gabriel condemns John, he condemns himself in the process. As a result, John comes to view himself as the "devil's son" and repudiates his subservience before his "father." Without this essentially negative, and ultimately socially derived, definition of himself, John finds himself in an existential void where "there was no speech or language, and there was no love."

Forced to reconstruct his identity, John progresses from this sense of isolation to a vision of the dispossessed with whom he shares his agony and his humanity. John's vision of the multitude whose collective voice merges with his own suggests suffering as the essential human experience, one obliterating both the safety and the isolation of imposed definitions. Significantly, this vision leads John to Jesus the Son rather than God the Father, marking an implicit rejection of Gabriel's Old Testament vengeance in favor of the New Testament commitment to an all-encompassing love. The son metamorphoses from symbol of limitation to symbol of liberation. Near the end of his vision, John explicitly rejects the separation of opposites—street and temple, white and black—encouraged by his social context: "The light and the darkness had kissed each other, and were married now, forever, in the life and the vision of John's soul." Returning to his immediate environment from the depths of his mind, John responds not to the call of Gabriel but to that of Elisha, a slightly older member of the congregation with whom he has previously engaged in a sexually suggestive wrestling match reminiscent of that in D. H. Lawrence's *Women in Love* (1920). John's salvation, then, may bring him closer to an acceptance of his own sensuality, to a definition of himself encompassing both temple and street. Baldwin ends the novel with the emergence of the newly "saved" John onto the streets of Harlem. His fate hinges on his ability to move ahead to the higher innocence suggested by his vision of the dispossessed rather than submit to the experiences that have destroyed and deformed the majority of the saints.

ANOTHER COUNTRY

Another Country, Baldwin's greatest popular success, analyzes the effects of deforming pressure and experience on a wide range of characters, black and white, male and female, homosexual and heterosexual. To accommodate these diverse consciousnesses, Baldwin employs the sprawling form usually associated with political rather than psychological fiction, emphasizing the diverse forms of innocence and experience in American society. The three major sections of *Another Country*—"Easy Rider," "Any Day Now," and "Toward Bethlehem"—progress generally from despair to renewed hope, but no single consciousness or plot line provides a frame similar to that of *Go Tell It on the Mountain*. Rather, the novel's structural coherence derives from the moral concerns present in each of the various plots.

Casting a Melvillean shadow over the novel is the black jazz musician Rufus Scott, who is destroyed by an agonizing affair with Leona, a white southerner recently arrived in New York at the time she meets him. Unable to forge the innocence necessary for love in a context that repudiates the relationship at every turn, Rufus destroys Leona psychologically. After a period of physical and psychological destitution, he kills himself by jumping off a bridge. His sister Ida, an aspiring singer, and his friend Vivaldo Moore, an aspiring white writer, meet during the last days of Rufus's life and fall in love as they console each other over his death. Struggling to overcome the racial and sexual definitions that destroyed Rufus, they seek a higher innocence capable of countering Ida's sense of the world as a "whorehouse." In contrast to Ida and Vivaldo's struggle, the relationship of white actor Eric Jones and his French lover Yves seems edenic. Although Baldwin portrays Eric's internal struggle for a firm sense of his sexual identity, Eric and Yves's shared innocence at times seems to exist almost entirely outside the context of the pressures that destroyed Rufus. The final major characters, Richard and Cass Silenski, represent the cost of the American Dream. After Richard "makes it" as a popular novelist, the couple's personal relationship decays, precipitating Cass's affair with Eric. Their tentative reunion after Richard discovers the affair makes it clear that material success provides no shortcut to moral responsibility.

Baldwin examines each character and relationship in the context of the institutional pressures discouraging individual responsibility. His portrait of Rufus, the major accomplishment of *Another Country*, testifies to a moral insight and a raw artistic power resembling that of Wright and Émile Zola. Forgoing the formal control and emotional restraint of his earlier novels, Baldwin opens *Another Country* with the image of Rufus as a man who "had fallen so low, that he scarcely had the energy to be angry." Both an exceptional case and a representative figure, Rufus embodies the seething anger and hopeless isolation that render Baldwin's United States a landscape of nightmare. Seeing his own situation as unbearable, Rufus meditates on the fate of a city tormented by an agony like his own: "He remembered to what excesses, into what traps and nightmares, his loneliness had driven him; and he wondered where such a violent emptiness might drive an entire city." Forcing readers to recognize the social implications of Rufus's situation, Baldwin emphasizes that his specific situation originates in his own moral failure with Leona. Where Gabriel

Grimes remained insulated from his immorality by arrogance and pride, Rufus feels the full extent of his self-enforced damnation. Ironically and belatedly, his destitution clarifies his sense of the extent of his past acceptance of the social definitions that destroy him.

Wandering the streets of Manhattan, Rufus feels himself beyond human contact. Desperately in need of love, he believes his past actions render him unfit for even minimal compassion. His abuse of Leona, who as a white woman represents both the "other" and the source of the most obvious social definitions circumscribing his life as a black male, accounts for his original estrangement from family and friends, who find his viciousness uncharacteristic. All, including Rufus, fail to understand soon enough that his abuse of Leona represents both a rebellion against and an acceptance of the role dictated by racial and sexual definitions.

Separated from the psychological source of his art—jazz inevitably rejects the substructure of Euro-American definitions of reality—Rufus falls ever further into a paranoia that receives ample reinforcement from the racist context. Largely by his own choice, he withdraws almost entirely from his acquaintances, both black and white. Once on the street following Leona's breakdown, he begins to recognize not only his immediate but also his long-term acceptance of destructive definitions. Thinking back on a brief same-sex affair with Eric to which he submitted out of pity rather than love, Rufus regrets having treated his friend with contempt. Having rejected the "other" in Eric and Leona, Rufus realizes he has rejected a part of himself. He consigns himself to the ranks of the damned, casting himself beyond human love with his plunge off the bridge.

While not absolving Rufus of responsibility for his actions, Baldwin treats him with profound sympathy, in part because of his honesty and in part because of the enormous power of the social institutions that define him as the "other." Throughout *Another Country*, Baldwin emphasizes that white heterosexual males possess the power of definition, although their power destroys them as surely as it does their victims. Television producer Steve Ellis, a moral cripple embodying the basic values of the American economic system, nearly destroys Ida and Vivaldo's relationship by encouraging Ida to accept a cynical definition of herself as a sexual commodity.

Vivaldo, too, participates in the cynicism when he visits the Harlem prostitutes, indirectly perpetuating the definitions that reduce black people to sexual objects and thus implicating himself in Rufus's death. In fact, every major character with the exception of Eric bears partial responsibility for Rufus's destruction, since each at times accepts the definitions generating the cycle of rejection and denial. The constituting irony, however, stems from the fact that only those most actively struggling for moral integrity recognize their culpability. Vivaldo, who attempts to reach out to Rufus earlier on the night of his suicide, feels more guilt than Richard, who simply dismisses Rufus as a common "nigger" after his mistreatment of Leona.

This unflinching portrayal of moral failure, especially on the part of well-meaning liberals, provides the thematic center of *Another Country*. Baldwin concludes the novel with the image of Yves's reunion with Eric, who is apparently on the verge of professional success with a starring role in a film of a Fyodor Dostoevski novel. This combination of personal and financial success seems more an assertion of naïve hope than a compelling part of the surrounding fictional world. The majority of the narrative lines imply the impossibility of simple dissociation from institutional pressure. Ultimately, the intensity of Rufus's pain and the intricacy of Ida and Vivaldo's struggle overshadow Eric and Yves's questionable innocence. As Ida tells Vivaldo, "Our being together doesn't change the world." The attempt to overcome the cynicism of this perception leads to a recognition that meaningful love demands total acceptance. Ida's later question "How can you say you loved Rufus when there was so much about him you didn't want to know?" could easily provide the epitaph for the entire society in *Another Country*.

JUST ABOVE MY HEAD

In *Just Above My Head*, Baldwin creates a narrator, Hall Montana, capable of articulating the psychological subtleties of *Go Tell It on the Mountain*, the social insights of *Another Country*, and the political anger of *Tell Me How Long the Train's Been Gone*. Like other observer-participants in American literature, such as Nick Carraway in F. Scott Fitzgerald's *The Great Gatsby* (1925) and Jack Burden in Robert Penn Warren's *All the King's Men* (1946), Hall tells both his own story and that of a more publicly prominent figure, in this case his brother Arthur, a gospel singer who dies two years prior to the start of the novel.

Significantly, *Just Above My Head* also reconsiders Baldwin's own artistic history, echoing countless motifs from his earlier writings. Though not precisely a self-reflexive text, *Just Above My Head* takes on added richness when juxtaposed with Baldwin's treatment of religious concerns in *Go Tell It on the Mountain*, the homosexuality theme in *Giovanni's Room*, the relationship between brothers and the musical setting in "Sonny's Blues," racial politics in *Blues for Mister Charlie* and *Tell Me How Long the Train's Been Gone*, the Nation of Islam in *The Fire Next Time* and *No Name in the Street*, and, most important, the intermingled family love and world politics in *If Beale Street Could Talk*. Baldwin's reconsideration of his own history, which is at once private like Hall's and public like Arthur's, emphasizes the necessity of a continual reexamination of the nature of both self and context in order to reach higher innocence.

Similarly, Hall's resolve to understand the social and existential meaning of Arthur's experience originates in his desire to answer honestly his children's questions concerning their uncle. Refusing to protect their original innocence—an attempt he knows would fail—Hall seeks both to free himself from the despair of experience and to discover a mature innocence he can pass on to the younger generation. Tracing the roots of Arthur's despair to pressures originating in numerous limiting definitions and failures of courage, Hall summarizes his, and Baldwin's, social insight:

> The attempt, more the necessity, to excavate a history, to find out the truth about oneself! is motivated by the need to have the power to force others to recognize your presence, your right to be here. The disputed passage will remain disputed so long as you do not have the authority of the right-of-way. . . . Power clears the passage, swiftly: but the paradox, here, is that power, rooted in history, is also, the mockery and the repudiation of history. The power to define the other seals one's definition of oneself.

Recognizing that the only hope for meaningful moral freedom lies in repudiating the power of definition, Hall concludes: "Our history is each other. That is our only guide. One thing is absolutely certain: one can repudiate, or despise, no one's history without repudiating and despising one's own."

Although Baldwin recognizes the extent to which the definitions and repudiations remain entrenched in institutional structures, his portrayal of Hall's courage and honesty offers at least some hope for moral integrity as a base for social action. If an individual such as Hall can counteract the pressures militating against personal responsibility, he or she may be able to exert a positive influence on relatively small social groups such as families and churches, which in turn may affect the larger social context. Nevertheless, Baldwin refuses to encourage simplistic optimism. Rather than focusing narrowly on Hall's individual process, he emphasizes the aspects of the context that render that success atypical. Although Hall begins with his immediate context, his excavation involves the Korean War, the Civil Rights movement, the rise of Malcolm X, and the role of advertising in American culture. Hall's relationships with his family and close friends provide a Jamesian frame for the Dreiserian events of the novel, somewhat as John's conversion frames the historical "Prayers of the Saints" in *Go Tell It on the Mountain. Just Above My Head*, however, leaves no ambiguity concerning the individual's ability to free him- or herself from history. Only a conscious decision to accept the pain and guilt of the past promises any real hope for love, for the higher innocence. Similarly, Baldwin reiterates that, while the desire for safety is understandable, all safety is illusion. Pain inevitably returns, and, while the support of friends and lovers may help, only a self-image based on existential acceptance rather than repudiation makes survival possible.

Arthur's death, occupying a thematic and emotional position similar to the death of Rufus in *Another Country*, provides the point of departure for Hall's excavation. A gifted gospel singer as a teenager, Arthur rises to stardom as the "emperor of soul." Despite his success, however, he never frees himself from doubts concerning his own identity or feels secure with the experience of love. Even though his parents offer him a firm base of love and acceptance, Arthur feels a deep sense of emotional isolation even as a child, a sense reinforced by his observa-

tions of life in Harlem and, later, in the South. Though he accepts his own homosexuality with relatively little anxiety, his society refuses him the freedom necessary for the development of a truly satisfying emotional life. The edenic innocence of Eric and Yves in *Another Country* clearly fails to provide a sufficient response to the institutional context of *Just Above My Head*.

Arthur's childhood experiences provide clear warnings against the attempt to maintain innocence through simplistic self-definition. Julia Miller, like John in *Go Tell It on the Mountain*, undergoes a salvation experience and embarks on a career as a child evangelist. Encouraged by her parents, friends of the Montanas who rely on their daughter for economic support, she assumes a sanctimonious attitude, which she uses to manipulate her elders. Arthur's parents deplore the indulgence of Julia, unambiguously rejecting the idea that her religious vocation lifts her beyond the "naughty" street side of her personality. Ultimately, and in great pain, Julia confronts this truth. After her mother's death, she discovers that her father, Joel, views her primarily as an economic and sexual object. His desire to exploit her earning potential even when she says she has lost her vocation reflects his underlying contempt for the spirit. This contempt leads to an incestuous rape that destroys Julia's remaining innocence and drives her to a life as a prostitute in New Orleans. Eventually, Julia recovers from this brutalization, but her example provides a clear warning to Arthur against confusing his vocation as a gospel singer with a transcendence of human fallibility.

The experiences of the members of Arthur's first gospel group, the Trumpets of Zion, reveal how institutions infringe even on those not actively committed to simplifying definitions. At one extreme, the social definitions establish a context that accepts and encourages murder—symbolic and real—of the other. Peanut, a member of the Trumpets and later Arthur's companion on the road, vanishes into the Alabama night following a civil rights rally, presumably murdered by whites seeking to enforce the definition of blacks as "niggers." Equally devastating, although less direct, is the operation of the context on Red, another member of the Trumpets, who turns to drugs in an attempt to relieve the pain of the Harlem streets.

Even Hall finds himself an unwilling accomplice to the imposition of social definitions when he is drafted and sent to Korea. Powerless to alter the institutional structure, Hall recognizes, and tells Arthur, that the American military spreads not freedom but repudiation in the developing world. Hall's subsequent employment by an advertising agency involves him in another aspect of the same oppressive system. Viewed as an anomaly by his employers, as an atypical high-class "nigger," Hall nevertheless participates in the creation of images designed to simplify reality for economic gain, which will be used to strengthen the oppressive system. The juxtaposition of Julia's false innocence with the destructive experiences of Peanut, Red, and Hall protects Arthur against the urge to dismiss any aspect of his awareness. A large part of his power as a singer derives from his recognition of the reality of both street and temple, expressed in his ability to communicate sexual pain in gospel songs and spiritual aspiration in the blues.

Arthur, then, appears ideally prepared for the responsible exercise of existential freedom. His failure even to survive underscores the destructive power of the corrupt institutional context. The roots of Arthur's doom lie in his homosexual relationship with Crunch, the final member of the Trumpets. Highly desirable physically, Crunch feels locked into a definition of himself as a sexual object prior to his involvement with Arthur. In its early stages, Arthur and Crunch's love, like that of Yves and Eric in *Another Country*, seems an idyllic retreat, a spot of innocence in the chaos of experience. The retreat, however, proves temporary, in part because Crunch cannot free himself from the urge for self-simplification and in part because of the continuing presence of the outside world. Uneasy with his sexual identity, Crunch becomes involved with Julia when he discovers the extent of her father's abuse. Arthur recognizes that Crunch is not abandoning him by reacting to Julia's pain and accepts the relationship. Granted sufficient time for adjustment, Arthur and Crunch seem capable of confronting their experience and forging a higher innocence as the basis for a lasting love. The time does not exist, however. Crunch is drafted and sent to Korea. Separated from Arthur's reassurance and tormented by self-doubt, Crunch never fully accepts his sexuality. After his return to Harlem, he and Arthur gradually lose contact.

The repeated losses—of Peanut, Red, and Crunch—create a sense of isolation that Arthur never overcomes. The expectation of loss periodically overpowers his determination to communicate, the determination that makes him a great singer. Even during periods of real joy, with his French lover Guy in Paris or with Julia's brother Jimmy, who is both his pianist and his lover, Arthur suffers acute emotional pain. Attempting to survive by rededicating himself to communication, to his artistic excavation of history, Arthur drives himself past the limits of physical and psychological endurance. He dies in the basement bathroom of a London pub after a lovers' quarrel, clearly only temporary, with Jimmy. By concluding Arthur's life with an image of isolation, Baldwin emphasizes the power of limiting definitions to destroy even the most existentially courageous individual.

Arthur's death, however, marks not only a conclusion but also the beginning of Hall's quest for the higher innocence that he, along with his wife Ruth, Julia, and Jimmy, can pass on to the younger generation. This higher innocence involves both individual and social elements, ultimately demanding the mutual support of individuals willing to pursue excavation of their own histories. This support expresses itself in the call-and-response dynamic, a basic element of African American oral culture that Arthur employs in his interaction with audiences while singing. As Baldwin re-creates the traditional form, the interaction begins with the call of a leader who expresses his own emotional experience through the vehicle of a traditional song that provides a communal context for the emotion. If the members of the community recognize and share the experience evoked by the call, they respond with another traditional phrase that provides the sense of understanding and acceptance that enables the leader to go on. Implicitly, the process enables both individual and community to define themselves in opposition to dominant social forces. If the experience of isolation is shared, it is no longer the same type of isolation that brought Rufus to his death. In *Just Above My Head*, the call-and-response rests on a rigorous excavation requiring individual silence, courage, and honesty expressed through social presence, acceptance, and love. Expressed in the interactions between Arthur and his audiences, between Hall and his children, between Baldwin and his readers, this call-and-response provides a realistic image of the higher innocence possible in opposition to the murderous social definitions.

As in John's vision in *Go Tell It on the Mountain* and Rufus's self-examination in *Another Country*, the process begins in silence, which throughout Baldwin's novels offers the potential for either alienation or communication. The alienating silence coincides thematically with institutional noise—mechanical, social, political. The majority of Americans, Baldwin insists, prefer distracting and ultimately meaningless sounds to the silence that allows self-recognition. Only individuals sharing Arthur's willingness to remove himself from the noise can hope to hear their own voices and transform the silence into music. Every moment of true communication in *Just Above My Head* begins in a moment of silence that effectively rejects the clamor of imposed definitions. The courage needed for the acceptance of silence prepares the way for the honest excavation of history that must precede any meaningful social interaction. The excavation remains a burden, however, without that interaction. No purely individual effort can alter the overwhelming sense of isolation imposed by social definitions. The individual stage of the process merely heightens the need for acceptance, presence, and love. Arthur sounds the call amid the noise; he cannot provide the response. Perhaps, Baldwin indicates, no one, not even Jimmy, can provide a response capable of soothing the feeling of isolation emanating from early experiences. Nevertheless, the attempt is vital. Julia recognizes both the necessity and the limitation of presence when she tells Hall of her relationship with Jimmy: "I don't know enough to change him, or to save him. But I know enough to be there. I *must* be there."

If presence—being there—is to provide even momentary relief, it must be accompanied by the honest acceptance underlying love. Refusing to limit his acceptance, Hall answers his son Tony's questions concerning Arthur's sexuality with complete honesty. Understanding fully that his acceptance of Arthur entails an acceptance of the similar complexity in himself and in Tony, Hall surrenders his voice to Jimmy's, imaginatively participating in a love that repudiates social definition, that rises up out of the silence beyond the noise. Implicitly, Hall offers both Tony and his daughter Odessa the assurance of presence, of acceptance, of love. They need not

fear rejection if they have the courage to accept their full humanity. The assurance cannot guarantee freedom, or even survival. It can, and does, intimate the form of mature innocence in the world described by the composite voice of Baldwin, Jimmy, and Hall, a world that "doesn't have any morality. Look at the world. What the world calls morality is nothing but the dream of safety. That's how the world gets to be so fucking moral. The only way to know that you are safe is to see somebody else in danger—otherwise you can't be sure you're safe."

Against this vicious safety, a safety that necessitates limiting definitions imposed on others, Baldwin proposes a responsibility based on risk. Only by responding to the call sounding from Arthur, from Jimmy and Hall, from Baldwin, can people find freedom. The call, ultimately, emanates not only from the individual but also from the community to which he or she calls. It provides a focus for repudiation of the crushing definitions. Hall, using Jimmy's voice, describes the call: "The man who tells the story isn't *making up* a story. He's listening to us, and can only give back, to us, what he hears: from us." The responsibility lies with everyone.

Craig Werner

OTHER MAJOR WORKS

SHORT FICTION: *Going to Meet the Man*, 1965.

PLAYS: *The Amen Corner*, pr. 1954; *Blues for Mister Charlie*, pr., pb. 1964; *A Deed from the King of Spain*, pr. 1974.

POETRY: *Jimmy's Blues: Selected Poems*, 1983.

SCREENPLAY: *One Day, When I Was Lost: A Scenario Based on "The Autobiography of Malcolm X,"* 1972.

NONFICTION: *Notes of a Native Son*, 1955; *Nobody Knows My Name: More Notes of a Native Son*, 1961; *The Fire Next Time*, 1963; *Nothing Personal*, 1964 (with Richard Avedon); *No Name in the Street*, 1971; *A Rap on Race*, 1971 (with Margaret Mead); *A Dialogue*, 1975 (with Nikki Giovanni); *The Devil Finds Work*, 1976; *The Evidence of Things Not Seen*, 1985; *The Price of the Ticket*, 1985; *Conversations with James Baldwin*, 1989; *Collected Essays*, 1998; *Native Sons: A Friendship That Created One of the Greatest Works of the Twentieth Century—"Notes of a Native Son,"* 2004 (with Sol Stein).

CHILDREN'S LITERATURE: *Little Man, Little Man*, 1975.

BIBLIOGRAPHY

Balfour, Lawrie Lawrence, and Katherine Lawrence Balfour. *The Evidence of Things Not Said: James Baldwin and the Promise of American Democracy.* Ithaca, N.Y.: Cornell University Press, 2001. Explores the political dimension of Baldwin's essays, stressing the politics of race in American democracy.

Campbell, James. *Talking at the Gates: A Life of James Baldwin.* New York: Viking Press, 1991. Good narrative biography is organized into five sections, each focusing on a particular period of Baldwin's life. Places Baldwin's work within the context of his times. Includes detailed notes and bibliography.

Fabré, Michel. "James Baldwin in Paris: Love and Self-Discovery." In *From Harlem to Paris: Black American Writers in France, 1840-1980.* Chicago: University of Illinois Press, 1991. Discusses Baldwin's Paris experiences. Brings biographical details to the European experiences of the bicontinental playwright, who owed France "his own spiritual growth, through the existential discovery of love as a key to life." The notes offer interview sources of quotations for further study.

Harris, Trudier, ed. *New Essays on "Go Tell It on the Mountain."* New York: Cambridge University Press, 1996. Collection of essays examines the composition, themes, publication history, public reception, and contemporary interpretations of Baldwin's first novel. Some of the essays discuss Baldwin's treatment of God, the American South, and homosexuality in the novel.

Kinnamon, Keneth, ed. *James Baldwin: A Collection of Critical Essays.* Englewood Cliffs, N.J.: Prentice Hall, 1974. A good introduction to Baldwin's early work featuring a collection of diverse essays by such well-known figures as Irving Howe, Langston Hughes, Sherley Anne Williams, and Eldridge Cleaver. Includes a chronology of important dates, notes on the contributors, and a select bibliography.

Leeming, David. *James Baldwin: A Biography.* New York: Alfred A. Knopf, 1994. A biography of Baldwin written by one who knew him and worked with him for the last quarter century of his life. Provides extensive literary analysis of Baldwin's work and relates his work to his life.

McBride, Dwight A., ed. *James Baldwin Now.* New York: New York University Press, 1999. Collection of essays reevaluates Baldwin's work, stressing the usefulness of interdisciplinary approaches in understanding Baldwin's appeal, political thought and work, and legacy. The contributors maintain that Baldwin was not an exclusively gay, expatriate, black, or activist writer but instead was a complex combination of all of those things.

Miller, D. Quentin, ed. *Re-viewing James Baldwin: Things Not Seen.* Philadelphia: Temple University Press, 2000. Collection of essays explores the ways in which Baldwin's writing touched on issues that confront all people, including race, identity, sexuality, and religious ideology. Works analyzed include the novels *Giovanni's Room, Another Country,* and *Just Above My Head.*

Scott, Lynn Orilla. *James Baldwin's Later Fiction: Witness to the Journey.* East Lansing: Michigan State University Press, 2002. Analyzes the decline of Baldwin's reputation after the 1960's, the ways in which critics have often undervalued his work, and the interconnected themes in his body of work.

Sylvander, Carolyn Wedin. *James Baldwin.* New York: Frederick Ungar, 1980. Good overview of Baldwin's work provides an aesthetic perspective, a bibliographical summary, and an analysis of individual works, with greatest emphasis given to Baldwin's plays, novels, and short stories.

Troupe, Quincy, ed. *James Baldwin: The Legacy.* New York: Simon & Schuster, 1989. Contains eighteen essays by and about Baldwin, five of which were written for this collection, and homage and celebration from many who were profoundly influenced by him, including Pat Mikell's account of Baldwin's last days in St. Paul de Vence. With a foreword by Wole Soyinka.

Weatherby, W. J. *James Baldwin: Artist on Fire.* New York: Donald I. Fine, 1989. Lengthy personal reminiscence of Baldwin by a close friend who calls his biography a portrait. Based on conversations with more than one hundred people who knew Baldwin. Rich in intimate detail; reveals the man behind the words.

J. G. BALLARD

Born: Shanghai, China; November 15, 1930
Died: London, England; April 19, 2009
Also known as: James Graham Ballard

PRINCIPAL LONG FICTION

The Drowned World, 1962
The Wind from Nowhere, 1962
The Drought, 1964 (republished as *The Burning World*)
The Crystal World, 1966
Crash, 1973
Concrete Island, 1974
High Rise, 1975
The Unlimited Dream Company, 1979
Hello America, 1981
Empire of the Sun, 1984
The Day of Creation, 1987
Running Wild, 1988 (novella)
The Kindness of Women, 1991
Rushing to Paradise, 1994
Cocaine Nights, 1996
Super-Cannes, 2000
Millennium People, 2003
Kingdom Come, 2006

OTHER LITERARY FORMS

J. G. Ballard was a prolific short-story writer; his stories fill more than twenty collections, though some are recombinations of stories in earlier collections, and the American and British collections constitute two series in which the same stories are combined in different ways. He also wrote occasional essays on imaginative fiction and on surrealist painting—he contributed an introduction to a collection of work by Salvador Dalí, for example. Many of these essays are collected in *A User's Guide to the Millennium: Essays and Reviews* (1996). The best of Ballard's short fiction is to be found in two retrospective collections: *Chronopolis, and Other Stories* (1971) and *The Best Short Stories of J. G. Ballard* (1978).

ACHIEVEMENTS

J. G. Ballard is one of a handful of writers who, after establishing early reputations as science-fiction writers, subsequently achieved a kind of "transcendence" of their genre origins to be accepted by a wider public. In Ballard's case, this transcendence was completed by the success of *Empire of the Sun*, which was short-listed for the Booker Prize and won the Guardian Prize before being boosted to best-seller status by a film produced by Steven Spielberg. In 1996, maverick film director David Cronenberg turned Ballard's cult classic *Crash* into an equally disturbing film noir that quickly found a dedicated audience (the film was released in the United States in 1997).

For a time in the early 1960's, Ballard seemed to constitute a one-man avant-garde in British science fiction, and his influence was considerable enough for him to become established as the leading figure in the movement that came to be associated with the magazine *New Worlds* under the editorship of Michael Moorcock. Ballard's interest in science-fiction themes was always of a special kind; he was essentially a literary surrealist who found the near future a convenient imaginative space. His primary concern was the effect of environment—both "natural" and synthetic—on the psyche, and he therefore found it appropriate to write about gross environmental changes and about the decay and dereliction of the artificial environment; these interests distanced him markedly from other modern science-fiction writers and helped him to become a writer sui generis.

Following the success of *Empire of the Sun* Ballard became a prominent figure in the British literary landscape, cast by critics and journalists as an eccentric cynic playing a role akin to that of the court jesters of legend, who were supposed to whisper the reminder "Remember that thou art mortal" into the ears if their dictatorial employers. In a democratized modern world "ruled" by the middle class in their capacity as voters, consumers, and complainers, Ballard provided steely reminders not merely of the fragile mortality of everything they hold precious but also of the thinness of the veneer of glamour protecting the delusion that their goods are actually good and their values actually valuable.

BIOGRAPHY

James Graham Ballard was born and reared in Shanghai, China, where his father—originally an industrial chemist—was involved in the management of the Far East branch of a British firm of textile manufacturers. The Second Sino-Japanese War had begun, and Shanghai was effectively a war zone by the time Ballard was seven years old; all of his early life was affected by the ever-nearness of war. After Japan's entry into World War II and its invasion of Shanghai, Ballard was interned in a prisoner-of-war camp. This was in the summer of 1942, when he was eleven; he was there for more than three years.

Ballard later said that his experience of the internment camp was "not unpleasant"—it was simply a fact of life that, as a child, he accepted. Children were not generally mistreated by the guards, and the adults made sure that the children were adequately fed, even at their own expense. He later observed that his parents must have found the regime extremely harsh. Although his family members were among the fortunate few who avoided malaria, his sister nearly died of a form of dysentery.

After his release, Ballard went to England in 1946. His family stayed in the Far East for a while, and his father did not return until 1950, when he was driven out of China by the Communist victory. Ballard recalled that after spending his early years in "Americanized" Shanghai, England seemed very strange and foreign. He went to Leys' School in Cambridge for a while, then went to King's College, Cambridge, to study medicine. His ultimate aim at this time was to become a psychiatrist. At Cambridge he began writing, initially intending to maintain the activity as a hobby while he was qualifying. In fact, he dropped out of his course after two years and subsequently went to London University to read English. The university seems to have found him unsuitable for such a course, and he left after his first year.

He then embarked on a series of short-term jobs, including working for an advertising agency and selling encyclopedias. Eventually, to end this aimless drifting, he enlisted in the Royal Air Force and was sent for training to Moosejaw, Saskatchewan, Canada. He was not suited to the air force either, but while in Canada he began reading magazine science fiction, and while waiting for his discharge back in England he wrote his first science-fiction story, "Passport to Eternity" (it was not published for some years). Shortly after this, in 1955, he married and began working in public libraries in order to support his family.

In 1956, Ballard began submitting short stories to Ted Carnell, editor of the British magazines *New Worlds* and *Science Fantasy*. Carnell was not only enthusiastic about Ballard's work but also helpful in finding Ballard a new job working on a trade journal. Eventually, Ballard became assistant editor of *Chemistry and Industry*, a job he held for four years. He moved in 1960 to the small Thames-side town of Shepperton, which he would make his permanent home. By this time he had three children and was struggling to find time to devote to his writing.

J. G. Ballard. (Getty Images)

During a two-week annual holiday he managed to write *The Wind from Nowhere*, the publication of which in the United States represented something of a breakthrough for him—the same publisher began to issue a series of collections of Ballard's short stories, and the income from these books allowed him to become a full-time writer. His wife died in 1964, when his youngest child was only five years old. As a result, he began to combine his career as a writer with the exacting pressures of being a single parent. The fame that followed the success of *Empire of the Sun* seems not to have disturbed his lifestyle at all.

For a reader curious about Ballard's life upon his move from China to England, his 1991 novel *The Kindness of Women* offers an enticing mix of autobiography and imagination. While the book covers real-life events and includes details such as Ballard's car crash, his subsequent exhibition of crashed cars at an avant-garde gallery in London, and his experimentation with hallucinogenic drugs in the 1970's, it should not be mistaken for genuine autobiography. Composite characters and imagined or greatly exaggerated events abound in the work, and most real-life characters are given new names, with the prominent exception of the protagonist, called Jim Ballard.

Unlike this novel's character, Ballard seems to have spent a lot of his creative energy on his imaginative writing. In addition to producing a steady output of original novels and short stories, Ballard long remained an active writer of essays and book reviews, which made his a familiar voice in British literary circles. He was stubbornly committed to—or, at least, anchored in—his adopted town of Shepperton until his death in April, 2009.

ANALYSIS

J. G. Ballard's first seven novels can be sorted easily into two groups. The first four are novels of worldwide disaster, while the next three are stories of cruelty and alienation set in the concrete wilderness of contemporary urban society. All of his novels are, however, linked by a concern with the disintegration of civilization; the principal dynamic of his work has been the movement of that disintegration from a (symbolic) global scale, initially to very intimate local scales and then to somewhat broader but still rather claustrophobic communities.

Ballard's early disaster stories follow a well-established tradition in British imaginative fiction. British science-fiction writers from H. G. Wells to John Wyndham have seemed to be fascinated by the notion of the fragility and vulnerability of the human empire and have produced many careful and clinical descriptions of its fall. The earlier works in this tradition are didactic tales, insisting on the vanity of human wishes and reveling in the idea that when the crunch comes, only the tough will survive. Ballard, in contrast, is quite unconcerned with drawing morals; his disaster stories are not social Darwinist parables or fatalistic accounts of the ultimate futility of human endeavor—although unsympathetic critics have sometimes read them in the latter light—but attempts to reexamine and reevaluate possible strategies of psychological survival in relation to various circumstances, ranging from the extreme and the extraordinary to the stiflingly mundane. His main concern is always the existential readjustments that his characters are forced to make when faced with the subjection of their world to unwonted pressure. His early novels construe the problem of catastrophic change largely in terms of adaptation, while his later ones suggest that careful social insulation from change is itself a catastrophe that requires similar processes of adaptation.

In one of his earliest essays on science fiction—a guest editorial he contributed to *New Worlds* in 1962—Ballard committed the heresy of declaring that H. G. Wells was "a disastrous influence on the subsequent course of science fiction." He suggested that the vocabulary of ideas to which science-fiction writers and readers had become accustomed should be thrown overboard, and with it the genre's customary narrative forms and conventional plots. It was time, he said, to turn to the exploration of inner space rather than outer space and to realize that "the only truly alien planet is Earth." He offered his opinion that Salvador Dalí might be the most pertinent source of inspiration for modern writers of science fiction. The rhetorical flourishes that fill this essay caution readers against taking it all too seriously, but, in the main, this is the prospectus that Ballard actually followed.

In the first phase of his career, Ballard assiduously practiced what he preached, shaking off the legacy of H. G. Wells, dedicating himself to the exploration of inner space and the development of new metaphysical (particularly metapsychological) systems and steering well clear of the old plots and narrative formulas. In so doing, he made himself one of the most original science-fiction writers of his generation before leaving the genre behind. In such mind-period novels as *Crash*, *Empire of the Sun*, and *The Day of Creation* he attempted to extrapolate his thesis by demonstrating the essential alienness of the planet on which we live. The novels of his third phase, such as *Super-Cannes* and *Kingdom Come*, have taken the process a stage further, by demonstrating that the actual ambitions and habits of humankind, although—by definition—not describable as "alien," are nevertheless sufficiently grotesque to be absurdly self-defeating.

THE WIND FROM NOWHERE

In *The Wind from Nowhere*, which is considerably inferior to the three other disaster novels, a slowly accelerating wind plucks the human-made world apart. No one can stand firm against this active rebellion of nature—neither the American armed forces nor the immensely rich industrialist Hardoon, who seeks to secrete himself within a gigantic concrete pyramid, which the wind eventually topples into an abyss. *The Wind from Nowhere* has a whole series of protagonists and shows the catastrophe from several viewpoints. This was one of the well-tried methods of retailing disaster stories, but it was unsuited to Ballard's particular ambitions, and in the other novels of this early quartet he employed single protagonists as focal points—almost as measuring devices to analyze in depth the significance of parallel physical and psychological changes.

THE DROWNED WORLD

In *The Drowned World*, Earth's surface temperature has risen and is still gradually rising. Water released by the melting of the polar ice caps has inundated much of the land, and dense tropical jungle has spread rapidly through what were once the temperate zones, rendering them all but uninhabitable. Ballard suggests that the world is undergoing a kind of retrogression to the environment of the Triassic period. The novel's protagonist is Robert Kerans, a biologist monitoring the changes from a research station in partially submerged London.

The psychological effects of the transfiguration first manifest themselves as dreams in which Kerans sees "himself" (no longer human) wandering a primitive world dominated by a huge, fierce sun. These dreams, he concludes, are a kind of memory retained within the cellular heritage of humankind, now called forth again by the appropriate stimulus. Their promise is that they will free the nervous system from the domination of the recently evolved brain, whose appropriate environment is gone, and restore the harmony of primeval protoconsciousness and archaic environment. Kerans watches other people trying to adapt in their various ways to the circumstances in which they find themselves, but he sees the essential meaninglessness of their strategies. He accepts the pull of destiny and treks south, submitting to the psychic metamorphosis that strips away his humanity until he becomes "a second Adam searching for the forgotten paradises of the reborn sun."

When it was published, *The Drowned World* was sufficiently original and sophisticated to be incomprehensible to most of the aficionados of genre science fiction, who did not understand what Ballard was trying to do or why. A minority, however, recognized the novel's significance and its import; its reputation is now firmly established as one of the major works of its period.

THE DROUGHT

In *The Drought* (later republished as *The Burning World*), the pattern of physical change is reversed: Earth becomes a vast desert because a pollutant molecular film has formed on the surface of the world's oceans, inhibiting evaporation. The landscape is gradually transformed, the concrete city-deserts becoming surrounded by seas of hot sand instead of arable land, while the shores of the oceans retreat to expose new deserts of crystalline salt. The soil dies and civilization shrivels, fires reducing forests and buildings alike to white ash. Ransom, the protagonist, is one of the last stubborn few who are reluctant to join the exodus to the retreating sea. From his houseboat he watches the river dwindle away, draining the dregs of the social and natural order. He lives surrounded by relics of an extinguished past, bereft of purpose and no longer capable of emotional response.

Eventually, Ransom and his surviving neighbors are driven to seek refuge in the "dune limbo" of the new seashore and take their places in a new social order dominated by the need to extract fresh water from the reluctant sea. Here, he finds, people are simply marking time and fighting a hopeless rearguard action. In the final section of the story, he goes inland again to see what has become of the city and its last few inhabitants. They, mad and monstrous, have found a new way of life, hideous but somehow appropriate to the universal aridity—which is an aridity of the soul as well as of the land.

THE CRYSTAL WORLD

In *The Crystal World*, certain areas of Earth's surface are subjected to a strange process of crystallization as some mysterious substance is precipitated out of the ether. This is a more localized and less destructive catastrophe than those in *The Drowned World* and *The Drought*, but the implication is that it will continue until the world is consumed. The initially affected area is in Africa, where the novel is set. The central character is Dr. Sanders, the assistant director of a leper colony, who is at first horrified when he finds his mistress and some of his patients joyfully accepting the process of crystallization within the flesh of their own bodies. Eventually, of course, he comes to realize that no other destiny is appropriate to the new circumstances. What is happening is that time and space are somehow being reduced, so that they are supersaturated with matter. Enclaves from which time itself has "evaporated" are therefore being formed—fragments of eternity where living things, though they cannot continue to live, also cannot die, undergoing instead a complete existential transubstantiation. Here, metaphors developed in *The Drought* are literalized with the aid of a wonderfully gaudy invention.

The transformation of the world in *The Crystal World* is a kind of beautification, and it is much easier for the reader to sympathize with Sanders's acceptance of its dictates than with Kerans's capitulation to the demands of his dreams. For this reason, the novel has been more popular within the science-fiction community than either of its predecessors. It is, however, largely a recapitulation of the same theme, which does not really gain from its association with the lush romanticism that occasionally surfaces in Ballard's work—most noticeably in the short stories set in the imaginary American West Coast artists' colony Vermilion Sands, a beach resort populated by decadent eccentrics and the flotsam of bygone star cults who surround themselves with florid artificial environments.

CRASH

Seven years elapsed between publication of *The Crystal World* and the appearance of *Crash*. Although Ballard published numerous retrospective collections in the interim, his one major project was a collection of what he called "condensed novels"—a series of verbal collages featuring surreal combinations of images encapsulating what Ballard saw as the contemporary zeitgeist. In the world portrayed in these collages, there is a great deal of violence and perverted sexual arousal. Ubiquitous Ballardian images recur regularly: dead birds, junked space hardware, derelict buildings. Mixed in with these are secular icons: the suicide of entertainer Marilyn Monroe, the assassination of President John F. Kennedy, and other personalities whose fates could be seen as symbolic of the era in decline.

The theme of *Crash* is already well developed in the condensed novels, which were collected in the United Kingdom under the title *The Atrocity Exhibition* (1969) and in the United States under the title *Love and Napalm: Export U.S.A.* Cars, within the novel, are seen as symbols of power, speed, and sexuality—a commonplace psychoanalytic observation, to which Ballard adds the surprising further representation of the car crash as a kind of orgasm. The protagonist of the novel, who is called Ballard, finds his first car crash, despite all the pain and attendant anxiety, to be an initiation into a new way of being, whereby he is forced to reformulate his social relationships and his sense of purpose. Ballard apparently decided to write the book while considering the reactions of members of the public to an exhibition of crashed cars that he held at the New Arts Laboratory in London.

Although it is mundane by comparison with his previous novels—it is certainly not science fiction—*Crash* is by no means a realistic novel. Its subject matter is trauma and the private fantasization of alarming but ordinary events. The hero, at one point, does bear witness to a transformation of the world, but it is a purely subjective one while he is under the influence of a hallucinogen. He sees the landscapes of the city transformed, woven into a new metaphysics by the attribution of a new context of significance derived from his perverted fascination with cars and expressway architecture.

CONCRETE ISLAND *and* HIGH RISE

The two novels that followed *Crash* retain and extrapolate many of its themes. *Concrete Island* and *High Rise* are both robinsonades in which characters become Crusoes in the very heart of modern civilization, cast away within sight and earshot of the metropolitan hordes but no less isolated for their proximity. In *Concrete Island*, a man is trapped on a traffic island in the middle of a complex freeway intersection, unable to reach the side of the road because the stream of cars is never-ending. Like Crusoe, he sets out to make the best of his situation, using whatever resources—material and social—he finds at hand. He adapts so well, in the end, that he refuses the opportunity to leave when it finally arrives.

The high-rise apartment block that gives *High Rise* its title is intended to be a haven for the well-to-do middle class, a comfortable microcosm to which they can escape from the stressful outside world of work and anxiety. It is, perhaps, too well insulated from the world at large; it becomes a private empire where freedom from stress gives birth to a violent anarchy and a decay into savagery. If *Concrete Island* is spiritually akin to Daniel Defoe's *Robinson Crusoe* (1719), then *High Rise* is akin to William Golding's *Lord of the Flies* (1954), although it is all the more shocking in translocating the decline into barbarism of Golding's novel from a remote island to suburbia, and in attributing the decline to adults who are well aware of what is happening rather than to children whose innocence provides a ready excuse. As always, Ballard's interest is in the psychological readjustments made by his chief characters and the way in which the whole process proves to be ultimately cathartic.

A major theme in the condensed novels, which extends into the three novels of the second group, is what Ballard refers to as the "death of affect"—a sterilization of the emotions and attendant moral anesthesia, which he considers to be a significant trend induced by contemporary lifestyles. The greatest positive achievement of the characters in these novels is a special kind of ataraxia—a calm of mind rather different from the one Plato held up as an ideal, which allows one to live alongside all manner of horrors without being unusually moved to fear or pity.

THE UNLIMITED DREAM COMPANY

Another gap, though not such a long one, separates *High Rise* from *The Unlimited Dream Company*, a mes-sianic fantasy of the redemption of Shepperton from suburban mundanity. Its protagonist, Blake, crashes a stolen aircraft into the Thames River at Shepperton. Though his dead body remains trapped in the cockpit, he finds himself miraculously preserved on the bank. At first he cannot accept his true state, but several unsuccessful attempts to leave the town and a series of visions combine to convince him that he has a specially privileged role to play: He must teach the people to fly, so that they can transcend their earthly existence to achieve a mystical union with the vegetable and mineral worlds, dissolving themselves into eternity as the chief characters do in *The Crystal World*. Although the name of the central character is significant, the book also appears to be closely allied with the paintings of another artist: the eccentric Stanley Spencer, who lived in another Thames-side town (Cookham) and delighted in locating within its mundane urban scenery images of biblical and transcendental significance.

The kind of redemption featured in *The Unlimited Dream Company* is as ambivalent as the kinds of adaptation featured in Ballard's earlier novels, and its promise does not carry the same wild optimism that similar motifs are made to carry in most science-fiction and fantasy novels. It is perhaps best to view *The Unlimited Dream Company* as one more novel of adaptation, but one that reverses the pattern of the earlier works. Here, it is not Blake who must adapt to changes in the external world but Shepperton that must adapt to him—and he, too, must adapt to his own godlike status. Blake is himself the "catastrophe" that visits Shepperton, the absolute at large within it whose immanence cannot be ignored or resisted. If the novel seems to be upbeat rather than downbeat, that is mainly the consequence of a change of viewpoint—and had the readers who thought *The Drowned World* downbeat been willing to accept such a change, they might have been able to find that novel equally uplifting.

HELLO AMERICA

Although *The Unlimited Dream Company* does not represent such a dramatic change of pattern as first appearances suggest, *Hello America* is certainly, for Ballard, a break with his own tradition. There is little in the novel that seems new in thematic terms, although it recalls his short stories much more than previous novels, but there is nevertheless a sense in which it represents a radical departure. The plot concerns the "rediscovery" in the twenty-second century of a largely abandoned America by an oddly assorted expedition from Europe. What they find are the shattered relics of a whole series of American mythologies.

The central character, Wayne, dreams of resurrecting America and its dream, restoring the mythology of technological optimism and glamorous consumerism to operational status. He cannot do so, of course, but there is a consistent note of ironic nostalgia in his hopeless ambition. What is remarkable about the book is that it is a confection, an offhand entertainment to be enjoyed but not taken seriously. From Ballard the novelist, this is totally unexpected, though his short fiction has frequently shown him to be a witty writer and a master of the ironic aside.

EMPIRE OF THE SUN

This change of direction proved, not unexpectedly, to be a purely temporary matter—a kind of brief holiday from more serious concerns. *Empire of the Sun* recovers all the mesmeric intensity of Ballard's earlier work, adding an extra turn of the screw by relating it to historically momentous events through which the author had actually lived.

Although the book's young protagonist is named Jim and is the same age as Ballard was when he was interned by the Japanese, *Empire of the Sun*—like *Crash* before it—is by no means autobiographical in any strict sense. Jim's adventures are as exaggerated as the fictional Ballard's were, but the purpose of the exaggeration is here perfectly clear: What seems from an objective point of view to be a horrible and unmitigated catastrophe is to Jim simply part of the developing pattern of life to which he must adapt himself and that he takes aboard more or less innocently. From his point of view, given that the internment camp *is* the world, and not (as it is from the point of view of the adult internees) an intolerable interruption of the world, it is the behavior of the British prisoners that seems unreasonable and hostile, while the Japanese guards are the champions of order.

The world does not begin to end for Jim until the war comes toward its close and the orderliness of camp life breaks down; what others see as a source of hope and a possibility of redemption from their living hell is for Jim something else entirely, to which he reacts in character-

istically idiosyncratic fashion. The frightful irony of all this is, as usual, overlaid and disguised by a straight-faced matter-of-factness that forbids the reader to cling to the conventional verities enshrined in an older, inherited attitude toward the war with Japan.

THE DAY OF CREATION

The Day of Creation returns to the Africa of *The Crystal World*, this time disrupted by the seemingly miraculous appearance of a new river; the "discoverer" of the river, Dr. Mallory of the World Health Organization, hopes that it may restore edenic life to territory spoiled for millennia by drought and ceaseless petty wars. Mallory's odyssey along the river, upon which he bestows his own name, might be seen as an inversion of Marlow's journey in Joseph Conrad's *Heart of Darkness* (1902), the mysteriously silent girl Noon being a hopeful counterpart of Conrad's soul-sick Kurtz; the redemption promised by the river is a temporary illusion, however, and Noon herself may be only a figment of Mallory's imagination.

RUNNING WILD

The novella *Running Wild*, thinly disguised as a mass-murder mystery in which the entire adult population of a small town is massacred, is another playfully ironic piece, though rather less gaudy than *Hello America*—appropriately, in view of its setting, which is a cozy suburban landscape of the home counties. It is more a long short story than a short novel, but it carries forward the argument of *High Rise* as well as that of Ballard's brief black comedies such as "The Intensive Care Unit."

THE KINDNESS OF WOMEN

The Kindness of Women revisits the semiautobiographical subject matter that Ballard introduced with *Empire of the Sun*. The novel opens amid the Japanese invasion of Shanghai in 1937, an event Ballard himself witnessed as a boy. His protagonist's carefree adolescence is literally shattered by a bomb blast, when the Japanese air raid surprises a boy, again named Jim Ballard, as he strolls down the middle of Shanghai's amusement quarter. Moving from 1937 directly to Jim's arrival in post-World War II Great Britain, *The Kindness of Women* accompanies its protagonist to way stations modeled after significant events in the author's life, mixing imagination and autobiographical material. While

The Kindness of Women covers terrain familiar to readers of Ballard's work, it nevertheless manages to shed fresh light on the author's recurring obsessions, themes, and symbols, such as ubiquitous instances of downed aircraft, drained swimming pools, and concrete flyovers encircling Heathrow Airport.

RUSHING TO PARADISE

Rushing to Paradise has been represented as a satire on the follies of the environmentalist movement, but it is a more complicated text than that. Antihero Dr. Barbara Rafferty is on a quest to establish a South Sea sanctuary for the albatross on an island wrested from the French government. The novel suggests that this is really Rafferty's private attempt to build a murderous playground where she can live out psychosexual needs of her own. This boldly unconventional idea is obviously linked to Ballard's familiar suggestion of the dominance of the psychological over the material. The novel's invention of new psychological disorders and obsessions, and its iconoclastic depiction of an environmentalist physician who develops into a quasi commandant presiding over a disused airfield and ruined camera towers, clearly gives *Rushing to Paradise* the surrealist streak common to Ballard's fiction.

Perhaps not surprisingly, *Rushing to Paradise* largely failed to connect with a larger audience. Even though the novel's premise of renewed French nuclear testing in the South Seas uncannily anticipated the real-life development of such tests in the mid-1990's and thus predicted the future, something rarely accomplished by traditional science-fiction texts, many readers apparently could not forgive Ballard his choice of an environmentalist woman as the novel's surreal centerpiece. Ballard's idiosyncratic characters, which had alienated science-fiction fans when *The Drowned World* was published, managed again to distance his work from readers unwilling to engage the author on his own unique artistic grounds.

COCAINE NIGHTS

Cocaine Nights won more critical acclaim than its predecessor by virtue of its apparent imaginative restraint. It tells the story of Charles Prentice's quest to exonerate his brother Frank, who is held in a Spanish jail after being charged with a murder to which he has confessed. Prentice's investigation draws him into the social orbit of a rogue tennis instructor and self-appointed

leader of a group of thrill-seeking English people who combat terminal boredom by committing imaginative crimes and outrageous acts of vandalism. With its earnestly tongue-in-cheek thesis that only flamboyant criminal behavior can energize the somnolent resort community of terminally exhausted upper-middle-class retirees, Ballard's novel casually defies the expectations of middle-class readers accustomed to the flatteries of "realistic" fiction.

SUPER-CANNES

Following the publication of *Cocaine Nights*, Ballard appeared to decide that, as his plots were largely incidental to the narrative decor and thematic underpinnings of his work, he might as well stick to the same one—although there is a sense in which this is a reversion to his earliest strategy, the group forming his first four disaster novels having displayed the same fundamental constancy. *Super-Cannes* repeats the formula of an amateur investigation into a distressing but seemingly inexplicable crime, with the investigation gradually revealing a kind of general social conspiracy in which no one is innocent. The setting this time is the purpose-built community of Eden-Olympia, near the French resort of Cannes; one of Eden-Olympia's social architects describes it as an experimental laboratory in which "to hothouse the future." Inevitably, given Ballard's worldview, this hothousing has produced bizarre and avid mutant growths, which have absorbed the protagonist's missing wife and are about to consume him.

MILLENNIUM PEOPLE

Millennium People moves the plot formula of *Cocaine Nights* and *Super-Cannes* back to England—more specifically, to the suburban commuter belt surrounding London. This time, it is the protagonist's ex-wife who is the victim, killed by a bomb at Heathrow Airport, and the secret conspiracy based in the hypothetical upmarket community of Chelsea Marina is orchestrated by the nihilistic revolutionism of a disgraced pediatrician. In some ways the novel is reminiscent of *High Rise*, but the inciting factor of social isolation that plays a key role in the earlier novel is missing; *Millennium People* is not at all comparable to a robinsonade, as it assumes a much broader and more fundamental social malaise that is rooted in the continuity of communication rather than in its absence.

KINGDOM COME

Like *Millennium People*, *Kingdom Come* replays the amateur investigation plot formula in an English setting within a stone's throw of London's orbital motorway, the M25. This time, the core of the setting is a massive shopping mall, the Metro-Centre. Surrounding residential areas have been subject to a wave of faux nationalism operated by gangs of youths descended from late twentieth century "football hooligans" whose quasi-tribal organizations employed soccer team as totems. These gangs have gradually transformed themselves into a quasi-fascist movement whose bid for power takes the form of their holding the entire Metro-Centre hostage, imposing on their victims an ultraregimented code of behavior adopting and adapting the title of Consumerism. As the "hostages" adapt, courtesy of a large-scale occurrence of Stockholm syndrome, a new society does indeed seem to be in the making, including such strange echoes of tribalism as Heathrow Airport cargo cults.

Kingdom Come is the most successful of the cluster of Ballard's investigation novels, although—precisely for that reason—when it was published its surrealism made some readers and critics so profoundly uncomfortable that they rejected it as merely absurd. The scenario is, indeed, a contorted caricature of everyday manifestations of consumerism and a wild exaggeration of the potential of gang violence, but the essence of Ballard's literary strategy has always been the use of extreme exaggerations and distortions to reach, touch, and twist the tender hearts of the objects of his attacks.

Brian Stableford

OTHER MAJOR WORKS

SHORT FICTION: *Billenium*, 1962; *The Voices of Time*, 1962; *The Four-Dimensional Nightmare*, 1963; *Passport to Eternity*, 1963; *The Terminal Beach*, 1964; *The Impossible Man*, 1966; *The Disaster Area*, 1967; *The Overloaded Man*, 1967; *The Atrocity Exhibition*, 1969 (also known as *Love and Napalm: Export U.S.A.*); *Chronopolis, and Other Stories*, 1971; *Vermilion Sands*, 1971; *The Best Short Stories of J. G. Ballard*, 1978; *Myths of the Near Future*, 1982; *Memories of the Space Age*, 1988; *War Fever*, 1990; *The Complete Short Stories*, 2001.

NONFICTION: *A User's Guide to the Millennium: Essays and Reviews*, 1996; *Miracles of Life: Shanghai to Shepperton, an Autobiography*, 2008 (autobiography).

MISCELLANEOUS: *J. G. Ballard: Quotes*, 2004.

BIBLIOGRAPHY

Baxter, Jeanette. *Contemporary Critical Perspectives: J. G. Ballard*. London: Continuum Books, 2008. Provides a general overview of Ballard's work, paying more attention than most such books to the author's journalism and short fiction, and grounding discussion of the novels in the concerns revealed by those works.

Brigg, Peter. *J. G. Ballard*. San Bernardino, Calif.: Borgo Press, 1985. One of the most exhaustive booklength discussions available of the author and his work. Considers Ballard primarily as a science-fiction writer, analyzing his work within that framework.

Delville, Michel. *J. G. Ballard*. Tavistock, England: Northcote House, 1998. Offers an introductory overview of Ballard's work.

Gasiorek, Andrzej. *J. G. Ballard*. New York: Manchester University Press, 2005. Discusses Ballard's fiction from his earliest work onward. Argues that Ballard's sojourn in the science-fiction field is excusable because his works deny and undermine all the genre's precepts.

Jones, Mark. "J. G. Ballard: Neurographer." In *Impossibility Fiction*, edited by Derek Littlewood. Atlanta: Rodopi, 1996. Asserts that Ballard's fiction is characterized by the recurring theme of the author's description of the human mind as a kind of geographic landscape. Praises Ballard for his radical, surrealist descriptions of a new relationship between mind and reality.

Luckhurst, Roger. *"The Angle Between Two Walls": The Fiction of J. G. Ballard*. New York: St. Martin's Press, 1997. Comprehensive study of Ballard's work through the late 1990's provides thorough discussion and analysis of his fiction. Well researched and very informative.

Orasmus, Dominika. *Grave New World: The Decline of the West in the Fiction of J. G. Ballard*. Warsaw: University of Warsaw Press, 2007. Interesting study presents an Eastern European perspective on Ballard's catastrophism and images of decadence.

Pringle, David. *Earth Is the Alien Planet: J. G. Ballard's Four-Dimensional Nightmare*. San Bernardino, Calif.: Borgo Press, 1979. First attempt at an overview of Ballard's science fiction, written by a devoted admirer of the author, remains an excellent introduction to Ballard's work. Discusses literary context, symbolism, and key returning themes and motifs in his texts.

Stephenson, Gregory. *Out of the Night and into the Dream: A Thematic Study of the Fiction of J. G.*

Ballard. New York: Greenwood Press, 1991. Focuses on Ballard's idiosyncratic use of science-fiction motifs. Comprehensive index aids readers in tracking thematic patterns.

Vale, V., and Andrea Juno, eds. *J. G. Ballard*. San Francisco: RE/Search, 1984. Gaudy but highly informative celebration of the author's work contains valuable interviews, an illustrated autobiography, and a selection of the author's fiction and critical writing. Full of photographic and literary material on and by Ballard and about his subjects. Includes a chronological list of Ballard's short stories.

HONORÉ DE BALZAC

Born: Tours, France; May 20, 1799
Died: Paris, France; August 18, 1850
Also known as: Honoré Balzac; Lord R'Hoone; Horace de Saint Aubin

PRINCIPAL LONG FICTION

La Comédie humaine, 1829-1848 (17 volumes; *The Comedy of Human Life*, 1885-1893, 1896 [40 volumes]; also known as *The Human Comedy*, 1895-1896, 1911 [53 volumes]; includes all titles listed below)

Les Chouans, 1829 (*The Chouans*)

Physiologie du mariage, 1829 (*The Physiology of Marriage*)

Gobseck, 1830 (English translation)

La Maison du chat-qui-pelote, 1830, 1869 (*At the Sign of the Cat and Racket*)

Le Chef-d'œuvre inconnu, 1831 (*The Unknown Masterpiece*)

La Peau de chagrin, 1831 (*The Wild Ass's Skin*; also known as *The Magic Skin* and *The Fatal Skin*)

Sarrasine, 1831 (English translation)

Le Curé de Tours, 1832 (*The Vicar of Tours*)

Louis Lambert, 1832 (English translation)

Maître Cornélius, 1832 (English translation)

La Femme de trente ans, 1832-1842 (includes *Premières fautes*, 1832, 1842; *Souffrances inconnues*, 1834-1835; *À trente ans*, 1832, 1842; *Le Doigt de Dieu*, 1832, 1834-1835, 1842; *Les Deux Rencontres*, 1832, 1834-1835, 1842; and *La Vieillesse d'une mère coupable*, 1832, 1842)

Eugénie Grandet, 1833 (English translation, 1859)

Le Médecin de campagne, 1833 (*The Country Doctor*)

La Recherche de l'absolu, 1834 (*Balthazar: Or, Science and Love*, 1859; also known as *The Quest of the Absolute*)

Histoire des treize, 1834-1835 (*History of the Thirteen*; also known as *The Thirteen*; includes *Ferragus, chef des dévorants*, 1834 [*Ferragus, Chief of the Devorants*; also known as *The Mystery of the Rue Solymane*]; *La Duchesse de Langeais*, 1834 [*The Duchesse de Langeais*]; and *La Fille aus yeux d'or*, 1834-1835 [*The Girl with the Golden Eyes*])

Le Père Goriot, 1834-1835 (*Daddy Goriot*, 1860; also known as *Père Goriot*)

Melmoth réconcilié, 1835 (*Melmoth Converted*)

Le Lys dans la vallée, 1836 (*The Lily in the Valley*)

Histoire de la grandeur et de la décadence de César Birotteau, 1837 (*History of the Grandeur and Downfall of César Birotteau*, 1860; also known as *The Rise and Fall of César Birotteau*)

Illusions perdues, 1837-1843 (*Lost Illusions*)

Splendeurs et misères des courtisanes, 1838-1847, 1869 (*The Splendors and Miseries of Courtesans*; includes *Comment aiment les filles*, 1838, 1844 [*The Way That Girls Love*]; *À combien l'amour revient aux vieillards*, 1844 [*How Much Love Costs Old Men*;] *Où mènent les mauvais chemins*, 1846 [*The End of Bad Roads*]; and *La Dernière Incarnation de Vautrin*, 1847 [*The Last Incarnation of Vautrin*])

Pierrette, 1840 (English translation)

Le Curé de village, 1841 (*The Country Parson*)

Mémoires de deux jeunes mariées, 1842 (*The Two Young Brides*)

Une Ténébreuse Affaire, 1842 (*The Gondreville Mystery*)

Ursule Mirouët, 1842 (English translation)

La Cousine Bette, 1846 (*Cousin Bette*)

Le Cousin Pons, 1847 (*Cousin Pons*, 1880)

OTHER LITERARY FORMS

In addition to his fiction, Honoré de Balzac (BAHL-zak) wrote several plays, including *Cromwell* (wr. 1819-1820, pb. 1925), *Vautrin* (pr., pb. 1840; English translation, 1901), and *Le Faiseur*, also known as *Mercadet* (pr. 1849; English translation, 1901), but he was not a playwright and generally devoted time to the theater only when he felt that there was a good profit to be made with little effort. Likewise, many of the articles and essays that Balzac wrote between 1825 and 1834, published in such journals as *Le Voleur, La Mode, La Caricature, La Silhouette*, and *La Revue de Paris*, were composed to enable the author to acquire ready money. Balzac's letters to the Polish baroness Evelina Hanska, to his family, and to Madame Zulma Carraud were published after the novelist's death.

ACHIEVEMENTS

The Human Comedy, Honoré de Balzac's masterwork, is one of the greatest literary achievements of all time. It contains many novels beyond those listed above, the bulk of which were written between 1830 and 1847. Before 1829, Balzac wrote under various pseudonyms—notably "Lord R'Hoone" and "Horace de Saint Aubin"—and frequently composed novels in collaboration with other writers. These twenty or so early volumes, which include *Sténie: Ou, Les Erreurs philosophiques* (1936; Sténie: or, philosophical errors), *Falturne* (1950), *Le Centenaire: Ou, Les Deux Beringheld* (1822; *The Centenarian: Or, The Two Beringhelds*, 1976), and *La Dernière Fée* (1823; the last fairy), were later renounced by Balzac, and rightly so, for they were written in haste and were obvious attempts to exploit the current taste for gothic melodrama and romantic adventures.

BIOGRAPHY

Honoré Balzac was born in Tours, France, on May 20, 1799, of bourgeois parents. He was to acquire the predicate of nobility—the name by which he is known today—when, in 1831, in tribute to his official commitment to embark on the writing of *The Human Comedy*, he dubbed himself Honoré *de* Balzac. This change of name is symptomatic of Balzac's lifelong craving to be an aristocrat and to enjoy the deep respect and the want-for-nothing lifestyle that accompanied that status.

The eldest of four children, Balzac was treated very coldly by his parents, who entrusted him to the care of a wet nurse for four years, then sent him to board with a family of strangers for two years, and finally had him attend for seven years a boarding school in Vendôme. Balzac's childhood years were loveless and painful, which probably encouraged him to turn inward toward dreams and fantasies. By 1816, Balzac had finished his studies in Vendôme, albeit with far less than a brilliant record, and was sent off to Paris to study jurisprudence, his mother ordering him to "shape up" and work very hard. At the age of twenty, however, Balzac declared to his family his surprising intention to become a writer, not a lawyer. When his parents skeptically agreed to his wishes, Balzac was permitted to live in Paris for two years, where he was set up in a poorly furnished apartment and was given a deliberately insufficient allow-

Honoré de Balzac. (Library of Congress)

ance, which was intended to demonstrate to this way-ward son the harsh economic facts of life.

Between 1819 and 1829, Balzac was forced to earn a living from writing, a situation that led him to compromise his literary genius for money; when this endeavor proved inadequate, he was not too proud to undertake other occupations. In an effort to ensure his freedom to write, Balzac became a bookseller, then a printer, then a journalist. All of these enterprises, however, ultimately failed. His most notorious business venture occurred in 1838, when he speculated on Sardinian silver mines. Everything Balzac tried to do as a businessman only drove him deeper into debt, a state of affairs that he often transposed to the realm of his fiction; yet even when Balzac was at the mercy of creditors and in danger of being arrested, he remained, at bottom, optimistic. His new novel would rescue him, at least temporarily, from financial embarrassment, or his current business venture would surely make him wealthy, or, best of all, an aristocratic

lady—and there was nearly always a prospect—would soon become his wife and give him not only her love but also her fortune. Nearly all of the women who mattered to Balzac were, in fact, noble, from Madame Laure de Berny, who sacrificed both her morals and her money to help the budding genius to survive, to Madame Evelina Hanska, the Polish baroness who began by writing anonymous letters of admiration to the well-known author and eventually, after her husband's death and her daughter's marriage, consented to become Balzac's wife.

It is an irony that suitably parallels that of the fictional world portrayed in *The Human Comedy* that Balzac's marriage to this woman of his dreams occurred only five months before his death. Balzac died from what one may term outright exhaustion on August 18, 1850.

ANALYSIS

At the age of thirty, Honoré de Balzac resolved to become a great French writer. At first, he believed that he could accomplish this goal by emulating the Scottish writer Sir Walter Scott, whose historical novels were highly esteemed in France during the first half of the nineteenth century. Like Scott, Balzac would be a historian of social, psychological, and political life. Later, however, as Balzac explains in his preface to *The Human Comedy*, this idea was modified. Balzac finally saw his true and original role to be that of "the secretary of society" rather than that of a social historian; that is, instead of bringing the past to life, as Scott had done, Balzac chose to transcribe the life around him into fiction. In many ways, the author of *The Human Comedy* is faithful to this role, drawing a picture of French society at all levels from roughly 1815 until the end of Balzac's writing career in 1848.

THE HUMAN COMEDY

In his novels, Balzac reveals the driving passions and needs of a wide range of individuals in various social positions: noblemen and aristocratic ladies; politicians, bankers, businessmen, and moneylenders; scientists, doctors, and priests; lawyers, policemen, and criminals;

musicians, painters, sculptors, and writers. This picture of society delineates not only ambitious members of the bourgeoisie and proud aristocrats but also the environments in which they live and work, including the luxurious, exhilarating, and cutthroat life of Paris and the comparatively dull and inactive existence of small provincial French towns. The two thousand characters whom Balzac depicts in *The Human Comedy* are not, however, mere social types. On the contrary, Balzac's protagonists are, in general, strongly individualistic, some of them to the point of eccentricity.

Each novel of *The Human Comedy* contains a single story that may be read and appreciated for itself; at the same time, each story is linked to the whole. A protagonist encountered in one novel might very well appear again, like an old acquaintance, within the context of another novel and possibly a very different plot. The small number of characters who travel from one novel to another give unity to Balzac's works and at the same time convey the impression that the fictional world described in *The Human Comedy* is alive and infinite in scope.

With regard to tone, Balzac's plots embrace a wide range of attitudes: tragically sad or comically ironic, highly idealistic, fantastic, or romantic. The novelist, however, is judged to have excelled particularly as a realist in his candid portrayal of the tremendous will to power of human nature and of the influence of money on social behavior.

In Balzac's works, many of the characteristic impulses of the nineteenth century coincided and reinforced one another. Balzac's legendary energy, his enormous, hubristic ambition, his tireless interest in the world, and his sheer appetite for experience—all these elements worked together to produce a massive tapestry of an entire society, unmatched in scope and detail before or since the author's time.

Three themes in Balzac's fiction can be seen as reflections of the novelist's personality: The first of these is the theme of madness or monomania, the second is the large role given to money, and the third is the recurrent search of Balzac's characters for love and success. The madmen of *The Human Comedy* include some of Balzac's most original and memorable characters. These figures are generally obsessed by ideas that they try to make into reality and for which they sacrifice every-

thing. Although the individual obsessions of these protagonists vary, Frenhofer, the painter in *The Unknown Masterpiece*, Grandet, the miser in *Eugénie Grandet*, and Claes, the scientist in *The Quest of the Absolute*, are nevertheless shadows of Balzac, the author, who expresses through them his own obsession: the painstaking composition of *The Human Comedy*. Balzac wrote for hours, weeks, and months on end to prove his genius to the world. Everything was sacrificed for his literary task, including comfortable lodging, clothes, and the most insignificant of worldly amusements.

The monomaniacs of Balzac's creation are particularly interesting figures. They are intelligent and possess glorious ideas that, if they initially seem eccentric, at the same time denote genius. Their bold determination to accomplish all they have set out to do is admirable only to a point, however. Balzac always shows that the obsessions of his monomaniacs dehumanize them. When, for example, Claes in *The Quest of the Absolute* sacrifices the sustenance of his family in order to continue financing his experiments, Balzac pushes his protagonist's passion to an extreme. The manias of Balzac's characters slowly annihilate everything around them until, in the end, these figures appear so blinded by their passion that they are completely enslaved by it. The tragic depiction of Balzac's monomaniacs is undoubtedly one of the cornerstones of *The Human Comedy*. These characters, who first command one's admiration, then appeal to one's sympathy, and finally elicit one's scorn, cause one to ponder with Balzac the force of human thought and willpower. Moreover, by means of his monomaniacs, Balzac expresses his own obsession and his fear of it.

Another important theme of *The Human Comedy* is money, which, in Balzac's fictional world, dominates all other values. In a sense, Balzac's attitude toward money is ambivalent. On one hand, he often shows nostalgia for the neoclassic age, when, under the monarchy, a member of the nobility was assured a life of ease and intellectual grandeur. On the other hand, however, Balzac accepts and objectively portrays the bourgeois society of his day. It is a society whose wheels are oiled by money, but many of Balzac's heroes feel optimistically that, by means of their intelligence, they can succeed in conquering the cycle. Apparently, Balzac himself believed that the appearance of having money was enough to command respect and social acceptance. Sometimes when his characters wear expensive-looking clothes and ride about in fancy carriages, they are, in fact, engaged in a carefully calculated masquerade to fool society by using its own superficial code against it. Of course, some of Balzac's protagonists succeed in this way, but most of them fail—paralleling the novelist's career, in which successes were few and financial failures many. Balzac's most pointed criticism of the role of money in society is not, however, that it is the entry ticket to social success. In such novels as *Père Goriot* and *Eugénie Grandet*, Balzac portrays money in its most diabolical role, as a corrupter of the noblest of human feelings, love.

Balzac depicts two kinds of love in his novels. Ideal love is the quest of many protagonists of *The Human Comedy*, who suffer in its absence and fail to realize its glorious promise. Desirable women in Balzac's fiction are often much older than their aspiring lovers, leading biographers to speculate about Balzac's own mother's indifference toward him and about the novelist's first amorous adventure with Madame de Berny, who—when Balzac met her at the age of twenty-two—was twenty-two years older than he. Aristocratic and maternal women such as Madame de Mortsauf in *The Lily in the Valley* represent a supreme love the likes of which cannot be matched. The very ideal quality of this love, however, is perhaps what leads to its impossibility. Although Balzac's characters glimpse the perfect love object time and time again, the latter generally remains out of reach because of societal or financial constraints. In contrast, love, as Balzac portrays it in his fictional society, is a dangerous counterfeit. Coquettish females of *The Human Comedy*, such as Antoinette de Langeais in *The Duchess de Langeais* (a part of *The Thirteen*), provoke innocent gentlemen to fall in love with them only to cultivate their own egos. For the boldest male protagonists of *The Human Comedy*, love is like money, something to be used to advance oneself in society. Rastignac in *Père Goriot* and Raphaël de Valentin in *The Wild Ass's Skin*, for example, make the calculated decision to fall in love, one with a wealthy banker's wife and the other with an aristocratic lady. Family love and devotion are also shams, falling into insignificance when confronted by personal ambition and money.

THE WILD ASS'S SKIN

Balzac classified the novels of *The Human Comedy* into three large areas: "Studies of Social Manners," "Philosophical Studies," and "Analytical Studies." *The Wild Ass's Skin*, published in 1831, was placed into the category "Philosophical Studies," probably because of its fantastic theme, the possession of a magic skin. Like many of Balzac's best novels, however, *The Wild Ass's Skin* is actually a mixture of cold reality and fantastic illusion. The hero of the novel, Raphaël de Valentin, a downtrodden genius whom society persistently ignores, is clearly a figure with whom the novelist could identify. Balzac's protagonist has written a philosophical treatise titled "Théorie de la volonté" ("Theory of the Will"), a work whose exact contents are never revealed but whose significance for Balzac and for *The Human Comedy* is evident. Like his hero, Valentin, Balzac is engaged in an analysis of man's will. Valentin may appear to be more theoretical than the novelist, but both Balzac and his protagonist find the power of ideas at work in the mind to be a fascinating and dangerous study. One suspects that Valentin is actually an image of Balzac's own projected success as well as the foreboding prototype of his failure.

The destiny of Raphaël de Valentin follows a curve from failure to success and back to failure again. At the beginning of the book, Valentin thinks seriously about committing suicide for two reasons. First, he has suffered very deeply in his love for a beautiful but heartless coquette named Foedora. Second, he is destitute. Even though his "Theory" has finally been completed—a lifework that ought to be acknowledged as striking proof of his genius—societal acclaim is still denied him. When Balzac later explains in his epilogue to the novel that Foedora is actually a symbol of society, one understands that her indifference to Valentin includes not only a condemnation of a would-be lover but also a cruel underestimation of his intelligence, the hero's very raison d'être. The initial tragedy of Valentin is realistically portrayed as a battle between a sensitive romantic young man and Parisian society.

In the next phase of Valentin's destiny, however, one sees an abrupt transformation that at first appears to project Balzac's hero to the heights of success. Valentin acquires from a mysterious antiquarian a wild ass's skin. Because, as in a fairy tale, the magic skin grants its owner's every wish, Valentin need no longer be poor. Indeed, it is society's turn to court him! Now the Parisian society that Valentin previously hoped to please is depicted as thoroughly repulsive and morally corrupt. As a sign of Valentin's rejection of it, one of his wishes is that he may forget Foedora, the novel's symbol of society. One may find in Valentin's change of attitude toward society the novelist's own admission to himself that what he ultimately seeks—general recognition of his genius as a writer—simply does not exist in a world ruled by personal vanity and money. Now that Foedora has been forgotten, she is replaced in Valentin's heart by Pauline, a poor, innocent young girl who has always shown him true love and devotion.

This "happy ending" is short-lived, however. In the final phase of Valentin's destiny, Balzac returns to the philosophical theme of the human will. The wild ass's skin that Valentin possesses is not a blessing after all, but a curse. After each wish that it grants to its owner, the skin shrinks in dimension, its dwindling size quickly becoming a horrifying picture of the diminishing length of Valentin's life.

It is interesting to correlate this tragic depiction of Balzac's hero with the situation of the novelist himself. When Balzac wrote *The Wild Ass's Skin* in 1831, he was already aware that his enormous writing task would take him away from the world of reality and cause him to become a more firmly established inhabitant of his fictional world. After the protagonist of *The Wild Ass's Skin* has unmasked society, he attempts to withdraw from it. Perhaps, pen in hand, wearing his monk's cloak, Balzac, too, may have thought that he could escape to the fictional realm of his imagination. Eventually, however, reality always intervened and subjugated the writer to its practical demands. Hence, Balzac gives that part of himself that repudiates money and all those who worship it a kind of allowance analogous to money. Valentin must make fewer and fewer wishes and finally tries not to express any desires at all, simply in order to continue living.

In this complex novel, Balzac transposes into fiction his own misery, his maddening drive to succeed, his dreams and love for life, while giving the reader a survey of the themes that will permeate many novels of *The Human Comedy*: money, unrealized love, the drive to succeed, and madness.

THE VICAR OF TOURS

Balzac finished writing *The Vicar of Tours* in April, 1832. In this short novel, Balzac, like Gustave Flaubert in his famous short story "Un Cœur simple" ("A Simple Heart"), relates a story that superficially seems unworthy of mention. Balzac's hero, Birotteau, like Flaubert's heroine, Félicité, is rather simpleminded and lives an uneventful life. True to the nature of Balzac's most memorable heroes, however, Birotteau is quite different from Félicité in that, despite his lack of intelligence, he is ambitious. Furthermore, he is naïvely happy. Balzac alternately pities and ridicules his provincial priest, whose passion it is to possess the beautiful apartment of his colleague, Chapeloud. While pointing out that a desire for material wealth is not seemly for a priest, Balzac ironically pardons his hero, who is, after all, only human and whose ambition, as ambitions go, can only be termed petty.

When Birotteau's ambition is fulfilled upon the death of Chapeloud, the apartment becomes the subject of a war of wills involving not only Birotteau's spinster landlady, Mademoiselle Gamard, but eventually the whole town of Tours. Indeed, a political career in the highest echelons of the French government and the important advancement of a priest within the Catholic Church both end up having, in some way, a relationship to what begins as Birotteau's "insignificant" passion.

In some ways, Birotteau is the opposite of the typical Balzacian monomaniac. Happy to let everything be handled by his friends and incapable of understanding what is going on, he watches the battle rage around him. Birotteau would not purposely hurt a fly, and he does not have an inkling of why he is being attacked.

As in many novels of *The Human Comedy*, an important turn in the plot of *The Vicar of Tours* hinges on a legal document, in this case the apartment lease. Balzac's years as a law student often served him well, as he used his knowledge of the law in composing many of his plots. Essentially missing from this novel is one of Balzac's major themes, money. Nevertheless, the vanity of the characters in *The Vicar of Tours* and their drive for personal success and power are keenly developed subjects of satire and, at the same time, very realistic studies of human psychology and social behavior. Balzac classed *The Vicar of Tours* under the heading "Scenes of

Provincial Life," a subcategory of "Studies of Social Manners"—where the largest number of novels in *The Human Comedy* can be found.

LOUIS LAMBERT

Approximately three months after completing *The Vicar of Tours*, in July, 1832, Balzac finished *Louis Lambert*. This novel was eventually included with *The Wild Ass's Skin* and eighteen other novels in the category "Philosophical Studies," but its relationship to Balzac's "Studies of Social Manners" is strengthened through the device of recurring characters. One of the minor figures of *The Vicar of Tours* is an old woman, Mademoiselle Salomon de Villenoix, who befriends Birotteau and shows him a great deal of compassion. In *Louis Lambert*, the same woman plays a more important role, as Balzac describes Mademoiselle de Villenoix in her youth, when she was the ideal love object of Louis Lambert, the principal character of the novel.

The parallels between *The Wild Ass's Skin* and *Louis Lambert* are quite interesting. Like Raphaël de Valentin, Louis Lambert is a genius who composes a philosophical work on the will; the title of his work, "Traité de la volonté" ("Treatise on the Will"), is virtually identical to the title of Valentin's. Each of the two characters succeeds in finding an ideal woman whose name is Pauline: Pauline de Villenoix in *Louis Lambert* and Pauline de Witschnau in *The Wild Ass's Skin*. Finally, the tragedy of each of the genius heroes lies in the fact that he goes mad. The Paulines of the two novels react to the inexplicable madness of the men they love by devoting themselves totally to them, somewhat like nurses or angels of mercy.

The similarities between *Louis Lambert* and *The Wild Ass's Skin* give one a fairly clear idea of what must have been Balzac's attitude toward himself. The novelist instills in his heroes two great passions that are undoubtedly reflections of his own drives: to become a recognized genius and to be loved. In these two novels, Balzac appears to demonstrate his belief that love and genius cannot coexist and that when one attempts to blend them, they annihilate each other. In this sense, the madness that overcomes Balzac's protagonists represents a double failure. Both Lambert and Valentin fall short of attaining ideal love and also fail to develop the potential of their genius.

It is nevertheless true that Balzac shows the passions of Louis Lambert for love and for recognition of his genius somewhat differently from the way he portrays these passions in his earlier novel. In *Louis Lambert*, the novelist seems to indicate a preference for one of the two goals when he emphasizes Lambert's genius. From the beginning of the novel, Lambert is seen through the eyes of an admiring narrator who relates in retrospect the bitter experiences of school days shared with Balzac's genius hero. In detailing these experiences, Balzac transposes into fiction many of his own memories of the lonely years he spent as a boarder at the Collège de Vendôme. Both the narrator and Lambert are neglected by their parents, ostracized by their peers, punished by their teachers, and forbidden—as in a prison—to enjoy even the slightest amusement. The narrator admits to being inferior to Lambert, whose genius he sensed when they were in school together and whose insights, although they are now only half-remembered, had the power of truth.

At the end of the novel, Balzac intensifies sympathy for the plight of his genius hero gone mad by reproducing a series of philosophical fragments that, because they are written down by Lambert's loving companion, Pauline, are only sketchy transcriptions of his actual thoughts. It is not important that these fragments appear puzzling and in some cases absurd: Like the incomplete recollections of the narrator, they are powerfully evocative *because* they are fragmentary, tantalizingly so, suggestive of what the world lost when it lost the genius of Louis Lambert.

EUGÉNIE GRANDET

Before the publication of *Eugénie Grandet* in 1833, Balzac had continued to experiment in his novels with the theme of madness. In addition to *Louis Lambert*, Balzac had written other "Philosophical Studies" in the period 1830-1832 that expand on this theme, including *The Unknown Masterpiece* and *Maître Cornélius*. In *The Unknown Masterpiece*, Balzac portrays a painter, Frenhofer, whose madness manifests itself in his increasing inability to transpose the idealized feminine figure he imagines to a canvas. The hero of *Maître Cornélius* suffers from an insidious malady: When he sleepwalks, his unconscious self steals the money that, in reality, he is supposed to guard.

In *Eugénie Grandet*, however, the theme of madness reaches a turning point. Balzac's protagonist, Old Grandet, like Maître Cornélius, is a miser, but what distinguishes him from the latter is that his mania does not indicate total sickness or madness. Grandet's passion does not seem to debilitate him in any way. On the contrary, it is his raison d'être and is willfully and, one may even say, intellectually directed. Grandet, one of the most fascinating characters of *The Human Comedy*, is a full-blown monomaniac. What makes him so interesting is that he is not one-dimensional. Although Grandet's obsessive drive for money remains constant throughout the novel, he is not always seen in the same light. In relations with his wife, his cook, his small-town neighbors, and especially his daughter, Eugénie, Grandet sparks off a variety of reactions to his miserly behavior. At times he is admired and feared for his sharp intelligence; at other times he is condemned for his lack of understanding and unyielding ruthlessness.

Yet manifestations of Grandet's monomania do not, by themselves, dominate the novel. Rather, Grandet's avarice competes for importance with another, complementary plot: the awakening of Grandet's daughter to love. Indeed, in *Eugénie Grandet*, the three subjects that have been identified as key themes in Balzac's fiction—madness, money, and the search for love—converge. Grandet's obsession with money comes into conflict with Eugénie's equally strong impulse to love. While her father's nature is to hoard money even if it means that his family must be destitute, Eugénie finds in giving away all of her money to her beloved cousin, Charles, a supreme expression of love.

Balzac pits his young heroine against other adversaries as well: provincial opportunism, social morality, and Charles's ambitions. Using his innocent and naïve heroine as a foil, Balzac reveals the crass motives of provincial society, contrasting Eugénie's exceptional, giving nature with the self-interest of others who, like Eugénie's father, are motivated primarily by money. Balzac placed *Eugénie Grandet* into the subcategory of *The Human Comedy* titled "Scenes of Provincial Life."

PÈRE GORIOT

Published in 1835, *Père Goriot*, given its Parisian locale, could easily have been placed into the category of *The Human Comedy* called "Scenes of Parisian Life."

Balzac finally classified it, however, among his "Scenes of Private Life," which is an equally suitable designation for the novel. *Père Goriot* is a pivotal novel of *The Human Comedy* in several ways. First, with respect to Balzac's trademark, the use of recurring characters, nearly all the characters in this novel, whether their roles are large or small, can be found somewhere else in Balzac's opus, with the exception of Goriot himself. Some characters were already seen in works published before 1835; others would be developed in subsequent novels. Eugène de Rastignac, the young hero of *Père Goriot*, for example, appeared briefly as a friend of Raphaël de Valentin in *The Wild Ass's Skin*. Similarly, Goriot's older daughter, Anasthasie, was already portrayed in a short novel, *Gobseck*, published in 1830. The criminal Jacques Collin, alias Vautrin, who makes his debut in *Père Goriot*, would be given prominent roles in such later works as *Lost Illusions* and *The Splendors and Miseries of Courtesans*.

Balzac successfully interweaves three different plots in *Père Goriot*, their relationship being that the principal protagonists of all three live in the same Parisian boardinghouse, La Maison Vauquer. Eugène de Rastignac is an innocent provincial young man, new to Parisian manners but eager to learn. In a sense, Rastignac takes up the same crusade as does Raphaël de Valentin in *The Wild Ass's Skin*, in that he directs all his efforts toward "conquering" society—which means that, like Valentin, he strives to earn social acceptance and esteem. One notes, however, that Balzac does not make Rastignac a writer, like Valentin. Rather, shadowing another part of Balzac's own past, the young hero of *Père Goriot* is a poor law student.

Old Goriot himself is another inhabitant of La Maison Vauquer. He is a Balzacian monomaniac, a hero whose "madness" is self-willed and consciously directed. Goriot is not, however, another copy of Balzac's miser, Grandet; rather, Balzac opposes these two figures. Goriot is not a miser; he does not hoard money. On the contrary, he spends it on his two daughters, Anasthasie and Delphine. Whereas Grandet causes his family to live like paupers in order to continue amassing money, Goriot willingly strips himself of his means of sustenance in order to continue giving money to his daughters. Balzac's intent in portraying Goriot may have been to examine the power of money in a situation that contrasts directly with that of his miser, Grandet. Certainly, Balzac never found a more intense formula for tragedy than when he created his monomaniac Goriot, who attempts to link money and love.

The third major plot of *Père Goriot* centers on another inhabitant of La Maison Vauquer, Vautrin, who—unbeknown to the other boarders of Madame Vauquer's establishment—is an escaped convict wanted by the police. Vautrin's view of society is in absolute opposition to that of Rastignac; whereas the young man attempts to court social favor, Vautrin denounces everything to do with the social order, calling it a *bourbier*, or mud hole. Intelligent and cynical, Vautrin advocates a different sort of social conquest, namely, bold defiance and outright rebellion.

Unlike most of the preceding novels in *The Human Comedy*, *Père Goriot* is a novel with multiple heroes and multiple plots. Balzac offers the reader a fresco of social manners through characters who represent very different classes of society, from the aristocrat and the bourgeois to the criminal *révolté*. Balzac uses his technique of portraying protagonists from various contrasting angles—seen in *The Vicar of Tours* and in *Eugénie Grandet*—much more extensively in *Père Goriot*. Goriot, Goriot's daughters, Rastignac, Vautrin, and other characters as well are alternately judged to be admirable, honest, and powerful, and to be imperfect, deceitful, and helpless. Goriot, in particular, is delineated by means of a kaleidoscope of contrary impressions. He loves his daughters, but he also hates them. His love is fatherly and not so fatherly. He is both self-sacrificing and self-interested. In death, he curses his daughters and pardons them in the same breath. Clearly, in *Père Goriot*, Balzac reached maturity as a novelist.

COUSIN BETTE

Cousin Bette was published rather late in Balzac's career, in 1846, and was placed, along with a complementary work titled *Cousin Pons*, among the "Scenes of Parisian Life." In the ten years between the publication of *Père Goriot* and that of *Cousin Bette*, Balzac wrote approximately forty-five other novels, many of which continued to develop the three major themes in his fiction—madness, money, and the search for love and success.

It is interesting to see all three themes once again in-terwoven in *Cousin Bette*, albeit in a strikingly different manner. In one of the novel's subplots, a new type of monomania is depicted in Baron Hulot d'Evry, who is driven repeatedly to commit adultery although his actions are an embarrassment to himself, his wife, and his family. Balzac hints at Hulot's hidden motivation when he describes his protagonist's wife, Adeline, as a martyr figure, a religious zealot, and a model of propriety.

Elisabeth Fischer—called Cousin Bette—is aware that the Hulot family, headed by Adeline, receives her only out of family duty and that, as a poor relation, she is neither loved nor esteemed by them. Even though she realizes that the apparent good fortune and happiness of the Hulot family are a carefully contrived sham, Bette is jealous of her cousin Adeline for having always been prettier, wealthier, and more successful than she. Cousin Bette's vengeance against the Hulot family, which is the principal plot of the novel, incorporates all three of the major themes of Balzac's fiction. Because Cousin Bette has no money, no success, and no love, her maddened drive for vengeance is unleashed. Her desire for revenge becomes a mania, and she is soon driven to the point where there is absolutely no limit to what she will do to ruin her cousin's life, including finding new females to entice both the Baron and Adeline's proposed son-in-law, Steinbock.

As though to intensify the diabolical power of Cousin Bette, Balzac adds to it the equally unscrupulous machinations of his heroine's pretty neighbor, Valérie Marneffe. Valérie helps Bette carry out her revenge against the Hulot family, and Bette, in return, aids her neighbor in an enterprise to extract money from her many male admirers. Valérie, a beautiful and ambitious middle-class woman, discovers that she can find financial success by seducing men and making them pay for her love. It is interesting that when Valérie is given the chance to run away to South America with an exotic Brazilian nobleman who loves her sincerely, she refuses in order to continue the business of her lucrative and ego-building seductions. In *Cousin Bette*, the achievement of an ideal love, like that glimpsed in earlier novels such as *The Wild Ass's Skin* and *Louis Lambert*, is seen as utterly impossible.

In *Cousin Bette*, Balzac makes a mockery not only of love but also of monomania. Through a gross exaggeration, this eccentric passion no longer characterizes a single figure of the novel, as in *Eugénie Grandet* or *Père Goriot*. Rather, no fewer than three characters of the novel can be called monomaniacs: Cousin Bette, Valérie Marneffe, and Baron Hulot. It is true, however, that the two females are far more developed than Hulot. These two female protagonists, as they strengthen and complement each other, offer a hyperbolic image of monomania, parodying one of the trademarks of Balzac's fiction. By means of this parody, Balzac plainly shows that he has dissociated himself from his characters' plight. Perhaps he was able to satirize monomania because his career as a novelist was unquestionably successful, and he was beginning to receive some of the recognition he had always sought. Nevertheless, his own "mania" persisted: Until he simply became too sick to write, he continued to work on yet another novel in *The Human Comedy*, with ten more volumes projected and endless bills to pay.

Sonja G. Stary

OTHER MAJOR WORKS

SHORT FICTION: *Les Contes drolatiques*, 1832-1837 (*Droll Stories*, 1874, 1891).

PLAYS: *Vautrin*, pr., pb. 1840 (English translation, 1901); *La Marâtre*, pr., pb. 1848 (*The Stepmother*, 1901, 1958); *Le Faiseur*, pr. 1849 (also known as *Mercadet*; English translation, 1901); *The Dramatic Works*, 1901 (2 volumes; includes *Vautrin*, *The Stepmother*, *Mercadet*, *Quinola's Resources*, and *Pamela Giraud*); *Cromwell*, pb. 1925 (wr. 1819-1820).

NONFICTION: *Correspondance*, 1819-1850, 1876 (*The Correspondence*, 1878); *Lettres à l'étrangère*, 1899-1950; *Letters to Madame Hanska*, 1900 (translation of volume 1 of *Lettres à l'étrangère*).

BIBLIOGRAPHY

Beizer, Janet L. *Family Plots: Balzac's Narrative Generations*. New Haven, Conn.: Yale University Press, 1986. A careful study of the family and other hierarchies in Balzac's novels. Argues that the structure of the family itself is an ordering principle of the fiction. Introduction clearly situates this work in the tradition of Balzac criticism while making clear how it differs from earlier studies.

Bell, David F. *Real Time: Accelerating Narrative from Balzac to Zola*. Urbana: University of Illinois Press, 2004. Cites examples from novels and short stories to explore how the accelerated movement of people and information in the nineteenth century was a crucial element in the work of Balzac and three other French authors.

Bloom, Harold, ed. *Honoré de Balzac*. Philadelphia: Chelsea House, 2003. One in a series of books designed to introduce readers to the works of significant authors. In addition to Bloom's introductory overview, features essays analyzing *The Wild Ass's Skin*, *Cousin Pons*, *Eugénie Grandet*, *Père Goriot*, and *Cousin Bette*.

Festa-McCormick, Diana. *Honoré de Balzac*. Boston: Twayne, 1979. Provides an excellent introduction to the works of Balzac. Describes with much subtlety Balzac's evolution as a novelist and offers insightful comments on his representations of women. Contains a very well annotated bibliography.

Garval, Michael D. "Honoré de Balzac: Writing the Monument." In *"A Dream of Stone": Fame, Vision, and Monumentality in Nineteenth-Century French Literary Culture*. Newark: University of Delaware Press, 2004. Chapter on Balzac is part of a volume that describes how France in the nineteenth century developed an ideal image of "great" writers, viewing these authors' work as immortal and portraying their literary successes in monumental terms. The work as a whole traces the rise and fall of this literary development by focusing on Balzac, George Sand, and Victor Hugo.

Madden, James. *Weaving Balzac's Web: Spinning Tales and Creating the Whole of "La Comédie humaine."* Birmingham, Ala.: Summa, 2003. Explores how Balzac structured his vast series of novels to create continuity both within and between the individual books. Describes how internal narration, in which characters tell each other stories about other characters, enables the recurring characters to provide layers of meaning that are evident throughout the series.

Maurois, André. *Prometheus: The Life of Balzac*. Translated by Norman Denny. New York: Harper & Row, 1965. The standard biography of Balzac analyzes the author's formative years, his place in the Parisian literary circles of the 1830's and 1840's, and his long relationship with Evelina Hanska. Makes judicious use of Balzac's extant letters in order to give readers a sense of Balzac's personality.

Pritchett, V. S. *Balzac*. New York: Alfred A. Knopf, 1973. Beautifully illustrated book by an eminent writer and literary critic enables readers to understand the milieu in which Balzac wrote. Presents interpretations of Balzac's short stories and his novel *The Wild Ass's Skin* that are especially thought-provoking. Includes a good bibliography of critical studies on Balzac.

Robb, Graham. *Balzac: A Life*. New York: W. W. Norton, 1994. Detailed biographical account of the life and work of Balzac focuses on his philosophical perspectives as well as on his fiction. Speculates on the psychological motivations underlying his work.

Rogers, Samuel. *Balzac and the Novel*. Madison: University of Wisconsin Press, 1953. Thoughtful study of Balzac's narrative techniques and his use of recurring characters in *The Human Comedy*. Also de-scribes Balzac's portrayal of different social classes in his novels.

Thomas, Gwen. "The Case of the Missing Detective: Balzac's *Une Ténébreuse Affaire*." *French Studies* 48 (July, 1994): 285-298. Discusses how Balzac, in his novel *The Gondreville Mystery*, anticipates a number of the conventions that would come to be associated with the detective story. Argues that Balzac retains gaps and indeterminacies in his work and that his final revelation is a literary device rather than a logical conclusion.

Zweig, Stefan. *Balzac*. Translated by William Rose and Dorothy Rose, edited by Richard Friedenthal. New York: Viking Press, 1946. After Maurois, Zweig is the best biographer of Balzac. This fascinating book reads almost like a novel about the author's life. Zweig's tendency to offer his own interpretations of events makes his work more subjective than Maurois's, and perhaps less reliable in some particulars, but it remains an excellent introduction for the nonspecialist.

TONI CADE BAMBARA

Born: New York, New York; March 25, 1939
Died: Philadelphia, Pennsylvania; December 9, 1995
Also known as: Miltona Mirkin Cade

PRINCIPAL LONG FICTION

The Salt Eaters, 1980
Those Bones Are Not My Child, 1999

OTHER LITERARY FORMS

Toni Cade Bambara (bam-BAHR-ah) is best known for her short stories, which appear frequently in anthologies. She has also received recognition as a novelist, essayist, journalist, editor, and screenwriter, as well as a social activist and community leader. Her stories depict the daily lives of ordinary people who live in the African American neighborhoods of Brooklyn, Harlem, and other sections of New York City and the rural South. Although she wrote in other genres, her short stories established her reputation. In *Gorilla, My Love* (1972), a collection of fifteen stories, Bambara focuses on the love of friends and neighborhood as she portrays the positive side of black family life and stresses the strengths of the African American community. These fast-paced stories, characterized by her use of the black dialect of the street, are full of humorous exchanges and verbal banter. *The Sea Birds Are Still Alive* (1977) is a collection of short stories that reflect Bambara's concern with people from other cultures; the title story focuses on the plight of Vietnamese refugees at the end of the Vietnam War. *Deep Sightings and Rescue Missions: Fiction, Essays, and Conversations*, a collection of Bambara's writings, most of which never appeared before in print, was published posthumously in 1996.

ACHIEVEMENTS

Toni Cade Bambara received the Peter Pauper Press Award in Journalism from the *Long Island Star* in 1958, the John Golden Award for Fiction from Queens College in 1959, and the Theater of Black Experience Award in 1969. She was also the recipient of the George Washington Carver Distinguished African American Lecturer Award from Simpson College, *Ebony*'s Achievement in the Arts Award, and the American Book Award, for *The Salt Eaters*, in 1981. *The Bombing of Osage Avenue* won the Best Documentary of 1986 Award from the Pennsylvania Association of Broadcasters and the Documentary Award from the National Black Programming Consortium in 1986.

As an editor of anthologies of the writings of African Americans, Bambara introduced thousands of college students to the works of these writers. She was a founder of the Southern Collective of African American Writers and played a major role in the 1984 Conference on Black Literature and the Arts at Emory University.

During the last fourteen years of her life, Bambara devoted her energies to the film industry, writing screenplays.

BIOGRAPHY

Miltona Mirkin Cade was born in New York City on March 25, 1939, to Helen Brent Henderson Cade. She grew up in Harlem, Bedford-Stuyvesant, and Queens, where she lived with her mother and her brother, Walter. She credited her mother with "cultivating her creative spirit and instilling in her a sense of independence and self-sufficiency." In 1970, after finding the name Bambara written in a sketchbook in her grandmother's trunk, she legally changed her surname to Bambara. She received a bachelor's degree in theater arts and English literature from Queens College in 1959, and that same year her first short story, "Sweet Town," was published in *Vendome* magazine. After studying in Italy and Paris, she earned a master's degree in American literature at City College of New York and completed additional studies in linguistics at New York University and the New School for Social Research. She was a social worker for the Harlem Welfare Center and director of recreation in the psychiatric division of Metro Hospital in New York City. She also taught in the Search for Education, Elevation, Knowledge (SEEK) program at City College.

In 1970, under the name Toni Cade, she published *The Black Woman: An Anthology*, a collection of essays, short fiction, poetry, and letters exploring the experiences of black women, with emphasis on their involvement with the Civil Rights movement and the women's movement. In 1971 she edited *Tales and Stories for Black Folks*, a collection of writings from students in her composition class along with works of well-known authors.

As an assistant professor at Livingston College at Rutgers University from 1969 to 1974, Bambara was active in black student organizations and arts

Toni Cade Bambara. (Joyce Middler)

groups. She was a visiting professor in Afro-American Studies at Emory University and an instructor in the School of Social Work at Atlanta University. In 1973, on a visit to Cuba, Bambara met with the Federation of Cuban Women, and in 1975 she traveled to Vietnam. These experiences served to broaden Bambara's view of the importance of community involvement and political action and provided subject matter for the stories in *The Sea Birds Are Still Alive*.

Bambara and her daughter, Karma, lived in Atlanta from 1974 to 1986, during which time Bambara continued to be active in community political and artistic organizations, hosting potluck dinners in her home and organizing writers and artists in the community. In 1986 Bambara moved to Philadelphia, where she continued her active participation in the community and worked on *The Bombing of Osage Avenue*, a 1986 documentary film about the bombing of a house where a group of black nationalists lived. She also worked on a film about African American writer Zora Neale Hurston.

Bambara was known as a writer, civil rights activist, teacher, and supporter of the arts. Her work represents her dedication to the African American community and her desire to portray the ordinary lives of the people who live in those communities. As a lecturer and teacher she worked to raise the consciousness of other African Americans and to encourage a sense of pride in their heritage. Bambara died of cancer in a suburb of Philadelphia on December 9, 1995.

ANALYSIS

Toni Cade Bambara's work reflects her experiences with political action committees and her belief in the necessity for social responsibility. The political activism of the 1960's and 1970's provides the subject matter for her work, as she explores the consequences of the Civil Rights movement and divisions in the African American community. In describing this community, Bambara portrays the individual characters with affection and humor.

THE SALT EATERS

Set in the 1970's, Bambara's novel *The Salt Eaters* focuses on the effects of the Civil Rights movement on the inhabitants of the small town of Claybourne, Georgia. The plot centers on the attempted suicide of the novel's main character, Velma Henry, a community activist who has tried to kill herself by slitting her wrists and sticking her head in an oven. The other major character is Minnie Ransom, a conjure woman who uses her healing powers to restore Velma to health. Minor characters include Fred Holt, the bus driver; Obie, Velma's husband; and Dr. Julius Meadows. These members of the African American community are suffering from the fragmentation and alienation that have occurred in the wake of the Civil Rights movement. Velma has been so filled with rage that she has sought death as an answer to her pain. The novel traces Velma's journey from despair to mental and spiritual health. Bambara's own experiences with political activism provided her with the background for the events of the novel.

Throughout the novel, Bambara stresses the importance of choice. In the opening line, Minnie Ransom asks Velma, "Are you sure, sweetheart, that you want to be well?" Freedom of choice requires acceptance of responsibility. If Velma is to heal herself, she must make a conscious choice of health over despair. Characters in the novel are seen in relationship to the larger community. Godmother Sophie M'Dear reminds Velma that her life is not solely her own, but that she has a connection and obligation to her family and community. Other characters are reminded of their responsibility to others. When Buster gets Nadeen pregnant, her uncle Thurston arrives with a gun, ordering Buster to attend parenting classes. Doc Serge tells Buster that abortion is not a private choice but a choice that involves the whole community. The characters echo Bambara's belief that membership in a community entails responsibilities to that community.

For most of the novel Velma sits on a stool in a hospital, suffering from depression, overwhelming fatigue, and mental collapse. She remains immobile and seemingly frozen as scenes from the past and present play in her mind in no particular order. Other characters seem to whirl past Velma and blend into one another, reflecting the problems that have brought Velma to this hospital room. Bambara shows that these problems are a result of alienation from the community. Because of his light skin, education, and profession, Dr. Julius Meadows has lost touch with his roots. Through a chance encounter with two young black men, Julius begins his journey back to the black community. Reflecting on the encounter, Julius feels that "whatever happened, he wasn't stumbling aimlessly around the streets anymore, at loose ends, alone."

Meadows's journey back into the black community parallels Velma's journey to health. Alienation from the community had brought Velma to the brink of destruction, and realignment with the community heals her. Velma's journey is similar to the spiritual journey of Tayo, the Native American protagonist in Leslie Marmon Silko's *Ceremony* (1977). The horrors Tayo experienced as a prisoner of the Japanese during World War II and the sense of alienation he experiences when he returns to his Laguna reservation have nearly destroyed his will to survive. Through immersion in the Native American culture, traditions, beliefs, and stories, Tayo finds his way back to health. Like Tayo, as Velma embraces her cultural heritage, she begins to heal.

The predominant image in the novel is the vision of the mud mothers painting the walls of their cave. This recurring vision haunts Velma until she sees the cave as a symbol of cultural history and identity. Other characters reflect on the responsibility of the older generation to educate and nurture the children of the community. If the children are forgetting the values of the community, it is because the elders have failed in their responsibility to instill community values in the young.

Bambara demonstrates in the novel that to keep traditions alive, every generation has to be nurtured and educated, has to be taught the old stories. At times the novel seems to be a catalog of African American cultural history, which includes African tribal customs and rituals, slave ships, and names of famous leaders. In the early part of the novel, Ruby, one of the most politically active characters, laments the loss of leaders and causes: "Malcolm gone, King gone, Fanni Lou gone, Angela quiet, the movement splintered, enclaves unconnected." Near the end of the novel, Velma realizes how much she has learned from the leaders and influences that are part of her background, "Douglass, Tubman, the slave narratives, the songs, the fables, Delaney, Ida Wells, Blyden, Du Bois, Garvey, the singers, her parents, Malcolm, Coltrane."

Bambara enriches the novel with background from folk legends and literary works. At times she merely mentions a name, such as Shine, the famous African American trickster, or the legendary Stagolee, who killed a man for his hat. Fred's friend Porter, borrowing a term from Ralph Ellison's novel *Invisible Man* (1952), explains his feelings about being black: "They call the Black man the Invisible Man. . . . Our natures are unknowable, unseeable to them." The following lines show how Bambara packs cultural, historical, and political history into one sentence: "Several hotheads, angry they had been asleep in the Sixties or too young to participate, had been galvanized by the arrival in their midst of the legless vet who used to career around Claybourne fast and loose on a hot garage dolly."

In contrast to the positive images, Bambara shows the negative side of society in describing the "boymen" who hang around women in grocery stores begging for money in a ritual she calls "market theater." In another scene, Ruby complains about the way women have had to carry the burden of improving society, "taking on . . . drugs, prisons, alcohol, the schools, rape, battered women, abused children," while the men make no contribution.

One of the most distinctive aspects of Bambara's style is her use of black dialect, with its colorful vocabulary, playful banter, and unique phrasing and speech patterns. At times the rhythm and rhyme of phrases give a musical quality to the prose: "Cause the stars said and the energy belts led and the cards read and the cowries spread." At other times Bambara describes the atmosphere in musical terms: "the raga reggae bumpidity bing zing was pouring out all over Fred Holt" and "the music drifted out over the trees . . . maqaam now blending with the bebop of Minnie Ransom's tapes."

The major theme of the novel is that identification with one's cultural history can be liberating and empowering. In *The Salt Eaters*, loss of cultural identity has brought despair. Bambara provides flashbacks to the civil rights struggles of the 1960's and the legacy of slavery. As they fight for political power, African Americans must remember the past and maintain their best traditions. As Velma begins to heal, she thinks that she knows "how to build resistance, make the journey to the center of the circle . . . stay centered in the best of her people's traditions."

Judith Barton Williamson

OTHER MAJOR WORKS

SHORT FICTION: *Gorilla, My Love*, 1972; *The Sea Birds Are Still Alive: Collected Stories*, 1977; *Raymond's Run: Stories for Young Adults*, 1989.

SCREENPLAYS: *The Bombing of Osage Avenue*, 1986 (documentary); *W. E. B. Du Bois: A Biography in Four Voices*, 1995 (with Amiri Baraka, Wesley Brown, and Thulani Davis).

NONFICTION: "What It Is I Think I'm Doing Anyhow" in *The Writer on Her Work*, 1981.

EDITED TEXTS: *The Black Woman: An Anthology*, 1970; *Tales and Stories for Black Folks*, 1971; *Southern Exposure*, 1976 (periodical; edited volume 3).

MISCELLANEOUS: *Deep Sightings and Rescue Missions: Fiction, Essays, and Conversations*, 1996.

BIBLIOGRAPHY

Alwes, Derek. "The Burden of Liberty: Choice in Toni Morrison's *Jazz* and Toni Cade Bambara's *The Salt Eaters*." *African American Review* 30, no. 3 (Fall, 1996): 353-365. Compares the works of Morrison and Bambara, arguing that whereas Morrison wants readers to participate in a choice, Bambara wants them to choose to participate. Asserts that Bambara's message is that happiness is possible if people refuse to forget the past and continue to participate in the struggle.

Butler-Evans, Elliott. *Race, Gender, and Desire: Narrative Strategies in the Fiction of Toni Cade Bambara, Toni Morrison, Alice Walker*. Philadelphia: Temple University Press, 1989. In the first book-length study to treat Bambara's fiction to any extent, Butler-Evans uses narratology and feminism to explore Bambara's works as well as those of two other important female African American writers.

Collins, Janelle. "Generating Power: Fission, Fusion, and Post-modern Politics in Bambara's *The Salt Eaters*." *MELUS* 21, no. 2 (Summer, 1996): 35-47. Examines nuclear power as a key metaphor in the novel, noting how Bambara raises ecological and ethical concerns about nuclear energy. Argues that Bambara's nationalist and feminist positions inform the novel's text as the author advocates political and social change.

Evans, Mari, ed. *Black Women Writers (1950-1980): A Critical Evaluation*. Garden City, N.Y.: Anchor Press/Doubleday, 1984. In the essay "Salvation Is the Issue," Bambara says that the elements of her own work that she deems most important are laughter, use of language, sense of community, and celebration.

Holmes, Linda J., and Cheryl A. Wall, eds. *Savoring the Salt: The Legacy of Toni Cade Bambara*. Philadelphia: Temple University Press, 2007. Collection of insightful essays commemorates Bambara's life, her writings, and the importance of her contributions to African American literature. Contributors include Toni Morrison, Amiri Baraka, Ruby Dee, Nikki Giovanni, and Audre Lorde.

Shinn, Thelma J. "Orbiting Home: Toni Cade Bambara." In *Women Shapeshifters: Transforming the Contemporary Novel*. Westport, Conn.: Greenwood Press, 1996. Chapter on Bambara's novels is included in a larger examination of how twentieth century women authors transformed the novel's structure by combining the traditions of Romantic and realistic fiction.

Taylor, Carole Anne. "Postmodern Disconnection and the Archive of Bones: Toni Cade Bambara's Last Work." *Novel: A Forum on Fiction* 35 (Spring/Summer, 2002): 258-280. Discusses Bambara's self-referential storytelling in *Deep Sightings and Rescue Misions*, where the stories refer to their own creation, and in her last novel, *Those Bones Are Not My Child*, which refers to Bambara's own life as a mother, writer, activist, and filmmaker.

Vertreace, Martha M. *Toni Cade Bambara*. New York: Macmillan Library Reference, 1998. The first full-length resource devoted to the entirety of Bambara's career. Provides information useful for students of the author's works.

Willis, Susan. "Problematizing the Individual: Toni Cade Bambara's Stories for the Revolution." In *Specifying: Black Women Writing the American Experience*. Madison: University of Wisconsin Press, 1987. Clear and informative essay analyzes Bambara's work, focusing largely on *The Salt Eaters* while also commenting on her most important short fiction.

RUSSELL BANKS

Born: Newton, Massachusetts; March 28, 1940
Also known as: Russell Earl Banks

PRINCIPAL LONG FICTION

Family Life, 1975 (revised 1988)
Hamilton Stark, 1978
The Book of Jamaica, 1980
The Relation of My Imprisonment, 1983
Continental Drift, 1985
Affliction, 1989
The Sweet Hereafter, 1991
Rule of the Bone, 1995
Cloudsplitter, 1998
The Darling, 2004
The Reserve, 2008

OTHER LITERARY FORMS

Russell Banks has published several short-story collections, including *Searching for Survivors* (1975), *The New World* (1978), *Trailerpark* (1981), *Success Stories* (1986), and *The Angel on the Roof: The Stories of Russell Banks* (2000). His poetry has been collected in *Fifteen Poems* (1967), *30/6* (1969), *Waiting to Freeze* (1969), and *Snow: Meditations of a Cautious Man in Winter* (1974). His account of the American experience—a commentary on the country's literature, film, politics, and history—appears in *Dreaming up America* (2008).

ACHIEVEMENTS

As several critics have observed, Russell Banks's novels explore the struggles of New England's white working class with a sharp eye and unrelenting focus. In part, his achievement derives from his own experience, including the torment of dealing with a broken family and an inchoate rage at a world that boxes in the individual and makes him or her feel alienated from the middle class and the privileged.

BIOGRAPHY

Russell Earl Banks grew up in a working-class family, the oldest of four children. His alcoholic father left the family when Banks was twelve years old. The family then moved from Newton, Massachusetts, to Barnstead, New Hampshire. Angry and directionless, sixteen-year-old Banks stole a car, yet he was a good student and won a full scholarship to attend Colgate University. He soon dropped out, feeling uncomfortable among middle-class students, and went to work as a plumber (his father had been a pipe fitter). The twenty-year-old Banks tried to join Fidel Castro's army in Cuba. Failing to do so, he married Darlene Bennett in June, 1962, and fathered the first of four daughters. The marriage failed and Banks moved on. He divorced Bennett and married Mary Gunst. This time, his mother-in-law, spotting his talent, supported his education at the University of North Carolina at Chapel Hill. He graduated Phi Beta Kappa in 1967. His second marriage ended in 1977.

Chapel Hill proved a turning point in the novelist's life. Banks discovered the joys of writing (concentrating mainly on poetry and short fiction) and became engaged with politics. In 1982, he began teaching composition courses; he also married Kathy Walton, an editor. The couple divorced in 1988. He then married Chase Twichell, a poet, in 1989.

Banks's early novels focus on characters living the kind of hard New England life that Banks himself had experienced. Critics describe his early stories and novels as bleak. His main characters are hard to like and rarely are successful. However, the dark energy of his work has been compared to that of Edgar Allan Poe and Herman Melville.

Not until *Continental Drift*, Banks's fifth novel, did he begin to receive attention as a major writer. This ambitious work features a complex social canvas of characters based on Banks's New England experience. The novel also has a more accessible style—leaner and stronger—than earlier experimental novels such as *Family Life* and *Trailerpark*.

ANALYSIS

Russell Banks's novels explore how individuals and communities suffer through and attempt to master their own lives. In *The Sweet Hereafter*, for example, four narrators confront the meaning of a tragic bus accident that took the lives of fourteen children and changed their Adirondack community forever. Banks pursues a similar narrator-main character symbiosis in *Affliction*, the story of Rolfe Whitehouse's quest to piece together the events leading up to his brother's disappearance. The same theme runs through *Cloudsplitter*, in which John Brown's son Owen recounts his troubled relationship with his father and the events driving the Brown family toward the fatal raid in 1859 on the Harper's Ferry armory, which was to be Brown's crowning blow against slavery. Owen feels compelled to retell and analyze his father's life.

The hero of *Hamilton Stark* has been described as a misanthropic pipe fitter, apparently modeled on Banks's father. The narrator who seeks to understand Stark has been compared to Nick Carraway of F. Scott Fitzgerald's *The Great Gatsby* (1925), which is high praise indeed and indicative of Banks's ability to not only submerse himself in his characters but also provide a perspective on them.

Stories in Banks's novels are usually filtered through the perspective of a narrator attempting to establish or reconnect with the main characters. Thus, the narrative of a Banks novel is itself an act of reconstruction: Getting the story in the proper order obsesses the narrator, whose own fate depends on understanding the lives of those who have touched him or her.

CONTINENTAL DRIFT

This novel focuses on two main characters who leave home to start a new life in Florida. Bob Dubois, thirty years old and living in New Hampshire, and Vanise Dorsinville, a young Haitian mother who emigrates to America, both seek a kind of visionary future that will lift them out of the rut of materialism and the day-to-day routines of their lives. What unites them is Banks's austere, unsentimental prose.

As the novel's title suggests, these two lives seem part of a broader movement, the ever-shifting versions of the American Dream to pursue happiness and find a better life. Banks's ability to imagine these different lives in extraordinary detail and from a panoramic perspective earned the plaudits of critics who suggested the author's work was now entering the mainstream of American fiction.

CLOUDSPLITTER

In this historical novel, Owen Brown narrates the story of his father's life and his own ambivalent feelings about the course of events that led to the raid on the government armory at Harper's Ferry, Virginia. The raid was the doomed culmination of a plan to foment a slave uprising that would (the Browns and their followers hoped) ultimately result in the abolition of slavery. The novel's structure reflects Banks's well-established method of making his novels as much about the teller as the tale.

Although Owen was not actually at his father's side in the raid at Harper's Ferry, Banks's decision to use him as the narrator proves ingenious, since Owen is free to describe his father and events from his own unique perspective that cannot be contradicted by the historical record. Owen is writing a memoir to understand his own involvement with his father and with history. He supplies a psychodynamic description of himself and his father that is beyond what is permissible in historical accounts.

Russell Banks. (© Miriam Berkley)

At first deeply disturbed by his father's rigid inflexibility and willingness to shed the slaveholders' blood, Owen becomes his father's most faithful disciple, abandoning him only when it becomes clear that the Harper's Ferry raid cannot succeed. Owen, who is subject to temptations of the flesh and to a conflicted attitude about race, exposes the wide range of emotions that his father abjures in his single-minded plan of attack on slavery. John Brown hardens himself into a symbol, and Owen confesses his failure to do likewise. However, Owen's very lack of fanaticism—or rather his embrace and then rejection of his father's extremism—makes Owen's narrative redolent of the human contradictions and tensions that John Brown steeled himself against.

Cloudsplitter is steeped in the antebellum period, providing vivid scenes not only of John Brown and his cohort but also of Frederick Douglass, who admires Brown yet counsels him that his raid cannot succeed.

THE DARLING

In *The Darling*, Dawn Carrington narrates her life story, including her years as a revolutionary in the Weather Underground, as the wife of a Liberian cabinet minister, and as a farmer in upstate New York. Born Hannah Musgrave in a well-to-family (her father is a famous pediatrician reminiscent of Dr. Benjamin Spock), she describes a fierce idealistic streak that is temporarily suspended when she becomes a government official's wife but is aroused once again when Charles Taylor, her husband's colleague, launches an uprising against Liberia's corrupt, dictatorial regime. Unfortunately, Taylor ignites a wave of bestial violence that is even worse than the depredations of his predecessors, and Carrington consequently is forced to reassess the trajectory of her life and how she could have so misjudged events and her own complicity in the horrors of history.

Like many of Banks's other narrators, Carrington is not very likeable. In fact, she is quite cold and rather inhuman in her overweening concern with saving humanity while contributing to situations that result in the sacrifice and suffering of those close to her. She is a fascinating narrator, though, precisely because she does not pity or excuse her excesses. In retrospect, she recounts the folly and callousness involved in many of her relationships.

The novel takes its place among Banks's stories exploring migratory characters seeking new visions of themselves through traveling to new lands. A failed revolutionary at home (Carrington was living underground when she escaped with her friend Zack to Liberia), she cannot content herself with the routines of a politician's life and thus is lured back into the world of revolutionary politics she thought she had abjured. Given her sorry record of radical failure, the term she uses for herself, "the darling," is ironic.

Critics were impressed with Banks's ability to write from a woman's perspective—not only about radical politics but also about Carrington's experience as a lover and mother (she gives birth to two sons who become victims of the Liberian civil war). Also, Banks describes U.S. involvement in Liberian politics with a sure hand. The scenes of the Liberian civil war are gruesome and stark, giving the novel an austere, documentary feel.

THE RESERVE

The novel is set in an exclusive community, The Reserve, in the Adirondacks. It is the preserve of old-money investors who have built cottages around two lakes but otherwise have made every effort to ward off the modern world. A strict set of rules governs the way that property can be used, allowing for the persistence of an unspoiled nature. Guides take visitors in and out of The Reserve, but nonlocals must stay at the clubhouse.

It is the 1930's and Jordan Groves, an artist modeled after Rockwell Kent, famous for his illustrations of William Shakespeare and Moby Dick, finds the finicky exclusivity of The Reserve an affront. He flies into the community to see Dr. Cole, an art collector. Making a dramatic landing on the lake near the doctor's cottage—which means Jordan has already broken The Reserve's rules concerning modes of transportation—Jordan becomes entranced with the doctor's divorced daughter, the beautiful Vanessa, a Fitzgeraldesque character whose emotional instability is reminiscent of the famous Zelda Fitzgerald, about whom her husband wrote in *Tender Is the Night* (1934).

The daring Vanessa provokes the married Jordan into taking her away in his plane. Rather like Ernest Hemingway's character Robert Jordan, the hero of *For Whom the Bell Tolls* (1940), Banks's Jordan recklessly allows

Vanessa to fly the plane, but he returns her to The Reserve, having determined this time not to be unfaithful to his wife, although he finds Vanessa sorely tempting.

Vanessa's world comes apart when her father dies from a heart attack. Hysterical over fears that her mother will have her committed, she pursues Jordan, who on a visit to Dr. Cole's cottage becomes implicated in the death of Vanessa's mother, the result of an unfortunate accident that Vanessa now wants Jordan and her father's guide, Hubert St. Germain, to cover up.

The plot is further complicated because Hubert has been having an affair with Jordan's wife, whom Jordan has taken for granted. Shattered by this infidelity, Jordan decides to join his friend John Dos Passos in Spain, where Jordan will fly planes for the Spanish Republic against Francisco Franco's Fascist rebellion. Inevitably, Jordan's action calls to mind Hemingway's Jordan, although Banks's literary allusion is sardonic. While his Jordan will be hailed as a hero, the novel reveals a rather cold, self-absorbed man who has much in common with Banks's other major characters, those other darlings who put themselves at the center of history with rather alarming results.

This highly romantic yet unsentimental novel cunningly explores the interactions of egos and events. Once again, Banks probes the psychology of radicalism and finds it wanting. What makes his case against Groves especially compelling is Bank's deft portrayal of the simple but sound Hubert as well as of the other guides and working people in Depression era America who do not have the luxury of indulging in Groves's pretensions.

This meticulously researched novel oscillates between starkly different settings—the Adirondacks and Spain—recalling Banks's similar strategies in *Continental Drift* and *The Darling*. In both cases, the characters are strongly defined by their period—their choices the result of a concatenation of events over which they can exert little control. In this respect, Banks's sensibility seems similar to the determinist ethos of the real John Dos Passos's great U.S.A. trilogy.

Carl Rollyson

OTHER MAJOR WORKS

SHORT FICTION: *Searching for Survivors*, 1975; *The New World*, 1978; *Trailerpark*, 1981; *Success Stories*, 1986; *The Angel on the Roof: The Stories of Russell Banks*, 2000.

POETRY: *Fifteen Poems*, 1967 (with William Matthews and Newton Smith); *30/6*, 1969; *Waiting to Freeze*, 1969; *Snow: Meditations of a Cautious Man in Winter*, 1974.

NONFICTION: *The Autobiographical Eye*, 1982 (David Halpern, editor); *The Invisible Stranger: The Patten, Maine, Photographs of Arturo Patten*, 1999; *Dreaming up America*, 2008.

EDITED TEXT: *Brushes with Greatness: An Anthology of Chance Encounters with Greatness*, 1989 (with Michael Ondaatje and David Young).

BIBLIOGRAPHY

Charles, Katie. "The Best Novels You've Never Read." *New York*, June 4, 2007. Banks's novel *The Darling* is included in this critical analysis of some of the best underrated and unknown novels.

Hutchison, Anthony. "Representative Man: John Brown and the Politics of Redemption in Russell Banks's *Cloudsplitter*." *Journal of American Studies* 41, no. 1 (April, 2007): 67-82. Examines the issue and representation of race in Banks's novel *Cloudsplitter*. Hutchison argues that Banks captures the time's sense of disillusionment among Americans of all races and ethnicities.

Niemi, Robert. *Russell Banks*. New York: Twayne, 1997. An introductory study, part of the reliable Twayne's American Authors series. This volume provides critical analyses of Banks's fiction and a brief biography, chronology, and annotated bibliography.

Trucks, Rob. *The Pleasure of Influence: Conversations with American Male Fiction Writers*. West Lafayette, Ind.: NotaBell Books, 2002. A collection of comprehensive interviews of American male writers of fiction, including Banks, who discuss their literary influences and their own works.

JOHN BANVILLE

Born: Wexford, Ireland; December 8, 1945
Also known as: Benjamin Black

PRINCIPAL LONG FICTION

Nightspawn, 1971
Birchwood, 1973
Doctor Copernicus, 1976
Kepler, 1981
The Newton Letter, 1982 (novella)
Mefisto, 1986
The Book of Evidence, 1989
Ghosts, 1993
Athena, 1995
The Untouchable, 1997
Eclipse, 2000
Shroud, 2003
The Sea, 2005
Christine Falls, 2006 (as Benjamin Black)
The Silver Swan, 2007 (as Black)
The Lemur, 2008 (as Black)

OTHER LITERARY FORMS

The first book that John Banville (BAN-vihl) published was a collection of short stories, *Long Lankin* (1970), and he has written a small amount of uncollected short fiction. He has also written two plays and has collaborated in writing television adaptations of his novels *The Newton Letter* and *Birchwood*.

ACHIEVEMENTS

John Banville is one of the most original and successful Irish novelists of his generation. His work has received numerous awards, including the prestigious James Tait Black Memorial Prize, the American-Irish Foundation Award, the GPA Prize, and the Man Booker Prize. Reviewers have treated each of Banville's new works with increasing respect for the author's ambition, verbal felicity, and individuality, and Banville has inspired a sizable amount of critical commentary. The development of his career coincides with a period of restlessness and experimentation in Irish fiction.

Not the least significant of Banville's achievements

is that he has availed himself of the artistic example of such postwar masters of fiction as Jorge Luis Borges, Gabriel García Márquez, and Italo Calvino. By admitting such influences, as well as those of the great Irish modernists James Joyce and Samuel Beckett, Banville's fiction has embodied a new range of options for the Irish novel and has provided an international dimension to an often provincial literary culture.

BIOGRAPHY

John Banville was born in Wexford, the seat of Ireland's southeasternmost county, on December 8, 1945. He was educated locally, first at the Christian Brothers School and, on the secondary level, at St. Peter's College. After school, he worked for Aer Lingus, the Irish airline. Subsequently, he worked in England for the post office and, briefly, for a London publisher. Returning to Ireland, he worked as a subeditor for the *Irish Press*, a national daily, and then later went to work at the *Irish Times*, where he served as literary editor from 1988 to 1999. The recipient of numerous awards, he also spent a semester in the International Writing Program at the University of Iowa. In 2005, he received the prestigious Man Booker Prize for his novel *The Sea*.

ANALYSIS

John Banville's subject matter and methods of artistic execution form the basis of his reputation for originality. In the context of contemporary fiction, Banville is notable for his commitment, for his felicity of phrase, and for his relationship to an important fictional genre, the historical novel. He has communicated, through both his artistic strategies and his choices of material, some of the main questions faced by contemporary fiction—communicated them perhaps too conspicuously and with an ease and self-possession uncharacteristic of many contemporary writers. Some readers may find that Banville's manner is paradoxically at odds with his central themes.

Banville's short stories, his novella *The Newton Letter*, and his novels constitute a remarkably unified and consistent body of work. From the outset of his career, he has shown immense artistic self-possession and an equally assured possession of his themes. Over the years, his style, while not remaining constant, has undergone comparatively little change. It is therefore possible to speak of Banville in terms of a completeness and typicality that most novelists of his age are still in the process of discovering.

The unity and integrity that are the most striking features of Banville's career and oeuvre become more striking still by virtue of their being so thematically important in his work. Fascination with the spectacle of the mind in the act of creation is a major concern of this author, and his career may be described in terms of an increasingly deliberate and far-reaching series of attempts to articulate this subject. This preoccupation has given his work a range, ambition, and commitment to large concepts that are extremely rare in modern Irish fiction and only slightly less rare in contemporary fiction generally.

In addition, the manner in which Banville elaborates his interest in humanity's creative dimension commands more critical attention than it has received. For example, his fiction is suffused with hints suggesting links among artistic strategies, scientific inquiry, and historical actuality. From these, it is possible to detect a rudimentary, though sustained, critique of traditional epistemological procedures. To complement this critique, the typical Banville protagonist either discovers unsuspected modes of perception or believes that he has no choice but to set out deliberately to discover them.

Together with the intellectual commitment implicit in such concerns, Banville's work possesses a typically complete and essentially unchanging aesthetic apparatus through which ideas and fiction's critique may be perceived. Since it is central to Banville's artistic vision that fiction's critique of conceptual thinking be considered inevitable and unavoidable, his novels' aesthetic apparatus is largely premised on techniques of doubleness, repetition, echoes, and mirrors. Protagonists often have problematic brothers or missing twins. Personal experience finds its counterpart in historical events. The result is a paradox: The duplicitous character of experience, which renders humanity's possession of its existence so frail and tentative, impels people, precisely because of that very frailty, to anchor themselves in the presumed security of defined abstractions.

Despite the presence of these thematic concerns throughout Banville's output, and despite the fact that his treatment of them has always been marked more by an ironic playfulness than by earnest sermonizing, his first two works of fiction are somewhat callow. In particular, *Nightspawn*, the story of an Irish writer's adventures in Greece on the eve of the colonels' coup, treats the material with a kind of relentless playfulness that is both tiresome in itself and in questionable taste. Despite the author's admitted—though not uncritical—affection for this novel, and despite its containing in embryonic form the concerns that beset all of his work, *Nightspawn*, as perhaps its title suggests, is an example of a young writer allowing his wonderfully fertile imagination to run to baroque lengths.

BIRCHWOOD

It is more appropriate, therefore, to begin a detailed consideration of John Banville's fiction with his second

John Banville. (Getty Images)

novel, *Birchwood*. Like *Nightspawn*, this novel is written in the first person—arguably Banville's preferred narrative mode. In *Birchwood*, Gabriel Godkin, the protagonist, tells in retrospect the story of his dark heritage and his efforts to escape it. Again, as in *Nightspawn*, much of the material has baroque potential, which the novel's middle section, depicting Gabriel's adventures with the circus of a certain Prospero, accentuates rather than dispels.

The circus escapade shines in the novel like a good deed in an evil world. While Gabriel is within the protected ring of the circus troupe, he seems to be essentially immune from the troubles of his past and from the state of famine and unrest that consumes the country through which the circus travels. Thanks to Prospero, he is islanded and becalmed in the surrounding tempest. Even under such conditions of childish play, however, the world is not a safe place. Adult imperfections continually intrude. Crimes are committed in the name of love; futile and obsessive hostilities break out. Innocent Gabriel flees the disintegrating circle—it seems appropriate to think of the circus in etymological terms, since circle and ring possess strong connotations of unity and completeness.

Gabriel forsakes the circus in a state of rather paranoid distress and finds himself, still more distressingly, to have come full circle, back to where he started. Now, however, he finds himself compelled to face his origins, which lie in the house of doom that gives this novel its title. The first part of the novel gives the history of the Godkin family. Like the circus sequence, this opening section of *Birchwood* owes more to imagination than it does to actuality. Many readers will be reminded of both Edgar Allan Poe and William Faulkner by Banville's combination of brooding atmosphere and theme of cultural decay on which this section is premised. Banville's farcical tone, however, without prejudicing young Gabriel's sensitivity, prevents the heavy-handedness and extravagance to which the gothic nature of his material is in danger of giving rise. The seriousness with which the elder Godkins take their insecurities is rendered laughable by the incompetence that ensues from their transparent intensity.

Gabriel, however, for all of his alienation from his heritage's inadequacies, finds it impossible to do other than to confront them. In a novel that satirically articulates the cultural shibboleth of bad blood, Gabriel feels compelled to carry out an act of blood that will purge his house of the usurper. The usurper in question is Gabriel's twin brother, Michael. The novel ends with Gabriel in sole possession of Birchwood.

This turn of events, however, does not mean that Gabriel is able, or intends, to restore the house to its former glory, a glory in which he never participated. As a writer, he seems to have the objective of reclaiming the house as it really was rather than imagining it as something other, something that imaginative treatment would make easier to assimilate. In this objective, students of Irish literature may see a critique of the lofty status often accorded the Big House in the poetry of William Butler Yeats. An appreciation of Banville's fiction does not require that he be seen as a defacer of the cultural icons of a previous generation. Nevertheless, the status of the Big House in *Birchwood*, coupled with themes of survival, inheritance, and artistic expression, offers a sense of the oblique manner in which this author regards his own cultural heritage while at the same time situating his regard in the wider, more generic contexts of such concerns as individuality, history, the role of the artist, and the nature of the real.

Given the significant, if problematic, status of the Big House in modern Irish literature (Big House being the generic name given to the imposing mansions of the socially dominant, landowning Anglo-Irish class), the degree to which *Birchwood* avoids a specific historical context is noteworthy. The work provides a sufficient number of clues (the famine and unrest already mentioned, the frequent mention of "rebels" in the first part of the novel) to suggest that the locale is Ireland. A larger historical context is obviated, however, by the obsessive, and more psychologically archetypal, quality of Gabriel's sense of his personal history. The result is a novel that is ultimately too reflexive, private, and inward looking to be entirely satisfactory.

DOCTOR COPERNICUS

It may be that the author himself reached the same conclusion, given that in his next two novels, *Doctor Copernicus* and *Kepler*, a specific and detailed sense of history is an important dimension of events. *Doctor Copernicus* inaugurates Banville's most important and ambitious project, and the one on which his long-term international reputation will probably be based. This project consists of four books dealing with the nature of the creative personality, conceived of in terms of the scientific imagination. A subtitle for the series might be "The Scientist as Artist," meaning that Banville considers the accomplishments of Copernicus, Kepler, and Isaac Newton (subject of *The Newton Letter*) in the field of scientific inquiry to be comparable to what an artist might produce. The series concludes with *Mefisto*, which both crystallizes and challenges the assumptions of its predecessors. The most fundamental link joining the four books is chronological, *Mefisto* being set in contemporary Ireland. Although other, more sophisticated connections may be made among the four novels, each may also be read independently.

Doctor Copernicus is a fictionalized biography of the astronomer who revolutionized humanity's sense of its place in the order of creation. The biography is presented in such a way as to dramatize the crucial tensions between Copernicus and the history of his time. Beginning with the astronomer's unhappy childhood, the novel details the essentially flawed, anticlimactic, unfulfilling (and unfulfillable) nature of human existence as Copernicus experiences it. The protagonist's character is conceived in terms of his inability to give himself fully to the world of men and women and affairs, whether the affairs are those of state or of the heart.

Sojourning in Italy as a young man, Copernicus has a homosexual affair that temporarily makes him happy. He lacks the self-confidence and will to believe in his happiness, however, and rejects it in an attack of spleen and confusion. Later in his career, he is required to take a political role, negotiating with Lutheran enemies of the Catholic Church and administering Church properties. Although he discharges his obligations in a responsible manner, it is perfectly clear that, given the choice between being a man of his time or being a student of the stars in their eternal courses, Copernicus prefers the latter isolated, impersonal service. The imperfections of the world—not only in the aggregate, demonstrated by the machinations of history, but also intimately, embodied by the astronomer's syphilitic brother, Andreas—prove emotionally insupportable, philosophically unjustifiable, and morally anesthetizing. Finding no basis for

unity and completeness in the sorry state of mortal humans, Copernicus takes the not particularly logical but impressively imaginative step of considering the heavens.

The astronomer's declared intention in pursuing this line of inquiry is not to bring about the revolution that history commemorates in his name. On the contrary, Copernicus sees his pursuits as conservative, intended to assert a model of order, design, and harmony where it cannot be said for certain one exists. Copernicus's efforts are fueled by his will and spirit, and the intensity of his commitment should not be underestimated because his results are stated in mathematical terms. What his conclusions provide is the fiction of order, a fiction posited on the conceit of mathematics being essentially a rhetoric—a product of mind, not an offspring of matter. Indeed, as Copernicus's career in the world of things and people suggests, his fiction elicits worldlings' assent all the more urgently for being necessarily untrue.

KEPLER

Banville's approach as a biographer in *Doctor Copernicus* is strictly chronological, which gives the novel both scope and a sense of the inevitability of the protagonist's development. Copernicus's integrity, continually challenged, is nourished by the inevitable nature of his spiritual needs and tendencies; in *Kepler*, the approach is fundamentally the same. Instead of providing a chronology of Kepler's life, however, Banville concentrates on the astronomer's productive years, using flashbacks to illuminate and enlarge aspects of the protagonist's character, as the need arises. This approach shifts the narrative emphasis from the protagonist's temperament, as it was in *Doctor Copernicus*, to the protagonist's working conditions. The effect of this modulation in authorial standpoint is to give historical circumstances greater prominence than in the earlier work and thus provide, from an aesthetic perspective, an image of humankind in the world that reverses the one provided in *Doctor Copernicus*.

Kepler is far more life-loving (which Banville communicates as far more capable of love) than his predecessor. He is far more attuned to the eddies and quicksands of the historical forces of his time, consciously aligning himself with one set of forces rather than another instead of disdainfully and brokenheartedly attempting to rise above the forces, as Copernicus tries to do. Kepler's astronomy, therefore, is presented as, in his own eyes, the opposite of Copernicus's model of conservation. Much of Kepler's achievement, in fact, is based on his critique of his predecessor's findings.

In addition, Kepler's generally worldly disposition leads him to develop practical applications of astronomical researches. When most successful in his own eyes, however, constructing his geometrical model of planetary harmony, he is unwittingly failing. His model is adequate to his own need of it but is not, by virtue of that adequacy, foolproof. The reader is given a strong sense that the model that Kepler's discoveries serve introduces as many errors as it corrects in Copernicus's model. In Copernicus's case, the model is the necessary transmutation of sorrow; in Kepler's case, it is the necessary transmutation of joy. Despite fate's cruel blows, Kepler asserts that the world should be considered part of a harmoniously integrated system. Because of fate's cruel blows, Copernicus asserts the same theory.

It would be invidious to conclude that one of these heroic figures suffers more than the others. Banville is at pains, as the dramatic structure of *Kepler* demonstrates, to point out that the astronomer's faith in the world proves to be as destructively alienating as Copernicus's skepticism. The spectacle—which concludes the novel—of this great scientific visionary spending his time and energy attempting to bring his debtors to account is a painfully ludicrous commentary on the all-too-understandable vanity of human wishes as well as a cogent expression of Banville's own perspective on his material.

THE NEWTON LETTER

In the novella *The Newton Letter* Banville changes his approach without quite changing his theme, returning once more to an ironic treatment of the Big House theme. Here the scenario is not biography but failed biography. The protagonist is not the great scientist but the apparently less-than-great modern writer attempting to recapture the scientist's life. This short work gives an inverted picture of the procedures that seem natural in the two earlier works in the series. The presupposition of expository coherence leading to insight and comprehension that is crucial, however unspoken, to the fictionalized biographies becomes a subject open to criticism in

The Newton Letter—open, like the procedures of Copernicus and Kepler, to the charge of fiction.

In addition, the fictional biographer (the protagonist of *The Newton Letter*) is failing to complete his work because of Newton's failure to pursue his research. By this means, the interrelationship between fiction and reality, and the possibility that these terms interchangeably reflect dual perspectives on immutable phenomena, is brought yet more clearly to the forefront of Banville's concerns.

Indeed, as in the case of the earlier novels of the series, life keeps interrupting the Newton biographer. The country house to which he has retreated in order to complete his work, while not possessing the menace and uncertainty of Birchwood, distracts and ultimately ensnares him, so that he is forced to choose between the demands of completeness (his work) and the obligations of incompleteness (his life). The biographer's failed project becomes a synonym for his mortal destiny.

MEFISTO

Banville's rejection of the biographical approach to the life of the mind is completed in the final volume of the series, *Mefisto*, in which the protagonist, a mathematician named Gabriel Swan, writes his own story. With this formal development, the procedure of both *Doctor Copernicus* and *Kepler* is completely inverted, and the value of the project, both from a biographical and from a scientific point of view, is most rigorously challenged. One reason it is possible to make such a claim is that *Mefisto* reaches back beyond its three predecessors to *Birchwood*, to which it bears some strong resemblances.

The most obvious novelty of *Mefisto*, however, is that it does not deal with a historical twentieth century scientist. Most of Banville's readers were not prepared for this development, which is a tribute to Banville's own conception of his project's integrity. It is unlikely, however, that the question of integrity is the only one at issue here. On one hand, this development is typical of the sly and slapstick humor that pervades Banville's work. On the other hand, the fictitiousness of *Mefisto*'s protagonist is an obvious expression of the status of failure in Banville's oeuvre, the failure from which the artist is obliged to begin and that his work, by attempting to mask or redeem it, merely makes more obvious. In addition, given that *Mefisto* has a historical context about which it is possible to say much, and that it is a novel that brings to an end a series of works in which historical events are given a prominent and influential place, it must be considered provocative and instructive that *Mefisto* eschews explicit information of a historical nature.

Mefisto is a novel of missing parts. It lacks a specific sense of time and space, though the alert reader will find part 1 of the novel set in a market town in provincial Ireland and part 2 in an Irish city that is presumably Dublin. The hero, Gabriel (a name that, in a novelist as self-conscious as Banville, must be an echo of the protagonist of *Birchwood*, particularly since in part 1 there is a dilapidated, Birchwood-like house), is a mathematician of genius, but it is difficult to deduce what his branch of mathematics is.

It is Gabriel's misfortune to believe that there can be a redemptive function in his symbols and abstractions. He mistakenly believes that, because of the light he finds shining in the purity of math, he can rescue damsels in distress—in genuine distress, like the drug-besotted Adele in part 2. This belief is cultivated by the jauntily cynical and amoral Felix, who fills the role of Mephistopheles, Gabriel's dark angel. There is enough twinning and doubling in the novel to suggest that Felix may also be Gabriel's stillborn twin brother. Events prove both the hopelessness and the inevitability of Gabriel's outlook. First, Gabriel is severely burned—the potential fate, no doubt, of all who make Mephistophelian contact. Second, he is brokenhearted by his failure to rescue Adele. The end of the novel, however, finds him rededicating himself to his vision of mathematics, to the rhetoric of perfection and security that it symbolizes.

The combination of failure and rededication on which *Mefisto* ends is an illuminating gloss on one of Banville's most crucial themes. Echoing a pronouncement of Samuel Beckett, Banville believes that the artist necessarily has failure for a theme and that the artist's work articulates that theme's pressing reality. On the other hand, Banville is still romantic enough to conceive of his theme in terms of world-changing, concept-forming figures. His work is thus also preoccupied with the meaning of success, which in turn is linked to ideas of progress, clarity, precision, and enlightenment. Failure

is relativized by success, and success by failure. The sense of doubleness and unity suggested by such a conclusion is typical of Banville's outlook.

THE BOOK OF EVIDENCE

Binary interplay is very much to the fore in Banville's most commercially successful novel, *The Book of Evidence*. This work takes the form of a first-person account of a vertiginous fall from grace undertaken by a lapsed mathematician, Freddie Montgomery, while Freddie is awaiting trial. In financial straits, Freddie decided to steal a painting, and in order to do so he murdered an innocent bystander, a servant. No good comes of these actions, unless it is to reveal to the scapegrace protagonist the necessity that his nature acknowledge limits and that the limits are those enjoined by the existence of others. As Freddie perceives, his failure to imagine the lives of others leads him into reckless disregard of those lives. His crime is this failure. Through the comprehensiveness and comprehension of his narrative, Freddie arrives at a perspective on his actions that he had previously lacked, having been hitherto driven to act by cupidity, fear, and callowness.

In a reflexive turn typical of Banville, Freddie's book becomes more substantial than his life. For all its narrative discontinuities, the story remains a simple one, reminiscent of a ballad, providing *The Book of Evidence* with an unlikely kinship to *Long Lankin*, the stories in which are premised on a ballad. This formal association also suggests *The Book of Evidence*'s indebtedness to two classics of jail literature, both by Oscar Wilde: *De Profundis* (1905; a first-person attempt at vindication) and *The Ballad of Reading Gaol* (1898; with its refrain, "For each man kills the thing he loves," which is clearly the case of Freddie and the stolen painting). Such objective possibilities of order counterpoint Freddie's subjective flouting of law—not merely the law of the land, which is held at such a distance in *The Book of Evidence* as to seem beside the point, but laws more fundamentally pertaining to the viability of the project of being human, with its obligations to others, obligations that in the distorted form of financial indebtedness to hoodlums motivate Freddie's murderous actions.

While conceptually and stylistically *The Book of Evidence* is at least the equal of Banville's earlier attainments, it also articulates much more decisively than does

Mefisto the author's sense of contemporary social reality. Its uniformly favorable critical reception suggests that it is a work that will contribute to Banville's gaining the wider readership that his originality, commitment to large questions, and aesthetic poise deserve.

ATHENA

Athena completes the trilogy begun with *The Book of Evidence* and continued with the ethereal *Ghosts*. Each novel centers on Freddie, here referred to only as Morrow, and once again Banville sets the action in another decaying house, portentously located on Rue Street. Morrow's criminal past reasserts itself as he falls in with Morden, an enigmatic figure who commissions the protagonist to catalog and evaluate eight Flemish paintings. The narrative is then punctuated by detailed descriptions of seven of these paintings, each of which is a fraud.

As he becomes more enmeshed in Morden's machinations, Morrow enters a hypnotic and masochistic relationship with another mysterious figure, a woman known only as A. Gradually the mystery evaporates—Morden and A. are siblings working for Da, their father, and Morrow is little more than a useful and available tool. Like Banville's earlier novels, *Athena* is driven by the self-conscious ruminations of the principal character, and like those other protagonists, Morrow is obsessed with the gulf between chaotic, shoddy reality and the perfection of art and the imagination. He longs for order, the model of which he finds in art, but his actions lead repeatedly to more frustration and havoc. The novel positively brims with allusions to other paintings and novels, and thus the self-conscious and ironic practices of the early novels are maintained. Along with *The Newton Letter*, *Athena* arguably ranks among Banville's best novels for its inventiveness and epistemological probity.

THE UNTOUCHABLE

In his work *The Untouchable*, Banville returns to the historical concerns that characterize so many of his earlier works. Here, Victor Maskell, narrator, art scholar, and former spy, is a thinly disguised version of Anthony Blunt, the British traitor who joined a spy ring while a student at Cambridge University in the 1930's. The novel is set in the 1970's, when Blunt was exposed, but again another subjective narrator shuttles back and forth through time in a mélange of history and personal reflection. The story takes the reader through Maskell's boyhood, years at Cambridge, and years during World War II, when his involvement with the Russians deepens in spite of his skepticism of their social project.

Like Morrow, Maskell is dedicated to art and ascends to the influential position of Keeper of the Royal Pictures, confessing that art is the only thing of any importance or stability in his life. Art in fact become a lens through which he views and evaluates himself, whereby he is alternately creator and created, forever suspended on his own perfect Grecian urn. However, the single painting around which he has organized his life, and which he purchased as a young man, French classical artist Nicolas Poussin's *The Death of Seneca*, may be a forgery, thus making his whole life a fraud. Like earlier Banville characters, Maskell is a searcher, seeking a fixed sense of identity that is forever out of reach. Once again, the subjective narrator is a self-betrayed figure, one whose most clever deceptions and stratagems rebound disastrously on him; once again readers encounter a profoundly lonely, alienated character.

THE SEA

Banville continues his consideration of old age, memory, and guilt in the Booker Prize-winning *The Sea*, which many critics consider his finest novel. After the death of his wife, Anna, from cancer, art critic Max Morden abandons his home and relocates to the Cedars, a seaside boardinghouse where, as a child many years earlier, he had encountered the affluent Grace family. Morden is working desultorily on an analysis of the French artist Pierre Bonnard. The novel moves fluidly among three time periods: Morden's present as a widower; his married life, focusing on the period leading up to his wife's death; and the summer long ago when he was befriended by the Graces.

The Graces—the ominously masculine father, the alluring mother, the uncanny twins, Chloe and Myles, and the ineffectual governess, Rose—represent a life utterly foreign and attractive to Max, an only child being raised by a single mother. He develops a passionate crush on Mrs. Grace that reaches its climax when he is afforded a voyeuristic peep up her skirt as she reclines on the ground; eventually these feelings are redirected toward Chloe, with whom he shares a first kiss and some other exploration. Looking back on his suddenly empty life,

Morden replays the seminal events of that singular summer in an attempt to understand how that child has become the bitter, bereft old man he is. His entire present must be reexamined through the lens of that summer long past, including his relationship with his daughter Claire, who has sacrificed a promising career as an art historian under the influence of a suitor of whom Max disapproves. *The Sea* looks backward over Banville's earlier novels through his playful, mysterious use of character names form earlier works and the work's relentless, reluctant uncovering of a long-submerged mystery.

CHRISTINE FALLS

In *Christine Falls*, Banville—writing under the pseudonym Benjamin Black—moves firmly into the genre of mystery and detective fiction. Set in the 1950's, the novel introduces the protagonist Quirke, a pathologist in a Dublin hospital. After discovering his brother-in-law, Malachy Griffin, in the act of tampering with the death record of a young woman who has died in childbirth, Quirke begins to unravel a story that soon goes far beyond the question of the woman's death and her baby's fate. Eventually the mystery involves the Catholic Church, orphanages in both Ireland and the United States, the notorious convent laundries that employed and imprisoned young women, and Quirke's own position within his adopted family.

In this novel Banville shows a willingness to explore multiple points of view, adhering more to the conventions of the popular mystery genre than to the techniques of his earlier novels. The fallible and self-deceptive Quirke is very much a Banville protagonist, however; his alienation and his reluctant (but inevitable) pursuit of truths about himself are themes that *Christine Falls* shares with many of Banville's other novels.

George O'Brien; David W. Madden
Updated by James S. Brown

OTHER MAJOR WORKS

SHORT FICTION: *Long Lankin*, 1970 (revised 1984).

PLAYS: *The Broken Jug*, pb. 1994 (adaptation of Heinrich von Kleist's *Der zerbrochene Krug*); *God's Gift*, pb. 2000 (adaptation of Kleist's *Amphitryon*).

SCREENPLAYS: *Reflections*, 1984 (adaptation of his novel *The Newton Letter*); *Birchwood*, 1986 (adaptation

of his novel); *The Last September*, 1999 (adaptation of Elizabeth Bowen's novel).

TELEPLAY: *Seaview*, 1994.

NONFICTION: *Prague Pictures: Portraits of a City*, 2003.

BIBLIOGRAPHY

Booker, M. Keith. "Cultural Crisis Then and Now: Science, Literature, and Religion in John Banville's *Doctor Copernicus* and *Kepler*." *Critique* 39, no. 2 (Winter, 1998): 176-192. Examines how Banville uses the complex parallels between science and literature as a way of exploring and representing reality in his renderings of the lives of the scientists in the two novels.

Deane, Seamus. "'Be Assured I Am Inventing': The Fiction of John Banville." In *The Irish Novel in Our Time*, edited by Patrick Rafroidi and Maurice Harmon. Lille, France: Publications de l'Université de Lille, 1975. Presents an excellent discussion of Banville's first three works of fiction. Deane, one of Ireland's leading critics, is particularly insightful concerning the reflexive elements in *Long Lankin*, *Nightspawn*, and *Birchwood*. Concludes with a challenging critique of the cultural significance of Banville's work.

D'Haen, Theo. "Irish Regionalism, Magic Realism, and Postmodernism." In *International Aspects of Irish Literature*, edited by Toshi Furomoto et al. Gerrards Cross, England: Smythe, 1996. Compares Banville's *Birchwood* and Desmond Hogan's *A Curious Street* to demonstrate the postmodern and Magical Realist qualities of each. Such features express the marginality of Ireland and of the Irish to Europe's dominant beliefs in Banville's fiction.

D'hoker, Elke. *Visions of Alterity: Representation in the Works of John Banville*. Atlanta: Rodopi, 2004. Scholarly work presents detailed readings of Banville's most important novels, focusing on their philosophical dimension. Includes bibliography and index.

Imhof, Rüdiger. *John Banville: A Critical Introduction*. Enlarged ed. Dublin, Ireland: Wolfhound Press, 1997. Early study of Banville's works discusses the novels up to and including *Mefisto*; additional material added for this enlarged edition addresses *The*

Book of Evidence, *Ghosts*, and *Athena*. Provides an intellectual guide to Banville's fictional preoccupations as well as a full bibliography.

Irish University Review 11 (Spring, 1981). Special issue on Banville presents a number of critical overviews, a bibliography, a wide-ranging interview with Banville, and the transcript of a talk he gave at the University of Iowa's Writers' Workshop—a rare formal statement on fiction and authorship.

Jackson, Tony E. "Science, Art, and the Shipwreck of Knowledge: The Novels of John Banville." *Contemporary Literature* 38, no. 8 (1997): 510-533. Examines Banville's postmodern sensibility in five novels. Basing his argument on Friedrich Nietzsche's theories about the indeterminacy of truth, Jackson demonstrates that scientific truths in Banville's novels can never explain everything and that art fills the gaps for which history and science cannot account.

McIlroy, Brian. "Pattern in Chaos: John Banville's Scientific Art." *Colby Quarterly* 31, no. 1 (1995). Uses examination of *Doctor Copernicus*, *Kepler*, *The Newton Letter*, and *Mefisto* to show how Banville illustrates the similarities between scientific and artistic methods of thinking and discovery. Also discusses the ways in which history, politics, religion, and sex influence scientific inquiry and art.

McMinn, Joseph. *The Supreme Fictions of John Banville*. New York: St. Martin's Press, 1999. Presents critical commentary on all of Banville's works of fiction through *The Untouchable*. Includes an introduction that places Banville's work within the context of American, Irish, and European writing.

Murphy, Neil. *Irish Fiction and Postmodern Doubt: An Analysis of the Epistemological Crisis in Modern Fiction*. Lewiston, N.Y.: Edwin Mellen Press, 2004. Discusses the works of Banville and two other Irish novelists, Neil Jordan and Aidan Higgins, in the context of postmodernist fiction. Relates the authors' works to Irish and international literary traditions. Includes bibliography and index.

PAT BARKER

Born: Thornaby-on-Tees, near Middlesborough, England; May 8, 1943

Also known as: Patricia Margaret Barker

PRINCIPAL LONG FICTION

Union Street, 1982
Blow Your House Down, 1984
The Man Who Wasn't There, 1984
The Century's Daughter, 1986
Regeneration, 1991
The Eye in the Door, 1993
The Ghost Road, 1995
The Regeneration Trilogy, 1996 (includes previous 3 novels)
Another World, 1998
Border Crossing, 2001
Double Vision, 2003
Life Class, 2007

OTHER LITERARY FORMS

Although Pat Barker has published book reviews and the short story "Subsidence" (2003), about the Iraq War, she is known primarily as a novelist.

ACHIEVEMENTS

Pat Barker is considered one of the premier British novelists to begin a career in the 1980's. Critics praised her early novels for their gritty portraits of working-class life. The first novel, *Union Street*, received the Fawcett Prize in 1983. However, it was her novels about the psychological damage of combat in World War I that earned her the greatest accolades. The second novel of her Regeneration trilogy, *The Eye in the Door*, brought her the Guardian Fiction Prize and Northern Electric Special Arts Prize, both in 1993. Its sequel, *The Ghost Road*, won the prestigious Booker Prize for Fiction in 1995, and she was named the Bookseller's Association Author of the Year in 1996. Subsequently, *The Ghost Road* was twice named among the all-time best Booker Prize novels.

Barker was awarded honorary degrees from English universities in Teesside, Napier, Hertfordshire, and Durham, as well as the Open University. She was made an honorary fellow of the London School of Economics in 1996. Two of her books were made into films, *Union Street* (renamed *Stanley and Iris*, 1989) and *Regeneration* (1997).

BIOGRAPHY

Pat Barker was born in Thornaby-on-Tees in Yorkshire, England, on May 8, 1943. She did not know her father, who was in the military during World War II, and after her mother started a second family when Barker was seven, she was raised by her grandmother and grandfather. Her grandfather, a laborer, was a wounded World War I veteran, and her grandmother worked in a fish-and-chips restaurant. Her grandmother took an interest in spiritualism and encouraged Barker to read from her books, as well as from the encyclopedia and various works of literature. From her grandparents she acquired a love of language and storytelling.

After finishing secondary school for girls, Barker attended the London School of Economics. She received a bachelor of science degree in 1965 and taught history, politics, and English to adult classes until 1970. She also enrolled for study at Durham University. She married David Barker, a professor of zoology, in 1978. They had one son, John, and a daughter, Annabel, who also became a novelist.

Barker's early unpublished work includes novels of manners about the English middle class. She was resigned to remaining unpublished until she took a writing course from the novelist Angela Carter. Carter encouraged Barker to write about her working-class background and helped her find a publisher for the result: *Union Street*. Coming out in 1982, the novel was well received by critics, and she was named one of Great Britain's best young writers by the Book Marketing Council and the literary journal *Granta*. *Granta* later placed her on its list of Twenty Best British Novelists. In 2003, Barker was named a Commander of the British Empire.

Pat Barker. (AP/Wide World Photos)

ANALYSIS

Pat Barker's novels are emotionally wrenching. As many critics have observed, Barker's frank realism and attention to historical detail can equally satisfy and repel readers, often in the same passages. Barker brings readers' attention to bear on terrible hazards: war, insanity, rape, murder, illicit sexuality, dysfunctional families, and child abuse. The prospect of violence—individual or communal, physical or psychological—gives great force to her plots. Moreover, she typically uses a third-person narrative point of view of limited omniscience. Shifting section by section from the inner thoughts of one character to another both enhances the immediacy of their experiences and constructs multiple perspectives on their temperaments. The effect is intimate and entangling.

Barker's acute ear for dialects and individual quirks of speech is the hallmark of her realism. Through dialogue she creates lifelike characters from a variety of backgrounds: for instance, working-class women in *Union Street*; prostitutes in *Blow Your House Down*; common soldiers, medical personnel, and upper-class poets in the Regeneration trilogy; and artists in *Double Vision* and *Life Class*. In fact, it is primarily through dialogue in the Regeneration trilogy that Barker conveys the brilliance of a psychologist during his treatment of his patients. Likewise, dialogue contributes to the uncompromising horror of the rape of a prostitute in *Blow Your House Down* and the eerie savageness in children in *Another World*, *The Man Who Wasn't There*, and *Border Crossing*.

The historical accuracy of the novels set wholly or in part during World War I received wide praise. Not only is Barker starkly vivid in portraying the confusion and shock of combat, she also depicts the struggles of physicians and psychologists to treat the wounded. She mixes historical people with fictional characters with flawless credibility and captures larger social anxieties, such as the fear gripping English women during the murderous career of the "Yorkshire ripper," who figures in *Blow Your House Down*.

Sexuality is another focus of Barker's unflinching realism, and often she treats it as a form of violence, yet there are also examples of principal characters growing closer emotionally because of sex, even when extramarital, as is the case with Billy Prior and Sarah Lumb in *The Eye in the Door* and Paul Tarrant and Elinor Brooke in *Life Class*.

In addition to love between characters in troubled times, Barker examines the dynamics of troubled families in ordinary times. Her early novels feature families comprising a mother and her children, the father either absent or unknown, as in *Union Street* and *The Man Who Wasn't There*. In *Another World*, however, Barker considers the problems of a husband and wife who both have children from previous marriages. The children are secretive, prone to deception and violence, and manipulative; the parents must handle them with great care to avoid alienating each other.

The resolutions to Barker's novels eschew completeness and closure; instead, characters make accommodations that set the terms for their future. In some cases, this means a compromise with beliefs. In the Regeneration trilogy, for example, a celebrated poet compromises his conviction that the war is wrong and returns to duty in combat. He later becomes a spokesperson for the generation nearly obliterated by the war. In other cases, the compromise means choosing among loved ones. In *Another World*, parents Nick and Fran must each send away the child from a previous marriage in order for their current marriage to succeed and their common son to survive. In most cases, there is death and guilt, if not despair.

The Regeneration trilogy

The Regeneration trilogy centers on the work of pioneering psychologist W. H. R. Rivers in treating shell shock, now known as post-traumatic stress disorder, late in World War I. The trilogy focuses on Rivers and several of his patients and their friends, some of whom, like Rivers, are historical figures, in particular the poets Siegfried Sassoon, Wilfred Owen, and Robert Graves. Several themes thread through the sequence, including antiwar protest, the origin and purpose of war literature, the horror of combat and its effects on the mind, techniques of psychoanalysis, sexuality, insanity, and relations between officers and enlisted men on the front lines. Barker particularizes these themes by switching among point-of-view characters in her third-person narrative voice; however, much of the story's tension emerges through dialogue.

Regeneration, the first novel of the trilogy, finds Sassoon, an army officer, confined to Craiglockhart mental hospital for denouncing the war. There, he witnesses great suffering among fellow patients, one of whom is Lieutenant Billy Prior. Prior has ceased speaking as a result of the horrors of combat and because of his anger at the conduct of the war. He is one of Barker's purely fictional characters, a man of the lower classes who has struggled into the officer ranks, usually reserved for the upper classes, thanks to his attention to duty, and his bisexuality. The reader finds that the war also exhausts Rivers as he works tirelessly to restore his patients' health so they can return to duty. He tricks Prior into speaking again and argues with Sassoon about a man's moral relation to the war and Sassoon's homosexuality. Sassoon discovers a true poet in Owen, another patient, and helps him draft one of the war's most famous poems, "Anthem for a Doomed Youth," which graphically portrays death in combat.

The Eye in the Door begins in April, 1918. It follows Sassoon's experiences on the front lines following his decision to return to combat in France, and Rivers's continuing treatment of Owen and other patients. However, Prior assumes a central place in the story. The novel examines his homosexual and heterosexual encounters and his romance with Sarah Lumb, a woman working at an armaments factory. At the same time, Barker evokes the intensity of social tumult stirred up by a right-wing politician's campaign to stigmatize and punish homosexuals and pacifists.

The Ghost Road maintains the focus on Prior. He becomes engaged to Lumb and eventually passes the evaluation of the medical board and returns to combat. So does Owen, after writing some of the most moving poetry ever about young men in war. Both die in a final campaign. Contrasting with them are Sassoon, now relegated to a minor character, and Graves, who takes a position at a training school rather than return to combat. Rivers comes to recognize that he has assumed the role of a father to his patients, and the fate of many of them in combat deeply disturbs him and causes him to reflect on the nature of his youth, his early experiences as a field anthropologist in the South Pacific, and therapy.

ANOTHER WORLD

Another World also examines the psychological effects of combat in World War I. However, the novel's primary theme is the intrafamily animosities that can lead to tragedy.

In Nick's family, tensions are rife and worsening. His wife, Fran, has a troubled eleven-year-old boy from a previous relationship. Nick, a psychology professor, likewise has a thirteen-year-old daughter. Together, they have a two-year-old son, and Fran is pregnant. None of them likes the arrangement, but Fran and Nick are determined to make the family a success. They have moved into a large Victorian house to that end, only to discover that a two-year-old boy had been murdered there two generations earlier by jealous half-siblings. Fran and Nick also uncover a chilling, pornographic portrait of the original family, a portrait that reminds them of themselves.

To make matters worse, Nick's beloved grandfather,

Geordie, is dying of cancer. He is 101 years old and a veteran of World War I. Post-traumatic stress disorder still gives him horrible nightmares, which make a living hell of his final days. As Nick fears that his stepson and stepdaughter may repeat the house's tragic past by harming their younger brother, Geordie dies a tortured, lingering death, and afterward a horrible secret surfaces. The old man's nightmares come not just from combat but from knowing that he murdered his own wounded brother. Ostensibly, the act was to save the brother from pain, but in reality, Geordie hated him.

Geordie's death and the revelation bring perspective to Nick on his own family problems. He and Fran arrange a solution to their family troubles, however temporary, realizing the primary danger lies in parental distraction, hypocrisy, self-absorption, and self-pity.

LIFE CLASS

Life Class addresses the role of art in World War I. It follows the experiences of three students at the Slade, a celebrated London arts academy overseen by Henry Tonks, a historical figure who was both a surgeon and artist.

Told in a third-person omniscient point of view, the novel opens with Paul Tarrant leaving the school in disgust after Tonks criticizes his drawings. Uncertain of his talent and future, he has an affair with a married model, but he is really in love with another student, Elinor Brooke, a woman intent upon making her own way in the world despite family disapproval and skimpy prospects for women artists. Also in love with her is Kit Neville, who has already gained a reputation as an artist despite being expelled from Slade by Tonks.

When war breaks out, Neville and Tarrant, both unfit for active duty, join the Red Cross. Tarrant becomes an ambulance driver, a grueling and dangerous job, and is wounded. Neville serves as liaison at a hospital for prisoners of war. Both struggle to capture in their art what they experience. Neville employs a dashing narrative style that enhances his reputation. Tarrant concentrates on the horror of the wounds that he has witnessed, and although his vivid, tortured paintings win Tonks's grudging approval, they seem too horrible to be shown in public. Meanwhile, Brooke swears not to let the war influence her work. After she takes a risky trip to a village near the front to visit Tarrant, her paintings of the people she encounters, however, help her to mature her style. Thus, the war moves young artists in divergent directions as they struggle to make art relevant in a war whose corruption, violence, and chaos overwhelms them and causes them to drift emotionally from one another.

Roger Smith

BIBLIOGRAPHY

Brannigan, John. *Pat Barker*. New York: Manchester University Press, 2005. Brannigan considers all of Barker's novels in a critical assessment of their social realism, their examination of gender roles, their treatment of memory, and their narrative style.

Falcus, Sarah. "A Complex Mixture of Fascination and Distaste: Relationships Between Women in Pat Barker's *Blow Your House Down*, *Liza's England*, and *Union Street*." *Journal of Gender Studies* 16 (November, 2007): 249-261. Falcus's thesis is that Barker's early novels portray women as trapped in imprisoning roles by their gender yet bonding with each other. Falcus examines that bonding in the light of feminist theory.

Fraser, Kennedy. "Ghost Writer." *The New Yorker*, March 17, 2008. Kennedy considers the influence of spiritualism in Barker's family background on her Regeneration trilogy and other novels.

Harris, Greg. "Compulsory Masculinity, Britain, and the Great War: The Literary-Historical Work of Pat Barker." *Critique* 39 (Summer, 1998): 290-305. Examines how the Regeneration trilogy frames gender roles during World War I through the psychological work of the character Dr. Rivers.

Kemp, Peter. "War Has Been Her Greatest Obsession, and It Looms Large in Her New Novel—But Is This Pat Barker's Last Battle?" *Sunday Times*, July 1, 2007. Based on an interview with Barker, Kemp writes of the author's reasons for returning to World War I as subject matter, and of her interest in artists of the day. Includes biographical information.

Monteith, Sharon. *Pat Barker*. Tavistock, England: Northcote House, 2002. In a critical overview, Monteith contends that Barker's fiction combines both individual character and the national mentality in considering the psychological effects of gender and violence in communities under stress from war, crime, or poverty.

Westman, Karen. *Pat Barker's "Regeneration": A Reader's Guide*. New York: Continuum, 2001. Following a short biographical chapter that also recounts the history of the writing of the three novels, Westmann addressed the themes of the Regeneration trilogy in detail. Includes a short bibliography.

DJUNA BARNES

Born: Cornwall-on-Hudson, New York; June 12, 1892
Died: New York, New York; June 18, 1982
Also known as: Djuna Chappell Barnes

PRINCIPAL LONG FICTION

Ryder, 1928
Nightwood, 1936

OTHER LITERARY FORMS

Although primarily known for her singular novel *Nightwood*, Djuna Barnes wrote in many genres throughout her long life. She initially earned her living in New York City as a freelance reporter and theater critic, publishing articles in the *Brooklyn Daily Eagle*, *New York Morning Telegraph*, *Vanity Fair*, *The New Yorker*, *New York Press*, *The Dial*, and other periodicals. Her artistic skills showed in her drawings, some of which appeared as early as 1915 in *The Book of Repulsive Women*, her first published chapbook. Her artwork also appeared as illustrations for *Ladies Almanack*, a roman à clef about lesbian circles in Paris, a book she cleverly structured in the format of an almanac. Another collection of her drawings was published in 1995 as *Poe's Mother: Selected Drawings of Djuna Barnes*. Her first collection of short stories, *A Book* (1923), was reissued as *A Night Among the Horses* in 1928 with a number of additional stories.

Barnes also was a dramatist. Her one-act plays were performed at the Provincetown Playhouse in Greenwich Village, New York City. She wrote and rewrote the full-length verse drama, *The Antiphon*, over a twenty-year period before poet T. S. Eliot, in his position as a literary editor with publisher Faber and Faber, approved the manuscript for publication. The action of the play occurs in a fictional township in England during World War II, as family members from America reunite; family drama ensues. Their memories of love and aggression probably reflect Barnes's own upbringing and family dynamics.

Barnes's last book before she died was *Creatures in an Alphabet* (1982), a collection of short rhyming poems. Since her death in 1982, collections of her journalism, short fiction, poetry, short plays, previously published work, and manuscript selections have appeared, confirming her versatile talents in many literary and artistic forms.

ACHIEVEMENTS

Djuna Barnes was initially known as a literary modernist, someone who wrote formally and linguistically complex and allusive works. In the 1970's, critics began to examine her work in the context of feminist studies and feminist literary theory. They also began researching Barnes, long known for her role in the American expatriate literary scene in Paris in the 1920's. Like Gertrude Stein, Barnes is now appreciated as a formative figure in studies of modernism and of lesbian and gay cultural history. The concessions she made to adhere to U.S. censorship regulations are less widely known, but the published typescript of *Nightwood* shows what Eliot deleted while editing. *Ryder*, in this regard, also was problematic, and Barnes used asterisks in the text to indicate the changes that she was forced to make.

Because her protagonists often refer to individuals that Barnes knew from her years in Paris or from childhood, her books lend themselves to biographical, psychobiographical, and life-writing approaches. Barnes was knowledgeable about women's rights, and her fiction investigates the nature of sexuality, gender, sexual expression, equality, and choice. Barnes received rec-

Djuna Barnes. (Courtesy, New Directions Publishing)

ognition for her role in American literature when she was elected in 1961 to the National Institute of Arts and Letters.

BIOGRAPHY

As a child, Djuna Chappell Barnes received no formal education, but she was educated at home in Cornwall-on-Hudson. She was one of five children in a difficult and polygamist family structure. She left for New York City after a brief and inappropriate marriage and then studied art at the Pratt Institute (1912-1913) and the Art Students League (1915-1916). While living in Greenwich Village, she became a reporter and covered political issues such as women's suffrage (her grandmother had been a suffragist), and wrote popular feature stories and conducted interviews.

Barnes moved to Paris and by the early 1920's was well established in expatriate circles on the Left Bank. She came to know James Joyce, Stein, Eliot, and many others. Memoirs from this period describe her as a dramatic, striking woman with an acerbic wit and strong will. Her *Ladies Almanack* both celebrates and satirizes the women she knew in Natalie Clifford Barney's lesbian salon on the rue Jacob, which met regularly to read writings by women. Barnes lived in Paris for about twenty years, primarily with her lover Thelma Wood. Other individuals close to her were Peggy Guggenheim, who helped support her; Emily Holmes Coleman, a writer and exhaustive diarist; and Robert McAlmon, who was responsible for privately printed *Ladies Almanack*.

Barnes also spent time in the early 1930's at the Guggenheim manor house, Hayford Hall, in the English countryside, with Guggenheim, Coleman, writer Antonia White, and an array of male and female visitors. Hayford Hall was a supportive and lively community, and the living arrangements gave Coleman the opportunity to read and critique the manuscript of *Nightwood*. Coleman's diaries reveal something most readers of Barnes do not know: Coleman's resourceful determination and urging letters were instrumental in convincing Eliot to accept the manuscript for publication by Faber and Faber and to write his somewhat ambiguous introduction.

With the onset of World War II, Barnes returned to New York and moved to a small apartment on the historic Patchin Place in Greenwich Village. She lived there for decades, eventually in failing health and famously unreceptive to visitors, including scholars. She sold her correspondence and manuscripts to the McKeldin Library at the University of Maryland in College Park in 1972 but destroyed parts of her personal archive. According to various accounts, Barnes's neighbors at Patchin Place could smell smoke coming from her apartment, and they knew that she was methodically burning information she did not want to become part of her history and legacy.

ANALYSIS

The difficulties of negotiating identity in a culture whose moral values and cultural expectations are powerful and repressive run throughout Djuna Barnes's canon, from her satirical and witty works to the profoundly serious and dark *Nightwood*. Emotions, which run high through the generations of the families she depicts, are reflected in the struggles, violence, or loyalties of individuals. Characters across a broad Euro-American landscape try to locate and free themselves from old patterns of quest and fulfillment, seeking authentic channels of emotional and sexual intimacy. Barnes's work incorporates multiple levels of meaning and multiple layers of figurative allusiveness, which make it challenging for readers to distinguish truth from falsehood and sincerity from fabrication; the characters themselves may not articulate their positions and often may not know themselves.

From the vantage point of the early twenty-first century Barnes remains a modernist concerned with literary innovation, but she is indisputably a saboteur of traditional culture, a woman who extended her writing beyond traditional modernism and who lived according to her own standards. Like other women writers of the period, such as H. D., Jean Rhys, Anaïs Nin, and Gertrude Stein, she cared about women's freedom and was certainly a feminist. It could be said, however, that her greatest allegiance was to language, to creating it and controlling it either through elaborate expression or declared silence.

RYDER

Published in 1928 with the author's own illustrations, Barnes's first novel, *Ryder*, is an elaborately structured story about the Ryder family, extending through four generations up to the early twentieth century. There are many family members, some of whom appear briefly while others, like the patriarch and polygamist Wendell Ryder (based on Barnes's father), loom large. The book sold well for a time, but the complexities of its language (Chaucerian, Elizabethan, and Rabelaisian) and harsh portrayal of family relationships failed to sustain a readership.

Highly ambitious, *Ryder* works through literary pastiche and satire, relying also on quick changes of style, tone, and narrative points of view. On some levels it resembles a family chronicle, but it progresses episodically with part of its energy created by many embedded genres, including letters, poems, ghost stories, lullabies, parables, and epigrams. The book creates tension between patriarchy and matriarchy and gradually foregrounds women's struggles for autonomy and integrity through the mothers and daughters it portrays.

NIGHTWOOD

Nightwood is Barnes's major work of fiction and is undoubtedly the book on which her strong reputation will continue to be based. Its literary style is dazzling, and its language is highly structured. Although like other modernist masterpieces, it brilliantly undermines traditional elements of plot, character development, and linearity. The story is minimalist, taking place primarily in Europe between the two world wars and projecting a landscape of postwar disillusionment. The characters attempt to move beyond their individual despair to find new communities.

At the center is Robin Vote, whose silences make her unknowable and protean, regardless of where and with whom she goes. Felix Volkbein, a supposed Old World aristocrat, marries Robin in anticipation of producing strong progeny, but Robin leaves him and her young son and goes off with Nora Flood, the "Westerner" from the United States. Nora is devoted to Robin even after Robin abandons her. She follows Robin in her wanderings and witnesses Robin's horrific breakdown in the final chapter. Nora carries the weight of loyalty and has the equilibrium of balanced self-knowledge. In contrast, Robin is forever in flux, the "eternal momentary," and thus a source to be pursued and repeatedly lost.

The person who reigns over events is Dr. Matthew O'Connor, who functions as a modern-day Tiresias, imparting advice to the individuals who seek him out for predictions and wisdom from his private *quartier* in Paris. Matthew comes to occupy the center stage of *Nightwood* as chronology recedes and long monologues replace direct narrative action. Matthew's monologues respond to each character's questions and their own respective monologues. Increasingly, the doctor exposes his uncertain identity and own collection of self-performances.

In the chapter "Go Down, Matthew," Matthew explains the message that Robin's abandonments suggest: Life is not to be known or understood, despite the relentless attempts. Whatever one does, individually or coupled or communally, life will not reveal itself, and whatever stories the narrative seems to tell, the accounting is flawed, merely one of many possible and impossible fabrications. There are formulas for actions and prescriptions for truths, and they all fall into dissolu-

tion. These revelations have repercussion within the plot and beyond it, repercussions for *Nightwood* as a literary text: Structure rebounds on itself, and then order blurs into different orders or into disorder. In other words, *Nightwood* incorporates some of the familiar modernist conclusions, but it does so with Barnes's unique genius.

The last few pages of the novel, titled "The Possessed," depict the most pessimistic scene in the book. Robin, who has quested through marriage, childbirth, motherhood, and bisexuality, makes her way to Nora's country property in the United States. Reaching a decaying chapel on the property reminiscent of the one in Eliot's modernist poem *The Waste Land* (1922), Robin collapses and swings at Nora's dog, both of them barking before going entirely silent. The scene is open to different interpretations but is surely a reckoning of the woman, and women, whose socialized and rebellious sides fight one another in a psychic and mythic war of attrition. There are many ways to approach and understand *Nightwood*. What is unlikely to change is *Nightwood*'s central position in the evolving history of prose narrative.

Miriam Fuchs

OTHER MAJOR WORKS

SHORT FICTION: *A Night Among the Horses*, 1929; *Spillway*, 1962; *Smoke, and Other Early Stories*, 1982; *Collected Stories*, 1996.

PLAYS: *Three from the Earth*, pr., pb. 1919; *The Antiphon*, pb. 1958; *At the Roots of the Stars: The Short Plays*, 1995.

POETRY: *The Book of Repulsive Women*, 1915 (includes drawings); *Collected Poems: With Notes Toward the Memoirs*, 2005.

NONFICTION: *Interviews*, 1985 (journalism); *I Could Never Be Lonely Without a Husband*, 1987 (Alyce Barry, editor); *New York*, 1989 (journalism).

CHILDREN'S LITERATURE: *Creatures in an Alphabet*, 1982.

MISCELLANEOUS: *A Book*, 1923 (enlarged edition published as *A Night Among the Horses*, 1929; abridged as *Spillway*, 1962); *Ladies' Almanack*, 1928; *Selected Works*, 1962; *Poe's Mother: Selected Drawings of Djuna Barnes*, 1995 (Douglas Messerli, editor).

BIBLIOGRAPHY

Benstock, Shari. *Women of the Left Bank, 1900-1940*. Austin: University of Texas Press, 1986. Classic biocritical study of women artists, writers, and intellectuals. Chapter seven covers Barnes's life and writing while she lived on the Left Bank of Paris, a thriving center for American expatriates.

Broe, Mary Lynn, ed. *Silence and Power: A Reevaluation of Djuna Barnes*. Carbondale: Southern Illinois University Press, 1991. Pivotal collection of essays that emphasize the feminist and communal aspects of Barnes's life.

Chait, Sandra M., and Elizabeth M. Podnieks, eds. *Hayford Hall: Hangovers, Erotics, and Aesthetics*. Carbondale: Southern University Illinois Press, 2005. Critical essays examine the characters living and learning at Hayford Hall, the Devonshire estate in England where Barnes lived for a time.

Fuchs, Miriam. "Djuna Barnes and T. S. Eliot: Resistance and Acquiescence." *Tulsa Studies in Women's Literature* 12, no. 2 (Fall, 1993): 288-313. Uses unpublished correspondence to map the collaborative dynamics between Barnes and poet T. S. Eliot.

_____. "The Triadic Association of Emily Holmes Coleman, T. S. Eliot, and Djuna Barnes." *ANQ: A Journal of Short Articles, Notes, and Reviews* 12, no. 4 (Fall, 1999): 28-39. Examines Emily Holmes Coleman's unpublished diary entries to relate the drama behind T. S. Eliot's decision to publish Barnes's novel *Nightwood*.

Herring, Phillip F. *Djuna: The Life and Work of Djuna Barnes*. New York: Viking Press, 1995. A useful, comprehensive, and critical biography of Barnes that traces her inspirations and influences. Herring examined private papers and manuscripts and interviewed family and friends for this scholarly but accessible work.

Kannenstine, Louis F. *The Art of Djuna Barnes: Duality and Damnation*. New York: New York University Press, 1977. The first university press study of Barnes, which aligns Barnes with James Joyce. A groundbreaking work that nevertheless has been criticized by feminist and other scholars.

Review of Contemporary Fiction 13, no. 3 (Fall, 1993). Special issue on Barnes's fiction. Features papers presented at the Djuna Barnes Centennial Conference at the University of Maryland in 1992.

Warren, Diane. *Djuna Barnes' Consuming Fictions*. Cornwall, England: Ashgate, 2008. Study that positions itself in relation to ongoing dialogues and debates about Barnes's work. Emphasizes her ideas of identity, language, and culture.

JULIAN BARNES

Born: Leicester, England; January 19, 1946
Also known as: Julian Patrick Barnes; Dan Kavanagh

PRINCIPAL LONG FICTION

Duffy, 1980 (as Dan Kavanagh)
Metroland, 1980
Fiddle City, 1981 (as Kavanagh)
Before She Met Me, 1982
Flaubert's Parrot, 1984
Putting the Boot In, 1985 (as Kavanagh)
Staring at the Sun, 1986
Going to the Dogs, 1987 (as Kavanagh)
A History of the World in 10½ Chapters, 1989
Talking It Over, 1991
The Porcupine, 1992 (novella)
England, England, 1998
Love, etc., 2000
Arthur and George, 2005

OTHER LITERARY FORMS

In addition to his fiction writing, Julian Barnes has served as a journalist and columnist for several British newspapers and magazines. He has published numerous essays, book reviews, short-story collections, and auto-biographical works.

ACHIEVEMENTS

Julian Barnes is one of a number of British writers born after World War II who gravitated toward London and its literary scene. Reacting to the certainties and assumptions of the previous generation, these writers have often resorted to irony and comedy in viewing the contemporary world. Some have experimented with the form of the traditional novel. Barnes's early novels are narrative and chronological in approach, but his fifth book, *Flaubert's Parrot*, combines fact and fiction, novel and history, biography and literary criticism. For that work he was nominated for Great Britain's most prestigious literary award, the Booker Prize, and was awarded the Geoffrey Faber Memorial Prize. He has also won literary prizes in Italy, France, Austria, and elsewhere, and he received the E. M. Forster Award from the American Academy of Arts and Letters in 1986.

BIOGRAPHY

Born in the English Midlands city of Leicester just after World War II to parents who taught French, Julian Patrick Barnes studied French at Magdalen College, Oxford, from which he graduated with honors in 1968 with a degree in modern languages. After he left Oxford, his abiding interest in words and language led him to a position as a lexicographer for the *Oxford English Dictionary Supplement*. In 1972 Barnes became a freelance writer, preferring that parlous profession to the law. During the 1970's and 1980's, he wrote reviews for *The Times Literary Supplement* and was contributing editor to the *New Review*, assistant literary editor of the *New Statesman*, and deputy literary editor of the *Sunday Times* of London. For a decade he served as a television critic, most notably for the *London Observer*; his commentary was noted for being witty, irreverent, and provocative.

Influenced by the French writer Gustave Flaubert, particularly his concern for form, style, and objectivity, Barnes produced serious novels that continued to exhibit his fascination with language and literary experiments, in contrast with the more traditional narrative approach and narrow subject matter of many twentieth century English novelists. Under the pseudonym Dan Kava-

nagh, Barnes also published a number of detective novels, less experimental in style, although the major protagonist of these books is gay.

By the 1990's Barnes had become one of Britain's leading literary figures. His literary reviews appeared in many of the leading publications in both his own country and the United States. He also wrote brilliant journalistic pieces on various topics—political, social, and literary—some of them appearing in *The New Yorker*. Many of these essays have been collected and published in *Letters from London* (1995). Barnes's long-standing fascination with France was revealed in his collection of short stories *Cross Channel* (1996), a series of tales about Englishmen and -women and their experiences of living and working in France.

In the mid-1990's Barnes accepted a one-year teaching position at Johns Hopkins University, in part, he said, to increase his knowledge of American society, the United States being second only to France among Barnes's foreign fascinations. After a several-year novelistic hiatus, in 1998 he published *England, England*, which, like *Flaubert's Parrot*, was short-listed for the Booker Prize, Britain's premier literary award, a recognition Barnes again received in 2005 with *Arthur and George*. In 2008, Barnes's ruminations on familial dying, death, and the hereafter, *Nothing to Be Fearful Of*, received wide critical acclaim.

ANALYSIS

In all of his works Julian Barnes has pursued several ideas: Human beings question, even though there can be no absolute answers; humanity pursues its obsessions, with the pursuit often resulting in failure. His novels have at the same time evolved in form and approach—the earliest are more traditional and conventional; the later works are more experimental. Barnes's wit, irony, and satire, his use of history, literary criticism, myth, and fable, his melding of imagination and intellect, and his continuing risk in exploring new forms and methods make him one of the most significant English novelists of his generation.

METROLAND

Barnes's first novel, *Metroland*, is orthodox in technique and approach; divided into three parts, it is a variation on the traditional bildungsroman, or coming-of-age novel. In part 1, the narrator, Christopher Lloyd, and his close friend, Toni, grow up in 1963 in a north London suburb on the Metropolitan rail line (thus the title), pursuing the perennial adolescent dream of rebellion against parents, school, the middle class, and the establishment in general. Convinced of the superiority of French culture and consciously seeking answers to what they believe to be the larger questions of life, they choose to cultivate art, literature, and music in order to astound what they see as the bourgeoisie and its petty concerns.

Part 2, five years later, finds Christopher a student in Paris, the epitome of artistic bohemianism, particularly when compared to his life in Metroland. It is 1968, and French students are demonstrating and rioting in the streets for social and political causes. None of this touches Christopher; he is more concerned about his personal self-discovery than about changing or challenging the wider world.

Nine years later, in part 3, set in 1977, Christopher is back in Metroland, married to Marion, an Englishwoman of his own class, with a child, a mortgaged suburban house, and a nine-to-five job. Toni, still a rebel, chides Christopher for selling out to the enemy. Ironically, however, Christopher is content with life in Metroland. He consciously examines and questions his present circumstances but accepts their rewards and satisfactions.

Questioning and irony are continuing themes in all of Barnes's novels, as is the absence of significant character development except for the leading figure. Toni, Christopher's French girlfriend Annick, and Marion, his English wife, are not much more than supporting figures. Relationships are explored through Christopher's narration alone, and Christopher finds himself, his questions, and his life of most concern and interest to him.

BEFORE SHE MET ME

Before She Met Me is also a story of an individual's attempt to relate to and understand his personal world. Graham Hendrick, a forty-year-old professor of history, has recently remarried. Now beginning a new life, happy with Ann, his new wife, and outwardly contented, both personally and professionally, Hendrick seems to be an older variation of Christopher and his self-satisfied middle-class existence. As in his first novel, Barnes includes a bohemian writer, Jack Lupton, as a foil for Hendrick's respectable conformity.

Before they were married, Ann acted in several minor films, and after viewing one of them, Hendrick, the historian, begins to search out his wife's past. At first his quest seems based on simple curiosity; soon, however, Ann's history begins to take over Hendrick's present life. Losing his professional objectivity as a historian, succumbing to jealousy, compulsively immersing himself in Ann's past, blurring the distinction between the real Ann and her image on the screen, Hendrick becomes completely obsessed. Seeing the present as a world without causes, Hendrick finds his crusade in the past, and that crusade is no longer public but private. Bordering on the melodramatic, *Before She Met Me* is the story of the downward spiral of an individual who can no longer distinguish fantasy from reality.

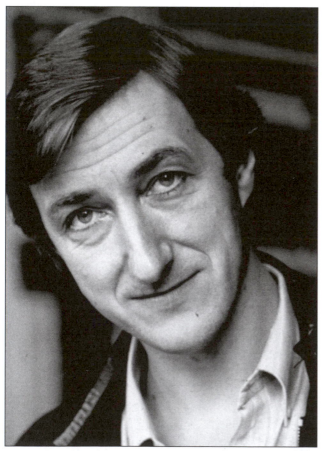

Julian Barnes. (© Miriam Berkley)

Did the love affairs Ann had on the screen replicate her private life off camera? Are her past love affairs continuing in the present?

Barnes poses the question, not only for Hendrick, caught up in his obsession, but also for the reader: What is reality, and can one discover the truth? Like *Metroland*, this novel has many comic and witty moments but ultimately ends tragically. Ann and Lupton had an affair that has since ended, but Hendrick, in his obsessive quest, falsely concludes that it continues; he murders Lupton and then, in Ann's presence, he takes his own life. Although told in the third person, *Before She Met Me* centers on the plight of a single figure questioning his world. Hendrick and his compulsions dominate the novel: His first wife, their child, Ann, and Lupton are figures perceived through his persona.

FLAUBERT'S PARROT

With his third novel published under his own name, *Flaubert's Parrot*, Barnes received considerable praise as a significant writer of fiction, less parochial in form and technique than most English novelists of his time. His first book published in the United States, *Flaubert's Parrot* was the recipient of numerous prizes. It too is a novel of questions and obsessions that unite the past and present, but in its collage of literary techniques, it is not a traditional narrative novel, including as it does fiction, biography, history, and literary criticism. As in his earlier works, Barnes focuses on a single individual in the novel; Geoffrey Braithwaite is an English medical doctor in his sixties, a widower, with a long-standing interest in the French writer Gustave Flaubert. Barnes also has been a student of French and admirer of Flaubert, and early in *Metroland* Christopher reads a work by Flaubert; several critics have examined the possible relationships among the author and his fictional figures Braithwaite, Christopher, and Hendrick.

Told in the first person, *Flaubert's Parrot* examines Braithwaite's attempt to discover which of two different stuffed parrots on exhibit in competing Flaubert museums is the one that sat on Flaubert's desk when he wrote his short story "Un Cœur simple" ("A Simple Heart"). In the story, an old servant, Félicité, is left after fifty years of service with only a parrot as a companion. When the parrot dies, Félicité has it stuffed. As her health fails, she confuses the parrot with the Holy Ghost, traditionally represented as a dove. On her deathbed she believes that she sees a giant parrot above her head. Braithwaite's quest to determine which is the real parrot allows him, and Barnes, to pursue with wit and irony numerous aspects of Flaubert's biography: his published works, including *Madame Bovary* (1857), his ideas for works he did not write, his travels, his use of animals in his writings, and his lovers. The novel includes chronologies, a dictionary, and an examination paper.

Flaubert's Parrot is not concerned only with Braithwaite's interest in Flaubert's past and the two surviving stuffed parrots. As the doctor pursues Flaubert and his parrot, he also begins to reveal his own history. Braithwaite's wife had frequently been unfaithful to him, as Emma Bovary was to her husband Charles, and she had eventually committed suicide. As Braithwaite explores the relationship between Flaubert and his fiction, seeking to know which is the real parrot, he also attempts to understand the realities of his own life and his connection with the fictional Charles Bovary. He becomes obsessive about discovering the truth of the parrots, but he is also obsessive about discovering his own truth. The difficulty, however, is that truth and reality are always elusive, and the discovery of a number of small realities does not result in the illumination of absolute truth. In the course of his discussions, Braithwaite muses on the incompetence even of specialists in ferreting out the truth; he criticizes a prominent scholar of Flaubert, whom he accuses of pronouncing French badly, of mistakenly identifying a portrait as Flaubert and of being unable to specify the color of Emma Bovary's eyes.

Flaubert's parrot, too, is seen as a symbol of this dichotomy of fact and fiction. The parrot can utter human sounds, but only by mimicking what it hears; still, there is the appearance of understanding, regardless of whether it exists. Is a writer, such as Flaubert, merely a parrot, writing down human sounds and observing human life without understanding or interpretation? At the end of Braithwaite's search for the real stuffed parrot used by Flaubert while writing his short story, the doctor discovers that dozens of stuffed parrots exist that Flaubert could have borrowed and placed on his desk. Braithwaite's quest has thus been one of many with no resolutions, posing questions without final answers.

STARING AT THE SUN

Staring at the Sun, Barnes's fourth novel published under his own name, exhibits a stronger narrative line than *Flaubert's Parrot*, but as in the story of Braithwaite, narrative here is not the primary concern of the author; questions remain paramount. The central figure is a lower-middle-class woman, Jean Serjeant, significantly unlike earlier Barnes protagonists because she is naïve and unsophisticated, lacking any intellectual pretensions. The tone of Barnes's portrayal of Jean contrasts sharply with the wit and irony featured throughout *Flaubert's Parrot*. Even Jean asks questions, however, such as what happened to the sandwiches Charles Lindbergh did not eat when he flew over the Atlantic Ocean in 1927, and why the mink is so tenacious of life (a statement from a print that hung in her bedroom when she was a child). Those questions have no answers, and Jean muses that questions that do have answers are not real questions.

The novel begins in 1941, with a prologue set during World War II. Sergeant-pilot Prosser is flying back across the English Channel to his base from France, just before dawn. The sun rises from the waves on the eastern horizon, captivating Prosser's attention. Shortly after, he reduces his altitude when he sees smoke from a steamship far below. As he flies at the lower altitude, the sun comes up again from the sea into his view, and for the second time in a single morning he watches the sun's ascent. He calls this event an ordinary miracle, but he never forgets it. Neither does Jean, after Prosser relates it to her a few months later while temporarily billeted in her parents' home. Prosser soon disappears from Jean's life but not from her memories: He kills himself, she later discovers, by flying directly into the sun. She marries Michael, a policeman who has no time for or interest in questions.

After twenty years of marriage, at the age of forty, Jean becomes pregnant for the first time. She leaves Michael in order to discover what she calls a more difficult, first-rate life; she is more on a quest for self than seeking an escape from her unsatisfactory husband. When her son, Gregory, is old enough to be left alone, Jean begins to travel widely, often by airplane. She pursues her own Seven Wonders of the World. While visiting the Grand Canyon, she observes an airplane flying below the canyon's rim. At first it seems to her to be against nature, but she concludes instead that it is against reason: Nature provides the miracles, such as the Grand Canyon and the double rising of the sun. As the novel proceeds, Jean becomes more like Barnes's other figures and less like her naïve and unsophisticated young self.

Gregory also parallels Barnes's earlier intellectual characters and their questions that can yield no conclusive answers. Afraid of death but contemplating suicide, he meditates on the existence of God. He posits fourteen possible answers, but no final truth. The last part of the novel is set in the future, a world of intrusive and obtrusive computers. All the world's knowledge has been incorporated into the General Purposes Computer (GPC), open to everyone. The computer, however, cannot answer why minks are so tenacious of life. A special informational program, TAT (The Absolute Truth), is added to the GPC, but when Gregory asks TAT whether it believes in God, the computer answers that his question is not a real question, and when he asks why it is not a real question, TAT again responds that Gregory's second question is also not a real question. Only "real" questions, it appears, can be answered by computers. In what she believes will be the last incident in her long life, in 2021, Jean, at the age of ninety-nine, accompanied by Gregory, makes a final flight, observing the sun this time as it sets in the west rather than as it rises in the east, as it had done twice during Prosser's "ordinary miracle" so many years before.

A HISTORY OF THE WORLD IN 10½ CHAPTERS

In *A History of the World in 10½ Chapters*, Barnes continued his experimentation in form and style. Unlike his earlier novels, this one has no central character. Instead, the reader is presented with a number of chapters or stories, ostensibly historical, that are loosely connected by several common themes. The first tale or fable is a revisionist account of the story of Noah's Ark. Narrated by a woodworm, the story portrays Noah as a drunk, humanity as badly flawed, and God and his plan as leaving much to be desired. Human beings fare equally poorly in the other chapters, and the Ark returns in later stories: A nineteenth century Englishwoman searches for the Ark on Mount Ararat; a twentieth century American astronaut, also seeking the Ark, finds a skeleton that he identifies as Noah's but that is really the bones of the woman explorer; another chapter discusses the Ark in the form of the raft of the *Medusa*, painted by Théodore Géricault.

In this novel Barnes raises the question of how one turns disaster into art, or how one turns life into art. In a half chapter, or "Parenthesis," he discusses history and love:

> History isn't what happened. History is just what historians tell us. . . . The history of the world? Just voices echoing in the dark, images that burn for a few centuries and then fade; stories, old stories that sometimes seem to overlap; strange links, impertinent connections.

Barnes connects love to truth, but truth, objective truth, can never be found. Still, Sisyphus-like, one must constantly toil to find it. So it is with love: "We must believe in it, or we're lost." *A History of the World in 10½ Chapters* does not always succeed: The stories do not always relate to one another successfully, and the tone at times fails to achieve the ironic brilliance of *Flaubert's Parrot*.

TALKING IT OVER

Talking It Over is superficially a less ambitious novel than *A History of the World in 10½ Chapters*. The novel features three characters: Stuart, a decent, dull banker; his wife, Gillian; and Stuart's old friend, Oliver, a flashy, cultured language instructor who falls in love with Gillian, who eventually leaves Stuart for Oliver. The characters are perhaps predictable, as is the eventual outcome, but Barnes's technique reveals the same events narrated by all three characters, who speak directly in monologues to the reader. Considered something of a minor work by critics, the novel again shows considerable verbal felicity, and in spite of the seeming predictability of the plot and the ordinariness of the characters, by the end the reader comes to appreciate their quirks and foibles.

ENGLAND, ENGLAND

After the publication of *Talking It Over*, it was several years before Barnes's next full-length novel appeared, in 1998: *England, England*. In the interim he had written a novella, *The Porcupine*, set in an Eastern European country in the aftermath of the fall of Communism. In it Barnes notes how difficult it is to escape from the past, from history, and from its illusions and delusions,

and he asks what one will escape to—to what new illusions and imaginings. *England, England* is also a meditation on history. A serious novel with a comedic and satirical core, it features Sir Jack Pitman, a larger-than-life, egocentric businessman who builds a historical Disneyland-style theme park on the Isle of Wight, off England's southern coast. Here tourists can enjoy and experience all of England's past and present in the same place, from the real king and queen, who have moved from the real England to "England, England," to a new Buckingham Palace, a half-sized Big Ben, cricket matches, the cottage of William Shakespeare's wife Anne Hathaway, Stonehenge, poet William Wordsworth's daffodils, and every other event or place that in popular belief represents the English past. In time, this new England—"England, England"—becomes more successful, economically and in all other ways, than the country that inspired it.

Parallel to Pitman's story is that of Martha Cochrane, a leading member of his staff who briefly replaces him after discovering Pitman's unusual sexual proclivities. She, too, has had a difficult relationship with history, realizing that even personal reminiscences, like broader history, lack objective reality, and that even historical memories are in reality imaginative constructs. The past becomes what we want it to be, or what we fear it was. Eventually, in old age, Cochrane escapes the present, returning to the former England, which itself has retreated into a largely preindustrial, rural past and is now called Anglia. The question becomes, Can history go backward? Is Cochrane's Anglia any more authentic than Pitman's theme park? Was old England itself ever more "real" than Pitman's "England, England," or was it, too, just an assembly of illusions and delusions?

LOVE, ETC.

Love, etc. returns to the characters who inhabit *Talking It Over* after a ten-year interval. Gillian and Oliver have returned to England from France, where Gillian has become the family's breadwinner; Oliver is as irreverent as ever but a failure in achieving his ambitions, including that of screenwriter. They have had two children. Stuart had moved to the United States, married again, again unsuccessfully, and established several businesses, more successfully; he has returned to London, where he inserts himself in the lives of Gillian and

Oliver, without, however, knowing precisely what motivates him or with what ultimate aim.

As in *Talking It Over*, the story is told in the first person by the various characters, who include, in addition to the principals, Gillian's mother, Stuart's American ex-wife, and a young female assistant at Gillian's art business. As in director Akira Kurosawa's film *Rashomon* (1950), each character's perception of reality differs from that of the others, notably at the conclusion, when Stuart and Gillian have sex after Stuart has retreated to bed. Afterward, Stuart believes the sex was consensual, but to Gillian it was rape. As the novel ends, however, for Gillian the supposed rape has turned into something else, including the possibility that the world will turn again and it will be Oliver who will be on the outside looking in.

ARTHUR AND GEORGE

In *Arthur and George*, Barnes turns to an actual historical event as inspiration. Arthur is Arthur Conan Doyle, the creator of the famous literary character Sherlock Holmes, and George is George Edalji. George's father is a Church of England vicar, a Parsee from India, and his mother is Scottish. As Doyle rose in the world, and as his literary fame led to social and economic success, Edalji pursued his own more limited goal, that of becoming a solicitor, the lowest plank in England's hierarchical legal structure. Although Edalji saw himself as the quintessential Englishman, his mixed family background made him an anomaly in his small rural village. A loner, focused on his professional ambition, he did not make friends readily. A series of savage attacks on animals saw Edalji arrested, tried, convicted, and sentenced to seven years in prison for the crimes. There was a considerable public outcry about the trial and subsequent sentence, and after three years Edalji was freed from prison but not exonerated, and his conviction was allowed to stand.

In the eyes of many readers of his Sherlock Holmes stories, Doyle himself was Holmes's alter ego and a brilliant detective in his own right, and he received numerous pleas for assistance in solving readers' personal dilemmas. Most of these he ignored, preferring travel, playing golf and cricket, tending his terminally ill wife, balancing a long-term romantic relationship, and becoming increasingly fascinated by spiritualism and the occult. However, during a time when Doyle's life was in disarray after his first wife died, he received a letter from Edalji, asking for his assistance. Edalji hoped for Doyle's help in gaining a pardon that would allow him to take up his profession again. Doyle responded, convinced that Edalji was an innocent victim of racial bigotry, something that Edalji denied. In *Arthur and George*, Doyle is taken over by the persona of the fictional Holmes and pursues the truth in order to establish Edalji's innocence and to gain compensation for the three years in prison that the young solicitor had endured.

Real life, however, even in a novel, is not like fiction, and the best that Doyle's campaign was able to accomplish was an admission by the government that Edalji's trial was unjust; the government refused to pay compensation because it claimed that Edalji's attitude contributed to his conviction. This Doyle saw as sheer hypocrisy, but of course that is often the response of government officials when caught out of bounds. For Edalji, it was a partial victory, and he was able to resume his profession as a solicitor. He was also a privileged guest at Doyle's wedding reception, and although apparently Edalji and Doyle never met again, Edalji much later attended a spiritualist memorial service for Doyle at London's Royal Albert Hall.

Barnes has stated that the novel's quotations of all letters save one, of all court proceedings, and of newspaper and magazine reports are reproduced from actual historical records, although of course the dialogue and thoughts of the characters are fiction. *Arthur and George* follows the technique employed in *Love, etc.* in having the story related alternately from Doyle's and then from Edalji's perspective, although in the third person rather than in the first person of the earlier novel. Also, when Doyle becomes the detective in pursuit of Edalji's innocence, Barnes's literary style and technique brilliantly mimics Doyle's own in his Sherlock Holmes stories. Finally, authors create fictional worlds in their novels, but they are also products of their own real world. Racial divisions such as those in early twentieth century England, as portrayed in *Arthur and George*, continue to be of commanding importance in England, particularly since the events of September 11, 2001.

Eugene Larson

OTHER MAJOR WORKS

SHORT FICTION: *Cross Channel*, 1996; *The Lemon Table*, 2004.

NONFICTION: *Letters from London*, 1995 (essays); *Something to Declare: Essays on France*, 2002; *The Pedant in the Kitchen*, 2003; *Nothing to Be Frightened Of*, 2008.

TRANSLATION: *In the Land of Pain*, 2002 (of Alphonse Daudet's unpublished notes).

BIBLIOGRAPHY

Carey, John. "Land of Make-Believe." *The Sunday [London] Times*, August 23, 1998. Carey, a leading British academic and a literary critic, discusses *England, England* as an unusual combination of the comic and the serious, a philosophical novel that posits important questions about reality.

Guignery, Vanessa. *The Fiction of Julian Barnes*. London: Palgrave Macmillan, 2006. Provides an excellent assessment of Barnes's literary works, including his novels, and presents a compilation of the interpretation of Barnes's works by other critics.

Higdon, David Leon. "'Unconfessed Confessions': The Narrators of Graham Swift and Julian Barnes." In *The British and Irish Novel Since 1960*, edited by James Acheson. New York: St. Martin's Press, 1991. Argues that the fiction of Swift and Barnes defines what is meant by British postmodernism. Asserts that the works of the two authors share themes of estrangement, obsession, and the power of the past.

Locke, Richard. "Flood of Forms." *The New Republic* 201 (December 4, 1989): 40-43. Locke, a professor of comparative literature, places Barnes's interest in form and style in the context of modern literature, beginning with Gustave Flaubert. Summarizes all of Barnes's novels, focusing particularly on *A History of the World in 10½ Chapters*.

Mosely, Merritt. *Understanding Julian Barnes*. Columbia: University of South Carolina Press, 1997. Provides a general introduction to Barnes's life and work, briefly discussing his novels, stories, and nonfiction. Includes a bibliography of criticism of Barnes's fiction.

Pateman, Matthew. *Julian Barnes*. Tavistock, England: Northcote House, 2002. Presents an insightful scholarly interpretation of Barnes's novels through *Love, etc.*

Rubinson, Gregory J. *The Fiction of Rushdie, Barnes, Winterson, and Carter: Breaking Cultural and Literary Boundaries in the Work of Four Postmodernists*. Jefferson, N.C.: McFarland, 2005. Examines how Barnes and three other important postmodern authors—Salman Rushdie, Jeanette Winterson, and Angela Carter—use literary devices to challenge culturally accepted ideas about such subjects as race and gender. Include index.

Stout, Mira. "Chameleon Novelist." *The New York Times Magazine*, November 22, 1992. Offers a brief biographical sketch, covering Barnes's childhood, his circle of friends, and his marriage to agent Patricia Kavanagh, and then discusses Barnes's experiments with various narrative forms and his common themes of obsession, dislocation, death, art, and religion.

PÍO BAROJA

Born: San Sebastián, Spain; December 28, 1872
Died: Madrid, Spain; October 30, 1956
Also known as: Pío Baroja y Nessi

PRINCIPAL LONG FICTION

La casa de Aizgorri, 1900
Aventuras, inventos y mixtificaciones de Silvestre Paradox, 1901
Camino de perfección, 1902 (*Road to Perfection*, 2008)
El mayorazgo de Labraz, 1903 (*The Lord of Labraz*, 1926)
Aurora roja, 1904 (*Red Dawn*, 1924)
La busca, 1904 (*The Quest*, 1922)
Mala hierba, 1904 (*Weeds*, 1923)
La lucha por la vida, 1904 (collective title for previous 3 novels; *The Struggle for Life*, 1922-1924)
La feria de los discretos, 1905 (*The City of the Discreet*, 1917)
Paradox, rey, 1906 (*Paradox, King*, 1931)
La ciudad de la niebla, 1909
Zalacaín el aventurero, 1909 (*Zalacaín the Adventurer*, 1997)
César o nada, 1910 (*Caesar or Nothing*, 1919)
El árbol de la ciencia, 1911 (*The Tree of Knowledge*, 1928)
Las inquietudes de Shanti Andía, 1911 (*The Restlessness of Shanti Andía, and Other Writings*, 1959)
El mundo es ansí, 1912 (English translation, 1970)
Memorias de un hombre de acción, 1913-1935 (22 volumes)
La sensualidad pervertida, 1920
La leyenda de Juan de Alzate, 1922 (*The Legend of Juan de Alzate*, 1959)
El cura de Monleón, 1936

OTHER LITERARY FORMS

Pío Baroja (bah-ROH-hah) wrote short stories, essays, memoirs, and verse in addition to his many novels.

Some of his novels are written in dialogue; in fact, Anthony Kerrigan presents *The Legend of Juan de Alzate* as a play in his introduction to *The Restlessness of Shanti Andía, and Other Writings*. Among Baroja's last books are his seven volumes of *Memorias* (1955), in which he availed himself of whole sections lifted from his fiction, which is, in turn, often autobiographical.

Baroja's first book was a collection of short stories, *Vidas sombrías* (1900; somber lives), which demonstrated a sympathetic tenderness for his characters that would diminish as his literary career advanced. Some of the stories are very short slice-of-life vignettes, and others concern the supernatural, such as "El trasgo" (the goblin) and "Medium." Some explore the psychology of women: "Agueda" treats the romantic stirrings in the mind of a disabled girl in the manner of Tennessee Williams's *The Glass Menagerie* (1944), and "Lo desconocido" ("The Unknown") probes the sudden and temporary urge of a bourgeois woman, traveling on a train with her husband, to flee the confines of the coach into the fascination of the night beyond. Others of these early stories contain the nuclei of future novels, such as "Un justo" (a just man), which prefigures *El cura de Monleón* and "Los panaderos" (the bakers), which anticipates the trilogy *The Struggle for Life*.

Baroja's second collection of short stories, *Idilios vascos* (1901-1902; Basque idylls), includes "Elizabide el vagabundo" (the love story of a vagabond), remarkable for its happy ending; a thirty-eight-year-old bachelor returns to Spain from Uruguay, falls in love, and to his surprise, finds that his love is reciprocated.

Baroja's essays do not differ substantially from his novels in view of the fact that he never hesitates to pack his novels with his own opinions. Baroja is not noted for the depth of his philosophical thinking, and he failed to assimilate with genuine understanding much of the material that he cites from the great philosophers.

In the book-length essay *Ciudades de Italia* (1949; cities of Italy), Baroja expresses his fear that the work will be a *chapuza* (botch-job) because he is not an art lover, a good tourist, or an aesthete. Art, as Baroja had told his readers years before, is child's play in comparison to the serious business of philosophy. Neither is he a lover of Italy; although he would have preferred to visit the United States or Germany, he chose Italy because it was cheaper to visit.

El tablado de Arlequín (1901; harlequinade) is an ongoing diatribe against Spaniards for their abulia. *Juventud, egolatría* (1917; *Youth and Egolatry*, 1920) summarizes the author's views on politics, religion, sex, morality, literature, and a host of other topics; the volume also contains a brief study of three of his ancestral clans—the Goñis, the Zornozas, and the Alzates, the humorous tone of which cannot disguise the pride Baroja takes in the contemplation of his own lineage.

Nuevo tablado de Arlequín (1917; new harlequinade) contains a brief history of Baroja's native Basque village, Vera del Bidasoa, and a long apologia for the German cause in World War I. *Vitrina pintoresca* (1935; picturesque showcase) treats a potpourri of topics ranging from the Jesuits, the Jews, and the Masons to the rivers of Spain, haunted houses, and the demons of carnival.

Baroja's attempts at poetry appear in *Canciones del suburbio* (1944; songs from the outskirts), published at the end of his career, not without the author's misgivings. This book is scarcely to be judged by the standards of serious poetry but is valuable inasmuch as it sheds light on Baroja the person. Indeed, Camilo José Cela considers the poems the best single book through which to become acquainted with their author.

ACHIEVEMENTS

Gerald Brenan dubbed Pío Baroja the greatest of Spanish novelists, second only to Benito Pèrez Galdós. Pedro Salinas called the gallery of Baroja's characters

Pío Baroja. (Popperfoto/Getty Images)

"perhaps the richest" of Spanish literature. In 1972, G. G. Brown wrote that Baroja's influence on the modern Spanish novel has been greater than that of all of his contemporaries put together, and added that although non-Spanish readers may find this "puzzling," Baroja's popularity in Spain is an "indisputable fact." Brown's aside is clearly directed at those English-language critics who have been cool in their appraisal of Baroja's art.

Critic Gregorio Marañon attributed to Baroja a major role in forging a social conscience in the middle-class Spanish youth of his generation. Marañon characterized the books of Baroja's Madrid trilogy, *The Struggle for Life*, as three breaches in the wall of self-absorption that blinded the Spanish bourgeoisie to the misery amid which the majority of their compatriots lived. Although the *generación del 98*, or Generation of '98, counted among its numbers figures more intellectual than Baroja, he is the only one of them to have a significant following. Cela declared that the entire post-Civil War novel springs from his works and decried the fact that Baroja was not awarded the Nobel Prize. Indeed, the influence of Baroja is to be found in subsequent novels by such authors as Cela, Juan Antonio Zunzunegui, Miguel Delibes, José María Gironella, Ignacio Aldecoa, and Luis Martín-Santos.

Furthermore, Baroja stands apart from the nineteenth century realistic novelists who strived to arrange the elements of their fiction into interpretive patterns from which their readers could glean transcendent meaning. Through the example of his fiction, which chronicles the random inconsequentiality of his characters' lives, Baroja can therefore be credited, as Brown observes, with an attempt to reform what for thirty centuries has been seen as one of the principal functions of art—to organize experience into meaningful patterns.

Among American authors who profited from reading Baroja are John Dos Passos and Ernest Hemingway. Dos Passos, who wrote about Baroja in *Rosinante to the Road Again* (1922), was especially influenced by Baroja's anarchic tendencies, at least until the time of his disenchantment with the political Left in the later 1930's and, like Baroja, he wrote many of his novels in trilogies. Hemingway, who cherished Baroja's commitment to narrative brevity, paid homage to the Basque octogenarian at his deathbed; in his personal correspondence he deplored

the fact that publisher Alfred Knopf had "dropped" Baroja when he did not sell well in the United States.

Although Baroja encouraged the myth of his simple and unappreciated bohemian existence, this is not quite the case. At the time of his death, he left behind the not unimpressive sum of 750,000 pesetas, and in 1934, he was elected to the Royal Spanish Academy.

BIOGRAPHY

Pío Baroja y Nessi was the third son of Serafín Baroja y Zornoza (1840-1915) and Carmen Nessi y Goñi (1849-1935). The young Baroja was extremely knowledgeable about his ancestry and careful to note that he was seven-eighths Basque and one-eighth Italian; his mother's surname, Nessi, was of Italian origin. His father was a mining engineer with a literary bent who was more concerned with what his friends thought of him than with the esteem of his family. An older brother, Ricardo Baroja (1871-1953), a painter and inventor, also was a writer. In 1879, the senior Baroja took his family to live in Madrid, then they moved to Pamplona; in 1886, they moved once again to Madrid.

Although not an exceptional student, Baroja entered the School of Medicine in Madrid at the age of fifteen and by 1891 completed his medical studies in Valencia. Two years later, he completed his thesis and obtained a position as practitioner in the Basque village of Cestona. The pettiness of small-town life and the suffering and the poverty that he was forced to witness daily disgusted him, and he decided to abandon his medical career. What he did not abandon, however, was the medical knowledge he had acquired; his novels are peopled with a host of doctors, and his dialogue bristles with the names and exploits of the heroes of medicine and physiology.

Baroja returned to Madrid to help his brother manage the family bakery, which allowed him to become familiar with the lower social orders of Madrid, a subject that would provide material for some twenty novels of his own creation. His venture into business was not successful, and it has been suggested that Baroja's hostility toward socialism may stem from his difficulties while running the bakery with the unions to which his employees belonged.

In 1898, Spain suffered the fiasco of the Spanish-American War, and in its soul-searching wake was born the Generation of '98. Although he is generally considered to have been a member of this group, Baroja himself denied any such affiliation: He scorned the artistic artifice of Ramón María del Valle-Inclán, disagreed with José Ortega y Gasset regarding the purpose of the novel, and resented the self-importance of Miguel de Unamuno y Jugo. Toward the popular novelist Vicente Blasco Ibáñez he harbored a deep loathing.

In 1899, Baroja made his first visit to Paris, and by 1900, when he published his first book, he was writing for such periodicals as *El país*, *El imparcial*, and *Revista nueva*. After purchasing a home in his native Basque village of Vera del Bidasoa in 1912, he divided his time between there and his home in Madrid, which he shared with his mother. He never married but had a number of liaisons that proved unsatisfactory. Although he grudgingly gave his support to Francisco Franco as the lesser of two evils at the outbreak of the Spanish Civil War, he left Spain voluntarily for Paris in the summer of 1936 and did not return until 1940.

During Baroja's final days, Ernest Hemingway, who had recently won the Nobel Prize, paid Baroja a visit. He brought with him a pair of socks and a bottle of his favorite whiskey, and told Baroja that the prize rightfully belonged to him. *Time* magazine, in October, 1956, recorded Baroja's succinct but unfortunately apocryphal reaction to such lavish praise: "Caramba." The less romantic truth is that in his arteriosclerotic haze, Baroja could do no more than respond to this tribute with an uncomprehending stare.

ANALYSIS

Near the end of his life, Pío Baroja listed those historical personalities who had sustained his interest the longest: the naturalist Charles Darwin; the chemist Louis Pasteur; the physiologist Claude Bernard; the philosophers Friedrich Nietzsche, Arthur Schopenhauer, and Immanuel Kant; and the poets Lord Byron, Giacomo Leopardi, and Gustavo Adolfo Bécquer. His writing was permanently influenced by such French and Spanish serial writers as Xavier de Montepin and Manuel Fernández y González and by the Spanish picaresque novel. He admired Charles Dickens but not William Makepeace Thackeray, Stendhal but not Gustave Flaubert, Paul Verlaine but not Marcel Proust, and

Giacomo Leopardi but not Alessandro Manzoni. Despairing of the world's capacity to produce writers of the highest caliber continually (his motto was "Nothing new under the sun"), he declared that the likes of Fyodor Dostoevski and Leo Tolstoy would not be seen again.

Baroja was as misanthropic and pessimistic as his mentor Schopenhauer and, also like the German philosopher, has been characterized as a misogynist. Baroja's references to the ignorance, greed, and superficiality of Spanish women are legion, yet his misogyny seems to be an ancillary property of his all-embracing misanthropy rather than an independent prejudice. Baroja's pessimism is reflected in his diction—in the frequent appearance of such words as *imbécil*, *estúpido*, and *absurdo*, as well as a bevy of more colorful words such as *energúmeno* (madman) and *gaznápiro* (simpleton). One of his favorite words for everything is *farsante* (farcical).

Baroja boasted that he used no word in his novels that was not appropriate in conversation, yet this does not preclude experimentation with unusual words that caught his fancy, for example, *cachupinada* (entertainment) and *zaquizamí* (garret). His love of the colorful is evident in the phrase he used to characterize himself—*pajarraco del individualismo* (big, ugly bird of individualism). Despite Baroja's commitment to the colloquial mode, he generally avoided slang unless it was for the purpose of local color in dialogue. In *The Struggle for Life* trilogy especially, his dialogue is strewn with italicized vocabulary peculiar to the low life of Madrid, for example, *aluspiar* (to stalk), *diñar* (to die), *jamar* (to eat). The practice of italicizing the vocabulary of the low life would be accepted and used even more by his follower Juan Antonio Zunzunegui, who came to occupy Baroja's vacant chair in the Royal Spanish Academy.

Baroja had an ear for pronunciation as well. When he returned to the Basque country after several years in Madrid as a child, he was ridiculed for his Madrilenian accent, and, on occasion, he notes this accent in his characters. He also had a penchant for decorating his prose with the lyrics of traditional songs not only in Basque but also in the other peninsular dialects; even in his essay on Italy, lyrics in the Italian dialects are cited. Indeed, refrains and simple repetitions for musical effects are typical of all of his prose.

Contemptuous of stylistic preciosity, he defended his

right as a novelist to be terse and even ungrammatical. Because he avoided grammatical convolutions so consistently, his works are easier reading than many other Spanish classics and are, therefore, very popular in introductory literature courses wherever in the world that Spanish is taught.

Long non-Spanish names that point to the incontestable Basque origin of the characters that they denote are frequent in Baroja's novels. His fascination with anthropology is obvious in his abundant use of ethnological designations (for example, *samnita*, the name of a pre-Roman tribe of southern Italy, is used generally as "stalwart" in *Lord of Labraz*) and in his sweeping generalizations about race (for example, Sacha in *El mundo es ansí* observing that there is not a significant difference between northern and southern Spaniards, as there is among Italians). Baroja's use of the novel as a forum to hold forth on just about anything brings about many allusions to figures from the past, not only political leaders and writers but also physiologists, philosophers, painters, and anthropologists, who are more often German, French, or Italian than Spanish.

Baroja's sensitivity to the suffering in life and his abhorrence of human cruelty and hypocrisy made him a severe judge of the human condition. He hated religion, which he believed is a dangerous illusion foisted on Europeans by the Semites. His novel *El cura de Monleón*, which deals with a Basque priest's loss of faith, is unfortunately unsuccessful because Baroja, as an unbeliever, simply could not understand the depth of emotion such a loss of faith would entail for a priest. God is conceived as *patoso*, a bungler who, if he exists at all, is to be found in the scientific laboratory. Just as fiercely, Baroja abhorred the laws of the state, and his novel *Red Dawn* explores the world of anarchy and anarchists. Like the author himself, the protagonist of *Red Dawn*, Juan Alcazán, is a humanitarian, rather than a doctrinal, anarchist; Baroja himself never dared to act on any of the anarchistic tendencies that he felt.

All Baroja's novels contain adventure, and if his adventuresome characters do not overcome the obstacles with which they are confronted, it is because they lose faith in life and fall victim to abulia. César Moncada, for example, in *Caesar or Nothing*, tries to imitate Cesare Borgia, but his Machiavellian goals fail in the face of his

innate pessimism. At the age of seventy, Baroja said that he still felt, as he had at the age of fifteen, a distant enthusiasm for adventure without really believing in it.

Baroja's fiction embraces a wide geographic purview. Some novels portray the Basque provinces of Spain, whose countryside he considered the purest and most authentic in Europe, isolated from the cement-and-cinema falsity of contemporary "civilization." Some portray the low life of Madrid (for example, *The Struggle for Life*), others have the Carlist Wars as a backdrop (for example, *Zalacaín el aventurero* and the Aviraneta series), and Andalusia is represented with originality in *The City of the Discreet*. Still others take place outside Spain (for example, *La ciudad de la niebla*, that is, London) or have as protagonists characters who are not Spanish (for example, Sacha Savarof, a Russian medical student who is observed in France, Switzerland, Italy, Russia, and Spain in *El mundo es ansí*).

PARADOX, KING

Paradox, King, a novel almost exclusively in dialogue, is one of Baroja's most highly acclaimed creations. Written in two weeks, it is a masterful combination of satire and fantasy, of misanthropy and humor. The restless Silvestre Paradox, a poverty-stricken inventor, joins an expedition to Africa organized to establish a Jewish colony, and is accompanied by a colorful group of naturalists, soldiers, and adventurers. The ship that takes them to Africa is wrecked in a storm and the survivors are taken captive in Bu-Tata, capital of the kingdom of Uganga. Once the captives conciliate the initially hostile natives, Paradox is proclaimed King, and the group institutes a European form of government that emphasizes complete freedom and dispenses with laws, schools, and teachers. At length, the French feel obliged to intervene; they bring "civilization" to Africa in the form of tuberculosis, alcoholism, and prostitution. The hospital fills up with epidemic victims, and Princess Mahu is driven to dancing nude in a nightclub.

Baroja uses the peculiarities of his characters to satirize his own aversions. There is, for example, the overbearing feminist Miss Pich, who insists that Socrates, William Shakespeare, and King David were women; her "fate" is to be raped by savages. The cynicism of *Paradox, King* concerning the lack of commitment among educators, theologians, and scientists, and the notion that humans can never escape the evils of civilization, even in a utopia, are totally in keeping with the fundamentals of Baroja's thinking.

THE TREE OF KNOWLEDGE

Like *Paradox, King*, Baroja's other masterpiece, *The Tree of Knowledge*, which the author believed was his best philosophical novel, emphasizes dialogue. The novel also contains the author's most successfully drawn protagonist, Andrés Hurtado, a sad and sensitive man whose pastimes, reading, attitudes, and sympathies closely parallel Baroja's own. Hurtado goes to Madrid to study medicine and is soon disillusioned by the inadequacy of his professors and the coldness of the hospital staff. Neither does his family afford him any relief from his pessimism, since he is incompatible with his father; he adores his little brother, Luisito, but the child soon dies of tuberculosis.

Once he becomes a doctor, Hurtado accepts a post in an isolated village, where he observes the same crassness and inhumanity as he had observed in the city. When he returns to Madrid, as he must, he meets Lulu, a woman of humble origins, and they marry. Hurtado considers himself unfit for fatherhood and knows that Lulu is not robust, but she becomes pregnant in defiance of biological probability. Just when marriage seems to have saved Hurtado from despair, Lulu dies, and Hurtado, refusing to confront an intolerable reality, decides to commit suicide.

ZALACAÍN EL AVENTURERO

Another popular novel, regarded by Baroja as one of his best, is *Zalacaín el aventurero*. Instinctively rather than intellectually philosophical in the manner of Hurtado, Zalacaín emerges as a hero unfettered by convention who tests his destiny. An orphan, Zalacaín comes under the influence of his cynical old uncle, Tellagorri, who comes to appreciate Zalacaín when he sees evidence of the boy's pluckiness. Zalacaín grows up to be successful in all of his endeavors, in war, in his career as a smuggler, and with women. At length, he dies in a dispute instigated by his wealthy brother-in-law, Carlos Ohando, who is resentful of Zalacaín for earning the love of his sister Catalina. The hero's violent death is consistent with the romantic conception of the novel, and the three roses laid on his grave by Linda, Rosita, and Catalina further suggest the hero of a romantic ballad.

THE RESTLESSNESS OF SHANTI ANDÍA

Baroja's early novel *The Restlessness of Shanti Andía*, belatedly translated into English some five decades after its original publication, is a complicated tale of maritime adventure that takes place in the idyllic Basque fishing village of Lúzaro. Shanti is torn by his loyalty to the Basque countryside and to the sea and is, as Beatrice Patt observes, a collector of adventures lived by others. He idolizes his dead uncle, Juan de Aguirre, a sea captain whose mysterious voyages made him a village myth. Much of the novel is taken up by Shanti's attempts to unravel his uncle's past, which involves tales of piracy, mutiny, buried treasure, and the slave trade. As pessimistic as Andrés Hurtado, Shanti comes across as a passive observer before the action-filled drama of someone else's heroics, a drama that he himself must narrate.

Although Baroja's dissatisfaction with human, and especially Spanish, society is everywhere evident in his fiction, the fast pace of his narrative and the lyric description that provides a background of poetry and almost druidic awe before the phenomena of nature keep his novels from being morbid. Those who dislike Baroja have chosen to emphasize his nonconformist and anarchistic nature, his melancholy, and the illogic of some of his pet arguments, while his admirers have chosen to emphasize the author's gentle nature hidden behind a defensive mask of sarcasm, a pose that he himself delighted in keeping alive. Nevertheless, there is little in his nearly one hundred books that escaped the severity of his uncompromising judgment against the false world of convention and complacency that engulfs the lives of most people and seals them off forever from compassion.

Jack Shreve

OTHER MAJOR WORKS

SHORT FICTION: *Vidas sombrías*, 1900; *Idilios vascos*, 1901-1902.

POETRY: *Canciones del suburbio*, 1944.

NONFICTION: *El tablado de Arlequín*, 1901; *Juventud, egolatría*, 1917 (*Youth and Egolatry*, 1920); *Nuevo tablado de Arlequín*, 1917; *La caverna del humorismo*, 1919; *Momentum catastrophicum*, 1919; *Divagaciones apasionadas*, 1924; *Entretenimientos*, 1927; *Aviraneta: O, La vida de un conspirador*, 1931;

Vitrina pintoresca, 1935; *Pequeños ensayos*, 1943; *Ciudades de Italia*, 1949; *La obsesión del misterio*, 1952; *Memorias*, 1955 (7 volumes).

MISCELLANEOUS: *Obras completas*, 1946-1951 (8 volumes).

BIBLIOGRAPHY

Barrow, Leo L. *Negation in Baroja: A Key to His Novelistic Creativity*. Tucson: University of Arizona Press, 1971. Explores the novelist's technique of "creating by destroying" as a rebellion against conventional Western values. Discusses the style, dialogue, atmosphere, characterization, and landscape in his novels to explain how Baroja uses fiction to express his philosophical, political, and social attitudes.

Devlin, John. *Spanish Anticlericalism: A Study in Modern Alienation*. New York: Las Americas, 1966. Links Baroja with other prorepublican writers whose works exhibit strong anticlerical bias. Locates the source of his disdain for religion in the agnosticism that underlies his novels.

DuPont, Denise. *Realism as Resistance: Romanticism and Authorship in Galdós, Clarín, and Baroja*. Lewisburg, Pa.: Bucknell University Press, 2006. Explores the boundaries between realism and Romanticism in novels by three Spanish authors: Baroja's *The Struggle for Life*, Leopoldo Alas's *La regenta*, and Benito Pérez Galdós's first series of *Episodios nacionales*. All three novels feature quixotic characters who act as authors, which DuPont traces to the influence of an earlier Spanish author—Miguel de Cervantes.

Landeira, Ricardo. *The Modern Spanish Novel, 1898-1936*. Boston: Twayne, 1985. A chapter on Baroja surveys the novelist's achievement and discusses *Paradox, King* and the other novels in the trilogy dealing with "The Fantastic Life." Considers the novel the bitterest of the three in attacking social ills.

Murphy, Katharine. *Re-Reading Pío Baroja and English Literature*. New York: Peter Lang, 2004. Murphy points out the many structural similarities between Baroja's early fiction and the novels of his contemporaries in England and Ireland, most notably Joseph Conrad, Thomas Hardy, E. M. Forster, and James Joyce. Her examination focuses on how Baroja and the English-language authors treat human consciousness, the identity and role of the artist, European landscapes, and questions of form, genre, and representation.

_____. "Subjective Vision in *El árbol de la ciencia* and *Jude the Obscure*." *Bulletin of Spanish Studies* 79, no. 2/3 (March, 2002): 331-353. Murphy compares Baroja's novel to Hardy's *Jude the Obscure*, examining how both novels use a single-consciousness technique that reflects the modernist interest in subjective experience. She also finds similarities between the two novels' creation of characters who cannot be explained by the reader or the author.

Patt, Beatrice P. *Pío Baroja*. New York: Twayne, 1971. Excellent introduction to the writer and his works. Briefly discusses Baroja's attitudes toward the church and state. Reviews Baroja's use of extended dialogue in *Paradox, King*; points out how it permits him to introduce personal prejudices into a work he considered "half-fantasy, half-satirical poem."

Reid, John T. *Modern Spain and Liberalism*. Stanford, Calif.: Stanford University Press, 1937. Extensive study of Baroja's novels as documents chronicling the social and political climate in his country. Claims the novelist intends that his works serve as statements of the principles of liberalism that counter the fascist tendencies of his homeland.

Turner, Harriet, and Adelaida López de Martínez, eds. *The Cambridge Companion to the Spanish Novel: From 1600 to the Present*. New York: Cambridge University Press, 2003. Essays trace the development of the Spanish novel, including Baroja's *The Tree of Knowledge*, *El mundo es así*, and other novels. Situates him within the broader context of Spanish literature.

JOHN BARTH

Born: Cambridge, Maryland; May 27, 1930
Also known as: John Simmons Barth

PRINCIPAL LONG FICTION

The Floating Opera, 1956
The End of the Road, 1958
The Sot-Weed Factor, 1960
Giles Goat-Boy: Or, The Rev. New Syllabus, 1966
Chimera, 1972 (3 novellas)
Letters, 1979
Sabbatical: A Romance, 1982
The Tidewater Tales: A Novel, 1987
The Last Voyage of Somebody the Sailor, 1991
Once upon a Time: A Floating Opera, 1994
Coming Soon!!!, 2001
The Development, 2008

OTHER LITERARY FORMS

While John Barth's novels have ensured his eminence among contemporary American writers, his works of short fiction have been no less influential or controversial. In addition to his novels, Barth has published a collection of shorter works, *Lost in the Funhouse* (1968), the technical involutions of which plumb the nature of narrative itself and disrupt conventional relationships between teller and tale. Barth has also published two essays of particular significance. In "The Literature of Exhaustion," he discusses those writers whose suspicion that certain forms of literature have become obsolete is incorporated both thematically and technically in the fiction they produce. He highlights the successes of Jorge Luis Borges, Vladimir Nabokov, and Samuel Beckett in the face of apparent artistic impasse; they acknowledge and push beyond the boundaries staked out by their literary predecessors and employ a potentially stifling sense of "ultimacy" in the creation of new work, so that their forms become metaphors for their aesthetic concerns. "The Literature of Replenishment" seeks to correct any misreading of the former essay as a complaint that contemporary writers have little left to accomplish save the parody of conventions that they arrived upon too late to

benefit from themselves. Barth's method is to define and legitimate postmodernism by placing its most interesting practitioners—he singles out Italo Calvino and Gabriel García Márquez for praise—in a direct line of succession that may be traced through the great modernists of the first half of the twentieth century back to eighteenth century novelist Laurence Sterne and sixteenth century writer Miguel de Cervantes. "The Literature of Replenishment" makes clear that Barth is not averse to admitting realistic elements into his fictional worlds, provided they do not constrain the imagination. Both of these essays are collected in *The Friday Book: Essays and Other Nonfiction* (1984). *The Friday Book* and its companion volume, *Further Fridays: Essays, Lectures, and Other Nonfiction* (1995), also contain many essays dealing with Barth's affection for and interest in his native state of Maryland.

ACHIEVEMENTS

Perhaps John Barth's method is a mark of a growing receptivity among readers and critics to formally venturesome fiction; perhaps it is merely a result of the writer's inevitable passage from unexpected new voice to mature artist. Whatever the case, Barth infiltrated the literary establishment with relative ease, with no perceptible compromise. He became the foremost existential novelist in the United States, but his approach to the rather somber question of the arbitrariness of moral values and the absence of intrinsic meaning has always been richly overlaid with humor that is at times intricate and esoteric and often expansive and full of delight in its own verbal virtuosity. Barth has shown a career-long obsession with mythology, with how classical tales may be reconstituted in and provide resonance for contemporary fiction, and with how the novel may continue to respond to the age-old and seemingly insatiable need for the coherent pleasures of narrative.

Barth continues to have his detractors, whose accusations typically focus on his tendency to overwork his jokes (a condemnation that often attends *Giles Goat-Boy*) or to surrender to vulgar effects (as in his revisionist history of John Smith's encounter with Pocahontas in *The Sot-Weed Factor*). Nevertheless, few would dispute Barth's stature as the most widely appreciated postmodernist, a designation that he embraces despite its connotation of self-absorption and unreadability. Barth won the National Book Award in 1973 for *Chimera*.

BIOGRAPHY

John Simmons Barth was born on May 27, 1930, in Cambridge, Maryland, the contemporary and historical environs of which have provided the setting for much of his writing. He attended Cambridge High School, after which he accommodated his passion for jazz and the drums with a brief stay at the Juilliard School. His unspectacular showing there led him to enroll at Johns Hopkins University, a move made possible when he won a scholarship he had forgotten he had applied for. He achieved the highest grade point average in the university's College of Arts and Sciences upon receiving the bachelor of arts degree in 1951.

To pay off tuition debts and support his wife (Harriet Anne Strickland, whom he had married in 1950), Barth took a job in the Classics Library, where he first became absorbed in the Asian tale cycles that would later inform the style and content of his own fiction. During this period came his first publications in student literary magazines, including one story, "Lilith and the Lion," the appearance of which in *The Hopkins Review* when Barth was twenty may rightly be considered his first professional work. His master's project was *The Shirt of Nessus*, a novel based on a love triangle including a father and son and populated by rapists, murderers, bootleggers, and lunatics; Barth confesses it a miscarriage, and he says it now rests in the Dorchester marshes on Chesapeake Bay.

Having received his master of arts degree in the spring of 1952, he began studying for a Ph.D. in the aesthetics of literature while tutoring and teaching freshman composition courses, until the cost of supporting both his family (his third child was born in January, 1954) and his education compelled him to teach full time. He took a

John Barth. (Teturo Maruyama)

position at Pennsylvania State University in 1953; his experience with freshman composition there would eventually find its way into *The End of the Road*. (He did not earn his doctorate until 1969, from the University of Maryland.) While at Penn State, Barth began a series of one hundred stories in the bawdy manner of Giovanni Boccaccio's *Decameron: O, Prencipe Galeotto* (1349-1351; *The Decameron*, 1620), detailing the history of Dorchester County. He abandoned the project within a year, but fifty of the proposed hundred stories were completed; a handful were published separately, and others later were incorporated into *The Sot-Weed Factor*.

Barth advanced from instructor to associate professor at Penn State, where he taught until 1965, and it was during this twelve-year period that he established his reputation. In the fall of 1954, Barth found a photograph of an old showboat; borrowing something of the conversational style of Laurence Sterne's *The Life and Opinions of Tristram Shandy, Gent.* (1759-1767) and some plot devices from *Dom Casmurro* (1899; English translation, 1953), by the Brazilian novelist Joaquim Maria Machado de Assis, he began *The Floating Opera* in January, 1955. It was completed in three months, but several publishers rejected it, and Appleton-Century-Crofts demanded many revisions before publishing it in 1956. By the fall of 1955, however, Barth was already at work on *The End of the Road*. Like *The Floating Opera*, with which it is often associated as a philosophical companion piece, it was finished in three months. It was ultimately published by Doubleday in 1958.

The Floating Opera was nominated for a National Book Award, which it failed to win; neither this work nor its successor sold well. Barth was denied a Guggenheim grant in 1958, but his school's research fund did provide $250 to send him to Maryland to gather information for his next project. He had expected *The Sot-Weed Factor* to be another three-month venture, but that mammoth refurbishing of the eighteenth century picaresque turned out to be nearly three years in the writing. That novel, too, met with relative public indifference, but it later became his first major critical success when it was released in paperback in 1964.

Giles Goat-Boy was begun in 1960, and it would be six years from inception to publication. In 1965, Barth left Penn State for a full professorship at the State University of New York in Buffalo. *Giles Goat-Boy* introduced Barth to the best-seller lists in 1966, but he was already at work on *Lost in the Funhouse*, a brain-teasing, technically probing collection of multimedia pieces that came out in 1968, for which Barth received his second unsuccessful nomination for a National Book Award.

His next book did earn that elusive honor, however; *Chimera*, Barth's most direct confrontation of ancient narrative in the form of three metafictions, won the National Book Award in 1973. In that same year, Barth changed locale once more, accepting a post at his alma mater, Johns Hopkins. It was not until 1979 that his next book, *Letters*, was published. Instead of creating a new form, Barth decided, as he had done in *The Sot-Weed Factor*, to resuscitate a traditional one—in this case, the epistolary novel. *Letters* plumbs the author's personal literary history as well, for its principal correspondents are characters from Barth's earlier novels.

Whether the familiar hybrid of writer-teacher nourishes or diminishes creativity will not be decided on the basis of one man's example, but Barth has found the academic atmosphere to be not only hospitable to his talents but also generous as an occasion and setting for his fiction: Two of his novels are set specifically in college

communities, and the theme of education—be it in a school, under the auspices of a spiritual adviser, or in the shifting, multifarious outside world of affairs—has been repeatedly highlighted in Barth's work. In 1970, soon after he and his first wife were divorced, Barth married Shelly Rosenberg, a former student of his at Penn State whom he had reencountered after some years. Shelly Barth, a high school literature teacher, is often alluded to in the various heroines in Barth's later works, many of which feature an enriching second marriage that helps frame the novel's story. From the 1970's onward, Barth taught writing at Johns Hopkins University. In August, 1979, he bought a weekend and summer residence on Langford Creek in Dorchester County, Maryland, where he did most of his writing. As with his fictional protagonists, traveling, especially sailing, became one of his favorite avocations. In 1992, Barth formally retired from teaching at Johns Hopkins. He was, however, named professor emeritus there and continued to teach writing seminars occasionally.

ANALYSIS

The literary historian and the literary technician meet in the novels and attitudes of John Barth. Barth's eagerness to affirm the artificiality of the art he creates enables him to strip-mine the whole range of narrative that precedes his career for usable personalities and devices; similarly, by beginning with the premise of literature as a self-evident sham, he greatly enlarges the field of possibility within his own fictions, so that outrageous plot contrivances, protean characters (or characters who are essentially banners emblazoned with ruling philosophies), and verbal acrobatics all become acceptable. Barth's general solution for handling the fracture between art and reality is not to heal it but rather to heighten his readers' awareness of it. This is why, despite his penchant for intellectual confrontation and long interludes of debate in his novels, Barth most often looks to humor—jokes and pranks, parody, and stylistic trickery—to make the philosophy palatable.

Barth meticulously reconstructs the fabric and feel of allegory (*Giles Goat-Boy*) or of the *Künstlerroman* (*The Sot-Weed Factor*), then minimizes the appropriateness of such patterns in the contemporary world by vigorously mocking them. He takes on formidable intellectual questions—the impossibility of knowing external reality, the unavailability of intrinsic values, the fragility of the self in an incurably relativistic universe—but chooses to do so in, to borrow one of his own most durable metaphors, a funhouse atmosphere. In fact, in Barth's fiction, abstract discussion is consistently revealed as a dubious alternative to passionate participation in life. Given the ambiguous state of the self, exposure to the world could be fatal if not for the strategy of fashioning and choosing from among a variety of masks that afford the beleaguered self a sense of definition and a schedule of valid responses to whatever situations the world presents. The willful choosing of masks is Barth's main theme; it suggests that the alternative to despair in the face of universal chaos and indifference is the responsibility to exercise one's freedom, much as artists exercise their creative faculties in writing and editing tales that satisfy them. In this sense, Barth's heroes are artists of the self who view the elasticity of character as a challenge to their mythmaking abilities and who treat their private lives as fictions that are amenable to infinite revision.

THE FLOATING OPERA

"Good heavens," complains Todd Andrews in *The Floating Opera*, "how does one write a novel! I mean, how can anybody stick to the story, if he's at all sensitive to the significance of things?" The doubts and false starts that frustrate the progress of this protagonist's "Inquiry"—a hodgepodge of papers contained in peach baskets in his hotel room, for which, life being on so tenuous a lease from eternity, he pays rent on a daily basis—reflect those that would potentially stymie Barth himself, were he not to make them part of his subject. Like his narrator/alter ego in *The Floating Opera*, Barth contends with the problem of making art out of nihilism. In Andrews's hands, that problem takes the shape of a book-long (and, he confesses, lifelong) obsession with how, and whether, to live. There is little of traditional suspense to propel the narrative; after all, this is an examination of a decision *not* to commit suicide, so that Andrews's private undertaking of Hamlet's well-known question has led him to accept life, at least provisionally and despite its absence of intrinsic value.

The quality of life is described by the title of the novel and symbolized by the barge show—part vaudeville,

part minstrel show—that flashes in and out of view as it moves along the river. No other image in literature so effectively captures the idea of Heraclitean flux: The "performance" is never the same for any two spectators, nor can one resume watching it at the same place in the show as when it last passed by. Furthermore, the nature of this floating phenomenon is operatic: sentimental, bizarre, wildly melodramatic, and often simply laughable. The players are amateurish, and they are best appreciated by an unrefined audience, people who are not bothered by the gaps in their understanding or by the unevenness of the performance. Andrews entertains the notion of building a showboat that has a perpetual play going on, and the novel itself is the alternative result; like the floating extravaganza, it is "chock-full of curiosities" and considers every possible taste: games, violence, flights of fancy and philosophy, legal and sexual intrigue, war and death, artwork and excrement. The implication here, as emphasized by T. Wallace Whittaker's rendition of William Shakespeare (one of the more delicate turns on the bill, to please the ladies), is that not only are all people players on a stage but also they are apparently purposeless, scriptless players at that.

There is something of the floating opera in the stylistic range of the novel as well. Todd Andrews is a monologist in the comic, voluble tradition of Tristram Shandy. In fact, both men write autobiographical inquiries into the strangeness of the human condition that digress and associate so frequently that they are destined to become lifeworks; both are artists racing against death to create, although Andrews is as likely to be felled by rational suicide as by his heart murmur; and both combine intellectual pursuits with technical "entertainments" (which include, in Barth's novel, repeated paragraphs, a double column of narrative "options," and a reproduction of the handbill announcing the schedule of events in "Adam's Original and Unparalleled Ocean-Going Floating Opera").

Motivation sets these two narrators apart, however, for if Tristram is compelled by life's delights, Andrews is alienated by its absurdity. Andrews is engaged in a search for purpose; his life hangs in the balance. His Inquiry began as his attempt to come to terms with his father's suicide in 1930, an event too complex to chalk up to an escape from debts incurred after the stock market crash of 1929. It then absorbed a letter to his father that, with the obsessive diligence of Franz Kafka in a similar enterprise, Andrews had begun in 1920 and continued to redraft even after his father's death. The Inquiry continued to blossom until, by the time the novel opens in 1954, it is autobiography, journal, and religious/philosophical treatise all in one, and it floats by at the moment of focus on Andrews's decision (made on one of two days in June, 1937), after a failed effort, not to commit suicide. (Todd Andrews admonishes readers not to confuse his first name with its meaning of "death" in German; his name, which misspells the German word, is more aptly read as "almost death.")

Given the kinds of experience Andrews relates, his final acceptance of life is rather surprising. His father's suicide is but one of a series of incidents that suggest that life may not be worth the salvaging effort. Sexuality, for example, is represented by his wonder at the ridiculousness of the act when, at age seventeen, he spies himself in a mirror in the midst of intercourse, and later, when his five-year affair with Jane Mack is revealed to have been directed by her husband, Harrison. Andrews's most profound confrontation with his own self, during World War I, reveals him to be "a shocked, drooling animal in a mudhole." When an enemy soldier stumbles upon him, the two share their terror, then silent communion and friendship—and then Andrews stabs him to death. All actions are equally pointless; all commitments are arbitrary; all attempts to solve human incomprehension are laughable.

From rake to saint to cynic, Andrews endures without much joy as an expert lawyer, although he does admit to a certain detached interest in the law's arbitrary intricacies, epitomized in the search for the legitimate will among the seventeen left to posterity by Harrison Mack, Sr., which, when found, decides the fate of more than one hundred pickle jars brimming with his excrement. Andrews is actually comfortable enough living in the Dorset Hotel among a collection of society's aged cast-offs, until a casual reference by his mistress to his clubbed hands initiates a kind of Sartrean nausea at the utter physical fact of himself; his growing detestation of that mortal coil, coupled with an absolute conviction that all value is artificially imposed, leads him to the brink of suicide, in the form of a scheme to blow up the opera boat

(which, in the restored 1967 edition of the novel, would include hundreds of spectators, with the Macks and Jeannine, their—or possibly Andrews's—daughter among them).

What stays him is the revelation that, if all values are arbitrary, suicide is not less arbitrary; furthermore, even arbitrary values may offer a way to live. This uneasy treaty with a relativistic universe is Andrews's provisional conclusion to the Inquiry, for the suicide does not come off. Some accident—a psychological shudder, an instinct beyond the intellect's dominion, or a spasm of sentimental concern for the little girl who had suffered a sudden convulsion—disrupts the plan, so the novel's philosophical journey concludes in the anticlimax promised by the narrator at the outset. If Barth frustrates some readers by forsaking the questions he has so fastidiously prepared them for, they must understand that the willingness to handle the sublime and the ridiculous alike with a shrug of good humor is part of the point: In the end, even nihilism is shown to be yet one more posture, one more mask.

THE END OF THE ROAD

In his next novel, *The End of the Road*, Barth's speculations on the nature and necessity of masks becomes more formulaic, although with somewhat bleaker results for his hero. Jake Horner—the name is borrowed from William Wycherley's sly seducer in his play *The Country Wife* (pr., pb. 1675)—suffers from "cosmopsis," a disease of hyperconsciousness: the awareness that one choice is no more inherently valid or attractive than another. When a nameless black doctor materializes near a bench at Pennsylvania Station, he discovers Jake as hopelessly rooted to the spot as the statuette Jake keeps of the tortured Laocoön. The doctor recognizes his paralysis and initiates a program of therapy that forces his patient into action. He explains that no matter how arbitrary the system of "choosing" that he advocates may appear, "choosing is existence: to the extent that you don't choose, you don't exist." All of Jake's subsequent activities—the plot of the novel—represent his execution of the doctor's precepts.

At the outset, Jake's quest is meticulously prescribed *for* him. He is advised to begin with simple, disciplined choices between well-defined alternatives; should he happen to get "stuck" again beyond his mentor's reach, he is to choose artificially according to Sinistrality, Antecedence, and Alphabetical Priority. He is made to worship the hard facts of an almanac and to travel in straight lines to scheduled locations; because it is a monument to fixity, he is to devote himself to teaching of prescriptive grammar at Wicomico State Teachers College. In short, Jake is to undergo Mythotherapy: the regular assignment of roles to the befuddled ego in order to facilitate participation in the world.

Once Jake's quest is complicated by relationships that overextend the narrative "masks" behind which he operates, that neatly contrived therapy proves insufficient. Joe and Rennie Morgan, characters analogous to Harrison and Jane Mack in *The Floating Opera*, confuse his roles: Joe is a strident god whose rational self-control and mechanical theorizing make him his wife's mentor and Jake's intimidator; Rennie's sexuality and mixture of admiration and helplessness toward her husband are provocative, but she involves Jake in a script he cannot handle. His "road" grows tortuous and overwhelming, as his strictly plotted career is diverted into adulterous liaisons and philosophical tournaments, deceit and death. The profundity of his relapse into irresponsibility is much greater this time, however, for he is not the only one victimized by it. By failing to control his roles at critical times, he becomes the instrument of Rennie's death: Rennie will not lie to ensure a safe operation, and Jake's frantic role-playing in order to secure an abortion ends in a grisly death at the hands of Jake's doctor. The reality of Rennie's bleeding on the table is one that, unlike his callous affair with the lonely Peggy Rankin, Jake cannot manipulate or evade; it is the end of the road for him as a free agent in the world. Because he apparently requires further training in order to function successfully, he escapes with the doctor to a new site of the Remobilization Farm.

Of course, Jake's intellectual adversary fares little better under the pressure of real events. Joe Morgan personifies Todd Andrews's supposition that an arbitrary value could be transformed into the "subjective equivalent of an absolute" that might then provide the coherent way of life so crucial to a man who deifies the intellect. Both Jake and Joe begin from the premise of relativism, which explains their mutual attraction, but while Jake tends to succumb to "weatherlessness" (a numbness incurred by the randomness of events and the loss of an essential I), Joe is smug about the rational system by which he and his wife abide. That self-assurance sanctions Rennie's being exposed to Jake's influence and provokes Jake to undermine Joe. When Joe is revealed as something less than pure mind and standards (Jake and Rennie spy him through a window masturbating, grunting, picking his nose), the god loses his authenticity, and the affair merely emphasizes Joe's fall from eminence. Rennie does bring her guilt to Joe, but he returns her to Jake to reenact the betrayal until she can account for it rationally. In the same way, Joe refuses to face up to the fact of Rennie's death, which was indirectly engineered by his experimental obsession, and proves himself to be far more comfortable in handling abstract ideas than in facing up to the welter of uncertainties beyond his field of expertise.

The road's end serves as a final blessing to Jake; the conclusion of the novel is not the completion of a quest but a relief from it. Since the turbulence of the world of affairs has proved unmanageable, he capitulates and numbly offers his "weatherless" self up to the auspices of the doctor, the price for performing Rennie's abortion. Jake retreats into submission after a disastrous initiation into the world.

THE SOT-WEED FACTOR

In his next two novels, Barth grants his philosophical preoccupations the panoramic expansiveness and formal openness of a Henry Fielding or François Rabelais, as if seeking epic dimension for what might well be considered in his first novels to be merely the idiosyncrasies of constipated personalities. *The Sot-Weed Factor* features a riotously inventive plot and a cast of characters that includes poets and prostitutes, lords and brigands, landowners and Indians, merchants and thieves, but the triumph of the novel is in its authentic language and texture: For some eight hundred pages, Barth's novel impersonates one of those sprawling eighteenth century picaresque English novels, complete with protracted authorial intrusions, outrageous coincidences, dizzying turns of plot, and a relish for lewd humor.

Barth borrows a satiric poem on colonial America by Ebenezer Cooke (1708) for the foundation of his novel and resuscitates Cooke himself to be his hero. Barth's Eben Cooke is a timid, awkward fellow who, unlike

Andrews and Horner, maintains a steadfast virginity—sexual, social, and political—in a world teeming with sin and subterfuge. His adherence to a chosen mask—that of poet laureate of Maryland—with its requisite responsibilities, keeps him on course. Until he happens upon that identity, Eben is overwhelmed by "the beauty of the possible," so much so that he cannot choose among careers. A broad education shared with his twin sister, Anna, at the hands of the ubiquitous Henry Burlingame serves to increase his wonder rather than to specify a direction, so that readers discover him as a young man who haunts the London taverns, somewhat ill at ease among more raucous peers. He cannot muster an identity reliable enough to survive the pressure of alternatives.

What could have become a lifelong "cosmopsic" stagnation is interrupted by an encounter with a whore, Joan Toast; instead of having sex, Eben chooses to defend his innocence, for he sees in it a symbolic manifestation of his ultimate role. He exalts the deliciously earthy Joan into a bodiless goddess of verse; it is this indifference to reality that will enable him to survive, if not to transcend, the subversive and often grotesque facts of the New World, and the astounding contrasts between the poet's rhapsodizing and the world's stubborn brutishness provide much of the novel's ironic humor.

That confrontation with the New World is set into motion by Eben's father, who, when advised of his son's failure to lead a useful life in London, commands Eben to set off for the father's tobacco (sot-weed) estate in Maryland. Armed with a sense of his true calling, Eben wins from Lord Baltimore an agreement to write the "Marylandiad," a verse epic glorifying the province he knows nothing about, and is granted the laureateship in writing. The balance of *The Sot-Weed Factor* is a prolonged trial of Eben's confidence: His initiation into political intrigue and worldly corruption lays siege to his high-flown illusions about humankind. The people he meets are rapacious victimizers, ravaged victims, or crass simpletons, and Eben's promised land, his Malden estate, turns out to be an opium den and brothel. One illusion after another is stripped away, until the poet's tribute to Maryland is metamorphosed into the bitter satire on the deformities of America and Americans found in the poem by the historical Cooke.

Eben would not survive the conspiracies and ugli-

nesses of reality were it not for the tutelage and example of Henry Burlingame. Whereas Eben labors to maintain one role—his "true" self—after years of aimlessness, Burlingame accepts and celebrates a series of roles, for he argues that, in a world of "plots, cabals, murthers, and machinations," an elastic personality will prove most useful. Therefore, he ducks in and out of the novel unpredictably, assuming a variety of guises (including that of John Coode, Baltimore's devilish enemy, Lord Baltimore himself, and even Eben Cooke) as the situation demands. Eben's discussions with his mentor, although they do not cause him to forsake his belief in the essential truth of man's perfectibility and of his own career, do instruct him in how to dissemble when necessary, as exemplified during the voyage to America, when an exchange of roles with his servant, Bertram, proves expedient. In a sense, *The Sot-Weed Factor* boils down to the contrast and the tentative accommodations made between the ideal and the real, or between innocence and experience, as represented by the virgin-poet, who is linked to a past (his father) and to a future (his commission), and by the orphaned jack-of-all-trades, who embraces adventures and lovers with equal vivacity.

The Sot-Weed Factor insists on no conclusive resolution between these attitudes; as is the custom throughout Barth's fiction, the struggles between theoretical absolutes must end in compromise. If Eben's first problem is to rouse himself out of languor, his second is to realize the inadequacy of a single, unalterable role. Accordingly, Eben repudiates his sexual abstinence in order to wed the diseased, opium-addicted Joan Toast—his ruined Beatrice, who has followed him secretly to America—and so accepts a contract between the ideal and the actual. Similarly, Burlingame can only win and impregnate his beloved Anna after he completes his search for his family roots, which is to say, after he locates a stable identity. The novel ends in good comic fashion: Lovers are finally united; plot confusions are sorted out. Significantly, however, Barth adds twists to these conventions, thereby tempering the comic resolution: Joan dies in childbirth, and Burlingame disappears without trace. Barth replicates the eighteenth century picaresque novel only to parody it; he seduces readers into traditional expectations only to undermine them.

For many readers, the most satisfying passages in

The Sot-Weed Factor are not the philosophical or the literary exercises but rather the bawdy set pieces, the comic inventories and the imaginative diaries; nor should any discussion of this novel neglect to mention the war of name-calling between whores, or the "revisionist" rendition of Captain Smith's sexual assault on the otherwise impregnable Pocahontas. Barth has written of his enjoyment of Tobias Smollett's *The Adventures of Roderick Random* (1748) for its "nonsignificant surfaces," and in such glittering surfaces lie the charms of *The Sot-Weed Factor* as well. Fiction invades history and finds in its incongruities and intricacies of plot, character, and motivation a compatible form. Of all the deceptions perpetrated in the novel, perhaps none is so insidious as that of American history itself—the ultimate ruse of civilization, an imperfect concealment of savagery and selfishness. To remain innocent of the nature of history is irresponsible; Eben Cooke's practiced detachment, as implied by his virginity, is morally unacceptable. This lesson enables him to mature both artistically and ethically, and to dedicate himself to the world of which he claims to be poet laureate.

GILES GOAT-BOY

Following immediately upon his satire of the historical past is Barth's satire of the future—a computer narrative. The novel-long analogy ruling *Giles Goat-Boy* transforms the universe into a university; this Newest Testament portrays a world divided (between East and West Campus) and waiting for the Grand Tutor, the Savior of the academic system, to protect Studentdom from the satanic Dean o' Flunks.

Barth provides Giles, an amalgam of worldwide messiah-heroes, as the updated instrument of human destiny. Giles (Grand-Tutorial Ideal, Laboratory Eugenical Specimen) is the child of the prodigious WESCAC computer and a virgin, who later appears as Lady Creamhair. Raised as a goat (Billy Bocksfuss) by an apostate scientist-mentor, Max Spielman, he eventually leaves the herd to join humanity as a preacher of the Revised New Syllabus on the West Campus of New Tammany College. The novel traces his attempts to verify and institute his claim to be Grand Tutor. Such a task entails a loss of innocence comparable in kind (although far more extensive in its implications for humanity) to those undertaken by his predecessors in Barth's canon. In *Giles*

Goat-Boy, the initiation into complexity assumes a mythical overlay, as the hero passes from his exotic birth to his revelation of purpose in the womb of WESCAC (in whose mechanical interior he and Anastasia, a student who serves as Female Principle, come together) to a series of "assignments" through which he must prove his worth to his role as lawgiver and deposer of the false prophet, Harold Bray, and, finally, to his sacrificial death for the sake of humankind.

Giles's career invokes Lord Raglan's systematic program for the stages of the hero's life, yet readers are irresistibly drawn to make correlations between the novel's allegorical personalities and events and their counterparts in journalistic reality. East and West Campus are barely fictional versions of the Soviet Union and the United States, with the hydrogen bomb, in the form of WESCAC, the source of their power struggle. John F. Kennedy, Nikita S. Khrushchev, Joseph McCarthy, Albert Einstein, and other contemporary world figures populate the novel, as do such ancient luminaries as Moses, Socrates, and Christ himself (Enos Enoch, accompanied by Twelve Trustees). These textures give *Giles Goat-Boy* the authority of sociopolitical history, but as is the case in *The Sot-Weed Factor*, Barth's penchant for discovering his own artifice casts a thick shadow of unreliability over the proceedings. For example, readers must share in the doubts over Giles's legitimacy, both filial and messianic: Not only do many people fail to accept his Grand Tutorhood (he predicts betrayal by the masses, who will drive him out on a rusty bicycle to his death on Founder's Hill) but also he himself is never completely certain that his words have not been programmed into him by WESCAC. The document itself—the pages before the readers—brought to "J. B." by Giles's son, is framed by disclaimers, editorial commentaries, footnotes, and postscripts, so that, finally, the "true text" is indistinguishable from the apocrypha. Moreover, Barth's liberal infusion of verse, puns, allusions, and stylistic entertainments strains the heroic conventions that he has assembled from a great variety of literary and mythic sources. In short, the quality of revelation as espoused by Gilesianism is consistently affected by the doubt and self-effacement implied in the structure of the narrative.

Despite Barth's typical supply of structural equivocations, *Giles Goat-Boy* is the author's most ambitious attempt to recognize correspondences between factual and fictional accounts, between politics and mythology, between public and personal history. If the hero's quest leads him into a world of complexity, there is at least, by virtue of these correspondences, the promise of insight. Under Burlingame's direction in *The Sot-Weed Factor*, readers learn that the human personality, correctly apprehended, is a compendium of various, even contradictory, selves; in *Giles Goat-Boy*, this lesson is applied to the whole history of human learning and progress. Only when Giles accepts the all-encompassing nature of truth—PASS ALL and FAIL ALL are inextricably connected, not separable opposites but parts of a mystical oneness—does he mature into effectiveness. His passage through experience will include failure, but failure will guarantee growth, itself evidence of passage. Giles is a condenser in whom worldly paradoxes and dichotomies—knowledge and instinct, asceticism and responsibility, Spielman and Eirkopf, West and East Campus, and all other mutually resistive characters and systems of thought—manage a kind of synthesis. Keeping in mind that Giles's story originates from a fundamental willingness to accept his humanity over his "goathood," one comes to appreciate that, although the novel is a satiric fantasy, it is inspired by the same receptivity to experience and the same optimistic energy in the face of desperate circumstances that are exalted by the tradition of quest literature.

The image of Giles and Anastasia united in WESCAC is the philosophical center of the novel; at this climactic moment, flesh is integrated with spirit, animal with human, and scientific hardware with "meaty tubes," all in the service of the improvement of the race. The gospel of *Giles Goat-Boy* is that the very impulse to enter the labyrinth is an affirmation, however unlikely the hero's chances against the beasts and devils (such as Stoker, the gloomy custodian of the power station) who reside within. Giles's victory is a transcendence of categories, a faith in the unity of the universe, and that revelation is enough to overcome the lack of appreciation by the undergraduates. No obstacle or imposture of the dozens that antagonize the hero obscures the meeting of goat-boy with computer; the circuitry of myth remains intact, even in this age of broken atoms.

LETTERS

"When my mythoplastic razors were sharply honed, it was unparalleled sport to lay about with them, to have at reality." So proclaims Jake Horner in *The End of the Road* while praising articulation as his nearest equivalent to a personal absolute. The narrative impulse is the principal source of faith for Barth's array of protagonists, insofar as faith is possible in an undeniably relativistic environment. In *Letters*, Barth allows those characters a fuller opportunity to engage in an authorial perspective. *Letters* solidifies Barth's associations with modernists such as James Joyce and Samuel Beckett; here Barth takes license not only with established literary forms—specifically, the epistolary novel—but also with his private literary past, as he nonchalantly pays visits and respects to old fictional personalities. Because *Letters*, by its very form, intensifies one's awareness of the novel as a fabricated document (and, for that matter, of characters as collections of sentences), it is Barth's most transparently metafictional work; as the novel's subtitle unabashedly declares, this is "an old time epistolary novel by seven fictitious drolls and dreamers each of which imagines himself actual." *Letters* breaks down into seven parts, one for each letter of the title, and covers seven months of letter writing. Place the first letter of each of the eighty-eight epistles in *Letters* on a calendar so that it corresponds with its date of composition, and the title of the novel appears; like Joyce's *Ulysses* (1922), *Letters* testifies to the diligence, if not to the overindulgence, of the craftsman.

Among these letter writers are a group recycled from previous works as well as two figures, Germaine Pitt (Lady Amherst) and the Author, newly created for this book. In spite of Barth's assertions to the contrary, an appreciation of these characters is rather heavily dependent on a familiarity with their pre-*Letters* biographies: Todd Andrews emerges from *The Floating Opera* as an elderly lawyer who writes to his dead father and is drawn to incest while enjoying one last cruise on Chesapeake Bay; Jacob Horner remains at the Remobilization Farm to which he had resigned himself at the conclusion of *The End of the Road*, and where his latest Information Therapy demands that he write to himself in an elaborate reconstitution of the past; Ambrose Mensch, the now-mature artist out of "Lost in the Funhouse," directs his correspondences to the anonymous "Yours Truly" whose message he found in a bottle years earlier and constructs his life, including an affair with Germaine Pitt, in accordance with Lord Raglan's prescription for the hero. Readers also meet descendants of previous creations: Andrew Burlingame Cook VI busily attempts to shape the nation's destiny in a Second American Revolution, and Jerome Bonaparte Bray, a mad rival to Barth himself who may be a gigantic insect, seeks to program a computer-assisted novel, *Numbers*, to compete with the authority of the one that treated him so shabbily.

The third level of writers in *Letters* includes the two who have no prior existence in Barth's works: Germaine Pitt, a colorful widow who had been the friend of James Joyce, H. G. Wells, Aldous Huxley, and other literary notables, anxiously campaigns as acting provost to ensure the prestige of her college against the administrative dilutions and hucksterism of one John Schott; the Author enters the novel as Pitt's own alternative candidate for an honorary doctorate (which Schott proposes to give to the dubious activist, State Laureate A. B. Cook VI), and he writes to everyone else in the vicinity of *Letters*.

The most consistent theme tying the letters and authors together is the conflict between restriction and freedom. The setting is the volatile United States of the 1960's, when sexual, moral, political, and even academic norms underwent the most serious reevaluation in American history. Obviously, Barth's creative history is the most evident aspect of this theme, and the repetitions and echoes among his novels and within *Letters* seduce readers into joining his search for pattern in the flux of human affairs. The ambiguous nature of history itself has also been one of his most durable themes—a chapter in *The Sot-Weed Factor* examines the question of whether history is "a Progress, a Drama, a Retrogression, a Cycle, an Undulation, a Vortex, a Right- or Left-Handed Spiral, a Mere Continuum, or What Have You"—and the suggestion here is that any sort of orthodoxy can be revealed, especially in times of social crisis, as fictional. Student protests against the establishment are replicated in the antagonism between characters and an established text; the societal disruptions in the novel disrupt and contaminate the narrative.

A. B. Cook VI, one of the novel's seven correspondents, is the descendant of Ebenezer Cooke in *The Sot-*

Weed Factor. Taking his cue from his ancestor, he is involved in the political intrigues of his own time, but he also attempts to rewrite history, providing alternative versions of storied events in the American past. The history of the Cook family is an antiestablishment one, filled with various attempts to launch the "Second American Revolution." This involves both rolling back the original American Revolution (for instance, during the War of 1812 the Cooks are on the British side) and extending it by making the United States more democratic. The Cooks, for instance, frequently ally with Native American peoples.

In contrast to Cook's historical vision stands the aesthetic one of Ambrose Mensch. Mensch is the prototypical modern artist as presented in modern novels by writers such as James Joyce and Thomas Mann. His goal in life is to mold his own experience into a finished object, remote from the contingencies of time and place. Barth recognizes that both Cook's and Mensch's visions are partial. To bring together the two polarities, his instrument is Germaine Pitt, Lady Amherst, who serves in many ways as the muse of the book. Germaine reconciles art and history and shows the way for the novel, and life itself, to have a productive future.

In contrast to Samuel Richardson's definitive use of the epistolary form, *Letters* is populated by characters who are more than vaguely aware of their unreality and therefore of the need to bargain with Barth for personal status and support. When the Author intrudes as a character, no convention is above suspicion; although he describes himself as turning away from the "fabulous irreal" toward "a détente with the realistic tradition," if this novel is the result, it is a severely qualified détente, indeed. Perhaps the structural "confusion" of the novel explains the smugness of Reg Prinz, an avant-garde filmmaker who wants to create a version of all of Barth's books in a medium that he feels to be superior and more up-to-date. What had been a playful interest in the relationships among creative media in *Lost in the Funhouse* has escalated in *Letters* into a battle for aesthetic dominance between the word-hating Prinz and the word-mongering Barth. (That Prinz is a prisoner of the novel, of course, enables Barth to sway the outcome of this battle, at least temporarily.)

Letters, like history itself, concludes in blood and

ambiguity; one suspects that Barth means to undergo a catharsis of the books and characters that have obsessed him and that continue to infiltrate his creative consciousness. It is testimony to Barth's ability to elicit admiration for his craft that readers do not leave *Letters*—or, for that matter, most of his works of fiction—with a sense of defeat. The keynote of Barth's literary career is exuberance; if nihilism and existential gloom have been the author's thematic preoccupations, their potentially numbing effects are undercut by his cleverness, his stylistic ingenuity, and his campaign for the rewards of narrative.

SABBATICAL

Barth's *Sabbatical* continues to bend philosophy into escapade. Subtitled *A Romance*, *Sabbatical* is rather a postmodernization of romance: All the well-established Barthian formal intrigues, ruminative digressions, plot coincidences (the married pair of main characters, in the same vein as *The Sot-Weed Factor*, are both twins), and other examples of literary self-consciousness complicate the vacation cruise of Fenwick Scott Key Turner, a former agent of the Central Intelligence Agency (CIA) and a contemporary novelist, and his wife, Susan, herself an established academic and critic. The nine-month sea journey—a frequent theme for Barth—leads to the birth of the novel itself, in whose plot the narrating "parents" seek clues to some conspiratorial CIA "plot" against them. (Fenwick has written an exposé that makes his "life as voyage" a perilous journey indeed—even when he is on sabbatical.) So the creative couple prepare, nurture, take pride in, and exhaustively analyze their verbal offspring while the real world blows into their story from the shore in another dizzying mixture of fact and fiction.

As readers have come to expect from Barth, however, the imagination is exalted above and beyond its moorings in the "real world," all the while calling attention to its own altitude. As Fenwick declares to his loving coauthor: "I won't have our story be unadulterated realism. Reality is wonderful; reality is dreadful; reality is what it is." The intensity, the scope, and the truth of reality are more appropriately the province of experimental technique.

THE TIDEWATER TALES

The Tidewater Tales is closely related to *Sabbatical*. Fenwick Scott Key Turner reappears in the guise of Franklin Key Talbott, and Carmen B. Seckler has be-

come the main character Peter Sagamore's mother-in-law, Carla B. Silver. Following the theme of twins in *Sabbatical*, Peter's wife, Katherine, is eight and a half months pregnant with twins. In fact, much of the plot consists of Peter and Katherine sailing around in their sloop *Story* while waiting for Katherine's pregnancy to come to term.

The sloop's name is an obvious reference to both Peter's and Katherine's (and Barth's) profession. Peter is a writer, and Katherine is an expert in oral history—a storyteller. The intricate narratives become a line of stories within stories as Barth concentrates on capturing all of reality within his fictive form.

THE LAST VOYAGE OF SOMEBODY THE SAILOR

The Last Voyage of Somebody the Sailor is a retelling of the Arabic short-story cycle *The Arabian Nights' Entertainments*, also known as *The Thousand and One Nights* (fifteenth century), with an interesting difference. Whereas traditionally the Arabian Nights stories have been valued as exotic fantasies wholly divergent from conventional modern realism, Barth demonstrates that what is usually considered realism can often also be considered fantastic. When Somebody (also known as Simon Behler), a modern-day sailor whose biography parallels Barth's own to some degree, arrives in medieval Baghdad, his stories of American boyhood, sexual awakening, and marital trouble are seen as amazing and weird by his Arabian audience, for whom the "marvelous" is all too familiar. Although this novel may lack the psychological depth of some of Barth's earlier works, such as *The End of the Road*, it does attempt a serious moral critique. Somebody's Arabian equivalent is the renowned sailor Sindbad, who initially appears to be a hero but whose avarice and cruelty are soon found out and duly punished. Somebody marries the beautiful princess Yasmin, with whom he has a happy relationship (though readers are perpetually reminded that it is a fictional one). Somebody's better-adjusted, more-humane kind of heroism is eventually celebrated by the Arabian Nights society, and thus the novel becomes an even happier version of Mark Twain's time-travel novel *A Connecticut Yankee in King Arthur's Court* (1889).

ONCE UPON A TIME

Once upon a Time is a hybrid of fiction and autobiography. Barth gives readers a bare-bones account of his life and career, sometimes fleshed out with extended anecdotes. Interspersed with this, however, are scenes of voyages to the Caribbean and back as well as meditations on the nature of storytelling itself. The strongest fictional element of the book is a totally invented character, Jay Scribner, who serves as Barth's alter ego. He is a more outwardly vigorous and outspoken figure who bounces off the character of the author. Scribner at once comments on and frames Barth's own sensibility. As the book proceeds on its jaunty course, Barth appends footnotes of what is going on, politically and otherwise, in the "real" world. The gently made point of the narrative is that autobiography is as much a fiction as fiction itself. What is real and what is imaginary (especially in the life and mind of a novelist) are always intertwining and cannot be separated from each other definitively—nor would readers in search of truly enlightening entertainment want such a thing to occur.

Arthur M. Saltzman
Updated by Nicholas Birns

OTHER MAJOR WORKS

SHORT FICTION: *Lost in the Funhouse*, 1968; *On with the Story*, 1996; *The Book of Ten Nights and a Night: Eleven Stories*, 2004; *Where Three Roads Meet*, 2005.

NONFICTION: *The Friday Book: Essays and Other Nonfiction*, 1984; *Further Fridays: Essays, Lectures, and Other Nonfiction*, 1995.

BIBLIOGRAPHY

Bowen, Zack. "Barth and Joyce." *Critique* 37 (Summer, 1996): 261-269. Discusses how Barth followed James Joyce in the grandness of his narrative scheme, his ironic focus on a region, and his personal overtones in his fiction. Explores Barth's anxiety about this influence.

_____. *A Reader's Guide to John Barth*. Westport, Conn.: Greenwood Press, 1994. Provides a concise overview of Barth's first ten books of fiction through *The Last Voyage of Somebody the Sailor*. Contains good bibliographies, a brief biographical sketch, and an interesting appendix, "Selected List of Recurrent Themes, Patterns, and Techniques."

Clavier, Berndt. *John Barth and Postmodernism: Spatiality, Travel, Montage*. New York: Peter Lang, 2007. Analyzes Barth's work from a perspective of postmodernism and metafiction, focusing on theories of space and subjectivity. Argues that the form of montage is a possible model for understanding Barth's fiction.

Fogel, Stan, and Gordon Slethaug. *Understanding John Barth*. Columbia: University of South Carolina Press, 1990. Presents a comprehensive interpretation of Barth's works from *The Floating Opera* to *The Tidewater Tales*. Includes both primary and secondary bibliographies, index divided by works, and general index.

Harris, Charles B. *Passionate Virtuosity: The Fiction of John Barth*. Urbana: University of Illinois Press, 1983. Contains separate chapters analyzing *The Floating Opera*, *The End of the Road*, *The Sot-Weed Factor*, *Giles Goat-Boy*, and *Chimera*. Includes exhaustive chapter endnotes, secondary bibliography, and index.

Schulz, Max F. *The Muses of John Barth: Tradition and Metafiction from "Lost in the Funhouse" to "The Tidewater Tales."* Baltimore: Johns Hopkins University Press, 1990. Focuses on the themes of "romantic passion and commonsense love" in Barth's work, with an emphasis on "the textual domestication of classical myths." Includes endnotes and index.

Scott, Steven D. *The Gamefulness of American Postmodernism: John Barth and Louise Erdrich*. New York: Peter Lang, 2000. Applies postmodernist theories to an analysis of Barth's work. Addresses the motifs of play and games in American postmodernist fiction generally and focuses on "gamefulness" in the writings of Barth and Erdrich.

Waldmeir, Joseph J., ed. *Critical Essays on John Barth*. Boston: G. K. Hall, 1980. Early critical work collects essays that provide a general overview of Barth's novels as well as essays focusing on *The Sot-Weed Factor*, *Giles Goat-Boy*, and other early novels. Includes chapter endnotes and index.

Walkiewicz, E. P. *John Barth*. Boston: Twayne, 1986. Very useful resource for the biographical details it provides. Includes a chronology of Barth's life and work, supplemented by primary and secondary bibliographies as well as notes and an index.

DONALD BARTHELME

Born: Philadelphia, Pennsylvania; April 7, 1931
Died: Houston, Texas; July 23, 1989

PRINCIPAL LONG FICTION

Snow White, 1967
The Dead Father, 1975
Paradise, 1986
The King, 1990

OTHER LITERARY FORMS

Donald Barthelme (bawr-TEHLM) became known first as a short-story writer, perhaps because the third of his long works appeared only three years before his death and the fourth was posthumous. For some commentators, as a result, Barthelme's name is still primarily associated with short stories—the more so because even his long fiction tends to be composed of the same fragments as his short. Barthelme was also the author of a children's book titled *The Slightly Irregular Fire Engine: Or, The Hithering Thithering Djinn* (1971).

ACHIEVEMENTS

Donald Barthelme was one of the great innovators in fictional techniques of the post-World War II era of American literature. Drawing on the technical discoveries of the Anglo-American modernist authors (including T. S. Eliot, Gertrude Stein, James Joyce, and Samuel Beckett), he developed a type of fiction that was largely structured on principles other than plot and character, the building blocks of nineteenth century "realistic" fiction. His fragmentary, collagelike splicing of historical and literary references expresses a certain world-weariness as well as a sense that history does not advance. Nevertheless, the irony expressed by this style softens a bit in the later works.

In addition to winning the National Book Award for his children's book in 1972, Barthelme was the recipient of a Guggenheim Fellowship (1966). He also won the PEN/Faulkner Award for Fiction for *Sixty Stories* (1981), one of the two collections of selected stories to appear during his lifetime.

BIOGRAPHY

Donald Barthelme was born in Philadelphia, where his parents were students at the University of Pennsylvania. A few years later, the family moved to Houston, where his father became a professor of architecture at the University of Houston. In high school, Barthelme wrote for both the school newspaper and the school literary magazine. In 1949, he entered the University of Houston, majoring in journalism. During his sophomore year (1950-1951), he was the editor of the college newspaper, the *Cougar*. During this year he also worked as a reporter for the *Houston Post*.

In 1953, Barthelme was drafted into the U.S. Army, arriving in Korea the day the truce was signed, at which

Donald Barthelme. (Bill Wittliff)

point he became the editor of an Army newspaper. Upon his return to the United States, he once again became a reporter for the *Houston Post* and returned to the University of Houston, where he worked as a speech writer for the university president and attended classes in philosophy. Although he attended classes as late as 1957, he ultimately left without taking a degree. When he was thirty years old, he became the director of Houston's Contemporary Arts Museum.

In 1962, Barthelme moved to New York to become the managing editor of the arts and literature magazine *Location*. His first published story appeared in 1961; his first story for *The New Yorker* appeared in 1963. After that time, most of his works appeared first in this magazine, and eventually Barthelme's name became almost a synonym for an ironic, fragmentary style that characterized its pages in the late 1960's and early 1970's.

Barthelme taught for brief periods at Boston University, the State University of New York at Buffalo, and City College of New York, where he was distinguished visiting professor of English from 1974 to 1975. He was married twice. His only child was a daughter, Anne Katharine, born in 1964 to his first wife, Birgit. It was for Anne that he wrote *The Slightly Irregular Fire Engine*. At the time of his death from cancer on July 23, 1989, he was survived by his second wife, Marion.

ANALYSIS

For the reader new to Donald Barthelme, the most productive way to approach his works is in terms of what they are not: looking at what they avoid doing, what they refuse to do, and what they suggest is not worth doing. Nineteenth century literature, and indeed most popular ("best-selling") literature of the twentieth century, is principally structured according to the two elements of plot and character. These Barthelme studiously avoids, especially in his earlier works, offering instead a collage of fragments whose coherence is usually only cumulative, rather than progressive. Some readers may find the early works emotionally cold as a result, given that their unity is to be found in the realm of the intellect rather than in that of feeling.

This style has resulted in the frequent classification of Barthelme as a postmodernist author, one of a generation of American writers who came to international prominence in the late 1960's and 1970's and who include Thomas Pynchon, John Barth, John Hawkes, William H. Gass, Ishmael Reed, and Kurt Vonnegut. This label indicates, among other things, that Barthelme's most immediate predecessors are the modernist authors of the early years of the century, such as T. S. Eliot, James Joyce, and Franz Kafka. Yet critics have split regarding whether Barthelme is doing fundamentally the same things as the earlier modernist authors or whether his works represent a significant development of their method.

Barthelme clearly diverges from the modernists in that he seems to lack their belief in the power of art to change the world; his most characteristic stance is ironic, self-deprecating, and anarchistic. Since this ironic posture is productive more of silence than of talk, or at best produces parodic talk, it is not surprising that Barthelme began his career with shorter pieces rather than longer ones. Further, it does not seem coincidental that the novels *Paradise* and *The King* were produced in the last years of his life, by which point his short stories had become slightly less frenetic in pace.

SNOW WHITE

Barthelme's longer works seem to divide naturally into two pairs. The earlier two are dense reworkings of (respectively) a fairy tale and a myth. The second pair are more leisurely, the one involving autobiographical elements, the other making a social point. Barthelme's first longer work, *Snow White*, is reasonably easy to follow, largely by virtue of the clarity with which the author indicates to the reader at all points what it is that he is doing—or, rather, what he is avoiding, namely, the fairy tale evoked by the work's title. Every reader knows the characters of this fairy tale; in fact, all of them have their equivalents in the characters of Barthelme's version, along with several others unaccounted for in the original. In Barthelme's version of the story, Snow White is twenty-two, lives with seven men with whom she regularly has unsatisfying sex in the shower, and seems to have confused herself with Rapunzel from another fairy story, as she continually sits at her window with her hair hanging out. Her dwarfs have modern names such as Bill (the leader), Clem, Edward, and Dan, and they suffer from a series of ailments, of which the most important seems to be that Bill no longer wishes to be touched.

During the day the seven men work in a Chinese baby-food factory.

The closest thing this retelling of the myth has to a prince is a man named Paul, who does not seem to want to fulfill his role of prince. Avoiding Snow White, he spends time in a monastery in Nevada, goes to Spain, and joins the Thelemite order of monks. Ultimately he ends up near Snow White, but only as a Peeping Tom, armed with binoculars, in a bunker before her house. Barthelme's version of the wicked queen is named Jane; she writes poison-pen letters and ultimately makes Snow White a poisoned drink. Paul drinks it instead, and he dies.

The underlying point of the contrast generated by these modernized versions of the fairy-tale characters is clearly that which was the point of Joyce's version of *Ulysses* (1922), namely, that there are no more heroes to-day. This in fact is the crux of the personality problems both of Paul, who does not want to act like a prince though he is one, and Snow White, who is unsure about the nature of her role as Snow White: She continues to long for a prince but at the same time feels it necessary to undertake the writing of a lengthy (pornographic) poem that constitutes her attempt to "find herself."

THE DEAD FATHER

The Dead Father, Barthelme's second long work, may be seen in formal terms as the author's overt homage to the fictions of the Anglo-American modernists, most notably Stein, Joyce, and Beckett. Certain of its sections appear to be direct appropriations of the formal innovations of Joyce's *Ulysses*. The result is a complex overlayering of techniques that seems as much about literary history as about any more objective subject matter. The text presupposed by this novel is that of the Greek story of Oedipus, and of Sigmund Freud's treatment of it. Freud's version insists on the potentially lethal effects of an overbearing father and suggests that sons must symbolically kill their fathers to attain independence. Without an understanding of the association of father with threat, the plot of this novel can make little sense.

Nineteen men are pulling the Dead Father—who in fact is not really dead until the end, and perhaps not even then—across the countryside by a cable. The Father is huge, like Joyce's Humphrey C. Earwicker from *Finnegans Wake* (1939), covering a great expanse of countryside. There are four children, named Thomas, Edmund, Emma, and Julie, who accompany the Father on his journey to his grave. Along the way his children cut off his leg and his testicles and demand his sword. This does not stop the Dead Father's sexual desires; one of the objectionable aspects of the old man is clearly the fact that he has not ceased to function as a male. An encounter with a tribe known as the Wends, who explain that they have dispensed with fathers entirely, develops the background situation.

The plot is discernible only in flashes through the dense thicket of fragmentary conversations and monologues. The narration of the journey is constantly being interrupted by textual digressions. One of the most developed of these is a thirty-page "Manual for Sons" that the children find and that is reprinted in its entirety in the text. The complexity of this work is undeniable. It differs from *Snow White* in that the underlying mood does not seem to be that of alienation: The power of the Father is too great. Yet it may be that the use of so many modernist techniques splits the technical veneer of the book too deeply from the deeper emotional issues it raises.

PARADISE

Barthelme's third long work, *Paradise*, comes the closest of the four to being a traditional novel. It is set in a recognizable place and time (Philadelphia and New York in the last quarter of the twentieth century) and uses the author's standard plot fragmentation to express the state of mind of its protagonist, an architect named Simon, who is going through a sort of midlife crisis. Simon has taken in three women, with whom he sleeps in turn; this arrangement solves none of his problems, which have to do with his previous marriage, his child by that marriage, his other affairs, and the drying up of his architectural inspiration. A number of chapters are set in the form of questions and answers, presumably between Simon and his analyst.

In this work, Barthelme draws on his knowledge of the Philadelphia architectural scene (especially the works of architect Louis Kahn) and seems to be expressing some of his own reactions to aging in the personality of the protagonist. This is certainly the easiest of the four novels for most readers to like.

THE KING

Barthelme's final long work, *The King*, once again returns to a literary prototype, this time the Arthurian romances. Like the characters in *Snow White*, Barthelme's Arthur, Guinevere, Lancelot, and knights are twentieth century characters; unlike the earlier ones, they are particular public personages, identified with the king and queen of England during World War II. (At the same time, their language and exploits situate them in the Celtic legends, or at least the Renaissance retelling of these by Sir Thomas Malory.) Barthelme is exploiting his usual anachronistic confusion of times here, yet his purpose in this work seems not to be merely that of comedy. While readers can be distanced from the categories of "friends" and "enemies" that the characters use in their aspect as figures in Arthurian romance, it is more difficult to be this distanced from a conflict still as much a part of contemporary culture as World War II. Barthelme's point seems to be that carnage is carnage and war is war, and that from the point of view of a future generation even twentieth century people's moral certainty regarding this more recent conflict will seem as irrelevant and incomprehensible as that of Arthur and his knights.

Though Barthelme never abandons his concern with form over the course of his four novels, it seems clear that the second pair deals with issues that the average educated reader may find more accessible than those treated in the first two. Moving from the textual ironies of the first and second to the more measured plotting of the third and fourth, Barthelme's novels show signs of a gradual emotional warming process for which many readers may be thankful.

Bruce E. Fleming

Other major works

SHORT FICTION: *Come Back, Dr. Caligari*, 1964; *Unspeakable Practices, Unnatural Acts*, 1968; *City Life*, 1970; *Sadness*, 1972; *Amateurs*, 1976; *Great Days*, 1979; *Sixty Stories*, 1981; *Overnight to Many Distant Cities*, 1983; *Forty Stories*, 1987; *Flying to America: Forty-Five More Stories*, 2007 (Kim Herzinger, editor).

CHILDREN'S LITERATURE: *The Slightly Irregular Fire Engine: Or, The Hithering Thithering Djinn*, 1971.

MISCELLANEOUS: *Guilty Pleasures*, 1974; *The Teachings of Don B.: Satires, Parodies, Fables, Illustrated Stories, and Plays of Donald Barthelme*, 1992 (Kim Herzinger, editor); *Not-knowing: The Essays and* *Interviews of Donald Barthelme*, 1997 (Kim Herzinger, editor).

BIBLIOGRAPHY

Barthelme, Helen Moore. *Donald Barthelme: The Genesis of a Cool Sound*. College Station: Texas A&M University Press, 2001. The author, a senior university lecturer, was married to Barthelme for a decade in the 1950's and 1960's. She traces his life from his childhood in Houston to his development as a writer.

Daugherty, Tracy. *Hiding Man: A Biography of Donald Barthelme*. New York: St. Martin's Press, 2009. Argues that Barthleme was writing in the modernist tradition of Samuel Beckett and James Joyce, and that he used advertisements, sentences from newspaper articles, instruction guides, and popular and commercial elements in order to make literature, not to subvert it.

Hudgens, Michael Thomas. *Donald Barthelme, Postmodernist American Writer*. Lewiston, N.Y.: Edwin Mellen Press, 2001. This volume in the series Studies in American Literature examines Barthelme's novels *The Dead Father* and *Snow White* and his short story "Paraguay." Includes bibliographical references and an index.

Klinkowitz, Jerome. *Donald Barthelme: An Exhibition*. Durham, N.C.: Duke University Press, 1991. Klinkowitz is easily the best informed and most judicious scholar and critic of contemporary American fiction in general and Barthelme in particular. Building on his Barthelme chapter in *Literary Disruptions* (below), he emphasizes the ways in which Barthelme reinvented narrative in the postmodern age and places Barthelme's fiction in aesthetic, cultural, and historical context.

_____. *Literary Disruptions: The Making of a Post-Contemporary American Fiction*. 2d ed. Urbana: University of Illinois Press, 1980. Informed, accurate, and intelligent, this work is the necessary starting point for any serious study of Barthelme and his work. The emphasis is on Barthelme's interest in structure, his revitalizing of exhausted forms, his words as objects in space rather than mimetic mirrors, and the imagination as a valid way of knowing the world.

McCaffery, Larry. *The Metafictional Muse: The Works*

of Robert Coover, Donald Barthelme, and William H. Gass. Pittsburgh, Pa.: University of Pittsburgh Press, 1982. After situating the three writers in their historical period, McCaffery provides excellent readings of individual works. Views Barthelme as a critic of language whose "metafictional concerns are intimately related to his other thematic interests."

Molesworth, Charles. *Donald Barthelme's Fiction: The Ironist Saved from Drowning*. Columbia: University of Missouri Press, 1982. Objecting to those who emphasize the experimental nature of Barthelme's fiction, Molesworth views Barthelme as essentially a parodist and satirist whose ironic stance saves him from drowning in mere innovation.

Nealon, Jeffrey T. "Disastrous Aesthetics: Irony, Ethics, and Gender in Barthelme's *Snow White*." *Twentieth Century Literature* 51, no 2. (Summer, 2005): 123-141. Nealon analyzes the ironic perspective in *Snow White*, demonstrating how Barthelme uses irony to reawaken the aesthetic experience. He argues that the beginning of the novel may cause readers to examine the failure of aesthetics and its relation to gender.

Patteson, Richard, ed. *Critical Essays on Donald Barthelme*. New York: G. K. Hall, 1992. A collection of critical essays on Barthelme from book reviews and academic journals. Provides an overview of critical reaction to Barthelme in the introduction. Essays explore Barthelme's use of language, his fragmentation of reality, his montage technique, and his place in the postmodernist tradition.

Trachtenberg, Stanley. *Understanding Donald Barthelme*. Columbia: University of South Carolina Press, 1990. A basic guide to Barthelme's body of work, including brief discussions of his biography and major writings. Includes an excellent annotated bibliography.

H. E. BATES

Born: Rushden, Northamptonshire, England; May 16, 1905

Died: Canterbury, Kent, England; January 29, 1974

Also known as: Herbert Ernest Bates; Flying Officer X

PRINCIPAL LONG FICTION

The Two Sisters, 1926
Catherine Foster, 1929
Charlotte's Row, 1931
The Fallow Land, 1932
The Poacher, 1935
A House of Women, 1936
Spella Ho, 1938
Fair Stood the Wind for France, 1944
The Cruise of the Breadwinner, 1946
The Purple Plain, 1947
Dear Life, 1949
The Jacaranda Tree, 1949
The Scarlet Sword, 1950
Love for Lydia, 1952
The Feast of July, 1954
The Nature of Love: Three Short Novels, 1954
The Sleepless Moon, 1956
Death of a Huntsman: Four Short Novels, 1957
The Darling Buds of May, 1958
A Breath of French Air, 1959
When the Green Woods Laugh, 1960
The Day of the Tortoise, 1961
A Crown of Wild Myrtle, 1962
Oh! To Be in England, 1963
A Moment in Time, 1964
The Distant Horns of Summer, 1967
A Little of What You Fancy, 1970
The Triple Echo, 1970

OTHER LITERARY FORMS

H. E. Bates published approximately four hundred short stories in magazines, newspapers, special editions, and collections; in fact, he is probably better known as a short-story writer than as a novelist. Many of his more successful efforts were long stories, and so it is natural that he eventually turned to the novella as a favorite medium. His works in this form were published most often in collections but occasionally appeared as independent works, as with *The Cruise of the Breadwinner* and *The Triple Echo*. His first published work was a one-act play, *The Last Bread* (pb. 1926), and throughout his career he aspired to write for the stage, though with little success. His play *The Day of Glory* (pb. 1945) had a short run in 1945.

A major portion of Bates's nonfiction works consist of essays on nature and country life. In this form he excelled, bringing to his subject a deep knowledge and understanding based on a lifetime of country living. In addition, he produced three volumes of children's books, a memoir of his mentor Edward Garnett, and a highly regarded though unscholarly study titled *The Modern Short Story: A Critical Survey* (1941). His autobiography is in three volumes: *The Vanished World* (1969), *The Blossoming World* (1971), and *The World in Ripeness* (1972).

ACHIEVEMENTS

From the publication of *The Two Sisters* in 1926 until the outbreak of World War II, H. E. Bates was known principally to literati in Great Britain and the United States as an accomplished writer of stories and novels about rural England. In spite of good reviews in the highbrow and popular press and the enthusiastic recommendations of such critics and colleagues as David Garnett, Geoffrey West, Richard Church, Edward O'Brien, and Graham Greene, Bates's books sold moderately at best—not more than a few thousand copies each. The one exception to this general neglect came in 1938 with *Spella Ho*, which was well received in England and serialized in condensed form in *The Atlantic*.

When war broke out, Bates was recruited for the Royal Air Force (RAF) and given a commission unique in literary and military history: to write short stories about the air war and the men who fought it. The result was two best sellers, *The Greatest People in the World, and Other Stories* (1942) and *How Sleep the Brave, and Other Stories* (1943); paperbound copies sold in the hundred of thousands. Following these, and coincident with

a change of publishers, Bates produced a string of best-selling novels about the war: *Fair Stood the Wind for France*, *The Purple Plain*, *The Jacaranda Tree*, and *The Scarlet Sword*. To many critics of the time, it appeared that Bates had capitulated to popular taste, but shortly afterward he published his finest novel, *Love for Lydia*.

During the 1950's, Bates's reputation assured substantial fees for his magazine stories, but his artistic reputation was more enhanced in this period by the novellas, a number of which recaptured rural life in prewar England. Versatility, however, was his new trademark, as the fiction embraced an ever-widening variety of characters, moods, and settings. In 1958, Bates returned to the ranks of the best sellers with *The Darling Buds of May*, a farce about the uninhibited Larkin family and modern country life. Four additional Larkin novels followed and were equally successful commercially but inferior artistically.

In 1973, Bates was made a Commander of the Order of the British Empire, but by the time of his death in 1974, he had slipped into obscurity once again. Popular interest in his work was revived within a few years of his death, however, stimulated in part by well-received British television series adapted from *Love for Lydia*, *Fair Stood the Wind for France*, *The Darling Buds of May*, and several stories and novellas. Films have been adapted from some of his novels and stories as well. The full measure of Bates's achievement has only begun to be appreciated.

BIOGRAPHY

Herbert Ernest Bates was born on May 16, 1905, in Rushden, Northamptonshire, England's center of shoe and boot manufacture. His father, employed in the boot factories since boyhood, vowed that his children would never follow the same career; accordingly, Herbert and his brother and sister, Stanley and Edna, were reared in strict Methodist respectability and educated at local schools. In his early years, Bates reacted strongly against the red-brick ugliness of his hometown, preferring country life with his maternal grandfather, George Lucas. Lucas was by far the most significant influence on Bates's life and fiction, instilling in him a passion for nature and a lifelong interest in rural affairs.

A bright student, Bates won a scholarship to nearby

Kettering Grammar School, where he performed indifferently until he met Edmund Kirby, an English master lately returned from World War I. Inspired and encouraged by Kirby, Bates resolved to become a writer, and though he could have attended university, he chose not to, electing instead to try newspaper writing and then clerking in a warehouse. There in his spare time he wrote a sprawling novel that Kirby advised him to burn. Undeterred, he tried a second, *The Two Sisters*, which traveled to ten publishers before being read by Jonathan Cape's great discoverer of new talent, Edward Garnett. Garnett recognized, where others had not, the sensitivity, feeling for character, and gift for nature writing that are the hallmarks of all Bates's fiction.

Having no university connections and never comfortable in London, Bates stayed in Rushden and continued his literary apprenticeship under Garnett and Kirby. Even before this, he had discovered in the Continental masters, especially Anton Chekhov, Ivan Turgenev, Leo Tolstoy, and Guy de Maupassant, the models for his own short fiction. Other influences were Stephen Crane, Ernest Hemingway, Thomas Hardy, and W. H. Hudson. Reading constantly and writing regularly, Bates remained in Rushden until his marriage in 1931. Virtually all his stories and novels of this period are set in and around Rushden and neighboring Higham Ferrers, and much of this work is autobiographical.

In 1931, Bates married Marjorie "Madge" Cox, and the couple made their home in a former barn in Little Chart, Kent, where they remained until Bates's death. Madge has been called "the perfect wife" for Bates; as one observer has noted, "She made his writing possible by creating an island of stability and calm in which he could work." The move to Kent made no immediate impact on Bates's fiction, as he continued to write stories and novels set in Northamptonshire. By the outbreak of World War II, he had exhausted his store of Midlands material, but induction into the RAF gave him a whole new set of experiences and widened the scope of his fic-

H. E. Bates. (Popperfoto/Getty Images)

tion. The stories written for the RAF were first published under the pseudonym "Flying Officer X," but when their authorship became public, Bates's name became a household word. *Fair Stood the Wind for France* was inspired by snippets overheard in barracks and pubs about airmen downed over France. The three war novels that followed in quick succession derived from Bates's postings to Burma and India. Royalties from these books made the Bates family (by now grown to six with the births of two girls and two boys) financially secure for the first time. Of nearly equal importance was an operation that Bates underwent in 1947 that relieved him of a lifetime of acute intestinal pain.

Bates's financial security and good health may have contributed to a burst of creativity, for *Love for Lydia* and a fine collection of short stories, *Colonel Julian, and Other Stories* (1951), quickly followed. Inspiration for *Love for Lydia* came from Bates's early Northamptonshire experiences, but the stories show an expanded awareness of contemporary matters. In 1956, however, *The Sleepless Moon* was greeted with such savagery from reviewers that Bates vowed never to write another novel. Unlike Hardy, Bates broke his vow, but with the exception of *The Distant Horns of Summer*, he avoided serious long fiction thereafter, concentrating instead on humor (the Larkin novels) and popular materials. For aesthetic outlets, he turned to the short story and the novella.

During the last two decades of his life, Bates remained a very private man. Never given to literary cliques or socializing among the arty crowd, he lived quietly in Little Chart. He traveled extensively to France and Italy but otherwise stayed close to home, indulging his passion for gardening and family life, and writing daily from early morning until noon. In 1966, he suffered a severe heart attack, followed by pneumonia, but recovered sufficiently to return to writing. His last works of importance are his three-volume autobiography and *The Triple Echo*, a novella. He died in 1974 in a Canterbury hospital of causes never revealed.

ANALYSIS

H. E. Bates's primary concern as a writer was for the individual and the forces that threaten his or her happiness or fulfillment. Bates is not, however, a political, social, moral, or philosophical theorist; ideas as such play almost no part in his fiction. Most of his protagonists are "ordinary" people—farmers, laborers, waitresses, housewives, children, pensioners, and young men of no particular education or accomplishments.

Curiously, Bates approaches his material from two very different, almost contradictory, points of view. Many of the stories and a few of the lesser novels are essentially Romantic in outlook, glorifying nature, promoting individual achievement and freedom, assuming the essential goodness of people. On the other hand, many of his stories and novellas, and virtually all of his most successful novels, are naturalistic in their portrayal of individuals at the mercy of forces they cannot understand or control, of nature as indifferent or even hostile, or of life itself as an almost Darwinian struggle. These two viewpoints coexist from the very beginning and contribute to Bates's great versatility. At the same time, the style is always clear and straightforward, uncomplicated by the experimental techniques of modern writing, the story line remaining strong and simple. These features of style and plot, together with the generally rural

settings of his fiction, make Bates appear somewhat anachronistic among contemporaries whose themes and techniques are more "modern." Although Bates broke no new ground for fiction, he kept vigorous the historical trends of Continental and American story writing, while in the novel he continued along lines suggested by Joseph Conrad and Thomas Hardy.

THE POACHER

The most ambitious of Bates's early novels, *The Poacher*, is essentially a Bates family history in which the central figure, Luke Bishop, is modeled on Grandfather Lucas, and Bates and his father are seen in Eddie Vine and his father, Walter. Luke Bishop is born about 1860 to a shiftless, poaching, shoemaker father whose ways he follows until the father is killed by a gamekeeper and Luke marries. Like Grandfather Lucas, he takes a small farm on poor soil and wrests from it a living, growing produce, grain, pigs, and chickens. Meanwhile, industry moves to Nenweald (Rushden), ending the freewheeling days of the cottage shoemakers, and brings with it the railroad, shops, and a new social tone of middle-class respectability. Bishop's wife, who becomes a schoolmistress, embodies these new values, while Bishop clings to the old, imparting them to Eddie. At age sixty, Luke is convicted of poaching and jailed. After serving his jail sentence, he returns to Nenweald only to realize that he no longer belongs there or anywhere; his world has vanished in the steam of factories and railroad engines and in the smoke of World War I.

The Poacher is a powerful and moving personal history that seeks neither glamour nor pity for its central character but takes an unflinching look at the changes in England's farms and small towns between 1880 and 1920. Bates is at his best in the taut, swift scenes of poaching and in re-creating the inner life of his unimaginative, uncouth, and bewildered protagonist. Essentially passive, Bishop is unable to cope with the changes that swirl around him; he is a product of the nineteenth century, ignored by "progress" and changes in mores. Through Bishop, Bates engages the reader's sympathy for those trampled by such progress, but because the novel's point of view is restricted, Bishop's story is not fully integrated into its setting. At times the novel seems claustrophobic, at the edges of the reality it attempts to re-create. It is less effective as social commentary than as personal history; nevertheless, Luke Bishop is a vivid human presence, representing a vigorous but now departed way of life.

Spella Ho

In the dramatic opening scene of *Spella Ho*, Bates's most successful prewar novel, Bruno Shadbolt watches his mother die of cold and consumption in an unheated hovel standing in the shadow of Spella Ho, a mansion of fifty-three chimneys. Throughout, the ugly, illiterate, determined, amoral Shadbolt and the aristocratic mansion are the poles between which the action moves. The story traces Shadbolt's slow and uneven rise from carter to wealthy industrialist. Along the way, he is aided by four women who change him in various ways—educating him, teaching him manners, altering his tastes—but who paradoxically leave untouched his essential nature, his monomaniacal drive to overcome poverty and anonymity.

In his pursuit of wealth and self-fulfillment, Shadbolt represents nineteenth century industrialists at their worst, but Bates's novel is not a one-sided attack on Victorian greed and materialism. By raising himself, Shadbolt brings prosperity and change to Nenweald (Rushden), providing jobs, goods, housing, transportation, and services to people who eagerly desire them. If Shadbolt's factories exploit workers and despoil the countryside, they also transform the local standard of living. In taking this evenhanded approach, Bates is not so much interested in being fair to England's captains of industry as he is in exploring a final crushing irony: that Shadbolt's legacy will be judged in the end as a monstrosity of ugliness and filth, while nothing of his personal triumph or his finer side will remain. Even Spella Ho, which he buys and restores, testifies not to his achievement but to that of refined aristocrats.

In addition to Shadbolt, the novel features a convincing cast of minor characters, individually rendered in detail. Once again, however, Bates fails to place his characters and action in a convincing context; for a novel concerned with social change, *Spella Ho* is curiously weak in period details. Between its opening in 1873 and its close in 1931, the novel changes little in scenery. The factories, gasworks, bus lines, and houses that Shadbolt builds are said to transform Nenweald utterly, but these changes are merely glimpsed. Once again, therefore,

Bates provides a character study of great passion and interest, a fascinating grotesque utterly authentic in personality. In addition, there are vivid and arresting portraits of late Victorian individuals and types, but the characters move through a vague world on which their impact is somehow strangely slight.

Love for Lydia

For more than a decade after *Spella Ho*, Bates focused in his novels on materials related to World War II. When he returned to his older material, therefore, it was with new eyes and understanding, fortified by advances in technique. *Love for Lydia* is unquestionably Bates's finest novel. On one level it parallels F. Scott Fitzgerald's *The Great Gatsby* (1925) as a hymn to the Jazz Age as lived in the small towns of England. The main characters are young people: Lydia Aspen, heir to a considerable fortune and aristocratic heritage; Richardson, young Bates thinly disguised; Tom and Nancy Holland, son and daughter of solid English farmers; Blackie Johnson, a mechanic and taxi driver; and Alec Sanderson, a small-town playboy of great charm but weak character. Lydia has been reared by her father, unusually sheltered and alone; when he dies, she moves to Evensford (Rushden, once again) to live with her aunts, who encourage her to gain experience of life. She and Richardson fall in love. There is a great deal of essentially innocent dancing and drinking, but Lydia's beauty is fatal: Sanderson, believing that Lydia has rejected him, accidentally drowns while drunk; Tom becomes her new love, only to die by accident or suicide of a shotgun blast. Richardson leaves to work in London, and for two years Lydia stumbles through a cloud of alcohol and dissipation. When Richardson returns, she is recovering in a sanatorium. Eventually they are reconciled.

The self-absorbed period of the 1920's, with its burst of promiscuity and hedonism, is the perfect setting for this exploration of the valuable and permanent qualities desired in human relationships. Love of self, love of life, and romantic love compete, capsizing friendships, shattering values, and upsetting traditional social arrangements until some balance can be restored. Self-absorption turns Lydia into a kind of Circe, destroying those who love her, and the quiet, uncertain Richardson into a morose, sarcastic loner. Healing comes when these two learn to give of themselves, as when Lydia can accept

Blackie's friendship and Richardson finally puts aside his wounded pride to offer Lydia the affection she needs.

Unlike Bates's naturalistic novels of the 1930's, *Love for Lydia* is dominated by the interrelationships of its characters. Events are controlled not by unseen forces but by the emotions of the characters, who are responsible for their actions and yet are victims of their own weaknesses and strengths. People in this novel are also fully a part of the world around them: Evensford breathes with its own life of dirty alleys and greasy shops, while, as always in Bates's fiction, the countryside throbs with life. In an unusual reversal, winter is the time of rebirth—the season when Lydia first joins the world and the season in which, three years later, she and Richardson are reunited. Bates thus deals not so much with the malaise of the age as with personal choices and the tendency of people to allow the worst in themselves to rule the better.

THE DISTANT HORNS OF SUMMER

The Distant Horns of Summer deals with a rather different theme—the nature of "reality." The novel centers on a young girl, Gilly, only seventeen, who has been hired by the parents of five-year-old James to look after the boy for the summer. James, like many children, lives most happily in a make-believe world in which his two friends are Mr. Pimm and Mr. Monday, two elderly men who in James's imagination treat him as a grown-up. Gilly takes the job in part to escape a man with whom she had fallen in love while working in a shop, only to fall in love with a tourist calling himself Ainsworth. He betrays her, of course, and when she tries to locate him, she finds that he, in a sense, does not exist, since she calls him by his assumed name. At the same time, James wanders off and loses himself literally and figuratively in his own world. When Gilly reports him missing, the police concern themselves more with the imaginary Pimm and Monday than with the real boy; a Miss Philpot, slightly dotty and never entirely sober, constructs her own version of events and concludes that Gilly is a nymphomaniac. Even when James is found, the confusions are unresolved.

Bates's exploration of reality has none of the philosophical seriousness of Samuel Beckett's novels; as always, it is with the particular individuals and experiences that he is concerned. Much of the novel is thus told through the eyes of young James, whose childish confu-

sions about what is "true" and what is not are entirely natural; but James, like children generally, knows quite well what is make-believe and what is not. He resents Ainsworth's unconvincing attempts to talk about Mr. Pimm and Mr. Monday, just as he is deeply hurt when he discovers that the camera Ainsworth lends him has no film. His pain at this discovery is as real as Gilly's when she learns that Ainsworth is an impostor whose affection for her is merely a pose. "Things are not as they seem" is not an abstract proposition but a concrete issue leading to betrayal and pain.

The characters of Gilly, James, and Ainsworth are convincingly drawn, and even the novel's minor figures are sharply etched and lifelike. As is always true of Bates's work, the style is bright and clear, the descriptive passages are full of sharp detail, and the dialogue is natural and idiomatic. Like the Kentish summer in which it is set, the novel radiates a mellow ripeness and melancholy that could be mistaken for romantic lassitude were it not that Bates infuses everything with intense vitality.

NOVELLAS

No discussion of Bates's fiction can afford to ignore the author's mastery of the short-novel form. With the short-story writer's gift of sketching character swiftly yet fully, and his ability to portray rural settings, Bates creates a number of memorable pieces focusing primarily on character. The earliest of these is *Seven Tales and Alexander* (1929), a romantic, idyllic re-creation of the days when young Bates and Grandfather Lucas would pick fruit to sell at market. Closer to the novella form per se is *The Cruise of the Breadwinner*, a chilling study of bravery and coming to manhood during World War II.

In the 1950's, Bates turned increasingly to this form, publishing two collections. From one of these comes *Dulcima*, a curious story of sexual exploitation centering on Dulcima, a heavy-legged, ungainly woman who attaches herself to a lonely old farmer, cheats him of his money, and taunts him with references to a boyfriend who does not exist. The vain and miserly farmer who thus allows himself to be deluded participates in his own destruction. *An Aspidistra in Babylon*, the title story of a collection published in 1960, reverses the plot of *Dulcima*, portraying the seduction of a young girl by a dashing soldier. Told through the girl's eyes, the story centers on trust—hers for the soldier, the soldier's aunt's for her. She is both betrayer and betrayed, stealing from the old woman to finance an elopement with the soldier, who spends the money on another woman.

The most unusual of Bates's novellas is among his last—*The Triple Echo*. Set during World War II, it features a young wife whose husband has been captured by the Japanese and a young soldier who eventually goes AWOL (absent without leave). The wife has been turned by farm drudgery into a man, dressing and acting like one. The soldier, to avoid detection by the military police, disguises himself as her sister. Sex roles reverse with the complexity of a Shakespearean comedy, but the story does more than explore androgyny, for beneath it runs an antiwar strain, a suggestion that such unnatural role reversals are part of the ruin of war.

The enduring qualities of Bates's fiction have little to do with the themes he explores, for he is not a modern "problem" writer. Rather, his fiction commands attention because of its style, its treatment of nature, and its explorations of individual characters. Bates writes in the purest English, with a sparkling clarity and sure sense of rhythm. Except in the earliest works, his stories and novels are presented vividly, pictorially, directly; there is always an immediacy and sensuousness about his work. He has been compared favorably and accurately with the Impressionist painters, whose works he collected. Most especially, when he writes of nature, whether a bright summer day, a dreary wintry rain, or a brilliant early spring afternoon, his prose quivers with life and brilliant images. Occasionally he tends toward lushness, but restraint, understatement, and quick, sure strokes are his characteristic virtues.

Bates's characters are similarly drawn: They spring from the page whole and solid. Seldom are they sophisticated or intellectual; more often they are inarticulate, emotional, bewildered. Even in the novels, characters seldom develop or reveal complex layers of themselves; rather, they struggle as best they can with what emotional and intellectual equipment they have. Perhaps for this reason, Bates is not an intellectual's writer; his tendency is to look past the beauties of style and the flashes of insight for something that is not there. What is present, however, is fiction of high quality, waiting to receive the attention it deserves.

Dean R. Baldwin

OTHER MAJOR WORKS

SHORT FICTION: *The Seekers*, 1926; *Day's End, and Other Stories*, 1928; *Seven Tales and Alexander*, 1929; *The Black Boxer: Tales*, 1932; *Thirty Tales*, 1934; *The Woman Who Had Imagination, and Other Stories*, 1934; *Cut and Come Again: Fourteen Stories*, 1935; *Something Short and Sweet: Stories*, 1937; *Country Tales: Collected Short Stories*, 1938; *The Flying Goat: Stories*, 1939; *My Uncle Silas: Stories*, 1939; *The Beauty of the Dead, and Other Stories*, 1940; *The Greatest People in the World, and Other Stories*, 1942; *The Bride Comes to Evensford, and Other Tales*, 1943; *How Sleep the Brave, and Other Stories*, 1943; *Dear Life*, 1949; *Colonel Julian, and Other Stories*, 1951; *The Daffodil Sky*, 1955; *The Sleepless Moon*, 1956; *Death of a Huntsman: Four Short Novels*, 1957 (also known as *Summer in Salandar*, 1957); *Sugar for the Horse*, 1957; *The Watercress Girl, and Other Stories*, 1959; *An Aspidistra in Babylon: Four Novellas*, 1960 (also known as *The Grapes of Paradise*, 1960); *The Golden Oriole: Five Novellas*, 1961; *Now Sleeps the Crimson Petal, and Other Stories*, 1961 (also known as *The Enchantress, and Other Stories*, 1961); *Seven by Five: Stories, 1926-1961*, 1963 (also known as *The Best of H. E. Bates*, 1963); *The Fabulous Mrs. V.*, 1964; *The Wedding Party*, 1965; *The Four Beauties*, 1968; *The Wild Cherry Tree*, 1968; *The Good Corn, and Other Stories*, 1974; *The Yellow Meads of Asphodel*, 1976.

PLAYS: *The Last Bread*, pb. 1926; *The Day of Glory*, pb. 1945.

NONFICTION: *Through the Woods*, 1936; *Down the River*, 1937; *The Modern Short Story: A Critical Survey*, 1941; *In the Heart of the Country*, 1942; *Country Life*, 1943; *O More Than Happy Countryman*, 1943; *Edward Garnett*, 1950; *The Country of White Clover*, 1952; *The Face of England*, 1952; *The Vanished World: An Autobiography*, 1969; *The Blossoming World: An Autobiography*, 1971; *The World in Ripeness: An Autobiography*, 1972.

BIBLIOGRAPHY

Alderson, Frederick. "Bates Country: A Memoir of H. E. Bates." *London Magazine* 19 (July, 1979): 31-42. Presents a personal account of Alderson's friendship with Bates, including their times together in the

Royal Air Force during World War II. Comments on Bates's writings, calling his style "impressionistic."

Baldwin, Dean R. *H. E. Bates: A Literary Life*. Selinsgrove, Pa.: Susquehanna University Press, 1987. Biography has proved to be a more reliable source of information about Bates than his own three-volume autobiography. Includes extensive commentary on his novels and short stories.

_____. "H. E. Bates: *The Poacher*." In *Recharting the Thirties*, edited by Patrick J. Quinn. Selinsgrove, Pa.: Susquehanna University Press, 1996. Discussion of Bates's 1935 novel *The Poacher* is included in an essay collection that seeks to refamiliarize readers with British authors who have been largely ignored since their major works first appeared in the 1930's. The essay is preceded by a brief biographical sketch of Bates.

Eads, Peter. *H. E. Bates: A Bibliographical Study*. 1990. Reprint. London: Oak Knoll Press and the British Library, 2007. Provides a good collection of biblio-graphical material on Bates and offers full details of first editions of all Bates's works, adding comments from reviews and the writer's autobiography.

Evenson, Brian. "H. E. Bates." In *British Novelists Between the Wars*, edited by George M. Johnson. Vol. 191 in *Dictionary of Literary Biography*. Detroit, Mich.: Gale Group, 1998. Essay on Bates provides biographical information, analysis of his work, and a bibliography.

Frierson, William. *The English Novel in Transition, 1885-1940*. New York: Cooper Square, 1965. Discusses the influence of Anton Chekhov, Thomas Hardy, and D. H. Lawrence on Bates's work and argues that pessimism is the most fundamental connective thread in his fiction.

Vannatta, Dennis. *H. E. Bates*. Boston: Twayne, 1983. Good introductory work provides less biographical information than Baldwin's biography (cited above) but more critical commentary. Includes useful bibliography of primary and secondary sources.

ANN BEATTIE

Born: Washington, D.C.; September 8, 1947

PRINCIPAL LONG FICTION

Chilly Scenes of Winter, 1976
Falling in Place, 1980
Love Always, 1985
Picturing Will, 1989
Another You, 1995
My Life, Starring Dara Falcon, 1997
The Doctor's House, 2002

OTHER LITERARY FORMS

In addition to her novels, Ann Beattie (BEE-tee) has published nonfiction as well as numerous volumes of short stories, including *Distortions* (1976), *The Burning House* (1982), *What Was Mine, and Other Stories* (1991), and *Follies: New Stories* (2005). She has also published two children's books: *Goblin Tales* (1975) and *Spectacle* (1985).

ACHIEVEMENTS

Hailed by many as the spokesperson for her generation, Ann Beattie has won numerous awards for her novels and short stories focusing on vapid, upper-middle-class characters. Along with several scholastic honors, Beattie has received a literary award from the American Academy and Institute of Arts and Letters, a Distinguished Alumnae Award from American University, and the PEN/Bernard Malamud Award. A member of the International Association of Poets, Playwrights, Editors, Essayists, and Novelists (PEN) and of the Authors Guild, in 1992 she was elected to the American Academy and Institute of Arts and Letters.

BIOGRAPHY

The daughter of an administrator in the U.S. Department of Health, Education, and Welfare, James A. Beattie, and Charlotte Beattie (née Crosby), Ann Beattie was born in Washington, D.C., in 1947 and grew up in the city's suburbs. As a child, she was encouraged to paint, read, and write. An avid scholar, she enrolled at American University in Washington, D.C., in 1966 and received her B.A. only three years later, in 1969. During this short tenure, she edited the university literary journal and was chosen by *Mademoiselle* magazine to be a guest editor in 1968. After her graduation, Beattie entered the M.A. program at the University of Connecticut as a graduate assistant to study eighteenth century literature. She received her degree in 1970 and began to work toward a doctorate; however, she quickly became frustrated and turned to writing short stories. It was then that— encouraged by her mentor, author John O'Hara— she submitted several stories to small-press literary journals. She achieved moderate success with these publications, and in 1974, her story "A Platonic Relationship" was published by *The New Yorker*. Later that same year, *The New Yorker* printed two more of Beattie's short stories, a signal of her arrival in the literary world. She quit the university to concentrate on her writing.

Beattie later served on the faculties of several universities as a writing instructor. In 1972 she married David Gates, a fellow University of Connecticut student; they were divorced in 1980. In 1985, a mutual friend introduced Beattie to the painter Lincoln Perry, a visiting professor at the University of Virginia, where Beattie had taught several years before. They were married in 1988. After several years in Charlottesville, they moved to Maine, where Beattie continues to write.

Ann Beattie. (Benjamin Ford)

ANALYSIS

Although Ann Beattie's fiction has often been criticized as pointless and depressing, there is a method to the author's seeming madness. Her stories and novels are not a mix of ennui and untapped angst but rather detailed examinations of the lives of several apparently different but uniquely similar people. No one specific character is repeated in any story, but some character types, such as the Vietnam War veteran, appear in different versions and perform different functions—as plot catalysts, for

example. At the same time, all of Beattie's characters share the same vague feelings of discontent and lack of fulfillment, the knowledge that something is missing in their lives.

CHILLY SCENES OF WINTER

Initially, a Beattie character may seem feisty and self-assured, even defensive about his or her lack of enthusiasm. In Beattie's first novel, *Chilly Scenes of Winter*, one player remarks, "You could be happy, too, Sam, if you hadn't had your eyes opened in the 60's." The promise of a better life that was given to these characters has transmogrified into unhappiness and loneliness without relief. Beattie's novels are, accordingly, laced with irony. It is the acknowledgment of this transgression through the use of irony that provides a saving grace for the stories and novels. The main character in *Chilly Scenes of Winter* is granted all that he wishes; in the end, however, all he wants is to escape his gratification.

Charles, the protagonist, is in love with Laura, a married woman. His desire for her eventually dominates his life, so that he is unable to function without that desire or—as he would believe—without her. Charles's obsession with Laura colors his relationship with his own family: his mother, Clara; her second husband, Pete; and Charles's sister, Susan. Even though his sister has accepted Pete, Charles refuses to acknowledge him as a replacement for their father, a man whose good qualities are magnified by the virtue of his death. Charles regards Pete as both a loser and a catalyst for Clara's chronic hypochondria. He claims that Pete refuses to accept life as it is, instead continuing to make excuses for Clara's instability. The irony is that what Charles so clearly perceives as Pete's faults are really his own. Charles cannot—or will not—admit that he, too, fantasizes about the woman he loves and constructs absurd ideas about her that are founded on nothing but his own imagination. Charles will never be able to have a normal life with Laura, just as Pete will never be able to have one with Clara.

Running throughout the novel is the idea that marriage itself is not a desirable norm. Sam, Clara's friend, comments, "It's nuts to get married," and indeed none of the relationships in *Chilly Scenes of Winter* seems to bode well for the participants. Pete and Clara's marriage is tainted by her mental illness, Jim and Laura's seems emptied by their lack of interest, and Charles and Laura's relationship is adulterous (and thus cannot be acknowledged).

The lack of sanction for Charles's love is typical of his whole existence. Nothing in his life lives up to his expectations, so he wanders pathetically, searching for both the ideal and the unreal. He is terrified of discovering a truth in his miserable existence, and this fear prevents him from completing his quest for love and a meaningful life. Charles is consumed by the thought that he will develop an "inoperable melanoma," even though there is no indication that he will; it is merely a phrase he has overheard in a hospital room. After Laura leaves Jim, Charles refuses to contact her; he will only drive past her house, hoping for a signal that will never be given.

FALLING IN PLACE

In contrast to a world where the characters are forced to wander endlessly, searching for a direction, the players in *Falling in Place* are given a very clear signal when a significant event occurs. The story opens with John Knapp; his estranged wife, Louise; their children, Mary and John Joel; and John's mistress, Nina. During the week, John lives with his mother, ostensibly to be close to his job in New York City but really to be far away from Louise and the children and closer to Nina. Naturally, this situation affects his children, and they become bitter and distanced not only from their father but also from their mother. Instead of swimming in a maelstrom of their own emotions, however, the characters in *Falling in Place* actually reach out to others and are influenced by them. John Joel's deviant friend Parker brings the action of the novel to a head: He provides John Joel with a handgun, and the latter proceeds to shoot his sister Mary in the side. When asked why he shot her, John Joel explains to his father, "She was a bitch."

Perhaps this phrase succinctly sums up Beattie's child characters in the story. Instead of behaving like real children, their circumstances force them to become miniature adults, faced with adult problems and desires. John Joel has an eating disorder, his friend Parker smokes a pack of cigarettes a day, and cold Mary dreams of sacrificing her virginity to singer Peter Frampton. They are a sad band of children, imitating the worst habits of their adult counterparts in the worst possible way. John Joel mouths adult words and defines his teenage sister in adult terms.

Finally, John and Louise divorce, freeing themselves and their children to pursue meaningful existences. None, however, really believes that he or she will be able to attain such an existence. At one point, John complains to Mary, "Don't you think I might already realize that my existence is a little silly?" Mary replies, "That's what *Vanity Fair* is like. Things just fall into place." John wonders if his daughter's advocacy of predestination seals her fate or if she simply cannot, or will not, try to imagine a future over which she has any control. Mary is not, however, the only member of her family who refuses to admit to a future. After Nina and John finally unite, Nina begs him to consider her wants: "Acres of land. Children. A big house. Try to *realize* what you love." John only replies, "You're what I want."

John, then, refuses to realize, to make real, his existence with Nina and any sort of happiness they might have. He and his fellow characters are moderately pleased with their ties to the past and present; one boasts of a once-removed acquaintance with singer Linda Ronstadt. Not one of them, however, will consider the effect of his or her present actions on the future. No one wants to be responsible for shaping a future; all merely accept whatever happens as a logical consequence of an illogical life.

LOVE ALWAYS

In contrast, the characters in *Love Always* begin by rejoicing that they are "beating the system." Hildon and his former-student friends run a slick journal titled *Country Daze*, the success of which, Hildon maintains, is "proof positive that the whole country is coked-out." Because the United States, or at least the readership of *Country Daze*, has gone to rack and ruin, Hildon and associates decide that their behavior does not have to measure up to any modern-day standards. Hildon continues his long-standing affair with coworker and advice columnist Lucy, despite his marriage. Lucy's fourteen-year-old niece, Nicole, is taking a brief vacation with her aunt from her role as a teenage junkie on a popular soap opera.

Nicole is yet another of Beattie's adult children, like John Joel and Mary in *Falling in Place*. She serves as a foil for the adults in her world who are childishly hiding from the responsibilities and terrors of the outside world in a world of their own devising. Nicole's aunt, Lucy, writes her column under the name Cindi Coeur. Ironically, she does not wear her heart on her sleeve but rather flees from mature relationships. Lucy is equally unhappy about Nicole's adult behavior, but she does not know what to do about it.

PICTURING WILL

In the mid-1980's the direction of Beattie's fiction began to change. Although the characters in her novels were still passive and directionless, they also experienced instances of redemption, primarily through a commitment to other human beings that no one in the earlier works seemed willing or able to make. A great many of the characters in the novels from *Picturing Will* onward do fail both themselves and others, however. In *Picturing Will*, for example, the needs of the five-year-old

protagonist, Will, are ignored by both of his divorced parents. His mother, Jody, is more interested in becoming a famous photographer than in taking care of her son, and his shiftless father, Wayne, would rather drink and womanize than pay attention to Will. The real hero of the story is Jody's lover, and later her second husband, Mel Anthis. It is Mel who sacrifices his own literary ambitions to dedicate his life to child rearing, thus ensuring that Will becomes the secure man and the loving husband and father that readers meet at the end of the novel.

ANOTHER YOU

In *Picturing Will*, Mel is introduced as a caring person, capable of loving a woman as difficult as Jody, and his affection for Will is believable. In the protagonist of *Another You*, however, a striking change in personality occurs, one that promises redemption. At the beginning of the book, Marshall Lockard seems much like the passive characters in Beattie's earlier novels, except that he is quite content with his purposeless life; in fact, Marshall has deliberately arranged his way of life. As an English professor at a small New Hampshire college, he can live vicariously through literary characters, and he has so well mastered the art of sarcasm that he can repel his students at will. Because his wife, Sonja, believes him too vulnerable to be subjected to any emotional stress, it is she, not Marshall, who goes to the nursing home to visit Marshall's stepmother, who reared him and loves him dearly. Although Sonja has become bored enough with this well-ordered existence to indulge in a little adultery with her employer, she does not mean for her husband to find out about it.

Despite all his precautions, however, Marshall is drawn into the untidy world. It all begins with a simple request from one of his students: She wants him to speak to someone on campus about her friend, who is claiming that she was assaulted by Marshall's colleague Jack MacCallum. Soon Marshall finds himself kissing the student and worrying about repercussions, explaining to the police why MacCallum was stabbed by his pregnant wife in the Lockard home, and dealing with his stepmother's death and his wife's infidelity, not to mention the two students' having fabricated their story and the supposed victim's turning out to be a narcotics agent. Marshall is so shaken by these heavy blows of reality that he decides to go to Key West, visit his older brother

Gordon, and ask about some events in their childhood that have always haunted him. Although only the reader—not Marshall—finds out the truth, simply by confronting the issue Marshall gains new strength. Instead of becoming another drifter in Key West, he heads back to New Hampshire, cold weather, and real life, hopefully with Sonja.

MY LIFE, STARRING DARA FALCON

In Beattie's early works, the characters are often far more interested in the lives of celebrities, such as Janis Joplin and Lucille Ball, than in their own lives. After all, it is much less risky to invest in a tabloid than in another person. A similar kind of vicarious existence is the subject of *My Life, Starring Dara Falcon*. Here, however, the protagonist, Jean Warner, is so young and so malleable that this is obviously a coming-of-age novel. Beattie even reassures her readers of a happy ending by beginning the book two decades after most of its events and by showing the narrator as a happily married, mature woman who understands herself and others. Readers thus know from the outset that Jean did escape from her husband's large extended family, which smothered her rather than giving her the security she sought, from a rather dull husband who is ruled by his family, and, most important, from the manipulations of the Machiavellian Dara Falcon.

In both *My Life, Starring Dara Falcon* and *Another You*, the protagonists begin as passive creatures who live vicariously through others, but they can and do choose to change, first by coming to terms with their own identities, then by daring to care about others. If in her early works Beattie showed what was wrong with the members of her generation, in her later works she offers hope to them and, indeed, to all of us.

THE DOCTOR'S HOUSE

Even a madman sounds sane, it is said, if one accepts his basic premise. No matter how bizarre or inappropriate one's actions, the indefensible can be easily explained and appear rational and responsible, providing the storyteller is willing to omit personal eccentricities and character flaws in the telling. In *The Doctor's House*, Beattie presents three unreliable narrators: Andrew, his little sister Nina, and their mother. The three storytellers present their narrations in a seemingly candid, honest manner. Though they often describe the same events,

their accounts differ greatly. The differences can be found primarily in the roles and motivations of the other players in the story. There are four main players, but the reader hears from only three.

The fourth player is the father, the doctor, in whose house all four live together and are forever emotionally scarred. The doctor, Frank, is cruel and sadistic, verbally torturing his wife and children. All three storytellers avoid Frank, which is easy to do because he is a doctor and finds many opportunities to be away from home. Frank is a womanizer; he regularly cheats on his wife, having affairs with his nurses, patients, and family friends. Frank and his wife have separate bedrooms, and he visits his wife's bedroom periodically only to confess his inadequacies and infidelities, crying at her feet and begging her forgiveness. Frank's wife is never identified by name, even in her own narrative. Frank refers to her always as "Mom," and the children seldom refer to her at all, except in the most unflattering ways.

Mom is an alcoholic, consuming bottles of liquor every day and passing out behind her closed bedroom door. Andrew and Nina fend for themselves, avoiding their father and ignoring their mother. The brother and sister become completely interdependent, fellow survivors who cling to each other in order to cope in a terribly dysfunctional family. Frank berates Andrew, calling his son a homosexual. Andrew is the "man" of the house, protecting his sister and indulging his mother. Andrew grows up to be a womanizer like his father, unable to commit or take any responsibility for his actions. He is charming and lovable though shallow and self-centered. As an adult, Andrew contacts all of his old girlfriends from high school, reliving his misspent youth and extending his quest for physical intimacy without emotional connections.

Nina, the book's first narrator, lives alone, her husband having been killed in an car accident. She lives in self-imposed isolation, admitting only Andrew and a few old friends into her well-ordered, safe world. Nina edits other people's writing for a living, rewording their sentences and correcting their mistakes, adding meaning by filling in holes.

Jennifer L. Wyatt; Rosemary M. Canfield Reisman
Updated by Randy L. Abbott

OTHER MAJOR WORKS

SHORT FICTION: *Distortions*, 1976; *Secrets and Surprises*, 1978; *Jacklighting*, 1981; *The Burning House*, 1982; *Where You'll Find Me, and Other Stories*, 1986; *What Was Mine, and Other Stories*, 1991; *Park City: New and Selected Stories*, 1998; *Perfect Recall: New Stories*, 2001; *Follies: New Stories*, 2005.

NONFICTION: *Alex Katz*, 1987.

CHILDREN'S LITERATURE: *Goblin Tales*, 1975; *Spectacle*, 1985.

EDITED TEXT: *The Best American Short Stories 1987*, 1987.

BIBLIOGRAPHY

Beattie, Ann. "An Interview with Ann Beattie." Interview by Steven R. Centola. *Contemporary Literature* 31 (Winter, 1990): 405-422. Provides biographical information and background on Beattie's fiction. Beattie discusses herself as a feminist writer and how she goes about creating credible male protagonists. Discusses *Falling in Place*, *Love Always*, *Chilly Scenes of Winter*, and *Picturing Will*.

Montresor, Jaye Berman, ed. *The Critical Response to Ann Beattie*. Westport, Conn.: Greenwood Press, 1993. Collection of essays presents contemporary reviews of Beattie's novels and collections of short stories as well as scholarly and academic analyses of her work by various critics. Novels discussed include *Chilly Scenes of Winter and Picturing Will*.

Murphy, Christina. *Ann Beattie*. Boston: Twayne, 1986. Provides a good general introduction to Beattie's work. Discusses her major stories, illustrating her central themes and basic techniques, and examines the relationship of the stories to her novels. Also addresses Beattie's place in the development of the contemporary American short story.

Porter, Carolyn. "The Art of the Missing." In *Contemporary American Women Writers: Narrative Strategies*, edited by Catherine Rainwater and William J. Scheick. Lexington: University Press of Kentucky, 1985. Argues that Beattie economizes not by developing a symbolic context, as James Joyce and Sherwood Anderson did, but rather by using the present tense and thus removing any temptation to lapse into exposition, forcing the background to emerge from dialogue of character consciousness.

Stein, Lorin. "Fiction in Review." *Yale Review* 85, no. 4 (1997): 156-165. Presents an excellent summary of Beattie's early fiction and then analyzes *My Life, Starring Dara Falcon*. Asserts that the novel has generally been underrated by critics.

Trouard, Dawn, ed. *Conversations with Ann Beattie*. Jackson: University Press of Mississippi, 2007. Collection reprints interviews with the author from 1979 to 2004, including an interview conducted by Trouard. Beattie addresses her sense of contemporary American life and misconceptions regarding her work; she also compares writing to photography. Includes chronology and index.

Wyatt, David. "Ann Beattie." *Southern Review* 28, no. 1 (1992): 145-159. Presents evidence that a marked alteration occurred in Beattie's fiction in the mid-1980's. Instead of withdrawing from life and its dangers, her characters began to choose to care about other people and to commit themselves to creativity. A perceptive and convincing analysis.

Young, Michael W., and Troy Thibodeaux. "Ann Beattie." In *A Reader's Companion to the Short Story in English*, edited by Erin Fallon et al. Westport, Conn.: Greenwood Press, 2001. Focuses on Beattie's short stories but includes informative biographical material on the author.

SIMONE DE BEAUVOIR

Born: Paris, France; January 9, 1908
Died: Paris, France; April 14, 1986
Also known as: Simone Lucie-Ernestine-Marie-Bertrand de Beauvoir

PRINCIPAL LONG FICTION

L'Invitée, 1943 (*She Came to Stay*, 1949)

Le Sang des autres, 1945 (*The Blood of Others*, 1948)

Tous les hommes sont mortels, 1946 (*All Men Are Mortal*, 1955)

Les Mandarins, 1954 (*The Mandarins*, 1956)

Les Belles Images, 1966 (English translation, 1968)

OTHER LITERARY FORMS

Simone de Beauvoir (duh boh-VWAHR) is best known for her social and political philosophy, especially her contributions to feminism. Foremost among her nonfiction works is her four-volume autobiography, *Mémoires d'une jeune fille rangée* (1958; *Memoirs of a Dutiful Daughter*, 1959), *La Force de l'âge* (1960; *The Prime of Life*, 1962), *La Force des choses* (1963; *Force of Circumstance*, 1964), and *Tout compte fait* (1972; *All Said and Done*, 1974). Equally important is her monumental sociological study on women, *Le Deuxième Sexe* (1949; *The Second Sex*, 1953). Two other sociological works follow *The Second Sex*, the first on China, *La Longue Marche* (1957; *The Long March*, 1958), and the second on the aged, *La Vieillesse* (1970; *The Coming of Age*, 1972). *Les Bouches inutiles* (1945), her only play, has not been translated into English. She also published two collections of short stories, *La Femme rompue* (1967; *The Woman Destroyed*, 1968) and *Quand prime le spirituel* (1979; *When Things of the Spirit Come First: Five Early Tales*, 1982). Her most important philosophical essays include *Pyrrhus et Cinéas* (1944), *Pour une morale de l'ambiguïté* (1947; *The Ethics of Ambiguity*, 1948), *L'Existentialisme et la sagesse des nations* (1948), and *Privilèges* (1955; partial translation "Must We Burn Sade?," 1953). A number of her other essays appeared in newspapers and journals. She also wrote a chronicle of her travels in the United States, *L'Amérique au jour le jour* (1948; *America Day by Day*, 1953); a powerful account of her mother's illness and death, *Une Mort très douce* (1964; *A Very Easy Death*, 1966); and a tribute to Jean-Paul Sartre, *La Cérémonie des adieux* (1981; *Adieux: A Farewell to Sartre*, 1984).

ACHIEVEMENTS

Simon de Beauvoir was a presence in French intellectual life during the second half of the twentieth century. She is one of the foremost examples of existentialist *engagement* and its most respected moral voice; the breadth of her writing alone secures de Beauvoir a prominent position in twentieth century letters. Her novels, especially *She Came to Stay*, *The Blood of Others*, and *The Mandarins* (for which she won the Prix Goncourt in 1954), pose some of the central philosophical and ethical questions of our time, exploring the problems of social morality, political commitment, and human responsibility. Along with her autobiography, her novels chronicle the time before and after World War II and the experiences that made her one of the most influential writers of the twentieth century.

De Beauvoir wrote numerous articles for *Les Temps modernes*, a periodical founded and directed by Sartre, and she was a member of its editorial board. In 1973, she became the editor of the journal's feminist column. *The Second Sex*, her carefully documented study of the situation of women, became one of the major theoretical texts of the women's movement. Always an activist for women's rights and social justice, she demonstrated against France's restrictive abortion laws and signed the "Manifeste des 343," a document listing women who admitted having had abortions. She was president of Choisir (1971) and of the Ligue des Droits des Femmes (1974), an organization devoted to fighting sex discrimination. De Beauvoir was also one of the founders of the feminist journal *Questions féministes*. Her indictment of social injustice is evidenced by *The Coming of Age*, her defense of a free press (the Maoist underground newspaper *La Cause du peuple*), and her political actions.

BIOGRAPHY

Simone Lucie-Ernestine-Marie-Bertrand de Beauvoir was born in Paris on January 9, 1908. Her father, Georges de Beauvoir, came from a wealthy family and was a lawyer by profession. A religious skeptic, he was openly contemptuous of the bourgeoisie and encouraged his daughter in intellectual pursuits. In contrast, her mother, Françoise, came from a provincial town, received her education in convents, and was a devout Catholic. Under her mother's supervision, the young de Beauvoir was educated at a conservative Catholic school for girls, the Cours Désir.

In *Memoirs of a Dutiful Daughter*—which covers the years from 1908 to 1929—de Beauvoir describes her early piety, her subsequent disenchantment with Catholicism, and the beginning of her rebellion against her middle-class background. Influenced by early readings

Simone de Beauvoir. (Archive Photos)

of Louisa May Alcott and George Eliot, she decided at age fifteen that she wanted to be a writer. After leaving the Cours Désir, she pursued the study of literature at the Institut Catholique in Paris. In 1926, she attended the Sorbonne and studied philosophy, Greek, and philology. Three years later, after a year at the prestigious École Normale Supérieure, she passed the examination for the *agrégation de philosophie*, the highest academic degree conferred in France.

In 1929, de Beauvoir met the writer-philosopher Jean-Paul Sartre and began an association with him that lasted until his death in April, 1980. The years from 1929 to 1944 are chronicled in the second volume of her autobiography, *The Prime of Life*. Having completed her academic degrees, she was assigned a series of teaching positions, first in Marseilles and later in Rouen and Paris. Her first novel, *She Came to Stay*, appeared in 1943; it established her as a writer, and she stopped teaching. During the war years, she became interested in political action. By the end of World War II, de Beauvoir and Sartre were labeled "existentialists," and their success and celebrity were assured. In 1947, de Beauvoir was invited on a lecture tour of the United States (described in *America Day by Day*) and began a four-year affair with American writer Nelson Algren.

During the postwar years, de Beauvoir became increasingly preoccupied with the problems of the intellectual in society, and she continued to examine the relationship between freedom and social commitment. In *Force of Circumstance* (which spans the years 1944 to 1962), the third volume of her autobiography, political events such as the Korean War and the Algerian crisis occupy progressively more space. She saw Sartre destroy his health to work on *Critique de la raison dialectique, I: Théorie des ensembles pratiques* (1960; *Critique of Dialectical Reason, I: Theory of Practical Ensembles*, 1976) and became painfully aware of human mortality and solitude. Old age and death are themes that run through de Beauvoir's work from this period, such as *The Woman Destroyed, The Coming of Age*, and the last volume of her autobiography, *All Said and Done*. In spite of this, the general tone of *All Said and Done*—as well as of the frequent interviews de Beauvoir gave—is one of a woman content to have achieved her existentialist project before her death in 1986.

ANALYSIS

Simone de Beauvoir's novels are grounded in her training as a philosopher and in her sociological and feminist concerns. *She Came to Stay*, *The Blood of Others*, *All Men Are Mortal*, and *The Mandarins* all revolve around the questions of freedom and responsibility and try to define the proper relationship between the individual and society. Her characters search for authenticity as they attempt to shape the world around them. Their education is sentimental as well as intellectual and political. While most of her heroes accommodate themselves successfully to reality, the same may not be said of her heroines. In the later novels, *The Mandarins* and *Les Belles Images*, her female characters, who are successful by worldly standards, suffer a series of psychological crises. As they undertake what the feminist critic Carol Christ has called spiritual quests, they often face suicide and madness. The existentialist enterprise of *engagement*, or commitment with a view of defining the self through action, seems more possible for the men in her novels than for the women. Jean Leighton has observed the absence of positive heroines in de Beauvoir's work: Woman seems condemned to passivity while man's fate is one of transcendence. Arguments from *The Second Sex* and from de Beauvoir's philosophical essays echo in the novels. The tension between the author's philosophical ideas and their potential realization by the women characters is clearly visible in her fiction.

SHE CAME TO STAY

De Beauvoir's first novel, *She Came to Stay*, is an imaginative transposition of her relationship with Olga Kosakiewicz. In 1933, de Beauvoir and Sartre had befriended Kosakiewicz, one of de Beauvoir's students. They had attempted a ménage à trois; *She Came to Stay* is the story of its failure.

The heroine of the novel, Françoise Miquel, is a young writer who has lived with Pierre Labrousse, a talented actor and director, for eight years. They feel that their relationship is ideal because it allows them both a great deal of freedom. Françoise befriends Xavière, a young woman disenchanted with provincial life, and in-

vites her to Paris, where she will help Xavière find work. Once in Paris, Xavière makes demands on the couple and is openly contemptuous of their values. Pierre becomes obsessed with Xavière; Françoise, trying to rise above the jealousy and insecurity she feels, struggles to keep the trio together. Out of resentment, Françoise has an affaire with Gerbert, Xavière's suitor. The novel ends as Xavière recognizes Françoise's duplicity; Xavière has now become the critical Other. Unable to live in her presence, Françoise turns on the gas and murders her.

She Came to Stay is a meditation on the Hegelian problem of the existence of the Other. The novel plays out the psychological effects of jealousy and questions the extent to which coexistence is possible. Critics such as Hazel Barnes and Carol Ascher have noted the close ties between de Beauvoir's first novel and Sartre's *L'Être et le néant* (1943; *Being and Nothingness*, 1956), published in the same year. Both texts deal with the central existentialist theme of letting others absorb one's freedom.

Despite Françoise's apparent independence, she needs Pierre to approve her actions and give them direction. Françoise's self-deception and the inauthenticity of her life anticipate de Beauvoir's analysis of *l'amoureuse*, the woman in love, in *The Second Sex*. Confronted with a rival, Françoise becomes aware that her self-assurance and detachment are illusory. Her growth as a character occurs as she sheds the unexamined rational premises she holds about herself and her relationship with Pierre. The gap between the intellect and the emotions continues to widen until it reaches a crisis in the murder of Xavière. Françoise is finally forced to confront her long-concealed hatred. In spite of its often stylized dialogue, *She Came to Stay* is a lucid, finely executed study of love and jealousy and one of de Beauvoir's finest novels.

THE BLOOD OF OTHERS

Although de Beauvoir was later to consider her second novel overly didactic, *The Blood of Others* is one of the best novels written about the French Resistance. The book opens with the thoughts of Jean Blomart as he keeps vigil over his mistress Hélène, who is dying from a wound received during a mission. The novel proceeds by flashback and alternates between the stories of Jean, a Resistance hero, and his companion Hélène. The son of a wealthy bourgeois family, Jean is plagued by feelings of guilt over his comfortable situation. He takes a job as a worker and tries to lead a life of uninvolvement. His attempted detachment is based on his belief that he can thus avoid contributing to the unhappiness of others. Passive at the outbreak of the war, he is finally drafted. Upon his return to Paris, he realizes that his detachment is actually a form of irresponsibility. He organizes a resistance group and becomes its leader. As he watches the dying Hélène, he questions whether he has the right to control the lives of his comrades. Although he is doomed to act in ignorance of the consequences of his decisions, he decides that he nevertheless has an obligation to act. The novel ends with Hélène's death and Jean's renewed commitment to the Resistance.

If *The Blood of Others* is the story of Jean's *engagement*, it is also the story of Hélène's political awakening. Like him, she is politically indifferent until a young Jewish friend is in danger of deportation. She then turns to Jean and becomes an active member of his group. In contrast with most of de Beauvoir's women, Hélène is one who, in her political commitment, manages to define herself through her actions rather than through her emotional attachments.

The Blood of Others presages the discussion of individual freedom in *The Ethics of Ambiguity*. In both the novel and the philosophical essay, the problem of the Other is interfaced with the question of social responsibility. With its emphasis on the denial of freedom during the Nazi occupation of France, the novel underscores the necessity of political action to ensure individual freedoms. The closed space of the love triangle in *She Came to Stay* is replaced by the larger obligations of the individual to a historical moment. *The Blood of Others* conveys the problematic quality of ethical decisions; as Robert Cottrell has noted, it evokes "the sense of being entrapped, of submitting to existence rather than fashioning it." Nevertheless, *The Blood of Others* is a more optimistic book than *She Came to Stay* in its portrayal of the individual working toward a larger social good.

ALL MEN ARE MORTAL

Individual actions are seen against a series of historical backdrops in *All Men Are Mortal*. The novel traces the life of Count Fosca, an Italian nobleman who is endowed with immortality. At the request of Régine, a successful young actress, he recounts his varied careers through seven centuries. A counselor to Maximilian of Germany and then to Charles V of Spain, he discovers the Mississippi, founds the first French university, and becomes an activist in the French Revolution. Like other existentialist heroes, Fosca paradoxically admits that only death gives life meaning. His goal of building an ideal, unified humanity remains unrealized as violence and useless destruction prevail.

Fosca's story is framed by that of Régine, who is embittered by her life and haunted by death. When she learns of Fosca's immortality, she thinks that she can transcend death by living forever in his memory. Like the women in love in de Beauvoir's preceding novels, Régine depends on others to give her life meaning. The story ends with Régine's cry of despair as she understands the futility and vanity of human action.

All Men Are Mortal takes up the theme of the uncertain outcome of individual actions and gives it a more decidedly pessimistic turn. This theme is modified somewhat by the more optimistic section on the French Revolution. Here, Fosca follows the career of one of his descendants, Armand. Armand's zeal in fighting for the Republican cause leads Fosca to modify his skepticism about human progress and to take comfort in the solidarity he experiences with Armand and his friends.

Fosca's discovery of the rewards of comradeship is very similar to that of Jean Blomart. Although Fosca's individual actions are either undercut by the presence of others or lost in history, actions taken by the group seem to have a more powerful impact on reality. Like *The Blood of Others*, *All Men Are Mortal* predicts de Beauvoir's later Marxist sympathies and reflects her growing politicization. Both Jean and Fosca tend to break with the solipsistic tendencies of the characters in *She Came to Stay* and move in the direction of greater social commitment. The context of the action in *All Men Are Mortal* is wider than in the preceding novels from a narrative and political point of view. It is perhaps its vast historical scope that makes *All Men Are Mortal* the least satisfying of de Beauvoir's novels. Philosophical speculations on love, history, and death dominate the narrative; the characters are lifeless and seem caught in a series of historical still lifes.

THE MANDARINS

The Mandarins, de Beauvoir's finest novel, covers the period from 1944 to the early 1950's and focuses on the relationship between political commitment and literature. The narrative voice shifts between Henri Perron, a novelist, journalist, and Resistance hero, and Anne Dubreuilh, a respected psychiatrist and the wife of Robert Dubreuilh, a prominent writer.

Robert, initiated into political activism during his years in the Resistance, believes that literature must now take second place to political concerns. He engages himself wholeheartedly in founding the S.R.L., an independent leftist political party. The problems that Robert confronts as a political figure point to the painful reality of making decisions that are not always satisfactory. He draws Henri into politics by convincing him that his newspaper, *L'Espoir*, should be the voice of the S.R.L. When they receive news of Soviet labor camps, they try to decide if they should publish the information. Knowing that they will play into Gaullist hands and alienate the Communists to whom they are sympathetic, they reluctantly decide to print the story.

For Henri, questions of political commitment after the war are more problematic. He would like *L'Espoir* to remain apolitical and is nostalgic for the prewar years, when literature and politics appeared to be mutually exclusive interests. Henri tries to act in good faith, but because of his sensitivity to others, he often opts for the less idealistically pure solution. He is reluctant to break with Paule, his mistress of ten years, and he protects acquaintances who collaborated with the Germans because he fears that, like Paule, they could not survive without his help. Throughout the novel, he is torn between politics and a desire to return to literature. He gradually faces the impossibility of "pure" literature. At the end of the novel, having lost *L'Espoir*, he and Robert decide to found a new journal of the Left.

The questions that de Beauvoir examines through Robert and Henri have a striking immediacy that captures the problem of the intellectual in the modern world. Much of the action in *The Mandarins* is a fictionalized account of her experiences as a member of the intellectual Left during the postwar years. Critics have sought to identify Sartre with Robert, Albert Camus with Henri, and de Beauvoir herself with Anne. In *Simone de Beauvoir and the Limits of Commitment* (1981), Anne Whitmarsh notes that there is much of Sartre's experiences with the Rassemblement Démocratique Révolu-

tionnaire in Robert's ties with the S.R.L. and that some of the early problems facing *Les Temps modernes* are reflected in the debates on the political role of *L'Espoir*.

The problems faced by the male characters are less pressing for Anne. Married to a man twenty years older, she seems out of touch with herself and her surroundings. Her work as a psychiatrist fails to occupy her fully, and her relationship with her unhappy daughter, Nadine, gives Anne little satisfaction. Encouraged by Robert, she accepts an invitation to lecture in the United States. In Chicago, she experiences an emotional awakening when she falls in love with Lewis Brogan, an up-and-coming writer. Her visits to Brogan are described in a highly lyric style full of images of country life and nature. The physical and affective aspects of her life with Brogan form an effective counterpoint to the intellectual character of her relationship with her husband. The shifting loyalties she experiences for both men give Anne's narrative a schizophrenic quality.

Back in Paris, Anne tries to help Paule, who has suffered a nervous breakdown. Paule rarely leaves her apartment and is unable to function without Henri. Anne sends her to a psychiatrist, who "cures" her by having her forget the past. Like Françoise and Régine, Paule represents the temptation of living through others. In Paule's case, however, the dependence reaches an existential crisis from which she never fully recovers. Paule's illness is mirrored in Anne as the psychiatrist herself plunges into a long depression. When Brogan ends their relationship, she contemplates suicide. Thinking of the pain her death would cause Robert and Nadine, she decides to live. Despite this decision, Anne's alienation from her family and indeed from her own being is more acute than ever.

Anne's emotional awakening and Paule's mental breakdown leave them both as only marginal participants in life. Neither woman achieves the transcendence that characterizes the life of her male counterpart. As Robert and Henri accommodate themselves to political realities, they become more integrated into society. The female quest for self-knowledge acts as a negative counterpoint to the male quest. The final scene is not unlike a collage in which the two parts of the composition are radically divided. The enthusiasm of Henri and Robert as they search for an appropriate title for their journal is juxtaposed to Anne's stillness; she sits off to the side, withdrawn, and hopes that her life may still contain some happiness.

LES BELLES IMAGES

Les Belles Images is one of de Beauvoir's most technically innovative novels. Laurence, the main character, is a young woman who writes slogans for a French advertising agency. She is married to a successful young architect and has two daughters. Catherine, her eldest daughter, is beginning to question social values. Laurence comes from the same mold as de Beauvoir's other heroines. She is, for all appearances, a confident young woman, but her facade of well-being dissolves to reveal an individual profoundly alienated from herself and her society. *Les Belles Images* is the story of Laurence's progressive withdrawal from society. Her interior journey ends in a mental and physical breakdown.

The novel is set in Paris during the 1960's. Some friends have gathered at the fashionable home of Dominique, Laurence's mother. Laurence, uninterested in the group, leafs through a number of magazines containing the *belles images*, or beautiful pictures, she is paid to create. The dialogue among the guests is filtered through Laurence, who then adds her own reflections. The conversations are trite and filled with clichés; like the slogans Laurence invents, they conceal the real problems of war, poverty, and unhappiness. The discrepancy between the advertisements and the things they represent precipitates Laurence's budding consciousness of herself as yet another *belle image*. Laurence's perception of the inauthenticity of her own life and of the lives of the people around her results in illness. Having already suffered a nervous breakdown five years before, she becomes anorexic and unable to relate to the artificial world around her.

Through her daughter Catherine, Laurence faces her unresolved feelings toward her childhood. She recalls the lack of emotional contact with her mother in a series of flashbacks in which she appears dressed as a child in a publicity snapshot. At the insistence of Laurence's husband, Catherine has been sent to a psychiatrist because she is overly sensitive to social injustices. Laurence sees the treatment that Catherine receives as an attempt to integrate her daughter into the artificial bourgeois world. At the novel's end, Laurence emerges from her illness to save her daughter from a fate similar to hers. Like other de Beauvoir heroines, Laurence chooses her illness as a means of escaping certain destructive social myths. Her breakdown, rather than the result of an original flaw discovered within herself, is an indication of the failure of society as a whole. Against the inauthentic world of the other characters, Laurence's illness appears as a victory and an occasion for emotional growth. Much like Anne in *The Mandarins*, Laurence is a voice from the outside who sees the social games and reveals them for what they are.

All of de Beauvoir's novels examine the relationship between the self and the Other that is at the heart of existentialist philosophy. In her early novels—*She Came to Stay, The Blood of Others*, and *All Men Are Mortal*—there is often an explicit existentialist premise underlying the action. In her later works, *The Mandarins* and *Les Belles Images*, the philosophical message, although still present, is clearly subordinated to the narrative. De Beauvoir's conclusions in *The Second Sex* appear to have led her to a closer examination of the lives of her female characters. Her later fiction adds another dimension to the quests for authenticity that mark her early production. For her heroes, the quest usually ends in some type of existentialist commitment; for her heroines, the quest seems to involve a withdrawal from harmful social myths. If at times the quests border on madness or isolation, they do so without losing their striking immediacy or their profound sense of reality. Like other great twentieth century quests, de Beauvoir's novels chart a journey into the heart of contemporary alienation.

Carole Deering Paul

OTHER MAJOR WORKS

SHORT FICTION: *La Femme rompue*, 1967 (*The Woman Destroyed*, 1968); *Quand prime le spirituel*, 1979 (*When Things of the Spirit Come First: Five Early Tales*, 1982).

PLAY: *Les Bouches inutiles*, pb. 1945.

NONFICTION: *Pyrrhus et Cinéas*, 1944; *Pour une morale de l'ambiguïté*, 1947 (*The Ethics of Ambiguity*, 1948); *L'Amérique au jour le jour*, 1948 (travel sketch; *America Day by Day*, 1953); *L'Existentialisme et la sagesse des nations*, 1948; *Le Deuxième Sexe*, 1949 (*The Second Sex*, 1953); *Privilèges*, 1955 (partial translation

"Must We Burn Sade?," 1953); *La Longue Marche*, 1957 (travel sketch; *The Long March*, 1958); *Mémoires d'une jeune fille rangée*, 1958 (4 volumes; *Memoirs of a Dutiful Daughter*, 1959); *La Force de l'âge*, 1960 (memoir; *The Prime of Life*, 1962); *La Force des choses*, 1963 (memoir; *Force of Circumstance*, 1964); *Une Mort très douce*, 1964 (*A Very Easy Death*, 1966); *La Vieillesse*, 1970 (*The Coming of Age*, 1972); *Tout compte fait*, 1972 (memoir; *All Said and Done*, 1974); *La Cérémonie des adieux*, 1981 (*Adieux: A Farewell to Sartre*, 1984); *Lettres à Sartre*, 1990 (2 volumes; Sylvie Le Bon de Beauvoir, editor; *Letters to Sartre*, 1992); *Lettres à Nelson Algren: Un Amour transatlantique, 1947-1964*, 1997 (Sylvie Le Bon de Beauvoir, editor; *A Transatlantic Love Affair*, 1998; also known as *Beloved Chicago Man: Letters to Nelson Algren, 1947-1964*, 1999); *Philosophical Writings*, 2004 (Margaret A. Simons, editor).

EDITED TEXTS: *Lettres au Castor et à quelques autres*, 1983 (2 volumes; volume 1, *Witness to My Life: The Letters of Jean-Paul Sartre to Simone de Beauvoir, 1926-1939*, 1992; volume 2, *Quiet Moments in a War: The Letters of Jean-Paul Sartre to Simone de Beauvoir, 1940-1963*, 1993).

BIBLIOGRAPHY

Appignansei, Lisa. *Simone de Beauvoir*. London: Penguin Books, 1988. Provides a significant appraisal of de Beauvoir's concept of the independent woman. Aptly explicates de Beauvoir's existentialist ethics and her suppositions of woman's subjectivity.

Bair, Deirdre. *Simone de Beauvoir: A Biography*. New York: Summit Books, 1990. This work, which some critics have termed the definitive study of de Beauvoir, covers her philosophical life and her inquiry into the nature of woman. It also focuses on her relationship with John-Paul Sartre.

Brown, Catherine Savage. *Simone de Beauvoir Revisited*. Boston: G. K. Hall, 1991. Contains chapters on de Beauvoir's life, on her role as a woman writer, and on her early fiction and drama, later fiction, philosophical and political studies, and memoirs. Aims to present a focused study and criticizes the emphasis on anecdotal reports and biography in other works on de Beauvoir.

Card, Claudia, ed. *The Cambridge Companion to Simone de Beauvoir*. New York: Cambridge University Press, 2003. Collection of essays focuses on de Beauvior's philosophy, including an analysis of the philosophy in her fiction. Includes a chronology, introductory overview, bibliography, and index.

Fallaize, Elizabeth. *The Novels of Simone de Beauvoir*. New York: Routledge, 1988. Contains separate chapters on *She Came to Stay*, *The Blood of Others*, *All Men Are Mortal*, *The Mandarins*, and *Les Belles Images*. Includes an introduction, biographical notes, and a bibliography.

Moi, Toril. *Simone de Beauvoir: The Making of an Intellectual Woman*. Cambridge, Mass.: Blackwell, 1997. Two chapters in this study are of particular interest regarding de Beauvoir's fiction. Chapter 3 recounts the hostile reception of de Beauvoir's work by those in France and elsewhere who did not believe that de Beauvoir, as a woman, had the intellectual strength and integrity of male philosophers, and chapter 4 examines *She Came to Stay*.

Rowley, Hazel. *Tête-à-Tête: Simone de Beauvoir and Jean-Paul Sartre*. New York: HarperCollins, 2005. Chronicles the relationship between de Beauvoir and Sartre, offering insights into their commitment to each other, their writing, their politics, and their philosophical legacy.

Sandford, Stella. *How to Read Beauvoir*. New York: W. W. Norton, 2007. Provides an introductory overview to de Beauvoir's philosophy. Cites excerpts from de Beauvoir's books to explain her examination of identity, gender, sexuality, old age, and other topics.

Simons, Margaret A., ed. *Feminist Interpretations of Simone de Beauvoir*. University Park: Pennsylvania State University Press, 1995. Collection contains essays on *The Second Sex*, de Beauvoir's relationship with Sartre, *The Mandarins*, and the author's views on the Algerian war. Includes bibliography and index.

Whitmarsh, Anne. *Simone de Beauvoir and the Limits of Commitment*. New York: Cambridge University Press, 1981. Contains succinct discussions of de Beauvoir's long fiction, including a section summarizing her fictional works. Biographical notes and bibliography add to this volume's usefulness.

SAMUEL BECKETT

Born: Foxrock, near Dublin, Ireland; April 13, 1906
Died: Paris, France; December 22, 1989
Also known as: Samuel Barclay Beckett

PRINCIPAL LONG FICTION

Murphy, 1938

Malone meurt, 1951 (*Malone Dies*, 1956)

Molloy, 1951 (English translation, 1955)

L'Innommable, 1953 (*The Unnamable*, 1958)

Watt, 1953

Comment c'est, 1961 (*How It Is*, 1964)

Mercier et Camier, 1970 (*Mercier and Camier*, 1974)

Le Dépeupleur, 1971 (*The Lost Ones*, 1972)

Company, 1980

Mal vu mal dit, 1981 (*Ill Seen Ill Said*, 1981)

Worstward Ho, 1983

OTHER LITERARY FORMS

Samuel Beckett produced work in every literary genre. His first book, published in 1931, was the critical study *Proust*, and during the next fifteen years, Beckett published a number of essays and book reviews that have yet to be collected in book form. After struggling with an unpublished play titled *Eleutheria* in the late 1940's (which was eventually published in 1995), he began publication of the series of plays that are as important as his novels to his current literary reputation. These include, notably, *En attendant Godot* (pb. 1952; *Waiting for Godot*, 1954), *"Fin de partie," suivi de "Acte sans paroles"* (pr., pb. 1957; music by John Beckett; *"Endgame: A Play in One Act," Followed by "Act Without Words: A Mime for One Player,"* 1958), *Krapp's Last Tape* (pr., pb. 1958), *Happy Days* (pr., pb. 1961), and many short pieces for the stage, including mimes. In addition to these works for the stage, he wrote scripts for television, such as *Eh Joe* (1966; *Dis Joe*, 1967); scripts for radio, such as *All That Fall* (1957; revised 1968); and one film script, titled *Film* (1965). Most, but not all, of Beckett's many short stories are gathered in various collections, including *More Pricks than Kicks* (1934), *Nouvelles et textes pour rien* (1955; *Stories and Texts for Nothing*, 1967), *No's Knife: Collected Shorter Prose, 1947-1966* (1967), *First Love, and Other Shorts* (1974), *Pour finir encore et autres foirades* (1976; *Fizzles*, 1976; also known as *For to Yet Again*), and *Collected Short Prose* (1991). Beckett's poetry, most of it written early in his career for periodical publication, has been made available in *Poems in English* (1961) and *Collected Poems in English and French* (1977). Many of the various collections of his short pieces mix works of different literary genres, and Richard Seaver has edited a general sampling of Beckett works of all sorts in an anthology titled *I Can't Go On, I'll Go On: A Selection from Samuel Beckett's Work* (1976).

ACHIEVEMENTS

Samuel Beckett did not begin to write his most important works until he was forty years of age, and he had to wait some time beyond that for widespread recognition of his literary achievements. By the time he received the Nobel Prize in Literature in 1969, however, he had established a solid reputation as one of the most important and demanding authors of plays and novels in the twentieth century.

In the 1930's, when he began to write, Beckett seemed destined for the sort of footnote fame that has overtaken most of his English and Irish literary companions of that decade. His work appeared to be highly derivative of the avant-garde coterie associated with *Transition* magazine and especially of the novels of James Joyce, who as an elder Irish expatriate in Paris befriended and encouraged the young Beckett. By the time Beckett was forty years old and trying to salvage a literary career disrupted by World War II, his anonymity was such that his own French translation of his first novel, *Murphy*, had sold exactly six copies. At the same time he presented his skeptical Paris publisher with another manuscript.

Nevertheless, it was at that time—the late 1940's—that Beckett blossomed as a writer. He withdrew into a voluntary solitude he himself referred to as "the siege in the room," began to compose his works in French rather than in English, and shed many of the mannerisms of his

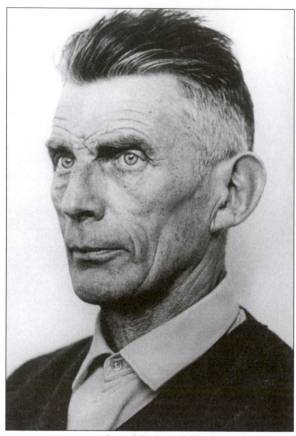

Samuel Beckett. (© The Nobel Foundation)

Disagreements about the nature of particular works and skepticism about the bulk of commentary generated by very brief prose fragments have also inevitably accompanied this rather sudden enshrinement of a difficult and extremely idiosyncratic body of work. However, even the most antagonistic later analyses of Beckett's novels grant them a position of importance and influence in the development of prose fiction since World War II, and they also accept Beckett's stature as one of the most important novelists since his friend and Irish compatriot James Joyce.

BIOGRAPHY

Samuel Barclay Beckett was born in Foxrock, a modestly affluent suburb of Dublin, Ireland. He gave Good Friday, April 13, 1906, as his birth date, but some convincing contrary evidence suggests that this particular day may have been chosen more for its significance than for its accuracy. His parents, William and Mary (May) Jones Roe, belonged to the Protestant middle class known as Anglo-Irish in Ireland. Beckett's childhood, in contrast to the unpleasant imagery of many of his novels, was a relatively cheery one of genteel entertainment at the family home, Cooldrinagh, private education at Portora Royal School in county Fermanagh, and greater success on the cricket green than in the classroom.

Beckett matriculated to Trinity College, Dublin, in 1923, and there he developed his first literary interests. He completed a curriculum in Romance languages at Trinity, and this led to an appointment as lecturer at the École Normale Supérieure in Paris after graduation in 1927. In Paris, Beckett began to associate with the bohemian intellectual circles of French, English, and American writers for which the city was then famous. Beckett returned to Dublin for a brief time in 1930 for graduate work and a teaching position at Trinity, but within a few months he returned to the Continent for travel throughout Germany and France and an extended reunion with his friends in Paris, including James Joyce. His first works of fiction, the stories in *More Pricks than Kicks* and the novel *Murphy*, are set in Dublin and its environs, but their intellectual preoccupations and bohemian antagonism toward middle-class complacency derive more from the environment of Paris than that of Ireland.

At the outbreak of World War II, Beckett was a per-

earlier work. The immediate result was the trilogy of novels that constitute his most important achievement in prose fiction: *Molloy*, *Malone Dies*, and *The Unnamable*. This period also produced *Waiting for Godot*, and it was this play that first brought Beckett fame. *Waiting for Godot*, considered a formative influence on the Theater of the Absurd, stimulated the first serious critical treatments of Beckett's work. Although Beckett himself attached more importance to his novels than to his plays, it was not until the 1960's that critics went beyond his plays and began to bring his prose works under close scrutiny. Then, as now, most criticism of Beckett's fiction focused on the trilogy and the austere prose fiction in French that followed it.

In the years since then, Beckett's novels have risen in critical estimation from essentially eccentric if interesting experiments to exemplars of self-referential "postmodern" fiction commonly cited by literary theorists.

manent resident of Paris. As an Irish citizen, he could have returned home, but instead he took refuge in the French countryside from the Nazi occupation of Paris. There, he assisted the Resistance and began to write the novel *Watt*, which marks a movement toward the style of his major fiction in its strangely dislocated senses of time and place. After the war, Beckett was decorated with the Croix de Guerre for his assistance to the French underground, and this award is generally cited as evidence of an essential humanism underlying the frequently misanthropic tenor of his novels. All evidence suggests, however, that the experience of the war increased Beckett's antagonism toward social affiliations and his skepticism about humanistic values.

Beckett returned to Paris after the war, and from 1946 to 1950, he retired into the "siege in the room," his most fertile period in a long literary career. By the time *Waiting for Godot* established his reputation, he had already developed the reclusive lifestyle that he maintained in his years of fame despite persistent media attention. He was married to longtime companion Suzanne Deschevaux-Dumesnil in secrecy in London in 1961, and he refused to attend the award ceremony for his Nobel Prize in Literature in 1969. He died in Paris on December 22, 1989.

ANALYSIS

It was a matter of some pleasure to Samuel Beckett that his work resists explication. His most important novels and plays are artfully constructed contemplations on their own form rather than commentaries on the familiar world of causal relationships and social contingencies. His most important novels abandon progressive narrative for the more difficult and subtle suggestiveness of haunting images, deliberate enigmas, and complexly ironic epigrams.

Although Beckett's work defies criticism, the author issued critical statements and congenially submitted to interviews with critics, managing to transform both sorts of critical occasions into intellectual performances as provocative, and occasionally as humorous, as his fiction. Two particular comments by Beckett, out of many stimulating ones, may serve as instructive introductions to the body of his prose works. In his first published book, *Proust*, Beckett wrote that artistic creation is es-

sentially an excavatory process, comparable to an attempt to reach an ideal, impossibly minuscule, core of an onion. Beckett's novels relentlessly pursue this sort of process, stripping away layers of assumptions about the self and the world, peeling away conventional modes of thought to reach a pure essence of existence free of the inevitably distorting effects of intellect, logical structure, and analytic order. This image of the onion is a rich one because it communicates the sense in Beckett's work that this excavatory process is unending, that disposal of each mode of thought reveals yet another, even more resistant, habit of mind. Beckett himself often spoke of his novels as a series, and it is this progressive penetration through one form of thought to another that marks the stages in the series.

Thirty years after *Proust*, Beckett submitted to an unusually provocative interview with Tom Driver that was published in *Columbia University Forum* in the summer of 1961. In this interview, he dwelled specifically on form. After contrasting the orderly form of most art to the intransigently chaotic nature of existence, he said: "The Form and the chaos remain separate. The latter is not reduced to the former. . . . to find a form that accommodates the mess, that is the task of the artist now." Beckett's novels reveal three stages in this attempt to discover a literary form that will accommodate the chaotic nature of existence. In the first stage, represented by *Murphy* and *Watt*, the process is a destructive one of ridiculing literary convention by parody and satire to suggest an as yet undiscovered alternative form of expression. In the second stage, represented by the trilogy, the attempt to give voice to that alternative takes the form of the disordered and at times deliberately incoherent monologues of individual narrators. In the third stage, represented by *How It Is* and the subsequent short prose pieces, the process takes the form of presenting metaphorical worlds that accommodate their own chaos.

This last stage, especially, is marked by the unpleasant emphasis on miserable degradation and the recurring private images that have given Beckett an undeserved reputation for misanthropy and deliberate obscurity. These charges are effectively rebutted by his own stated sense of "the task of the artist now." Beckett's works do not provide relaxing reading experiences. They are designed to disorient, to dislocate, and to thwart intellectual complacency. The formidable difficulties they present to the reader, however, are essential records of the intellectual ambience of advanced mid-twentieth century thought.

MURPHY

Beckett's earliest fiction, the stories in *More Pricks than Kicks*, describes the passive resistance to social conformity and death under anesthesia of a protagonist named Belacqua (an allusion to Dante). Beckett's first novel, *Murphy*, presents the same resistance and senseless death in the story of Murphy, given the most common surname in Ireland. Murphy is the first of numerous Beckett protagonists who seek to relinquish all ties to their environment and their compulsion to make sense of it. The centerpiece of *Murphy* is an analysis of the discrete zones of the character's mind in the sixth chapter. The third and last of these zones is a darkness of selflessness in which mind itself is obviated. It is this zone beyond consciousness that most Beckett protagonists seek; it is their failure to reach it that creates the tension in most of Beckett's fiction.

Murphy is surrounded by representatives of two frames of reference that prevent his withdrawal from the world. The first is nationality, represented here by character types such as the drunken Irish poet Austin Ticklepenny and monuments to national ideals such as the statue of Cuchulain in the Dublin General Post Office. The second frame of reference is erudition, represented here by a plethora of arcane references to astronomy, astrology, philosophy, and mathematics. Assaulted by these adjuncts of identity, Murphy remains unable to disengage himself fully from the world, to withdraw completely into the third zone of his mind.

The problem that Beckett confronts in *Murphy* is central to all of his novels: to define consciousness in a novel without the usual novelistic apparatus of recognizable environment, nationality, and psychology. The novel only approaches such a definition in the chapter on Murphy's mind and in the image of an eerily withdrawn character named Mr. Endon. Elsewhere, Beckett is able to suggest an alternative only by destructive means: by heaping scorn on things Irish, by deflating intellectual pretensions, and by parodying novelistic conventions. These forms of ridicule make *Murphy* Beckett's most humorous and accessible novel. The same reliance on ridicule, however, ensures that *Murphy* remains derivative of the very forms of thought and literature it intends to challenge.

WATT

Although it was not published until 1953, after *Molloy* and *Malone Dies*, *Watt* was written a decade earlier and properly belongs among Beckett's early novels. It is a transitional work, written in English, in which one can observe intimations of the central concerns of the trilogy of novels written in French.

Like Murphy, Watt is an alienated vagabond seeking succor from the complexities of existence. In the opening and closing sections of this four-part novel, Watt's world is a recognizably Irish one populated with middle-class characters with small social pretensions. In the central two sections, however, Watt works as a servant on the surreal country estate of a Mr. Knott. *Watt* most resembles Beckett's later fiction in these central sections. In them, Watt ineffectually attempts to master simpler and simpler problems without the benefit of reliable contingencies of cause and effect or even the assurance of a reliable system of language. The structure of the novel is ultimately dislocated by the gradual revelation that the four parts are not in fact presented in chronological order and that they have been narrated by a character named Sam rather than by an omniscient narrator. Sam's account proves unreliable in particulars, thus completing the process by which the novel undermines any illusion of certainty concerning the interaction of the characters Watt ("What?") and Knott ("Not!").

Watt, like *Murphy*, relies on satire of literary precedents and disruption of novelistic conventions. There are allusions in the novel to the work of William Butler Yeats and James Jones and to the poet Æ (George William Russell), to cite only the Irish precedents. The great disruption of novelistic conventions is effected by "Addenda" of unincorporated material at the end of the text and by pedantic annotations throughout the novel. Nevertheless, *Watt* does look ahead to *Molloy* in its central sections, dominated by episodic problems such as the removal of Knott's slops and the attempt of the wretched Lynch family to have the ages of its living members total exactly one thousand. The full emergence of this sort of episodic narrative in Beckett's fiction, however, seems to have required the focus of attention on language itself (rather than on literary conventions). That was one important effect of Beckett's decision to begin to compose novels in French rather than in English.

MERCIER AND CAMIER

Mercier and Camier, although published in 1970, was written in French in 1946, soon after Beckett returned to Paris at the end of the war. Like *Watt*, it is best placed among Beckett's works by date of composition rather than publication. Written at the outset of the "siege in the room" that produced Beckett's major novels, it illuminates the process by which the style of the trilogy emerged from concentration on elements of composition rather than on the social concerns that dominate most conventional novels.

Mercier and Camier is an account of an aimless journey by two decrepit characters out of and back into a city that resembles Dublin. A witness-narrator announces his presence in the opening sentence but remains otherwise inconspicuous. The descriptions of the two characters' generally enigmatic encounters with others, however, are periodically interrupted by subtly disported tabular synopses that call attention to the arbitrary features of the narrator's accounts. The novel is thus a shrewdly self-conscious narrative performance, with the emphasis falling on the telling rather than on the meaning of the tale.

The belated publication of *Mercier and Camier* was a welcome event because the work represents what must have seemed to Beckett an unsatisfactory attempt to open the novel form to accommodate the "mess" he finds dominant in the world. His composition of the novel in French produced a spare prose style and calculated use of language that would prove essential to his later fiction. Like *Watt*, however, the novel retained a peripheral witness-narrator; this may have been one of the sources of Beckett's dissatisfaction with the novel, for immediately after *Mercier and Camier* he shifted to the monologue essential to the three works that followed.

Beckett's major accomplishment in prose fiction is the trilogy of novels begun with *Molloy*, written in French in 1947 and 1948. All three are narrative monologues, all seek to explain origins, and all expose various forms of self-knowledge as delusions. Thus, they approach that ideal core of the onion in their quest for explanations, and they assert the governing "mess" of in-

coherence, which continues to resist artificial, if comforting, intellectual fabrications.

MOLLOY

In structure, *Molloy*, translated into English by Beckett in collaboration with Patrick Bowles, is the most complex work in the trilogy. The first part of the novel is the narrative of the derelict Molloy, who discovers himself in his mother's room and attempts unsuccessfully to reconstruct his arrival there. The second part is the narrative of the Catholic and bourgeois detective Jacques Moran, who has been commissioned by an authority named Youdi to write a report on Molloy. As Moran's report proceeds, he gradually begins to resemble Molloy. His narrative ends with the composition of the sentence with which it began, now exposed as pure falsehood.

Molloy and Moran are counterparts whose narratives expose the alternative fallacies, respectively, of inward and outward ways of organizing experience. Molloy's self-involved preoccupations, such as his chronic flatulence, function as counterparts of Moran's more social preoccupations, such as Catholic liturgy and his profession. Both are left in unresolved confrontation with the likelihood that the ways they have attempted to make sense of their origins and present circumstances are pure sham. The special brilliance of *Molloy* is the manner in which this confrontation is brought about by the terms of each narrator's monologue. The prose style of the novel is dominated by hilarious deflations of momentary pretensions, ironic undercutting of reassuring truisms, and criticism of its own assertions. It is in this manner that *Molloy* manages to admit the "mess" Beckett seeks to accommodate in the novel form: Its compelling and humorous narratives effectively expose the limits rather than the fruits of self-knowledge.

MALONE DIES

Malone Dies is the purest of the narrative performances of Beckett's storytellers. In it, a bedridden man awaits death in his room and tells stories to pass the time. His environment is limited to the room, the view from a window, and a meager inventory of possessions he periodically recounts with inconsistent results. Beyond these, he is limited to the world of his stories about a boy named Sapo, an old man named MacMann, an employee in an insane asylum named Lemuel, and others. All are apparently fictions based on different periods in Malone's own life. At the end of the novel, Malone's narrative simply degenerates and ends inconclusively in brief phrases that may suggest death itself or simply the end of his willingness to pursue the stories further.

It is essential to the novel that Malone criticize his own stories, revise them, abandon them, and rehearse them once again. His predicament is that he knows the stories to be false in many respects, but he has no alternative approach to the truth of his own origins. Like Beckett, Malone is a compulsive composer of fictions who is perpetually dissatisfied with them. As a result, *Malone Dies* is one of the most completely self-critical and self-involved novels in the twentieth century stream of metafictions, or novels about the nature of the novel. It demonstrates, with bitter humor and relentless self-examination, the limits of fiction, the pleasure of fiction, and the lack of an acceptable substitute for fiction.

THE UNNAMABLE

In *The Unnamable*, Beckett pursues the preoccupations of *Molloy* and *Malone Dies* to an extreme that puts formidable difficulties before even the most devoted reader of the modern novel. In *Molloy* the focus is on two long narrative accounts, in *Malone Dies* it narrows to concentrate on briefer stories, and in *The Unnamable* it shrinks further to probe the limits of language itself, of words and names. As the title suggests, these smaller units of literary discourse prove to be just as false and unreliable as those longer literary units have proven to be in Beckett's previous two novels. In *The Unnamable*, there is no character in the ordinary sense of the term. Instead, there are only bursts of language, at first organized into paragraphs, then only into continuous sentences, and finally into pages of a single sentence broken only by commas.

The premise of the novel is that a paralyzed and apparently androgynous creature suspended in a jar outside a Paris restaurant speaks of himself and versions of himself labeled with temporary names such as Mahood and Worm. As he speaks, however, he is diverted from the content of his speech by disgust with its elements, its words. The names of Murphy, Molloy, and Malone are all evoked with complete disgust at the complacent acceptance of language inherent in the creation of such literary characters. *The Unnamable* thus attempts to chal-

lenge assumptions of literary discourse by diverting attention from plot and character to phrase and word. It is tortuous reading because it calls into question the means by which any reading process proceeds.

The preoccupation with speaking in the novel leads naturally to a corollary preoccupation with silence, and *The Unnamable* ends with a paradoxical assertion of the equal impossibility of either ending or continuing. At this point, Beckett had exhausted the means by which he attempted to admit the "mess" into the form of the novels in his trilogy. He managed to proceed, to extend the series of his novels, by exploring the richness of metaphorical and generally horrific environments like that of the unnamable one suspended, weeping, in his jar.

HOW IT IS

Beckett's critics commonly refer to the series of prose fictions begun with *How It Is* as "post-trilogy prose." The term is useful because it draws attention to the methods of Beckett's works as well as their chronology. Even in the midst of the incoherence of *The Unnamable*, there are references to the familiar world, such as the fact that the narrator is located in Paris. In *How It Is* and the works that followed, however, the environment is an entirely metaphorical and distinctly surreal one. Without reference to a familiar world, these works are governed by an interior system of recurrent images and memories. *How It Is* marks the beginning of this final stage in the series of Beckett's works, and so its French title, *Comment c'est*, is an appropriate phonetic pun meaning both "how it is" and *commencer*, or "to begin."

In *How It Is*, the speaker, named Bom, is a creature crawling in darkness through endless mire, dragging with him a sack of canned provisions, and torturing and being tortured by other creatures with their indispensable can openers. His narrative takes the form of brief, unpunctuated fragments separated by spaces on the page. Each fragment is of a length that can be spoken aloud, as it ideally should be, and the style may be in part a product of Beckett's experience in the production of plays. There is a second character, named Pim, against whom the narrator tends to define his own status. The novel, which many prefer to term a prose poem, is thus broken into three parts: before Pim, with Pim, and after Pim.

The Bom and Pim interaction is an excruciating account of misery in a netherworld of darkness and slime. It is related entirely in retrospect, however, and the changing relationships of domination and subordination are less important than the manner in which the language of the fragments creates its own system of repetitions and alterations of phrases. *How It Is* dramatizes, in fact, how it *was* for Bom, and in place of clear references to the familiar world, it offers a verbal model for the mechanics of memory. This remains a consistent, if extraordinarily complex, extension of Beckett's attempt to accommodate the "mess" of chaos in the novel form. Its extremely calculated prose creates a sense of the consistent, but inexplicable and ultimately uninformative, impingement of the past on the present.

THE LOST ONES

The Lost Ones is a representative example of Beckett's prose fiction immediately following *How It Is*. He composed many brief prose pieces in this period, abandoned most of them, and resurrected them for publication at the urging of enthusiastic friends. Most are published in collections of his short works. *The Lost Ones*, however, is a more sustained narrative performance (sixty-three pages in the American edition). It was abandoned in an incomplete form in 1966 but retrieved and supplemented with an effective conclusion in 1970. It has also gained greater attention than most of Beckett's works from this period because of an innovative stage adaptation by the Mabou Mines Company in New York City in 1973.

The Lost Ones is unique among Beckett's works because it focuses on a group rather than on an individual. In fifteen unnumbered passages of prose, it describes the workings of a huge cylinder populated by male and female figures who maneuver throughout its various areas by means of ladders. The prose style is remarkably understated in comparison to the painful, if metaphorical, imagery of *How It Is*, and the primary action is the continual reorganization of this closed set of persons according to an entropic process of diminishing energies. Mathematical computation, a motif in many of Beckett's novels, is a primary feature in *The Lost Ones*. As language does in so many of Beckett's earlier novels, numerical calculations prove an inadequate means of organizing experience in this work, and the crucial final paragraph added in 1970 is a fatalistic exposure of the worthlessness of these computations as indications of the past, present, or future of this surreal environment. As in many of Beckett's later prose pieces, the metaphorical environment created by the prose is open to many interpretive referents. The text is subtly allusive—the French title, for example, evokes Alphonse de Lamartine—and the viability of literature as an effective indication of past, present, or future is among the possible subjects of this spare and immensely suggestive text.

COMPANY

With the exceptions of *The Lost Ones* and other aborted works, nearly twenty years elapsed between the writing of *How It Is* and the next of Beckett's prose fictions to approach the novel in form if not in length. *Company* ended this relative silence, during which Beckett produced a variety of works in other genres. Like *How It Is* and the intervening works, *Company* presents a generally metaphorical environment and a consistent emphasis on the workings of memory. Unlike Beckett's other late works, however, it was composed in English and apparently generated out of contemplation of distinctly autobiographical images.

Company is a narrative by a figure immobilized on his back in darkness. Despite this surreal premise, it dwells on images of a familiar, suggestively Irish environment marked by features such as Connolly's store and the Ballyogan Road. It thus combines the astringency of Beckett's "post-trilogy prose" with the references to an identifiable world common in the trilogy. It is, however, far from a regression from experimental form or an abandonment of the attempt to accommodate the "mess" in a novel. Instead, it represents the fruit of Beckett's years of careful manipulation of a spare prose style in his second language. Like *How It Is*, *Company* concentrates on the inexplicable workings of memory. Unlike *How It Is*, the novel does so in a passive and restrained mixture of nostalgic and ironic images free of the vulgar and painful hostility of that earlier novel. In less flamboyant ways than Beckett's earlier works, *Company* also manages to underscore its own nature as an artificial, literary construction. Its governing metaphor of "company" manages to encompass both the memories surrounding the narrator and the meeting of author and reader of a literary text.

ILL SEEN ILL SAID

Company was followed by *Ill Seen Ill Said*, a series of paragraphs consisting primarily of sentence fragments. They describe a woman and her attempt to capture the details of her environment. The devotion to detail is such that vocabulary, rather than image, tends to capture attention, frequently because of intentional neologisms, interior rhymes, and sporadic echoes. It is more an evocation of a mood than a plotted novel, one that reveals the author, having rid himself of complacent use of language in earlier works, as a prose stylist with marked affinities to a poet. *Ill Seen Ill Said*, despite the disparagement of voice in its title, marks the emergence in Beckett's works of a devotion to pure sensation unmodulated by systems of logic or desire. It is in this respect that *Ill Seen Ill Said* is a necessary and inevitable extension of "the task of the artist now" addressed in a long series of novels. Rather than suggesting an alternative literary expression by destructive irony or subverting complacency by incoherent monologue, it attempts to present consciousness free of artificial order in a distinctly lyrical form of prose fiction.

In an early essay on the Irish poet Denis Devlin published in *Transition* in 1938, Beckett offered this dictum: "Art has always been this—pure interrogation, rhetorical question less the rhetoric." Like so many of his statements on other writers, this has a special relevance to Beckett's own literary career. Over a period of a half century, he produced fictions that relentlessly question assumptions of intellectual and literary order. He did so with a single-minded devotion to what he took to be "the task of the artist now" and so compiled an oeuvre that is unique in the twentieth century in its concentration on a central purpose and in its literary expression of the great philosophical preoccupations of its time. Beckett's work has been discussed by critics in reference to other innovative thinkers of the century as disparate as Albert Einstein, Sigmund Freud, and Jean-Paul Sartre. In addition to fueling the literary debates of his time, Beckett's work may be said to have created, in part, contemporary literary theories such as structuralism and deconstruction. Despite their formidable difficulties, then, Beckett's novels have an indisputable importance to anyone seriously interested in the intellectual climate of the twentieth century.

John P. Harrington

OTHER MAJOR WORKS

SHORT FICTION: *More Pricks than Kicks*, 1934; *Nouvelles et textes pour rien*, 1955 (*Stories and Texts for Nothing*, 1967); *No's Knife: Collected Shorter Prose, 1947-1966*, 1967; *First Love, and Other Shorts*, 1974; *Pour finir encore et autres foirades*, 1976 (*Fizzles*, 1976; also known as *For to Yet Again*); *Four Novellas*, 1977 (also known as *The Expelled, and Other Novellas*, 1980); *Collected Short Prose*, 1991.

PLAYS: *En attendant Godot*, pb. 1952 (*Waiting for Godot*, 1954); *"Fin de partie," suivi de "Acte sans paroles,"* pr., pb. 1957 (music by John Beckett; *"Endgame: A Play in One Act," Followed by "Act Without Words: A Mime for One Player,"* 1958); *Krapp's Last Tape*, pr., pb. 1958; *Act Without Words II*, pr., pb. 1960 (one-act mime); *Happy Days*, pr., pb. 1961; *Play*, pr., pb. 1963 (English translation, 1964); *Come and Go: Dramaticule*, pr., pb. 1965 (one scene; English translation, 1967); *Not I*, pr. 1972; *Ends and Odds*, pb. 1976; *Footfalls*, pr., pb. 1976; *That Time*, pr., pb. 1976; *A Piece of Monologue*, pr., pb. 1979; *Ohio Impromptu*, pr., pb. 1981; *Rockaby*, pr., pb. 1981; *Catastrophe*, pr. 1982; *Company*, pr. 1983; *Collected Shorter Plays*, 1984; *Complete Dramatic Works*, 1986; *Eleutheria*, pb. 1995.

POETRY: *Whoroscope*, 1930; *Echo's Bones and Other Precipitates*, 1935; *Poems in English*, 1961; *Collected Poems in English and French*, 1977.

SCREENPLAY: *Film*, 1965.

TELEPLAYS: *Eh Joe*, 1966 (*Dis Joe*, 1967); *Tryst*, 1976; *Shades*, 1977; *Quad*, 1981.

RADIO PLAYS: *All That Fall*, 1957 (revised 1968); *Embers*, 1959; *Words and Music*, 1962 (music by John Beckett); *Cascando*, 1963 (music by Marcel Mihalovici).

NONFICTION: *Proust*, 1931; *The Letters of Samuel Becket: Vol. 1, 1929-1940*, 2009 (Martha Dow Fehsenfeld and Lois More Overbeck, editors).

TRANSLATION: *An Anthology of Mexican Poetry*, 1958 (Octavio Paz, editor).

MISCELLANEOUS: *I Can't Go On, I'll Go On: A Selection from Samuel Beckett's Work*, 1976 (Richard Seaver, editor).

BIBLIOGRAPHY

Acheson, James. *Samuel Beckett's Artistic Theory and Practice: Criticism, Drama, and Early Fiction.* New

York: St. Martin's Press, 1997. An examination of Beckett's literary viewpoint as it expressed itself in his drama and early fiction. Chapter 6 focuses on the trilogy—the novels *Molloy*, *Malone Dies*, and *The Unnamable*. Includes bibliography and index.

Alvarez, Alfred. *Beckett*. 2d ed. London: Fontana, 1992. A short, lively, and sometimes opinionated discussion of Beckett by a critic who does not altogether trust the author and who knows how to argue not only for his strengths but also against his limitations. Contains a good short discussion of the intellectual climate that precipitated absurd literature.

Bair, Deirdre. *Samuel Beckett: A Biography*. 1978. Reprint. New York: Simon & Schuster, 1993. Although Beckett was often reluctant to talk about himself, he cooperated with Bair. This work is among the fullest versions of a life of Beckett in print, and to know his life is to understand his art. The criticism of the specific texts is often limited, but Bair is very good at putting the work in the context of Beckett's very odd life. Contains good illustrations.

Cronin, Anthony. *Samuel Beckett: The Last Modernist*. New York: HarperCollins, 1996. Fully documented and detailed biography describes Beckett's involvement in the Paris literary scene, his response to winning the Nobel Prize, and his overall literary career.

Ellman, Richard. *Four Dubliners: Wilde, Yeats, Joyce, and Beckett*. New York: George Braziller, 1988. Examines the Irish roots in Beckett's novels and plays and their subsequent influence on Irish writing. A lively and interesting study of four Irish writers, suitable for all students.

Esslin, Martin, ed. *Samuel Beckett: A Collection of Critical Essays*. Englewood Cliffs, N.J.: Prentice Hall, 1965. Collection of major essays by some of the most widely respected Beckett critics. Includes essays on all phases of his work, not only by English-speaking critics but also by European writers, who see Beckett not as a writer in English but as a part of the European tradition.

Hill, Leslie. *Beckett's Fiction: In Different Worlds*. New York: Cambridge University Press, 1990. Focuses on Beckett's novels from *Murphy* to *Worstward Ho*. Includes a preface that briefly characterizes previous criticism as reductive. Includes notes and bibliography.

Kenner, Hugh. *A Reader's Guide to Samuel Beckett*. London: Thames and Hudson, 1973. This essential companion for anyone determined to make some kind of sense of the works of Beckett comments clearly and simply on the individual texts.

_____. *Samuel Beckett: A Critical Study*. Berkeley: University of California Press, 1968. Work by probably the best commentator on Beckett is lively, imaginative, and extremely good at placing Beckett in the Irish tradition as well as assessing his part in the movement of experimental literature.

Knowlson, James. *Damned to Fame: The Life of Samuel Beckett*. New York: Simon & Schuster, 1996. Comprehensive biography presents a great deal of material on Beckett's life that was not previously available. Includes detailed notes and bibliography.

McDonald, Rónán. *The Cambridge Introduction to Samuel Beckett*. New York: Cambridge University Press, 2006. Chapter 4 of this succinct overview of Beckett's life and works focuses on his prose fiction, including the novels *Murphy*, *Watt*, *Molloy*, *Malone Dies*, *The Unnamable*, and *How It Is*.

Pattie, David. *The Complete Critical Guide to Samuel Beckett*. New York: Routledge, 2000. Reference volume combines biographical information with critical analysis of Beckett's literary works, including the novels *Murphy*, *Watt*, *Mercier and Camier*, and *How It Is*.

Pilling, John, ed. *The Cambridge Companion to Beckett*. New York: Cambridge University Press, 1994. Comprehensive reference work provides considerable information about the life and works of Beckett, including analysis of his novels. Includes bibliography and indexes.

APHRA BEHN

Born: Kent, England; July(?), 1640
Died: London, England; April 16, 1689
Also known as: Ayfara Amis; Aphara Amis;
 Astrea; Aphra Bayn; Aphra Johnson

PRINCIPAL LONG FICTION

Love Letters Between a Nobleman and His Sister,
 1683-1687 (3 volumes)
Agnes de Castro, 1688
*The Fair Jilt: Or, The History of Prince Tarquin
 and Miranda*, 1688
Oroonoko: Or, The Royal Slave, a True History,
 1688
*The History of the Nun: Or, The Fair Vow-
 Breaker*, 1689
The Lucky Mistake, 1689
The Nun: Or, The Perjured Beauty, 1697
The Adventure of the Black Lady, 1698
The Wandering Beauty, 1698

OTHER LITERARY FORMS

As a truly professional writer, perhaps the first British female to have written for profit, Aphra Behn (bayn) moved easily through the various literary genres and forms. Her plays include *The Forced Marriage: Or, The Jealous Bridegroom* (pr. 1670); *The Amorous Prince: Or, The Curious Husband* (pr., pb. 1671); *The Dutch Lover* (pr., pb. 1673); *The Town Fop: Or, Sir Timothy Tawdry* (pr. 1676); *Abdelazer: Or, the Moor's Revenge* (pr. 1676); *The Rover: Or, The Banished Cavaliers* (*Part I*, pr., pb. 1677; *Part II*, pr., pb. 1681); *Sir Patient Fancy* (pr., pb. 1678); *The Roundheads: Or, The Good Old Cause* (pr. 1681); *The City Heiress: Or, Sir Timothy Treat-All* (pr., pb. 1682); *The Lucky Chance: Or, An Alderman's Bargain* (pr. 1686); *The Emperor of the Moon* (pr., pb. 1687); *The Widow Ranter: Or, The History of Bacon of Virginia* (pr. 1689); and *The Younger Brother: Or, The Amorous Jilt* (pr., pb. 1696).

Although Behn enjoyed only mild success as a poet, her verse was probably no better or worse than that of a large number of second-rank versifiers of the Restoration. Behn's best poetry can be found in the song "Love in fan-

tastic triumph sate" (1677), from her tragedy *Abdelazer*, and in a metrical "Paraphrase on Oenone to Paris" for Jacob Tonson's volume of Ovid's *Epistles* (1680). The remainder of her verse includes a long, amorous allegory, *A Voyage to the Isle of Love* (1684); an adaptation of Bernard de Fontenelle's epic that she titled *A Discovery of New Worlds* (1688); and two occasional pieces, "A Pindarick on the Death of Charles II" (1685) and "A Congratulatory Poem to Her Most Sacred Majesty" (1688).

ACHIEVEMENTS

Aphra Behn's achievement as a novelist should be measured principally in terms of the modest gains made by the novel form in England during the seventeenth century. Prior to *Oroonoko*, the English novel lingered in the shadows of the theater. The small reading public contented itself with works such as John Lyly's *Euphues, the Anatomy of Wit* (1578), Sir Philip Sidney's *Arcadia* (1590), Thomas Lodge's *Rosalynde: Or, Euphues Golden Legacy* (1590), Thomas Nashe's *The Unfortunate Traveller: Or, The Life of Jack Wilton* (1594), and Thomas Deloney's *The Pleasant History of John Winchcomb in His Younger Days Called Jack of Newbery* (1597; better known as *Jack of Newbery*)—all long, episodic stories, sprinkled with overly dramatic characterization and improbable plot structures. In *Oroonoko*, however, Behn advanced the novel to the point where her more skilled successors in the eighteenth century could begin to shape it into an independent, recognizable form.

Behn possessed the natural gifts of the storyteller, and her narrative art can easily stand beside that of her male contemporaries. A frankly commercial writer, she simply had no time, in pursuit of pleasure and the pen, to find a place in her narratives for intellectual substance. Nevertheless, she told a story as few others could, and the force of her own personality contributed both reality and a sense of immediacy to the still inchoate form of seventeenth century British fiction.

BIOGRAPHY

The details of Aphra Behn's birth are not known. The parish register of the Sts. Gregory and Martin Church,

Wye, England, contains an entry stating that Ayfara Amis, daughter of John and Amy Amis, was baptized on July 10, 1640. Apparently, John Johnson, related to Lord Francis Willoughby of Parham, adopted the girl, although no one seems to know exactly when. Ayfara Amis (some sources spell her first name as Aphara) accompanied her adoptive parents on a journey to Suriname (later Dutch Guiana) in 1658, Willoughby having appointed Johnson to serve as deputy governor of his extensive holdings there. Unfortunately, the new deputy died on the voyage; his widow and children proceeded to Suriname and took up residence at St. John's, one of Lord Willoughby's plantations. Exactly how long they remained is not clear, but certainly the details surrounding the time Behn spent at St. John's form the background for *Oroonoko*.

Biographers have established the summer of 1663 as the most probable date of Behn's return to England. By 1665, Behn was again in London and married to a wealthy merchant of Dutch extraction who may well have had connections in, or at least around, the court of Charles II. In 1665 came the Great Plague and the death of Behn's husband; the latter proved the more disastrous for her, specifically because (again for unknown reasons) the Dutch merchant left nothing of substance to her—nothing, that is, except his court connections. Charles II, in the midst of the first of his wars against Holland, hired Behn as a secret government agent to spy on the Dutch, for which purpose she proceeded to Antwerp, a Belgian city near the border with Holland. There she contacted another British agent, William Scott, from whom she obtained various pieces of military information, which she forwarded to London. Although she received little credit for her work, and even less money, Behn did conceive of the pseudonym Astrea, the name under which she published most of her poetry.

The entire adventure into espionage proved a dismal failure for Behn; she even

had to borrow money and pawn her valuables to pay her debts and obtain passage back to England. Once home, early in 1667, she found no relief from her desperate financial situation. Her debtors threatened prison, and the government refused any payment for her services. Prison followed, although the time and the exact length of her term remain unknown. Some of Behn's biographers speculate that she was aided in her release by John Hale (d. 1692)—a lawyer of Gray's Inn, a wit, an intellectual, a homosexual, the principal subject of and reason for Behn's sonnets, and the man with whom she carried on a long romance. When she did gain her release, she determined to dedicate the rest of her life to writing and to pleasure, to trust to her own devices rather than to rely on others who could not be trusted.

Behn launched her career as a dramatist in late De-

Aphra Behn. (Library of Congress)

cember, 1670, at the new Duke's Theatre in Little Lincoln's Inn Fields, London. Her tragicomedy *The Forced Marriage* ran for six nights and included in the cast the nineteen-year-old Thomas Otway (1652-1685), the playwright-to-be only recently arrived from Oxford. Because of the length of the run, Behn, as was the practice, received the entire profit from the third performance, which meant that she could begin to function as an independent artist. She followed her first effort in the spring of 1671 with a comedy, *The Amorous Prince*, again at the Duke's; another comedy, *The Dutch Lover*, came to Drury Lane in February, 1673, and by the time of her anonymous comedy *The Rover*, in 1677, her reputation was secure. She mixed easily with the literati of her day, such as Thomas Killigrew, Edward Ravenscroft, John Wilmot, Earl of Rochester, Edmund Waller, and the poet laureate John Dryden, who published her rough translations from Ovid in 1683. With her reputation came offers to write witty prologues and epilogues for others' plays as well as what she wanted more than anything—money. A confrontation with the third earl of Shaftesbury and the newly emerged Whigs during the religious-political controversies of 1678, when Behn offended Charles II's opponents in a satiric prologue to an anonymous play, *Romulus and Hersilia*, brought her once again to the edge of financial hardship, as she was forced to abandon drama for the next five years.

Fortunately, Behn could fall back on her abilities as a writer of popular fiction and occasional verse, although those forms were not as profitable as the London stage. Her series *Love Letters Between a Nobleman and His Sister* and *Poems upon Several Occasions* (1684) were well received, but the meager financial returns from such projects could not keep pace with her personal expenses. When she did return to the stage in 1686 with her comedy *The Lucky Chance*, she met with only moderate success and some public abuse. *The Emperor of the Moon*, produced the following season, fared somewhat better, although by then the London audience had lost its stomach for a female playwright—and a Tory, at that. She continued to write fiction and verse, but sickness and the death of her friend Edmund Waller, both in October, 1688, discouraged her. Five days after the coronation of William III and Mary, on April 16, 1689, Behn died. She had risen high enough to merit burial in Westminster Abbey; John Hoyle provided the fitting epitaph: "Here lies proof that wit can never be/ Defense enough against mortality."

ANALYSIS

In the early twentieth century, Vita Sackville-West, in trying to estimate Aphra Behn's contribution to English fiction, asked, "What has she left behind her that is of any real value?" Sackville-West bemoaned Behn's failure in her fiction to reflect fully London life, London characters, London scenes; her attention to exotic themes, settings, and characters merely debased and wasted her narrative gifts. Such a judgment, while plausible, fails to consider Behn's fiction in its historical and biographical context. Her tales abound with German princes, Spanish princesses, Portuguese kings, French counts, West Indian slaves, and various orders of bishops, priests, and nuns, yet Behn's *real* world was itself highly artificial, even fantastic: the intrigue of the Stuart court, the ribaldry of the London stage, the gossip of the drawing room, the masquerade, and the card parlor. Behn, in her real world, took in the same scenes as did John Dryden, Samuel Pepys, and the earl of Rochester. Thus it may be too hasty to assert that her fiction neglects her actual experience in favor of fantastic and faraway window dressing.

In *Agnes de Castro*, Behn lets loose various powers of love, with the result that her heroines' passions affect the fortunes of their lovers. Thus, Miranda (*The Fair Jilt*) reflects the raving, hypocritical enchantress whose very beauty drives her lovers mad, Ardelia (*The Nun*) plays the capricious lover whose passion carries her through a series of men as well as a nunnery, and Agnes de Castro presents a slight variation on these others in that she is a product of circumstance: She is loved by the husband of her mistress.

Another primary theme in Behn's work is that of the noble savage, which has traditionally been assigned to *Oroonoko*, as has the subordinate issue of antislavery in that same novel. In 1975, Professor George Guffey suggested a withdrawal from the feminist-biographical positions on Behn's work from which the noble savage/ antislavery ideals spring and a movement toward "a hitherto unperceived level of political allusion." Guffey did not label *Oroonoko* a political allegory but did suggest that readers should look more closely at events in England between 1678 and 1688. Guffey maintained that the novelist deplores not the slavery of a black, noble savage but the bondage of a *royal prince*—again a reference to the political climate of the times. The interesting aspect of Guffey's analysis is that his approach lends substance to Behn's principal novel and to her overall reputation as a literary artist, and it parries the complaint that she failed to echo the sound and the sense of her own age.

In 1678, Sir Roger L'Estrange published *Five Love Letters from a Nun to a Cavalier*, a translation of some fictional correspondence by the minor French writer Guilleraques. Behn used the work as a model for at least three of her prose pieces: *Love Letters Between a Nobleman and His Sister*, *The History of the Nun*, and *The Nun*. For the latter two, the novelist took advantage, at least on the surface, of the current religious and political controversies and set forth the usual claims to truth.

THE HISTORY OF THE NUN

There may be some validity to the claim that *The History of the Nun* exists as one of the earliest examinations by a novelist into the psychology of crime and guilt. The events of the novel proceed reasonably enough at the outset but become less believable; by the conclusion, the events appear to be exceedingly unreal. Despite this difficulty, the novel does have some value. Behn demonstrates her ability to develop thoroughly the key aspects of the weaknesses and the resultant sufferings of the heroine, Isabella. Behn immediately exposes the concept that "Mother Church" can take care of a girl's problems, can easily eradicate the desires of the world from her heart and mind, and can readily transform a passionate maiden into a true, devoted sister of the faith. In addition, despite her wickedness, Isabella is very much a human being worthy of the reader's understanding. At every step, the girl pays something for what she does; with each violation against the Church and each crime of passion, she falls deeper into the darkness of her own guilt. What she does, and how, is certainly contrived, but how she reacts to her misdeeds reflects accurately the guilty conscience of a believable human being.

THE NUN

Behn's second "Nun" novel, not published until 1697, certainly leads the reader through a more complicated plot entanglement than the 1689 story, but it contains none of the virtue exhibited in the earlier work. The interesting aspect of *The Nun*'s plot is that Behn kills the heroine, Ardelia, first; only afterward do the principal rivals, Don Sebastian and Don Henriques, kill each other in a fight. The interest, however, is only fleeting, for those events do not occur until the end of the novel. All that remains of the bloody situation is Elvira, Don Sebastian's unfaithful sister. After weeping and calling for help, she is seized with a violent fever (in the final paragraph) and dies within twenty-four hours. Certainly, Behn's ingenuity in this piece demands some recognition, if for no reason other than her adeptness, as James Sutherland has put it, at "moving the pieces around the board."

AGNES DE CASTRO

Because of the relative sanity of its plot, in contrast to the two previous tragedies, *Agnes de Castro* comes close to what Behn's feminist supporters expect of her. In other words, in this piece, pure evil or a series of tragic events cannot be blamed entirely on love or on reckless female passion. Although Don Pedro genuinely loves his wife's maid of honor, Agnes, she, out of loyalty to her mistress, refuses to yield to his passion. Such action encourages the other characters to exhibit equal degrees of virtue. Constantia, Don Pedro's wife, seems to understand that the power of Agnes's charms, although innocent enough, is no match for her husband's frailty of heart over reason. Thus, she resents neither her husband nor her maid; in fact, she is willing to tolerate the presence of Agnes to keep her husband happy.

The novel, however, does not exist as a monument to reason. Something must always arise, either in politics or romance, to disrupt reasonable people's attempts at harmony. In the novel, a vengeful woman lies to Constantia and plants the idea in her mind that Agnes and Don Pedro are plotting against her. The woman's report breaks Constantia's trust in her husband and her maid, and the honest lady dies of a broken heart. The novel, however, remains believable, for Behn simply emphasizes the frailty of honor and trust in a world dominated by intrigue and pure hatred. Given the political and religious climates of the decade, the setting and the plot of *Agnes de Castro* are indeed flimsy facades for the court and coffeehouse of seventeenth century London.

THE FAIR JILT

Although in *The Fair Jilt* Behn continued to develop the conflict between love and reason, the novel has attracted critical attention because of its allusions to the writer's own experiences. Again, Behn lays claim to authenticity by maintaining that she witnessed parts of the events the novel relates and heard the rest from sources close to the action and the characters. In addition, the events occur in Antwerp, the very city to which the novelist had been assigned for the performance of her spying activities for Charles II's ministers.

From the outset of the novel, Behn establishes the wickedness of Miranda, who uses her beauty to enchant the unsuspecting and even tempts the weak into committing murder. Obviously, had Behn allowed her major character to succeed in her evil ways, nothing would have been gained from the novel. What results is the triumph of the hero's innate goodness; as weak as Prince Tarquin is, he endures. His loyalty and devotion outlast and, to a certain extent, conquer Miranda's wickedness.

OROONOKO

Behn's literary reputation today rests almost totally on a single work, *Oroonoko*. The novel succeeds as her most realistic work, principally because it recounts the specifics of seventeenth century Suriname with considerable detail and force. Behn installs her hero amid the splendor of a tropical setting, a Natural Man, a pure savage untouched by the vices of Christian Europe, unaware of the white man's inherent baseness and falsehood.

In lashing out at the weaknesses of her society, Behn does not forget about one of her major concerns—love. Oroonoko loves the beautiful Imoinda, a child of his own race, but the prince's grandfather demands her for his own harem. Afterward, the monarch sells the girl into slavery, and she finds herself in Suriname, where Oroonoko also is brought following his kidnapping. The prince embarks on a term of virtuous and powerful adventures in the name of freedom for himself and Imoinda, but his captors deceive him. Thereupon, he leads a slave revolt, only to be captured by the white scoundrels and tortured. Rather than see Imoinda suffer dishonor at the hands of the ruthless white planters and government officers, Oroonoko manages to kill her himself. At the end, he calmly smokes his pipe—a habit learned from the Europeans—as his captors dismember his body and toss the pieces into the fire.

The final judgment on Behn's fiction may still remain to be formulated. Evaluations of her work have tended to extremes. Some critics assert that Behn's novels, even *Oroonoko*, had no significant influence on the development of the English novel, whereas others argue that the author's limited attempts at realism may well have influenced Daniel Defoe, Samuel Richardson, Henry Fielding, and others to begin to mold the ostensibly factual narrative into the novel as the form is recognized today. From Behn came the background against which fictional plots could go forward and fictional characters could function. Her problem, which her successors managed to surmount, was her inability (or refusal) to make her characters and events as real as their fictional environments. That fault (if it was a fault) lay with the tendencies and the demands of the era in which she wrote, not with the writer. Indeed, it is hardly a failure for a dramatist and a novelist to have given to her audiences exactly what they wanted. To have done less would have meant an even quicker exit from fame and an even more obscure niche in the literary history of her time.

Samuel J. Rogal

OTHER MAJOR WORKS

PLAYS: *The Forced Marriage: Or, The Jealous Bridegroom*, pr. 1670; *The Amorous Prince: Or, The Curious Husband*, pr., pb. 1671; *The Dutch Lover*, pr., pb. 1673; *Abdelazer: Or, The Moor's Revenge*, pr. 1676; *The Town Fop: Or, Sir Timothy Tawdry*, pr. 1676; *The Rover: Or, The Banished Cavaliers, Part I*, pr., pb. 1677, *Part II*, pr., pb. 1681; *Sir Patient Fancy*, pr., pb. 1678; *The Feigned Courtesans: Or, A Night's Intrigue*, pr., pb. 1679; *The Young King: Or, The Mistake*, pr. 1679; *The Roundheads: Or, The Good Old Cause*, pr. 1681; *The City Heiress: Or, Sir Timothy Treat-All*, pr., pb. 1682; *The Lucky Chance: Or, An Alderman's Bargain*, pr. 1686; *The Emperor of the Moon*, pr., pb. 1687; *The Widow Ranter: Or, The History of Bacon of Virginia*, pr. 1689; *The Younger Brother: Or, The Amorous Jilt*, pr., pb. 1696.

POETRY: *Poems upon Several Occasions, with "A Voyage to the Island of Love,"* 1684 (including adaptation of Abbé Paul Tallemant's *Le Voyage de l'isle d'amour*); *Miscellany: Being a Collection of Poems by Several Hands*, 1685 (includes works by others).

TRANSLATIONS: *Aesop's Fables*, 1687 (with Francis Barlow); *Of Trees*, 1689 (of book 6 of Abraham Cowley's poem *Sex libri plantarum*).

MISCELLANEOUS: *The Case for the Watch*, 1686 (prose and poetry); *La Montre: Or, The Lover's Watch*, 1686 (prose and poetry); *Lycidus: Or, The Lover in Fashion*, 1688 (prose and poetry; includes works by others); *The Lady's Looking-Glass, to Dress Herself By: Or, The Art of Charming*, 1697 (prose and poetry); *The Works of Aphra Behn*, 1915, 1967 (6 volumes; Montague Summers, editor).

BIBLIOGRAPHY

Altaba-Artal, Dolors. *Aphra Behn's English Feminism: Wit and Satire*. Cranbury, N.J.: Associated University Presses, 1999. Examines Behn's writings from the perspective of feminism. Includes bibliography and index.

Anderson, Emily Hodgson. "Novelty in Novels: A Look at What's New in Aphra Behn's *Oroonoko*." *Studies in the Novel* 39, no. 1 (Spring, 2007): 1-16. Explores the aspects of novelty in novels through a focused reading of *Oroonoko*. Argues that the novel demonstrates a concern for didacticism and its own newness that was characteristic of many eighteenth century novels.

Carnell, Rachel K. "Subverting Tragic Conventions: Aphra Behn's Turn to the Novel." *Studies in the Novel* 31, no. 2 (Summer, 1998): 133-151. Discusses Behn's experiments with the novel form and the strategies she employed to counter the blatantly misogynistic resistance to her participation in political exchange.

Hughes, Derek and Janet Todd, eds. *The Cambridge Companion to Aphra Behn*. New York: Cambridge University Press, 2004. Replete with tools for further research, this is an excellent aid to any study of Behn's life and work. Includes two essays discussing various aspects of her novel *Oroonoko*.

Link, Frederick M. *Aphra Behn*. New York: Twayne, 1968. Provides a comprehensive survey of Behn's novels, plays, poems, and translations, with the plays

receiving the greatest attention. Includes a chronology, notes, bibliography, and index.

Rivero, Albert J. "Aphra Behn's *Oroonoko* and the 'Blank Spaces' of Colonial Fictions." *Studies in English Literature, 1500-1900* 39, no. 3 (Summer, 1999): 443-462. Discusses Joseph Conrad's *Heart of Darkness* (which first appeared as a serial in 1899 and was published in book form in 1902) and Behn's *Oroonoko*. Both works feature characters that begin as civilized and go spectacularly native, and both attempt to preserve hierarchies of race and class while representing the impossibility of doing so in chaotic colonial settings.

Sackville-West, Victoria. *Aphra Behn: The Incomparable Astrea*. New York: Russell & Russell, 1927. Brief study of Behn's life relies heavily on biographical passages in Behn's novels. Whereas Sackville-West finds her subject engaging as a woman, she does not wholeheartedly admire Behn's writing. An appendix lists Behn's works and production or publication dates.

Spencer, Jane. *Aphra Behn's Afterlife*. New York: Oxford University Press, 2000. Examination of Behn's works, including *Oroonoko*, emphasizes Behn's influence. Features a discussion of the author's reputation as a novelist. Includes bibliography and index.

Todd, Janet. *The Secret Life of Aphra Behn*. New Brunswick, N.J.: Rutgers University Press, 1996. Speculative biographical work includes an introduction that summarizes efforts to study Behn's work and life, her place in literature, her ability to write in so many different genres, and the biographer's efforts to overcome the paucity of facts available. Features bibliographies of works written before and after 1800.

_____, ed. *Aphra Behn Studies*. New York: Cambridge University Press, 1996. Collection of essays is divided into four parts: Part 1 concentrates on Behn's plays, part 2 on her poetry, part 3 on her fiction, and part 4 on her biography. Includes an introduction outlining Behn's career.

Wiseman, Susan. *Aphra Behn*. 2d ed. Tavistock, England: Northcote House, 2007. Biography examines Behn's life and work. Discusses her works in all genres, including her novels *Oroonoko* and *Love Letters Between a Nobleman and His Sister*.

SAUL BELLOW

Born: Lachine, Quebec, Canada; June 10, 1915
Died: Brookline, Massachusetts; April 5, 2005
Also known as: Solomon Bellows; Solly

PRINCIPAL LONG FICTION

Dangling Man, 1944
The Victim, 1947
The Adventures of Augie March, 1953
Seize the Day, 1956
Henderson the Rain King, 1959
Herzog, 1964
Mr. Sammler's Planet, 1970
Humboldt's Gift, 1975
The Dean's December, 1982
More Die of Heartbreak, 1987
A Theft, 1989
The Bellarosa Connection, 1989
The Actual, 1997 (novella)
Ravelstein, 2000
Novels, 1944-1953, 2003 (includes *Dangling Man*, *The Victim*, and *The Adventures of Augie March*)
Novels, 1956-1964, 2007 (includes *Seize the Day*, *Henderson the Rain King*, and *Herzog*)

OTHER LITERARY FORMS

In addition to his many novels, Saul Bellow published short stories, plays, and a variety of nonfiction. His stories have appeared in *The New Yorker*, *Commentary*, *Partisan Review*, *Hudson Review*, *Esquire*, and other periodicals, and his collections of short stories include *Mosby's Memoirs, and Other Stories* (1968) and *Him with His Foot in His Mouth, and Other Stories* (1984). His full-length play *The Last Analysis* was produced for a short run on Broadway in 1964, and three one-act plays, *Orange Soufflé*, *A Wen*, and *Out from Under*, were staged in 1966 in the United States and Europe. Another one-act play, *The Wrecker*, was published, though not staged, in 1954. Throughout his career, Bellow wrote numerous articles on a variety of topics. In 1976, he published an account of his trip to Israel, *To Jerusalem and Back: A Personal Account*.

ACHIEVEMENTS

Often described as one of America's most important novelists, Saul Bellow earned enormous critical praise and a wide readership as well. He was awarded the Nobel Prize in Literature in 1976. His popularity is, perhaps, surprising, because his novels do not contain the usual ingredients one expects to find in best-selling fiction—suspense, heroic figures, and graphic sex and violence. In fact, his novels are difficult ones that wrestle with perplexing questions, sometimes drawing from esoteric sources such as the anthroposophy of Rudolf Steiner and the psychology of Wilhelm Reich. One of America's most erudite novelists, Bellow often alluded to the work of philosophers, psychologists, poets, anthropologists, and other writers in his fiction. He once stated that modern novelists should not be afraid to introduce complex ideas into their work. He found nothing admirable about the anti-intellectualism of many modern writers and believed that most of them failed to confront the important moral and philosophical problems of the modern age. Opposed to the glib pessimism and the "complaint" of the dominant tradition of modern literature, Bellow struggled for affirmation at a time when many writers viewed such a possibility as merely an object of ridicule.

In contrast to many other American writers, who produced their best work when they were young and then wrote mediocre or poor fiction as they grew older, Bellow is known for the consistent high quality of his work. Moreover, his fiction reveals an immense versatility. In his work, one finds highly structured Flaubertian form as well as picaresque narrative, naturalistic realism as well as romance.

Bellow earned a reputation as a master of narrative voice and perspective, a great comic writer (perhaps the best in America since Mark Twain), and a fine craftsman whose remarkable control of the language allowed him to move easily from the highly formal to the colloquial. Most important, his novels illuminate the dark areas of the psyche and possess immense emotional power. Bellow once complained that many contemporary authors and critics are obsessed with symbolism and hidden meanings. A literary work becomes an abstraction for them, and they contrive to evade the emotional power inherent in literature. Bellow's novels do not suffer from abstraction; they deal concretely with passion, death, love, and other fundamental concerns, evoking the whole range of human emotions for his readers.

BIOGRAPHY

Saul Bellow was born Solomon Bellows (he later dropped the "s" from his last name) in Lachine, Quebec, Canada, on June 10, 1915, the youngest of four children. Two years before, his parents, Abraham and Liza (Gordon) Bellows, had emigrated to Canada from St. Petersburg, Russia. The family lived in a very poor section of Montreal, where Bellow learned Yiddish, Hebrew, French, and English. In 1923, Bellow was diagnosed with tuberculosis and spent half a year in Montreal's Royal Victoria Hospital. When he was nine years old, the family moved to Chicago, where they lived in the tenements of Humboldt Park.

In 1933, after graduating from Tuley High School, Bellow entered the University of Chicago. Two years later he transferred to Northwestern University, where he received a bachelor's degree with honors in sociology and anthropology. In 1937, he entered the University of Wisconsin at Madison to study anthropology but left school in December to marry Anita Goshkin and to become a writer. He was employed briefly with the Works Progress Administration Writers' Project and then led a bohemian life, supporting himself with teaching and odd jobs. During World War II, he served in the merchant marine and published his first novel, *Dangling Man*.

After publishing his second novel, *The Victim*, Bellow was awarded a Guggenheim Fellowship in 1948, which enabled him to travel to Europe and work on *The Adventures of Augie March*, parts of which he published in various periodicals before publishing the novel in 1953. This third novel won the National Book Award for fiction in 1953 and established Bellow as one of America's most promising novelists.

After his return from Europe in 1950, Bellow spent a large part of the next decade in New York City and Duchess County, New York, teaching and writing before moving back to Chicago to publish *Herzog*. While *Seize the Day* and *Henderson the Rain King* did not re-

ceive the critical attention they deserved, *Herzog* was an enormous critical and financial success, even becoming a best seller for forty-two weeks and selling 142,000 copies, making Bellow wealthy for the first time in his life. *Herzog*, which prompted several thousand readers to send letters to the author pouring out their souls, is not only Bellow's masterpiece but also the most autobiographical of his novels. The impetus for the novel was the breakup of his second marriage, to Sondra Tschacbasov, because of her affair with his best friend, the writer Jack Ludwig. Although the novel reveals all of the important episodes of Bellow's life up to the time of the writing of *Herzog*, its primary focus is on the triangle of Herzog (Bellow), an academic suffering from writer's block, his beautiful and strong-willed wife Madeleine (Sondra), and the flamboyant charlatan Valentine Gersbach (Ludwig). The shameless Gersbach pretends to be Herzog's best friend and even provides marital counseling for the despondent husband while cuckolding him.

The next two novels, *Mr. Sammler's Planet* and *Humboldt's Gift*, helped increase Bellow's reputation but also created some controversy. *Mr. Sammler's Planet* was critical of the excesses of the late 1960's, and some complained that Bellow had become a reactionary. Although Bellow opposed the Vietnam War, he found it difficult to identify with the "counterculture." *Humboldt's Gift* disturbed some critics, who complained that Bellow's interest in the ideas of Austrian social philosopher Rudolf Steiner indicated that he was becoming an escapist; it was a mistaken assumption. An ardent supporter of Israel, Bellow traveled to that country in 1975 and published an account of his journey, *To Jerusalem and Back*. In 1976 he was awarded the Nobel Prize in Literature. Winning the Nobel Prize did not result in a loss of Bellow's creativity, and he published important books in the 1980's and 1990's, especially *The Dean's December*, *More Die of Heartbreak*, and *The Actual*, which challenge conventional thinking on political, aesthetic, and philosophical matters. His final novel, *Ravelstein*, published in 2000, prompted controversy, as it revealed that Bellow's close friend Allan Bloom (Abe Ravelstein in the novel) was gay and probably died as a consequence of acquired immunodeficiency syndrome (AIDS).

Bellow was married five times; he had three sons by his first three wives and, at the age of eighty-four, a daughter by his fifth wife. After living in Chicago for many years, he moved to Massachusetts in 1994, where he became a professor of literature at Boston University. Bellow died in Brookline, Massachusetts, in 2005 at the age of eighty-nine.

ANALYSIS

Saul Bellow's mature fiction can be considered a conscious challenge to modernism, the dominant literary tradition of the age. Bellow viewed modernism as a "victim literature" because it depicts alienated individuals who are conquered by their environments. According to Bellow, this "wasteland" tradition originated in the middle of the nineteenth century with the birth of French realism and culminated in the work of Samuel Beckett and other nihilistic contemporary writers. This victim literature reveals a horror of life and considers humanist values useless in a bleak, irrational world. Modernism assumes that the notion of the individual self that underlies the great tradition of the novel is an outmoded concept and that modern civilization is doomed.

FIRST NOVELS

Bellow's first two novels owe a large debt to the wasteland modernism that he would explicitly reject in the late 1940's. *Dangling Man* is an existentialist diary that owes much to Fyodor Dostoevski's *Notes from the Underground* (1864). The demoralized protagonist, Joseph, is left "dangling" as he waits to be drafted during World War II. A moral casualty of war, he has no sense of purpose and feels weary of a life that seems boring, trivial, and cruel. Excessively self-conscious and critical of those around him, he spends most of his time alone, writing in his journal. He can no longer continue his past work, writing biographical essays on philosophers of the Enlightenment. Although he is alienated, he does realize that he should not make a doctrine out of this feeling. The conclusion of the novel reveals Joseph's ultimate failure to transcend his "victimization"; he is drafted and greets his imminent regimentation enthusiastically.

Bellow's next novel, *The Victim*, also depicts a passive protagonist who is unable to overcome his victimization. As Bellow admitted, the novel is partially modeled on Dostoevski's *The Eternal Husband* (1870) and

Saul Bellow. (© The Nobel Foundation)

uses the technique of the doppelgänger as Dostoevski does in *The Double* (1846). Bellow's novel presents the psychological struggle between Asa Leventhal, a Jew, and Kirby Allbee, his Gentile "double." A derelict without a job, Allbee suggests that Leventhal is responsible for his grim fate. Leventhal ponders the problem of his guilt and responsibility and tries to rid himself of his persecuting double. Despite his efforts to assert himself, he is still "dangling" at the end of the book—still a victim of forces that, he believes, are beyond his control.

THE ADVENTURES OF AUGIE MARCH

After his second novel, Bellow became disenchanted with the depressive temperament and the excessive emphasis on form of modernist literature. He had written his first two novels according to "repressive" Flaubertian formal standards; they were melancholy, rigidly structured, restrained in language, and detached and objective in tone. Rebelling against these constricting standards, Bellow threw off the yoke of modernism when he began to write his third novel. The theme, style, and tone of *The Adventures of Augie March* are very different from those of his earlier novels, for here one finds an open-ended picaresque narrative with flamboyant language and an exuberant hero who seeks to affirm life and the possibility of freedom. Whereas the environment has a profound influence on Joseph and Asa Leventhal, Augie refuses to allow it to determine his fate. During the course of many adventures, a multitude of Machiavellians seek to impose their versions of reality on the good-natured Augie, but he escapes from them, refusing to commit himself.

With his third novel, then, Bellow deliberately rejected the modernist outlook and aesthetic. The problem was to find an alternative to modernism without resorting to glib optimism. It seems that he found an alternative in two older literary traditions—in nineteenth century English Romantic humanism and in a comedy that he considered typically Jewish. Unlike the fiction of the modernists, which denigrates the concept of the individual, Bellow's fiction asserts the potential of the self and its powerful imagination, which can redeem ordinary existence and affirm the value of freedom, love, joy, and hope.

While comedy in Bellow's fiction is a complex matter, its primary function seems to be to undercut the dejection that threatens his heroes. The comic allows Bellow's protagonists to cope with the grim facts of existence; it enables them to avoid despair and gain a balanced view of their problematic situations. Comedy, the spirit of reason, allows them to laugh away their irrational anxieties. Often Bellow seems to encourage his worst anxieties in order to bring them out into the open so that he can dispose of them through comic ridicule.

SEIZE THE DAY

Whereas *The Adventures of Augie March* presents Bellow's alternative to a "literature of victimization," his subsequent novels can be regarded as probing, exploratory studies in spiritual survival in a hostile environment. *Seize the Day* is a much more somber novel than *The Adventures of Augie March*. Bellow felt that his liberation from Flaubertian formalism had gone too far, and that he must use more restraint in his fourth novel.

He realized that Augie was too effusive and too naïve. The protagonist of *Seize the Day* is similar to the protagonists of the first two novels, but while Tommy Wilhelm is a "victim," Bellow's attitude toward him is different from his attitude toward Joseph and Asa Leventhal. In his fourth novel, Bellow sought to show the spiritual rebirth of such a "victim."

The short novel, divided into seven parts, presents the day of reckoning in the life of Wilhelm, a forty-four-year-old former salesman of children's furniture whose past consists of a series of blunders. Living in the Hotel Gloriana (which is also the residence of his wealthy father, Dr. Adler), Wilhelm feels that he is in a desperate situation. He is unemployed and unable to obtain money from his unsympathetic father. He gives his last seven hundred dollars to be invested for him by the mysterious psychologist Dr. Tamkin, a man who has become not only his surrogate father and financial adviser but also his instructor in spiritual and philosophical matters. Furthermore, Wilhelm's wife, Margaret, from whom he is separated, is harassing him for money. Depressed and confused by the memories of his failures in the past and absorbed by his problems in the present, Wilhelm needs love and compassion. Dr. Adler, Dr. Tamkin, and Margaret all fail him.

Seize the Day is a harsh indictment of a money-obsessed society, where a father is unable to love a son who is unsuccessful. Tamkin's speech on the two souls, no doubt the most important passage in the novel, helps clarify Bellow's social criticism. The psychologist argues that there is a war between a person's "pretender soul," the social self, and the "real soul." When the pretender soul parasitically dominates its host, as is common in modern society, the individual becomes murderous. If the individual is true to the real soul, however, and casts off the false pretender soul, he or she can learn to love and "seize the day."

Bellow shows that all of the characters in the novel are products of an exploitative, materialistic society—all are dominated by their pretender souls. Dr. Adler has fought his way up the economic ladder to success. Revered by the residents of the Hotel Gloriana, he is full of self-love. He desires to spend his remaining years in peace and refuses to acknowledge his paternal obligation to his desperate son. Wilhelm's appeals for money are actually pleas for some sign of paternal concern. He provokes his father, trying to disturb the polite barrier of aloofness that the old man has constructed to prevent any kind of real communication between father and son. While Wilhelm is a difficult son for a father to cherish, Dr. Adler is a coldhearted man who has no real affection for his son, or for anyone else except himself. When, at the end of the novel, Wilhelm begs his father for some kind of sympathy, the hard-boiled Adler brutally rejects him, revealing his hatred for his "soft" son.

Dr. Adler's failure as a father results in Wilhelm's turning to the strange psychologist Dr. Tamkin. Down on his luck, Tamkin is a confidence man hoping to make easy money. He is another one of Bellow's eccentric fast-talkers, full of fantastic stories and philosophical and psychological insights. Wilhelm is attracted to Tamkin not only because he is a father figure who promises to save him from his dire financial crisis but also because he is one man in a cynical society who speaks of spiritual matters. The direct result of Tamkin's advice is the loss of Wilhelm's money, but while the doctor is a phony whose flamboyant personality enables him to dupe the naïve ex-salesman, he does indirectly allow Wilhelm to obtain a kind of salvation.

Wilhelm is the only character in the novel who is able to forsake his pretender soul. He is a product of society as the other characters are, but he is different from them in his instinctive distaste for the inveterate cynicism at the heart of society. Accepting society's definition of success, he considers himself a failure. He suffers immensely and constantly ponders his life and his errors in the past, yet while he can at times degenerate into a buffoon indulging in self-pity and hostility, he is also attracted to the idealism that Tamkin occasionally expounds.

A significant moment occurs near the end of the novel when Wilhelm suddenly feels a sense of brotherhood with his fellow travelers in the New York subway. For once he has transcended his self-absorption, though he is immediately skeptical of this intuitive moment. At the very end of the novel, another heightened moment occurs in which he does make the breakthrough foreshadowed in the subway scene. Having lost all of his money, he pursues into a funeral home a man who resembles Tamkin. Suddenly he finds himself confronting a corpse, and he begins to weep uncontrollably. He weeps not merely out of self-pity, as some have suggested, but for humankind. Understanding that death and suffering are an inextricable part of the human condition, he feels humility and is able to overcome his excessive self-absorption. He is finally able to cast off his pretender soul. The work concludes with a powerful affirmation and suggests an alternative to the spiritual death of a materialistic, predatory society.

HENDERSON THE RAIN KING

Bellow's next novel, *Henderson the Rain King*, is the first fully realized work of his maturity. It is Bellow's first novel of which one can say that no other writer could have conceived it, much less written it. Although it has some characteristics of the picaresque, the fable, and the realistic novel, *Henderson the Rain King* assumes the most widely used form for longer works during the English Romantic era—the quest romance. The tone of the novel is somewhat different from that typically found in the quest romance, however; it is exuberant and comic, and the book is full of wit, parody, farce, and ironic juxtapositions.

The novel might be seen as Bellow's version of Joseph Conrad's *Heart of Darkness* (1902). Like Conrad's Marlow, Eugene Henderson recalls his journey into the heart of Africa and his bizarre adventures there, which culminate in his meeting with a Kurtz-like instructor who has a profound influence on him. Whereas Kurtz reveals to Marlow the human potential for degradation, Dahfu conveys to Henderson the human promise of nobility. With its allusions to William Wordsworth, Samuel Taylor Coleridge, Percy Bysshe Shelley, and William Blake, the novel affirms the possibility of the individual's regeneration by the power of the human imagination; it is a trenchant rejection of Conrad's pessimism.

The novel can be divided into three basic parts: Chapters 1-4 depict Henderson's alienation; chapters 5-9 present his journey to the African tribe of the Arnewi; and chapters 10-22 portray his journey to the African tribe of the Wariri and his spiritual regeneration. The first section presents Henderson's discursive recollections of his life before he set out for Africa, in which he attempts to reveal the reasons for the journey. While these chapters provide a plethora of information about him, he is never able to articulate the reasons for his "quest," as he calls it.

Bellow is suggesting in this section that there are no clear-cut reasons for the African journey. Henderson leaves his wife and family for the African wilderness because of his dissatisfaction with his meaningless existence. A millionaire with tremendous energy but no scope for it, Henderson has spent most of his life suffering or making others suffer. Middle-aged, anxious about his mortality, and unable to satisfy the strident inner voice of "I want, I want," he leaves for Africa, hoping to burst "the spirit's sleep," as he phrases it, echoing Shelley's *The Revolt of Islam* (1818).

With his loyal guide Romilayu, he first visits the Arnewi tribe. These people are "children of light" who represent a healthy existence; they are gentle, peaceful, and innocent. Queen Willatale, who rules the tribe, informs Henderson that man wants to live—"grun-tu-molani." It is an important message for Henderson, but he soon demonstrates that he is unable to follow Willatale's wisdom. Desiring to help the tribe, whose water supply has been infested by frogs, he decides to kill the creatures. His bomb is too powerful and destroys the cistern as well as the frogs. Henderson has violated the code of the Arnewi, who abhor violence and have love for all living creatures.

After Henderson leaves the Arnewi, he visits the Wariri, "the children of darkness," who are violent and hostile, reminiscent of the predatory society of Bellow's earlier novels. He does meet one extraordinary individual, however, and establishes a friendship with him. King Dahfu is a noble man who completes Henderson's education begun with the Arnewi. He perceptively observes that Henderson's basic problem is his avoidance of death: He is an "avoider." Dahfu helps him by persuading him to go down into a lion's den to overcome his anxiety over mortality. Dahfu believes, too, that Henderson can absorb qualities of the lion and slough off his porcine characteristics. Dahfu is another one of Bellow's eccentric teachers who speaks both wisdom and nonsense. His greatest importance for Henderson is that he embodies the nobility of human beings, who can by the power of the imagination achieve spiritual regeneration. At the end of the novel, Henderson finally bursts the spirit's sleep and leaves Africa for America. He has a sense of purpose and can love others. He plans to become a physician and will return home to his wife.

HERZOG

Herzog is by most accounts Bellow's best and most difficult novel. It is a retrospective meditation by a middle-aged professor who seeks to understand the reasons for his disastrous past. A complex, discursive work, pervaded by sardonic humor, it defies traditional labeling but owes a debt to the novel of ideas, the psychological novel, the epistolary novel, and the romantic meditative lyric. *Herzog* is a meditative work in which the protagonist compulsively remembers and evaluates his past, striving to avoid complete mental breakdown. There are reminiscences within reminiscences, and the story of Moses Herzog's life is related in fragments. Bellow's method enables the reader to see how Herzog's imagination recollects and assembles the fragments of the past into a meaningful pattern.

Distraught over his recent divorce from his second wife, Madeleine, Herzog has become obsessed with writing letters to everyone connected with that event as well as to important thinkers, living and dead, who concern him. He associates his domestic crisis with the cultural crisis of Western civilization, and therefore he ponders the ethics of Friedrich Nietzsche as well as those of his psychiatrist, Dr. Edvig. Herzog's letter writing is both a symptom of his psychological disintegration and his attempt to meditate on and make sense of suffering and death.

At his home in the Berkshires, Herzog recalls and meditates on the events of his recent past; the five-day period of time that he recalls reveals the severity of his psychological deterioration. His mistress, Ramona, believes that a cure for his nervous state can be found in her Lawrentian sexual passion, but he considers her "ideology" to be mere hedonism; impulsively, he decides to flee from her to Martha's Vineyard, where he has friends. After arriving there, the unstable professor leaves almost immediately and returns to New York. The next evening he has dinner with Ramona and spends the night with her, waking in the middle of the night to write another letter. The following morning he visits a courtroom while waiting for a meeting with his lawyer to discuss a lawsuit against Madeleine. Hearing a brutal child-abuse and murder case causes the distraught professor to associate Madeleine and her lover with the brutal child murderers; he flies to Chicago to kill them. As he spies on them, he realizes his assumption is absurd and abandons his plan. The next morning he takes his young daughter Junie for an outing but has a car accident and is arrested by the police for carrying a gun. He confronts an angry Madeleine at the police station and manages to control his own temper. Later, he is released and returns to his run-down home in the Berkshires, and the novel ends where it began.

Interspersed within these recollections of the immediate past are memories of the more distant past. By piecing these together, one learns the sad story of Herzog's domestic life. Feeling a vague dissatisfaction, the successful professor divorced his first wife, Daisy, a sensible midwestern woman, and began affairs with a good-natured Japanese woman, Sono, and the beautiful, bad-tempered Madeleine. After marrying Madeleine, Herzog purchased a house in the Berkshires, where he intended to complete his important book on the Romantics. Soon they returned to Chicago, however, where both saw a psychiatrist, and Madeleine suddenly announced that she wanted a divorce. The shocked Herzog traveled to Europe to recuperate, only to return to Chicago to learn that Madeleine had been having an affair with his best friend and confidant the whole time their marriage had been deteriorating.

Herzog's grim past—his disastrous marriages and the other sad events of his life that he also recalls—becomes emblematic of the pernicious influence of cultural nihilism. Herzog is devoted to basic humanist values but wonders if he must, as the ubiquitous "reality instructors" insist, become another mass man devoted to a brutal "realism" in the Hobbesian jungle of modern society. His antipathy for the wastelanders' cynicism is strong, but he knows his past idealism has been too naïve. Repeatedly, the "reality instructors" strive to teach ("punish") Herzog with lessons of the "real"—and the "real" is always brutal and cruel. Sandor Himmelstein, Herzog's lawyer and friend, proudly announces that all people are "whores." It is an accurate description not only of Himmelstein but also of his fellow reality instructors. Their cynical view is pervasive in modern society, in which people play roles, sell themselves, and seduce and exploit others for their own selfish ends.

The turning point of the novel is Herzog's revelation in the courtroom episode. Intellectually, he has always

known about evil and suffering, but emotionally he has remained innocent. His hearing of the case in which a mother has mistreated and murdered her son while her lover apathetically watched is too much for him to bear; here is a monstrous evil that cannot be subsumed by any intellectual scheme. In a devastating moment the professor is forced to realize that his idealism is foolish.

At the end of the novel, Herzog has achieved a new consciousness. He recognizes that he has been selfish and excessively absorbed in intellectual abstractions. A prisoner of his private intellectual life, he has cut himself off from ordinary humanity and everyday existence. He sees that his naïve idealism and the wastelanders' cruel "realism" are both escapist and therefore unacceptable attitudes; they allow the individual to evade reality by wearing masks of naïve idealism or self-serving cynicism. The exhausted Herzog decides to abandon his compulsive letter writing and to stop pondering his past. The threat of madness has passed, and he is on the road to recovery.

Mr. Sammler's Planet

Mr. Sammler's Planet is a meditative novel of sardonic humor and caustic wit. The "action" of the novel centers on the protagonist's recollection of a brief period of time in the recent past, though there are recollections of a more distant past, too. Once again the mental state of the protagonist is Bellow's main concern. Like Herzog, Artur Sammler has abandoned a scholarly project because he finds rational explanations dissatisfying; they are unable to justify suffering and death. The septuagenarian Sammler is yet another of Bellow's survivors, a lonely humanist in a society populated by brutal "realists."

This seventh novel, however, is not merely a repetition of Bellow's previous works. Sammler is detached and basically unemotional, yet he reveals a mystical bent largely absent in Bellow's other protagonists. He is drawn to the works of Meister Eckhart and other thirteenth century German mystics. While he does not literally believe in their ideas, he finds reading their works soothing. His religious inclination is a recent phenomenon. Sammler had been reared in a wealthy, secular Jewish family in Kraków, Poland. As an adult, he became a haughty, cosmopolitan intellectual, useless to everyone, as he readily admits. On a visit to Poland in 1939, when the Germans suddenly attacked, he, his wife, and others were captured and ordered to dig their own graves as the Nazis waited to murder them. Although his wife was killed in the mass execution, miraculously Sammler escaped by crawling out of his own grave. After the war ended, Sammler and his daughter Shula were rescued from a displaced persons camp by a kind nephew, Dr. Elya Gruner, who became their patron.

The experience of the Holocaust destroyed what little religious inclination Sammler possessed, but in his old age he has become concerned with his spiritual state. Unfortunately, it is difficult to pursue spiritual interests in a materialistic society hostile to them. The basic conflict in the novel is between Sammler's need to ponder the basic questions of existence—a need accentuated by the dying of the noble Gruner—and the distractions of modern-day society. In the primary action of the novel, Sammler's main intention is to visit the dying Gruner, who finds Sammler a source of great comfort. Several "accidents" distract Sammler from his goal, and on the day of his nephew's death, he arrives too late.

The "accidents" that encumber Sammler reveal clearly the "degraded clowning" of contemporary society. Sammler is threatened by a black pickpocket who corners the old man and then exposes himself. In the middle of a lecture he is shouted down by a radical student who says that Sammler is sexually defective. His daughter Shula steals a manuscript from an Indian scholar, and Sammler must waste precious time to recover it. Even Gruner's self-centered children, who have little compassion for their dying father, distract Sammler by their thoughtless actions.

Opposed to Gruner, who is part of the "old system" that esteems the family, the expression of emotion, and the traditional humanist values, is the contemporary generation, a kind of "circus" characterized by role-playing, hedonism, amorality, self-centeredness, and atrophy of feeling. Despite its flaws, Bellow sympathizes with the "old system." The novel concludes after Sammler, despite the objections of the hospital staff, goes into the postmortem room and says a prayer for Gruner's soul.

HUMBOLDT'S GIFT

As in Bellow's previous novels, the tension and the humor of *Humboldt's Gift* have their origins in the protagonist's attempt to free himself from the distractions of contemporary society and pursue the needs of his soul. The protagonist, Charlie Citrine, strives to define for himself the function of the artist in contemporary America. He tries to come to terms with the failure and premature death of his onetime mentor, Von Humboldt Fleisher, who had the potential to be America's greatest modern poet but achieved very little. Charlie wonders if the romantic poet can survive in a materialistic society; he wonders, too, if he can overcome his fear of the grave and exercise his imagination. A writer who has squandered his talent, Charlie has intimations of terror of the grave and intimations of immortality. He spends much time reading the anthroposophical works of Rudolf Steiner; although he is skeptical of some of Steiner's more esoteric teachings, he is sympathetic to the spiritual worldview of anthroposophy, even finding the notion of reincarnation persuasive.

The primary nemesis of Charlie's spiritual life is Ronald Cantabile, a small-time criminal. Renata, Charlie's voluptuous mistress, Denise, his ex-wife, and Pierre Thaxter, a confidence man, are also major distractions. When Charlie, on the advice of a friend, refuses to pay Cantabile the money he owes him from a poker game, the criminal harasses him. In fact, the proud, psychopathic Cantabile refuses to leave Charlie alone even after he agrees to pay him the money. He continually humiliates Charlie and even tries to involve him in a plot to murder the troublesome Denise.

Denise, Renata, and Thaxter also distract Charlie from pondering the fate of Humboldt and meditating on fundamental metaphysical questions. Hoping Charlie will return to her, Denise refuses to settle her support suit and continues to demand more money. When Charlie is forced to put up a two-hundred-thousand-dollar bond, he is financially ruined, and the loss of his money results in the loss of the voluptuous Renata, who decides to marry a wealthy undertaker. A third disillusioning experience involves Thaxter, who has apparently conned Charlie. Charlie had invested a small fortune in a new journal, *The Ark*, which was supposed to restore the authority of art and culture in the United States. Thaxter, the editor of *The Ark*, never puts out the first issue and has, it appears, stolen the money. His confidence game symbolizes America's lack of respect for art and culture, impractical subjects in a practical, technological society.

Charlie does, however, overcome these "distractions." Humboldt's posthumously delivered letter, accompanied by an original film sketch (his "gift") and a scenario that the two had written at Princeton years before, provides the genesis for Charlie's salvation. The original film idea and the scenario of their Princeton years enable Charlie to attain financial security, but, more important, Humboldt's letter provides the impetus for Charlie's decision at the end of the novel to repudiate his past empty life and pursue the life of the imagination. Humboldt's ideas, bolstered by the poetry of Blake, Wordsworth, and John Keats, enable Charlie to avoid the fate of the self-destructive artist. He decides to live in Europe and meditate on the fundamental questions—in short, to take up a different kind of life.

When, at the end of the novel, Charlie gives Humboldt and the poet's mother a proper burial, Bellow suggests that Charlie's imagination is ready to exert itself and wake him from his self-centered boredom and death-in-life. The final scene of the novel promises Charlie's spiritual regeneration.

THE DEAN'S DECEMBER

Bellow's 1982 novel *The Dean's December* is "a tale of two cities," Chicago and Bucharest, in which the protagonist, a dean at an unnamed college in Chicago, ponders private and public problems. Albert Corde experiences at first hand the rigid penitentiary society of the Communist East as well as the anarchic society of the non-Communist West, which seems on the verge of disintegration. The novel is a protest against the dehumanization of the individual. The East has enslaved its population, while the West has "written off" its doomed "Underclass." Like *Humboldt's Gift*, this novel can be seen as a kind of retrospective crisis meditation in which the protagonist attempts to come to terms with an immensely complex and threatening "multiverse," as Augie March calls it.

The complicated plot defies a succinct summary, but the basic situation can be outlined. The dean and his wife, Minna, arrive in Romania to visit her dying mother. Corde tries to help his despairing wife, who is unable to reconcile herself to the grim reality of her mother's death. He also ponders the controversy that he has provoked in Chicago. The dean has published two articles in *Harper's* in which he has commented on the

political and social problems of the city. The articles outrage the powerful members of Chicago society, and the administration of his college disapproves of the controversy that the dean has provoked. Moreover, Corde creates another controversy when he pressures the police to solve the murder of a white graduate student, Rickie Lester. A sensational trial, a "media circus," is the result of the dean's search for justice.

While, more than any other novel by Bellow, *The Dean's December* is concerned with contemporary public issues, especially the vile conditions of the inner city, it is also concerned with the spiritual state of the individual. In fact, Bellow suggests that there is a connection between the spiritual malady of the individual and the spiritual anarchy of society. The novel is a protest against not only people's lack of political freedom but also the spiritual enslavement that is the result of their inability to see clearly and to experience reality. Corde implies that this inability to experience reality is largely a product of "seeing" the world with a kind of reductive journalism completely lacking in imagination. Disgusted with contemporary journalism that provides only substitutes for reality, Corde intends to incorporate "poetry" into writing. The novel suggests that in Corde's kind of poetic vision there is hope for the spiritual rebirth of the individual and society.

MORE DIE OF HEARTBREAK

Three years after the publication of his collection *Him with His Foot in His Mouth, and Other Stories*, Bellow published *More Die of Heartbreak*. This comic novel does not have a highly structured plot; rather, it might be best described as an elaborate monologue from the overstimulated mind of the bachelor narrator, Kenneth Trachtenberg. Kenneth, an expert in Russian history and culture, is preoccupied with his uncle, Benn Crader, a renowned botanist. The only important "action" in the novel revolves around the attempt of Dr. Layamon, his daughter Matilda, and her fiancé Benn Crader to "extort" money from Benn's relative, Harold Vilitzer, a political racketeer in bad health. Years before, Vilitzer had cheated the Crader family in a real estate deal. The greedy Dr. Layamon sees his daughter's marriage to Benn as a marvelous opportunity to acquire a fortune if Benn will agree to pressure Vilitzer for the money the corrupt politician stole from the Crader family. Although he wants to please his beautiful fiancé and her father, Benn is not enthusiastic about the plan. As the narrator suggests, Benn is a man who should be in search of "higher meanings." At the end of the novel, Benn flees from the Layamons to the North Pole to carry out his research. The implication is that now he will be able to pursue his neglected aesthetic and metaphysical goals.

A THEFT

After being rejected by two periodicals because it was "too long," the short novel *A Theft* was published in 1989 as a paperback original. Like so many of Bellow's works, the plot of this 109-page novel is subordinate to Bellow's interest in character. Just as *Seize the Day* might be considered an intimate psychological exploration of Wilhelm, *A Theft* is a detailed exploration of the soul of the heroine, Clara Velde. Clara was brought up on old-time religion but has led a disorganized life, including disappointing love affairs, suicide attempts, and four marriages. Her fourth marriage is not successful, and she is actually in love with an "old flame," Ithiel Regler, a Henry Kissinger-like high-powered adviser to statesmen. For Clara, transcendent love between her and Ithiel is symbolized by an emerald ring that he gave her years ago. When this ring is stolen, Clara finds herself in a troubling search for it and experiences a kind of spiritual quest as well. She feels a special sense of kinship with her self-possessed au pair, Gina. In its epiphany-like quality, the conclusion of the novel is reminiscent of *Seize the Day*.

THE BELLAROSA CONNECTION

Another paperback original, the short novel *The Bellarosa Connection* is narrated by the wealthy founder of the Mnemosyne Institute in Philadelphia. The institute instructs businesspeople and others in the use of memory. The narrator, a retired widower, focuses his immense powers of recollection on two relatives who haunt him—Harry and Sorella Fonstein. Harry narrowly escaped the Nazi death camps, thanks to the Broadway producer Billy Rose, who made use of his gangster connections in Italy to help Fonstein and others escape to freedom. Billy Rose's generosity is particularly noteworthy, the narrator implies, because the Broadway producer has a sleazy reputation.

In the United States, Harry marries the intelligent, capable Sorella and becomes successful but is frustrated by

Rose's repulsing Harry's repeated attempts to meet him and express his gratitude. The central scene of the novel is the dramatic encounter between Sorella and Rose, in which the determined woman attempts to coerce the stubborn producer into meeting her husband by threatening to reveal sordid details of Rose's private life. Despite Sorella's "blackmail," Rose refuses to meet Harry.

Bellow in this short novel is pondering how the assimilation of Jews into American life can corrupt not only their values but also their souls. Sorella reflects: "The Jews could survive everything that Europe threw at them. I mean the lucky remnant. But now comes the next test—America." Apparently the United States proves "too much" for at least some of them.

THE ACTUAL

The novella *The Actual* is narrated by Harry Trellman, an introspective man in his sixties who grew up in a lower-middle-class Jewish neighborhood in Chicago. His father was a simple carpenter; his mother's family was wealthy. Harry was put in an orphanage despite the fact that both his parents were alive because his hypochondriacal mother did not have the time to care for him; she spent much time abroad and in the United States at various sanitariums looking for a cure for her disease of the joints. The bills for sojourns abroad and at home were paid by the mother's family; her brothers were successful sausage manufacturers who could pay for the cures she took at Bad Nauheim or Hot Springs, Arkansas. After the Korean War, the government sent Harry to study Chinese at a "special school." He spent a number of years in the Far East, the final two in Burma, where he made business connections, and then returned to Chicago, where he had "unfinished emotional business."

Although the precise source of Harry's income is not clear, apparently he is well-off. Semiretired and without financial concerns, Harry is nevertheless far from being content. For more than four decades he has loved Amy Wustrin, whom he first knew in high school. When Harry returned to Chicago after his Far East sojourn, he and Amy met again. Despite for Harry a momentous sexual encounter in which he kissed Amy "under the breast and inside the thigh," the relationship did not progress. After divorcing her first husband, Amy married Jay Wustrin, Harry's best friend in high school. Neither Jay nor Amy paid much heed to the marriage vows, and the result was a bitter divorce that culminated in Jay's playing tapes in divorce court of Amy's adulterous lovemaking in which one could hear her orgasmic cries. None of this disheartening history dampened Harry's ardent love for Amy.

Harry and Amy are brought together by the ninety-two-year-old billionaire Sigmund Adletsky, for whom Amy is working as an interior decorator and Harry as adviser in his "brain trust." Harry accompanies Amy in her emotionally arduous task of exhuming Jay's body from his cemetery plot next to the grave of Amy's mother so that Amy can bury her father there. (A practical joker with nihilistic proclivities, Jay had purchased the plot from Amy's father.) In the grave scene that concludes the novel, the withdrawn intellectual Harry takes decisive action by confessing his love for Amy and asking her to marry him. This scene is reminiscent of the conclusion to *Humboldt's Gift*, when the protagonist in the cemetery achieves an epiphany and the work ends with the implication that the protagonist, keenly aware of mortality and the death-in-life of his past existence, will be spiritually reborn.

RAVELSTEIN

Bellow's final novel, *Ravelstein*, is heavily autobiographical and explores the relationship between the narrator Chick (Bellow) and his good friend Abe Ravelstein, a fictional portrait of Allan Bloom, whose book *The Closing of the American Mind* (1987) was a surprise best seller and made the University of Chicago professor wealthy and famous. This novel prompted some controversy when it was published because it revealed that Bloom was gay and probably died of complications from AIDS. Some people felt that Bellow acted unethically by "outing" Bloom and invading his privacy. Bellow seems to have anticipated this objection to the writing of *Ravelstein*, for early in the novel the dying Ravelstein encourages his friend Chick to write a book about him after he dies and be as ruthless as Chick wants in exposing his flaws and weaknesses. It is likely that the iconoclastic Bloom encouraged Bellow to write a candid book about him that would eschew all romanticizing and sentimentality.

The form of the novel owes debts to the genres of biography, memoir, and roman à clef. In addition to the narrator and Ravelstein, other characters in the novel also have real-life counterparts, including Bellow's fifth wife, Janis Freedman, as Rosamund; his Romanian-born fourth spouse, Alexandra Tulcea, as Vela; the conservative thinker Leo Strauss as Davaar; the sociologist Edward Shils as Rakhmiel Kogon; former assistant secretary of state Paul Wolfowitz as Philip Gorman; and political scientist Werner Dannhauser as Ravelstein's close friend Morris Herbst.

Unlike *The Victim* or many of Bellow's other stories, plot is unimportant in this novel; portrayal of character and the exploration of ideas are the primary interests. Bellow is concerned, too, with exploring the interior life of the narrator, who is preoccupied with the problem of nihilism in its various forms and disguises. The narrator wrestles with the problem of how a good person should react to evil in the modern world. Chick seems to regard Ravelstein as his mentor—this dying intellectual comes to embody Jewish humanism that places the highest importance on the worth of human life and the value of the individual; in contrast is the murderous nihilism of the World War II period that resulted in the horrors of the Holocaust. The meandering meditative mind of the narrator repeatedly returns to the anti-Semitism of the twentieth century, which represents the evil that is the opposite of the goodness that Ravelstein embodies.

Ravelstein is a death-haunted book that describes not only the final illness of the narrator's dear friend but also the illness that comes very close to killing the narrator. Like Bellow, who nearly died from an illness similar to the narrator's, the narrator survives to write this portrait of his friend. The book concludes with the narrator's recollection of his and Ravelsteins's discovery of a huge flock of tropical parrots surviving in the midwestern winter. This epiphany suggests that the narrator has finally reconciled himself to the profound loss of his friend and that he can affirm existence in all its inexplicable strangeness and mysterious beauty.

Allan Chavkin

OTHER MAJOR WORKS

SHORT FICTION: *Mosby's Memoirs, and Other Stories*, 1968; *Him with His Foot in His Mouth, and Other Stories*, 1984; *Something to Remember Me By: Three Tales*, 1991; *Collected Stories*, 2001.

PLAYS: *The Wrecker*, pb. 1954; *The Last Analysis*, pr. 1964; *Under the Weather*, pr. 1966 (also known as *The Bellow Plays*; includes *Out from Under, A Wen*, and *Orange Soufflé*).

NONFICTION: *To Jerusalem and Back: A Personal Account*, 1976; *Conversations with Saul Bellow*, 1994 (Gloria L. Cronin and Ben Siegel, editors); *It All Adds Up: From the Dim Past to the Uncertain Future*, 1994.

EDITED TEXT: *Great Jewish Short Stories*, 1963.

BIBLIOGRAPHY

Atlas, James. *Bellow: A Biography*. New York: Random House, 2000. Full and accessible biography was written with the cooperation of its subject. Includes bibliography and index.

Bach, Gerhard, ed. *The Critical Response to Saul Bellow*. Westport, Conn.: Greenwood Press, 1995. Substantial collection presents two to five reviews and essays on each of Bellow's novels. Includes an informative editor's introduction, a chronology, and an interview with Bellow.

Bigler, Walter. *Figures of Madness in Saul Bellow's Longer Fiction*. New York: Peter Lang, 1998. Examines the psychological makeup of Bellow's characters. Includes bibliographical references.

Bloom, Harold, ed. *Saul Bellow*. New York: Chelsea House, 1986. Omnibus of reviews and essays on Bellow's work gives a good sense of the early critical responses. Includes commentary by writers such as Robert Penn Warren, Malcolm Bradbury, Tony Tanner, Richard Chase, and Cynthia Ozick.

Cronin, Gloria L. *A Room of His Own: In Search of the Feminine in the Novels of Saul Bellow*. Syracuse, N.Y.: Syracuse University Press, 2001. Approaches Bellow's novels from the perspective of French feminist theory, providing many provocative insights on gender in the works and analyzing Bellow's characters with attention to the nuances of language. Unlike some critics, Cronin avoids a reductionist reading of Bellow's work that sees the novels as the product of a biased male point of view.

Freedman, William. "Hanging for Pleasure and Profit: Truth as Necessary Illusion in Bellow's Fiction." *Papers on Language and Literature* 35 (Winter, 1999): 3-27. Argues that Bellow's realism is a search for truth, not the discovery of it. Discusses how Bellow deals with the question of whether the individual is isolated or a member of a human community. Contends that for Bellow the value of literature is the ceaseless search for truth in a world that promises truth but seldom provides it.

Halldorson, Stephanie S. *The Hero in Contemporary American Fiction: The Works of Saul Bellow and Don DeLillo*. New York: Palgrave Macmillan; 2007. Juxtaposition of the works of two major American writers who are rarely linked results in an insightful examination of the meaning of the hero and the antihero in modern culture.

Kiernan, Robert. *Saul Bellow*. New York: Continuum, 1989. Provides a useful chronology of Bellow's life and production. Traces the writer's development from *Dangling Man* to *More Die of Heartbreak*. Among the best books on Bellow for the general reader.

Leroux, Jean-Francois. "Exhausting Ennui: Bellow, Dostoevsky, and the Literature of Boredom." *College Literature* 35, no. 1 (Winter, 2008): 1-15. Explores the theme of ennui, a major element in Bellow's work, and the influence of the novels of Fyodor Dostoevski on Bellow's outlook.

Miller, Ruth. *Saul Bellow: A Biography of the Imagination*. New York: St. Martin's Press, 1991. Traces Bellow's travels, linking the author's life to his work. Contains useful appendices, a bibliography, a listing of interviews, and a table of contents from *The Noble Savage*, a journal edited by Bellow.

JUAN BENET

Born: Madrid, Spain; October 7, 1927
Died: Madrid, Spain; January, 1993
Also known as: Juan Benet Goitia

PRINCIPAL LONG FICTION

Volverás a Región, 1967 (*Return to Región*, 1985)
Una meditación, 1970 (*A Meditation*, 1982)
Una tumba, 1971 (novella)
Un viaje de invierno, 1972
La otra casa de Mazón, 1973
En el estado, 1977
Del pozo y del Numa: Un ensayo y una leyenda, 1978 (novella)
El aire de un crimen, 1980
Saúl ante Samuel, 1980
En la penumbra, 1983 (novella)
Herrumbrosas lanzas, I-VI, 1983
El caballero de Sajonia, 1991 (novella)

OTHER LITERARY FORMS

Although best known for his novels, Juan Benet (buh-NEHT) gained recognition as a superb essayist and short-story writer as well. His essays range in scope from music to linguistics, but his most perceptive writings are those on literary theory: *La inspiración y el estilo* (1965), *Puerta de tierra* (1970), *El ángel del Señor abandona a Tobías* (1976), and *La moviola de Eurípides* (1982). Above all, Benet articulates a literary posture that underscores the importance of style and enigma in the creation of fiction.

Benet's short stories have been collected in several volumes, including *Nunca llegarás a nada* (1961), *Cinco narraciones y dos fábulas* (1972), *Sub rosa* (1973), and *Trece fábulas y media* (1981). For the most part, the stories parallel his longer fiction in style and theme, though they are often more playful in tone. Benet also wrote four plays—*Max* (pb. 1953), *Agonía confutans* (1969), *Anastas: O, El origen de la constitución* (pb. 1970), and *Un caso de conciencia* (1970)—but none was performed during his lifetime with either critical or commercial success.

ACHIEVEMENTS

Juan Benet can perhaps be regarded most accurately as a novelist's novelist (or a critic's novelist) who wrote difficult works for a minority public. Indeed, his fiction rarely permits even the most experienced reader to feel at ease. After finishing a Benet work, one is left with the disquieting thought that one has missed the point or that there are many more points than one could possibly imagine—or, worse yet, that there is no point at all. Benet challenges his readers to rethink critical traditions that demand decisive meanings or that wrest from analysis unresolved ambiguities. His is a pluralistic fiction, a narrative of ideas forged with a style at once intricate and dense.

Despite the professed irritation of many critics with the difficult nature of his fiction, Benet gained recognition as one of Spain's most distinguished contemporary writers. He was one of the first novelists of the post-World War II era to break with neorealism in Spain and to offer a more subjective and experimental fiction in its place. Since 1969, when *A Meditation* was awarded the prestigious Premio Biblioteca Breve, Benet became one of the most prolific writers of his time. He continued to garner literary prizes (including the important Premio de la Crítica for *Herrumbrosas lanzas, I-VI*) and was invited to lecture throughout Western Europe and the United States. Perhaps more important, he began to have a profound influence on younger writers seeking new directions for the Spanish novel. Benet's fiction served as an imposing symbol of innovation and change in postwar Spain, and the unique vision that he brought to his craft propelled him to the forefront of his profession even as he remained aloof from the literary and critical establishment.

BIOGRAPHY

Juan Benet was born Juan Benet Goitia in Madrid on October 7, 1927, to Tomas Benet and Teresa Goitia. Benet was one of those extraordinary individuals who successfully cultivated his talents in two often conflicting pursuits: the scientific rigor of modern engineering and the aesthetic demands of creative writing. He was an avid reader in his youth and came to know intimately such master novelists as Stendhal, Gustave Flaubert, Fyodor Dostoevski, and Miguel de Cervantes. By the age of twenty, he was a regular participant in the literary *tertulias* of novelist Pío Baroja, one of the few modern Spanish writers whom Benet admired. He did not discover his true literary mentor (and his desire to be a writer), however, until 1947, when in a bookstore in Madrid he stumbled upon the work of William Faulkner. Faulkner's influence on Benet was decisive, and much of Benet's stylistic complexity, as well as his tragic vision of time and history, is rooted in Faulkner's mythical Yoknapatawpha County and the decadent American South that Faulkner meticulously created.

Benet graduated from the School of Engineering in Madrid in 1954 and served as a civil engineer and contractor throughout the Iberian Peninsula. Much of his early work, however, was centered in the northwestern provinces of León and Asturias, where he constructed roads and dams for the Spanish government. Isolated in the mountains for long periods of time, with only his work crew as company, Benet read classical philosophy and wrote fragments of fiction that would later appear in his novels. In 1963, while supervising construction of a dam on the Porma River, he began to revise a manuscript titled "El guarda," which four years later would become his first published novel, *Return to Región*. Over the next decade Benet successfully balanced his career as an engineer with his newly won fame as a novelist. His stature as an author continued to grow not only in Spain but also elsewhere in Europe and in the Americas.

In the last part of his life he devoted nearly all of his time to writing, even though he insisted in 1967, shortly after the publication of *Return to Región*, that he was an author only by avocation. Thus, Benet's engineering past must be viewed as crucial to his development as a novelist. His work in remote areas of Spain not only afforded him time to think and write but also

presented him with the physical and psychological ambience for his mythical Región, the fictional setting for nearly all of his long fiction and microcosm of postwar Spain.

ANALYSIS

Juan Benet falls chronologically into the group of writers commonly known as the Generation of '50. The realistic orientation and engagé approach to literature espoused by these writers (including Jesús Fernández Santos, Juan Goytisolo, Luis Goytisolo, and Rafael Sánchez Ferlosio) became the predominant literary force in Spain for nearly three decades following the Spanish Civil War (1936-1939). For the most part, novelists of this period defined their task as the verbal reproduction of a familiar reality, the shared world of reader and writer. The most important Spanish fiction written during the 1950's and early 1960's thus portrays everyday events in conventional novelistic forms.

Despite Benet's chronological affiliation with the writers of this period, he represents a direct antithesis to their fundamental literary canons. Indeed, his negative assessment of neorealistic fiction and his emphasis on style and enigma made him one of the most original

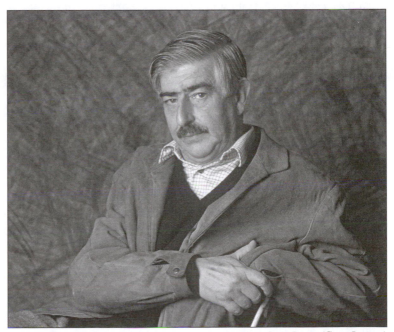

Juan Benet. (Getty Images)

Spanish writers of the twentieth century. His first collection of short stories, *Nunca llegarás a nada*, clearly transgresses the canons of social realism and foreshadows the tone, style, and thematic concerns that Benet develops more intensely in his long fiction. Rather than record the observable in his narrative, Benet seeks instead to probe beneath the surface of reality and explore what he terms "the zone of shadows." The abstruse and often inaccessible fiction that results has set Benet radically apart from the neorealism of the early postwar period as well as from the more experimental writing of the 1970's.

With the exception of *En el estado*, Benet set all of his novels in Región, a mythical region created in the fashion of Faulkner's Yoknapatawpha County or Gabriel García Márquez's Macondo. This private narrative world stands as the most explicit symbol of the ruin and despair that form the central motif of Benet's fiction. First created in 1961 in the short story "Baalbac, una mancha," Región did not achieve full realization until *Return to Región*, in which its geographic and enigmatic peculiarities are presented in detail. From one point of view, Región is the aggregate of characters, events, and social themes that, in Benet's view, constitute twentieth century Spanish society. More important than the social background, however, is the enigmatic reality of Región itself, portrayed by Benet on varying levels of complexity. On one hand, he depicts Región and the surrounding area with scientific precision. In fact, Región is described in such detail that the captivated reader searches to locate it on a map of Spain. Its flora and fauna, its landscape, and even its geological formation are portrayed with equal exactness of description, thus creating a reality that appears both authentic and identifiable in the physical world outside the text.

Benet establishes the real in Región in order to undermine it, however—to place in doubt its correspondence with the everyday world of observable reality. For the most part, he achieves this not explicitly, through use of the supernatural, but more subtly, by means of conflicting descriptions and recurrent suggestions of the unreal. In the first place, he portrays Región in a full state of decadence, surrounded by hostile landscapes and immersed in a threatening temperate zone. The entire area is a massive labyrinth of streams, valleys, forests, and deserts that have a life and meaning of their own. Throughout

his fiction, but most forcefully in *Return to Región*, Benet constructs an ambience in which he underscores the extreme and contrasting elements of the physical environment: desert/luxuriant vegetation; heat/cold; mountain/valley; rivers/dried-up streams; life/death. Nature serves to deter outsiders (known as intruders) from entering Región, and the unwary visitor often falls victim to the hostility of the area, never to be seen or heard from again.

Within the hostile physical world of Región, Benet creates a complementary reality characterized by the enigmatic and the inexplicable. For example, mysterious wildflowers grow only on the soil of tombs; strange sounds and lights terrify travelers at night; a mythical woodsman, Numa, guards the forest of Mantua and kills with a single shot any intruder who crosses its boundaries. On a rational level, Benet explains neither the origins nor the ultimate consequences of these and a host of similar elements that constitute the world of Región. They inhere in the murky area beneath the surface of reality and frequently defy logical explanation.

RETURN TO REGIÓN

Nearly all of Benet's long fiction is cast in a similar stylistic and thematic mold. Both the consistency and the complexity of his fiction can be shown most succinctly through a discussion of the Región trilogy, *Return to Región, A Meditation*, and *Un viaje de invierno*. Although the latter two works were published without delay and received immediate attention from critics, *Return to Región*, first novel of a then unknown writer, was sold to Ediciones Destino only after a long process of submissions and rejections. Symptomatic of the Spanish literary scene of the time, one of Benet's rejection letters assured him that because his novel lacked dialogue the public would not read it. *Return to Región* is now considered one of the most important Spanish novels of the postwar era.

What traditionally has been called plot does not exist in *Return to Región*. Instead, the novel consists of a complex framework of third-person narration and pseudo-dialogues between the two principal characters, Doctor Sebastián and Marré Gamallo. Daniel Sebastián is an aging doctor who has been living in solitude for nearly a quarter of a century in Región, with little else to do but drink, remember, and care for a child driven insane by the absence of his mother. One evening he is visited by a woman, Marré Gamallo, and throughout the night the two characters carry on a soliloquy-like dialogue in which they evoke their pasts and examine their destinies. During the Spanish Civil War, the woman was the lover of Sebastián's godson, Luis I. Timoner, and this love represented for her the only happiness in her lifetime. She has returned to Región in search of the fulfillment that she lost when Luis fled into the mountains near the end of the war. For his part, Doctor Sebastián awakens the phantasmagorical events of his past and remembers in particular his unfulfilled passion for María Timoner, Luis's mother. Through the memories of Sebastián and his visitor, and with the additional comments of the third-person narrator, the reader is able to reconstruct the fragmented history of the ruination of Región and its habitants.

Much of the narrative of *Return to Región* is devoted to the creation of a milieu that became the cornerstone of Benet's fiction: the pervasive desolation of Región. Within this atmosphere, the threatening physical reality of the area not only stands as a striking tableau of ruin but also permeates the inhabitants through a process of antipathetic osmosis: A direct relationship exists between the geographic location, climatic conditions, and physical ruin of the town and the spiritual malaise of Región's inhabitants. The moral dilapidation of Doctor Sebastián, for example, resembles the condition of his decaying house, and María Timoner is compared to the withered leaves of the black poplar trees. Both characters are submerged in the hellish atmosphere of the moribund province, with scant hope for redemption.

Like many twentieth century writers, Benet deliberately fragments his narratives into puzzlelike structures that do not yield their meaning to a passive reader. Although the chronological duration of *Return to Región* is only one night, the psychological time spans nearly four decades, from 1925 to an unspecified present during the 1960's. Hence the temporal focus continually shifts, and time periods are fused so that the past is felt not as distinct from the present but as included in it and permeating it. Benet achieves this linkage primarily through the uncertain crucible of memory. During the course of their conversation, Dr. Sebastián and Marré Gamallo recapture a complex past that is patently destructive and capa-

ble of overwhelming any sense of hope in the present or future. In essence, the two characters possess a past that "was not." That is to say, there exists little from their previous lives that can be remembered in a positive sense. They resemble the characters in Faulkner's *The Sound and the Fury* (1929), to whom nothing can happen because everything has already happened. As one of the children in Faulkner's novel declares: "I am not is, I am was." The elusive present and nonexistent future thus stand helpless before the past, which engenders stagnation and despair rather than growth and fulfillment. Benet's novel affirms the destructive power of time at every turn of the page, and his characters regress toward a past that exists only to remind them that they are condemned to a life of nothingness.

Throughout his numerous theoretical essays on literature, Benet argues that style is the central component of fiction. Once a writer has developed a highly personal and fluid style, he or she is able to transcend the purely informational aspects of the novel—plot, setting, characters—and produce work of more lasting value. For Benet, the world was an enigma that he sought to penetrate and subsequently portray in his fiction. On one level, therefore, language serves as a means of discovery: The more developed a writer's style, the more perceptive will be the discovery. It is important to point out, however, that for Benet discovery was merely a prerequisite of creation. The writer does not merely represent what he or she perceives but rather invents a singular fictional reality through the skillful use of language. Style therefore serves as an enabling device that reifies imagination and affords new ways of knowing the world.

Benet's style is perhaps best described as labyrinthine. His sentences are frequently the length of a full page or more and include parentheses, parentheses within parentheses, and subordinate clauses that unite to form a syntactical webwork. Benet's style is, in fact, a persistent maze of obstacles replete with complex obtrusions, delays, ambiguous interpolations, and confusions. When used by the third-person narrator of *Return to Región*, the baroque sentences increase the enigmatic nature of the particular reality at hand. The narrator eschews words and linguistic structures that portray a world imitative of our own; hence, everything associated with what he says becomes part of a rarefied atmosphere aimed at precluding complete and rational understanding. A similar method defines the nature of the characters. Essentially stylized creations, their dialogue is the antithesis of realistic speech patterns. The conversation of Doctor Sebastián and Marré Gamallo, for example, is indistinguishable from the discourse of the narrator. The reader thus grows confused as one narrative voice blends into another and is lost amid the complicated labyrinth of words. Much of Benet's style and technique, it seems, is part of a deliberate plan to withhold meaning from the reader. As a result, the world of Región remains ambiguous and mysterious within the language that creates and sustains its very existence.

A MEDITATION

A Meditation, Benet's second novel, displays many of the stylistic and philosophical traits evident in *Return to Región* but represents a more ambitious undertaking than the earlier work. Written in the first person, *A Meditation* is precisely what the title suggests: a meditation on the past that covers a time span of nearly fifty years, from 1920 to the late 1960's. Although the novel is composed of an artistically manipulated structure rather than a loosely formed stream of consciousness, the events and characters that are presented do not appear in a specific chronological arrangement. Instead, the unnamed narrator evokes a succession of fragmented memories that frequently remain vague and incomplete. The novel consists of one long paragraph, a feature that Benet stressed by submitting it to the publishers on a long, unbroken roll of paper rather than in the normal fashion of sequentially typed pages. The linear, uncut nature of the manuscript, however, by no means resembles the internal structure and content of the novel. In the manner of Marcel Proust and Faulkner, Benet's nameless narrator scrutinizes the past in an attempt to recover and understand the nature of his family, friends, and previous existence in the vicinity of Región.

The traditional use of plot, which in *Return to Región* is reduced to a minimum, regains significance in *A Meditation*. There is no dramatic development and subsequent denouement, however, and the sequence of events in the novel could easily be rearranged. As the narrator's mind wanders through the past, certain incidents and characters are summoned into consciousness and placed in view of the reader. No single event or character, however, is presented in its entirety during a specific moment in the novel. Instead, Benet creates a maze of interpenetrating segments that represent the narrator's voluntary and involuntary memory and the desire for a "remembrance of things past."

Benet's treatment of time and memory in *A Meditation* clearly resembles the temporal concerns evident in *Return to Región*. In both novels, time plays an integral part in the psychological and physical ruin of Región and its inhabitants and serves as a point of departure for philosophical speculation. In *A Meditation*, however, the reflections on time by the first-person narrator are actually reflections on the writing of the novel itself. Since the narrative consists of the recollection and subsequent expression of past events, any kind of temporal speculation must necessarily reflect on the construction of the work. Time and recollection, which form the intrinsic essence of the novel, thus play equal roles in both its form and its content.

While memory provides the means for examining or recovering the past, the whole notion of time—past, present, future—embodies a fundamental thematic preoccupation of *A Meditation*. In addition to its role in the structure of the narrative, which consists of the continual amassing of fragmented memories, time is treated concretely in the form of Cayetano Corral's clock and in abstraction by means of the narrator's numerous digressions. The mysterious clock, which has been in Cayetano's possession for several years, does not run. Although he has worked on the clock since he gained possession of it, he is less concerned with repairing its mechanical parts than with understanding its function: the making of time. He fails in his efforts because, as the entire novel aims to show, time is not measured by the rhythmic pulsating of the clock but by the mechanism of the human psyche. In all of Benet's fiction, time becomes above all that which destroys: The past is an absence that creates a void for the present as well as the future. Although the first-person narrator of *A Meditation* indeed evokes past events, and in the process creates a self as a product of that past, the novel affirms the way in which Benet's characters do not grow and change through time in a positive sense but rather remain stagnant within the ruin that they inevitably embody.

Benet's style in *A Meditation* is similar to that of *Re-*

turn to *Región* but more complex. In some respects, the novel resembles Marcel Proust's *À la recherche du temps perdu* (1913-1927; *Remembrance of Things Past*, 1922-1931), especially in narrative structure and technique. The influence of Faulkner, however, remains predominant in Benet's complex use of language. Like the American author, Benet frequently amasses words in a manner that has caused some critics to charge him with prolixity. Many of Benet's sentences cover several pages, and it becomes a difficult task to remain attentive to the assorted ideas contained in one of the narrator's thought patterns. On the other hand, Benet's peripatetic style is crucial to the content and structure of the novel and to the complicated way in which he formulates his meditation. Benet's sentences are perhaps best defined as saturated solutions: Images and topics are juxtaposed through the transcendent life of the mind, which continually explores obscure and enigmatic elements of reality.

One of the recurrent stylistic features of Benet's fiction, and one particularly important in *A Meditation*, is the presentation of contradictory suggestions within a single context. Just as William Faulkner employs oxymoronic or near-oxymoronic terms in many of his novels, so Benet utilizes contradictory statements to keep his narratives in a state of flux or suspension, thus inspiring uncertainty and confusion in the reader. The oxymoronic descriptions that Benet employs in *A Meditation* are constructed by the simultaneous suggestions of disparate or contrasting elements and therefore create a sharp polarity or tension. Both objects and characters are portrayed in this fashion and form part of the essential paradox of the novel. On one hand, Benet achieves a kind of order and coherence by virtue of the clear and sharp antitheses that the contrasts involve. On the other hand, however, such descriptions create disorder and incoherence by virtue of their qualities of irresolution and contradiction. Hence, the reality of *A Meditation*, evoked through the uncertain authority of memory and conveyed by the uninhibited flow of language, is the enigmatic domain of the human psyche.

UN VIAJE DE INVIERNO

Many critics consider *Un viaje de invierno* (a winter journey), the final novel of the Región trilogy, to be Benet's most abstruse piece of fiction. Once again, the reader must penetrate a world created by marathon sentences, a complex framework of recurring images, an ambiguous temporal structure, and an interrelated series of events that remain essentially unexplained in terms of motivation and ultimate resolution. Although *Un viaje de invierno* represents Benet's maximum effort to eliminate plot as an integral part of the novel, most of the narrative revolves around the uncertain configuration of a fiesta. Demetria holds the affair each year, ostensibly to honor the return of her daughter Coré, who annually spends six months away from Región; the novel begins with the writing and mailing of the invitations and ends with a vague description of the party. Any attempt, however, to comprehend the complex reasons for holding the celebration or to untangle the temporal confusion that surrounds the event encounters intransigent opposition. Demetria is unable to determine the number of guests she has invited, and she does not know how many attend, as she has never been to the party herself. Coré does not appear in the narrative, and the party is painted in such mysterious, rarefied tones that one is only able to guess at its implied meaning: for Demetria, an opportunity to exercise her will; for the guests, an ephemeral mitigation of their loneliness and a flight from the pain of daily life.

Arturo, the other principal figure of the novel, works as Demetria's servant. He has apparently (although we do not know for certain) worked as a handyman at other homes in the area, and each change of job brings him closer to the source of the Torce River. Arturo himself knows little about his past, except that for nearly all of his life he has labored on the farms along the Torce valley and has slowly journeyed up the river. It is a "winter's journey," as the title of the novel indicates, one that seems to lead him inescapably toward death, yet the impetus for the journey is shrouded in mystery and borders on the magical. Arturo's future was determined early in his youth when one evening he listened to a waltz (*el vals K*) in the music conservatory where his mother worked as a cleaning woman. In the same way that Doctor Sebastián in *Return to Región* is condemned to suffer in Región after reading his future on the telegraph wheel, Arturo is destined to seek meaning in life at the head of the Torce River. The meaning that he seeks, of course, is correlated with death, toward which he inevitably and mysteriously journeys. This fatalistic destiny represents the future of nearly all of Benet's characters and inheres in the atmosphere of ruin and anguish that pervades his fiction.

As in his first two novels, Benet's style in *Un viaje de invierno* creates an uneasy and portentous mood. His style in the latter work, however, seems based on a more studied attempt to avoid translating sensation into perception. A cognitive knowledge of something, be it of a character, an object, or a particular ambience, is of secondary importance to the pure consciousness of it. In this sense, Benet can be viewed as an idealist: Because one's consciousness seizes nothing but manifestations, reality is illusory. Indeed, when reading *Un viaje de invierno*, the reader senses that he or she is before the dream of reality instead of reality itself. For example, neither Coré nor Amat (Demetria's absent husband) ever appears as a concrete being in the novel; rather, both exist only as manifestations of Demetria's nostalgic memory. Demetria herself, whose existence is never seriously doubted, embodies Benet's predilection for the intangible and the ethereal. She is known to the inhabitants of Región by more than one name (Demetria, Nemesia, Obscura), and Benet never ascribes concrete physical characteristics to her. Her hand, for example, is *impalpable*, and she speaks words that sound without resonance. Her voice has no pitch or tone, and when she touches Arturo, he senses, yet does not feel, her hands. In short, Benet's method of portraying Demetria and the other figures of the novel points to the notion that we can discern only the image of something and not the thing itself.

The ethereal essence of his characters, however, in no way alleviates their existential despair. As in his previous novels, this despair in large part stems from the oppressive power of time. One is never aware in *Un viaje de invierno* of a pure present, and a specific past is not very often exclusively defined. In fact, Benet seems purposely to create a timeless vision of reality in which past and present are interfused to form a vague series of occurrences that defy order and reason. This notion of temporal uncertainty bears directly on the title of the novel as well as one of its central motifs: the journey. Nearly all of the characters set out on journeys—to Central Europe, to the Torce River, to town, and so on. In one fashion or another, however, all of the trips revolve around the fiesta. Because the party cannot be located in time by any of the characters, it becomes clear that they undertake their journeys in order to exist in a temporal vacuum where past, present, and future do not possess any reality.

Like the characters in the earlier novels of the trilogy, however, the characters of *Un viaje de invierno* are trapped by the past, even as time moves forward and passes them by. If life consists of a continuation of the past into an ever-growing and expanding present, then the characters of *Un viaje de invierno* can have no hope for the future. Their lives are defined by a temporal vortex in which being is divorced from the linear progression of time. Although the fiesta represents for the characters an opportunity to grasp Martin Heidegger's "silent strength of the possible," they are ensnared by stagnation, where meaning remains elusive. This is the ultimate message of Benet's fiction, one that is affirmed even as he conceals it in the contradictory and enigmatic world of Región.

David K. Herzberger

OTHER MAJOR WORKS

SHORT FICTION: *Nunca llegarás a nada*, 1961; *Cinco narraciones y dos fábulas*, 1972; *Sub rosa*, 1973; *Cuentos completos*, 1977; *Trece fábulas y media*, 1981; *Una tumba, y otros relatos*, 1981.

PLAYS: *Max*, pb. 1953; *Agonía confutans*, pb. 1969; *Teatro*, 1970 (includes *Anastas: O, El origen de la constitución, Agonía confutans*, and *Un caso de conciencia*).

NONFICTION: *La inspiración y el estilo*, 1965; *Puerta de tierra*, 1970; *El ángel del Señor abandona a Tobías*, 1976; *En ciernes*, 1976; *¿Qué fue la guerra civil?*, 1976; *La moviola de Eurípides*, 1982; *Artículos, 1962-1977*, 1983; *Sobre la incertidumbre*, 1983; *Cartografía personal*, 1997; *La sombra de la guerra*, 1999.

TRANSLATION: *A este lado del Paraíso*, 1968 (of F. Scott Fitzgerald's novel *This Side of Paradise*).

BIBLIOGRAPHY

Cabrera, Vincente. *Juan Benet*. Boston: Twayne, 1984. Good introductory study examines Benet's works as a whole, including his novels.

Compitello, Malcolm Alan. *Ordering the Evidence: "Volverás a Región" and Civil War Fiction*. Barcelona: Puvill Libros, 1983. Illuminates the historical aspects of *Return to Región* in terms of the Spanish Civil War.

Ferrán, Ofelia. *Working Through Memory: Writing and Remembrance in Contemporary Spanish Narrative*. Lewisburg, Pa.: Bucknell University Press, 2007. Benet's novels are among those analyzed in a study of Spanish literature published from the 1960's through the 1990's. Demonstrates how these novels explore present memory as a way for Spaniards to recover from the traumatic and repressive past of the Spanish Civil War and the regime of Francisco Franco.

Herzberger, David K. *The Novelistic World of Juan Benet*. Clear Creek, Ind.: American Hispanist, 1976. Analyzes Benet's novels by examining them in the light of the author's own theories.

Manteiga, Roberto C., David K. Herzberger, and Malcolm Alan Compitello, eds. *Critical Approaches to the Writings of Juan Benet*. Hanover, N.H.: University Press of New England, 1984. Collection of critical essays on Benet's work includes a foreword in which the author explains his works in an international context.

Margenot, John B., III. "Character Questing in Juan Benet's *Volverás a Región*." *Modern Language Studies* 19, no. 3 (Summer, 1989): 52-62. Analyzes the novel in terms of a mythical quest by its characters, focusing on the characters' physical movement to Región as well as their psychological exploration through time and memory.

_____, ed. *Juan Benet: A Critical Reappraisal of His Fiction*. West Cornwall, Conn.: Locust Hill Press, 1997. Collection of essays aims to reevaluate Benet's work from the perspective of the late twentieth century. Includes bibliographical references and index.

Rodríguez, Joe. "Reason, Desire, and Language: Reading Juan Benet's Trilogy as a Relational Totality." *Bulletin of Spanish Studies* 83, no. 2 (March, 2006): 241-263. Focuses on three of Benet's novels—*Return to Región, A Meditation*, and *Un viaje de invierno*—describing their narrative techniques and their relationships to one another.

Turner, Harriet, and Adelaida López de Martínez, eds. *The Cambridge Companion to the Spanish Novel: From 1600 to the Present*. New York: Cambridge University Press, 2003. Collection of essays tracing the development of the Spanish novel includes a discussion of Benet's novels *Return to Región, A Meditation*, and *Saúl ante Samuel*, among others.

Walkowiak, Marzena M. *A Study of the Narrative Structure of "Una meditación" by Juan Benet*. Lewiston, N.Y.: Edwin Mellen Press, 2000. In-depth study of *A Meditation* explains the novel's complex world by exploring its narrative structure and plot, the role of its characters, the narrator's point of view, and its treatment of time and space. Places the book within the context of post-World War II political and literary developments within Spain.

ARNOLD BENNETT

Born: Shelton, near Hanley, England; May 27, 1867
Died: London, England; March 27, 1931
Also known as: Enoch Arnold Bennett; Sal Volatile

PRINCIPAL LONG FICTION

A Man from the North, 1898
Anna of the Five Towns, 1902
The Grand Babylon Hotel, 1902 (also known as *T. Racksole and Daughter*)
The Gates of Wrath, 1903
Leonora, 1903
A Great Man, 1904
Teresa of Watling Street, 1904
Sacred and Profane Love, 1905 (also known as *The Book of Carlotta*)
Hugo, 1906
The Sinews of War, 1906 (with Eden Phillpotts; also known as *Doubloons*)
Whom God Hath Joined, 1906
The City of Pleasure, 1907
The Ghost, 1907
Buried Alive, 1908

The Old Wives' Tale, 1908
The Statue, 1908 (with Phillpotts)
The Glimpse, 1909
Clayhanger, 1910
Helen with the High Hand, 1910
The Card, 1911 (also known as *Denry the Audacious*)
Hilda Lessways, 1911
The Regent, 1913 (also known as *The Old Adam*)
The Price of Love, 1914
These Twain, 1915
The Lion's Share, 1916
The Pretty Lady, 1918
The Roll-Call, 1918
Lilian, 1922
Mr. Prohack, 1922
Riceyman Steps, 1923
Elsie and the Child, 1924
Lord Raingo, 1926
The Vanguard, 1927 (also known as *The Strange Vanguard*, 1928)
Accident, 1928
Piccadilly, 1929
Imperial Palace, 1930
Venus Rising from the Sea, 1931

OTHER LITERARY FORMS

In addition to fifteen major novels, Arnold Bennett published thirty-three novels generally considered potboilers by his critics. Some of these Bennett himself regarded as serious works; others he variously called fantasias, frolics, melodramas, or adventures. His total published work exceeds eighty volumes, including eight collections of short stories, sixteen plays, six collections of essays, eight volumes of literary criticism, three volumes of letters, six travelogues, and volumes of autobiography, journals, and reviews, as well as miscellaneous short articles, introductions, pamphlets, "pocket philosophies," and a few poems. Much of the content of his journals has never been published. In addition, Bennett collaborated in the production of five films and operas, three of which were adapted from his plays and novels. Four of his plays and novels have been adapted for film by other screenwriters, and two of his novels have been adapted for the stage.

ACHIEVEMENTS

Although Arnold Bennett won only one major literary award, the James Tait Black Memorial Prize for *Riceyman Steps*, his contribution to the history of the novel exceeds that accomplishment. Bennett's early novels played an important role in the transition from the Victorian to the modern novel. A somewhat younger contemporary of Thomas Hardy, Henry James, and Joseph Conrad, Bennett helped to displace the "loose, baggy" Victorian novel and to develop the realistic movement in England. With fine detail he portrayed the industrial Five Towns, his fictional version of the six towns of pottery manufacturing in England's Staffordshire County.

His early career was strongly influenced by the aestheticism in form and language found in works by Gustave Flaubert, Guy de Maupassant, and Ivan Turgenev, and he admired the naturalism of Honoré de Balzac, Émile Zola, and Edmond de Goncourt and Jules de Goncourt. Later, however, he rejected what he called the "crudities and . . . morsels of available misery" of naturalism and, while retaining an interest in form and beauty, he came to feel that aesthetics alone is an empty literary goal and that the novelist must combine "divine compassion," believability, and the creation of character with the "artistic shapely presentation of truth" and the discovery of "beauty, which is always hidden." With these aims in mind, he chose as the subject of his best works that which is beautiful and remarkable about the lives of unremarkable, middle-class people.

Although his novels rarely sold well enough to earn him a living, Bennett's best novels were highly regarded by critics and fellow authors. He carried on a correspondence of mutual encouragement and criticism with Conrad and H. G. Wells; some of these letters have been published. Conrad, a master of style, wrote: "I am . . . fascinated by your expression, by the ease of your realization, the force and delicacy of your phrases." Despite their acclaim for Bennett's best work, however, even Bennett's admirers regretted his propensity to write potboilers for money.

Because of the volume of his work, Bennett is remembered today as a novelist, but in his lifetime his income derived from his equally prodigious output of plays and journalism; his "pocket philosophies" and critical reviews also won him enormous public prestige. During the 1920's he was virtually the arbiter of literary taste, a reviewer who could make or break a book's sales or a newcomer's career. He was among the first to praise the literary merits of such controversial newcomers as D. H. Lawrence, T. S. Eliot, William Faulkner, Virginia Woolf, and James Joyce. Bennett regarded himself less a novelist than a professional writer who should be able to, and did, undertake any genre with competence and craftsmanship. (The exception was poetry; he never wrote poetry to meet his own standards.) His reputation suffered in the latter part of his career for those very qualities, which too often fell short of genius and inspiration. He did reach the level of greatness occasionally, however, and his literary reputation is firmly established with the inclusion of *The Old Wives' Tale* in most lists of the great English novels.

BIOGRAPHY

Enoch Arnold Bennett was born on May 27, 1867, in Shelton, Staffordshire County, England, near the six towns that constitute the Potteries region in central England, the scene of much of Bennett's early work. His father, Enoch Bennett, was successively a potter, a draper, a pawnbroker, and, eventually, through hard work and study, a solicitor. Bennett attended the local schools, where he passed the examination for Cambridge University. He did not attend college, however, because his autocratic father kept him at home as clerk in the solicitor's office.

As a means of escape from the grime and provincialism of the Potteries district, Bennett began writing for the *Staffordshire Sentinel* and studying shorthand. The latter skill enabled him to become a clerk with a London law firm in 1888. In London, he set about seriously to learn to write. He moved to Chelsea in 1891 to live with the Frederick Marriott family, in whose household he was introduced to the larger world of the arts. His first work published in London was a prizewinning parody for a competition in *Tit-Bits* in 1893; this work was followed by a short story in *The Yellow Book* and, in 1898, his first novel, *A Man from the North*. He became the assistant editor and later the editor of the magazine *Woman*, writing reviews pseudonymously as "Barbara," a gossip and advice column as "Marjorie," and short sto-

ries as "Sal Volatile." It is generally thought that this experience provided Bennett with good background for female characterization.

As he became better known as a journalist, Bennett began writing reviews for *The Academy* and giving private lessons in journalism. In 1900, his journalistic income allowed him to establish a home at Trinity Hall Farm, Hockliffe, in Bedfordshire. He brought his family to Hockliffe after his father had been disabled by softening of the brain, the condition that eventually killed him. Bennett wrote prodigiously there, producing not only his admired *Anna of the Five Towns* but also popular potboilers and journalism, including the anonymous "Savoir-Faire Papers" and "Novelist's Log-Book" series for *T. P.'s Weekly*. This production financed some long-desired travel and a move to Paris in 1903.

Bennett lived in France for eight years, some of the busiest and happiest of his life. Shortly after his arrival, he observed a fat, fussy woman who inspired the thought that "she has been young and slim once," a thought that lingered in his mind for five years and inspired his masterwork, *The Old Wives' Tale*. Meanwhile, he continued writing for newspapers and magazines, including the first of his series "Books and Persons," written under the nom de plume "Jacob Tonson" for *The New Age*. Between 1903 and 1907 he also wrote ten novels. In 1907, he married Marguerite Soulié, an aspiring actor who had worked as his part-time secretary. From the beginning of the marriage, it was evident that the two were incompatible, but Marguerite did provide him with an atmosphere conducive to his undertaking the novel that had germinated for so long and that he felt beforehand would be a masterpiece. He determined that *The Old Wives' Tale* should "do one better than" Guy de Maupassant's *Une Vie* (1883; *A Woman's Life*, 1888), and his careful crafting of the book was recognized by critics, who immediately acclaimed it as a modern classic.

Before Bennett moved back to England in 1913, he wrote six more novels, three of which are among his best: *Clayhanger, The Card*, and *Hilda Lessways*. In 1911, he traveled in the United States, where his books were selling well and were highly respected. After that tour, he moved to the country estate Comarques at Thorpe-le-Soken, Essex, where he had access to the harbor for a yacht, his means of gaining what relaxation he could. The yacht was important to Bennett because he had suffered since youth from a variety of ailments, mostly resulting from his high-strung temperament. He had a serious stammer or speech paralysis, which exhausted him in speaking; he also had compulsive personal habits and suffered from a liver ailment and chronic enteritis, which restricted his diet and caused great discomfort when he ate incautiously. As he grew older, he suffered increasingly from excruciating neuralgia, headaches, and insomnia, almost without relief near the end of his life.

Except for the yacht, his recreation was to write; he probably wrote his light works as a relief from the tension of the serious novels, yet he demanded good style from himself even for them. His craftsmanship was conscious and intense, and his drive to produce great quantity while still maintaining quality undoubtedly sapped his strength, both physically and psychologically, and contributed to his death at the age of sixty-three.

Bennett's physical maladies were probably exacerbated by World War I and the collapse of his marriage. Although he continued his usual pace of writing during the war—five more novels in the period 1914 through 1919—much of his energy was spent in patriotic activities, ranging from entertaining soldiers to frontline journalism. From May 9, 1918, until the end of the war, he served as volunteer director of British propaganda in France. He refused knighthood for his services.

After the war, he tried to restore his depleted finances by writing plays, which had been more remunerative than novels, but the later ones were unsuccessful. In 1921, he and his wife separated. He gave her a settlement so generous that for the rest of his life he was under pressure to publish and sell his writing. Contemporary critics believed that these years of low-novel production marked the end of his creativity. Bennett surprised his critics, however, with *Riceyman Steps*, which was critically acclaimed and was awarded the James Tait Black Memorial Prize. This was followed by *Lord Raingo* and *Imperial Palace* as well as by six less distinguished novels and one unfinished at his death. Bennett's creative resurgence may have resulted in part from his relationship with Dorothy Cheston, who bore his only child, Virginia, in 1926. His journalistic career had never waned, and in the 1920's he continued his "Books and Persons" series in the *Evening Standard*, with a prestige that influenced the reading public and allowed him to promote the careers of many young authors. Bennett's health was steadily deteriorating, however, and in March, 1931, he died in his Chiltern Court flat from typhoid fever.

ANALYSIS

As a self-designated professional author, Arnold Bennett not only wrote an extraordinary quantity in a great variety of genres but also created a broad range of themes and characters. It is difficult to detect a common approach or theme in a corpus of forty-eight novels that include

Arnold Bennett. (Library of Congress)

fantasy, realism, romance, naturalism, satire, symbolism, comedy, tragedy, melodrama, Freudian psychology, allegory, economics, regionalism, cosmopolitanism, politics, medicine, and war. Nevertheless, in spite of this diversity, Bennett is generally esteemed for his realistic novels, which are considered his serious work. In most, if not all, of these fifteen novels, certain related themes recur, rising from the author's youthful experiences of growing up in Burslem under the domination of his father. His desire to escape the intellectual, aesthetic, and spiritual stultification of his Burslem environment led Bennett to examine a cluster of themes related to escape: rebellion against the ties of the home conflicting with love for one's roots, aspiration versus complacence and philistinism, fear of failure to escape and fear of failure after escape, and the problem of coping with success if it comes. Another cluster of themes relates to his conflict with his father and the shock of his father's debilitating illness and death: the generation gap, emotional repression by dominating parents, the cyclical influence of parents on their children, a soul parent who vies in influence with the natural parent, degeneration and illness, the pathos of decrepitude in old age, and awe at the purpose or purposelessness of life.

A MAN FROM THE NORTH

A Man from the North, Bennett's first novel, includes the themes of aspiration, emotional repression, the soul parent, illness and death, and failure after escape. It is the story of Richard Larch, an aspiring writer from the Potteries, who goes to London to experience the greater intellectual and moral freedom of a cosmopolis. There he meets his soul father, Mr. Aked, a journalist and failed novelist who introduces Larch to the drama—the "tragedy"—of ordinary lives. Aked, however, is an unsuccessful guide; he dies. Larch is also unable to succeed; he eventually marries a woman he does not love and settles down to the sort of life Aked had described. It is the story of what Bennett himself might have been if he had not succeeded after leaving Burslem.

ANNA OF THE FIVE TOWNS

Anna of the Five Towns, in contrast, is the story of the failure to escape. Anna is repressed by her overbearing and miserly father; under the influence of her soul mother, Mrs. Sutton, she learns to aspire to a few amenities, such as new clothes for her wedding, but these as-

pirations come too late to change her life significantly. Accepting the values of the community rather than escaping them, she marries Henry Mynors, her more prosperous suitor, rather than Willie Price, the man she loves in her own way.

Although the themes of *A Man from the North* and *Anna of the Five Towns* are similar, they differ in that Anna stays and copes with her environment with some success. She does not escape Bursley (Bennett's fictional name for Burslem), but she escapes her father's control and improves her perceptions of beauty and human relationships to some degree. The books also differ in that *A Man from the North* presents an unrelentingly grim memory of Burslem. Later, however, Bennett read George Moore's *A Mummer's Wife* (1884), and its section on Burslem showed him that "beauty, which is always hidden," could be found in the lives of the townspeople and in art expressing those lives. Bennett thus returned to the locale for *Anna of the Five Towns*, and although the portrayal is still grim, Anna's life has tragic beauty. Anna rebels against the ties of home, but she also has some love for her roots there, in the person of Willie Price.

THE OLD WIVES' TALE

Between *Anna of the Five Towns* and *The Old Wives' Tale*, Bennett wrote eleven minor novels, some of which were serious and some not, but each taught him something that contributed to the greatness of *The Old Wives' Tale*. Several of them were light comedies, and in writing these Bennett developed the assured comic touch that marks even his serious novels. Three of them were Five Towns novels about female characters from various segments of Bursley society; in these he developed those skills in characterizing women that were so admired in his finest novels. These skills were honed during his time in France, where Bennett learned a great deal about the literary presentation of sex. During these years, Bennett said, he learned more about life than he had ever known before.

When Bennett was ready to write his masterpiece, *The Old Wives' Tale*, he had reached full artistic maturity and was at the height of his literary power. He had published one critically acclaimed novel and several others that had allowed him to improve his characterization, especially of women, to temper his realism with humor, and to perfect his themes in various plots. His dislike of Burslem's grime and provincialism had been balanced by compassion for the town's inhabitants and awareness of what beauty and aspiration could be found there. His personal involvement in the town had been modified by his experiences in London and Paris, so that he could be objective about the sources of his material. This balance of technique and emotion is reflected in the structure of *The Old Wives' Tale*. The novel counterpoints the lives of two sisters, Constance and Sophia Baines, the first of whom stays in Bursley while the second leaves but later returns. Their stories parallel not only each other but also those of preceding and succeeding generations. In fact, the first section of the book is subtitled "Mrs. Baines" (Constance and Sophia's mother).

In section one, *The Old Wives' Tale* takes up in midcareer one generation's old wife, with a husband so ill that the wife is running his draper's business and rearing two young daughters. As the girls grow up, Mrs. Baines finds them increasingly hard to handle. During a town festival in which an elephant has to be executed for killing a spectator, Mr. Baines dies. Shortly afterward, Sophia elopes with Gerald Scales, a traveling salesman, and Constance marries Samuel Povey, the former shop assistant, whom Mrs. Baines considers "beneath" her. When Samuel and Constance take over the business, introducing progressive marketing methods, Mrs. Baines retires to live with her elder sister and dies soon thereafter. The story of Mrs. Baines, then, is the end of the life of a woman who "was young and slim once," although she is not depicted so and that part of her life is understood only by later comparison with the stories of her daughters.

The cycle of Mrs. Baines continues with Constance, who represents the person who stays in Bursley, held by the roots of the past. As Mrs. Baines's successor, Constance marries a husband whose aspiration is to improve, not to leave, Bursley, and they run the business with a combination of youthful progressiveness and family tradition. Constance and Samuel have a son, Cyril. After a scandal in which Samuel's cousin is executed for murdering his alcoholic wife, Samuel dies. Constance continues the business for a while, unresponsive to further progressive business practices, and spoils her son until he becomes hard for her to manage. She is finally forced

to retire from business by changes in the business structure of Bursley, and Cyril escapes from her and Bursley to London to study art. As a result, Constance comes to depend emotionally on Cyril's cousin, Dick.

Sophia, the rebel against Bursley, finds a soul mother in the schoolteacher who introduces her to a world of wider intellectual aspiration. In her eagerness to experience more than Bursley offers, however, she elopes with Gerald, a salesman, who represents sophistication and romance to her. They go to France, where they squander their money and slip into mutual disillusionment and recrimination. After observing the public execution of the murderer of a courtesan, Sophia becomes ill, and Gerald abandons her. She eventually acquires a boardinghouse in Paris, where she supports several dependents and survives the Siege of Paris through single-minded hoarding and hard work. She becomes a reclusive fixture on her street, much like Constance on her square in Bursley. When she becomes ill and the business becomes hard for her to manage, she sells it and returns to Bursley to grow old and die.

Each daughter's life recapitulates Mrs. Baines's life in certain respects. Each marries, loses a husband, succors children or other dependents, runs a business, gradually loses control over her life (the change marked in each case by a symbolic execution), loses health and strength, and retires to die as a burdensome old woman like the one Bennett saw in the Paris restaurant. Further, although they are not women, the two Povey young men, Cyril and his cousin Dick, recapitulate the early years of Sophia and Constance: Cyril, the rebel who leaves Bursley but does not succeed; and Dick, the stay-at-home progressive idealist. At the end, Dick is engaged to marry a slim, young counterpart to Constance, who will no doubt carry on the cycle.

The thematic repetitions found in *The Old Wives' Tale* are not so obvious as the preceding discussion may make them appear, of course; variations of individual character allow the reader a sense of more difference than similarity. The variations also mark a further step in Bennett's use of his themes. Constance and Sophia are not so warped by Bursley as is Anna in *Anna of the Five Towns*; in fact, Sophia, who escapes, is warped more than Constance, who stays. Both derive strength from their roots, and while neither can be said to escape or to achieve happiness or grace in living, both transcend Bursley more successfully than do other townspeople. The theme of their decrepitude in old age is a separate one, also used in some of Bennett's other novels, but not related to the escape and success themes. The Baineses are grouped in other Five Towns stories with those who succeed on Bursley's terms. Beginning in 1906 in *Whom God Hath Joined*, in the collection of short stories *The Matador of the Five Towns* (1912), and in *The Old Wives' Tale*, Bennett placed a growing emphasis on those members of Burslem society who have some education, culture, and sophistication. Perhaps Bennett had been reassured by his personal success that his childhood in Burslem could be accepted.

CLAYHANGER

Whether or not it is true that Bennett had come to accept his past, it is certainly true that his next serious book, *Clayhanger*, was his most nearly autobiographical. After the completion of the trilogy of which *Clayhanger* was the first volume, Bennett turned from the Five Towns to London as the setting for his novels. The Clayhanger trilogy is the story of a man who at first is defeated in his desire to escape Bursley. Having been defeated, however, he learns from his soul father to rise above Bursley's philistinism. Over the years, he breaks one after another of his bonds to Bursley until he has succeeded in escaping intellectually, and, eventually, he completely abandons the Five Towns.

Much of this story occurs in the third volume of the trilogy, *These Twain. Clayhanger* itself is the story of the generational conflict between Edwin Clayhanger and his father, Darius. The conflict is similar to the one between Anna and her father in *Anna of the Five Towns* and that between Sophia and Mrs. Baines in *The Old Wives' Tale*, but in *Clayhanger* it is much more intense and more acutely observed. Edwin is sensitively introduced in the first two chapters; he has within him "a flame . . . like an altar-fire," a passion "to exhaust himself in doing his best." He is rebelling against his father, whose highest aspiration for his son is to have him take over his printing business.

The advancement of the theme in *Clayhanger* over its treatment in the earlier novels is that the generational conflict is presented sympathetically on both sides. In chapters 3 and 4, Darius is portrayed as sensitively as

Edwin has been previously. In an intensely moving chapter, his childhood of promise, stifled at seven years of age by poverty and abusive child labor, is described. Because Darius as a "man of nine" was unable to "keep the family," they were sent to the poorhouse. They were rescued from this degradation by Darius's Sunday school teacher (his soul father), who had recognized the boy's promise and who secured Darius a decent job as a printer's devil. This background of deprivation and emotional sterility prevents Darius from expressing his softer emotions, such as his love for Edwin. The reader thoroughly empathizes with Darius's total dedication to the business he built and by which he supports his family; it is no wonder that he can conceive nothing nobler for Edwin than to carry on this decent business. Because Darius can never discuss his traumatic childhood experiences, Edwin never understands him any more than Darius understands Edwin.

In his desire to hold on to his son and keep him in the family business, Darius simply ignores and overrides Edwin's inchoate talent for architecture. Later, he uses Edwin's financial dependence to squelch the young man's desire to marry Hilda Lessways, whom Edwin has met through the architect Osmond Orgreave. Although Edwin resents his father's domination, he cannot openly rebel; he feels inadequate before his father's dominance, and he looks forward to the day when he will have his vengeance. That day comes when Darius becomes ill with softening of the brain, the same ailment that killed Bennett's own father. The progression of the illness and Edwin's emotions of triumph, irritation, and compassion are exquisitely detailed. Even after Darius's death, however, Edwin is not free from his father's presence, for he becomes increasingly like his father, learning to take pride in the business and tyrannizing his sisters and Hilda, with whom he is reconciled at the end of the book. *Clayhanger* thus concludes with the apparent defeat of aspiration by the cycle of parental influence. The hope of eventual success is raised, however, by the death of Darius, that primary symbol of Bursley repression, and the return of Hilda, the symbol of aspiration.

HILDA LESSWAYS

In *Hilda Lessways*, the second book of the trilogy, Bennett picks up Hilda's parallel story of generational conflict with her mother and cultural conflict with

Turnhill, another of the Five Towns. Hilda's story is far less compelling than Edwin's, however, and adds little to the plot development. More important, its structure repeats what Bennett did successfully in *The Old Wives' Tale*: It contrasts two efforts to cope with Bursley, which provide for a double perspective on the problem, and then brings them together for the denouement made possible by that combined perspective. The double perspective also allows Bennett to maintain his characteristic objectivity and touch of humor.

THESE TWAIN

These Twain is the last Five Towns novel; it presents the marriage of Edwin and Hilda. Through a series of adjustments and small victories, the two are able to achieve social success in the Five Towns, which allows them to wean themselves emotionally from the Potteries and leave forever. The *Clayhanger* trilogy thus deals with escape and success rather than some aspect of failure as in the earlier novels.

In changing his fictional settings from Bursley to London or the Continent, Bennett also extended his themes from success or failure in escaping poverty and provincialism to success or failure in handling the accomplished escape. Perhaps that is another reason, aside from the reasons usually offered, for Bennett's long period of low productivity and substandard potboilers from 1915 to 1922. Between *Anna of the Five Towns* and *The Old Wives' Tale*, Bennett had a similar period of low-quality work during which he perfected skills that made the Five Towns novels great. Similarly, in his postwar characters Audrey Moze, George Cannon, G. J. Hoape, Lilian Share, and Mr. Prohack, Bennett experimented with stories of people who must cope with financial or social responsibilities for which they may have been poorly prepared. Also in these stories he experimented more boldly with varieties of sexual relationships: in *The Lion's Share*, implied lesbian sexuality; in *The Pretty Lady*, prostitution; in *Lilian*, the keeping of a mistress. Furthermore, although these next qualities do not show up clearly in the low-quality work of this period, the use of symbols and psychological insight must have been developing in Bennett's mind. These qualities emerge rather suddenly and very effectively in the novels beginning with *Riceyman Steps*. They may account for some of the high acclaim that novel received after the period of

reorientation, but the adapted themes were perfected by 1923 as well.

RICEYMAN STEPS

The themes in *Riceyman Steps* are variations on those of the Five Towns novels, not departures, which might seem necessary to a metropolitan setting. The decayed and grimy industrial area of Clerkenwell is in many respects Bursley resituated in London. Henry Earlforward, the miser, represents Bursley's industrial materialism. Henry, like Edwin Clayhanger, has succeeded in that environment; he has a well-respected bookstore that offers him financial self-sufficiency. Unlike Edwin, however, Henry's complacent rootedness to Clerkenwell progressively cuts him off from grace, beauty, then love, and finally even life. His wife, Violet, also has financial security, but because she fears the loss of her success, she has become almost as miserly as he.

Both Henry and Violet are described as sensual; Henry's rich red lips are mentioned several times, and Violet, formerly a widow, wears red flowers in her hat. Money, however, is the chief object of their eroticism. Henry's miserliness is his passion, and he gives Violet her own safe as a wedding gift. Violet becomes "liquid with acquiescence" after seeing the hoarded disorder of Henry's house, and she urges him to bed after he has shown her the gold coins in his private safe. The passion for money soon overrides the related passion of human love. Henry and Violet lock doors more tightly about themselves to protect their treasures until each of them is figuratively shut into a private, iron-walled safe. Starving emotionally and intellectually in their isolation, they finally starve themselves physically as well, rather than spend money for adequate food. Here, aspiration gone awry, the fear of failure and the inability to cope with success become literally debilitating diseases. Violet dies of a tumor and malnutrition and Henry of cancer. After death, they are scarcely missed, the ultimate symbols of the stultification that Bennett's characters strive with varying success to escape.

FINAL YEARS

After *Riceyman Steps*, Bennett's next few novels—*Lord Raingo*, *Accident*, and *Imperial Palace*—continue the themes of coping with success, and the protagonists are given increasing ability to handle it. Much as Clayhanger finally overcomes the problems of escape,

Evelyn Orcham in *Imperial Palace* is the culminating figure in Bennett's second cluster of themes. Ironically, Bennett died shortly after he had resolved the problems underlying the themes of his serious novels.

All of Bennett's serious works are firmly rooted in the realistic tradition (although he used more symbolism than has generally been recognized), and the author excelled in the presentation of detail that makes his themes and characters credible. In the late years of his career, Bennett was criticized by Virginia Woolf for portraying people's surroundings, rather than the people themselves, and forcing his readers to do his imagining for him, even though he believed that the creation of characters was one of the three most important functions of a novel. Woolf's criticism was sound enough to do serious damage to Bennett's standing as a major novelist, and it has been the keystone of critical opinion on Bennett ever since. A sense of environmental impact, however, has always been accepted as an important means of characterization in realistic literature. Woolf's criticism says as much about changing styles in literature as it does about the merits of Bennett's fiction. More important, it was a criticism aimed at Bennett's total canon, given that his potboilers had not yet died of their natural ailments when Woolf wrote. Sophia and Constance Baines, Edwin and Darius Clayhanger, and Henry Earlforward are finely articulated, memorable characters. Bennett's sense of place, characters, and universality of themes combine to make his finest novels memorable; *The Old Wives' Tale* is sufficient to secure Bennett's stature as one of the outstanding novelists of his era.

Carol I. Croxton

OTHER MAJOR WORKS

SHORT FICTION: *The Loot of Cities*, 1905; *Tales of the Five Towns*, 1905; *The Grim Smile of the Five Towns*, 1907; *The Matador of the Five Towns*, 1912; *The Woman Who Stole Everything*, 1927; *Selected Tales*, 1928; *The Night Visitor*, 1931.

PLAYS: *Polite Farces for the Drawing-Room*, pb. 1899; *Cupid and Commonsense*, pr. 1908; *What the Public Wants*, pr., pb. 1909; *The Honeymoon: A Comedy in Three Acts*, pr., pb. 1911; *The Great Adventure: A Play of Fancy in Four Acts*, pr. 1912; *Milestones: A Play in Three Acts*, pr., pb. 1912 (with Edward Knoblock); *The Title*, pr., pb. 1918; *Judith*, pr., pb. 1919; *Sacred and Profane Love*, pr., pb. 1919; *Body and Soul*, pr., pb. 1922; *The Love Match*, pr., pb. 1922; *Don Juan*, pb. 1923; *London Life*, pr., pb. 1924 (with Knoblock); *Flora*, pr. 1927; *Mr. Prohack*, pr., pb. 1927 (with Knoblock); *The Return Journey*, pr. 1928.

NONFICTION: *Journalism for Women*, 1898; *Fame and Fiction*, 1901; *How to Become an Author*, 1903; *The Truth About an Author*, 1903; *Things That Interested Me*, 1906; *Things Which Have Interested Me*, 1907, 1908; *The Human Machine*, 1908; *Books and Persons: Being Comments on a Past Epoch, 1908-1911*, 1917; *Literary Taste*, 1909; *Mental Efficiency, and Other Hints to Men and Women*, 1911; *Those United States*, 1912 (also known as *Your United States*); *Paris Nights*, 1913; *From the Log of the Velsa*, 1914; *The Author's Craft*, 1914; *Over There*, 1915; *Things That Have Interested Me*, 1921, 1923, 1926; *Selected Essays*, 1926; *Mediterranean Scenes*, 1928; *The Savour of Life*, 1928; *The Journals of Arnold Bennett*, 1929, 1930, 1932-1933.

BIBLIOGRAPHY

Anderson, Linda R. *Bennett, Wells, and Conrad: Narrative in Transition*. New York: St. Martin's Press, 1988. Explores the work of Bennett, H. G. Wells, and Joseph Conrad, all of whom began to write in the 1890's. Describes how these authors were forced to respond to a major redefinition in the concept of the novel during that period.

Batchelor, John. *The Edwardian Novelists*. New York: St. Martin's Press, 1982. After quoting Virginia Woolf's reservations about Bennett's fiction, Batchelor compares the two novelists, especially in terms of their treatment of women as being socially conditioned. Discusses *Clayhanger*, *A Man from the North*, *Anna of the Five Towns*, and *The Old Wives' Tale* as well as Bennett's acclaimed short story "The Death of Simon Fuge."

Broomfield, Olga R. R. *Arnold Bennett*. Boston: Twayne, 1984. Offers thorough criticism and interpretation of Bennett's work. Includes bibliography and index.

Drabble, Margaret. *Arnold Bennett: A Biography*. 1974. Reprint. Boston: G. K. Hall, 1986. Drabble, a respected British novelist in her own right, draws from

Bennett's journals and letters to focus on his background, childhood, and environment, all of which she ties to his literary works. Includes profuse illustrations, an excellent index, and a bibliography of Bennett's work.

Koenigsberger, Kurt. *The Novel and the Menagerie: Totality, Englishness, and Empire*. Columbus: Ohio State University Press, 2007. Imaginative literary study traces the relationships of zoos and other animal collections to the narratives in domestic English novels, including those of Bennett, which are discussed in a chapter titled "Elephants in the Labyrinth of Empire: Arnold Bennett, Modernism, and the Menagerie." Maintains that writers have drawn on menageries as means of representing the dominance of the British Empire in the daily life of England.

Lucas, John. *Arnold Bennett: A Study of His Fiction*. London: Methuen, 1974. After a brief review of criticism of Bennett's works, Lucas examines the author's fiction, devoting lengthy treatments to his major novels, addressing them in terms of character and plot. Ardently defends Bennett's realism, which Lucas regards as equal to that of D. H. Lawrence. Includes copious quotations from Bennett's work.

McDonald, Peter D. *British Literary Culture and Publishing Practice, 1880-1914*. New York: Cambridge University Press, 1997. Examines the early careers of Arnold Bennett and other writers who published from 1880 to 1914 to trace the transformation of British literary culture.

Owen, Meirion. "The Resonance of Bennett's *Anna of the Five Towns* to Woolf's *To the Lighthouse*." *Notes and Queries* 54, no. 2 (June, 2007): 160-163. Charts the similarities between the novels by Bennett and Virginia Woolf, demonstrating how images of women painters and mutilated mackerel appear in both books and discussing how the two authors influenced each other.

Roby, Kinley. *A Writer at War: Arnold Bennett, 1914-1918*. Baton Rouge: Louisiana State University Press, 1972. Although primarily biographical, this book also offers valuable insights into Bennett's work during and after World War I. Defends Bennett's post-1914 work, contending that it was influenced by Bennett's exhaustion of his Five Towns material, by his steadily deteriorating relationship with his wife, and by the war itself. Includes an excellent index.

Squillace, Robert. *Modernism, Modernity, and Arnold Bennett*. Lewisburg, Pa.: Bucknell University Press, 1997. Argues that Bennett saw more clearly than his novelist contemporaries the emergence of the modern era, which transformed a male-dominated society to one open to all people regardless of class or gender. Very detailed notes and a bibliography acknowledge the work of the best scholars.

THOMAS BERGER

Born: Cincinnati, Ohio; July 20, 1924
Also known as: Thomas Louis Berger

PRINCIPAL LONG FICTION

Crazy in Berlin, 1958
Reinhart in Love, 1962
Little Big Man, 1964
Killing Time, 1967
Vital Parts, 1970
Regiment of Women, 1973
Sneaky People, 1975
Who Is Teddy Villanova?, 1977
Arthur Rex, 1978
Neighbors, 1980
Reinhart's Women, 1981
The Feud, 1983
Nowhere, 1985
Being Invisible, 1987
The Houseguest, 1988
Changing the Past, 1989
Orrie's Story, 1990
Meeting Evil, 1992

Robert Crews, 1995
Suspects, 1996
The Return of Little Big Man, 1999
Best Friends, 2003
Adventures of the Artificial Woman, 2004

OTHER LITERARY FORMS

Thomas Berger has published numerous articles, reviews, and short stories in magazines such as the *Saturday Evening Post*, *Esquire*, *Harper's*, and *Playboy*. He has written four plays, two of which, *The Burglars: A Comedy in Two Acts* (pb. 1988) and *Other People*, have been published; *Other People* was also produced in 1970 at the Berkshire Theatre Festival in Massachusetts. Berger's radio play *At the Dentist's* was produced by Vermont Public Radio in 1981.

ACHIEVEMENTS

Thomas Berger is one of the most productive, most respected, and most challenging literary figures in the United States. His novels, including the highly acclaimed *Little Big Man* and critically and popularly successful works such as *Who Is Teddy Villanova?* and *Neighbors*, seem sure to earn for him a lasting place in American letters. His Reinhart series is one of the most singular and significant accomplishments of postwar American literature, forming as it does both a sociological epic and an index to the changing face of the American novel in the second half of the twentieth century. The Reinhart series stands—along with John Updike's Rabbit novels and Phillip Roth's Zuckerman novels—as one of the most noteworthy and respected multivolume narratives in postwar American fiction. Acknowledged as a masterful prose stylist, Berger writes novels that are aggressively intelligent without being ostentatiously "difficult," works that are often hilariously funny without losing their serious bite.

In 1970, Richard Schickel correctly identified Berger as "one of the most radical sensibilities now writing in America" and bemoaned the fact that Berger had not received the recognition he deserved. More than a decade later, Thomas R. Edwards intensified this complaint with the charge that the failure to read and discuss Berger's work is no less than "a national disgrace." Reviewing *Neighbors* for the *Chicago Tribune*, Frederick

Busch may have best summed up Berger's stature as a novelist when he said, "This is a novel by Thomas Berger, and everything he writes should be read and considered." In 2003, award-winning novelist Jonathan Lethem, in his introduction to the reprint of Berger's *Meeting Evil*, added his voice to those of the readers, reviewers, and critics who celebrate Berger as "one of America's three or four greatest living novelists."

BIOGRAPHY

Thomas Louis Berger was born in Cincinnati, Ohio, on July 20, 1924, and grew up in the nearby suburban community of Lockland. Disenchanted after a short bout with college, Berger enlisted in the U.S. Army, serving from 1943 to 1946 and entering Berlin in 1945 with the first American Occupation troops; his experiences gave him some of the background for his first novel, *Crazy in Berlin*.

After the war, Berger returned to college, receiving his B.A. at the University of Cincinnati in 1948. He continued his studies as a graduate student in English at Columbia University (1950-1951), where he completed course work for an M.A. and began a thesis on George Orwell, which he never completed. Instead, Berger turned his attention to the writers' workshop at the New School for Social Research. In that workshop, under the aegis of Charles Glicksberg, Berger began to write short stories. "I produced one story a week for three months, most of them melancholy in tone, maudlin in spirit, and simple of mind," he has recounted, "Hemingway then being my model." Berger dismisses his short fiction, explaining, "The marathon is my event, and not the hundred-yard dash." Despite this assessment, Berger's short fiction has appeared in magazines ranging from the *Saturday Evening Post* to *Harper's*, *Esquire*, *Playboy*, and *North American Review*.

From 1948 through 1951, Berger supported his writing by working as a librarian at the Rand School of Social Science. In 1951-1952, he was a staff member of *The New York Times Index*, and the following year he was a copy editor for *Popular Science Monthly*. In 1956 Berger and his wife toured Western Europe, including France, Italy, Austria, and Germany. Revisiting the scene of his army experience in Germany allowed him the emotional distance to abandon his work in progress and to begin and complete his first published novel, *Crazy in Berlin*. Until 1964 and the publication of his third novel, *Little Big Man*, Berger had to supplement the income from his fiction with freelance editing. From 1971 to 1973, Berger wrote a characteristically idiosyncratic film column for *Esquire*, managing to discuss almost everything *but* the major motion pictures of the day.

In 1950, Berger married Jeanne Redpath, an artist he met at the New School. In the fifteen years from 1965 to 1980, Berger and his wife moved twelve times, the places they lived including New York City; Bridgehampton on Long Island; Mount Desert, Maine; Malibu, California; London, on two separate occasions; and the Hudson riverbank in Rockland County, New York. In addition to a lectureship at Yale in 1981-1982, Berger has been a distinguished visiting professor at Southampton College, and during the 1970's and early 1980's he gave readings at more than twenty universities. In 1986 he was awarded an honorary doctor of letters degree by Long Island University.

Thomas Berger. (© Jerry Bauer)

ANALYSIS

The dust-jacket blurb written by Thomas Berger for *Who Is Teddy Villanova?* reviews the general scheme of his career, pointing out that each of his novels "celebrates another classic genre of fiction: the western [*Little Big Man*], the childhood memoir [*Sneaky People*], the anatomical romance [*Regiment of Women*], the true-crime documentary [*Killing Time*], and the Reinhart books [*Crazy in Berlin*, *Reinhart in Love*, and *Vital Parts*] together form a sociological epic." *Who Is Teddy Villanova?* extended this pattern to the classic American hard-boiled detective story, *Arthur Rex* extended it to Arthurian romance, *Neighbors* traces its lineage most directly to Franz Kafka, and *Reinhart's Women* continues the Reinhart series. In similar fashion, *The Feud* offers Dreiserian slice-of-life naturalism, *Nowhere* celebrates the utopian fantasy, *Being Invisible* acknowledges its precursors in the invisibility narratives of both H. G. Wells and Ralph Ellison, *The Houseguest* revisits the banal menace of *Neighbors*, presenting a self-made hollow man in the tradition of F. Scott Fitzgerald's *The Great Gatsby* (1925), and *Changing the Past* shares assumptions with Robert Louis Stevenson's *The Strange Case*

of Dr. Jekyll and Mr. Hyde (1886) and with the "three wishes" narrative tradition.

In *Orrie's Story*, Berger "reinvents" the Greek tragedy of the Oresteia, setting it in postwar America. *Robert Crews* is obviously Berger's take on Daniel Defoe's *Robinson Crusoe* (1719), and *Meeting Evil* moves from the Kafkaesque presentation of the banality of evil to the moral imperative of responding to evil that is deadly. *Suspects* renews Berger's fascination with the interplay of law enforcement with criminals in general and with police procedurals in particular. *The Return of Little Big Man* goes back to the world and time of *Little Big Man*, updating Jack Crabb's adventures through the final vanishing of the Old West as it is replaced by the simulations of Buffalo Bill's Wild West Show and the 1893 World's Columbian Exposition. *Best Friends* is a more gentle and hopeful take on the doubling of "kicker and kickee" that has long been one of Berger's central concerns. *Adventures of the Artificial Woman*, which Berger considers a "literary conceit" rather than a true novel, blends themes from Mary Wollstonecraft Shelley's *Frankenstein* (1818) with themes from George Bernard Shaw's

Pygmalion (pb. 1912). The mistaken notion that these "celebrations" of classic novel forms are really parodies has dogged Berger's career, but unlike parodies, his novels start from rather than aim toward literary traditions; Berger achieves a testing and broadening of possibilities rather than a burlesquing of limitations. If anything, his celebrations serve as kinds of "deparodizations," twisting genres already self-conscious to the point of parody in ways that radically defamiliarize them. The variety of Berger's novels, a range with perhaps no equal in contemporary American literature, underlines the precision of his craft while distracting readers from the steadiness and the seriousness of his purpose.

Most critics have failed to consider that Berger's manipulations of novel forms are ultimately self-exploring and reflexive literary experiments. He tries to make of each novel an "independent existence," an alternative verbal reality that he hopes the reader will approach "without the luggage of received ideas, a priori assumptions, sociopolitical axes to grind, or feeble moralities in search of support." This verbal world both owes its existence to a number of traditional and arbitrary literary conventions of representation and seeks to remind the reader that the working of those conventions is of interest and significance in itself—not only as a means to the representation of reality.

Failing to appreciate the independent existence of Berger's fictional worlds, reviewers have misread *Little Big Man* as an indictment of American abuse of Native Americans, *Regiment of Women* as a polemic for or against the women's movement, *Neighbors* as a critique of suburban life, and so on. Such a topical approach to these novels ignores the possibility that Berger's real theme is language, and that underlying the manically different surfaces of his novels is a constant preoccupation with the ways in which problems of human existence stem from the confusion of language with reality. Again and again, Berger's novels find new ways to suggest that the structures and institutions that order and give meaning to existence are much less important than the ways in which one talks about them, and that the ways one talks about those organizing beliefs inevitably have been designed by someone to influence or manipulate someone else's perception and judgment. Reinhart's ex-wife spells this out for him when she chides, "It ought to begin

to occur to you that life is just a collection of stories from all points of self-interest."

Put another way, the persistent goal of Berger's novels is to shift our attention from the purportedly real world we live in to the ways in which that world is conventionally perceived as a construct of language. This effort proceeds from the assumption that what we have been told about reality (received ideas) and what we tell ourselves about reality (our personal myths) have become more "official" or persuasive than experience itself, that language has been so twisted, so manipulated as to refer more to itself than to the material world to which it ostensibly refers. It is in this sense that Berger cheerfully warns that we should not confuse fiction with life, because "the latter is false," and it is in this spirit that he reminds the readers of *Killing Time* that his novel "is a construction of language and otherwise a lie."

Accordingly, the lives of Berger's characters are affected more by words than by actions. Victimized by definitions that exclude or threaten them, by rhetoric that makes them lose sight of physical facts, and by language designed more to preclude than to encourage clear thinking, his characters are enslaved by language. For this reason, the plot of a Berger novel typically chronicles the efforts of the protagonist to free him- or herself from someone else's verbal version of reality. In this way, Jack Crabb in *Little Big Man* bounces back and forth not only between white and Plains Indian cultures but also between competing codes of conduct designed to legitimate all manner of cruelty. Berger shows how Jack's greatest problems are actually matters of definition, as he inevitably finds himself defined as white when the situation is controlled by Native Americans and as Native American when the situation is controlled by whites. All of Berger's novels explore the processes of victimization, as all of Berger's protagonists struggle, whether consciously or unconsciously, to free themselves from the inexorable tendency to think of themselves as the victims of outrages and impositions both humorously small and tragically large.

While Berger refuses to subscribe to any single codified philosophy, whether romantic, existential, or absurd, his characters do live in worlds that seem to operate largely on Nietzschean principles. As Frederick Turner has observed, Berger's moral stance is consistently "beyond sentimentality, beyond classic American liberalism," concerning itself with fundamentals rather than with surfaces. Like philosopher Friedrich Nietzsche, Berger assumes that "there are higher problems than the problems of pleasure and pain and sympathy," though few of his characters would subscribe to this view—their pleasure, their pain, and their sympathy being of paramount importance to them.

Those characters are a string of outrageously impossible but compellingly plausible individuals who seem, in Berger's words, to be "persistent liars" and "monsters of one persuasion or another." Berger is uniformly fond of these "monsters," and his characters can never be branded as "good" or "evil," since all are as appealing in their often bizarre excesses as they are sadly humorous in their deficiencies. Most important, all of Berger's characters *do their best*. They may trick, abuse, and betray one another, but in a world where understanding seems full of drawbacks and the irresponsible consistently victimize those who feel obligations, they are finally no more nor less than normal. In the courtroom of his novels, Berger refuses to become either judge or advocate, choosing instead to establish a dialectic of wildly opposing viewpoints. He explains that his job is to maintain these characters in equilibrium, a concern of "art and not politics or sociology."

No analysis of Berger's novels would be complete without mentioning the delights of his prose style. Berger is one of a handful of American writers, contemporary or otherwise, for whom the sentence is an event in itself. His style challenges the reader with precise but often elaborate or serpentine sentences, reflecting his conviction that "the sentence is the cell beyond which the life of the book cannot be traced, a novel being a structure of such cells: most must be vital or the body is dead." What sentence vitality means to Berger can be seen in the way he elaborates the commonplace metaphor of the "ham-fisted" punch in *Who Is Teddy Villanova?*

> He had struck me on the forehead, that helmet of protective bone, an impractical stroke even for such stout fingers as his, had he not turned his hand on edge and presented to my skull the resilient karate blade that swells out between the base of the smallest digit and the wrist: in his case, the size and consistency of the fleshy side of a loin of pork.

This marvelous punch knocks out Russell Wren, Berger's private-eye narrator, who comes to with this equally meticulous and mannered realization:

> My loafers were in a position just ahead of his coal-barge brogans, a yard from where I slumped; meanwhile, my feet, twisted on their edges and crushed under the crease between thigh and buttock, were only stockinged: he had knocked me out of my shoes!

Leonard Michaels described this style as "one of the great pleasures of the book . . . educated, complicated, graceful, silly, destructive in spirit," and his comment applies to all of Berger's novels. Noting that he looks for himself through the English language, Berger states that for him language is "a morality and a politics and a religion."

CRAZY IN BERLIN

In Berger's first novel, *Crazy in Berlin*, the twenty-one-year-old Carlo Reinhart, a U.S. Army medic in occupied Berlin, struggles to reconcile the conflicting claims of Nazism, Judaism, Communism, Americanism, and his own German heritage—all overshadowed by the more fundamental concepts of friendship, victimization, and survival. This first of the Reinhart novels also features the points of view of a manic series of contradictory characters, including an American intelligence officer who is an idealistic Communist, a Russian officer who wants to become a capitalist, and a cynical former Nazi now working as a Russian agent.

REINHART IN LOVE

In the second Reinhart novel, *Reinhart in Love*, Berger's bumbling protagonist is discharged from the army, in which he had been happy, and returns to civilian life, which he finds singularly disastrous. His comic misadventures are guided by Claude Humbold, a wonderfully devious real estate agent/con man for whom Reinhart reluctantly works; by the enterprising and calculating Genevieve Raven, whom he is tricked into marrying; and by Splendor Mainwaring, his black friend whose special talent is getting Reinhart into impossible situations.

LITTLE BIG MAN

Had Berger never written anything but *Little Big Man*, he would have earned a respected place in American literary history. This story of Jack Crabb's life in both the Cheyenne and white cultures of the historical as well as the dime-novel Old West has been called variously "the best novel about the West," "a Barthian western," and "a seminal event in what must now seem the most significant cultural and literary trend of the last decade—the attempt on many fronts to develop structures, styles, ways of thinking that are beyond any version of ethnocentrism." The story has been transcribed ostensibly from the tape-recorded reminiscences of "the late Jack Crabb—frontiersman, American Indian scout, gunfighter, buffalo hunter, adopted Cheyenne—in his final days upon this earth." That Jack's final days come 111 years after his first, and that he also claims to have been the sole white survivor of the Battle of the Little Bighorn, raises obvious questions about the truth of his account. Furthermore, Jack's narrative comes to the reader through the patently unreliable editorship of "Ralph Fielding Snell," a fatuous, gullible, self-professed "man of letters" who also happens to mention that he has suffered three or four nervous breakdowns in the past few years. Against these reflexive, metafictional devices, Berger balances the disarming realism of Jack Crabb's narration, its tone resonating with the wondering honesty and credibility of Huck Finn.

Frederick Turner has noted that part of the real power of this narration is derived from Jack's coming "to understand both myth and history as radically human constructs." What Turner means by "radically human constructs" can be understood from the way in which *Little Big Man* combines very different rhetorics or "codes" for talking about the Old West. Indeed, Jack's narrative consists of excerpts from and imitations of actual histories of the West, autobiographies, dime novels, Native American studies, and other codes that are mixed together in unpredictable combinations. This jumbling of codes and vocabularies (for example, Jack may mingle the crassest of frontier expressions with terms such as "colloquy," "circumferentially," "hitherto," or "tumult") exposes the perceptual biases of the "official" codes that have been developed for talking about the Old West—whether by Zane Grey, Francis Parkman, or L. A. Hoebel (an expert on Cheyenne culture). Jack begins to realize that even when his situation seems to be defined by bullets or arrows, the real conflict lies in the clash between the often antithetical ways in which he

must think of himself, whether he is to define himself and act according to Cheyenne terms, cavalry terms, capitalist terms, journalistic terms, and so on.

Accordingly, the panorama of Jack's adventures, ranging from his adoption by the Cheyenne to his gunfight with Wild Bill Hickok to his being the only white survivor of Custer's Last Stand, is shadowed by the panorama of his changing narrative styles: Not only does Berger pack every classic Western theme into the novel, but he also fills it with subtly varied "codes" that make it—like all of his novels—at least in part an exploration of the workings of language. The genius of this novel is that its metafictional devices are so well woven into the fabric of Jack's fascinating story that they have eluded all but a handful of readers, reviewers, and scholars. By any standards, *Little Big Man* is a masterpiece, one of the most delightful novels ever written.

THE RETURN OF LITTLE BIG MAN

Who, remembering Ralph Fielding Snell's comment in the epilogue to *Little Big Man* that Jack Crabb's tape-recorded memories did not stop with the Battle of the Little Bighorn, would not like to know what further adventures Jack might have had, particularly as Snell hints that they included both more time witnessing the gunfighting culture of the Old West and time spent touring with Buffalo Bill's Wild West Show? Who would not want to see how Berger would return to his best-known character to tell the rest of his amazing story? In this fine sequel, Berger deftly resurrects Jack's inimitable voice and wondering vision and turns both toward chronicling the birth of a new century in which simulacra such as Buffalo Bill's Wild West Show replace the Old West, the 1893 Chicago World's Fair offers glimpses of America's technologized future, and an indomitable New Woman captures Jack's heart and his story.

KILLING TIME

Killing Time is a kind of reflexive, even self-destructive murder mystery. Based in part on accounts by Frederic Wertham in *The Show of Violence* (1949) and Quentin Reynolds in *Courtroom* (1950) of an actual sensational murder case in 1937, *Killing Time* tells the story of Joseph Detweiler, "an awfully nice guy" who is also a psychopathic murderer. The novel opens with the discovery that someone has murdered three people in an apartment. The plot seems to be developing into a routine murder mystery or police procedural as the investigative machinery goes into action, but the murderer, Joe Detweiler, turns himself in even before police suspicions about him crystallize. The balance of the novel, therefore, focuses on Detweiler's conversations with the police and his lawyer. Berger's book declines, however, to become a courtroom drama and proceeds instead through a variety of conventions, from the detective story and the psychological thriller to the courtroom drama and other well-codified genres.

Although Joe is a multiple murderer and is quite mad, all other personalities in *Killing Time* lack character in comparison. Joe is the criminal, but he alone among the policemen, lawyers, and judges truly believes in law and justice. His philosophy is bizarre, but Joe manages to change the perspectives of all those who know him. What really separates Joe from those around him is his profound mistrust of language. He sees actions as truth, while language is just "talking about talk."

To a significant extent, Berger is "talking about talk" in *Killing Time*, just as he is exploring the nature of language and the nature of fiction, for this is a supremely reflexive novel. The book is full of fictions within its larger fictional frame; all the characters apart from Joe are cast as conscious and unconscious makers of fiction. For example, Joe's lawyer derives his greatest satisfaction from "a favorable verdict returned by a jury who knew it had been hoaxed," and he explains to Joe that in the courtroom, "reality is what the jury believes." By presenting character after character whose verbal deceptions and artistry are obviously analogous to the techniques of the novelist (one character even becomes a novelist), and by putting his characters in situations analogous to that of the reader of a novel, Berger reminds his reader that the novel is just as much a hoax as any of those created by its characters. As Berger most bluntly states in the front of the book, "A novel is a construction of language and otherwise a lie."

VITAL PARTS

Vital Parts, the third Reinhart novel, picks up the adventures of its protagonist in the 1960's, as the forty-four-year-old Reinhart rapidly adds to the list of windmills with which he has unsuccessfully tilted. Bob Sweet, a flashy boyhood acquaintance, replaces Claude Humbold as Reinhart's business mentor, luring him into

his most dubious venture to date: a cryonics foundation for freezing the dead. His tough-minded wife, Genevieve, and his surly hippie son, Blaine, both despise him, while Winona, his fat, unhappy, sweetly innocent daughter, worships him. Caught in a cultural crossfire, Reinhart threatens to succumb to the pressures and perversities of modern life.

REGIMENT OF WOMEN

Berger's next novel, *Regiment of Women*, managed to offend reviewers and readers on both sides of the women's movement when it was published in 1973. A dystopian novel set in America in the year 2047, the book presents a society in which traditional male and female roles have been completely reversed. Women not only control the corporate, artistic, legal, and military machinery of this society but also sexually dominate it, strapping dildos over their pants to assault men. In such an inverted society, to be "manly" is to wear dresses and makeup, to hold only powerless jobs, to have silicone breast implants, and to be emotionally incapable of rational thought or significant action. To be "effeminate" is to bind breasts, to wear false beards, to dress in pants and suits, to be rough, physical, aggressive, and to have a reduced life expectancy caused by stress.

Berger's protagonist in this future world is a twenty-nine-year-old insecurity-riddled male secretary named Georgie Cornell. An unlikely sequence of events lands him first in prison, arrested for wearing women's clothing (slacks, shirt, tie, and coat) and incorrectly suspected of being a men's liberation agent. Driven to discover accidentally that he is physically stronger than his female captors, Georgie escapes and is promptly appropriated as an agent/hero by the men's liberation underground. For the rest of the novel, Georgie struggles to discover his "natural" identity, a process that forces him to cast off received idea after received idea, discarding sexual generalizations to forge a particular definition of self. He is joined in this "rebellion" by a female FBI agent so demented that she wants only to be "masculine"—to wear dresses and makeup, to be gentle and sensitive.

Despite its topical focus, *Regiment of Women* is fundamentally concerned not with sexual roles but with the more basic problem of the hypostatizing power of language. From start to finish, the novel reminds the reader that Georgie's reality has been almost completely gloved by language, and, in so doing, also calls attention both to the way language operates in the reader's reality and to the ways in which a novelist manipulates language to create an independent "reality." At the bottom of this concern with language and rhetoric lies Berger's belief that victimization in any realm starts as a linguistic phenomenon in which the generalizations and attendant rhetoric of some self-interest part company with the particulars of immediate experience. Accordingly, *Regiment of Women* is a book much more concerned with the discovery of true individuality and freedom and with the workings of language than with sexual politics.

SNEAKY PEOPLE

Berger's seventh novel, *Sneaky People*, is easily his most gentle (although much of its action concerns plans for a murder). *Sneaky People* reveals Berger's ear for the American vernacular as it chronicles the coming-of-age of a young boy, Ralph Sandifer, in a dreamy small-town world where nothing is as bucolic as it seems. Ralph's father owns a used-car lot and plans to have one of his employees murder Ralph's mother. The drab, mousy-seeming mother secretly writes and sells pornography of the most lurid sort. Indeed, this is a book that seems to say that it is "sneaky" acts that best reveal character, and it is a book that is itself something of a sneaky act and continues Berger's obsession with the nature of language.

Berger has described *Sneaky People* as "my tribute to the American language of 1939—to be philologically precise, that of the lower-middle class in the eastern Middle West, on which I am an authority as on nothing else." The characters in this novel speak the vital, unleveled, pretelevision American vernacular of the 1930's, and the prose style of *Sneaky People* is in a sense the real subject of the book, reflecting Berger's belief that "the possibilities for wit—and thus for life—decline with the homogenization of language."

WHO IS TEDDY VILLANOVA?

Berger's mastery of and play with prose style reaches its most exuberant high in *Who Is Teddy Villanova?*, which invokes the conventions of the hard-boiled detective novel but also defies almost all of the expectations that attend those conventions. *Who Is Teddy Villanova?* gives evidence of Berger's great respect for the masters of this genre—Dashiell Hammett, Raymond Chandler,

and Ross Macdonald—but it also adds a number of outlandish twists, most prominent among them being a first-person narrator who introduces himself with "Call me Russell Wren" and who tells his story "in a rococo style reminiscent by turns of Thomas De Quincey, Thomas Babington Macaulay, and Sir Thomas Malory." Wren is a former instructor of English more concerned with finding readers for the play he is writing than with finding out why a series of thugs and policemen brutalize him either in search of or in the name of a mysterious Teddy Villanova, about whom Wren knows absolutely nothing. The novel follows Wren through one misadventure after another as he pursues the elusive Villanova with Ahab's passion and some curiously "fishy" metaphors (a huge thug slips through a doorway "as deftly as a perch fins among subaqueous rocks").

In truth, Wren does confuse his own small-fish situation with that of Herman Melville's great quest, and his confusion is symptomatic of a more profound problem: When faced with experience, Wren always tries to organize it in terms of the fictional worlds of literary and television private eyes. Like Ralph Fielding Snell in *Little Big Man*, another preposterous "man of letters," Wren perpetually falls victim to his own linguistic hypostatizations as he persistently confuses the literary life of fictional detectives with his own situation. A detective who questions him observes, "I suspect you are living the legend of the private eye, which I confess I had always believed mythical." Wren's narrative style is governed by his immersion in the literary myth of the private eye, and his prose style is governed by his pseudointellectual background, producing such wonderfully incongruous lines as "This wench is my ward. . . . Toy with her fine foot if you like, but eschew her quivering thigh and the demesnes that there adjacent lie." The result is humorously self-conscious, almost forcing the reader to step back from the action of the novel and consider its implications for the act of reading and for language use itself.

ARTHUR REX

Its dust jacket announces that *Arthur Rex* is "Thomas Berger's salute to the Age of Chivalry from his own enmired situation in the Time of the Cad," and this novel has been prominently praised as "the Arthur story for our times." Berger brings to the legend of King Arthur both a profound respect for its mythic power and a modern perspective on the nature of its myth, as can be seen in a comment by Sir Gawaine, when, late in his life, he is asked if he does not long for the old days of action. Gawaine answers no, explaining,

> I am happy to have had them in my proper time, but of a life of adventure it can be said that there is no abiding satisfaction, for when one adventure is done, a knight liveth in expectation of another, and if the next come not soon enough he falleth in love, in the sort of love that is an adventure, for what he seeketh be the adventure and not the lovingness. And methinks this sequence is finally infantile, and beyond a certain age one can no longer be interested in games.

Berger's version of the Arthur legend in no way diminishes the glory of Arthur's attempt or the measure of his achievement, and it equally honors the stylistic achievement of Sir Thomas Malory's telling of the legend. Berger does devote greater attention to the cause of Arthur's final tragedy, which centers in his account on the erosion of the innocent belief that life can be governed by the simple principle of opposing good to evil. Complexity finally overwhelms Arthur; to Launcelot, he sadly admits that "evil doing hath got more subtle, perhaps even to the point at which it cannot properly be encountered with the sword." What Arthur does not realize is that strict adherence to a rigid code of conduct may create more problems than it solves, threaten order more than ensure it. Only too late do Arthur and some of his wiser knights begin to understand that the Code of Chivalry, like any inflexible system of abstract principles, comes into conflict with itself if pursued too blindly. In Berger's hands, Arthur's most anguishing discovery is not that he has been betrayed by his queen and his most trusted knight but that his philosophy has been shallow, because "to the profound vision there is no virtue and no vice, and what is justice to one, is injustice to another."

Arthur recognizes the flaw in his great dream, but Berger makes it clear that Arthur's legend is not to be judged by the success or failure of that dream. The Lady of the Lake assures the dying Arthur that he could not have done better in his life than he did, and the ghost of Sir Gawaine offers to his king the Round Table's poignant epitaph: "We sought no easy victories, nor won any. And perhaps for that we will be remembered."

NEIGHBORS

Earl Keese, Berger's protagonist in *Neighbors*, is a quiet, reasonable, forty-nine-year-old suburbanite who tells people that his home sits "at the end of the road," because that phrase sounds less "dispiriting" than "dead end." In fact, his life has long since reached its apparent dead end, and it takes the arrival of mysterious and maddening new neighbors, Harry and Ramona, to confront Keese with a sequence of situations so outrageous that he can no longer maintain the hoax of his previously complacent life. Not only do Harry and Ramona (zany versions of Nietzsche's "free spirits") fail to observe the social amenities, but they also seem committed to deliberate provocation, pushing him to see how far he will go to avoid humiliation.

Their visits increasingly seem like motiveless assaults, as their comings and goings produce a series of off-balance events that gradually strip Keese of his easy social assumptions and habitual responses. As his bizarrely embarrassing experiences increasingly blur the line between comedy and nightmare, his relations with all those around him begin to undergo subtle changes. He realizes that his life has grown so stale that Harry and Ramona's aggravations may actually offer him a salvation of sorts—the chance to take control of and give style to his life. As Keese finally admits to Harry, "Every time I see you as a criminal, by another light you look like a kind of benefactor."

Madcap physical changes punctuate the plot—entrances, exits, fights, a damaged car, a destroyed house—but for all its action, *Neighbors* might best be described as a series of functions of language: puns, platitudes, theories, definitions, excuses, accusations, rationalizations, promises, questions, threats—all acts performed with words. Keese knows better than to trust completely what he sees (he suffers from "outlandish illusions"), but he uncritically does believe his ears, consistently confusing rhetoric with reality, mistaking verbal maps for the territory of experience. In fact, *Neighbors* may offer the most verbal world Berger has created; like *Little Big Man*, it is a book in which language becomes the only operating reality. Vocabularies from law and ethics intertwine throughout the novel, and Berger does not fail to exploit the incongruities of the two lexicons. Terms having to do with guilt, justice, punishment, revenge, motive, confession, blame, crime, and accusation appear on virtually every page, resonating at once with the rhetoric of the courtroom and with that of Franz Kafka's *The Trial* (1925). Keese's "guilt" is not unlike that of Kafka's Joseph K., and the slapstick humor of this book records a deadly serious philosophical trial.

REINHART'S WOMEN

In *Reinhart's Women*, the now fifty-four-year-old Reinhart finally discovers something he can do well: cook. The novel finds Reinhart ten years after his divorce from Genevieve, living with and supported by his daughter, Winona, now a beautiful and successful fashion model. His son, Blaine, last seen as a surly radical in *Vital Parts*, is now a surly, snobbish, and successful stockbroker, unchanged in his disdain for his father. Having finally admitted that he is hopeless as a businessman, Reinhart has withdrawn from the world and contents himself with managing his daughter's household and with cooking "in a spirit of scientific inquiry." Actually, cooking has become for him an aesthetic philosophy, and for the first time in his life he does not "feel as if he were either charlatan or buffoon." "Food," Reinhart notes, "is kinder than people."

Long completely at the mercy of unmerciful women, particularly his mother and his ex-wife, Reinhart can now even take in stride the news that his daughter is having a lesbian affair with a successful older businesswoman. Age has taught him that "the best defense against any moral outrage is patience: wait a moment and something will change: the outrage, he who committed it, or, most often, oneself."

Winona's lover (a female version of the con men who have always directed Reinhart's forays into business) contrives to lure Reinhart back into the world, first as a supermarket product demonstrator, then as a guest "chef" for a spot appearance on a local television show, and the novel closes with the strong prospect of his own show: "Chef Carlo Cooks." His apparent successes, however, are not confined to the kitchen, as Reinhart escapes the gentle and loving tyranny of his daughter, emerges unscathed from an encounter with his ex-wife, and begins a promising relationship with a young woman who seems in many ways a female version of himself—intelligent, considerate, awkward. In fact, Reinhart begins to gather around him a small band of

kindred souls, hoping to buy and run a quaint small-town café. Once again the lure of business proves irresistible for Reinhart, and once again the prospect of disaster cannot be discounted, but this time the odds seem more in Reinhart's favor. Jonathan Baumbach has summed up this addition to the Reinhart books as "Berger's most graceful and modest book, a paean to kindness and artistry, a work of quiet dazzle."

Berger's first novel, *Crazy in Berlin*, started Reinhart, "a stumbling American Odysseus," on what Berger has termed "his long career of indestructibility." The subsequent novels in the series—*Reinhart in Love, Vital Parts*, and *Reinhart's Women*—follow Reinhart as he grows older and, ultimately, wiser. Said by one critic to be "a clowning knight errant, pure of heart—that is, a custodian of our conscience and of our incongruities," Reinhart is an incurable idealist who really has no faith in idealism. Complexity, Reinhart's essence, is also his nemesis: He can always see both sides to every argument, feel responsibility for any injustice, and though he realizes that "true freedom is found only by being consistent with oneself," he has a very hard time figuring out how to do this, particularly in the novels before *Reinhart's Women*. Essentially, Reinhart seeks a consistent rationale for his unimpressive, awkward, but indomitable individuality. Combining the features of "a big bland baseball bat" with those of "an avatar of Job the beloved of a sadistic God," Reinhart can never shake the suspicion that he does not fit anywhere but is nevertheless responsible for the general confusion that surrounds and usually engulfs him.

Reinhart is as ill suited for despair, however, as he is for success. Although reminded by a successful acquaintance that he is "redundant in the logistics of life," he can never really be disillusioned, even though his dreams steadily fall prey to the practical opportunism of those around him. No match for a mother who can tell him, "If I ever thought you had truck with Filth, I'd slip you strychnine," or a shrewish wife whose advice to him is "If you're going to be an ass-kisser, then you ought to at least kiss the asses of winners," Reinhart can recognize the distinction between his secular search for a Holy Grail and the social meliorism that passes for idealism. Like all of Berger's characters, Reinhart never gives up: An indomitable toughness underlies his numerous weaknesses, and whatever the situation, he always muddles through, scarred but undaunted.

THE FEUD

In 1984, Berger almost gained the kind of critical recognition he has so long deserved as literary judges selected *The Feud* for the 1984 Pulitzer Prize—only to have their selection overruled in favor of William Kennedy's *Ironweed* (1983) by the Pulitzer administrative committee. What the vagaries and politics of literary prize determination should not obscure is the fact that Berger's twelfth novel (described by Berger as "my most modest work, a little memoir of the place and time of my youth" and "as a kind of Dreiserian slice of life") is a masterpiece of precision that posits its richly textured semblance of small-town life in 1930's America with a perfectly controlled minimum of exposition and a sense of quiet, timeless authority. In its narrowest sense, *The Feud* chronicles the sudden eruption and three-day playing out of an intense feud between two small-town families, the Beelers and the Bullards. Fueled by misunderstanding, misplaced pride, pathological insecurity, small-town xenophobia, self-serving interpretations of events, and the convergence of an incredible sequence of coincidences, this feud is finally remarkable for nothing quite so much as its representation of the way things actually happen in life. The action—both humorous and tragic—of this novel quickly reveals that the dynamics of feuding, quaint though the term may sound, is one of the received structures of human experience, a mold just waiting to be filled—whether by Montagues and Capulets, Hatfields and McCoys, or Beelers and Bullards.

CHANGING THE PAST

Berger's re-creation of the "you have three wishes but be careful what you wish for" story may be one of his most underappreciated novels and is one of his most intensely self-reflexive. Berger is a novelist known for his own approaches to "changing the past," whether it is the "historical" past of *Little Big Man* and *The Return of Little Big Man* or the legendary past of *Arthur Rex* and *Orrie's Story*. Of course, he is also a writer who programmatically changes the past of literary tradition as he consistently reinvents classic novel and literary forms. This novel allows him to imagine the consequences of an "infinitely malleable" past in which changing events

seems not to free his protagonist from the larger destiny of his character.

ORRIE'S STORY

Orrie's Story re-creates much of the ambience of *The Feud* and *Sneaky People* but sets within that 1930's and 1940's small-town world the classic story of Orestes, son of Agamemnon and Clytemnestra, who must kill both Clytemnestra and her lover, Aegisthus, to avenge his father's murder by them. In the *Oresteia* (458 B.C.E.) of Aeschylus, a tragedy already recast in the American Civil War era by Eugene O'Neill's *Mourning Becomes Electra* (pr., pb. 1931), Berger has discovered another of the timeless stories of inescapable situations that have always informed and been reinterrogated by his writing. Matching the precision and control of *The Feud* and echoing its mastery of the American idiom, *Orrie's Story* may be Berger's best-written and most starkly powerful novel.

The Feud, *Being Invisible*, *The Houseguest*, and *Orrie's Story* all offer new twists to Berger's fascination with issues of discriminating "kickers" from "kickees," victims from victimizers, the disparate responses of humans confronted by the complexities of responsibility. While *Nowhere*—which continues the misadventures of Russell Wren, protagonist of *Who Is Teddy Villanova?*, as he finds himself transported to the ironic utopia of a quirky kingdom apparently modeled on American film musicals—raises issues usually larger than those facing the individual, it continues Berger's unsentimental confrontation with the essential insolubility of human problems. As Berger's protagonist in *Changing the Past* finally discovers after trying on and discarding a number of wishful alternative versions of his own past, "Life is taking your medicine."

MEETING EVIL

In his introduction to the 2003 paperback edition of *Meeting Evil*, Jonathan Lethem groups it along with *Neighbors* and *The Houseguest* as Berger's "novels of menace," provisionally adding *Best Friends* as a "gentle capstone" to these books that all explore the interplay of victim with victimizer. This may be Berger's most intensely moralistic novel, since its deadly evil provocateur, Richie, confronts solid and somewhat dull good citizen John Felton with a situation beyond the redress of language or irony, compelling him finally to act in the only way that can "meet" Richie's threat. Another way of looking at this novel would be to group it with *Orrie's Story* and with *Changing the Past* as Berger's determined attempt to free himself from the received idea among reviewers that he is a "comic" novelist. These, despite humorous moments, are grim novels, and *Meeting Evil* is possibly the most grim of them all, as it offers no wiggle room in Felton's ultimate moral responsibility.

ROBERT CREWS

For the main characters in *Robert Crews* and *Suspects*, the medicine of life, while bitter, offers the possibility of some kind of redemption. The former novel is Berger's reworking of Defoe's *Robinson Crusoe*; however, Berger's eponymous hero is a far remove from Defoe's shipwrecked Christian incipient capitalist. Crews is an alcoholic parasite who is slowly drinking himself to death. Lost in some unidentified northern woods after a plane crash, with far fewer supplies than even Crusoe is provided with, Crews slowly and surely proves himself capable of surviving in what he calls "a state of nature." He saves not only himself but also his "Friday," a woman fleeing from an abusive husband. Although not quite as blameless as some others of Berger's "kickees," Crews is able at the end to approach what one critic has called the "esteem, apparent honor, and comradeship" that some Berger victim-protagonists attain. Crews's hold on them is precarious but, one at least hopes, lasting.

SUSPECTS

In *Suspects*, Berger provides the reader with two bungling protagonists: Nick Moody, an alcoholic detective investigating a murder case, and Lloyd Howland, brother-in-law and uncle of the two victims. The novel itself takes the form of the small-town police procedural, as in books by Hillary Waugh and K. C. Constantine. In this case, however, Berger, instead of recasting or reworking the mode, deepens it, particularly in his presentation of character. Almost every character, major or minor, from the real culprit to a rookie police officer introduced near the end, is fleshed out and given three dimensions. Even so, Berger probes several characteristic concerns: the workings of fate, miscommunication between human beings, and the instability of language.

Lloyd finds himself a suspect because of a series of incongruous yet logical steps in a chain of circum-

stances, "an unbroken progress he was powerless to alter." He keeps losing jobs, primarily because he is a typical Berger "kickee." His victimization is caused by the misinterpretation of his actions by those around him: When he tries to return a box opener to his boss, he is perceived as wielding a threatening weapon. The main crime in the novel is also committed because the victim's actions are misconstrued by the murderer (although in this case the error is much more willfully perverse). Both Lloyd and Nick Moody find themselves in their present circumstances because they cannot come up with an adequate definition for the word "love." This imprecision of definition in Lloyd's case makes him unable to have sex with someone with whom he is friends, and in Moody's case it leads to broken marriages and a strained relationship with his son. At the end of the novel, it is Lloyd's reaching out to Moody that saves the detective from committing suicide. It is unsure whether Lloyd will make the police force or Moody will quit drinking, but at least a hint of redemption is offered.

ADVENTURES OF THE ARTIFICIAL WOMAN

In one sense, *Adventures of the Artificial Woman* is as artificial as its animatronic main character, since Berger never intended the work to be published as a novel, thinking of it as a "literary conceit," a novelette he hoped would be published with a collection of his short stories. Its ostensible protagonist is Phyllis, a robot so lifelike she can pass for human, whose striking looks and capacity for intellectual growth lead her through a series of sex-worker jobs to acting jobs and finally to her greatest and most unsustainable job as president of the United States. Phyllis's all-too-likely adventures and moral-by-design nature afford Berger the opportunity to take broad satirical swipes at a number of human vagaries and at the humbug and posturing so firmly imbricated in contemporary media and political culture—and to confront Ellery, her creator, with the age-old moral responsibility of parent to child, creator to created creature.

Brooks Landon
Updated by William Laskowski

OTHER MAJOR WORKS

PLAYS: *Other People*, pr. 1970; *The Burglars: A Comedy in Two Acts*, pb. 1988.

RADIO PLAY: *At the Dentist's*, 1981.

BIBLIOGRAPHY

Landon, Brooks. *Thomas Berger.* Boston: Twayne, 1989. First book-length study of Berger draws from the author's correspondence with Berger to support the thesis that the interpretation of Berger's novels is the study of his style. Begins with a brief overview of Berger's career and then analyzes, by conceptual grouping, Berger's first fifteen novels.

Lethem, Jonathan. Introduction to *Meeting Evil*, by Thomas Berger. New York: Simon & Schuster, 2003. Presents a brilliant analysis of Berger's career, discussing his unique strengths as a writer and his place in American letters.

Madden, David W. *Critical Essays on Thomas Berger.* New York: G. K. Hall, 1995. Solid collection includes a valuable overview of Berger criticism by the editor, a lengthy interview with Berger, and the text of Berger's play *Other People.* Gerald Weales's 1983 essay "Reinhart as Hero and Clown," reprinted here, is perhaps still the best single discussion of the Reinhart books available.

Malone, Michael. "Berger, Burlesque, and the Yearning for Comedy." *Studies in American Humor* 2 (Spring, 1983): 20-32. One of the most instructive essays in the two-volume *Studies in American Humor* special issue on Berger, this piece offers a persuasive analysis of Berger's complexity that also considers why his achievements have not been better celebrated. Malone claims that whatever the novel form, Berger writes comedy, as opposed to comic novels.

Wallace, Jon. "A Murderous Clarity: A Reading of Thomas Berger's *Killing Time.*" *Philological Quarterly* 68 (Winter, 1989): 101-114. Offers superb analysis of the philosophical implications of Berger's use of sources in *Killing Time.* Wallace is one of the few critics to recognize the interpretive importance of Berger's style.

Wilde, Alan. "Acts of Definition: Or, Who Is Thomas Berger?" *Arizona Quarterly* 39 (Winter, 1983): 314-351. Instructive essay on Berger's work offers a phenomenology that recognizes the inseparability for the author of the concepts of freedom and self-definition. Wilde finds in Berger's novels, however, a "fear of otherness" that just as easily may be termed "fascination."

GEORGES BERNANOS

Born: Paris, France; February 20, 1888
Died: Neuilly-sur-Seine, France; July 5, 1948
Also known as: Paul Louis Georges Bernanos

PRINCIPAL LONG FICTION

Sous le soleil de Satan, 1926 (*The Star of Satan*, 1927; better known as *Under the Sun of Satan*, 1949)

L'Imposture, 1927 (*The Imposter*, 1999)

La Joie, 1929 (*Joy*, 1948)

Un Crime, 1935 (*A Crime*, 1936)

Journal d'un curé de campagne, 1936 (*The Diary of a Country Priest*, 1937)

Nouvelle Histoire de Mouchette, 1937 (*Mouchette*, 1966)

Monsieur Ouine, 1943, 1955 (*The Open Mind*, 1945)

Un Mauvais Rêve, 1950 (*Night Is Darkest*, 1953)

OTHER LITERARY FORMS

Georges Bernanos (behr-NAH-nohs) wrote one play, *Dialogues des Carmélites* (1949; *The Fearless Heart*, 1952), which he intended to be a film scenario. His short stories include "Madame Dargent," which appeared in 1922; "Une Nuit" (a night), in 1928; and "Dialogue d'ombres" (dialogue of shadows), in 1928. This last short story lends its title to a collection of Bernanos's short fiction, published in 1955. His hagiographical works include *Saint Dominique* (1926), *Jeanne, relapse et sainte* (1929; *Sanctity Will Out*, 1947), and *Frère Martin: Essai sur Luther* (1951; *Brother Martin*, 1952).

Bernanos wrote many essays and political articles, which are available in the following collections: *Le Crépuscule des vieux* (1956; the twilight of the aged), containing essays from 1909 to 1939, and *Français, si vous saviez* (1961; Frenchmen, if you knew), containing essays from 1945 to 1948. Although there is no complete collection of his correspondence, the most important letters are found in *Georges Bernanos: Essais et témoignages* (1949) and in many issues of *Bulletin de la Société des amis de Georges Bernanos*. A six-volume edition of his works, *Œuvres de Bernanos*, was published in 1947. His fiction is collected in *Œuvres romanesques, suivies de "Dialogues des Carmélites"* (1961).

ACHIEVEMENTS

Although Georges Bernanos was a prolific author, with eight major novels and numerous political and journalistic essays to his credit, his reputation will probably always rest on *Diary of a Country Priest* and, to a lesser extent, *The Fearless Heart*, set to music in an opera by Francis Poulenc. Bernanos's earlier works, such as *Under the Sun of Satan*, *L'Imposture*, and *Joy*, are dense, analytical, and disunited. His later works, including *The Open Mind* and *Mouchette*, are, despite their poetry and single vision, rather impenetrable to general readers. In *Diary of a Country Priest* and *The Fearless Heart*, however, Bernanos's characters attain a heroism that is self-giving, capable of overcoming fear and attaining self-acceptance.

It is perhaps this human dimension of Bernanos's heroes that most attracts the public. Bernanos was oriented toward the human limitations of humankind, rejecting the Nietzschean superman. Like Honoré de Balzac, he explored the social dimension of human relations rather than political theories, although much of his early journalistic work was intended to support the Action Française movement, and social themes constitute a large segment of his novels. His aim was to preserve the freedom of modern humans, who, in Bernanos's view, had become the slave of "civilization." Like Charles-Pierre Péguy, he deplored the corruptive power of money, of a world wrapped in paper. He mistrusted the machine and modern industrialism. He detested mediocrity and chose as his heroes young people with the ability to save a decadent and paralyzed society.

With his invectives against modern society symbolically expressed in the parishes of Ambricourt and Fenouille, which are drowned in a sea of "ennui," Bernanos, like Péguy, takes his place in "la vieille France," the France of days gone by, of Saint Louis, Joan of Arc, and Pierre Corneille. Yet, as Hans Urs von Balthasar observes, Bernanos is a very modern writer, for he loves the past only to appreciate the future. He loves the monarchy, not because of a desire to return to the past, but because it represents a certain order that is absent from the modern world.

Not only Bernanos's penetration of a changing social order but also his powerful characterization lead the reader to see in him a disciple of Balzac, whom he greatly admired. Where Balzac's description passes from the exterior to the interior, however, Bernanos's is primarily interior—although not without characteristic physical description: the unkempt cassock of the Curé of Ambricourt or his beautiful eyes, the nose and nudity of the Mayor of Fenouille. Brian Fitch observes that Bernanos always writes the same novel; consequently, his heroes, like Balzac's, reappear throughout his oeuvre. Although Bernanos gives them different names, they are the same person. Chevance and Ambricourt are descended from Donissan; Saint-Marin and Monsieur de Clergerie seem like brothers. Mouchette resembles her namesake in *Under the Sun of Satan*—as Bernanos himself put it—in "the same tragic solitude in which I saw both live and die."

Perhaps Bernanos's most outstanding achievement derives from his deep spiritual dimension. He is a Christian prophet and visionary in the line of Léon Bloy, with whom he did not wish to be identified, and Péguy, whom he greatly admired. A contemporary of Paul Claudel and François Mauriac, Bernanos subscribed neither to Claudel's triumphalistic Catholicism nor to Mauriac's sexual preoccupations. Perhaps his sensibility is most akin to that of Fyodor Dostoevski, from whom he differs not in content but in style, presenting his characters in an analytical and spiritual rather than a dramatic and social setting. Bernanos faced the problem of the de-Christianization of the modern world, of a selfish and

Georges Bernanos. (Time & Life Pictures/Getty Images)

most all of Bernanos's novels. Bernanos was influenced both by his mother's staunch piety and by his father's anti-Semitism. Although Bernanos was an avid reader, his childhood was marked by frequent changes in schools, for he was not a model student. He formed close ties, however, with some of his teachers—such as Abbé Lagrange at Bourges and later Dom Besse—and always showed great enthusiasm for spiritual pursuits.

In 1906, Bernanos became strongly attracted to Charles Maurras's militant royalist movement, Action Française, to which he adhered faithfully until the beginning of the 1930's. From 1906 to 1913, he pursued both a *licence* in letters and one in law at the Institut Catholique in Paris. In 1913, he moved to Rouen, where he became editor in chief of the local royalist newspaper *L'Avant-garde de Normandie*. It was there that he met his future wife, Jeanne Talbert d'Arc, a direct descendant of Joan of Arc's brother. They were married in 1917, while Bernanos was still engaged in military service during World War I. It was to prove a happy and fruitful marriage—six children were born to the couple between 1918 and 1933—although it was marked by many illnesses and financial difficulties.

Bernanos's first job, as an insurance inspector, was to be of short duration; after 1926, he devoted himself exclusively to writing, following the success of his first novel, *Under the Sun of Satan.* Although he continued his support of Maurras until 1931, he, like Péguy, was greatly disillusioned to see that his ideal, embodied in the Action Française, was to deteriorate into expediency. Also like Péguy, Bernanos was not without a certain hubris in his loyalty to the movement, as Balthasar notes; he manifested the self-righteousness he so criticized in others. During this period, financial pressures and inner tensions caused Bernanos frequently to uproot his family, and he settled for a time in Majorca in Spain. A motorcycle accident in 1933 left him disabled for life. In 1938, he finally left the Continent for Brazil, where he remained until 1945, returning home at the invitation of Charles de Gaulle. Despite his absence from his native country during World War II, Bernanos remained true to his great passion, France, through his frequent polemics and articles. Yet soon after his return, in 1946, he refused membership in the French Legion of Honor for the third time.

apathetic society alienated from God and from itself. Yet, unlike most writers of the 1920's and 1930's, Bernanos was a prophet of hope and salvation, which he believed would be realized through redemptive suffering and Christian love. Most of all, he was, as Balthasar says, the prophet of divine grace—not that of Jansenistic predestination, but that which connotes true freedom for the human being. His awareness of God is profound and almost mystical; grace, for Bernanos, is "la douce pitié de Dieu," the gentle pity of God.

BIOGRAPHY

Although the life of Georges Bernanos, born Paul Louis Georges Bernanos, began and ended in Paris, the word "restless" best describes the many wanderings that led him to towns and cities in France, Spain, South America, and Africa. Possibly of Spanish descent, his father, Émile Bernanos, was an interior decorator of good business ability. The family, which included Bernanos's sister, Thérèse, spent the summers at Fressin, in Pas-de-Calais, and the north of France was to be the scene for al-

Although Bernanos's restlessness continued (the following year would see him in Tunisia, doing work on behalf of Action Française), he completed one of his major works at this time, *The Fearless Heart*. With his own death imminent, the work became his spiritual testament, confronting the fear of death and the fear of loss of honor with sublime courage. Bernanos died at the American Hospital in Neuilly-sur-Seine, a Paris suburb, on July 5, 1948.

ANALYSIS

As a novelist preoccupied with spiritual conflicts, Georges Bernanos repeatedly explored the symbolic contrast between the innocent vulnerability of childhood and the corrupt world of humanity. Bernanos's children and adolescents are of two types: the suffering adolescent and victim, and the innocent young girl. Mouchette, "Sainte Brigitte du néant" (Saint Brigitte of the void), crushed by society and family, and Steeny of *The Open Mind*, who emerges from his childhood innocence, belong to the first category: We also find adults who have experienced humiliation in childhood, such as Monsieur Ouine or Mouchette's mother, so like one of Dostoevski's suffering women. Perhaps the best illustration of the second type, the innocent young girl, is Chantal de Clergerie, whom Bernanos modeled on Saint Thérèse of Lisieux.

Bernanos also creates adult heroes who are granted the fresh spiritual vision of a child, often at the moment of death, such as the Curé of Ambricourt and Chevance and, to a lesser degree, the ascetic Donissan. Always indifferent to the approval of society and to their own pleasure, they are nevertheless deeply aware of good and evil. Such is the Curé of Ambricourt, who reads the souls of Chantal and her mother. Like Saint Thérèse of Lisieux, these characters show the spirit of hope, abandonment to God, and self-acceptance.

Just as children and motifs of childhood appear throughout Bernanos's fiction, so too does the symbolic figure of the priest; the role of the priest, like that of the child, is to dramatize the spiritual conflict that is at the heart of human experience. Bernanos's priests also fall into two categories: the self-effacing and the self-assured. Those in the first category are apparently lacking in intelligence; they are unattractive, like Donissan, Chevance, and the Curé of Ambricourt. They are, however, endowed with supernatural lucidity and clairvoyance, which is different from psychological insight, for it is manifested in a love of souls most consumed by evil. At the same time, the priest himself suffers from a slow and consuming agony. Gaëton Picon maintains that Bernanos chose a priest-hero because such a figure represents the only person in the modern world capable of accepting the spirituality rejected by contemporary civilization. He does so in his solitude and silence, yet he is totally involved in the process of Salvation. He is thus the model for all human beings, who should be instruments of grace for one another.

The second type of priest, who is self-assured, robust, and intellectual, is seldom the sacerdotal ideal. Cénabre, in *L'Imposture* and *Joy*, is a man who has lost his faith but who ironically studies the lives of the saints. The Curé of Fenouille, though ascetic, is not expansive or loving; consequently, he embodies the emptiness of his "dead parish." Finally, Monsieur Ouine is an antipriest, a caricature of the sacerdotal vocation who is unable to give a firm answer, as his name (*oui*, "yes"; *ne*, "no" or "not") indicates. He experiences agony, as do the Curé of Ambricourt and Chevance, but his self-seeking prevents that agony from becoming redemptive.

Suffering and agony are the lot of both the good and the evil characters in Bernanos's novels. The Curé of Ambricourt suffers from the loss of God; Chantal de Clergerie, as Albert Béguin observes, goes to the heart of the agony of Christ. Monsieur Ouine suffers from his emptiness; Mouchette, from her humiliation. Death, usually violent, comes to at least one and often several characters in each of Bernanos's novels. Many die by suicide, just as contemporary civilization pushes people toward spiritual suicide. This suicide is one of despair in Doctor Delbende, of pride in Fiodor, of humiliation in Mouchette, of passion in Hélène and Eugène Devandomme. Murder claims Chantal de Clergerie and Jambe-de-Laine; death, after a spiritual agony, comes to the Curé of Ambricourt.

This somber world of violence reflects the inner world of satanic thirst and spiritual emptiness that is particularly evident in modern society. It is personified in Satan, who, in Bernanos's first novel, is incarnated as a crafty horse dealer; it is internalized in the unbelieving

Cénabre; and it is obliquely suggested in the seductive Ouine. The omnipresent parish represents the modern world. Ambricourt is devoured by ennui, or apathy; Fenouille is a "dead parish" (the original title of *The Open Mind*). Bernanos saw mediocrity and self-righteousness as the greatest of modern evils, the cancers that devour society. Like Péguy, Bernanos deplored the de-Christianization of France and the irresistible attraction to Satan.

The satanic world appears as a hallucination, *un mauvais rêve* (a bad dream), as one novel is titled. *The Open Mind* reads like a nightmare; many scenes in *Mouchette* are hallucinatory, such as the young girl's conversation with the old woman who keeps vigil over the dead (her suicide is like a rhythmic drowning). Henri Debluë sees the dream as one of Bernanos's principal motifs, yet it is not always a bad dream. With Balthasar, Debluë believes that the good dream gives an existential dimension to Bernanos, representing his desire for Being—which, for Bernanos, is the human community in Christ.

UNDER THE SUN OF SATAN

Begun in 1919 and written in cafés and trains, *Under the Sun of Satan* was finally published in 1926. It is composed of three apparently disconnected parts, although many critics, including Claudel, see in it an inherent unity. Bernanos did not write the novel in its final order; he completed the last part first and the second part, the account of Donissan's meeting with the Devil, last. The model for the hero Donissan is Saint Jean-Baptiste-Marie Vianney, Curé of Ars (1768-1859). The novel was an immediate success; as William Bush observes, the unusual incarnation of Satan appealed to a public that was weary of escapism as found in André Gide and Marcel Proust.

The subject of the novel, according to Bernanos, is "the sun of Satan in whose black light mankind basks." The hero, Donissan, is guilty of sin in wanting to know if God is really in command and if Satan can be conquered. He realizes his error in the third part of the story, when he is unable to bring a dead child back to life because he wanted the miracle, not for the honor of God, but for himself. He dies shortly afterward and the reader is led to believe that he has come to a true knowledge of God and himself.

Bernanos was faced with the challenge of integrating

this conclusion into the rest of the story, which he had begun with a character who was to haunt him for a long time and to whom he was to return later, Mouchette. One of his suffering adolescents, the Mouchette of *Under the Sun of Satan* is the victim of greedy parents and an apathetic society. She commits double adultery, murders her first lover, and, after a nervous collapse, gives birth to a stillborn child. It is not until the second part that the reader sees the results of her crimes, for which she is only partially responsible.

It is in fact the second part, "The Temptation of Despair," that links parts 1 and 3. It introduces readers to the awkward, overly ascetic Abbé Donissan, who one night gets lost on the way to a neighboring village and encounters the Devil, a crafty horse dealer, eventually the reflection of Donissan's own face. After a sinister conversation with his enemy, Donissan realizes that he has the gift of reading souls. His most important meeting is with Mouchette, whose secrets he reveals. Although there is no indication of a change of heart in Mouchette, her dying request to be brought into the Church and Donissan's rapid compliance seem to indicate an exchange of grace between the suffering victim and the saintly priest, a theme that was to characterize many of Bernanos's works.

DIARY OF A COUNTRY PRIEST

Composed rapidly between 1934 and 1936, at the same time that Bernanos was writing about a contrasting theme in *The Open Mind*, *Diary of a Country Priest* was unreservedly acclaimed as a masterpiece. Unlike its predecessors, *L'Imposture* and *Joy*, it is remarkable for its unity. The entire story is in diary form, told from the first-person point of view, which gives the story a compelling directness. Written with gentleness and simplicity, it does not have the extravagance of *Under the Sun of Satan*. It was Bernanos's favorite novel, and it has maintained its popularity; in 1936, it received the Grand Prix du Roman of the French Academy.

Like all of Bernanos's parishes, Ambricourt represents the modern world, dying of apathy. The Curé himself is dying of a cancer that he does not know he has, aggravated by an alcoholic heritage and his own poor nutrition habits. He is unattractive, awkward, and ill at ease. The self-righteous, like the Count of the neighboring château, scorn him, yet tormented sinners and God-seekers that recall Dostoevskian characters—Doctor Delbende, the Countess, the companion of Louis Dupréty, the defrocked priest—all seek him, for they instinctively realize his innate goodness.

The turning point of the story is the interview of the Curé with the Countess, a selfish woman, disappointed in marriage, who lives in the past with her memories of her dead child. She has thus alienated her living child, Chantal, as well as her husband, who seeks the affection of the governess, much to the distress and jealousy of Chantal. Yet the priest fearlessly reveals to the Countess her sin, enabling her to accept herself. The emotional stress proves too great for her, however, and she dies. The priest, unable to reveal the conversation, is falsely accused by the family of complicity in her death. Although the priest also confronts Chantal without a similar acknowledgment on her part, the reader is led to believe that this tormented adolescent, too, may have found grace through the self-sacrifice of the saintly priest.

It is perhaps in the final exchange between the Curé of Ambricourt and his former classmate, Louis Dupréty, that the mystery of grace is revealed most clearly. The Curé of Ambricourt learns of Dupréty's impending death and is forced to spend the night with him. It is in this situation that the agony of death overcomes Dupréty, and he realizes that simple acceptance of oneself is all that God requires of him. In perfect self-abandonment and trust, he receives absolution from the defrocked priest, for, as he says in the concluding words of the novel, "Everything is grace."

THE OPEN MIND

Unlike Bernanos's other novels, except, perhaps, *Mouchette*, *The Open Mind* is a story without hope. Even the history of its composition was marked by frustration. Bernanos began it in 1931 and, while he was writing it, suffered his rupture with Maurras, the motorcycle accident that disabled him for life, financial disasters, and the loss of a great part of the manuscript. He finished the novel in 1940, at the beginning of the Occupation. It was published in Brazil, with many typographical errors and omissions. Only in 1955, when Béguin carefully edited the text after consulting Bernanos's manuscripts, was a definitive edition published by the Club des Libraires de France.

Béguin considers *The Open Mind* to be Bernanos's greatest work, and indeed, while writing it, Bernanos himself planned it as his masterpiece. Here, Béguin argues, Bernanos pushed his exploration of the interior world to the furthest possible limit. A novel that treats extreme acts, including seductions, murders, suicides, and deeds of madness, it derives its unity from its hallucinatory manner rather than from its plot. The hero, Monsieur Ouine, based on Gide, is an ambiguous person who, as his name indicates, says yes and no (*oui, ne*) at the same time. Although he does not really dominate the story, he provides the conclusion. According to Bush, he and most other characters of the novel seem to symbolize the decay of modern civilization, the aimlessness of society, and the apathy of a de-Christianized world.

A difficult work for the general reader, *The Open Mind* has a complex plot in which the horrors of violence and seduction are suggested rather than developed. The story is set in Fenouille, in the Artois district, and revolves mainly around Philippe, or Steeny, one of Bernanos's suffering adolescents, who is disillusioned with his ailing mother and her intimate companion, Miss. The same Miss seems to make advances to Steeny, as does the neighboring Madame de Néréis, or Jambe-de-Laine, mistress of the château of Wambescourt. Finally, Monsieur Ouine, a retired professor of languages who lives at the château, tries to win Steeny. The confused youth, with a desire for love and a nostalgia for innocence, becomes accidentally involved in the murder of a young farm boy, probably committed by Monsieur Ouine. This murder precipitates the double suicide of the two lovers, Hélène and Eugène Devandomme, the lynching of Jambe-de-Laine, and the probable suicide of the Mayor.

It is in the conversations of the priest with Monsieur Ouine and later with the Mayor, in the priest's sermon, and in Monsieur Ouine's final words to Steeny before his death that we probe the complexity of these characters' personalities. All three have a nostalgia for goodness. The Curé is even ascetic and intellectual, but love of God and service to others are not among his virtues. He lacks the childlike spiritual insight of the Curé of Ambricourt, conceived by Bernanos at the same time. The Mayor is sensual and clever but not simple and trusting. Monsieur Ouine, the victim of an unhappy childhood and a premature seduction, gives the impression of "calm and lucid acceptance," yet he is destroyed by his intellectual perversion, not unlike Cénabre. It is thus by negative images that Bernanos focuses on the need for hope, the spiritual freshness of childhood, and the exchange of grace. Without them, life becomes an infernal hallucination, as in the town of Fenouille.

Bernanos's desire to bring sinners and the suffering back to community in Christ is the source of his hope. As a prophet of divine grace, he evokes redemption through an exchange between two human beings. The agony of Donissan brings light to Mouchette, who, although she kills herself, asks to be brought into the church to die. Chevance entrusts Chantal with his joy to save Cénabre. The Curé of Ambricourt brings the Countess to an acknowledgment of her sin and is himself given final absolution by a defrocked priest. Blanche de la Force receives the ultimate grace of martyrdom through the Prioress's offering of herself. It is thus through human means that God operates in grace, for Bernanos's theology is based on the Incarnation. It is a down-to-earth mysticism, profoundly Christian yet articulating the universal human need for forgiveness and salvation.

Irma M. Kashuba

OTHER MAJOR WORKS

SHORT FICTION: *Dialogue d'ombres*, 1955.

PLAY: *Dialogues des Carmélites*, pb. 1949 (*The Fearless Heart*, 1952).

NONFICTION: *Dominique*, 1926; *Noël à la maison de France*, 1928; *Jeanne, relapse et sainte*, 1929 (*Sanctity Will Out*, 1947); *La Grande Peur des bien-pensants*, 1931; *Les Grands Cimetières sous la lune*, 1938 (*A Diary of My Times*, 1938); *Nous autres français*, 1939; *Lettre aux anglais*, 1942 (*Plea for Liberty*, 1944); *La France contre les robots*, 1947 (*Tradition of Freedom*, 1950); *Les Enfants humiliés*, 1949 (included in *Tradition of Freedom*, 1950); *Georges Bernanos: Essais et témoignages*, 1949; *Frère Martin: Essai sur Luther*, 1951 (*Brother Martin*, 1952); *Le Crépuscule des vieux*, 1956 (wr. 1909-1939); *Français, si vous saviez*, 1961 (wr. 1945-1948); *Correspondance*, 1971 (2 volumes; Jean Murray and Albert Béguin, editors); *Lettres rétrouvées, 1904-1948*, 1983 (Jean-Loup Bernanos, editor).

MISCELLANEOUS: *Œuvres de Bernanos*, 1947 (6 volumes); *Œuvres romanesques, suivies de "Dialogues des*

Carmélites," 1961; *The Heroic Face of Innocence: Three Stories*, 1999.

BIBLIOGRAPHY

Balthasar, Hans Urs von. *Bernanos: An Ecclesial Existence*. Translated by Erasmo Leiva-Merikakis. San Francisco, Calif.: Ignatius Press, 1996. Balthasar, a theologian, analyzes Bernanos's works. He describes Bernanos as a "deeply prayerful, practicing sacramental Catholic" who made everything he wrote an "ecclesial existence that has been given form."

Blumenthal, Gerda. *The Poetic Imagination of Georges Bernanos: An Essay in Interpretation*. Baltimore: Johns Hopkins University Press, 1965. Focuses primarily on *The Diary of a Country Priest*, but Blumenthal's discussion of Bernanos's mystical explanation of human behavior can be applied to all of the author's work.

Brée, Germaine, and Margaret Guiton. "Private Worlds." In *An Age of Fiction: The French Novel from Gide to Camus*. New Brunswick, N.J.: Rutgers University Press, 1957. A literary history that places Bernanos within the context of twentieth century French novelists. Brée and Guiton view Bernanos's reticence and revelation as complementary.

Bush, William. *Georges Bernanos*. New York: Twayne, 1969. This volume in the Twayne Authors' series provides an overview of Bernanos's life and work. Bush suggests that totalitarian order was a major preoccupation of Bernanos.

Curran, Beth Kathryn. *Touching God: The Novels of Georges Bernanos in the Films of Robert Bresson*. New York: Peter Lang, 2006. French filmmaker Bresson adapted two of Bernanos's novels to the screen: *The Diary of a Country Priest* and *Mouchette*. Curran explains how both Bernanos and Bresson articulate grace and redemption in their work through the suffering and death of their protagonists.

Fraser, Theodore P. *The Modern Catholic Novel in Europe*. New York: Twayne, 1994. Fraser traces the development of the modern European Catholic novel from nineteenth century France through the Vatican II reforms of the 1960's. Chapter 2 focuses on Bernanos and other French novelists.

Molnar, Thomas. *Bernanos: His Political Thought and*

Prophecy. 1960. Reprint. New Brunswick, N.J.: Transaction, 1997. An examination of Bernanos's conservative political and social views. Includes a new introduction by the author.

Schroth, Raymond A. *Dante to "Dead Man Walking": One Reader's Journey Through the Christian Classics*. Chicago: Loyola Press, 2001. Schroth, a Jesuit priest and college professor, provides overviews of fifty literary works, including *The Diary of a Country Priest*, to discover what each book says about Christian faith and doctrine.

Tobin, Michael R. *Georges Bernanos: The Theological Source of His Art*. Montreal: McGill-Queen's Uni-

versity Press, 2007. A biography and a literary critique of Bernanos's work. Tobin analyzes the themes of Bernanos's novels and other works to demonstrate how the incarnation of God in Jesus Christ was the fundamental theological truth common to all of his writings.

Whitehouse, J. C. *Vertical Man: The Human Being in the Catholic Novels of Graham Greene, Sigrid Undset, and Georges Bernanos*. London: Saint Austin Press, 1999. Whitehorse analyzes and compares the works of the three novelists, concentrating on how they depict the relationship of the individual human being with his or her God.

THOMAS BERNHARD

Born: Heerlen, the Netherlands; February 9 or 10, 1931
Died: Gmunden, Austria; February 12, 1989
Also known as: Nicolaas Thomas Bernhard

PRINCIPAL LONG FICTION

Frost, 1963 (English translation, 2006)
Verstörung, 1967 (*Gargoyles*, 1970)
Das Kalkwerk, 1970 (*The Lime Works*, 1973)
Korrektur, 1975 (*Correction*, 1979)
Ja, 1978 (*Yes*, 1991)
Die Billigesser, 1980 (*The Cheap-Eaters*, 1990)
Beton, 1982 (*Concrete*, 1984)
Der Untergeher, 1983 (*The Loser*, 1991)
Holzfällen: Eine Erregung, 1984 (*Woodcutters*, 1987; also known as *Cutting Timber: An Imitation*, 1988)
Alte Meister, 1985 (*Old Masters*, 1989)
Auslöschung: Ein Zerfall, 1986 (*Extinction*, 1995)
In der Höhe: Rettungsversuch, Unsinn, 1989 (*On the Mountain: Rescue Attempt, Nonsense*, 1991)

OTHER LITERARY FORMS

Thomas Bernhard (BEHRN-hahrt) published at a prolific pace after the appearance of his first book, a vol-

ume of poems, in 1957. In addition to his novels, he wrote several volumes of poetry as well as many dramatic works of varying style and popularity, and he was widely acknowledged as one of the leading contemporary playwrights in German. Perhaps Bernhard's most important work, equal in power to his fiction, is his five-volume autobiographical sequence, which covers his life from his earliest years to the age of nineteen: *Die Ursache: Eine Andeutung* (1975; *An Indication of the Cause*, 1985), *Der Keller: Eine Entziehung* (1976; *The Cellar: An Escape*, 1985), *Der Atem: Eine Entscheidung* (1978; *Breath: A Decision*, 1985), *Die Kälte: Eine Isolation* (1981; *In the Cold*, 1985), and *Ein Kind* (1982; *A Child*, 1985); the last volume is chronologically the first. Bernhard made programmatic statements only reluctantly, sometimes in terse and often provocative newspaper and radio interviews; the most important formulations in this regard are his acceptance speeches for several prestigious literary awards.

ACHIEVEMENTS

In the mid-1960's, critics and the German-speaking public began to take a serious interest in Thomas Bernhard, recognizing in his work an original voice and an extraordinary, if uncompromisingly bleak, vision. This critical fascination with Bernhard has, in the main, withstood the test of time, but the interest and reactions the author evokes are negative as often as they are positive. George Steiner, for example, has called Bernhard "the most original, concentrated novelist writing in German," linking him with "the great constellation of [Hugo von] Hofmannsthal, [Franz] Kafka, [Robert] Musil," yet Steiner has also said that Bernhard's later works betray a lack of new insight, that originality gave way to formulaic themes and clichés.

It can be said that Bernhard always appealed to a rather limited audience. His work presents the same kind of resistance to facile understanding as that of Samuel Beckett; his literary practice is not straightforward or discursive; his somewhat stock themes are by no means uplifting. Thus, while his readership has never been large, particularly in the English-speaking world (where many novels and plays have been translated but have been almost uniformly ignored by critics and readers alike), he received virtually every significant Austrian and German literary award, including the Georg Büchner Prize, considered the pinnacle of literary recognition in Germany.

Biography

Thomas Bernhard was born in Heerlen (near Maastricht) in the Netherlands on February 10, 1931, of Austrian parents. His ancestors were Austrian peasants, innkeepers, and butchers in Salzburg and Upper Austria, but he spent his earliest childhood years living with his grandparents in Vienna. He later moved with them to Traunstein, in Bavaria, and in 1943 he was sent to a boarding school in Salzburg. There he experienced not only humiliations at the hands of his teachers and fellow pupils but also the air raids and bombings of the city along with the chaotic end of World War II. In 1947— soon after his family had moved to Salzburg—Bernhard left the school to take up an apprenticeship in a grocer's shop in the worst part of Salzburg. This act signified not only a decision to abandon his formal education but also a rejection of the conventional career and existence that he felt were being imposed on him from outside. His early and chosen path was thus away from the normative to the periphery of society, a descent into an abyss that reflected his own inner state. In 1948, a serious illness brought Bernhard close to death, and he had to spend a good deal of time in a tuberculosis sanatorium; it was there that he began to write.

In 1949, Bernhard suffered a serious emotional blow—the death of his grandfather, the Austrian writer Johannes Freumbichler, a man who had a profound influence on Bernhard's intellectual development. It was Freumbichler who became the model on which Bernhard patterned the male protagonists of many of his works. In 1950, Bernhard was keenly affected by the death of his mother, to whom he was very close. In the years from 1952 to 1957, Bernhard studied the plastic arts, music, and drama at the Mozarteum in Salzburg, and from 1953 to 1955, he was also a legal correspondent for the Socialist newspaper *Demokratisches Volksblatt*. He traveled to Yugoslavia and Sicily before his first volume of poetry appeared in 1957, and in the same year, he completed his music studies. In 1960 and 1961, he was in London, working both as a legal corre-

Thomas Bernhard. (Courtesy, Teos)

spondent and as a librarian. In 1962 and 1963, Bernhard lived in Poland, and in the latter year, his first major prose work, *Frost*, appeared. After 1965, Bernhard lived as an independent writer on a farm in Ohlsdorf, near Gmunden, Upper Austria. He died there of a heart attack on February 12, 1989; he was fifty-eight years old.

ANALYSIS

Thomas Bernhard's work can be characterized as a series of variations on certain recurring themes and situations. While this consistency gives his work a certain formal cohesion, it also, quite naturally, leads many critics to fault him for sterility of imagination or manic obsessiveness. The almost overwhelming negativity of Bernhard's novels is autobiographical, rooted in the agony of the author's own existence. Bernhard himself stated that, for him, writing was both a search for the origins of his personal disaster and an attempt—an ultimately Sisyphean attempt—to maintain equilibrium in the face of despair. Writing for Bernhard was thus a form of therapy, but therapy conducted in a never-ending session, because there would be no ultimate healing. In a television interview, Bernhard once compared himself to a surgeon who desperately performs a series of operations on himself to rid his body of cancerous growths, growths that reappear as fast as they are removed. The metaphor of disease and the hopelessness implied by Bernhard's comparison are both reminiscent of Kafka.

In the prototypical situation of Bernhard's fiction, an individual—normally a man—receives a "shock" of some sort, whether in the form of a personally catastrophic experience or in an existential moment of loss. In any event, the victim is left emotionally and psychologically deranged, unable to carry on as before and confronted overwhelmingly by a sense of mortality, by the fatal inevitability of death. This individual situation, in turn, is implicitly elevated to an absolute and universal condition, so that there remains but one vantage point for viewing the panorama of human existence: the finality of death. As Bernhard said in his scandalous speech on the occasion of his acceptance of the Austrian State Prize for Literature, "When one thinks about death, everything in human life seems ridiculous."

A somewhat natural adjunct to this situation is the theme of language or, more correctly, the failure and futility of language. Often in Bernhard's fiction one encounters men who are absorbed in a study of some sort, a study that is to reach fruition by being written down, expressed in a personal act of creation. This attempt to assert oneself in the face of death's inevitable destruction is, of course, almost always unsuccessful. The psychological cripples who are Bernhard's protagonists often despair of the efficacy of language as a communicative vehicle and retreat to a life of total introspection, devoting themselves instead to meditating on topics such as madness, the relationship between the individual and the state, disease, and death.

This critical attitude toward language places Bernhard in an Austrian tradition the roots of which can be traced to Hugo von Hofmannsthal and Ludwig Wittgenstein. The former's despairing "Ein Brief" (1902; "Letter of Lord Chandos," 1952) was one of the earliest literary expressions of loss of faith in language and remains one of the most powerful; Wittgenstein's philosophical reflections on language and its limits had a profound formative influence on Bernhard. As a result, Bernhard is caught in a literary cul-de-sac from which there seems to be no escape: Much of the tension that imbues his work derives from the paradox that he is a writer who is impelled constantly to question his medium. On one hand, he conveys meaning, he communicates by means of his writing, but on the other hand, he constantly retracts this possibility and declares that language cannot bring people into contact with one another or the world of things; on the contrary, it merely emphasizes the painful isolation of the individual speaker: "I speak the language which only I understand, just as each of us understands only his own language." It has been suggested, therefore, that Bernhard's "antiliterature" is obsessed less with the theme of death qua death than it is with the death of meaning.

FROST

When it appeared in 1963, Bernhard's first novel, *Frost*, caused a sensation. Although some critics pronounced the book "disgusting" and the author "only of regional Austrian interest," Carl Zuckmayer wrote in *Die Zeit* on June 21, 1963, that the novel was "one of the most stirring and urgent prose works" he had encountered in years. Focusing fixedly on the themes of sickness and death in its long, involved, and almost breathless sentences, *Frost* set the tone for what was to follow in Bernhard's compulsive fiction.

In effect, *Frost* functions as a bildungsroman in reverse. The protagonist, a medical student completing his *Famulatur*, or clinical internship, is charged with the task of observing and reporting on a painter named Strauch, a man who has retreated to the remote mountain village of Weng, has burned all of his paintings, and is in the process of a complete mental collapse. The assignment, therefore, is quite literally part of the student's education, and he fully intends to carry out his study with an objective and critical attitude. The young intern quickly discovers, however, that he will have to report on ontological more than on medical problems, and he slowly but surely begins to abandon his detached viewpoint for a more subjective one. What the medical student, the narrator of the novel, experiences can be described as a nightmarish sequence of intimate glimpses into the personality of the painter Strauch, as a terrifying fairy tale minus the traditional happy ending. The painter drags him about in the snow while explicating his philosophy of decay, confronting the young student with memories of ghostly accidents, putrescent funerals, and rotting war dead dotting wasted landscapes.

Feeling himself becoming "sucked in" by all of this, the narrator attempts at first to resist the perverse attraction of Strauch's monologues (which constitute a large portion of the text of *Frost*) because he knows that they are the product of a diseased mind. The painter talks incessantly of himself, of his hallucinations, his paranoia, his severing of contact with the outside world, his complete lack of interest in anything but his own psyche. He is "a person living a precarious existence in the world of the imagination," an individual in a state of complete and admittedly unproductive detachment. Isolation, the goal of total encapsulation within himself, is the painter's obsession, and he constantly returns to the image of the absolute and final cold, the coming frost that will deprive everything of life. It will be a time when "the stars will flash like nails closing the lids of heaven," when the apocalyptic cold will be inside and outside all landscapes and all animals and people populating them.

By the end of the novel, the medical student has lost his power to stand firm in his own identity and can only

conduct his "scientific" reporting in the language and idiom of his case history: "He simply slips his vulnerability into me in the form of sentences, like slides into a projector, which then casts these terrors on the ever present walls of my (and his) self." Unlike the typical protagonist of the bildungsroman, therefore, the medical student in *Frost* has not gained in self-realization and has not become more well balanced; on the contrary, his progression is a regression, because he has fallen prey to a mentor from whom he is ultimately indistinguishable.

This development has implications for the narrative perspective of *Frost*, implications that Bernhard develops in his later novels. Because the medical-student narrator of *Frost* surrenders his objectivity in describing the fate of the painter Strauch, the reader is also left somewhat at a loss to assess and interpret the narrative. All seems dispassionately presented and objectively recorded, but can one trust a narrator who becomes subsumed in the personality of a deranged monomaniac? The question grows even more acute in Bernhard's subsequent work.

GARGOYLES

Bernhard's second novel, *Gargoyles* (the German title, *Verstörung*, which the distinguished translators Richard Winston and Clara Winston chose to ignore, suggests "bewilderment" or "derangement"), is in several respects an extension or continuation of *Frost*. The motto for the work is a dictum from Blaise Pascal's *Pensées* (1670; *Monsieur Pascal's Thoughts, Meditations, and Prayers*, 1688; best known as *Pensées*), "The eternal silence of these infinite spaces terrifies me," and the theme of isolation and the inability to communicate is introduced at every turn. The novel is sustained (or, in the opinion of some critics, fails to be sustained) by an extremely pared-down plot in which action is reduced to a minimum. A doctor's son has returned home from university studies, and in an attempt to bridge their mutual estrangement, the doctor takes the son with him on his rounds. Together, they visit patients, all of whom are in various stages of physical decay or mental torment, such as the industrialist who has shut himself up in his house, where he perpetually writes and summarily destroys what he has written, and the young boy, crippled and insane, who is kept in a cage in a bedroom, where his atrophied body gives off a foul odor.

The bulk of the novel, however, is devoted to the final patient, a prince by the name of Saurau who lives in a castle high on a mountain. The meandering outpourings of this aristocrat are reminiscent of Arthur Schopenhauer—all that Saurau touches upon is tainted with negativity. Saurau's remarks cover everything from technology to psychology and are constantly shifting and a bit out of focus, but his long monologue is galvanized by three central themes: decay and corruption (in the state, Europe, and the world); the violence of nature; and the self-destructive essence of all human relationships, particularly familial ones (Saurau's father has committed suicide, and Saurau anticipates that his own son will do the same). Saurau summarizes, in a sense, his philosophical outlook when he states that "mankind is nothing more than a collective community of dying which is now in the billions and spread out over five continents." Much like Strauch in *Frost*, he has limited his contact with the outside world to reading newspapers and resolutely awaits "the final end." Appropriately enough, the novel "concludes" in midsentence.

Saurau's long monologue constitutes approximately the final third of the novel. Once again, as in *Frost*, the narrative perspective becomes dominated not by a "trustworthy" chronicler (the doctor's son) but by a transmitter who shatters the foundation of traditional realistic narration: the ability to distinguish competently between inner and outer reality and to comment on both. The reader is left immersed in a psyche that cannot maintain borders between inner and outer worlds and thus gains no insight into "universal connections," only into the phantasies and derangements of a sick, self-ensconced mind.

It is small wonder, therefore, that Bernhard's second novel brought him little critical acclaim. Although some critics acknowledged a "persuasive stylistic power . . . that embraces characters and objects as well as locales and landscapes involved," many others could comment only on Bernhard's "extraordinary one-sidedness," on his extremely negative themes and characters, or on his "unstructured, plotless outpourings," which "quickly pall upon a reader through their repetitiousness." For these reasons, perhaps, Bernhard made some rather significant formal changes in his next novel, *The Lime Works*.

THE LIME WORKS

With the publication of *The Lime Works* in 1970, Bernhard achieved a literary tour de force that must have been surprising even to him: The novel brought him instant and almost unanimous recognition as a major figure in contemporary German literature, reversing to a large extent the negative critical reception of *Gargoyles* and bringing him, in the same year, the ultimate German literary award, the Georg Büchner Prize.

This stunning reversal can be attributed, in part, to two felicitous formal changes. First, *The Lime Works* employs a narrative perspective that is notably different from that in the earlier novels. Unlike *Frost* and *Gargoyles*, in which the student narrators gradually lose control of the narratives, *The Lime Works* is distinguished by a marked distancing of narration that is present from the outset, a remoteness that is reinforced by an almost constant use of the subjunctive mood; the narrator here does nothing but quote other observers (thus making his reporting second- or even thirdhand). The result is an intentional and extreme indirectness, combined with an obsessive exactitude of narrative detail. This formal technique, in turn, is meant to amplify one of the novel's central themes (and one of Bernhard's personal tenets): the complexity, intractability, and inherent duplicity of language. This "language problem," already alluded to in *Frost*, becomes in *The Lime Works* the ultimate undoing of Konrad, the novel's central character. A second formal change to be noted is less complex in nature but is certainly significant to the reader: *The Lime Works* is structurally taut and possesses, unlike Bernhard's first two novels, a true "ending." This work is free of much of the somewhat gratuitous prose of *Frost* and *Gargoyles*, and the conclusion, although known from the beginning, is artistically and psychologically satisfying.

In terms of its themes and its minimal action, *The Lime Works* is vintage Bernhard. Konrad has led a life of isolation in "a state of almost complete estrangement from his brothers and sisters, parents, relations, and finally from his fellow human beings." Although he is married, this relationship, too, is one of lonely distance and separation, because the marriage has degenerated into a series of ritualized obsessions and mutual irritations. The reports with which the reader is presented attempt to trace, at times in a fragmented or even contradictory manner, the harried existence of the Konrads, who have moved about from place to place in search of seclusion. They finally retire to a lime works that Konrad has known since childhood, a place where he can devote himself to writing down his great "study" of human hearing.

At once, he sets about isolating himself by planting shrubs all around the works and by discouraging contact with the outside world, since his work demands that he be "completely isolated and free of people." Intrusions from the consumer society, from other people, and even from his wife are, however, continual and unavoidable. He nevertheless tries to maintain, in the face of these disturbances, "the highest degree of uninterrupted intellectual and physical self-control," but he is confronted by an inner problem that is even more insuperable than these constant outside irritations: his inability to set thoughts down on paper. Although he feels he has good ideas, he is trapped in "the powerlessness of his own being"; he cannot shed the conviction that "words ruin everything you think." Increasingly driven to distraction and a sense of futility, Konrad eventually loses what is left of his mental equilibrium and kills his wife.

Bernhard parallels the violence of his story with a prose style that is similarly aggressive. The reader is virtually assaulted by a language that is whipped up to greater and greater extremes of expression, and by repetitions of emphatic words. This violent style gives the uncanny impression that language itself is attempting to work out its own obsessions. Convinced as he is that the perception of mental or physical reality cannot be captured in words, Bernhard paradoxically thematizes the impossibility of adequate linguistic representation, and this in a prose that is extremely successful as literary art. Implicit here as well is a continuation of the antagonism between author and reading public that has found expression since the advent of Romanticism: Because the author believes that his readership will not be able to accept the consequences of his attack on a normative and socially functional language that this same readership employs, he resorts to a radical preoccupation with his own linguistic development, to a solipsistic forging of deeper inroads into his self. This nexus of concerns found full-blown and direct expression in Bernhard's subsequent novel, *Correction*.

CORRECTION

Formally and thematically, *Correction* is once again a logical extension of Bernhard's previous work. Narrative "structure" is here rarefied almost to the point of obliteration, however, because the first-person narrator of this novel without chapters and paragraphs does not even make the pretense of telling a story; he is present merely to "sift and sort" the posthumous notes and jottings of the work's protagonist, Roithamer, a brilliant Austrian scientist who has committed suicide immediately before the narrative begins. The narrator, Roithamer's friend, has been named the executor of Roithamer's papers, and in the first section of this novel in two parts (the only formal division of any kind in the work), he recalls in a personal manner his friendship with Roithamer, which began when they were boys. These recollections are supplemented with entries from the scientist's journals and notebooks, however, and in the second section of the novel, the narrator's voice gradually gives way almost entirely to the voice of Roithamer speaking through his papers, a device familiar to readers of Bernhard. Once again, therefore, a narrative shift or fusion makes it possible for three voices to speak in an intertwined and almost indistinguishable manner: Bernhard himself, the original narrator, and the work's central character, Roithamer, into whose mind the reader is perforce propelled. By the end of the novel, this last voice dominates, so that Roithamer's pain and obsessions become the reader's as well.

These obsessions are an admixture of Thomas Bernhard and Ludwig Wittgenstein. "Bernhardesque" is the loathing for Austria (here more scathingly expressed than in any of Bernhard's previous novels), "a permanent condition of perversity and prostitution in the form of a state, a rummage sale of intellectual and cultural history." At a deeper level, attributable to Bernhard is the conviction that a dedicated life of thought or mental activity is at once the only posture of existence worth adopting and a self-destructive modus vivendi. Shared by Bernhard and Wittgenstein, on the other hand, is a belief that could be described as the novel's cardinal theme: the fact that every individual is at birth cast into a world that person has not created; there is a great gulf between what an individual is and what he or she is forced to be, and language, the only means of overcoming this chasm, is a hopelessly inadequate tool for the task.

Finally, the links between Roithamer and Wittgenstein will be clear to anyone familiar with the philosopher's life and works. The fundamental similarity between the two is their tortured, obsessive probing of language and the limits of thought, but there are many other links as well. Roithamer, like Wittgenstein, has studied and taught in England, and he also inherits a large fortune that he summarily gives away. His family, too, has a history of suicide, and, like Wittgenstein, Roithamer spends a great deal of time and energy designing a novel and somewhat bizarre house for his sister, in this case a conical construction that becomes the novel's central metaphor. The neurasthenic protagonist decides to do this because such a structure would be tantamount to the physical reification of an idea wholly his own, the product and symbol, as it were, of his autonomous thinking. The realization of this idea becomes, in fact, a unique edifice, but one that his sister cannot comprehend. Despite the fact that her brother has attempted to "think" her reality and embody it in a house ideally suited to her, the experiment is doomed to fail simply because the gap between people is unbridgeable. The sister dies as soon as the house is completed, and Roithamer is forced to reassess his attempt, the failure of which signifies and affirms his own isolation and estrangement. He determines that it is language itself that is responsible for the impossibility of mutual understanding—or of doing anything right, for that matter: "Everything is always different from the way it has been described, the actual is always different from the description." Hence, any utterance or communication is in constant need of correction—"and then I will correct the correction and correct again the resulting corrections and so forth"—an obvious no-win situation that ultimately drives one to the ultimate correction, suicide. Roithamer takes his life by hanging himself in a forest that he has known since boyhood, a step not unlike the self-enclosure of Konrad in the lime works he had known as a child.

CONCRETE

While *Correction* brought to a culmination of sorts the formal and thematic development begun in *Frost*, it by no means exhausted Bernhard's invention. The short novel *Concrete* belies the charge, frequently heard after publication of *Correction*, that Bernhard was merely repeating himself. Although it employs the narrative strategies and obsessive motifs that came to be the staples of the Bernhardian world, *Concrete* is significantly different from its predecessors in both tone and content.

"From March to December, writes Rudolph . . .": Thus begins the long first sentence of *Concrete*, providing the narrative with the barest of frames; the last sentence in the book begins: "I drew the curtains in my room, writes Rudoph . . . ." Everything in between is the first-person narration of Rudolph; the entire novella consists of a single, unbroken paragraph.

In many ways, Rudolph is a typical Bernhardian protagonist. For years, he has been making notes for a study of the composer Felix Mendelssohn, but he has yet to begin the actual writing, let alone complete the project. Rudolph rails against his sister, whose business acumen (she is a real estate agent who deals only in high-priced properties) and Viennese social connections he despises; he also directs his invective against many other targets, including dog lovers, pretenders to culture, and the state of Austria.

All of this will be familiar to Bernhard's readers, but such a summary can be misleading. Rudolph is a more human figure than his counterparts in *The Lime Works* and *Correction*, and his diatribes are accordingly more entertaining. While his narrative is considerably shorter than those of his predecessors, it embraces a much wider range of experience. In contrast to the relentless prose and claustrophobic atmosphere of *Correction*, *Concrete* is highly readable and often blackly comic. Nowhere is this opening out of the narrative more apparent than in the story-within-the-story that gives *Concrete* its title. Late in the book, Rudolph, who suffers from sarcoidosis, takes a trip to Palma, Majorca. There he recalls a young woman, Anna Härdtl, whom he met in Palma on his previous visit, some eighteen months before. Her husband fell or jumped to his death from the balcony of their hotel; he is buried in Palma with a woman, a complete stranger, in "one of the above-ground seven-tier concrete tombs which are common in Mediterranean countries owing to a shortage of space."

There is a marked contrast between Anna Härdtl's tragic story, presented in indirect discourse as Rudolph remembers their encounter, and the litany of Rudolph's complaints and vituperations that has preceded it—a contrast that Rudolph himself seems to recognize. He is free, as ordinary people such as Anna Härdtl are not, to maintain a proud and contemptuous isolation, untroubled by the exigencies of making a living. In the degree of self-awareness and genuine growth achieved by its protagonist, in its strangely engaging tone, and in its accomplished metamorphosis of the classical form of the short novel, *Concrete* testifies to the vitality of Thomas Bernhard's art.

N. J. Meyerhofer

OTHER MAJOR WORKS

SHORT FICTION: *Amras*, 1964 (English translation, 2003); *Prosa*, 1967; *Ungenach*, 1968; *An der Baumgrenze: Erzählungen*, 1969; *Ereignisse*, 1969; *Watten: Ein Nachlass*, 1969 (*Playing Watten*, 2003); *Gehen*, 1971 (*Walking*, 2003); *Midland in Stilfs: Drei Erzählungen*, 1971; *Der Stimmenimitator*, 1978 (*The Voice Imitator*, 1997); *Three Novellas*, 2003 (includes *Amras*, *Playing Watten*, and *Walking*).

PLAYS: *Der Rosen der Einöde*, pb. 1959 (libretto); *Ein Fest für Boris*, pr., pb. 1970 (*A Party for Boris*, 1990); *Der Ignorant und der Wahnsinnige*, pr., pb. 1972; *Die Jagdgesellschaft*, pr., pb. 1974; *Die Macht der Gewohnheit*, pr., pb. 1974 (*The Force of Habit*, 1976); *Der Präsident*, pr., pb. 1975 (*The President*, 1982); *Die Berühmten*, pr., pb. 1976; *Minetti: Ein Porträt des Künstlers als alter Mann*, pr. 1976; *Immanuel Kant*, pr., pb. 1978; *Vor dem Ruhestand*, pb. 1979 (*Eve of Retirement*, 1982); *Der Weltverbesserer*, pb. 1979 (*The World-Fixer*, 2005); *Am Ziel*, pr., pb. 1981; *Über allen Gipfeln ist Ruh: Ein deutscher Dichtertag um 1980*, pb. 1981 (*Over All the Mountain Tops*, 2004); *Der Schein trügt*, pb. 1983 (*Appearances Are Deceiving*, 1983); *Ritter, Dene, Voss*, pb. 1984 (English translation, 1990); *Der Theatermacher*, pb. 1984 (*Histrionics*, 1990); *Elisabeth II*, pb. 1987; *Heldenplatz*, pr., pb. 1988; *Histrionics: Three Plays*, 1990.

POETRY: *Auf der Erde und in der Hölle*, 1957; *In hora mortis*, 1957 (English translation, 2006); *Unter dem Eisen des Mondes*, 1958; *Die Irren-die Häftlinge*, 1962; *Contemporary German Poetry*, 1964 (includes selections of his poetry in English translation).

SCREENPLAY: *Der Italiener*, 1971.

NONFICTION: *Die Ursache: Eine Andeutung*, 1975 (*An Indication of the Cause*, 1985); *Der Keller: Eine Entziehung*, 1976 (*The Cellar: An Escape*, 1985); *Der Atem: Eine Entscheidung*, 1978 (*Breath: A Decision*, 1985); *Die Kalte: Eine Isolation*, 1981 (*In the Cold*, 1985); *Ein Kind*, 1982 (*A Child*, 1985); *Wittgensteins Neffe: Eine Freundschaft*, 1982 (*Wittgenstein's Nephew: A Friendship*, 1986); *Gathering Evidence*, 1985 (English translation of the first five autobiographical works listed above; includes *An Indication of the Cause, The Cellar: An Escape, Breath: A Decision, In the Cold*, and *A Child*).

BIBLIOGRAPHY

Bernhard, Thomas. "Meet the Author." *Harper's Magazine* 315, no. 1997 (August, 2007): 18-20. Interview with Bernhard in which he comments on the purpose of art, expresses his disgust for literary critics, and maintains that he is not interested in his own fate or in the fate of his books.

Dowden, Stephen D., and James N. Hardin, eds. *Understanding Thomas Bernhard*. Columbia: University of South Carolina Press, 1991. Collection of essays explores the themes and approaches of Bernhard's works, among them the novels *Frost, Gargoyles, The Lime Works, Correction, Old Masters*, and *Extinction*. Includes bibliography and index.

Honegger, Gitta. *Thomas Bernhard: The Making of an Austrian*. New Haven, Conn.: Yale University Press, 2001. The first comprehensive biography of Bernhard in English examines the complex connections of Bernhard's work with the geographic, political, and cultural landscape of twentieth century Austria.

Indiana, Gary. "Thomas Bernhard." *Artforum* 8, no. 3 (Fall, 2001): 17-24. Provides a profile of Bernhard, a time line of the important events in his life, a reader's guide to his work, and excerpts from several pieces.

Konzett, Matthias. *The Rhetoric of National Dissent in Thomas Bernhard, Peter Handke, and Elfriede Jelinek*. New York: Camden House, 2000. Analyzes how the three Austrian writers created new literary strategies in order to expose and dismantle conventional ideas that impede the development of multicultural awareness and identity.

_____, ed. *A Companion to the Works of Thomas Bernhard*. Rochester, N.Y.: Camden House, 2002. Collection of essays examines numerous aspects of

Bernhard's work, including its aesthetic sensibility, its impact on Austrian literature, its relation to the legacy of Austrian Jewish culture, and its cosmopolitanism.

Long, Jonathan James. *The Novels of Thomas Bernhard: Form and Its Function*. Rochester, N.Y.: Camden House, 2001. Intended as an accessible introduction to Bernhard's novels for English-speaking audiences. Focuses on Bernhard's later novels but also analyzes the novels written in the 1960's and 1970's.

Martin, Charles W. *The Nihilism of Thomas Bernhard: The Portrayal of Existential and Social Problems in His Prose Works*. Atlanta: Rodopi, 1995. Traces how Bernhard uses nihilism in his work, examining the works chronologically from 1963 until 1986. Notes that although at one point Bernhard sought to transcend his own nihilism, he ultimately concluded that nihilism was a necessary response to the reality of Austrian society and to his personal problems.

WENDELL BERRY

Born: Henry County, Kentucky; August 5, 1934
Also known as: Wendell Erdman Berry

PRINCIPAL LONG FICTION

Nathan Coulter, 1960 (revised 1985)
A Place on Earth, 1967 (revised 1983)
The Memory of Old Jack, 1974
Remembering, 1988
A World Lost, 1996
Jayber Crow, 2000
Hannah Coulter, 2004
Andy Catlett: Early Travels, 2006

OTHER LITERARY FORMS

Wendell Berry has published widely in most major genres—poetry, short fiction, and nonfiction prose (notably the essay) as well as long fiction. In addition to his novels and novellas, Berry is the author of several short-story collections and additional short stories about the Port William Membership. He has also published essay collections, nonfiction works, and numerous volumes of poetry.

ACHIEVEMENTS

The author of more than forty books, Wendell Berry has been the recipient of many honorary degrees and writing awards, including the T. S. Eliot Award, the Aiken Taylor Award for poetry, and the John Hay Award of the Orion Society.

BIOGRAPHY

Wendell Erdman Berry was the first of four children born to a respected Kentucky family with deep farming roots in Henry County. His father was an attorney and one of the founders of the Burley Tobacco Growers Cooperative. Growing up during the 1930's in a tobacco-growing community, Berry always wanted to become a farmer. He attended the local New Castle Elementary School, though he was a reluctant student who would rather be outdoors, wandering the local countryside. As a teenager, he was particularly drawn to Curran's Camp, a fishing camp on the Kentucky River owned by his bachelor uncle.

Both Wendell and his brother John attended Millersburg Military Institute and the University of Kentucky in Lexington. Finding the university a welcome respite from the rigors of a military academy, Berry majored in English and began to take an interest in creative writing. He met Tanya Amyx in Lexington, and they were married in 1957. A creative-writing fellowship led Berry to Stanford University in 1958 to study with Wallace Stegner.

Returning from California in 1960, Berry and his family farmed for a year in Kentucky before Berry was awarded a Guggenheim Fellowship, which enabled the family to travel to Europe and live in Florence and the French Riviera while Berry worked on his second novel, *A Place on Earth*. An offer to direct the freshman writing program at the Bronx campus of New York University

Wendell Berry. (© Dan Carraco, courtesy of North Point Press)

brought the family back to the United States in 1962, but Berry found urban life uncongenial, so they returned to Lexington when Berry accepted a teaching position at the University of Kentucky in 1964. He was still drawn to his childhood roots in Henry County, and, after a year, the Berrys were able to purchase some land in Port Royal and move to Lane's Landing Farm, which became their home. Berry taught at the University of Kentucky until his retirement in the late 1990's, and he has continued writing and farming since that time.

ANALYSIS

Wendell Berry is perhaps the most prominent farming and agrarian writer in the United States in the period beginning in the late twentieth century. Throughout his long and prolific career, virtually everything Berry has written has in some way either celebrated or advocated the values of traditional farming and rural life. As novelist Wallace Stegner noted, it is hard to decide in which genre Berry writes best. As one of Stegner's creative-

writing students at Stanford, Berry shares affinities with other West Coast writers, such as Gary Snyder, Ken Kesey, and Ernest J. Gaines, but his vision is primarily that of a Kentucky regional writer and a southern agrarian.

Berry's novels and short stories recount the saga of the Port William Membership, a fictional rural Kentucky community of small tobacco farmers and their families. All of his novels, except for *Remembering*, are set in the lower Kentucky River Valley, where Berry has spent most of his life. Much of his fiction evokes an elegiac sense of a rural community and a way of life gradually lost to the changing economics of the modern American consumer culture. Berry's pastoral, agrarian vision is not merely nostalgic, however; it is wed to a clear sense of environmental stewardship and responsibility to the land and to small-scale, local economics. His characters struggle to maintain community on all levels—social, economic, and environmental. Berry's fictional vision encompasses the unity of people, place, and the natural world.

More than anything else, Berry's novels are a continuous saga of a region—the Kentucky River Valley—and a rural way of life between the two world wars. His major character in these Port William Membership stories is the community itself, composed for the most part of decent, unassuming people trying to maintain their farming culture against the outside forces of war and economic and social change. Their major crop was burley tobacco, a demanding crop that bound families together in seasonal labor. World War II was the great watershed that marked the end of a self-sufficient rural economy and the agrarian lifestyle it nurtured. Young men were drawn off to war, leaving behind women, children, and the elderly to work the farms as best they could.

Berry's novels are largely the story of the decline and fall of this rural, agrarian culture and its impact on the Port William Membership; hence his tone is wistful and his themes are of recurring loss: elderly parents, sons killed in war, farms neglected or mismanaged, community and cultural continuity gone. Berry's fictional world is populated mainly by three families—the Coulters, the Catletts, and the Beechums—with their quirks and eccentricities, along with other rural townsfolk. His novels are often thinly plotted and episodic, with few major characters, relying on tone and description to convey the essence of the story. Berry's muted realism and lack of melodrama convey a sense of the ordinary pace of premechanized Kentucky rural life, although the absence of thematic conflict does not encourage strong character or plot development. To some degree, these limitations are those of choice rather than ability, given the regional focus of Berry's fiction.

The initial conflicts of pioneering and settlement of Kentucky were followed by the slow development of a rural culture based on the cultivation of tobacco and livestock. The wilderness was gradually subdued by human effort, but the culture was careless and wasteful with natural resources. With so much land there for the taking, settlers saw no need to conserve the soil or prevent erosion. A continual theme throughout Berry's novels is cultural and environmental conservatism—and the natural and cultural costs of failing to learn to conserve the land. He regrets the American failure to create an enduring agrarian culture with strong local roots and a sense of history. Neither religion nor culture encouraged a sense of affection or respect for the land. His characters are warped by their harsh work ethic, their greed, their ignorance and indifference. Berry imposes his strong personal vision on his fictional world, blending storytelling with cultural history, a strong regional focus, and a clear environmental philosophy. His creative approach is to some degree recursive, returning to the same families in different episodes in successive novels.

NATHAN COULTER

Berry's first novel, *Nathan Coulter*, evolved from an early short story, "The Brothers," written during his undergraduate years at the University of Kentucky. First published in 1960, it was later revised and shortened for reissue in 1985. The initial sales were disappointing, although the novel received some favorable reviews. It was compared with other regional "tobacco novels," although it is really more of a coming-of-age story of two brothers, Nathan and Tom Coulter, who are forced to deal with their father's harsh rejection of them after their mother's death. The revised version of *Nathan Coulter* eliminates the last three chapters of the earlier book and ends with Grandpa Coulter's death, providing greater focus and unity. Each of the five sections of the novel is built around a central episode in the lives of the brothers:

their mother's death, after which they live with their grandparents; Tom's courtship, which separates him from his younger brother, Nathan; the burning of their father's barn after it is struck by lightning; Tom's leaving home after a fight with his father; and the death of the boys' grandfather, old Dave Coulter, which brings Nathan to the verge of manhood. The novel is narrated in the first person by Nathan, the younger brother, encouraging the reader to empathize with him.

Berry's first novel presents a starkly realistic, unsentimental portrait of a boy's coming-of-age on a Kentucky tobacco farm before the age of mechanization. Berry presents a harsh, patriarchal world of unrelenting toil and obsessive work ethic among three generations who cannot get along because of their fierce pride and independence. Grandpa Coulter and his son Jarrat, the boys' father, are linked by their stubborn pride and irritability, which makes life miserable for those around them. Berry presents a hard, male world in which women are absent or subordinate—a Calvinistic world of work and self-deprivation. There is an implicit division between those who respect the land (and themselves) and those who abuse it or who are obsessively bound to it. Despite their constant labor, the Coulter men have lives that seem harsh and unattractive. The kind and unambitious Uncle Burley, Jarrat's brother, serves as a foil to Grandpa Dave and Jarrat and offers an alternative way of living in family and community.

A PLACE ON EARTH

Berry's second novel, *A Place on Earth*, was begun at Stanford in 1960 and published in 1967. The original version, as Berry has admitted, was overwritten and needed to be revised and edited. Before the novel was reissued in 1983, Berry cut about a third of its length, reorganized it into five major sections, and added chapter titles.

A Place on Earth is the portrait of Port William, Berry's fictional community, toward the end of World War II, from late winter to fall, 1945. It is the story of a rural community's loss and atonement, through war, flood, and suicide, set against the natural rhythm of the seasons. The protagonist, Mat Feltner, learns that his son Virgil has been reported missing in action in Europe, and for the next six months, Mat, his wife Margaret, and their daughter-in-law Hannah struggle to accept their loss. Virgil's death is paralleled by the death of Annie Crop, a sharecropper's child swept away in a flood. Ernest Finley, Mat's cousin, a crippled war veteran and carpenter, takes his life when his infatuation with Ida Crop is gently rebuffed. The townsfolk of the Port William Membership learn to accept these deaths within the larger natural rhythm of the seasons and of rural life.

Berry presents credible portraits of his rural characters—especially the older men, the village elders Mat Feltner, Frank Lathrop, Jack Beechum, Burley Coulter, and Jayber Crow, who struggle to maintain their way of life—but the novel lacks strong dramatic or psychological conflict. Once again, Berry's major concern is the struggle by the older generation to maintain traditional farming practices in the face of war and loss. With the death of his son, Mat Feltner wonders who will farm and inherit his land. Jack Beechum also searches for a tenant to keep his farm from being sold off by his wealthy daughter and her banker husband. Work and love are the focal points of Berry's agrarian moral order: Characters are measured by their success or failure in farming and holding on to their land. The town's celebration of Japan's surrender marks the end of World War II and the beginning of the inevitable changes that peacetime will bring to the Port William Membership.

THE MEMORY OF OLD JACK

In Berry's third novel, *The Memory of Old Jack*, he turns to the story of Jack Beechum, a character introduced as an old man in *A Place on Earth*. Told retrospectively from the third-person point of view, it is the story of Jack's life and his attachment to his farm, with an unhappy marriage to Ruth Lightwood, who does not share his love of the land. Through the concentration on Jack's character and his conflicts, this novel gains a unity and focus absent in Berry's first two novels. Jack's story is told through his own recollections on a warm September day in 1952, as his friend Wheeler Catlett takes the ninety-two-year-old Jack from his boardinghouse in town out to his farm.

Jack's memories reach back to the end of the Civil War, when, after his parents' death, he was befriended by Ben Feltner, who taught him to farm. Jack's loveless marriage to Ruth Lightwood is the great regret of his life. Her desire for wealth and prestige forced him to overex-

tend himself and almost lose his farm to debt. Cold and disapproving toward Jack, Ruth encourages their daughter Clara's disapproval of her father. Never having had a son, Jack turns to his lawyer, Wheeler, and to his young tenant farmer, Elton Penn, as spiritual heirs. In his will, Jack arranges with Wheeler to leave enough money for Elton to buy his farm, so that Clara and her husband cannot sell it. Jack's life unites love and work, but his love is for his farm, not his family.

REMEMBERING

Berry's next two works are about episodes in the life of Andy Catlett, farmer and son of Wheeler Catlett, a character who resembles Berry himself in some ways. *Remembering* recounts a crisis in Andy Catlett's life that takes place during a lecture tour he is making as an agricultural journalist, shortly after he has lost his hand to a corn picker and has become estranged from his wife and family. During a long night in a San Francisco hotel, he reexamines his life. As he remembers formative incidents from his childhood and the mentors who have influenced him, he regains his faith and purpose. Central to his conversion is a recollected interview with two farmers—an Amish man and a corporate farmer—whose contrasting values and scale of farming dramatize Berry's traditional agrarian philosophy. Andy returns home from his abortive trip to be reconciled with his wife and his sense of place as a traditional farmer.

A WORLD LOST

A World Lost, a more polished work, returns to Andy's childhood, during the summer of 1944, to recount the story of his uncle's murder and Andy's subsequent quest to understand the crime. It is a rich, meditative work that traces a boy's attempts to comprehend the mysteries of the adult world. Andy's uncle Andrew is a rich and complex character, a heavy drinker and womanizer, a practical joker, and a storyteller, who compensates for his unhappy marriage and unfulfilling job as a salesman through his close relationship with his nephew. Young Andy does not fully understand the sexual aura that draws women to his uncle and results in his being shot over a jest he makes to Cap Harmon's daughter in a restaurant. Andy's determination to uncover the secret of his uncle's murder takes him on an odyssey from childhood to adulthood and results in some of Berry's best fictional writing.

JAYBER CROW

Perhaps Berry's most important novel, *Jayber Crow* chronicles the life story of an orphan and preministerial student who becomes Port William's bachelor town barber, church janitor, and gravedigger during the years from 1937 through 1969. Berry's use of the first-person narrative point of view allows Jayber the dual roles of participant/observer and insider/outsider as he lovingly recounts the lives of the Port William Membership. Through his observations of the lives that unfold around him, Crow reflects on the meaning of religion, faith, prayer, love, marriage, vocation, and farming. The thirty-two episodic chapters unfold in roughly chronological order. Two chapters, "A Little Worter Drinking Party" (chapter 10) and "Don't Send a Boy to Do a Man's Work" (chapter 21) are rich enough to stand alone as humorous tales.

The marriage theme is central to the novel and involves two contrasting stories. The most important involves Jayber's lifelong infatuation with and admiration for Mattie Keith, who eventually marries her childhood sweetheart, Troy Chatham, in what turns out to be a mismatched and unhappy marriage. Jayber watches Mattie's suffering and pledges an unspoken devotion to her that resembles courtly love. The Chathams' marriage slowly unravels through the strains and misjudgments stemming from Troy's ambition to become a successful agribusinessman and his subsequent neglect and indifference toward his wife and children. The symbol of their failed marriage is Troy's sale of the Nest Egg, Mattie's land inheritance, to pay his farm debts. Troy and Mattie's incompatibility is paralleled by the marital estrangement of Roy and Cecelia Overhold. In each case, false pride, ambition, and anger lead to loneliness and unhappiness. In contrast, Jayber admires the successful marriage of Athey and Della Keith and the common-law relationship of Burley Coulter and Kate Helen Branch, both of which are based on shared values and mutual love.

The second major story involves Jayber's working out of his life and destiny following his rejection of what he realizes is a mistaken call to the ministry. Sent to the Good Shepherd Orphanage after the death of his foster parents, Jayber falls under the influence of Brother Whitespade, a harsh and dominating superintendent who urges Jayber to become a minister; he is then influenced by Dr. Ardmire, his New Testament professor at Pigeonville College, who dissuades him with enigmatic answers to Jayber's questions about prayer and belief. After leaving Pigeonville for the state university in Lexington, where he learns barbering to support himself, Jayber discovers that he is not suited for teaching either and drops out to return home. He settles in Port William and discovers a secular vocation to be the town's barber and to live out the answers to his religious questions. During his lifetime, Jayber witnesses the slow decline of his rural community from the impact of outside social and economic forces and endures the loss of the woman he had loved from afar.

HANNAH COULTER

A recollection of the memories of a twice-widowed farm wife, *Hannah Coulter* picks up the story of Hannah Feltner, a character introduced in *A Place on Earth*. In 1945, Hannah was a newly married war widow with an infant daughter, living with her in-laws, her husband, Virgil, having disappeared after the Battle of the Bulge. *Hannah Coulter* is a story of gratitude for the abundant life Hannah has made after her second marriage in1948 to Nathan Coulter, a young World War II veteran who returned to Port William to farm. Told retrospectively from the first-person point of view, Hannah's life has been a process of coming to know her story and its meaning.

In the year they were married, Hannah and Nathan bought the old Cuthbert farm and began to make their life together, restoring the rundown farm to productivity and raising their three children there. They gradually fit the pattern of their lives to the history of the place. They were careful and thrifty in gradually repairing their home and barns and reclaiming their land from prior abuse and neglect. Hannah recalls the support of neighbors and community during tobacco harvest and the gradual decline of the old customs as farming became increasingly mechanized in the decades after the war. Their three children all sought careers away from the farm, and Hannah finds herself the last Coulter in Port William after her husband's death from cancer in 2001, though some hope remains when her grandson Virgie comes home to start a new life. *Hannah Coulter* is a snapshot of the vanished family farm, its seasonal rhythms, and the abundant life that it once supported.

ANDY CATLETT

A first-person narrative account of nine-year-old Andy Catlett's post-Christmas visits to both sets of his grandparents, *Andy Catlett* provides a contrasting picture of small-town and country life in rural Kentucky in 1943. Andy's first solo bus trip away from home serves as a rite of passage for him. Berry continues his saga of the Port William Membership in these sketches of holiday traditions and winter tobacco-curing work as seen through the eyes of a small boy learning the responsibilities of adulthood under the careful tutelage of his grandparents. Berry's familiar townspeople—the Catletts, the Coulters, and the Feltners—appear from a slightly different perspective. This charming boy's book provides some interesting glimpses of rural customs, culture, and traditions as well as some insights into race relations in Kentucky during the pre-Civil Rights period.

Berry emphasizes the importance of the extended family and the continuity of generations as Andy enjoys a respite from his parents' firmness in the company of his indulgent grandparents. Abundant holiday meals of hearty country food are described in great detail. Traditional gender roles and division of labor are emphasized, with the men outdoors doing farm chores and the women indoors busy with domestic chores. Not quite ready to enter the men's world yet, Andy wanders back and forth between the kitchen and the barn. The impacts of the technological transition to electricity and the advent of the automobile are starting to be felt, as the rhythms of life in town quicken as electricity arrives. Andy's memories serve as a nostalgic glimpse into a now-vanished rural way of life.

Andrew J. Angyal

OTHER MAJOR WORKS

SHORT FICTION: *The Wild Birds*, 1986; *Fidelity*, 1992; *Watch with Me*, 1994; *Three Short Novels*, 2002; *That Distant Land: The Collected Stories*, 2004.

POETRY: *November Twenty-six, Nineteen Hundred Sixty-three*, 1963; *The Broken Ground*, 1964; *Openings*, 1968; *Findings*, 1969; *Farming: A Hand Book*, 1970; *The Country of Marriage*, 1973; *An Eastward Look*, 1974; *Horses*, 1975; *Sayings and Doings*, 1975; *To What Listens*, 1975; *The Kentucky River: Two Poems*, 1976; *There Is Singing Around Me*, 1976; *Three Memorial Poems*, 1976; *Clearing*, 1977; *The Gift of Gravity*, 1979; *A Part*, 1980; *The Wheel*, 1982; *Collected Poems, 1957-1982*, 1985; *Sabbaths*, 1987; *Traveling at Home*, 1989; *Sabbaths, 1987-1990*, 1992; *Entries*, 1994; *The Farm*, 1995; *The Selected Poems of Wendell Berry*, 1998; *A Timbered Choir: The Sabbath Poems, 1979-1997*, 1998; *Given: New Poems*, 2005.

NONFICTION: *The Long-Legged House*, 1969; *The Hidden Wound*, 1970; *The Unforeseen Wilderness*, 1971; *A Continuous Harmony*, 1972; *The Unsettling of America*, 1977; *The Gift of Good Land*, 1981; *Recollected Essays, 1965-1980*, 1981; *Standing by Words*, 1983; *Home Economics*, 1987; *Harland Hubbard: Life and Work*, 1990; *What Are People For?*, 1990; *The Discovery of Kentucky*, 1991; *Standing on Earth*, 1991; *Sex, Economy, Freedom, and Community*, 1993; *Another Turn of the Crank*, 1995; *Life is a Miracle: An Essay Against Modern Superstition*, 2000; *The Art of the Commonplace: The Agrarian Essays of Wendell Berry*, 2002 (Norman Wirzba, editor); *In the Presence of Fear: Three Essays for a Changed World*, 2002; *Citizenship Papers: Essays*, 2003; *Blessed Are the Peacemakers: Christ's Teachings of Love, Compassion and Forgiveness*, 2005; *Standing by Words: Essays*, 2005; *The Way of Ignorance, and Other Essays*, 2005; *Conversations with Wendell Berry*, 2007 (Morris Allen Grubbs, editor).

BIBLIOGRAPHY

Altherr, Thomas L. "The Country We Have Married: Wendell Berry and the Georgian Tradition of Agriculture." *Southern Studies* 1 (Summer, 1990): 105-115. Examines the influence of Vergil's *Georgics* (c. 37-29 B.C.E.; English translation, 1589) on Berry's treatment of agriculture.

Angyal, Andrew J. *Wendell Berry*. New York: Twayne, 1995. Introductory work provides a brief biography of the author as well as critical interpretation of his fiction. Includes chronology, bibliography, and index.

Freeman, Russell G. *Wendell Berry: A Bibliography*. Lexington: University of Kentucky Libraries, 1992. Serves as a good resource for information on the history of Berry's nonstop, multigenre publishing career.

Freyfogle, Eric T. "The Dilemma of Wendell Berry." *University of Illinois Law Review* 2 (1994): 363-385.

Presents a detailed study of the moral implications of Berry's cultural criticism, especially in his fictional works.

Goodrich, Janet. *The Unforeseen Self in the Works of Wendell Berry*. Columbia: University of Missouri Press, 2001. Interesting work takes a fresh approach to Berry's writings. Argues that whether Berry is writing poetry or prose, he is reimagining his own life and thus belongs to the tradition of autobiography.

Hicks, Jack. "Wendell Berry's Husband to the World: *Place on Earth*." *American Literature* 51 (May, 1979): 238-254. One of the best critical overviews available of Berry's earlier work. Examines the farmer-countryman vision in Berry's fiction and traces thematic connections among Berry's essays, poetry, and fiction.

Knott, John R. "Into the Woods with Wendell Berry." *Essays in Literature* 23 (Spring, 1996): 124-140. Draws on both Berry's fiction and his poetry to explore the role of the wilderness in his works, noting the more hopeful tone of later volumes.

Nibbelink, Herman. "Thoreau and Wendell Berry: Bachelor and Husband of Nature." *South Atlantic Quarterly* 84 (1985): 127-140. Contrasts Henry David Thoreau's love of wilderness with Berry's preference for cultivated land in terms of the bachelor-husband metaphor.

Peters, Jason, ed. *Wendell Berry: Life and Work*. Lexington: University Press of Kentucky, 2007. Collection of critical essays examines Berry's life, career, works, philosophy, and legacy as an agrarian writer and thinker. Includes chronology, selected bibliography, and index.

Slovic, Scott. "Coming Home to 'The Camp': Wendell Berry's Watchfulness." In *Seeking Awareness in American Nature Writing: Henry Thoreau, Annie Dillard, Edward Abbey, Wendell Berry, Barry Lopez*. Salt Lake City: University of Utah Press, 1992. Presents a fine appreciation of Berry's naturalist, ecological vision. Included in a larger study that places Berry within an important American literary tradition.

Smith, Kimberly K. *Wendell Berry and the Agrarian Tradition: A Common Grace*. Lawrence: University Press of Kansas, 2003. Detailed study focuses on the influence of Berry's thought and work on modern ecological agrarianism through his support of small farming and traditional agrarian values.

VICENTE BLASCO IBÁÑEZ

Born: Valencia, Spain; January 29, 1867
Died: Menton, France; January 28, 1928

PRINCIPAL LONG FICTION

Arroz y tartana, 1894 (*The Three Roses*, 1932)
Flor de mayo, 1895 (*The Mayflower: A Tale of the Valencian Seashore*, 1921)
La barraca, 1898 (*The Cabin*, 1917; also known as *The Holding*, 1993)
Entre naranjos, 1900 (*The Torrent*, 1921)
Sónnica la cortesana, 1901 (*Sonnica*, 1912)
Cañas y barro, 1902 (*Reeds and Mud*, 1928)
Los muertos mandan, 1902 (*The Dead Command*, 1919)
La catedral, 1903 (*The Shadow of the Cathedral*, 1909)
El intruso, 1904 (*The Intruder*, 1928)
La bodega, 1905 (*The Fruit of the Vine*, 1919)
La horda, 1905 (*The Mob*, 1927)
La maja desnuda, 1906 (*Woman Triumphant*, 1920)
La voluntad de vivir, 1907
Sangre y arena, 1908 (*The Blood of the Arena*, 1911; better known as *Blood and Sand*, 1913)
Luna Benamor, 1909 (includes short stories; English translation, 1919)
Los Argonautas, 1914

Los cuatro jinetes del Apocalipsis, 1916 (*The Four Horsemen of the Apocalypse*, 1918)

Mare Nostrum, 1918 (English translation, 1919)

Los enemigos de la mujer, 1919 (*The Enemies of Women*, 1920)

El paraíso de las mujeres, 1922 (*The Paradise of Women*, 1922)

La tierra de todos, 1922 (*The Temptress*, 1923)

La reina Calafia, 1923 (*Queen Calafia*, 1924)

El papa del mar, 1925 (*The Pope of the Sea: An Historic Medley*, 1927)

A los pies de Venus, 1926 (*The Borgias: Or, At the Feet of Venus*, 1930)

En busca del Gran Kan, 1929 (*Unknown Lands: The Story of Columbus*, 1929)

El Caballero de la Virgen, 1929 (*The Knight of the Virgin*, 1930)

El fantasma de las alas de oro, 1930 (*The Phantom with Wings of Gold*, 1931)

Other literary forms

In addition to his novels, Vicente Blasco Ibáñez (BLAHS-koh ee-BAHN-yays) wrote early romances, including such works as the novella *El conde Garci-Fernández* (1928), *¡Por la patria! (Romeu el guerrillero)* (1888), *La araña negra* (1928; a collection of short fiction), and *¡Viva la república!* (1893-1894). Blasco Ibáñez later repudiated these early romances as unworthy of preservation. Blasco Ibáñez also wrote short stories and novelettes, including *Fantasías, leyendas, y tradiciones* (1887), *El adiós a Schubert* (1888; stories of a distinctly romantic nature and quite different from the author's mature pieces), and, later *Cuentos valencianos* (1896), *La condenada* (1899), *El préstamo de la difunta* (1921), *Novelas de la costa azul* (1924), and *Novelas de amor y de muerte* (1927). His nonfiction includes *Historia de la revolución española, 1808-1874* (1890-1892), *París: Impresiones de un emigrado* (1893), *En el país del arte* (1896; *In the Land of Art*, 1923), *Oriente* (1907), *Argentina y sus grandezas* (1910), the thirteen-volume *Historia de la guerra europea de 1914* (1914-1919), *El militarismo mejicano* (1920; *Mexico in Revolution*, 1920), the three-volume *La vuelta al mundo de un novelista* (1924-1925; *A Novelist's Tour of the World*, 1926); *Una nación secuestrada: Alfonso XIII desenmascarado* (1924; *Alfonso XIII Unmasked: The Military Terror in Spain*, 1924), *Lo que será la república española: Al país y al ejército* (1925), *Estudios literarios* (1933), and *Discursos literarios* (1966); and one play, *El juez* (pb. 1894). Translations of many of Blasco Ibáñez's short stories have been collected in *The Last Lion, and Other Tales* (1919) and *The Old Woman of the Movies, and Other Stories* (1925).

Achievements

Vicente Blasco Ibáñez is probably the most widely read Spanish novelist, both in Spain and abroad, except for Miguel de Cervantes. Certainly he was one of the most prolific writers his country ever produced (his collected works run to forty volumes) a result of his extraordinarily dynamic and energetic nature and of his determination to show both the positive and the negative aspects of Spain to his countrymen and to the world.

Blasco Ibáñez has not received a balanced judgment from literary critics. Most have offered exaggerated praise or scorn for his works or have ignored him altogether. For many years, many Spanish critics denied the value of his novels because they rejected his radical political ideas, they envied his financial success, or they held a low opinion of his literary origins. (Blasco Ibáñez did not participate in some of the stylistic renovations of the *generación del 98*, or the Generation of '98, adhering instead to many of the realistic-naturalistic practices of the nineteenth century, thought by many to be out of date.) While Blasco Ibáñez's attacks on the Spanish political scene and eventual millionaire status led to ostracism by his Spanish contemporaries, such English-speaking critics as William Dean Howells, Havelock Ellis, Walter Starkie, Gerald Brenan, A. Grove Day, and Edgar Knowlson, Jr., offered a fairer perspective.

Certainly there are significant defects in some of Blasco Ibáñez's works. Without question, his early Valencian novels represent his greatest achievement, revealing a powerful double legacy that cannot be ignored: a pictorial, concrete, at times poetic style of strength and beauty, and a striking portrayal of human action. Later in his career, as Blasco Ibáñez strayed farther and farther from the format and the setting he knew best, the aesthetic value of his novels declined dramatically. While a definitive study of his total literary production remains to be done, analyses of individual novels have at least offered glimpses into the genuine artistry of his best works.

BIOGRAPHY

Vicente Blasco Ibáñez was born in a room over a corner grocery in Valencia on January 29, 1867. From his parents, he inherited the vigor of the Aragonese peasants, and from an impoverished childhood, he gained the spirit of struggle and defiance. During his early years, the lad of sturdy build, brown eyes, and curly hair could be seen more often walking the beach of nearby Cabañal or talking to fishermen and sailors than sitting at his desk in school. By the age of fourteen, he had written a cloak-and-dagger novel, by age fifteen had published a short story in the Valencian dialect, and by age sixteen had run away from the University of Valencia to Madrid. There, while doing secretarial work for the aging writer Manuel Fernández y González, he gained the inspiration for his first series of lengthy writings—a dozen romances that he later repudiated. By age seventeen, he had published a poem advocating chopping off all the crowned heads of Europe, starting with Spain.

The death of Alfonso XII in 1885 marked the young writer's start as republican conspirator and frequent political prisoner. After completing his law degree in 1888 and his first forced exile in France (brought on by increasingly anti-clerical speeches), Blasco Ibáñez married his cousin, María Blasco del Cacho, who was to endure his tempestuous nature and stormy career. They had five children before their separation immediately prior to the outbreak of World War I. On November 12, 1894, Blasco Ibáñez released the first issue of *El pueblo*, a journal that he was to run virtually single-handedly and in which many of his best works would appear in serial form. It was into this

enterprise that he poured all of his energy and stamina, as well as the entirety of his parents' inheritance.

Blasco Ibáñez proved to be a born leader of crowds, self-assured, fluent in his oratory, with a booming voice whose warmth quickly dispelled any first impression of coldness that might have been caused by his pointed beard, his mustache, and his aquiline nose. As time passed, he grew to be increasingly impulsive and impatient to eliminate the stupidity, ignorance, and laziness around him. Antireligious in a city venerated as the repository of the Holy Grail, and republican in a region noted for its conservative monarchism, he never avoided the chance for an iconoclastic stance.

Nevertheless, his election as the Valencian representative for the journal *Las cortes* in 1898 was the first of many. To his growing political fame was added an international literary reputation with the French translation of *The Cabin* in 1901. In 1904, he abandoned his home at La Malvarrosa on the Valencian shore to take up residence in Madrid and other Spanish cities.

The year 1909 found Blasco Ibáñez making two trips to Argentina, first to give lectures and subsequently to

Vicente Blasco Ibáñez. (AP/Wide World Photos)

supervise the development of some new settlements. There he remained, fighting harsh climates and jungle dangers, until economic difficulties led him back to Europe immediately prior to World War I. Shortly afterward, he launched into a campaign to help the Allies, in the form of *Historia de la guerra europea de 1914*, speeches throughout neutral Spain, and several novels, of which *The Four Horsemen of the Apocalypse* had the greatest political and financial impact. When unexpected wealth poured in from this work's reprints, translations, and film rights, he moved to the French Riviera, where most of his last novels were written.

By 1925, Blasco Ibáñez had undertaken a triumphant tour of the United States, composing lengthy travel literature based on a six-month luxury-liner trip around the world, when he received news of the death of his wife. Within months, he married the daughter of a well-known Chilean general and soon thereafter, in failing health, retired to his Riviera home to churn out his final writings. The night before his sixty-first birthday, weakened by pneumonia, diabetes, and overwork, he died uttering the words "my garden, my garden," a reflection of his ardent desire to have his Menton garden resemble those of his beloved Valencia. In his will, he bequeathed his home to "all the writers of the world" and insisted that he not be buried in a nonrepublican Spain. On October 29, 1933, two years after the proclamation of the Second Republic, his body was moved to Valencia amid the impassioned eulogies of those who had scorned him years before. More than forty-seven years later, as renovations were undertaken on the Blasco Ibáñez home at La Malvarrosa, the first international symposium on Don Vicente's works was held, and a determination to rectify the critical neglect of his work was voiced.

Blasco Ibáñez was a man of action first and a writer second. His works bear a profound and constant autobiographical stamp—the mark of a rebel, a revolutionary journalist, a colonizer, a sailor, a fighter for the cause of peasants, fishermen, and slum dwellers, and an exile who attacked his government yet remained loyal to Spanish traditions, as reflected in his tireless efforts to glorify his country's imperial past and to combat the anti-Spanish legend. It is with at least some justification that he is remembered by many of his countrymen more for his life than for his writings.

ANALYSIS

Following Vicente Blasco Ibáñez's first romances, five phases can be distinguished in the course of his prolific career. Into the first fall his Valencian works, from *The Three Roses* (which he considered his first novel) through *Reeds and Mud* and including two collections of stories, *Cuentos valencianos* and *La condenada*. Within this group, three works can be considered the novelist's masterpieces: *The Mayflower*, *The Cabin*, and *Reeds and Mud*. Second are his novels of social protest, written between 1903 and 1905 and dealing with the Catholic Church (*The Shadow of the Cathedral*, set in Toledo, and *The Intruder*, set in the Basque provinces) or with the exploitation of workers in vineyards and in large cities (*The Fruit of the Vine* and *The Mob*, set in Jérez de la Frontera and Madrid, respectively). "Art," the author explains, "should not be simply a mere manifestation of beauty. Art should be on the side of the needy defending forcefully those who are hungry for justice." Nevertheless, interminable didactic monologues, long ideological question-and-answer dialectics, and overtly symbolic characterization lessen the aesthetic worth of these works.

The third phase comprises psychological novels in which the author stresses character development within specific settings: *Woman Triumphant* (Madrid), *La voluntad de vivir* (the aristocracy of Madrid and Paris), *Blood and Sand* (bullfighting in Seville and Madrid), *The Dead Command* (Balearic Islands), and *Luna Benamor* (Gibraltar). While some of these works are admirable for their characterization and for their descriptions of landscape and local customs, they are clearly inferior to the Valencian writings. Fourth are cosmopolitan and war novels, including *Los Argonautas* (a detailed account of a transatlantic journey, envisioned as the first in a series of works dealing with Latin America) and several novels written to defend the Allied cause: *The Four Horsemen of the Apocalypse*, *Mare Nostrum*, *The Enemies of Women*, *The Temptress*, and *Queen Calafia*. These novels proved to be as popular as they were lacking in artistic merit. Finally, Blasco Ibáñez's fifth phase includes historical novels of Spanish glorification, ranging from the account of Pope Benedict XIII's life to the voyages of Columbus and a love story set in Monte Carlo.

In some ways, Blasco Ibáñez is a transitional figure between the age of the realistic novel (1870-1900) and the Generation of '98. Works such as *The Fruit of the Vine* and *The Mob* demonstrate his participation in the ninety-eighters' preoccupation with Spanish social issues, and most of his works, particularly in his early periods, reveal the extraordinary sensitivity to landscape that Pío Baroja's generation would display. Blasco Ibáñez's regionalistic *costumbrismo* and use of descriptive detail are techniques that relate him to the earlier generation of Benito Pérez Galdós and José María de Pereda.

It was Blasco Ibáñez who introduced the *pueblo*, rather than the middle class, as a frequent source for the novel's protagonist, a character who struggles heroically against his environment and his own animal instincts. A convincing narrative action of sharp contrasts; a pictorial, concrete, sensual, often impressionistic realism of strength and beauty; and an admirable tightness and unity of plot are the features that set the Valencian novels apart as his most accomplished works.

Blasco Ibáñez was not a contemplative man, and his themes, while relevant and often powerful, are not complex or subtle. His modes of characterization, his third phase notwithstanding, are a far cry from the probing, individualizing approach of most of the late nineteenth century realists. His figures lack depth, are often excessively masculine and melodramatic, and seldom rise above mere types. They can be divided into two classes: good and bad. These opposites are inevitably caught up in an eternal struggle with each other or with nature. There are few inner battles of conscience, few motivations aside from those of glory, power, sexual gratification, or mere survival. Nevertheless, Blasco Ibáñez's main type—the man of action, passion, animal instinct, and rebellion—is a graphic and powerful creation, made convincing by the sheer force of his portrayal, if not by any unique identity.

Batiste (*The Cabin*), Retor (*The Mayflower*), Toni (*Reeds and Mud*), and, in later novels, Sánchez Morueta (*The Intruder*), Gallardo (*Blood and Sand*), Centauro (*The Four Horsemen of the Apocalypse*), Ferragut (*Mare Nostrum*), and Renovales (*Woman Triumphant*) are such characters, presented in deliberate (albeit artificial) contrast to their opposites; these are weak and lazy types, such as Tonet (*The Mayflower*) and the other Tonet

(*Reeds and Mud*). Blasco Ibáñez's women are also one-sided—oppressed and overworked domestics, conventional society figures, or women of action and conquest. The last group would include Dolores (*The Mayflower*), Neleta (*Reeds and Mud*), Leonora (*The Torrent*), Doña Sol (*Blood and Sand*), and la Marquesita (*The Fruit of the Vine*). Finally, one should note that, even if Blasco Ibáñez did not create great characters, he was able to succeed in capturing dramatically the heterogeneity of the masses. Pimentò of *The Cabin*, who represents the people of the region around the Valencian *huerta*, is one striking example of this skillful portrayal.

Although Blasco Ibáñez has often been referred to as the Spanish Zola, he rejected the naturalists' pseudo-scientific, analytical approach and emphasis on crude detail, came to mitigate the impression of fatalistic determinism through his admiration of humankind's will to fight and a suggestion of optimism, and, finally, often presented a lighter, less objective, and more poetic tone than is the norm in Émile Zola's novels. Nevertheless, there are many moments in Blasco Ibáñez's work when a strong measure of pessimism and philosophical determinism or the use of unpleasant language and description demonstrate the influence of French naturalism.

Finally, one should not forget that Blasco Ibáñez produced some of the finest Spanish short stories of the modern era. One has only to look at the moving portrait of the protagonist of "Dimoni" to realize the author's skill in this genre. John B. Dalbor, the major critic to have undertaken detailed studies of these pieces, believes that many of the stories are in fact superior to the author's novels and that the very best of these stories are to be found in the collections *Cuentos valencianos*, *La condenada*, and *El préstamo de la difunta*. In the Valencian novels, Blasco Ibáñez's descriptive power—tumultuous, exuberant, dramatic, and exact—is most evident, a talent that sprang from keen observation and an uncanny ability to improvise.

THE MAYFLOWER

These virtues are evident in Blasco Ibáñez's second novel, *The Mayflower*, set in the fishing village of Cabañal; the descriptions of regional scenes and customs and many of the characters are typically drawn from observation at first hand. The plot concerns the struggles of the poor fishermen of the Valencia area.

Pascualet, called "El Retor" because of his benign clerical appearance, works and saves so that some day he can afford his own boat and free himself from the demands of another captain. His spendthrift brother, Tonet, is lazy and hates manual labor. When their father is killed at sea, their mother, Tona, cleverly converts her husband's boat into a beach tavern, where she earns a meager but adequate living for the family. El Retor goes to sea as an apprentice, but Tonet turns to drink and women until he leaves for service in the navy. By this time, a child, Roseta, has been born of Tona's affair with a passing *carabinero*. When Tonet returns to find that his brother has married the seductive Dolores, he soon agrees to marry Rosario, who has waited for him for many years. Soon Tonet renews (unbeknown to El Retor) his previous youthful encounters with Dolores, and battles between the sisters-in-law increase in frequency and intensity, despite the attempts at reconciliation managed by the ancient village matriarch, Tía Picores. A boy born to El Retor and Dolores is actually Tonet's child.

After years of hard work and saving, and after a tense smuggling adventure that results in a considerable profit, El Retor is able to arrange for the building of the finest vessel ever seen in the village, named *Flor de Mayo* after the brand of tobacco that had been smuggled into Spain on the earlier trip. Prior to the ship's second sailing, Rosario reveals to El Retor that for years his brother has had an affair with Dolores and that his son is really Tonet's offspring. After a night of shock and humiliation and after refusing for the moment to avenge the affront by his brother, El Retor sets sail in one of the worst storms to afflict the coast of Cabañal. In a suspenseful and tumultuous final chapter, El Retor confronts his brother on board the *Flor de Mayo*, extracts a confession from him, and then refuses to give him the boat's single life jacket. Instead, he puts it on the boy and tosses him overboard. The lad is thrown upon the rocks, and the ship is ripped apart by the fury of the wind. Dolores and Rosario, watching the action from the shore, mourn their loss, and old Tía Picores shouts a final condemnation of the people of Valencia, who are ultimately responsible for the deaths the women have witnessed.

Blasco Ibáñez's viewpoint is usually one of relative neutrality and omniscience, and, as is the case with other Valencian novels, he frequently transports the reader through the minds of the various characters. Some subjective authorial control, however, is evident in the progressively dominant tone of fatalism, the use of situational irony, and moments of open humor.

The style is natural and spontaneous, at times distinctly colloquial. The reader is most impressed by the fresh, graphic, highly sensuous descriptive passages, lyric moments in which a vivid plasticity and an appeal to the senses predominate. Indeed, it seems logical that Blasco Ibáñez dedicated the novel to his childhood friend Joaquín Sorolla, the artist whose vivid transcription and dazzling colors are reflected in the novelist's prose. The reader is immersed in descriptions of Cabañal and of the sea. One can envision the dawn after a night of rain, hear the distant whistle of the first trains leaving Valencia, and smell the wet earth of the village streets and the strong odors (presented in naturalistic fashion) of the local fish market. Animal images abound, and the leitmotifs of human bestiality and the human-sea relationship are the two main elements around which the novel's symbolism is constructed. (The sea itself, for example, represents the inexorable force of destiny.)

The characters are generally flat, since Blasco Ibáñez's frequent suggestion of naturalistic predestination precludes any substantial psychological development. Rather, the author was more interested in description and in constructing a rapid, suspenseful plot line for the daily readers of *El pueblo*, in which the work first appeared. Tonet is pleasure-loving, unrepentant, lazy, and self-centered. His brother El Retor is the first of Blasco Ibáñez's strong heroes, trustworthy, naïve, hardworking, and stubborn. In the last two chapters, an introspective glimpse into his musings is of a kind almost unique among the Valencian novels; a long interior monologue suggestive of Miguel de Unamuno y Jugo's later portraits of inner conflict and uncertainty reveals that, if it were not for the pressures of time and the force of his own tumultuous nature, Blasco Ibáñez might have created psychological portraits of considerable depth. Finally, of some importance is the way in which the author develops the entire *pueblo* as a kind of mass character, accustomed to the hell of life's struggle and to the constant challenge of death.

The central thematic statement of the novel concerns humankind's futile fight against the bestiality of human instincts and the powerful forces of nature. Secondary themes include a condemnation of excessive pride, a parody of religious rituals, and criticism of the villagers' exploitation by the people of Valencia.

The novel's structure is built around two main lines of action: El Retor's attempts to escape from poverty and the adulterous relationship between Tonet and Dolores. As in a number of the later Valencian works, the plot follows a regular, unified pattern: several expository chapters, consisting of an episodic introduction and two chapters of retrospective background; after that, the main action develops as a rectilinear, basically causal progression, within which the main costumbristic "digressions" become integral parts of the whole (the market scene, the Good Friday procession, the smuggling expedition, and the blessing of the boats). The unity of *The Mayflower*, like that of the other novels of the period, derives above all from the fact that Blasco Ibáñez wrote with a clear goal: to capture a people and a region. The powerful descriptions and vigorous, dramatic depiction of the villagers' primitive and difficult existence are the narrative manifestations of this purpose and represent those aspects of the work that are of greatest value.

THE CABIN

Blasco Ibáñez's third Valencian novel, *The Cabin*, was his first universally acclaimed masterpiece. It developed as the final version of a short story that he composed while hiding from the police during four days in 1895. The plot is extremely simple, lacking any kind of secondary complication and moving without distraction toward the final tragedy. In the village of Alboraya, in the *huerta* region north of Valencia, Tío Barret is evicted by a usurious landlord, whom Barret then kills in a burst of anger. For ten years, the villagers prevent anyone from working the land, as revenge for Barret's fate and as a warning to other landowners against mistreatment of the *huertanos*. Nevertheless, Batiste and his family arrive to restore the property and its shack. Pimentô, the village bully and loafer and a local warden for the rationing of irrigation use, causes Batiste to lose his water rights.

Meanwhile, other members of the family suffer: The daughter Roseta's romance with the butcher's apprentice is destroyed, and the three boys must fight their way home from school every day. The youngest son is

thrown into a slimy irrigation ditch, which leads to his death. At this point, the villagers seem to repent of their actions and take charge of the funeral. Soon, however, Batiste is lured into a tavern fight with Pimentô, which leads to their shooting each other. On the night Pimentô dies from his wounds, Batiste awakens to find the cabin on fire. As the shack burns, the villagers leave the family to their plight.

The style of *The Cabin* exhibits those attributes already mentioned. Moments of naturalistic delineation and melodramatic animal imagery are perhaps more frequent than in *The Mayflower*, and the color red becomes particularly prominent (linking images of blood, earth, the irrigation water, the fire, the tavern atmosphere, and so on). Batiste (the stoic, hardworking protagonist typical of Blasco Ibáñez's works) and Pimentô (the cowardly incarnation of collective egotism and laziness) are opposite, unidimensional poles of character presentation. The latter figure and the various representatives of the village "chorus" exemplify well the author's powerful glimpses of mass psychology.

Structurally, the novel demonstrates a typical plan: three introductory chapters concerning the arrival of Batiste and then the past tragedy of Tío Barret, four of increasing conflict, and three final chapters in which the boy's funeral suggests a momentary peace and the final disaster is presented. Each of the ten chapters is built tightly into an organic whole, yet each demonstrates a kind of aesthetic autonomy, focusing on a single incident or anecdote. A strict causal line and the careful use of foreshadowing, contrast, and leitmotif add to the impression of structural unity. Finally, cyclical factors are evident, as Barret's story at the start and Batiste's fate at the end are meant to appear similar.

A sense of fatalism and inevitability, similar to that of *The Mayflower*, is created as thematic statements are made in condemnation of the landowners' exploitation and the hypocrisy and pride of the villagers, and in support of the will to struggle for individual liberty and the need to curb one's bestial instincts, to fight against nature and the influence of collective heredity.

The novel, then, is concerned with humankind's courageous attempts to overcome nearly insurmountable obstacles. This struggle is presented on two main levels, one socioeconomic and regional, the other of universal dimensions. Batiste finds work but discovers that he must betray his fellow *huertanos* in breaking the boycott against using forbidden lands. Blasco Ibáñez, however, is ambiguous in his loyalties; one first feels sympathy for the tenant farmers as Tío Barret's eviction is described, only to have one's allegiance shift to a man fighting against the farmer's prejudice and conservatism. The author admires worker solidarity but also respects Batiste's determination to better himself. This confusion, R. A. Cardwell believes, "might be counted the major flaw of the novel." The ending is also ambiguous.

At first glance the ending seems to demonstrate Blasco Ibáñez's pessimism about the power of society and tradition in thwarting individual enterprise, but on a deeper level it may suggest the author's optimism about a person's capacity for courageous struggle and a faint hope for eventual success. This ambiguity, in turn, relates to the universal level of meaning inherent in this and other Valencian novels. Humanity will continue to fight throughout the cyclical pattern of human existence. Blasco Ibáñez's novel thus suggests (albeit subtly) the final stage of the realistic movement of the 1890's, in which the materialistic naturalism of the previous decade gave way to idealistic themes of the need for human understanding and sympathy.

Within the trajectory of the Valencian works themselves, *The Cabin* seems to represent a middle position between the emphasis on socioeconomic concerns of *The Three Roses* and a later emphasis on the way a person acts when confronted by the universal laws of an all-powerful nature. *Reeds and Mud*, with its extraordinary depiction of such natural forces, is the most powerful expression of this subsequent focus.

REEDS AND MUD

While not recognized as such by all the critics, Blasco Ibáñez's last Valencian novel, *Reeds and Mud*, is probably his single greatest literary achievement. "It is the one work," the author confided to his friend Camilo Pitollet, "which holds for me the happiest memories, the one which I composed with the most solidity, the one which I think is the most rounded." The novel is one of the most thorough adaptations by any major Spanish writer of the tenets of French naturalism.

The scene is set between 1890 and 1900 in the swamplike region of the Albufera lake near Valencia, an area known to Blasco Ibáñez's non-Valencian readers for its rice fields and plentiful game birds. The narrative itself is constructed on three levels: first, the story of three generations—the old fisherman Tío Paloma, his hardworking son, Toni, and his rebellious, irresponsible grandson, Tonet; second, the lush, all-pervading atmosphere of the Albufera; and third, a constant, "transcendent" feeling of the power of destiny, the irrevocable pressures of an abstract, deterministic force.

The plot demonstrates the sharp singleness of effect that one generally finds in a short story and traces the love affair between Tonet and Neleta from childhood to disaster, years later. While the lad is away at war, the latter marries a sickly but rich tavern owner, Cañamèl, to escape her impoverished existence. The subsequent illicit love affair between Tonet and Neleta leads to a series of events in which humans are again shown to be defenseless against the destructive forces of nature and animal instinct. Tonet suffers an emotional breakdown. Cañamèl dies after specifying in his will that Neleta cannot retain their property if she remarries or associates in an intimate way with another man. After Neleta gives birth to Tonet's child, she refuses to see her lover openly and orders him to abandon the child in the city across the lake, to escape further suspicion of violating the terms of the will. Instead, fear, remorse, and accidents of fate lead Tonet to throw the infant into the lake. When his dog later discovers the baby's corpse, Tonet seeks escape from life's misery in suicide.

Blasco Ibáñez's skillful shifts in point of view contribute a great deal to the novel's sense of realism. Such shifts frequently reveal a single incident from several different perspectives. Despite the strong measure of objectivity and the relative lack of overt authorial comment, Blasco Ibáñez's humor breaks through now and then as a means of comic relief from the growing tension of the plot line; this is noticeable, for example, in the juvenile enthusiasm of Don Joaquín during a hunting incident and Sangonera's "religious love affair" with the three *pucheros*. Above all, *Reeds and Mud* includes Blasco Ibáñez's most striking descriptive passages, revealing the freshness, the spontaneity, the richness and sensual power that constitute his most significant artistic contribution.

As always with the Valencian novels, no figures are

presented in great depth. Each seems to represent dominant passions or vices: laziness (Tonet), drunkenness (Sangonera), avarice (Neleta), the will to work and struggle (Toni), hatred for the changing times (Paloma), and so on. Certainly, all the characters are seen to blend in naturalistic fashion into the landscape around them (although they stand alongside nature rather than being consistently overpowered by it). Tonet is a victim of his own weaknesses: his indifference, his laziness, his hypocrisy, his yearning for adventure, and (under the influence of Neleta) his greed. Caught between the philosophies of his father and grandfather, Tonet is unable to shake off his inertia to make any decision regarding his life. Neleta comes also to represent the force and fecundity of nature. Sangonera, one of Blasco Ibáñez's most memorable types, is at the same time comic and pathetic, a kind of nineteenth century hippie or a modern version of the Golden Age *gracioso*, the comic "servant" who nevertheless is able to utter some very wise convictions. Toni corresponds to Batiste of *The Cabin* and to El Retor of *The Mayflower*, demonstrating the persistence, hard work, self-denial, and undying spirit of struggle that the author so admired.

Thematically, *Reeds and Mud* reveals the fullness of Blasco Ibáñez's acceptance of many tenets of the naturalists' philosophy. The human battle against the bestiality of human instincts and the powerful forces of nature is once again shown to be futile. Precluding an entirely naturalistic interpretation, however, are such factors as the exaltation of Paloma's and Toni's respective kinds of strength, the absence of heredity as a significant force, and a few elements of sheer coincidence in the plot line. (The plot itself does not reveal the strict logic of *The Cabin*; Tonet's suicide, for example, is not really the necessary outcome of causal factors.) Other related but minor thematic concerns again include the condemnation of egotism and envy and a criticism of humankind's drive to accumulate material goods at the expense of nature.

The novel's structure follows Blasco Ibáñez's typical pattern. The main action builds to three peaks, in scenes of adultery, infanticide, and suicide. As usual, a series of techniques is employed to achieve the effect of extraordinary unity: causal links of plot; the skillful integration into the narrative of the main costumbristic scenes (in this case, there are three—the raffle of the best fishing lo-cations, the Fiesta del Niño Jesús, and the hunting expeditions, or *tiradas*); parallels and corresponding incidents; and the skillful use of timing, contrast, and the repetition of leitmotifs. In *Reeds and Mud*, Blasco Ibáñez succeeds most fully in achieving the aim of the Valencian novels: the lifelike rendering (rather than didactic or moralistic evaluation) of a region—its people, its customs, its ambience.

THE FOUR HORSEMEN OF THE APOCALYPSE

Although far inferior artistically to the best of his Valencian novels, Blasco Ibáñez's greatest popular success was *The Four Horsemen of the Apocalypse*. Here the protagonist, Julio Desnoyers, is an elegant young Argentine whose father, a Frenchman, had migrated to Argentina because of the Franco-Prussian War of 1870-1871. After making his fortune in South America, the elder Desnoyers takes his family to Paris. Julio decides to marry Margarita Laurier, a frivolous divorcée, but the outbreak of World War I produces a profound change in the thinking of both. Margarita abandons her interests in fashion and social activities and dedicates herself to the wounded soldiers as a nurse. Julio enlists and sacrifices his life fighting the Germans.

The title derives from the biblical book of Revelation, which describes the four scourges of plague, war, hunger, and death—forces that, the elder Desnoyers prophesies, will walk the earth again. The novel was written as an instrument of propaganda for the Allied cause, and its major weakness is its heavy-handed and exaggerated condemnation not only of the German military establishment but also of the German people and the entirety of German culture. An extraordinarily detailed and vivid account of the Battle of the Marne is the novel's one positive achievement.

Blasco Ibáñez's works are, to say the least, uneven. While his later novels will doubtless continue to be read for years, it is his early masterpieces that earn for him a major place in modern Spanish literature. When adequate studies of his novels are produced and acceptable translations of his best works appear, the world will acknowledge his magnificent descriptions of land and sea and of regional life around Valencia and his powerful portraits of individuals struggling against overwhelming internal and external obstacles.

Jeremy T. Medina

OTHER MAJOR WORKS

SHORT FICTION: *Fantasías, leyendas, y tradiciones*, 1887; *El adiós a Schubert*, 1888; *Cuentos valencianos*, 1896; *La condenada*, 1899; *Luna Benamor*, 1909 (includes the novel of the same title; English translation, 1919); *The Last Lion, and Other Tales*, 1919; *El préstamo de la difunta*, 1921; *Novelas de la costa azul*, 1924; *The Old Woman of the Movies, and Other Stories*, 1925; *Novelas de amor y de muerte*, 1927.

PLAY: *El juez*, pb. 1894.

NONFICTION: *Historia de la revolución española, 1808-1874*, 1890-1892; *París: Impresiones de un emigrado*, 1893; *En el país del arte*, 1896 (*In the Land of Art*, 1923); *Oriente*, 1907; *Argentina y sus grandezas*, 1910; *Historia de la guerra europea de 1914*, 1914-1919 (13 volumes); *El militarismo mejicano*, 1920 (*Mexico in Revolution*, 1920); *Una nación secuestrada: Alfonso XIII desenmascarado*, 1924 (*Alfonso XIII Unmasked: The Military Terror in Spain*, 1924); *La vuelta al mundo de un novelista*, 1924-1925 (3 volumes; *A Novelist's Tour of the World*, 1926); *Lo que será la república española: Al país y al ejército*, 1925; *Estudios literarios*, 1933; *Discursos literarios*, 1966.

MISCELLANEOUS: *Obras completas*, 1923-1934 (40 volumes); *Obras completas*, 1964-1965 (3 volumes).

BIBLIOGRAPHY

Anderson, Christopher L. *Primitives, Patriarchy, and the Picaresque in Blasco Ibáñez's "Cañas y barro."* Potomac, Md.: Scripta Humanistica, 1995. Anderson reevaluates the novel *Reeds and Mud*, focusing on the portrayal of its female characters, whom he considers within the context of a male-dominated society.

Anderson, Christopher L., and Paul C. Smith. *Vicente Blasco Ibáñez: An Annotated Bibliography, 1975-2002.* Newark, Del.: Juan de la Cuesta, 2005. Extensively annotated compilation of writings by and about Blasco Ibáñez that updates Paul Smith's *Vicente Blasco Ibáñez: An Annotated Bibliography* (1976), which lists works published between 1882 and 1974.

Day, A. Grove, and Edgar C. Knowlton. *V. Blasco Ibáñez.* New York: Twayne, 1972. Survey of Blasco Ibáñez's life and canon that includes a discussion of his revolutionary influences, cosmopolitan experiences, interest in social protest and human psychology, glorification of Spain, and intense dislike of Germans.

Howells, William Dean. "The Fiction of Blasco Ibáñez." *Harper's* 131 (1915): 956-960. Howells, an American novelist and literary critic, praises Blasco Ibáñez's literary skill.

Medina, Jeremy T. *The Valencian Novels of Vicente Blasco Ibáñez.* Valencia, Spain: Albatros Ediciones, 1984. A study of five novels with themes relating to Valencia: *The Three Roses*, *The Mayflower*, *The Cabin*, *The Torrent*, and *Reeds and Mud*. Medina has written two other studies of Blasco Ibáñez's novels, both published by Albatros Ediciones. These studies are *The "Psychological" Novels of Vicente Blasco Ibáñez* (1990) and *From Sermon to Art: The Thesis Novels of Vicente Blasco Ibáñez* (1998).

Oxford, Jeffrey Thomas. *Vicente Blasco Ibáñez: Color Symbolism in Selected Novels.* New York: Peter Lang, 1997. Analyzes the use of color in some of Blasco Ibáñez's novels, arguing that although he was a naturalist, he often depicted life in a subjectively artificial way that belied the naturalists' attempt to objectively portray reality.

Swain, James O. *Vicente Blasco Ibáñez, General Study: Special Emphasis on Realistic Techniques.* Knoxville: University of Tennessee Press, 1959. A critical study of Blasco Ibáñez's work, with one chapter focusing on the realistic images of war in *The Four Horsemen of the Apocalypse.*

ROBERTO BOLAÑO

Born: Santiago, Chile; April 28, 1953
Died: Barcelona, Spain; July 15, 2003
Also known as: Roberto Bolaño Ávalos

PRINCIPAL LONG FICTION

Consejos de un discípulo de Morrison a un fanático de Joyce, 1984 (with Antoni García Porta)
La pista de hielo, 1993
La senda de los elefantes, 1993 (also known as *Monsieur Pain*, 1999)
Estrella distante, 1996 (*Distant Star*, 2004)
La literatura Nazi en América, 1996 (*Nazi Literature in the Americas*, 2008)
Los detectives salvajes, 1998 (*The Savage Detectives*, 2007)
Amuleto, 1999 (*Amulet*, 2006)
Nocturno de Chile, 2000 (*By Night in Chile*, 2003)
Una novelita lumpen, 2002
2666, 2004 (English translation, 2008)

OTHER LITERARY FORMS

Roberto Bolaño (boh-LAWN-yoh) was primarily a poet. He published his first chapbook, *Reinventar al amor* (reinventing love), in 1976. In 1979, he edited a collection of poetry, *Muchachos desnudos bajo el arcoiris de fuego* (naked guys under a rainbow of fire), which reflects the work of an aesthetic movement he cofounded. He continued writing and publishing poetry until his death. Bolaño also wrote reviews, journalistic columns, critical articles, commentaries on literature and society, and autobiographical essays. Some of these are collected in the volume *Entre paréntesis: Ensayos, artículos, y discursos, 1998-2003* (2004; in parentheses: essays, articles, and speeches).

ACHIEVEMENTS

The publication of *Los detectives salvajes* in 1998 made Roberto Bolaño a sensation among readers of the Spanish language, as did the novel's 2007 translation, *The Savage Detectives*, for English readers. In 1999, the novel earned him the prestigious Rómulo Gallegos Prize, the Spanish equivalent of the Pulitzer Prize, as well as the Herralde Prize the same year. Among his other awards is the Municipal Prize of Santiago for the short-story collection *Llamadas telefónicas* (1997; phone calls). Many critics consider him the greatest Latin American fiction writer of the second half of the twentieth century, particularly because he departed from the tradition of Magical Realism of writers such as Gabriel García Márquez.

BIOGRAPHY

Roberto Bolaño was born Roberto Bolaño Ávalos on April 28, 1953, in Santiago, Chile. His father was a truck driver and amateur boxer, and his mother was a mathematics teacher. The family lived in a series of small cities in south-central Chile before moving to Mexico City, Mexico, in 1968.

Bolaño thrived in the Mexican capital, reading voraciously and eclectically, and he dropped out of school to immerse himself in political and literary culture. He was especially devoted to poetry. Very much in the spirit of the hippie era, he joined a Mexican communist group and traveled to El Salvador to take part in the leftist ferment there. In 1973, he returned to Chile to support the Socialist government of President Salvador Allende. Not long afterward, General Augusto Pinochet Ugarte staged a coup. Bolaño was briefly placed under arrest.

In 1974, Bolaño was again in Mexico City, where he cofounded the reactionary literary movement infrarealism, which was influenced by Dadaism and the French Surrealist poet André Breton. Intent upon disrupting the staid establishment poetry of the era, Bolaño and his friends soon became notorious for disrupting poetry readings by shouting out their own poetry from the audience.

Infrarealism, however, proved short-lived. The movement's brief life, and a failed romance, led Bolaño to leave Mexico in 1977. After a year traveling through France, Spain, and North Africa, he settled for a while in Barcelona. He worked as an itinerant laborer in a variety of jobs—including salesman, night watchman, dock worker, and grape picker—and continued to write poetry.

Roberto Bolaño. (AP/Wide World Photos)

In 1982, Bolaño married Carolina Lopez, a Catalonian, and settled in the resort town of Blanes on the Catalonian coast. In 1984, he published his first novel, *Consejos de un discípulo de Morrison a un fanático de Joyce* (advice of a disciple of Morrison to a Joyce fanatic). He and his wife had a son, Lautaro, in 1991 and later a daughter, Alexandra. To earn a living for his family, which he called his "only motherland," Bolaño concentrated on writing fiction. He became a prolific writer, able to devote himself to the craft for long periods of time. By 1996, he was publishing at least one novel every year, as well as poems, essays, and newspaper columns.

Widely considered a major new writer, Bolaño remained a maverick, outspoken and often caustic. Nevertheless, his reputation steadily grew. At the same time, his health declined. Aware that he was dying, he rushed to complete his last novel to ensure financial security for his family. He passed away on July 15, 2003, in Barcelona. His novel *2666* was edited by his literary executor, Ignacio Echevarría, and published in 2004. In its original edition, the novel is more than eleven hundred pages

long, and it became an immediate success. It was hailed by some critics as one of the most significant fictional works in a generation of Latin Americans.

ANALYSIS

Roberto Bolaño was a writer's writer. Literature was his subject matter. The fictions that people make out of their own lives constitute his primary theme, and the dangers of those fictions, especially as manifest in obsession, ambition, and self-deception, provide the narrative suspense of his plots. Moreover, he readily displays his debt to his favorite authors: Nicanor Parra of Chile, Jorge Luis Borges, Julio Cortázar of Argentina, Thomas Pynchon of the United States, and James Joyce of Ireland. Scores more are mentioned in his works, and he includes in his fiction discussion of topics such as aesthetics and literary movements, their contests, prizes, and films. Each novel opens a panorama on modern literature.

Bolaño himself frequently appears as a character in his fiction under his own name, as "B," or as his alter ego, Arturo Belano. He draws much of his material from his own experience and that of people he knew. *The Savage Detectives*, for instance, borrows from his times with friends in Mexico City, so much so that its second section is practically a roman à clef. This foundation in actual history helps give his fiction its exuberant immediacy and restlessness. Nearly all of his characters live a wandering existence, and the hint is that those who settle down lose the vitality that sets them apart, for better or worse. Many fictional characters also appear in more than one novel, and passages in some novels give rise to later novels, as is the case with *Distant Star*, which expands on the ending of *Nazi Literature in the Americas*.

Bolaño makes use of several genres, mixing them so that his narratives emerge from literary conventions but are not bound by them. The pursuit of a mystery is central to his plots, through detectives such as Romero in *Nazi Literature in the Americas*, amateur detectives such as Belano and Ulises Lima, or scholars such as those in the first section of *2666*. There are also scenes appropriate to satire, crime thrillers, romantic comedy, and the coming-of-age novel. Many stories are told by first-person narrators, a technique that intensifies the immediacy of the narratives. Other times, however, Bolaño creates a prismatic effect: Such novels as *The Savage Detectives* use dozens of narrators, so that a story is not so much told as pieced together from every available viewpoint.

Bolaño undermines conventions and foils the expectations of genre. His protagonists end up antiheroes, usually near death or left in fear and doubt at a novel's end. The effect is to remove literature from its usual status as an artifact, an entertainment created by satisfying typical plot and character patterns, and to impel readers to see the characters as not simply literary creations but also possible lives. Accordingly, Bolaño's fiction expresses human relationships and thereby reflects society—politics in particular. Having himself lived through political turmoil, he is able to investigate the mechanics of moral failure and competition for power under the guise of ideology. Above all, Bolaño possesses a superior ability among modern writers to involve readers in the chancy, vital world of his tales.

THE SAVAGE DETECTIVES

The Savage Detectives recounts the history of avantgarde poets from 1975 in Mexico City until 1996 in Africa. Their literary movement, visceral realism, begins with a mischievous revolutionary fervor but spins apart through jealousy, murder, exile, despair, insanity, and, in a very few cases, self-discovery. Although the underlying plot line is straightforward, the narrative structure and multiple points of view belong uniquely to this novel. The book is divided into three sections that present the story out of temporal order.

The section "Mexicans Lost in Mexico" concerns the last two months of 1975 and takes place wholly in Mexico City. It is told through the diary entries of Juan García Madero, a seventeen year old whose ambition is to study literature and become a poet. He encounters two older poets, Belano and Lima. They are the leaders of the visceral realism movement, which is defined mostly by its vigorous opposition to mainstream Mexican literature. By chance the pair discovers that another poet, Cesárea Tinajero, also had used the term "visceral realism" to describe a literary movement. Tinajero was a shadowy figure from the 1920's, known for a single published poem. Belano and Lima decide to track her down, along with García Madero and Lupe, a prostitute on the run from her pimp.

The novel's long middle section, "The Savage Detectives," leaps forward in time, after Belano and Lima have fled to Europe in 1976. It comprises a series of testimonies about Lima and Belano by former visceral realists and some older literati, whom the pair interviewed about Tinajero. The reader learns that Lima and Belano live like lost souls, bouncing from one place to another in Nicaragua, France, Spain, Austria, and Israel. Lima eventually turns up again in Mexico City, years later and a broken man. Belano, although continuing to write, develops a mortal illness and goes to Africa as a correspondent, hoping to be killed in action. He is last seen near Monrovia, Liberia, in 1996, trying to evade a rebel army.

The final section, "The Sonora Desert," reverts to García Madero's diary, which records the events of the first six weeks of 1976. Belano, Lima, Lupe, and García Madero speed north in a borrowed car, pursued by Lupe's pimp and his henchman. The four find Tinajero in a border town of down-and-out killers. Her life having turned into a long decline into poverty, she is killed by Lupe's pursuers before Belano and Lima can interview her about visceral realism. The four fugitives then split up. García Madero finds and reads Tinajero's secret notebooks. Expecting access to the thoughts of a brilliant literary rebel, the notebooks disappoint him, and he is forced to see beyond his own ambition to become a poet. An earlier character's observation about his own literary experience applies to García Madero as well: "It gave us a glimpse of ourselves in our common humanity. It wasn't proof of our idle guilt but a sign of our miraculous and pointless innocence." These words define the true savagery of *The Savage Detectives*.

BY NIGHT IN CHILE

By Night in Chile opens with Father Sebastián Urrutia Lacroix on his deathbed confessing to the reader that although once at peace with himself, he is no longer. He is tormented by accusations from a mysterious "wizened youth" and struggles to justify his life. What follows, printed in a single paragraph, is a turbulent montage of images, anecdotes, stories, allegories, laments, and delusions.

After seminary, Urrutia allies himself to Chile's preeminent critic, an old-fashioned example of the Western literati: effete, independently wealthy, and sterile. Through him, young Urrutia socializes with the cultural elite (meeting such luminaries as Pablo Neruda), eventually becoming a prominent critic and university professor himself. However, he is suborned by politics and sent on a seriocomic mission to save the Catholic Church by agents of Opus Dei and a second mission to educate the generals of the ruling military junta about communism.

Urrutia comes to recognize that his appreciation of Chile's underlying culture, like that of many of his literary compatriots, is selective, often precious, and self-deceiving. He asks piteously, "Is it *always* possible for a man to know what is good and what is bad?" He understands at last that the answer is no and that he, like other intellectuals, has let himself be used, out of vanity, by those in power for the maintenance of power. He recognizes, further, that the wizened youth tormenting him is in reality the withered remnant of his own conscience.

NAZI LITERATURE IN THE AMERICAS

Nazi Literature in the Americas has the appearance of a biographical encyclopedia. The entries, varying in length from half a page to nearly thirty pages, discuss writers from throughout the two continents and from early in the twentieth century to as late as 2029. They are writers of nearly all genres. Through most of the book the tone is detached, judicious, and scholarly. Gradually, however, as Bolaño discusses thirty-one authors with fascist sensibilities under thirteen headings, it becomes clear to the reader that he is far from detached and that his purpose is ridicule. Moreover, he becomes involved in their world despite himself.

All these writers yearn for an autocracy that is based, variously, on race, creed, ideology, or class. While espousing family values and other standards of conduct, few of the writers practice what they preach. Herein lies the book's mordant humor. The writers are violent (soccer thugs, mercenaries, torturers, and murderers), sexually promiscuous and deviant, sometimes ignorant, and treacherous. The last of them is a figure of horror.

Chilean Carlos Ramírez Hoffman is a military pilot who creates poetic skywriting over Santiago. He is also a member of a death squad; he murders several people and tortures others, then he disappears. At this point Bolaño enters the novel as a character. Abel Romero, a private investigator on the trail of Ramírez Hoffman, asks for Bolaño's help. Together they track him down, but Bolaño begs Romero not to kill Ramírez Hoffman: "'He can't hurt anyone now,' I said. But I didn't really believe it. 'Of course he could. We all could. I'll be right back,' said Romero." The ending insists that literature, even that by the lunatic fringe, has a way of turning personal.

Roger Smith

OTHER MAJOR WORKS

SHORT FICTION: *Llamadas telefónicas*, 1997; *Putas asesinas*, 2001; *El gaucho insufrible*, 2003 (includes short stories and essays); *Last Evenings on Earth*, 2006; *El secreto del mal*, 2007.

POETRY: *Reinventar al amor*, 1976; *Fragmentos de la universidad desconocida*, 1993; *Los perros románticos: Poemas, 1980-1998*, 2000 (*The Romantic Dogs, 1980-1998*, 2008); *Tres*, 2000.

NONFICTION: *Entre paréntesis: Ensayos, artículos, y discursos, 1998-2003*, 2004.

EDITED TEXT: *Muchachos desnudos bajo el arcoiris de fuego*, 1979.

BIBLIOGRAPHY

Andrews, Chris. "Varieties of Evil." *Meanjin* 66 (September, 2007): 200-206. Andrews discusses Bolaño's portrayal of state-sponsored crime in Latin America in his works of fiction.

Corral, Will H. "Portrait of the Writer as a Noble Savage." *World Literature Today* 80 (November/December, 2006): 4-8. A concise but comprehensive literary biography of Bolaño that discusses the influences on his choice of subjects and styles for his works of fiction.

Deb, Siddhartha. "The Wandering Years: Roberto Bolaño's Nomadic Fiction." *Harper's*, April, 2007. In this magazine article, Deb analyzes the types of protagonist included in Bolaño's novels *Distant Star* and *By Night in Chile*.

Ocasio, Rafael. *Literature of Latin America*. Westport, Conn.: Greenwood Press, 2004. A good, updated survey of modern Latin American poetry and fiction.

Zalewski, Daniel. "Vagabonds: Roberto Bolaño and His Fractured Masterpiece." *The New Yorker*, March 26, 2007. Zalewski provides much biographical information on Bolaño in this magazine article to aid readers in an examination of the novel *The Savage Detectives*.

HEINRICH BÖLL

Born: Cologne, Germany; December 21, 1917
Died: Merten, West Germany (now in Germany);
  July 16, 1985
Also known as: Heinrich Theodor Böll

PRINCIPAL LONG FICTION

Der Zug war pünktlich, 1949 (*The Train Was on
  Time*, 1956)
Wo warst du, Adam?, 1951 (*Adam, Where Art
  Thou?*, 1955)
Nicht nur zur Weihnachtszeit, 1952
Und sagte kein einziges Wort, 1953 (*Acquainted
  with the Night*, 1954)
Haus ohne Hüter, 1954 (*Tomorrow and
  Yesterday*, 1957)
Das Brot der frühen Jahre, 1955 (*The Bread of
  Our Early Years*, 1957)
Billard um halbzehn, 1959 (*Billiards at Half-Past
  Nine*, 1961)
Ansichten eines Clowns, 1963 (*The Clown*, 1965)
Ende einer Dienstfahrt, 1966 (*End of a Mission*,
  1967)
Gruppenbild mit Dame, 1971 (*Group Portrait
  with Lady*, 1973)
*Die verlorene Ehre der Katharina Blum: Oder,
  Wie Gewalt entstehen und wohin sie führen
  kann*, 1974 (*The Lost Honor of Katharina
  Blum: Or, How Violence Develops and Where
  It Can Lead*, 1975)
Fürsorgliche Belagerung, 1979 (*The Safety Net*,
  1982)
Der Vermächtnis, 1982 (*A Soldier's Legacy*,
  1985)
Frauen vor Flusslandschaft, 1985 (*Women in a
  River Landscape*, 1988)
Der Engel Schwieg, 1992 (wr. 1950; *The Silent
  Angel*, 1994)
Kreuz ohne liebe, 2003

OTHER LITERARY FORMS

Although Heinrich Böll (bohl) is known chiefly for
his novels and short stories, he also wrote plays, essays,

and poems, and he was an active lecturer, critic, and
translator. His essays on literature (which include discussions of Fyodor Dostoevski, Thomas Wolfe, François Mauriac, Mary McCarthy, and Aleksandr Solzhenitsyn) show his familiarity with European and American
literature. In his essays on politics, Böll was an outspoken critic of trends in modern German society. Together
with his wife, Böll translated works by Irish, English,
and American authors into German, including works by
John Synge, Brendan Behan, and J. D. Salinger. A comprehensive ten-volume edition of Böll's works was published in Germany beginning in 1977. The first five volumes contain novels and stories; the second five contain
radio plays, dramas, film texts, poems, essays, reviews,
speeches, commentaries, and interviews.

ACHIEVEMENTS

Heinrich Böll is probably the best-known twentieth
century German writer in Germany and abroad. In Germany, his work is popular at all levels of society. His
books have been widely translated into many languages.
Böll was the Western author most frequently published
and read in the Soviet Union. Until 1951, however, he
was virtually unknown. In that year, Gruppe 47 awarded
him its Literature Prize for his story "Die schwarzen
Schafe" ("The Black Sheep"). After that, Böll received
many prizes, including the Nobel Prize in Literature in
1972. The Swedish Academy praised Böll for his broad
perspective on his time and for his sensitive characterizations, acknowledging his contribution to the renewal
of German literature after the Nazi era. In 1969, Böll was
elected president of the West German PEN Club, evidence of the respect that other writers had for him. He
was elected president of the International PEN Club in
1971, the first German to be so honored, and he served in
that position until May, 1974. In 1974, Böll received the
Carl von Ossietzky Medal from the International League
of Human Rights in recognition of his concern for human rights. He was made an honorary member of the
American Academy of Art and Literature and of the
American National Institute of Art and Literature in the
same year. Böll's outspoken criticisms of the social

abuses he perceived in modern German society provoked widespread debate.

Biography

Heinrich Theodor Böll was born in Cologne, Germany, on December 21, 1917. On his father's side, his ancestors were ship carpenters who emigrated from England centuries before, Catholics fleeing persecution under the reign of Henry VIII. On his mother's side, his ancestors were Catholic farmers and brewers. Böll's father was a cabinetmaker. In an autobiographical sketch of 1958 titled "Über mich selbst" ("About Myself"), Böll describes the hunger, poverty, and unemployment in Germany during the inflationary years of the 1920's, topics that frequently recur in his works. He remembers the first money he received—a note for one billion marks with which he managed to buy a stick of candy. In an autobiographical sketch published in 1981, *Was soll aus dem Jungen bloss werden? Oder, Irgendwas mit Büchern* (*What's to Become of the Boy? Or, Something to Do with Books*, 1984), Böll describes his childhood and youth during the years when Adolf Hitler was in power and his strong opposition to the Nazis. Whenever possible, he avoided participating in the Hitler Youth.

In an interview with the critic Horst Bienek in 1961, Böll said that he began to write when he was seventeen or eighteen. He wrote four, five, or perhaps six novels at this time, three of which were burned in Cologne during World War II. In the same interview, Böll acknowledged his debt to many writers, among them Karl May, Marcel Proust, Johann Peter Hebel, Dostoevski, Jack London, Ernest Hemingway, Albert Camus, Graham Greene, William Faulkner, Thomas Wolfe, Adalbert Stifter, Theodor Fontane, and Joseph Roth. When Böll left school in 1937, he became an apprentice in the book trade in Bonn. In the winter of 1938, he was drafted into the German labor service. He began to study German literature at the University of Cologne, but his studies were interrupted when he was called for military service in 1939. Although he was strongly opposed to the war, Böll had to serve as an infantryman in the German army for six years on the eastern and western fronts and was wounded four times.

In 1942, Böll married Annemarie Cech, who later be-

came a teacher of English. During the war, Böll deserted twice and was finally captured by the Americans. Böll draws on his firsthand experiences of the war in his early novels and stories. On his return from a prisoner-of-war camp in 1945, Böll worked briefly in the family carpentry shop until he found a job with the Cologne Bureau of Statistics. He also resumed his studies. After 1951, he earned his living as a writer. In the mid-1950's, Böll visited Ireland for the first time and liked it so much that he bought some property there. Thereafter he returned to reside in his native city of Cologne (often used as the setting of his novels) with his wife and three sons. He died in Merten, West Germany, on July 16, 1985.

Analysis

Serious moral commitment is the essence of Heinrich Böll's writing. In an essay of 1952 titled "Bekenntnis zur

Heinrich Böll. (© The Nobel Foundation)

Trümmerliteratur" ("In Defense of Rubble Literature"), Böll praises Charles Dickens for the same commitment. Dickens wrote about the social abuses he saw in English schools, prisons, and poorhouses and, by depicting these abuses, helped to bring about change. Böll believed that literature can change society by making people more aware of the world in which they live. In his 1958 essay "Die Sprache als Hort der Freiheit" ("Language as the Stronghold of Freedom"), he says that words contain enough dynamite to destroy whole worlds. It is for this reason that dictatorships fear the printed word almost more than armed resistance. Böll's early works show the senseless destruction of war and the hardships of the immediate postwar years in Germany, whereas his later works focus on contemporary German society. He had hoped that the experience of the Hitler years would change society for the better; instead, he saw the same opportunism, love of power, militarism, and greed that existed before the war.

In addition to having a strong sense of the moral and political responsibility of the writer, Böll believed that the writer should be humane and compassionate. In his works, Böll's sympathy for his fellow human beings is always evident. He is especially sympathetic toward ordinary, unheroic people who are often victimized by a cruel society. These are the kinds of people Böll chose for his protagonists. Böll's moral earnestness does not, however, preclude a sense of humor. His works are frequently humorous or satiric, although his satire is rarely vituperative.

ADAM, WHERE ART THOU?

In his interview with Horst Bienek, Böll said that his early novel *Adam, Where Art Thou?* was still one of his favorite works. It is the only one of Böll's novels that deals exclusively with World War II. In it, Böll draws extensively on his experiences as a soldier. The novel is structured episodically: The nine episodes are loosely connected by the figure of the soldier Feinhals, who is not, however, the protagonist. In some chapters, Feinhals plays only a peripheral role, and in two chapters he does not appear at all. Minor characters in one chapter become the central characters in another. As the name "Adam" in the title suggests, Böll's focus is on the suffering of humankind rather than on a specific individual. The novel is a strong denunciation

of war, typical of Böll's attitude toward war throughout his work. Böll depicts war as senseless, boring, and sordid.

The action of *Adam, Where Art Thou?* takes place mostly behind the lines, in military hospitals and hospital clearing stations, where Böll can bring the suffering caused by the war into sharper focus. Since the novel describes the retreat of the German army from the eastern front between 1944 and 1945, the loss of life is particularly senseless, because the outcome of the war is no longer in doubt. The individuals he depicts have no power to shape their own destinies; rather, they are hopelessly trapped in the war. In the tragic love affair between Feinhals and the Jewish-Catholic schoolteacher Ilona, Böll shows how the war disrupts personal relationships. This relationship has no chance to grow: Ilona is deported to a concentration camp, where she is killed, and Feinhals is picked up by the military police and sent to the front.

At the beginning of the novel, Böll quotes Antoine de Saint-Exupéry, who wrote that war is a disease, like typhoid. Even nature appears to be infected and hostile: The sun bathes everything in a bloody red or resembles a burning iron egg, about to wreak destruction like a shell or a grenade; melons rot like corpses in the fields. Chapter 3 depicts life in a military hospital and its evacuation as the Russians approach. Life for those working in the hospital is a dreary routine. In order to tolerate the daily boredom, Corporal Schneider has an elaborate ritual of drinking before he begins work. Böll also describes the turmoil of the retreat in this chapter. Even though the officers had known earlier about the retreat, they had not thought to tell the doctor, who had performed major surgery on two wounded soldiers that morning. Because moving these patients would cause their deaths, the doctor and Corporal Schneider choose to stay behind with them. Schneider goes out to meet the Russians carrying a Red Cross flag. Ironically, he is not killed by the Russians but by a German shell, supposedly a dud, on which he accidentally treads. The explosion makes the Russians think they are being attacked, and they shell the hospital, killing the doctor and his two patients, before they realize that nobody is returning their fire. Despite the quiet heroism of the doctor and Schneider, the patients die.

In chapter 7, Böll depicts the concentration camp where Ilona is killed. It is the only time in Böll's works that a concentration camp appears. The commandant, Filskeit, is the epitome of what Hannah Arendt has termed "the banality of evil." He is strict, industrious, ambitious, and reliable; he does not drink, smoke, or consort with women; he respects all authority, and he has a firm belief in Nazi ideology. Although he does not like killing, he obediently carries out his orders, lacking any compassion or humaneness. He has a passionate love for music, especially for choral singing, yet instead of making him more human, his love of art has made him even more inhuman; in his treatise on the relationship between race and choir, he makes art serve Nazi ideology. His choral performances are technically perfect but completely sterile. When new prisoners are brought to the camp, Filskeit makes them sing for him; those who sing well escape the gas chamber for a while and sing in his choir. When Ilona is brought before him, she sings the All-Saints Litany. Ilona's love of music is contrasted with Filskeit's: Music for her expresses beauty, joy, and faith, not the technical perfection that Filskeit demands. Filskeit cannot endure the purity of Ilona's singing and the faith it reveals, and he brutally kills her.

The senselessness of war is particularly evident in the novel's last two episodes. In chapter 8, a bridge is blown up in a tiny village. German soldiers are sent to guard the area, but nothing ever happens, and the soldiers eat and drink and laze away the time. Finally, it is decided that the bridge will be rebuilt. The engineer and his workers arrive and the bridge is rebuilt with model efficiency and speed; soon after it is completed, it is blown up again to halt the Russian advance. Chapter 9, which is rather melodramatic, shows Feinhals arriving home in his native village, which lies between the American and the German lines. He has survived the war and deserted the army. A vindictive German sergeant decides to shell the village to punish the inhabitants for their lack of patriotism (they are flying white flags). On the threshold of his home, Feinhals is hit by a shell and dies thinking, "How absolutely senseless," a reflection of Böll's own attitude to the war.

BILLIARDS AT HALF-PAST NINE

Although Böll also denounces World War II and the Nazi era in *Billiards at Half-Past Nine*, he widens his scope to show a panorama of German history from 1907 to 1958. In his interview with Horst Bienek, Böll said that the novel was inspired by a historical event. In 1934, the Nazi military leader Hermann Göring had four young Communists beheaded in Cologne; the youngest of the four was only seventeen or eighteen years old—the same age Böll was when he started to write. This event gives rise in the novel to the story of Ferdi Progulske, who tries to assassinate the Nazi gymnastics teacher Wakiera with a homemade bomb and is beheaded for this deed. Another source of inspiration for the novel was a famous altarpiece by Jan and Hubert van Eyck that Böll saw in Ghent; this work, known as *Adoration of the Lamb*, is a polyptych in the center of which is the Lamb of God.

The novel focuses on the lives of the Fähmel family, and the action takes place on one day, September 6, 1958, Heinrich Fähmel's eightieth birthday. Heinrich and Johanna Fähmel represent the older generation, the members of which grew up in the Wilhelmine years and experienced World War I. Böll uses flashbacks in the form of recollections to depict the earlier lives of his characters. Heinrich Fähmel arrived in Cologne for the first time in 1907 and immediately began to create a role for himself as a successful architect. He won a commission to build Saint Anthony's Abbey, married Johanna Kilb, and became through his marriage a member of the patrician class. For fifty years he has played the same role, but eventually that role traps him. When he reminisces about his past life on his eightieth birthday, he realizes that he should not have followed the rules of the establishment but should have protested against the Wilhelmine and Hitler governments. His wife, Johanna, did protest. During World War I, she criticized the emperor and German militarism; during World War II, she protested against the deportation of the Jews. In order to protect her, Heinrich had her committed to a mental institution in 1942. The sanatorium has been a refuge from reality for Johanna for sixteen years. When she leaves it to attend her husband's eightieth birthday party, she shoots at a minister because she thinks of him as the murderer of her grandchildren. She still sees the same militarism and love of power that she had criticized earlier. Her attempt to shoot the minister is a futile gesture of protest against the people in power.

Heinrich and Johanna's son, Robert Fähmel, represents the generation that grew up under Hitler. He has withdrawn completely from life. Like his father, he is an architect, but he never spends more than an hour a day in his office and conducts all of his business by mail. Since the end of the war, Robert has been playing billiards each morning at the Prince Heinrich Hotel in an attempt to escape from modern society. While he plays billiards, he talks about his past life with the bellboy, Hugo, and listens to what Hugo tells him about his life. The reasons for this strange behavior gradually become apparent. During the Hitler years, Robert had protected his friend Schrella from being victimized by the Nazis Nettlinger and Wakiera; this led to his involvement in a group of people who refused to partake of the "host of the beast." Among them he met Schrella's sister, Edith, who bore his child and whom he later married.

Robert was part of the plot to kill the Nazi sadist Wakiera, for which the high school student Ferdi was arrested and beheaded. Schrella and Robert had to flee, and Robert escaped to Holland. He was allowed to return on the condition that he join the army when he finished his studies. In the army, Robert became a demolitions expert, the opposite of his profession as an architect, and in revenge destroyed buildings to protest the murder of innocent people during the war. At the end of the war, he destroyed the abbey that his father had built. When Schrella returns to Germany after twenty-three years of exile and attends Heinrich's party, he criticizes Robert for his withdrawal from society. Robert's decision to adopt Hugo, the bellboy, at the story's end shows that he has come to terms with his wasted life and intends to become involved again.

Böll employs a symbolic contrast between lambs and buffalo to characterize German society during the fifty-year span of the novel. The lambs are the good and innocent people such as Schrella, Edith (who is killed in the bombardments), and all the people who helped Robert while he was in exile and who were arrested and killed because of it. The lambs are those who keep their integrity and who are persecuted and killed by the buffalo. The majority of people in society are buffalo, people such as Nettlinger and Wakiera, who beat Robert and Schrella with barbed-wire whips, and Robert's brother Otto, who became a Nazi and would have denounced his own mother. These buffalo, who represent the martial spirit and the love of power, still exist in modern Germany. Hugo, for example, is persecuted because of his lamblike qualities.

The representatives of the modern generation are Robert's children, Joseph and Ruth, and Joseph's fiancé, Marianne. On his grandfather's eightieth birthday, Joseph, who is rebuilding Saint Anthony's Abbey, learns that his father was responsible for destroying it and wonders whether he should tell his grandfather. Heinrich, however, has already realized who has destroyed his masterpiece and is not upset, because he now realizes that people are more important than buildings. Finding out about his father's action makes Joseph think about his own life. The question of whether he will build or destroy is left open at the end.

The conclusion of the novel is both optimistic and pessimistic. The Fähmel family and the people associated with them—Schrella, Hugo, Marianne, and Robert's secretary Leonore—have been drawn close together. They form a tight circle of people who uphold idealism and humane values; they are an isolated circle of lambs in a world of buffalo. They cannot, however, change society; they can preserve their values only by withdrawing from the world. Society on the whole has not changed for the better, Böll implies. Former Nazis such as Nettlinger are still in power, militarism still flourishes, and society is still inhumane: The buffalo are still in the majority and continue to persecute the lambs.

THE CLOWN

In *The Clown*, Böll's criticism of trends in modern German society becomes sharper. The protagonist, Hans Schnier, a twenty-seven-year-old clown who has just given a disastrous performance, is spending a lonely night in his apartment. The "action" of the novel is restricted to this single night, during which Hans telephones many of the people he knows, although (as in *Billiards at Half-Past Nine*) Böll uses extensive flashbacks in the form of recollections to relate Hans's past experiences. Some years earlier, Hans fell in love with Marie Derkum, a Catholic, left high school for her, and became a clown. To the annoyance of his wealthy family, Hans refused to adopt a middle-class profession. For five years, Hans was a successful clown, showing the absurdities of daily life in his act. He lived with Marie and traveled around with her. Marie then joined a group of progressive Catholics, after which their relationship deteriorated. Marie wanted Hans to marry her and sign papers promising to rear their children as Catholics. Although Hans refused at first, he eventually agreed. This, however, did not satisfy Marie: She accused him of agreeing to her demands merely to keep her rather than being convinced of the "justness of abstract principles of order." Marie left him and married Heribert Züpfner, one of the prominent Catholics in the German establishment. After that, Hans began to drink heavily, which ruined his clown act. In his apartment on the night covered in the novel, Hans makes a series of phone calls in a state of controlled desperation. He tries to win back Marie—with no success. The telephone is a symbol of his isolation, of the lack of real communication between people. At the end of the novel, Hans paints his face white and goes to the Bonn railway station to play his guitar and beg.

Böll's focus on a group of progressive Catholics for criticism in this novel caused Catholic groups in Germany to take offense. Böll attacks not only Catholics, however, but also any group that values dogma more than individual human lives. The progressive Catholics in the group are narrow, self-sufficient, and hypocritical. Because they are tied to dogma, they lack all compassion and humaneness. During a gathering of this group, which Hans and Marie attend, the prominent Catholic Sommerwild tells about a Catholic writer who lived for a long time with a divorced woman. When he married her, an eminent church dignitary asked whether he could not have kept her as his concubine. All the Catholics laugh at this story. Hans is shocked by the cynical attitude toward human relationships that he finds in this group. He believes in the sanctity of relationships; the formality of a marriage license means nothing to him. He believes that his relationship with Marie is a marriage because of the commitment and love they have for each other. Like the progressive Catholics, Hans's brother Leo, who is studying to be a priest, places the letter of the law above human considerations. He will not leave the seminary to come to Hans's aid because it is against the rules.

Böll also attacks the ease with which people adapt to the prevailing ideology. One such example is Hans's mother. During the war, she was a racist and used such Nazi slogans as "our sacred German soil" (an ironic phrase, because the Schnier family makes its wealth from digging up the coal under the sacred German soil). In the last months of the war, she encouraged her daughter Henrietta to volunteer for antiaircraft duty, thereby causing Henrietta's death. Hans's alienation from society began when his sister died. Now Mrs. Schnier is president of the Executive Committee of the Societies for the Reconciliation of Racial Differences.

Despite her wealth, Mrs. Schnier is stingy. As a child, Hans was often hungry; on one occasion, Hans saw his mother go down to the storeroom to eat the food she would not give to her children. Böll also presents examples of other born conformists. The fascist writer Schnitzler makes people believe that he was censored for his resistance to Hitler, which was not the case; he is now indispensable at the Foreign Office. Because the teacher Brühl never joined the Nazi Party (although his sympathies were with the Nazis), he now has the reputation of a man with a courageous political past and is a professor at a teacher training college. The ruthless Hitler Youth leader, Herbert Kalick, has recently been awarded a medal for his work in spreading democratic ideas among young people in Germany.

Böll also criticizes the greed and commercialism in West German society. Hans's father represents big business in Germany. Like Hans's mother, his father is also mean and refuses to help his son financially, and he is too concerned with prestige and respectability. Böll does not spare the German Democratic Republic: Hans was once invited to perform there, but when the Communists discovered that he wanted to perform "The Party Conference Elects Its Presidium" instead of anticapitalist skits, he had to leave on the next train.

The spontaneous and naïve Hans considers adapting to society and playing the role of the hypocrite but decides to keep his integrity: He refuses to compromise his ideals and adapt to social norms. Instead, he completely rejects German society; in his radical alienation from society he resembles Dostoevski's underground man, an indication of the impact that Dostoevski had on Böll's writing. Hans protests against the hypocrisy, sterile dogma, materialism, and opportunism of modern society. The clown, who as an outsider can be sharply critical of society, symbolizes Hans's protest. The conclusion of the novel is more pessimistic than that of *Billiards at Half-Past Nine*. Hans does not have a circle of friends and family—he is alone at the end, a beggar by choice.

GROUP PORTRAIT WITH LADY

Like *Billiards at Half-Past Nine, Group Portrait with Lady* shows a panorama of German history in the twentieth century. Böll's main focus in the novel is on the 1930's and 1940's, after which the focus shifts to the 1970's. The novel is made up of reports about Leni Pfeiffer, née Gruyten, a woman of forty-eight. The narrator, a character called the "author," gradually reconstructs Leni's life. He searches for material; interviews friends, relatives, and enemies of Leni; and comments on the reports. The many people he interviews form a cross section of German society, from millionaires to garbage workers, and through these interviews the reader is given a picture not only of Leni but also of the commentators themselves. The "author" is not objective, because he confesses that he loves Leni.

The novel highlights main events in Leni's life. She was born in Cologne in 1922. In 1938, she was dismissed from a Catholic high school and began to work in her father's engineering firm. During the war, her brother, Heinrich, and her cousin, Erhard, were shot by the Germans for trying to sell an antitank gun to the Danes, a futile act of protest against the Nazi regime. In 1941, Leni married Alois Pfeiffer, who was killed three days later. When her father was arrested in 1943 for illegal business dealings, Leni was left penniless and began making wreaths in a cemetery nursery. There she met Boris Lvovich Koltovsky, a Soviet prisoner of war, and they fell in love. During the heavy bombardments of the city in 1944, they met secretly in the underground vaults of the cemetery. In 1945, Leni gave birth to their son, Lev. When the Allies occupied the city, Boris was arrested on suspicion of being a German soldier. He was put to work in a French mine, where he died in an accident. Leni continued to work and look after her son.

Like most of Böll's protagonists, Leni is a naïve, innocent figure who refuses to conform to social norms. She is generous and compassionate to everyone and is perplexed by the evil in people. Leni has a healthy and natural attitude toward sexuality, which Böll contrasts with society's hypocritical attitude toward the body. Be-

cause Leni maintains her integrity and refuses to conform, society persecutes her. Long after the war, in 1970, her neighbors hate her because she lets rooms cheaply to foreign workers and because she is expecting her Turkish lover's child. Whenever she ventures out of her apartment, her neighbors verbally abuse her, calling her a whore—some would even like to see her gassed, an indication that people are just as inhumane as they were during the Nazi era.

In this novel, Böll is sharply critical of racism. He satirizes the Nazi belief that the Slavs were subhuman. It is the Soviet prisoner Boris, with his knowledge of German literature, who ironically reminds the Germans of their humanistic tradition, perverted by the Nazis. The dummy company that Leni's father forms to swindle the government and avenge himself on the Nazis for killing his son reminds people of the great Russian literary tradition, because he names his fictitious workers after great Russian writers and characters in their works. The racism in Germany during the war years is still evident in modern German society; only the target of the racism has changed: Now the foreign workers are the deprived and misused members of society.

Böll's attack on greed, commercialism, and opportunism is particularly severe in this novel. Pelzer, the owner of the nursery where Leni worked, is an unscrupulous opportunist who profits from war. In World War I, he stole gold from the teeth of dead American soldiers. After the war, he joined the Communist Party for a time; when it became expedient, he joined the Nazi Party instead. When he was supposed to arrest prominent people, he let them go if they paid him. During World War II, he made money from wreaths, increasing his profit by reusing wreaths. Just before the Americans arrived in Cologne, he resigned from the Nazi Party and was thus allowed to stay in business. Pelzer is now very wealthy from his various business dealings. Böll does not, however, portray Pelzer entirely negatively: Pelzer's love of money stems from the poverty he endured as a youth. He also tried to protect Leni and Boris during the war.

Hoyser, Leni's father's former head bookkeeper, has no redeeming qualities and is the epitome of crass commercialism. During the war, Leni had allowed the Hoysers to live in her house rent-free. When she could not repay the money she had borrowed from Hoyser, he repossessed her house and immediately began charging her rent. At the end of the war, he made a profit by buying property cheaply from former Nazis, who in turn had stolen the property from Jews. Hoyser and his grandchildren decide at the end of the novel to evict Leni because she is letting rooms cheaply to foreigners. The Hoysers' lives revolve entirely around money, to the absolute exclusion of compassion.

As in his other novels, Böll is very critical of German society. Some hope, however, lies in the new generation, as represented here by Lev. He is in prison for crudely forging checks to try to get Leni's house back from the Hoysers. Lev is alienated from bourgeois society. At school, Lev was cruelly taunted for being illegitimate, and he purposely pretended to be stupid to show his contempt for the educational system (his true intelligence is evidenced by his fluent command of Russian and his sensitive understanding of German literature). As a child, Lev had a passion for cleanliness, and he is now a garbage worker; Böll's satiric message is that society needs to be cleansed. Lev has rejected middle-class society and values and has chosen to live as an outsider. Among the foreign garbage workers, he finds community and solidarity (the garbage workers cause a traffic jam with their trucks to prevent Leni's eviction). Hope also lies in the group of Leni's friends who work together to help her. As in *Billiards at Half-Past Nine*, however, the community of like-minded, idealistic people is helpless to change society; the members of the group can retain their integrity only on the fringes of society.

THE LOST HONOR OF KATHARINA BLUM *and* THE SAFETY NET

The Lost Honor of Katharina Blum and *The Safety Net* also focus on modern German social problems. In *The Lost Honor of Katharina Blum*, Böll shows how the media psychologically destroy an individual through sensationalistic and untruthful reporting. In addition to attacking irresponsible journalistic practices, Böll criticizes society for tolerating and indeed thriving on media spectacles. In *The Safety Net*, Böll deals with the problems of terrorism in a democratic society. His belief in the moral responsibility of the writer is as strong in these later works as it was in his earlier ones. Throughout his works, Böll is concerned with the individual who struggles to retain integrity in a basically hostile world. The critic Marcel Reich-Ranicki has summed up Böll's achievement succinctly, saying that without wanting to do so, Böll represents German literature of the twentieth century: He is a poet but also more than a poet, because he speaks against all forms of tyranny in the world.

Jennifer Michaels

OTHER MAJOR WORKS

SHORT FICTION: *Wanderer, kommst du nach Spa . . .*, 1950 (*Traveller, If You Come to Spa*, 1956); *So ward Abend und Morgen*, 1955; *Unberechenbare Gäste*, 1956; *Doktor Murkes gesammeltes Schweigen und andere Satiren*, 1958; *Der Fahnhof von Zimpren*, 1959; *Erzählungen, Hörspiele, Aufsätze*, 1961; *Entfernung von der Truppe*, 1964 (*Absent Without Leave*, 1965); *Eighteen Stories*, 1966; *Absent Without Leave, and Other Stories*, 1967; *Children Are Civilians Too*, 1970; *Die Verwundung und andere frühe Erzählungen*, 1983 (*The Casualty*, 1986); *Veränderungen in Staech: Erzählungen, 1962-1980*, 1984; *The Stories of Heinrich Böll*, 1986.

PLAYS: *Ein Schluck Erde*, pb. 1962; *Aussatz*, pb. 1970.

POETRY: *Gedichte*, 1972; *Gedichte mit Collagen von Klaus Staeck*, 1980.

SCREENPLAY: *Deutschland im Herbst*, 1978.

NONFICTION: *Irisches Tagebuch*, 1957 (*Irish Journal*, 1967); *Brief an einen jungen Katholiken*, 1961; *Frankfurter Vorlesungen*, 1966; *Aufsätze, Kritiken, Reden*, 1967; *Hierzulande*, 1967; *Neue politische und literarische Schriften*, 1973; *Schwierigkeiten mit der Brüderlichkeit*, 1976; *Einmischung erwünscht*, 1977; *Missing Persons, and Other Essays*, 1977; *Gefahren von falschen Brüdern*, 1980; *Spuren der Zeitgenossenschaft*, 1980; *Was soll aus dem Jungen bloss werden? Oder, Irgendwas mit Büchern*, 1981 (*What's to Become of the Boy? Or, Something to Do with Books*, 1984); *Vermintes Gelände*, 1982; *Bild, Bonn, Boenisch*, 1984.

MISCELLANEOUS: *Heinrich Böll Werke*, 1977-1979.

BIBLIOGRAPHY

Conard, Robert C. *Heinrich Böll*. Boston: Twayne, 1981. Written before Böll's death and thus incomplete in a number of respects, this book is nevertheless one of the best introductions to and studies of Böll's work readily available to the general reader. Includes chronologies and helpful bibliographies, though many of the sources listed are in German.

_____. *Understanding Heinrich Böll*. Columbia: University of South Carolina Press, 1992. Provides a general introduction to Böll's life and work, with chapter 4 focusing on his major novels, including *Billiards at Half-Past Nine*, *The Clown*, *Group Portrait with Lady*, and *The Lost Honor of Katharina Blum*.

Crampton, Patricia, trans. *Heinrich Böll, on His Death: Selected Obituaries and the Last Interview*. Bonn: Inter Nationes, 1985. Brief volume presents a collection of short elegiac essays as well as Böll's last interview. Offers many perceptive and impressionistic insights into both the man and the writer. Includes about a dozen photographs of Böll in his last years.

Ludden, Teresa. "Birth and the Mother in Materialist Feminist Philosophy and Contemporary German Texts." *Women* 17, no. 3 (Winter, 2006): 341-354. Provides a critical analysis of the treatment of childbirth in works by Böll and two other novelists, with particular emphasis on the birth scenes in *Group Portrait with Lady*, Günter Grass's *Die Blechtrommel* (1959; *The Tin Drum*, 1961), and Patrick Süskind's *Das Parfüm: Die Geschichte eines Mörders* (1985; *Perfume: The Story of a Murderer*, 1986).

Macpherson, Enid. *A Student's Guide to Böll*. London: Heinemann Educational Books, 1972. Brief introductory work is intended for students of German literature. In addition to devoting chapters to the novels and short stories, discusses Böll's critical writings and lectures for the light they shed on his narrative practice.

Reid, J. H. *Heinrich Böll: A German for His Time*. New York: Berg, 1988. Quoting Böll's remark that writers must be understood as products of their time, Reid examines Böll as just that, tracing the political and social currents that shaped his work. Perceptive and evenhanded, this study is less concerned with belles lettres than with ideologies and political history. The short stories find mention and commentary chiefly as expression of Böll's ideas. An excellent bibliography, largely in German, reflects the book's main concern.

_____. "Private and Public Filters: Memories of War in Heinrich Böll's Fiction and Nonfiction." In *European Memories of the Second World War*, edited by Helmut Peitsch, Charles Burdett, and Claire Gorrara. New York: Berghahn Books, 1999. A study of Böll's work is included in this examination of how German, French, and Italian literature reflects Europeans' changing memories of World War II.

Zachau, Reinhard K. *The Narrative Fiction of Heinrich Böll*. New York: Cambridge University Press, 1997. Presents a study of Böll's work in its social context in the second German Republic. Includes several essays on Böll's major works, focusing on their literary traditions as well as on the link in his work between moral/aesthetic issues and sociopolitical issues.

ARNA BONTEMPS

Born: Alexandria, Louisiana; October 13, 1902
Died: Nashville, Tennessee; June 4, 1973
Also known as: Arna Wendell Bontemps

PRINCIPAL LONG FICTION

God Sends Sunday, 1931
Black Thunder, 1936
Drums at Dusk, 1939

OTHER LITERARY FORMS

Arna Bontemps (bahn-TAHM) was a prolific author and editor. He wrote or cowrote many children's books, biographies, and histories, and he edited or coedited more than a dozen works, including African American poetry anthologies, histories, slave narratives, and a folklore collection. His short stories were collected in *The Old South* (1973), and his poetry collection, *Personals*, appeared in 1963. He and Countée Cullen adapted Bontemps's novel *God Sends Sunday* for the New York stage in 1946 as *St. Louis Woman*. Bontemps's forty-two-year correspondence with writer Langston Hughes was published in 1980.

ACHIEVEMENTS

Arna Bontemps's finely honed poems quietly reflect his lifelong Christian beliefs. After winning several prizes for his poems and short stories in the 1920's and 1930's, Bontemps was granted the first of two Rosenwald Fellowships in Creative Writing in 1939 (the other came in 1943). In 1949 and 1954 he received Guggenheim Fellowships for creative writing. He was given the Jane Addams Children's Book Award in 1956 for *The Story of the Negro* (first published in 1948), which was also named a Newbery Honor Book in 1949. In 1969 he was appointed writer-in-residence at Fisk University, and in 1972 he was named honorary consultant to the Library of Congress in American cultural history. Beginning in the 1960's he became a popular national speaker, and he always offered encouragement to struggling African American writers. Wherever he served as a teacher, he was loved and respected by his students.

BIOGRAPHY

Arna Wendell Bontemps, whose parentage was Louisiana Creole, was born in the front bedroom of his maternal grandfather's comfortable home at the corner of Ninth and Winn Streets in Alexandria, Louisiana. The house is still standing, though it has been moved; in 1992 it became the site of the Arna Bontemps African American Museum. Bontemps's father, a skilled stonemason, bricklayer, and former trombonist with a New Orleans marching band, moved with his wife, children, and in-laws to California following a racial incident in Louisiana. The elder Bontemps also served as a Seventh-Day Adventist preacher after he abandoned Catholicism.

Bontemps's earliest childhood was spent happily in his grandparents' house in Alexandria. Later, in California, he was greatly influenced by a great-uncle, Uncle Buddy, who came from Alexandria to stay with his relatives in California. Though Uncle Buddy was a down-at-the-heels alcoholic, he nevertheless represented for young Bontemps the essence of Louisiana culture, folklore, and history with his colorful stories and speech. Self-educated, intelligent, and articulate, Uncle Buddy was a good reader and storyteller and awakened in his grandnephew a love of hearing and telling stories and of reading and reciting poetry. Most important, Uncle Buddy reminded young Bontemps of his Louisiana and southern roots, which were later to be a great literary storehouse for the budding author.

Bontemps's mother died when he was ten years old, and he and his sister went to live on his grandmother's farm near Los Angeles. Bontemps completed his secondary schooling at a private boarding school and his bachelor's degree at the University of the Pacific. After college he went to New York City, where he joined the Harlem Renaissance, which was in full swing, and began a close, lifelong friendship with writer Langston Hughes.

Bontemps taught school in New York, married Alberta Jones when he was twenty-four, and subsequently fathered six children. In 1931 Bontemps and his family moved to Alabama, where he taught in a junior college and observed southern behavior and customs. The family left Alabama in 1934 because of a hostile racial climate following the trial of the Scottsboro Nine, black men who were unjustly convicted of raping two white women, and moved into Bontemps's father's small house in California. There the author worked on his second novel, frequently writing outdoors with his small portable typewriter on a makeshift desk.

By 1943 he had moved to Chicago, where he earned a master's degree in library science. Accepting an appointment as full professor and head librarian at Fisk University in Nashville, Bontemps served there until the mid-1960's, when he accepted a professorship in history and literature at the University of Illinois at Chicago Circle. He also served as curator of the James Weldon Johnson Collection.

He retired in 1969 to work on his autobiography, which remained unfinished at his death. In 1972 he published *The Harlem Renaissance Remembered* and returned to visit his birthplace in Louisiana. After his death on June 4, 1973, he was honored at both Protestant and Catholic memorial services.

ANALYSIS

Although he lived and taught in many regions of the United States, Arna Bontemps always identified with the South and set most of his fictional works there. Bontemps greatly valued his African American inheritance and tried to increase both racial pride and interracial understanding through his many books about African American figures, life, and culture.

GOD SENDS SUNDAY

In God Sends Sunday, set in the 1890's, Bontemps depicts a diminutive black jockey, Little Augie, who lives on a Red River plantation in Louisiana with his older sister. Because he was born with a caul over his face, he is thought to be lucky. He discovers a talent for riding horses, which serves him well when he escapes to New Orleans on a steamboat and becomes a jockey. With his success, Augie grows rich, arrogant, and ostentatious. He falls in love with a beautiful young mulatto, Florence Desseau, but learns, to his sorrow, that she is the mistress of his rich white patron. Going to St. Louis to find a woman like Florence, Augie falls in with a crowd of prostitutes, gamblers, and "sugar daddies," one of whom he murders when the man bothers Augie's woman. When he returns to New Orleans, he at last has

Florence as his lover. She deserts him, however, taking his money and possessions. Augie's luck fades, and he declines rapidly into penury and alcoholism. In California, Augie commits another "passion murder" and escapes to Mexico.

This novel exhibits a remarkable joie de vivre among its black characters, but they are primarily caricatures within a melodramatic plot. Bontemps uses black dialect and folklore effectively, however, especially the blues, for which Augie has a great affection.

BLACK THUNDER

Bontemps's second novel, first published in 1936, was reissued in 1968 with a valuable introduction by Bontemps in which he describes finding a treasured store of slave narratives in the Fisk Library and reading the stories of slave insurrectionists Nat Turner, Denmark Vesey, and Gabriel Prosser. Bontemps identified Prosser as the slave-rebel-hero whose yearning for freedom most greatly resembled his own.

Arna Bontemps. (Library of Congress)

Black Thunder is generally acknowledged by readers and critics alike to be Bontemps's best novel; it has even been called the best African American historical novel. The French Revolution and the slave rebellion in Santo Domingo provide significant background as the story dramatizes an enslaved people's long-restrained desire for freedom. Bundy, an old black peasant, longs for the freedom that the legend of Haitian liberator Toussaint-Louverture has inspired in many slaves. When Bundy is viciously flogged to death, Gabriel Prosser, a strong young coachman, feels driven to seek freedom for himself and his people. This feeling is even held by already freed slaves, such as Mingo, a leather worker, who plays a major role in the rebellion effort. The white Virginians, both patricians and common folk, hold Creuzot, a French painter, and Biddenhurst, a British lawyer, responsible for the slaves' disquiet. Moreover, as they do not believe the slaves to be human, members of the white population cannot understand why the slaves would want freedom. The whites' interpretation of the Bible supports their racist beliefs.

Gabriel, too, is deeply religious, though not fanatical, and often echoes scripture. He believes that God will free his people because Armageddon is at hand. He plans, with the assistance of free blacks, slaves, and a few sympathetic whites, to capture the arsenal at Richmond in order to seize the weapons and overpower the city. Unfortunately, a monsoonlike rainstorm on the night of the rebellion causes a delay in the insurrection. Bontemps's powers as a prose artist are especially strong as he describes, in haunting cadences, the revolt's defeat by nature's wrath. The slaves believe that ill luck and fateful weather led to the revolt's collapse, but in actuality two elderly, spoiled house servants betrayed the cause. The collapse of the rebellion marks the climax of the story; what follows tells of the insurrectionists' capture and execution. Bontemps makes astute use of court records as he dramatizes Gabriel's trial.

Bontemps is in firmer control of his literary material in *Black Thunder* than in his other novels. All his characters—white planter-aristocrats, free blacks, and French zealots—are drawn with objectivity and restraint. Pro-freedom views are not praised at the expense of anti-freedom beliefs. Furthermore, the novel's characters, even minor ones, are richly complex. For example, Ben

and Pharaoh, the betrayers of the rebellion, evidence conflicting loyalties both to their aristocratic masters and to their African American brothers. In a memorable interior monologue, Ben condemns himself for the narcissism that made his own survival more important to him than that of his fellow slaves. His ironic curse is that he must live under the threat of a horrible revenge at the hands of his own people.

Bontemps's special achievement in *Black Thunder* is the skill with which he integrates Gabriel's revolt into the fabric of Virginian, and American, life by using a documentary style of exposition. While Virginia legislators debate further segregation of blacks as a way of dealing with race issues, quoted reports from Federalist newspapers oppose the liberal ideas of former president Thomas Jefferson and attribute Gabriel's revolt to Jefferson's evil influence. These same newspapers support the presidential campaign of John Quincy Adams.

Even more impressive is Bontemps's use of interior monologues and passages that present the points of view of several individual characters, Caucasian and African American. First- and third-person perspectives are blended in order to present both objective and subjective forces. Bontemps's careful synthesis of history and imagination helps him demonstrate the universal, age-old struggles of humankind to surmount barriers of race, class, and caste and gain equality, liberty, respect, and security. Because Bontemps allows Gabriel to maintain and even increase his integrity, he becomes a truly tragic figure who is, at the end of the novel, "excellent in strength, the first for freedom of the blacks, . . . perplexed but unafraid, waiting for the dignity of death."

DRUMS AT DUSK

Drums at Dusk, like *Black Thunder*, is a historical novel in which Bontemps makes use of slave narratives and legal records to establish background for the black rebellion leading to Haiti's independence and Toussaint-Louverture's ascendancy. Bontemps centers the story on a young girl of French ancestry, Celeste Juvet, and Diron de Sautels, an aristocratic young Frenchman who claims membership in Les Amis des Noirs, embraces enthusiastically the ideas of writers of the French Revolution, and works as an abolitionist. Celeste and her grandmother reside on a large plantation where the owner's cousin, Count Armand de Sacy, abuses ailing slaves and mistreats his mistresses, abandoning them at his uncle's. De Sacy is deeply disliked, and when several slaves foment an insurrection, the aristocrats are overturned and rebel leaders successfully seize power.

Diron de Sautels's radical opinions influence young blacks, and they fight with three other groups for political control of Santo Domingo: rich aristocrats, poor whites, and free mulattos. *Drums at Dusk* describes with melodramatic sensationalism the sybaritic lives of the wealthy and their sexual exploitation of light-skinned black women. Moreover, the novel describes graphically the heinous conditions on the slave ships and the terrible treatment of slaves on many of the plantations. The patricians' cruelty and abuse lead to a rapid spread of liberal ideology and the rise of such leaders as Toussaint-Louverture.

In spite of its faults, Bontemps's last novel, like his second one, emphasizes the universal need and desire for freedom, which he intimates is as necessary for the survival of human beings as water, air, food, and shelter.

Philip A. Tapley

OTHER MAJOR WORKS

SHORT FICTION: *The Old South*, 1973.

PLAYS: *St. Louis Woman*, pr. 1946 (with Countée Cullen).

POETRY: *Personals*, 1963.

NONFICTION: *Father of the Blues*, 1941 (with W. C. Handy; biography); *They Seek a City*, 1945 (with Jack Conroy; revised as *Anyplace but Here*, 1966); *One Hundred Years of Negro Freedom*, 1961 (history); *Free at Last: The Life of Frederick Douglass*, 1971; *Arna Bontemps-Langston Hughes Letters: 1925-1967*, 1980.

CHILDREN'S LITERATURE: *Popo and Fifina: Children of Haiti*, 1932 (with Langston Hughes); *You Can't Pet a Possum*, 1934; *Sad-Faced Boy*, 1937; *The Fast Sooner Hound*, 1942 (with Jack Conroy); *We Have Tomorrow*, 1945; *Slappy Hooper: The Wonderful Sign Painter*, 1946 (with Conroy); *The Story of the Negro*, 1948; *Chariot in the Sky: A Story of the Jubilee Singers*, 1951; *Sam Patch*, 1951 (with Conroy); *The Story of George Washington Carver*, 1954; *Lonesome Boy*, 1955; *Frederick Douglass: Slave, Fighter, Freeman*, 1959; *Famous Negro Athletes*, 1964; *Mr. Kelso's Lion*, 1970; *Young Booker: Booker T. Washington's Early Days*, 1972; *The*

Pasteboard Bandit, 1997 (with Hughes); *Bubber Goes to Heaven*, 1998.

EDITED TEXTS: *The Poetry of the Negro*, 1949 (with Langston Hughes; revised 1971); *The Book of Negro Folklore*, 1958 (with Hughes); *American Negro Poetry*, 1963; *Great Slave Narratives*, 1969; *Hold Fast to Dreams*, 1969; *The Harlem Renaissance Remembered*, 1972.

BIBLIOGRAPHY

Canaday, Nicholas. "Arna Bontemps: The Louisiana Heritage." *Callaloo* 4 (October-February, 1981): 163-169. Canaday traces the significant influence of Bontemps's great-uncle from Louisiana, Buddy (Joe Ward), on the author's novel *God Sends Sunday*.

James, Charles L. "Arna Bontemps: Harlem Renaissance Writer, Librarian, and Family Man." *New Crisis* 109, no. 5 (September/October, 2002): 22-28. Profile of Bontemps describes his family and educational backgrounds, discusses the reasons his parents left Louisiana, and addresses the author's experience of racism. Includes photographs.

Jones, Kirkland C. "Bontemps and the Old South." *African American Review* 27, no. 2 (1993): 179-185. Addresses the fact that the Old South is employed more extensively in Bontemps's fiction than in that of any other Harlem Renaissance writer. Points out how the South is the setting for several of his novels and argues that his novel about Haiti, *Drums at Dusk*, is "in some ways his Southernmost piece of fiction."

_____. *Renaissance Man from Louisiana: A Biography of Arna Wendell Bontemps*. Westport, Conn.: Greenwood Press, 1992. The first full-scale biography of Bontemps treats the author's life and career in detail but only cursorily analyzes or evaluates the writings. Includes chronology, photographs, bibliography, and index.

Reagan, Daniel. "Voices of Silence: The Representation of Orality in Arna Bontemps' *Black Thunder*." *Studies in American Fiction* 19 (Spring, 1991): 71-83. Examines the use of African American vernacular traditions in *Black Thunder* and concludes that the novel's significant statements of black cultural identity occur in the oral discourse that Bontemps portrays through figurative language.

Scott, William. "'To Make up the Hedge and Stand in the Gap': Arna Bontemps's *Black Thunder*." *Callaloo* 27, no. 2 (Spring, 2004): 522-541. Analyzes *Black Thunder* to show how Bontemps's novel about the Gabriel Prosser slave revolt expresses Prosser's belief that in order to bridge the gap from the experience of slavery to an experience of freedom it was necessary to promise a passage from slavery to freedom.

Stone, Albert. *The Return of Nat Turner: History, Literature, and Cultural Politics in Sixties America*. Athens: University of Georgia Press, 1992. Examines how the Nat Turner rebellion and other slave revolts have been represented in American literature. A chapter titled "The Thirties and the Sixties: Arna Bontemps' *Black Thunder*" analyzes Bontemps's successful synthesis of history and his own imagination in that novel.

Thompson, Mark Christian. "Voodoo Fascism: Fascist Ideology in Arna Bontemps's *Drums at Dusk*." *MELUS* 30, no. 3 (Fall, 2005): 155-177. Contends that Bontemps's novel about a revolt in Haiti, in which he sought to depict the origins of black revolution and political power by creating a strong and charismatic leader, is in actuality an apology for fascism.

ELIZABETH BOWEN

Born: Dublin, Ireland; June 7, 1899
Died: London, England; February 22, 1973
Also known as: Elizabeth Dorothea Cole Bowen

PRINCIPAL LONG FICTION

The Hotel, 1927
The Last September, 1929
Friends and Relations, 1931
To the North, 1932
The House in Paris, 1935
The Death of the Heart, 1938
The Heat of the Day, 1949
A World of Love, 1955
The Little Girls, 1964
Eva Trout, 1968

OTHER LITERARY FORMS

The first seven novels that Elizabeth Bowen (BOH-uhn) produced were republished by Jonathan Cape in Cape Collected Editions between the years 1948 and 1954, when Cape also republished four of her short-story collections: *Joining Charles* (1929), *The Cat Jumps, and Other Stories* (1934), *Look at All Those Roses* (1941), and *The Demon Lover* (1945). Other collections of her short stories are *Encounters* (1923), *Ann Lee's, and Other Stories* (1926), *Stories by Elizabeth Bowen* (1959), and *A Day in the Dark, and Other Stories* (1965). *The Demon Lover* was published in New York under the title *Ivy Gripped the Steps, and Other Stories* (1946); this work, as the original title indicates, has supernatural content that scarcely appears in Bowen's novels. Bowen's nonfiction includes *Bowen's Court* (1942), a description of her family residence in Ireland; *Seven Winters* (1942), an autobiography; *English Novelists* (1946), a literary history; *Collected Impressions* (1950), essays; *The Shelbourne: A Center of Dublin Life for More than a Century* (1951), a work about the hotel in Dublin; *A Time in Rome* (1960), travel essays; and *Afterthought: Pieces About Writing* (1962), which collects transcripts of broadcasts and reviews. A play that Bowen coauthored with John Perry, *Castle Anna*, was performed in London in March, 1948.

ACHIEVEMENTS

Considered a great lady by those who knew her, Elizabeth Bowen draws an appreciative audience from readers who understand English gentility—the calculated gesture and the controlled response. Bowen's support has come from intellectuals who recognize the values of the novel of manners and who liken her work to that of

Jane Austen and Henry James. Her contemporaries and colleagues included members of the Bloomsbury Group and scholars of Oxford University, where the classical scholar C. M. Bowra was a close friend. Many readers know Bowen best through her novel *The Death of the Heart* and her short stories, especially "The Demon Lover," "Joining Charles," and "Look at All Those Roses," which are frequently anthologized in college texts. Bowen was made a Commander of the Order of the British Empire in 1948, and she was awarded an honorary doctor of letters degree at Trinity College, Dublin, in 1949, and at Oxford University in 1957. She was made a Companion of Literature in 1965.

BIOGRAPHY

Although born in Ireland, Elizabeth Dorothea Cole Bowen came from a pro-British family who received land in county Cork as an award for fighting with Oliver Cromwell in 1649. The family built Bowen's Court in 1776—what the Irish call a "big house"—as a Protestant stronghold against the mainly Catholic Irish and lived there as part of the Anglo-Irish ascendancy. Bowen was educated in England and spent some summers at Bowen's Court. Not until after the Easter Rising in 1916 did she come to realize the causes of the Irish struggle for independence, and in writing *Bowen's Court* she admitted that her family "got their position and drew their power from a situation that shows an inherent wrong."

Her barrister father, when he was nineteen, had disobeyed forewarnings and carried home smallpox, which eventually killed his mother and rendered his father mad. Preoccupied with the desire for a son, Bowen's father nearly lost his wife in the attempt to have one in 1904, and, burdened with the debts of Bowen's Court, he suffered severe mental breakdowns in 1905 and 1906 and again in 1928. He was the cause of Elizabeth's removal to England, where, as an Irish outcast, her defense was to become excessively British. Living in a series of locations with her mother, she was kept uninformed of family circumstances; as an adult, her novels provided for her an outlet for her sense of guilt, the result of her feeling responsible for the unexplained events around her. Her lack of roots was intensified with the death of her mother in 1912.

Bowen studied art, traveled in Europe, and worked as

Elizabeth Bowen. (Library of Congress)

an air-raid warden in London during World War II. In 1923, she married Alan Charles Cameron, who was employed in the school system near Oxford, and they lived there for twelve years. She inherited Bowen's Court in 1928 when her father died, and in 1952, she and her husband returned there to live. Bowen's husband, however, died that year. Bowen sold the home in 1960 and returned to Oxford.

Bowen's career as a novelist spanned years of drastic change, 1927 to 1968, and, except for *The Last September*, she wrote about the present; her war experiences are reflected in the short-story collection *The Demon Lover* and in the novel *The Heat of the Day*. After 1935, she also wrote reviews and articles for the *New Statesman* and other publications, for the Ministry of Information during World War II, and for *The Tatler* in the 1940's, and she helped edit *The London Magazine* in the late 1950's. Afflicted with a slight stammer, Bowen lectured infrequently but effectively; transcripts of two of her BBC broadcasts, "left as they were spoken," may be read in *Afterthought*. After a visit to Ireland in 1973, Bowen died in London, leaving an unfinished autobiographical work, *Pictures and Conversations* (1975).

ANALYSIS

Elizabeth Bowen had a special talent for writing the conversations of children around the age of nine, as is evident in *The House in Paris*. Somewhat corresponding to her personal experience, her novels often present a homeless child (usually a girl), orphaned and shunted from one residence to another, or a child with one parent who dies and leaves the adolescent in the power of outwardly concerned but mainly selfish adults. Frequently, management by others prolongs the protagonist's state of innocence into the woman's twenties, when she must begin to assert herself and learn to manage her own affairs. (At age twenty-four, for example, Eva Trout does not know how to boil water for tea.) On the other side of the relationship, the controlling adult is often a perfectly mannered woman of guile, wealthy enough to be idle and to fill the idleness with discreet exercise of power over others. The typical Bowen characters, then, are the child, the unwanted adolescent, the woman in her twenties in a prolonged state of adolescence, and the "terrible woman" of society. Young people, educated haphazardly but expensively, are culturally mature but aimless. Genteel adults, on the other hand, administer their own selfish standards of what constitutes impertinence in other persons; these judgments disguise Bowen's subtle criticism of the correct English.

Typical Bowen themes include those of loss of innocence, acceptance of the past, and expanding consciousness. The pain and helplessness attendant on these themes and the disguise of plentiful money make them unusual. Although Bowen writes about the privileged class, three of her four common character types do not feel privileged. To handle her themes, Bowen frequently orders time and space by dividing the novels into three parts, with one part set ten years in the past and with a juxtaposition of at least two locations. The ten-year lapse provides a measure of the maturity gained, and the second location, by contrast, jars the consciousness into reevaluation of the earlier experience.

THE HOTEL

The fact that the Bowen women often have nothing to do is very obvious in *The Hotel*, set in Bordighera on the Italian Riviera, but of greater interest is the fact that, like Ireland, Bordighera is another place of British occupancy. The hotel guests' activities are confined to walking, talking, taking tea, and playing tennis. Mrs. Kerr is the managing wealthy woman who feeds on the attentions of her protégé, Sydney Warren, and then abandons Sydney when her son arrives. At age twenty-two, Sydney, for lack of better purpose, studies for a doctorate at home in England. Back in Italy, she becomes engaged to a clergyman as a means of achieving an identity and popularity, but her better sense forces reconsideration, and she cancels the engagement and asserts her independence.

THE LAST SEPTEMBER

The Last September, set in 1920, when the hated British soldiers (the Black and Tans) were stationed in Ireland to quell rebellion, shows Sir Richard and Lady Myra Naylor entertaining with tennis parties at their big house. Like Bowen, who wrote in *Afterthought* that this novel was "nearest my heart," Lois Farquar is a summer visitor, aged nineteen, orphaned, asking herself what she should do. An older woman tells her that her art lacks talent. Almost engaged to a British soldier, Gerald Lesworth, she might have a career in marriage, but Lady Naylor, in the role of graceful-terrible woman, destroys the engagement in a brilliant heart-to-heart talk in which she points out to Lois that Gerald has no prospects.

As September closes the social season, Gerald is killed in ambush, and as Lois—much more aware now and less innocent—prepares to depart for France, her home, Danielstown, is burned down; this loss signals her separation from the protected past.

TO THE NORTH

After *Friends and Relations*, Bowen entered the most fruitful part of her career. Her next four novels are generally considered to be her best work. *To the North* has rather obvious symbolism in a protagonist named Emmeline Summers, whose lack of feeling makes her "icy." She runs a successful travel agency with the motto "Travel Dangerously" (altering "Live Dangerously" and "Travel Safe"); the motto reflects both her ability to understand intellectually the feelings of others through their experience and her orphan state in homelessness. Emmeline tries to compensate for her weaknesses by imposing dramatic opposites: Without a home of her own, she overvalues her home with her widowed sister-in-law, Cecilia Summers; frequently called an angel, she has a fatal attraction to the devil-like character Markie Linkwater. When Cecilia plans to remarry (breaking up the home), when Markie (bored with Emmeline) returns to his former mistress, and when Emmeline's travel business begins to fail rapidly because of her preoccupation with Markie, she smashes her car while driving Markie north; "traveling dangerously" at high speeds, she becomes the angel of death.

The cold of the North suggested by the novel's title also touches other characters. Lady Waters, who offers Emmeline weekends on her estate as a kind of second home, feeds mercilessly on the unhappiness of failed loves and gossip. Lady Waters tells Cecilia to speak to Emmeline about her affair with Markie and thereby initiates the fateful dinner party that leads to the accident. Pauline, the niece of Cecilia's fiancé, is the orphaned adolescent character on the verge of becoming aware of and embarrassed by sex. Bowen describes Emmeline as the "stepchild of her uneasy century," a century in which planes and trains have damaged the stability and book knowledge of sexual research (indicated by the reading of Havelock Ellis), thereby freeing relationships but failing to engage the heart. The travel and the lack of warmth make the title a metaphor for the new century's existence. With her tenuous hold on home, love, and career, Emmeline commits suicide.

THE HOUSE IN PARIS

The House in Paris is set in three locations that reflect different aspects of the protagonist, Karen Michaelis: England, the land of perfect society; Ireland, the land of awareness; and France, the land of passion and the dark past. Parts 1 and 3 take place in a single day in Paris; part 2 occurs ten years earlier, during four months when Karen was age twenty-three. The evils of the house in Paris become apparent in the flashback and can be appreciated only through recognition of the terrible woman who runs it, Mme Fisher, and the rootlessness of the foreign students who stay there. Among other students, Mme Fisher has had in her power Karen and her friend Naomi Fisher (Mme Fisher's daughter), and the young

Max Ebhart, a Jew with no background. Ten years later, when Max wants to break his engagement with Naomi to marry another, Mme Fisher interferes, and he commits suicide.

The book begins and ends in a train station in Paris. In part 1, Leopold (age nine and the illegitimate child of Karen and Max Ebhart) and Henrietta Mountjoy (age eleven and the granddaughter of a friend of Mme Fisher) arrive on separate trains—Henrietta from England in the process of being shuttled to another relative, and Leopold from his adoptive parents in Italy to await a first acquaintance with his real mother. Leopold and Henrietta, meeting in the house in Paris, become symbolic of the possibility that, with Mme Fisher bedridden for ten years (since Max's suicide) and now dying, the future will be free of the mistakes of the past. Mme Fisher, in an interview with Leopold, tells him that the possibility of finding himself "like a young tree inside a tomb is to discover the power to crack the tomb and grow up to any height," something Max had failed to do.

Dark, egotistic, self-centered, and passionate like his father, Leopold constructs imaginatively a role for his unknown mother to play and then breaks into uncontrollable weeping when a telegram arrives canceling her visit. The mature and implacable Henrietta, orphaned like Leopold but accustomed to the vicissitudes of adult life, shows him how to crack out of the tomb of childhood. In part 3, quite unexpectedly, Ray Forrestier, who had given up diplomacy and taken up business to marry Karen in spite of her illegitimate child, urges a reunion with her son Leopold, takes matters into his own hands, and brings Leopold to Karen.

THE DEATH OF THE HEART

The three-part structure of Bowen's novels is most fully realized in *The Death of the Heart*. The parts of this novel are labeled "The World," "The Flesh," and "The Devil," and they follow the seasons of winter, spring, and summer. The world of Windsor Terrace, the Quaynes' residence in London, is advanced and sterile. Portia enters into this world at age fifteen, an orphan and stepsister to the present Thomas Quayne. Thomas's wife, Anna, who has miscarried twice and is childless, secretly reads Portia's diary and is indignant at the construction Portia puts on events in the household. Portia sees much "dissimulation" at Windsor Terrace, where doing the "right" thing does not mean making a moral choice. As one of Bowen's radical innocents who has spent her youth in hotels and temporary locations, Portia says no one in this house knows why she was born. She has only one friend in this, her first home: Matchett, the head servant, who gives Portia some religious training. Of the three male friends who wait upon Anna—St. Quentin Martin, Eddie, and Major Brutt—Portia fastens on the affections of Eddie.

Spring, in part 2, brings a much-needed vacation for the Quaynes. Thomas and Anna sail for Capri, and Portia goes to stay with Anna's former governess at Seale-on-Sea. At the governess's home, dubbed Waikiki, Portia is nearly drowned in sensuality—the sights, smells, sounds, and feelings of a vulgar and mannerless household. Portia invites Eddie to spend a weekend with her at Seale-on-Sea, which further educates her in the ways of the flesh.

On her return to London in part 3, Portia's more open nature is immediately apparent to Matchett, who says she had been "too quiet." The Devil's works are represented both obviously and subtly in this section, and they take many identities. St. Quentin, Anna, Eddie, even the unloving atmosphere of Windsor Terrace make up the Devil's advocacy. St. Quentin, a novelist, tells Portia that Anna has been reading Portia's diary, a disloyalty and an invasion of privacy with which, after some contemplation, Portia decides she cannot live. Herein lies the death of her teenage heart, what Bowen calls a betrayal of her innocence, or a "mysterious landscape" that has perished.

Summer at Windsor Terrace brings maturity to Portia as well as to others: Anna must confront her own culpability, even her jealousy of Portia; St. Quentin, his betrayal of Anna's reading of the diary; Thomas, his neglect of his father and his father's memory. Even Matchett takes a terrified ride in the unfamiliar cab, setting out in the night to an unknown location to pick up Portia. They all share in the summer's maturation that Portia has brought to fruition.

William Shakespeare's Portia prefers mercy to justice, paralleling the Portia in this novel. Bowen's Portia observes everything with a "political seriousness." The scaffolding of this novel supports much allusion, metaphor, and drama—all artfully structured. The world, the flesh, and the Devil as medieval threats to saintliness are reinterpreted in this context; they become the locations of the heart that has been thrust outside Eden and comprise a necessary trinity, not of holiness but of wholeness. This novel earns critics' accord as Bowen's best.

THE HEAT OF THE DAY

In *The Death of the Heart*, ranked by many critics as a close second in quality to *The Heat of the Day*, Bowen uses World War II to purge the wasteland conditions that existed before and during the years from 1940 through 1945. Middle-class Robert Kelway has returned from the Battle of Dunkirk (1940) with a limp that comes and goes according to the state of his emotions. At the individual level, it reflects the psychological crippling of his youth; at the national level, it is the culmination of the condition expressed by the person who says, "Dunkirk was waiting there in us."

Upper-class Stella Rodney has retreated from the privileges of her past into a rented apartment and a war job. Having grown impassive with the century, divorced, with a son (Roderick) in the army, she has taken Robert as her lover. She has become so impassive, in fact, that in 1942, a sinister and mysterious government spy named Harrison tells her that Robert has been passing information to the enemy, and she says and does nothing.

Critics have commented frequently on this novel's analogies to William Shakespeare's *Hamlet, Prince of Denmark* (pr. c. 1600-1601), an obvious example being Holme Dene (Dane home), Robert Kelway's country home. Psychologically weak, Robert is ruled by his destructive mother, who also had stifled his father and planted the seeds of Robert's defection from English ways. While Stella visits Holme Dene and learns to understand Robert, her son visits a cousin who tells him that Stella did not divorce her husband, as was commonly thought, but rather was divorced by him while he was having an affair, although he died soon after the divorce. Roderick, however, has managed to survive Stella's homelessness with a positive and manly outlook; when he inherits an estate in Ireland, he finds that it will give him the foundation for a future.

EVA TROUT

In *Eva Trout*, the various autobiographical elements of Bowen's work come to life: Bowen's stammer in Eva's reticence, the tragic deaths of both parents, the transience and sporadic education, the delayed adolescence, the settings of hotels and train stations. Eva Trout lives with a former teacher, Iseult Arbles, and Iseult's husband, Eric, while she waits for an inheritance. She turns twenty-four and receives the inheritance, which enables her to leave their home, where the marriage is unstable, and buy a home of her own filled with used furniture. She also escapes the clutches of Constantine, her guardian, who had been her father's male lover.

Eva discovers that a woman with money is suddenly pursued by "admirers," and Eric visits her in her new home. Eva subsequently lets Iseult think that Eric has fathered her child, Jeremy, whom she adopts in the United States. After eight years in American cities, where Eva seeks help for the deaf-mute Jeremy, Eva and Jeremy return to England. From England, they flee to Paris, where a doctor and his wife begin successful training of Jeremy. Back in England, Eva attempts the next phase of reaching security and a normal life. She seeks a husband and persuades the son of Iseult's vicar to stage a wedding departure with her at Victoria Station. All her acquaintances are on hand to see the couple off, but Jeremy— brought from Paris for the occasion—playfully points a gun (which he thinks is a toy) at Eva and shoots her. In the midst of revelry, on the eve of her happiness, Eva drops dead beside the train.

Eva Trout makes a poignant and haunting last heroine for the Bowen sequence. This novel offers Bowen's final bitter statement on the elusiveness of security and happiness.

Grace Eckley

OTHER MAJOR WORKS

SHORT FICTION: *Encounters*, 1923; *Ann Lee's, and Other Stories*, 1926; *Joining Charles*, 1929; *The Cat Jumps, and Other Stories*, 1934; *Look at All Those Roses*, 1941; *The Demon Lover*, 1945 (also known as *Ivy Gripped the Steps, and Other Stories*, 1946); *The Early Stories*, 1951; *Stories by Elizabeth Bowen*, 1959; *A Day in the Dark, and Other Stories*, 1965; *Elizabeth Bowen's Irish Stories*, 1978; *The Collected Stories of Elizabeth Bowen*, 1980.

PLAYS: *Castle Anna*, pr. 1948 (with John Perry).

NONFICTION: *Bowen's Court*, 1942; *Seven Winters*, 1942; *English Novelists*, 1946; *Collected Impressions*, 1950; *The Shelbourne: A Center of Dublin Life for More than a Century*, 1951; *A Time in Rome*, 1960; *Afterthought: Pieces About Writing*, 1962; *Pictures and Conversations*, 1975; *The Mulberry Tree: Writings of Elizabeth Bowen*, 1986.

CHILDREN'S LITERATURE: *The Good Tiger*, 1965.

BIBLIOGRAPHY

Bennett, Andrew, and Nicholas Royle. *Elizabeth Bowen and the Dissolution of the Novel: Still Lives*. New York: St. Martin's Press, 1994. Asserts that Bowen was one of the most important authors in English in the twentieth century and that her work has been undervalued. A good source of information about Bowen's novels and their influence.

Bloom, Harold, ed. *Elizabeth Bowen: Modern Critical Views*. New York: Chelsea House, 1987. Collection of eleven essays surveys the range of Bowen criticism. Includes excerpts from important book-length critical works on Bowen. Supplemented by an extensive bibliography.

Corcoran, Neil. *Elizabeth Bowen: The Enforced Return*. New York: Oxford University Press, 2004. Analyzes several of Bowen's novels by showing how these and other of her works focus on three themes that are central to Bowen's writing: Ireland, children, and war.

Craig, Patricia. *Elizabeth Bowen*. Harmondsworth, England: Penguin Books, 1986. Short biographical study is indebted to Victoria Glendinning's work cited below, although it draws on later research, particularly on Bowen's Irish connections. Offers perceptive readings of Bowen's stories and novels and includes a useful chronology.

Ellmann, Maud. *Elizabeth Bowen: The Shadow Across the Page*. Edinburgh: Edinburgh University Press, 2003. Examination of Bowen's life and writings uses historical, psychoanalytical, and deconstructivist approaches to interpret her works. Focuses on analysis of Bowen's novels but also explicates some of her short stories and nonfiction.

Glendinning, Victoria. *Elizabeth Bowen*. New York: Alfred A. Knopf, 1977. Comprehensive biography by an author who is well versed in the complexities of Bowen's Irish context and details them informatively. Establishes and assesses Bowen's standing as an eminent English novelist of the 1930's. Also candidly discusses Bowen's private life, making full use of Bowen's numerous autobiographical essays.

Hoogland, Renée C. *Elizabeth Bowen: A Reputation in Writing*. New York: New York University Press, 1994. Views Bowen's work from a lesbian feminist perspective, concentrating on the ways in which Bowen's fiction explores the unstable and destabilizing effects of sexuality.

Jordan, Heather Bryant. *How Will the Heart Endure: Elizabeth Bowen and the Landscape of War*. Ann Arbor: University of Michigan Press, 1992. Focuses primarily on Bowen's novels and argues that war was the most important influence on Bowen's life and art. Discusses how two of her most common fictional motifs—of houses and ghosts—reflect war's threat to cultural values and its blurring of the lines between reality and fantasy.

Lee, Hermione. *Elizabeth Bowen: An Estimation*. London: Vision Press, 1981. Comprehensive and sophis-ticated study makes large claims for Bowen's work. Asserts that she is both the equal of her Bloomsbury contemporaries and an important exponent of the European modernism deriving from Gustave Flaubert and Henry James. Also incisively analyzes Bowen's concentration on the intersection of the cultural and the psychological.

Rubens, Robert. "Elizabeth Bowen: A Woman of Wisdom." *Contemporary Review* 268 (June, 1996): 304-307. Examines the complex style of Bowen's work as a reflection of her personality and background; discusses her romanticism and her rejection of the dehumanization of the twentieth century.

Walshe, Eibhear, ed. *Elizabeth Bowen Remembered*. Dublin: Four Courts Press, 1998. Collection of essays drawn from the annual lectures at the church where Bowen was buried. In addition to a brief biography, includes discussions of Bowen's use of Irish locales, motifs of gardens and gardening, and the Anglo-Irish tradition in Bowen's writing.

PAUL BOWLES

Born: New York, New York; December 30, 1910
Died: Tangier, Morocco; November 18, 1999
Also known as: Paul Frederic Bowles

PRINCIPAL LONG FICTION

The Sheltering Sky, 1949
Let It Come Down, 1952
The Spider's House, 1955
Up Above the World, 1966

OTHER LITERARY FORMS

Paul Bowles (bohlz) is probably critically appreciated best for his short fiction, even though he is also known for his novels. Famous as a translator especially of Moroccan fiction, he translated from Arabic, French, and Spanish and wrote poetry, travel literature, and even music, to which he devoted himself during the 1930's. His autobiography, *Without Stopping*, was well received when it was published in 1972.

ACHIEVEMENTS

Paul Bowles has a unique place in American literature. As an exile, he shared with 1920's expatriate novelist Gertrude Stein, among others, a distanced perspective on his native culture. Through his translations, he earned an international reputation as an author with a North African sensibility. His fiction reflects a world akin to that written about by existentialists Jean-Paul Sartre or Albert Camus, and indeed he has been described as America's foremost existentialist writer, a label more likely to restrict him to a time period than to characterize his fiction accurately. Although his nihilism does appear to be somewhat overblown, it also has a modern application, reflecting as it does a dark vision of the world as contemporary as the times demand.

Bowles became a guru of sorts to the Beat generation, although Bowles's attraction for them had as much to do with his writings about drugs as it did with his generally pessimistic philosophy. Never an author of wide appeal, he has nevertheless had a loyal following among those interested in experimental and avant-garde writing. His work reflected a steady maturation, his 1982 experimental work *Points in Time* receiving praise from, among others, Tobias Wolfe, who wrote that the book was a completely original performance. Perhaps in the last analysis, Paul Bowles will be best remembered for his originality, his willingness to challenge definitions and the status quo in his fiction. With every work, he tried to forge new ground.

BIOGRAPHY

Paul Frederic Bowles spent most of his adult life living abroad, in permanent exile, mostly in Morocco, although for brief periods he also lived in France, Mexico, and South America. Admonished as a young man by his disapproving father that he could not expect merely to sit around and loaf as a writer when at home, Paul Bowles found places where he could sit and invite his soul.

He was born in the Jamaica section of New York City, the only child of a dentist and a mother who was a former schoolteacher. He was a precocious child and began writing at an early age. By the time he was in grade school, he had also begun composing music, a passion that occupied him more than did writing until after World War I. Immediately after high school, he attended very briefly the School of Design and Liberal Arts before enrolling in the fall of 1928 as a freshman at the University of Virginia, a choice made primarily because it was the school attended by Edgar Allan Poe. In March, he left the university and ran off to Paris, where he was already known as the writer whose poem "Spire Song" had been published in Eugène Jolas's little magazine *transition*. Bowles returned home the next fall and went to work for Dutton's bookstore while trying to write a novel in his spare time. In the spring, he returned to Virginia to complete his freshman year, at which point he ended forever his college career.

By 1929, Bowles had met and been encouraged by American composer Aaron Copland to pursue a career as a composer by returning to Paris to study with Nadia Boulanger, which he did in the spring of 1931. His second Paris sojourn began his literary life when he met and became friends with Gertrude Stein, who took him under her ample wing and tutored him in writing. It was Stein's companion Alice B. Toklas who suggested that Bowles and Copland, who had joined him abroad, live someplace warm, and she suggested Morocco, to which the two composers moved in the late summer of 1931. It was the beginning of Bowles's love affair with North Africa and his life as a writer: From Tangier, Bowles sent Stein his first prose efforts and received back from her the encouragement to continue writing, although, as he admitted later, it was not until the 1940's, while watching his wife, Jane, compose her first novel, that he began to work seriously at the writer's trade.

From 1931 to 1933, Bowles traveled between Europe and North Africa, gathering the impressions that would later shape his first novel, *The Sheltering Sky*. In 1933 he moved to New York City, where he made a living writing music reviews for the *Herald Tribune* and composing theater music for works by Orson Welles, Lillian Hellman, Tennessee Williams, and others.

In 1938 Bowles married Jane Auer, and the couple moved to Mexico in 1940, where Jane Bowles wrote *Two Serious Ladies* (1943), the novel that inspired Paul Bowles to take his literary craft seriously, and where Paul composed his opera *The Wind Remains*, which premiered in New York in 1943. The opera's failure deepened Bowles's interest in pursuing fiction writing.

That same year the Bowleses moved back to New York. There, in 1947, Paul Bowles had an overpowering dream of Tangier. The dream inspired him to begin *The Sheltering Sky* and prompted his return to North Africa, where he traveled for a year seeking material for the novel in progress. Jane joined him in 1948, and the two settled in Tangier, where they would become the center of a lively artistic community that included writers William S. Burroughs and Brion Gysin and visitors Tennessee Williams and Truman Capote.

The Sheltering Sky was published in October of 1949, and by December it was on *The New York Times* bestseller list. That same month, Bowles plunged into his second novel, *Let It Come Down*. Appearing in 1952, it did not receive the popular success or critical acclaim of his first novel, beginning a pattern that would persist throughout his literary career.

While working on novels, short stories, and poems, Bowles became interested in the tales of Moroccan oral storytellers, which he began to translate. By the 1960's, he was translating Moroccan writers as well.

Jane Bowles's declining literary career came to a close with her stroke in 1957. While she survived the illness, its debilitating effects stopped her writing and increased her problems with depression. By 1967 she had been committed to a psychiatric hospital in Spain, and she died in 1973. Reacting to Jane's death, Paul Bowles did little writing for nearly a decade, although he still actively translated. The 1982 critically acclaimed appearance of *Points in Time*, an avant-garde approach to history, marked Bowles's return to writing.

Public interest in Bowles increased dramatically with the 1990 release of a film version of *The Sheltering Sky* directed by Bernardo Bertolucci, in which Bowles had a minor part, and with the 1995 Lincoln Center Paul Bowles celebration and symposium, which Bowles at-

Paul Bowles. (Cherie Nutting)

tended despite failing health. On November 18, 1999, Bowles died in Tangier.

ANALYSIS

Because of his small output of novels as well as his problematic relationship with American writing, Paul Bowles has not achieved a firmly established reputation as a novelist. A writer who always attracted attention, and serious attention at that, Bowles has not been accorded sufficient critical notice for his significance as a writer to be measured. To paraphrase Johannes Willem Bertens, one of his most perceptive critics, who has written on the critical response to Bowles's work, Bowles as a novelist can be classified in three categories: Romantic, existentialist, and nihilist. As a Romantic, Bowles saw the modern world in a disjunctive relationship with nature, and that vision pushed him to depict the march of Western progress in very pessimistic terms, which accounts for one of his most frequently recurring themes, namely, that of a sophisticated Westerner confronting a less civilized and more primitive society in a quest of self-discovery. Such Romantic attitudes suggest the reasons for labeling Bowles as an existentialist. The search for an authentic life amid the self-doubts and the fragile, provisional nature of the civilized instincts, as Theodore Solotaroff has described it, places Bowles squarely within the existentialist tradition made more formal and philosophical by such writers as Camus and Sartre.

The search for values in a world without God, a world with an ethical vacuum, suggests the third possible interpretation of Bowles's fiction, that of nihilism. There are those critics, especially Chester E. Eisinger, who understand the novelist's universe as totally without hope, a region devoid of meaning and purpose and thereby representing a nihilistic philosophical position. This position is worked out through the clash between civilizations, or rather through the tension between civilization and the savage. Even Bowles himself remarked that life is absurd and the whole business of living hopeless, a conviction he shared with most of his central characters, thereby giving credence to any nihilistic interpretation of his fiction. Whichever position one takes, the central details of Bowles's novels remain the same: A Westerner, often an intellectual, searches through an Eastern, less civilized culture for meaning and direction, usually finding neither by the end of the book.

THE SHELTERING SKY

The Sheltering Sky is both Paul Bowles's first novel and his best-known novel. It is a book in which the author set forth those topics or themes that he would pursue throughout the rest of his fiction with almost obsessive tenacity. The story follows an American couple, Port and Kit Moresby, who have traveled to Morocco in search of themselves and to reinvigorate their marriage after years of indifference. The couple appear in Oran shortly after World War II and there experience a series of devastating events that eventually kill Port and destroy the mental stability of his wife, Kit.

Soon after their arrival, Port insists that they travel inland into the desert. Kit is opposed, so Port, accompanied by an Australian photographer and her son, depart, leaving Kit with Tunner, their American friend, who is to escort her on the night train later that day. Bored by the ride, Kit wanders into the fourth-class, or native, section of the train and passes a frightening night among the Arabs, later sleeping with Tunner. Meanwhile, Port has come to the realization that he desires a reconciliation with his wife. The novel follows this hapless pair as they progress farther and farther into the heart of the country, leaving civilization more distantly behind them. Port contracts typhoid and dies, leaving his wife alone to face the rigors of the desert. She is picked up by a passing caravan and made the sexual slave of the leaders of the group. She is both entranced and repulsed by the experience and is soon completely disoriented by her subjugation. Finally, she is rescued by a member of the American embassy only to disappear once again, this time for good, into the Casbah, or native quarter, in Oran.

The Sheltering Sky is considered Bowles's most uncompromisingly existential work and has been read by the critics along this line, with the fragile and provisional nature of civilized instincts being put to the test against the brutality and savagery of the primitive desert. Not only does Port test his febrile psyche against overwhelming powers of the North African terrain but also he must face the fact that he harbors in himself no reserves, no hope— for it is all too late—of anything better. Unable to commit himself to his wife, or to anything else for that matter, Port is left with a void that, in the end, exacts a heavy

price, leaving him utterly alone and unequipped to face the hostile environment. So, too, Kit is stripped of her defenses and forced back on herself, only to discover that she has no inner resolve either. In the end, these two civilized Americans lack the inner strength to combat the primitive forces, both within and without, which they encounter in their North African adventures.

The novel offers a convincing portrait of the disintegration of a couple of innocents thrust into a cruel environment for which they are totally unprepared. The writing in places is luminescent, the locale wonderfully realized—so much so that the novel's shortcomings pale by comparison, leaving a work, if flawed, at least magnificently so, and convincing in its portrait of nihilism in the modern world.

LET IT COME DOWN

Bowles's second novel, *Let It Come Down*, continues an existentialist quest by following Nelson Dyer, an American bank clerk, who throws over his job to join an old acquaintance who lives in Tangier and who offers Dyer a position in the travel agency he runs there. When he arrives, Dyer finds that his friend Jack Wilcox does not operate a successful agency and in fact seems to possess a mysterious source of income. As the story advances, Dyer's relationship with Wilcox takes on a Kafkaesque tone, as he is obviously not needed at the agency.

Out of money and in desperate need of a job, Dyer accepts an offer to help in a money scheme by transporting cash between a local bank and a shop. Realizing that he is being used for illegal purposes, Dyer takes the money he has been given and flees Tangier, only to discover that he is utterly helpless in a country where he neither speaks the language nor understands the customs. After he has killed his native guide, the novel concludes with Dyer alone and hunted in a foreign country but curiously pleased with his state of affairs as an isolated individual.

Once again, Bowles has thrust an upper-middle-class American into a North African environment and allowed him to become submerged in the native and alien culture. With his loss of identity, Dyer discovers something far more authentic about himself as he is systematically stripped of his civilized supports and is forced to fall back on what little reserves he possesses as an individual human being. This peeling away of the veneer of civilization reveals underneath an emptiness and void that leaves the protagonist, like Port Moresby, totally unprepared for the unfamiliar culture into which he is thrust. Under such pressure, he collapses and must seek refuge in internal strength, of which he possesses precious little. His plunge into an exotic culture, instead of rejuvenating him, debilitates his vigor, leaving him in a weakened if also enlightened condition.

As with other American writers, such as Edgar Allan Poe and Herman Melville, Bowles wrote of the exhaustion exacted by primitive cultures on the more civilized. It is a reversal of the romantic notion that cultured humans, tired of their culture, can find rejuvenation through immersion in a more savage environment. Instead, like Joseph Conrad's heroes, Dyer finds only confusion and despair. At least, it may be argued, he discovers the truth, however unpalatable it might be, and the conclusion of the novel leaves him possessed of a dark actuality, if robbed of a comforting illusion.

THE SPIDER'S HOUSE

Bowles's next novel, *The Spider's House*, was set in 1954 against the political upheaval caused by the deposition of Morocco's hereditary ruler, Sultan Mohammed, by the colonial regime of the French. The fiction traces the tension caused by the collapse of the traditional way of life of the native inhabitants of the city of Fez through a fifteen-year-old boy, Amar, who, halfway through the novel, is befriended by John Stenham, an expatriate American writer, who has fallen in love with an American woman tourist named Lee Burroughs. By the conclusion of the novel, John leaves Fez with Lee, abandoning Amar to deal with the destruction of his way of life any way he can.

Although it is not a political novel, *The Spider's House* uses the tensions of the French colonial rule not only to highlight the theme of the disintegration of Muslim culture under the French but also to provide a backdrop against which to play out the drama of the on-again, off-again love affair between Lee and John. Amar is from a devout family but one that is not caught up in the political conflicts between the Istiqlal, the Nationalist party, with their use of terror, and the colonials. Both the French and the Nationalists are bent on stopping the ritual religious festival of *Aid el Kabir*, and Amar, who has been forbidden to leave the Medina where his family re-

sides, gets caught outside the city's walls and is rescued by Lee and John, who have been observing the unfolding cycle of violence that is developing between the French and the Moroccans. John helps Amar return to his family through the city's walls, and Amar offers to take the couple to see the religious celebration in a village outside Fez. The Americans are fascinated by the exotic quality of the Arab life around them and agree to accompany Amar. The festival turns out badly for them, however, when Lee is shocked and repulsed by the rituals of the feast. After a quarrel, Lee and John decide that they are beginning a love affair.

Meanwhile, Amar has received a large sum of money from Lee so that he can join the Nationalists in their fight against the French. Still apolitical, Amar again gets caught up in the action of the revolution and is manipulated by the Istiqlal, barely avoiding capture by the French. At the end of the novel, he wants to rejoin John and Lee but is rebuffed by the novelist, who is set on going off with his new lover. The fiction concludes when Amar is abandoned by his newly won friend in the political turmoil of a struggle he barely understands.

As the critics have pointed out, *The Spider's House* contains a nostalgia for a past that does not belong either to John Stenham or to Bowles, but it is a longing that is nevertheless keenly felt. It has also been described as a deeply religious book, one in which Bowles mourns for a lost religious belief no longer possible in Western civilization, with its emphasis on the rational and the scientific. Certainly, the book focuses on the consequences of destroying a traditional way of life and on a myopic colonialism that blunders along in an attempt to apply Western methods to a totally unsuitable situation. It is the story of all colonial experiences in which a foreign power tries to forge a new life for a people it only partially understands, which accentuates one of the main achievements of the book, the faithful rendering of the North African landscape with its traditions and cultures.

UP ABOVE THE WORLD

For his fourth novel, Bowles shifted his location to South America and his plot to that of the detective novel. Although seen by many critics as genre fiction of the whodunit variety, *Up Above the World* is a far cry from a run-of-the-mill thriller. It is, in fact, a deeply psychological study of the disintegration of another couple, Taylor and Day Slade, who, much in the same vein as the Moresbys, undergo a tragic transformation that ultimately destroys them.

The Slades arrive by ship in an unidentified South American country at the port town of Puerto Farol. A woman whom they had befriended on the ship is found dead in her hotel room—murdered, it is discovered later, at the behest of her son by a thug named Thorny. The son, Grover Soto, afraid that the Slades have been a witness to the killing, hunts down the couple, who have by now taken a train to the interior of the country. The Slades are finally subjected to the use of drugs and a variety of brainwashing techniques in order to erase the memory of Mrs. Rainmantle, the murdered woman, from their minds. While recuperating at the ranch of Grover Soto, Day sees some written instructions that were to have been destroyed, and in a moment of panic, Soto drugs and then kills Taylor. As the novel concludes, he is about to do the same with Day.

The novel is a psychological thriller much in the vein of Graham Greene's "entertainments," a lesser work not demanding the exertion either to read or to write that a more serious novel requires. Certain themes and characters immediately label the book as one of Bowles's, however. Echoes of his earlier novels appear in the wandering Americans confronting themselves amid the exotic background of a less civilized and unknown world, their eventual disintegration as they experience an alien culture, and the search for meaning in what appear to be meaningless lives. Even the appearance of chance events, encounters onto which critics have latched to tie the volume to the thriller genre, are also present in his earlier work. The big difference in *Up Above the World* is the novel's compactness. It is streamlined, and in that sense it provides a faster, perhaps more accessible read, but it is a novel no less interesting for all that.

The critics, especially Bertens, have been particularly hard on this book, largely because of its thriller status, which is unfair, given that the novel goes beyond the requirements of mere genre fiction and into a netherworld of the truly black. In many ways, this book is Bowles's most pessimistic and most nihilistic, and, writing in the thriller vein, Bowles has made a contribution to the American fictional form most foreboding and dark, a form, in short, closest to his own hopeless vision.

Bowles's fiction will remain attractive both to the few who truly admire advanced writing and thinking and to a general reading audience. It is unfortunate that Bowles's reputation as a writer's writer has limited the enjoyment of his work by the public, as he not only deserves a wider readership but also has much to offer the general reader. Too easily dismissed as the product of an expatriate writer and therefore of little interest to students of American literature, Bowles's work is nevertheless central to the American literary experience, dealing as it does with the protagonist facing the frontier on the edge of civilization, a position that recalls that of Melville's Ishmael, James Fenimore Cooper's Natty Bumppo, and even Mark Twain's Huck Finn. Finally, critics and the public alike need to read Bowles's fiction for its relevant encounters between modern humankind and an increasingly mechanistic and depersonalized world, a place truly of nihilism and despair.

Charles L. P. Silet
Updated by John Nizalowski

OTHER MAJOR WORKS

SHORT FICTION: *The Delicate Prey, and Other Stories*, 1950; *A Little Stone: Stories*, 1950; *The Hours After Noon*, 1959; *A Hundred Camels in the Courtyard*, 1962; *The Time of Friendship*, 1967; *Pages from Cold Point, and Other Stories*, 1968; *Three Tales*, 1975; *Things Gone and Things Still Here*, 1977; *Collected Stories, 1939-1976*, 1979; *Midnight Mass*, 1981; *In the Red Moon*, 1982; *Call at Corazón, and Other Stories*, 1988; *A Distant Episode: The Selected Stories*, 1988; *Unwelcome Words*, 1988; *A Thousand Days for Mokhtar, and Other Stories*, 1989; *The Stories of Paul Bowles*, 2001.

POETRY: *Scenes*, 1968; *The Thicket of Spring: Poems, 1926-1969*, 1972; *Next to Nothing*, 1976; *Next to Nothing: Collected Poems, 1926-1977*, 1981.

NONFICTION: *Yallah*, 1957; *Their Heads Are Green and Their Hands Are Blue*, 1963; *Without Stopping*, 1972; *Points in Time*, 1982; *Days: Tangier Journal, 1987-1989*, 1991; *Conversations with Paul Bowles*, 1993 (Gena Dagel Caponi, editor); *In Touch: The Letters of Paul Bowles*, 1994 (Jeffrey Miller, editor).

TRANSLATIONS: *The Lost Trail of the Sahara*, 1952 (of R. Frison-Roche's novel); *No Exit*, 1958 (of Jean-

Paul Sartre's play); *A Life Full of Holes*, 1964 (of Driss ben Hamed Charhadi's autobiography); *Love with a Few Hairs*, 1967 (of Mohammed Mrabet's fiction); *The Lemon*, 1969 (of Mrabet's fiction); *M'Hashish*, 1969 (of Mrabet's fiction); *The Boy Who Set the Fire*, 1974 (of Mrabet's fiction); *The Oblivion Seekers*, 1975 (of Isabelle Eberhardt's fiction); *Harmless Poisons, Blameless Sins*, 1976 (of Mrabet's fiction); *Look and Move On*, 1976 (of Mrabet's fiction); *The Big Mirror*, 1977 (of Mrabet's fiction); *The Beggar's Knife*, 1985 (of Rodrigo Rey Rosa's fiction); *Dust on Her Tongue*, 1989 (of Rey Rosa's fiction); *Chocolate Creams and Dollars*, 1992 (of Mrabet's fiction).

EDITED TEXT: *Claudio Bravo: Drawings and Paintings*, 1997 (revised 2005).

MISCELLANEOUS: *Too Far from Home: The Selected Writings of Paul Bowles*, 1993; *The Paul Bowles Reader*, 2000.

BIBLIOGRAPHY

Caponi, Gina Dagel. *Paul Bowles*. New York: Twayne, 1998. Provides an excellent introduction to Bowles and his writings. After a brief chronology and biography, Caponi explores the breadth of Bowles's canon through various critical lenses: existentialism, postcolonial literature, detective fiction, surrealism, extraordinary consciousness, travel writing, and historical fiction.

_____. *Paul Bowles: Romantic Savage*. Carbondale: Southern Illinois University Press, 1994. Biographical and critical study of Bowles's life and art examines the sources of his fiction, his major themes and techniques, and his methods of story composition.

_____, ed. *Conversations with Paul Bowles*. Jackson: University Press of Mississippi, 1993. Collection of reprinted and previously unpublished interviews reveals Bowles's own opinions about his life and art. Bowles often tended to give perverse responses to interview questions, but he still communicated a great deal about the relationship between himself and his work. He claimed that the man who wrote his books did not exist except in the books.

Dillon, Millicent. *You Are Not I: A Portrait of Paul Bowles*. Berkeley: University of California Press,

1998. Biography traces the relationship between the author and his wife Jane Auer Bowles. Dillon reevaluates the views she expresses in her biography of Jane Bowles and provides her own speculations on Paul Bowles's life and work.

Green, Michelle. *The Dream at the End of the World: Paul Bowles and the Literary Renegades in Tangier*. New York: HarperCollins, 1991. Presents a lively account of the artistic and socialite sets that congregated in Tangier in the 1940's and 1950's. Investigates the life of Bowles and those who came to stay with him in Morocco, providing some interesting background details for readers of Bowles's fiction. Includes photographs and index.

Lacey, R. Kevin, and Francis Poole, eds. *Mirrors on the Maghrib: Critical Reflections on Paul and Jane Bowles and Other American Writers in Morocco*. Delmar, N.Y.: Caravan Books, 1996. Collection of critical essays on the Bowleses and the Beats explores the relationship between the concept of otherness and Morocco. Includes a number of essays by Moroccan critics, who provide a North African viewpoint on the strengths and weaknesses of Bowles's depiction of their homeland.

Patterson, Richard. *A World Outside: The Fiction of Paul Bowles*. Austin: University of Texas Press, 1987. Comprehensive, scholarly examination of Bowles's work provides extensive discussion of *The Sheltering Sky*. Includes informative endnotes and index.

Pounds, Wayne. *Paul Bowles: The Inner Geography*. New York: Peter Lang, 1985. Serves as a good introduction to Bowles and his use of landscape. Demonstrates the connection between setting and the spiritual states of Bowles's characters.

Sawyer-Laucanno, Christopher. *An Invisible Spectator: A Biography of Paul Bowles*. New York: Weidenfeld & Nicolson, 1989. Very readable account of the writer's life offers some intriguing speculation on the connections between events in Bowles's life and the plots of his stories. Includes notes, a select bibliography that lists Bowles's major works in literature and music, and an index.

KAY BOYLE

Born: St. Paul, Minnesota; February 19, 1902
Died: Mill Valley, California; December 27, 1992

PRINCIPAL LONG FICTION

Plagued by the Nightingale, 1931
Year Before Last, 1932
Gentlemen, I Address You Privately, 1933
My Next Bride, 1934
Death of a Man, 1936
Monday Night, 1938
Primer for Combat, 1942
Avalanche, 1944
A Frenchman Must Die, 1946
1939, 1948
His Human Majesty, 1949
The Seagull on the Step, 1955
Three Short Novels, 1958 (includes *The Crazy Hunter, The Bridegroom's Body*, and *Decision*)
Generation Without Farewell, 1960
The Underground Woman, 1975
Process, 2001 (wr. c. 1925)

OTHER LITERARY FORMS

Although she published many novels, Kay Boyle was recognized principally for her shorter works. First published in the small magazines of the 1920's, her early stories were collected in *Wedding Day, and Other Stories* (1930) and *The First Lover, and Other Stories* (1933). Active as an editor and critic on small magazines such as *Contempo* and on progressive political journals, Boyle also translated the works of such European writers as Joseph Delteil, Raymond Radiguet, and Marie-Louise Soupault. Two volumes of her short stories, *The Smoking Mountain: Stories of Postwar Germany* (1951) and *Nothing Ever Breaks Except the Heart* (1966), reflect wartime and postwar Europe. Collected in *Fifty Stories* (1980), Boyle's short fiction appeared in American periodicals for decades.

Boyle's poetry, also first published in small magazines, was collected in *A Glad Day* (1938) and *Collected Poems* (1962). Her volume of poetry titled *American*

Citizen Naturalized in Leadville, Colorado (1944), based on the experience of an Austrian refugee in the U.S. military, is dedicated to writer Carson McCullers, "whose husband is also overseas," and *Testament for My Students, and Other Poems* (1970) concerns "that desperate year, 1968." *This Is Not a Letter, and Other Poems* (1985) appeared fifteen years later.

As a European correspondent after World War II, Boyle wrote nonfiction prose of both journalistic and literary distinction, including her reportage of the war crimes trial of Heinrich Babb for *The New Yorker* and her essays on civil rights and the military establishment. Her edited volume *The Autobiography of Emanuel Carnevali* (1967) and her chapters in Robert McAlmon's *Being Geniuses Together, 1920-1930* (1968) capture the literary underground of that period, and a subsequent collection, *The Long Walk at San Francisco State, and Other Essays* (1970), reflects the antiwar movement of the 1960's. Boyle also published three illustrated children's novels: *The Youngest Camel* (1939, 1959) and the Pinky novels (1966 and 1968).

ACHIEVEMENTS

The 1930's, declared her vintage period by critics, brought Kay Boyle an O. Henry Award for the title story of *The White Horses of Vienna, and Other Stories* (1936), followed in 1941 by another for "Defeat," a story on the French collapse that also appeared in her novel *Primer for Combat*. Published widely in *Harper's, The New Yorker, Saturday Evening Post*, and *The Atlantic Monthly*, and with her short works collected in *Thirty Stories* (1946), Boyle won the praise of contemporaries as the "economical housewife of the short story technique."

BIOGRAPHY

The cross between Kay Boyle's midwestern roots and cosmopolitan experience produced the distinctive flavor of her work. Although born into an upper-class family in St. Paul, Minnesota, Boyle spent her early years not in the Midwest but in the eastern United States, France, Austria, and Switzerland, and especially in the mountains, which become a symbol of human transcendence in her work. The active and involved nature of her childhood is expressed in her love of horses, riding, and skiing, and its aesthetic and creative aspect in the family custom of gathering sketches and stories between marbled covers for gift books. Katherine Evans Boyle, the "shining light" to whom Boyle dedicated her first works, provided an image of strength and purpose, introducing her daughter to the most avant-garde of European art and literature as well as the most progressive of American populist politics. Kay Boyle's grandfather, Jesse Peyton Boyle, a dynamic, charismatic St. Paul businessman whom the author later called a "charming reactionary," was a model of the aggressive, compelling patriarch, in contrast to the more vulnerable and intuitive male figure typified by her father, Howard Peyton Boyle.

The next years saw Boyle return to the Midwest and then to the Greenwich Village literary and political cir-

cles that would provide her with friends and supporters. A series of financial reversals brought the family to Cincinnati, where Howard Boyle became established in the retail automotive business. After a brief stay at Shipley, Kay Boyle studied violin at the Cincinnati Conservatory and architecture at Ohio Mechanics Institute, later calling hers "no education at all," saying that she had never been "properly through the eighth grade" and had instead pursued writing on her own, a training she advocated later for her students as well. Less than twenty years old, Boyle moved to New York City, attended a few classes at Columbia University, worked as a secretary, and met Greenwich Village literati of a progressive bent. In the space of her short stay, she worked for *Broom*, a journal of European and American experimentalism, and became acquainted with Harriet Monroe's *Poetry* magazine; with Lola Ridge, whose Gaelic ancestry she shared; and with William Carlos Williams, who became her friend and mentor. Described as a shy, timid ingenue, Boyle appears in Williams's memoirs attending Fourteenth Street parties with John Reed, Louise Bryant, Jean Toomer, Kenneth Burke, and Hart Crane.

The 1920's was another expatriate decade for Boyle. In 1921, she married Richard Brault, a French student whom she had met in Ohio, and she returned with him to his family's provincial seat. Williams recalls meeting a lonely and isolated Boyle in the vicinity of Le Havre, in which atmosphere her first two novels take place. When the marriage deteriorated and ended a few years later, Boyle remained in Paris and the Riviera, playing a central role in the literary underground of American exiles and the European avant-garde. Centered on the publication of small magazines, these groups brought Boyle together with Ernest Walsh, the effervescent poet, critic, and editor of *This Quarter*, the lover and compatriot whose death from lung injuries incurred as a pilot Boyle recounts in *Year Before Last*.

The aesthetic of Boyle's group, represented by *Transition* magazine and Eugene Jolas, was eclectic, drawing on the work of Ernest Hemingway, James Joyce, Gertrude Stein, Ezra Pound, William Carlos Williams, and Carl Sandburg. Experi-

Kay Boyle. (Library of Congress)

mental, antirational, and antirealist, this loosely knit group ascribed to an informal creed known as Orphism, set down in the 1929 manifesto "The Revolution of the Word," signed by Boyle, Laurence Vail, Hart Crane, and others interested in representing a primarily interior reality in a rhythmic, "hallucinatory" style cognizant of current psychological and anthropological lore and inimical to standard realism and the genteel tradition. It was in this milieu that Boyle developed the lyrical subjectivism reflected in her early poems and stories, a quality she found in D. H. Lawrence and Arthur Rimbaud, Walt Whitman and Edgar Allan Poe, Stein and Joyce.

Following Walsh's death and the birth of her first child, Sharon, Boyle, out of money and dispirited, joined a communal art colony led by Raymond Duncan, brother of dancer Isadora Duncan; his personal charisma and exploitative idealism are reflected in a number of Boyle's novelistic relationships in which one will is subsumed in another. Rescued from this amalgam of Jean-Jacques Rousseau, Leo Tolstoy, and pseudoanarchistic principles by Caresse and Harry Crosby, whose unconventional sun religion and Black Sun Press were underground institutions, Boyle spent her next years in the French and British settings that are reflected in the novels of the period. In 1931, she married the scholar and poet Laurence Vail, and in the following years she had three more daughters, Apple-Joan, Kathe, and Clover.

Emerging aboveground in the late 1930's with a Simon & Schuster contract, Boyle published a major short-story collection, *The White Horses of Vienna, and Other Stories*, which introduced the Lipizzaner horses that became an important symbol in her later works. Three highly praised short novels and two longer ones followed, including her own favorite, *Monday Night*, and she received a Guggenheim Fellowship to pursue the metaphor of aviation for human history. Before the fall of France to the Nazis in 1939, she wrote about the collapse of Europe's democracies before fascism. Boyle's war novels of that period are usually set in small French villages and involve expatriated women who become entangled in the political choices of various men, usually Austrians made nationless by the Anschluss.

As the settings of her fiction moved from the interior to the external world, Boyle's style became more suited to the wider audiences of such magazines as the *Satur-day Evening Post* and her works became more popular. This development, decried by some critics, damaged her standing in literary circles in a way that it did not for other authors—such as Katherine Anne Porter, Boyle's friend—who kept their hackwork clearly separate from their artistic lives. The conflict between resistance and collaboration addressed in her novels surfaced in Boyle's private life as well when Vail, whose sentiments are possibly expressed by several characters in *Primer for Combat*, disapproved of her efforts to secure visas for Jewish refugees, citing the "historical necessity" of fascism. Following their divorce, Boyle married Baron Joseph von Franckenstein, an Austrian refugee whose experiences are reflected in *American Citizen Naturalized in Leadville, Colorado*, in *His Human Majesty*, and in the general situation of Austrian antifascists in the continental novels of the war period.

After the fall of France, Boyle's popular novels *Avalanche* and *A Frenchman Must Die* brought the Resistance experience to American audiences. Perhaps because of an establishment bias against best sellers, against explicitly political intent, or, in some cases, against the notion of a woman writing about war and the "masculine side of the male character," as one critic stated, and surely because of their superficial and rather formulaic character, these novels received negative reviews from Diana Trilling, Edmund Wilson, and *The New Yorker*. Despite this criticism, Boyle continued to address the question of individual political choice in short novels such as *Decision*, set in post-Civil War Spain, and in *The Seagull on the Step*, which points out the growing inappropriateness of American occupation policy. After the war, Boyle's work became even more journalistic as she took on the role of European correspondent, chiefly in occupied Germany, where her husband directed Amerika Dienst, an International Information Agency service, and Boyle reported on the war crimes trial of Heinrich Babb. She also commented on European moral and political conditions in her short stories of the period, developing as she did so a vision of German and European history that she would use in later novels and in a planned nonfiction project. Like Thomas Mann, Ignazio Silone, and other antifascist intellectuals, Boyle addressed the vulnerabilities that continued to expose Western democracies to the totalitarian threat explored by Erich Fromm, Hannah Arendt, and many others.

Returning in 1953 to an America caught up in the events of McCarthyism, Boyle lost her job with *The New Yorker*, while von Franckenstein, a war hero captured and tortured in Nazi Germany during his career with the OSS and an able civil servant, was removed from his State Department post for his "questionable" loyalty in associating with Boyle, who was deemed a security risk. After frequent testimony by both before Internal Security committees, von Franckenstein was reinstated in 1957. In 1958, the first American edition of Boyle's *Three Short Novels*, including *The Crazy Hunter*, *The Bridegroom's Body*, and *Decision*, appeared, followed by *Generation Without Farewell*, her most ambitious postwar novel.

Following von Franckenstein's death from cancer in 1963, Boyle continued her political commitment and her writing during the anti-Vietnam War movement, a cause in which her earlier analysis of French colonialism and European fascism made her especially active. Supporting the use of civil disobedience to protest military recruitment and induction as well as weapons research and manufacture, she organized protest groups and petitions and traveled with one such group to Cambodia, where they brought the war there to media attention. She spent Christmas Eve of 1967 in jail for her part in a sit-in at an Oakland military induction center, an experience she later drew upon in her novel *The Underground Woman*. As a teacher of creative writing at San Francisco State University, she courted dismissal to join a student protest. For her part in the protest, Boyle received a forty-five-day jail sentence, which was suspended until the following Easter. Because she spent her time in jail with regular prisoners rather than with other political protesters, Boyle became further convinced of the inequities of the American social system. While she was incarcerated, she discovered that she had breast cancer, something she had long feared.

In June of 1968, Boyle published her version of Robert McAlmon's 1934 memoir, *Being Geniuses Together, 1920-1930*, hoping to introduce his writing to a wider audience. She revised McAlmon's work, adding alternate chapters presenting her own commentary and memories of the period. Boyle's writing was praised, but she also received criticism for romanticizing many incidents. During the same year, Boyle covered the trial of Huey Newton, the Black Panther leader who was accused of killing one policeman and injuring another. Boyle was an ardent supporter of the Black Panther Party, fully accepting the organization's view that the police department was a racist institution, determined to eliminate black activists. *The Long Walk at San Francisco State, and Other Essays* discusses her stands on social protest.

During the 1970's, Boyle returned to writing poetry. She also developed an interest in the role of women in Ireland. The book she planned on these women never materialized, but she did publish a story about Ireland, "St. Stephen's Green," in *The Atlantic Monthly* in 1980. In 1978, she was inducted into the American Academy of Arts and Letters and received the San Francisco Art Commission Award of Honor. Boyle retired from teaching in 1980, the year in which *Fifty Stories* appeared. Publication of the collection sparked renewed interest in her writing, and in 1982, *Three Short Novels* was reissued with an introduction by the Canadian writer Margaret Atwood. In 1986, Boyle received the Los Angeles Times Robert Kirsch Award for her outstanding body of work. In 1992, Boyle was a strong supporter of Bill Clinton's campaign for the U.S. presidency. She died on December 27, 1992.

Analysis

Perhaps more consistently and tenaciously than any other twentieth century American writer, Kay Boyle sought to unite the personal and the political, the past and the present, the feminine and the masculine. Recognized in both literary and popular realms, her rich oeuvre unites the American and the European experiences of twentieth century history.

Helpful though it may be as an outline, the conventional division of Boyle's achievement into an aesthetic period before 1939 and a polemical period after may obscure Boyle's constant focus on the dialectic between subject and object. In the exploration of personal experience, her intense imaginative reconstruction posits the integration of conflicting aspects of the self, the struggle between self-abnegation and self-assertion, and the liberation of the individual from repressive aspects of personal or family relationships. Usually presented as a union of archetypally masculine and feminine characteristics in an individual or in a couple, often a pair of same-sex friends, Boyle's image of the completed self is one of growth beyond confining roles.

In her exploration of the self as a political creature, Boyle asserts the life-affirming potential of the individual and the community against destructive authoritarian or absolutist constructs, whether within the family or in the larger society. In her intense evocation of personal awakening to political morality, Boyle's synthesis reaches beyond the narrowly ideological to affirm the human search for tenderness in a landscape that, although distorted by repression, gives hope for regeneration. Like Thomas Mann, Ignazio Silone, and André Malraux, Boyle seeks to integrate the individual psyche into the larger social milieu, to make the self meaningful in history, exercising the responsibility that Mann called for when he said that had the German intellectual community remained accountable, Nazism would have been prevented.

Using modernist techniques to refute contemporary nihilism, Boyle restores perspective to the confrontation between the individual sensibility and a complex, often hidden, social reality. Her decision to address a broad audience on political as well as personal themes, sometimes seen as a "betrayal" of her talent, might be understood more fully as a commitment to the exercise of moral responsibility through literature. Exploring the need to unite discordant psychic and political elements and to assert the life-affirming, Boyle provides in her work a model of balanced wholeness in the larger as well as the smaller world.

PLAGUED BY THE NIGHTINGALE

Boyle's first novel, *Plagued by the Nightingale*, which Hart Crane admired, introduced an expatriate American bride to her husband's family in their decaying French provincial seat. A crippling congenital disease afflicting all the family males, an emblem of general social decay, prevents the young husband, Nicole, from asserting independence, and requires the family to be always on the lookout to perpetuate itself. Bridget, the young wife, and Luc, a family friend whose energy and vivacity have earmarked him for marriage to one of Nicole's three sisters, are alternately drawn into and re-

pelled by the patriarchal family's power to protect and engulf. By making the birth of an heir the condition upon which the young couple's inheritance depends, Nicole's father threatens to bring them entirely within the control of the patriarchal family. Freeing both herself and Nicole from the grasp of this decaying culture, Bridget chooses to bear a child not by Nicole, whose tainted genes would continue the cycle, but by Luc, a vigorous outsider whose health and vitality promise liberation and autonomy.

Although ostensibly a narrative of personal life, this first novel becomes political in its exploration of the relationship between the self and the family, the will to immerse oneself in the group or to aspire to self-determination. The decaying and yet compelling power of the patriarchal family becomes a metaphor for Western culture itself in its paralyzing traditionalism and sacrifice of the individual to authority.

YEAR BEFORE LAST

Continuing this exploration of personal experience in search of security and selfhood, *Year Before Last* recounts Hannah's final year with her lover Martin, a poet and editor who is terminally ill with a lung disease. In the conflict between Martin's former lover, Eve, who is his partner in the publication of the small magazine that is truly the group's creative life, and Hannah, self-sacrifice and self-assertion in pursuit of love and art are polarized. Eve, "strong and solitary" yet unfulfilled, and Hannah, vulnerable, nurturing, yet unaffirmed, both seek realization through Martin ("What are we but two empty women turning to him and sucking him dry for a taste of life?"), only to find it in themselves as they join in his care. They are complementary aspects of the self united to assert the primacy of love and art. In this resolution of two opposing sets of personal qualities, here presented as a bond between two women in support of a positive male, the self is empowered in the larger world of artistic creation.

MY NEXT BRIDE

This resolving dyad of two women appears in slightly different guise in *My Next Bride*, the final novel of this early self-exploratory group. Victoria, left emotionally and materially destitute, joins an art colony whose tunic-wearing, dancing anarchists are led by a charismatic, idealistic, but ultimately exploitative male, Sorrel, the reverse of the vital, creative male seen in Martin. Searching for security and idealism, Victoria falls instead into complete self-abnegation in a series of underworld trials, including prostitution and abortion, that represent total abandonment of selfhood and self-determination. She finally returns to herself with the support of two friends, one of whom becomes her lesbian lover and symbolizes the union of the submissive and the assertive, the passive and the active, that appears in Boyle as an emblem of the healed psyche. Boyle's treatment of homosexual themes, especially her use of the homosexual couple as an image of the completed self, is remarkable for its freedom from negative stereotypes.

GENTLEMEN, I ADDRESS YOU PRIVATELY

In *Gentlemen, I Address You Privately*, Boyle breaks free from the reconstruction of her own experience to enter a totally imaginative landscape with a mythic quality never so markedly present before, a quality that comes to dominate the best of her later work. Here, the dyad is of two men, one a cleric cut off from experience in the contemplative heights of art and religion, the other a sailor plunged entirely into atavistic life at sea. Deserting cell and ship alike, they enter the human world, descending from Mont St. Michel (like all Boyle's mountains, a symbol of the transcendent and the ideal) to the muck of a squatter's hut, where they hide out as farmhands. In the common-law marriage of Quespelle, a brutal peasant who delights chiefly in killing rabbits, and Leonie, a madonna-like yet buddingly fertile female akin to William Faulkner's Lena Grove, the destructive and nurturing forces of the real world appear. This sharply polarized image of the human family, brutal masculinity and submissive femininity, proves too dualistic for reproduction and growth. A more positive figure of the male is posited in Munday, the gentle, intuitive aesthete who acts in defense of the old dog Quespelle intends to shoot, the bedraggled horse, the rabbits, and finally Leonie. Quespelle leaves for the city, and Munday is left with Leonie. The two have a "new taste for life," transformed by the love that "binds the two . . . together, hand and foot, and then sends [them] out, away from any other comfort"; Adam and Eve emerge from paradise to establish the human community in this Faulknerian affirmation of the self in opposition to both authoritarian families and absolute ideas.

THE CRAZY HUNTER

This liberation is again apparent in Boyle's better-known short novels *The Crazy Hunter* and *The Bridegroom's Body*, set in a Lawrentian English countryside where life must break free of repressive families and social structures. In *The Crazy Hunter*, Nan must assert herself against the control of her mother, Mrs. Lombe, so she purchases a gelding against her mother's wishes but is disappointed when the horse suddenly goes blind. In condemning the horse to be shot, Mrs. Lombe becomes the authoritarian hunter whose presence is strong in Boyle's novels, her destructive power threatening both her husband, Candy, and Nan, who must assume her mother's strength without her repressiveness. Nan, in teaching the horse to jump at risk to her own life, and Candy, putting his body between the veterinarian's pistol and the horse's flying hooves, establish the father's legitimate power and the daughter's liberation from the mother's control in defense of vital yet vulnerable life. The horse, which becomes for Boyle a symbol of this life force, retains its conventional identification with passion and strength while taking on more complex qualities of aspiration, idealism, and vulnerable beauty. Usually regarded as a primarily masculine symbol, the horse in Boyle's work is strongly associated with the gentle, intuitive male or with the female, and particularly with emerging female sexuality.

THE BRIDEGROOM'S BODY

In *The Bridegroom's Body*, the repressive domination associated with the mother and confined to the immediate family in *The Crazy Hunter* becomes patriarchal in its extension to the entire community in the country estate of the Glouries. A remote, rainy, brooding, and yet potentially fertile land, the estate is dominated by predatory hunters led by Lord Glourie, an insensitive, uncommunicative sportsman, an upper-class Quespelle, whose chief interests are hunting and drinking with other hunters. This predatory patriarchy is mirrored in the natural world by Old Hitches, chief of the swans, whose dominance is threatened by the Bridegroom, a young swan who has set up his nest in defiance of the patriarch and in assertion of a more gentle and intuitive male potency.

Lady Glourie, an energetic, forceful woman in her tweeds and sturdy shoes, struggles to maintain life in an atmosphere completely lacking in spiritual and emotional fulfillment by caring for the sick sheep, the swan master's pregnant wife, and the Bridegroom himself. An isolated figure made illegitimate and ineffective by the hunters, she longs for a female friend. Her hopes rise only to be dashed when Miss Cafferty, the nurse called to care for the pregnant woman, proves not a comradely version of Lady Glourie but rather her total opposite— young, conventionally attractive in her bright green dress, and seemingly vulnerable to male approval. Miss Cafferty eventually vindicates herself, however, imploring Lady Glourie to "see her own beauty," her strength against the "butchers, murderers—men stalking every corner of the ground by day and night." This plea leaves Lady Glourie with the "chill" that Boyle expresses as the promise of regeneration, of union between the two versions of female strength, which have as yet "no record, no sign, no history marked on them."

DEATH OF A MAN

Death of a Man, influenced by Boyle's own experiences in the Tyrol, is a love story set against the backdrop of the growing influence of the Nazi Party in Austria. Personal desires and needs are set against the uncontrollable influences of the political conflicts in Europe during the years prior to World War II. Like the short story "The White Horses of Vienna," the novel reflects the political unrest in Austria during the 1930's. Growing economic difficulties and dissatisfaction with the government led many Austrians to view favorably the political agenda of the Nazi Party. In fact, the novel received several negative reviews for what many critics considered a sympathetic portrayal of the Nazis.

Like many of Boyle's heroines, the main character, Pendennis, is an expatriate American who has no real roots in either her family or her country. She is bored by her husband, an Englishman whom she feels lacks passion and who is unable to provide her with the love and belonging she craves. Instead, she is fascinated by Dr. Procheska, a handsome man whose passion and compassion are matched by his strong political principles and devotion to the Nazi cause. Politics drives them apart because the Nazi leader in the area disapproves of this relationship, which distracts the doctor from his political commitment. Eventually the two come to realize that love should transcend politics; however, history overrules them. They end up in passing trains, Pendennis re-

turning to Procheska's village to find him, Procheska fleeing to Italy as the Nazis are being arrested or driven out of Austria after one of their party members has assassinated the head of government.

MONDAY NIGHT

Recognizing the destructive power of authoritarian personal and political ideologies in a more overtly public way, the psychological detective story *Monday Night* places the search of two American exiles, Wilt and Bernie, against a collapsing moral order in prewar Europe. Wilt and Bernie pursue the case of Monsieur Sylvestre, a chemist whose testimony holds such sway in the courts that he alone has convicted a series of young men of murder in several mysterious deaths by claiming to have found traces of poisonous substances in the victims' "viscera." The Americans learn that Sylvestre himself is the murderer; this "misanthropy too savage to be repudiated" is motivated by the fact that the young men, like the Bridegroom, affirm some kind of spontaneous and generous emotional life with their families, a life Sylvestre himself has repudiated by rejecting his lover and their young son and follows by expunging himself from his world. Against the backdrop of a brisk arms business carried on with both sides in the Spanish Civil War and instances of French chauvinism and contempt for foreign nationals and their own people in a series of fixed bicycle races, one French spokesman pleads for moral action against destructive totalitarianism ("It is you who could stop it if you, your country really cared"), for "everlasting and violent freedom" against the dead authoritarianism represented by Sylvestre. Expressing the terror of vulnerable humanity, Wilt, awakened to a moral apprehension, questions, "Is it possible that a madman whose passion it has been to toy with human life and with the honor and liberty of countless victims was put in a position of highest authority?"

DECISION

This individual moral awakening to larger choice underlies all of Boyle's "war" novels of the 1940's. In the acclaimed short novel *Decision*, a detached journalist is awakened to the modern hell of fascist Spain through her chance encounter with two young men, republicans under surveillance, executed for their part in a Madrid prison hunger strike. The human capacity for resistance, expressed by a republican flamenco singer with the phrase "you get up on stage and bellow your heart out," is found in an even more life-affirming form in women, whose "power of the weak," to use Elizabeth Janeway's term, means that

> we, as women, have learned and forgotten more than they have ever set down in books. . . . we are sustained in our weakness by something they never even heard a whisper of . . . by a consecration to the very acts of hope, tenderness, love, whatever the name may be, which no man [that is, no fascist] has any share in.

In an awakening not narrowly political but moral in Hannah Arendt's sense, the narrator believes "at that instant . . . in each individual death, and the look of the sky as it must have been to them then, at the last trembling moment of defiance."

This apprehension of personal and political commitment exists in all of Boyle's longer war novels. Set usually in mountain villages in the Savoy or the Tirol, where the ambiguity of the national identity makes choice necessary, these novels posit some encounter between an American woman exile and one or more men, often Austrian skiers, whose stateless position requires choice of a personal nationality. This interplay occurs in the context of the village and the larger nation, where alternating mendacity and heroism, resistance and collaboration, illustrate the consequences of such choices. In the short novel *1939*, Ferdl Eder's failed attempts to join the French army, frustrated by chauvinistic discrimination against foreigners, leave him with no recourse but to accept the hated German passport; he leaves his American lover, who has herself abandoned a secure marriage to assert her choice.

PRIMER FOR COMBAT

Primer for Combat, the most involved of this group of Boyle's works, expresses the need for what Phyl, the American woman, calls "participation . . . in the disaster. In humanity's disaster." Against a tapestry of characters in a French village during the first days of the Occupation, in an introspective diary format, Boyle, in a manner reminiscent of Ignazio Silone and André Malraux, posits complex relationships among fascism, colonialism, classism, and democracy and self-determination as they are internalized in personal commitment. Phyl is awakened from the moral torpor of her fascination with the Austrian Wolfgang, whose opportunistic collaboration she comes to recognize by contrast with Sepp von Horneck, another Austrian, who, refusing to exchange liberation for reconstruction, escapes to join the Gaullist forces. Ultimately, Phyl's choice is not between men but between models of human action, acquiescence, or self-assertion. "I have found my own people," she says; "I have found my own side, and I shall not betray them." Fascism is located not within the political but within the personal realm, "not a national indication but an internal one." *Primer for Combat*, the best of Boyle's war novels, synthesizes the contradiction between the personal and the political.

HIS HUMAN MAJESTY

With *His Human Majesty*, Boyle abandons popular adventure and returns to serious literature. Although set during wartime, the novel deals with the theme of individual sin and redemption. In 1943, Boyle began writing a series of short stories about the American ski troops who were training in Leadville, Colorado. The stories were never completed, and eventually she turned the material into a two-part novel focusing on universal human facts about honor, truth, and loyalty. The title is taken from William Blake's mythic poem about sin and redemption, *Jerusalem: The Emanation of the Giant Albion* (1804-1820).

The main character in the novel, Fennington, a ski trooper, is the protagonist in both parts. In the first section, "Enemy Detail," he is portrayed as an aloof idealist. He avoids most of the others in his unit, finding them coarse and shallow. He occupies his time reading a one-hundred-year-old diary written by Augusta Tabor, an early settler. His one friend, Pater, is a newspaper reporter who is married to a Hollywood star. When Fennington meets Pater's wife, he falls in love with her, thereby betraying his friendship. Driven by guilt, he volunteers for a dangerous mission to rescue two stranded travelers, only to discover that they are Pater's wife and a German prisoner of war she was helping to escape. The rescue attempt proves too late, and Pater's wife dies. Fennington thus loses both his self-respect and the woman he loves.

"Main Drag," the second section, opens by describing the tensions and prejudices in camp. The flaws and weaknesses of the troopers and the townspeople are revealed. Eventually, Fennington meets the descendant of Augusta Tabor. When she receives word that her husband has been killed in the war, Fennington comforts her. The two kiss, discovering that love provides the only hope for the future. Leadville becomes a microcosm, exposing the evil and weaknesses of the larger society; however, acts of compassion and bravery can help to alleviate humanity's trials and sorrows. The novel ends with an emphasis on the need for commitment. For Boyle, individual redemption is found in love.

GENERATION WITHOUT FAREWELL

In two novels addressing the postwar period of occupation, *The Seagull on the Step* and *Generation Without Farewell*, Boyle's vision of the dialectic between the personal and the political becomes more fully a clash between the human and the totalitarian impulses in the heart and in history. In *Generation Without Farewell*, like *His Human Majesty* a study of the human response to authoritarianism, hunters stalk their prey in an occupied German village. Both Germans and Americans, led by the American Colonel Roberts, the universal authoritarian, hunt a wild boar believed to be hidden in the seemingly primeval forest surrounding the village. An expression of the people's will to survive and affirm the positive aspects of their nationality against the dead hand of their Nazi past, the boar is identified by an American observer, Seth Honerkamp, with an antifascist spirit and the great composers of the past.

Jaeger, an anti-Nazi German searching for his roots in a past not distorted by fascism, sees in the hunt his people's historic tendency to create an "other" whose extermination becomes an obsession, destroying human liberty and ultimately the very source of the culture. The will to liberty breaks free, however, when Robert's wife, Catherine, and daughter, Milly, both expressions of the reproductive and nurturing power contained in the Demeter-Persephone myth so pervasive in Boyle's work, join Jaeger and Christoph Horn. Horn is Milly's lover, whose identification with the Lipizzaner horses in his care connects him with the most fertile and, at the same time, the most transcendent elements of the national spirit they represent. This identification is shared by Milly, whose pregnancy by Horn parallels the mare's pregnancy in a particularly female vision of the survival and continuity of the culture itself. Although the repres-

sive qualities of both German and American authority unite in the hunt for the boar, an attempt to ship the horses to Brooklyn, and an epidemic of polio—the essentially American disease that fatally strikes Horn despite Jaeger's and Honerkamp's efforts to secure an iron lung—Catherine joins Milly to protect the coming child, leaving a revitalized Jaeger and Honerkamp to continue their pursuit for the life-affirming aspects of both German and American cultures.

THE UNDERGROUND WOMAN

The myth of the sorrowing mother in search of her daughter appears again in *The Underground Woman*. Against the background of the American antiwar movement, Athena Gregory's psychic restoration is connected to a vision of human transcendence expressed in a community of women. Athena, a university classics teacher, her husband lost to cancer and her daughter to a satanic cult, finds herself jailed during a sit-in at an induction center. Through a process of bonding not only with the other war protesters but also with the black, Hispanic, and poor white women there, she finds personal and political transformation in an intense female friendship with Calliope, another older woman whose intuitive, emotional nature balances Athena's own rational, analytic one. She also forms a friendship with a young woman musician, who replaces Athena's daughter Melanie, irrevocably lost to a cult serving Pete the Redeemer, an exploitative, charismatic leader who demands complete surrender of the will.

Released from jail and from her mourning, Athena asserts her new self in a symbolic defense of all daughters when she successfully resists Pete's attempt to commandeer her home. In this affirmative vision of female power, Athena resolves the conflict between her two selves—the respectable, aboveground Athena, sprung from Zeus's head and heir to his rationality, and the more emotional, intuitive "underground woman"—as she joins Calliope to save the deer from the hunters and the Hispanic prostitute's children from the state. In this late novel, Kay Boyle's vision of personal and political self-affirmation advances the dialectic between subjective experience and objective reality that marks her work from the beginning.

Janet Polansky
Updated by Mary E. Mahony

OTHER MAJOR WORKS

SHORT FICTION: *Short Stories*, 1929; *Wedding Day, and Other Stories*, 1930; *The First Lover, and Other Stories*, 1933; *The White Horses of Vienna, and Other Stories*, 1936; *The Crazy Hunter, and Other Stories*, 1940; *Thirty Stories*, 1946; *The Smoking Mountain: Stories of Postwar Germany*, 1951; *Nothing Ever Breaks Except the Heart*, 1966; *Fifty Stories*, 1980; *Life Being the Best, and Other Stories*, 1988.

POETRY: *A Glad Day*, 1938; *American Citizen Naturalized in Leadville, Colorado*, 1944; *Collected Poems*, 1962; *Testament for My Students, and Other Poems*, 1970; *This Is Not a Letter, and Other Poems*, 1985; *Collected Poems of Kay Boyle*, 1991.

NONFICTION: *Breaking the Silence: Why a Mother Tells Her Son About the Nazi Era*, 1962; *Being Geniuses Together, 1920-1930*, 1968 (with Robert McAlmon); *The Long Walk at San Francisco State, and Other Essays*, 1970; *Words That Must Somehow Be Said: The Selected Essays of Kay Boyle, 1927-1984*, 1985.

CHILDREN'S LITERATURE: *The Youngest Camel*, 1939, 1959; *Pinky, the Cat Who Liked to Sleep*, 1966; *Pinky in Persia*, 1968.

EDITED TEXTS: *365 Days*, 1936 (with others); *The Autobiography of Emanuel Carnevali*, 1967; *Enough of Dying! An Anthology of Peace Writings*, 1972 (with Justine van Gundy).

BIBLIOGRAPHY

Elkins, Marilyn, ed. *Critical Essays on Kay Boyle*. New York: G. K. Hall, 1997. Collection of reviews and critical essays on Boyle's work includes contributions by William Carlos Williams, Katherine Anne Porter, and Malcolm Cowley. Among the topics addressed in the critical essays are Boyle's novels *My Next Bride*, *Death of a Man*, and *Monday Night*.

Hollenberg, Donna. "Abortion, Identity Formation, and the Expatriate Woman Writer: H. D. and Kay Boyle in the Twenties." *Twentieth Century Literature* 40 (Winter, 1994): 499-517. Discusses the theme of self-loss through the roles of marriage and motherhood in Boyle's early works. Shows how expatriation gave Boyle some psychic space to explore the impact of gender roles on her aspirations and addresses how inadequate maternal role models affected her identity as an artist.

Lesinska, Zofia P. *Perspectives of Four Women Writers on the Second World War: Gertrude Stein, Janet Flanner, Kay Boyle, and Rebecca West*. New York: Peter Lang, 2002. Examines the works that Boyle and three other women writers created during the 1930's and World War II. Maintains that these writers transcended the conventions of war writing, which had traditionally focused on diplomacy and military campaigns. Instead, their work emphasized the importance of social, cultural, and political histories, narrating these stories with a sense of empathy for the nonvictorious.

Mellen, Joan. *Kay Boyle: Author of Herself*. New York: Farrar, Straus and Giroux, 1994. Draws on personal conversations with Boyle and her family to discuss the autobiographical nature of Boyle's writing and lays bare much of Boyle's own mythologizing of her life in her autobiographical writing.

Moore, Harry T. "Kay Boyle's Fiction." In *The Age of the Modern and Other Literary Essays*. Carbondale: Southern Illinois University Press, 1971. Attributes Boyle's lack of success, despite her supreme talent, to timing. Examines her 1960 novel *Generation Without Farewell* and argues that it far surpasses other contemporary novels about postwar Germany.

Porter, Katherine Anne. "Kay Boyle: Example to the Young." In *The Critic as Artist: Essays on Books, 1920-1970*, edited by Gilbert A. Harrison. New York: Liveright, 1972. Porter, a well-regarded novelist, examines how Boyle fit in the literary context of her time. Focuses on the novel *Plagued by the Nightingale* and on some of Boyle's short stories.

Spanier, Sandra Whipple. "'I Can't Go on, I'll Go On': Kay Boyle's Lullaby of Incarceration and Cancer." *Prairie Schooner* 72, no. 2 (Summer, 1999): 5-23. Spanier, author of a biography of Boyle (below), focuses on Boyle's battle against breast cancer and how the disease affected Boyle's life. Includes excerpts of letters that Boyle sent to friends in which she describes her disease and its impact.

_____. *Kay Boyle: Artist and Activist*. Carbondale: Southern Illinois University Press, 1986. The first critical biography and major work on Boyle is heavily annotated and thorough. Examines all of Boyle's writings, locating central themes and concerns that create a single coherent body of work. Supplemented by illustrations and by select but extensive primary and secondary bibliographies.

Yalom, Marilyn, ed. *Women Writers of the West Coast: Speaking of Their Lives and Careers*. Santa Barbara, Calif.: Capra Press, 1983. This volume grew out of a series of public dialogues with a handful of women authors. The entry on Boyle, however, came from an offstage conversation Boyle had with photographer Margo Davis in March, 1982. Boyle recalls her involvement in the antiwar movement in the 1960's, her life in Paris, being blacklisted in the 1950's, her writing, and the authors whom she admires. A valuable source of background information on Boyle.

T. CORAGHESSAN BOYLE

Born: Peekskill, New York; December 2, 1948
Also known as: Thomas John Boyle; T. C. Boyle

PRINCIPAL LONG FICTION

Water Music, 1981
Budding Prospects: A Pastoral, 1984
World's End, 1987
East Is East, 1990
The Road to Wellville, 1993
The Tortilla Curtain, 1995
Riven Rock, 1998
A Friend of the Earth, 2000
Drop City, 2003
The Inner Circle, 2004
Talk Talk, 2006

OTHER LITERARY FORMS

In addition to his novels, T. Coraghessan Boyle has published several collections of mostly satirical short stories that generally address the same themes seen in his longer fiction.

ACHIEVEMENTS

T. Coraghessan Boyle's novels have been praised for their originality, style, and comic energy. At a time when his contemporaries seem obsessed with the mundane details of everyday life—presented in a minimalist style— Boyle approaches fiction as an iconoclastic storyteller who embraces and borrows from the entire history of narrative literature, celebrating the profane, often-

absurd complexities of human endeavors. His first collection of short stories won the St. Lawrence Award for Short Fiction, *Water Music* received the Aga Khan Award, and the PEN/Faulkner Award for Fiction was given to *World's End*. Boyle also has been a recipient of the PEN short story award. A film adaptation of *The Road to Wellville* by director and screenwriter Alan Parker was released in 1994.

BIOGRAPHY

Born into a lower-middle-class family in Peekskill, New York, in 1948, Thomas John Boyle was a rebellious youth who played drums, sang in a rock-and-roll band, and drove fast cars. He did not get along with his father, a school-bus driver whose alcoholism killed him at age fifty-four in 1972. Boyle's mother, a secretary, was also an alcoholic and died of liver failure. Assuming the name T. Coraghessan Boyle at the State University of New York at Potsdam, Boyle studied saxophone and clarinet until he realized that he lacked the necessary discipline for music and drifted into creative writing. After college, to avoid military service during the Vietnam War, he taught English for two years at Lakeland High School in Shrub Oak, New York, while increasing his use of drugs, including heroin.

In 1972, Boyle entered the creative-writing program at the University of Iowa, where he studied under Vance Bourjaily, John Cheever, and John Irving. He also studied nineteenth century English literature and received a Ph.D. in 1977, with a short-story collection, later pub-

T. Coraghessan Boyle. (Courtesy, Allen & Unwin)

lished as *Descent of Man* (1979), serving as his dissertation. He became head of the writing program at the University of Southern California and settled in Woodland Hills, a suburb of Los Angeles, with his wife, Karen Kvashay (whom he met when they were both undergraduates), and their children, Kerrie, Milo, and Spencer. In 1992 the Boyles moved to Montecito, near Santa Barbara, and a 1909 house designed by Frank Lloyd Wright.

ANALYSIS

T. Coraghessan Boyle's novels concern the misconceptions that people of different sexes, races, nationalities, and backgrounds have about one another and the misunderstandings—some violent—that result. The clashes between Britons and Africans in *Water Music*, drug entrepreneurs and Northern California rednecks in *Budding Prospects*, Indians and Dutch settlers in New York in *World's End*, Americans and a half-American Japanese in *East Is East*, privileged white Southern Californians and destitute illegal Mexican immigrants in *The*

Tortilla Curtain, environmentalists and timber companies in *A Friend of the Earth*, hippies and straights in *Drop City*, and a deaf woman whose identity has been stolen and law-enforcement authorities in *Talk Talk* all allow Boyle to satirize the prejudices, eccentricities, and excesses of several cultures as well as groups within those cultures. Boyle's ironic fiction is populated by a multitude of diverse characters, all convinced that theirs is the only possible way of perceiving and dealing with a complex, changing, often-hostile world. Boyle alternates the viewpoints of these protagonists to present events and issues from all possible sides and increase the irony of the situations. He writes both in a straightforward, economical style and in more ornate prose resembling that of such popular writers as John Barth and Thomas Pynchon. Far from being didactic, Boyle's serious fiction entertains through masterful storytelling and through the author's control of his vivid style.

WATER MUSIC

Water Music alternates between the stories of Scottish explorer Mungo Park and London criminal Ned Rise until their destinies converge in Africa. Park (1771-1806), the first white man to see the Niger River, wrote a best-selling account of his adventures, *Travels in the Interior Districts of Africa* (1799), led a larger expedition into the interior of Africa, and drowned in the rapids of the Niger during an attack by natives. Boyle uses the fictionalized Park and the lowborn Rise to contrast the levels of English society and attitudes toward the British Empire.

Park, a public hero, is less than heroic as imagined by Boyle. He thinks he has had unique experiences because he is unable to recognize the humanity of the Africans he encounters. He selfishly ignores Ailie, his long-suffering fiancé and later devoted wife, thinking nothing of leaving her behind for years while he strives for glory. Park is less concerned with any benefits to humankind resulting from his expeditions than with mere adventure and fame. This need leads him to distort and romanticize his experiences in his writings. The irony of these exploits is that Park would be totally lost without the assistance of such nonwhites as Johnson, born Katunga Oyo. Sold into slavery in America, Johnson learns to read, wins his freedom, becomes a highly respected valet in London, and translates Henry Fielding's *Amelia* (1751) into Mandingo before returning to Africa. His earthy yet sophisticated realism contrasts strongly with Park's muddled idealism. Park's moral blindness suggests some of the causes of the collapse of the Empire.

Ned Rise, on the other hand, is a victim in the tradition of the picaros created by Fielding, Daniel Defoe, and Charles Dickens. (Dickens's mixture of colorful characterizations, humor, and moral outrage, as well as his use of odd names, seems to be a major influence on Boyle.) Rise is stolen from his mother at birth and forced to become a beggar when old enough. He has his right hand mutilated by a cleaver, is nearly drowned, is robbed, is wrongfully imprisoned and hanged—coming back to life as he is about to be dissected—loses his true love, Fanny Brunch, is imprisoned again, and is shipped to Africa to become part of Park's fatal expedition. Park's Britain represents culture and privilege; Ned's stands for the poverty and depravity at the extreme other end of the social scale. The ironically named Rise learns to survive, however.

In the tradition of such classics of the American picaresque novel as John Barth's *The Sot-Weed Factor* (1960) and Thomas Berger's *Little Big Man* (1964), *Water Music* is an enormously entertaining black comedy, a deliberately anachronistic, self-conscious narrative that frequently calls attention to its form and style. Boyle's delight in being a literary show-off, a tendency he has subdued as his career has progressed, led some of the novel's reviewers to dismiss it as a stunt, but *Water Music* quickly developed a cult following and has come to be seen as a clear announcement of the debut of an original, irreverent talent.

BUDDING PROSPECTS

Boyle presents another ill-conceived adventure, though on a much smaller scale, in *Budding Prospects: A Pastoral*. Its thirty-one-year-old protagonist, Felix Nasmyth, is a chronic failure given another shot at success by the mysterious Vogelsang, a Vietnam War veteran and sociopath. With the assistance of Boyd Dowst, holder of a master's degree in botany from Yale University, Felix is to grow marijuana in rural Northern California. Vogelsang promises the desperate Felix that he will earn half a million dollars from the enterprise.

Felix and his inept friends Phil and Gesh experience culture shock in isolated Willits, a town whose aggressively antagonistic citizens consider themselves morally superior to the rest of the decadent world. Obstacles to raising a productive marijuana crop include rain, fire, a hungry bear, a 320-pound alumnus of the state mental hospital's violent ward, and John Jerpbak, a menacing policeman who, like everyone in Willits, knows what Felix is doing. The comedy of *Budding Prospects* results from the dogged perseverance of Felix and friends in this doomed endeavor.

Beside his usual theme of individuals out of their element in a strange environment, Boyle offers a satire of the American free-enterprise system. As he interprets it, the system is motivated primarily by greed, with success coming less through intelligence or hard work than through luck. The dubious morality of Felix's project only adds to the irony. He and his friends want to get rich quickly and are honest only in admitting that they care about nothing but money. That they work harder to fail in an illegal business than they would to earn money honestly is yet another irony in a highly ironic tale. Felix's unreliable narration as he constantly compares himself to the pioneers who settled America adds comic hyperbole. Such humor keeps Boyle's examination of the materialistic side of the American Dream from being preachy.

WORLD'S END

Boyle returned to a larger canvas with *World's End*, his most ambitious and least comic novel, a consideration of America's self-destructive impulse. The Van Brunts, Dutch settlers in what is now northern Westchester County, New York, in the late seventeenth century, experience conflicts with a hostile nature and the voracious Van Warts, the patroons who own the land they farm. The lives of the Van Brunts become intertwined with those of the Kitchawanks, their Indian neighbors. The greedy machinations of the Van Warts lead to misery for the settlers and Indians and death for several of them.

Boyle alternates chapters about these characters with chapters dealing with their twentieth century descendants, including Jeremy Mohonk, the last of the Kitchawanks, whose efforts to regain his birthright (stolen by the Van Warts) earn for him seventeen years in prison. Truman Van Brunt betrays his friends and relatives to save himself, just as one of the original Van Brunts had done. The protagonist of the twentieth century chapters is Walter Van Brunt, reared by communists after Truman runs away and his mother dies. In the late 1960's, Walter is torn between the countercultural life led by his friends and the wealth and social position of the Van Warts. After losing his wife when she finds him in bed with Mardi Van Wart and losing both his feet in separate motorcycle accidents, Walter tracks down his lost father in Barrow, Alaska, to discover that Truman has spent years researching his family's history to justify his actions. Walter returns home thoroughly disillusioned, and Jeremy Mohonk gains revenge against his enemies by impregnating the wife of the current Van Wart, ironically allowing the despised line to continue.

In *World's End*, Boyle shows how people of different races, sexes, and social and economic backgrounds exploit, betray, and fail one another. The characters either are desperate to control their destinies or consider themselves the victims of fates they are incapable of overcoming. Almost everyone is self-deluding, from the right-wing fanatic Dipe Van Wart, in his pathetic attempts to resist change, to Walter, who sees himself as an alienated, existential antihero in the tradition of Meursault in Albert Camus's *L'Étranger* (1942; *The Stranger*, 1946). Walter thinks that his life will fall into place if he can understand his father, but finding Truman leads only to confusion.

As Boyle rifles English literary traditions as part of his satire in *Water Music*, in *World's End* he draws on the mythical views of America espoused by such writers as Washington Irving, James Fenimore Cooper, Nathaniel Hawthorne, Herman Melville, and William Faulkner. From the destruction of the virgin wilderness to the exploitation of the Indian to the curses inflicted on several generations of characters to fatal obsession with the inexplicable, the novel is virtually a catalog of traditional American literary themes.

World's End represents a new maturity in Boyle as an artist. In this novel he eschews the too-easy irony and too-obvious satire that occasionally weaken his earlier fiction, while he confirms his skill at storytelling. Though *World's End* is a sprawling novel with more than one hundred characters, Boyle exerts masterful control over his complicated, overlapping plots, expecting his readers to share his joy in the manipulation of so many coincidences, parallels, and ironies.

EAST IS EAST

The inability of people of different backgrounds to understand one another is even more at the center of *East Is East* than it is in Boyle's other novels. Hiro Tanaka, a twenty-year-old cook on a Japanese ship, jumps overboard off the coast of Georgia. Hiro, another Boyle orphan, has never known his father, an American rock musician who loved and left Hiro's mother, an eventual suicide. Ostracized by Japanese society for being half American, Hiro longs to lose himself in the great melting pot but unfortunately washes ashore on isolated Tupelo Island, site of Thanatopsis House, an artists' colony.

After a series of confused encounters with the natives, Hiro finds refuge in the cottage of Ruth Dershowitz. A mediocre writer from California, Ruth is at Thanatopsis thanks to her being the lover of Saxby Lights, son of Septima Lights, the colony's founder. Ruth pities the hungry, frightened fugitive from immigration authorities but also longs to incorporate Hiro into a short story with which she is having difficulty. Saxby finds out about Hiro, who is imprisoned, escapes to the Okefenokee Swamp, and is arrested again when near death.

Both the white and the black residents of Tupelo Island are frightened by their Japanese visitor, who is equally bewildered by them. Detlef Abercorn, the immigration official sent to find Hiro, is from Los Angeles and feels totally alienated in the South. An albino, he, like Hiro, has never truly fit in anywhere. Abercorn is assisted by Lewis Turco, a veteran of covert operations in Southeast Asia, who prides himself on being in control in any environment, but he is so paranoid that he creates nothing but chaos. No one in *East Is East* understands or trusts anyone else. The writers, painters, sculptors, and composers at Thanatopsis, who should be able to transcend the cultural differences that handicap the others, are instead so self-absorbed and crippled by petty jealousies that they are totally ineffective as human beings.

Hiro is another Boyle innocent destroyed by his inability to deal with the world's complexities and hostilities and by his own foolishness. Hiro has a system of beliefs—based on Japanese writer Yukio Mishima's theory of the samurai—to help guide him, but Mishima's teachings prove tragicomically ineffective in the Georgia swamps. Hiro trusts Ruth, to a degree, because he has no one else, and although she genuinely wants to help, her needs must come first. Ruth, the most fully developed female character in Boyle's early novels, ironically finds success through being caught harboring an illegal immigrant, for she then lands a book contract to tell her story. In this novel, the unscrupulousness of supposedly sensitive artists is as much the target of Boyle's satirical ire as are cultural differences.

THE ROAD TO WELLVILLE

Similar to each other in scheme and scope, *The Road to Wellville* and *Riven Rock* elaborate the wry appraisal of human nature and American values found in *Budding Prospects* and *East Is East* in period tales whose vivid historical tableaux call to mind Boyle's achievement in *Water Music* and *World's End*. *The Road to Wellville* is a farcical examination of the career of Dr. John Harvey Kellogg, inventor of cornflakes and other "gastrically correct" natural foods. A devout vegetarian and zealous promoter of physical culture, Kellogg opens his Battle Creek Sanitarium to men and women at the beginning of the twentieth century, hoping to win them over to his vision of a healthier lifestyle through carefully restricted diets, vigorous exercise regimens, and crackpot medical interventions that include yogurt enemas and sinusoidal baths.

Kellogg's "Temple of Health," as some deem it, is a magnet for celebrities, socialites, eccentrics, and connivers who represent a cross section of Boyle's America. Among them is Eleanor Lightbody, an independent woman and self-proclaimed "Battle Freak" whose sense of liberation is tied to her willing embrace of Kellogg's instruction. Intelligent and principled, Eleanor is blind to the absurdity of Kellogg's methods and to the misery they cause her sickly husband, Will, who suffers the increasingly dangerous indignities of rehabilitation at the sanitarium out of love for his wife. Boyle interweaves the adventures of the Lightbodys with those of Charlie Ossining, a likable scalawag who has squandered the money given him by a patron to establish a competing health-food company in Battle Creek. Ossining's inept efforts to duplicate Kellogg's products through cheap and eventually devious means offer a comic reflection on the underside of entrepreneurialism and the free-enterprise system.

The most interesting character is George Kellogg, one of Dr. Kellogg's numerous adopted children and a symbol of the Kellogg method's failure. George spends most of the novel dissipated and disorderly, deliberately embarrassing his father to extort money from him. He embodies the tendency toward entropy that undermines the best-laid plans in all of Boyle's novels and the irrepressible primitive appetites that get the better of even the most sophisticated characters.

RIVEN ROCK

Boyle develops these character types and traits further in *Riven Rock*. Set at approximately the same time as *The Road to Wellville*, *Riven Rock* portrays another American captain of industry whose personal shortcomings reflect an inherent flaw in the human condition. Stanley McCormick, heir to the McCormick Reaper fortune, is afflicted with an apparently hereditary schizophrenia that manifests as sexual psychopathy. He spends most of the novel locked away at Riven Rock, a family retreat in Santa Barbara, deprived of the company of women—his wife included—because a mere glimpse of a woman provokes him into profane and lewd attacks. In flashbacks, Boyle portrays Stanley as a naïve and sensitive young man who has perhaps been driven mad by the pressure of family responsibilities, and almost certainly by the insensitivity of the women in his life, including his domineering mother and his crusading wife.

As in his other panoramic novels, Boyle refracts the central conflicts and issues through the experiences of a number of characters. Chief among these is Stanley's wife, Katherine, a caring but ambitious woman who bears a striking resemblance in her attitudes to Eleanor Lightbody of *The Road to Wellville*. Educated and fiercely independent, Katherine is dedicated to Stanley's rehabilitation partly out of affection, but also as part of her selfish quest to have a child and know the fulfilled expression of her privilege and will. Edward O'Kane, Stanley's nurse and caretaker, complements Katherine. Sexually profligate and perpetually hostage to his lusts, he impregnates several women over the course of the novel, which leads to repeated comic complications with their families and his employer. In their own ways, Katherine and O'Kane embody the same appetites that govern Stanley. Boyle emphasizes this point through the efforts of Stanley's doctors to cure him by studying the insatiable sex drives of monkeys brought to the secluded estate. *Riven Rock* is possibly Boyle's most direct attempt to present the competing interests and compelling drives behind a culture and citizens as an expression of Darwinian biological imperatives.

The anger in Boyle's novels is tempered by the comedy. Even a relatively somber work such as *World's End* has moments of sublime silliness, as Dipe Van Wart fights middle-age depression by eating dirt from beneath his ancestral home—a fitting comic metaphor for his family's neuroticism and mindless consumption of the land. Boyle's fiction is also notable for the diversity of his style, which changes not only from novel to novel but also from chapter to chapter. Boyle understands well how to play on the natural rhythms of convoluted sentences and when to resort to the subtler joys of simpler ones, has a vocabulary rivaling Vladimir Nabokov's, and delights in parody. *East Is East* offers the mock Faulkner appropriate to a comic novel set in the South, but it avoids the overkill occasionally seen in Boyle's short stories and earlier novels. *The Road to Wellville* and *Riven Rock* are kaleidoscopic narratives in the style of Charles Dickens and William Makepeace Thackeray; their broad historical context accommodates their sweeping social satire. Most important is Boyle's ability to create believable, usually sympathetic, characters caught in absurd quests for truths they are incapable of understanding.

A FRIEND OF THE EARTH

A Friend of the Earth is both a satire of environmentalism and an attack on those who stand by while the planet is being decimated. Boyle tells parallel stories about Ty Tierwater and Andrea, his second wife. In the 1989-1997 chapters, Ty, owner of a shopping center established by his late father, is converted to saving nature from the excesses of human greed by the charismatic Andrea. In 2025-2026, all their work has been wasted, with the United States experiencing extreme weather conditions, especially blazing heat and endless rain. Forests are barren and most animal species extinct. After many years apart, Andrea is reunited with her seventy-five-year-old husband, who cares for a menagerie of exotic animals rescued by legendary rock star Maclovio Pulchris on his Northern California estate. The twentieth century chapters explain how Ty, Andrea, and the earth came to be the way they are.

In 1989, Sierra, Ty's teenage daughter from his first marriage, has an epiphany while taking part in a protest against a logging operation's destruction of the Oregon forests. Her commitment to the cause leads her to spend three years squatting in a redwood. Meanwhile, Ty goes to prison, first for kidnapping Sierra after she is taken from him by the authorities and later for setting fire to logging equipment. His increasing fanaticism places a huge strain on his relationship with Andrea.

Boyle is that rare writer who cares passionately about social and political issues yet is never didactic. Rather than lecturing about environmental causes, he makes the reader care about his fully developed, deeply flawed characters. As his career has developed, Boyle has become increasingly skilled at descriptive writing, and the passages in *A Friend of the Earth* about the effects of the high temperatures and resulting sandstorms, the muddy terrain left by the rains, the tree Sierra sees as almost human, and the confusion of the soon-to-be-extinct animals underscore what the characters say about their cause.

Boyle's vivid vision of the near future is pessimistic. Eating and drinking options are limited, with catfish the only available fish species and sake the only alcoholic drink. Outbreaks of a super flu are a constant threat. Baby boomers such as Ty and Andrea are left without Social Security and carry out tenuous existences. Only the ultrarich can live what once passed for normal lives. Environmental organizations such as Earth First!, which Andrea has helped guide, have failed miserably. Solace comes only through family, friendship, and love.

DROP CITY

Boyle returns to the milieu of *Budding Prospects* with *Drop City*. Paulette Starr, who calls herself Star, and her friend Ronnie Sommers, who prefers Pan, travel west from New York in 1970 to join the Drop City commune near Sonoma, California. Star and Ronnie feel at home in the ostensibly utopian community created by Norm Sender, though they find themselves growing apart. Ronnie wants to experience everything possible, while the less adventurous Star begins a relationship with the more stable Marco Connell.

Boyle alternates between the lives of the characters in Drop City and the lives of a completely different set of outsiders in Boynton, Alaska. Living alone in a remote wilderness, Cecil "Sess" Harder, a fur trapper, is the winner when Anchorage native Pamela McCoon comes to Boynton to audition three potential suitors. Sess has a live-and-let-live attitude toward everything but bush pilot Joe Bosky, who once stole Sess's girlfriend, shot his sled dogs, and makes obscene advances to Pamela. When Drop City begins collapsing into anarchy, Norm decides to move the group to Alaska, where the two strands of the story merge. While many in Boynton are horrified by the hippies, Sess and Pamela are more sympathetic, becoming friends with Star and Marco, while Ronnie gravitates to Joe, with dire results.

As Boyle contrasts the two communities, it becomes increasingly clear that he favors Sess's more workman-like existence. The self-obsessed Drop City residents are too casual and undisciplined to survive the harsh Alaskan winter. They would rather smoke marijuana, have sex, and listen to music than try to ensure there is enough food for everyone. When Norm leaves, the leaderless community becomes even more chaotic. Sess and Pamela, on the other hand, know how to adjust to the demands of their lonely isolation. They have chosen to exist apart from others, knowing what sacrifices and skills are needed. Star and Marco can prosper only by following their examples.

A gentler satire than usual for Boyle, *Drop City* is another of his examinations of the American quest for individual freedom and the pitfalls awaiting those who embark on such an adventure. The communal scenes recall *The Road to Wellville*, while the scenes set in the Alaskan wild resemble *A Friend of the Earth*. Although nature (rivers, mountains, wild animals) has been a consistent concern of Boyle's from the beginning of his career, none of his novels has captured nature's haunting beauty and primitive danger as well as *Drop City*.

Michael Adams
Updated by Stefan Dziemianowicz

OTHER MAJOR WORKS

SHORT FICTION: *Descent of Man*, 1979; *Greasy Lake, and Other Stories*, 1985; *If the River Was Whiskey*, 1989; *Without a Hero*, 1994; *T. C. Boyle Stories: The Collected Stories of T. Coraghessan Boyle*, 1998; *After the Plague: Stories*, 2001; *Tooth and Claw*, 2005.

EDITED TEXT: *Doubletakes: Pairs of Contemporary Short Stories*, 2003.

BIBLIOGRAPHY

Boyle, T. Coraghessan. "According to Boyle." Interview by Louisa Ermelino. *Publishers Weekly*, June 19, 2006. Boyle discusses the inspiration and research for *Talk Talk* and his love for language.

_____. "Rolling Boyle." Interview by Tad Friend. *The New York Times Magazine*, December 9, 1990. Boyle portrays himself as a missionary for literature who promotes himself to ensure that his work is read. He comments on the new maturity and reality in some of his fiction but admits that the absurd and bizarre are more natural for him.

_____. "T. C. Boyle: Errant Punk." Interview by Gary Percesepe. *Mississippi Review* 35 (Fall, 2007): 21-43. Boyle talks about the themes of his novels and about being a creative-writing student and teacher.

Hicks, Heather. "On Whiteness in T. Coraghessan Boyle's *The Tortilla Curtain*." *Critique* 45 (Fall, 2003): 43-64. Discusses Boyle's treatment of ethnic identity and compares it with that of William Faulkner in *Light in August* (1932).

Hume, Kathryn. *American Dream, American Nightmare: Fiction Since 1960*. Urbana: University of Illinois Press, 2000. Boyle's work is discussed in an extensive study of the tension between utopian and dystopian tendencies in late twentieth century American fiction.

Kammen, Michael. "T. Coraghessan Boyle and *World's End*." In *Novel History: Historians and Novelists Confront American's Past (and Each Other)*, edited by Mark C. Carnes. New York: Simon & Schuster, 2001. Discusses Boyle's fictional use of history and historical characters, particularly in *World's End*. Followed by a response from Boyle.

Schäfer-Wünsche, Elisabeth. "Borders and Catastrophes: T. C. Boyle's California Ecology." In *Space in America: Theory, History, Culture*, edited by Klaus Benesch and Kerstin Schmidt. Atlanta: Rodopi, 2005. Compares Boyle's treatments of environmental issues in *The Tortilla Curtain* and *A Friend of the Earth*.

Schenker, Daniel. "A Samurai in the South: Cross-Cultural Disaster in T. Coraghessan Boyle's *East Is East*." *Southern Quarterly* 34 (Fall, 1995): 70-80. Presents an in-depth analysis of the cultural clashes and intransigence that inform the tragicomic vision of Boyle's novel.

Vaid, Krishna Baldev. "Franz Kafka Writes to T. Coraghessan Boyle." *Michigan Quarterly Review* 35 (Summer, 1996): 533-549. Using the form of a letter from Franz Kafka, Vaid discusses Boyle's work, investigates the similarity between the two writers, and argues that the reader could grow as tired of Kafka's logic as of Boyle's broad panoramas.

MALCOLM BRADBURY

Born: Sheffield, South Yorkshire, England;
September 7, 1932

Died: Norwich, Norfolk, England; November 27, 2000

Also known as: Malcolm Stanley Bradbury

PRINCIPAL LONG FICTION

Eating People Is Wrong, 1959
Stepping Westward, 1965
The History Man, 1975
Rates of Exchange, 1983
Cuts: A Very Short Novel, 1987 (novella)
Doctor Criminale, 1992
To the Hermitage, 2000

OTHER LITERARY FORMS

A prolific writer, Malcolm Bradbury was a highly regarded literary critic whose output of scholarly nonfiction and edited work exceeds his output of novels. He is also well known for his television work, including teleplays, television miniseries, original episodes for television series, and adaptations for television. In addition, Bradbury wrote short stories, poetry, stage revues, and satirical essays.

ACHIEVEMENTS

Known first for his satirical campus novels and later for his merging of realism and postmodernism in fiction as well as his literary criticism, Malcolm Bradbury combined his literary work with his academic career. He was a cofounder of the internationally recognized writing program at the University of East Anglia in England, where he was a professor of American studies and a teacher of creative writing. The literary history of America and the importance and vitality of the contemporary novel were his areas of interest, and his contribution to both fields was significant. His novel *The History Man* won the Heinemann Prize from the Royal Society of Literature in 1975 and his novel *Rates of Exchange* was nominated for the Booker Prize. Bradbury also won awards for his television screenplays, adaptations, and episodes. He was made a Commander of the Order of the British Empire in 1991, for his services to literature, and was knighted in 2000.

BIOGRAPHY

Malcolm Stanley Bradbury was born in Sheffield, England, on September 7, 1932, the son of Arthur, a railwayman, and Doris Bradbury. The young Bradbury suffered from a heart condition that kept him off the playing fields during his school years. Instead, he spent his time in libraries. His academic diligence and love for literature contributed to his becoming first in his family to be a university student. He attended the University of Leicester and graduated in 1953 with first-class honors. Bradbury received an M.A. from the University of London in 1955, and then went on to study at Indiana and Yale universities in the United States before receiving his Ph.D. in American studies from the University of Manchester, England, in 1962.

Bradbury had a major heart operation in 1958 and completed his first novel, *Eating People Is Wrong*, while in the hospital. In 1959, he married Elizabeth Salt, a librarian, with whom he had two sons, Matthew and Dominic, and began his teaching career as a tutor of adult education at the University of Hull. From 1961 to 1965,

Malcolm Bradbury. (Getty Images)

he taught at the University of Birmingham. While there, he published humorous essays, sketches, and reviews; became friends and sometimes collaborated with fellow novelist David Lodge; and wrote a critical study of Evelyn Waugh.

In 1965, the year his second novel, *Stepping Westward*, was published, Bradbury moved to the University of East Anglia, where he would spend the rest of his academic career. In 1970, he cofounded a writing program there that would become the training ground for such Booker Prize novelists as Ian McEwan and Kazuo Ishiguro. Bradbury retired from academic life in 1995.

In the ten years between *Stepping Westward* and his third novel, *The History Man*, Bradbury wrote a collaborative book of poems and three important works of literary criticism. *The History Man*, Bradbury's best-known novel, marked a turning point in his fiction career. The

work won the Heinemann Prize from the Royal Society of Literature, was adapted for television, and stimulated interest in his two earlier novels. In a period of extraordinary productivity, Bradbury followed *The History Man* with a collection of stories and parodies, more literary criticism, a work on Saul Bellow, and the first of his works for television. Bradbury's fourth novel, *Rates of Exchange*, was published in 1983. Its setting in Eastern Europe and its protagonist, a linguistics professor who is a cultural exchange visitor for the British Council, reflect Bradbury's travels and busy schedule as a guest lecturer and speaker at scholarly conferences. *Rates of Exchange* was short-listed for the Booker Prize and made into a television series.

In addition to his teaching and lecturing schedule, Bradbury wrote dozens of award-winning television adaptations and episodes, short humorous fiction, edited works, and scholarly criticism throughout the 1970's, 1980's, and 1990's. *Doctor Criminale*, his fifth novel, was published in 1992. His sixth novel, *To the Hermitage*, appeared shortly before his death from heart failure in 2000.

ANALYSIS

Appearing at roughly ten-year intervals, each of Malcolm Bradbury's satirical campus novels can be considered a commentary on its decade. One of Bradbury's concerns as a novelist and critic is the dialogue between realism and postmodernism, as he strives to conserve tradition while experimenting with postmodernist forms. This tension can be seen in each individual novel even while the trend of his forty years of fiction writing moves from the most realistic in *Eating People Is Wrong* to the most experimental in *To the Hermitage*.

EATING PEOPLE IS WRONG

Written for the most part while Bradbury was still a student, *Eating People Is Wrong* is his first satirical campus novel. The protagonist, Professor Stuart Treece, is head of the English department at an unnamed provincial university in 1950's England. Though he is still young, he finds his prewar, liberal, humanist values outdated in the modern postwar world. From a humble background and educated at London University rather than Cambridge or Oxford, he is not sure where he fits in his world. Intelligent in his field of eighteenth century literature, Treece is characterized by a self-deprecating irony. He is all too aware of his failings; nevertheless, he is unable to act decisively.

Emma Fielding is a graduate student who is Treece's liberal mirror image and becomes his lover. Like him, she is a fair-minded person whose dominant characteristics are doubt and indecision. She is unable to finish her thesis on fish imagery in William Shakespeare or to reject any of her inappropriate suitors.

Louis Bates is a working-class undergraduate who is self-centered and takes himself too seriously. He falls in love with Emma, a situation that provides much of the comedy in the novel. Both Treece and Emma feel morally obliged to take Louis seriously in spite of his absurdity. Treece and his colleague, Dr. Viola Masefield, become romantically entangled. She is Treece's foil and opposite, always up-to-date but rather shallow.

Much of the humor of the novel derives from its social commentary on the life, faculty, and student body of the provincial university. There is much interior monologue and many comic scenes. The ending is deliberately ambiguous. Louis discovers Treece and Emma's affair, attempts suicide, and is sent to an insane asylum. Treece lies in a hospital bed, suffering from a vague illness, possibly his existential identity crisis. He and Emma are forced to take responsibility for Bates's attempted suicide, and they find themselves left only with their guilt.

STEPPING WESTWARD

James Walker, the protagonist of Bradbury's 1965 transatlantic novel, is a British novelist who accepts an invitation to become writer-in-residence at an American university. Like Stuart Treece in *Eating People Is Wrong*, Walker is a liberal humanist who is unfocused, caught not only between the conservative past and a present devoid of either historical or moral compass but also two worlds.

Another campus satire, *Stepping Westward* begins with a meeting of the creative-writing fellowship committee at Benedict Arnold University. The energetic and egotistical Bernard Froelich, who is writing a book that includes Walker, successfully lobbies to bring him to the university. The American antagonist is the arch-conservative department chair, Harrison Bourbon.

The satire of campus politics is one of the threads

of the novel. The closing scene is another meeting of the creative-writing fellowship committee. This time Froelich, who always gets what he wants, has succeeded in driving out Bourbon and manages to fund a literary journal that he will edit and in which he will publish his often-rejected works.

Walker, who has left his wife and daughter behind in England, becomes involved with the American student Julie Snowflake, a typical American girl who is writing a thesis about Walker. Thus, the rather passive Walker is seen always through the eyes of others. America, at first only an abstract idea for Walker, gradually becomes concrete through a variety of American characters and voices.

Although attracted to America, Walker refuses to take a loyalty oath and ultimately returns to England. He had experimented with new energy and ideas in the United States, but he found them lacking in morality and a sense of history. He instead embraces the solidity and reality of England. As with *Eating People Is Wrong*, the ending to *Stepping Westward* is ambiguous. Both countries and cultures have limitations. For Walker, England lacks imagination, whereas the United States lacks substance.

THE HISTORY MAN

The setting of *The History Man* is the University of Watermouth, a university that is managed like a factory, a modernist setting without tradition. The novel is framed by campus parties given by Howard Kirk, a fashionably radical sociology professor who has just finished his third book, and his wife Barbara.

The History Man is Bradbury's 1970's novel; the sexual revolution is in full flower. Kirk is a manipulator and an opportunist, a Don Juan notorious for his affairs, which extend to giving good grades to female students with whom he is sleeping. He persecutes a conservative student and lobbies against allowing a conservative scholar to speak on campus. While still a comedy, this novel is darker than the previous two. Kirk succeeds in seducing the one sympathetic character, Annie Callendar, who is a liberal humanist of the Stuart Treece or Emma Fielding variety. Her views are noble, but in Kirk's world, no longer viable. The novel ends as an indictment of the university setting where a character such as Kirk can prosper.

Unlike James Walker in *Stepping Westward*, Kirk has succeeded in escaping the past. The novel is written in the present tense, thus eliminating any sense of history. The narration is almost entirely from the outside, with no interior monologue or omniscient narrator. It presents the characters only through their speech and actions, which creates a mechanical, inhuman effect that is chillingly contemporary. *The History Man* is richly ambiguous, both comic and cruel. It reveals a society at the crossroads between liberal realism and shallow and amoral postmodernism.

RATES OF EXCHANGE

As in other Bradbury novels, *Rates of Exchange* is witty and satirical, a commentary on the critical conflict between realism and postmodernism. It is a comedy about language and academic travel, an extended metaphor in which rates of exchange represent not only the literal exchange of currency but also various figurative exchanges: cultural, narrative, sexual, and linguistic. The protagonist, Dr. A. Petworth, is a linguist who has traveled to a fictional Eastern European country called Slaka on a cultural exchange program to give a lecture entitled "The English Language as a Medium of International Communication."

Much of the humor of the novel revolves around language, specifically the broken English spoken by Slaka's inhabitants, and the misunderstandings caused by meanings lost in translation. At times the novel parodies the language and style of travel guides and narratives; at other times the narrative takes on the vocabulary and style of Petworth's professional lexicon and his linguist's frame of reference. Thus, language itself becomes a subject of the work.

Another theme of the novel is style: Petworth is a linguist who lacks both literary and personal style, while the novelist Katya Princip, with whom he becomes romantically involved, is a stylish dresser with a literary style, magical realism. Like Stuart Treece and James Walker, Petworth is a rather vague and ineffectual character without a clear identity. Indeed, one of the comic motifs of the novel is the mispronunciation of Petworth's name—Pitwit, Petwurt, Pervert—and that his hosts have him confused with another professor of the same name.

Rates of Exchange is filled with playful literary allusions and postmodern self-references. *The History Man*

is mentioned when Petworth shops for something to read at the airport. The confusion between Bradbury and his friend and fellow-writer, Lodge, also is referenced in the story. As in *Stepping Westward*, the novel ends with the confused and mediocre protagonist returning to a passive life in England.

DOCTOR CRIMINALE

The protagonist of *Doctor Criminale* is a television journalist, reflecting Bradbury's own preoccupation of the 1980's and 1990's. Francis Jay is on a quest to uncover the background of one of the major figures of contemporary thought, Dr. Bazlo Criminale. Doctor Criminale is a colossal figure—a poet, biographer, novelist, thinker, arranger of conferences—known by all. However, he also is shadowy, a "vague and placeless creature, the European intellectual." No one knows where he comes from.

Jay travels widely in search of Doctor Criminale, attending various academic conferences as part of his search. Eventually, Jay finds him behind the Iron Curtain, having discovered that the great man is deeply compromised. (One of the themes of the novel is the necessary compromise of modern life.) Jay himself is a Bradburian hero, a liberal humanist who must integrate postmodern values into his own life and work.

TO THE HERMITAGE

To the Hermitage is a large and ambitious work that weaves together two parallel narrative threads in two different time periods. The first thread begins with the arrival of Denis Diderot, the great Enlightenment philosopher, at the court of Catherine the Great of Russia. The second thread is the tale of a novelist and literary critic who travels to St. Petersburg in 1993 to participate in the Diderot Project, an academic gathering on the life and work of the philosopher.

The novel is a satire of contemporary literary criticism and a contrast between the order of the Age of Reason and the disorder of both the 1993 coup against Boris Yeltsin and the state of literary criticism in academia. In a classic Bradbury comic scene, an American deconstructionist literary critic in a baseball cap declaims against the idea of the Age of Reason while the conference collapses into drunken disorder. *To the Hermitage* brings together the three threads of Bradbury's career: modern critical theory, academics, and the novel.

Susan Butterworth

OTHER MAJOR WORKS

SHORT FICTION: *Who Do You Think You Are? Stories and Parodies*, 1976.

PLAYS: *Between These Four Walls*, pr. 1963 (with David Lodge and Jim Duckett); *Slap in the Face*, pr. 1965 (with Lodge, Duckett, and David Turner); *Inside Trading*, pr. 1996.

POETRY: *Two Poets*, 1966 (with Allan Rodway).

SCREENPLAY: *Cold Comfort Farm*, 1995 (adaptation of Stella Gibbons's novel).

TELEPLAYS: *Love on a Gunboat*, 1977; *The Enigma*, 1980 (based on a story by John Fowles); *Standing for Henry*, 1980; *The After Dinner Game: Three Plays for Television*, 1982 (with Christopher Bigsby); *Rates of Exchange*, 1984 (adaptation of his novel); *Blot on the Landscape*, 1985 (based on the novel by Tom Sharpe); *Imaginary Friends*, 1987 (based on the novel by Alison Lurie); *Porterhouse Blue*, 1987 (based on the novel by Sharpe); *Anything More Would Be Greedy*, 1989; *The Gravy Train*, 1990; *The Green Man*, 1990 (adaptation of Kingsley Amis's novel); *The Gravy Train Goes East*, 1991; *Cold Comfort Farm*, 1995 (based on the novel by Stella Gibbons); *An Autumn Shroud*, 1996 (based on the novel by Reginald Hill); *Ruling Passion and Killing Kindness*, 1997 (based on the novels by Hill).

NONFICTION: *Phogey! Or, How to Have Class in a Classless Society*, 1960; *All Dressed up and Nowhere to Go: The Poor Man's Guide to the Affluent Society*, 1962; *Evelyn Waugh*, 1964; *What Is a Novel?*, 1969; *The Social Context of Modern English Literature*, 1971; *Possibilities: Essays on the State of the Novel*, 1973; *The Outland Dart: American Writers and European Modernism*, 1978; *The Expatriate Tradition in American Literature*, 1982; *All Dressed up and Nowhere to Go*, 1982 (revised edition of *Phogey!*, 1960, and *All Dressed up and Nowhere to Go*, 1962); *Saul Bellow*, 1982; *The Modern American Novel*, 1983; *Why Come to Slaka?*, 1986; *Mensonge: Structuralism's Hidden Hero*, 1987 (also known as *My Strange Quest for Mensonge*); *No, Not Bloomsbury*, 1987; *The Modern World: Ten Great Writers*, 1988; *Unsent Letters: Irreverent Notes from a Literary Life*, 1988 (revised 1995); *From Puritanism to Postmodernism: The Story of American Literature*, 1991 (with Richard Ruland); *The Modern British Novel*, 1993

(revised 2001); *Dangerous Pilgrimages: Transatlantic Mythologies and the Novel*, 1995.

EDITED TEXTS: *Forster: A Collection of Critical Essays*, 1966; *E. M. Forster: "A Passage to India"—A Casebook*, 1970; *The American Novel and the Nineteen Twenties*, 1971 (with David Palmer); *Victorian Poetry*, 1972 (with Palmer); *Modernism: 1890-1930*, 1976 (with James McFarlane); *The Novel Today*, 1977; *The Contemporary English Novel*, 1979 (with Palmer); *An Introduction to American Studies*, 1981, 1989, 1998 (with Howard Temperley); *Contemporary American Fiction*, 1987 (with Sigmund Ro); *The Penguin Book of Modern British Short Stories*, 1987; *New Writing*, 1992 (with Judy Cooke); *New Writing Two*, 1993 (with Andrew Motion); *Present Laughter: An Anthology of Modern Comic Fiction*, 1994; *Class Work: The Best of Contemporary Short Fiction*, 1995; *The Atlas of Literature*, 1998.

MISCELLANEOUS: *Liar's Landscape: Collected Writing from a Storyteller's Life*, 2006 (Dominic Bradbury, editor).

BIBLIOGRAPHY

Acheson, James. "The Small Worlds of Malcolm Bradbury and David Lodge." In *The British and Irish Novel Since 1960*, edited by James Acheson. New York: St. Martin's Press, 1991. Critics often couple Bradbury with his friend and sometime-collaborator David Lodge, as their criticism is similar and their fiction is related by their university setting, themes, and tone.

_____. "Thesis and Antithesis in Malcolm Bradbury's *The History Man*." *Journal of European Studies* 33 (March, 2003): 41-52. Thirty years after its publication, *The History Man* continues to be Bradbury's best-known and most discussed novel. Acheson examines the novel in detail.

Bigsby, Christopher, and Heide Zeigler, eds. *The Radical Imagination and the Liberal Tradition: Interviews with English and American Novelists*. London: Junction Books, 1982. Bradbury discusses his work in an interview with his University of East Anglia colleague, Christopher Bigsby.

Burton, Robert S. "A Plurality of Voices: Malcolm Bradbury's *Rates of Exchange*." *Critique* 28 (1987):

101-106. A linguistic analysis of the semiotics and language use of *Rates of Exchange*.

Connery, Brian A. "Inside Jokes: Familiarity and Contempt in Academic Satire." In *University Fiction*, edited by David Bevan. Amsterdam: Rodopi, 1990. A pointed discussion of Bradbury's role in the genre of satirical campus fiction.

Haffenden, John. *Novelists in Interview*. London: Methuen, 1985. In his interview with Haffenden, Bradbury explains the literary theory behind his fiction and discusses the ideas and voice of *The History Man*.

Widdowson, Peter. "The Anti-History Men: Malcolm Bradbury and David Lodge." *Critical Quarterly* 26, no. 4 (1984): 5-32. A critical dissection of the work of Bradbury and Lodge. Asks whether their works are postmodern or reflections of a bourgeois capitalism.

RAY BRADBURY

Born: Waukegan, Illinois; August 22, 1920
Also known as: Ray Douglas Bradbury

PRINCIPAL LONG FICTION

Fahrenheit 451, 1953
Dandelion Wine, 1957
Something Wicked This Way Comes, 1962
Death Is a Lonely Business, 1985
A Graveyard for Lunatics: Another Tale of Two Cities, 1990
Green Shadows, White Whale, 1992
From the Dust Returned: A Family Remembrance, 2001
Let's All Kill Constance, 2003
Farewell Summer, 2006
Now and Forever: "Somewhere a Band Is Playing" and "Leviathan '99," 2007

OTHER LITERARY FORMS

Ray Bradbury's principal literary form has been the short story, and he has published several important collections, including *Dark Carnival* (1947), *The Illustrated Man* (1951), *The Golden Apples of the Sun* (1953), and *I Sing the Body Electric!* (1969). Two important extensive collections of his short stories are *The Stories of Ray Bradbury* (1980) and *Bradbury Stories: One Hundred of His Most Celebrated Tales* (2003). In addition to his short stories and novels, he has published in a wide variety of literary forms, from light verse and poetry to plays for radio, television, films, and the stage. One of his notable screenplays, which he wrote in collaboration with the director John Huston, is *Moby Dick* (1956). His poetry has been collected in such volumes as *The Complete Poems of Ray Bradbury* (1982) and *I Live by the Invisible: New and Selected Poems* (2002). A representative example of his nonfiction is the widely and well-reviewed *Zen in the Art of Writing: Essays on Creativity* (1989).

ACHIEVEMENTS

Although Ray Bradbury became arguably the best-known science-fiction writer in the United States, the majority of his work, which ranges from gothic horror to social criticism, centers on humanistic themes. Aficionados of the genre have criticized his science-fiction stories for their scientific and technological inaccuracies, a criticism he shrugs off, stating that his dominating concerns are social, cultural, and intellectual issues, not scientific verisimilitude. His stories, which often explore the dehumanizing pressures of technocracies and the mesmerizing power of the imagination, are widely anthologized and translated into many foreign languages. His ascent from pulp magazines to literary respectability has been intermittently recognized with several awards, including appearances in Martha Foley's annual best American short-story collections, two O. Henry Prizes, the Benjamin Franklin Magazine Award, the National Institute of Arts and Letters Award, an Academy Award nomination, an Emmy Award for his television adaptation of his 1972 children's book *The Halloween Tree*, and a Golden Eagle Award for his 1961 screenplay *Icarus Montgolfier Wright*.

In 2000 the National Book Foundation honored Bradbury with a medal for Distinguished Contribution to American Letters, and in 2004 President George W. Bush presented him with the National Medal of Arts. In 2007 he received a special citation from the Pulitzer Board for his outstanding work in science fiction and fantasy, and the French paid tribute to him with the medal of Commandeur, Ordre des Arts et des Lettres. Bradbury has been honored with a star on the Hollywood Walk of Fame, and his hometown of Waukegan, Illinois, has named a park for him. Astronomers have named an asteroid in his honor, and a crater on the Moon is named for his novel *Dandelion Wine*. His best novels are cautionary tales of the dangers of unrestricted scientific and technological progress, and his work has a strong moral core, encouraging the hope that humanity will deal creatively and ethically with the new worlds it seems driven to construct.

BIOGRAPHY

Ray Douglas Bradbury was born on August 22, 1920, in Waukegan, Illinois. His father, Leonard Spaulding Bradbury, whose distant ancestor Mary Bradbury was among those tried for witchcraft in Salem, Massachusetts, in the seventeenth century, was a lineman with the Waukegan Bureau of Power and Light; his mother, Esther Marie (née Moberg) Bradbury, emigrated to the United States from Sweden when she was a child. When he was three years old, his mother took him to his first film, *The Hunchback of Notre Dame* (1923), and he was frightened and entranced by Lon Chaney's performance in this film and, later, in *The Phantom of the Opera* (1925). As a child, Bradbury passed through a series of enthusiasms, from monsters to circuses to dinosaurs and eventually to the planet Mars. His development through childhood was aided by an older brother and by an aunt, Neva Bradbury, a costume designer, who introduced him to the theater and to the stories of Edgar Allan Poe.

In 1932, Bradbury's family moved to Arizona, where they had previously spent some time in the mid-1920's, largely because of his father's need to find work. In 1934

the family left behind both Arizona and Waukegan, settling in Los Angeles, which became Bradbury's permanent home. He attended Los Angeles High School and joined the Science Fiction Society (he had earlier begun reading Hugo Gernsback's magazine *Amazing Stories*, which, he said, made him fall in love with the future). After graduation, Bradbury worked for several months in a theater group sponsored by the actor Laraine Day, and for several years he was a newsboy in downtown Los Angeles. He took these jobs to support his writing, an avocation that he hoped would soon become a vocation.

His poor eyesight prevented him from serving in the military during World War II, which left him free to launch his writing career. During the early 1940's he began to publish his stories in such pulp magazines as *Weird Tales* and *Amazing Stories*, but by the late 1940's his work was appearing in such mass-market magazines as *Collier's*, the *Saturday Evening Post*, *The New Yorker*, *Harper's Magazine*, and *Mademoiselle*. Because these magazines paid well, he was able, on September 27, 1947, to marry Marguerite Susan McClure, a former English teacher at the University of California in Los Angeles. He continued, during the 1950's, to write for the pulp and mass-market magazines, and he routinely collected his stories for publication in books. In the mid-1950's he traveled to Ireland in connection with a screenplay of *Moby Dick* that he wrote with John Huston. Upon his return to the United States, Bradbury composed a large number of television scripts for such shows as *Alfred Hitchcock Presents*, *Suspense*, and *The Twilight Zone*. During the late 1950's and early 1960's, Bradbury's stories and novels focused mostly on his midwestern childhood—for example, *Dandelion Wine* and *Something Wicked This Way Comes*, the latter his favorite book.

During the 1960's and 1970's, Bradbury's output of fiction decreased, and his ideas found outlets in such forms as plays, poems, and essays. He also became involved in a number of projects such as "A Journey Through United States History," the exhibit that occupied the upper floor of the United States Pavilion for the New York World's Fair in the mid-1960's. Because of this display's success, the Walt Disney organization hired him to help develop the themes for Spaceship Earth, an important part of Epcot Center at Disney

World in Florida. Bradbury also helped design a twenty-first century city near Tokyo. In the 1980's he continued to diversify his activities by collaborating in projects to turn his novel *Fahrenheit 451* into an opera and his novel *Dandelion Wine* into a musical, and he developed a series, *Ray Bradbury Theater*, that ran on cable television from 1986 to 1992 and has continued its influence on DVD.

In 1990 Bradbury published *A Graveyard for Lunatics* with the publishing house Alfred A. Knopf, but after 1992 Avon became his publisher because Bradbury was unhappy that Knopf had allowed several of his books to go out of print and had been dilatory in publishing his new works. Avon has kept his backlist in print and has brought out such short-story collections as *Quicker than the Eye* (1996) and *Driving Blind* (1997).

In 1999 a stroke temporarily interfered with Bradbury's writing, and as he regained his ability to walk with a four-pronged cane, he also returned to creating stories, now aided by one of his daughters, who transcribed his telephone-dictated works. His poststroke novels include *From the Dust Returned* and *Farewell Summer*. As his health improved, he traveled to various ceremonies honoring him not just for his contributions to science fiction and fantasy but also to American literature. In 2004 he made news with his impassioned objection to the misuse of the title of his novel *Fahrenheit 451* for the title of Michael Moore's documentary film *Fahrenheit 9/11*. Deaths of family members and friends along with his own health problems have heightened Bradbury's awareness of his own race with death, a theme that is prominent in his twenty-first century short stories and novels.

Ray Bradbury. (Thomas Victor)

ANALYSIS

Paradoxically, Ray Bradbury's stories look both backward and forward. For him, each story is a way of discovering a self, and the self found in one story is different from the self found in another. Bradbury, like all human beings, is made of time, and human beings, like rivers, flow and change. Adapting the ancient Greek phi-losopher Heraclitus's famous statement that one cannot step into the same river twice, one could say that no person ever steps twice into the same self. Sometimes Bradbury discovers a self in the past, and sometimes, particularly in his science fiction, he discovers a self in the future. Several critics have pictured him as a frontiersman, ambivalently astride two worlds, who has alternately been attracted to an idealized past, timeless and nostalgic, and to a graphic future, chameleonic and threatening. This creative tension is present both in his own life and in the generation of Americans he likes to depict. It is also intimately connected with the genre—science fiction—with which he became so closely identified.

Bradbury has been called a romantic, and his romanticism often surfaces in the themes he investigates: the conflict between human vitality and spiritless mechanism, between the creative individual and the conforming group, between imagination and reason, between intuition and logic, between the innocence of childhood and the corruptions of adulthood, and between the shadow and the light in every human soul. His stories make clear that, in all these conflicts, human beings, not machines, are at the center of his vision. An ambivalence about technology characterizes his life and work. For example, he never learned to drive, even while spending most of his life in Los Angeles, a city that has made the automobile not only an apparent necessity but also an object of worship. He also refused to use a computer, and he successfully avoided flying in an airplane for the first six decades of his life. Each of these attitudes is rooted in some profoundly emotional experience; for example, he never learned to drive because, as a youth, he witnessed the horrible deaths of five people in an automobile accident. Because of his emphasis on basic human values against an uncritical embracing of technical progress, because of his affirmation of the human spirit against modern materialism, and because of his trust in the basic goodness of small-town life against the debilitating indifference of the cities, several critics have accused him of sentimentality and naïveté. Bradbury has responded by saying that critics write from the head, whereas he writes from the heart.

The poetic style that he developed is admirably suited to the heartfelt themes that he explores in a cornucopia of highly imaginative stories. He cultivated this style through eclectic imitation and dogged determination. As an adolescent, he vowed to write several hundred words every day, for he believed that quantity would eventually lead to quality. Experience and the example of other writers would teach him what to leave out. According to Bradbury, his style was influenced by such writers as Charles Dickens, Mark Twain, Thomas Wolfe, and Ernest Hemingway. On another occasion, however, he stated that his style came as much from silent-film actor Charles Chaplin as from Aldous Huxley, as much from Tom Swift as from George Orwell, as much from cowboy actor Tom Mix as from Bertrand Russell, and as much from Edgar Rice Burroughs as from C. S. Lewis.

Bradbury was also influenced by such poets as Alexander Pope, Gerard Manley Hopkins, and Dylan Thomas, and such dramatists as William Shakespeare

and George Bernard Shaw. Furthermore, and surprisingly, such painters as El Greco and Tintoretto and such composers as Wolfgang Amadeus Mozart and Joseph Haydn showed him how to add color and rhythm to his writing. According to him, all these influences—writers, poets, painters, and musicians—gloried in the joy of creating, and their works overflow with animal vigor and intellectual vitality. Their ardor and delight are contagious, and their honest response to the materials at hand calls forth a similar response in their readers, viewers, and listeners. This enchanting of the audience, similar to casting a magic spell, is what Bradbury attempts to do with his kaleidoscopic style: to transform colorful pieces of reality into a glittering picture that will emotionally intensify the lives of his readers.

Bradbury's writing is profoundly autobiographical, and childhood, adolescent, and adult experiences generated many of his stories. Graham Greene once said that there is always one moment in childhood when the door opens and lets the future in. Actually, for Bradbury, there were many such moments. He once said that everything he had ever done—all his activities, loves, and fears—were created by the primitive experiences of monsters and angels he had when he was five years old. He also said, however, that the most important event in his childhood occurred when he was twelve years old, at a carnival, when the performance of a magician, Mr. Electrico, so energized his imagination that he began to write stories to communicate his fervid visions to others.

Several critics have detected a decline in the quality of Bradbury's later work, but the standard he set in the 1950's was very high. Because he has worked in so many different literary forms, and because, within each of these forms, his treatment of a potpourri of subjects has been equally variegated, it is difficult to make neat generalizations about this author's oeuvre. The public has recognized Bradbury as the world's premier science-fiction writer, but only a third of his work has been in the genre. Certainly, his science-fiction stories have revealed that cultivated and craftsmanlike writing is possible in what was seen, before he began to publish, as a vulgar genre. Within the science-fiction community, however, sharp differences of opinion exist about Bradbury's contributions. A sizable segment sees his work as reactionary, antitechnological, and anti-utopian.

As one of these critics has put it, Bradbury is a science-fiction writer for people who do not really like science fiction. On the other hand, a large group, which includes a significant segment of the literary community (viewing him as one of their own), sees him as a humanist and a regional writer. This group draws some good arguments from Bradbury's stories: For example, even when he writes about Mars, the planet symbolizes for him the geography—emotional and intellectual—of the American Midwest. In this sense, his regionalism is one of the mind and heart.

Actually, both sides of this debate can find evidence for their views in Bradbury's motley work. He can be both enthusiastic about a future transformed by technology and critical of the dangers posed by technocracies. Ultimately, for Bradbury, technology is a human creation, and it is therefore subject to the labyrinthine goods and evils of the human heart. Although his best work is deeply humanistic and includes a strong critique of unrestrained technology, he is no Luddite. It is true that the technological society has produced many problems—pollution, for example—but human beings love to solve problems; it is a defining characteristic of the species.

Those who see only Bradbury's critique of technology view him as a pessimistic writer. In the proper light, however, his work is really profoundly optimistic. His fiction may rest upon the gloomy foundation of the Fall, but, in traditional theology, the counterpart of the Fall is Redemption, and Bradbury believes that human beings will renew themselves, particularly in space, which he sees as modern humankind's religious quest. Space, then, is Bradbury's new wilderness, with an infinity of new challenges. In that inexhaustible wilderness, human beings will find themselves and be saved.

DARK CARNIVAL

Numerous Bradbury stories, including several in his first collection, *Dark Carnival*, have as their provenance specific childhood events. For example, "The Small Assassin," which metamorphoses some of his childhood experiences and fears, tells of a newborn infant, terrified at finding himself thrust into a hostile world, taking revenge on his parents by first terrorizing, then murdering them. This story also reveals that Bradbury's view of childhood innocence is more complex than many critics realize, for, in Bradbury's view, beneath the facade of innocence lies a cauldron of sin—a dark vision of the human condition that some critics have called Calvinistic. Another tale, "The Lake," is based on Bradbury's experience as a seven-year-old, when his cousin nearly drowned in Lake Michigan. These and other early stories, which he first published in such pulp magazines as *Weird Tales*, *Amazing Stories*, and *Astounding Science Fiction*, served as his apprenticeship, an opportunity to perfect his style, deepen his vision, and develop the themes on which he would play variations in his later, more accomplished short stories, novels, poems, and dramas.

One of these early themes that also haunted his later fiction is alienation. Bradbury himself experienced cultural alienation when he traveled to Mexico in 1945. Americans were then mostly Protestant, individualistic, and preoccupied with getting ahead. Mexicans, on the other hand, were mostly Catholic, communalistic, and preoccupied with death. On his trip to Guanajuato, northwest of Mexico City, Bradbury was both horrified and fascinated by the catacombs, with their rows of propped-up mummified bodies. A story collected in *Dark Carnival*, "The Next in Line," grew out of this experience. In this story, a young American wife finds herself, after her traumatic ordeal in the Guanajuato crypts, alienated both from the strange Mexican society and from her own body, which she obsessively realizes is a potential mummy. Bradbury uses the metaphor of death to help the reader comprehend one reality, life, in terms of another, death. Metaphor thus becomes a medicine, a way of healing ourselves by envisioning ourselves into new modes of experiencing, learning, and surviving.

THE MARTIAN CHRONICLES

Although, at first glance, many of Bradbury's early stories seem notable for their great variety, he did deal, especially in his stories about Mars, with a set of conflicts that had a common theme, and so, when an editor suggested in 1949 that he compose a continuous narrative, he took advantage of the opportunity, since several of his stories about the colonization of Mars by Earthlings lent themselves to just such a treatment. Using the chronological frame of 1999 to 2026, Bradbury stitched these stories together with bridge passages that gave the book a semblance of unity. (It also presented categorizers of his works with a problem: Some have listed the book as a novel, others as a short-story collection.) Many critics have called *The Martian Chronicles* (1950) Bradbury's masterpiece, a magical and insightful account of the exploitation of a new frontier, Mars, by Earthlings whose personalities appear to have been nurtured in small midwestern American towns. By placing these normal human beings in an extraordinary setting, Bradbury was able to use the strange light of an alien world to illuminate the dark regions of human nature.

The apparatus of conventional science fiction makes an appearance, including monsters and supermachines, but Bradbury's basic intent is to explore the conflicts troubling postwar America: imperialism, alienation, pollution, racism, and nuclear war. He therefore depicts not a comforting human progress but a disquieting cycle of rises and falls. He also sees the Martian environment, itself transformed by human ingenuity, transforming the settlers. Thus his ultimate view seems optimistic: Humanity will, through creative adaptation, not only survive but also thrive. In *The Martian Chronicles* Earthlings metamorphose into Martians, an action that serves as a Bradburian metaphor for the human condition, which is to be always in the process of becoming something else.

Even though scientists criticized *The Martian Chronicles* for its portrayal of Mars as a planet with a breathable atmosphere, water, and canals (known by astronomers in 1950 to be untrue), and even though science-fiction devotees found Bradbury's portrayal of Martian colonies implausible, the book was a triumphant success, largely, some have suggested, because of these "weaknesses." Bradbury's Mars mirrored the present and served as the stage on which his eccentric characters—the misfits, opportunists, and romantics—could remake Mars in their own images (only to find themselves remade by Mars in the process). *The Martian Chronicles* has proved to be enduringly popular. It has passed through several editions, sold millions of copies, and been translated into more than thirty foreign languages.

THE ILLUSTRATED MAN

Another book of interlinked stories, *The Illustrated Man*, followed soon after the publication of *The Martian Chronicles*. In *The Illustrated Man* the device linking the stories together is the tattoo art on the skin of one of the characters. Bradbury sets some of his stories on Mars,

and a few bear some relation to the cycle of stories in *The Martian Chronicles*. By the early 1950's, Bradbury was a well-established writer, able to place his stories in both pulp and popular magazines and able to profit again when his collections of these stories were published as books. His fourth collection, *The Golden Apples of the Sun*, abandoned the frame narrative that he had been using and instead simply juxtaposed stories from a wide variety of genres—science fiction, fantasy, crime, and comedy.

John Huston, the film director, was impressed by a dinosaur story that Bradbury had written and asked him to come to Ireland to develop a screenplay for Huston's film about another great beast, *Moby Dick*. Bradbury's experiences in Ireland in 1953 not only led to an excellent screenplay but also gave him material for several stories and plays about the Irish. Furthermore, the trip gave him the chance to meet the English philosopher Bertrand Russell and art historian Bernard Berenson, two of his heroes. Berenson had written a fan letter to Bradbury in which he praised the American's attitude toward writing as a "fascinating adventure."

FAHRENHEIT 451

During this most prolific period in Bradbury's literary life, he also published the book that would generate, along with *The Martian Chronicles*, his greatest success and influence. The story that came to be called *Fahrenheit 451* went through several transformations. In 1947 he had written a short story, "Bright Phoenix," in which the residents of a small town counter government book-burning edicts by memorizing the banned books. In 1951 he expanded this idea into a long story, "The Fireman," which appeared in *Galaxy Science Fiction*. A fire chief informed him that book paper first bursts into flame at 451 degrees Fahrenheit, which gave him the title for his novel-length story set in a future totalitarian state. Some critics interpreted this dystopian novel as an attack against McCarthyism, then at the height of its power, but the book also attacks the tyrannical domination of mass culture, especially in this culture's tendency to eschew complexity of thought and to embrace the simple sentiments of pressure groups. The central irony of the novel concerns firefighters whose job is to set fires (burn books) rather than to extinguish them.

Bradbury, a lifelong book lover, used *Fahrenheit 451*

to show how important books are to freedom, morality, and the search for truth. The novel concludes with Montag, a fireman who has rejected his role as book burner, joining a community that strives to preserve books by memorizing them. Some critics have pointed out that this new society, where individuals abandon their identities to "become" the books they have memorized, inculcates a mass behavior as conformist as the one from which they and Montag have escaped, but Bradbury would respond that this new culture allows for a multiplicity of ideas and attitudes and thus provides the opportunity for human creativity to shape a hopeful legacy for the next generation.

DANDELION WINE

From the mid-1950's to the mid-1960's, Bradbury's writings tended to center on his midwestern childhood, without being camouflaged by science-fiction or fantasy settings. His novel *Dandelion Wine* is a nostalgic account of a small Illinois town in the summer of 1928. Again, as was the case with so much of his earlier work, this novel was composed of previously published stories, and the superficial unity that Bradbury imposed on the material was not sufficiently coherent to satisfy some critics. Another similarity to his previous work was his theme of the twin attractions of the past and the future. The twelve-year-old hero finds himself between the secure, uncomplicated world of childhood and the frightening, complex world of adulthood. Despite the loneliness, disease, and death that seem to plague adults, the young man, like the colonists in *The Martian Chronicles*, must transform his past to create his future. Critics accused Bradbury of sentimentality in *Dandelion Wine*, pointing out how depressed and ugly Waukegan, Illinois—the model for Green Town—was at this time. Bradbury answered that he was telling his story from the viewpoint of the child, and factories, trains, pollution, and poverty are not ugly to children. Adults teach children what is ugly, and their judgments about ugliness are not always sound. For a child, as for Bradbury, Green Town was like William Butler Yeats's Byzantium, a vision of creativity and a dream for action.

SOMETHING WICKED THIS WAY COMES

Bradbury returned to some of these themes in another novel, *Something Wicked This Way Comes*, in which a father tries to save his son and his son's friend from the evil embodied in a mysterious traveling carnival. The friend, Jim Nightshade (a name indicative of the symbolic burden the characters in this novel must bear), is particularly susceptible to the carnival's temptations, since his shadow side is so powerful. The father ultimately achieves victory by using the power of laughter as his weapon; however, the father also points out that human victories are never final and that each individual must constantly struggle never to permit the good that is in him or her to become a passive rather than an activating force. The potential for evil exists in every human being (a Christian idea, original sin, that surfaces in many of Bradbury's stories), and unless humans keep their goodness fit through creativity, evil will take over. For Bradbury, love is the best humanizing force that human beings possess.

Something Wicked This Way Comes marked a turning point in Bradbury's career. After this work failed to enhance his status as a significant American novelist, he turned increasingly to plays, poems, and essays. His turn to drama was essentially a return, since he had acted, as a boy, on the stage and on radio, and since he had written several plays when he was young (they were so bad that he vowed never to write plays again until he learned to write competently in other forms). Many of his plays are adaptations of his stories, and most of them have been staged in California, though a few have had productions Off-Broadway in New York. The majority of his plays have been published. His first collection, *The Anthem Sprinters and Other Antics*, appeared in 1963 (the "anthem sprinters" are Irishmen who flee from motion-picture theaters before the national anthem is played). Although his short-story writing diminished during the 1960's, it did not vanish, and in 1969 he published another collection, *I Sing the Body Electric!*, which was a miscellany of science-fiction and fantasy stories.

Throughout his life, Bradbury has also been an avid reader of poetry. He has often made use of poetic diction in his stories, but, as in the case of his playwriting, he refrained from publishing his poetry until late in his career, because he wanted it to be accomplished and stylistically refined. Heavily indebted to Gerard Manley Hopkins, Dylan Thomas, Walt Whitman, and others, his poetry has not had the success of his stories. Much of the poetry, whimsical in tone, can be categorized as light verse.

THE TOYNBEE CONVECTOR

In 1988 Bradbury published his first new collection of short stories in eighteen years, *The Toynbee Convector* (a retrospective of one hundred stories, *The Stories of Ray Bradbury*, was published in 1980). As in some of his other collections, the stories of *The Toynbee Convector* contain a number of genres, subjects, and themes. The title story centers on a returned time traveler (the convector is his time machine, named for the historian Arnold Toynbee). He enthralls people with his message that, in the future world he visited, most of Earth's problems have been solved: The planet's waters have been cleansed, the dolphins and whales have been preserved, and the Moon and Mars have been colonized. In the story's concluding twist, however, it turns out that the time traveler had faked his trip to provide twentieth century humans with hope. Again, the reader encounters one of Bradbury's favorite themes: A lie can create a reality. In this story, a lie was needed to shake the world from its despair. For Bradbury, then, lies are like dreams, in that they are truths waiting to be born.

GREEN SHADOWS, WHITE WHALE

During the last decade of the twentieth and the first decade of the twenty-first century, Bradbury published four novels and three novellas as well as a graphic novel. Like his previous writings, these stories are rooted in his childhood experiences, or in his relationships with other writers, both living and dead, or in films. For example, in *Green Shadows, White Whale*, he fictionalizes his mid-1950's experiences in Ireland while working with John Huston on the screenplay for *Moby Dick*. Unlike the motion picture, this memoir, which interweaves facts and fabrications, is lighthearted, emphasizing the tall tales of the eccentrics in Heeber Finn's pub rather than the quest for a perfect script. Some critics have described this novel as the "most entertaining" of Bradbury's career and his vignettes of the Irish as perceptively humorous, but others have found it disappointing, complaining that the Irish characters, situations, and stories are stereotypical and that the "Irish green" disproportionately overshadows the "white whale."

AHMED AND THE OBLIVION MACHINES

Many of Bradbury's creative efforts throughout his life have appealed to adolescents as well as adults, and in *Ahmed and the Oblivion Machines* (1998) he wrote "a fable for adults and children alike" (the "oblivion machines" are unsuccessful aircraft of the past). This novella's central character is a twelve-year-old Arab boy whose fall from a camel accidentally separates him from his father's caravan. Before finding his way back to his father, Ahmed experiences several adventures that help him to understand who he truly is and what humankind should be. His guide in his desert wanderings is a god, whose statue Ahmed's tears vivify. This god not only teaches Ahmed to fly but also teaches him to interpret history correctly. Because this is a fable, this knowledge will enable Ahmed to create a world better than his father's. Critics have tended to compare this novella unfavorably with Bradbury's earlier fables, finding the story line weak and the symbolism either arcane or overelaborate.

FROM THE DUST RETURNED

Published on Halloween, 2001, *From the Dust Returned* provides another example of how Bradbury often constructs his novels from previous short stories. For more than fifty years he had made the Elliots, a family of supernatural eccentrics, central characters in a series of stories. Using the device of a family gathering at a vacated midwestern mansion, eerily depicted on the dust jacket by a Charles Addams painting, Bradbury stitches old and new stories together through an investigation of the family's history, meaning, and destiny. Unlike many of his other horror tales, this story's tone is blithesome, and the Thousand Times Great Grandmother, the green-winged uncle, the sleeping and dream-traveling daughter, and assorted other extramundane relatives, along with an adopted earthly son, are all meant to inspire affection rather than fear. Some commentators have situated this novel among Bradbury's "most enduring masterworks," and others have asserted that some of the individual stories rank with his best. On the other hand, some critics have detected in this novel a deterioration of the once-lauded Bradburian style, citing numerous solecisms, absurd images, and overwritten passages.

CRUMLEY MYSTERIES

During the decade 1980-1990, Bradbury returned to the literary forms that had made him famous. He published a novel, *Death Is a Lonely Business*, his first in twenty-three years, in 1985. This novel and *A Graveyard for Lunatics*, published in 1990, make use of some of the same characters, and both are detective stories with a strong dose of fantasy. In 2003 he completed what had become a trilogy with *Let's All Kill Constance*, which he began in a hospital while recuperating from a stroke. All three novels have a common setting (Southern California) and such recurring characters as the nameless writer-narrator and his detective friend Elmo Crumley.

The story of the final novel, with its tongue-in-cheek tone, begins on a stormy night in Venice, California, in 1960, when a Hollywood has-been frantically knocks on the writer's door. The once-glamorous, now lusterless Constance Rattigan believes her life is in danger, because she has received a 1900 Los Angeles telephone directory with red markings indicating not only already dead Hollywood stars but also those who are about to die, including Constance. After leaving the directory and her address book with the writer, she disappears. With the help of Crumley, the narrator travels around Los Angeles, warning and interviewing other possible victims. In the course of these peregrinations the narrator paints a squalid picture of the ruthless, greedy, and heartless Hollywood scene.

Several reviewers found the clash of genres in the first two novels—detective and fantasy—too disorienting to make the stories effective, but others found Bradbury's re-creation of a bygone era in Southern California history appealing. Critical response to the last novel of the trilogy was largely favorable, although some have called it the weakest member of the trilogy, while others have noted numerous flaws in Bradbury's writing, which the charitable have attributed to his ill health.

FAREWELL SUMMER

Among the novels of Bradbury's late period, *Farewell Summer* was the most eagerly anticipated, as it is the sequel to the much-loved *Dandelion Wine*, published nearly fifty years before. Following this gestation, which has been called one of the longest in literary history, the sequel, though it makes use of material removed from the original manuscript of *Dandelion Wine*, profits from the life experiences that Bradbury had in the interim. *Farewell Summer* was written by a man approaching death who has existential knowledge that life, in the end, takes away youth, love, friends, and happiness, leaving nothing but darkness. However, in

telling this story he hopes that his spirit will in some way live on.

The story takes place in Green Town, Illinois, during an Indian summer in October, 1929, and it centers on a conflict between a thirteen-year-old boy, Douglas Spaulding, and an elderly "school board despot," Calvin C. Quartermain. The conflict begins when the sound of Doug's cap-pistol accidentally precipitates the death of an old man, and Quartermain is determined to discover the "killer" among the group of "rebellious rapscallions." Making use of American Civil War imagery and an elegiac tone, Bradbury describes intergenerational battles that occur in relation to the courthouse clock and a haunted house on the edge of a ravine. Both the clock and the house are part of the "immense frightening machinery of the Enemy" because of their connections to death. In the story's resolution the boys repair the clock that they had stopped, and Quartermain has a birthday party for a girl who gives Doug his first kiss. In the final part of the novel, titled "Appomattox," Quartermain and Doug meet to share the lessons that this "civil war" has taught them. Many readers and critics have described *Farewell Summer* as moving, unforgettable, and wise, though some have asserted that it lacks the enchantment of *Dandelion Wine*.

NOW AND FOREVER

In 2007 Bradbury published two novellas under the cover title *Now and Forever*. Like several of his books of the new century, this one also includes discussions of the provenance of each story. The first novella, *Somewhere a Band Is Playing*, owes its origin to Bradbury's time in Tucson, Arizona, as a child and his encounters with actor Katharine Hepburn in his life and in her 1955 film *Summertime*. In 1956, when he started writing the story, he intended it as a starring vehicle for the actor, but by the time he completed it, Hepburn, one of the novella's dedicatees, was gone. Nefertiti, the most intriguing resident of the unmapped Summerton, Arizona, would have been the Hepburn role, and her relationship with the visiting journalist, James Cardiff, is, along with the town itself, the focus of the story. Cardiff discovers that the town has no children, doctors, or dead bodies in the cemetery. He falls in love with the ageless "Nef" and is confronted with the agonizing choice between remaining in Summerton forever or returning to the joys and sufferings of his conventional mortal life. Although this novella was conceived by a young writer, it was finished by an old man attempting to age gracefully.

Time and death are also themes in the second novella in *Now and Forever, Leviathan '99*. This story derives from Bradbury's experiences while he was writing the screenplay for *Moby Dick*. He here transforms Herman Melville's story into a science-fiction adventure. The spaceship *Cetus* replaces the *Pequod*, and a planet-destroying comet stands in for the great white whale. Melville's narrator, Ishmael, becomes the astronaut Ishmael Hunnicut Jones, the South Pacific island native Queequeg becomes the alien Quell, and Ahab becomes a monomaniacal, blind starship captain. Before its incarnation as this novella, *Leviathan '99* had been a radio drama starring Christopher Lee as the captain. In another version it had been a poorly received play, and Bradbury hoped that this new telling would be successful. On the whole, these novellas have met with favorable critical response, with some reviewers praising their imaginative visions that have assumed an honored place in the ever-growing Bradburian canon.

Robert J. Paradowski

OTHER MAJOR WORKS

SHORT FICTION: *Dark Carnival*, 1947; *The Martian Chronicles*, 1950 (revised 1997); *The Illustrated Man*, 1951; *The Golden Apples of the Sun*, 1953; *The October Country*, 1955; *A Medicine for Melancholy*, 1959; *Twice Twenty-Two*, 1959; *The Machineries of Joy*, 1964; *Autumn People*, 1965; *Vintage Bradbury*, 1965; *Tomorrow Midnight*, 1966; *I Sing the Body Electric!*, 1969; *Long After Midnight*, 1976; *"The Last Circus," and "The Electrocution,"* 1980; *The Stories of Ray Bradbury*, 1980; *Dinosaur Tales*, 1983; *A Memory of Murder*, 1984; *The Toynbee Convector*, 1988; *Quicker than the Eye*, 1996; *Driving Blind*, 1997; *One More for the Road: A New Short Story Collection*, 2002; *The Best of Ray Bradbury: The Graphic Novel*, 2003; *Bradbury Stories: One Hundred of His Most Celebrated Tales*, 2003; *The Cat's Pajamas*, 2004; *Summer Morning, Summer Night*, 2008.

PLAYS: *The Anthem Sprinters and Other Antics*, pb. 1963; *The World of Ray Bradbury: Three Fables of the Future*, pr. 1964; *The Day It Rained Forever*, pb. 1966;

The Pedestrian, pb. 1966; *Dandelion Wine*, pr. 1967 (adaptation of his novel); *Madrigals for the Space Age*, pb. 1972; *The Wonderful Ice Cream Suit, and Other Plays*, pb. 1972; *Pillar of Fire, and Other Plays for Today, Tomorrow, and Beyond Tomorrow*, pb. 1975; *That Ghost, That Bride of Time: Excerpts from a Play-in-Progress*, pb. 1976; *The Martian Chronicles*, pr. 1977 (adaptation of his story collection); *Fahrenheit 451*, pr. 1979 (musical; adaptation of his novel); *A Device Out of Time*, pb. 1986; *On Stage: A Chrestomathy of His Plays*, 1991.

POETRY: *Old Ahab's Friend, and Friend to Noah, Speaks His Piece: A Celebration*, 1971; *When Elephants Last in the Dooryard Bloomed: Celebrations for Almost Any Day in the Year*, 1973; *Where Robot Mice and Robot Men Run Round in Robot Towns: New Poems, Both Light and Dark*, 1977; *The Bike Repairman*, 1978; *Twin Hieroglyphs That Swim the River Dust*, 1978; *The Aqueduct*, 1979; *The Haunted Computer and the Android Pope*, 1981; *The Complete Poems of Ray Bradbury*, 1982; *Forever and the Earth*, 1984; *Death Has Lost Its Charm for Me*, 1987; *Dogs Think That Every Day Is Christmas*, 1997 (illustrated by Louise Reinoehl Max); *With Cat for Comforter*, 1997 (illustrated by Louise Reinoehl Max); *I Live by the Invisible: New and Selected Poems*, 2002.

SCREENPLAYS: *It Came from Outer Space*, 1952 (with David Schwartz); *Moby Dick*, 1956 (with John Huston); *Icarus Montgolfier Wright*, 1961 (with George C. Johnson); *The Picasso Summer*, 1969 (with Ed Weinberger).

NONFICTION: *Teacher's Guide to Science Fiction*, 1968 (with Lewy Olfson); *"Zen and the Art of Writing" and "The Joy of Writing": Two Essays*, 1973; *Mars and the Mind of Man*, 1973; *The Mummies of Guanajuato*, 1978; *The Art of the Playboy*, 1985; *Zen in the Art of Writing: Essays on Creativity*, 1989; *Yestermorrow: Obvious Answers to Impossible Futures*, 1991; *Bradbury Speaks: Too Soon from the Cave, Too Far from the Stars*, 2005.

CHILDREN'S/YOUNG ADULT LITERATURE: *Switch on the Night*, 1955; *R Is for Rocket*, 1962; *S Is for Space*, 1966; *The Halloween Tree*, 1972; *Fever Dream*, 1987; *Ahmed and the Oblivion Machines: A Fable*, 1998.

EDITED TEXTS: *Timeless Stories for Today and Tomorrow*, 1952; *The Circus of Dr. Lao, and Other Improbable Stories*, 1956.

BIBLIOGRAPHY

Bloom, Harold, ed. *Ray Bradbury*. New York: Chelsea House, 2001. Critical essays cover the major themes in Bradbury's works, looking at, among other topics, his Martian stories, his participation in the gothic tradition, the role of children in his work, and his use of myth.

_____. *Ray Bradbury's "Fahrenheit 451."* New York: Chelsea House, 2001. Eight essays address various aspects of one of Bradbury's most important novels. Includes an informative editor's introduction, a chronology, and a bibliography.

Eller, Jonathan R., and William F. Touponce. *Ray Bradbury: The Life of Fiction*. Kent, Ohio: Kent State University Press, 2004. Described as "the first comprehensive textual, bibliographical, and cultural study of sixty years of Bradbury's fiction," this book makes use of manuscripts, correspondence, charts, and graphs to bring out the interconnections among the many versions that led to Bradbury's published works and the events in his life. Includes index.

Greenberg, Martin Henry, and Joseph D. Olander, eds. *Ray Bradbury*. New York: Taplinger, 1980. Anthology of Bradbury criticism includes essays that defend Bradbury against the charge that he is not really a science-fiction writer but an opponent of science and technology; others defend him against the charge that his work is mawkish. Includes extensive bibliography and index.

Mogen, David. *Ray Bradbury*. Boston: Twayne, 1986. Provides a brief introduction to Bradbury's career, focusing on analyses of the literary influences that shaped the development of his style and the themes that shaped his reputation. Includes detailed notes, bibliography, and index.

Reid, Robin Ann. *Ray Bradbury: A Critical Companion*. Westport, Conn.: Greenwood Press, 2000. Offers biographical information as well as critical discussion of Bradbury's major works and their critical reception. Includes bibliography and index.

Touponce, William F. *Naming the Unnameable: Ray Bradbury and the Fantastic After Freud*. Mercer Island, Wash.: Starmont House, 1997. Argues that the psychoanalytic ideas of Sigmund Freud and Carl Jung are helpful in plumbing the effectiveness of much of Bradbury's work (though in a letter to the author, Bradbury himself denies any direct influence, saying he has "read little Freud or Jung"). Asserts that Bradbury has produced stories of a modern consciousness that often forgets its debt to the unconscious.

Weist, Jerry. *Bradbury: An Illustrated Life—A Journey to Far Metaphor*. New York: William Morrow, 2002. Celebratory book, with an introduction by Bradbury, has, as its principal attraction, its numerous illustrations, carefully chosen and presented by an auction-house expert in science-fiction and fantasy collectibles. Includes index.

Weller, Sam. *The Bradbury Chronicles: The Life of Ray Bradbury*. New York: William Morrow, 2005. Authorized biography, based on extensive research in Bradbury's personal archives and on many interviews, presents an inspirational account of the highly imaginative writer. Includes detailed bibliographic notes, selected bibliography, and index.

MARION ZIMMER BRADLEY

Born: Albany, New York; June 3, 1930
Died: Berkeley, California; September 25, 1999
Also known as: Marion Zimmer

PRINCIPAL LONG FICTION

The Door Through Space, 1961
"The Planet Savers" and "The Sword of Aldones," 1962
The Bloody Sun, 1964
Star of Danger, 1965
The Winds of Darkover, 1970
The World Wreckers, 1971
Darkover Landfall, 1972
Hunters of the Red Moon, 1973 (with Paul Edwin Zimmer)
The Spell Sword, 1974
The Heritage of Hastur, 1975
The Shattered Chain, 1976
The Forbidden Tower, 1977
The House Between the Worlds, 1980
Two to Conquer, 1980
Sharra's Exile, 1981
The Mists of Avalon, 1983
Thendara House, 1983
Web of Light, 1983
The Firebrand, 1987
Witch Hill, 1990
Renunciates of Darkover, 1991
The Forest House, 1993
The Forest of Darkover, 1993
Rediscovery: A Novel of Darkover, 1993
Towers of Darkover, 1993
Glenraven, 1996 (with Holly Lisle)
Witchlight, 1996
Gravelight, 1997
Lady of Avalon, 1997
The Shadow Matrix: A Novel of Darkover, 1997
Heartlight, 1998
In the Rift, 1998 (with Lisle)
Traitor's Sun: A Novel of Darkover, 1998
Priestess of Avalon, 2000 (with Diana L. Paxson)
The Fall of Neskaya, 2001 (with Deborah J. Ross)

Zandru's Forge, 2003 (with Ross)
Flame in Hali, 2004 (with Ross)
The Alton Gift, 2007 (with Ross)

OTHER LITERARY FORMS

Although Marion Zimmer Bradley is known primarily as a novelist, she also wrote some short fiction as well as nonfiction, publishing several collections of short stories and a few essays. In addition to her writing, Bradley made a name for herself as an editor. She founded *Marion Zimmer Bradley's Fantasy Magazine* in 1988, and she also edited numerous anthologies, notably the Darkover anthologies and the Sword and Sorceress series. The Sword and Sorceress series has continued since her death as Marion Zimmer Bradley's Sword and Sorceress.

ACHIEVEMENTS

Marion Zimmer Bradley was one of the most prolific female science-fiction and fantasy authors, with more than sixty novels to her name and others written under pseudonyms. Although she was nominated for both the Hugo Award and the Nebula Award, science fiction's highest honors, she never won either, despite the fact that her novels contributed to the growth of science fiction and fantasy in numerous ways. After her death, she was honored with a World Fantasy Award for Life Achievement in 2000.

In her fiction, Bradley pushed the boundaries of sexual taboos, especially concerning homosexuality, with her sympathetic homosexual characters. It could also be argued that she, like fellow fantasy writer Andre Norton, served as a role model for many women who wanted to write science fiction and fantasy. As an editor, Bradley published many authors' debut stories and helped other women writers become established in what had traditionally been a male-oriented field. Her lasting contributions to the field of science fiction and fantasy are the Darkover and Avalon series, both of which continue after her death. Twenty-seven Darkover novels were published under her name, some of which were under way when she died and completed by others.

BIOGRAPHY

Marion Zimmer was born in Albany, New York, in 1930. As a teen, she was a science-fiction and fantasy fan. She made her first amateur sale to a fiction contest in *Fantastic/Amazing Stories* in 1949. That same year, she married Robert Alden Bradley. Her oldest son, David, was born in 1950. Bradley wrote during these early years, but only for fanzines and school magazines. Her first professional sale came in 1953, when she sold a short story to *Vortex Science Fiction.*

Bradley's first novel was published in 1961. In 1962, she published two novels together, including the first novel set on the planet Darkover. The Darkover novels eventually became her best-known works. She published several more novels in the 1960's, while going to college; some of her work at this time was done under various pseudonyms. She graduated from Hardin-Simmons University in Texas in 1964 with a B.A., and in 1966-1967 she did graduate work at the University of California, Berkeley. During this time she and Robert Bradley divorced. She then married Walter Breen, with whom she had two children, Patrick and Moira.

During the 1970's, Bradley published an average of two books per year, usually a Darkover novel and another novel. The Darkover series generated fan groups specifically dedicated to that series. Also in the 1970's, Bradley became a pastoral counselor in California and began to study religion and counseling. Her writing career continued to flourish in the 1980's. In 1983, she published *The Mists of Avalon*, a best seller. In 1980, she became an ordained priest of the Pre-Nicene Catholic Church and established the Centre for Nontraditional Religion. Religious themes also appear in her novels.

In the late 1980's, Bradley began editing her own magazine as well as anthologies. She helped nurture up-and-coming writers, particularly female authors. In her magazine and the Sword and Sorceress anthologies, she made an effort to publish first-time authors. In 1990, Bradley divorced Breen. Her writing and editing career continued, although she had some health problems. She died in 1999 after suffering a major heart attack, leaving behind many works in progress that were completed by other authors.

ANALYSIS

Marion Zimmer Bradley's early years fit the conventional mold of the science-fiction and fantasy genres in which she was publishing. However, as she matured as a writer, she explored unconventional themes, particularly in the areas of religion and sexuality. She also moved away from hard science fiction into more traditional fantasy. Many of her characters possess psychic abilities or other kinds of powers that set them apart from others. Most of the criticism published on Bradley's work has focused on her as a woman writer and as a creator of female characters who is concerned with women's issues. Among her most memorable female characters are Morgaine from *The Mists of Avalon* and the members of her female sisterhoods, such as the Free Amazons of Darkover. Although Bradley did not call herself a feminist, she has been both criticized and applauded by others who have applied that label to her.

DARKOVER LANDFALL

Darkover Landfall is not the first book Bradley published about Darkover, but it is the first book in the chronological order of that series. *Darkover Landfall* details the origin of humans on the planet Darkover. A colonization ship, heading for another planet, crashes on the inhospitable planet. While trying to repair their ship, the crew and colonists are exposed to the Ghost Wind, a natural occurrence that spreads a psychoactive pollen over the crash party. The pollen activates latent psychic abilities, but, even more distressingly, it lowers sexual inhibitions. Various sexual unions occur among the survivors. Eventually, they realize that they will have to make their home on the world.

The plot is a fairly conventional one for a science-fiction novel. This book shows Bradley's interest in and use of psychic abilities in her novels. On a nonconventional level, the book, without giving details, explores alternate sexualities and alternate standards of marriage and partnerships. For the colonists to ensure a broad gene pool, everyone must have children with different partners. The biggest controversy raised by the novel when it appeared, however, stemmed from the fact that Camilla Del Rey, the first officer, is forbidden to have an abortion when she wishes one. If it had not been for the crash, her peers would have had no problem with her choice, but because the colonists know that fertility and infant survival rates will be low for the first several years on their new planet, they force her to have the child. This position, although defended in the world of the book, sparked controversy and ire among Bradley's fans, feminists, and other writers. It was not until her later books that Bradley changed their minds.

THE SHATTERED CHAIN

The Shattered Chain is another Darkover novel, but it differs from earlier works because it focuses on the Free Amazons, or Renunciates, of Darkover. Centuries after the crash of the starship, Darkover has become a planet with a harsh caste system and a mostly feudal political and economic system. Women have few or no rights in most of this society. The exception is the Free Amazons. The Free Amazons have renounced their allegiance to and reliance on their former families and men. They renounce marriage, swearing an oath that they will give themselves to men and will have children only when they want to. They are often ridiculed by Darkoveran society. This novel in many ways answers the criticisms leveled at Bradley after the publication of *Darkover Landfall*. In this novel, the women are the protagonists and the capable characters.

The story is told in three sections, with twelve years separating part 1 from part 2. Parts 1 and 2 focus on rescues. In the first part, Rohanna Ardais, a telepathic noblewoman, hires the Free Amazons to rescue her abducted kinswoman because the men in her family have given up on her. Melora, Rohanna's cousin, is trapped in a Dry Town. In the Dry Towns, all women are chained, wearing the outward sign that they belong to the men. The Free Amazons rescue Melora and her daughter Jaelle so that Jaelle will not be chained. In part 2, Magda Lorne, a Terran sociologist, impersonates a Free Amazon to ransom her male friend, Peter Haldane, from a thief. She meets the grown Jaelle and her band and is forced to pledge the oath of the Amazons. She then realizes that she believes the oath. Part 3 focuses on the ramifications of Magda and Jaelle's oath.

While the first two parts of this novel carry most of the action for the story, it is the last section that reveals Bradley's themes. Throughout part 3, the three female protagonists confront the choices they have made and the prices they have paid or will pay. Rohanna renounced her freedom of choice for security in marriage.

Jaelle gained her freedom but renounced the ability ever to marry. Magda has to renounce her Terran allegiance to live as a Free Amazon. Bradley's point is that what is important is the choice—a woman should always have a choice in what she does. Rohanna did not have that choice and learns to live with it. Jaelle did have that choice but realizes it requires a price. She eventually chooses to live as a freemate with Peter Haldane. That she wants to give herself to a man is her choice as well.

There is a brief mention of the theme of fate in this novel, a theme Bradley explores in greater depth in later works. It seems to be pure chance that Magda meets Jaelle on her way to free Haldane. However, Lady Rohanna does not think it mere coincidence that Haldane looks exactly like Rohanna's son or that Magda meets Jaelle, the one person who could uncover her masquerade as a Free Amazon. Bradley suggests that there is a higher power at work. While feminists hated *Darkover Landfall*, many hailed *The Shattered Chain* as a feminist novel. Reviewer Joanna Russ, critical of the earlier work, later included *The Shattered Chain* in a listing of books depicting feminist utopias. In her later works, Bradley continued her exploration of the theme of woman's choice.

THE MISTS OF AVALON

While she will be known forever among the science-fiction community for creating Darkover, Bradley is known to a wider literary audience for *The Mists of Avalon*. This novel, impressive in length, could be considered her magnum opus. It stayed on *The New York Times* best-seller list for months following its publication in 1983 and was Bradley's first and most successful crossover mainstream novel.

The themes that Bradley explores in *The Shattered Chain* reappear in *The Mists of Avalon*. This is the story of the women of the Arthurian legend and their struggles with fate, religion, and the social strictures of their time. The novel deals with the matter of choice, or lack thereof. Although it is principally the story of Morgaine and Gwenhwyfar, it also gives some attention to Igraine, the mother of Morgaine and Arthur; Viviane, the Lady of the Lake; Morguase, Morgaine's aunt and the mother of Gawaine; and Nimue, daughter of Lancelot and the nemesis of the Merlin, Kevin Harper. Through these women, Bradley reconfigures the Arthurian legends into a woman's history and story.

Bradley reimagines the thematic conflict of the legend. In the book, the old ways of the Goddess religion are dying out because of the encroachment of Christianity. The Lady of the Lake is the high priestess of the Goddess faith, with Avalon as her seat of power. The Merlin is the chosen messenger of the gods. Viviane, the Lady of the Lake, and Taliesin, the Merlin, plan to put Uther on the throne of Britain so that he can protect the people from both the Saxons and the Christians. They further arrange that Uther's son Arthur should be king of both Britain and Avalon. Their plans go awry when Gwenhwyfar turns out to be overly pious and converts Arthur to Christianity.

Morgaine is raised on Avalon as priestess of the Goddess and vows to do the Goddess's will. However, when Viviane arranges for Arthur and Morgaine to participate in the ancient rites and have sexual intercourse, Morgaine feels betrayed and leaves Avalon. She joins Arthur's court, though she never gives up her ways. She continually tries to make Arthur be true to his oath to Avalon. In Bradley's version of the legend, this is the source of the conflict between Arthur and Morgaine—the struggle of one religion over another. Mordred, the son of Arthur and Morgaine, is also incorporated into this struggle, as he has been raised in Avalon and sees himself as the one to return Britain to its old ways. To do so, he must remove his father. Morgaine never hates Arthur in this version; in fact, the siblings love each other. Morgaine has always been Arthur's first love.

The conflict between the religions spurs social conflict as well. Under the old ways, women had the choice of whom they would mate with or love. The priests bring patriarchy and the concept of adultery. Bradley makes it clear that few of these women have choices. Igraine, at the age of fifteen, is given in marriage to the old duke of Cornwall. Morgaine is given to Arthur in the rites. Gwenhwyfar is given to Arthur as part of a deal for horses. Arthur later arranges a marriage for Morgaine with the aged Uriens, king of North Wales. The women do what is expected of them, however much they internally question these rules. In addition to having no social choices, Bradley suggests, the women have no choices at all. Viviane and Morgaine both have the Sight, a gift from the Goddess that gives them knowledge of the future. The implication is that everyone has a destiny to be

carried out, and there is little that can be done to change that destiny.

The success of *The Mists of Avalon* may be attributed to many things. First, the Arthurian legend holds a certain mystique of its own, and Bradley captures that sense of awe in her own way. Second, Bradley manages to portray the conflict that many women feel with traditional Judeo-Christian religions. Bradley, through Gwenhwyfar, often mentions how priests teach that sin came into the world through a woman, and therefore all women are evil. Morgaine's character dismisses that notion with contempt, and even Gwenhwyfar seems to finally reject it, entering the embrace of the Goddess in the aspect of the Virgin Mary.

LATER WORKS

Bradley reimagined another classic work in her 1987 novel *The Firebrand*, a retelling of the fall of Troy as told from Kassandra's point of view. The novel had some success, but it did not achieve the critical acclaim of *The Mists of Avalon*. Part of this could be that the source work did not resonate as strongly as the Arthurian literature with contemporary readers. Also, the thematic conflict of the older Goddess religion with Christianity is obviously absent from a book on the fall of Troy.

In 1993, Bradley returned to the Avalon series with a prequel, *The Forest House*, set in Briton during the Roman occupation. The title refers to the dwelling of the Druid priestesses who were resistant to the Roman occupation. The conflict revolves around a priestess in love with a young Roman during the collapse of the Roman Empire. Reviewers considered it a good companion novel to *The Mists of Avalon*, though it again did not receive as much critical attention as the earlier novel.

Bradley continued to write more stories in the Avalon series with *Lady of Avalon* and *Priestess of Avalon*. She died before she could complete the last novel, and it was finished by fantasy novelist Diana L. Paxson. Bradley's last two Avalon novels explore the same themes as the earlier books. Since Bradley's death, Paxson has continued writing in the series with such novels as *The Ancestors of Avalon* (2004), which links Avalon to Atlantis, and *Ravens of Avalon* (2007), which focuses on the historical figure of Queen Boudica.

P. Andrew Miller

OTHER MAJOR WORKS

SHORT FICTION: *The Dark Intruder, and Other Stories*, 1964; "A Sword of Chaos," 1981; "The Lesson of the Inn," 1981; *The Best of Marion Zimmer Bradley*, 1985; *Lythande*, 1986.

NONFICTION: "Responsibilities and Temptations of Women Science Fiction Writers," 1985.

CHILDREN'S LITERATURE: *The Brass Dragon*, 1970.

EDITED TEXTS: *Sword and Sorceress: An Anthology of Heroic Fantasy*, 1984-2003 (series); *Snows of Darkover*, 1994.

BIBLIOGRAPHY

Arbur, Rosemarie. *Marion Zimmer Bradley*. Mercer Island, Wash.: Starmont House, 1985. Provides a great overall look at Bradley's work, with biographical and chronological overviews as well as analyses of the fiction, divided into types such as Darkover, non-Darkover science fiction, and fantasy.

Hildebrand, Kristina. *The Female Reader at the Round Table: Religion and Women in Three Contemporary Arthurian Texts*. Uppsala, Sweden: Uppsala University Library, 2001. Places Bradley's work within the context of the history of the Arthurian legends and women's literature in general.

Kaler, Anne K. "Bradley and the Beguines: Marion Zimmer Bradley's Debt to the Beguinal Societies in Her Use of Sisterhood in Her Darkover Novels." In *Heroines of Popular Culture*, edited by Pat Browne. Bowling Green, Ohio: Bowling Green State University Popular Press, 1987. Discusses Bradley's use of elements from real medieval societies of women in creating her Darkover novels.

King, Betty. *Women of the Future: The Female Main Character in Science Fiction*. Metuchen, N.J.: Scarecrow Press, 1984. Provides background on how women characters have been portrayed in science fiction, placing Bradley's work in historical perspective.

Paxson, Diana L. "Marion Zimmer Bradley and *The Mists of Avalon*." *Arthuriana* 9, no. 1 (Spring, 1999): 110-126. The author who has continued the series of Avalon books examines the biographical roots of Bradley's female spirituality in *The Mists of Avalon*.

Riggs, Don. "The Survival of the Goddess in Marie de France and Marion Zimmer Bradley." *Journal of the Fantastic in the Arts* 9, no. 1 (1998): 15-23. Compares the depictions of the goddess in twelfth century writer Marie de France's *Lanval* and in Bradley's *The Mists of Avalon*.

Roberson, Jennifer, ed. *Return to Avalon: A Celebration of Marion Zimmer Bradley*. New York: DAW Books, 1996. Collection of appreciative essays—written primarily by other female luminaries writing in the science-fiction and fantasy genres—provides information about Bradley's fiction.

Russ, Joanna. "Recent Feminist Utopias." In *Future Females: A Critical Anthology*, edited by Marleen S. Barr. Bowling Green, Ohio: Bowling Green State University Popular Press, 1981. Draws comparisons among many different feminist utopias created in works of fiction, including Bradley's *The Shattered Chain*.

Schwartz, Susan M. "Marion Zimmer Bradley's Ethic of Freedom." In *The Feminine Eye*, edited by Tom Staicar. New York: Frederick Ungar, 1982. Discusses the portrayal of women in the Darkover novels, particularly *The Shattered Chain*. Examines Bradley's themes of choice and the price of choice and also emphasizes the importance of risk taking and choices involving tests of will and courage in the Darkover novels.

Tober, Lee Ann. "Why Change the Arthur Story? Marion Zimmer Bradley's *The Mists of Avalon*." *Extrapolation* 34, no. 2 (Summer, 1993): 147-157. Argues the feminist significance of Bradley's novel as an inversion of the male-centered Arthur legend.

JOHN BRAINE

Born: Bradford, Yorkshire, England; April 13,
   1922
Died: London, England; October 28, 1986
Also known as: John Gerard Braine

PRINCIPAL LONG FICTION

Room at the Top, 1957
The Vodi, 1959 (also known as *From the Hand
   of the Hunter*, 1960)
Life at the Top, 1962
The Jealous God, 1965
The Crying Game, 1968
Stay with Me till Morning, 1970 (also known as
   The View from Tower Hill, 1971)
The Queen of a Distant Country, 1972
The Pious Agent, 1975
Waiting for Sheila, 1976
Finger of Fire, 1977
One and Last Love, 1981
The Two of Us, 1984
These Golden Days, 1985

OTHER LITERARY FORMS

Although John Braine was first and foremost a novelist, he also received recognition for his contributions as a television reporter for *The Spectator*, as a film critic for the *Daily Express*, and as a book reviewer for *The People*. His only stage drama, *The Desert in the Mirror* (pr. 1951), was unsuccessful, but he won two national awards for British television adaptations of his novels: *Man at the Top* (1970, 1973) and *Waiting for Sheila* (1976). The seriousness of Braine's concern with the general problems facing the novelist is clear in his two most significant nonfiction works: *Writing a Novel* (1974) and *J. B. Priestley* (1978). In the former, he establishes guidelines for the aspiring novelist and shows how a professional writer who cannot afford to make wrong decisions "manufactures books according both to British and American readers." In the latter, Braine celebrates the life and career of a man to whom he felt closer than he did to "any other living writer."

ACHIEVEMENTS

John Braine's reputation is that of a frank, serious, tough-minded novelist writing from an Irish-Catholic, lower-middle-class background. His experiences in urban, industrialized Bradford, in the rural area of West Riding, and in the upper-middle-class environment of suburban London also figure prominently in his novels. Through all of his novels runs the theme of the stature of the self. He depicts real characters who have allowed their jobs, social positions, material ambitions, class membership, purely physical tendencies, and social and cultural ideals to subvert their essential sensitive and loving selves. His novels belong thematically to a tradition of realistic fiction (associated particularly with England) that tries to find a public significance in personal experience.

Braine's often vitriolic criticism of English society and the frequently harsh reality of his novels have had a marked influence on contemporary British fiction. This influence began in 1957 when his first novel, *Room at the Top*, became an instant success and brought him international recognition. Together with Kingsley Amis, Alan Sillitoe, John Osborne, John Wain, and other contemporaries, Braine ushered in with this novel a new generation of writers whose concerns led commentators to identify them as "Angry Young Men"—an epithet suggesting writers of social protest or critics of humankind's plight in the modern world. Their works shared a commonality of theme and style: a realistic portrayal of working-class or lower-middle-class life in England, a preference for provincial backgrounds, an antihero who directs his protests against the class structure and the welfare state, and an unadorned use of everyday language.

Through his hero, Joe Lampton, Braine made a conspicuous contribution to that gallery of "angries": Driven by ambition, envy, and greed, Joe possesses no admiration or liking for the class into which he is gatecrashing. He wants its advantages and privileges but not its conventions. Had *Room at the Top* appeared before Amis's *Lucky Jim* (1954) or Osborne's play *Look Back in Anger* (pr. 1956), Braine's name might be better known today than those of his contemporaries. Praised for its vitality, honesty, and realism, and criticized for its sentimentality and weak construction, Braine's first novel has the mixture of strengths and weaknesses characteristic of this new generation of writers.

Although *Room at the Top* was one of the most discussed—and probably one of the most praised—novels of 1957, some critics were less than enthusiastic about the promise of this new writer, and they surfaced to review his next two novels. Neither the sequel, *Life at the Top*, nor the intervening novel, *The Vodi*, enjoyed the same popularity and prestige. In considering the former, some critics felt that Braine was merely capitalizing on the success of his first novel; in the words of the reviewer for *Saturday Review*, *Life at the Top* was "disappointingly close, both in theme and in treatment, to the serials that appear in slick magazines." As for *The Vodi*, a number of critics felt that Braine's skillful storytelling and compassionate insight into human suffering failed to compensate for such technical defects as disparity of tone, obscure details, uneven pace, and lack of climactic power. The reviewer for *The Times Literary Supplement* wrote that the book succeeded "not where it [tried] to be new but where it [did again] what was well done in *Room at the Top*."

Admirers of Braine's work were delighted to find that his succeeding novels were not imitations of anything he had written before. Many saw *The Jealous God* as an important turning point in his career. His control of characters, refined style, exploration of a religious theme, and command of point of view and focus dispelled fears that he was a one-novel writer. *The Crying Game*, on the other hand, was praised as an exposé of the decadent urban life but was criticized for weak conflicts and insufficient distance between author and hero. Others found the writing to be hasty and the characters unpleasant. On this disappointing novel with virtually no story, Anthony Burgess commented, "The hedonism is too often self-conscious, . . . and the narrative style gives off the stale apple smell of old popular magazines."

Braine wrote eight more novels that met with varying critical success. As an analysis of marital discord, *Stay with Me till Morning* was deemed repetitious and ambiguous, perplexing many critics. Just as unclear, perhaps, was *The Queen of a Distant Country*. Some critics found

the novel's conversations about writers and the writer's world to be authentic, while other commentators held that this was an extremely pompous and self-indulgent book about Braine himself. *The Pious Agent* and *Finger of Fire* were judged to be routinely competent exercises in the spy genre; some felt that they were saved only by Braine's characterization and smooth, sophisticated style. *Waiting for Sheila*, on the other hand, was seen as a working model for Braine's own novelistic methods. It was praised for its plotting, characterization, and celebration of sex, but reviewers regretted that Braine had not allowed himself to be carried away in a longer, in-depth study of decadent London. The London *Sunday Times* called *One and Last Love* "a rhapsody" and "deliberately provoking." Reviewers felt that Braine's narrative power and his ability to evoke people and places, past memories and present experience, remained as vivid as ever in this, the most autobiographical of his novels.

Throughout his life, Braine remained capable of surprises. Among British novelists of the post-World War II era, he is distinguished by his stubborn integrity and by his craftsmanship.

BIOGRAPHY

John Gerard Braine was born April 13, 1922, in the Nonconformist city of Bradford, Yorkshire. His parents, Fred and Katherine, were lower-middle-class Catholics and therefore part of a distinguishable minority. His father was a works superintendent for the Bradford Corporation, his mother a librarian whose Irish Catholic family had relocated, along with a colony of Irish, to Yorkshire during the potato famine of the 1840's. With an attitude much like that of the headmaster's wife toward her students in Cyril Connolly's *Enemies of Promise* (1938), Braine's mother expected great things of her son; she "supercharged" him, to use Connolly's word, and he responded, both as a student and later as a professional writer.

Braine's formal education, while it lasted, was very good. From 1927 to 1933 he attended the state-run Thackley Boarding School, where, along with his exposure to Charles Dickens and Thomas Babington Macaulay, he found the predominantly Protestant, working-class atmosphere an asset to an aspiring writer; as he later observed, "One is pitchforked into the only tenable position for a writer; on the outside, looking in." After passing his examinations with honors, he graduated in 1933 to St. Bede's Grammar School, Heaton, and for the first time was made aware of "a split between the social world of home and school." At Thackley, Braine had been "a mildly mixed-up little boy"; at St. Bede's, he found himself "wildly at variance with the whole world" as he knew it. In adult life, his recurring nightmare was of being back at St. Bede's and aware of improperly done homework, wasting time, allowing people to get ahead of him, guilt, and, above all, physical pain. Although he left school at sixteen without graduating, five years later he received his school certificate by correspondence courses. Braine had no regrets about either school, however, for the experiences gave him what he needed: the essentials of English grammar and lessons about the world in which he lived, "which meant knowing about what had happened in the past."

For the next two years, Braine drifted in typical success-story pattern from one dull job to another—as an assistant in a furniture shop, a secondhand bookshop, and a pharmaceutical laboratory, as well as a "progress chaser" in a piston ring factory. In 1940, he became a librarian at the Bingley (Yorkshire) Public Library and—with time out as a telegrapher in the Royal Navy (1940-1943), a freelance writer in London (1951-1953), a patient suffering from a recurrence of tuberculosis (between 1952 and 1954), and a student at library school—worked as a librarian until 1957. In that year, the success of *Room at the Top* finally made it possible for him to quit his job and devote all his time to writing. He was then undeniably confirmed in his vocation as a writer.

Although Braine claimed he could not remember ever wanting to be anything but a writer, his struggle toward that goal had little of the heady directness that characterizes Joe Lampton's shortcut to the top. The writer in him first broke loose in 1951, when he left behind the security of a home, job, and family tradition in business to pursue the vocation of a freelance writer in London. He knew he was a writer, though to prove it he had published only one story and a few poems and articles (the latter in the *Tribune* and the *New Statesman*) and had written a play, *The Desert in the Mirror*, which was produced in 1951 in Bingley. Although he was attracted by a desire for independence, the excitement of the "big city," and the illusion of bohemianism, the most important reason for his move was the feeling that he had about Bingley in particular and the North of England in general, "the feeling that there was something to be said." Only by leaving the North could he see it clearly enough to write about it. "It was like stepping away from an oil painting: when one's too near, one can see only a collection of smudges."

He gained the confidence to begin what later became *Room at the Top* (originally titled "Born Favourite") when literary agent David Higham read Braine's profile of his Irish grandmother in the *New Statesman*. Paul Scott, then in charge of fiction at Higham's, told Braine

John Braine. (Getty Images)

he should write a novel, that the novel was his "true medium." In September, Turnstile Press offered him an advance subject to a synopsis and a sample chapter; not until 1953, however—after Turnstile's rejection, his mother's death, treatment for tuberculosis, and four more rejections—was the novel accepted for publication. Looking back on this period in his life, Braine considered that the sacrifices he made were necessary ones: "What gave my novel edge and urgency was my consciousness of what I had sacrificed in order to write it." In the foundations of *Room at the Top* are buried his despair on first arriving in London, his tears after the failure of *The Desert in the Mirror*, and his agony when Turnstile rejected the novel. "There had to be suffering, there had to be failure, there had to be total commitment." Indeed, this commitment continued as Braine went on to write twelve more novels before his death in 1986. In each of the novels, the reader finds a preoccupation with those things with which Braine was most familiar: Northern England, Catholicism, and the relationships between men and women.

ANALYSIS

"What I care about the most," John Braine wrote in the 1960's, "is telling the truth about human beings and the world they live in. . . . And every word I write is a celebration of my love for the created world and everyone and everything within it." In *Room at the Top*, *The Jealous God*, and *Waiting for Sheila*, Braine demonstrates the kind of truth telling he describes, a truth telling distinguished by exact observations, honesty of vision, and a clear and workmanlike style. Typically, his heroes are harried by a desire for personal affirmation, a desire they can seldom articulate or suppress. Worldly success, sensual gratification, and especially money are the only ends they know or can name, but none of these slakes their restlessness. Braine's heroes grapple desperately for money, they lacerate themselves climbing to success, yet they remain sullen and bewildered, always hopeful for some unexpected sign by which to release their bitter craving for a state of grace or, at least, illumination. In the midst of humanity's inevitable corruption and consequent need for redemption, Braine implies a vision much like that of J. B. Priestley: "a vision of a just society, a civilized and harmonious whole, a society in which there would be no alienation."

Braine's assault on British life begins with *Room at the Top*, a familiar "rags-to-riches" story about an individual who has glimpses of life beyond the reach of his environment, his struggle to achieve, his success after the sacrifice of his own soul. To this pattern Braine adds another theme: Any society is corrupt that demands the sacrifice of integrity as the price of success. Joe Lampton, as narrator, thus represents in the modern British novel a new species: the predatory, northern, working-class hero with long-range ambitions to achieve lusty affluence.

A significant departure for Braine is evident in his fourth novel, *The Jealous God*, in which he draws on his experiences as a Catholic to trace the influence of the Church on the personal life of a deeply religious yet sensual man. Unlike Joe Lampton, whose ambitions are material, Vincent Dungarvan has spiritual ambitions. Superimposed on this material is a study of an overpowering mother-son relationship; all of this gives new life to what E. M. Forster called "the undeveloped heart."

Waiting for Sheila, on the other hand, looks at an aspect of sex that is a major theme in other Braine novels as well: what it means to be a man. With its tragic implications, vivid class consciousness, and powerful portrayal of upper-middle-class life in a London suburb, *Waiting for Sheila* typifies the realistic impulse behind all of Braine's writing as he catches the wave of a permissive society.

ROOM AT THE TOP

About *Room at the Top*, Kenneth Allsop quotes Braine as saying: "In the Welfare State the young man on the make has to be a bit tougher and learn how to fiddle more cleverly. My job in writing about Joe Lampton was to look at him clearly." Like all of his novels, this one is rich in class overtones. Braine's working-class hero comes to a large provincial town from a slummy outpost of depression, demanding more than a minimum of material comforts and a chance to sneer at the pretension of the bourgeoisie. Lampton demands the best—"an Aston-Martin, 3-guinea linen shirts, a girl with a Riviera suntan"—and gets it by marrying a rich man's daughter. His triumph over his upbringing and his natural instincts is, however, a sour one; the price of his success is the abandonment of his true love relationship with an older woman and her subsequent suicide, a catastrophe for which his arrival at the top proves no compensation.

Braine's Yorkshire heritage is a strong presence in the novel. The speech, landscape, and people of his home county reflect a conscious provincialism in much of his work. Here Bradford shows up as the archetypal industrial city, which "more than any other in England is dominated by a success ethos." Warley, like Bradford, is a drab, soot-covered city where human life is secondary to trade, where there is little culture, and where the population is divided between the very rich and the very poor.

The novel also invites comparisons with the works of Horatio Alger. Like the typical Alger hero, Joe Lampton achieves his ambition not by hard work or even by ruthlessness, but by being lucky enough to attract the attention of a rich man. Whereas the Alger hero does this by saving the rich man's daughter from some menace, Lampton does it by impregnating the rich man's daughter, a girl he does not love. Moreover, whereas Alger leaves the reader with the assurance that his hero is going to live happily ever after, at the end of *Room at the Top*, the reader knows very well that Lampton is bound to lead a miserable life. Powerful in scheme, plot, and, narrative thrust, *Room at the Top* is a moral fable about ambition that very much epitomizes its age.

THE JEALOUS GOD

Essentially a variation on the eternal love triangle, Braine's fourth novel, *The Jealous God*, dramatizes the conflicts among an unmarried Catholic man (Vincent Dungarvan), a divorced Protestant woman with whom he has an affair (Laura Heycliff), and the teachings of the Catholic Church. This time, Braine portrays the everyday working-class life of the Irish in a smoke-gray mill town in the North of England. Unlike *Room at the Top*, *The Jealous God* never visits the modern industrial world of Warley, with its struggles for economic and social success. Here, Braine's concerns are spiritual, not material.

Like Joe Lampton, the hero is still an outsider, but this time he is a Catholic history teacher who finds himself torn between his vocation and the novelty of sex. Also unlike Lampton, he is, at thirty, still a virgin, a nonsmoker, and almost a teetotaler. Although his ardently Catholic mother hopes he will enter the clergy to make up for his father's failure, Dungarvan is sidetracked by his affair with Laura Heycliff, a pretty librarian, and then by his sister-in-law, Maureen, who seduces him. Unlike

Lampton, for whom sex is as simple and desirable as money, Dungarvan has a complicated conception of the ideal relationship between the sexes. Unlike Lampton, too, he is not a character type; neither conformist nor rebel, he is himself—confused, full of conflicts, hard to get along with, but himself.

WAITING FOR SHEILA

A mixture of romantic novel, egocentric narrative, fantasy, and explicit sexual document, Braine's ninth novel, *Waiting for Sheila*, once again dissects the trappings of success as modern society has come to view it. Jim Seathwaite, a northerner, is a familiar hero to readers of *Room at the Top*. He moved to a southern Surrey suburb, became successful as general manager of Droylsden's department store, and married Sheila, the chairman's former secretary. The usual Braine touch of price tags places the Seathwaites in the "made it" grade: They own a five-bedroom, two-bath home with all of the modern conveniences, including a professionally landscaped garden. Beneath Jim Seathwaite's veneer, however, as the reader comes to learn, is an inadequate man scarred by a wartime childhood during which his mother was unfaithful to his father, who died the day he discovered her infidelity. Braine's innovative use of the theme of the unfaithful wife (rather than the more common theme of the unfaithful husband) is but one of several departures in this novel.

Waiting for Sheila is deceptively simple in style and structure. For example, throughout the book Braine observes the unities: The reader does not leave Seathwaite's home; the action occurs within a few hours. Braine tells the story in the first person, in a stream-of-consciousness narrative—another departure for him—from the point of view of a thirty-year-old neurotic who has a conscience. He is sitting in solitude and drinking himself stupid while recalling his childhood, his adolescence, and his early manhood in one long, Freudian confession. Almost like a patient on a psychiatrist's couch, he hints at first and then finally reveals the truth: His wife is also unfaithful, and he feels as helpless as did his father. The reader learns that he finds in the lascivious Sheila the earth mother and bitch-lover he sensed first, at seven, in his mother—a self-indulgent beauty who drove his working-class father to drink and a muddy grave. Another theme in the work is thus that of the nuances and compromises of marriage—a general theme with which Braine is concerned in all of his books.

If he has never been short of detractors, Braine has had his defenders, too. Over the course of his writing career his reputation grew as a middlebrow writer who had mastered the basics of his craft. Few modern writers have had a firmer sense of milieu. His ear for dialogue was accurate, and his grasp of narrative technique impressive. With his talent, his tolerance of human foibles, and his total commitment to writing, Braine has been a significant figure in modern British fiction, an honest and perceptive observer of the social scene.

Dale Salwak

OTHER MAJOR WORKS

PLAY: *The Desert in the Mirror*, pr. 1951.

NONFICTION: *Writing a Novel*, 1974; *J. B. Priestley*, 1978.

BIBLIOGRAPHY

Allsop, Kenneth. "The Neutralists." In *The Angry Decade: A Survey of the Cultural Revolt of the Nineteen-Fifties*. 1958. Reprint. Wendover, England: John Goodchild, 1985. Considers the works of Kingsley Amis and John Wain before examining Braine's *Room at the Top*. Also provides biographical information on Braine and evaluates his goals as a writer.

Carpenter, Humphrey. *The Angry Young Men: A Literary Comedy of the 1950's*. London: Allen Lane, 2002. Entertaining book discusses Braine, Kingsley Amis, John Osborne, and the other writers dubbed the Angry Young Men. Carpenter maintains that the supposed movement of angry young men in literature and drama was a creation of the media.

Fjagesund, Peter. "John Braine's *Room at the Top*: The Stendhal Connection." *English Studies* 80, no. 3 (June, 1999): 247. Points out similarities between Braine's novel, published in 1957, and Stendhal's *Le Rouge et le noir* (1830; *The Red and the Black*, 1898). Compares the protagonists of the two novels and argues that these men are responding to similar dilemmas within their respective historical periods.

Hewison, Robert. "All the Rage." *New Statesman*, January 23, 2006. Presents a historical overview of the Angry Young Men and the cultural revolution they unleashed in Great Britain in the mid-1950's. Describes how the work of Braine, Harold Pinter, John Osborne, and Alan Sillitoe was a reaction to their family backgrounds and was heavily influenced by the modernism of 1950's Europe.

Karl, Frederick R. "The Angries." In *A Reader's Guide to the Contemporary English Novel*. Rev. ed. New York: Farrar, Straus and Giroux, 1972. Attacks the writers associated with the Angry Young Men movement, maintaining that their novels are poorly executed and their heroes boring. Karl reserves his harshest judgment for Kingsley Amis's *Lucky Jim* and derides *Room at the Top* and *The Vodi* as trite and formulaic.

Laing, Stuart. "*Room at the Top*: The Morality of Affluence." In *Popular Fiction and Social Change*, edited by Christopher Pauling. New York: St. Martin's Press, 1984. Well-rounded article traces the novel's critical success and analyzes historical, social, and political changes in postwar Britain that are reflected in the novel's themes and the relationships between characters.

Lee, James Ward. *John Braine*. New York: Twayne, 1968. Provides a good overview of Braine's work, beginning with an introduction that considers Braine in the context of other authors categorized as Angry Young Men. Devotes a chapter to analysis of *Room at the Top* and three later novels. Includes a brief selected bibliography.

Salwak, Dale. *Interviews with Britain's Angry Young Men*. San Bernardino, Calif.: Borgo Press, 1984. Braine recalls how he got started as a writer and comments on some of the values in his work, his mother's influence on his success, themes in some of his novels, and a work then in progress, the novel *One and Last Love*. He also provides some perspective on his being grouped with the Angry Young Men.

Schoene-Harwood, Berthold. *Writing Men: Literary Masculinities from Frankenstein to the New Man*. Edinburgh: Edinburgh University Press, 2000. Traces how masculinity has been depicted in literature from the nineteenth century to the end of the twentieth century. Part 2 contains a detailed analysis of *Room at the Top*.

RICHARD BRAUTIGAN

Born: Tacoma, Washington; January 30, 1935
Died: Bolinas, California; September, 1984
Also known as: Richard Gary Brautigan

PRINCIPAL LONG FICTION

A Confederate General from Big Sur, 1964
Trout Fishing in America, 1967
In Watermelon Sugar, 1968
The Abortion: An Historical Romance, 1971
The Hawkline Monster: A Gothic Western, 1974
Willard and His Bowling Trophies: A Perverse
    Mystery, 1975
Sombrero Fallout: A Japanese Novel, 1976
Dreaming of Babylon: A Private Eye Novel 1942,
    1977
The Tokyo-Montana Express, 1980
So the Wind Won't Blow It All Away, 1982
An Unfortunate Woman, 2000 (wr. 1982; first
    published in French as *Cahier d'un Retour de*
    Troie, 1994)

OTHER LITERARY FORMS

Richard Brautigan (BRAWT-ih-gehn) began his literary career as a poet. "I wrote poetry for seven years," he noted, "to learn how to write a sentence." Though a poet for many years, Brautigan maintained that his ambition was to write novels: "I figured I couldn't write a novel until I could write a sentence." Although most of Brautigan's later work was in novel form, he continued to publish poetry and also produced a collection of short stories (*Revenge of the Lawn: Stories 1962-1970*, 1971).

ACHIEVEMENTS

Short-story writer, novelist, and poet, Richard Brautigan created a stream of works that resist simple categories—in fact, defy categorization altogether. Much of his popularity can be attributed to his peculiar style, his unconventional plots, simple language, and marvelous humor, which together provide a melancholy vision of American life and the elusive American Dream.

Much of Brautigan's work involves the search for simplicity—an expansion of the Emersonian search for pastoral America. Yet, the complacent rural life is no longer available in Brautigan's world: All the trout streams have been sold to the highest bidder, all the campgrounds are already filled, in fact overflowing; yet, the search must go on for new places where the imagination can still roam free—to a pastoral America where the individual can escape the suffocating din of technocracy.

Brautigan's work evolved into a new, unorthodox version of the American novel. His experimentation with language, structure, characterization, plot, and motif broke new ground. Because of this, many critics have been unable to characterize his work with ease. Unable to pinpoint his exact standing, they have dismissed him as a counterculture phenomenon, a faddish nonentity. Although Brautigan's oeuvre is indeed very uneven, his best work is genuinely original and ensures him a lasting place in American literature.

BIOGRAPHY

Richard Gary Brautigan was born and reared in the Pacific Northwest. The son of Bernard F. Brautigan and Lula Mary Keho Brautigan, he spent his early years in Washington and Oregon. His literary career took hold when, in 1958, he moved to San Francisco, California, and began writing poetry in the company of Lawrence Ferlinghetti, Robert Duncan, Philip Whalen, and Michael McClure. The company he kept led to his initial identification as a Beat poet, but Brautigan's unique and now well-known style defied the classification.

Resisting crass commercialism and the profits linked with corporate America, Brautigan's first books were published primarily for the benefit of his friends and acquaintances. Success finally forced him to allow a New York publication of his work in the 1960's, however, and Grove Press published his *A Confederate General from Big Sur*. Shortly after his change of allegiance from Four Seasons Foundation in San Francisco to Grove Press in New York, Brautigan was invited to become poet-in-residence at Pasadena's California Institute of

Technology. Although he had never attended college, he accepted the invitation and spent the 1967 academic year at the prestigious school.

In 1957, Brautigan married Virginia Diorine Adler. They had one daughter, Ianthe, and later were divorced. In his later years, Brautigan divided his time among three places: Tokyo, San Francisco, and, when in retreat or fishing, a small town in Montana. He died in 1984, an apparent suicide.

ANALYSIS

Richard Brautigan's novels are generally characterized by the appearance of a first-person narrator (sometimes identified in the third person as Brautigan himself) who presents an autobiographical, oftentimes whimsical story. Brautigan's work employs simple, direct, short, and usually repetitive sentences. In his best work, he has an uncanny ability to create vibrant and compelling scenes from apparently banal subject matter. It is the voice of the "I," however, that carries the Brautigan novel, a voice that often unifies virtually plotless and quite heterogeneous materials.

A CONFEDERATE GENERAL FROM BIG SUR

Brautigan's first published novel, *A Confederate General from Big Sur*, is perhaps his funniest. A burlesque of American society long after the Civil War, the story is told by Jesse, a gentle, shy, withdrawn narrator (not unlike Brautigan himself) who meets Lee Mellon, a rebel, dropout, and activist living in San Francisco. Lee soon moves to Oakland, California, where he lives, rent-free, at the home of a committed mental patient. The story then moves to Big Sur along the central coast of California, where Lee and Jesse live in a cabin, again owned by a mental patient. As Jesse and Lee figure out how to cope with life and no money, they find a fortune of six dollars and some loose change, get rip-roaring drunk in Monterey, and discover Elaine and a great deal of money. Johnston Wade, a crazed insurance man, arrives on the scene, informing everyone that he is fleeing from his wife and daughter (they want to commit him to a mental institution). He leaves as abruptly as he arrived, remembering an important business appointment he must keep. The book ends, as it must, without ending.

Richard Brautigan. (Library of Congress)

In *A Confederate General from Big Sur*, Brautigan is facing the question of how to cope with civilization. The flight from technology toward wilderness holds risks of its own. Brautigan offers no answers. Human life is not unlike that of the bugs sitting on the log Jesse has thrown into the fire. They sit there on the log, staring out at Jesse as the flames leap around them.

The theme of the novel is the ambition to control one's life and destiny. The ownership of the Big Sur log cabin by a mental patient and Johnston Wade's own mental aberrations only serve to illustrate the fleeting control all people have over their lives. Brautigan introduces Wade to burlesque the myth of American destiny. He is a parody, a ridiculous image of American business and technocracy: the self-made man running away from his wife and child who suddenly remembers an important business engagement.

IN WATERMELON SUGAR

Although not published until 1968, *In Watermelon Sugar* was written in 1964, during Brautigan's evolution from poet to novelist. The book reflects this evolutionary change, for in many ways it is more poetic than novelistic in its form. The story is that of a young man who lives in a small community after an unspecified cataclysm. In the first of the three parts of the book, the shy and gentle narrator tells the reader about himself and his friends. Their peaceful life was not always so, he explains, and he tells about iDEATH, a central gathering place that is more a state of mind than an actual physical location. In the second part of the novel, the narrator has a terrible dream of carnage and self-mutilation. The third part of the book begins with the narrator's awakening, strangely refreshed after the terrible dream. The gentle, leisurely pace of the first part then restores itself.

In Watermelon Sugar is like Aldous Huxley's *Brave New World* (1932), a utopian novel of the Garden of Eden, springing forth out of the chaos of today's world. It is Brautigan's vision of the rustic good life in postindustrial society. From watermelons comes the juice that is made into sugar, the stuff of the lives and dreams of the people of iDEATH. By controlling their own lives, by creating their own order, the people of iDEATH recover society from chaos. The sense of order and recurrence is set in the very first line of the book, which both begins and ends "in watermelon sugar." That phrase is also used as the title of the first part of the book, as well as the title of the first chapter. Like a refrain, it sets a pattern and order in a world in which people live in harmony with nature and with their own lives.

THE ABORTION

Like several of Brautigan's books, *The Abortion: An Historical Romance* spent some time in the library of unpublished books that it describes, where dreams go (and can be found). The world of *The Abortion* is that of a public library in California: not an ordinary library, but one where losers bring the books they cannot publish. Again, Brautigan's narrator is a shy, introverted recluse—the librarian, unnamed because he is ordinary, like the people who bring their books to the library to have them shelved. Brautigan himself visits the library at one point in the novel to bring in *Moose*; he is tall and blond, with an anachronistic appearance, looking as if he would be more comfortable in another era. That circumstance is certainly the case with the narrator as well.

There is less action in *The Abortion* than in most of Brautigan's novels; the book plods along slowly, mim-

icking its central theme, which is that a series of short, tentative steps can lead one out of a personal and social labyrinth and toward the promise of a new life. Before the reader knows it, however, the librarian is out in the rain with a girl; she gets pregnant; and they journey to Tijuana so she can have an abortion. The girl is called Vida, and she represents life in the twentieth century. The librarian struggles with his inner self, afraid to move from the old ways, afraid to let go of his innocence. Brautigan contrasts him with his partner, Foster, a wild caveman who takes care of the books that have been moved from the library to dead storage in a cave. Foster is loud and outgoing—the opposite of the timid librarian—and he thinks of the library as an asylum.

With Vida, the librarian becomes embroiled in a quest for survival. Vida brings him out of the library into the world of change and conflict. He is frightened by it, but, step by tentative step, he confronts it.

The Abortion is a commentary on American culture. Brautigan draws a loose parallel between the library and American history: The librarian narrator is the thirty-sixth caretaker of the library; at the time the book was written, there had been thirty-six presidents of the United States. The origins of the mysterious library go back into the American past as well, just as Brautigan himself appears as an anachronism from an earlier, easier time.

While Brautigan laments the times gone by and yearns for the "good old days" and the leisurely pace of the library, he also holds out hope for a fresh alternative. American culture has nearly been destroyed—the beauty queen named Vida hates herself, and bombs and industrial technocracy threaten lives and deaden spirits. Strangely enough, by destroying life—by the abortion—one can begin anew, start a new life. The narrator and Vida share this hopefulness, which was widespread in the counterculture when *The Abortion* was published.

THE HAWKLINE MONSTER

With *The Hawkline Monster: A Gothic Western*, Brautigan began a series of novels that adapt the conventions of genre fiction in a quirky, unpredictable manner. Not strictly parodies, these hybrids sometimes achieve wonderful effects—odd, unsettling, comical—and sometimes fall flat. Combining the gothic novel, the Western, and a dash of romance, *The Hawkline Monster* is set in eastern Oregon during 1902 and centers on a magical Victorian house occupied by two equally baffling Victorian maidens with curious habits. The unreality of the situation does not affect the two unruffled Western heroes of the book, however, who methodically go about their task of killing the Hawkline Monster. The problem is not only to find the monster but also to discover what it is; the ice caves under the house complete the unreality of the situation. Brautigan moves lyrically from the mundane to the magical in this fusion of the real and the surreal.

TROUT FISHING IN AMERICA

Trout Fishing in America, Brautigan's most famous novel and his best, is a short, visionary inscape of the American nightmare. Brautigan has created a tragic symbol of what has happened to America: The trout streams are all gone, the campgrounds are full; escape to the American pastoral is no longer possible. Yet Brautigan assures his readers that all is not lost—there is still a place where they can find freedom. If all the land is being used and one cannot physically escape the city, then one must escape to the pastoral realm of one's imagination. Trout fishing, Brautigan insists, is thus a way of recapturing the simple while remaining aware of the complex.

Trout Fishing in America, like much of Brautigan's work (including his last novel, *So the Wind Won't Blow It All Away*), is autobiographical. The gentle, withdrawn narrator uses trout fishing as a central metaphor. A victim of the technological world, the narrator creates his own watery realm, complete with its own boundaries—a place where he can find solace from the technological stranglehold. His vision implies that all people have a fundamental right to the abundant richness and good life that America can provide but that are denied to many because the bankrupt ideas of the past still hold sway. Aware of the complexities of American life, Brautigan seems to be exhorting his readers to recapture the simple life, to escape the confinement of the city for the freedom of the wilderness. If that wilderness in the actual sense is cut off and no longer accessible; if all the trout streams have been developed, disassembled, and sold; if the horizon is now not new but old and despoiled; if the parks are already overcrowded; if there is no other way, then one must escape through the imagination.

SO THE WIND WON'T BLOW IT ALL AWAY

In *So the Wind Won't Blow It All Away*, Brautigan gives readers a glimpse of what post-trout-fishing-in-America life has become. Billed as an "American tragedy," *So the Wind Won't Blow It All Away* focuses on the tragedy that America and American life have become: "dust . . . American . . . dust."

Written, as are most of his novels, in the first person, Brautigan's novel is the memoir of an anonymous boy reared in welfare-state poverty somewhere in the Pacific Northwest. Unloved but tolerated by his mother, the boy, with his family, goes from town to town, meeting an odd assortment of minor characters. Although undeveloped, these characters serve to carry the novel's theme and serve as victims of the technocracy America has become. There is an old pensioner who lives in a packing-crate shack; adept at carpentry, the old man built a beautiful dock and boat and knows all the best fishing spots on the pond near his home, but he does not use his knowledge or equipment. A gas-station attendant who cares nothing about selling gas but likes to sell worms to fishermen also appears on the scene. There is a thirty-five-year-old alcoholic who traded ambition for beer; charged with the safety of the sawmill, the man dresses in finery (although readers are told that his appearances are not true to life), cares nothing about his job, and is continually encircled by boys who swoop like vultures to take his empty bottles back to the store for credit. Like America itself, the guard has brittle bones resembling dried-out weeds. Finally, Brautigan introduces a husband and wife who, each night, carry their living room furniture to the pond, set it up, and fish all night.

Brautigan presents America as having come to the end of its greatness, like the end of a summer afternoon. The technological success that spurred the country to greatness has resulted in its downfall. The husband and wife have changed all their electrical lamps to kerosene and await the cool evening with its refreshing possibilities, but as they patiently fish in the wrong spot, America goes on, killing its imagination with the technology of mindless television.

So the Wind Won't Blow It All Away ends with the horrible climax of the death of a boy, shot by mistake in a dying orchard. With that end, however, is the beginning of a new life, for, though the orchard has been left alone to die, new fruit will grow. The novel recalls the message of *The Abortion*: The substitutions of the confinement of the city for the freedom of the wilderness, and of television for imagination, are choices people have. With this novel, Brautigan returned to the successful themes of his earliest novels, warning that to go on will result only in dust.

David Mike Hamilton

OTHER MAJOR WORKS

SHORT FICTION: *Revenge of the Lawn: Stories 1962-1970*, 1971.

POETRY: *The Return of the Rivers*, 1957; *The Galilee Hitch-Hiker*, 1958; *Lay the Marble Tea: Twenty-four Poems*, 1959; *The Octopus Frontier*, 1960; *All Watched over by Machines of Loving Grace*, 1967; *The Pill Versus the Springhill Mine Disaster*, 1968; *Please Plant This Book*, 1968; *Rommel Drives on Deep into Egypt*, 1970; *Loading Mercury with a Pitchfork*, 1976; *June 30th, June 30th*, 1978.

MISCELLANEOUS: *The Edna Webster Collection of Undiscovered Writings*, 1995.

BIBLIOGRAPHY

Abbott, Keith. *Downstream from "Trout Fishing in America."* Santa Barbara, Calif.: Capra Press, 1989. Abbott recounts his memories of Brautigan from their first meeting in San Francisco in 1966 through the Montana years and back to 1982 in San Francisco. Abbott's last chapter, "Shadows and Marble," is a critical essay devoted to Brautigan's language and strategy of fiction.

Barber, John F., ed. *Richard Brautigan: Essays on the Writings and Life*. Jefferson, N.C.: McFarland, 2007. The thirty-two essays in this book are written by friends and colleagues of Brautigan who knew and respected the author and his writing. Many of the pieces here are previously unpublished, while others have appeared in literary journals. Altogether, they serve as a loving tribute to Brautigan, who was greatly admired by the essayists on both a personal and a literary level. Includes previously unpublished photographs and artwork.

Boyer, Jay. *Richard Brautigan*. Boise, Idaho: Boise State University Press, 1987. Short study of Brau-

tigan offering criticism and interpretation. Boyer describes how *Trout Fishing in America* sought to use the imagination to transcend reality. Includes a bibliography.

Bradbury, Malcolm. *The Modern American Novel*. New York: Oxford University Press, 1983. Chapter 7, "Postmoderns and Others: The 1960's and 1970's," cites Brautigan, placing him in the genre of writers who "celebrated the hippie youth spirit." Bradbury gives succinct but insightful critical commentary on Brautigan's novels. He sees Brautigan as much more than a hippie writer, whose spirit of "imaginative discovery" spawned a number of literary successors.

Brautigan, Ianthe. *You Can't Catch Death: A Daughter's Memoir*. New York: St. Martin's Press, 2000. Brautigan's daughter recalls her childhood spent bouncing between her two bohemian parents' homes. She describes her father, who committed suicide when she was twenty-four years old, as a "dignified, brilliant, hysterically funny, and sometimes difficult" man.

Chénetier, Marc. *Richard Brautigan*. New York: Methuen, 1983. A semiotic examination of Brautigan's approach to structure and elements of style that generate meaning. This slender volume touches on several works, with particular attention to *Trout Fishing in America*.

Foster, Edward Halsey. *Richard Brautigan*. Boston: Twayne, 1983. This blend of biography and criticism deals primarily with Brautigan's work within his own cultural ambience, referring to other contemporary fiction, the Beat movement, and Zen Buddhism as an overall influence. Not always flattering, Foster discusses most of Brautigan's novels and short fiction.

Iftekharuddin, Farhat. "The New Aesthetics in Brautigan's *Revenge of the Lawn: Stories 1962-1970*." In *Creative and Critical Approaches to the Short Story*, edited by Noel Harold Kaylor. Lewiston, N.Y.: Edwin Mellen Press, 1997. This essay deals primarily with Brautigan's short stories. Iftekharuddin's discussion of literary innovation and his treatment of other Brautigan critics make this an important contribution.

Mills, Joseph. *Reading Richard Brautigan's "Trout*

Fishing in America." Boise, Idaho: Boise State University Press, 1998. A brief volume in the Boise State University Western Writers series, providing a critical analysis of the novel. Includes a bibliography.

Stull, William L. "Richard Brautigan's *Trout Fishing in America:* Notes of a Native Son." *American Literature* 56 (March, 1984): 69-80. Stull approaches general themes in *Trout Fishing in America* by examining some of the book's many allusions to other

literature and Americana. A good introduction to the novel and to Brautigan.

Wright, Lawrence. "The Life and Death of Richard Brautigan." *Rolling Stone*, April 11, 1985. A biographical sketch, noting Brautigan's early fame and cult following, the fading of his reputation, and his suicide. Notes that when friends describe him, he seems two different people; at one point he was diagnosed as a paranoid schizophrenic.

HERMANN BROCH

Born: Vienna, Austria; November 1, 1886
Died: New Haven, Connecticut; May 30, 1951
Also known as: Hermann Joseph Broch; Vergil Bertrand

PRINCIPAL LONG FICTION

Die Schlafwandler, 1931-1932 (*The Sleepwalkers*, 1932)
Die unbekannte Grösse, 1933 (*The Unknown Quantity*, 1935)
Der Tod des Vergil, 1945 (*The Death of Virgil*, 1945)
Die Schuldlosen, 1950 (*The Guiltless*, 1974)
Der Versucher, 1953 (revised as *Demeter*, 1967, *Bergroman*, 1969, and *Die Verzauberung*, 1976; English translation, *The Spell*, 1986)

OTHER LITERARY FORMS

Although his fame and reputation as a writer rest on his two major novels, *The Sleepwalkers* and *The Death of Virgil*, Hermann Broch (brawk) was in fact a multifaceted author of truly eclectic interests—interests ranging from literature per se in almost every genre to literary criticism, from philosophical and sociopolitical essays to incisive psychological studies of mass hysteria. Broch's earliest publications were poems and essayistic studies submitted to some of the local journals in Vienna. A sonnet, "Mathematisches Mysterium" (mathematical mysterium), and two essays—one a review of

Thomas Mann's novella *Der Tod in Venedig* (1912; *Death in Venice*, 1925)—appeared as early as 1913 in the liberal journal *Der Brenner*, which was noted for publishing such influential writers of the period as Karl Kraus, Mann, Georg Trakl, Franz Werfel, and Stefan Zweig.

In fact, it was the essay, as a vehicle for the expression of both literary and philosophical thought, that would become Broch's preferred medium over the years, although one that was long overshadowed in the minds of the reading public by his two major novels. At the end of World War I, in 1919, Broch published the essay "Konstitutionelle Diktatur als demokratisches Rätesystem" (constitutional dictatorship as a democratic soviet-system), which outlines his belief that a sort of Nietzschean will to power was required if constitutional governments were to bring about a true democracy based on humanist, egalitarian ideals. Other important essays of the early 1930's by Broch include his "Logik einer zerfallenen Welt" (logic of a fallen world) and "Das Böse im Wertsystem der Kunst" (evil in the value system of art); both indicate their author's lifelong search for human values in a world gone awry.

One of Broch's more incisive essays to appear in English was titled "The Style of the Mythical Age," published in 1947; in the early 1950's there followed such essays as "Einige Bemerkungen zum Problem des Kitsches" (observations on the problem of kitsch), "Hofmannsthal und seine Zeit" (Hofmannsthal and his age), and "Study on Mass-Hysteria," posthumously published in 1959. Broch's essays occupy two volumes of the ten-volume edition of his collected works, *Gesammelte Werke*, published by Rhein Verlag of Zurich over a nine-year period beginning in 1952: The first volume of essays, published in 1955, bears the title *Dichten und Erkennen: Essays I* (poetry and perception); the second volume, also published in 1955, is titled *Erkennen und Handeln: Essays II* (perception and deed).

Broch also tried his hand at drama, writing three plays between 1933 and 1934. His first play, *Die Entsühnung* (pb. 1933; *The Atonement*, 1972), premiered at the prestigious Schauspielhaus in Zurich, Switzerland, on May 15, 1934, under the title . . . *Denn sie wissen nicht, was sie tun* (for they know not what they do). It deals with workers' problems and stems from Broch's experience as a skillful and respected mediator in labor disputes within the textile industry. As one indication of the continuing interests even in Broch's minor works, this early play was successfully adapted for radio by Ernst Schonwiese in 1961.

Broch's second work for the theater, *Es bleibt alles beim Alten* (1934; the same old thing), was a musical farce written with his son, Hermann Friedrich Broch de Rothermann (1910-1994). Broch's third work in this genre bore the rather baroque title *Aus der Luft gegriffen: Oder, Die Geschèfte des Baron Laborde* (1934; pulled out of thin air: or, the affairs of Baron Laborde); once again, Broch's son was named coauthor, though the actual extent of his participation is in dispute. It was apparently the father's wish that his son embrace a theatrical career, so he listed him as a collaborator in the writing of these plays. It is interesting to note that, in a later version of this play, Broch replaced both his name and his son's name with the pseudonym Vergil Bertrand—a name made up of those of two of the chief protagonists in *The Death of Virgil* and *The Sleepwalkers*, respectively.

Finally, Broch was also a skillful writer of short stories; a collection, *Short Stories*, edited by Eric Herd, appeared in 1966. Some of Broch's most famous stories are "Der Meeresspiegel" (1933; "The Ocean's Mirror"); "Die Heimkehr des Vergil" (1933; "The Homecoming of Virgil"), which foreshadows the larger novel of 1945; and "Der Steinerne Gast" (1941; "The Stony Guest"), the germinal story of the novel *The Guiltless*.

ACHIEVEMENTS

Hermann Broch must surely be counted among such other major German novelists of the twentieth century as Franz Kafka, Mann, Robert Musil, Heinrich Böll, and Günter Grass, alongside such other creative artists as Wassily Kandinsky, Gustav Klimt, Oskar Kokoschka, Gustav Mahler, Egon Schiele, and Arnold Schönberg—in terms of both the committed humanist stance he assumes in his writing and the purely technical mastery of his craft.

In this latter regard, Broch has been compared justifiably to James Joyce and William Faulkner in his use of interior monologue and stream of consciousness to capture the reality of life—and death—that he perceived all around him. For Broch, such techniques reflect the age in which he matured. William James's *Principles of Psychology*, which includes a chapter titled "The Stream of Thought," had been published in 1890. It was James who had advanced the concept of stream of consciousness, as later adapted for fiction. Sigmund Freud's *Die Traumdeutung* (*Interpretation of Dreams*), which called attention to the irrational inner life of humans, appeared in 1900, and his *Zur Psychopathologie des Alltagslebens* (*Psychopathology of Everyday Life*) was published in 1904. Albert Einstein's theory of relativity, which called into question the very certainty with which humans could know the "real" world, was published in 1905. All these works fostered, indeed necessitated, a preoccupation with subjective truth on the part of intellectuals of the day.

Given his early training as an engineer and his more than passing interest in science, Broch was acutely conscious of such revolutionary theories concerning reality and was able to translate the scientific and psychological principles being developed at that time into viable literary devices. His most successful literary endeavor, *The Death of Virgil*, is a compelling tour de force, lyric in its elegiac sense of loss, dreamlike in its irreal transcendence of time and space, yet actual in its uncompromising depiction of the artist's fate.

Broch's lifework was the quest for meaning in a world in which all certainties were open to question. Though he did not begin his full-fledged literary career until he was in his forties, he was spiritually a part of that generation of apocalyptic writers and artists who bore witness to the crisis facing Western European culture in the first decades of the twentieth century. While other artists of the day may have contributed their share to the erosion of cultural values (the Dadaists, for example) or sought order and meaning in an irrational realm beyond the visible world of shared human experience (the Surrealists), Broch, to his credit, stood firmly in this maelstrom of eroding values, seeking to recover a sense of absolute totality in the simultaneity of universal human actions. To perceive reality, to plot an ethical course of behavior based on one's perceptions, and to act with conviction for the betterment of humanity was Broch's sustaining motivation in all of his writing, regardless of genre.

Finally, insofar as Broch reached maturity as an author well after such spiritual contemporaries as Kafka (1883-1924), Rainer Maria Rilke (1875-1926), and Hugo von Hofmannsthal (1874-1929), Broch must be

regarded as a vital link to such important Austrian writers as Thomas Bernhard and Peter Handke—writers who are similarly concerned with the debilitating effect of modern civilization on the individual psyche, writers committed as Broch was to sociopolitical, cultural critique, using literary methods that owe their effectiveness in part to extraliterary disciplines such as psychology, sociolinguistics, and cultural anthropology.

BIOGRAPHY

Hermann Joseph Broch was born in Vienna, Austria, on November 1, 1886, the first son of Joseph Broch, a wealthy Jewish textile manufacturer, and Johanna, née Schnabel, who came from an old and affluent Viennese Jewish family. Three years later, Broch's brother, Friedrich, was born.

In a symbolic sense, Hermann Broch was very much a child of his times. He grew up in fin de siècle Europe, experiencing all the hopes and fears, the sense of irrevocable loss coupled with the dreams of unlimited fulfillment, then manifest. It was a time of transition, of outward progress, yet it was a time when people began to call into question the very basis of life, which for centuries had rested upon a foundation of unshakable absolutes. To an entire generation that prided itself on its modernity, the nineteenth century must have seemed strangely anachronistic; the fin de siècle was a period of uncertainty and anxiety—the "gay apocalypse," as Broch himself termed it—one that seemed relativistic and devoid of absolutes. As such, it would leave its stamp on all of Broch's writing, ultimately finding its most eloquent expression in *The Death of Virgil*. Further, it is this crisis in values that accounts in large measure for the boundary situations of all of Broch's fictional characters.

It was in this fragile world that Broch entered adulthood. In 1903, he graduated from the public school system and advanced to the Vienna Institute for Weaving Technology. Further study followed at the Textile Institute in Mülhausen (Alsace-Lorraine)—a period in Broch's life that would provide the background for the third part of *The Sleepwalkers*. Upon graduating in September of 1907 with a degree in textile engineering, Broch journeyed to the United States for two months to familiarize himself with cotton farming and milling pro-

Hermann Broch. (Getty Images)

cedures in the South, particularly in New Orleans, Louisiana. Upon his return to Austria, Broch entered his father's firm and became active in its management. As an administrator in the local textile union, Broch also gained a reputation for his equitable decisions in labor disputes. The plight of the worker in a society, changed overnight by rapid industrialization, was familiar to Broch from not only personal experience but also his reading of German naturalists such as Gerhart Hauptmann, Arno Holz, Johannes Schlaf, and Hermann Sudermann.

In 1908, Broch served for a time as a volunteer with the military stationed in Zagreb. In December of 1909, he married Franziska von Rothermann, despite the objections of both families. He continued to work in his father's firm, educating himself by reading widely in many fields. From 1915 to 1921, he pursued more formal studies in logic, mathematics, and physics at the University of Vienna, all the while working on a personal theory of values and his own philosophy of history. He began to immerse himself in ideas of Immanuel Kant, Søren Kierkegaard, Friedrich Nietzsche, Arthur Schopenhauer, Karl Kraus, and Otto Weininger. Oswald Spengler's *Der Untergang des Abendlandes* (1918-1922; *The Decline of the West*, 1926-1928), in particular, prompted Broch to develop his ideas on the necessity of the heroic quest on the part of the isolated and alienated individual if humankind should rise from the abyss of shattered values. Paradoxically, for Broch, the search for personal values served only to exacerbate the collapse of communal values. Years later, as a refugee from Adolf Hitler's Third Reich, Broch would seek a resolution of this paradox in the individual's pursuit of universal humanist goals.

During World War I, Broch served as an administrator for the Austrian Red Cross until he was discharged for medical reasons in 1916. He assumed control of his father's business and continued to write essays on philosophical and sociopolitical issues. As an indication of the direction his thought took at this time, one finds Broch turning for publication to such journals as *Die Rettung* and *Der Friede*. It was also at this time that Broch began to gain entry into the leading literary and intellectual circles active in Vienna at this time: the circles around Freud, the acerbic critic Karl Kraus, the writer Robert Musil, and the philosopher Ludwig Wittgenstein.

The crisis in values that began to manifest itself in nearly every phase of human endeavor during the hectic 1920's proved especially critical for Broch. His twelve-year marriage to von Rothermann ended in divorce in 1922, after a year's separation. The fear of impending inflation as well as a desire to devote more and more time to purely intellectual pursuits prompted Broch to give up the directorship of the family firm in 1927. From 1927 to 1931, he enrolled in courses at the University of Vienna, studying mathematics, philosophy, philology, and psychology. He began writing in earnest, seeing in literature the chance to resolve those of life's questions incapable of being answered adequately by rational science alone. His first major success, *The Sleepwalkers*, was completed during these years.

In later years, particularly after the publication of *The Death of Virgil*, Broch would once again return to his roots in science, devoting his attention almost exclusively to the social sciences. He came to view science as a sort of metapolitics, better able to redeem humankind than art, having grown skeptical once again of the efficacy of art to explain life, to posit values adequately for the masses. Ironically enough, it is in his most ambitious work, *The Death of Virgil*, that Broch eloquently expresses in art his apprehension and uncertainties about art. So great, in fact, was his conviction in this regard that he went so far as to associate the art for art's sake aesthetic of a poet such as Stefan George, for instance, with that sort of pseudo-art that has come to be known as kitsch. The personal crisis in his life worsened and, in 1928, he sold the family textile mills, despite the opposition of relatives, and returned to the University of Vienna to pursue a doctorate in philosophy and mathematics.

The situation for Jews grew worse daily—the first laws against the Jews were passed in 1933—and study at the university became increasingly difficult (even though Broch had converted to Catholicism in the early twentieth century). In 1935, he moved to Mösern near Seefeld in the Tyrolean Alps to work on his so-called mountain novel, *Bergroman*. It is a work that attempts to express the demoniac personality of the protagonist, who captivates an entire village, subjecting it entirely to his will. It was meant to present in miniature an idea of the mass hysteria of the fascist era. In its setting, the novel owes much to Mann's *Der Zauberberg* (1924; *The*

Magic Mountain, 1927), though it is fragmentary and far inferior to Mann's monumental effort. Broch had met Mann in 1932 and had been influenced by him as early as the first decade of the century. He wrote a review of Mann's *Death in Venice* in 1913 and would undoubtedly have been familiar with Mann's first major success as a writer, *Buddenbrooks* (1900), which details the decline and fall of one family amid that of an entire age and way of life. Personal matters deteriorated for Broch during the late 1930's. He was arrested and held in detention by the Gestapo; through the intervention of such well-known figures as Joyce and Mann, Broch's release was secured and permission was granted for him to emigrate.

Traveling by way of England and Scotland, Broch finally arrived in New York on October 9, 1938, to begin a new life. While in England, he received assistance from the PEN Club of London, which enabled him to continue work on *The Death of Virgil*. Once in the United States, Broch was aided by the American Guild for German Cultural Freedom in New York and by the Oberlaender Trust of Philadelphia. Other grants that he received over the years came from the American Academy of Arts and Letters, the John Simon Guggenheim Memorial Foundation (1939) for work on *The Death of Virgil*, the Rockefeller Foundation (1942), and the Bollingen Foundation (1946-1947), the latter two being granted so that Broch could continue his research in mass psychology. Offers also came in from major universities. Broch worked at the Princeton Office of Public Opinion Research and accepted a professorship in German literature at Yale University. In addition, he received an invitation to teach at East Germany's prestigious Jena University, but he declined this offer to continue his work at Yale.

With the publication in 1945 of *The Death of Virgil*, Broch's place in the history of German—and world—literature was secure. His reputation during his last years in the United States grew steadily, though it never rivaled that of such other noted émigrés as Bertolt Brecht and Mann. In 1950, Broch was nominated by the Austrian delegation of the PEN Club, an international writers' association, as well as by literary circles in the United States, for the Nobel Prize in Literature. Thus, Broch was on the threshold of a much-deserved worldwide recognition when he succumbed to a heart attack on May 30, 1951, in New Haven, Connecticut; burial followed in nearby Killingworth.

ANALYSIS

THE SLEEPWALKERS

Hermann Broch's first novel, *The Sleepwalkers*, is a psychological-historical novel that explores the gradual disintegration of values beginning in the latter half of the nineteenth century and culminating in the Armageddon that was World War I. The work is a trilogy whose main sections bear the names and the worldviews of each section's protagonist: "Pasenow, or the Romantic," "Esch, or the Anarchist," and "Huguenau, or the Realist."

Specifically, the work depicts the degeneration of German society from 1888 to 1918—a thirty-year period of crucial and inevitable change, as Hannah Arendt describes it in her 1949 article "The Achievement of Hermann Broch":

> 1888, when the Romantic finds himself in the not yet visible decay of the old world; 1903, when the Anarchist gets entangled in the prewar confusion of values; 1918, when the Realist becomes the undisputed master of a nihilistic society.

Part 1 of *The Sleepwalkers* presents the reader with the fragile world of the Junker Joachim von Pasenow, a Romantic in the sense that he inhabits an otherworldly realm of sterile conventions and anachronistic Prussian values, a realm of facades and titular masks whose symbol is the uniform. The protagonist is a man of honor, a believer in order and tradition. He loses his brother, Helmuth, in a senseless duel over family honor and so assumes responsibility for the family estate. In his task of maintaining the property and privileges of the landed aristocracy to which his family belongs, he is helped by his close friend, Eduard von Bertrand, who has risen to become a leading industrialist in Berlin. The first part comes to a close with Pasenow's marriage to Elisabeth, who, as the daughter of a wealthy neighbor, is well within Pasenow's social circle. The founding of this new family, particularly after the birth of a child, seems to promise the continued growth and prosperity of Pasenow's class and way of life. As Broch's readers will come to discover, this is not to be.

In part 2, a petit bourgeois bookkeeper by the name of

Esch makes his appearance. A malcontent, he is called an anarchist because, unlike Pasenow, he has lost faith in the old values and is seeking a new faith at any cost. Yet, like the hero of part 1, Esch is presented as a victim of circumstances, of a process of general social and cultural decline destined to run its full course. Having become a small-time variety-show entrepreneur, Esch, who is a social climber, will use any means at his disposal to get ahead—bribery and blackmail included. He is an impetuous man, settling accounts with real or imagined adversaries in confrontations contrived and acted out in his mind. Such interior dialogues only exacerbate Esch's inability to act. Though drawn to political agitators, his attraction, like his dreams, is so unrefined as to inhibit effectively any consequent action. Rather, Esch destroys things and people who are seen to stand in his way. Foremost among them is Pasenow's friend, Bertrand, whom Esch tries to blackmail for his homosexuality. Bertrand, a man positively portrayed as someone in charge of his fate, a man against whose actions those of the other characters are to be gauged, commits suicide rather than submit to the intrigues of a person such as Esch. His death must be viewed as the death of all that is decent and worthwhile in the novel. At the close of part 2, Esch takes the widow Hentjen in marriage in a near parody of Pasenow's marriage at the close of part 1.

In part 3, the reader is confronted with the total triumph of amorality. Although Huguenau, the realist, is the nominal hero of this last section, he shares center stage with Pasenow, who has gone on to become a major in the war and is now governor of the town in which Esch is serving as editor of a Socialist newspaper. Through a twist of fate—Pasenow publishes an idealistic article in Esch's paper—the two men become allied across class boundaries and against Huguenau, who, after deserting from the same army in which Pasenow had served so honorably, has become a successful businessman. He is a realist in the sense that his approach to every situation in life is cold, methodical—in short, businesslike. Such a worldview allows Huguenau to manipulate life dispassionately to his own advantage. Huguenau ends up slandering Pasenow and murdering Esch—both of whom, like sleepwalkers, are oblivious to events around them—yet still manages to become a leading member of the society that has emerged after the war.

The destinies of Pasenow and Esch are those of Romantic tradition and mere anarchy: the Romantic past is over; anarchy, as a precondition for the emergence of a new social order, has spent its energy. The fascist state is being born. On a technical level, the form of the novel perfectly reflects its content. Traditional nineteenth century epic narration—reminiscent, for example, of the mature Theodor Fontane—dominates the first portion of the novel. Gradually, however, this ordered, objective style becomes transformed into a more subjective narrative style. The tightly woven and objectively related plot incidents of part 1 give way to the imaginative musings of Esch in part 2, where stream of consciousness and interior dialogue mirror the growing emphasis on subjective reality and its concomitant skepticism, prevalent around the beginning of the twentieth century.

In part 3, the narration has become even more fragmented; it has disintegrated into a series of epic, dramatic, or lyric episodes bound loosely by the destinies of Pasenow, Esch, and Huguenau. Through the juxtaposition of seemingly objective dialogue and stream of consciousness, Broch skillfully plays off one view of reality against another. The resulting discrepancy between outer and inner reality reveals, according to Arendt, "the fundamental fragility of the time, the insecurity and convulsiveness of those who were its representatives." Through his use of various narrative perspectives to relate main and subordinate plot lines, Broch creates multiple levels of action and reality as his characters emerge, recede, and interact with one another. This technique effectively reflects the general collapse of an integrated worldview and results in a true multiple perspective, each character, each social sphere declaring its own relative values to be absolute.

THE DEATH OF VIRGIL

The Death of Virgil, which was recognized with both Guggenheim and Rockefeller awards, was originally written in the form of an eighteen-page story in 1936. The story was modified and lengthened as a direct result of Broch's detention and the very real threat of death at the hands of the Nazis in 1938. As Theodore Ziolkowski points out, "Whereas [Broch] had previously considered Vergil primarily as a prototype of the artist in a valueless society, he now devoted his attention to the *death* of Vergil." Broch himself said of the genesis of the work that "*Virgil* was not written as a 'book,' but (under Hitler's threat) as my private discussion with death." Broch continued to work on *The Death of Virgil* after his release from prison—revising and expanding the work's central idea—and by 1940, he had compiled the major part of the novel. He continued to refine the work until 1945, when it was published simultaneously in English and German. As the title indicates, the story deals with the death of the poet Vergil; his meditations on self and society, art and human activity, and life and death constitute the bulk of the novel.

The story takes place in the year 19 B.C.E., in the ancient port city of Brundisium in Italy; in an obvious parallel to Joyce's *Ulysses* (1922), the work covers only the final eighteen hours of Virgil's existence. This unity of time and place indicates the hero's (and the author's) anguished quest for unity, despite all of life's apparent dissonance, despite the chaos that death seems to herald. It is this nearness to death that sets life into sharp focus for author and hero alike.

The plot is straightforward and easily summarized. The work opens with the dying poet's return from Greece to Italy with the imperial navy. What follows and what takes up the greater part of five hundred pages until Virgil's death is anything but straightforward. Broch has created an intensely lyric work that, in its approximation of poetic, even musical form and structure, has expanded the very notion of the modern novel.

Broch himself described his work as being

> a poem, though not in the sense of a single lyrical outburst and also not in the sense of a poem cycle on a central theme, yet a poem and moreover, one that extends in a single breath over more than five hundred pages.

The entire work, in fact, is one long interior monologue, in which the thoughts and visions, the feverish dreams and repressed fears of Virgil are all called forth from the depths of his subconscious; in order to capture their reality and truth, the poet must articulate them by means of language.

The point of view throughout is that of Virgil himself, a poet, paradoxically enough, in despair of poetry. In the face of his imminent death, Virgil comes to question the relevance, the validity, indeed the morality of his entire lifework. Is a life given over to purely contemplative activity enough to justify it, given the need for committed action in a valueless world marked by enmity, war, poverty, and death? It is on his way from the ship to the emperor's palace that Virgil encounters all the ill-fated members of humanity. Where, he wonders, is the dignity and meaningfulness of life? Where is the beauty that he desperately sought to reproduce in poetry? Has he not, in his work, neglected fully half of life's total reality: namely, its horror, its evil, its ugliness? These are existential questions that the poet Rilke posed in his *Die Aufzeichnungen des Malte Laurids Brigge* (1910; *The Notebooks of Malte Laurids Brigge*, 1930) and in his *Duineser Elegien* (1923; *Duino Elegies*, 1931) and that Kafka raised in many of his diary entries and letters.

In fact, Kafka's request to his longtime friend and literary executor, Max Brod, to destroy his works after his death finds its parallel in Broch's novel when Virgil reveals to friends his wish to destroy the *Aeneid*. His reasons are that as a work of art, of beauty, it fails to represent the totality of truth and reality adequately; because it is "only" beautiful, he feels it to be of little benefit to humankind. Kafka's doubts were those of Broch as well, as evidenced in part by Broch's lifelong vacillation among a wide variety of forms: short story, drama, poetry, novel, philosophical essay, sociological case study, and so on. In *The Death of Virgil*, however, Broch confronted the problem of artistic validity head-on, and in so doing, he created a soul-searching work of literature, which, had he written nothing else, would have sufficed to add his name to the history of world literature. As Broch himself put it, expressing a kinship with Kafka, "We live and write, and that's all."

Broch completed his monumental novel precisely at a time in history when humanity seemed to have reached its lowest point. With death and destruction all around him, Broch, with all the conviction he could muster as a humanist, posited life and human creativity as counterweights. Virgil gives in to the pleas of his friend, Emperor Octavianus Augustus, and entrusts his *Aeneid* to him for safekeeping. He does so because he comes to realize that it is the task of the poet to offer humans, if ever so vaguely, a small glimpse of the eternal, which is theirs—and perhaps theirs alone—to perceive. As the harbinger of eternal, metaphysical order, Virgil sees the poet as the spiritual counterpart to Emperor Augustus, who embodies the temporal order.

Structurally, the novel is divided into four parts: "Water, the Arrival"; "Fire, the Descent"; "Earth, the Expectation"; and "Air, the Homecoming." Each section thus corresponds to a phase in the hero's perception of creation. In part 1, Virgil becomes aware of life's polarities while aboard the ship taking him back to Italy. He becomes conscious of the contrast between the limitless heavens above and the dark, murky, unfathomable waters below; he sees the noble passengers above deck and the pitiful slaves below; there is the sea itself signifying life and man's seemingly endless journey toward a shore that represents for the poet his inevitable death, his homecoming. On his journey through the dark and narrow streets of Brundisium, he sees the slums of the poor, which contrast sharply with the emperor's palace. For Virgil, it is his arrival at the threshold of self-awareness that serves as a catalyst for all the self-doubts faced and ultimately resolved in the rest of the novel.

Book 2 depicts in rhapsodic monologues and long lyric sequences Virgil's descent into the hellfire of self-recrimination. Book 3, which is the most narrative section of the work, presents in Virgil's discussions with his friends the poet's earthly expectations for himself as a poet, for his art, and his subsequent despair over his actual achievements. Part 4 brings a resolution to all of Virgil's doubts. Through his debate with Augustus, he comes to realize that a greater sacrifice is needed for him *not* to burn the *Aeneid*. Destruction of the work would bring fleeting self-satisfaction. Allowing it to exist elevates this work of aesthetic beauty to the status of all of those creative works that bear witness to one man's less-than-perfect quest for unity and truth.

In a final, grand vision leading from death's door back through life to birth and beyond into the order-generating act of creation itself, Virgil comes to realize the totality of life, precisely in the affirmation of all of life's apparently irreconcilable opposites, including life and death themselves. It is a vision of life that nearly defies verbal articulation. For this reason, Broch described the novel's structure in musical terms, comparing it to a traditional symphony in four movements. He even ascribed musical designations to three of the four sections: 1—"andante"; 2—"adagio"; and 4—"maestoso." Language as music is what Broch had in mind—music not only because of language's sonorous qualities but also, and more important, because of the lyric language's universal, timeless power to enchant.

It is the language that Hofmannsthal sought to describe in his famous *Brief des Lord Chandos an Francis Bacon* (1905; first published as "Ein Brief" in *Der Tag*, 1902; *The Letter of Lord Chandos*, 1952) and to which Rilke gave voice in his *Duino Elegies* and *Sonette an Orpheus* (1923; *Sonnets to Orpheus*, 1936). It is lyric language, self-reflective in its anxious attempt to crystallize the most fleeting of life's moments, the moment between that which has not yet dawned and that which is irrevocably lost—Broch's famous "no longer and not yet." In *The Death of Virgil*, Broch has captured many such moments in the life and gentle death of a man who, like himself, sought to understand life and death, to perceive their meaning, to discover their intrinsic order and unity, and then to create the language commensurate to the task of conveying his vision to others.

Thomas Di Napoli

OTHER MAJOR WORKS

SHORT FICTION: *Methodologische Novelle*, 1933; *Methodisch konstruiert*, 1949; *Short Stories*, 1966 (E. W. Herd, editor).

PLAYS: *Die Entsühnung*, pb. 1933 (also known as *. . . Denn sie wissen nicht, was sie tun*; English translation, *The Atonement*, 1972).

NONFICTION: "James Joyce und die Gegenwart," 1936 ("James Joyce and the Present Age," 1949); *Dichten und Erkennen: Essays I*, 1955; *Erkennen und Handeln: Essays II*, 1955; *Brief*, 1957; *Massenpsychologie*, 1959; *Hofmannsthal und seine Zeit*, 1964 (*Hugo von Hofmannsthal and His Time: The European Imagination, 1860-1920*, 1984); *Zur Universitätsreform*, 1969; *Gedanken zur Politik*, 1970; *Hermann Broch-Daniel Brody: Briefwechsel, 1930-1951*, 1970 (Bertold Hack and Marietta Kleiss, editors); *Menschenrecht und Demokratie*, 1971; *Briefe über Deutschland, 1945-1949*, 1986; *Geist and Zeitgeist: The Spirit in an Unspiritual Age*, 2002 (John Hargraves, editor).

MISCELLANEOUS: *Gesammelte Werke in zehn Bänden*, 1952-1961 (10 volumes); *Die Heimkehr*, 1962; *Kommentierte Werkausgabe in dreizehn Bänden*, 1974-1981.

BIBLIOGRAPHY

Bartram, Graham, and Philip Payne. "Apocalypse and Utopia in the Austrian Novel of the 1930's: Hermann Broch and Robert Musil." In *The Cambridge Companion to the Modern German Novel*, edited by Graham Bartram. New York: Cambridge University Press, 2004. *The Sleepwalkers* and *The Death of Virgil* are analyzed and placed within the wider context of 1930's Austrian literature in this essay about novelists Broch and Robert Musil.

Broch de Rothermann, H. F. *Dear Mrs. Strigl: A Memoir of Hermann Broch*. Translated by John Hargraves. New Haven, Conn.: Beinecke Rare Book & Manuscript Library, Yale University, 2001. Broch's son recalls his father's personal life. Describes Broch's relationship with his father, his exile in the United States, and other aspects of Broch's often difficult life. In both English and German.

Halsall, Robert. *The Problem of Autonomy in the Works of Hermann Broch*. New York: Peter Lang, 2000. Halsall argues that concerns about autonomy are central to understanding Broch's literature and philosophy and demonstrates how these concerns are evident in his novels, including *The Sleepwalkers* and *The Guiltless*. Includes bibliographical references and an index.

Hargraves, John A. *Music in the Works of Broch, Mann, and Kafka*. Rochester, N.Y.: Camden House, 2001. Although this book examines music as an aspect of the work of three German writers, Hargraves's study concentrates on Broch, arguing that of the three writers, Broch was the most interested in expressing the primacy of music in his writing. Essays discuss Broch's discursive writings on music and the musical elements in several of his novels.

Horrocks, David. "The Novel as Parable of National Socialism: On the Political Significance and Status of Hermann Broch's *Bergroman*." *Modern Language Review* 86, no. 2 (April, 1991). A critical study of *The Spell*, focusing on themes of Nazism. Horrocks examines why Broch portrayed the rise of Nazism in an oblique way and the novel's significance as a political statement.

Lützeler, Paul Michael. *Hermann Broch: A Biography*. Translated by Janice Furness. London: Quartet, 1987. Lützeler, who has edited the seventeen-volume collected works of Broch and written extensively on his life, provides a comprehensive general biography. Includes an index.

_____, ed. *Hermann Broch, Visionary in Exile: The 2001 Yale Symposium*. Rochester, N.Y.: Camden House, 2003. Contains papers delivered at an international symposium that present a wide range of interpretations of Broch's work. Several papers analyze various elements of *The Sleepwalkers*, *The Death of Virgil*, *The Guiltless*, and Broch's early novels.

Simpson, Malcolm R. *The Novels of Hermann Broch*. Las Vegas, Nev.: Peter Lang, 1977. A useful general introduction to Broch, providing an interpretation of each of his novels in relation to the author's life. Evaluates Broch's literary status and contribution to the modern novel.

Strelka, Joseph P. "Hermann Broch." In *Major Figures of Modern Austrian Literature*, edited by Donald G. Dariau. Riverside, Calif.: Ariadne Press, 1988. An overview of Broch's life and work is included in this collection of essays about Austrian authors who began their literary careers before World War II, were driven into exile after Austria was annexed to Germany, and became prominent figures after the war.